W9-BYK-605

Selecting Effective Treatments

3rd Ed

2007

San Francisco CA
John Wiley + Sons

L Seligman
L W Reichenberg

JOSSEY-BASS

Selecting Effective Treatments

A Comprehensive, Systematic Guide to Treating Mental Disorders

Third Edition

Linda Seligman and Lourie W. Reichenberg

John Wiley & Sons, Inc.

Published by Jossey-Bass.
A Wiley Imprint
989 Market Street, San Francisco, CA 94103-1741 www.josseybass.com

Wiley Bicentennial logo: Richard J. Pacifico

Jossey-Bass books and products are available through most bookstores. To contact Jossey-Bass directly call our Customer Care Department within the U.S. at 800-956-7739, outside the U.S. at 317-572-3986, or fax 317-572-4002.

Jossey-Bass also publishes its books in a variety of electronic formats. Some content that appears in print may not be available in electronic books.

Library of Congress Cataloging-in-Publication Data

Seligman, Linda.
Selecting effective treatments : a comprehensive, systematic guide to treating mental disorders / Linda Seligman and Lourie W. Reichenberg. – 3rd ed.
p. ; cm.
Includes bibliographical references and indexes.
ISBN 978-0-7879-8868-5 (pbk.)
1. Mental illness–Treatment. 2. Psychiatry–Differential therapeutics. 3. Psychotherapy. I. Reichenberg, Lourie W., date. II. Title.
[DNLM: 1. Mental Disorders–therapy. WM 400 S465s 2007]
RC480.S342 2007
616.89′14–dc22

2007019068

Printed in the United States of America
THIRD EDITION

PB Printing 10 9 8 7

CONTENTS

Preface ix

1 **Introduction to Effective Treatment Planning** 1

The Importance of Systematic and Effective Treatment Planning • Research on the Effectiveness of Psychotherapy • Determinants of Treatment Outcome • An Integrated Model for Treatment Planning • The Client Map • Dimensions of Treatment Planning • Examples of Treatment Planning: Anne and Bettie

2 **Mental Disorders in Infants, Children, and Adolescents** 52

Overview of Mental Disorders in Infants, Children, and Adolescents • Mental Retardation • Learning, Motor Skills, and Communication Disorders • Pervasive Developmental Disorders • Attention-Deficit and Disruptive Behavior Disorders • Feeding and Eating Disorders of Infancy or Early Childhood • Tic Disorders • Encopresis • Enuresis • Separation Anxiety Disorder • Selective Mutism • Reactive Attachment Disorder • Stereotypic Movement Disorder • Additional Mental Disorders Diagnosed in Children and Adolescents • Treatment Recommendations: Client Map • Recommended Reading

3 **Situationally Precipitated Disorders and Conditions** 155

Overview of Situationally Precipitated Disorders and Conditions • Adjustment Disorders • Other Conditions That May Be a Focus of Clinical Attention • Treatment Recommendations: Client Map • Recommended Reading

4 Mood Disorders 180
Overview of Mood Disorders • Major Depressive Disorder • Dysthymic Disorder • Depressive Disorder Not Otherwise Specified • Bipolar Disorders • Cyclothymic Disorder • Treatment Recommendations: Client Map • Recommended Reading

5 Anxiety Disorders 233
Overview of Anxiety Disorders • Panic Disorder • Phobias • Obsessive-Compulsive Disorder • Posttraumatic Stress Disorder and Acute Stress Disorder • Generalized Anxiety Disorder • Treatment Recommendations: Client Map • Recommended Reading

6 Disorders of Behavior and Impulse Control 290
Overview of Disorders of Behavior and Impulse Control • Substance-Related Disorders • Eating Disorders • Sexual and Gender Identity Disorders • Impulse-Control Disorders Not Elsewhere Classified • Sleep Disorders • Treatment Recommendations: Client Map • Recommended Reading

7 Disorders in Which Physical and Psychological Factors Combine 387
Overview of Disorders in Which Physical and Psychological Factors Combine • Somatoform Disorders • Factitious Disorders • Delirium, Dementia, and Amnestic and Other Cognitive Disorders • Mental Disorders Due to a General Medical Condition • Treatment Recommendations: Client Map • Recommended Reading

8 Personality Disorders 418
Overview of Personality Disorders • Paranoid Personality Disorder • Schizoid Personality Disorder • Schizotypal Personality Disorder • Antisocial Personality Disorder • Borderline Personality Disorder • Histrionic Personality Disorder • Narcissistic Personality Disorder • Avoidant Personality Disorder • Dependent Personality Disorder • Obsessive-Compulsive Personality Disorder • Personality Disorders Not Otherwise Specified • Treatment Recommendations: Client Map • Recommended Reading

9 Disorders Involving Impairment in Awareness of Reality: Psychotic and Dissociative Disorders 486
Overview of Psychotic and Dissociative Disorders • Psychotic Disorders • Dissociative Disorders • Treatment Recommendations: Client Map • Recommended Reading

10 The Future of Diagnosis and Treatment Planning 528
New Understanding of Diagnosis • Changes in Treatment • Social and Cultural Influences • Recommended Reading

References 542

About the Authors 597

Name Index 599

Subject Index 613

This book is dedicated to my father, Irving Goldberg (1904-1994), who always encouraged my writing and scholarship, and to my mother, Florence Scolnick Goldberg (1908-1996), who was never quite sure why I wanted to write books but was proud of me anyhow.

—LS

To my father, who always encouraged me, my husband, Neil, who is always supportive, and my son, Al, who always understands.

—LWR

PREFACE

The landmark research of Smith, Glass, and Miller (1980), along with other research, gave the definitive affirmative answer to the question of whether psychotherapy has any value. Research in the decade that followed turned to differential therapeutics, seeking to determine which approaches to psychotherapy are effective in treating which mental disorders, under what conditions, with which clients, and to what ends.

Our understanding about the differential diagnosis of mental disorders has advanced greatly since then. In 2000, these advances culminated in the publication of the fourth edition text revision of the *Diagnostic and Statistical Manual of Mental Disorders*, or *DSM-IV-TR*. But understanding of differential therapeutics has lagged behind. Many books have been published that focus on one particular disorder, espouse one preferred mode of treatment, or offer a compendium of articles by different authors, but few volumes have presented a systematic, research-based approach to the treatment of mental disorders. As a result, approaches to treatment are often haphazard, with clinicians relying on familiar or comfortable models rather than on treatments that have demonstrated the greatest effectiveness.

Our goal in the writing of this third edition of *Selecting Effective Treatments* was to cite the most up-to-date and empirically based treatments for mental disorders while maintaining the format and integrity of previous editions.

ENHANCEMENTS TO THE THIRD EDITION

Knowledge about differential therapeutics for mental disorders certainly has advanced since the 1990s, when the previous edition of this book was published. Mental health professionals have a better understanding of the etiology, presentation, risk factors, prevalence, effective treatments, and prognosis for the major mental disorders. Knowledge has expanded particularly in terms of understanding of pervasive developmental disorders, bipolar disorders, disorders of childhood, schizophrenia spectrum disorders, and eating disorders, among others. This, the third edition of *Selecting Effective Treatments*, updates our knowledge of the diagnosis and treatment of mental disorders.

All sections of this book have been revised to reflect current information. Of course, chapter revisions are particularly extensive in those areas where our knowledge has grown the most. Many enhancements have been made to the third edition, including expanded information on assessment, the spectrum concept of mental disorders, suicide risk factors, and new approaches to treatment. Suicide risk factors have received attention because suicide is a growing public health concern, a leading cause of death for the elderly and young adults, and a symptom of many mental disorders. We also have expanded greatly the sections on diagnosis and treatment of depression, borderline personality disorder, the schizophrenia spectrum disorders, and the bipolar disorders. A new section discusses treatment approaches for people who are dually diagnosed with a substance use disorder and a mental disorder.

AUDIENCE

Most of the existing books on treatment of mental disorders have been written from a medical perspective, but most treatment of mental disorders is provided by psychologists, counselors, social workers, and psychiatric nurses. Therefore, this book fills a gap in the literature by focusing on the needs of these nonmedical mental health practitioners and by recognizing the increasingly important part they play in treating mental disorders. The book is also addressed to students in these fields who have at least a basic understanding of approaches to counseling and psychotherapy.

Clinicians, researchers, and educators in the mental health fields should all be able to use this book in their work. Clinicians in particular who read the book can expect to gain a deeper understanding of the complexities of diagnosis, as well as of the latest edition of the *Diagnostic and Statistical Manual of Mental Disorders (DMS-IV-TR)*. In addition, clinicians will be able to develop sound treatment plans and will gain greater confidence and credibility, which should help them treat their clients more knowledgeably and more effectively.

Some information has been provided about the usefulness of medication for the various mental disorders; this information is included primarily to help clinicians determine when a referral for medication is in order and to assist them in anticipating the impact that medication is likely to have on their clients.

This book also should help clinicians deal with managed care organizations (MCOs). Treatment of mental disorders is now generally overseen by MCOs, and, in order to provide the best help possible to their clients, clinicians must be knowledgeable about dealing with MCOs. *Selecting Effective Treatments* should enable clinicians both to make more accurate diagnoses and to provide treatments that are likely to be effective. This book will help them explain their choice of treatment approach to their clients, to their supervisors and colleagues, and to MCOs. This in turn should make it more likely that their clients will receive third-party payments that will enable them to afford the counseling and psychotherapy they need.

ORGANIZATION

Selecting Effective Treatments, Third Edition, does not restrict clinicians to a narrow range of approaches, nor does it advocate for one particular theoretical model. Research does not support such a circumscribed view of therapy, and such an approach would not promote the optimal use of each therapist's special talents. Rather, this book seeks to increase clinicians' understanding of the symptoms and dynamics of mental disorders and to provide a range of treatment options for each disorder, allowing clinicians to blend their own therapeutic strengths and preferences with those approaches that have demonstrated effectiveness. New approaches to treatment included in the third edition include motivation enhancement therapy, dialectical behavior therapy, emotion-focused therapy, and mindfulness and other Eastern-influenced strategies that have received empirical support for their effectiveness in the treatment of specific mental disorders.

As professors, therapists, and researchers ourselves, we recognize the need for practitioners and students to have a comprehensive, user-friendly text. Such a text should not only provide the latest empirical research but also present it so that readers can visualize disorders and begin to develop their own treatment plans that are both evidence based and practical.

Chapter One provides introductory information about diagnosis and treatment of mental disorders, as well as the DO A CLIENT MAP format of treatment planning. Chapters Two through Nine begin with a case study, continue with a description as well as a summary of research on the effective treatment of each disorder covered in the chapter, and end with a Client Map, a comprehensive model of treatment planning developed by Linda Seligman, which can be adapted to any diagnosis. This format has been used throughout all three editions of this book and offers what we think is an effective and efficient approach to diagnosis and treatment.

In Chapters Two through Nine, the mental disorders have been grouped into eight broad categories. Within each of these chapters, the material on each mental disorder generally has been organized into six sections:

- A description of the disorder
- An overview of the characteristics that typify people with that disorder
- A review of assessment tools available for the disorder
- An overview of the qualities of style and personality that typify clinicians likely to be successful in treating the disorder
- A review of the research on effective treatment of the disorder
- Information on the prognosis for the disorder

Chapter Ten identifies and discusses emerging trends in the ever-evolving fields of diagnosis and treatment of mental disorders.

ACKNOWLEDGMENTS

Of course, no project of this size could be accomplished without the help and support of others. We are deeply grateful to Genilee Swope Parente for her generous assistance with reference checking, to Jossey-Bass for ushering the book through the production process, and to our husbands, Robert Zeskind and Neil Reichenberg, without whose enduring encouragement and support this work would not have been possible.

Linda Seligman, Ph.D., L.P.C.
Lourie W. Reichenberg, M.A., L.P.C.

CHAPTER ONE

Introduction to Effective Treatment Planning

A usually quiet and withdrawn young woman became verbally abusive to her supervisor and warned him that if she were not promoted to a job commensurate with her outstanding abilities, she was going to "come back with a gun." A few weeks earlier, she had had a brief consultation with a psychiatrist, who diagnosed her as having a major depressive disorder and prescribed antidepressant medication.

A man who had been a capable and hardworking accountant was referred to an employee assistance counselor because of a sudden and extreme decline in his performance. After some brief and unsuccessful efforts were made to remotivate the man, he was fired from his job.

A woman had been treated with years of unsuccessful psychoanalysis, during which she had been told that her difficulty in concentrating and her chaotic lifestyle reflected her efforts to avoid dealing with her early losses.

THE IMPORTANCE OF SYSTEMATIC AND EFFECTIVE TREATMENT PLANNING

Poor clinical understanding, inaccurate diagnosis, and inappropriate treatment contributed to all of the situations just described. The first woman had a history of both manic and depressive episodes; in fact, she had a bipolar disorder, and the antidepressant medication she was given contributed to the development of another manic episode. The man was suffering from a cognitive disorder resulting from a head injury incurred in a cycling accident. The second woman had attention-deficit/hyperactivity disorder and eventually responded well to a combination of behavior therapy and medication. These examples, based on actual clients, make clear the importance of accurate diagnosis and treatment planning.

The primary goal of diagnosis and treatment planning is to help psychotherapists from all disciplines — psychologists, counselors, social workers, psychiatrists, and psychiatric nurses — make sound therapeutic decisions so that they can help their clients ameliorate their difficulties, feel better about themselves and their lives, and achieve their goals.

A need for accountability as well as for treatment effectiveness mandates systematic treatment planning. As health care costs have risen, the growth and impact of managed care have escalated, and third-party payers increasingly require mental health professionals to describe and justify their treatment plans. Case managers, who are usually mental health practitioners themselves, review treatment plans and determine whether they are appropriate. Clearly the therapist's knowledge of treatment planning is an essential element of people's ability to receive the psychotherapy they need.

Requests for accountability also come from mental health agencies and clinics; from counseling centers at schools, hospitals, and residential facilities where therapy is done; and from funding agencies. Financial support is rarely adequate for mental health services in these settings, and therapists often must provide documentation of the services' effectiveness before they can obtain continued funding.

Unfortunately, treatment planning is sometimes viewed as a process that must be carried out for no better reason than to satisfy bureaucratic requirements. On the contrary, the fundamental reason for treatment planning is to facilitate effective delivery of mental health services. The purpose of this book, as the Preface has outlined, is to provide the most up-to-date information available on differential therapeutics — that is, the study of which treatment approaches are most likely to be effective in treating each of the mental disorders. This book seeks to facilitate the process of treatment planning by linking knowledge about treatments to information about diagnoses, usually made according to the guidelines in the *Diagnostic and Statistical Manual of Mental Disorders*, now in its fourth edition text revision, known as *DSM-IV-TR* (American Psychiatric Association, 2000).

This book is not designed to present a rigid formula for treatment planning; the state of the art does not allow that, and, even if it were possible, it probably would not be desirable. Therapeutic effectiveness depends not only on the application of well-supported methods of intervention but also on such indefinable and complex ingredients as the therapist's style, the expertise and training of the therapist, the personalities of therapist and client, their demographic characteristics, and the alliance between the two of them. Therefore, this book presents information not just on the mental disorders and their appropriate treatment but also on the probable nature of the people suffering from each disorder, those characteristics of the therapist that are likely to contribute to effective treatment, and the prognosis for the treatment of each disorder.

In therapy many roads can be taken to the same goal. This book seeks to point out which roads are likely to be smooth and rewarding and which are full of ruts and barriers. Plotting the actual course is up to the therapist and the client. Systematic treatment planning allows the clinician to map the therapeutic journey, revise the route as necessary, and repeat the trip with others if it turns out to be worthwhile, all without compromising the spontaneity of the traveler or the guide.

RESEARCH ON THE EFFECTIVENESS OF PSYCHOTHERAPY

The overall effectiveness of psychotherapy has long been established. As the meta-analytic review by Smith, Glass, and Miller (1980) concluded, "The average person who received therapy is better off at the end of it than 80 percent of those who do not" (p. 87). Lambert and Cattani-Thompson (1996) sum up the research by stating, "The research literature clearly shows that counseling is effective in relation to no-treatment and placebo conditions. The effects of counseling seem to be relatively lasting. These effects are attained in relatively brief time periods, with the percentage of clients who show substantial improvement increasing as the number of counseling sessions increases" (p. 601). So the overall verdict on the outcome of psychotherapy is positive: for most people, therapy is more effective at ameliorating emotional disorders than is no treatment at all. These conclusions do not pertain only to the treatment of adults; according to Mash (2006), great strides have been made in the past decade in developing effective intervention and prevention programs for children as well.

In the past twenty years, the movement toward effective treatments has resulted in the identification of certain treatments that work particularly well with certain disorders. In 1995, the American Psychological Association identified eighteen treatments shown to be empirically supported through randomized controlled trials for use with specific disorders — cognitive-behavioral therapy for bulimia, exposure therapy for specific phobia, and exposure and response prevention for obsessive-compulsive disorder (OCD), to name just a few (Task Force on Promotion and Dissemination of Psychological Procedures, 1995).

But the literature reminds us that clinical efficacy and clinical effectiveness are two different things. The efficacy of therapy relates to the results shown in the setting of a research trial, whereas clinical effectiveness is the outcome of the therapy in routine practice.

Matching therapy to specific disorders would seem to be the answer to improving effectiveness. Yet research has not fully supported this method, which suggests that effective therapy is more complicated and involves a host of variables that have more of a synergistic relationship than simply matching people with appropriate treatment.

Comparative research is needed, and should explore both the relative advantages and disadvantages of alternative treatment strategies for people with different disorders and the therapeutically relevant qualities of the client, the therapist, and their interaction. Study of the therapeutic process contains many challenges, however, and even the best-defined therapy is difficult to reproduce because of its interactive nature. Other challenges inherent in the process of conducting research on therapy's effectiveness include the large number of client-related variables, variations in therapists' expertise, variations in the severity of disorders, participant and observer bias, the questionable ethics of establishing true control and placebo groups with people who have emotional disorders, and the difficulty of assessing how much progress has been made.

DETERMINANTS OF TREATMENT OUTCOME

Psychotherapy outcome is determined primarily by four clusters of variables:

1. Therapist-related variables, including such factors as personality, age, gender, ethnicity, education and training, theoretical orientation, ability to inspire trust and hope, facility for communicating empathy and caring, and treatment style (Wampold, 2001; Wampold & Brown, 2005). Therapist competence and ability to form an alliance has a particularly strong relationship to better therapeutic outcomes.
2. Client-related variables, including demographic factors, diagnosis and symptoms, motivation for and expectations of treatment, history, support systems, ability to form relationships and collaborate with the therapist, personality, and the natural course of the client's disorder (Bohart & Tallman, 1999).
3. The therapeutic alliance, including the ability of the therapist and the client to agree on goals and treatment procedures, the match between therapist- and client-related variables, and their collaboration and interaction (Norcross, 2002).

4. Treatment variables, including the theories that guide the treatment, the strategies used, medication, the treatment setting and context, the frequency and duration of treatment, and such adjuncts to treatment as self-help groups (Nathan & Gorman, 2002).

Maximization of the therapy's effectiveness should take account of all four clusters of variables.

This chapter presents an integrated model for treatment planning that will help therapists think systematically about that process and explore the factors to be considered in structuring treatment. These factors include, among others, the modality of treatment (group, individual, or family), the theoretical framework for treatment, the duration of treatment, and the treatment setting. The chapter goes on to summarize the available research on the first three clusters of variables related to outcome (therapist-related variables, client-related variables, and the therapeutic alliance).

The chapters that follow focus primarily on the fourth cluster of variables (treatment variables), to help therapists deepen their understanding of the mental disorders discussed in *DSM-IV-TR* and their effective treatment. Because this book is designed to help clinicians move beyond the assumption that therapy is effective and on to an understanding of what works for whom, the large and growing body of literature on that subject is reviewed here. Some of the conclusions drawn from the literature are tentative, but they should provide a basis for future research into treatment planning, as well as for the development of effective treatment plans.

AN INTEGRATED MODEL FOR TREATMENT PLANNING

The integrated model presented here in skeleton form lists the five major elements (items I through V) that structure the information in the following eight chapters. When clinicians assess particular clients or disorders, they often do not have information about all the categories and subcategories in this outline, but effective use of the model does not depend on complete information. Indeed, gaps in the therapist's knowledge, as well as in the information available on a client, can actually be used to guide the development of a treatment plan and to indicate areas needing further research or investigation.

I. *Description of the Disorder.*

   A. *Diagnosis.* The *Diagnostic and Statistical Manual of Mental Disorders* (*DSM-IV-TR*; American Psychiatric Association, 2000) is the accepted system for classifying mental disorders in the United States, as well as in many other countries. Its nomenclature will be used as the standard throughout this book. Other diagnostic manuals are available, including the *Psychodynamic Diagnostic Manual* (PDM Task Force, 2006) and the *ICD-10 Classification of Mental and Behavioural Disorders* (World Health Organization, 2005). However, they have not attained widespread use and acceptance in the United States.

B. *Epidemiology.* Epidemiology includes both the incidence (number of new cases) and the prevalence (number of existing cases at a given time) of a disorder. Acute disorders tend to have a higher incidence; chronic disorders, a higher prevalence. Approximately 46.4 percent of Americans will have some type of mental disorder during their lifetimes (Kessler, Berglund, et al., 2005). In general, the more common the disorder and the better established the diagnosis, the more is known about its treatment, because of the greater opportunity for research on the disorder.

C. *Primary and secondary symptoms.* A mental disorder typically includes a cluster of symptoms, both primary and secondary (or underlying). The primary symptoms are those that must be present to meet the criteria for diagnosis according to *DSM-IV-TR*, the major source of information on symptoms of mental disorders. Comparison of a disorder's criteria with a person's presenting symptoms is important in individualizing a treatment plan so that it meets the needs of that particular person. For example, two people may both be diagnosed with major depressive disorders. However, if one is suicidal and presents a danger to the self, whereas the other complains primarily of guilt and problems in eating, sleeping, and concentration, their treatment plans will differ. Treatment for the first person will emphasize safety; for the second, cognitive therapy to address the guilt, and relaxation and imagery to treat the vegetative symptoms related to sleeping and eating may be the most important interventions.

D. *Typical onset, course, and duration of the disorder.* This information can be useful to clients as well as to the clinician who is engaged in treatment planning. Disorders vary widely in terms of their course. For example, some disorders, such as schizophrenia, are often chronic and need extended follow-up; others, such as major depressive disorder, tend to run a circumscribed course but frequently recur.

II. *Typical Client Characteristics.* The purpose of this section is to provide typical profiles of people with particular mental disorders. These profiles can facilitate diagnostic interviewing, alerting clinicians to client patterns that are likely to be present. By comparing these profiles with information gathered on individual clients, therapists can also identify areas that need exploration and can gain insight into clients' readiness for treatment, types of treatment that are most likely to be effective, adjunct and referral sources that may be useful, and prognoses. The following client characteristics, among others, are typically relevant to treatment.

A. *Genetic and other predisposing factors.* In this section, the etiologies of mental disorders are discussed. Many disorders tend to follow a genetic or familial pattern; these disorders or related ones are often found in a client's family. Schizophrenia and bipolar disorders are examples of disorders that are heritable. Identification of these patterns enables clinicians to plan treatments that take account of environmental or family dynamics contributing to the development of a disorder. A family history of a disorder may also imply a biological element to its transmission, suggesting that medication may be especially useful. In addition, developmental patterns (such as the age at which a disorder is most likely to emerge) and predisposing factors (such as a precipitating incident or a background common to those who suffer from the disorder) also provide data useful in determining treatment plans. That information can also facilitate the formulation of plans to prevent relapse.
B. *Demographics.* Information about such variables as the typical socioeconomic environment, partner status, age, and family constellation of someone with a given disorder is included in this section. Information on multicultural background, including age and ethnicity, also is presented in this section.
C. *Source of referral and apparent motivation for treatment.* Clues to a person's probable response to treatment are often provided by the nature of the referral. For example, a person who has sought therapy on the recommendation of a career counselor with whom she has worked successfully is likely to have a greater motivation to change than is someone who has been ordered into treatment by the courts. People's reports of their motivation and desire for change also are relevant to treatment planning.
D. *Treatment history.* Information on previous treatment and its outcome is important in determining what treatments are likely to be helpful. A long treatment history, especially one including numerous treatment failures, suggests a poor prognosis, but perhaps that outcome can be averted if a treatment is provided that is different from those that have failed. Clinicians should familiarize themselves with the ways people have responded to treatment in the past, building on what was successful and avoiding what was ineffective.
E. *Personality profile.* Clients' personality profiles are obtained through psychological assessment, interviews, and observation by clinicians. Typical interpersonal and intrapsychic dynamics of clients with each mental disorder will be considered throughout this book, including such characteristics as cognitions, affect, behavior, defenses, and lifestyle.

F. *Developmental history.* A review of the client's background, including such areas as family relationships, work history, social and leisure activities, and medical conditions, usually provides valuable information on that person's strengths and areas of difficulty. If the client's successes and failures, support systems, and coping mechanisms are considered when treatment is planned, the treatment is likely to be more effective. Also, viewing people broadly and in context facilitates use of available resources, such as a supportive spiritual community, and helps clinicians avoid pitfalls to treatment, such as peers who encourage drug and alcohol use as well as antisocial behavior.

III. *Preferred Therapist Characteristics.* This section reviews the available information on therapist-related variables that are relevant to the treatment of a particular disorder or client. Such information may include the therapist's experience, theoretical orientation, and training; the therapist's personal and professional qualities; and the relationship between the client's and the clinician's personalities and backgrounds.

IV. *Intervention Strategies.* In this section, what is known about the effective treatment of a disorder is reviewed. Recommendations about treatment strategies are made, and areas where information is lacking are discussed.

A. *Approaches to psychotherapy and counseling.* This section contains a review of the literature on those approaches to therapy that seem to work best with the mental disorder under consideration. The following dimensions of the therapeutic process are important in treatment planning and, depending on the information available, will be discussed in detail in subsequent chapters:

- Psychotherapeutic theories and strategies
- Therapist's implementation of these theories and strategies (including level of directiveness, exploration, support, structure, and confrontation)
- Balance of focus — affective, behavioral, cognitive
- Modality of treatment — individual, family, group (Seligman, 2004)

B. *Medication.* This section considers the question of whether medication enhances or is necessary in the treatment of a particular disorder. Although the focus of this book is the treatment of mental disorders by nonmedical clinicians who emphasize psychotherapy or counseling rather than drugs to effect change, a combination of medication and psychotherapy is typically more effective for some disorders than either one alone. Nonmedical therapists must be aware of these findings so that they can refer clients with such disorders for medical evaluation and provide treatment in collaboration with a psychiatrist or other medical specialist.

C. *Duration and pacing of treatment.* This section focuses on the typical length of treatment necessary for ameliorating symptoms of a disorder and on the swiftness of the therapeutic pace.
D. *Treatment setting.* Inpatient settings, partial hospitalization or day treatment, and outpatient settings all have their place in the treatment of mental disorders. Which setting is preferred or needed for each disorder will be discussed.
E. *Adjunct services.* These services include social and personal growth activities, support and self-help groups (such as Alcoholics Anonymous), leisure and exercise groups, professional and governmental services (such as legal aid and subsidized housing), and psychoeducational services (such as assertiveness training and education on effective parenting) that may enhance the effectiveness of psychotherapy.

V. *Prognosis.* This section provides information on how much change or improvement can be expected in a person experiencing the disorder under consideration, how rapidly progress is likely to occur, the likelihood of relapse, and the overall prognosis. Accurate assessment of prognosis depends on both the nature of the mental disorder and the motivation and resources of the person with the disorder. The severity of the client's disorder, of course, is relevant to outcome. In general, the more severe and long-standing the disorder, the poorer the prognosis. Disorders that are mild and short in duration and that have a clear precipitant tend to have better prognoses. For example, people with circumscribed, reactive, brief, situational problems, such as adjustment disorders and some mood and anxiety disorders, tend to have better treatment outcomes. In contrast, people with personality disorders, schizophrenia, and other disorders that are enduring and pervasive and that do not have an apparent precipitant typically respond to treatment more gradually and in more limited ways.

THE CLIENT MAP

The major elements of the treatment plan discussed in this chapter have been expanded and organized into a structured and systematic model for treatment planning — the Client Map. The steps of this treatment plan are represented by the acronym formed from the first letter in each of the twelve steps in this model: DO A CLIENT MAP. This acronym facilitates recall of the parts of the plan, reflects the plan's purpose, and guides its development. A clinician who supplies information about the following twelve items will have created the Client Map, a structured treatment plan for working with a particular client:

DO A CLIENT MAP

Diagnosis

Objectives of treatment

Assessments (for example, neurological tests, personality inventories, and symptom checklists)

Clinician characteristics

Location of treatment

Interventions to be used

Emphasis of treatment (for example, level of directiveness; level of supportiveness; cognitive, behavioral, or affective emphasis)

Numbers (that is, the number of people in treatment: individual, family, or group)

Timing (frequency, pacing, duration)

Medications needed

Adjunct services

Prognosis

The format represented by the DO A CLIENT MAP acronym is used throughout this book to illustrate the process of treatment planning for sample cases.

DIMENSIONS OF TREATMENT PLANNING

In general, treatment planning moves from the nature of the disorder through consideration of the client's characteristics and on to the treatment approach. That will be the sequence followed throughout most of this book. In the present section, however, the focus will be primarily on approaches to treatment and their impact on mental disorders. The parts of the Client Map considered here are diagnosis, objectives of treatment, assessments, clinician characteristics, location, interventions, emphasis, numbers, timing, medications, and adjunct services. Because information on diagnosis, assessments, interventions, and prognosis are specific to each disorder, they will be discussed separately, and at length, in the chapters relating to each disorder.

Diagnosis (DO A CLIENT MAP)

Effective treatment planning begins with the development of an accurate multiaxial assessment, made according to the guidelines in the *DSM*. Such an assessment includes information on people's mental disorders, any relevant medical conditions, their stressors, and their overall levels of coping and adjustment as reflected by the Global Assessment of Functioning Scale. The diagnosis is the foundation for treatment planning. Once the diagnosis has been made, clinicians can move ahead to develop a complete and effective treatment plan.

Development of such a plan must take into consideration a number of variables. One of the most important considerations is to identify treatments that are likely to be effective in ameliorating the symptoms of the client's disorder. Ideally, clinicians should select treatment approaches that have received empirical support. That is not always possible, of course. Although empirically supported treatments have been identified for many disorders, especially the anxiety and mood disorders, eating disorders, and substance use disorders (Nathan & Gorman, 2002; Roth & Fonagy, 2005), a concise list of effective treatments for every disorder does not exist. In some cases, many diverse treatments have been found to be equally effective for a particular disorder; in other cases, no treatment approaches have received strong research support. We will focus on what has been proven efficacious as well as what seems most likely to be effective in order to help readers achieve the best possible treatment options in the therapy they provide.

In 1995, the Division 12 Task Force of the American Psychological Association published guidelines for identifying empirically supported treatments (Task Force on Promotion and Dissemination of Psychological Procedures, 1995). As mentioned earlier, included with the criteria was a list of eighteen treatments that the task force identified as having empirical support for use in treatment of particular diagnoses or specific populations. Each of the eighteen treatments had been tested in randomized controlled trials and implemented using a treatment manual.

This research raised concerns about the applicability of these findings to people with diverse backgrounds and those with comorbid conditions. Questions also were raised about the use of manualized treatments and the impact and importance of the therapeutic alliance (Levant, 2005). A flurry of research since that time has focused on common factors that account for much of the variance across disorders, as well as the effect of the therapeutic alliance. Both of these important topics are discussed later in this chapter.

As research continues to explore the appropriate use of specific approaches to particular clients and disorders, the use of manualized therapy, providing clear and specific treatment guidelines and interventions, has increased. Well over 130 different manualized treatments for specific disorders now claim to be empirically validated (Chambless & Ollendick, 2001). Although some studies indicate that the use of manuals reduces variability in outcomes (Crits-Christoph et al., 1991), other research indicates that even with manual-based treatments, therapist effects on outcome are often large (Malik, Beutler, Alimohamed, Gallagher-Thompson, & Thompson, 2003). Ahn and

Wampold (2001) concur. They write that strict adherence to a treatment manual can lead to "ruptures in the alliance and, consequently, poorer outcomes" as well as thwart the therapist's ability to adapt treatment to the "attitudes, values, and culture of the client, a necessary aspect of multicultural counseling" (p. 255). Clinicians should use sound clinical judgment and flexibility, rather than rigid application of manuals (Levant, 2005).

A growing number of studies, to be discussed in later chapters, assess the effectiveness of therapies for adults, children, and adolescents with particular disorders (Barlow, 2004; Mash & Barkley, 2006; Nathan & Gorman, 2002). Although some studies focus on only one or two approaches, others provide useful information on the effectiveness of various psychotherapies. In general, the desirable treatment approaches for a particular client or disorder are those that demonstrate a high likelihood of addressing relevant problems; maximize the client's motivation; help the therapist and the client achieve the treatment goals; overcome obstacles; consolidate gains; and reduce the likelihood of a relapse (Beutler & Consoli, 1993).

People with more than one diagnosis are typically challenging clients. People's cognitive and processing abilities, their premorbid functioning, and their access to resources all affect their response to treatment (Sachse & Elliott, 2001). Typically, a person who was at a lower level of functioning before therapy will still be at a lower level after therapy than a person who was at a higher level of functioning before therapy, even though both may have improved.

Also important in understanding psychopathology and treatment selection is the client's development and life stage. A growing number of studies discuss developmental processes, such as attachment, socialization, gender identity, and moral and emotional development. Understanding the client's stage of development is particularly important when treating children, adolescents, families, and older adults (Levant, 2005). Also important is knowing when a person developed a particular disorder and understanding the impact of that disorder on the person's development. People with long-standing disorders, for example, may well have failed to meet important developmental milestones, especially in self-direction and socialization.

Objectives of Treatment (DO A CLIENT MAP)

Decisions on treatment objectives or goals should be made in collaboration with the client. Using the best available information — considering costs, benefits, resources, and options — the therapist and the client work together to create a treatment plan. An active, involved client is crucial to the success of treatment (Levant, 2005). No matter how wisely the therapist selects an intervention strategy, and no matter how abundantly the therapist demonstrates the personal and professional qualities that are positively correlated with a good outcome, therapy is unlikely to be effective if the client is not ready or able to benefit from the therapeutic strategy and the therapist's positive qualities. In fact, the key to therapeutic effectiveness often is found in the client or in such client-related variables as expectations of therapy, motivation for change, degree of participation, and severity of the disorder, although it also can be found in the therapeutic alliance or the particular treatment approach that is used (Bowman, Scogin, Floyd, & McKendree-Smith, 2001; Lambert & Cattani-Thompson, 1996; Prochaska & Norcross, 2006). Attention should be given, then, to those qualities in clients that are correlated with effective treatment, as well as to clinician characteristics and treatment approaches, discussed later.

Client's Readiness for Change. Prochaska and Norcross (2006) address the importance of the person's readiness for change, which they describe as unfolding over five stages: precontemplation, contemplation, preparation, action, and maintenance. Each stage represents a period of time characterized by discrete attitudes, behaviors, and language on the part of the client. The person must achieve certain tasks before moving on to the next stage. The stages are as follows:

1. *Precontemplation.* People in this stage have no intention of changing their behavior. Although they might think about changing, or wish to change, they are unwilling to do anything that will promote change. In fact, they may be stuck in repetitive and ineffective thoughts and behaviors for years. To move beyond this stage, the person must recognize and admit there is a problem.
2. *Contemplation.* At this stage of change, the person is able to admit the problem, wants to change, and is willing to move beyond merely thinking about it. The task required to move to the next level of change is to take action — even a small first step — toward behavioral change.
3. *Preparation.* This is the stage in which behavior and intentions are aligned. The person is ready to make a change and begins to set goals and an action plan in preparation for moving on to the next stage.
4. *Action.* During this stage, people commit time and energy to modify their behavior and begin working to overcome their problems, to the point that their efforts become recognized by others. The action stage may last from one day to six months. During this time the person is acquiring skills and strategies to help prevent relapse.
5. *Maintenance.* Maintaining and continuing behavioral change for longer than six months is the hallmark of the maintenance stage.

Prochaska and Norcross warn that the process of change is not linear; rather, it is more like a spiral, with a person cycling and recycling through the five stages. For example, when people are trying to change unhealthy behaviors such as smoking, drug use, or overeating, relapse and cycling through the stages of change are common. However, recognizing a person's pretreatment stage of change is important to effective treatment and prognosis.

These researchers and others have developed models for matching the therapist's style to the client's readiness. According to Prochaska and Norcross (2006), clients with very low levels of readiness need therapists who can focus on consciousness raising, dramatic relief, and environmental evaluation. To facilitate movement from precontemplation to the contemplation stage involves increased use of cognitive, affective, and evaluative processes.

Client's Perceptions of Psychotherapy. The research suggests that people who perceive their therapists as helping them, who have positive perceptions of their therapists' skills and facilitative attitudes, and who see themselves engaged in teamwork with their therapists are likely to show more benefits from therapy than people who do not share those perceptions. Therefore, clients' perceptions of the therapeutic process seem to play a very important role in determining outcomes.

Client's Expectations for Treatment. People enter therapy with a broad range of expectations and attitudes. The well-known self-fulfilling prophecy seems to hold true: people who expect positive and realistic outcomes from therapy, and whose expectations are congruent with those of their therapists, are more likely to achieve those outcomes, whereas negative expectations lead people to abandon efforts to reach their goals. Meyer and colleagues (2002) report that therapists who instill hope and promote the client's positive expectations of treatment foster increased client participation in treatment and a reduction in symptoms. They conclude that "expectations of treatment effectiveness are powerful predictors of outcome in psychotherapy" (p. 1051) and are an important part of building a positive therapeutic alliance.

At least some portion of the positive effect of therapy comes from what is known as the Hawthorne effect. Many people have been shown to improve simply as a result of having special attention paid to them (Prochaska & Norcross, 2006). The special attention paid to a client by a mental health professional can improve self-esteem, reduce anxiety, and promote improvement. Thus, empirical research is needed if one is to conclude that the effectiveness of any particular treatment methodology is more than just the result of person-to-person contact.

Assessments (DO A CLIENT MAP)

The development of a treatment plan for a given client begins with a thorough understanding of that person. Formats for intake interviews and mental status examinations are readily available elsewhere (Seligman, 2004) and are beyond the scope of this volume, but a brief and useful overview of relevant aspects of the client is provided by Strub and Black (2000). They suggest gathering data on the following dimensions:

- Description of presenting concerns
- Demographic characteristics
- Mental status
- Cultural and religious background
- Physical characteristics and abilities; medical conditions
- Behavior
- Affect and mood
- Intelligence; thinking and learning style
- Family composition and family background
- Other relevant past history and experiences
- Social behavior
- Lifestyle
- Educational and occupational history
- Family history of psychiatric illness
- Any other relevant areas

Clinicians also should collect and review any relevant records and prior assessment information (for example, psychological tests and medical evaluations). Most therapists seem to be making increased use of diagnostic interviews, inventories, and rating scales. In the preliminary stages of therapy, these help the clinician gather information on the client's diagnosis and dynamics. In the termination stages, they provide information on progress and outcome. The literature offers many objective and projective assessment tools, developed in recent years, that can play an important role in deepening understanding of clients (Strub & Black, 2000). The following are some of the most useful:

- Structured diagnostic interviews, such as the NIMH Diagnostic Interview Schedule, the Schedule for Affective Disorders and Schizophrenia, the Brief Psychiatric Rating Scale, and the Symptom Checklist-90-R
- General personality inventories, including the Minnesota Multiphasic Personality Inventory-2; the Millon Clinical Multiaxial Inventory-III; the Millon Adolescent Personality Inventory; the California Psychological Inventory; the Myers-Briggs Type Indicator; and the High School, Children's, and Early School Personality Questionnaire

- Inventories for assessing specific symptoms, including the Beck Depression Inventory-II, the Beck Anxiety Inventory, the Hamilton Rating Scale for Depression, the State-Trait Anxiety Inventory, the Michigan Alcoholism Screening Test, the Conners' Rating Scale, the Behavior Assessment System for Children-2, and the Eating Disorders Inventory

Inventories also may be used to assess other aspects of the person. These might include intelligence, aptitudes, achievement, interests, and values. Assessment is an important component of the treatment planning process and should be done with care. Effective treatment planning is unlikely unless the clinician has made an accurate diagnosis and has a good understanding of the client's development, concerns, strengths, and difficulties, acquired through a careful assessment.

Variables Related to the Client's Demographic and Personal Characteristics. On the National Comorbidity Survey Replication, a structured interview administered to a national sample of people over the age of eighteen, nearly 50 percent of respondents reported at least one mental disorder during their lifetimes, and close to 30 percent had experienced such a disorder during the previous twelve months (Kessler et al., 2005). Of those who had experienced at least one disorder, half experienced symptoms by the age of fourteen, and three-fourths by the age of twenty-four. The most common disorders included anxiety, mood, impulse-control, and substance use disorders. People who experience symptoms commonly delay seeking treatment. On average, people with mood disorders wait six to eight years before seeking treatment, and people with anxiety disorders wait nine years to as long as twenty-three years before seeking treatment (Wang et al., 2005).

What distinguishes people who seek help for their concerns and who benefit in the process from people who do not? Those who do seek treatment are more likely to be female, college educated, and from the middle to upper classes, and they are more likely to have reasonable expectations for how therapy can help them. People who continue in therapy tend to be more dependable, more intelligent, better educated, less likely to have a history of antisocial behavior, and more anxious and dissatisfied with themselves than those who leave therapy prematurely (Garfield, 1986).

Those who leave treatment early are more likely to be ambivalent about change and seeking help. Principe, Marci, and Glick (2006) found that 40 percent of clients at community mental health centers and 20 percent seen in private practice terminated therapy in the first two visits. Because the therapeutic alliance forms early in treatment (Horvath and Laborsky [1993] found that it peaked at the third session), it is essential for clinicians to instill hope and the expectation of a positive therapeutic outcome early in treatment (Meyer et al., 2002).

Many personal characteristics in clients are correlated with outcomes. Orlinsky, Grawe, and Parks (1994) found that people who are open, in touch with their emotions, and able to express their thoughts and feelings in therapy are more likely to have positive treatment outcomes. Meyer and colleagues (2002) found that clients were more likely to improve if they were actively engaged in therapy, regardless of which therapeutic intervention was used. The likelihood of a positive outcome is also increased if the client demonstrates good ego strength and can take responsibility for problems rather than viewing them as external sources of difficulty (Sachse & Elliott, 2001). Moreover, according to Miller and Rollnick (2002), motivated people as well as people with positive pretreatment functioning, who are aware of their difficulties and have positive expectations of change, stable lifestyles, and good support systems seem better able to make good use of therapy.

Research on the relationship between outcomes and clients' personal characteristics is suggestive but not yet conclusive. Overall, however, indications are that therapy is particularly effective with white females who are intelligent, motivated, expressive, and not severely dysfunctional. Therapy can be very helpful to people who do not fit this description, of course, but these findings point out some of psychotherapy's limitations, as well as the difficulty of adapting the therapeutic process to the needs of a particular client.

Clinician Characteristics (DO A CLIENT MAP)

Such therapist variables as empathic understanding, affirmation of the client, credibility, clinical skills, the ability to engage and focus the client, and the capacity to focus the client on affective experiences had been explored in more than two thousand process-outcome studies by 1994 (Orlinsky et al., 1994) and probably at least as many since that time. These factors are similar to those proposed by Carl Rogers (1951, 1965) as necessary and important to therapy and are generally associated with positive treatment outcomes. Following are descriptions of some of the most important of these therapist characteristics.

Empathy. Not just rote repetition of a client's words, true empathy involves compassion and an attitude of profound interest — almost as if the therapist were stepping into the other person's psychological shoes. In *A Way of Being*, Rogers (1980) wrote about empathy: "It means entering the private perceptual world of the other ... being sensitive, moment by moment, to the changing felt meanings which flow in this other person" (p. 142). When clients feel truly heard, they are more likely to be comfortable exploring their feelings on a deeper level. With appropriate empathy, therapists are able to choose interventions that are appropriate for the client's needs at that time. Greenberg,

Watson, Elliott, and Bohart (2001, p. 382) identify ways in which empathy contributes to outcome:

1. Feeling understood increases client satisfaction and thereby increases self-disclosure, compliance with the therapist's suggestions, and feelings of safety.
2. Empathy provides a corrective emotional experience.
3. Empathy promotes exploration and the creation of meaning, facilitating emotional reprocessing.
4. Empathy contributes to the client's capacity for self-healing.

Unconditional Positive Regard. The therapist's regard for the client remains constant and positive. It is unconditional, nonjudgmental, and not based on anything the client might do or say but rather reflects appreciation and caring for another human being. The therapist shows this regard for a client through the use of empathy and understanding.

Congruence. The therapist is genuine and real and does not put up a false professional front or façade (Rogers, 1957). Congruence is evident among the therapist's thoughts, emotions, and behaviors.

Bowman and colleagues (2001) report that it is the therapeutic alliance and "the complex interactions involving client, therapist, and treatment variables [that] probably account for most variance in psychotherapy outcome" (p. 147). The therapist factors discussed here, and later in this chapter, are critical in developing a sound therapeutic alliance.

Demographic Variables. Therapist demographic variables appear to be weaker predictors of outcome than client variables (Bowman, Scogin, Floyd, & McKendree-Smith, 2001). In a study comparing three treatment modalities — cognitive-behavioral therapy, interpersonal therapy, and medication — such therapist variables as age, gender, race, religion, and clinical experience were not found to be related to therapeutic effectiveness (Wampold & Brown, 2005).

In a meta-analysis on the effect of therapist gender on psychotherapy outcome, Bowman and colleagues (2001) looked at more than sixty studies and concluded that the gender of the therapist has little effect on outcomes. However, a recent study indicates that female clients prefer female therapists and that female therapists tend to form stronger therapeutic alliances with their clients than do male therapists (Wintersteen, Mensinger, & Diamond, 2005). Although the gender of the therapist may be important to some clients and is worth considering (especially in short-term counseling where rapid establishment of a positive therapeutic alliance is important), research has failed to demonstrate that gender matching leads to improved outcomes or reduced dropout rates (Cottone, Drucker, & Javier, 2003; Sterling, Gottheil, Weinstein, & Serota, 1998).

The literature also found no clear evidence that the therapist's age affects therapeutic outcomes (Butcher, Mineka, & Hooley, 2006). In general, clients seem to prefer clinicians who are mature enough to have had considerable experience in their field and who understand clients' age-related and developmental issues but who do not seem so old as to be out of touch with modern developments in the profession.

Ethnic and Cultural Diversity. The ethnic and cultural match between client and therapist has also been the focus of much attention. Socioeconomic status and race appear to bear little relationship to therapeutic outcomes. Garb (1998) notes that social class effects were not significant in children's ratings of therapists.

Nor does the race of the therapist appear to affect therapeutic outcomes. However, Thompson, Bazile, and Akbar (2004) found that African American clients prefer to see African American therapists rather than European American therapists, and an earlier study (Lambert, 1982) noted that African American clients tend to leave therapy at higher than usual rates when they are working with European American therapists. These studies suggest that race may be a factor in determining length of treatment, if not therapeutic outcomes. Moreover, according to Hess and Street (1991), "Several studies have demonstrated that subjects express a greater preference for, engage in more self-exploration with, and are better understood by counselors of their same ethnic background than by those whose background differs from their own" (p. 71).

Degree of assimilation to the majority culture seems to be a moderating variable in the relationship between clients' and their therapists' ethnicity and therapeutic outcomes. Coleman, Wampold, and Casali (1995) conclude that clients who are not highly assimilated to the majority culture have more negative attitudes toward therapy and are more likely to prefer ethnically similar therapists. By contrast, according to Sue, Ivey, and Pedersen (1996), clients who are highly assimilated to the majority culture sometimes feel stereotyped if they are automatically assigned to ethnically similar therapists. In some cases, ethnic matching between client and therapist does seem to be indicated and may result in greater trust and understanding between client and therapist (Thompson et al., 2004; Wong, Kim, Zane, Kim, & Huang, 2003), but the research generally suggests that therapists who attend to issues of culture as well as to their clients' wants and expectations in therapy are likely to be successful with both ethnically similar and ethnically different clients.

Experience and Professional Discipline. Research on the link between therapist experience or expertise and outcome has yielded inconclusive results. Two studies found that expertise was more important than theoretical orientation (Eells, Lombard, Kendjelic, Turner, & Lucas, 2005). However, two other studies that compared experienced clinicians to graduate students on their ability to conduct assessments of personality and psychopathology found no significant difference in their abilities. This was true regardless of whether the clinicians were conducting interviews, gathering biographical information, or administering and interpreting the Rorschach or the MMPI. Although these studies were conducted with clinical and counseling psychologists, Garb's research (1998) focused on social workers and other mental health professionals indicates similar results.

Beutler, Crago, and Arizmendi (1986) found no relationship between the therapist's professional discipline and therapeutic outcomes. In fact, Berman and Norton (1985) found that, overall, professionals and paraprofessionals were equally effective.

Nevertheless, Greenspan and Kulish's study (1985) of 273 clients who terminated treatment prematurely, but after at least six months, indicates that therapists with Ph.D. degrees and personal experience of psychotherapy have lower rates of premature termination by clients than do therapists with M.D. or M.S.W. degrees. Seligman (1995), however, reports that psychologists, psychiatrists, and social workers do not differ in their therapeutic effectiveness. So far, no clear and conclusive relationship has been found between the length of the therapist's training, the therapist's personal experience of psychotherapy, and the therapist's professional discipline, on the one hand, and therapeutic outcomes, on the other.

Since 1950, more than two thousand research studies have been conducted on therapists' personal characteristics and styles. The following characteristics, attitudes, and approaches on the part of therapists have been found to be correlated with therapists' effectiveness (Bowman et al., 2001; Greenberg et al., 2001; Lambert & Barley, 2001; Lambert & Cattani-Thompson, 1996; Meyer et al., 2002; Orlinsky, Grawe, & Parks, 1994):

- Communicating empathy and understanding to clients
- Having personal and psychological maturity and well-being
- Manifesting high ethical standards
- Being authoritative rather than authoritarian, and freeing rather than controlling of clients

- Having strong interpersonal skills; communicating warmth, caring, respect, acceptance, and a helping, reassuring, and protecting attitude; affirming rather than blaming clients
- Being nondefensive; having a capacity for self-criticism and an awareness of their own limitations, but not being easily discouraged; continuously searching for the best ways to help clients
- Empowering clients and supporting their autonomy and their use of resources
- Being tolerant of diversity, ambiguity, and complexity; being open-minded and flexible
- Being self-actualized, self-fulfilled, creative, committed to self-development, responsible, and able to cope effectively with their own stress
- Being authentic and genuine and having credibility
- Focusing on people and processes, not on rules
- Being optimistic and hopeful, having positive expectations for the treatment process, and being able to engender those feelings in clients
- Being actively engaged with and receptive to clients, and giving some structure and focus to the treatment process

These findings support the importance of the core conditions first identified by Rogers (1951, 1965) as necessary for effecting improvement, regardless of the therapist's theoretical orientation. The findings suggest that the therapist who is emotionally healthy, active, optimistic, expressive, straightforward yet supportive, involved, and in charge of the therapeutic process, and who is also able to temper that stance with encouragement of responsibility on the part of the client, is the one most likely to achieve a positive outcome.

Location (DO A CLIENT MAP)

Research on selection of treatment settings is fairly limited. In general, the treatment location will be determined by the following seven considerations (Seligman, 2004):

1. Diagnosis, and the nature and severity of the symptoms
2. Danger that clients present to themselves and others
3. Objectives of treatment
4. Cost of treatment, and the client's financial resources and insurance coverage

5. Client's support systems, living situation, and ability to keep scheduled appointments
6. Nature and effectiveness of previous treatments
7. Preferences of the client and of significant others

When therapists are choosing among treatment options, Johnson, Rasbury, and Siegel (1997) recommend that the following four considerations be taken into account:

1. Finding the least restrictive setting
2. Selecting a setting that provides the most optimal therapeutic care for the particular person and disorder
3. Matching the person's needs with the specific treatment provided (settings without enough resources and those that are overly restrictive may be nontherapeutic)
4. Choosing the most cost-effective treatment (for example, if a day treatment program will suffice, inpatient or residential treatment should not be considered)

Often placement will be determined or limited by insurance providers or financial considerations. Clearly, decisions regarding the best placement for an adult, adolescent, or child will require weighing a variety of complicated and interrelated factors.

The decision about the treatment setting, like many of the other decisions that must be made as part of treatment planning, calls on clinical judgment because the literature gives only sketchy guidelines. Options typically include inpatient treatment (such as a hospital or residential treatment program), day treatment program, or outpatient treatment.

Residential Treatment. Residential treatment centers are the most restrictive environment for treating mental disorders. Placement is usually for an extended period of time, often a year or more, and most residential treatment centers are typically not located in the person's community; thus family and home visits are often not possible or are of limited duration. These programs provide a highly structured environment and may be appropriate for people with psychotic disorders, significant mental retardation, substance dependence, and other severe disorders. Residential treatment programs are sometimes necessary in the treatment of children with severe or profound mental retardation, conduct disorders, or psychotic disorders that do not respond to outpatient or pharmacological interventions. These children often exhibit chronic behavior problems, such as running away, substance use, and aggression (Johnson et al., 1997).

Inpatient Hospitalization. Inpatient hospitalization is considerably shorter than residential treatment. Hospital stays range from overnight to less than a month in most cases. Inpatient treatment programs are usually highly structured and oriented toward a rapid diagnosis and crisis stabilization. Inpatient hospitalization may be appropriate for people who pose a danger to themselves or to others and who have severe mental disorders. The following list provides examples of situations in which inpatient care might be considered:

- Suicide attempts or severe depression
- Eating disorders in which a person cannot maintain body weight
- Psychosis or irrational or bizarre thinking that makes a person a danger to self or others
- Sexual abuse or neglect of a child, or a home environment that makes it unsafe for the child to remain in the home

People with drug or alcohol problems who are physiologically dependent on harmful substances also may need a period of inpatient treatment. However, unless detoxification is needed, treatment of substance dependence can often be accomplished through day treatment or intensive outpatient programs, combined with the client's participation in self help groups.

People are often discharged from a hospital to a less restrictive setting (generally an outpatient or day treatment program) as soon as warranted. Some studies indicate that a brief hospital stay followed by aftercare is more therapeutic than a longer stay. In general, the most efficient, least confining treatment setting should be used to reduce the stigma associated with treatment, maintain the client's independence and connection to the community, and reduce costs.

Partial Hospitalization. Day treatment and partial hospitalization programs permit people to live at home while attending a highly structured program focused specifically on their needs (such as schizophrenia, substance use, eating disorders, dual diagnosis, and others). Day treatment programs are less costly than inpatient hospitalization and often serve as transitions from inpatient or residential treatment settings to outpatient treatment. At the end of the day treatment program, stepped-down, half-day programs or weekly group meetings commonly are used to consolidate the gains that have been made.

Outpatient Treatment. Far more people will be treated for mental disorders in outpatient settings than will be seen in inpatient or day treatment settings. A wide variety of outpatient treatment programs are available including private practice, community mental health centers (which also usually offer inpatient treatment), and agencies focused on specific populations (for example, women, children, people from a particular cultural or ethnic background) or problems (for example, anxiety disorders, phobias, relationship conflicts, or career concerns).

Current Trends. As for where treatment actually tends to take place, a variety of surveys indicate that admission to psychiatric hospitals has decreased substantially in the past forty-five years and that stays are much shorter than they were in the past (Butcher et al., 2006). The trend toward shorter inpatient stays pertains to adults, adolescents, and children alike. Managed care and the development of medications that effectively control the symptoms of severe disorders have contributed to the reduction in hospitalization. The introduction of managed care has resulted in a shift away from inpatient services to outpatient, day treatment, and community-based services (Ross, 2001). In six states, psychiatric readmission rates were higher under managed care, leading the U.S. Department of Health and Human Services to conclude that "increased hospital readmission rates may indicate persons with severe mental illness are being released from inpatient care too quickly" (U.S. Department of Health and Human Services, Office of Inspector General, 2000, p. 1). At the same time, shorter hospital stays have prevented some unnecessary and costly treatments and have enabled some people to live their lives more fully.

Interventions (DO A CLIENT MAP)

Once the clinician has identified the treatment setting for a particular person, the next step probably will be to determine the specific approaches and strategies that will guide treatment. A vast array of psychotherapeutic approaches is available to clinicians. According to Stricker and Gold (2006), more than four hundred different schools of psychotherapy have been advanced. However, few meaningful differences in outcomes seem to exist among therapies; on the contrary, therapies seem to have more similarities than differences. Earlier in this chapter, the overall effectiveness of psychotherapy was discussed. The findings of Lambert, Shapiro, and Bergin (1986) seem typical: outcome research suggests that 66 percent of clients improve, 26 percent are unchanged, and 8 percent are worse after therapy.

Once it was established that most people benefit from psychotherapy, the fundamental question became, "What forms of psychotherapy are most effective, and what are the common ingredients of their greater effectiveness?" Although conclusive answers still are not available, a considerable body of research concludes that such factors as the establishment of a healing process, a positive and collaborative therapeutic alliance, the client's hopefulness and belief that treatment can help, a credible treatment approach to address the client's symptoms, and the development of the client's self-efficacy and problem solving are key components of any successful therapy (Ahn & Wampold, 2001; Frank & Frank, 1991; Lambert & Bergin, 1994; Rogers, 1957; Rosenzweig, 1936; Wampold, 2001). Wampold (2001) conducted a meta-analysis of the literature and found that as much as 70 percent of the outcome variance between different models of therapy was attributable to these common factors shared by all successful therapies.

As we have seen, the differences in outcome are due more to the therapist, the client, and their alliance than to the particular theoretical model being used. Of course, the treatment approach and the strategies used do make an important contribution to outcome. The ability to maximize the effectiveness of psychotherapy, then, requires an understanding not only of therapeutic approaches and strategies but also of the client and clinician variables.

Theoretical Approaches. This chapter will now look at the most common theoretical orientations in practice today. A brief description of each, as well as of its application and effectiveness, is provided.

Psychoanalysis. Few studies are available on the effectiveness of classical psychoanalysis, partly because the lengthy and intense nature of the process means that each analyst can treat only a small number of clients. Therapists have generally been moving away from prolonged psychoanalysis and other treatments of long duration and toward the development of briefer psychotherapies. Nevertheless, a thirty-year study on the effectiveness of psychoanalysis was conducted by the Menninger Foundation in the 1980s. A high percentage (63 percent) of those who had been selected for psychoanalysis had good or moderate outcomes. Readers are referred to the Psychotherapy Research Project (Wallerstein, 1986) for further details.

Psychodynamic psychotherapy. As the use of long-term psychodynamic approaches has declined, brief psychodynamic psychotherapy has gained in popularity. The psychodynamic approach to treatment borrows heavily from the psychoanalytic model, but treatment with this approach takes less time, is more directive, and incorporates the use of other treatment techniques, such as cognitive therapy (Seligman, 2006).

Ideal clients for brief psychodynamic psychotherapy are motivated to change; willing to make a commitment to therapy; psychologically minded; able to tolerate and discuss painful feelings; intelligent; and in possession of good verbal skills, flexible and mature defenses, a focal issue; and have had at least one meaningful childhood relationship (Messer, 2001; Messer & Warren, 1995).

Typical outcomes of brief psychodynamic therapy include symptom relief, improved relationships, better self-esteem, greater insight and self-awareness, better problem-solving ability, and a sense of accomplishment (Budman, 1981). The approach provides a corrective emotional experience for people who are not severely dysfunctional but who may be suffering from depressive disorders, anxiety disorders (especially PTSD), adjustment disorder, stress, bereavement, and mild to moderate personality disorders (Goldfried, Greenberg, & Marmar, 1990). This approach is not recommended for treatment of severe depression that seems to have a biochemical basis, for psychotic disorders, for long-term substance misuse, and for borderline or other severe personality disorders.

Interpersonal psychotherapy (IPT) is an empirically validated form of brief psychodynamic therapy that has proven as effective as medication and cognitive therapy in the treatment of depression (Craighead, Hart, Craighead, & Ilardi, 2002; Sinha & Rush, 2006). Based on the work of Harry Stack Sullivan, IPT was designed by Gerald Klerman and colleagues specifically for the treatment of depression. It is a focused, time-limited treatment approach that emphasizes social and interpersonal experiences (Seligman, 2006). IPT has been successfully adapted for use with adolescents to decrease interpersonal problems and reduce substance use (Mufson, Dorta, Moreau, & Weissman, 2004). Readers are referred to Chapter Four for a more complete examination of IPT.

Behavior therapy. Many studies over the last thirty years have substantiated the value of behavior therapy. For example, exposure therapy has proven its effectiveness in the treatment of PTSD (Prochaska & Norcross, 2006). Exposure also is helpful in relieving symptoms of OCD. Systematic desensitization is helpful in treating symptoms of specific phobias and agoraphobia. Flooding, along with medication, has been shown to effect significant improvement in agoraphobia, although this approach must be used with great caution.

Behavior therapy also is effective in the treatment of conduct disorder, behavioral difficulties associated with mental retardation, enuresis, substance-related disorders, and family conflicts. Other disorders, including impulse-control disorders, sexual dysfunctions, oppositional defiant disorder, paraphilias, some sleep disorders, anxiety disorders, and mood disorders, are also likely to respond well to behavior therapy (Nathan & Gorman, 2002; Roth & Fonagy, 2005).

People most likely to benefit from behavior therapy are those who are motivated to change, follow through on homework tasks or self-help programs, and have friends and family members who are supportive of their efforts to change. The literature contains many positive reports of behavior therapy's effectiveness.

Nevertheless, assessment of the effectiveness of this treatment approach is complicated by its many strategies and variations. Duration of treatment and specific techniques are critical variables in the determination of the effectiveness of behavior therapy. For example, one two-hour session of in vivo exposure seems to be more effective than four half-hour sessions, and flooding can actually increase anxiety if it is not maintained long enough for the anxiety reaction to subside. Moreover, in the treatment of phobias, OCD, and sexual disorders, performance-based in vivo exposure methods are likely to be more effective than methods employing imaginal symbolic procedures. Support is better than confrontation in promoting clients' adherence to treatment plans in behavior therapy, but more research is needed before it can be determined exactly how this powerful treatment approach can best be used.

Cognitive and cognitive-behavioral therapy. Cognitive therapy, developed by Beck and his colleagues (Beck, Rush, Shaw, & Emery, 1979), has gained widespread acceptance for its effectiveness in the treatment of anxiety disorders, eating disorders, conduct disorder, substance-related disorders, personality disorders, and depression (Beck, 2005; Hollon & Beck, 2004).

Cognitive therapy assumes that people's thoughts are a dynamic representation of how they view themselves, their world, their past, and their future (in other words, their phenomenal field). Cognitive structures are viewed as the major determinants of people's affective states and behavioral patterns. Through cognitive therapy, people become aware of their cognitive distortions and correct their dysfunctional automatic thoughts and schemas, a correction that leads to overall improvement. The focus of treatment is on the present, and between-session tasks are important.

Cognitive therapy is often combined with behavior therapy, with the early rivalry between these two approaches having evolved into mutual appreciation and recognition of the value of their integration. Indeed, the efficacy of cognitive-behavioral therapy (CBT) in alleviating many disorders has been well documented (Hollon & Beck, 2004). CBT has been found to be as effective as medication in the treatment of depression and actually offers long-term advantages over medication in the reduction of relapse rates (Craighead, Hart, et al., 2002). White and Barlow (2002) report a meta analysis that included forty-three controlled studies of treatment for panic disorder with agoraphobia. The results showed that CBT was associated with the largest effect size. CBT also is the treatment of choice for treating bulimia (Wilson & Fairburn, 2002; Wilson, 2005).

Criticism of CBT has focused on concern that the therapy is a quick fix and does not involve insight or depth. Yet research indicates that CBT has lasting effectiveness, in some cases at least as long as seven years after the conclusion of therapy.

Other types of cognitive-behavioral therapies, such as rational emotive behavior therapy (REBT), developed by Ellis (Ellis & Greiger, 1996), and dialectical behavior therapy (DBT), created by Linehan (1993) in her work with clients with borderline personality disorder (BPD), have also achieved some success. Based on cognitive-behavioral therapy, DBT integrates considerable support and insight-oriented therapy into treatment (Seligman, 2006). Current research on the use of DBT with adolescents and others with suicidal ideation, depression, and self-harming behavior indicates that DBT is effective in reducing hospitalization rates, self-harming behaviors such as cutting, and depression (American Psychiatric Association, 2001; Meyer & Pilkonis, 2006; Robins, Ivanoff, & Linehan, 2001). DBT has also been adapted for treating eating disorders, antisocial personality disorder, and substance use comorbid with BPD (Rizvi & Linehan, 2001).

REBT has had little empirical research behind it, and appears to be less effective than exposure-based therapies for the treatment of some anxiety disorders, including agoraphobia, social anxiety, and OCD (Butcher et al., 2006). However, Johnson, Devries, Ridley, Pettorini, and Peterson (1994) conclude that REBT is successful in reducing depression, automatic negative thinking, irrational thinking, and general pathology in people with mild to moderate unipolar depression. REBT may be most helpful in teaching fairly healthy people to cope with stress.

Humanistic-experiential therapy. Humanistic-experiential therapies, beginning with Carl Rogers's person-centered therapy (1951, 1965), emphasize the importance of client experience to effect change. Humanistic therapies assume that people value self-determination and the ability to reflect on a problem, make choices, and take positive action. Humanistic-experiential therapists serve as facilitators or coaches to help people become aware of their feelings, label them, understand them, and develop new feelings and behaviors as a result. Enhancing their emotion processing skills helps people master and modulate their emotional arousal and ultimately expand their awareness and self-esteem (Gendlin, 1996; Greenberg & Watson, 2005).

Humanistic-experiential therapies include person-centered therapy, Gestalt therapy, process-experiential therapy, emotion-focused therapy, relationship enhancement therapy for couples, and motivational interviewing. Process-experiential therapy (PE) combines Gestalt therapy (Perls, 1969) with person-centered therapy. PE shows promise as the number of outcome studies increase.

PE seems to be particularly helpful in treating depression, anxiety, trauma, and relationship difficulties.

Motivational interviewing is a form of treatment developed by Miller (1983) as a way to help people resolve their ambivalence about change and commitment to treatment. It is based on the supportive and empathic style of person-centered therapy, which had its origins in the work of Carl Rogers. Motivational interviewing is most often used at the beginning of treatment for substance-related disorders. Roth and Fonagy (2005) report that it seems to work best when paired with a more extensive treatment approach, rather than used as a single intervention. Several studies have found that adding motivational interviewing to a substance use treatment program leads to higher retention rates during treatment and decreases relapse at three-month follow-up (Connors, Walitzer, & Dermen, 2002).

Until recently, little controlled research was available on the effectiveness of humanistic therapies, but as the number of controlled outcome studies increases, evidence suggests that these treatment approaches are effective in reducing symptoms and improving functioning in a range of problems, including alcohol misuse, anxiety disorders, personality disorders, interpersonal relationships, depression, coping with cancer, trauma, marital difficulties, and sometimes even schizophrenia (Bozarth, Zimring, & Tausch, 2001; Cain & Seeman, 2001; Elliot, 2001; Gottman, Coan, Carrere, & Swanson, 1998; S. Johnson, 2004).

In the largest meta-analysis of humanistic therapy outcomes, Elliott (2001) examined nearly one hundred studies and found reinforcement of the major conclusions reached by two earlier studies (Elliott, 1995; Greenberg, Elliott, & Lietaer, 1994). Humanistic therapies are effective; they are more effective than no treatment; and posttreatment gains remain stable at twelve-month follow-up. Elliott notes that CBT shows a modest superiority to person-centered therapy and nondirective supportive treatments, but that more process-directive therapies, such as Gestalt therapy, emotion focused therapy for couples, and process-experiential therapies, "are at least equivalent in effectiveness to CBT and may eventually turn out to be slightly superior" (p. 72). Elliott concludes that "with specific problems or particular groups, person-centered therapies proved to be as viable as the more goal-oriented therapies" (p. 168).

Other approaches to psychotherapy. Although most of the empirical research on psychotherapy's effectiveness has focused on the psychodynamic, behavioral, humanistic, and cognitive approaches, research is growing in other areas.

Lack of empirical research does not mean that a particular therapy is ineffective. On the contrary, research consistently indicates that no one theoretical orientation is significantly more effective than another overall. Other approaches that may also be effective include the following:

- *Adlerian* approaches, which have recently grown in popularity, are particularly useful in treating behavioral disorders of children, family and other interpersonal conflicts, mild depression and anxiety, and concerns focused on goals and direction.
- *Existential psychotherapy* is best suited to relatively well-functioning people with mild depression, mild anxiety, or situational concerns that raise questions about the meaning and direction of their lives. It is often useful for people coping with life-threatening illnesses as well as those struggling to find purpose in their lives.
- *Eastern-based therapies*. Therapies that synthesize Asian and Western perspectives are increasing in use. Transpersonal psychology has integrated many Asian theories and techniques into therapy. Many clinicians view meditation and yoga as integral to stress reduction and calming the mind and include them in their treatment plans. Walsh (2000; Walsh & Shapiro, 2006) notes that hundreds of studies have been conducted on these practices and that Asian therapies are second only to behavior therapies in the amount of empirical research on their effectiveness. Many Western therapies have begun to incorporate Eastern ideas, such as mindfulness (Linehan, 1993); acceptance (Eifert & Forsyth, 2005); emotional transformation (Goleman, 2003); and focusing, altruism, and service (Walsh, 2000). Indeed many clinical practices now offer meditation and yoga as part of a holistic approach to treatment. Walsh and Shapiro (2006) report research indicating that the following difficulties benefit from the practice of mindfulness meditation: insomnia, eating disorders, anxiety, panic and phobic disorders, aggression, and substance misuse.
- *Integrated approaches*. An integrative approach is one that combines treatment approaches and strategies in a logical, systematic way so as to maximize the chances of a positive therapeutic impact. This is different from a cookbook approach that specifies the use of certain types of therapy for certain disorders and is different from an eclectic approach that employs a fairly random and unsystematic array of interventions. Surveys of practice reflect a shift toward integrated or eclectic treatment. Nearly 30 percent of psychologists, 37 percent of counselors, and 34 percent of social workers describe their primary theoretical orientation as integrated or eclectic (Prochaska & Norcross, 2006).

Again, because no one therapeutic orientation has been found to be more effective than others, clinicians with a solid background in one primary theoretical orientation can draw from other theories and interventions to create treatment plans that seem most helpful for the current needs of a particular client (Seligman, 2006), or they can combine two complementary approaches into a new integrated treatment — for example, the blending of behavior therapy with experiential therapy in the creation of acceptance and commitment therapy (Eifert & Forsyth, 2005).

As we have seen, the existence of so many common factors in therapy suggest that there are not really hundreds of discrete approaches to psychotherapy but instead are many variations on a far smaller number of well-established themes. The existence of so many commonalities among therapeutic approaches raises an interesting issue: Are the differences among therapies genuine, and do these therapies have differential effectiveness? Or is any apparent differential effectiveness among therapies due more to particular therapists' effectiveness, if not to the chemistry of particular therapeutic relationships? Let's turn now to look in more detail at a very powerful factor in the success of therapy — the therapeutic alliance.

The Therapeutic Alliance. Discussion of interventions is not complete without discussion of the therapeutic alliance. Interventions to develop this alliance should be included in the treatment plan and are essential in shaping an effective approach to treatment.

In recent years, the therapeutic alliance has become one of the most researched variables in psychotherapy, with literally thousands of articles in the literature investigating aspects of the synergistic relationship that develops between the therapist and the client. Martin, Garske, and Davis (2000) believe that this interest has increased over the past twenty years as part of the effort to explain not only why therapy works but also why research consistently finds little difference in outcomes across therapeutic modalities.

A comprehensive review of the research surrounding the effect of the therapeutic alliance was conducted by the Division 29 Task Force of the American Psychological Association. The division's Steering Committee concluded (American Psychological Association Task Force Steering Committee, Division 29, 2001) that the empirical research supports the fact that the alliance works in conjunction with variables (such as therapist and client characteristics, and the selection of interventions) to create effective therapy; that therapist behaviors that enhance the alliance should be included in practice and treatment guidelines; and that tailoring the relationship to the needs of the client enhances treatment effectiveness.

Specific elements of the therapeutic relationship found to be "demonstrably effective" (therapeutic alliance, cohesion in group therapy, empathy, goals consensus, and collaboration); and "promising and probably effective" (positive regard, congruence/genuineness, feedback, repair of alliance ruptures, self-disclosure, management of countertransference, and quality of relational interpretations) (p. 495). These elements are provided mainly by the therapist and are common to almost all psychotherapeutic approaches. The Division 29 Task Force recommends practitioners incorporate these elements into their treatment of clients and "make the creation and cultivation of a therapy relationship characterized by the elements found to be demonstrably and probably effective ... a primary aim in the treatment of patients" (p. 496).

To what extent the therapeutic alliance contributes to successful outcomes in therapy remains a mystery, confounded by definitions of variables, theoretical definitions, and research methodology. Research studies rate the alliance as responsible for anywhere from less than 10 percent to as much as 30 percent of the variance in therapeutic outcome (Horvath & Laborsky, 1993; Lambert & Barley, 2001; Martin et al., 2000). Martin and colleagues conducted a meta-analytic review of seventy-nine studies of the therapeutic alliance and found that although the alliance had only a modest effect on outcomes (0.22), the effect is consistent across large numbers of studies and is not linked to many other variables. The authors validate the hypothesis that "the alliance may be therapeutic in and of itself" (p. 446).

In other words, if a good alliance is formed between client and therapist, the client will experience the relationship as therapeutic regardless of which treatment approach is used. Krupnick and colleagues (1996) found that even when the primary intervention is medication, the therapeutic alliance is still important to outcomes.

Establishing an alliance. Nelson and Neufeldt (1996) found that the development of a productive working alliance is facilitated by role induction (helping people learn how to be clients and to make good use of their sessions), by open disclosure of the therapist's background and procedures, by the therapist's and the client's agreement on realistic goals and tasks, and by the therapist's asking the client for feedback. Role induction also seems helpful in the development of attitudes in clients that are conducive to a positive outcome. In role induction, clients are oriented to the therapeutic process and are given clear information on what is expected of them, what the therapist can offer, and what therapy will probably be like. The client's engagement in the therapeutic process is a variable that is correlated with a positive therapeutic outcome. Miller, Hubble, and Duncan (1997) emphasize the importance of the client having a positive perception of the therapist, believing that the focus is on his or her goals and expectations, and of being comfortable with the pace of treatment; also important is the ability of the client and the therapist to view themselves as engaged in a common endeavor likely to succeed.

Research consistently indicates that the therapeutic alliance is a necessary but not sufficient condition for effecting desired changes and positive therapeutic outcomes. Horvath and Symonds (1991) conclude that a successful therapeutic alliance makes it possible for the client to accept and follow the treatment faithfully and bridges the gap between process and outcome. The conditions conducive to a positive therapeutic alliance have been discussed earlier in this chapter, but therapists should not limit their attention to those conditions; they should also attend to clients' preferences.

Bordin (1979) suggests three important aspects of the therapeutic alliance:

1. An affective bond between the client and therapist
2. Agreement between client and therapist about the goals of treatment
3. A sense of working collaboratively on the problem

The alliance across various therapies and modalities. Research consistently shows the importance of the therapeutic alliance in achieving good outcomes across all treatment methodologies (Barber, Connolly, Crits-Christoph, Gladys, & Siqueland, 2000). A review of empirical studies of cognitive-behavioral therapy (Keijsers, Schaap, & Hoogduin, 2000) notes two clusters of therapist behaviors that are associated with successful outcomes in CBT: the conditions of warmth, empathy, positive regard, and genuineness, first set forth by Rogers, and the formation of a positive and collaborative therapeutic alliance.

Forming a therapeutic alliance when working with families requires different skills from when working with individuals, and often involves establishing multiple alliances across a multigenerational system. Beck, Friedlander, and Escudero (2006) note that no single alliance should be considered in isolation because "a therapist's alliance with each family member affects and is affected by the alliance with all other family members" (p. 355).

Multiple studies on the alliance between therapist and families have found that a strong alliance was more likely to occur if the following conditions were met:

- The family agreed with the therapist on goals, had confidence that treatment would bring about positive change, and developed a good emotional connection with the therapist.
- The therapist promoted rapport and exhibited warmth.
- The therapist was optimistic and had a sense of humor.
- The therapist was active in sessions (Beck, Friedlander, & Escudero, 2006).

Reinforcing findings from individual therapy, Quinn, Dotson, and Jordan (1997) showed that a strong therapeutic alliance was more important than technique in family therapy and that the client's perception, rather than the therapist's perception, is the best predictor of treatment outcome. However, in their study of family research, Quinn and colleagues found that the woman's perception of the alliance was more important than the man's perception in predicting outcome.

Conversely, a weak alliance between the family system and the therapist was found when a family member had distrust of the counseling process or when there was disagreement over goals. Robbins, Turner, and Alexander (2003) showed that much like that in individual therapy, the therapeutic alliance in family therapy is also created early on — in the first three or four sessions — and is also predictive of outcome.

Clients' perceptions of the alliance. Clients' perceptions of the quality of the therapeutic alliance are formed early and tend to be stable. They are more highly correlated with therapeutic outcome than therapists' or observers' perceptions of the quality of the therapeutic alliance (Martin et al., 2000). Because clients who rate the alliance as positive are more likely to stay in therapy, to have positive outcomes, and to rate therapy as helpful, establishing an effective therapeutic alliance should be one of the most important, if not the most important, goals of the therapist from the beginning of treatment.

No Treatment. Sometimes the best intervention is no intervention at all. Despite the demonstrated effectiveness of therapy, an estimated 5 to 10 percent of people who receive psychotherapy deteriorate during treatment (Lambert & Ogles, 2004). Although little research is available on the negative effects of psychotherapy, no treatment may be the best recommendation for the following people:

- People at risk for a negative response to treatment (for example, people with severe narcissistic, borderline, obsessive-compulsive, self-destructive, or oppositional personality patterns)
- People with a history of treatment failures
- People who want to support a lawsuit or a disability claim and thus may have an investment in failing to make progress
- People at risk for no response (for example, people who are poorly motivated and not incapacitated, people with malingering or factitious disorder, and those who seem likely to regress as a result of the therapeutic process)
- People likely to show spontaneous improvement (for example, healthy people in crisis or with minor concerns)

- People likely to benefit from strategic use of the no-treatment recommendation (for example, people with oppositional patterns who are refusing treatment and people whose adaptive defenses would be supported by a recommendation of no treatment)

The no-treatment recommendation is intended to protect clients from harm, prevent clients and therapists from wasting their time, delay therapy until clients are more receptive to it, support prior gains, and give people the message that they can survive without therapy. Although this option may make theoretical sense, clinicians do not seem to use it with any frequency, at least partly because of the great difficulty of predicting who will not benefit from therapy and the risk involved in discouraging people from beginning therapy when they may really be able to make good use of it. Nevertheless, therapists may want to give more consideration to this recommendation, especially in light of the current emphasis on short-term productive treatment.

Emphasis (DO A CLIENT MAP)

The multitude of approaches to psychotherapy reflects only one aspect of the diversity that exists in treatment interventions. Variation in the implementation of therapies also greatly increases the diversity of approaches. Clinicians adapt models of psychotherapy to their own personal styles and individualize treatments to meet the needs of particular clients. Therefore, the application of an approach to psychotherapy differs from one therapeutic relationship to another. The dimensions discussed in this section reflect some of the ways to adapt treatment to an individual.

Directive Versus Evocative. The directive approach can be viewed as encompassing cognitive and behavior therapies and such techniques as systematic desensitization, flooding, positive reinforcement (including token economies, contingency contracting, and extinction), strategic techniques (such as suggestion, paradox, and metaphor), humor, homework tasks, and bibliotherapy (Malik et al., 2003). In all these approaches the therapist assumes an authoritative stance, clearly defines target concerns, and designs a specific program to change overt and covert symptoms.

A study by Malik and colleagues (2003) found that psychodynamic therapy was the least directive of eight therapies examined. Psychoanalysis is characterized by a therapist who is clearly an authority figure, but such psychoanalytic techniques as free association are evocative or experiential. The focused-expressive therapies, such as humanistic, experiential, or person-centered models, were also low on directiveness and high on evocativeness, focusing on the therapist-client interaction and encouraging clients to choose their own topics or modes of processing. Those approaches emphasize such processes as catharsis and abreaction, ventilation, empathy and reflection of feeling, support, affection, praise, and unconditional positive regard.

Two clients are used here to illustrate how treatment emphasis differs, depending on the client. Both Anne and Bettie have similar presenting problems. Each is a woman in her early twenties who has sought counseling after a broken engagement, but their circumstances and their views of therapy are very different and thus warrant different levels of directiveness.

Anne is in her second month of an unplanned pregnancy. She is receiving little help from her family or from her former fiancé. She is unemployed and is living with a single friend who has two children. Anne is not sure what she wants to do about her pregnancy and has been using alcohol as a way to avoid thinking about her difficulties. She has not had previous therapy and is uncertain of why the nurse with whom she spoke at an abortion clinic has referred her to a counselor, although she is motivated to get some help.

Bettie's situation is quite different. Although she too is depressed that her former fiancé ended their engagement, she views this as a time to review her goals. She believes that she focused too much of her time and energy on her fiancé and has neglected her career and her education. She is interested in returning to college, learning more about some of her aptitudes and preferences, and establishing a better balance between her social life and her career. At the same time, she is angry that she feels a need for therapy, and her disappointment in her former fiancé has led her to feel mistrustful of others.

Anne does not have the leisure or the sense of direction for an evocative approach. She needs a directive therapist, not to tell her what to do about her pregnancy, but to give her a structure for expediting her decision making and helping her gain some control of her life. In addition, her use of alcohol is endangering her unborn child and creates urgency in this situation. Bettie, by contrast, would be more amenable to experiential or person-centered therapy, which would afford her the opportunity to engage in self-examination and goal setting.

In general, a directive approach has been correlated with a focus on goal attainment and with lower than average levels of therapeutic alliance (Malik et al., 2003). Alternatively, an evocative approach seems more likely to be successful with people who are self-directed and more able to participate in a sound alliance between client and therapist (Beutler & Consoli, 1993; Malik et al., 2003).

Exploration Versus Support. This is another dimension that has received little but theoretical examination in the literature. Nevertheless, it is often cited as an important aspect of treatment (Rockland, 2003; Wallerstein, 1986).

The dimension of exploration versus support, like the dimension of directiveness versus evocativeness, exists on a continuum. Approaches that emphasize exploration typically are probing, interpretive, and analytical, stressing the importance of insight, growth, and an understanding of past influences and patterns. By contrast, approaches that emphasize support tend to be present-oriented, symptom-focused, and more action-oriented. Psychoanalysis and psychodynamic psychotherapy, using such techniques as free association, analysis of transference, examination of dreams, and interpretation, emphasize exploration. The other end of the continuum is represented by the behavioral model, with its focus on the present, on circumscribed and measurable changes, and on reinforcement of positive coping mechanisms. Person-centered counseling, although less action-oriented, also reflects a supportive approach in which client strengths and self-direction are reinforced.

Models at each end of the continuum, of course, as well as those in the middle, inevitably include both exploration and support. They are distinguished by the balance between exploration and support rather than by the absence of one or the other. Rockland (2003), for example, outlines a psychodynamic approach to supportive therapy that provides both supportive and exploratory interventions. By tailoring the appropriate levels of support to the client's needs, Rockland focuses on improving ego functioning, reality testing, and clarity of thought, rather than attempting to resolve unconscious conflicts.

One of the few studies of this dimension of therapy was conducted by Wallerstein (1986), who concluded that insight is not always necessary for change. In 45 percent of the cases he examined, changes that were achieved seemed to go beyond the amount of insight that was attained, whereas insight surpassed discerned change in only 7 percent of these cases. Overall, Wallerstein concluded, supportive therapy was more effective in these cases than had been expected, and it did not seem to be less effective than exploratory therapy.

Bettie and Anne, the clients discussed earlier, need different levels of exploration. Bettie, a strong client who is interested in personal growth and introspection, is a good candidate for an approach that is at least moderately probing in nature, such as brief psychodynamic therapy. Anne, by contrast, needs a more supportive approach that will help reduce the stress she is experiencing and enable her to draw on her existing strengths to cope with her situation.

Other Aspects of Emphasis. Other aspects of emphasis include the balance of treatment focus on past, present, and future and the relative attention paid to developing the therapeutic alliance, among others. Emphasis also entails considering how to adapt a treatment approach to a specific person. For example, a clinician may use CBT with many clients but will apply that approach differently for each one. When considering emphasis in developing treatment plans, then, clinicians should also give some thought to what elements of the chosen theoretical orientation will be emphasized and which will be downplayed as treatment progresses. For example, CBT with Anne might focus primarily on behavior, whereas CBT with Bettie probably would pay more attention to thoughts.

Although most therapists probably make intuitive judgments of whether their clients will benefit from high or low levels of exploration and high or low levels of support, and of which aspects of treatment to stress, more research on these dimensions would facilitate effective treatment planning.

Numbers (DO A CLIENT MAP)

The therapist must also decide who will be treated. Some disorders, such as OCD, are best resolved with individual therapy; others, such as oppositional defiant disorder or substance use disorders, are best treated with a family therapy component. Group treatment is another consideration.

Individual Psychotherapy. Individual psychotherapy certainly has demonstrated its effectiveness. Individual therapy seems to be the modality of choice for people whose intrapsychic difficulties cause them repetitive life problems, for people in crisis or with urgent concerns, for people with problems that might cause them distress or embarrassment in a group setting, and for people who are vulnerable, passive, and low in self-esteem (Clarkin, Frances, & Perry, 1992). Although individual therapy is generally a safe choice, it does have certain limitations. It does not offer the client the opportunity to receive feedback from anyone but the therapist, it gives the therapist only one source of information about the client, it encourages transference reactions, it affords little chance to address family dynamics, and it offers only a limited opportunity to try out new interpersonal behaviors in therapy sessions.

Group Psychotherapy. Group therapy has been shown to be effective for a variety of different problems (Pines & Schlapobersky, 2000), including substance-related disorders, eating disorders, and borderline personality disorder (Linehan, 1993). In the past, efforts were made to determine what makes group therapy effective and to compare the impact of group and individual therapy. Studies of therapeutic factors and processes contributing to clients' improvement, such as self-disclosure, insight, catharsis, interaction, and acceptance/cohesiveness, all yielded ambiguous results. Perhaps both the nature of the group and the client- and therapist-related variables are so powerful in determining outcome in both group and individual treatment that few conclusions can be drawn about group therapy in general (Bloch, Crouch, & Reibstein, 1981). More recent research tends not to distinguish between individual and group formats in determining empirically supported treatments (Chambless & Ollendick, 2001; Malik et al., 2003).

Group therapy does, however, seem to be effective from both cost and outcome standpoints. In general, studies find its impact to be comparable to that of individual therapy. Fenster (1993) suggests that group psychotherapy usually should be the treatment of choice for interpersonal problems, including loneliness, competitiveness, shyness, aggressiveness, and withdrawal, as well as for people who have problems with intimacy and authority. Group therapy offers an environment more like everyday life and therefore provides an arena for interaction and learning from others. Group therapy can promote self-esteem, reduce resistance, and diffuse feelings of differentness and shame.

In deciding whether a particular person is likely to benefit from group psychotherapy, therapists need to consider not only the impact of the group on the client but also the impact of the client on the group. Ideal clients for group therapy seem to be those who are motivated, aware of their interpersonal difficulties, capable of taking some responsibility for their concerns, and able to give and accept feedback. People who are extremely aggressive, confused, self-centered, or fearful of others may have a harmful impact on group interaction and are unlikely to derive much benefit from that process. If group therapy is used at all with clients like these, it probably should be deferred until they have made noticeable progress in individual or family psychotherapy.

Therapy groups may be either heterogeneous (composed of people with different problems) or homogeneous (composed of people with similar problems). People with similar disorders and problems can often learn coping skills from each other, benefit from feedback and modeling, and receive support and validation. Heterogeneous groups often focus on group interaction and help people build interpersonal skills.

Couples and Family Therapy. Research has demonstrated that couples therapy and family therapy are effective in general and may be superior to alternative treatment modalities for some problems and disorders (Accordino & Guerney, 2001; Pinsof & Wynne, 2000). Johnson and Boisvert (2001) report that the empirically supported interventions for couples include emotion-focused couples therapy (Greenberg & Johnson, 1988; S. Johnson, 2004) and relationship enhancement therapy (Guerney, 1977, 1994).

Family therapy, of course, is often indicated for problems that stem from, are affected by, and have an impact on the family system. Empirical research has found specific types of family therapy to be an integral part of the successful treatment of many disorders, including schizophrenia, major depressive disorder (Evans et al., 2005) and anorexia nervosa (Wilson & Fairburn, 2002). Children and adolescents seen for therapy will usually have family therapy as a component of their treatment, especially for conduct disorder, oppositional defiant disorder, and ADHD (Anastopoulos & Farley, 2003). People with disorders that seem to have a genetic or familial component, such as substance-related disorders, bipolar disorders (Miklowitz & Goldstein, 1997; Sachs, 2004), and OCD, are also likely to benefit from family therapy. Additional information on each of these disorders and the integration of family therapy into treatment planning is delineated in the relevant chapters of this book.

Research continues on the appropriate uses of these treatment modalities, but most of the information in the literature about the respective strengths and benefits of the three primary modalities of therapy — individual, group, and family — is inferential. The following list summarizes this information, showing the client groups for which each of the modalities is recommended:

Individual Counseling	*Group Therapy*	*Family Therapy*
Highly anxious, withdrawn, isolated, or introverted clients; people who have difficulty with ambiguity; people seeking help with intrapsychic concerns; extremely suspicious, guarded, hostile, paranoid, or destructive people who have difficulty with trust; people seeking independence and individuation; people with very	Anxious clients with authority concerns; people with pervasive personality dysfunction who have made progress in individual therapy; people with interpersonal concerns; people who may feel stigmatized or scapegoated as a result of individual therapy (such as the identified patient in a family); people who are likely to give the	People who have problems with family structure and dynamics; people with intergenerational or other family conflicts; families with communication problems; families needing consolidation; acting-out adolescents; families with limited resources, when more than one family member needs help; families with no

intimate or idiosyncratic concerns; people with concerns of very long duration in which improvement rather than maintenance is sought; people in crisis	therapist excessive power; people who need reality testing and group feedback; people with specific behavioral concerns (such as eating disorders or alcohol dependence) that are shared with other group members; people with limited financial resources; people who have been through traumatic experiences that also have been experienced by others in their treatment group	severe pathology; children; families with a member who has a chronic or recurrent mental disorder

Timing (DO A CLIENT MAP)

The typical client is seen once a week for a session of forty-five to fifty minutes in length, but the frequency of therapy sessions can vary. One session every other week is often used in supportive therapy, particularly toward the end of treatment, whereas clients in psychoanalysis commonly have five sessions per week. The duration of therapy also varies widely, of course, and is often difficult to predict.

The limited research comparing long-term treatment with short-term treatment is either specific to one treatment modality and one disorder (such as dialectical behavior therapy for borderline personality disorder) or combines many studies across a broad range of disorders. For example, Hansen and Lambert (2003) looked at nearly five thousand people in various outpatient settings and found that half achieved significant change in fifteen to nineteen sessions. A similar study of seventy-five people estimated that eleven sessions was the average number for 50 percent of the people to achieve significant change (Anderson & Lambert, 2001).

Bloom (2001) reviewed outcome studies on a single session of treatment. The results indicated that only clients with relationship problems benefited from a single in-depth treatment session. A study by Kadera, Lambert, and

Andrews (1996) found that the average time for recovery was eleven sessions (with 76 percent of those who would recover doing so by thirteen sessions), and that all who were going to recover had done so by twenty-five sessions.

Overall, approximately 50 percent of clients showed measurable improvement after eight sessions of therapy, 75 percent after twenty-six sessions, and 85 percent after one year of treatment (Howard, Kopta, Krause, & Orlinsky, 1986). Orlinsky and Howard (1986) conducted meta-analyses of studies that looked at the relationship between length of therapy and therapeutic outcome. They concluded that the total number of sessions — and, to a lesser extent, duration of treatment — are positively correlated with therapeutic benefit. Not all studies show the same relationship, however, and a small number show a curvilinear relationship between outcome and number of sessions.

Research has yet to indicate an optimum length of treatment for specific disorders. Relevant studies are informative but incomplete. Clearly, more empirical research is necessary to determine the most effective length of treatment for people with specific disorders. Typically, short-term therapy is not just less long-term therapy; the goals, the treatment interventions, the disorders, and the clients themselves are likely to differ. Therefore, research must consider presenting problems, diagnoses, client profiles, and other variables when the research question is one of determining outcomes on the basis of therapy's duration.

Today's emphasis on short-term therapy has increased the importance of studying approaches to brief treatment and determining the people for whom they are suitable. Many studies have demonstrated that short-term treatment can have a significant and lasting positive impact, but that is only the case for some clients and some disorders (Bloom, 2002; Cameron et al., 1999; Lambert & Anderson, 1996). Roberts (2002), for example, found that brief therapy is indicated in the immediate aftermath of a crisis, such as a suicide attempt, trauma, or national disaster such as occurred on September 11. Bloom (2002) reviewed fifty-nine outcome studies on the effectiveness of brief therapy and found that four to sixteen sessions of therapy benefited people who had anxiety disorders. Short-term cognitive therapy seems to be appropriate when problems are related to stress, dysfunctional behaviors, academic problems, interpersonal difficulties, and career concerns (Littrell, Malia, & Vanderwood, 1995), and brief psychodynamic psychotherapy is suitable for both chronic and nonchronic depression (Luborsky et al., 1996). In fact, 10 to 18 percent of clients improve before the first session of therapy just by virtue of having made contact with a potential source of help (Howard et al., 1986).

When determining whether brief therapy will be appropriate, Lambert and Anderson (1996) suggest that the following criteria should be considered:

- The nature and severity of the disorder
- The client's readiness to change
- The client's ego strength
- The client's motivation for an enduring therapeutic relationship
- The client's ability to relate to the therapist

Other researchers confirm that a thorough assessment at the beginning of treatment is essential to determine appropriateness of fit for brief therapy (Corcoran & Boyer-Quick, 2002). In general, clients with fewer symptoms and better pretreatment functioning achieve better results faster than those with more serious disorders (Roth & Fonagy, 2005).

Typically people who are motivated, who do not have personality disorders, and who have a focal concern or crisis, a positive history, good ego functioning, and a sound ability to relate well to others and express their emotions make good clients for short-term therapy.

People for whom short-term therapy usually is not indicated are those who are very hostile, paranoid, or psychotic or who have long standing, severe problems. Eating disorders, bipolar disorders, dysthymic disorder, borderline personality disorder, and antisocial personality disorder are examples of disorders that generally do not respond well to short-term therapy.

In general, short-term therapy seems likely to be effective with a substantial percentage of clients (approximately 75 percent); in fact, time-limited treatment can encourage people to be more focused and to make more rapid progress. Again, however, candidates for this approach to treatment must be carefully selected.

Medications (DO A CLIENT MAP)

As already mentioned, this book is directed primarily toward nonmedical clinicians, who do not themselves prescribe medication as part of the treatment they provide. Nevertheless, nonmedical clinicians who understand the role that medication can play in the treatment of mental disorders can determine when a client's progress might be accelerated by a referral for a medication evaluation and collaboration with a physician, usually a psychiatrist. For clients who are taking medication for mental disorders, ongoing assessment of medication compliance often is an important part of psychotherapy and reflects a holistic approach to treatment (Pratt & Mueser, 2002).

Research indicates that the combination of psychotherapy and medication can increase the effectiveness of treatment for some disorders (Jindal & Thase, 2003). For example, people with schizophrenia who receive medication as well as other interventions have reduced symptom levels, improved executive function, and lower rates of relapse and rehospitalization. Baker, Patterson, and Barlow (2002) and Evans and colleagues (2005) report that medication can enhance the effectiveness of cognitive-behavioral interventions in the treatment of severe anxiety and panic disorders.

Kendall and Lipman (1991) found that psychotherapy and medication can have a synergistic relationship, especially in the treatment of major depressive disorder. The medication acts first and, by energizing clients and promoting some optimism, enables them to make better use of psychotherapy; the impact of the therapy in turn promotes compliance with the recommended drug treatment. According to these researchers, antidepressant medications are particularly helpful in reducing the likelihood of relapse and in treating vegetative symptoms, while the psychotherapy aids with many facets of adjustment and coping. Although the effects of the therapy may take longer to appear than the effects of the medication, the effects of the therapy are likely to last longer.

Medication, combined with therapy, seems particularly useful for disorders involving debilitating anxiety, endogenous (melancholic) depression, mania, or psychosis. Therapy alone may be all that is needed in treating problems involving adjustment, behavior, relationships, mild to moderate anxiety, reactive depression, and some personality disorders. Many disorders in the second group, however, such as eating disorders, some personality disorders, and impulse-control disorders, are often accompanied by underlying depression. Medication is increasingly being used along with therapy to enhance the impact of psychotherapy on the primary diagnosis by alleviating the underlying symptoms.

Psychotropic medications can be divided into the following five groups (Preston, O'Neal, & Talaga, 2005):

1. *Antipsychotic medications*. These drugs are primarily for the treatment of schizophrenia and other disorders involving delusions and hallucinations. People with Tourette's disorder, pervasive developmental disorders, and severe cognitive disorders also can benefit from these drugs. This category includes the phenothiazines (such as Thorazine, Prolixin, Mellaril, and Stelazine); such antipsychotic drugs as clozapine (Clozaril), haloperidol (Haldol), and risperidone (Risperdal); and newer atypical antipsychotic medications with better tolerability and fewer extrapyramidal symptoms, including ziprasidone (Geodon), olanzapine (Zyprexa), and aripiprazole (Abilify).

2. *Antidepressant medications*. These drugs fall into the following groups:

a. Tricyclic and heterocyclic antidepressants, which facilitate the treatment of moderate to severe major depressive disorder (especially with melancholia); enuresis; trichotillomania; panic attacks; bipolar depression; and eating, sleep, and obsessive-compulsive disorders. Examples of this type of drug include imipramine (Tofranil), clomipramine (Anafranil), and amitriptyline (Elavil).

b. Monoamine oxidase inhibitors (MAOIs), such as phenelzine (Nardil) and tranylcypromine (Parnate), which are often effective with atypical depressions, severe phobias, anxiety disorders, panic disorder, obsessional thinking, hypochondriasis, and depersonalization disorder. They are also used to treat disorders that have not responded to other antidepressant medication.

c. Selective serotonin reuptake inhibitors (SSRIs) are effective in the treatment of depression, as well as of such disorders as eating and somatoform disorders that are accompanied by underlying depression. They may also be effective in reducing anxiety, especially when it is combined with depression. This category includes fluoxetine (Prozac), sertraline (Zoloft), citalopram (Celexa), fluvoxamine (Luvox), and paroxetine (Paxil).

d. Serotonin and norepinephrine reuptake inhibitors (SNRIs) affect levels of both serotonin and norepinephrine. SNRIs include venlafaxine (Effexor), duloxetine (Cymbalta), and mirtazapine (Remeron). SNRIs may be more effective than SSRIs in the treatment of severe depression (Preston et al., 2005).

e. Bupropion (Wellbutrin) is an atypical antidepressant that is frequently used in combination with an SSRI.

3. *Mood stabilizers*. Lithium, the best-known mood stabilizer, is effective in reducing symptoms of mania, depression, and mood instability. Newer mood stabilizers include topiramate (Topamax), divalproex (Depakote), and lamotrigine (Lamictal). They are used for treatment of bipolar disorders, cyclothymic disorder, and schizoaffective disorder.

4. *Benzodiazepine/antianxiety drugs*. These medications are used for reduction of anxiety, panic attacks, and insomnia. They also can facilitate withdrawal from drugs or alcohol and can enhance the impact of antipsychotic medication. Examples of these drugs are alprazolam (Xanax), lorazepam (Ativan), diazepam (Valium), and clonazepam (Klonopin). Some of these drugs are highly addictive and dangerous and so must be prescribed and used with great care.

5. *Other drugs.* Additional drugs helpful in the treatment of mental disorders include methylphenidate (Ritalin), atomoxetine (Strattera), and amphetamine mixed salts (Adderall) for the treatment of ADHD and naltrexone (ReVia) and Methadone for prevention of misuse of alcohol and narcotics, respectively. Benzodiazepines are sometimes helpful in the treatment of irritability and agitation associated with withdrawal from substances. If withdrawal is accompanied by psychosis or paranoia, antipsychotic medications may also be helpful.

Electroconvulsive therapy (ECT) also is mentioned here because of its beneficial use in the treatment of severe depression, particularly when psychotherapy and medication have failed, and especially when the depression is characterized by melancholia or accompanied by psychotic features. Although ECT has some worrisome side effects, these have been reduced over the years, and this treatment can bring benefit to people with treatment-resistant depression.

Adjunct Services (DO A CLIENT MAP)

Adjunct services can provide additional sources of support, education, and training. Parent skills training, for example, can be a useful adjunct to treatment for conduct disorder and reinforces what the child learns in therapy. Nutrition counseling can help people with eating disorders develop realistic goals that are appropriate to their weight and type of disordered eating. A person who has lost a family member to suicide might benefit by attending a peer support group with people with similar losses. And twelve-step programs such as Narcotics Anonymous or Alcoholics Anonymous can help people with substance-related disorders during the recovery process.

Adjunct services can also be suggested for family members. For example, families coping with a diagnosis of autism or a schizophrenia spectrum disorder might benefit from receiving psychoeducation about the disorder and attending caregiver support groups. Couples counseling or family counseling often helps family members understand the client better. For example, a woman with dependent personality disorder might benefit by participating in concurrent individual and couples counseling, to help her husband understand and support the changes she is trying to make.

All adjunct services should reinforce the goals the client is working on. Whether it is an exercise program, volunteer activities to improve socialization, bibliotherapy, or biofeedback to help people recognize bodily sensations, the types of services suggested should reinforce progress that a client is making in individual therapy. Between-session assignments can help clients get the most out of their sessions. For example, those who are technologically savvy might use computerized logs and journals to chart progress or participate in Internet support groups between therapy sessions to help them stay on task. The

Internet has become one of the leading providers of health care information, and clients can reinforce their efforts through special forums, support groups, and online resources relating to their areas of concern.

Near the conclusion of treatment, therapists might want to refer clients to adjunct services to begin work on secondary issues that have been raised in therapy but were not the central focus of attention. Referrals for marital counseling, family therapy, assertiveness training, or career counseling might be appropriate at this time, depending on the person's goals.

Myriad types of adjunct services are available to suit the distinct needs of each client and the timing of treatment. Less well functioning clients might need assistance in obtaining government services, such as legal aid or housing assistance, or referrals might be needed for inpatient hospitalization or day treatment. Therapists who creatively and diligently stay abreast of the available community resources will be able to refer clients to the appropriate services as needs arise.

Prognosis (DO A CLIENT MAP)

Prognosis refers to the likelihood that clients will achieve their objectives when treated according to the plan that has been developed to help them. Prognosis depends largely on two variables: the nature and severity of the disorders and problems and the client's motivations to make positive changes.

EXAMPLES OF TREATMENT PLANNING: ANNE AND BETTIE

Application of the preceding information on treatment planning to the cases of Bettie and Anne (discussed earlier in this chapter) should clarify the type of treatment likely to benefit each of them. This format, with examples of Client Maps for specific disorders, will be followed in subsequent chapters of the book.

Client Maps of Anne and Bettie

Although both women are coping with broken engagements, Anne is also dealing with an unplanned pregnancy, and she has used alcohol and avoidance as coping mechanisms. Bettie, by contrast, has more self-confidence and more personal resources, and she is able to view her unexpected change in plans as an opportunity for personal growth.

Both women probably would benefit from short-term therapy. Bettie should be seen weekly; she has significant concerns but is in no danger. Anne should be seen more frequently, until she has resolved her immediate crisis and dealt successfully with her alcohol use. Bettie is more self-directed. Although she does evidence some cognitive dysfunction, resistance, and mild depression,

Bettie may respond well to a modified form of person-centered therapy that encourages her to develop her self-confidence and her self-awareness and to establish goals and direction, as well as interpersonal skills. Anne, by contrast, is less motivated toward self-exploration and is primarily interested in resolving her immediate concerns. Her therapy will probably focus more on cognitive-behavioral areas, emphasizing decision making and behavioral change.

Anne seems likely to respond best to individual therapy because she is in crisis, must make a rapid decision about her pregnancy, and is not currently interested in personal growth and development. Bettie, however, would probably benefit from either individual or group psychotherapy, or from a combination of the two — perhaps short-term individual therapy followed by participation in a personal growth group for women or a psychotherapy group for young adults.

Neither Anne nor Bettie seems to need medication, although Anne's therapist should make sure that Anne is receiving any necessary medical care and is aware of the risks of her alcohol use. Both Anne and Bettie are capable of self-regulation and are in touch with reality. An outpatient treatment setting, such as a community mental health center or a private practice, seems an appropriate location for treatment. Adjunct services, such as Alcoholics Anonymous and even inpatient treatment, may be considered for Anne if her alcohol misuse is severe enough.

After their immediate concerns have been resolved, both Bettie and Anne may decide to continue treatment, but their goals are likely to differ. Bettie will probably seek to improve her relationship skills, clarify her goals and direction, and enhance her self-esteem. Anne will probably need to develop better coping mechanisms and greater independence and may need to look at past issues to understand and change her poor choices.

The research on therapeutic variables does not yield definitive descriptions of the exact types of psychotherapy that would be best for each of these women. Nevertheless, it does offer guidelines for designing a treatment plan likely to be effective for each of them. Following are Client Maps for Anne and Bettie.

Client Map of Anne

Diagnosis

Axis I: 296.23 Major depressive disorder, single episode, severe, without psychotic features

305.00 Alcohol abuse

Axis II: Dependent personality traits

Axis III: No known physical disorders or conditions, but pregnancy reported

Axis IV: End of engagement, unplanned pregnancy, housing problems, unemployed

Axis V: Global assessment of functioning (GAF Scale): current GAF = 45

Objectives of Treatment

Establish and maintain abstinence from alcohol

Provide direction and structure so client can determine best outcome of pregnancy

Reduce stress

Stabilize living situation

Locate suitable employment

Improve coping skills

Assessments

Thorough medical evaluation to determine impact of alcohol use on pregnancy

Michigan Alcohol Screening Test

Clinician Characteristics

Knowledgeable about the development and symptoms of alcohol abuse

Structured and directive

Skilled at setting goals and direction

Able to promote motivation, independence, and optimism

Location of Treatment

Outpatient

Consider inpatient treatment if alcohol abuse worsens

Interventions to Be Used

Motivational therapy at the start, to enhance compliance with treatment plan

Cognitive-behavioral therapy

Emphasis of Treatment

Initial directive and supportive emphasis

Emphasis on cognitions and behavior

Numbers

Primarily individual therapy

Timing

Rapid pace

Longer duration (more than six months) to address issues of relapse prevention and dependence

Twice weekly sessions until client is out of crisis and more stable

Medications Needed

None

Adjunct Services

Support group to develop social and coping skills and provide support

Homework assignments

Twelve-step program such as Alcoholics Anonymous or Women for Sobriety

Prognosis

Good (after client gets past crisis), assuming she is motivated to stop drinking and find adequate coping skills for dealing with her problems

Relapse common

Client Map of Bettie

Diagnosis

Axis I: 309.0 Adjustment disorder with depressed mood

Axis II: V71.09 No diagnosis on Axis II

Axis III: None reported

Axis IV: Problems with primary support group: end of engagement

Axis V: Global assessment of functioning (GAF Scale): current GAF = 77

Objectives of Treatment

Reduce stress and reinforce positive coping skills

Explore and determine goals and future direction

Develop relationship skills

Assessments

Myers-Briggs Type Indicator

Strong Interest Inventory

Clinician Characteristics

Supportive and exploratory

Skilled at fostering resilience

Able to promote exploration of long-term objectives

Location of Treatment

Outpatient

Interventions to Be Used

Initially cognitive-behavioral therapy

Process-experiential therapy

Emphasis of Treatment

Initial supportive emphasis

Emphasis on emotions and values

Numbers

Primarily individual therapy

Timing

Rapid pace

Short duration (less than six months)

Weekly sessions

Medications Needed

None

Adjunct Services

Career counseling

Referral to support group for women

Prognosis

Excellent

This chapter has presented an outline for a comprehensive treatment plan, the DO A CLIENT MAP. It has also reviewed the literature on the dimensions of effective therapy and on the contributions that the qualities of the therapist, the qualities of the client, and the interaction between therapist and client can make to therapeutic outcomes. The next eight chapters describe the various mental disorders and report on research of treatment approaches that have been found to be effective with those disorders. That information, in combination with the information presented in this chapter, should help clinicians maximize the success of their efforts to help clients in psychotherapy.

CHAPTER TWO

Mental Disorders in Infants, Children, and Adolescents

Shannon's first arrest occurred when she was nine years old and was caught stealing a videotape from a local store, but her parents had been receiving complaints about her since kindergarten. She frequently pushed and hit younger children and took their toys. She tore up flowers and bushes in the neighbors' gardens and threw eggs at their houses. When the neighbors complained to her parents, Shannon and some friends retaliated by stealing the neighbors' mailbox and breaking bottles in their driveway.

At school, Shannon had trouble staying in her seat. She frequently interrupted other children and the teacher. She rarely completed her schoolwork independently, and she often lost her assignments.

Shannon's parents were concerned, but they both had experienced similar problems in school, and both had left high school without graduating. Both were employed to support the family (Shannon and two older children), the mother as a school bus driver and the father as a mechanic. Parental supervision was limited; the oldest child, age sixteen, watched Shannon and her brother after school.

Shannon's history reflects symptoms of disruptive behavior and attention deficit. These are common symptoms of mental disorders among children and adolescents.

OVERVIEW OF MENTAL DISORDERS IN INFANTS, CHILDREN, AND ADOLESCENTS

The need for mental health services for the nation's youth is evident in the following statistics:

- 1.5 million children ages twelve to seventeen meet the criteria for admission to an alcohol treatment center (Substance Abuse and Mental Health Services Administration [SAMHSA], 2003).
- An estimated 12 percent of the sixty-three million children in the United States have a mental disorder (Oltmanns & Emery, 2007).
- In 2001, 23 percent of all victims of violent crime were children ages twelve to seventeen.
- Homicide and suicide are the second and third leading causes of death among young people ages fifteen to nineteen. (Accidental death is the first.)
- Firearms were the cause of death in more than 80 percent of teen homicides and about half of teen suicides (Centers for Disease Control and Prevention, 2003). One study found that more than 90 percent of children and adolescents who committed suicide had a mental disorder (Shaffer & Craft, 1999).

Research repeatedly indicates that the best way to reduce the incidence and severity of mental disorders is prevention. Therefore, early identification of both symptoms and strengths and effective treatment of emotional problems in young people are critical in reducing the overall prevalence and severity of mental disorders.

Unlike the mental disorders discussed in other chapters of this book, which are related to one another by their similarity of symptoms, those discussed in this chapter are linked by their early age of onset. This chapter addresses the thirteen major categories of disorders usually first diagnosed in infancy, childhood, or adolescence, as listed in the *Diagnostic and Statistical Manual of Mental Disorders (DSM-IV-TR)* (American Psychiatric Association, 2000). The chapter also briefly reviews childhood presentations of some disorders discussed elsewhere in the book. Although most of the disorders discussed in this chapter usually begin in childhood, many often continue into adulthood. Therefore, the information in this chapter will be relevant to all therapists.

Etiology of Mental Disorders in Young People

Many theories have been advanced about the etiology of childhood mental disorders. Psychodynamic theorists typically describe these disorders as developmental fixations or regressions and attribute them to early childhood conflicts, experiences, or problems in attachment. Medical models look for neurological or genetic causes. Behavior theory posits that these disorders are the results of learned experiences. Ecological and social learning theorists consider the impact of environmental factors on the child. Developmental theorists look at age-related patterns and deviations from those patterns.

All these theories are relevant to an understanding of the full spectrum of mental disorders found in young people. For example, mental retardation reflects a deviation from age-appropriate levels of cognitive development, and some of the pervasive developmental disorders are characterized by a regression in language and social development. Other disorders, such as Rett's disorder, have neurological, biological, or genetic determinants. Conduct disorder often is linked to chaotic and antisocial family patterns.

Attachment also has an impact on child development. Bowlby (1969, 1982) describes attachment as a process: a child produces behaviors in reaction to stress; these behaviors, in turn, elicit other behaviors from the caregiver that ideally provide a sense of security for the child, usually through physical closeness or proximity (Ainsworth, Blehar, Waters, & Wall, 1978). Bowlby's theory suggests that the quality of all subsequent interpersonal relationships is affected by the nature of attachment relationships formed during infancy. Findings suggest that insecure attachment during the early years can affect children's cognitive and social development, their relationships across the life span, and even their skills in parenting the next generation (Zeanah & Boris, 2000).

Children typically are referred for psychotherapy when their behaviors or symptoms interfere with their daily functioning or with the functioning of their families. Problems in school, such as inattention, misbehavior, or academic deficits, often prompt teachers or school counselors to suggest therapy. Academic problems often coexist with social-emotional problems, such as insecure attachment, inappropriate peer relationships, aggression, social isolation, low self-esteem, and lack of motivation. The family members of children with difficulties like these frequently experience considerable stress and change themselves and may be struggling with their own mental disorders. Therefore, the therapist working with a child usually has targets of intervention in addition to the child — namely, the school, the family, and the environment. The therapist needs to be knowledgeable about social, educational, and community resources for children and families. The therapist also needs to be an excellent diagnostician because comorbidity and confusing presentations (such as a depressive disorder masked by anger or a bipolar disorder that looks like hyperactivity) are common in childhood mental disorders.

Prevalence and Client Characteristics

As many as 20 percent of adolescents and children may have a mental disorder (U.S. Department of Health and Human Services [DHHS], 2006). This translates into 7.7 to 12.8 million children. Less than a third of those children are believed to be receiving the type of treatment they need (DHHS, 2006). An epidemiological study conducted by the National Institute of Mental Health (NIMH, 2005) estimates that half of all mental disorders begin by the age of fourteen. The National Comorbidity Survey Replication (Kessler, Berglund, et al., 2005) found that anxiety disorders have the highest lifetime prevalence rate (28.8 percent), followed by disruptive behavior and attentional disorders, including ADHD, conduct disorder, and oppositional defiant disorder (24.8 percent). Mood disorders (20.8 percent) and substance abuse disorders (14.6 percent) also are prevalent across the life span (Kessler, Berglund, et al., 2005).

In 2005, 16 percent of school-age children (four to seventeen years old) had parents who had talked to a health care provider or school personnel about their child's emotional or behavioral difficulties in the previous twelve months. However, only about 6 percent of these children received any mental health treatment (NIMH, 2005). Boys have more emotional difficulties than girls in this age group. Seven percent of boys received some type of mental health treatment or help with emotional concerns other than medication, compared to 3 percent of girls. Boys were also more likely to be prescribed medication for behavioral and emotional difficulties (NIMH, 2005).

Mental disorders appear to be "the chronic diseases of the young" (NIMH, 2005), beginning in childhood and adolescence and affecting the core areas of life, including educational achievement, relationships, and occupational success (Kessler, Berglund, et al., 2005). Failure to recognize and diagnose these disorders, as well as delays in treatment, can exacerbate the situation, leading to mental illness that is more severe and more resistant to treatment, as well as to the development of co-occurring (or comorbid) disorders as the adolescent moves into young adulthood. Left untreated, early-onset mental disorders can lead to school failure, long-standing mood disorders, substance misuse, instability, and violence (Kessler, Berglund, et al., 2005).

By definition, mental disorders in youth have an onset prior to the age of eighteen. Unlike adults, who usually come to therapists without a diagnosis, children often initially receive diagnoses in medical or educational settings. Their diagnoses usually address their major symptoms but may overlook comorbid disorders, so the therapist should be alert to additional symptoms or disorders that may require complex treatment planning.

Children with mental disorders vary in appearance. Some, for example, have obvious physical anomalies. Children with some disorders of neurobiological etiology, such as Rett's disorder or some types of mental retardation, typically have associated physical characteristics, such as microcephaly (small head), short stature, or atypical facial structure. By contrast, children with disorders of a psychosocial etiology, such as conduct or separation anxiety disorders, usually evidence no external physical symptoms.

Because children present differently in different settings, therapists should collect information from multiple sources in order to make accurate diagnoses. The collection of information should almost always include input from teachers and parents. A variety of checklists are available to assess behaviors. These inventories, including the Conners' Teacher and Parent Rating Scales (Conners, 1997), the Achenbach Child Behavior Checklist (Achenbach, 1991), and the Behavior Assessment System for Children, 2nd Edition (BASC) (Reynolds & Kamphaus, 2002) are usually used to facilitate the collection and organization of information. Each assesses such characteristics as anxiety, depressive symptoms, hyperactivity, inattention, impulsivity, atypical thoughts, aggressive or delinquent behaviors, and somatic complaints.

Therapy with children almost always involves contact with their families because a disorder and its concomitant behaviors will both affect and be affected by family life. The impact of financial and emotional stressors, transitions, and family relationships on a child's emotional health should all be assessed. Additional services may be required to provide treatment, support, and resources to siblings and parents, who may have their own emotional difficulties.

Preferred Therapist Characteristics

Therapists working with children should have a broad range of professional and personal skills. They must be patient and calm. They should have a clear understanding of their own values and of their own childhood and parenting experiences. As neutral adults, therapists typically are the focus of children's negative and positive reactions. Children may refuse to talk, make insulting and disparaging statements to their therapists, or even attack their therapists physically. Children may also relate to therapists in seductive or manipulative ways. Therapists' countertransference reactions to these behaviors may interfere with treatment unless therapists carefully monitor and understand their feelings and use them only in ways that are therapeutic. Therapists may also need to manage their own rage in response to child abuse and their need to save children from their caregivers.

In addition to basic psychotherapy skills, therapists who work with children must have sound knowledge of human development over the life span. One of therapists' most important tasks will be to distinguish between age-appropriate and atypical behaviors: some of the disorders discussed in this chapter are characterized by behaviors that may be developmentally appropriate at some ages but clinically significant at others. In diagnosing attention-deficit/hyperactivity disorder (ADHD), for example, one task of the clinician is to determine how much activity is typical for the client's chronological age.

Collaboration with other professionals is another important task for therapists working with children. Young people who come for therapy may also have been seen by physicians, psychiatrists, school counselors, social workers, speech therapists, and family therapists. Ongoing consultation and collaboration with other professionals will be crucial to providing the most effective and efficient treatment. At the same time, however, too many helpers can fragment the treatment, so therapists may need to assume a case management role in order to coordinate services for children and their families and in order to ensure that all the treatment providers have shared and congruent goals.

Parenting a child with a mental disorder can evoke feelings of failure, frustration, sadness, anger, and helplessness. The child's needs may also overwhelm the family, impairing its functioning and family relationships. Therefore, therapists working with children must give empathy and support to families as well as guidance about parenting, information about the particular disorders involved, and referrals for family therapy and other ancillary services.

Intervention Strategies

Treatment planning for children is a very complex task; individual psychotherapy is rarely the sole treatment modality. Children experience at least two systems — the family and the school — that affect their behaviors and emotional well-being. A therapist may be seeing a child for individual therapy while the child also is involved in special education, family therapy, medical treatment, and the juvenile justice system. Treatment of the child will usually require contact and cooperation with all the agencies and professionals concerned.

Interventions that take into account the child's stage of development, level and stage of change, demographic factors (for example, race, ethnicity, and socioeconomic status), and such personality traits as impulsivity and coping style have been found to improve treatment outcomes and reduce dropout rates (Gintner, 2004; Prochaska & Norcross, 2006). Cultural variables should also be taken into account when diagnosing mental disorders and developing treatment plans for children (Paniagua, 2001).

Direct intervention strategies may include individual, group, and family therapy or consultation, as discussed in the following paragraphs. Other sections of this chapter discuss in greater detail treatment modalities effective for specific disorders.

Individual Therapy. Johnson, Rasbury, and Siegel (1997) suggest that the structure of individual therapy — regularly scheduled sessions of fixed length and frequency that are conducted at a stable location — is in itself an important intervention. This kind of structure can give children a positive experience with clear limits and boundaries, as well as an environment in which trust and safety can readily be established.

Because adolescents are usually able to participate in traditional talk therapy, individual therapy for adolescents is similar to therapy for adults. Cognitive-behavioral, psychodynamic, person-centered, integrative, and other approaches can be used with adolescents who have sufficient ego strength and cognitive functioning to benefit from these methods of intervention. If the adolescent has significant expressive language disorders or mental retardation, however, some accommodations may be necessary so that accessible interventions can be provided.

Play Therapy. Play is often the therapeutic modality used to help children express themselves and modify their behaviors. Play therapy can be conducted in either group or individual treatment settings. Play therapists have an assortment of toys, games, and art supplies and assume that children will seek out the toys and activities that are relevant to their emotional needs. In the same way that physical, cognitive, and social-emotional development follow predictable patterns, play progresses through developmental stages. An understanding of the stages of play can provide therapists with a useful frame of reference for understanding children.

The process of play therapy varies and will depend on the theoretical orientation of the therapist. In person-centered play therapy, for example, children are allowed free expression in their play, and therapists reflect feelings, assuming that this process will be therapeutic in itself and that children have the ability to solve their own problems (Hollins, 2001; Johnson, 2001). In psychodynamic play therapy, therapists interpret the symbolism in the play; the assumption here is that unconscious material is brought into consciousness so that the child's ego is able to resolve unconscious psychic conflicts. Social learning theorists view play therapy as an opportunity for therapists to teach prosocial play behaviors and for children to practice appropriate social interactions.

Group Therapy. Published outcome studies indicate that group therapy is the most frequently offered treatment modality for children and adolescents (Weisz & Hawley, 2002). Research indicates that elementary school-age children tend to profit most from homogeneous groups that address a specific problem, whereas adolescents can benefit from groups that focus on a variety of issues (Thompson, Rudolph, & Henderson, 2003). A number of empirically supported treatments have been delivered in group format, including treatments for depression, anger, and anxiety disorders such as posttraumatic stress disorder (Gintner, 2004). Group therapy can address behavioral difficulties, educational and social problems, and intrapsychic issues. The group format usually involves shared discussion about the personal issues of group members, an exchange of feedback, and opportunities for peer support, modeling, and behavioral rehearsal.

Many approaches to group therapy have been developed on the basis of different theoretical models, as well as on the basis of children's varying needs. For example, person-centered group therapy may be effective for children with mild behavior problems or emotional immaturity (Johnson et al., 1997). Children with severe disruptive behavior disorders, however, typically require groups that have more structure and emphasize behavioral change. Other types of structured groups are those established with the purpose of helping members work toward a common goal. For example, groups to teach adolescents to cope with depression would include a carefully sequenced set of lessons. Impulse control, anger management, and problem solving are other areas in which structured therapeutic groups can benefit young clients. Training in these areas, based on cognitive-behavioral theory, teaches such skills as recognizing and labeling affect, managing stress, using relaxation techniques, understanding appropriate interpersonal distance, starting and stopping conversations, identifying problems, and evaluating alternative solutions.

Not all children should be involved in group therapy, however. Yalom (1995) recommends screening children for group readiness, and Dishion, McCord, and Poulin (1999) suggest that the problem behaviors of adolescents with conduct disorder may actually increase with exposure to others who have similar problems. Moreover, children who are actively experiencing psychotic thoughts are usually not appropriate candidates for group therapy.

Family Interventions. On the assumption that a child's or an adolescent's behavior is shaped by the family, therapists often involve families in treatment. The goal of this kind of intervention is to change those interactions among family members that may be contributing to or sustaining a troubled child's difficulties. Structural family therapy, for example, seeks to develop appropriate boundaries between family members and subsystems. Another therapeutic goal in this model of therapy is the empowering of adults to take on the responsibilities of parenting. Interactional models focus on improving communication skills among family members. The parents, the troubled child, and the siblings may be guided in making "I" statements and in rephrasing content or expressing emotions in constructive ways; modeling and role playing are often used to achieve this goal. The particular approach to family therapy will be determined by the nature of the family's dynamics and difficulties and the child's disorder.

Clinical research supports family involvement for a variety of childhood problems, including autism, conduct disorder, oppositional defiant disorder, ADHD, eating disorders, and substance use disorders (Gintner, 2004; Kazdin & Weisz, 2003). Younger children also fare better with increased family or parental involvement. Of individual, group, and family modalities, family therapy is the most underused and has a higher dropout rate (Gintner, 2004). Therapists who implement family therapy should address the issue of participation up front and discuss barriers that may preclude parent and family participation. Family patterns of dysfunction may need to be addressed through couples counseling or individual counseling.

Parental psychoeducation may also be used to complement a child's treatment. In this approach, information is presented to the parents about their child's disorder, and methods are suggested for creating positive change. Psychoeducation often involves a prescribed curriculum, presented over a series of sessions.

The issue of confidentiality with children is complicated because the family is an integral part of the treatment, if only in a supportive way (for example, in family members' provision of transportation or payment). Therapists need to clarify the boundaries and limits of confidentiality with the child as well as with the other family members before therapy begins. What information will be communicated to parents, as well as how that communication will occur, should be agreed on during the planning phase of treatment. These negotiations will be especially important when the child is a mature adolescent.

Other Treatment Modalities. Behavioral change programs for use at home or in school are frequently an integral part of psychotherapy with children. Symptoms that may require this type of intervention include repetitive or habitual behaviors, impulsive or off-task behaviors that interfere with the completion of schoolwork, and self-injurious behaviors. Behavioral interventions require carefully planned collaboration and are rarely effective without the support and involvement of the adults in a child's daily life.

Psychotropic medication is increasingly used with children; psychostimulants for ADHD are particularly common. The positive effects of stimulant medication have been documented repeatedly, but its use continues to be a source of debate among physicians and psychotherapists (Erk, 2004). Antidepressant medication is often prescribed for children with mood disorders, including bipolar disorder. Although the use of selective serotonin reuptake inhibitors (SSRIs) for depression in children must be carefully overseen by parents and professionals because of a small risk of increased suicidal ideation early in treatment, empirical evidence supports the effectiveness of this medication in treating depression (Field & Seligman, 2004). Other medications used to treat childhood mental disorders include neuroleptics, such as haloperidol (Haldol; for tic or psychotic disorders), and atypical antipsychotics. Therapists working with children should be aware of the potential drug therapies and their side effects.

Residential or day treatment programs and hospitalization are interventions for severe disorders in young clients. These may be necessary for children who pose a danger to themselves or to others. Residential treatment programs are sometimes used in the treatment of children with severe or profound mental retardation, conduct disorder, severe eating disorders, substance use disorders, or psychotic disorders that do not respond to outpatient or pharmacological interventions.

Prognosis

Outcome research for mental disorders in children and adolescents is fairly limited and rarely encompasses the full range of treatments available or comorbid disorders. Most research provides information only on short-term outcomes; additional longitudinal research is needed. Further information will be provided throughout this chapter on effective treatments for specific mental disorders in young people.

One weakness of outcome research is that it tends to focus on behavioral or cognitive-behavioral interventions (Weisz & Hawley, 2002); there has been little research on nonbehavioral approaches. Readers should keep this limitation in mind when outcome research for specific disorders is discussed in the relevant sections of this chapter.

MENTAL RETARDATION

Description of the Disorder

Mental retardation has a pervasive impact on cognitive, emotional, and social development. Historically, mental retardation has been diagnosed from results of individual intelligence tests, such as the Wechsler intelligence scales and the Stanford-Binet Intelligence Scales; level of social functioning has also been incorporated into the diagnosis. According to *DSM-IV-TR* (American Psychiatric Association, 2000), the criteria for diagnosis of mental retardation includes onset prior to age eighteen, below-average intellectual functioning (IQ below 70), and impaired adaptive functioning in at least two important areas, such as communication, social skills, and work. The impact of this disorder on a child's life and the prognosis for improvement in functioning are significantly correlated with the degree of intellectual impairment. Performance on standardized IQ tests determines the subcategory of retardation. An inventoried IQ score in the range of 50–55 to 70, two to three standard deviations below the mean, reflects *mild* mental retardation. An IQ score in the range of 35–40 to 50–55, or three to four standard deviations below the mean, reflects *moderate* mental retardation. An IQ score in the range of 20–25 to 35–40, or four to five standard deviations below the mean, reflects *severe* mental retardation. An IQ score below the range of 20–25 reflects *profound* mental retardation. Because of the many physical anomalies that may be associated with severe and profound levels of retardation, children with those low levels of functioning usually can be identified during infancy. In contrast, mild to moderate levels of retardation may not be diagnosed until children begin school.

The evaluation of functioning or adaptive behavior is a less precise process. Such assessment tools as the Vineland Adaptive Behavior Scales are often used to quantify these skills. These scales provide an assessment of a person's life skills on the basis of reports made by caretakers and teachers, or on the basis of direct observations made by the evaluator. The scales provide an assessment of communication, social functioning, daily living, and motor skill development. Wide variations in a child's functioning raise questions about distorted reporting or about the possibility that cultural factors are interfering with functioning.

Mental retardation usually is diagnosed during infancy or childhood. Recent estimates suggest that approximately 1 to 3 percent of the general population can be diagnosed with mental retardation (Mash & Wolfe, 2005). Boys are three times more likely than girls to be diagnosed with mental retardation, which may in part be accounted for by fragile X syndrome — the most common cause of inherited mental retardation (Mash & Wolfe, 2005). Approximately 40 to 60 percent of people with mental retardation have identifiable biological causes for the disorder, such as genetic and chromosomal abnormalities, prenatal and perinatal difficulties, or acquired childhood diseases (Handen & Gilchrist, 2006). Down syndrome is the most widely known genetic type of mild or moderate retardation. Severe and profound retardation commonly have neurological origins and may be associated with more than two hundred physical disorders, including cerebral palsy, epilepsy, and sensory disorders (Baumeister & Baumeister, 1995).

Psychosocial and familial factors account for nearly half of people diagnosed with mental retardation. This subtype is characterized by lack of identifiable biological causes and is thought to be the result of some combination of domestic violence, maternal substance misuse, child abuse, parental cognitive dysfunction, and lack of stimulation or other environmental deprivation. Mild and moderate mental retardation are more common among children of low socioeconomic status (SES) and children from minority groups (Mash & Wolfe, 2005). This correlation with SES has led to questions about the validity of these diagnoses. The issue is confounded by the fact that children with mild retardation often demonstrate age-appropriate behaviors at home but developmentally inappropriate behaviors at school. Brooks-Gunn, Klebanov, Smith, Duncan, and Lee (2003) undertook a study of IQ and SES and found that differences between African American and white children were reduced by 71 percent when SES was accounted for. As the population of the United States becomes increasingly diverse, therapists will need to exercise caution in diagnosing mental retardation. The therapist should make a thorough examination of clients' cultural and socioeconomic contexts and of their nonacademic functioning. The therapist will also have to determine whether the assessment tools being used are culturally biased.

Typical Client Characteristics

The characteristics of children, adolescents, and adults with mental retardation vary greatly and depend on their level of impairment and on their environment. Because of their cognitive limitations, these people tend to be concrete in their thinking, reasoning, and problem solving. Developmental delays are common, with such milestones as walking and talking generally appearing later than average. Learning of new tasks requires more practice and guidance for people with mental retardation than for their chronological counterparts.

The American Association on Mental Retardation (AAMR, 2002) developed a multifaceted diagnostic approach that takes into account a person's ability and level of support needed rather than IQ when defining mental retardation. The largest classification, comprising 85 percent of people with this disorder, are people with mild mental retardation. Children with mild levels of retardation may not exhibit atypical behaviors in all environments. They often master self-care, as well as social and job skills. Children with mild levels of retardation may demonstrate highly adaptive behaviors in nonacademic settings. Their cognitive deficits may become apparent only when they are placed in situations that require higher-order reasoning skills, such as reading, writing, or mathematics. To learn these skills, the children usually require special education, which adapts the curriculum to their learning needs.

People with moderate mental retardation comprise approximately 10 percent of those with mental retardation. Children diagnosed with moderate mental retardation may achieve intellectual levels as adults of the average four- to seven-year-old child (Butcher, Mineka, & Hooley, 2006). Even though their rate of learning is slow, they may learn to read and write, obtain a full understanding of spoken language, and be partially responsible for self-care. However, due to poor motor skills, lack of coordination, bodily deformities, and sometimes an angry or hostile temperament, they may not be able to achieve complete independence.

A child with a severe level of retardation will frequently exhibit significant motor deficiencies in addition to cognitive impairment. The child may require a wheelchair for mobility and may require assistance with feeding, toileting, and self-care. Speech and language deficiencies may necessitate a facilitated communication device, such as a picture board or word cards. People with severe mental retardation comprise 3 to 4 percent of those with mental retardation. They are generally diagnosed at a very young age because of developmental delays and physical anomalies (Mash & Wolfe, 2005).

Profound mental retardation is rare, comprising only 1 to 2 percent of people with mental retardation. Because of severe cognitive impairments, these individuals are capable of learning only basic self-care behaviors and are likely to need lifelong care. Epilepsy, congenital heart defects, and other medical conditions are likely to co-occur in this population.

Comorbid psychological and physical disorders are common among people with mental retardation. Thirty to 50 percent of children with mental retardation experience serious emotional difficulties in addition to their disorder (Handen & Gilchrist, 2006). Most common are ADHD, oppositional defiant disorder, conduct disorder, anxiety disorders, and depression. Johnson (2002) notes that these disorders may be the most common reasons why children are placed in special educational settings.

In recent years, fetal alcohol syndrome has received increasing attention from the medical and research communities. Children with this medical condition often develop mild mental retardation. Co-occurring disorders and symptoms include ADHD, decreased impulse control, and diverse learning problems. Despite public education programs about the dangers of alcohol use during pregnancy, the incidence of fetal alcohol syndrome is five to twenty cases per ten thousand births (Weber, Floyd, Riley, & Snider, 2002).

Preferred Therapist Characteristics

Therapists working with people diagnosed with mental retardation must be able to establish realistic goals and accept limited progress. They must be knowledgeable about human development and the correlation between intellectual level and development in thinking, communication, and social and motor skills. They should exhibit patience and genuineness in their interactions with people with mental retardation.

Therapists must also have excellent collaborative skills because often multiple services are provided by a variety of agencies (Handen & Gilchrist, 2006). Harbin, McWilliam, and Gallagher (2000) identify four key elements in creating interventions for people with mental retardation: early intervention to reduce dysfunction, a family-centered approach, integration of therapy into the child's environment, and inclusion of the child within the academic and social environment.

The presence of comorbid disorders is particularly likely in people with severe and profound levels of retardation and will necessitate a team-based treatment approach. Moreover, stress and problems in the family or the environment tend to exacerbate the symptoms of mental retardation, decreasing the person's ability to cope, and these factors also require identification and amelioration. Therapists must work closely with the families of people with mental retardation, so therapists' understanding and appreciation of the particular challenges that parents experience in bringing up a child with mental retardation will facilitate the ongoing treatment of this population.

People with mental retardation probably will need treatment into adulthood to help them achieve as much independence as possible. Therefore, therapists may serve as long-term case managers, coordinating a variety of services and playing a role as advocates for these clients.

Intervention Strategies

Early intervention is essential to the effective treatment of children with mental retardation. Special education, home health care, language stimulation, and social skills training at an early age can have a great impact on treatment outcomes. A developmental approach, which takes account of children's cognitive age rather than their chronological age and sets goals on the basis of individual abilities and needs, is crucial to working with children with mental retardation.

Many people with mild or moderate levels of retardation have the potential to function in socially appropriate ways if they are provided with adequate training. Handen and Gilchrist (2006) suggest that parent training, community-based treatment, and individual psychotherapy can all be effective in promoting these clients' positive self-regard and improving their social and occupational skills.

Feldman and Werner (2002) developed a weekly, in-home parent training program that focused on reducing stress and improving behavior problems at home. The program lasted for three to six months and was successful in meeting its stated objectives. The value of community-based treatment resources, such as occupational therapy, group support, and recreational facilities, are also substantiated by empirical evidence that documents the benefits of community-based support for families and for children diagnosed with mental retardation (Handen & Gilchrist, 2006).

Individual psychotherapy has also been found to improve functioning. A behavioral approach is most often used to help people diagnosed with mental retardation develop appropriate social interaction and self-help skills, such as dressing, taking a bus, and grocery shopping. Learning skills for self-help and daily living is a critical goal for children and adults with mild to moderate levels of mental retardation and can make the difference between a life of dependence and a life of productivity.

Most children with severe and profound levels of retardation will ultimately reside in public institutions. Therapists involved in their treatment can contribute to these people's quality of life by helping them develop recreational interests and interpersonal relationships. Sturmey (1995) used behavior management strategies with adults with profound levels of retardation; when the number of positive social interactions initiated by the staff was increased, the maladaptive behaviors of adults with mental retardation were significantly decreased.

Behavior modification has long been viewed as the treatment modality of choice for mental retardation and has been especially helpful in decreasing self-injurious behaviors (SIBs). Kahng, Iwata, and Lewin (2002) report that SIBs generally respond well to behavioral treatment, with a success rate of 80 percent. Four studies that combined reinforcement with antecedent manipulation actually reduced SIBs by 100 percent (Kahng, Iwata, & Lewin, 2002). The effectiveness of behavioral interventions increases when the treatment is designed to meet the specific needs of the individual.

Hurley (1989) identifies a variety of therapeutic adaptations that may need to be implemented in work with this population. These adaptations include therapists' matching their approach to the cognitive and developmental levels of the client, being directive and concrete, taking an eclectic approach to the choice of treatment modalities, involving the family, and recognizing their personal biases about people with mental retardation. Another accommodation is to reduce the length of sessions to thirty to forty-five minutes to address the needs of people with short attention spans. Sessions that are shorter and more frequent also address the need of many people with mental retardation to have information repeated to facilitate their learning.

Family counseling may be indicated, to improve parent-child interactions and educate families about services available in the community. Families of children with mental retardation could benefit from supportive therapy, particularly when the initial diagnosis is made and at times when changes or adaptations for the child are required. Marital problems are common among parents of children with mental retardation and may also require intervention, as may issues of loss and grief that are similar to those experienced by parents during bereavement.

Hizen parenting skill training, a program similar to the parent management training model developed by Patterson (1982), was introduced to a group of Japanese parents of children with mental retardation (Menta, Ito, Okuma, & Nakano, 1995). In a ten-session psychoeducational format, the parents were given information on child development and on basic techniques of behavior change, including positive and negative reinforcement and shaping. The group members also provided support for one another. The children's skills and behavior problems, and the mothers' parenting skills and levels of stress and depression, were measured as dependent variables at the beginning of the training and at regular intervals during the subsequent year. Improvements were noted in all the dependent variables.

Psychopharmacology plays an increasingly important role in the control of such symptoms as aggression, agitation, and hyperactivity associated with mental retardation (Handen & Gilchrist, 2006). Lithium and antipsychotic medications have been used to reduce aggressive behaviors and SIB in children with mental retardation. Psychostimulants for ADHD (which affects 9 to 16 percent of children with mental retardation) are often prescribed to control hyperactivity and improve concentration. Response rates range from 45 to 66 percent (Aman, Armstrong, Buican, & Sillick, 2002). Despite the lack of studies on its effectiveness, the nonstimulant ADHD medication atomoxetine (Strattera) has been used with some success. Strattera has few side effects and does not cause seizures, as do some other drugs for ADHD (Mash & Wolfe, 2005).

As mentioned earlier, case management for people with mental retardation is often an important part of treatment planning, particularly for adolescents and young adults. Advocacy with schools, agencies, and families and facilitation of appropriate job placement are tasks that may be included in a treatment plan, as may coordination of a multimodal treatment team.

Prognosis

Mental retardation has implications for a person's entire life span. Adults with a mild level of retardation often live independently and maintain jobs with minimal supervision. People with a moderate level of retardation may ultimately be able to live independently in group-home settings and gain employment in sheltered workshops. Social skills training, career counseling, and development of self-awareness skills may all facilitate these clients' efforts at being independent. Therapists working with children and adults who have severe and profound levels of mental retardation may be able to effect many positive changes. For example, behavioral techniques to reduce SIB have been proven to be effective. Regardless of the degree of retardation, therapists can make a difference in improving the lives of people diagnosed with mental retardation.

LEARNING, MOTOR SKILLS, AND COMMUNICATION DISORDERS

Description of the Disorders

Learning, motor skills, and communication disorders are identified in children whose levels of functioning are significantly below expectations in the pertinent skill areas. The expectations are based on the children's age, cognitive abilities, and education, and whether their level of functioning is judged to be interfering with their achievement or daily activities. According to *DSM-IV-TR*, a determination that a child's level of functioning is significantly below expectations is made if the child's score on achievement tests is more than two standard deviations below the child's IQ. Functioning is measured with such standardized assessments as the Woodcock Johnson-III Tests of Achievement

(Woodcock & Johnson, 2001) or the Wechsler Individual Achievement Test, 2nd Edition (Wechsler, 2001).

Disorders of mathematics, reading, and written expression are characterized by significant difficulties in those areas of academic functioning. Students with learning disorders do not process information in a manner that facilitates participation in classroom learning. These disorders must be distinguished from underachievement caused by normal variations, lack of opportunity, poor teaching, or cultural factors. Deficiencies of vision or hearing should be ruled out as causes of impairment before learning disorders are diagnosed. The category of learning disorders not otherwise specified describes academic deficits that do not meet the criteria for specific learning disorders. This diagnosis may be used when a child exhibits academic deficits in more than one academic area, when the deficits do not reach the required degree of significance (two standard deviations below age- and ability-based expectations) or in a learning area not specifically named in the *DSM*.

Developmental coordination disorder is the diagnosis for motor coordination that is substantially below age- and intelligence-based expectations. This diagnosis should not be made if symptoms are due to a medical condition (American Psychiatric Association, 2000).

DSM-IV-TR describes four types of communication disorders: (1) expressive language disorder, (2) mixed receptive-expressive language disorder, (3) phonological disorder, and (4) stuttering. Children with the first two disorders demonstrate language development that is significantly below expectations based on nonverbal ability and that interferes with academic progress. The disorders are differentiated based on whether the child has the ability to perceive and understand basic language (expressive language disorder) or has difficulty with both expression and understanding (mixed receptive-expressive language disorder). Phonological disorder is ''failure to use developmentally expected speech sounds that are appropriate for age and dialect'' (American Psychiatric Association, 2000, p. 65); lisping is an example. Stuttering reflects problems with speech fluency that interfere with a child's ability to communicate or make good academic progress.

Learning, motor skills, and communication disorders currently are thought to be related to genetics, brain function, and environmental risk factors (Mash & Wolfe, 2005). Lead poisoning or head traumas in childhood may contribute to learning disorders. Silver (2006) also reports correlations between learning disorders and low birth weight, maternal smoking or alcohol use during pregnancy, and exposure to other toxins.

Family patterns of learning disabilities have long been recognized. Approximately 35 to 45 percent of boys with learning disorders have at least one parent who had similar learning problems, and studies have identified strong environmental factors combined with genetic factors as leading to development of learning disabilities (Lyon, Fletcher, Fuchs, & Chhabra, 2006). Environmental factors associated with learning disorders include low SES, poor self-esteem, depression, and perceptual deficiencies (Silver, 2006). As a result of these concomitant problems, differential diagnosis may be difficult, and treatment may require both educational and psychological interventions.

Typical Client Characteristics

DSM-IV-TR estimates that the prevalence of learning disorders ranges from 2 to 10 percent, with approximately 5 percent of students in public schools having a learning disorder. The disorders usually become evident in the early elementary school years. Children with these disorders often are unhappy in school, have negative self-images and social difficulties, and show increased likelihood of dropping out of school. Depression, as well as attention-deficit and disruptive behavior disorders, often coexist with learning disorders.

Reading disorders are found in approximately 4 percent of school-age children, making it the most common learning disability (Kamphaus, 2000); of that group, 60 to 80 percent are boys. Children with reading disorders may have difficulty decoding unknown words, memorizing vocabulary lists, and comprehending written passages. There is a growing body of research which indicates that early interventions can successfully improve reading, math, and writing skills (Lyon et al., 2006). Conversely, lack of interventions can lead to continued problems throughout adolescence and into adulthood.

According to *DSM-IV-TR* (American Psychiatric Association, 2000), approximately 1 percent of school-age children can be diagnosed with mathematics disorders. Children with mathematics-related deficiencies may have procedural, semantic memory, and visual-spatial problems that contribute to learning disabilities in mathematics (Geary, 2003). Frequent procedural errors can result from poor understanding of the concepts, the use of procedures more commonly employed by younger children, and difficulties in sequencing. Semantic memory problems can include memory deficits and difficulty retrieving facts. Problems with visual-spatial relations can cause children to misinterpret or misunderstand spatially represented information. Any combination of these problems, in addition to the child's own lowered expectations of math performance, can contribute to mathematics disorders (Geary, 2003).

Disorders of written expression are rarely found in isolation; another learning disorder is also present in most cases (American Psychiatric Association, 2000). The difficulties associated with disorders of written expression are typically reflected in multiple areas, which include handwriting, spelling, grammar, and the creation of prose.

Children with developmental coordination disorder usually appear clumsy and have delays in achieving developmental milestones. This disorder is often accompanied by a communication disorder.

Language disorders resemble learning disorders in terms of prevalence, gender ratio, and familial patterns. They typically appear during the preschool years. Although they often disappear spontaneously, they can still cause considerable academic and social impairment.

Preferred Therapist Characteristics

Therapists working with children who have learning disorders must be able to take a broad view of their clients, determining and assessing a range of possible contributing factors and coexisting mental disorders. Therapists should be able to evaluate children's perceptual and cognitive processes, as well as their emotional functioning. Children with significant language deficits may require nonverbal approaches to therapy, such as play therapy or activity-group therapy. Therapists should be able to work effectively as part of a treatment team that includes school; family; and occupational, physical, or language therapists.

Intervention Strategies

The primary interventions for children with learning disorders will occur at school. The major goal will be the remediation of learning and skill deficits. A child who demonstrates significant underachievement (more than two standard deviations below measured ability) may be eligible for special education. The Individuals with Disabilities Education Act of 1997 and the Reauthorized IDEA of 2004 (IDEA 2004) spell out services to all children with disabilities. Initially implemented in 1975 as Public Law 94–142, the Education for All Handicapped Children Act was renamed in 1990 as the Individuals with Disabilities Education Act and requires an individualized education plan, developed by the school according to the child's individual needs, as well as the provision that all children with learning disabilities must be educated in the least restrictive environment. IDEA 2004 includes a responsiveness to intervention approach to provide earlier identification of students with learning disabilities and a systematic, research-based approach to interventions.

The goals of psychotherapy for children with learning, motor skills, and communication disorders typically focus on improving self-confidence and interpersonal behaviors, and on school adjustment. Silver (2006) suggests that essential goals of treatment include identifying and building on the children's strengths as well as educating the children and their families about learning disorders and their impact on school, family, and social functioning. Parents often feel anger and disappointment about their children's academic performance, and those feelings must receive attention. Once academic issues are addressed, and once the family and the child have a better understanding of the learning disorder and its impact on them, the child's behavioral problems may disappear spontaneously (Silver, 2006).

Children with learning disorders frequently come for counseling because of problems with their interpersonal skills. The same perceptual difficulties that impair academic learning can interfere with a child's comprehension of social information and may result in inappropriate social behaviors (Silver, 2006). Therapy may be required to teach social skills. Lyon et al. (2006) and others describe social skills training programs with curricula based on cognitive-behavioral models. These training programs teach social skills, such as understanding social space; behaviors associated with making a personal approach; attending and communication skills; and understanding the nature of social interactions. The lessons are primarily didactic but are typically given in small-group settings so as to facilitate practice and feedback.

Counselors and therapists are sometimes asked to instruct children in learning strategies. Children with learning disorders frequently demonstrate distinctive preferences in learning style and may need individualized help in acquiring new ways to learn. Clinicians can use cognitive-behavioral approaches to help children understand their learning strengths and weaknesses and build on their abilities.

Therapists may also need to serve as advocates for children with their schools. This role may require a therapist to explain the learning strategies likely to work best for a particular child and to recommend an appropriate educational placement for the child.

Therapists are especially likely to see children with learning or related disorders if there is a coexisting mental disorder. Treatment plans should take into account not just the coexisting mental disorder but also the academic, interpersonal, family, and self-esteem issues that typically accompany learning problems.

People in other professions also contribute to the treatment of children with learning and related disorders. Communication and coordination disorders are almost always addressed through school-based programs. Children are routinely screened by speech and language therapists, who identify speech disorders and design treatments for correcting them. Motor skills disorders are addressed by other specialists, usually occupational or physical therapists, who use exercises to improve muscle tone, balance, range of motion, and fine motor coordination. Occupational therapists sometimes teach keyboarding skills, which facilitate a child's communication with teachers and with other children. Computer technology offers an invaluable aid for children with motor skills disorders.

Prognosis

Although some early learning deficits are related to developmental delays and can improve with maturation, many such deficits continue to have a negative impact on functioning throughout adolescence and adulthood. Learning disorders and related disorders, left undiagnosed and untreated, can lead to extreme frustration, loss of self-esteem, inadequate education, underemployment, and more serious mental disorders. Proactive interventions, including psychotherapy, individualized teaching strategies to accommodate different learning styles, and social skills training, can have a significant positive impact on children with these disorders (Silver, 2006).

PERVASIVE DEVELOPMENTAL DISORDERS

Description of the Disorders

The prevalence of autism spectrum disorders (pervasive developmental disorders) is approximately one in every five hundred children (NIMH, 2004). *DSM-IV-TR* describes four pervasive developmental disorders (PDDs) differentiated by age, pattern of onset, and nature of symptoms:

1. Autistic disorder
2. Rett's disorder
3. Childhood disintegrative disorder
4. Asperger's disorder

A fifth type listed by *DSM-IV-TR* is pervasive developmental disorder not otherwise specified. All five have a great impact on neurological, emotional, and linguistic development and, in some cases, physical development.

Degree of impairment and prognosis vary considerably for each disorder. Typically, children with Rett's disorder and childhood disintegrative disorder regress over time, whereas those with autistic disorder and Asperger's disorder may improve. An accurate diagnosis will aid in the development of appropriate treatment plans.

Children with PDDs typically have deficits in socialization, communication, and behavior (American Psychiatric Association, 2000; Baird et al., 2001; NIMH, 2004). They tend to avoid contact with others, and they have poor social skills, as well as a limited capacity for empathy. Their speech is often limited or atypical, and they have difficulty sustaining a conversation. Most lack initiative and may exhibit rigid, stereotyped, repetitive behaviors, such as rocking, flapping, or head banging. Children diagnosed with PDDs tend to under- or overreact to sensory stimuli and have difficulty with change and variations from their regular routines. Many children with PDDs can also be diagnosed with mental retardation, although some high-functioning children have cognitive abilities in the average or superior range (Baird et al., 2001). Moreover, a variety of general medical conditions, including chromosomal abnormalities and chronic infections, often can be found in children with PDDs.

Genetic and environmental factors have been found to play a role in the development of PDDs. Rett's disorder, in particular, is caused by a genetic mutation of the MeCP2 gene located on the X chromosome (Colvin et al., 2003). Fragile X syndrome (a chromosomal disorder more common in males) has been found in as many as 25 percent of cases of autistic disorder (Kabot, Masi, & Segal, 2003). Autistic disorder and Asperger's disorder have been found to occur more frequently in family members than in the general population. Research shows that when a family has one child with autism, the risk of having a second child with the same disorder is one hundred times greater than in the general population (Baird et al., 2001).

Such conditions as ADHD, obsessive-compulsive disorder (OCD), mental retardation, learning disorders, and stereotypic movement disorders frequently coexist with PDDs. These co-occurring disorders make differential diagnosis difficult, especially in young children and in children with severe disability or superior intelligence (Baird et al., 2001).

The PDDs have many similarities, but each is diagnosed on the basis of distinguishing characteristics. Discussion of these follows.

Autistic Disorder. Autistic disorder, found in two to twenty of every ten thousand people, is characterized by significant deficits in socialization, communication, and behavior (American Psychiatric Association, 2000). Social difficulties are reflected by limited initiation of social interaction or conversation, lack of interest in other people, dysfunctional emotions, poor skills in imitating affective expressions, and limited empathy. Children with autistic disorder are often found to lack motivation to respond to social and environmental input (Koegel, Koegel, & Brookman, 2003).

Although the number of children diagnosed with this disorder appears to be on the rise, many attribute the increase to better detection and early diagnosis rather than to an actual increase in the occurrence of the disorder (Koegel et al., 2003). Autistic disorder is four to five times more prevalent in males than in females and has been found in families of all ethnic, racial, and socioeconomic backgrounds (American Psychiatric Association, 2000).

The degree of impairment in communication skills varies widely among people with autistic disorder. Some are mute, whereas others do eventually develop age-appropriate language skills; nearly all, however, have problems with the use of narrative language and with comprehension, and they tend to show abnormalities in spoken language. These problems further impair their socialization.

Children with autistic disorder rarely engage in make-believe play that mimics human activity. Their play more often exhibits repetitive, stereotyped interactions with inanimate objects — for example, lining their toys up in a row rather than engaging in imaginative play. As these children grow older, this play activity may evolve into obsessional interest in mechanical objects, time schedules, or factual data. Children with autistic disorder may also exhibit characteristic physical movements (hand flapping, rocking), fascination with moving things (such as ceiling fans and light switches), aggressive and hyperactive behavior, abnormalities in sleeping and eating, and a preoccupation with some narrow interest (lights, trains, meteorology).

Another characteristic of autistic disorder is onset before the age of three. Infants with autistic disorder can often be distinguished from other children by such symptoms as deficits in pointing ability, reluctance to look at others, and inability to orient to their names (Kabot et al., 2003). Sleeping and eating disorders are also common. Some studies indicate that a period of normal development in infants followed by regression around the age of fifteen to nineteen months is common in as many as 40 percent of cases (Kabot et al., 2003). Mental retardation accompanies this diagnosis in 75 to 80 percent of children (NIMH, 2004). Nearly a third of children develop seizures. Tuberous sclerosis is also common (NIMH, 2004).

Children with autistic disorder are particularly likely to have relatives who have affective disorders. Anxiety is common (Koegel et al., 2003), and bipolar or major depression is found in about one-third of the families of people with autism (DeLong, 1994; Kabot et al., 2003). Gillberg, Gillberg, and Steffenberg (1992) have found that children with autistic disorder are often firstborn or only children.

Rett's Disorder. Rett's disorder was first identified in 1966 by Dr. Andreas Rett. This neurodevelopmental disorder is characterized by a period of normal development during the first five to forty-eight months of life. This period is followed by progressive loss of abilities and ultimately by severe or profound retardation (Colvin et al., 2003). Recent research has traced the cause of Rett's disorder to a specific defective gene located on the X chromosome. This disorder is rare, and is estimated to affect one to four in ten thousand females (Newsom & Hovanitz, 2006). Males have not been found to have Rett's disorder.

Children with this disorder exhibit deceleration of head growth, stereotypical hand movements (usually hand wringing or hand washing), lack of social involvement, poorly coordinated gait or trunk movements, mental retardation, and severely impaired receptive and expressive language development (American Psychiatric Association, 2000). Other symptoms, such as seizures, delays in physical growth, and scoliosis, vary with the individual and with age. Forty percent of people with Rett's disorder never develop clear nonverbal communication, whereas others are able to use eye movements and body language to communicate (Colvin et al., 2003). People with this disorder remain severely functionally dependent.

Childhood Disintegrative Disorder. Children diagnosed with childhood disintegrative disorder manifest apparently normal development until at least the age of two. At some point between the ages of two and ten, however, they exhibit significant regression of functioning in at least two of the following areas:

- Language
- Social skills
- Elimination
- Play
- Motor skills

Children with this extremely rare disorder eventually exhibit social, communication, and behavioral deficits that are similar to those of children with autistic disorders. Severe mental retardation also usually accompanies childhood disintegrative disorder. This disorder is more common among males (American Psychiatric Association, 2000).

Asperger's Disorder. Like autistic disorder, Asperger's disorder is typified by impaired social skills and repetitive or stereotypical behaviors. Unlike autistic disorder, however, Asperger's disorder typically does not involve significant delays or impairment in the development of language, oral communication, or cognitive functioning (American Psychiatric Association, 2000). Children with this disorder also often develop age-appropriate self-help skills. Although these children have limited skills in social interaction, they may seek out interpersonal situations. This is one of the characteristics that sets Asperger's disorder apart from the other PDDs (Smith-Myles & Simpson, 2002).

Asperger's disorder is estimated to affect about forty-eight in every ten thousand children (Smith-Myles & Simpson, 2002). The disorder is at least five times more common in males, and onset is somewhat later than an autistic disorder (American Psychiatric Association, 2000). There also appears to be elevated incidence of Asperger's disorder among family members.

Typical Client Characteristics

Children with PDDs are characterized by their atypical social behaviors. They generally exhibit flat affect, poor eye contact, and minimal social speech. They do not demonstrate the social behaviors that one expects in children of their age. They typically do not seek parental attention and do not engage in imitative or interactive play (Baird et al., 2001). Although the quality of their social skills continues to be weak, their social skills may improve with age or circumstances. Other characteristics of people with PDDs vary and depend on the specific disorder; most of the available research focuses on autistic disorder and Asperger's disorder.

Autistic speech usually reflects such atypical features as echolalia or rote repetition of what others have said. Older children with autism may develop fairly complex speech, but they continue to have difficulty participating in social conversation because they miss social and conversational cues. Children with autistic disorder and Asperger's disorder often have difficulty with transitions or changes in routine. Their stereotypic behaviors may become exaggerated at times of transition or when they experience increased stress.

Good verbal abilities, average to above-average intelligence, and less severe symptoms may actually mask the extent of social dysfunction found in people with Asperger's disorder (Mayes & Calhoun, 2004). Like children with autistic disorder, children with Asperger's have difficulty reading social cues. People with Asperger's disorder tend to be self-centered and are often loners. These traits interfere with their ability to form meaningful relationships. Although they may seek out social contact, they do not know how to participate in the usual give-and-take of communication (McConnaughy, 2005; Smith-Myles & Simpson, 2002).

Repetitive behaviors are manifested differently in children with autism and those with Asperger's. A person with autism tends to exhibit repetitive motor behaviors related to an object — for example, banging a drum repeatedly. Alternatively, a person with Asperger's disorder is more likely to be preoccupied with one subject, becoming an expert in a particular area of interest, such as dinosaurs or the solar system (Smith-Myles & Simpson, 2002).

Having a first-degree relative with a PDD typically has a profound impact on the family. Nearly all parents of children with autistic disorder were found to have clinically significant levels of stress related to the challenges of having a child with a severe disability (Koegel, 2000; Koegel et al., 2003). Siblings often have peer problems, feel lonely, and are concerned about their brother or sister who has the disorder (Bagenholm & Gillberg, 1991). Marital difficulties commonly develop as the parents of the child focus their energies on the often fruitless search for a remedy.

Assessment

A diagnosis of PDD can be facilitated by the use of screening instruments and more in-depth behavioral assessments. Kabot et al. (2003) suggest that the use of such instruments in conjunction with parental reports of the child's developmental and behavioral progress can improve the effectiveness of the rating scales. A number of screening tools are available that distinguish children with autism and other PDDs from the general population. The Pervasive Development Disorders Screening Test II, the Autism Screening Questionnaire, and the Pervasive Developmental Disorders Questionnaire have all been found to be effective (Baird et al., 2001; Kabot et al., 2003).

The Checklist for Autism in Toddlers (CHAT; Baron-Cohen, Allen, & Gillberg, 1992) identifies early signs of the disorder by assessing imaginative play, social interest, social play, indication of interest through pointing, and following of another's gaze. The CHAT had a positive predictive value of 83 percent for autism and other PDDs in one study in which it was part of a two-stage screening process (the first stage identified children with profound sensory and motor impairment). The M-CHAT, a version of the screening tool, has recently been developed to discriminate between PDDs and development and language delays. The M-CHAT has not yet been evaluated as a general population screening tool (Baird et al., 2001).

The Pervasive Developmental Disorder Screening Test II (PDDST-II) was developed by Siegel (1999) to screen for autism spectrum disorders in primary care and other settings. The PDDST-II is not available in printed form. It consists of a parental report measure that the parents complete in the clinician's office (Eaves & Ho, 2004). Another instrument currently being developed for early screening is the Screening Tool for Autism in Two-Year-Olds (STAT; Stone, Coonrod, Turner, & Pozdol, 2004). The STAT is designed to differentiate between children with autism and those with other developmental disorders.

After a child has been screened for PDDs, a more extensive assessment is needed. The National Research Council (NRC, 2001, p. 214) recommends a "multidisciplinary evaluation of social behavior, language, and nonverbal communication, adaptive behavior, motor skills, atypical behaviors, and cognitive status by a team of professionals experienced with autism spectrum disorders." A variety of assessment instruments have been created that measure degree and severity of autism symptoms in children. For example, the Childhood Autism Rating Scale (CARS; Schopler, Reichler, De Vellis, & Daly, 1991) is the most widely used (Kabot et al., 2003). It assesses children's performance in fifteen different domains: relating to people, imitation, emotional response, body use, object use, adaptation to change, visual response, listening response, sensory response, fear or nervousness, verbal communication, nonverbal communication, activity level, intellectual functioning, and general impressions. The CARS severity rating also can be used to assess longitudinal progress.

The Autism Diagnostic Interview-Revised (ADI-R) provides a more detailed assessment after a screening tool has determined that more in-depth assessment is needed. The ADI-R (Lord & Rutter, 1994) demonstrates reliability and validity with preschool children. It requires considerable time to administer the five-part questionnaire. The Autism Behavior Checklist (ABC) is one of the oldest rating scales, but according to Kabot it lacks "sensitivity and specificity" and is considered to have limited usefulness (Kabot et al., 2003, p. 29).

Separate scales have been developed to measure symptom severity in school-age children with Asperger's disorder. The Gilliam Asperger's Disorder Scale (GADS) has been shown to be both reliable and valid (Kabot et al., 2003). A population screen was developed by Ehlers and Gillberg (Ehlers, Gillberg, & Wing, 1999), and other scales, such as the Australian Scale for Asperger's Syndrome and the Autism Spectrum Quotient, are available, although they are relatively new and have not been systematically evaluated (Baird et al., 2001).

Preferred Therapist Characteristics

Given the growing number of young children who are being diagnosed with PDDs, therapists working with children must be familiar with the range of symptoms associated with these disorders and be able to make appropriate referrals for assessment, intervention, and educational planning. Therapists can play an important role as part of a multidisciplinary team, supporting families through the assessment process and helping develop behavioral interventions that suit the child's particular needs and learning style (Kabot et al., 2003). At present, treatments and prognoses for the different types of PDD vary greatly but are generally guarded at best.

Intervention Strategies

Early intervention and intensive, behaviorally based treatment are key to developing positive outcomes in PDDs (Kabot et al., 2003; Lovaas & Smith, 2003). Although there is no single best treatment option for children with PDDs, Kabot et al. (2003) conducted an analysis of the peer-reviewed literature and found agreement among the professionals that highly structured, specialized programs work best. They also found the following components to be important in early interventions for autism spectrum disorders:

- Screening should be conducted at the earliest age possible.
- Interventions must be intensive.
- Programs should include parent training and support.
- Interventions should focus on improving social and communication skills.
- Individual goals and objectives should be set.
- Training should emphasize generalizability to other areas.

Because of the pervasive nature of the symptoms, treatment is multifaceted and usually requires collaboration by many health care providers (Kabot et al., 2003). Children with PDDs are usually involved in special education, speech and language therapy, and physical therapy. Those with Rett's disorder or childhood disintegrative disorder may also be under the care of physicians, neurologists, or other medical specialists. Consultation with other service providers, as well as case management of this broad spectrum of services, may fall to the therapist.

Autistic Disorder. Current findings indicate that programs that provide at least twenty to twenty-five hours per week of intensive engagement are the most effective. Typical goals of behavioral treatment are to increase communication skills, enhance learning, and reduce behaviors that prevent learning from taking place (for example, repetitive or ritualistic behaviors, tantrums, aggression). The interventions most effective with these clients are structured and are based on the child's interests, teach tasks as a series of simple steps, engage the child's attention, and provide positive reinforcement for behavior (NIMH, 2004). Parental involvement plays a major role in treatment outcomes.

One model program, the UCLA Young Autism Project, provides forty hours a week of one-to-one behavior modification for children under the age of four for a period of three years (Lovaas & Smith, 2003). Goals of the program include the diminishing of negative behaviors (such as rocking, flapping, and repetitive noises) and the increasing of socially appropriate skills (such as making eye contact, answering social questions, and engaging in play). At the end of the program, many children achieve average levels of intellectual and academic functioning; others make fewer gains. A previous study of an earlier program reported that 47 percent of the children were able to enter a regular first-grade class and demonstrated considerable gains in IQ scores; a positive long-term impact of this treatment has also been reported (McEachin, Smith, & Lovaas, 1993), although other researchers have not been able to replicate these results. The costs and the intensity of such programs are high but must be weighed against the potential costs of lifelong residential placement.

Koegel (2000) reports that when pivotal response interventions (PRI) for autism target two key areas of the child's functioning — motivation and child initiations — upwards of 85 percent of children under the age of five who are diagnosed with autistic disorder can learn to use verbal language as their primary mode of communication. PRI have also been found to improve academic performance and reduce aggressive, self-stimulating, and self-injurious behaviors. In this approach, parents are trained as interventionists who work with the child throughout the day. Such parent education programs have been found to be effective in increasing communication skills, decreasing disruptive behaviors, and increasing generalizability of treatment gains (Koegel et al., 2003). In addition, such programs have also been shown to reduce parental anxiety and increase parental feelings of empowerment.

Other approaches have also demonstrated some effectiveness. One study found that children who received behaviorally based treatment made more progress than children who were given a more eclectic approach (Eikeseth, Smith, Jahr, & Eldevik, 2002). Smith analyzed twelve peer-reviewed outcome studies and found that mean gains in IQ scores were higher in the nine behavioral programs than in the other programs (reported in Kabot et al., 2003). Campbell, Cueva, and Hallin (1995) found that children with autistic disorders who had good cognitive abilities were able to benefit from a relationship-oriented and cognitive-behavioral model of individual counseling. By communicating understanding, the therapists built rapport and were then able to use cognitive-behavioral therapies to teach the children more adaptive methods of communication and social interaction. The model included teaching the children such communication skills as making eye contact and allowing an appropriate amount of personal space, as well as helping them understand typical topics of interest for children in their age group.

Asperger's Disorder. Because of their intelligence and level of independent functioning, children with Asperger's disorder often are not diagnosed until they enter school (Tsatsanis, Foley, & Donehower, 2004). Treatment interventions include individualized behavior therapy, group therapy in which children can practice their skills with peers, psychoeducation, and social skills training.

Assessment of social skills can help determine specific areas that require individualized attention. The social skills inventory developed by Taylor and Jasper (Maurice, Green, & Foxx, 1996) rates abilities on such traits as establishing eye contact, taking turns with toys, initiating greetings, and answering social questions. Displaying empathy, asking questions, and relating to peers are included in advanced skills assessment.

Adolescence is a difficult time for many children, and children with Asperger's are no exception. This is often a time of increased peer relationships, social pressure, and reduced self-esteem. Because of their reduced social abilities, adolescents with Asperger's disorder are particularly vulnerable. Social skills training that incorporates script fading, social stories, and role-playing new situations can be effective methods to help the adolescent develop conversation skills, understand appropriate social behavior, and reduce anxiety associated with social situations (Adams et al., 2004; Sarokoff, Taylor, & Poulson, 2001; Tsatsanis et al., 2004).

Overall Treatment Recommendations. In addition to behavioral treatment, people with PDDs typically require a variety of adjunct services, which may include speech and language training and residential placement. Medication is sometimes also helpful, particularly if SIB, tantrums, and severe aggression are not responsive to behavior modification. The medications used are those used to treat similar symptoms in other disorders — SSRIs for the treatment of anxiety, depression, or OCD; antipsychotic medication like haloperidol (Haldol) to treat severe behavioral problems; and anticonvulsants for the one in four children with PDDs who also have seizures (NIMH, 2004).

A variety of other innovative treatments have been used with these people, such as vitamins, gluten-free diets, sensory integration, and facilitated communication. To date the value of these treatments has not been conclusively demonstrated (Kabot et al., 2003).

"Parents are the point people who ensure continuity across the life span of the child" (Kabot et al., 2003, p. 30). As such, parents need education, advocacy training, and support. In addition to parents' primary role in the assessment of autism and other PDDs, parental involvement includes training to become co-therapists (Lovaas & Smith, 2003), attending meetings to assist in the development of individual treatment plans, and belonging to support groups. Family consultation, as well as supportive therapy for parents and siblings, should usually be included in the treatment of children with PDDs. Therapists work with parents to serve as advocates, coordinate services, and reduce family stress. Couples or sibling therapy can also be beneficial as a means of providing emotional support and useful information about the development of the disorder. The sense of isolation felt by families of children with PDDs may also be reduced if informative publications and networking resources are provided. The Autism Society of America has local chapters throughout the country, and the Rett's Syndrome Association disseminates information from its headquarters. Both groups also have sites on the Internet.

Prognosis

Lovaas (1987) found good outcomes for 47 percent of children with autistic disorder who received early intervention with intensive, behaviorally based therapy. In a review of outcome studies, Gillberg (1991) found that some children diagnosed with autistic disorder had become able to lead independent lives as adults, but that about two-thirds of children with the disorder went on to require care throughout their lives. Prognoses for people with the other PDDs are variable. For those with Asperger's disorder, the prognosis is excellent; many live independent lives. Residential treatment is probable for those with Rett's disorder and childhood degenerative disorder because of the progressive nature of these disorders. For all PDDs, early intervention appears to be the most important factor in a positive outcome (Baird et al., 2001; Lovaas & Smith, 2003; NIMH, 2004).

ATTENTION-DEFICIT AND DISRUPTIVE BEHAVIOR DISORDERS

Overview of the Disorders

Attention-deficit and disruptive behavior disorders listed in *DSM-IV-TR* include attention-deficit/hyperactivity disorder, conduct disorder, and oppositional defiant disorder, as well as disruptive behavior disorder not otherwise specified.

These disorders present therapists with a considerable challenge. Children with these concerns often have multiple disorders, need a variety of collaborative interventions across settings, and can retain symptoms of attention-deficit/hyperactivity disorder into adolescence and adulthood (Barkley, 2006).

Attention-deficit/hyperactivity disorder is found in as many as 50 percent of the children seen for psychotherapy (Barkley, 2006). Children with oppositional defiant disorder and conduct disorder often have comorbid attention deficits, and many children with attention-deficit disorder or conduct disorder have concomitant learning disorders, antisocial difficulties, low self-esteem, and depression. Thirty-seven percent may continue to exhibit myriad psychosocial difficulties across the life span (Anastopoulos & Farley, 2003; Erk, 2004) with as many as 5 to 10 percent developing more serious mental disorders, and 10 to 25 percent developing substance-related problems (Barkley, 2006). ADHD is a neurobiological disorder that cannot be prevented and currently has no cure (Erk, 2004; Kazdin, 2000). To be effective, early diagnosis and treatment interventions should focus on symptom management, address comorbid diagnoses, and continue as long as symptoms are present.

Attention-Deficit/Hyperactivity Disorder

Description of the Disorder

DSM-IV-TR divides attention-deficit/hyperactivity disorder (ADHD) into three subtypes:

1. Predominantly hyperactive-impulsive type
2. Predominantly inattentive type
3. Combined type

As many as 3 to 7 percent of school-age children have been diagnosed with ADHD, making it the most prevalent neurological disorder of childhood (Erk, 2004). Boys are more likely to develop the disorder than girls, by a 3:1 ratio (Smith, Barkley, & Shapiro, 2006). ADHD appears to occur across cultures and has been identified in almost every country in which it has been studied, including Japan, China, Turkey, South America, and the Middle East (Barkley, 2006; Erk, 2004).

The current research indicates that ADHD is a neurobiological or neurobehavioral disorder. Research has found that irregular metabolism of brain chemistry contributes directly to ADHD behavioral patterns. Premotor and superior prefrontal lobe regions of the brain, areas that are responsible for directing executive functioning and impulse control, appear to be much less active in people with ADHD (Smith et al., 2006). The disorder also has a strong genetic component, often appearing in several members of a family.

By definition, ADHD has an onset prior to age seven; is present in two or more settings (such as at home and in school); and interferes with social, academic, or occupational functioning. The person with this disorder also exhibits six or more symptoms of inattentiveness or hyperactivity-impulsivity that have persisted for at least six months (American Psychiatric Association, 2000). Symptoms of inattention include failure to give close attention to details, difficulty with focused or selective attention, poor follow-through on instructions, failure to finish work, difficulty organizing tasks, misplacement of things, distraction by extraneous stimuli, and forgetfulness. Hyperactive-impulsive characteristics are more visible, so the hyperactive-impulsive type of ADHD is usually identified at a younger age. Hyperactive-impulsive behaviors include fidgeting, running about, difficulty playing quietly, acting as if driven by a motor, talking excessively, blurting answers, and interrupting. Overall, people with ADHD have poorer inhibitory control than other people (Smith et al., 2006).

The process of diagnosing ADHD should include comprehensive behavioral, psychological, educational, and medical evaluations to rule out or identify physical, chemical, or environmental contributing factors (Barkley, 2006). Cognitive and achievement assessments, as well as parents' and teachers' input on behavior rating scales, are important for providing information from a variety of settings. The inclusion of a continuous performance test (CPT), a computerized test in which a child is asked to press a button when a specific letter follows another, can provide a measure of the person's ability to sustain attention and control impulsivity over time. A variety of CPTs, such as the Test of Variables of Attention (TOVA), help clinicians distinguish between the three subgroups of ADHD (combined type, predominantly inattentive type, and predominantly hyperactive-impulsive type).

Behavior checklists also provide an assessment of attentional patterns. The Conners' Rating Scales-Revised (Conners, 1997) offer long and short versions of child and adolescent, teacher, and parent rating scales for ADHD. The most commonly used rating scales for ADHD are the Achenbach Child Behavior Checklist (CBCL); Parent, Teacher and Youth Self-Report forms (Achenbach, 1991); and the Behavior Assessment System for Children, 2nd Edition (BASC-2; Reynolds & Kamphaus, 2002). All use a 4-point Likert-type scale to assess a range of behaviors. The Adult ADHD Self-Report Scale is a six-item self-report questionnaire developed by the World Health Organization to screen for adult ADHD (Kessler et al., 2005). A version of the Conners' Rating Scale is also available for adults. The Conners instrument is frequently used by physicians to monitor the effects of medication. The CBCL and the BASC-2 evaluate a broader spectrum of comorbid symptoms, such as depression, anxiety, atypical thoughts, and delinquent and withdrawn behaviors. The BASC-2 includes a scale that allows the therapist to check the validity of responses and facilitates assessment of the predominantly inattentive type of ADHD.

Although not offering conclusive diagnoses, magnetic resonance imaging (MRI) and positron emission tomography (PET) technology have been used to study neurological activity in people with ADHD. Preliminary results suggest that the appearance of significant brain abnormalities may ultimately allow the diagnosis of ADHD to be based on direct assessment of brain functioning. At this time, however, these procedures are being used solely for research purposes.

One difficulty with the diagnosis of ADHD is its reliance on a history derived from teachers' and parents' reports. Negative relationships between the child and these adults may skew these assessments. Moreover, the *DSM* requirement that the identified behaviors be more frequent and more severe than those found in children at comparable developmental levels is sufficiently vague to create diagnostic problems, particularly in children of preschool age. In recent years a dramatic increase in the diagnosis of ADHD in preschoolers has been reported, raising questions about what constitutes normal active behavior in preschoolers.

Typical Client Characteristics

As mentioned earlier, the current prevalence rates for ADHD range from 3 to 7 percent of children (American Psychiatric Association, 2000). Gender differences have shown that males with ADHD present with more aggressive and oppositional behavior than females, who are more likely to have symptoms of the inattentive type of ADHD. There is currently a lack of data comparing boys with ADHD to girls with ADHD, but research is being conducted on the effect of gender on the development and course of the disorder (Biederman, Faraone, Chu, & Wozniak, 1999).

Current research suggests a relationship among ADHD, oppositional defiant disorder (ODD), and conduct disorder (CD). ADHD is the most frequent condition co-occurring with conduct problems and frequently precedes the onset of ODD (Burns, Burns, & Walsh, 2002). Anxiety, depression, and tic disorders have often been found to coexist with ADHD as well, although the nature of the relationship is less clear.

Often the comorbid disorders are masked by the ADHD, but they may be persistent and have deleterious effects. For example, 30 to 50 percent of those with ADHD have co-occurring depression or anxiety. These disorders increase the risk of substance misuse or suicidal ideation or even death via suicide (Coleman & Webber, 2002). The effects of co-occurring conditions should not be underestimated, as they may persist after treatment for ADHD, as part of a cluster (sequelae) of difficulties the individual experiences.

Symptomatic behaviors vary and depend on the age at presentation and the type of ADHD. The symptoms of ADHD prior to age three may include behaviors that disrupt family life and are not conducive to preschool attendance.

Such symptoms include increased motor activity, excessive climbing, aggression, and destructiveness. Cantwell (1996) found that preschoolers usually do not outgrow such behavior. The common feature in elementary school-age children with ADHD is difficulty in sustaining attention, particularly during long, monotonous, repetitive tasks. (These children can usually focus their attention on tasks that include small instructional units or fast-paced multisensory presentations.) Other common symptoms include poor impulse control, restlessness, and overactivity. Children may also exhibit noncompliant and antisocial behaviors related to their impulsivity.

Impulsive behaviors typically impair functioning in many areas. They can result in poor interpersonal relationships and academic difficulties. Barkley (2006) reports that 25 to 40 percent of children with ADHD have comorbid learning disorders. Children with ADHD also are at greater risk for accidental injury and may experience significant sleep problems. As a result of all these difficulties, children with ADHD commonly manifest poor social skills and low self-esteem. Family conflict and discomfort at school also often accompany these children's behaviors, resulting in continued academic difficulties, with as many as 30 to 50 percent of children with ADHD being retained at least one grade in school and 25 to 36 percent never graduating from high school (Barkley, 2006).

Current research suggests that the symptoms of ADHD can persist across the life span. As many as 30 to 50 percent of children with ADHD will be symptomatic through adolescence and adulthood (Barkley, 2006). The symptoms of the disorder typically change, however. Hyperactivity is unusual among adolescents with ADHD; restlessness, poorly organized schoolwork, failure to complete independent work, and high-risk behaviors are more common indicators of this disorder in teenagers (Cantwell, 1996).

Difficulties that follow adolescents with ADHD into adulthood often result in underemployment in relation to their intelligence, education, and family backgrounds. They tend to change jobs frequently, have difficulty creating and maintaining stable relationships, and are more likely to be cited for traffic violations and motor vehicle accidents (Barkley, 2006). Adult symptoms can include restlessness, fidgety behavior, impulsivity, inability to concentrate, and short attention span, among others. Although many adults who have ADHD were never formally diagnosed in childhood, treatment for adults has been found to be effective in addressing these cognitive and behavioral symptoms. Depending on the frequency and severity of symptoms and the results of behavioral checklists, medication may be prescribed to accompany psychotherapy.

Hallowell and Ratey (1994) list the following twenty diagnostic criteria for a diagnosis of adult ADHD, with the presence of fifteen or more considered to be significant: a sense of not meeting one's goals, difficulty getting organized, chronic procrastination, multiple ongoing simultaneous projects, blurting out inappropriate comments, frequent searches for high stimulation, intolerance of boredom, distractibility, creativity, trouble following proper procedures, low frustration tolerance, impulsive behaviors, a tendency to worry, a sense of insecurity, mood swings, restlessness, a tendency toward addictive behavior, chronic problems with self-esteem, inaccurate self-observation, and a family history of ADHD or bipolar disorders (pp. 73–74).

Research has shown compelling evidence of a greater prevalence of ADHD among members of the same family. Smith and colleagues (2006) report that between 10 and 35 percent of first-degree relatives of children diagnosed with ADHD also exhibit characteristics of that disorder, and studies of twins confirm a genetic component of ADHD. First-degree relatives have also been found to have an elevated incidence of depression, alcohol misuse, conduct-related problems, and antisocial disorders (Biederman, Newcorn, & Sprich, 1991). Thus a child with ADHD often has a parent or sibling with the disorder, which may lead to a chaotic home environment and make it difficult for the parents to establish the clear guidelines needed by a child with ADHD. In addition, more severe behavioral problems create conflict in family relationships and strain family functioning (Orr, Miller, & Polson, 2005). A more stable family environment has been shown to have ameliorating effects on the long-term outcome of the disorder.

Preferred Therapist Characteristics

Hyperactive behavior typically affects the therapeutic relationship, just as it affects a person's daily life. The therapist needs to present a calm and patient demeanor, to avoid escalating the excitable behaviors of a person with ADHD. Many transference and countertransference issues can arise as a result of the emotional volatility in a person with this disorder. To be effective, therapists must be clear about their own emotional issues and able to distinguish them from those of the client.

Children with ADHD frequently experience negative interactions with others, particularly adults, as a result of their impulsive and sometimes noncompliant behaviors (Barkley, 2006). Consequently, the development of a trusting, accepting relationship with the therapist is a critical element of treatment. Therapy can be enhanced by the provision of a structured setting where boundaries of time and safety are clearly established by the therapist.

Therapists who work with people with ADHD need to have a working knowledge of the neurological and genetic components of the disorder. Therapists need to be able to educate parent and child about ADHD and to work collaboratively with others involved in the child's treatment, such as teachers, physicians, and family members. Therapists should be comfortable with using behavior management strategies and setting and enforcing limits and also be flexible enough to tailor treatment to meet the individual needs of the child.

They also need a clear developmental yardstick against which to measure problems and improvements in the child's behavior.

Intervention Strategies

ADHD is one of the most researched disorders of childhood. In an effort to provide responsible treatment interventions, several professional organizations (American Academy of Child and Adolescent Psychiatry [AACAP], 1997; American Medical Association [Goldman, Genel, Bezman, & Slanetz, 1998]; and the American Academy of Pediatrics, 2001) have published policy statements as a guideline for clinicians. Orr and colleagues (2005) found considerable consensus among the groups, including the following recommendations: assessment and diagnosis should include a medical/neurological exam; the developmental history should screen for a family history of ADHD and explore the nature of marital and parent-child relationships, and the mental and physical health of caregivers; parent and teacher reports (including interviews, grades, and behavior reports) and standardized rating scales should be gathered; and *DSM-IV-TR* criteria should be followed, including assessment for comorbid conditions. The assessment should also include clinician observation of the child's behavior.

Empirical support exists for the effectiveness of four approaches to treatment for ADHD: pharmacological treatment, parent training in child behavior management methods, teacher implementation of behavior management approaches, and a combination of these approaches in multimodal therapy (Smith et al., 2006). In general, to be most effective, a multimodal treatment strategy that combines stimulant therapy (medication), parent training and counseling, classroom interventions, and cognitive-behavioral therapy is recommended. Research indicates that when pharmacological treatment or behavioral treatment is removed, symptoms of ADHD return to pretreatment levels (Greenhill & Ford, 2002). Because it increases anxiety, stimulant medication is inappropriate in the treatment of some co-occurring disorders, such as anxiety (Smith et al., 2006) and must be recommended with care. A variety of studies, treatment packages, and options are available and are beyond the scope of this book. Readers are referred to the books listed at the end of this chapter for further details.

Therapists working with children with ADHD rely primarily on behavioral interventions to reduce behavioral problems and emotional difficulties. Behavioral treatments for children with ADHD are based on operant conditioning, the shaping of behavior through the use of positive reinforcers. ADHD is seen as a disorder of performance, rather than of knowledge or skills. Therefore, treatment most often is designed to improve attention and enhance motivation for these children to display their knowledge (Smith et al., 2006). To be effective, these interventions must be used across all environments (home, classroom, and therapy) and for months or even years (Smith et al., 2006). They are demanding of time and resources; they involve teaching, practice, encouragement, reinforcement, and monitoring; and they require cooperation on the part of teachers and parents.

Cognitive-behavioral models of treatment have been used to improve social skills in people with ADHD, with limited success. Evidence of CBT effectiveness is lacking at this time (Smith et al., 2006), and the research on social skills training is mixed. Dietary changes also have no compelling evidence of efficacy.

Social skills training programs teach behaviors that can improve interpersonal relationships. Such skills as identifying personal space, starting and maintaining a conversation, identifying the main idea of a conversation, and accepting and giving compliments are all addressed in these programs.

Negative behavior traits found in children with ADHD can disrupt the entire family system. Therefore, treatment should extend to parent training (PT) (Anastopoulos & Farley, 2003), to help parents manage their child's problem behaviors, and sometimes to family therapy. PT has been found to reduce parental stress and increase parental self-esteem and is effective as a preventive intervention in preventing escalation of ADHD symptoms along the developmental pathway to such comorbid disorders as ODD or CD (Anastopoulos & Farley, 2003; Smith et al., 2006). There are a variety of PT approaches, with most of them ranging from eight to twelve sessions and suitable for children between the ages of four and twelve.

Anastopoulos and Farley (2003) describe a parent training program that can be completed in eight to twelve sessions in a group or individual format of sixty to ninety minutes each. Components of the program include an overview of ADHD as well as education in the use of such behavior management techniques as positive reinforcement, response cost, setting up a token economy, and the use of time-outs. The program educates parents on how to handle child behavior problems in public and how to work with the schools. In addition to improving the child's behavior, PT has also been found to improve family functioning, decrease parental stress, and increase self-esteem. Although many different PT treatments exist, they all help educate parents about ADHD, promote awareness and encouragement of socially competent behavior, teach self-evaluation strategies, model good communication skills, and provide consistent rewards and consequences (Anastopoulos & Farley, 2003; Barkley, 2006; Smith et al., 2006).

One promising approach for children has been developed by Barkley (Smith et al., 2006). Because neurophysiological deficits, not poor parenting skills, are at the root of the child's problem, Barkley's approach educates parents on what and how to communicate with the child to best address the child's deficit in executive functioning. The program also includes a component that recognizes that many children with ADHD develop ODD. Barkley includes a training program for parents on contingency management techniques in an effort to prevent the development of ODD.

Due to their developmental stage, many adolescents do not respond well to PT. Clinicians might consider alternative treatments, such as problem-solving and communication training (Anastopoulos & Farley, 2003).

The combination of medication and PT is superior to medication alone in improving family functioning (Greenhill & Ford, 2002). Numerous online support groups, such as Children with Attention Deficit Disorders (www.chadd.org) and the Attention Deficit Disorder Association (ADDA; www.add.org), provide information and family support.

School interventions in the treatment of ADHD are important as well. Consistent and regular communication among parents, teachers, school counselors, and therapists is an integral part of treatment, so that desirable behaviors will be reinforced in multiple settings. Many children with ADHD qualify for additional resources at school, and the therapist can be instrumental in working collaboratively with the school and family in this process. Children with ADHD often exhibit disruptive behavior in classroom settings in which they are required to sit quietly or be attentive for extended periods of time. Classroom interventions usually consist of behavioral techniques that promote teachers' use of selective attending, ignoring of inappropriate behavior, the establishment of clear rules, rewards for success, daily progress notes, increased transition times, and matching of academic materials to the attention span and ability level of the child (Barkley, 2006). A meta-analysis on the effectiveness of seventy separate school intervention programs found that classroom behavioral and academic interventions can improve performance and behavior of children with ADHD, with the greatest improvements occurring with contingency management procedures and peer tutoring approaches (Smith et al., 2006). Effective contingency management strategies included token rewards, as well as group rewards for the entire class.

Other psychotherapeutic approaches have also played a role in the treatment of ADHD. Individual therapy can be instrumental in helping a child cope with academic, social, and family stressors. Counselors can model such traits as self-confidence, empathy, flexibility, resilience, and being nonjudgmental, which can become a part of the child's repertoire of coping skills (Erk, 2004). Treatment plans can address the individual needs of the child and address issues of low self-esteem, losses and disappointment, stress, or comorbid anxiety and mood disorders.

Individual therapy that focuses on improving communication skills, recognition of nonverbal messages, and appropriate approach behaviors has promoted social skill development in children with ADHD. Due to difficulties in executive functioning, children and adolescents with ADHD benefit from learning skills that help improve their daily functioning, such as time management, anger management, impulse control, and replacing negative messages with positive self-talk. However, research on social skills training has produced mixed results (Smith et al., 2006). Such variables as type of ADHD, co-occurring conditions, parent versus teacher ratings, and the presence of ODD have produced inconsistent results. Smith and colleagues note there may actually be an increase in negative and antisocial behaviors when children with ADHD, ODD, or CD are placed together in groups. Therefore, group therapy for children with ADHD is not recommended.

The use of psychostimulant medication for treatment of ADHD has increased fivefold since 1989 (Greenhill & Ford, 2002) and has been the focus of considerable research. Smith and colleagues (2006, p. 88) report that stimulant medications are "the most studied and the most effective treatment for the symptomatic management of ADHD." Recent research indicates the improved effectiveness of combining intensive behavior therapy with psychostimulant medication.

The Multimodal Treatment Study of ADHD (MTA; MTA Cooperative Group, 1999, 2004) is the largest study ever undertaken of one specific disorder. The MTA Study, along with the 1998 NIH Consensus Development Conference on ADHD and the publication of the *McMaster Evidence Based Review of ADHD Treatments*, provides convincing research for the effectiveness of stimulant treatments for the symptoms of ADHD (Greenhill & Ford, 2002). In nearly two hundred studies of psychostimulants (methylphenidate, amphetamines, or pemoline), 70 percent of children responded well to the medication, compared with 13 percent to placebo (Greenhill & Ford, 2002).

Effective drugs are thought to stimulate the production of the neurochemicals that facilitate brain functioning. Contrary to the popular misconception that these children are hypersensitive or hyperattentive, neurodevelopmental research suggests that ADHD is actually a problem of underarousal. Methylphenidate (Ritalin) is prescribed in more than 85 percent of the cases in which medication is recommended (Greenhill & Ford, 2002), with dextroamphetamine (Dexedrine) second and pemoline (Cylert) third. Approximately 80 percent of children with ADHD will respond positively to one of these medications (Greenhill & Ford, 2002). Atomoxetine (Strattera) was approved by the FDA in 2003 for use in children and adults with ADHD (Smith et al., 2006). Strattera is not a stimulant and therefore has no abuse potential. Other nonstimulant medications used in the treatment of ADHD include tricyclic antidepressants, buspirone (BuSpar), bupropion (Wellbutrin), and the antihypertensive drugs clonidine (Catapres) and guanfacine (Tenex). Safety and efficacy issues with regard to use of these medications in children have not been fully addressed.

Therapists may become involved in monitoring clients' reactions to medication and should be in contact with prescribing physicians. Additional research is needed on desired outcomes, as there is currently no standard of success.

Some look for a 25 percent reduction of ADHD symptoms, whereas others continue the dosage until the child's behavior in the classroom is not disruptive. The Abbreviated Conners' Teacher Rating Scale can be used to determine when a child's behavior has sufficiently improved.

Stimulant medications have been well researched and judged safe (Rapport & Moffitt, 2002). The most common side effects of stimulant medication for treating ADHD are decreased appetite and insomnia. Less common side effects include abdominal pain, headaches, and dizziness (Smith et al., 2006). Suppression of growth, particularly in older children, occurs rarely and generally remits when the medication is discontinued (Greenhill & Ford, 2002). In less than 1 percent of children, vocal or motor tics may develop. Medication for ADHD may be contraindicated when there is a history of tic disorders. Stimulants have similar efficacy from childhood through adolescence (Smith et al., 2006). Unfortunately, there is limited research available at this time on the effect of treating preschoolers with psychostimulants (Greenhill & Ford, 2002).

Not all children respond well to medication, and there has been some indication that those with coexisting anxiety are less likely to respond to methylphenidate (Ritalin) and experience more side effects. Greenhill and Ford (2002) suggest that characteristics of young age, low rates of anxiety, low severity of the disorder, and high IQ may predict good response. The decision to treat a child with medication should be based on the severity of the symptoms; on the preferences of the parents and the child; on the ability of the child, the parents, and the school to cope with the disorder; and on the success or failure of alternative treatment (Rapoport & Castellanos, 1996).

Prognosis

The long-term effectiveness of psychostimulants on ADHD symptoms in children has not been studied for longer than twenty-four months. Anecdotal evidence suggests that gains are lost when the medication is stopped and continue when it is restarted (Greenhill & Ford, 2002). Similar results have been noticed with behavioral and other nonpharmacological treatments (Hinshaw, Klein, & Abikoff, 2002). Although not curative, multiple treatment strategies, including pharmacological therapy, parent training, parent counseling, and classroom interventions, can help reduce related behavioral or emotional difficulties.

Studies cited earlier support the benefits of psychostimulant medication. Research also points to the additive effects of psychostimulant and cognitive-behavioral therapies, including parent training and clients' self-monitoring, to address certain variables — teacher-rated social skills, parent-child relations, reading achievement, and comorbid anxiety (Greenhill & Ford, 2002; Kazdin, 2000). Combined medication management and behavior therapy have not been shown to reduce the core symptoms of ADHD, but have been shown to improve positive functioning and other non-ADHD symptoms. Integrated treatments continue to be the accepted treatment approach for this disorder (Barkley, 2006; Coleman & Webber, 2002; Erk, 2004; Hinshaw et al., 2002).

Disruptive Behavior Disorders

DSM-IV-TR (American Psychiatric Association, 2000) describes two disruptive behavior disorders: conduct disorder (CD) and oppositional defiant disorder (ODD). These disorders include a spectrum of behaviors that occur in children and adolescents. Typical client characteristics and preferred therapists for each disorder will be discussed separately. The disorders will be considered together in the sections on intervention strategies and prognosis. The link between ODD and CD has been the topic of considerable research (Lavigne et al., 2001; Loeber, Burke, Lahey, Winters, & Zera, 2000).

Research suggests that ODD, CD, and antisocial personality disorder (discussed further in Chapter Eight) represent a continuum of behaviors. In other words, early onset and greater severity of symptoms of ODD increase the potential for a person to develop CD, and the early onset and severity of that disorder increase the likelihood of the symptoms' progressing into antisocial personality disorder. Biopsychosocial differences determine the pathway, with earlier onset of symptoms indicating a more severe course (McMahon, Wells, & Kotler, 2006).

Definition and treatment of ODD and CD have been the focus of numerous research studies. The literature indicates the following trends:

- There has been an increase in the number of crimes committed by female juveniles (McMahon et al., 2006).
- Since 2005, juvenile arrests for violent crimes have increased in medium-sized cities (Eggen, 2007).
- Violent crime is occurring at a younger age, with arrests increasing 45 percent for children ages seven to twelve from 1988 to 1997 (Snyder, 2001).
- Early-onset conduct problems in young children have been linked to more serious and violent offenses and criminal conviction rates in adulthood two to three times greater than late-onset conduct disorder (Moffitt, Caspi, Harrington, & Milne, 2002).

Description of the Disorders

Most of the treatment literature considers CD and ODD to be on a continuum of disorders that involve both externalizing disorders characterized by dysfunctional behavior (primarily found in boys) and internalizing disorders, characterized by anxiety and depression (primarily found in girls). CD and ODD are hierarchical and developmentally related (Loeber et al., 2000; Erk, 2004). From the standpoint of the therapist, the primary differences between these two disorders are that the symptoms for ODD are milder and the prognosis is more promising than for CD.

Conduct Disorder. Conduct disorder is one of the most frequently encountered diagnoses in settings that provide therapy to young people: one-third to one-half the children seen for treatment in mental health clinics present with symptoms of CD (Kazdin, 2002). Estimates of the prevalence of CD vary and depend on the population sampled. It has been estimated that between one and four million children and adolescents in the United States exhibit symptoms of CD (Chamberlain & Smith, 2003). The disorder is found among boys at a three to four times higher rate than among girls (Kazdin, 2002), though the gender ratio evens out in adolescence.

A diagnosis of CD is based not just on the presence of conduct-disordered behavior; as with all mental disorders, the disturbance must cause clinically significant impairment in social, academic, or occupational functioning. Diagnosis requires the presence of repetitive and persistent violations of the basic rights of others or violations of major age-appropriate societal norms or rules. *DSM-IV-TR* lists fifteen behaviors, divided into four main groups — aggression against people and animals, destruction of property, deceitfulness or theft, and serious violations of rules — that characterize conduct disorder. For a diagnosis of this disorder, three or more incidents reflecting these symptoms must have been present during the previous twelve months, with at least one during the previous six months.

Substantial research has identified numerous factors that increase a child's risk of developing CD, including child temperament, parenting factors, socioeconomic factors, prenatal complications, exposure to violence, and association with antisocial peers (Kazdin, 2002; McMahon et al., 2006). Noncompliant behavior — that is, a disregard for adults — is a key ingredient of the development of severe conduct problems at home, at school, and with peers. Research indicates that when treatment interventions address issues of noncompliance, improvement is made in all areas of behavior (McMahon et al., 2006).

CD is divided into childhood-onset and adolescent-onset types. A diagnosis of childhood-onset type is made when at least one manifestation of this disorder occurred prior to the child's reaching the age of ten. Adolescent-onset type is diagnosed if the characteristics of the disorder did not appear before age ten. According to Webster-Stratton and Reid (2003), the prognosis for the childhood-onset type is worse than for the adolescent-onset type; early-onset conduct disorder is frequently a precursor to serious illegal and harmful behaviors in adolescence and adulthood, including substance misuse, property crimes, and violence. Children with early-onset CD are also at increased risk for abuse by their parents, depression, dropping out of school, and other disorders (Webster-Stratton & Reid, 2003). By the time a child reaches the age of eighteen, CD has often evolved into the more serious and enduring diagnosis of antisocial personality disorder, particularly if the CD began early and continued through adolescence.

Comorbidity with other disorders often occurs and complicates the diagnosis of CD. Kazdin (2002) reports that diagnoses involving disruptive or externalizing behaviors, such as CD, ODD, and ADHD, often occur together. Between 45 and 70 percent of children with CD have ADHD; 84 to 96 percent of children with CD have also met the criteria for ODD; and CD is frequently comorbid with anxiety and mood disorders. The high rate of comorbidity of depression and CD increases the risk of serious outcomes, such as substance misuse and suicide. The suicide risk increases if the conduct-disordered person is female or has experienced a recent stressor, such as legal or disciplinary problems, school problems, or is not in a school or work situation (Evans et al., 2005; McMahon et al., 2006).

Co-occurring anxiety appears to have an ameliorating effect on aggression. One study (Hinshaw & Lee, 2003) reports that boys with co-occurring anxiety based on inhibition and fear are less aggressive than boys with CD alone. CD is also strongly associated with symptoms of mania (Evans et al., 2005), which often presents in childhood as irritable mood and includes symptoms of physical restlessness and poor judgment.

Academic difficulties and deficits, including grade failure, increased dropout rates, low verbal intelligence, poor reading skills, and other learning disorders also are commonly found in children with CD (Kazdin, 2002). In the assessment of CD clinicians should assess for all comorbid disorders, as treatment of all coexisting disorders is likely to improve prognosis (Evans et al., 2005).

Some researchers draw on attachment theory (Bowlby, 1969, 1982) and social learning theory in understanding behavioral disorders. Insecure attachment between parent and child has been linked to aggressive behavior, low self-esteem, poor coping skills, low socialization skills, and poor interpersonal relationships in the child as well as increased maternal stress, child abuse, and neglect (Brinkmeyer & Eyberg, 2003). This perspective has had an impact on treatment models, as will be seen in the section on interventions.

Oppositional Defiant Disorder. According to *DSM-IV-TR*, oppositional defiant disorder (ODD) is described as "a pattern of negativistic, defiant, disobedient, and hostile behavior toward authority figures that persists for at least 6 months" (American Psychiatric Association, 2000, p. 100). Characteristic behaviors include anger and hostility, resistance to adult authority, deliberately annoying others and being easily annoyed by others, and resentful and vindictive behavior. Children with ODD also tend to blame others for their own negative behavior. At younger ages, children may manifest ODD through temper tantrums, kicking, power struggles with parents, disobedience, screaming, and low tolerance for frustration (Mash & Wolfe, 2005). Common complaints from the parents of older children with this disorder are that the children argue, threaten, show disrespect for adults, destroy property in a rage, refuse to cooperate, and are stubborn.

These symptoms often appear to be an exacerbation of typical childhood misbehaviors. The diagnosis of ODD is made when these behaviors are of greater frequency, duration, and intensity than would be expected for the child's age and when they cause social, occupational, and academic impairment (American Psychiatric Association, 2000). Often these children come to the attention of school counselors and therapists when the oppositional behaviors interfere with functioning at school. Until then, parents may not recognize the behaviors as being unusual. Oppositional behaviors are sometimes reinforced: when a child acts inappropriately, an adult reacts with hostility or frustration, and the child responds by escalating the negative behaviors.

Estimates of the prevalence of ODD vary greatly: it is thought to occur in 2 to 16 percent of children (American Psychiatric Association, 2000). ODD is positively correlated with low SES, single-parent families, and urban location (Loeber et al., 2000). Physical abuse and multiple changing caretakers are also associated with the development of this disorder (Mash & Wolfe, 2005). This disorder usually begins by the age of eight, with peak prevalence occurring between the ages of eight and eleven (American Psychiatric Association, 2000). Before puberty, boys diagnosed with ODD outnumber girls, but the rates seem to equalize after the age of twelve.

Typical Client Characteristics

Conduct Disorder. The negative, hostile behaviors of children with CD often keep others away or evoke equally hostile responses, and a negative pattern often is perpetuated. Age-inappropriate stubbornness, hostility, defiance, and other oppositional behaviors may be noticeable as early as preschool (Mash & Wolfe, 2005) and cause difficulty in parent-child and teacher-student relationships. Inappropriate behaviors can be categorized as either overt or covert. Overt behaviors, such as theft, assault, and the setting of fires, have a direct impact on others. These behaviors are more often exhibited by males (American Psychiatric Association, 2000). Covert, or nonconfrontational, behaviors, exemplified by verbal fights, gossip, lying, shoplifting, or truancy, are more often exhibited by females with CD.

Children and adolescents with CD have difficulty developing satisfactory interpersonal relationships. They typically lack empathy, are hostile toward adults, dominate other children, and, as adolescents, are likely to have numerous sexual partners. These relationship deficits are thought to have a connection with early problems in attachment (Greenberg, Lengua, Coie, Pinderhughes, & Conduct Problems Prevention Research Group, 1999; McMahon et al., 2006), as well as an environmental component. For example, around the age of ten, children with behavior problems are typically rejected by their better-functioning peers and so gravitate toward associations with acting-out peers (McMahon et al., 2006).

Due to the high incidence of family risk factors, a multidimensional assessment that includes careful analysis of the families, environments, peer groups, and skills of those with CD is necessary to the development of appropriate treatment plans. Kazdin (2002) reports that parents of young people with CD have a high incidence of psychopathology themselves and that their symptoms commonly include depression, antisocial personality disorder, criminal behavior, and alcohol misuse. Mash and Wolfe (2005) also found an increased incidence of marital discord and unemployment in families of children with CD.

Research shows that such behavior tends to run in families, across generations (Mash & Wolfe, 2005), which suggests a genetic, perhaps neurobiological, component. Genetic influences contribute to such traits as difficult temperament, impulsivity, problems with executive functioning, and hyperactivity. Parent modeling of problem behavior also contributes. Harsh parenting as well as inconsistent use of punishment is often found, as well as poor supervision and child monitoring (McMahon et al., 2006). Family relationships are often strained and lacking in affection. Families may include a parent or an older sibling with antisocial behavior. Mothers are particularly likely to exhibit symptoms of depression, anger, and feelings of isolation. These parental characteristics are correlated with premature termination of the children's treatment and with increased likelihood that the children's disruptive behaviors will return after treatment has ended.

Modeling of poor behavior by parents, such as marital violence, paternal pet abuse, and paternal drinking are positively related to the symptom of fire setting; exposure to marital violence and harsh paternal and maternal parenting were associated with animal cruelty (Becker, Stuewig, Herrera, & McCloskey, 2004). Those who engage in fire setting are at three to four times increased risk for later arrest for a violent crime. Fire setting, cruelty to animals, and other dangerous and physically harmful behaviors are also predictors of poor long-term outcomes.

Children with CD often come from large families, live in substandard housing in areas with high crime rates, and attend school in disadvantaged settings (Kazdin, 2002; Loeber et al., 2000). In school settings, children who meet the criteria for CD typically have both academic and behavioral problems. Language-processing deficits are also common and may interfere with comprehension and with the processing of social information (Erk, 2004).

Aggression in childhood is viewed as part of a syndrome that typically continues on to norm-violating behaviors in adolescence (Kazdin, 2002). Children who begin to exhibit such behavior in childhood rather than adolescence are most likely to exhibit severe antisocial symptoms. Researchers have begun to organize clinically meaningful subgroups of aggressive children based on a continuum of types of behaviors. The continuum ranges from starting rumors, arguing, using slang, bullying, engaging in threatening behavior, and striking back in anger, to physical fighting (Lochman, Barry, & Pardini, 2003).

Bullying is a form of aggression that has been the subject of increasing attention and research. Bullying occurs primarily in school settings, and nearly 75 percent of children experience at least one bullying incident in any given year. Episodes of bullying occur alarmingly early in a child's experience, with 50 percent of children in kindergarten having experienced some form of bullying behavior by another child (McMahon et al., 2006). Bullying behavior peaks during the adolescent years and decreases during high school.

Oppositional Defiant Disorder. Young people diagnosed with ODD have low tolerance for frustration or delayed gratification. They expect their demands to be granted immediately. Many children with ODD exhibit aggressive behaviors. Although ODD is part of a spectrum or cluster of behavioral problems, most children with ODD do not subsequently develop conduct disorder. Even so, most children with CD started with a preexisting or co-occurring ODD and continued along the developmental pathway (Kazdin, 1995). These children are at risk for substandard academic performance and school suspension and expulsion, and have higher dropout rates (Roeser, Eccles, & Sameroff, 2000). Communication and learning disorders also are common in children with ODD and CD.

Comorbidity of ADHD and either ODD or CD is found in nearly 50 percent of children under the age of twelve who meet the criteria for ADHD (Pliszka, Carlson, & Swanson, 2001). Impulsive behaviors typical of children with ADHD may intensify oppositional behaviors and contribute to poor social judgment and faulty decision making. Mash (2006) warns that "when ADHD is present, the onset of conduct disorder is earlier, the developmental progression from less serious to more serious antisocial behavior is more rapid, and the risk of psychopathy may be greater" (p. 20) than if the child had had CD without ADHD. If ADHD is present, its treatment is essential to the successful treatment of both ODD and CD.

Assessment

The multiplicity of problems and contributing factors that are involved in these disorders, particularly in CD, makes their assessment and treatment extremely complex. Multiple systems and settings may be included in the assessment process. The assessment of children with CD, for example, may involve professionals from other agencies, such as law enforcement, the judicial system, and social services, as well as consultation with teachers and others in the school system. In almost all cases, a family interview is indicated.

Information regarding behaviors and attitudes observed at school should also be considered. Low self-esteem related to poor academic performance may exacerbate problems. The Conners' Teacher Rating Scale (Conners, 1997) and the teacher versions of the CBCL (Achenbach, 1991) and BASC (Reynolds & Kamphaus, 2002) enable teachers to provide information about children's aggressive behaviors, as well as any hyperactive, inattentive, somatic, depressive, and other behaviors. The importance of including reports from multiple informants in the diagnostic assessment of ODD and CD is highlighted by Hart and colleagues (1994), who found that reports from teachers have the strongest correlation with criterion behaviors observed in 177 boys between the ages of seven and twelve in a clinic setting; reports from parents and other children were less valid.

The first step in devising a treatment plan for young persons with CD or ODD is to assess the degree of danger the children pose to themselves or others and to evaluate the impact that the environment may be having on their continued development. Such behavior checklists as the Achenbach Child Behavior Checklist (CBCL; Achenbach, 1991) or the Behavior Assessment System for Children (BASC) (Reynolds & Kamphaus, 2002) are useful in identifying the parents' perceptions and the severity of the child's behaviors. If the client has a clear suicide plan or intends to harm others, parents or appropriate authorities must be notified, and residential treatment should be considered. The psychological status of the parents and the parents' perceptions of the child's behaviors may also be so impaired that the home is not an appropriate setting for the child. Alternative placement may be necessary if the child's relationship to the parent is aggressive or if the child is abused.

The therapist should also identify any co-occurring disorders that may contribute to or compound the effects of the primary disorder. The possibility of ADHD, learning disorders, depression, thought disorders, a history of abuse, substance use, neurological difficulties, and other medical conditions should always be considered. Psychological testing is recommended and should include assessment of cognitive, perceptual, and social-emotional functioning.

A neurologist can be consulted to rule out seizure activity, and a psychiatrist may be consulted regarding the advisability of medication. This lengthy diagnostic process can provide invaluable guidance in treatment.

Assessments for these disorders must be developmentally, culturally, and contextually sensitive (McMahon et al., 2006). Any assessment should take the child's age, developmental pathways, cultural and socioeconomic background, as well as family and peer influences, into account.

Preferred Therapist Characteristics

Working with a child with a disruptive behavior disorder can be challenging. Therapists should have a solid understanding of the multiple causal factors that lead to the development of these disorders and should have the ability to assess and treat comorbid disorders. Successful interventions usually will involve multiple professionals and community agencies working together toward an integrated treatment that includes the home, school, and community (McMahon et al., 2006).

Conduct Disorder. The most effective treatments for CD involve a collaborative decision-making approach to cognitive-behavioral interventions. Thus the therapist should have the ability to assess such family processes as the affective bond between the caregiver and child, parental discipline strategies, and the ability of the parents to apply and maintain consistent structure and discipline (Henggeler & Lee, 2003). Therapists may be called on to provide behavior therapy, anger management, social skills training, and parent education, and to help clients resurrect empathy that has been squashed since childhood or never learned (Hanna & Hunt, 1999).

Therapists who work with defiant, aggressive adolescents should take care to establish a respectful, empathic therapeutic relationship. Hanna and Hunt (1999) point to the importance of respect, humor, genuineness, and the use of concise language by therapists working with this population. Therapists should acknowledge the role of culture in their clients' lives and be aware of countertransference issues that may derail therapy. The client's disruptive, angry, callous, provocative, or intimidating behaviors may stir up unresolved conflicts or negative feelings from the therapist's own youth. Therapists should not engage in win-lose battles, should not trust the adolescents' portrayal of their own behavior, should not fear manipulation, and should not become intimidated when working with aggressive adolescents. Therapists may need to work with the legal system or with court-ordered services and so must have knowledge of those systems. Therapists' expertise appears to be an important predictor of successful treatment outcomes for clients with CD (Kazdin, 1993).

Oppositional Defiant Disorder. Clients with ODD typically transfer their negative feelings toward authority, as well as their perceptions of hostility in the environment, to their therapists. Therapists working with young clients diagnosed with ODD must have great patience and be cognizant of their own feelings about control, anger, defiance, and misbehavior. Therapists must also recognize their own countertransference issues so as to prevent them from having a negative impact on treatment (Hanna & Hunt, 1999).

Therapists for these children must be able to provide a consistent relationship during long-term treatment, if that kind of treatment is indicated. Therapists also need knowledge of behavior therapies, family therapy, and psychoeducation, and they may be called on to develop behavioral strategies for changing negative behaviors and to provide training in social skills and problem solving.

Intervention Strategies

More than fifteen hundred controlled outcome studies exist on the treatment of CD and ODD. In 1997, the American Academy of Child and Adolescent Psychiatry (AACAP) published clinical practice guidelines for the treatment of CD. Multiple research studies have identified the treatment of parents as a key factor in successful outcomes for young people with disruptive behavior disorders (Kazdin, 2003; Webster-Stratton & Reid, 2003).

One of the greatest challenges in treating young people diagnosed with CD or ODD is the frequency with which parents terminate treatment prematurely. Henggeler and Lee (2003) found that high levels of caregiver stress, substance misuse, and mental health problems were common barriers to effective family interventions. Parents who terminated treatment early reported continuing problems with their children's antisocial and aggressive behaviors, whereas the parents of children who had completed treatment reported an increase in functional behaviors at home, at school, and in the community. Still, one study indicated that even in the families that dropped out of treatment early, 34 percent reported they were currently functioning well and had made important changes during their treatment. Brinkmeyer and Eyberg (2003) found that much of the dropout rate during parent-child interaction therapy was unaccounted for by gender, age, IQ, child's diagnosis, maternal psychopathology, or number of parents in the home (Kazdin, 1990, 1997). Highly critical mothers and those with severe parenting stress were more likely to drop out, but the impact of other family factors on dropout rates was not explored.

Adding a treatment component that reduces parental stress has been shown to improve treatment outcomes and compliance (Kazdin, 2003). Addressing such nonparenting issues as job stress, health problems, family disputes, and external demands can also help reduce the number of families who terminate treatment prematurely.

Empirically supported treatments for families with a child who is diagnosed with CD or ODD include parent management training, multisystemic therapy, cognitive problem-solving skills training, functional family therapy, and brief strategic family therapy.

Kazdin (2002) has shown parent management training and multisystemic training to work well with conduct-disordered children. Kazdin suggests that his own work has shown that children with multiple risk factors, earlier onset of symptoms, severely aggressive behavior, and family adversity will have poorer treatment outcomes. It seems that for many childhood disorders, it is the synergistic effect of multiple risk factors that portends a poor prognosis.

One meta-analysis of psychotherapeutic interventions for ODD and CD does indicate that psychotherapy is significantly better than no treatment at all (Weisz, Weiss, Han, Granger, & Morton, 1995). The same meta-analysis has found that behavioral interventions generally yield outcomes that are more positive than those for nonbehavioral treatments, and that adolescent girls demonstrate better outcomes than those for children in any other age or gender group.

Parent Management Training (PMT). PMT is the most studied treatment for CD and provides clinical evidence that changing family interaction processes positively alters child behavior (Kazdin, 2002). PMT, developed by Patterson in 1982, is the model for many current training programs for parents. PMT is a cognitive-behavioral approach that teaches such skills as monitoring children's behaviors, maintaining discipline, and providing rewards. Outcome studies find that PMT reduces children's aggression and increases their prosocial behaviors (Webster-Stratton & Reid, 2003). These behaviors, once learned, can be generalized to school settings. Improvements in siblings' behavior and decreased maternal stress and depression have also been beneficial side effects of PMT (Kazdin, 2003). Longitudinal studies indicate that PMT has continuing effectiveness ten to fifteen years after the original training (Webster-Stratton & Reid, 2003).

Webster-Stratton and Reid (2003) developed a PMT-style program that uses videotaped vignettes, role playing, a discussion group for parents, and peer support. In the basic curriculum, parents learn to play with and praise their children, to set limits, and to provide discipline. The advanced curriculum teaches such concepts as time-outs, problem solving, anger management, and communication skills. Webster-Stratton reports clinically significant improvement at three-year follow-up in two-thirds of the children rated. A later version was developed for teacher training in schools.

Treatment manuals and parent training materials are often a part of PMT. Additional research indicates that video-based treatment, when combined with therapist-led discussion groups, leads to improvements that can still be measured at one- and three-year posttreatment intervals (Kazdin, 2002).

Multisystemic Therapy (MST). MST is a family- and community-based treatment for adolescents who present with such serious clinical problems as substance misuse, chronic antisocial behavior, serious mental health issues, and family dysfunction. MST addresses the multiple contexts in which CD is manifested. Therapists introduce individual, peer, and school interventions that involve some of the techniques already mentioned. Eight published outcome studies indicated that this approach, used with adolescents exhibiting violent criminal behaviors, has shown promise in the treatment of criminal behavior, substance abuse, and emotional disturbance. More than thirty states and several countries currently run licensed MST programs, and 1 percent of adolescent offenders at risk of incarceration in the United States have been treated with MST (Henggeler & Lee, 2003).

Problem-Solving Skills Training (PSST). It is clear that cognitive-behavioral approaches that teach problem-solving techniques decrease aggressive behaviors, but the effects are greatest in children who have achieved formal operational cognitive levels (generally by the age of eleven) and in adolescents with strong ego functioning (Durlak, Fuhrman, & Lampman, 1991; Kazdin, 1993, 2002). Dishion and Andrews (1995), focusing on high-risk children between the ages of eleven and fourteen, evaluated a variety of intervention models that included the use of groups for parents, groups for teenagers, combined parent and teen groups, and self-directed workbooks. All of these therapeutic interventions were effective, but those that featured parents' involvement demonstrated the most positive results. Webster-Stratton and Reid (2003) found that the most effective parent interventions included training in communication and problem solving.

PSST also teaches children to define a problem, identify goals, generate options, choose the best option, and evaluate the outcome. Techniques from social learning theory, such as modeling, role playing, reinforcement, and shaping of behaviors, enhance clients' ability to make decisions. PSST leads to significant reductions in parents' and teachers' ratings of children's aggressive behaviors, both immediately after treatment and one year later. Adding a parent training component further improves treatment outcomes (Kazdin, 2003). Kazdin (2002) studied the effectiveness of PSST in an elementary school classroom, and found that those who received the training exhibited less disruptive behavior and more prosocial behavior. The beneficial impact was still noticeable two years later and points to a school intervention that can be easily implemented and improves outcomes.

Functional Family Therapy. Functional family therapy, developed by Alexander and Parsons in 1982, is derived from parent management training as well as from communication training and behavioral, structural, and systems theories of family therapy. At its core, this therapy attempts to identify faulty or dysfunctional interactions in the family and replace them with more functional responses and behaviors. Functional family therapy attempts to reduce defensiveness and blame and increase positive interactions among family members. It has been implemented among adolescents with CD whose behaviors have resulted in court involvement. Outcomes include improved family communications and the clients' decreased involvement with the courts up to two-and-one-half years after treatment (Kazdin, 1997).

Functional family therapy has also been shown to alter conduct problems of varying severity and to lower recidivism rates for young people who break the law (Kazdin, 2002). This treatment modality, used with young people with ODD or CD, has been found superior to psychodynamic or person-centered treatment in controlled studies. Treatment outcomes include increased family communication and a lower incidence of contact with the court system.

Individual and Group Psychotherapy. Individual psychotherapy nearly always will be a part of the treatment plan for a young person diagnosed with CD or ODD. Milder forms of disruptive behavior disorders often respond well to individual therapy that includes consultation with parents and school. In these cases, treatment planning should include a prevention component. In addition to PSST (discussed earlier), anger management training and reality therapy have been shown to be effective with people with CD or ODD.

Reality therapy can provide a framework for challenging the distorted environmental perceptions often held by adolescents involved in or at risk for problem behavior. This approach, developed by Glasser (1990), is frequently used in day treatment or hospital settings. The therapeutic relationship and such techniques as contracting and the use of rewards and consequences help clients meet their needs in healthy, positive ways. Insight often improves after behavior has changed (Hanna & Hunt, 1999).

Anger management training is another cognitive approach that has received some support in the treatment of behavior problems. Lochman and colleagues (2003), for example, describe the Anger Coping and Coping Power programs, which teach elementary school-age children to use cognitive-behavioral strategies for coping with anger such as emotional awareness, relaxation techniques, perspective taking, social problem solving, and dealing with peer pressure. Goal setting was identified as an important determinant of treatment effectiveness.

Such treatment modalities as psychodynamic therapy, relationship-based treatment, and play therapy have been shown to be significantly less effective in treating CD (Kazdin, 2002, 2003). This may be because they fail to take into account and treat problems in multiple domains.

The use of group therapy to treat CD and ODD has demonstrated mixed results. Social skills training groups like those developed by Kazdin (2003) have been successful in decreasing the oppositional behaviors and increasing the prosocial behaviors of children with ODD. Therapy groups for adolescents with CD have been less successful. Treatment in hospitals, schools, and correctional facilities often include a group therapy component in which peers come together to talk about their problems. Kazdin (2003) warns that placing adolescents with CD together in groups could impede improvement because of the tendency for the group to bond and reinforce deviant behavior. To minimize contagion of acting-out behaviors, Lochman and colleagues (2003, p. 279) recommend the following course of action in anger control training:

- Use two group leaders in a small (four- to six-person) group environment.
- Set clear expectations.
- Develop consequences for negative behavior during group.
- Include positive feedback.
- Establish groupwide contingencies for positive reinforcement.
- Encourage prosocial activities outside of the group.

Pharmacological Interventions. Medication alone is ineffective in treating CD or ODD (AACAP, 1997; Kazdin, 2002). However, pharmacotherapy has been found to be beneficial in the treatment of specific symptoms, such as aggression, and of such comorbid conditions as ADHD, mood disorders (depression and bipolar disorder), anxiety, and paranoid ideation with aggressiveness. McMahon and colleagues (2006) note that lithium, clonidine, anticonvulsants, antidepressants, and psychostimulants such as Ritalin are commonly used in the treatment of people with disruptive behavior disorders.

Hospitalization and Day Treatment Programs. Sometimes a young person's behavior becomes sufficiently dangerous or uncontrollable, or the family dysfunction so severe, as to warrant the child's placement in a group home, hospital, or residential setting. AACAP (1997) notes that *DSM-IV-TR* criteria for CD are not often sufficient for hospitalization. However, additional symptoms, such as a substance-related disorder, self-destructive or suicidal behavior, or homicidal or aggressive behavior, may make hospitalization necessary, as might severe symptoms of comorbid depressive disorder, bipolar disorder, psychosis, or intermittent explosive disorder.

Inpatient, partial hospitalization, and residential treatment programs should provide detoxification from drugs or alcohol, as well as time and resources both for in-depth evaluation and for stabilization on medication. A therapeutic milieu that includes behavior modification, family therapy, parent training, and individual and group therapy should also be included for young people diagnosed with disruptive behavior disorders who are receiving intensive treatment.

Day treatment programs offer similar benefits to those available in hospital or residential settings, but they allow the young person to return home at night and are usually less costly than hospitalization. Day treatment programs typically are intensive, running from five to eight hours a day, five days per week. In addition to individual, group, and family therapy, these programs often include special education and behavioral consultation as part of individualized intervention plans. Day treatment programs have been found to reduce behaviors associated with CD and to improve social skills and family functioning (McMahon et al., 2006).

Prognosis

Many factors are associated with successful treatment of disruptive behavior disorders. The most effective treatment approaches are those that involve the child's peer groups, family, and school. In a meta-analysis of treatment for disruptive behavior disorders, McMahon (1994) found outcome to be related to accuracy in diagnosing comorbid disorders. The duration of treatment and the therapist's expertise in treating CD also seem to be important predictors of a successful outcome (Kazdin, 1993). Risk factors at onset of CD, such as early onset, severely aggressive behavior, and family adversity, can result in a poor long-term prognosis and influence responsiveness to treatment (Kazdin, 2003).

McMahon and colleagues (2006) stress that appropriate assessment and the selection of interventions that match the child's needs are key to effective treatments. Early intervention facilitates therapists' efforts to change cognitive structures, so that new ideas are generated and alternative choices are made. In many cases, early intervention also precludes the development of more severely disruptive behavior. In CD with late or adolescent onset, children can draw on a history of appropriate behaviors. In general, family-based therapy is better for younger children, whereas older children do better with multicomponent interventions.

Often these disorders are thought of as having poor prognoses and being costly to society because such a large number of these children remain involved with mental health agencies or the criminal justice system throughout the life span (Webster-Stratton & Reid, 2003). However, young people diagnosed with ODD or CD certainly can show a positive response to treatment. The most critical element of successful treatment for this population appears to be parents' participation in ongoing support and periodic retraining. Self-help movements like Tough Love can also be helpful to parents of children with disruptive behavior disorders. Prevention, both for high-risk children who have not yet met the criteria for ODD or CD and for those who have had these disorders but have improved through therapy, is also essential in reducing the incidence and severity of these disorders.

FEEDING AND EATING DISORDERS OF INFANCY OR EARLY CHILDHOOD

Description of the Disorders

The *DSM-IV-TR* category feeding and eating disorders of infancy or early childhood includes three disorders that interfere to a significant degree with a child's development, social functioning, or nutritional health: pica, rumination disorder, and feeding disorder of infancy or early childhood. The first two can also be diagnosed in adults but are much more common in children.

Pica is characterized by the consumption of nonnutritive substances for at least one month. The substances that are eaten vary across the life span. Infants and preschool children with this disorder typically eat such items as paint, paper, hair, or cloth. Older children typically eat insects, plants, clay, pebbles, or animal droppings. Soil, ice, clay, and hair are the most common substances eaten by adults who have pica (American Psychiatric Association, 2000; Roberts-Harewood & Davies, 2001). The diagnosis of pica should not be made if the eating habits are consistent with the cultural values and beliefs of the person and that person's family.

Pica often coexists with mental retardation or another disorder (often a neurological one). It becomes the focus of treatment only if it interferes with the person's functioning to a significant extent. Children with pica usually do not present for treatment until a medical complication has resulted. Lead poisoning is a common complication of eating paint chips. Other resulting medical problems include obstructed bowels, intestinal perforations, or infections. Although rare, repeated ingestion of hair (known as trichobezoar or Rapunzel syndrome) may result in the development of an intestinal hairball that must be surgically removed (Memon, Mandhan, Qureshi, & Shairani, 2003).

Pica is rare and is most often found in preschool children and among children with severe emotional disturbances. Onset is usually between the ages of twelve and twenty-four months. Prevalence of pica is significantly greater among children with mental retardation (as high as 30 percent in that population) or autistic disorder (as high as 60 percent). Its prevalence is also higher among children with behavior disorders and children from families with low SES (Kronenberger & Meyer, 2001). The disorder may also occur in pregnant women. One study of pregnant women found that 33 percent of the women with pica had a history of childhood pica, and 56 percent had a positive family history of the disorder, suggesting that the disorder may have a learned component (Roberts-Harewood & Davies, 2001).

Rumination disorder is found primarily in infants, with a typical age of onset of three to twelve months. This rare disorder is also found in older children and adults diagnosed with mental retardation (American Psychiatric Association, 2000). The symptoms include repeated regurgitation and remastication of food. The disorder develops after a period of normal eating and digesting and is not due to a general medical condition. Children with rumination disorder typically exhibit straining postures and sucking movements that facilitate the regurgitation. They appear to derive satisfaction from this activity, although they also are often irritable and hungry (American Psychiatric Association, 2000). Most children recover spontaneously from this disorder, but it should be taken seriously when it occurs, because death from malnutrition results in as many as 25 percent of cases (American Psychiatric Association, 2000).

Two subtypes of rumination disorder have been distinguished. The psychogenic subtype is reserved for those children who show no evidence of mental retardation. The etiology of psychogenic rumination is thought to be related to negative interactions between infants and caregivers, especially around feeding issues. The self-stimulating subtype is most likely to be found in children with mental retardation, whose ruminative behaviors are linked to cognitive rather than social deficits (Kronenberger & Meyer, 2001).

Feeding disorder of infancy or early childhood is diagnosed when a child exhibits persistent failure to eat adequately and has not gained age-appropriate weight or has lost a significant amount of weight over a period of at least one month. The symptoms must not be related to a general medical condition or to a lack of available food. Onset must be before the age of six years and usually occurs during the first year of life (American Psychiatric Association, 2000). This disorder can lead to a dangerous medical condition: nonorganic failure to thrive. Families of children with feeding disorder of infancy or early childhood often (but not always) exhibit such psychosocial contributory factors as low SES, emotional disorders in the parents, high environmental stress, and abuse and neglect of the child (Wilson, 2001). Feeding disorder of infancy or early childhood may be found in children who also have reactive attachment disorder that is linked to conflicts occurring in connection with feeding (Kronenberger & Meyer, 2001). Recent research notes a link between childhood failure to thrive and mothers who have eating disorders (Mash & Wolfe, 2005).

Accurate data about the prevalence of feeding disorders of infancy or early childhood is sparse because these disorders typically occur in conjunction with mental retardation, pervasive developmental disorders, or other mental disorders, and may not be coded separately. They are listed on Axis I only if they are prominent enough to require separate treatment.

Typical Client Characteristics

Children with rumination disorder, as already mentioned, usually have had a period of normal eating habits before the atypical eating behaviors appear. Mash and Wolfe (2005) note that the longer a child has pica and eats nonnutritive substances, the greater the likelihood that serious problems will develop. Untreated, this disorder may result in weight loss, malnutrition, and even death. Some parents report a sour odor from these children's regurgitations (Rapoport & Ismond, 1996). Children who have ingested chips of lead paint may exhibit the effects of lead poisoning, which include developmental delays, learning disabilities, and attention deficits (Pace & Toyer, 2000).

Children with feeding disorder of infancy or early childhood may be irritable and difficult to console. They may exhibit slowed growth patterns or sleep-wake cycle disturbances. Psychosocial problems, such as parental psychopathology, poor parent-child interactions, poverty, and neglect, are significant correlates of this disorder (Mash & Wolfe, 2005). Insecure attachment and a high incidence of negative interactions and emotions, including anger, sadness, and frustration, have been reported among children with the diagnosis of nonorganic failure to thrive related to feeding and eating disorders (Lyons-Ruth, Zeanah, & Benoit, 1996). An estimated 1 to 5 percent of pediatric hospital admissions are for failure to thrive. *DSM-IV-TR* reports that up to one-half of these admissions may reflect feeding disturbances unrelated to a medical condition (American Psychiatric Association, 2000).

Preferred Therapist Characteristics

Children with feeding and eating disorders usually first present in medical settings when physical conditions have developed from their impaired eating. Therefore, therapists affiliated with hospitals are most likely to see children with these disorders, although the parents of these children may be seen in any treatment setting.

Therapists working with this population must be at ease with potentially life-threatening situations. Therapists must also be good collaborators, able to consult with and contribute to a team of medical professionals. Training in family systems and cognitive-behavioral approaches can help therapists deal with the familial correlates of these disorders, as well as with parents' resistance and with their anger about feeling blamed for their children's symptoms.

The treatment of anorexia nervosa and bulimia nervosa is addressed in Chapter Six, but Wilson and Fairburn (2002) and others have identified children younger than ten who are restricting their diets because of concern about body fat. Therefore, therapists working with children who have eating problems should be knowledgeable about anorexia nervosa and bulimia nervosa.

Intervention Strategies

In addition to medical monitoring, the primary treatment modality for children with feeding and eating disorders is work with the family. Cognitive-behavioral and educational approaches are useful in addressing issues related to parenting. Provision of information on children's developmental and eating patterns is commonly the first step toward a positive outcome. Linscheid (1992) suggests providing the child with a parent substitute who can offer a warm, nurturing feeding environment while the parents receive counseling to address any issues that are interfering with their nurturing of the child.

Pica is often addressed through parent training in behavior management strategies. This kind of training promotes closer monitoring of the child's eating, as well as the use of behavioral rewards or consequences. Charts for recording the ingestion of appropriate foods can be developed and can be used with stickers or other rewards for the child's eating of appropriate nutritive substances. This approach is usually adequate for discouraging children from eating inappropriate substances (Kronenberger & Meyer, 2001).

A limited number of research studies have been conducted on the effect of vitamin and mineral supplements in the treatment of children with pica. Three promising studies indicate a reduction in symptoms of pica in children who were given a daily multivitamin or iron supplements (Pace & Toyer, 2000). More research is needed on the relationship between pica and nutrition.

Rumination disorder is addressed primarily through family interventions designed to improve the parent-child relationship and provide the child with consistent nurturance and responses. Cognitive-behavioral or educational therapies for parents, focused on attachment issues, child development, and parenting skills, can also be helpful. Parent-child therapy may be introduced to model and encourage more positive and supportive interactions between parent and child (Kronenberger & Meyer, 2001).

Other techniques have also proved helpful in treating rumination disorder. In life-threatening situations, behavior modification with aversive stimuli may be necessary. For example, Rapoport and Ismond (1996) describe a case in which mild electric shocks were applied to the leg of an infant when rumination behaviors were exhibited; the symptoms were arrested within one week. Researchers have found a relationship between the occurrence of rumination and the types of food provided (Linscheid, 1992); ruminating behaviors diminished in children with mental retardation when they were fed their preferred foods.

When feeding disorder of infancy or early childhood is accompanied by failure to thrive, the treatment is similar to that for reactive attachment disorder. If the disorder involves the child's refusal of food, then behavioral techniques can be helpful and may include positive reinforcement for eating, the modeling of positive eating behaviors, control of between-meal eating, and reduction of mealtime distractions (Kronenberger & Meyer, 2001).

Prognosis

In the majority of cases, feeding and eating disorders in young children remit after a few months of appropriate intervention. However, early feeding problems may contribute to the later development of eating disorders. Jacobi, Hayward, de Zwaan, Kraemer, and Agras (2004) conducted a meta-analysis of risk factors associated with eating disorders and reported one longitudinal study which indicated that pica and early digestive problems were related to later onset of bulimia (Marchi & Cohen, 1990); however, a second longitudinal study indicated that early feeding problems were unrelated to the development of either anorexia or bulimia nervosa in adolescence or childhood (Kotler, Cohen, Davies, Pine, & Walsh, 2001). Clearly, additional research is needed on the relationship between early childhood eating problems and later disordered or binge eating. Pica may persist for years, especially if it is present in conjunction with mental retardation. Rumination disorder in infants most often resolves by itself within a month or two, but chronic cases left untreated can result in death (American Psychiatric Association, 2000).

TIC DISORDERS

Description of the Disorders

The disorders discussed in this section are typified by "sudden, rapid, recurrent, nonrhythmic, stereotyped motor movement or vocalization" (American Psychiatric Association, 2000, p. 108). These symptoms typically worsen under stress and are less noticeable when the child is involved in an engrossing activity. The symptoms also diminish significantly during sleep. Examples of simple motor tics are eye blinking, neck jerking, facial grimacing, shrugging, or coughing. Simple vocal tics include clearing one's throat, grunting, sniffing, or barking. Complex motor and vocal tics incorporate complete actions or words that are repeated involuntarily and in rapid, staccato fashion. Complex motor tics include jumping, grooming, or smelling an object. A child with complex vocal tics may repeat sentences or phrases out of context. Other types of complex vocal tics include palilalia (repetition of one's own sounds or words) and echolalia (repetition of the sound, word, or phrase last heard). Despite its overuse in the media to represent Tourette's disorder, coprolalia (the use of socially unacceptable or obscene words) is found in only 10 to 20 percent of people with tics. Tic disorders are more common in boys.

A diagnosis of a tic disorder is appropriate only if the onset of the disorder occurs prior to the age of eighteen, if the symptoms are not the result of drugs or a medical condition (such as Huntington's disease), and if the symptoms cause significant distress or impairment (American Psychiatric Association, 2000). Towbin and Cohen (1996) report that tic disorders vary according to five properties:

1. Frequency (the number of tics that occur over a given period)
2. Complexity (the nature of the tic itself)
3. Intensity (the forcefulness of the tic; some tics are subtle, whereas others seem almost explosive or violent)
4. Location (the parts of the body affected by the tic)
5. Duration (the length of time that tics persist in each episode)

Assessment according to these properties can be helpful in determining what type of disorder is involved, the exacerbating factors, and the appropriate treatment and its impact.

Tic disorders have a higher incidence in children with certain coexisting disorders. The literature suggests that tic disorders are related to other disorders with neuropsychiatric components, including ADHD, learning disorders, pervasive developmental disorders, anxiety disorders, OCD, disruptive behavior disorders, and mood disorders (Storch et al., 2005). Jankovic (2001, p. 1186) reports that these coexisting disorders "often interfere more than tics do with overall functioning and with academic and work performance." Magnetic resonance imaging (MRI), biochemical, and genetic studies of people with Tourette's disorder have indicated that the disorder is an inherited, developmental disorder of synaptic neurotransmission (Jankovic, 2001). Motor tics can sometimes be a side effect of the psychostimulants used in the treatment of other disorders; therefore, many clinicians do not prescribe psychostimulant medication for children who have concurrent Tourette's disorder. The spectrum of tic disorders includes the following disorders.

Tourette's Disorder. Tourette's disorder, named after Gilles de la Tourette, who first identified it, is diagnosed on the basis of tics that occur many times a day and that combine multiple motor tics with one or more vocal tics. The motor and vocal tics need not occur simultaneously in order for this diagnosis to be made. The severity and the location of the tics may change over time, but the diagnostic criteria require that the symptoms occur for a period of at least one year, with no more than a three-month tic-free period (American Psychiatric Association, 2000). As many as 1 percent of children have Tourette's disorder, with boys outnumbering girls by a 4:1 to 6:1 ratio

(Kadesjo & Gillberg, 2000). People with this disorder usually also have relatives with the disorder.

Tourette's disorder often begins with intermittent, simple eye blinking. Tics initially may present only a few times each week or may be almost constant. Over time, the tic behaviors usually become persistent (of higher frequency or longer duration) and occur at multiple sites on the body. These involuntary movements have been reported to occur as frequently as one hundred or more times per minute (Berardelli, Curr, Fabbrini, Gillio, & Manfredi, 2003). The tics often interfere with academic or work performance as well as with social relationships. By the age of ten, children with Tourette's disorder may be aware of urges that forewarn them of impending tics; a tic itself may be described as an itch or a tickle. Because of these premonitions, adolescents and adults may perceive their tics as at least partly voluntary. Some report the ability to suppress their tics during the school day or while at work and then "release" their tics when they come home (Jankovic, 2001). Usually by adolescence or early adulthood, the frequency of the tics has been reduced, but cases of disabling Tourette's disorder have been found in adults.

Chronic Tic Disorder. Chronic tic disorder resembles Tourette's disorder except that it involves single or complex motor or vocal tics (not both). The symptoms are also of lesser intensity and frequency than in Tourette's disorder and are usually confined to the eyes, face, head, neck, and upper extremities. This disorder sometimes is comorbid with ADHD and is exacerbated by stress, excitement, boredom, fatigue, and exposure to heat (Jankovic, 2001). Chronic tic disorder has a duration of more than twelve months.

Transient Tic Disorder. Transient tic disorder resembles chronic tic disorder except for its duration: it lasts at least four weeks but no longer than one year. Emotional tension is often the cause of simple forms of transient tic disorder.

The prevalence of chronic tic disorder and transient tic disorder is not known. Many children with these disorders never come to the attention of the medical or mental health communities. Estimates suggest that the prevalence of Tourette's disorder is about 0.7 percent in school-age children, but estimates can range as high as 4.2 percent when all types of tic disorders are included (Jankovic, 2001). Research on the course of tic severity over the first two decades of life indicates that after a mean tic onset of 5.6 years of age, maximum tic severity usually peaks between 8 and 12 years of age and is frequently followed by a decline in symptoms (Leckman et al., 1998). The prevalence of tic disorder in early adulthood is half the rate in children. The research has implications for treatment, especially during the adolescent years when short periods of remission, from a few weeks to a year, may occur (American Psychiatric Association, 2000).

Typical Client Characteristics

In most children, tic disorders have an intermittent course — increasing in frequency and then waning at various intervals. Anxiety, stress, and fatigue are known to worsen all tic disorders (Bagheri, Kerbeshian, & Burd, 1999). Leckman and Cohen (1994) report cases of families who chastised children for tic-related behaviors and thereby increased stress, which in turn led to increased frequency and severity of tics; severe cases of Tourette's disorder may be related to this pattern of family dynamics. Tic disorders often have an impact on self-image and functioning. Social withdrawal may result from interactions with others who focus on and criticize the tic-related behaviors.

Tic disorders often co-occur with ADHD (50 percent of children with Tourette's have ADHD), learning disabilities (25 to 30 percent), and OCD (25 to 40 percent). Other behavior problems associated with Tourette's disorder include poor impulse control, anxiety and depression, inability to control anger, sleep problems, emotional outbursts, and self-injury (Bagheri et al., 1999; Jankovic, 2001).

Preferred Therapist Characteristics

Therapists working with children who have severe tic disorders need skills in establishing positive and supportive working relationships, both with these young clients and with their parents. Tourette's disorder in particular introduces stressors into family dynamics, and these stressors may in turn exacerbate the condition. Tourette's disorder is often a lifelong disorder that requires ongoing support and advocacy from the therapist.

Therapists should be adept at individualizing treatment for the child; have a working knowledge of behavioral techniques, including habit reversal training; and be capable of working with professionals in the educational and medical arenas.

Intervention Strategies

The treatments of choice for tic disorders currently include an initial psychodynamic approach (to identify any underlying stressors), cognitive-behavioral methods of stress management, education of children and families about the disorder, advocacy with education professionals, and collaborative work with physicians if pharmacological interventions are necessary (Bagheri et al., 1999; Jankovic, 2001). Choosing among these interventions to formulate an effective treatment plan requires careful analysis of the type of disorder that is involved, as well as analysis of any underlying stressors that may be exacerbating the disorder.

The initial goal of treatment is not to eliminate all tics completely, but to educate the child and the parents about the nature of the disorder and the influence that stress, anxiety, and fatigue can have on symptoms. Children should be helped to achieve a degree of control over tics that allows them to function as normally as possible (Jankovic, 2001).

After establishing a positive working relationship and having made efforts to educate the family about the disorder and the role that stress plays in exacerbating symptoms, the therapist should facilitate the collection of baseline data about the frequency of the tics. Sometimes the act of collecting the data is therapeutic in itself, and the frequency of the tics may diminish (Bagheri et al., 1999). Baseline data guide the behavioral and environmental interventions, which constitute the next step in treatment.

Therapists or school counselors can suggest classroom modifications to reduce stress. These may include development of clear expectations, a low student-teacher ratio, predictable schedules, and contracts specifying rewards for behavioral control. Flexibility is important; perhaps the child can be allowed to leave the classroom when a tic occurs, or maybe academic requirements can be adjusted. School curricula that accommodate a variety of learning styles can allow children with Tourette's disorder to use learning strategies that make use of their strengths.

Adolescents with this disorder benefit from career counseling, which can help them make plans to enter occupations in which they are likely to succeed (Towbin, Cohen, & Leckman, 1995). The creation of realistic expectations on the part of these adolescents, their parents, and their teachers may also be a treatment goal.

Behavioral techniques are often used to diminish tic-related behaviors. Self-monitoring, for example, involves children in recording the occurrence and frequency of tics (Kronenberger & Meyer, 2001). This approach is particularly helpful in children with multiple developmental problems and can be used to document the amount of progress that has been made (Bagheri et al., 1999). In relaxation training, children are taught to use such methods as progressive relaxation of muscle groups, deep breathing, or imagery before or during episodes of tics. Habit-reversal training uses reinforcement and other behavioral techniques to enable people with tic disorders to recognize premonitory urges, become aware of the presence of tics, monitor their own behaviors during stress-inducing situations, use relaxation techniques, and perform competing behaviors that are incompatible with the performance of the tic-related behavior (Piacentini & Chang, 2005). This approach has achieved significant success in the treatment of Tourette's disorder and in the treatment of chronic motor or vocal tic disorders, but care should be taken, as some children who undergo behavior modification to directly target symptoms of Tourette's disorder may have an increase of tic symptoms (Bagheri et al., 1999).

Children with Tourette's disorder sometimes benefit from individual therapy, especially in overall improvement in life satisfaction and social functioning (Deckersbach, Rauch, Bulhmann, & Wilhelm, 2006). Towbin et al. (1995) suggest that psychodynamic, cognitive, behavioral, and interpersonal treatment models may all be successful with particular constellations of symptoms. For example, a psychodynamic or cognitive approach may help a child explore events that have led up to episodes of tics, and an understanding of those events may provide insights that can allow increased control over symptomatic behaviors. As another example, because the stress created by negative family interactions can increase the frequency of tics, and because blame from family members and teasing from peers can cause a child with Tourette's disorder to assume the role of victim, interpersonal and family therapy can help the child and the family understand the disorder and the role that each family member plays in perpetuating negative dynamics and worsening the symptoms (Towbin et al., 1995). An adjunct to treatment that should be considered for the family is the Tourette's Syndrome Association, which provides many types of information, as well as family support networks all around the country (www.tsa-usa.org).

Tourette's disorder often has a negative impact on peer relationships, especially among children and adolescents. Children with Tourette's disorder typically benefit from participation in social skills training groups, similar to those used for children with learning disorders, that can help them develop skills in relaxation and play and can teach them appropriate behaviors for approaching others.

Pharmacological treatment usually is reserved for those people who do not respond well to behavioral and environmental interventions. Dopamine antagonist drugs (Haldol, Orap) and the atypical neuroleptic risperidone (Risperdal) are the most effective in terms of tic reduction, but serious side effects may include tardive dyskinesia, sedation, and tremors. For mild to moderate tics, or for those clients who want to avoid neuroleptic side effects, clonidine (Catapres) or guanfacine (Tenex) have been prescribed. Both are reported to reduce irritability and impulsivity and may reduce symptoms of ADHD as well (Bagheri et al., 1999). Especially in children, the use of multiple drugs should be avoided, if at all possible, to eliminate the risk of potential drug interactions and serious side effects.

Comorbid disorders must also be taken into account when treating those with tic disorders. The behaviors associated with comorbid ADHD, OCD, and anxiety and mood disorders make the treatment more challenging, and should be addressed through behavior therapy whenever possible.

Prognosis

Bagheri et al. (1999) report that behavioral interventions can result in 50 percent less medication being required. A growing body of research indicates that habit-reversal training (HRT) is effective in reducing tics. Deckersbach et al. (2006) showed reduced tic severity, improvements in life satisfaction, and improvement in psychosocial functioning during HRT therapy. Behavioral interventions have many benefits in the treatment of this disorder, but do require significant effort and time.

ENCOPRESIS

Description of the Disorder

Encopresis is defined by *DSM-IV-TR* as "repeated passage of feces into inappropriate places, whether intentional or involuntary" (American Psychiatric Association, 2000, p. 118). This diagnosis is applicable only if the person has a chronological or developmental level equivalent to at least four years of age and if the symptoms were present at least once a month for a minimum of three months. The symptoms must not be due to a general medical condition or to a reaction to medications. In order to establish an appropriate treatment plan, the therapist should determine whether the child has ever had an extended period of continence before the onset of encopresis.

Most children are developmentally, cognitively, and psychologically ready to achieve toilet training between twenty-four and thirty months of age (Kuhn, Marcus, & Pitner, 1999), and nearly all children in the United States are fully toilet trained by the age of five years. *DSM-IV-TR* states the prevalence of encopresis among five-year-olds as 1 percent. Encopresis is more common in boys, and the disorder is rare beyond the age of sixteen.

DSM-IV-TR (American Psychiatric Association, 2000) distinguishes between encopresis with constipation and overflow incontinence and encopresis without these symptoms. These distinctions usually reflect differences in etiology and subsequent treatment. Kuhn et al. (1999) suggest that children diagnosed with encopresis without constipation can be divided into four subgroups: those who fail to obtain initial bowel training, those who exhibit fear of the toilet, those who use soiling to manipulate, and those with chronic diarrhea or irritable bowel syndrome.

Encopresis with constipation often develops after an occurrence of severe constipation resulting from an illness or a change in the diet. The resulting impaction of fecal material can cause painful bowel movements, and anal fissures or irritations have also been reported as contributing factors (Cox, Sutphen, Borowitz, Kovatchev, & Ling, 1998). Children develop a fear response and withhold feces in order to avoid painful bowel movements. The child avoids using the toilet, parents respond with requests for more frequent toileting, and a parent-child conflict develops. The resistance and fecal soiling continue. This scenario accounts for the majority of cases of encopresis.

Encopresis without constipation seems better understood as the result of operant conditioning, in which the child receives reinforcement (usually increased attention from the parents) for soiling. Peterson, Reach, and Grube (2003) report significant emotional problems in approximately 20 percent of children with the disorder.

Typical Client Characteristics

Five to 20 percent of children exhibit encopresis without constipation. These children often have other significant mental disorders, such as mental retardation, conduct disorder, or oppositional defiant disorder. They typically are manipulative and receive secondary gains from the soiling.

Children with both types of encopresis may feel shame and low self-esteem related to their symptoms. Parental anger and rejection, as well as children's avoidance of social situations in which they may be embarrassed (such as overnight visits with friends), may further contribute to their distress and impairment. Smearing of feces (usually to hide the evidence) is sometimes present and can exacerbate negative family reactions.

Preferred Therapist Characteristics

The therapist will need good skills in establishing rapport with both the child and the parents and in collaborating with physicians. The child must feel secure with and trusting of the therapist in order for the treatment to be successful. Similarly, the relationship with the parents must enable them to feel support, as well as some relief from the guilt that parents of children with encopresis often experience.

Intervention Strategies

The effectiveness of encopresis treatment programs varies substantially by type. Cox et al. (2003) report the importance of identifying symptoms to determine whether a behavioral problem is present or whether the child's problems are "bowel-specific" (p. 376), as the latter may be more easily treated. The Virginia Encopresis Constipation Apperception Test (VECAT; Cox et al., 2003) shows promise as a tool to help determine symptoms and diagnose encopresis with and without constipation. Biofeedback, behavioral interventions, medical management, play therapy, and family-focused approaches have all been used in the treatment of encopresis.

Successful treatment of this disorder requires collaboration among parents, the child, the therapist, and the physician. Enhanced toilet training (ETT), which combines behavioral treatment (reinforcements, instructions and modeling, parent education) with medical management, has shown promise. A recent outcome study showed that ETT resulted in fewer symptoms compared with medical management alone, required fewer doses of laxatives, and resulted in longer intervals without symptoms (Ritterband et al., 2003).

An innovative Internet version of ETT was created by the University of Virginia and Vanderbilt University. The Web site (U-CAN-POOP-TOO) provides a wide range of treatment modules for encopresis, allowing children to select the modules most relevant to their needs. An animated guide walks children through the tutorials, modules, and follow-up pages, with an audio accompaniment to the text. The site is easily accessible to parents and children in the privacy of their homes, provides effective learning tools, and reduces barriers to treatment (visits to doctors, transportation, time away from work and school, fees). Ritterband et al. (2003) report a 70 percent cure rate (the number of children without any accidents postassessment) for the Web-based group versus 45 percent for the control group after three weeks of treatment. The authors of the study note that this is one of the first studies to empirically evaluate the use of an Internet program to help treat a medical condition. Internet treatments have significant potential benefits including increased accessibility, detailed information, privacy, and low-cost delivery. Finally, an animated, entertaining system may enhance compliance by children and be a positive adjunct to therapy.

Some children with encopresis are resistant to treatment. In cases like these, a behavioral assessment should be made to determine whether co-occurring aggression, oppositional behavior, or temper tantrums are hindering toilet training. In these cases, psychodynamic approaches may be useful. Cuddy-Casey (1997) used psychodynamic play therapy with a child who was both enuretic and encopretic and achieved resolution of the elimination disorders in thirteen sessions. She suggests that persistent elimination problems may reflect the child's power struggles with the parents or a history of toileting-associated trauma that may need intervention.

Mash and Wolfe (2005) report that optimal treatment for encopresis involves a combination of medical intervention and behavior modification. Positive reinforcement involving rewards for appropriate toilet use are likely to enhance any type of treatment chosen. To succeed, the overall treatment plan must be one to which the parents will subscribe and lend their support.

Prognosis

Encopresis may continue for some time, but it is rarely chronic. When symptoms are long lasting, as many as one in five children may develop psychological problems, but this is believed to be a result of encopresis, rather than the cause of it (Peterson et al., 2003). Early intervention and treatment clearly are key to a good prognosis.

ENURESIS

Description of the Disorder

Enuresis is the repeated voiding of urine into the bed or clothes and is considered to be clinically significant if it occurs at least twice per week during three consecutive months or if it interferes with the child's social or interpersonal functioning. In order for this diagnosis to be appropriate, the child must have both chronological and mental ages of at least five years, and the disorder must not be caused by a general medical condition.

The diagnosis, as well as its treatment and prognosis, will be clarified if the time of day when the symptoms typically appear can be determined. Diurnal enuresis occurs during the daytime and is considered to be related to poor toilet training, social anxiety, or preoccupation with other activities (American Psychiatric Association, 2000). Nocturnal enuresis is more common. It usually occurs during the first one-third of the night, occasionally during the REM stage of sleep, and may occur during deep sleep that prevents awareness of the need to urinate. Children with nocturnal enuresis may also experience episodes of sleepwalking, encopresis, and nightmares and may report dreams about urinating (Rapoport & Ismond, 1996).

Early incidents of nocturnal enuresis are often the result of the child's sleeping deeply, having a small bladder, and other symptoms the child will outgrow in the course of development. However, Kazdin (2000) notes that enuresis in middle and later childhood is a risk factor for the development of other emotional disorders and that parents ought to intervene if the situation has not remitted by then.

Secondary enuresis, which follows a period of appropriate bladder control, is most likely to develop between the ages of five and eight (American Psychiatric Association, 2000). The prevalence of the disorder decreases with age, with 15 percent experiencing spontaneous remission each year. Thus, nocturnal enuresis is found in 15 to 25 percent of five-year-old boys and girls; 8 percent of twelve-year-old boys; and only 1 to 3 percent of all adolescents (Thiedke, 2003). Only 1 percent of cases continue into adulthood.

Diurnal enuresis is more common among girls and is rarely seen after the age of nine (American Psychiatric Association, 2000). Contextual factors should be considered in cases of diurnal enuresis because it is often related to anxiety around missing school activities or to a reluctance to use school toilets (Rapoport & Ismond, 1996).

Typical Client Characteristics

Enuresis can lead to anxiety for the child and may cause embarrassment, particularly around the overnight visits to friends and family members. Children may also experience lowered self-esteem as a result of this disorder. Parental anger may contribute to these negative emotions. Miller found that 23 to 36 percent of parents had used punishment as the primary method of addressing their children's enuresis (Thiedke, 2003). Needless to say, punishment and shame are contraindicated and only serve to lower the child's self-esteem.

A family history of enuresis is a predictor for this disorder to occur in children. The likelihood of having enuresis is five to seven times greater in children with one parent who also had the disorder. Familial factors such as stress, social background, and changes in residence were not found to contribute to this disorder. The current research indicates that three variables are necessary for nighttime control of bladder functioning: normal bladder capacity, effective arousal from sleep when the bladder is full, and a decrease in nighttime urine production. An imbalance in any of these areas, which often occurs in children, is currently thought to be the cause of nocturnal enuresis (Houts, 2003). Research is also beginning to look at a chromosomal link to nocturnal enuresis. Additional studies will help determine treatments of the future.

Preferred Therapist Characteristics

The therapist should have a solid foundation in family dynamics and techniques of behavioral treatment. Much of the family's associated emotional distress can be alleviated if education about the disorder is provided, guilt is relieved, and symptoms are rapidly addressed with behavioral techniques that reduce the frequency of wetting. The therapist must be supportive and nonjudgmental about the causes of the disorder. Unless abuse or another severe problem or symptom is present, the focus should be on removing the symptoms of enuresis, not on exploring underlying emotional difficulties.

Intervention Strategies

The initial phase of treatment for enuresis involves establishing rapport with the family and the child. Education about enuresis and its treatment can diminish anxieties related to the disorder. The collection of baseline data may effect some change in the enuretic behaviors and will provide necessary information for measuring progress. Children are often asked to keep a voiding diary in which they log both daytime and nighttime urination patterns for one week. Following a medical checkup to rule out problems with bladder function, most children respond well to behavioral approaches to enuresis.

The enuresis alarm or some variation on it has been found to be the most effective and least expensive form of therapy (Houts, 2003; Lyon & Schnall, 2005; Thiedke, 2003). A popular version of this system involves an alarm worn on the body: a sensor is attached to a pad that is placed inside the child's pants, and the alarm is placed on the child's wrist or in a pocket. If the pad becomes wet, a sensor in the pad triggers the alarm and increases awareness of the need to urinate. This system may need to be used for up to fifteen weeks and can be useful both day and night. This system reportedly has a cure rate of 75 percent (Houts, 2003).

A variation on this system, called dry-bed training, was developed by Azrin, Sneed, and Foxx (1973). This version adds retention training (in which the children are taught to hold their urine for as long as possible during daytime hours) to the alarm-and-pad system. To date, it has been more successful than any other treatment modality. However, there is no evidence to show a remission benefit for dry-bed training without the alarm, indicating the key role for alarm therapy (Lyon & Schnall, 2005). Relapse is common, but repetition of the treatment usually brings about successful resolution of any relapse.

There is a 10 to 30 percent dropout rate in treatment of enuresis with alarms. Thiedke (2003) cites acting-out behavior on the part of the child, high levels of anxiety in the mother, a lack of concern about the condition on the part of the parents and the child, and other familial traits, such as low parental education level, high SES, and an unstable family situation, as contributing to poor compliance with behavioral alarms.

Full-spectrum home training (FSHT; Houts, 2003) has been developed over twenty years of research. This behavioral approach can be started with children as young as six; it combines basic urine alarm treatment, cleanliness training, retention control training, and overlearning to prevent relapse. Due to the commitment of time and the difficulty arousing a child when the alarm goes off in the middle of the night for the first four weeks, parents and children are asked to sign a contract (Houts, 2003). FSHT has been taught in group and individual formats with comparable outcomes. Separate groups should be formed for children twelve and older to reduce the embarrassment of being with younger children. Based on five outcome studies, 75 percent of children stopped bedwetting at the end of the average twelve-week training. At one-year follow-up, six out of every ten children remained permanently dry.

Drugs, including antidiuretics, tricyclic antidepressants, and anticholinergic medications that may increase bladder capacity, have been used to treat enuresis, but none has been shown to have enduring effects. A meta-analysis of desmopressin (DDAVP), the most frequently prescribed medication for nocturnal enuresis, showed the medication to reduce symptoms by one to two nights a week compared with a placebo (Lyon & Schnall, 2005). However, when treatment was discontinued, relapse rates ranged from 80 to 100 percent (Thiedke, 2003). The Cochrane Incontinence Group Trials compared DDAVP to alarms and found that the medication was more effective the first week. After three months, however, alarms were responsible for 1.4 fewer wet nights a week than medication (Lyon & Schnall, 2005).

Clearly a behavioral component is necessary for successful treatment of nocturnal enuresis. This is confirmed by several studies on combined treatment with desmopressin and conditioning alarms. Although the children initially improved during treatment using both methodologies, the use of alarms alone yielded higher improvement rates once the treatment stopped. Desmopressin may be a good choice, however, for situational use, such as for sleepovers, camping, and vacations (Lyon & Schnall, 2005).

Imipramine (Tofranil), an antidepressant, was found to reduce wetting frequency in 85 percent of children treated, but the symptoms returned within three months after the medication was discontinued (Lyon & Schnall, 2005). Given the potential side effects of this medication, it should be considered only after other options have been exhausted.

Alternative approaches to treatment have not been studied as extensively, but the following have been found to have a positive effect: acupuncture, retention control, biofeedback, caffeine restriction, hypnosis, and elimination diet. Children who continue to experience nocturnal enuresis, or those who are noncompliant with the alarm-and-pad treatment, may have behavioral problems that need to be addressed.

Prognosis

Spontaneous remission occurs in many children with enuresis. For those who do receive treatment, the classical conditioning method, represented by the enuresis alarm and dry-bed training or FSHT, has been found superior to no treatment at all, to psychodynamic psychotherapy, and to medication. A logical approach would be to combine behavior modification techniques with the alarm system, reserving the use of DDAVP for sleepovers or other appropriate occasions. Whatever the treatment plan, relapse prevention, follow-up, support, and encouragement are important components to reduce anxiety and improve self-esteem in the child.

SEPARATION ANXIETY DISORDER

Description of the Disorder

Separation anxiety disorder is the most common anxiety disorder among children, occurring in nearly 10 percent of children (Mash & Wolfe, 2005). The essential characteristic of this disorder is excessive distress upon separation from home or primary attachment figures. Manifestations of the distress may include worry about caretakers being harmed, reluctance or refusal to go to school or be separated from caregivers, fear about being alone, and frequent somatic complaints, such as headaches, stomachaches, and nausea and vomiting. Children with separation anxiety disorder often have difficulty at bedtime. They may express fear of going to sleep, request someone stay with them until they do, experience frequent nightmares, and attempt to sleep in their parents' bed. For diagnosis, *DSM-IV-TR* requires evidence of three or more of these symptoms for at least four weeks, with an onset prior to eighteen years of age.

In public, children with separation anxiety disorder may cling to their parents. They often visit the school health clinic with minor physical complaints, or they ask to call home and have their parents come to take them home (Popper & Gherardi, 1996). As these children mature, the symptoms may change, with absenteeism and somatic complaints being particularly prominent. Children with separation anxiety disorder frequently present with symptoms of other anxiety disorders and often report many specific fears, as well as feelings of sadness and of not being loved. The fear of getting lost is particularly common in these children (Albano, Chorpita, & Barlow, 2003). Separation anxiety disorder frequently coexists with major depressive disorder and ADHD. Communication disorders and reluctance to go to school are also common.

The etiology of separation anxiety disorder varies. In some cases it is precipitated by a stressful event, such as a significant loss, separation from loved ones, or exposure to danger. This disorder may also stem from an insecure attachment to the primary caregiver, or it may occur in families in which a parent is overly involved (Hudson & Rapee, 2001). Separation anxiety disorder has been associated with enmeshed family relationships. As with many of the other disorders seen in childhood, a careful analysis of contextual and interpersonal factors is important in making a diagnosis and developing treatment plans. Kendall, Aschenbrand, and Hudson (2003) suggest separate structured interviews with family members to rate the severity and onset of the distress.

Females seem more likely to present with this disorder than males, although some studies have found no gender differences. In older children, this disorder can be a contributing factor in refusal to go to school (Albano et al., 2003).

Typical Client Characteristics

Popper and Gherardi (1996) report that the peak prevalence of this disorder occurs before adolescence and seems to be related to issues surrounding increasing independence and resultant changes in family relationships. Albano and colleagues (2003) suggest that many children begin to exhibit these symptoms around the ages of five or six, when they enter school for the first time. Its onset is often subtle, with the child making innocent requests for physical closeness to the parent because of a physical complaint or a nightmare. The parent may unwittingly reinforce the fearful behavior by allowing the child to stay nearby. Stress may exacerbate the symptoms, and separation anxiety disorder can have a chronic course if not treated early. Children with separation anxiety disorder are at increased risk of developing other anxiety disorders in adolescence (Aschenbrand, Kendall, Webb, Safford, & Flannery-Schroeder, 2003). Early onset of separation anxiety disorder also appears to be predictive of adult panic disorders.

Children with this disorder sometimes have academic and social problems related to their absenteeism, as well as discomfort with other children. Their fears may preclude their participation in social activities including sleepovers, and their lack of participation interferes with their peer relationships.

Mothers of children with separation anxiety disorder have a high prevalence of anxiety or depressive disorders. Lower SES and lower levels of parental education also have been associated with greater prevalence of separation anxiety disorder. It also appears to be more common among white families (Albano et al., 2003), although Paniagua (2001) notes that internalizing disorders are often overlooked or misdiagnosed in children of color due to lack of understanding of cultural context or clinician bias.

Assessment

When treating anxiety disorders in childhood, therapists must assess the degree to which significant people in the child's life exacerbate or reduce the child's anxiety. Careful assessment of anxiety and avoidance behavior in daily life, as well as observations of the child interacting with the parents, is necessary.

Care should be taken to distinguish separation anxiety disorder from school refusal. As many as 75 to 80 percent of those who refuse to go to school also experience separation anxiety, yet the two groups have distinguishing characteristics (Coleman & Webber, 2002). Children with separation anxiety disorder are more likely to be female, prepubescent, and from families with lower SES. School refusers are more likely to be adolescent, male, and from families with higher SES. In addition, for separation anxiety disorder to be the diagnosis, the child must experience significant fear on separation from the attachment figure. For school refusal, the child is more likely to have anxiety or fear about a specific situation within the school setting (Coleman & Webber, 2002).

Preferred Therapist Characteristics

Therapists working with children who have separation anxiety should work to establish trust and build rapport, accepting the child where he or she is and remaining flexible enough to tailor the treatment program to fit the child's individual needs. The therapist should model appropriate social skills, self-talk, and behavior. The therapist will also be responsible for assigning homework, creating practice situations in session, and developing in vivo experiences. Therapists must also be adept at family counseling and capable of providing training and feedback to the parents, who may be overly anxious themselves.

In general, the literature supports the inclusion of parents in the treatment of children with mental disorders, as parental involvement generally increases treatment efficacy (Kendall et al., 2003). However, a relationship has been found between anxiety and overly involved parents. More research is needed to determine the degree to which parental involvement can improve or hinder treatment of separation anxiety disorder (Barrett & Shortt, 2003; Hudson & Rapee, 2001). Therefore, an integral part of the therapist's role is to determine if the parents are enmeshed with the child. The therapist is often the primary facilitator of the child's separation from the parent and must be confident and clear in that role. If the therapist presents any insecurity or uncertainty, the child and the parent may not receive the emotional support required for them to effect separation.

Intervention Strategies

Separation anxiety disorder can be classified as a phobic response, usually surrounding the fear of leaving the primary caregiver, but occasionally it is related to fear of social and school situations. Fears and phobias are acquired through classical conditioning. Such fears can be unlearned through the use of the behavioral technique of exposure therapy, in which the child systematically confronts the feared situation through graded exposure. The research shows this type of therapy to be highly effective in the treatment of phobias (Evans et al., 2005). Little research is available on treatment effectiveness specific to separation anxiety disorder, but growing empirical evidence indicates that cognitive-behavioral therapy is the treatment of choice for childhood anxiety. Consequently, the course of treatment for separation anxiety disorder almost always includes a cognitive-behavioral approach.

One treatment program that has been shown to be effective in as many as two-thirds of cases is the Coping Cat model, developed by Kendall (Kendall et al., 2003). The treatment program also has a beneficial effect on some comordid conditions in addition to separation anxiety disorder. Coping Cat is a multifaceted treatment program that includes education as well as cognitive, affective, sociological, parent and family, and behavioral elements. This cognitive-behavioral method builds on the therapist-child relationship and also provides psychoeducation on the physiological signs of excessive anxiety, normal anxiety, self-talk associated with anxiety, the use of relaxation to reduce anxiety, and behavioral skills. A key component is the hierarchical use of exposure tasks to provide real experiences with arousal and management of anxious distress. Generally, the first half of treatment is the educational phase and the second half is the exposure phase.

Therapists teach their young clients that having some anxiety is reasonable. Children learn to identify the cognitive process involved and develop coping skills so that they can meet their fears head-on, thereby making avoidance unnecessary. By first practicing in session and then rehearsing outside of session, the child develops confidence that the coping skills are working.

If school attendance is an issue and the symptoms are of brief duration, a return to school may be sufficient treatment. Children with chronic features of the disorder, however, such as a long history of absenteeism, many visits to the school clinic, or significant problems at school, may require additional treatment. School counselors may become involved in the development and implementation of a plan for returning the child to school or shaping attendance behaviors by rewarding progressive approximations (bringing the child to the perimeter of the school property, to the front door, and finally to the classroom, and gradually extending the time that the child remains at school). After the child's return to school, individual and family psychotherapy, in addition to ongoing school consultation, can be implemented to address any underlying anxieties that may continue and that may shift to another manifestation or to another child in the family.

Family therapy as part of the treatment plan is particularly important when enmeshment is contributing to the disorder or when maternal or paternal anxiety or depression contribute to the child's anxious behavior. Parents of children with separation anxiety disorder may be dependent on their children or may be emotionally immature themselves. The goal of therapy in these cases would be to reestablish appropriate hierarchies and boundaries between the family subgroups.

In 1996, the first randomized control studies on the effect of CBT plus parent involvement were conducted with anxious children. Family anxiety management training includes teaching parents coping skills to help them manage their own anxiety, training parents in contingency management, and providing parents with problem-solving and communication skills (Barrett & Shortt, 2003). After treatment, 88 percent of children were free of anxiety, and the positive effect of treatment was still found five to seven years later. Age and gender did appear to play a significant role in the treatment. Researchers found that CBT plus parental involvement was more effective in younger children (ages seven to ten) and girls. Older children and boys were as likely to benefit from individual therapy to reduce their anxiety as they were from family anxiety management training. In severe cases, hospitalization may be required in order to force the separation that parent and child may be unable to accomplish.

Such strategies as relaxation techniques and contracting for progressive improvement have also been used successfully in the treatment of separation anxiety disorder. Group work may also be indicated in the treatment of anxiety disorders, but has not been researched specifically for treatment of separation anxiety disorder.

Medication has been used in the treatment of separation anxiety disorder, although few studies are available on the effectiveness of medication for anxiety disorders in children. At this writing, studies are under way to compare Coping Cat treatment (CBT) with sertraline (Zoloft), the combination of the two, and a placebo pill. The study will include combined data from six different locations (Kendall et al., 2003).

Prognosis

Kendall and colleagues (2003) report that 65 to 75 percent of children treated with the Coping Cat program recovered from their symptoms and remained symptom free for a substantial period of time. The remaining 25 to 35 percent were typically older children who had more complicated cases and co-occurring disorders.

A significant number of adults with multiple anxieties report having had a history of childhood separation anxiety disorder, a finding which suggests that separation anxiety disorder is a precursor of later anxiety disorders, especially agoraphobia and panic disorders (Evans et al., 2005). Children with separation anxiety disorder are also at risk for developing mood disorders in adulthood (Evans et al., 2005), as well as for substance-related disorders (Kendall et al., 2003). Childhood anxiety frequently continues into adulthood and affects the person across the life span (NIMH, 2005).

SELECTIVE MUTISM

Description of the Disorder

Selective mutism is characterized by a person's consistently not speaking in some social contexts, such as school, although the person does speak in other contexts, usually at home (American Psychiatric Association, 2000). Symptoms are not due to unfamiliarity or discomfort with the language, nor are the symptoms the result of embarrassment over stuttering or another communication disorder. The minimum duration required for diagnosis of this disorder is one month. Black and Uhde (1995) found that 97 percent of people diagnosed with selective mutism also had comorbid symptoms of social phobias, and 30 percent had specific phobias. Developmental disorders, anxiety, and nocturnal enuresis are also commonly found in children with selective mutism.

Kronenberger and Meyer (2001) describe children with four subtypes of selective mutism:

1. Children who are shy and fearful, with significant stranger anxiety
2. Children who are noncompliant and hostile
3. Children whose mutism is the result of a traumatic or upsetting event or experience
4. Children who have a symbiotic relationship with the primary caretaker and who are manipulative and controlling, although they sometimes seem shy

Each of these subtypes presents a different clinical picture and may respond to different methods of intervention.

Selective mutism occurs in approximately 0.5 percent of all children (Bergman, Piacentini, & McCracken, 2002). Girls are slightly more likely to present with this disorder than boys. It usually begins before the age of five. Because their symptoms occur only in social situations, at school, or among strangers, children with selective mutism may frequently be misdiagnosed, or their symptoms may not interfere with the child's functioning until the start of preschool or elementary school. Although many parents report that their children function normally at home, these children often have academic and social difficulties at school, and teasing by peers is particularly common.

Typical Client Characteristics

In a study of Norwegian children, Kristensen (2000) found selective mutism to be comorbid with developmental disorders or delays nearly as frequently as with anxiety disorders. Many children with selective mutism met the criteria for an anxiety disorder (74 percent of those with selective mutism), developmental disorder or delay (68 percent), and an elimination disorder (31 percent).

Anxiety disorders tend to run in families, whether as a result of genetics, environment, or a combination of both. Various studies have found that parents of children with selective mutism score higher on assessments of social phobia, avoidant personality disorder (Black & Uhde, 1995), schizotypy in mothers, and anxiety in fathers (Kristensen & Torgersen, 2001), indicating that social anxiety in children with selective mutism usually is a family phenomenon.

Rettew (2000) suggests that symptoms of shyness, social anxiety, and avoidant personality disorder lie on a continuum.

Assessment

Early diagnosis and treatment of selective mutism are important. Assessment of selective mutism should include a complete family history of the child, including a multigenerational history of social anxiety and phobias as well as the chronology of the child's linguistic abilities as observed in a variety of settings (home, school, and social situations, such as parties and visits with extended family). Schwartz and Shipon-Blum (2005) suggest that a videotape of the child playing spontaneously at home with a parent or sibling can be helpful in ruling out a pervasive developmental disorder or language delay. A complete assessment should determine what, if any, precipitating factors led to the child's mutism, the role of anxiety or defiance in the child's behavior, the nature of the attachment to the primary caregiver, and whether the child's behavior reflects extreme shyness.

Childhood assessments of anxiety, such as the Multidimensional Anxiety Scale for Children or the Hamilton Anxiety Scale, can be helpful in determining the level of the child's anxiety (Morris & March, 2004; Schwartz & Shipon-Blum, 2005). The Beck Anxiety Inventory for Children may be helpful to establish a baseline or assess progress in ongoing therapy.

Preferred Therapist Characteristics

The therapist treating a child for selective mutism should be confident, consistent, calming, reassuring, and supportive. This stance is helpful to the parents, who are likely to be insecure and anxious themselves, and it will also help the child develop trust and feel comfortable speaking in novel settings. The therapist may coordinate an assessment with a speech and language specialist, as many children have co-occurring developmental delays. The therapist may need to serve as an advocate for the child, facilitating the establishment of a special education plan or initiating an evaluation of the child's school functioning, and so must be comfortable working collaboratively.

Intervention Strategies

Appropriate treatment for this disorder should initially emphasize reducing the child's level of anxiety, increasing the child's self-esteem, and improving behaviors in social settings. Teaching social and other skills can help reduce the child's feelings of fear and shyness and help the child learn to express needs more directly. As the child becomes less anxious, treatment will emphasize behavior therapy aimed at improving the child's comfort level in social environments.

Several approaches have been used in encouraging children diagnosed with selective mutism to talk. Stimulus fading, a method similar to systematic desensitization, has had success with children who speak in some situations. In this approach, a person with whom the child does speak (often the mother) accompanies the child to the site where the child is mute. The child is gradually introduced to the feared situation while the parent withdraws. The child may also be rewarded for increasing communication and social interaction. These behaviors can then be generalized through shaping and reinforcement techniques.

Play therapy can also be useful in treating this disorder, especially if the child will not speak to the therapist. The symbolic nature of play allows the child a nonverbal modality in which to safely process uncomfortable feelings and upsetting experiences that may be at the heart of selective mutism.

Cognitive-behavioral therapy has been found to be effective in treating selective mutism (Morris & March, 2004) by helping children reduce their anxious fears and develop positive thoughts. Given the role that families play in the perpetuation of this disorder, intervention with the family is usually indicated. Structural family therapy is a logical choice because of its goal of restructuring family roles and relationships. This approach can engage and empower the nonenmeshed parent (usually the father) and establish appropriate boundaries and family hierarchies, with the parents in charge of the family (Kronenberger & Meyer, 2001). In some cases marital therapy or individual therapy for one parent is indicated so that issues in the parental relationship to the child can be addressed.

School intervention is an important aspect of helping the child with selective mutism become comfortable speaking across settings. Cunningham has developed a school-based ten-stage program that teaches professionals, parents, and teachers to encourage the child to talk to teachers and peers. Resources are available for professionals, parents, and educators who wish to work collaboratively (McHolm, Cunningham, & Vanier, 2005).

Psychopharmacological strategies are also being used in the treatment of selective mutism. Morris and Marsh (2004) report strong evidence for the effectiveness of SSRIs in the treatment of childhood anxiety, but studies on the use of SSRIs to treat selective mutism are limited. One study indicated that when fluoxetine (Prozac) has been used, parents have reported improvement, but teachers and clinicians working with the children have not (Black & Uhde, 1994). Such strategies as relaxation and desensitization, used in treating anxiety disorders, have also been used with selective mutism (see Chapter Five for more information on relaxation techniques). However, family-based psychotherapy remains the most often used approach to treatment for selective mutism (Butcher et al., 2006).

Prognosis

Popper and Gherardi (1996) report that approximately half the children with selective mutism are able, after treatment, to talk in public by the age of ten. For young children with this disorder, then, the prognosis is relatively good; the prognosis is less optimistic for those who still exhibit symptoms beyond the age of twelve (Livingston, 1991). Family therapy, behavior modification, and pharmacotherapy with SSRIs are the most frequently used treatments for selective mutism. Early diagnosis and intervention are key to preventing long-term effects of this condition.

REACTIVE ATTACHMENT DISORDER

Description of the Disorder

The work of Bowlby (1969, 1982) and Ainsworth (Ainsworth et al., 1978) demonstrate the critical role of attachment in the normal socialization and biological development of children. Bowlby defined attachment theory as "a way of conceptualizing the propensity of human beings to make strong affectional bonds to particular others and of explaining the many forms of emotional distress and personality disturbance, including anxiety, anger, depression, and emotional detachment, to which unwilling separation and loss give rise" (1969, p. 127).

Attachment, then, is the emotional bond that exists between infant and caretaker. Biological maturation is strongly related to early attachment bonds. Development of the ability to modulate emotional arousal and self-soothe is dependent on having had a "safe base" or secure attachment with a primary caregiver. The way in which secure and insecure attachment patterns evolve and affect children's development is the focus of many studies that offer compelling evidence about the relationship between secure attachment and the development of security, self-image, and intimate relationships throughout the life span. Ainsworth's research on the Strange Situation (Ainsworth et al., 1978) further contributed to attachment theory. Both Bowlby and Ainsworth believed attachment to be a life-span concept.

Reactive attachment disorder (RAD) is an uncommon disorder that begins before the age of five, in which children manifest severe disturbance in social relatedness. Children with RAD are those whose attachment to their primary caregivers has been disrupted so that future relationships are also impaired. These children have experienced extremely poor care involving persistent disregard of their basic emotional or physical needs or repeated changes of primary caregiver, and it is this pathogenic care that has caused the disturbance in social functioning (American Psychiatric Association, 2000).

DSM-IV-TR delineates two subtypes of RAD. The inhibited type characterizes children who seem extremely withdrawn, unresponsive, or hypervigilant. The disinhibited type characterizes children who demonstrate no preferential attachment to any caregiver but instead are excessively social and seek comfort indiscriminately. Children with this type of RAD may even follow or seek solace from strangers.

The disinhibited type of RAD has often been found in children who have been institutionalized or maltreated. A study of children adopted out of institutions indicates that indiscriminate sociability is one of the most persistent social abnormalities (Zeanah et al., 2004) and may persist for years, even when children subsequently attach to new caregivers. The inhibited subtype is characterized by a failure to respond to or initiate social interactions in a developmentally appropriate way.

Children placed in foster care or institutional care settings are at increased risk for developing RAD (Wilson, 2001; Zeanah & Boris, 2000), as are children who experience severe trauma before the age of five (Sheperis, Renfro-Michel, & Doggett, 2003). However, the diagnosis does not apply to all children who may not have formed a secure attachment. Wilson (2001) describes the disorder as lying on a continuum of attachment problems with symptoms of increasing severity found in insecurely attached children.

Studies have considered the relationship of early attachment experiences to behaviors among preschool children. In many cases, children identified as hostile and aggressive have also manifested disordered attachment behaviors with their mothers. Therefore, RAD may reflect the roots of oppositional defiant disorder and conduct disorder (Lyons-Ruth et al., 1996), and early identification and treatment of RAD may prevent the later development of ODD and CD.

Typical Client Characteristics

Evidence that a child has problems with emotional attachment can appear before the first birthday and includes such symptoms as detached or unresponsive behavior, difficulty being comforted, severe colic, or feeding difficulties and failure to thrive. Little information is available on the prevalence of RAD, although Richters and Volkmar (1994) suggest it might be less than 1 percent. To date, most studies have focused on high-risk populations. For example, one study found that 38 percent of children who entered foster care before the age of four had signs of RAD (Zeanah et al., 2004).

Many symptoms, such as somatic complaints, disruptive behavior, and poor social relatedness, pose a challenge in diagnosis, as many symptoms of RAD are similar to the disruptive behavior disorders and pervasive developmental disorders, and can also be confused with symptoms of childhood bipolar disorder, anxiety, PTSD, and dissociative disorder (Hall & Geher, 2003; Hanson & Spratt, 2002; Sheperis, Renfro-Michel, & Doggett, 2003). *DSM-IV-TR* criteria exclude children with pervasive developmental disorders from also having a diagnosis of RAD. Strong links with later psychopathology have been found for infants who exhibit disorganized attachment (Green & Goldwyn, 2002).

Children with RAD are also at risk for language delays, difficulties in emotion regulation, and developmental delays, symptoms that can be mistaken for ADHD, especially in the school setting. Hall and Geher (2003) found that such behaviors as indiscriminate affection toward strangers, compulsive lying and stealing, and sexual behaviors differentiate RAD from ADHD. The symptoms of a child with RAD usually improve when that child is in a more favorable environment. Despite the overlap of symptoms, there is little empirical research on RAD and its comorbid disorders.

Assessment

No comprehensive and reliable test is available for the diagnosis of RAD. Rather, assessment is made based on semistructured interviews, global assessment scales, attachment-specific scales, and behavioral observations (Sheperis, Doggett, et al., 2003). The Child Behavior Checklist (Achenbach, 1991), the Behavior Assessment System for Children (BASC; Reynolds & Kamphaus, 2002), the Eyberg Child Behavior Inventory (ECBI; Eyberg & Pinkus, 1999), and the Sutter-Eyberg Student Behavior Inventory-Revised (SESBI-R; Eyberg & Pinkus, 1999) are among the most useful. Two scales directly related to RAD, the Reactive Attachment Disorder Questionnaire and the Randolph Attachment Disorder Questionnaire (Randolph, 1996), show potential but should not be used as the sole diagnostic instrument, as the first questionnaire was normed in Europe and the second does not measure the insecure attachment subtype (Sheperis, Doggett, et al., 2003).

The growing interest in examining attachment in older children and adults led to the creation of the Adult Attachment Interview (AAI) by George, Kaplan, and Main (1984). The instrument employs a sixty- to ninety-minute interview to assess adult attachment and provides information on how attachment experiences affected the person's development as an adult and parent.

Preferred Therapist Characteristics

Therapists working with children who have attachment disorder should understand the dynamics of the attachment process. Rebuilding a relationship between the child and the parents will be the primary goal of treatment. A psychodynamic or family systems conceptual framework for analyzing family dynamics is helpful in understanding this disorder and its treatment. One of the greatest challenges for therapists dealing with RAD is managing their own negative feelings toward the caregivers and remaining supportive and empathic while still establishing appropriate guidelines and boundaries for child care.

The therapist must also be able to consult with and contribute to a team of medical professionals.

Intervention Strategies

The goal of treatment for children with RAD is to improve the relationship between the child and the primary caregiver. The caregiver-child relationship forms both the basis for assessment of symptoms and the nexus for treatment of RAD (AACAP, 2005). Three modalities can help children with RAD and their caregivers develop more effective, positive interactions: working through the caregiver, working with the dyad (caregiver and child), or working with the child alone.

Of utmost importance is to ensure that the child has a caregiver who is emotionally available, sensitive, and responsive, and to whom attachment can develop (Robinson, 2002). The next step in treating children with RAD is to address those behaviors that interfere with the development of adequate and secure attachments (Hanson & Spratt, 2000; Hart & Thomas, 2000). Initially, psychoeducation for the caregivers will focus on parenting skills and on the nature of positive attachment behaviors.

Psychoeducation may be accompanied by parent-child dyad therapy, in which the therapist models positive interactions and facilitates parent-child play. At least two dyadic interactive therapy programs have been shown to be effective. Infant-parent psychotherapy seeks to improve the emotional communication between the child and caregiver (Lieberman, Silverman, & Pawl, 2000). The second program, interaction guidance, focuses on behavior and involves videotaping and shaping (McDonough, 2000). Both incorporate suggestion and positive reinforcement and highlight parenting strengths as observed in the session. Dyadic therapy may later be widened to include other family members. In accordance with attachment theory and the goal of improving the relationship between the child and the primary caregiver, individual therapy with the child should be considered only as an adjunct to dyadic therapy, especially with younger children (AACAP, 2005).

Additional treatment goals address the assessment and development of attachment behaviors in the parents. Caregiver characteristics that have been shown to be risk factors include depression, poverty, a history of abuse in the parent's own childhood, and lack of social support (Wilson, 2001). Any abusive or neglectful behaviors certainly must be modified, and quickly. Marital or individual psychotherapy may also be in order. An assessment of the parents' relationships to their individual families of origin can provide the therapist with a baseline assessment of the parents' levels and styles of attachment. Research using the Adult Attachment Interview (Cowan, Cohn, Cowan, & Pearson, 1996) shows significant links between parental attachment and a child's externalizing and internalizing behaviors. This kind of information can stimulate therapeutic discussions with the parents. A cognitive-behavioral framework can be used to identify inappropriate thoughts and actions in the parenting process, and psychodynamic therapy can address unresolved issues from childhood that are interfering with the ability to parent.

In aggressive or violent children, evidence-based treatments such as multisystemic therapy or parent training, which were discussed extensively in the previous sections on ODD and CD, may be considered. No data are available on the use of pharmacotherapy to treat RAD. Caution should be used in the consideration of such interventions, particularly in preschool-age children.

Interventions that involve physical restraint, "rebirthing," holding therapy, or regression therapy to create reattachment have not been empirically validated and have been associated with serious harm, including death. Both the American Psychiatric Association (2002) and AACAP (2003) have issued policy statements opposing coercion therapies for children with serious disturbances such as RAD.

Therapists must carefully monitor the family situations of children diagnosed with RAD. In some cases, where no gains or changes have been made to improve the quality of child care, or in cases where the children are so aggressive that they are unmanageable in the home, protective removal of the child may be warranted (AACAP, 2005); the options include placing the child in foster care, with a relative, or in respite care. Establishing a consistent, safe environment that provides positive care and nurturing is essential to the child's safety and the alleviation of this disorder.

Prognosis

Research has demonstrated a connection between insecure attachment and subsequent behavior and impulse-control problems, low self-esteem, poor peer relationships, psychiatric syndromes, criminal behavior, and substance abuse (Sheperis, Doggett, et al., 2003; Wilson, 2001; Zeanah & Emde, 1994). Clearly, early and effective intervention is indicated for RAD. Interventions based on attachment theory are relatively new, however, so only limited evaluation data are available. Nevertheless, the treatment of RAD offers many possibilities for future research and holds promise as a way to prevent later behavior disorders.

STEREOTYPIC MOVEMENT DISORDER

Description of the Disorder

Stereotypic movement disorder, according to *DSM-IV-TR*, is characterized by repetitive, apparently intentional, driven, nonfunctional, and often self-injurious behaviors, such as hand waving, rocking, head banging, or self-biting. These behaviors persist for at least four weeks and interfere with normal activities.

Comorbidity with mental retardation and pervasive developmental disorders is common (American Psychiatric Association, 2000; Rapoport & Ismond, 1996). Stereotypic movement disorder has also been identified in children diagnosed with anxiety disorders and mood disorders. As is true of most secondary disorders, stereotypic movement disorder should be diagnosed only if it is so severe as to warrant separate treatment.

Typical Client Characteristics

Children with stereotypic movement disorder exhibit the repetitive behaviors just described and may present with bruises, bite marks, cuts, and scratches (American Psychiatric Association, 2000). These behaviors are voluntary, although the children may report that they cannot stop them. The behaviors, sometimes manifested by children who have inadequate social stimulation (Rapoport & Ismond, 1996), often begin after a stressful event and may continue despite chastisement from family members and teasing by peers. The family histories of children with stereotypic movement disorder often include compulsive or other stereotypic behaviors (Rapoport & Ismond, 1996).

DSM-IV-TR reports that self-injurious behavior occurs at all ages and in both genders. Head banging is more prevalent in males at a ratio of 3:1; self-biting occurs more frequently in females.

Preferred Therapist Characteristics

Therapists working with children with stereotypic movement disorder should be aware of common comorbid disorders and their treatments. For example, childhood stereotypes (repetitive movements) may indicate an underlying disorder, such as autism or other pervasive developmental disorders or Tourette's syndrome. An adolescent or adult onset, however, might be an indication of stimulant abuse. Treatment should take into account the severity and cause of the disorder, and the age of the person.

Behavioral strategies are typically the first line of treatment, so therapists need a working knowledge of the basic elements of behavior change therapies. Skill in cognitive-behavioral and psychodynamic play therapy may also be helpful, as may family counseling and collaboration with physicians and educators. Therapists need to be calm and empathic with these clients, particularly if underlying anxiety or depression is present.

Intervention Strategies

Treatment for stereotypic movement disorder is similar to that used for behaviors associated with autism, tic disorders, and OCD. Applied behavior analysis has been shown to be clinically effective in reducing problem behavior and increasing appropriate skills for people with mental retardation, autism, and stereotypic behavior. Forty years of literature and three meta-analyses (Hagopian & Boelter, 2005) have concluded that treatments such as this, based on operant principles of learning, were effective in reducing problem behavior, including stereotypic behavior and self-injurious behavior, and in a variety of settings (home, schools, and hospitals).

In applied behavior analysis, baseline data are collected, both to determine the initial frequency and timing of the targeted behaviors and to evaluate progress. Then a behavioral plan is developed for modifying behaviors. The plan may follow a classical model or a model based on operant conditioning.

The classical paradigm for conditioning pairs the stereotypic behavior with some aversive stimulus or competing behavior. This type of aversion or competition is intended to decrease the frequency of the targeted behavior. For example, a rubber band may be placed around a child's wrist, and the child is given instructions to pluck the band each time the stereotypic behavior begins. As another example, tape may be placed over the thumb of a child in order to interfere with the automatic nature of chronic thumb sucking.

Operant conditioning uses both positive and negative reinforcers to change a targeted behavior. In the case of stereotypic movements, a chart may be developed and particular time periods may be delineated, with the child being rewarded with a sticker for each time period in which the behavior is not manifested; at the end of a week, the stickers can be redeemed for prizes. Therapists facilitate the development of these plans, but special education teachers often oversee their execution. Therefore, consultation between therapists and teachers may contribute to the effectiveness of the treatment.

If the stereotypic movements are related to a mood disorder or an anxiety disorder, play therapy may be the treatment of choice. These treatments can help children identify the sources of their discomfort. When their distress is alleviated, the children may not need to manifest behavioral expressions of their distress.

Prognosis

Little information is available about the prognosis for stereotypic movement disorder, perhaps because it is rarely the primary focus of treatment and usually accompanies more severe disorders. One study of behavior modification in autistic preschoolers showed a reduction in stereotypic behaviors at ages three and four, but not among two-year-olds, leading researchers to surmise that early and consistent intervention improves outcomes. Successful reduction of targeted behaviors via behavior modification is likely, although this disorder may persist for years, sometimes with changes in its nature. This outcome is especially likely in people with severe or profound levels of mental retardation (American Psychiatric Association, 2000).

ADDITIONAL MENTAL DISORDERS DIAGNOSED IN CHILDREN AND ADOLESCENTS

Many of the mental disorders considered in later chapters of this book are found in young clients, although they are far more prevalent in adults. The remainder of this chapter will discuss differences in the diagnosis and treatment of some of those disorders when they are found in children and adolescents. Discussion of some disorders will not follow the usual format of this book if information of particular relevance to children is unavailable in certain areas. Readers should also review later sections of this book to obtain a complete picture of these disorders.

Depression

Description of the Disorder

The diagnosis of depression in childhood requires an understanding of child development and of age-related differences in presentations of this disorder. Although reported feelings of sadness are characteristic of depression across all age ranges, children are more likely to mask their feelings rather than verbalize them. School-age children experiencing depression are less likely to appear sad but are more likely to be irritable and to present somatic complaints such as headaches, stomachaches, and fatigue (Field & Seligman, 2004).

Adolescents' symptoms of depression are similar to those of adults and include sad feelings, social withdrawal, and, in about 10 percent of cases, mood-congruent hallucinations. Adolescents are less likely than younger children to complain of physical problems and to cry, but irritability continues to be a characteristic complaint along with problems in relationships, impaired school performance, and substance misuse.

In young children, separation anxiety disorder often is characterized by features of depression, including crying, sulkiness, irritability, and a sad appearance. Clinicians should be sure that separation anxiety disorder is not misdiagnosed as a depressive disorder.

Typical Client Characteristics

Therapists working with children and adolescents often will encounter symptoms of depressive disorders. The prevalence rate of major depressive disorder in young people ranges from 1 to 3 percent among children and from 1 to 8 percent among adolescents (Field & Seligman, 2004, p. 241). Dysthymic disorder is slightly less common. Gender differences among children with symptoms of mood disorders have not been found. Nevertheless, the incidence of mood disorders in females doubles after puberty, suggesting a hormonal influence (Evans et al., 2005).

Assessment

Assessing the range of symptoms, degree of severity, and whether psychotic features accompany the mood disorder is important to accurate diagnosis and treatment. The Child Assessment Schedule (CAS), the Interview Schedule for Children (ISC), the Diagnostic Interview for Children and Adolescents (DICA), the Diagnostic Interview Schedule for Children (DISC), and the Children's Depression Rating Scale-Revised (CDRS-R) are useful in diagnosing depression in children (Field & Seligman, 2004). The Child Depression Inventory is the most widely used assessment of depression in children ages seven to seventeen (Silverman & Rabian, 1999). It has been extensively studied and is reported to have high stability and internal consistency.

Preferred Therapist Characteristics

Such traits as empathy and the ability to work collaboratively with parents are important when working with children with depression. Skillful recognition of suicidal ideation, good listening skills, and a nonjudgmental attitude are also important (Mackinaw-Koons & Fristad, 2004).

Intervention Strategies

Recommended treatment for children with mood disorders is similar to that for adults (see Chapter Four), but some programs and guidelines are especially pertinent to young clients with these disorders. Clarke and colleagues (2002), for example, designed the STEADY intervention model for adolescents with depression. This psychoeducational group training includes workbooks, readings, and quizzes to help adolescents track mood and activities, understand and comply with medication, set goals, and develop alternatives to negative thinking. The training takes place over six to nine sessions followed up with monthly phone calls and as many as six additional optional sessions as needed.

A combination of cognitive-behavioral therapy (CBT) and medication management was found to work best in the treatment of adolescent depression. NIMH funded the Treatment of Adolescents with Depression Study (TADS), which indicated a 71 percent positive response to combined treatment with CBT and fluoxetine (Prozac) compared with 61 percent who responded well to fluoxetine alone, 43 percent who responded well to CBT alone, and 35 percent who responded well to a placebo (Evans et al., 2005).

Although medications are being used effectively in the treatment of mood disorders among adults, little research is available on their effectiveness in children. When medication is used to treat mood disorders in children and adolescents, the child must be well monitored in order to prevent serious side effects. SSRIs in particular have been shown to increase the risk of suicidal ideation and behavior in children and adolescents, especially during the early months of treatment (Handen & Gilchrist, 2006). Since 2004, these medications have been required by the U.S. Food and Drug Administration to carry a black box warning label. Certainly, more research is needed in this area of pharmacology.

Suicide is a serious concern when working with children and adolescents diagnosed with mood disorders. Risk factors that increase the likelihood of a suicide attempt include previous history of attempted suicide, psychosis, mania, feelings of hopelessness, a recent loss, lower self-esteem, higher stress levels, and concurrent substance use. Psychological autopsy results indicate that depression has been present in as many as 85 percent of all suicide deaths (Haley, 2004).

Prognosis

Weisz and colleagues (1995) conducted a meta-analysis of outcome studies and found that children with depression who received psychotherapy were 77 percent more likely than controls to show improvement on posttreatment assessments and continued to be better off than 69 percent of the controls on follow-up assessments. Field and Seligman (2004) note that even with successful interventions, risk of relapse of depression in children and adolescents is high (40 to 60 percent). The risk of recurrence continues into adulthood. Comorbid disorders, such as ADHD, conduct disorder, personality disorders, and co-occurring substance-related disorders, can further complicate treatment of mood disorders in childhood and adolescence.

Bipolar Disorder

Description of the Disorder

Despite the fact that bipolar disorder has a relatively low occurrence in the population, a recent study indicates that the number of children diagnosed with bipolar disorder rose 26 percent from 2002 to 2004 ("Treating Children as Young as Four for Bipolar," 2005). The sudden increase raises questions about possible misdiagnosis and the potential for overprescribing medications. For example, symptoms overlap between the manic phase of a bipolar disorder and ADHD; this is particularly relevant considering that research indicates that 50 to 80 percent of children with bipolar disorder also have ADHD. Therapists should consider age of onset as well as family history of ADHD and bipolar disorder symptoms. Therapists also should be aware that the mood swings characteristic of most adolescents can be mistaken for a bipolar disorder.

Although the incidence of bipolar disorder is lower than depression, both conditions can have childhood or adolescent onset. Research conducted by the National Institute of Mental Health (2002) suggests that bipolar disorder affects 2 percent of the general population, 15 percent of whom manifest symptoms in childhood or adolescence.

Diagnosis of childhood bipolar disorder can be complicated by co-occurring disorders, by symptoms that mimic other disorders such as ADHD or conduct disorder, and by the fact that the symptoms of childhood mania often differ from the manic symptoms of adult bipolar disorder. Also, symptoms of mania in childhood often do not meet the one-week-duration criterion found in *DSM-IV-TR*. Bipolar disorder can become an extremely debilitating condition and is associated with high rates of suicide, the third leading cause of death in adolescents (National Center for Health Statistics, 2003).

Typical Client Characteristics

Children with bipolar disorder may exhibit emotional, cognitive, and physical symptoms. Bipolar rages or emotional storms that may last longer than thirty minutes are common. Such children frequently lack awareness of their surroundings or insight into their behavior. They also lack self-soothing skills (DuVal, 2005). Such rages are a symptom of mania (DuVal, 2005; NIMH, 2002). The symptoms of grandiosity, flight of ideas, hypersexuality, and decreased need for sleep are highly specific to bipolar disorder and can often distinguish bipolar disorder from ADHD. Time of onset is also important; ADHD generally appears at an earlier age.

In a review of ten years of research, Geller and Luby (1997) reported that childhood-onset bipolar disorder, rather than being episodic and acute, is more likely to be continuous, chronic, and rapid-cycling, and to include mixed or manic states. General agreement has not yet been reached about the definition and presentation of symptoms of mania in childhood. *DSM-IV-TR* requirements for mania are based on adult presentation. Strict adherence to the criteria eliminates those children from diagnosis who present without one euphoric symptom of mania (Hunt et al., 2005). Therapists may need to differentiate between euphoric symptoms of mania (grandiosity, pressured speech, and hypersexual behavior) and symptoms that are dysphoric in nature, such as irritability, anger, and aggression. Controversy has risen between experts, and this is borne out in the research, as some authors use a more expansive interpretation of the *DSM-IV-TR* criteria in the symptoms they include — increasing the diagnosis of bipolar disorder and inflating prevalence rates. Future research in this area will help clarify the issue. Until then, clinicians are wise to keep this controversy in mind when assessing children with symptoms of bipolar mania.

Assessment

A psychometric measurement has not been designed specifically for the diagnosis of bipolar disorder in children and adolescents. The Washington University Schedule for Affective Disorders and Schizophrenia for School-Age Children (K-SADS) has been used as a diagnostic tool and has a mania rating scale (K-SADS MRS) that provides good concurrent validity (Hunt et al., 2005; Pavuluri, Brimaher, & Naylor, 2005). Findling and colleagues (2005) reported that the Young Mania Rating Scale (YMRS) has been validated and is useful in distinguishing between bipolar disorder and other disorders, although Hunt and colleagues (2005) found it to be a helpful list of symptoms but not useful in distinguishing between diagnoses.

DSM-IV-TR indicates that adolescents with bipolar disorder are more likely to exhibit psychotic features, to have difficulties in school, to misuse substances, and to manifest antisocial behavior. Therapists should be aware that substance misuse and certain prescription drugs including antidepressants, stimulants used in the treatment of comorbid ADHD, and steroids may precipitate a manic episode (Botteron & Geller, 1995).

Preferred Therapist Characteristics

Mackinaw-Koons and Fristad (2004) found that parents of children with bipolar disorder often felt blamed, criticized, and responsible for their children's illnesses. Therefore, therapists should be both knowledgeable about pediatric bipolar disorder and able to separate the child from the symptoms.

In the same study, parents reported that symptoms of hypersexuality posed particular difficulties, for even in the absence of any allegations or basis for suspicion of abuse, therapists frequently assumed sexual abuse had occurred because the child was exhibiting sexually provocative behavior. Certainly, all suspected child abuse must be reported, but therapists need to recognize that hypersexuality is a frequent symptom of bipolar disorder. Care must be taken to distinguish bipolar symptoms from those of abuse (Mackinaw-Koons & Fristad, 2004).

Above all, therapist competence in the treatment of bipolar disorder in children is key to successful treatment. Given the paucity of research and literature, and the low prevalence rate, most mental health professionals may have seen few or no cases of pediatric bipolar disorder (Mackinaw-Koons & Fristad, 2004). Considering the potentially life-threatening nature of the illness, mental health providers must be willing to refer to a more experienced provider when necessary.

Intervention Strategies

Family education is an important component of treatment of bipolar disorder in children and can enhance medication compliance and relapse prevention. Miklowitz and Goldstein (1997) developed a manual-based version of family-focused therapy for adolescents with bipolar disorder. Family-focused therapy helps reduce symptoms, gives the child coping tools, decreases the level of expressed emotions from relatives, and improves family problem-solving skills. This therapy also helps the adolescent understand and accept the diagnosis of bipolar disorder, comply with medications, manage stress, reduce family tensions, and self-monitor symptoms to help prevent relapse (Pavuluri et al., 2004).

In child- and family-focused cognitive-behavioral therapy (CFF-CBT), Pavuluri and colleagues (2004) combine CBT and interpersonal psychotherapy to address the needs of the child and the family. CFF-CBT is presented as the RAINBOW program, representing the rainbow of moods the child experiences along with an easy-to-remember acronym of skills that are taught during therapy sessions (Routine; Affect regulation; I can do it; No negative thoughts; Be a good friend; Oh, how can we solve the problem?; and Ways to get support). Preliminary research shows that CFF-CBT decreased symptom severity and increased functioning in children. Parent satisfaction was also rated as high.

Multifamily psychoeducation groups have also been found to be helpful in the treatment of childhood bipolar disorder. Material about the disorder is taught and skills are practiced in weekly groups that include parents and children. Following the psychoeducation component, the groups break into separate parent and child groups to provide support and guidance (Miklowitz, 2004; Sachs, 2004).

Only lithium has been approved by the FDA for the treatment of bipolar disorder in adolescents twelve years of age or older; however, children of all ages are being prescribed lithium, anticonvulsants, antipsychotics, and electroconvulsive therapy (Weller, Danielyan, & Weller, 2004). Caution is advised in the use of these medications with young children and adolescents.

Psychosis

Description of the Disorder

Although rare, childhood-onset psychosis does occur. Fewer than one child in ten thousand develops schizophrenia, with boys being twice as likely as girls to develop the disorder (Asarnow & Asarnow, 2003). The *DSM-IV-TR* criteria for psychotic disorders in children are the same as those used for adults, with primary symptoms including hallucinations, delusions, loose associations, and illogical thinking (American Psychiatric Association, 2000). Prodromal symptoms may begin about two to six years before the onset of psychosis (Evans et al., 2005). Negative symptoms (cognitive slippage, decrease in executive functioning) occur before positive symptoms (delusions and hallucinations). Prodromal symptoms most likely to appear in adolescence include social withdrawal, a decline in academic functioning, odd behavior, and magical beliefs (Kopelowicz, Liberman, & Zarate, 2002). Irritability; lack of concern for appearance; sleep problems; mood changes; flat affect; inappropriate emotion; and decreased motivation, energy, and concentration are also common (Evans et al., 2005).

In adolescence, use of marijuana, alcohol, and stimulants (cocaine and amphetamines) has been found to increase the incidence of psychosis. These drugs are well documented to increase psychosis in vulnerable individuals (Kopelowicz et al., 2002).

Childhood-onset schizophrenia. Childhood-onset schizophrenia is rare (Kopelowicz et al., 2002). Symptoms are insidious in young children and may include illogical conversation or thought patterns, as well as magical thinking. Well-formed delusions and hallucinations are uncommon in childhood. The difficulty in applying this diagnosis to children is that loose associations and illogical thinking are not unusual before the age of seven (Volkmar, 1996). With older children, however, these symptoms should be taken quite seriously. (For additional information on psychotic disorders, see Chapter Nine.)

Research continues on brain development and schizophrenia in children, as does the search for a genetic component to psychosis. Adolescence is a time of tremendous brain development (Evans et al., 2005), and some research has found an increase in schizophrenia among adults who regularly used marijuana during that key period of neurological growth. More research is needed in this area.

Typical Client Characteristics

Childhood-onset schizophrenia is the most prevalent psychotic disorder in children. Onset before the age of six is extremely rare; nevertheless, Mash and Wolfe (2005) report that when onset of schizophrenia does occur in childhood, the symptoms are likely to persist through adolescence and into adulthood. Histories of adults diagnosed with schizophrenia often reveal the presence of unusual personality styles as well as language or motor problems in childhood (Evans et al., 2005).

Psychotic symptoms (delusions and hallucinations) usually respond to antipsychotic medication. Atypical antipsychotics are used most frequently (Evans et al., 2005). Executive functioning and cognitive symptoms take longer to resolve. The frequency of schizophrenia increases with the beginning of adolescence. The onset of the disorder is about five years later for females than males (Kopelowicz et al., 2002). Schizophrenia often is comorbid with developmental disorders, depression, and anxiety.

Preferred Therapist Characteristics

Training and experience are similar to those required for working with adults with psychotic disorders. Schizophrenia tends to be familial, and therapists need to be alert to the possibility that other family members may also have psychotic disorders. A difficult aspect of the work with a family that has a child with psychosis is helping the family members cope with the uncertain prognosis of the disorder.

Intervention Strategies

Family climate is one of the most powerful predictors of relapse in schizophrenia (Kopelowicz et al., 2002); families that exhibit high expressed emotion (highly critical, hostile, or overly involved) have higher relapse rates (Kazdin, 2002). Structured education and family interventions that reduce anxiety and stress, teach family members to be less critical and negative, and reduce excessive emotional involvement of family members are important to the creation of a low-stress environment in which the child can effectively reside. As is the case for adults, multiple treatment modalities are required. In addition to family therapy, treatment for children and adolescents with psychotic disorders may include cognitive-behavioral training, cognitive restructuring, social skills training, interpersonal psychotherapy, compliance therapy, and pharmacological management (Evans et al., 2005). Therapists may become involved in the development of educational plans, which should incorporate social and emotional goals. Social skills training involving the teaching of approach behaviors, interpersonal interaction, playing with peers, and effective communication should be included. Stress management interventions may also be useful to young people diagnosed with psychotic disorders, given that high levels of stress have been found to increase dysfunctional thought patterns and the likelihood of psychotic episodes. Modification of the home environment, promotion of a positive attitude on the part of the parents, and training of the parents in effective coping strategies are all likely to be helpful. Additional useful psychoeducational family interventions could include teaching communication and problem-solving skills and providing specific factual information about the disorder and its treatment.

Prognosis

Bellack and Mueser (1993) report a fairly positive prognosis for young people diagnosed with psychotic disorders. They have found that children who received family interventions in addition to medication had a relapse rate of only 17 percent, in comparison with a relapse rate of 83 percent among a control group in which children received medication only. Wyatt has found that early diagnosis and treatment can improve long-term outcomes in people with schizophrenia (Evans et al., 2005; Kopelowicz et al., 2002). Advances are being made in terms of research on genetic and environmental factors that contribute to schizophrenia. Recent research implicates dopamine levels in the brain as a key factor in the onset of psychosis. Future research will focus on preventive measures that reduce the symptoms or delay or defer the onset of this debilitating disorder.

Anxiety Disorders

The prevalence rate of anxiety disorders among children ranges from 3 to 6 percent, making them the third most common psychiatric disorders of childhood and adolescents (behind ADHD and ODD). More than half of these children will go on to experience a major depressive episode as part of their anxiety syndrome. The principal risk factor for the onset of a childhood anxiety disorder is having a parent with an anxiety disorder or a depressive disorder (Morris & March, 2004).

Assessment of childhood anxiety disorders can begin with such tools as the Child Behavior Checklist (CBCL; Achenbach, 1991), the Multidimensional Anxiety Scale for Children, the Children's Yale-Brown Obsessive-Compulsive Scale, or the Revised Children's Manifest Anxiety Scale (Reynolds, 1985; Barrett, Duffy, Dadds, & Rapee, 2001; Morris & March, 2004; Silverman & Rabian, 1999).

Substantial empirical support exists for exposure and response prevention therapy in the treatment of anxiety disorders in children. Additional treatment strategies include cognitive restructuring to correct distortions in thinking, behavior therapy, psychoeducation, social skills training, and medication. Typically, homework and office-based modeling techniques are used. Childhood-onset anxiety disorders are resistant to traditional insight-oriented therapy. Family interventions also play a critical role in the treatment of children (Abramowitz, Whiteside, & Deacon, 2005; Morris & March, 2004).

Following is a closer look at the most commonly occurring anxiety disorders of childhood: obsessive-compulsive disorder, generalized anxiety disorder, posttraumatic stress disorder, and phobias. Readers will find additional information on symptoms, assessment, and treatment in Chapter Five.

Obsessive-Compulsive Disorder

Evans et al. (2005) report that as many as 1 percent of children and adolescents meet the diagnostic criteria for obsessive-compulsive disorder (OCD), manifesting symptoms similar to those of adults with the disorder. Most children with OCD present with obsessions about germs or disease and exhibit concomitant rituals of washing or checking. Other common obsessions include concern about harm to the self or others, sexual themes, or forbidden thoughts. Common compulsions, in addition to washing and checking, include touching, counting, hoarding, and repeating.

Typical Client Characteristics

Younger children in particular may have more magical thinking and may have more superstitious OCD symptoms (Evans et al., 2005). Children with an early onset of OCD commonly have a family history of the disorder (Mash & Wolfe, 2005).

A high rate of comorbid disorders has also been reported, including tic disorders, ADHD, learning disorders, eating disorders, other anxiety disorders, and depression (Mash & Wolfe, 2005). Twenty percent of adolescents with OCD have comorbid disorders, such as other anxiety disorders and Tourette's disorder (Hinkle, 2004).

Often treatment is sought only after symptoms have become debilitating and have resulted in reduced self-esteem and loss of friends (Hinkle, 2004). Epidemiological studies have identified no differences in prevalence rates among various ethnic groups. However, cultural beliefs can affect the content of obsessions and compulsions (American Psychiatric Association, 2000).

Preferred Therapist Characteristics

Children with OCD frequently lack insight and may resist any change in their compulsive behaviors. As behavioral changes are introduced, oppositional behavior may be exhibited in response to any limits placed on the targeted behaviors. Therefore, therapists working with children with OCD need to be empathic yet confident in their skills and the treatment plans they develop; they need to set limits and reinforce homework compliance. Therapists must also provide support to the parents of children with OCD and be particularly aware of religious or spiritual rituals that may be mistaken for obsessions or compulsions of OCD (Hinkle, 2004; Paniagua, 2001).

Intervention Strategies

Childhood OCD is treated as an anxiety disorder, and cognitive-behavioral interventions are emphasized. Abramowitz and colleagues (2005) conducted a meta-analysis of eighteen studies of pediatric OCD treatment. Their analysis of the literature concludes that exposure and response prevention is superior to medication in the treatment of pediatric OCD. Symptoms of anxiety and depression were reduced and there were fewer residual symptoms compared to treatment with SSRIs. SSRIs, which have become the most frequently used treatment for children with OCD, were also effective in reducing obsessive and compulsive symptoms and should be considered when exposure and response prevention fails, is unavailable, or has been refused. However, symptom relapse was found when the medications were discontinued.

Fewer than 10 percent of children with OCD or Tourette's disorder have pediatric autoimmune neuropsychological disorders associated with streptococcal infections (PANDAS; Evans et al., 2005; Swedo, 2002). Five criteria are necessary for diagnosing PANDAS, which occur in two situations: a child develops tics, obsessions, and compulsions after a strep infection, or a child who has Tourette's syndrome or OCD may become worse after a strep infection. Although researchers do not fully understand the link between PANDAS and mental disorders, it may be important to recognize and identify these types of OCD and Tourette's disorder so that appropriate medical assessment for streptococcal infection and possible treatment measures can begin (Evans et al., 2005).

Prognosis

Complete remission for OCD in childhood is estimated to be in the range of 10 to 15 percent (Hinkle, 2004). Thus OCD remains a serious and chronic disorder for a large proportion of the children who develop symptoms. For additional discussion of the diagnosis and treatment of OCD, see Chapter Five.

Posttraumatic Stress Disorder. Posttraumatic stress disorder (PTSD) is common in children exposed to trauma and is strongly correlated to degree of exposure (Mash & Wolfe, 2005). The criteria for PTSD in children are the same as for adults. Children's distress may be manifested in slightly different ways, however, because of their different level of cognitive and emotional functioning. Nightmares are common among children with PTSD, although they may not be able to remember the content of the dreams. Avoidance of any event or place associated with the trauma, difficulty falling or staying asleep, irritability, exaggerated startle responses, and withdrawal behaviors are also typical of children with PTSD (Evans et al., 2005).

Traumatic loss, exposure to interpersonal or community violence, car accidents, and life-threatening medical illness have all been found to produce symptoms of PTSD in children. Kilpatrick and colleagues (2003) found that the six-month prevalence rate was 3.7 percent of boys and 6.3 percent of girls ages twelve to seventeen. Evans et al. (2005) reported on a survey of adolescents which found that 23 percent had been both a victim of violence and had witnessed a violent crime. Children who experienced such traumas commonly exhibited detachment, sadness, restricted affect, and dissociative episodes (Evans et al., 2005). Children exposed to repeated or chronic traumas, such as abuse, exhibited even more troubled behaviors.

Adolescent boys are more likely to be exposed to violence and assault, whereas girls are more likely to experience dating violence and rape (Evans et al., 2005). Adolescents exposed to severe trauma frequently experience difficulties with academic performance; increased sexual activity; substance misuse; and an increase in aggressive, reckless, or avoidant behavior (Evans et al., 2005). Depression and substance-related disorders were found to co-occur in nearly 75 percent of the adolescents diagnosed with PTSD (Kilpatrick et al., 2003).

Inappropriate sexual behaviors are often exhibited by children who have experienced sexual abuse. A study of one hundred sexually abused school-age children documented the effectiveness of a twelve-week CBT treatment that included gradual confrontation of traumatic thoughts, feelings, and memories (Evans et al., 2005). The treatment included exposure components and cognitive therapy.

Longitudinal studies of PTSD in childhood suggest it can become a chronic psychological disorder for some children, persisting well into adulthood and sometimes lasting a lifetime (Fletcher, 2003). Effective treatment of PTSD in children is similar to its treatment in adults. For more information, refer to Chapter Five.

Generalized Anxiety Disorder. Generalized anxiety disorder (GAD) is present in 3 to 6 percent of all children; average age of onset is between ten and fourteen years of age (Albano et al., 2003). Children with GAD have concerns about many aspects of their lives, usually schoolwork, appearance, money, or the future (Evans et al., 2005). These children typically exhibit excessive worry or anxiety, difficulty controlling the worry, trouble concentrating, apprehension over upcoming events, problems in sleeping, and muscle tension. They have difficulty relaxing and may exhibit exaggerated emotional responses to stressors. Frequently their anxiety is reflected in somatic complaints (Kronenberger & Meyer, 2001).

Comorbidity of GAD with other disorders, especially other anxiety disorders, major depressive disorder, and school refusal, is common (Evans et al., 2005). Specific phobias, problems with social adjustment, separation anxiety, and low self-esteem are also common. The prevalence of GAD is similar for both genders (Mash & Wolfe, 2005).

Assessment and treatment of children with GAD emphasizes behavioral strategies. Research to date shows that CBT is effective compared to the impact of conditions of no treatment provided to people in a control group or on a wait list (Evans et al., 2005; Kendall et al., 2003). The Revised Children's Manifest Anxiety Scale is often used in determining the extent of the anxiety and the specific issues that may underlie the disorder (Reynolds & Richman, 1978). This inventory provides a baseline that can be used to evaluate the success of treatment. The first approach to treatment is most often a plan for systematic desensitization. This plan can be designed by the therapist and implemented by the parents. Treatment should be tailored to the child's age and developmental needs. For example, CBT with family involvement has been found to be more effective in treating seven- to ten-year-olds with GAD than in treating eleven- to fourteen-year-olds (Evans et al., 2005).

Little data on the use of medication to treat GAD is available. Nevertheless, the use of such medications with children and adolescents has increased.

Phobias. Phobias are common among children, particularly specific and social phobias, although they rarely are presented for treatment. In most cases, the children simply avoid whatever situations produce the phobic responses. Animal phobias are common in young children. Older children are more likely to exhibit blood- and injury-related phobias that may cause extreme anxiety and interfere with normal functioning (Evans et al., 2005).

Treatment for phobias in children is similar to that for other anxiety disorders. Evans et al. (2005) report that modeling and reinforcement are the behavioral treatments most established and efficacious in the treatment of phobias. Additional information about phobias and their effective treatment is to be found in Chapter Five.

TREATMENT RECOMMENDATIONS: CLIENT MAP

This chapter has focused on disorders that usually begin before the age of eighteen, as well as disorders that typically begin later but sometimes manifest earlier. Beyond their early age of onset, these disorders vary widely, although most are reflected by behavioral difficulties. The following general treatment recommendations, organized according to the format of the Client Map, are provided for the disorders discussed in this chapter.

Client Map

Diagnosis

Disorders usually first diagnosed during infancy, childhood, or adolescence

Objectives of Treatment

Eliminate dysfunctional behavior

Improve academic functioning

Improve socialization and peer-group involvement

Promote family understanding of the disorder

Improve parenting and family functioning

Assessments

Assessment of intelligence, attention, and learning abilities

Assessment of behaviors, fears, mood, and other relevant symptoms

Clinician Characteristics

Skilled at providing support and building rapport while setting limits and overcoming resistance

Knowledgeable about developmental patterns and issues in children

Able to collaborate with family members, teachers, school counselors, and physicians

Location of Treatment

Usually outpatient

Day treatment centers increasingly available for troubled children

Interventions to Be Used

Behavior therapy, especially reality therapy, emphasizing strategies for behavior change

Cognitive therapy

Establishment of a baseline

Setting of realistic goals

Modification and tracking of behavior

Use of reinforcements and logical consequences

Education on the disorder for the child and the family

Training in communication and other skills

Play therapy (for young children)

Emphasis of Treatment

Structured but supportive

Primarily oriented toward the present

Numbers

Individual and family therapy

Peer-group counseling and play therapy possibly helpful

Timing

Usually medium-term therapy, with a rapid pace

Medications Needed

Usually recommended for ADHD, Tourette's disorder, OCD, psychotic disorders, and severe forms of other disorders

Adjunct Services

Parent education

Rewarding activities for children

Prognosis

Varies according to the disorder

Client Map of Shannon

This chapter began with a description of Shannon, a nine-year-old girl who, for several years, had been displaying a broad range of behavioral and academic problems. As is common among children with attention-deficit and disruptive behavior disorders, the parents had manifested similar symptoms as youngsters. Consequently, they had difficulty appreciating the severity of Shannon's symptoms and helping her modify her behavior. The following Client Map outlines the treatment recommended for Shannon.

Diagnosis

Axis I: 312.8 Conduct disorder, childhood-onset type, moderate

314.01 Attention-deficit/hyperactivity disorder, predominantly hyperactive-impulsive type, moderate

Axis II: V71.09 No diagnosis on Axis II

Axis III: None reported

Axis IV: Arrest, academic problems, lack of adequate supervision

Axis V: Global assessment of functioning (GAF Scale): current GAF = 50

Objectives of Treatment

Eliminate conduct-disordered behavior

Improve attention, academic skills, and grades

Assessments

Assessment of intelligence and learning abilities

Conners' rating scales

Clinician Characteristics

Skilled at building rapport, overcoming resistance, setting limits, using family interventions

Location of Treatment

Community mental health center

Interventions to Be Used

Reality therapy, emphasizing strategies for behavior change (to help client recognize the self-destructive nature of her behavior)

Contract for behavioral change

Help in recognizing triggers for impulsive behavior and substituting alternative behaviors

Training in healthy ways to meet her needs

Setting of realistic goals in family and school meetings (for help in improving attention and academic achievement)

Reinforcement for positive behaviors

Emphasis of Treatment

Structured but supportive, primarily present-oriented

Numbers

Individual therapy with family involvement

Counseling group at school (to help in improving social skills and reinforcing positive changes)

Consultation with school counselor, teachers, and representatives of the legal system (to provide the experience of consequences for theft but also an avenue for demonstrating sincere efforts to change)

Timing

Medium- or long-term treatment, weekly sessions, rapid pace

Medications Needed

Referral to a child psychiatrist for determination of whether medication is indicated for reducing symptoms of ADHD

Adjunct Services

Parent education

Involvement in some interesting, action-oriented pursuit likely to provide a success experience

Possible involvement in a Big Sister program

Prognosis

Good, with parental cooperation; otherwise, fair

Recommended Reading

Journals, including *Adolescence, Child Abuse and Neglect, Child Development, Developmental Psychology, Elementary School Guidance and Counseling, Journal of Abnormal Child Psychology, Journal of the American Academy of Child and Adolescent Psychiatry,* and *Journal of Clinical Child Psychiatry.*

Barkley, R. A. (2006). *Attention-deficit hyperactivity disorder: A handbook for diagnosis and treatment* (3rd ed.). New York: Guilford Press.

Barkley, R. A., & Murphy, K. R. (2006). *Attention deficit hyperactivity disorder: A clinical workbook* (3rd ed.). New York: Guilford Press.

Kazdin, A. E. (1995). *Conduct disorders in childhood and adolescence.* Thousand Oaks, CA: Sage.

Landreth, G. L. (Ed.). (2001). *Innovations in play therapy: Issues, process, and special populations.* Philadelphia: Brunner-Routledge.

Mash, E. J., & Barkley, R. A. (2006). *Treatment of childhood disorders* (3rd ed.). New York: Guilford Press.

CHAPTER THREE

Situationally Precipitated Disorders and Conditions

Beth H., a forty-seven-year-old divorced Jewish woman, sought counseling two weeks after a biopsy revealed that she had breast cancer. She reported that she had been consumed by fear and grief since her diagnosis and had been unable to make decisions about her treatment. The physicians had told her that she could choose either a mastectomy or a combination of removal of the tumor and the surrounding tissue along with thirty radiation treatments. Beth was terrified that the radiation itself would cause secondary cancers, and she viewed the mastectomy as the safer option. However, that choice was also frightening and confusing to her because she was apprehensive about the extensive surgery and the resulting physical changes. Beth had explored the possibility of reconstructive surgery concurrent with her mastectomy. Once again, however, she had been confronted with an array of choices, all of them with risks and drawbacks. Beth's physicians cautioned her that putting the surgery off too long might worsen her prognosis, but her anxiety and her sorrow were preventing her from making a decision. Despite these worries, Beth continued to fulfill all her personal and professional responsibilities satisfactorily.

Beth reported that her life had been difficult over the past year but that she had been managing to keep it all under control. She and her husband had divorced a year before, and Beth had just begun to socialize as a single person. She had a successful career as a benefits manager for a county government.

She also had a twelve-year-old daughter, Amanda, whom she described as the greatest joy in her life. She had several close women friends and maintained positive relationships with her father and her younger sister. She reported great enjoyment of outdoor activities, especially hiking, camping, and bird-watching.

Beth's diagnosis of cancer raised several powerful fears that were linked to her symptoms. Her mother had died of breast cancer at the age of fifty, and Beth feared that she too would die and not see her daughter grow up. She was also apprehensive that even if she did survive, the diagnosis and the subsequent surgery would prevent her from developing close intimate relationships and marrying again. She was terrified that her disease was hereditary and that her daughter would inherit this legacy. Finally, she was fearful that she would need chemotherapy after the surgery. Beth reported that she had successfully coped with many problems over the course of her life but had never before felt so hopeless and worried.

Beth is an emotionally healthy woman who has functioned well throughout her life. She has good relationships with family and friends, rewarding interests, and a usually optimistic view of her life and of herself. The diagnosis of breast cancer, however, especially coming not long after her divorce, raised many fears about her future and left her feeling anxious and discouraged. Beth was experiencing an adjustment disorder with mixed anxiety and depressed mood.

This chapter will focus on both adjustment disorder and other conditions that may be a focus of clinical attention (formerly known as the V-code conditions). These typically are the mildest categories of symptoms described in the fourth edition text revision of the *Diagnostic and Statistical Manual of Mental Disorders*, or *DSM-IV-TR* (American Psychiatric Association, 2000).

OVERVIEW OF SITUATIONALLY PRECIPITATED DISORDERS AND CONDITIONS

Description of the Disorders and Conditions

Both categories — adjustment disorders and other conditions that may be a focus of clinical attention (referred to in this chapter as conditions) — usually have an identifiable precipitant or cause and are often relatively mild and transient, especially if the person has no other mental disorders. Causes are most likely to be such common life events or circumstances as relocation, divorce, a death, or conflicts in a relationship. Any emotional symptoms that result are clearly connected to the precipitant, although the client may react with some generalized dysfunction.

Several other disorders in *DSM-IV-TR* (such as brief psychotic disorder and major depressive disorder without melancholic features) also tend to be precipitated by an external stressor, but the severe symptoms associated with those disorders may obscure the role of the precipitant. At least initially, the symptoms themselves rather than stressful life circumstances become the focus of treatment. For adjustment disorders and conditions, however, helping people address the precipitant and its impact on their lifestyle and adjustment are usually the primary focus of treatment; the emotional upset and dysfunctional behavior resulting from the precipitant receive secondary attention. In treating these disorders and conditions, clinicians commonly assume that if people can gain a realistic view of the precipitant, adapt to and manage the changes it has produced, and increase their sense of control, then any dysfunctional symptoms accompanying the stressful life change will correspondingly be alleviated, if not eliminated.

Sometimes clinicians have difficulty determining whether a person is experiencing a condition or an adjustment disorder. Adjustment disorders by definition result in noticeable impairment or dysfunction and/or marked distress beyond what would be expected in reaction to the stressor (American Psychiatric Association, 2000). Conditions are normal or expectable reactions to life events and are therefore not viewed as mental disorders, although the conditions are associated with some upset or dysfunction that may be alleviated by psychotherapy and may be associated with comorbid mental disorders. Beth, for example, was immobilized by symptoms of apprehension and depression, which reflected an adjustment disorder. Had she been saddened and worried by the diagnosis of cancer but nevertheless in control and able to make appropriate medical decisions, she would have been described as experiencing a condition, probably a phase of life problem.

Adjustment disorders and conditions tend to be relatively brief in duration. If there is a long-standing cause or precipitant, however (such as abuse, a long-standing and worsening medical illness, or treatment via neuroleptic medications), the adjustment disorder or condition may be enduring.

Following is a helpful five-level taxonomic structure (Strain, 1998) clarifying the relative levels of severity of these two categories:

1. Normal state
2. Problem-level (for example, the conditions)
3. Adjustment disorder
4. Minor disorder or not otherwise specified diagnosis
5. Major disorder

In other words, the conditions represent more dysfunction than what is considered normal, but not enough for a diagnosis of a mental disorder, whereas an adjustment disorder is viewed as the mildest type of mental disorder listed in *DSM-IV-TR*.

Typical Client Characteristics

Nearly everyone has experienced either an adjustment disorder or a condition or both. They occur at all levels of mental health, intelligence, affluence, and psychological sophistication. Their symptoms may be triggered by a broad range of transitions and changes, such as mistreatment and abuse, diagnosis of a life-threatening illness, or divorce, and may reflect and be related to common problems of living, such as occupational dissatisfaction, relationship conflict, or caretaking of an ill or elderly parent. Although few people go through life without experiencing a disturbing loss or life change, some people — especially those who have effective coping mechanisms and ways of handling stress, those who have support systems and confidants, those who have a record of successfully coping with previous stressors, and those whose overall functioning is good — are less likely to be troubled by these problems. People are also typically more successful at handling stressful life circumstances if those events are not severely disruptive and if there are not multiple stressors. The impact of stressors seems to be additive, so that a major stressor (such as diagnosis of a life-threatening illness) accompanied by several minor stressors (such as relocation and a new job) are probably going to have a much greater impact than an isolated major stressor.

Preferred Therapist Characteristics

People with adjustment disorders or conditions typically work best with therapists who are supportive, affirming, collaborative, and empathic and who provide the stimulus, direction, and decision-making and other skills needed for the clients to mobilize themselves and use their resources more effectively. Treatment is typically short term and focused on helping people cope more effectively with their stressful changes or circumstances. Therapists should be comfortable with brief, structured interventions that may involve teaching and referral to outside sources of help and information but that are unlikely to involve extended exploration. Therapists should also be comfortable dealing with persons in crisis who may be feeling overwhelmed, discouraged, and even suicidal. Because adjustment disorders and other conditions may stand alone or be accompanied by a broad range of other disorders, therapists need to be skilled diagnosticians so that they can determine quickly whether coexisting mental disorders are present that may interfere with the client's efforts to cope.

Intervention Strategies

Treatment for adjustment disorders and conditions varies and depends on the nature of the associated crisis or life circumstance and on the presence of any coexisting disorders. In general, however, treatment will be designed to help people achieve a clear understanding of what is going on in their lives, of their reactions to those situations, and of their options. People's current resources and coping mechanisms provide the foundation for treatment, and efforts will be made to increase clients' awareness of their existing strengths, to build on those strengths, and to help them develop new coping skills if those are needed. For example, people with a condition called partner relational problem might be taught how to improve their communication skills, clarify their expectations of their partners, seek a mutually agreed-on and rewarding relationship, and enhance their other relationships. People who have experienced the death of a loved one will usually need help in expressing and managing their grief; in dealing with the impact the loss has on their lives; and in establishing new and realistic goals, directions, friends, and activities.

Therapists will typically seek to build rapport quickly so that they can function as collaborators, helping and guiding people with adjustment disorders or conditions toward mobilizing their resources, gathering information, and coping effectively with stressors. Normalizing people's troubled reactions, if that is warranted, can be helpful. A support group composed of others who are dealing with similar life circumstances can reduce feelings of aloneness and differentness and can help people accept and understand their responses to the stressor, obtain information about it, and learn ways to cope effectively with it. Support groups for people coping with cancer, for people who have experienced the death of a loved one, for people going through marital separation or divorce, and many others are widely available and can greatly enhance the process of therapy.

Prognosis

The prognosis is excellent for returning people with adjustment disorders and conditions to their previous levels of functioning. In fact, some people seem to function even better afterward because they have gained self-confidence from handling their situation effectively and because they developed or improved their skills over the course of therapy. Therefore, treatment of adjustment disorders and conditions is often a growth-promoting experience for clients. However, if a stressor is unremitting, if the person is unsuccessful in coping with the stressor, or if the person has preexisting emotional difficulties, the symptoms may not abate or may even evolve into a more significant mental disorder.

ADJUSTMENT DISORDERS

Description of the Disorders

The category of adjustment disorders is the less prevalent of the two discussed in this chapter. According to *DSM-IV-TR*, "The essential feature of an adjustment disorder is a psychological response to an identifiable stressor or stressors that results in the development of clinically significant emotional or behavioral symptoms. The symptoms must develop within three months after the onset of the stressor(s)'' (American Psychiatric Association, 2000, p. 679). Precipitating stressors may be of any severity and may include traumas.

Adjustment disorders are one of the very few *DSM* diagnoses that are by definition time-limited. This diagnosis can be maintained for a maximum of six months after the termination of the precipitating stressor. If symptoms persist beyond this period, the diagnosis must be changed. However, because many precipitants (such as a disabling medical condition or a dangerous environment) are chronic and enduring, this diagnosis may be maintained for many months or even years. An adjustment disorder that remits within six months is described as acute; one that lasts longer is classified as chronic.

The category of adjustment disorders is sometimes thought of as a residual category, one that is not used if the symptoms also meet the criteria for another mental disorder. The diagnosis of adjustment disorder typically stands alone on Axis I of a multiaxial assessment, but it can be used along with the diagnosis of another mental disorder if the development of the adjustment disorder is separate from the development of the other mental disorder. For example, a person with a preexisting somatization disorder might develop symptoms of an adjustment disorder after a marital separation. In that case, both diagnoses would be listed.

A wide variety of stressors can precipitate an adjustment disorder. Stressors may be single events (such as the end of a relationship or the loss of a job) or multiple events (such as diagnosis of an illness and concurrent partner relational conflict). The stressors may be circumscribed events, recurrent events (such as relapses of an illness), or continuous circumstances (such as poverty or a conflicted relationship). The most common stressors for adults are partner relational difficulties, divorce or separation, financial problems, and relocation; for adolescents the most common stressors are school-related problems, relationship problems, and parental divorce or conflict (Butcher, Mineka, & Hooley, 2006). Because the impact of stressors tends to be additive, assessment should look beyond the presenting concern to determine what other circumstances may be affecting a person.

The reaction to the stressor, rather than the presence of the stressor itself, is what determines whether a person has an adjustment disorder. A significant stressor (such as the loss of one's home in a flood) may have little impact on one person, whereas a relatively minor stressor (such as the end of a brief dating relationship in adolescence) may evoke a very strong reaction in another person. An adjustment disorder seems particularly likely to develop when a stressor touches on an area of vulnerability for the client and leads to an adverse reaction.

Adjustment disorders differ from conditions in being characterized by impaired functioning or reactions exceeding those that would normally be expected — in other words, by a strong negative psychological response to a stressor. A condition, by contrast, refers to a context, a problem, or a situation rather than to excessive reactions and symptoms.

DSM-IV-TR specifies six types of adjustment disorders. When this diagnosis is made, the clinician should specify whether the type is adjustment disorder with depressed mood, with anxiety, with mixed anxiety and depressed mood, with disturbance of conduct, with mixed disturbance of emotions and conduct, or unspecified. Examples of the unspecified type include adjustment problems characterized by work inhibition or mild physical symptoms without an apparent medical cause. Depression and anxiety are the most common accompaniments of adjustment disorders in adults, whereas disturbances of conduct are particularly common among adolescents with adjustment disorders (Benton & Lynch, 2006). Such behaviors as vandalism, fighting, truancy, reckless driving, and other self-destructive acts are typical of youth with adjustment disorders, and this kind of disorder may be confused with conduct disorder if a careful history is not taken.

Adjustment disorders are common, estimated to range from 2 to 8 percent of the general population (American Psychiatric Association, 2000) to as high as 22 percent in clinical populations (Strain, 1998). Adjustment disorder with depressed mood is the most common subtype (11.6 percent), followed by adjustment disorder with anxious mood. Because many people with an adjustment disorder do not seek treatment and experience spontaneous remission of symptoms, its incidence is difficult to assess and may be considerably higher than these estimates.

The prevalence and severity of this type of disorder are typically greater in adolescents, with as many as one-third experiencing an adjustment disorder. Disappointment in relationships was found to be the most frequent stressor cited in adolescent adjustment disorder (Benton & Lynch, 2006).

No differences in prevalence rates of adjustment disorders have been found among races or genders (American Psychiatric Association, 2000; Benton & Lynch, 2006). Adolescent males with this diagnosis, however, seem to have the highest likelihood of committing suicide. Indeed, Portzky, Audenaert, and van Heeringen (2005) found that the suicidal process was shorter and without prior indication of emotional problems in adolescents with adjustment disorder compared to those with major depression. Deliberate self-harm behavior is found in adolescents with adjustment disorders, at a rate greater than for most other disorders. Self-poisoning was the most frequent self-harm behavior in the fifteen-to-nineteen age group. Even so, suicidal thoughts were admitted to in only 11 percent of adolescents with adjustment disorder. Clearly it is important to assess all people with adjustment disorders for suicidal ideation and plans, but this is especially important if the client is an adolescent male who has experienced a recent interpersonal loss or conflict.

Background and support make a difference in these people's lives. In a group of people with adjustment disorders who had attempted suicide, more than 50 percent came from unstable homes, were orphaned, or had experienced some type of emotional deprivation in childhood (Polyakova, Knobler, Ambrumova, & Lerner, 1998).

Typical Client Characteristics

Adjustment disorders occur in all types of people but seem to be diagnosed more frequently in those with above-average incomes (Benton & Lynch, 2006). Adjustment disorders also are particularly common among people who have little experience in dealing effectively with previous stressful events, have multiple stressors, or are coping with life-threatening illnesses. Indeed, one Japanese study identified adjustment disorder as the most commonly diagnosed mental disorder in the oncology setting (Akechi et al., 2004). Similarly, a high incidence of adjustment disorder was found among a sample of older adults anticipating cardiac surgery; 50.7 percent had an adjustment disorder related to their medical condition and its treatment. Other factors that seem to predispose people to develop an adjustment disorder include financial difficulties, a history of mood disorders or alcohol-related disorders, family conflict, poorly controlled physical pain, and feelings of loss of control.

No evidence exists to tie adjustment disorders to underlying organic or biological factors. Rather, the common link in the development of these disorders seems to be stress (Benton & Lynch, 2006). The most frequently co-occurring disorders with an adjustment disorder are personality, anxiety, mood, and substance use disorders. In children, adjustment disorders are most likely to co-occur with conduct or behavioral problems.

Assessment

No specific assessment tools exist for the diagnosis of adjustment disorders. Clinicians can gain a better understanding of intensity and severity of symptoms by using instruments designed to assess levels of stress, mild anxiety, or depression. Checklists can also be helpful in assessing client attitudes and progress, especially in employment-related issues. Tools that promote self-awareness and help clients clarify options can be useful — for example, developing a chronology of important life events and taking inventories of interests or marital satisfaction. The Myers-Briggs Type Indicator (Myers & McCauley, 1985) and the Lifestyle Assessment Questionnaire (National Wellness Institute, 1983) can also help people understand why they are having difficulty with particular situations, what resources they may be able to draw on, and what options they have.

Preferred Therapist Characteristics

Most people with adjustment disorders have a relatively high level of previous functioning. They probably are capable of handling the stressors themselves but are daunted by the stressors' suddenness or by their perceived lack of resources and their low self-esteem. Therapists should communicate confidence that with some support and direction, these people will be able to resolve their problems themselves. This optimistic attitude should strengthen people's coping mechanisms and encourage them to face the stressors with a hopeful outlook.

Intervention Strategies

Most adjustment disorders improve spontaneously without treatment when stressors are removed, attenuated, or accommodated, but therapy can facilitate recovery. It can hasten improvement, provide coping skills and adaptive mechanisms to avert future crises, and minimize poor choices and self-destructive behaviors that may have adverse consequences. As necessary, therapy also can address long-standing maladaptive emotional and behavioral patterns.

A flexible crisis-intervention model probably best characterizes the therapy usually recommended for the treatment of adjustment disorders. This model of therapy focuses both on relieving the acute symptoms that clients are experiencing and on promoting clients' adaptation to and ability to cope with the stressors. Therapy would also support the clients' strengths, paying little attention to past problems unless these problems suggest patterns that should be addressed in an effort to promote effective coping with current stressors. Education and information are usually part of the treatment and are intended to help people take a realistic look at their situations and become aware of options and resources that may be useful. Helping people develop the skills and attitudes they need to cope with future stressors also is an important element in treatment. The following are typical steps in short-term crisis intervention used to treat adjustment disorders (Butcher et al., 2006):

1. Clarifying and promoting understanding of the problem
2. Identifying and reinforcing the client's strengths and coping skills and teaching new coping skills if needed
3. Collaborating with the client to develop a plan of action that will mobilize and empower the client
4. Providing information and support to promote affective, cognitive, and behavioral improvement in the client
5. Terminating treatment, making appropriate referrals, and following up

The overriding goal of this brief, problem-focused orientation to treatment is to return people to previous or higher levels of functioning and to change some of their self-destructive behaviors and reactions so that the chances of a recurrence are reduced with the next life change.

A wide variety of interventions have been suggested for treatment of adjustment disorders. The specific interventions employed depend on the symptoms associated with the particular adjustment disorder as well as on the nature of the stressors, the strengths and challenges of the client, and the theoretical orientation of the therapist. For example, to cite just a few of the diverse approaches that can be used, people with depressive symptoms probably will respond to techniques borrowed from cognitive and interpersonal therapy (see Chapter Four), people experiencing anxiety probably will benefit from learning how to use relaxation techniques (see Chapter Five), and those with problems of conduct are likely to respond to behavior therapy (see Chapters Two and Six). Because approximately one-third of people with adjustment disorders, particularly adolescents, have suicidal thoughts, preventing suicide must of course be a priority of treatment (see Chapter Four). Such behavioral interventions as relaxation, bibliotherapy, assertiveness training, and visual imagery are often combined with cognitive interventions in the treatment of this disorder so that behaviors as well as beliefs can be changed.

An example of a cognitive-behavioral approach to treatment is suggested by Meichenbaum and Deffenbacher (1988), who developed stress inoculation training (SIT) in the late 1980s. SIT includes the following three overlapping phases:

1. Conceptualization: developing a warm, collaborative relationship through which the problem can be assessed and reconceptualized
2. Skill acquisition and rehearsal: developing coping strategies (for example, relaxation, communication skills, and decision-making)
3. Application and follow-through: applying coping strategies to current problems and taking steps to prevent relapse

Guidelines recently developed in the Netherlands for managing adjustment disorders in occupational and primary health care confirm the use of stress inoculation training and gradual exposure to increasing stress as a method to enhance the person's problem-solving capacity in relation to the work environment (van der Klink & van Dijk, 2003).

Brief psychodynamic psychotherapy also seems to be a useful approach in treating adjustment disorders. This approach does involve interpretation and the use of positive transference, two techniques that are usually associated with long-term treatment. However, because brief psychodynamic psychotherapy typically focuses on a single concern presented by the client, treatment can be both crisis-oriented (involving environmental manipulation and crisis resolution) and insight-oriented (promoting understanding of the connection between the impact of the crisis and the client's personality dynamics).

The therapist using brief psychodynamic psychotherapy typically is supportive, active, flexible, and goal-directed, working in a time-limited context (nearly always fewer than twenty-five sessions) to restore the client's previous level of equilibrium. This model seems particularly well suited to problems of acute onset experienced by people with positive prior adjustment and a good ability to relate to others and engage in a therapeutic relationship. Ideally, such clients are also verbal, psychologically minded, and highly motivated to benefit from treatment.

According to Bloom (2002), studies of treatment in which brief psychodynamic psychotherapy was used with children and adolescents experiencing adjustment disorders show that client improvement is superior to no intervention at all and that such therapies are as effective as time-unlimited interventions. One advantage of brief psychodynamic psychotherapy seems to be in quickening the pace of people's ability to deal with disconcerting life changes and in effecting immediate improvement.

Solution-focused therapy is another brief approach that is likely to be effective in the treatment of adjustment disorders. Developed by de Shazer (1991) and others, this approach emphasizes health, positive reframing, and rapid resolution of problems. Its hallmark is de Shazer's Miracle Question (p. 113): "Suppose that one night there is a miracle and while you were sleeping the problem that brought you to therapy is solved. How would you know? What would be different? What will you notice different the next morning that will tell you that there has been a miracle?" This question helps people focus on goals that are likely to lead to the resolution of the precipitants of their difficulties and to improvement in coping and feelings of empowerment.

Emotion-focused therapy can be particularly helpful in teaching clients with adjustment disorder to regulate the stress and the emotional distress that results from significant life changes. Through exercises that help people become more mindful of their feelings, able to express both positive and negative emotions in an appropriate manner, and tolerate and sit with their emotions, the therapist can help clients proactively work through their difficult emotions. Being able to recognize, express, tolerate, and regulate emotions is a valuable coping skill for clients who are going through a crisis or life transition (Greenberg, 2002).

The therapist's understanding of the specific nature of the crisis that led to the development of an adjustment disorder can guide the selection of appropriate treatment interventions. Environmental manipulation that is acceptable to the client, such as a change of residence, a job transfer, hired help for a new baby, or reorganization of shared duties at home or at work can be useful. Bibliotherapy — the assignment of books written by others who have knowledge about concerns similar to the client's — also can provide useful information and a clearer perspective. For example, excellent books are available on such specific stressors as cancer (Seligman, 1996), divorce (Margulies, 2001; Trafford, 1992; Viorst, 1998), and career changes (Bolles, 2006).

Group therapy can be a useful addition to treatment. It can provide a support system, teach and reinforce coping mechanisms, improve self-esteem, and promote reality testing through group members' sharing their perceptions of the client's situation. Groups composed of people going through similar life circumstances (cancer, marital separation or divorce, or bereavement, for example) can be particularly helpful. Group therapy typically does not provide crisis intervention, however, so it may not be a sufficient response to the urgency of a client's situation. A combination of group and individual therapy can be particularly useful to people with adjustment disorders: the individual therapy addresses the immediate crisis, and the group therapy provides support and an arena for testing new ideas and behaviors.

If a stressor directly or indirectly involves the client's family, at least a few sessions of family therapy may be useful in solidifying the support that the person is receiving, ensuring that the person's efforts to cope with the stressor are not being undermined by the family, and addressing any family circumstances that may be related to the stressful situation. Any problems involving secondary gains from the extra attention that people may be receiving when they are in crisis can also be identified and addressed in family therapy. The family can benefit from seeing that adjustment disorders occur when a psychosocial stressor challenges a person's capacity to cope. This may enable them to provide appropriate support and practical help to the person with the adjustment disorder.

Medication is usually not necessary in the treatment of adjustment disorders, although in some cases medication may help people manage anxiety or depression. Any use of medication should be time-limited and symptom-focused, and it should be perceived as secondary to the therapy, which promotes development of coping skills and seeks to prevent future emotional disorders.

People with adjustment disorders usually can be encouraged to resume their former lifestyle, to expect a return to normal functioning in a relatively short time, and to deal with the stressor as expeditiously as possible. Typically, the longer a person avoids dealing with a stressful situation, the more difficult it will be for the person to handle the situation effectively. Therefore, timing is an important variable in treatment. Early detection and treatment of adjustment disorders seem to enhance the prognosis, so it is unfortunate that many people with these relatively mild disorders do not seek treatment for their symptoms.

Prognosis

Of all the disorders, the prognosis for treatment of adjustment disorders is one of the most positive and is particularly good for adults. Those who are able to minimize disruptions to life roles, regulate emotional distress, and remain actively involved in aspects of life that hold meaning and importance to them will generally do well. A meta-analysis of people who developed adjustment disorders in response to a diagnosis of cancer, for example, showed that those who received problem-focused cognitive-behavioral therapy experienced significant positive changes in coping with cancer, developing a fighting spirit, reducing anxiety, and clarifying their perceptions of their problems, both at the conclusion of the eight-week intervention and at four-month follow-up (Meyer & Mark, 1995).

Although the overall prognosis for treatment of adjustment disorders is excellent, the prognosis is not as good for males and for people with behavioral symptoms or comorbid disorders. The literature suggests that adolescents with adjustment disorders frequently develop other, more severe, disorders (Benton & Lynch, 2006). Adolescent males in particular have been found to have increased suicidal ideation shortly after the occurrence of the relevant stressor (Portzky et al., 2005). This should be kept in mind during treatment.

People with adjustment disorders tend to seek subsequent psychotherapy. Whether this pattern reflects an incomplete recovery from the adjustment disorder, a subsequent adjustment disorder, the onset of another disorder, or simply a wish for more personal growth is not clear from the literature, but it does highlight the importance of including a preventive component in the treatment of adjustment disorders.

OTHER CONDITIONS THAT MAY BE A FOCUS OF CLINICAL ATTENTION

Description of the Conditions

The various conditions discussed here encompass concerns that may well be amenable to psychotherapy but that are not in themselves mental disorders (unlike adjustment disorders). People with these conditions may not have any mental disorders. They may have coexisting mental disorders that are unrelated to the condition, or they may have mental disorders that are related to the condition, but the condition is listed on the multiaxial assessment because it is severe and important enough to warrant separate attention.

These three possibilities can be illustrated by three hypothetical clients who seek counseling after losing a job. Each of these clients would be described as having an occupational problem (a condition). The first client is a well-functioning person with no coexisting mental disorders who lost her job because the company went out of business; now she needs help in locating new employment. She is coping well, but would benefit from some help in planning her job search and developing her job-seeking skills. The second person lost his job for the same reason and has no mental disorders related to his unemployment, but he reports that he cannot seek employment requiring outdoor work because of his extreme fear of snakes; he would be described as having an occupational problem and a coexisting but relatively unrelated mental disorder, specific phobia. The third person lost her job because her use of alcohol led to frequent absences; she would have a coexisting and related diagnosis of alcohol dependence.

Not all current stressors are listed as conditions on Axis I of a multiaxial assessment; Axis IV is the usual place to list the stressors. Axis I should be reserved for circumstances that have a significant or pervasive impact on a person's life and so merit special clinical attention.

DSM-IV-TR groups the conditions as follows.

Psychological Factors Affecting Medical Condition. In this condition, psychological symptoms, maladaptive behaviors, a mental disorder, or other psychological factors are having a negative impact on a person's medically verified physical illness (specified on Axis III). The psychological factor may be increasing the risk of complications. It may also be contributing to an exacerbation of the medical condition or a poor outcome of treatment for that condition. When this condition is listed, both the psychological factor and the medical condition are named. For example, if a person with lung cancer (coded on Axis III as neoplasm, malignant, lung, primary) continues smoking against medical advice, that person's multiaxial assessment would also include, on Axis I, maladaptive health behaviors affecting malignant lung neoplasm. The condition, of psychological factors affecting medical condition, often reflects a negative cycle in which a medical condition causes stress, physical discomfort, and worry, which in turn lead to emotions and behaviors that worsen the person's physical disorder.

Medication-Induced Movement Disorders. This category includes neuroleptic-induced Parkinsonism, neuroleptic malignant syndrome, neuroleptic-induced acute dystonia, neuroleptic-induced acute akathisia, neuroleptic-induced tardive dyskinesia, medication-induced postural tremor, and medication-induced movement disorder not otherwise specified. All these conditions describe symptoms that manifest themselves physiologically and are side effects of medication (usually neuroleptic drugs). Consequently, many people with these conditions have a comorbid diagnosis of a psychotic disorder. These movement disorders include a considerable array of symptoms, among them rigid muscle tone, a pill-rolling tremor, a masklike facial appearance (Parkinsonism), muscle contractions causing abnormal movements and postures (dystonia), restlessness and anxiety (akathisia), and involuntary movements of the face, tongue, or limbs (tardive dyskinesia). Many of these symptoms are irreversible.

Adverse Effects of Medication Not Otherwise Specified. This condition is similarly caused by medication. However, it encompasses symptoms other than movement, such as hypotension and sexual dysfunction.

Relational Problems. This broad category includes the following five conditions: (1) relational problems related to a mental disorder or general medical condition (such as an adolescent daughter's withdrawal from her mother who is coping with breast cancer), (2) parent-child relational problem, (3) partner relational problem, (4) sibling relational problem, and (5) relational problem not otherwise specified (such as problems with colleagues, friends, or in-laws). These descriptors are used to label interpersonal difficulties significant enough to warrant clinical attention. Such difficulties may be related to poor communication skills, weak parenting skills (such as difficulty in maintaining discipline), over- or underinvestment in relationships, lack of empathy and caring for others, or family changes and role conflicts.

Problems Related to Abuse or Neglect. Conditions in this category include physical abuse of child, sexual abuse of child, neglect of child, physical abuse of adult, and sexual abuse of adult. These descriptors are used both for the survivors and the perpetrators of abuse; different code numbers indicate the distinction. These conditions are often accompanied by coexisting and related mental disorders, such as antisocial personality disorder or alcohol abuse for the perpetrator and posttraumatic stress disorder or borderline personality disorder for the survivor. Nearly 30 percent of people who have been abused will become abusers themselves, so a person may have more than one condition from this section (Butcher et al., 2006).

Almost three million cases of child abuse and neglect are reported each year in the United States. In 2004, 872,000 children were officially found to have been abused or neglected (Department of Health and Human Services, 2006). Birth parents or other parental figures (stepparents, adoptive parents) are the main perpetrators of childhood abuse and neglect (Azar & Wolfe, 2006). Mothers are more likely to neglect their children, whereas fathers are more likely to abuse. Eighty-nine percent of sexual abuse, 58 percent of physical abuse, and 67 percent of emotional abuse is committed by males (Sedlak & Broadhurst, 1996).

People who have been abused manifest a broad range of reactions; no consistent pattern of postabuse adjustment has been identified. Some may emerge from the experience without significant emotional difficulties, but more commonly symptoms of depression, self-destructive behavior, hypervigilance and anxiety, withdrawal, repressed anger, substance misuse, dysfunctional and abusive relationships, shame, and low self-esteem are present.

The child's safety must be the first priority for therapists who work with children. With adolescents and older adults, establishing trust, providing support, and using more active therapeutic interventions have been shown to make a difference in restoring or preserving the emotional health of people who have been abused. Clearly, abuse and neglect are conditions that merit intensive treatment, both for the survivors and for the perpetrators.

Additional Conditions That May Be a Focus of Clinical Attention. This broad and diverse group includes the following twelve conditions:

1. *Noncompliance with treatment* is refusal to follow treatment recommendations for either a mental disorder or a medical problem. Many factors may contribute to the development of this condition. For example, the original medical or mental disorder may have been misdiagnosed or not fully explained to the person, so he or she may have little motivation to comply with treatment, or a mental disorder (perhaps even the one being treated) may be interfering with the person's interest in treatment. As another example, people with bipolar disorders sometimes enjoy their manic or hypomanic episodes and so resist treatment. The appeal of secondary gains may also counteract the benefits of successful treatment. A thorough evaluation of people with this condition, as well as a thorough evaluation of their families and their occupational and environmental contexts, is important to a full understanding of the dynamics of this condition.

2. *Malingering* is defined as the deliberate production of symptoms for the purpose of gaining some external benefit, such as a military discharge or disability payments. This condition sometimes accompanies a diagnosis of antisocial personality disorder. People with this condition are often involved in lawsuits or have other legal problems. They may be uncooperative and withholding in treatment in an effort to avoid full disclosure that might jeopardize external benefits. With malingering, as with many of the other conditions, a thorough understanding of the context is important, as is corroborative information from other sources if it can be obtained. The Structured Interview of Reported Symptoms (Rogers, Kropp, Bagby, & Dickens, 1992) is a useful tool for detecting feigned symptoms, as is the use of open-ended questions to elicit information. Clinicians seem skilled at detecting malingering, but this descriptor should still be used with caution.

3. *Adult, childhood, or adolescent antisocial behavior* is used to label both isolated acts and repeated patterns of antisocial behavior not due to a mental disorder. Patterns of antisocial behavior associated with this condition generally begin in adulthood and are accompanied by a relatively stable lifestyle, so that

the person does not meet the criteria for antisocial personality disorder. Clinicians should be careful to rule out not only antisocial personality disorder but also conduct disorder, substance use disorders, or another impulse-control disorder before concluding that this condition is present. People with this condition often have accompanying financial, occupational, and relationship problems and tend to misuse drugs and alcohol.

4. *Borderline intellectual functioning* is coded on Axis II and reflects an IQ in the 71–84 range, below normal but above the criteria for mental retardation. Interpersonal difficulties, adjustment difficulties, and other behavioral difficulties are often found in people with this condition, just as they are in people diagnosed with mental retardation.

5. *Age-related cognitive decline* is characterized by cognitive impairment and decline that are within normal limits. The decline is significant enough to cause distress but not significant enough to meet the criteria for dementia or another cognitive mental disorder. People with this condition may have difficulty remembering other people's names, keeping appointments, or solving complex problems, but they do not forget such information as their own names and addresses. Fears that they are developing dementia may lead them to seek assessment and treatment. Neurological and psychological evaluations, including assessment of memory and verbal fluency, can help determine whether this condition or a more serious disorder is present.

6. *Bereavement* is a response to the death of a loved one. Common symptoms include sadness, regret about actions taken around the time of the death, anxiety, mild somatic symptoms, loss of appetite, and difficulty sleeping. These symptoms may subsequently be diagnosed as a major depressive disorder if they are long-standing (usually more than two months), if they cause severe impairment, and if they include such signs of a major depression as strong feelings of guilt and worthlessness, suicidal ideation and preoccupation with death, psychomotor retardation, or loss of contact with reality (other than seeing or hearing the deceased). People with few support systems and those with coexisting medical problems are at particularly high risk for severe reactions to a death. Responses to death vary widely among cultures, so a client's background, ethnicity, and religious beliefs should be considered when a diagnosis related to a death is made.

7. *Academic problem* reflects difficulties in scholastic achievement that are not due to a mental disorder (such as a learning disorder, a communication disorder, or mental retardation). Children and adolescents, of course, are most likely to present with this condition, which may involve such issues as poor study skills, little interest in school subjects or achievement, or a poor image of their own academic abilities.

8. *Occupational problem* includes such concerns as career choice and dissatisfaction, job loss or change, demotion, or difficulty fulfilling the requirements of a job. High stress, reduced self-esteem, insecurity, anger, resentment, and fears about the future may accompany this condition (Seligman, 1994). Career counseling and assessment can be helpful both in clarifying the concerns of people with this condition and helping them resolve those concerns.

9. *Identity problem* encompasses a variety of doubts about self-image or direction and involves such issues as sexual orientation, morals and values, friendships, group loyalties, and long-term goals. These concerns are most likely to emerge during middle and late adolescence, but also are common in adults going through a sort of midlife reevaluation. People with an external locus of control, as well as those experiencing a life change, a family breakup, a loss, a challenging developmental task, or a values conflict with others, are especially prone to identity problems.

10. *Religious or spiritual problem* reflects issues related to a loss of faith, questions about religious beliefs or affiliation, problems associated with conversion to another faith, or other spiritual concerns. Consultation with a spiritual or religious adviser as well as with a psychotherapist may help people cope more successfully with these concerns. Religious and spiritual beliefs can be very important in helping people find meaning and direction in their lives and maintain good self-esteem and interpersonal relationships.

11. *Acculturation problem* focuses on issues related to a move from one culture to another. It may entail such concerns as balancing loyalty to one's culture of origin with an interest in adopting one's current culture, feeling alienated and isolated in the new culture, longing for one's former home or culture, or conflicts among family members who acculturate differently after immigration.

12. *Phase of life problem* includes such circumstances as illness, divorce, retirement, graduation, marriage, the birth of a baby, a relocation, or other life change. It is distinguished from an adjustment disorder in terms of the nature and severity of the person's reaction to the change; adjustment disorder reflects more difficulty and emotional dysfunction in response to the change.

The conditions just listed are problems in living that are experienced by most people. Often reactions to these conditions go untreated, and people manage to deal with them with varying degrees of success. People with these conditions who do not have coexisting mental disorders are typically in good contact with reality, and their reactions usually are consistent with the stressors or life circumstances they are experiencing. Nevertheless, they may be experiencing considerable unhappiness and dissatisfaction with their lives and may benefit from therapy.

Typical Client Characteristics

Because conditions can be found in the entire range of people, few generalizations can be made about people with conditions. Those who seek therapy are likely to have fewer support systems and less effective coping skills. Beyond that, however, all that can be said is that these people are struggling with particular life circumstances that can be addressed in therapy.

Preferred Therapist Characteristics

Therapist variables indicated for treatment of conditions vary little from those indicated for treatment of adjustment disorders. People probably will respond best to therapists who are supportive and flexible and yet who challenge them to grow and develop. Therapists should encourage these clients to take responsibility for their own treatment when that is possible, but should also provide direction, resources, and information as needed. The therapist should maintain an attitude that is optimistic and that anticipates fairly rapid progress. With the conditions, as with adjustment disorders, clinicians must be astute diagnosticians so that they can ascertain quickly whether coexisting mental disorders are present; that factor will determine the specific nature of a particular client's treatment.

Intervention Strategies

Treatment for the conditions usually is similar to treatment for adjustment disorders. The major difference is that less attention probably will be paid to the client's emotional, social, and occupational dysfunction, and more attention will be paid to the presenting concerns and the person's existing strengths and coping abilities, especially if no coexisting mental disorders have been identified. People can benefit from support and from the reassurance of having their reactions normalized. People experiencing conditions typically need education and information about their situation and about the options available to them. Environmental changes can be useful, as can the inclusion in therapy of others who are involved in the problem (for example, family members, friends, or business colleagues). Brief approaches to treatment are emphasized.

No controlled studies have been located on the treatment of the conditions generally, but suggestions can be inferred from studies of treatment for specific types of conditions and from information on the treatment of related disorders. Specific approaches to therapy have been developed or adapted to ameliorate some of the conditions. For example, a large body of literature is available on theories and strategies of career counseling that can guide therapy for people coping with occupational problems. Career counseling typically promotes values clarification, information seeking, and decision making; teaches such skills as interviewing and résumé writing; and promotes self-awareness and career maturity. Bibliotherapy (especially reading about occupations) and informational interviewing for the purpose of learning about job roles can accelerate the process of therapy.

Family therapy is likely to be useful for most people coping with relationship problems and family change and conflict. Many books are available to familiarize therapists and clients with patterns of family change and effective ways of dealing with those patterns. Among these are *Families and Change* (McKenry & Price, 2005), *The Divorce Remedy* (Weiner-Davis, 2002), and *The Seven Principles for Making Marriage Work* (Gottman & Silver, 2000).

Many books also are available to help people work through the process of loss and bereavement. For example, Elizabeth Kübler-Ross (1997, 2001, 2005) has written about the stages of grief and healing, and Pauline Boss has delved into the area of ambiguous loss in *Loss, Trauma, and Resilience* (2006).

An approach to both group and individual therapy that is cognitive-behavioral in nature and is geared to the developmental level of the client has been found effective in helping people with borderline intellectual functioning (Paxon, 1995). Multimodal therapy has also demonstrated effectiveness with these clients, as well as with people who have experienced abuse and neglect.

Strategies that address the mind-body connection, such as biofeedback, relaxation, and encouragement of a healthy lifestyle, can help people with psychological factors affecting a medical condition (Seligman, 1996). Collaborative treatment, in which therapist and physician work together, is indicated for these clients, as well as for people coping with medication-induced movement disorders.

People with long-standing antisocial behavior typically benefit from counseling in a homogeneous group setting. That environment can facilitate their receiving feedback and learning and practicing new ways to meet their goals and cope with stress.

Support groups can be particularly helpful to people coping with the conditions listed in *DSM-IV-TR;* sometimes these groups provide all the treatment that is needed. Therapy or self-help groups composed of people with similar life circumstances (such as bereavement, retirement, a recent divorce, a serious illness, or abuse) can be particularly useful in offering information and modeling coping mechanisms as well as in providing feedback and support.

Courses designed to develop such skills as parenting, assertiveness, and studying also can be useful to people with these conditions. The group environment of the classes can also offer support and encouragement while normalizing concerns.

Many people coping with these conditions will have coexisting mental disorders, of course, particularly people who are perpetrators or survivors of abuse or neglect. The treatments recommended for the coexisting mental disorders (see the relevant chapters in this book) should become part of the help that is provided to these people.

Prognosis

The prognosis for treatment of most of these conditions, if they stand alone, is quite good, although the diversity of conditions and of people manifesting these conditions mandates caution in generalizing. Typically, people who benefit the most from treatment are those who have the highest pretreatment levels of functioning and self-concept and are motivated to receive treatment. Borderline intellectual functioning, medication-induced movement disorder, and age-related cognitive decline are not likely to improve much in response to therapy, but treatment of these conditions may well have a positive impact on the outlook and coping abilities of people with these conditions. People with long-standing antisocial behavior also tend not to have a positive response to treatment. Nevertheless, most conditions that are short term and that have developed in response to specific precipitants (such as a death or a relocation) are likely to have an excellent prognosis, especially if they are not accompanied by other mental disorders.

TREATMENT RECOMMENDATIONS: CLIENT MAP

The following list organizes the recommendations made in this chapter for the treatment of situationally precipitated disorders (adjustment disorders and other conditions) according to the Client Map format.

Client Map

Diagnoses

Adjustment disorders

Other conditions that may be a focus of clinical attention

Objectives of Treatment

Increase knowledge and understanding of the situation

Promote information gathering

Enhance strengths

Improve coping, problem solving, and decision making

Relieve symptoms

Promote use of support

Restore at least prior level of functioning

Assessments

Measures of transient anxiety, depression, and stress

Problem checklists

Clinician Characteristics

Flexible yet structured

Present-oriented

Optimistic

Skilled in diagnosis and treatment of a broad range of disorders

Location of Treatment

Outpatient

Interventions to Be Used

Empowerment of client

Crisis intervention

Bibliotherapy

Brief psychodynamic psychotherapy

Cognitive-behavioral therapy

Brief solution-focused therapy

Emotion-focused therapy

Stress management

Strengthening and development of coping skills, such as assertiveness, decision making, communication, relaxation, reframing, and others

Other short-term or active approaches

Emphasis of Treatment

Moderate emphasis on support

Probing only when relevant to current concerns

Focus to be determined by specific precipitant and response

Numbers

Usually individual therapy

Concurrent or later group therapy sometimes indicated

Family sessions sometimes indicated

Timing

Usually brief duration and rapid pace

Timing may need modification in the presence of coexisting mental disorders

Medications Needed

Usually none

Adjunct Services

Inventories to clarify goals and direction

Education and information

Peer support groups composed of people with similar concerns

Possibly environmental manipulation

Prognosis

Excellent if cause or precipitant can be changed, especially if no underlying mental disorder is present and person has good premorbid functioning and self-esteem

Client Map of Beth H.

This chapter began with the case of Beth H., a forty-seven-year-old woman who had been diagnosed with breast cancer. Short-term counseling helped Beth decide to have a mastectomy, with immediate reconstruction, to facilitate her rapid return to work and help her maintain her positive body image. Fortunately, chemotherapy was not needed. Beth became involved with a support group that helped normalize her feelings and provided information, role models, and encouragement.

After the immediate medical crisis was over, Beth continued to receive therapy to help her establish rewarding goals and directions for herself and implement health- and lifestyle-related goals. Like most people with adjustment disorders, Beth needed only some short-term counseling to help her mobilize her resources, make decisions, and establish a rewarding direction for herself. The self-awareness, support systems, and coping strategies she gained from the therapeutic process should enable her to cope more effectively with future life transitions. This chapter concludes with a Client Map of Beth.

Diagnosis

Axis I: 309.28 Adjustment disorder with mixed anxiety and depressed mood

Axis II: V71.09 No diagnosis on Axis II

Axis III: 174.9 Neoplasm (malignant, breast)

Axis IV: Diagnosis and treatment of breast cancer, divorce

Axis V: Global assessment of functioning (GAF Scale): current GAF = 72

Objectives of Treatment

Reduce anxiety and depression related to cancer diagnosis

Help client make sound decisions about her medical treatment

Promote establishment of healthy patterns of eating, sleeping, exercise, and self-care

Continue client's efforts to cope with her divorce and develop a rewarding lifestyle

Help client resume previous level of functioning and maintain self-esteem

Assessments

Measure of Adjustment to Cancer Scale

Profile of Mood States

Clinician Characteristics

Supportive and accepting yet action-oriented

Knowledgeable about cancer and the mind-body-spirit connection

Location of Treatment

Outpatient

Interventions to Be Used

Cognitive-behavioral therapy, designed to promote a fighting spirit, normalize reactions, and empower the client

Bibliotherapy on treatment options and reactions to cancer

Analysis and modification of dysfunctional cognitions

Use of information-gathering and decision-making strategies

Identification and mobilization of previously successful coping mechanisms

Visual imagery and relaxation

Planning to improve wellness, socialization

Emphasis of Treatment

High emphasis on supportiveness

Moderate emphasis on directiveness

Focus on the present, with exploration of cognitions, behaviors, and affect, especially fears and coping skills

Numbers

Primarily individual therapy, with a few counseling sessions including client and her daughter

Timing

Short term

Weekly sessions

Rapid to moderate pace

Medications Needed

None

Adjunct Services

Support group for women coping with breast cancer

Prognosis

Excellent

Recommended Reading

Araoz, D. L., & Carrese, M. A. (1996). *Solution oriented brief therapy for adjustment disorders: A guide for providers under managed care.* New York: Brunner/Mazel.

Boss, P. (2000). *Ambiguous loss: Learning to live with unresolved grief.* Cambridge, MA: Harvard University Press.

Bridges, W. (2001). *The way of transition: Embracing life's most difficult moments.* Cambridge, MA: Perseus Press.

Crosson-Tower, C. (2005). *Understanding child abuse and neglect* (6th ed.). Boston: Allyn & Bacon.

Dalai Lama, & Cutler, H. C. (1998). *The art of happiness: A handbook for living.* New York: Riverhead Books.

Kushner, H. S. (2004). *When bad things happen to good people.* New York: Anchor Books.

Trafford, A. (1992). *Crazy time: Surviving divorce and building a new life* (Rev. ed.). New York: HarperCollins.

Viorst, J. (1998). *Necessary losses.* New York: Free Press.

CHAPTER FOUR

Mood Disorders

Karen C., a thirty-year-old married African American woman, was brought to a therapist by her mother. Karen reported feeling severe depression and hopelessness. She was barely able to care for her five-year-old child or her home, and she had not gone to her part-time job as an aide at her child's school for over two weeks. Her accompanying symptoms included significant weight gain, excessive fatigue and sleeping, and severe guilt.

Karen and her husband had been married for eight years. Karen's husband was in the military, which meant that he was frequently away from home. Karen had always found his absences difficult and had encouraged her husband to leave the service. He complained that she was too dependent on him, and he urged her to develop her own interests.

Apart from her work at their child's school, Karen had few outside activities, and she had few supports other than her mother, who had been widowed shortly after the birth of Karen, her only child. Karen's mother had not remarried. She told Karen that she had been so devastated by the death of Karen's father that she would never get involved with another man. The mother seemed to have experienced episodes of severe depression, although she had never received treatment for them.

Conflict had been increasing in Karen's marriage and had reached a peak about three weeks before, when Karen's husband left for an overseas tour of duty in what both viewed as a safe part of the world. Karen was fearful that he would become involved with another woman and never return home, even though her husband's behavior gave her no justification for her concerns. She berated herself for not being a good wife and stated that life was not worth living without her husband. The only bright spot for Karen over the past few weeks had come when she received a letter from him. She read it again and again and did feel better for a few hours, but her depression soon returned.

Karen's developmental history was unremarkable except for her having been ill quite often. After her graduation from high school, she had worked as a secretary and lived with her mother until her marriage. She had dated little before her marriage, but she did remember having felt very depressed at least once before in her life, when a young man she had dated a few times became engaged to another woman.

Karen is suffering from a severe depression that has impaired her level of functioning. A precipitant can be identified for Karen's current episode of depression, but her symptoms do not suggest either an adjustment disorder or a condition; her reactions show too much dysfunction to be reflective of either one. Instead, Karen is experiencing a mood disorder characterized by depression.

This chapter provides information on the diagnosis and treatment of the various types of mood disorders — major depressive disorder, dysthymic disorder, depressive disorder not otherwise specified, bipolar I disorder, bipolar II disorder, and cyclothymic disorder, all of which typically include significant depression. Although three of these disorders (bipolar I and II and cyclothymic disorder) also include inordinately elevated moods (mania or hypomania), the primary focus of the first section of the chapter will be depression, the common ingredient of all these disorders.

OVERVIEW OF MOOD DISORDERS

Description of the Disorders

Primary symptoms of depression are feelings of discouragement and hopelessness, a dysphoric mood, a loss of energy, and a sense of worthlessness and excessive guilt. Physiological (or vegetative) symptoms are common and typically include changes in appetite and sleep, with insomnia and loss of appetite the most common manifestations. Schatzberg (2005) reports that chronic pain symptoms frequently accompany depression and are often the reported reason for seeking help, especially in those who see a physician first. A physical examination sometimes is indicated to ascertain whether medical treatment is needed for the specific physical complaints.

In the 1970s, the professional literature commonly distinguished between exogenous or reactive depression, linked to an external event or situation, and endogenous, melancholic, or biochemical depression, having a physiological basis. Endogenous depressions are less common than reactive ones. With the third edition of the *DSM*, both forms of depression were encompassed by major depressive disorder. However, an understanding of these two types of depression is still useful.

Severe and reversed vegetative symptoms (increased appetite, oversleeping) are more common in endogenous depression than in reactive depression. Melancholia, or an absence of pleasure or interest, typically accompanies endogenous depression. Endogenous depressions are also far more likely than reactive ones to involve delusions or hallucinations, psychomotor retardation or agitation, extreme guilt, and worsening in the morning.

Atypical depression differs considerably from melancholic depression. Reverse vegetative symptoms (overeating and oversleeping) are characteristic of atypical depression (Matza et al., 2003). Despite its name, atypical depression was found in 36.4 percent of the depressed sample in the National Comorbidity Survey (Matza, Revicki, Davidson, & Stewart, 2003). The disorder is characterized by earlier age of onset and greater chronicity and is found in a high number of depressed women (70 percent of subjects in a study reported by Agosti and Stewart, 2001). Higher rates of paternal depression, childhood neglect, sexual abuse, suicidal thoughts and attempts, disability, and co-occurring disorders such as substance misuse, panic, and anxiety are seen in people with atypical depression. This disorder does not always respond to selective serotonin reuptake inhibitors (SSRIs) or tricyclic antidepressants. Rather, MAOIs have been found to be more effective. Research is currently being conducted on a patch delivery method of MAOIs that would reduce the unpleasant side effects.

The *DSM* also identifies another type of major depressive disorder, postpartum depression, beginning within four weeks of giving birth. Women are at increased risk of developing this disorder if they have a history of premenstrual depression, negative life events during pregnancy, partner relational problems, or inadequate social support after giving birth (Saxena & Sharan, 2006). Rapid intervention and follow-up preventive treatment are needed so that the depressed mother does not pose a danger to the child or to the parent-child relationship. Somerset and colleagues (2006) estimate the occurrence of postpartum depression to be in the range of 8 to 22 percent.

Depression can also be seasonal. Many people experience reduced energy and other symptoms of seasonal affective disorder (SAD), when the days grow shorter in the fall, with remission of symptoms in the spring. This type of depression can also occur during summer months. SAD is related to the amount of available natural light and linked to such biological phenomena as light sensitivity and problems in melatonin secretion. This seasonal pattern is present in 4 percent of the population of the United States, and is particularly common in women and young people, as well as in people living in northern climates

(Butcher et al., 2006). Additional symptoms include loss of interest in activities that were previously considered pleasurable, withdrawal from friends and family, carbohydrate craving, headaches, fatigue, and daytime hypersomnia (Terman, Terman, & Williams, 1998). Remission is sometimes followed by a period of elevated mood. Primary treatment for SAD is thirty-minute daily exposure to a fluorescent light box at 10,000 lux. Some people have seen a positive treatment response in one to four weeks. In some cases, light therapy in conjunction with medication can be even more effective (Terman et al., 1998). Rosenthal (2006) notes that psychotherapy and medication management can also be effective in treating SAD.

Suicidal ideation is a common symptom in depression, one that obviously requires attention. People with depression are at thirty times higher risk of suicide than people who are not depressed (Haley, 2004; Ohayon & Schatzberg, 2002; Schatzberg, 2005).

According to Wilhelm (2006), rates of completed suicide increase when people have any of the following:

- Melancholic or psychotic depression
- Chronic medical illness
- Personality disorders
- A co-occurring substance use disorder
- Little social support

Suicide rates are particularly high among the elderly (Penninx, 2006). White males between the ages of sixty-five and eighty-four have the second highest suicide rates (35 per 100,000); white males over the age of eighty-five have the highest rate, 51.7 per 100,000 (Hoyert, Heron, Murphy, & Kung, 2006).

Depression "is the most common indicator and the greatest predictor" of suicide (Carrier & Ennis, 2004, p. 97) and has been implicated in as many as 85 percent of suicidal deaths (Haley, 2004). Records reveal approximately 55,000 suicides and 200,000 suicide attempts annually in the United States. Suicide, like depression, seems to have a genetic or familial component: more than 11 percent of those who attempt suicide have a family member who has attempted or completed suicide (Maris, 2002). People suffering from depression may be in such severe emotional pain that they feel as if their symptoms will never end, and suicide may seem to be the only escape.

Therefore, depressed clients should always be asked about suicidal thinking. If suicidal ideation is present, information should be gathered about any plans that have been formulated, as well as about the availability of means. Preventing suicide must be a first priority, and if a threat of suicide is present, consideration should be given to hospitalization, to notifying friends and relatives (ideally with the client's consent), and to developing a written agreement with the client that is designed to ensure safety and provide alternatives to self-injury.

Psychotic features are reported in nearly 19 percent of people who meet the criteria for major depression, most often in people who are severely depressed and meet eight or nine of the *DSM-IV-TR* criteria for the disorder (Ohayon & Schatzberg, 2002). Even those who do not have hallucinations or delusions may have impaired reality testing. They typically feel bereft of supports and believe that those who care about them are undermining them or would be better off without them.

The following are some other secondary symptoms common in depression:

- *Emotional symptoms:* anxiety, anger and hostility, irritability and agitation, social and marital distress
- *Behavioral symptoms:* crying, neglect of appearance, withdrawal, dependence, lethargy, reduced activity, poor social skills, psychomotor retardation or agitation
- *Attitudinal symptoms:* pessimism, helplessness, thoughts of death or suicide, low self-esteem
- *Cognitive symptoms:* reduced concentration, indecisiveness, distorted thinking
- *Physiological symptoms:* sleep disturbances, loss of appetite, decreased sexual interest, gastrointestinal and menstrual difficulties, muscle pains, headaches

Typical Onset, Course, and Duration of Depression. A first episode of depression generally occurs during young or middle adulthood but may occur at any age, as can a recurrence. The initial episode of depression tends to occur earlier in women than in men; men are more likely to have an initial episode in midlife. Depression may also begin in childhood. In this case, it is often characterized by agitation rather than by overt sadness. Depression may be primary or secondary to a preexisting chronic mental or physical disorder (such as alcohol dependence). Depression often coexists with a personality disorder (most often borderline, histrionic, or dependent personality disorders) and, in children, with ADHD and disruptive behavior disorders. Depression has also been associated with abuse in childhood (Schatzberg, 2005).

Relevant Predisposing Factors. Depression can have many possible origins, dynamics, and precipitants. Familiarity with these and an ability to understand the determinants of a particular person's depression are essential to the formulation of an effective treatment plan. From a biopsychosocial perspective, a genetic predisposition toward depression, combined with negative life experiences and a pessimistic temperament, can contribute to depression. Beck and other cognitive theorists view depression as a result of faulty logic and misinterpretation, involving a negative cognitive set and core cognition. Behavioral theorists hypothesize that people who become depressed have poor interpersonal skills and therefore receive little positive social reinforcement. The interpersonal model explains depression as stemming from undue dependence on others as well as from conflict and poor communication in relationships. Biological approaches view depression as resulting from a dysregulation of serotonin and other neurotransmitters in the brain. Decreased prefrontal activity in the brains of people who are depressed has been well documented with PET scans (Schatzberg, 2005). Developmental models suggest that people who experience depression are more likely to have had difficult childhoods, early traumatic experiences, an inappropriate level of maternal care, low cohesion or adaptability in the family, and controlling or rejecting parents (Marecek, 2006).

The onset of depression often follows one or more traumatic or otherwise stressful life events, which frequently involve interpersonal loss. Stressors involving loss are strongly correlated to depression, whereas stressors involving threat or danger are more likely to precipitate anxiety (Kessler, 2006). Depression can be defined as a "maladaptive, exaggerated response to stress" (Korszun, Altemus, & Young, 2006, p. 41). Stressors may include problematic interpersonal relationships, career disappointments, and others (Whisman, Weinstock, & Tolejko, 2006). Indeed, the anticipation of an impending loss can trigger a return of unresolved feelings about an earlier loss and can precipitate depression. This pattern is particularly likely in people who have experienced a high number of significant negative life events (shame and humiliation, violence, trauma, and abuse).

According to Pettit and Joiner (2006), interpersonal factors are among the strongest predictors of depression chronicity. Perceived criticism, hostile communications, and interpersonal problems can be powerful predictors of relapse as well as of a poor response to treatment. Several authors (Coyne, 1976; Joiner, 2000) have identified another sort of self-propagatory process as contributing to depression. They found that people who were depressed emphasized negative self-evaluations and sought out confirmation from others to verify their own negative self-view. Not only does this process reinforce negative thoughts and exacerbate depressive symptoms, but the process itself may promote rejection and criticism from others. Weinstock and Whisman (2004) found that the seeking of negative feedback was directly correlated with depressive symptoms.

Depression sometimes has a genetic or familial component, particularly for those whose mothers were depressed (Goodman & Tully, 2006), although Kessler (2006) notes that a family history of anxiety, substance misuse, or other psychological disorder is just as likely to predict depression. Children of depressed parents typically have greater levels of depression themselves at every stage of development — infant, toddler, child, adolescent, and adult (Goodman & Tully, 2006). Earlier age of onset of depression, greater functional impairment, and recurrence are also correlated with parental depression.

Women are much more likely to experience depression than men, but whether this difference suggests a causative factor that is hormonal or environmental and social is unclear. Depression occurs in as many as 15 percent of women during pregnancy and postpartum, and the increasing rate of depression in women of childbearing years is cause for concern.

A growing body of literature on maternal depression shows adverse outcomes for children, beginning in the womb. Deficits in cognitive functioning, vulnerability to developing psychopathology, and early symptoms of depression have been found in children exposed prenatally to their mother's depression. These children also have an increased risk of having dysregulated neuroregulatory systems and frontal brain activity (Wadhwa et al., 2002).

Babies born to depressed mothers also will probably experience the negative effects of having a depressed parent. When compared to nondepressed mothers, depressed mothers display less positive affect, increased sadness or irritability, and negative and intrusive behavior toward their children. Rather than being consistent disciplinarians, depressed mothers are likely to alternate between lax and harsh discipline (Goodman & Tully, 2006).

In addition, people with depression often have a history of early developmental difficulties. Therefore, history taking should include questions about any possible familial background of depression and about childhood development. Information that reveals a family history of depression and a history of early developmental problems may help both the therapist and the client understand the nature and dynamics of the disorder.

Epidemiology. Mood disorders are among the top ten worldwide causes of disability (Sue, Sue, & Sue, 2006). Depressive disorders are the most common and, because of suicide, probably the most lethal of the mental disorders. Some ten million Americans and more than one hundred million people worldwide will experience depression in a given year. Although only 20 to 25 percent of those who experience clinical depression will actually receive treatment, a large percentage of the people who are seen by therapists are treated for mood disorders.

Depression has a broad range of severity. Most people with depression are able to carry on with their lives and may even succeed in concealing their symptoms from others. In some people, depression may be present for many years at a subclinical level, becoming a deeply ingrained part of the personality. People with severe depression, however, typically manifest significantly impaired functioning.

Approximately one in fifty depressed clients is hospitalized, and depression accounts for 75 percent of psychiatric hospitalizations. The exact number of hospitalizations for suicide attempts or suicidal ideation is unknown, but young people with the combination of a mood disorder and a substance-related disorder have particularly elevated suicide rates, as do people with concurrent diagnoses of a mood disorder and borderline personality disorder, or with depression accompanied by delusions, panic, or anxiety disorders.

The prevalence of clinical depression seems to be increasing, and its onset is occurring at an earlier age (Somerset, Newport, Ragan, & Stowe, 2006). Married women are more likely to be depressed than those who have never married; the opposite is true for men (Sue et al., 2006). Depression seems particularly common among married women of lower socioeconomic levels who are full-time homemakers with young children. Kessler (2006) notes that this difference could be due to related factors — for example, men become more depressed about finances, whereas women are more concerned about family and relationship issues. Some research indicates that women may be more vulnerable to stressful life events than men. Exposure to stressful life events is higher in those with depression compared to those without depression.

Typical Client Characteristics

Extensive research supports the theory that pessimism increases depressive symptoms (Girgus & Nolen-Hoeksema, 2006). Seligman (1990) has written about the importance of what he calls "learned helplessness" in the dynamics of depression. He theorizes that many people who are depressed have long-standing motivational, interpersonal, cognitive, and affective deficits, as well as low self-esteem, resulting from a long series of uncontrollable and painful events that seem to make them depression-prone. They tend to set unrealistic goals, have little sense of competence, and view others as more powerful and capable than themselves.

People suffering from depression frequently experience discord with their spouse or partner. One negative outcome of living with a depressed person is an increased burden on the partner caused by the depressed person's emotional strain, lack of energy, and fear of future relapse (Benazon & Coyne, 2000). Wives of depressed men reported taking on more household responsibilities than did husbands of depressed women. Spouses of depressed women tend to rate their wives more negatively on measures of depression, dependence, and detachment (Whisman et al., 2006). Couples, overall, exhibit more negative behavior and decreased problem-solving ability when one person is depressed. Interestingly, negative ratings continue even when depression remits. Spouses of depressed people are more negative and critical, which creates a negative feedback loop that ultimately increases relapse rates for depression (Whisman et al., 2006). Therefore, couples therapy may be an effective adjunct to individual therapy, especially for women who are depressed. Preventing relationship distress and divorce can be an effective prophylactic measure in warding off depression.

Girgus and Nolen-Hoeksema (2006) looked at cognitive variables in the development of depression, including thoughts about body image, self-esteem, and perceived self-efficacy. High self-esteem has an ameliorating effect on stress and depression. Self-efficacy is also believed to buffer stress. When stress is high, people with low self-esteem have more depression.

Women have a greater interpersonal orientation than do men. Many women experience sociotropy — heightened concern about what others think; this increases dependence on the approval of others and correlates with incidence of depressive episodes. Stressors in the interpersonal realm are associated with increased depression in women, as is unmitigated communion — going along with what other people think without expressing an opposing opinion. Girgus and Nolen-Hoeksema (2006) found that both of these traits occur more frequently in women than in men.

Assessment

The Beck Depression Inventory (BDI; Beck, Steer, & Brown, 1996), Hamilton Rating Scale for depression, and the Structured Clinical Interview for DSM (SCID; First, Spitzer, Gibbon, & Williams, 1997) are frequently used to assess depression. Co-occurring disorders should also be assessed, as well as the quality and stability of the client's strengths, support system, and relationships with others. Specific assessments for bipolar disorder and mania are presented in the bipolar section.

Preferred Therapist Characteristics

The Treatment of Depression Collaborative Research Program (Krupnick et al., 1996) of the National Institute of Mental Health indicates that the therapeutic alliance seems far more important than the intervention strategy in determining outcomes of treatment for depression. Even people in the placebo and clinical management conditions of that study demonstrated significant alleviation of depression, apparently because of the power of a positive therapeutic alliance. The quality of the alliance was important both early and late in treatment and for all groups, including those receiving psychotherapy and those receiving medication. Krupnick speculates that medication alone as a treatment for depression may not be effective because it often is not provided in the context of an ongoing positive therapeutic alliance.

Ideally, a therapist working with a person who is depressed should strongly communicate the core conditions of effective therapy (genuineness, caring, acceptance, empathy, and others discussed in Chapter One) and should be able to provide support, structure, reality testing, optimism, reinforcement, and a strong role model. Of course, the therapist needs to intervene actively if suicide is threatened.

Judith Beck (2005) emphasizes the importance of the therapist's assuming a directive role in treating depression and warns that a person-centered approach, in which all of the client's behaviors receive approval, can lead to a sense of helplessness in depressed clients, although their sense of responsibility may be increased. The therapist should avoid being threatened, gratified, or frustrated by the depressed client's dependence and neediness and should gradually promote the client's independence. Sometimes a person who is depressed directs anger and disappointment at the therapist and may invite rejection; the therapist should maintain objectivity despite the challenges presented by a depressed client.

Intervention Strategies

Depression takes many forms, and diagnosis of the particular form is crucial in determining the best treatment. In general, individual psychotherapy without medication is appropriate for treatment of mild to moderate depression that is uncomplicated by a bipolar pattern, by coexisting psychosis, by cognitive impairment, by mental retardation, or by misuse of substances (Young, Weinberger, & Beck, 2001). This is particularly true if the depression is reactive or exogenous (that is, if it has arisen in response to a troubling life circumstance). For severe or complex forms of depression, the combination of medication and psychotherapy is almost always recommended. Couples therapy and family therapy can enhance treatment by providing support to the family as well as by ameliorating any family conflict that may be contributing to the depression. Group therapy can be a helpful adjunct to individual therapy for people who are mildly depressed. However, it would not be appropriate as the primary mode of treatment for people with severe depression; their hopelessness and lack of energy make it difficult for them to engage actively in that process. Empirical research suggests the efficacy of cognitive-behavioral therapy and interpersonal therapy for the treatment of depression.

Cognitive and Cognitive-Behavioral Therapy. Cognitive-behavioral therapy and cognitive therapy are the most extensively evaluated forms of psychotherapy for depression. CBT has been found to be equal in effectiveness to tricyclic antidepressants and monoamine oxidase inhibitors (MAOIs; Craighead, Miklowitz, Frank, & Vaik, 2002). After treatment consisting of sixteen weeks of CBT, 50 to 70 percent of people with major depressive disorder no longer met the criteria for the disorder. At one-year follow-up, only 20 to 30 percent had relapsed. More research is needed regarding CBT and severe depression. However, some studies have found the combination of medication and CBT to be more effective than either intervention alone (Craighead, Miklowitz, et al., 2002). In addition, the medication-only group had a higher dropout rate.

The following features of the cognitive-behavioral approaches are instrumental in producing positive change (Craighead, Miklowitz, et al., 2002):

- They present a concrete rationale for depression and treatment, as well as a vocabulary for defining and describing the problem.
- They educate clients about the relationship between thoughts and feelings and teach self-monitoring skills for dysfunctional thoughts.
- They are highly structured and offer clear plans for change, giving people a sense of control.
- They provide feedback and support so that people can see change, receive reinforcement, and attribute improvement to their own efforts.
- They teach skills that increase personal effectiveness and independence.
- They include relapse prevention strategies.

Cognitive therapy may be more successful with some types of clients than with others. Cognitive-behavioral therapy was found to be particularly effective with young people, with 70 percent responding well to it (Kaslow & Thompson, 1998; Reinecke, Ryan, & DuBois, 1998).

Interpersonal Psychotherapy. Like CBT and cognitive therapy, interpersonal psychotherapy (IPT), based on the work of Harry Stack Sullivan and the psychodynamic therapists, and developed by Klerman, Weissman, Rounsaville, and Chevron (1984), has been empirically validated as effective in the treatment of severe depression as well as its milder forms (Craighead, Hart, et al., 2002). Klerman and his colleagues describe IPT as "a focused, short-term, time-limited therapy that emphasizes the current interpersonal relations of the depressed patient while recognizing the role of genetic, biochemical, developmental, and personality factors in causation and vulnerability to depression" (p. 5).

In the IPT model, depression is viewed as having three components: symptom function, social and interpersonal relations, and personality and character problems (Mufson, Dorta, Moreau, & Weissman, 2004). IPT focuses on the first two components while taking account of the third in the formulation of interventions. Proponents of IPT hold that four problem areas play key roles in depression: abnormal grief, nonreciprocal role expectations in significant relationships, role transitions (such as retirement or divorce), and interpersonal deficits (Craighead, Hart, et al., 2002). The IPT model has developed strategies for dealing with each of these focal problem areas and matches treatment to clients' concerns. In general, IPT concentrates on the clients' history of significant relationships, the quality and patterns of the clients' interactions, the clients' cognitions about themselves and their relationships, and the associated emotions. Clients are helped to increase optimism and acceptance, develop strengths and coping mechanisms, obtain relevant information on depression, and enhance their competence. IPT differs from the cognitive-behavioral approaches in that it uses little homework and places less emphasis on planning actions and assessing progress; it places more emphasis on insight, relationships, and clarification of patterns. Hollon (2000) notes that IPT is as effective as antidepressants in the reduction of acute depression in women, whereas other psychodynamic therapies have not been proven as effective (Sinha & Rush, 2006). Readers are referred to *A Comprehensive Guide to Interpersonal Psychotherapy*, by Weissman, Markowitz, and Klerman (2000), for a more extensive review of empirical studies on the effectiveness of IPT.

Other Treatments for Depression. A number of other treatments for depression show promise. Following are a few of these new treatment approaches:

Behavioral activation treatment. This treatment focuses on scheduling daily activities and engaging in alternative behaviors to help achieve goals, with less focus on cognitive changes. One study indicates that behavior activation therapy is as effective as medication and slightly better than cognitive therapy in relieving moderate to severe depression. Another study, by Hollon, Stewart, and Strunk (2006), shows the effects of behavior activation treatment to be as enduring as CBT and more enduring than medication.

Regular exercise. Running and other regular forms of exercise can also contribute to the relief of depression. Exercise is especially effective for atypical depression, which generally focuses on interpersonal losses.

Mindfulness. Mindfulness-based cognitive therapies have become popular in recent years. Rather than asking people to change their cognitions, mindfulness helps people become aware of their thoughts, feelings, and bodily sensations and learn to accept them. By viewing thoughts as merely thoughts, and not some directive that needs to be acted on or a faulty cognition that needs to be changed, people can become mindful of the thought in the moment and then let it pass. Several studies show promise for the use of mindfulness therapy in the treatment of recurrent depression (Ma & Teasdale, 2004; Teasdale et al., 2000).

Self-system therapy (SST). Another new approach specifically targets people with depression who have difficulty identifying and pursuing goals involving advancement, growth, and achievement. SST has been developed by Strauman and other researchers (2006) at Duke University specifically to treat the one-fifth of people with depression who fit that profile. SST is based on regulatory focus theory (Higgins, 1997), which states that people make decisions on the basis of one of two types of needs: (1) promotion (needs focused on nurturance) or

(2) prevention (needs based on security and protection). SST helps clients work both on prevention goals, which involve keeping bad things from happening, and on promotion goals, which involve making good things happen. SST draws on cognitive-behavioral therapy, but focuses more on helping the client develop skills and strategies to answer the following four questions:

1. What are your promotion and prevention goals?
2. What are you doing to attain them?
3. What is keeping you from making progress?
4. What could you do differently?

Initial research indicates that SST is as effective as CBT in the treatment of depression; in some cases, people made greater strides with SST. Additional research is necessary to compare the effectiveness of SST with that of other approaches in the treatment of depression. For now, SST is another option when therapists are trying to choose the best treatment for different types of depression (Strauman et al., 2006).

Other new approaches. A plethora of new approaches for the treatment of depression are currently being studied. For example:

- Some researchers have found that deprivation of one night's sleep reduces depression (Staner, Luthringer, & LeBon, 2006).
- Bright light therapy has recently been shown to be effective in treating nonseasonal depression, as well as seasonal affective disorder (Golden et al., 2005).
- Repetitive transcranial magnetic stimulation (rTMS), a noninvasive procedure that generates short magnetic pulses through a person's scalp, has shown some promise in treating medication-resistant depression (Avery et al., 2006). However, the Food and Drug Administration has not approved rTMS for any psychiatric disorders at this time.
- Other approaches, including brief and intensive hospitalization, guided imagery, social skills training, and flooding, have been used effectively to help people cope with sadness and move ahead with their lives.

Medication. Medication, of course, is often used for severe or treatment-resistant depression, although medication is not successful in alleviating symptoms in all clients. Moreover, problems associated with medication include clients' reluctance to take medication, potential suicidal ideation in children taking antidepressant medications, side effects, clients' inconsistent adherence to treatment, incomplete remission of symptoms, and high rates of recurrence when the medication is discontinued (Ohayon & Schatzberg,

2002). Seventy-five percent of people in the United States who are treated for depression receive antidepressant medication (Kluger, 2003). However, nearly one-third of the people who are prescribed medication take it for less than thirty days (Marecek, 2006). Therefore, the clinician should carefully consider whether a client should be referred for medication and, if so, should closely monitor its impact.

Common Ingredients of Treatments for Depression. Whether the therapist follows the cognitive model of Beck and his associates, the interpersonal model, or one of the other models, the treatments for depression discussed here include many common ingredients that are associated with their success. Therapists should promote a positive therapeutic alliance and encourage clients' active involvement in treatment, their realistic appraisal of alternatives, goal setting, a sense of mastery and improved self-esteem, better reality testing, clearer interpersonal boundaries, and a repertoire of problem-solving skills and coping mechanisms.

Therapy should be moderately high in directiveness, at least in the early stages of treatment. Therapists should gradually decrease directiveness over the course of treatment, however, to prevent clients from becoming too dependent and to increase client self-esteem. Supportiveness will also need to be fairly high initially; people who are depressed are in considerable pain, and a probing approach runs the risk of opening new painful areas. Clients also need considerable acceptance and positive regard at the start of treatment because of the fragility of their self-concepts. Nevertheless, a person-centered approach is not nearly as likely to reduce depression as is a process-experiential sort of approach. Judith Beck (2005) warns that "empathy alone can sometimes lead to clients feeling worse" (p. 80). She notes that therapists should couple empathy with statements that include hope for the future. Too much empathy can validate the hopelessness of the situation and encourage clients to believe that their problems cannot be solved.

The focus of the initial stages of treatment usually will be on cognitive and behavioral areas of concern rather than on affective areas. Affect certainly should receive some attention, but extensive discussion of depression tends to entrench its symptoms and contributes to the client's sense of discouragement and hopelessness; a focus on the cognitive or the behavioral area is more likely to mobilize the client.

Treatment will often be multifaceted and may involve individual and family treatment. The familial nature of some forms of depression provides an important rationale for family therapy. Other family members who manifest overt or underlying depression or who are at risk for developing such disorders may also benefit from therapy, and their improvement can in turn help relieve the client's depression (Craighead, Miklowitz, et al., 2002). Relapse in mood disorders, as in schizophrenia, is often related to high expressed emotion (criticism, hostility, or both) in the family, so therapy in which family members are taught communication skills can be helpful (Craighead, Miklowitz, et al., 2002; Miklowitz, 2002).

Treatment of depression will typically be provided one to two times a week in an outpatient setting and will be paced fairly rapidly, but not so rapidly as to threaten or discourage the client. Such inventories as the Beck Depression Inventory, as well as concrete, mutually agreed-on assignments, can give the client optimism and a sense of progress and direction. Therapy for depression tends to be short term (twelve to twenty sessions over a period of three to six months) and usually does not take as long as a year. The treatment of depression can also be enhanced by adjunct services to help people establish a sense of direction and become involved in rewarding activities (such as social groups and sports) likely to increase their sense of competence and confidence.

Prognosis

The prognosis for a positive response to treatment for depression is excellent; a high percentage of people improve, regardless of which of the treatments discussed here has been used. Prognosis is correlated with many factors, which include the severity of the depression, the existence of intact partner relationships, high learned resourcefulness, and absence of dysfunctional social relationships (Craighead, Miklowitz, et al., 2002).

Severe depression tends to be a self-limiting disorder and rarely lasts longer than six to twelve months, but depression has a high rate of relapse, especially during the first few months after treatment. At least one study indicates that combining medication with psychotherapy provides superior effectiveness to medication alone or psychotherapy alone (Craighead, Miklowitz, et al., 2002). Given the low rate of compliance with medication, psychotherapy may help increase adherence for those who continue treatment. An important part of any treatment for depression should include a relapse prevention component. Treatment should usually also involve follow-up sessions, perhaps at monthly intervals, to maintain progress and facilitate rapid treatment for relapses.

We will now consider the nature and treatment of the following mood disorders as defined by the fourth edition text revision of the *Diagnostic and Statistical Manual of Mental Disorders*, or *DSM-IV-TR* (American Psychiatric Association, 2000):

- Major depressive disorder
- Dysthymic disorder
- Depressive disorder not otherwise specified (NOS)

- Bipolar I and II disorders
- Cyclothymic disorder

All these disorders typically have depression as a prominent feature, but the depression varies in its intensity, duration, and pattern of onset. Bipolar disorders and cyclothymic disorder are also characterized by unpredictable shifts in mood, as well as by elevated moods.

The mood disorders section of *DSM-IV-TR* also includes bipolar disorder NOS, mood disorder due to a general medical condition, substance-induced mood disorder, and mood disorder NOS. Nearly all the major sections of *DSM-IV-TR* include substance-induced disorders, medical disorders due to a general medical condition, and NOS variations. Substance-induced disorders will be discussed in Chapter Six, and impulse-control disorders and mental disorders due to a general medical condition will be discussed in Chapter Seven; little attention will be paid in this book to the NOS disorders because of their variability and the lack of standard definitions.

MAJOR DEPRESSIVE DISORDER

Description of the Disorder

According to *DSM-IV-TR*, a major depressive episode is manifested by the presence of a depressed mood (dysphoria) or loss of enjoyment or interest in almost everything (anhedonia) and the presence of at least four of the following symptoms nearly every day for at least two weeks:

1. Significant weight or appetite change (found in over 70 percent of people with this disorder)
2. Insomnia or hypersomnia (found in nearly 90 percent)
3. Psychomotor retardation or agitation
4. Fatigue or loss of energy (found in 78 percent)
5. Feelings of guilt or worthlessness
6. Reduced ability to think or concentrate
7. Recurrent thoughts of death or suicide

These symptoms are accompanied by significant distress or impairment in functioning. Although depression usually is not difficult to identify, irritability sometimes masks depression in children and adolescents. Somatic complaints also may deflect attention from depression but are frequently associated with depression, as are sexual difficulties, excessive worry and ruminating, and problems of substance use.

A major depressive disorder consists of one or more major depressive episodes. In diagnosing a major depressive disorder, clinicians must make determinations related to the following factors:

1. *Severity:* mild, moderate, severe, in partial remission, or in full remission (no symptoms for two months or longer).
2. *Presence of psychotic features:* mood-congruent (consistent with the depressive attitudes), mood-incongruent, or none. (Psychotic features are found in 10 to 35 percent of people with major depressive disorder, at equal rates in men and women; Wilhelm, 2006).
3. *Chronicity:* persistent depression for at least two years.
4. *Presence of melancholic features:* depression of endogenous or biochemical origin suggested by loss of interest or pleasure, lack of reactivity to pleasurable events, and at least three of the following symptoms: (a) characteristically different quality of depression from that associated with a bereavement, (b) worsening of symptoms in the morning, (c) awakening typically at least two hours before usual time, (d) experience of psychomotor retardation or agitation, (e) significant weight loss or loss of appetite, (f) unwarranted guilt, (g) flat rather than reactive mood, (h) good response to medication, (i) lack of a clear precipitant, and (j) absence of a personality disorder. Depression with melancholic features has a stronger genetic link than other forms of depression (Butcher, Mineka, & Hooley, 2006).
5. *Presence of atypical features:* atypical depression improves in response to actual or anticipated positive events and is accompanied by at least two of the following characteristics: (1) weight gain or increase in appetite, (2) sleeping at least ten hours a day, (3) heavy feelings in arms or legs, and (4) prolonged pattern of sensitivity to rejection that is severe enough to cause impairment.
6. *Presence of postpartum onset:* begins within four weeks of giving birth. Postpartum depression is often accompanied by high anxiety, mood lability, and an increased rate of obsessional thoughts, often focused on the baby's well-being (Somerset et al., 2006). The illness has a 30 to 50 percent likelihood of recurrence with subsequent births (American Psychiatric Association, 2000).
7. *Presence of full interepisode recovery:* greater likelihood of recurrence and less likelihood of good response to treatment are associated with the absence of complete recovery between multiple depressive episodes. The pattern of multiple depressive episodes without full interepisode

recovery often reflects an underlying dysthymic disorder, discussed later in this chapter.

8. *Presence of seasonal pattern:* characterized by depression, usually of moderate severity, that begins at the same time each year for at least two years. Episodes of this nature outnumber any other type of depression the person has experienced.

Typical Client Characteristics

Symptoms of a major depressive disorder usually begin with dysphoria and anxiety and develop over several days or weeks, although the onset may be sudden and may closely follow a loss or other stressor. Without treatment, this disorder typically runs its course in about six months to one year, but residual symptoms can be present for two years or more, reflecting a chronic disorder. Overall impairment during episodes is typical and may be so severe as to prevent even minimal functioning. Constant feelings of lethargy and hopelessness may be present, and people typically have to struggle to perform daily routines or even to get dressed in the morning. Recurrence is a strong possibility with this disorder, and its likelihood increases with each subsequent recurrence.

Women have a 1.5 to 3 times higher prevalence rate of depression than men (Kessler, 2006). The rate of depression in women is so high that the World Health Organization estimates that major depression is the leading cause of disease-related disability among women internationally.

Approximately 10 percent of adults are diagnosed with a depressive disorder in any given year; 16 percent of people meet the criteria for major depressive disorder at some time in their lives (Kessler et al., 2003). The age of onset of major depressive disorder appears to be getting younger (Jackson & Williams, 2006; Somerset et al., 2006), with the greatest frequency of first episodes of depression occurring during the childbearing years for women (Somerset et al., 2006). From puberty until midlife, women experience depression at twice the rate of men, which has led researchers to investigate mood disorders in relation to hormones and the reproductive cycle, as well as looking at the relationship between gender and help-seeking behavior. Regardless of the cause, incidence of depression peaks in both men and women at midlife. As many as 15 percent of people with severe, prolonged major depressive disorder die as a result of suicide.

People with major depressive disorder typically have other emotional and family problems, including a family history of depression and alcohol misuse (Wilhelm, 2006). This relationship seems to hold true for women more than for men. At least 25 percent of people with major depressive disorder have a preexisting dysthymic disorder (a long-standing mild to moderate depression), a combination that is sometimes referred to as double depression. They also frequently have coexisting disorders, notably substance-related disorders, eating disorders, anxiety disorders, and personality disorders. Children with major depressive disorder are particularly likely to have a coexisting mental disorder. Overlap of depression and medical conditions is also high, as in Parkinson's disease, multiple sclerosis, epilepsy, dementia, cancer, metabolic illnesses, and other physical conditions (Dozois & Dobson, 2002). Clients beginning treatment for depression should also be referred for a physical examination. (Additional information on depression in children and adolescents is provided in Chapter Two.)

Several studies have found an association among cognitive thought patterns, stressful life events, and incidence of major depressive disorder and suggest that the combination of a stressor and a depression-prone personality has a high correlation with the onset of a major depressive disorder. Particularly likely to trigger a major depressive episode are stressors involving an interpersonal loss. Clinicians should bear in mind that drugs (both prescribed and street drugs) and alcohol also can precipitate depressive symptoms.

Girgus and Nolen-Hoeksema (2006) report that women who experience major depressive episodes have a sense of hopelessness, pessimism, and failure, and tend to be self-critical and vulnerable. Seligman (1990) and others have found that people experiencing depression are more likely to attribute their symptoms to negative life events rather than to their own internal cognitions. People who ruminate about their own behavior have more depressive symptoms. Indeed, reflection and brooding tend to increase depression because rumination is more likely to be focused on negative thoughts. People with depression also tend to be less successful at problem solving, to have distorted negative interpretations of events, and to amplify their negative emotions. Many studies confirm a connection between severe depression and a preexisting personality pattern that includes dependence, need for approval, anxiety, dysfunctional thinking, neuroticism, and a weak self-image (Widiger, Mullins-Sweatt, & Anderson, 2006).

Trauma has also been found to contribute to a vulnerability to depression across the life span. Traumatic events occurring early in life can alter neurobiological stress responses and increase vulnerability to major depressive disorder (Penza, Heim, & Nemeroff, 2006). Physical, sexual, and emotional abuse; accidents; physical illness; surgery; parental loss or separation; an unstable family life; inadequate parental care (perhaps due to the parent's own mental or physical illness); family violence; rejecting or inconsistent parenting; lack of family warmth; and insecure attachment can all leave people vulnerable to major depressive disorder. Substance misuse, comorbid mental disorders, and suicide attempts have also been shown to increase as a result of these factors.

Preferred Therapist Characteristics

Therapists most likely to be effective in treating people with major depressive disorder are those who are structured, focused on the present, and able to attend to interpersonal issues and deficits. They can establish clear and realistic goals with clients and encourage optimism and a higher level of activity.

Intervention Strategies

Clinicians often begin treating depression with psychotherapy alone, with the addition of medication if improvement is not noted after several months of psychotherapeutic treatment. Although medication seems to act more quickly on symptoms than psychotherapy does, it still may require three to five weeks for a therapeutic response, and the effects of the medication are generally not as enduring unless it is continued. Clients also tend not to be as accepting of medication as they are of psychotherapy, and the compliance rate is low.

Psychotherapy. As we have discussed earlier, such approaches as behavior therapy, cognitive-behavioral therapy, and interpersonal therapy are the ones most likely to be effective in the treatment of depression. Many studies, including two meta-analyses, have demonstrated that these approaches to treatment are likely to have a significant and relatively rapid impact on the symptoms of major depressive disorder (Craighead, Hart, et al., 2002). Craighead notes that "typically 50 to 70 percent of major depressive disorder patients who complete a course of CBT no longer meet the criteria for major depressive disorder at posttreatment" (p. 251). Cognitive-behavioral therapy has demonstrated a slight but not usually significant superiority to interpersonal therapy in the treatment of major depressive disorder, and both approaches have demonstrated a slight superiority over treatment by medication alone. Good results have been obtained in as few as eight sessions, but at least sixteen sessions seem indicated for the treatment of severe depression.

A meta-analysis by Gloaguen, Cottraux, Cucherat, and Blackburn (1998) reviewed all the clinical trials for depression conducted between 1977 and 1996 and concluded that cognitive therapy was superior to antidepressant medication and a variety of other psychotherapies in the treatment of mild or moderate depression. CBT was found to be equal to behavior therapy. Cognitive-behavioral therapy also appears to provide some protective effect against depression recurrence, as CBT's maintenance effects at one-year posttreatment were equal to or superior to one year of antidepressant medication and clearly superior to short-term (sixteen-week) medication treatment (Craighead, Hart, et al., 2002). CBT has been shown to reduce both symptoms of depression and relapse rates, after medication management has ended (Young et al., 2001).

Behavioral treatments, such as skills training, self-control training, problem-solving therapy, and contingency management, all have been found superior to minimal treatment and as effective as antidepressant medication in the treatment of depression (Sinha & Rush, 2006). Dialectical behavior therapy shows promise for the treatment of depression, but more research is needed on its effectiveness. Mindfulness-based cognitive therapy has been shown to reduce relapse in women with recurrent depressive episodes.

Medication. A variety of medications have been used in the treatment of major depressive disorder. The first-generation tricyclic antidepressants (TCAs) and MAOIs are less well tolerated and more dangerous on overdose and now have largely been replaced by SSRIs. Medication is generally indicated if depression is severe, recurrent, or chronic; if psychosis is present; and if psychotherapy alone has not helped (Dozois & Dobson, 2002; Nemeroff & Schatzberg, 2002).

Medication and therapy both have a place in the treatment of depression. The particular nature of the depression, however, and its accompanying symptoms suggest whether medication is likely to be helpful and, if so, which medication. The SSRIs — fluoxetine (Prozac), paroxetine (Paxil), sertraline (Zoloft), citalopram (Celexa), and fluvoxamine (Luvox) — work by blocking the reuptake of serotonin. Each SSRI has its own profile and side effects, which may include nervousness, sexual dysfunction, weight gain, nausea, diarrhea, and insomnia. Newer atypical antidepressants, such as venlafaxine (Effexor), trazadone (Desyrel), bupropion (Wellbutrin), and mirtazapine (Remeron), have been found to be more effective in cases of treatment resistant depression and the endogenous or melancholic subtype of major depressive disorder (Nemeroff & Schatzberg, 2002). Although little research is available, polypharmacy is also being used to create an antidepressant cocktail that often is more effective than an SSRI alone. Differences of efficacy, tolerability of side effects, exclusion of women of childbearing years from clinical trials (even though they have the highest rate of unipolar depression), and lack of information on comorbid medical disorders have all muddied the waters in research on the effectiveness of psychopharmacology for the treatment of mood disorders.

In general, medication is particularly indicated for people with endogenous (rather than reactive) depressions that include such symptoms as biological disturbances, a family history of depression, and lack of a clear precipitant. However, depressive disorders combined with somatization disorders or personality disorders tend not to respond as well to medication. When medication is needed, compliance with treatment and improvement in overall functioning can be enhanced by its combination with psychotherapy (Young et al., 2001).

Electroconvulsive Therapy. Electroconvulsive therapy (ECT) is also sometimes used to treat severe symptoms of major depressive disorder, particularly in those who present with psychosis or immediate suicide risk (Butcher et al., 2006). Kho, van Vresswijk, Simpson, and Zwinderman (2003) conducted a meta-analysis of fifteen controlled studies that compared ECT with other treatments for depression. The researchers concluded that a full course of ECT was more effective than medication or simulated ECT. Psychotic symptoms were found to be a predictor of better response.

Criteria for the use of ECT include a need for rapid symptom reduction, a history of good response to ECT, the client's preference for ECT, and the inappropriateness or ineffectiveness of medication or other treatment approaches. Although ECT has been greatly improved in recent years, both ECT and antidepressant medication have side effects, and their risks need to be weighed against their possible benefits.

Day Treatment Programs. Although the hospital may sometimes be the initial setting for treating people with severe depression, a trend toward using day treatment programs and residential crisis centers has developed. These programs typically are more cost-effective, and they seem to achieve slightly better short- and long-term outcomes for people whose depressions warrant close supervision, usually because they are suicidal, psychotic, or immobilized by depression (Sledge et al., 1996).

Light Therapy. Daily light therapy for at least four weeks has been shown to significantly reduce symptoms in seasonally related major depressive disorder, although some people with winter recurrences of depression benefit more from a combination of light therapy and medication or cognitive therapy (Rosenthal, 2006). Dietary changes, including avoidance of caffeine and alcohol and emphasis on complex carbohydrates (bread, pasta, potatoes), together with exercise, have been found to ease symptoms of seasonally related depression. These recommendations may also be beneficial in other types of depression.

Other Treatment Options. A range of other treatments also seem helpful in ameliorating depression. Sinha and Rush (2006) recommend investigation of the efficacy of alternative forms of treatment, such as acupuncture, stress management, yoga, and others. Exercise therapy also holds some promise in the treatment of this disorder, specifically in improving mood and possibly leading to remission of major depression in older adults (Sinha & Rush, 2006). Manber, Allen, and Morris (2002) reviewed alternative treatments and found that stress reduction methods that include yoga and mindfulness meditation appear to prevent relapse in individuals with a history of chronic, recurrent depression.

Prognosis

The prognosis for fairly rapid symptom relief of major depressive disorder through medication, psychotherapy, or both is good: nearly 70 percent of people treated for major depressive disorder experience remission of their symptoms within one year (Young et al., 2001). A good prognosis has been found to be positively associated with the number and supportiveness of social resources, with mild to moderate depression, with increased learned resourcefulness, and for those with intact partner relationships (Young et al., 2001).

Nevertheless, approximately one-third of people treated for major depressive disorder will not respond to the first treatment they receive (Craighead, Hart, et al., 2002). It is unclear if these severely depressed people will respond better to a second treatment modality. However, research has shown that those who do not initially respond to medication do often respond to a second drug.

For many people, recurrence of depression continues to be a problem. Indeed, as many as 50 percent will experience a relapse within ten years. Those who experience two episodes will have a 90 percent chance of having a third episode (Young et al., 2001). Those treated with CBT seem to do far better in terms of relapse than those treated with medication alone. Rates of recurrence are highest during the first four to six months after recovery and have a negative correlation with response to treatment. In other words, those people who have had a rapid and complete response to treatment are the ones least likely to have a recurrence.

Overall, then, the prognosis for recovery from a given episode of a major depressive disorder is good, but many factors contribute to a high likelihood of relapse. A poorer long-term prognosis exists for those whose depression is accompanied by psychotic features. A recurrence of depression for these people is likely to also include psychosis (Butcher et al., 2006). The prognosis is generally also worse for people with accompanying pervasive maladjustment. The prognosis for major depressive disorder is worsened by the presence of a coexisting general medical condition, by substance misuse, or by the presence of long-standing depression prior to treatment. Those with co-occurring personality disorders tend to have poor treatment responses to every treatment intervention except CBT (Craighead, Hart, et al., 2002). The elderly also have a particularly high rate of relapse.

Several approaches to treatment have been found to improve prognosis. Treatment of both initial and residual symptoms through CBT, either alone or in combination with medication, has been associated with a reduced rate of recurrence (Craighead, Hart, et al., 2002). Those with a low level of social dysfunction responded better to interpersonal psychotherapy than to other treatments. Poor response to IPT is seen in people with co-occurring panic disorder, cognitive dysfunction, and personality disorders. Future research should focus on which types of treatment will work best with particular clients and their specific symptoms and needs.

Extended treatment and follow-up can improve prognosis. For example, treatment may comprise six to eighteen weeks of intensive psychotherapy, four to nine months of less intensive relapse prevention, and maintenance and follow-up that may continue for years. Teaching people to recognize the early symptoms of depression, to reduce and manage stress, to increase the level of mastery and pleasure in their lives, and to make good use of support systems is also likely to reduce rates of recurrence.

DYSTHYMIC DISORDER

Description of the Disorder

Dysthymic disorder is characterized by the presence of chronic depression, usually mild to moderate in severity, on most days for at least two years. (In children and adolescents, a minimum duration of one year is required for diagnosis, and the primary manifestation of the disorder may be irritability rather than depression.) According to *DSM-IV-TR*, at least two of the following six symptoms also are present:

1. Poor appetite or overeating
2. Insomnia or hypersomnia
3. Low energy or fatigue
4. Low self-esteem
5. Difficulty in concentrating or decision making
6. A sense of hopelessness

Other common symptoms of dysthymic disorder include reduced activity and accomplishment, guilt and self-doubts, withdrawal from social and other activities, and vegetative symptoms (disturbances in eating, sleeping, and weight). Suicidal ideation and thoughts of death may be present but are less common in people with dysthymic disorder than in those with major depressive disorder.

People diagnosed with dysthymic disorder have not had manic or hypomanic episodes, and their symptoms are not due to substance use. They do manifest some distress or impairment as a result of their symptoms, but typically not as much as people diagnosed with major depressive disorder.

In establishing the diagnosis, the clinician also makes the following determinations about the disorder:

- *Age of onset:* most common periods of onset include late adolescence or early adulthood, with 50 percent having an onset before age twenty-one (Butcher et al., 2006).
- *Presence of atypical features:* described in the section on major depressive disorder

Dysthymic disorder generally has no clear point of onset or obvious precipitant. People with this disorder tend to maintain an acceptable level of social and occupational functioning and often conceal their symptoms from others but may experience mild to moderate impairment or limitations that are due to their depression. Sometimes people with this disorder grow so accustomed to their symptoms that they assume that the way they are feeling is normal; consequently, only a small percentage of people with this disorder seek treatment. Pettit and Joiner (2006) report that the average length of a dysthymic episode is ten years, but it can persist for twenty years or more (Butcher et al., 2006). People often only seek treatment for relief of related symptoms, such as a change in weight or a failure to achieve success in their careers. The possibility has been raised that dysthymic disorder is really a personality disorder rather than a mood disorder and is a pervasive, enduring, and potentially lifelong way of dealing with the world.

Dysthymic disorder is common, particularly among females. Lifetime prevalence rates are between 2.5 and 6 percent (Kessler, Berglund, et al., 2005). Among people sixty years of age and older, approximately 18 percent have been found to meet the criteria for this disorder, and in this group, the disorder is more common in men than in women by a 2:1 ratio (Kessler, 2006). Even among those who seem to recover from dysthymic disorder, nearly half may relapse within two years.

Typical Client Characteristics

Some researchers theorize that an episode of depression leaves a person vulnerable to future episodes, due to pessimism, negativity, lack of resilience, and chronic environmental stressors. One study showed that negative cognitive patterns are easily activated, and depression may be erosive. Men with dysthymic disorder are particularly likely to present with accompanying situational problems, usually in the areas of work or family.

Prior, comorbid, or familial mental disorders are common in people with dysthymic disorder. A coexisting or previous childhood mental disorder (such as conduct disorder, ADHD, or learning disorder) is often reported, as is a family history of depression. Dysthymic disorder frequently is accompanied by a personality disorder or by another physical or mental disorder. Anxiety, eating, and substance use disorders are particularly common. People with dysthymic disorder are also at considerably elevated risk for development of a subsequent major depressive disorder, and therapists should be alert to that possibility.

Personality patterns of people with dysthymic disorder tend to be similar to those of people with major depressive disorder. They typically are low in self-esteem and low in extroversion; they feel helpless and vulnerable, ruminate on interpersonal relations, and have difficulty handling stressful events or social disappointments (Pettit & Joiner, 2006). Underlying hostility and conflict avoidance may be present, as well as dependence and a low tolerance for frustration. People with dysthymic disorder may have a long-standing pattern of avoiding their difficulties by fleeing into overwork or excessive activity. Pettit and Joiner note that avoidance of conflict gradually results in losses of self-esteem, self-efficacy, and the possibility of obtaining relationships or jobs. People with dysthymic disorder are often divorced or separated and likely to come from lower socioeconomic groups. Somatic and physiological complaints (such as eating and sleeping problems) are common and may be the presenting problem when treatment is sought. Children with this disorder, like those with major depressive disorder, often are irritable and complaining.

In some ways, people with dysthymic disorder present more of a challenge to the therapist than do people with major depressive disorder. People with dysthymic disorder have been depressed for so long that they may not know how to be anything but depressed, and they may be resistant to and apprehensive about change. Secondary gains associated with their depression, such as attention and reduced demands, may reinforce their sad, helpless stance, and they may hesitate to relinquish those gains without the assurance of continuing rewards and attention. These clients also present some suicide risk. Although their depression is not as severe as in a major depressive disorder, they do have the resourcefulness and the energy to make a suicide attempt, whereas a severely depressed client may be too incapacitated even to attempt suicide.

Preferred Therapist Characteristics

The type of therapist recommended for people diagnosed with dysthymic disorder is quite similar to the type of therapist recommended for people with major depressive disorder. The establishment and maintenance of a strong working alliance are important in motivating people to continue and to comply with treatment. The therapist working with a person who has dysthymic disorder can be somewhat less supportive and more confrontational, however, and can expect clients to complete more extratherapeutic tasks because these people generally are less impaired and more resilient than those with major depressive or bipolar disorders.

Intervention Strategies

The psychotherapeutic approaches to treating major depressive disorder discussed earlier in this chapter also are recommended for the treatment of dysthymic disorder. These include cognitive, cognitive-behavioral, and interpersonal therapy, particularly in combination with the teaching of social skills and such related skills as assertiveness and decision making. Promoting the development of coping skills to address the client's sense of hopelessness and helplessness can also make a positive difference.

Although research specific to the treatment of dysthymic disorder is sparse, some information on its treatment is available. Seligman's positive psychology has been shown to reduce depression in people who are mildly depressed (Seligman, Steen, Park, & Peterson, 2005). Through positive interventions such as gratitude visits, keeping a positive journal, and identifying signature strengths and applying them in new ways, clients showed reduced scores on the Beck Depression Inventory and increased scores on the Steen Happiness Index (SHI). Although positive psychology has been shown to be effective in a limited sampling of mildly depressed people, additional research is necessary to determine the effectiveness of positive interventions on more serious depressive disorders. Nevertheless, therapists should assess a client's strengths and coping skills and incorporate these strengths into counseling objectives and treatment goals as part of overall strength-based interventions (Smith, 2006).

Gillies (2001) indicates that interpersonal therapy (IPT) is as effective for dysthymia as for major depressive disorder. IPT has also been shown to be effective in treating double depression (the combination of major depressive disorder and dysthymic disorder). Supportive therapy, positive psychology, and group therapy seem to play a greater role in the treatment of dysthymic disorder than in major depressive disorder. People with dysthymic disorder have more energy and a better level of functioning, so they are more able to engage and participate in group therapy and make use of supportive interventions. For older adults, interventions that focus on problems and solutions are more likely to be accepted than insight-oriented therapies (Karel, Ogland-Hand, & Gatz, 2002).

People who are depressed often have difficulties in their relationships. Craighead, Hart, and colleagues (2002) report that behavioral marital therapy (BMT) can be as effective as CBT in relieving symptoms of depression and marital distress. However, BMT has not been empirically validated in the treatment of severe depressive disorders. People who are depressed often have partners with emotional disorders, a finding that raises the question of whether difficult marriages contribute to the incidence of depression or whether people who are depressed select partners with similar traits. Regardless of the answer, family counseling in combination with individual therapy is indicated for many people with dysthymic disorder, as well as for people with other forms of depression.

Although people with dysthymic disorder have milder symptoms than people with major depressive disorder, successful treatment of dysthymic disorder often takes longer than treatment of shorter and more severe depressive disorders. People with dysthymic disorder have been depressed for so long that their impaired functioning may have had a profound impact on many areas of their lives, including work, relationships, and leisure activities, so they may need to restructure and repair their lives in these areas. Moreover, their long-standing depression probably has become so deeply entrenched that they lack the coping skills to overcome it on their own. Beck (2005) found that going over treatment goals and prioritizing them can often help when clients get stuck or fail to make progress. When therapists give clients the choice of whether to discuss skill development in session or to work on it outside of session, clients often report a greater sense of control and investment in the process. Some basic education and development may need to take place before the symptoms of the depression will remit.

Medication is often used in treatment of dysthymic disorder, as it is in treatment of major depressive disorder. However, the risk is high that clients will discontinue antidepressant treatment early on (Olfson, Marcus, Tedeschi, & Wan, 2006). One advantage of combining psychotherapy and medication is to afford an opportunity to educate clients on the importance of medication compliance and to provide continued encouragement toward that end. Current research is investigating the place of medication in the treatment of dysthymic disorder. SSRIs, in particular, have demonstrated effectiveness in the treatment of this disorder (Craighead, Hart, et al., 2002). For example, sertraline (Zoloft) has shown effectiveness in reducing symptoms, and one study showed paroxetine (Paxil) to be more effective than problem-solving psychotherapy in treating dysthymia (Williams, Barrett, & Oxman, 2000).

Despite the recent increased use of pharmacotherapy in combination with psychotherapy to treat dysthymic disorder, psychotherapy is still central because of the importance of improving overall functioning, promoting social and coping skills, and establishing a rewarding lifestyle. Especially given the research which shows that most people stop antidepressant medication in the first thirty days and that fewer than 30 percent continue medication beyond ninety days, combining talk therapy with pharmacotherapy seems to be prudent (Olfson et al., 2006).

Therapists working with people with dysthymic disorder seem to have a broader range of therapeutic options from which to choose than do therapists working with more severely depressed people. In general, psychotherapy aimed at treating dysthymic disorder is most effective if it is moderately supportive, moderately structured and directive, focused on cognitions and behavior more than on affect, and composed of an array of educational and psychotherapeutic interventions designed to modify cognitions, increase activity, and improve self-esteem and interpersonal skills. Treatment will also probably pay some attention to the past, in an effort to elucidate repetitive and self-destructive patterns and clarify the dynamics that are perpetuating the depression.

Prognosis

The spontaneous remission rate from dysthymia is less than 10 percent per year (American Psychiatric Association, 2000). The remission rate improves with treatment. Viable goals for treatment of dysthymic disorder include relief of depression and associated anxiety, amelioration of somatic and physiological symptoms, increased optimism and sense of control, and improved social and occupational functioning. Without treatment, the prognosis for dysthymic disorder is poor. In general, people with dysthymic disorder who can recall a healthier way of functioning, who have some good interpersonal skills and support systems, who have maintained a reasonably rewarding lifestyle, and whose depression is not deeply entrenched are likely to respond well to treatment. For people who do not meet those criteria, therapy may be long and difficult and perhaps unsuccessful. Setting limited goals and focusing on gains may help promote optimism in both the client and the therapist, even if a full recovery cannot be obtained.

DEPRESSIVE DISORDER NOT OTHERWISE SPECIFIED

Description of the Disorder

As is true of most other categories of mental disorder listed in *DSM-IV-TR*, a not otherwise specified (NOS) category is included at the end of the section on depression. This particular NOS category, however, unlike most others, is used often by clinicians because many manifestations of depression are not encompassed by the depressive disorders listed in the *DSM*. According to *DSM-IV-TR*, depressive disorder NOS is defined as a disorder with depressive features that do not meet the criteria for any other specific depressive disorder or adjustment disorder. This category can be used, for example, to describe a recurrent depression with episodes briefer than two weeks, premenstrual dysphoric disorder (depression associated with the menstrual cycle), depression occurring in the residual phase of a psychotic disorder, or a depression that is not severe enough to meet the criteria for major depressive disorder but is too brief for a diagnosis of dysthymic disorder. Treatment recommendations for the other types of depression provide the basis for determining the treatment of depressive disorder NOS, with treatment adapted to meet the needs of the particular client.

BIPOLAR DISORDERS

Description of the Disorders

Bipolar disorders are highly complex mood disorders that are distinguished by episodes of dysfunctional mood, potentially including major depressive episodes, mild-to-moderate depressive episodes, manic episodes, hypomanic episodes, and mixed episodes, often separated by periods of relatively normal mood. Despite the complexity of bipolar disorders, Jefferson (2003) reports that people are much more likely than in the past to be diagnosed accurately. Greater awareness of this disorder and its many manifestations has improved diagnostic accuracy.

Four types of bipolar disorder have been identified in *DSM-IV-TR:*

1. Bipolar I disorder
2. Bipolar II disorder
3. Cyclothymic disorder (considered separately later in this chapter)
4. Bipolar disorder NOS

Bipolar I disorder, by definition, must include at least one manic episode reflecting an extremely elevated mood. It also may include episodes of major depression and of hypomania (an elevated mood that is less severe than a manic episode). Bipolar I disorder typically includes disturbances of mood, cognition, and behavior, and may include psychotic symptoms, although the disorder is not the result of a psychotic disorder, nor is it superimposed on a psychotic disorder. The nature of a person's first episode tends to reflect the nature of the person's dominant type of episode for the illness; that is, a person who has an initial episode of depression as part of a bipolar I disorder has a 90 percent likelihood of subsequent episodes of depression. In men, the first episode of this disorder is usually a manic one; in women, it is more likely to be a depressive episode (American Psychiatric Association, 2000).

Bipolar II disorder is a "subtler, but equally distressing condition" compared to bipolar I disorder (Oakley, 2005, p. 1209). It differs from bipolar I disorder primarily in its lack of any manic episodes. It includes at least one hypomanic episode and at least one depressive episode and, like bipolar I disorder, causes considerable distress or impairment in functioning. Psychotic features are not found in bipolar II disorder. Symptoms of bipolar II disorder are often confused with histrionic and borderline personality disorders; all three disorders include symptoms of irritation, aggressiveness, and rage.

Manic Episodes (Found Only in Bipolar I). According to the *DSM*, a manic episode is a period of "abnormally and persistently elevated, expansive, or irritable mood'' lasting at least one week (American Psychiatric Association, 2000, p. 357). At least three of the following seven symptoms accompany the elevated mood:

1. Grandiosity
2. Reduced need for sleep
3. Increased talkativeness
4. Racing thoughts
5. Distractibility
6. Increased activity
7. Excessive pleasure-seeking, to a potentially self-destructive extent (for example, hypersexuality, excessive spending, or gambling)

A manic episode, like an episode of major depression, is typically quite severe and causes impairment in social and occupational functioning. People experiencing this phase of bipolar I disorder tend to have grandiose thoughts and feel they are powerful and destined for great success. They have little insight into the potential risks of their behavior or into the feelings of others, and they may become hostile and threatening if challenged. Symptoms of mania include changes in thinking, appearance, behavior, and energy level, as well as impaired judgment and the expression of dramatic emotions. Anger and aggression that occur when other people set limits are also common. Manic episodes frequently result in hypersexuality or promiscuous behavior, excessive spending or schemes that result in severe financial consequences, or delusions about the person's importance that may result in contacting public officials or in conflicts with the police. The judgment and impulse control of people experiencing a manic episode are poor, and they typically are hyperactive and distractible. Their speech tends to be loud, pressured, and intrusive. People experiencing manic episodes often have delusions or hallucinations (usually of a grandiose type), which may lead clinicians to misdiagnose them as having schizophrenia. The following is a description of one person whose experience typifies the manic phase of bipolar I disorder:

> Evelyn R. is a twenty-seven-year-old white woman with a stable marriage and work history. During a manic episode, she slept little, staying up most of the night to make plans for her future, which was to include the purchase of several houses, and love affairs with many of her coworkers and acquaintances. When her startled husband objected, she informed him that she was in the prime of her life and that he should stay out of her way. A brief period of hospitalization was required to prevent Evelyn from destroying her marriage and spending all the couple's resources.

Hypomanic Episodes. Hypomania, or partial mania, is similar to the symptoms of mania but without loss of reality testing, without psychosis (hallucinations and delusions), and without significantly impaired functioning (Oakley, 2005). These episodes resemble mild versions of manic episodes in terms of symptoms and accompanying mood. The symptoms of hypomania include increased energy, racing thoughts, less need for sleep, and more goal-directed behavior. Hypomanic episodes have a minimum duration of four days. Recognizing a hypomanic episode — which is, by definition, part of bipolar II disorder, and is also found in bipolar I — can be a challenge. Many people do not perceive hypomania as pathological, and therefore they do not present it as a problem. The therapist meeting initially with a person who is having a hypomanic episode may mistakenly think that the person is simply in a very good mood, but the mood's unremitting nature, its usual lack of a precipitant, and the person's history of dysfunctional mood episodes will distinguish a hypomanic episode from a normal cheerful mood.

Depression. The depressive phase of a bipolar disorder closely resembles the depression associated with a major depressive disorder, but with some differences. The depression associated with a bipolar disorder often entails less anger and somatizing and more oversleeping and psychomotor retardation. Episodes of bipolar depression also result in increased rates of suicide compared to major depressive disorder, an important distinction to note. Bipolar depression may include psychotic features, such as delusions and hallucinations. According to Baldessarini and Tondo (2003), bipolar and unipolar mood disorders with psychotic features are the most frequently occurring psychotic disorders.

The American Psychiatric Association guidelines on the management of bipolar disorders note that people with a bipolar I or II disorder who are experiencing a depressed mood are frequently misdiagnosed as having a unipolar major depressive disorder. As a result, they may receive inappropriate treatment (American Psychiatric Association, 2004a).

Episodes of mild to moderate depression are associated with cyclothymic disorder but not with bipolar I or bipolar II disorders. These episodes will be discussed further in the section on cyclothymic disorder.

Mixed Episodes. Forty percent of people with bipolar disorders experience mixed episodes (Miklowitz, 2006). In these episodes, the criteria for both a major depressive episode and a manic episode are met nearly every day for at least one week. Mixed states are often associated with increased suicide risk and a relatively poor response to treatment with lithium (Bowden, Kusumakar, MacMaster, & Yatham, 2002).

Duration of Episodes. The average duration of an episode of dysfunctional mood is two and a half to four months, but may be as short as a few days. The depressive phase tends to be the longest, with an average duration of six to nine months. The manic phase has an average duration of two to six weeks. An average of thirty-three months elapses between episodes of dysfunctional mood, but five years or more may elapse between the first and the second episode, with the time between episodes becoming shorter and the episodes themselves becoming longer as they recur. Typically, the pattern of the episodes' duration and frequency stabilizes by the fourth or fifth episode. Episodes tend to end abruptly. Without treatment, people with bipolar disorders typically have ten or more episodes over the course of their lives; the frequency of the episodes varies from three per year to one every ten years.

Specifiers. In diagnosing bipolar I or II disorders, the clinician should indicate the nature and severity of the current episode and should list the appropriate specifiers, including the following:

- *For all four types of episodes:* presence or absence of a seasonal pattern, psychosis, catatonic features, postpartum onset, rapid cycling, and interepisode recovery
- *For depressive episodes:* presence of melancholic features and atypical features (both discussed further in the section on major depressive disorder)

An additional course descriptor for bipolar I and II disorders is determination of the presence of rapid cycling. Rapid cycling, or switching between depression and mania, is found in 13 to 20 percent of people with bipolar disorder (Miklowitz, 2006) and is more frequent in females. Rapid cycling, by definition, includes four or more discrete episodes of depression, mania, hypomania, or a mixture of depression and mania (mixed episode) in a single year. Determining when one episode ends and another begins usually is difficult. Coryell (2002) notes that rapid cycling appears to be a transient state. Even so, this pattern is linked to increased dysfunction and to a poorer prognosis.

Prevalence. Lifetime prevalence rates for bipolar I and bipolar II disorders are 0.8 and 0.5 percent, respectively (Sue et al., 2006). Figures in the National Comorbidity Survey Replication (Kessler, Chiu, et al., 2005) indicate that 2.6 percent of the U.S. population has a bipolar disorder in a given year. Untreated, bipolar disorders carry a considerable risk of relapse and mortality. Statistics on the number of suicide attempts and completions indicate that as many as 50 percent of people with bipolar disorder attempt suicide, and nearly 20 percent complete it (Leahy, 2004). Although people with bipolar disorders are even more likely than people with major depressive disorder to commit suicide and to require hospitalization, fewer than one-third ever receive treatment (Craighead, Miklowitz, et al., 2002).

Both genders are equally represented among people with bipolar I disorder, but women are more likely than men to develop bipolar II disorder. Onset of a bipolar I disorder is usually earlier than for major depressive disorder, with over half experiencing onset before the age of thirty (American Psychiatric Association, 2000). Onset may occur any time after the age of five, although the incidence of bipolar I disorder peaks in the late teens and early twenties, and a first episode is unlikely before the age of twelve or after the age of fifty.

Typical Client Characteristics

Bipolar I disorder is a highly heritable illness, more so than bipolar II or major depressive disorder (unipolar depression) (Sue et al., 2006). Twin studies indicate a 65 to 75 percent concordance rate for monozygotic twins in comparison to 14 percent for dizygotic twins (Keck & McElroy, 2002). Lifetime prevalence of mood disorders among family members of people with bipolar I disorder are eight to ten times higher than in the general population. Similarly, 50 percent of people with bipolar I disorder have at least one parent with a mood disorder (Sachs, 2004).

Both bipolar I and bipolar II disorders can be exacerbated or triggered by a stressful life event. Other environmental contributors include families with high expressed emotion who are critical, hostile, or emotionally overinvolved (Craighead, Miklowitz, et al., 2002; Miklowitz, 2004). Such stressful family interaction patterns typically exacerbate a preexisting biological predisposition toward bipolar disorder and lead to emotional dysregulation. S. L. Johnson (2004) found that overactivity following positive life events and goal attainment can lead to a manic episode. Researchers theorize that the brains of people with bipolar disorder do not deactivate after an event, but instead continue on into euphoria and manic symptoms.

While experiencing hypomania, people typically are more goal-focused, productive, and cheerful, and have expansive moods. Such enthusiasm, however, is generally out of proportion to the event, and racing thoughts and flight of ideas that accompany hypomania can disrupt concentration. People in a hypomanic episode might be described as not being able to talk fast enough to keep up with their own thoughts. Irritability, being quick to find fault, and high energy may also be present. Hypomanic episodes often are missed in diagnosis, as many people who experience mild euphoria, greater productivity, and expansive moods are not likely to be troubled by them. However, as with mania, a greater risk of self-harm through injury or accident accompanies a hypomanic episode.

Bipolar disorder is the most likely of any Axis I disorder to be accompanied by a co-occurring substance-related disorder. Bipolar I co-occurs with substance abuse or dependence in 60 percent of cases; bipolar II, in 48 percent (Zarate & Tohen, 2002). Such dual diagnosis and treatment often provide a challenge for clinicians, as people with the combination of the two disorders have been shown to have worse outcomes, higher rates of mixed mood episodes, a shorter time to relapse, and a larger number of psychosocial difficulties.

Kessler and colleagues (1999) found that bipolar I disorder was comorbid with at least one other disorder 100 percent of the time. Other commonly co-occurring disorders include impulse-control disorders, personality disorders, anxiety disorders, and other disorders related to affect regulation (Miklowitz, 2006). Diagnosis of bipolar disorders can be complicated by the presence of comorbid disorders and is frequently misdiagnosed as a personality disorder. However, Miklowitz and others estimate that fewer than 28 percent of people with bipolar disorder meet the criteria for an Axis II personality disorder when they are in remission.

The co-occurrence of anxiety disorders, such as panic disorder, obsessive-compulsive disorder (OCD), and posttraumatic stress disorder (PTSD), with the bipolar disorders may indicate a possible link between the OCD spectrum disorders and bipolar disorders. Tourette's disorder also frequently occurs in people with bipolar disorders. Zarate and Tohen (2002) note a 13 to 23 percent comorbidity rate of bipolar disorders and impulse-control disorders (pathological gambling, intermittent explosive disorder, kleptomania, pyromania, and trichotillomania), and impulse-control disorders often precede the onset of a bipolar disorder. People with bipolar disorder are also more likely to have other comorbid mood disorders, most often dysthymic, cyclothymic, or schizoaffective disorder. Many people later diagnosed with bipolar I disorder had premorbid cyclothymic disorder involving unstable but less severe mood changes. Not only do these co-occurring disorders complicate the diagnosis of bipolar disorder, but their treatment often exacerbates the symptoms of bipolar disorder. For example, stimulants used to treat ADHD can trigger a manic episode, or anxiolytics used to treat panic disorder can decrease inhibitions and increase impulsivity.

Adolescents with bipolar disorders tend to have interpersonal and academic problems and can be misdiagnosed as having the more common conduct disorder or ADHD. In a study of adolescents with bipolar I symptoms, as many as 57 percent had co-occurring ADHD. The overlap of symptoms of ADHD and bipolar disorder — such as racing thoughts, impulsivity, distractibility, poor insight, impaired judgment, excessive activity, and impaired attention — also make differential diagnosis difficult. Bipolar disorders and ADHD differ in that ADHD generally has an early onset (before age seven), is chronic rather than episodic, and does not involve elevated moods or psychotic features

(Altman, 2004). ADHD, as well as conduct disorder and psychotic disorders, are all more likely to be comorbid with bipolar disorder than with unipolar depression.

One in three people with bipolar disorder has significant employment-related losses. Deficits in work-related functioning can continue one or even two years after a hospitalization due to a bipolar disorder (Craighead, Miklowitz, et al., 2002). In fact, only 20 percent of people with bipolar disorder are able to continue to work at expected levels in the first six months following an episode, and more than 50 percent have employment-related difficulty for the following five years.

The disorder also takes a toll on partner and family relationships. Marital distress is reported at a higher rate in people with bipolar disorder than in the general population (Craighead, Miklowitz, et al., 2002). According to Miklowitz (2002), criticism, high expressed emotion, overprotectiveness, lack of problem-solving skills, and problems with intimacy are often present in families of people with bipolar disorders.

Assessment

Considerable progress has been made in the past ten years in the diagnosis and treatment of bipolar disorders. However, accurate diagnosis of this complicated mood disorder is not always made on the first presentation, especially if the person presents with depression. Unless a history of manic episodes can be identified, the disorder probably will be misdiagnosed as a major depressive disorder rather than a bipolar disorder. Bipolar disorders are most easily diagnosed when people present with a sudden onset of severe mania lasting weeks or months (Oakley, 2005). When symptoms of mania are severe enough to induce psychosis, however, bipolar I disorder can be mistaken for schizophrenia.

Zarate and Tohen (2002) concluded that accurate differential diagnosis can only be done longitudinally, after careful consideration of family history, chronology of symptoms, response to treatment, and functioning between episodes.

Accurate diagnosis can be prolonged or delayed due to the difficulty in determining whether the psychosis accompanies depression, schizophrenia spectrum disorders, or the manic episode of a bipolar I disorder. In general, psychosis that accompanies bipolar I disorder is mood-congruent. For example, a grandiose and expansive mood might be accompanied by grandiose hallucinations or delusions.

For accurate diagnosis, clinicians must conduct a detailed history of prior mood episodes. A useful self-assessment tool for hypomanic symptoms, the Hypomania Checklist-32 (HCL-32), has been developed by Angst and colleagues (2005). Although the inventory requires more validation to determine whether it can accurately discriminate between subtypes of bipolar disorder, it is helpful as a hypomanic symptom checklist.

The need for assessment and management of suicide risk remains constant throughout treatment for bipolar disorder. Approximately 40 percent of people with bipolar disorder make at least one suicide attempt (Sachs, 2004). Therapists must remain vigilant and familiarize themselves with the risk factors for suicide:

- A prior history of suicide attempts is the biggest risk factor for future suicide.
- Suicide risk is highest in the first two years after onset of a bipolar disorder.
- Suicide occurs more frequently in the months immediately following release from a psychiatric hospital.
- Most suicide is associated with a current depressive or mixed episode.
- Suicide risk is higher if substance use is involved.
- Such co-occurring disorders as panic disorder, PTSD, ADHD, and borderline personality disorder increase risk.
- Four times as many males as females complete a suicide attempt, whereas women make more frequent attempts.

Preferred Therapist Characteristics

Craighead, Miklowitz, and colleagues (2002) note that the therapeutic alliance plays an important role in the successful treatment of people with bipolar disorders, just as it does in the treatment of those with depressive disorders. Therapists should form a true partnership with their clients for the purpose of monitoring medication, charting moods, educating clients about the diagnosis and its treatment, and helping clients make good use of what they learn through treatment.

Sachs (2004) discusses the importance of the therapist establishing a collaborative relationship with both clients and their psychiatrists to ensure that treatment goals include medication compliance. Medication nonadherence is an important issue for people with bipolar disorder and must be addressed. Despite the risk of relapse and serious symptoms, nearly 60 percent of people who take lithium to treat a bipolar disorder are only partially compliant with their medications.

Intervention Strategies

Goals for the treatment of bipolar disorders include alleviating acute symptoms; preventing future episodes of dysfunctional mood; and remedying any occupational, interpersonal, or other lifestyle problems that have resulted from the disorder. The nature and severity of the episode of dysfunctional mood, as well as the accompanying impairment, will guide the specific choice of treatment. Sachs (2004) recommends a collaborative care model in which psychiatrist, therapist, and family interact to ensure the client's safety, provide assessment information, and begin treatment. Preliminary research suggests that the combination of psychotherapy and medication for the treatment of bipolar disorder may be more beneficial than medication alone (Jones, 2004; Sachs, 2004).

Miklowitz (2006) describes the following three distinct phases of treatment for bipolar disorder:

1. *Acute phase.* This phase begins when the person meets the criteria for an episode (mania, hypomania, depression, or mixed) and treatment begins (Sachs, 2004). Bipolar symptoms, particularly those that are present during the manic phase, are sometimes so severe and so self-destructive that hospitalization is needed. The period of hospitalization is typically brief, lasting only until medication has had an opportunity to stabilize the client's mood.

Providing therapy during the acute phase is likely to be very difficult, especially when symptoms of euphoria and grandiosity increase resistance to the idea that treatment is necessary. The flight of ideas and high activity levels of people in a manic episode make analysis and clarification of concerns all but impossible. If therapy is attempted during the manic phase, it will probably have to be very structured and concrete, involving short, frequent sessions focusing more on behavior and milieu than on introspection and exploration of affect.

2. *Stabilization phase.* Miklowitz (2002) recommends that a relapse prevention plan be created when the client is stabilized. Timing is of utmost importance, as people who are experiencing a manic or hypomanic mood will have difficulty recognizing their crisis or moderating their euphoric and upbeat behavior. Miklowitz notes two predictors of rehospitalization for people with bipolar disorder: medication noncompliance and failure to recognize early signs of relapse. When clients are stabilized, work should begin on helping them identify prodromal symptoms, list preventive measures, and create a written plan or contract that details the procedures a significant and trusted other can follow to help them if relapse occurs. Indeed, because of the difficulty of treating people during the manic phase of a bipolar disorder, several authors have suggested that collaborative care contracts be created and signed when the person is between episodes. These contracts can be used to authorize treatment if the person develops manic symptoms at some future date. Such contracts identify behaviors that might indicate relapse, specify constructive behaviors,

and give a family member (or therapist) permission to seek treatment on the client's behalf should such previous efforts fail (Miklowitz, 2001; Sachs, 2004).

Much in the literature focuses on the importance of educating family members about bipolar disorder (Craighead, Miklowitz, et al., 2002; Miklowitz, 2004; Sachs, 2004). Especially when there is an acute onset, family members can be a stabilizing force in the person's life, overseeing medication compliance and monitoring safety plans. Separate education programs for family and partners of people with bipolar disorder can increase knowledge of resources and social supports, improve medication compliance, decrease family stress, ameliorate emotional difficulties, and improve coping strategies (Craighead, Miklowitz, et al., 2002).

During this phase, individual psychotherapy and family therapy can help people maintain medication compliance, recover from the symptoms of their disorder, restore a normal mood, and start to establish a framework that offers structure and support. The stabilization phase ends when the client has recovered from the acute episode (Sachs, 2004).

3. *Maintenance phase.* After people with bipolar disorders have moved into the maintenance phase of treatment, the focus turns to maintaining recovery and preventing another episode from occurring. Adjunct treatment to address family and relationship issues, as well as career and employment-related concerns, can begin. Sachs (2004) suggests that maintenance therapy should continue for at least one year following the first manic episode (and any subsequent episode). A history of three or more episodes would be an indication that long-term maintenance of bipolar disorder is needed.

Treatment during the normal or depressive phases of bipolar disorders generally can be very helpful if the guidelines discussed earlier for the treatment of depression are followed. Treatment usually will be more supportive and less confrontational than therapy for major depressive disorder, however, because medication is really the primary mode of treatment for bipolar I and II disorders. The relatively high level of functioning experienced by many people between episodes of a bipolar disorder suggests that less emphasis is needed on social skills, although educating people about the nature of their disorder is an important element of the treatment.

Medication. As mentioned earlier, medication is the primary mode of treatment for bipolar I and II disorders. Lithium has long been the standard treatment for bipolar disorders, and the response rates range from 60 to 80 percent (Delgado & Gelenberg, 2001). Lithium acts primarily on manic symptoms. However, lithium alone fails to produce a sustained remission (at least three years in duration) in approximately 75 percent of people with bipolar disorders, and the compliance rate for people with bipolar disorder who take lithium is worse than any other group of people taking any other drug (Sue et al., 2006).

Twenty years ago, lithium was the only medication option for people with bipolar disorder. Fortunately, positive results have been found with other classes of drugs, including anticonvulsants and atypical antipsychotics. The newer atypical antipsychotic drugs, such as olanzapine (Zyprexa), clozapine (Clozaril), risperidone (Risperdal), quetiapine (Seroquel), and ziprasidone (Geodon), generally have fewer side effects and extrapyramidal symptoms, although sedation, weight gain, and an increased risk of diabetes have been reported (Yatham & Kusumakar, 2002). At least one study has indicated that these medications reduce recurrence rates of mania when compared with placebo or with lithium or valproate treatment alone. However, additional research needs to be conducted on the long-term side effects of these newer drugs, as well as their usefulness in maintenance and relapse prevention.

The choice of medication — whether lithium, other antipsychotics, antidepressants, anticonvulsants, or other medications — depends on whether rapid cycling, psychotic features, depression, or severe mania are present (Jefferson, 2003). The choice of medication also varies according to the phase of treatment (acute, stabilization, or maintenance) (Miklowitz, 2006; Yatham & Kusumakar, 2002).

Nonadherence to drug treatment is related to clients' feelings about having moods curtailed by medication, missing the high or euphoric periods, and medication side effects, such as weight gain, sweating, and sexual dysfunction. A complete discussion of medication is beyond the scope of this book. Interested readers are referred to the American Psychiatric Association's *Practice Guideline for the Treatment of Patients with Bipolar Disorder* (2004a) or the three-part World Federation of Societies of Biological Psychiatry (WFSBP) guidelines for information on the biological treatment of bipolar disorders (Grunze et al., 2002, 2003, 2004).

Sometimes antidepressant medication or other activating drugs prescribed for unipolar depression can bring about mania, hypomania, or a mixed state in people who are susceptible to mood swings (Miklowitz, 2001). Such a state would not be diagnosed as a bipolar disorder, but would be considered a substance-induced mood disorder, unless symptoms lasted longer than a month after the medication is stopped or there is a prior history of manic symptoms (Miklowitz, 2006).

Psychotherapy. After clients become stabilized, psychotherapy can begin. Miklowitz (2001) suggests that the most important reasons for individual therapy for people with bipolar disorder are to help them cope with stress triggers, troubling life events, and disturbances in family functioning. Few controlled studies have been conducted on the types of psychotherapy that are most likely to be helpful in the treatment of bipolar disorders, but some research supports interpersonal psychotherapy (IPT) and IPT with social rhythm therapy (Craighead, Miklowitz, et al., 2002); family-focused psychoeducational treatment (FFT; Miklowitz & Goldstein, 1997); and cognitive-behavioral approaches, such as mania inoculation training (a type of therapy that builds on CBT and helps clients work on cognitive distortions that frequently occur with manic symptoms of grandiosity and narcissism). In mania inoculation training, clients learn that they are not all-powerful, nor are they powerless. They learn to see the ''normative middle'' (Leahy, 2004).

Interpersonal therapy. As in the treatment of unipolar depression, IPT has been shown to reduce the amount of time bipolar clients spend in the depressive phase (Frank, 1999). Also, people who stayed in IPT had fewer recurrences than those who switched from one mode of treatment to another. As in other areas of bipolar disorder, establishing routines and consistency seems to provide a protective factor.

Social rhythm therapy. Social rhythm therapy combines IPT with a focus on the person's circadian rhythms. Social rhythm therapy helps clients understand the effect of the sleep-wake cycle on their moods and to plan ahead for situations that might normally disrupt them (Frank, 2005; Frank & Swartz, 2004). Behavioral techniques that encourage people to chart the precipitants, nature, duration, frequency, and seasonality of their dysfunctional mood episodes can be effective in helping them recognize what might trigger future episodes. Maintaining a stable, balanced, and healthy lifestyle and minimizing and coping with stressors can also contribute to the prevention of dysfunctional mood episodes (Frank, 2005).

Family-focused therapy. Several studies show family therapy to be a helpful adjunct to medication in the treatment of bipolar disorder (Miklowitz, 2006). Two controlled studies found that family-focused therapy (FFT) was effective in lowering the frequency of relapse and increasing the length between episodes in people with bipolar disorder. FFT in combination with medication appears to ameliorate tension in the family. Miklowitz and Goldstein (1997) published a family-focused treatment manual for bipolar disorder in which they recommend educating the family and the client that bipolar disorder is an illness that probably will recur, and helping them recognize the biopsychosocial causes (for example, poor sleep hygiene, family criticism) and identify prodromal symptoms of mania and depression so that they can be prepared to address them.

Group therapy. Group therapy is usually not indicated for people experiencing a severe episode of a bipolar disorder, because the nature of their symptoms makes it difficult for them to engage in the group process. Nevertheless, group therapy has been found to enhance treatment compliance and may be useful during the recovery phase. Couples therapy has been associated with improved medication compliance and a better overall course for the disorder (Roth & Fonagy, 2005). Such self-help groups as the Depression and Bipolar Support Alliance (DBSalliance.org) and the Family-to-Family program of the National Alliance for the Mentally Ill (www.nami.org) can also be sources of support and information.

Other Treatments. ECT occasionally can play an important role in the treatment of bipolar disorders, especially for people who are actively suicidal or are agitated, who have psychotic depression, or for whom other treatments have failed (Yatham, Kusumakar, & Kutcher, 2002). The efficacy rate of ECT is reported to range from 50 to 100 percent in these cases.

Vagus nerve stimulation (VNS therapy) also has been approved by the FDA as an intervention for people who suffer from severe, treatment-resistant depression. In VNS, a device implanted into the chest sends electrical pulses to the vagus nerve in the neck, which in turn activates areas of the brain that lead to an improvement in mood. Treatment effectiveness has varied in initial studies, and more empirical data is needed (Feder, 2006).

Addressing Dual Diagnosis. People with bipolar disorders often have an unrecognized and untreated substance use disorder (Noordsy, McQuade, & Mueser, 2003). Substance use, especially when it co-occurs with psychosis, dramatically increases the risk of relapse and hospitalization for people with bipolar disorder. Substance misuse can also increase violence, aggression, and suicide risk in this population. Thus early detection and treatment not only of bipolar disorder but of co-occurring substance use disorders are cornerstones of effective treatment.

Sachs (2004) recommends that therapists make suicide assessment and substance use discussions a part of every phase of treatment, not only at intake, for people with bipolar disorders. Because most clients are not likely to bring up their problems of substance use, standardized self-report questionnaires can be useful. Self-report measures have been found to be more accurate than personal interviews (Noordsy et al., 2003).

Traditional treatment approaches have attempted to treat either the substance use disorder or the mental disorder, but not both disorders simultaneously. Indeed, many people with substance use and bipolar disorders are referred to rehabilitation programs that do not provide treatment for their bipolar disorder. In addition, many people with bipolar disorder are refused treatment at rehabilitation centers because of their mental disorder. According to Sachs, no empirical evidence exists to indicate that separate interventions are effective. The current mode of thinking is that both the substance use disorder and the bipolar disorder should be treated simultaneously.

People dually diagnosed with bipolar disorder and a substance use disorder should participate in integrated treatment consisting of relapse prevention, group therapy, psychoeducation on symptoms of bipolar disorder and triggers for substance misuse, encouragement and monitoring of medication compliance, urine screenings for drug use, and discussion of issues relevant to both disorders, such as recognizing signs of relapse, stress management and relaxation techniques, and cognitive-behavioral therapy to improve resistance to misusing substances (Sachs, 2004).

Prognosis

Bipolar disorders present an even greater risk of recurrence than major depressive disorder, and without treatment that risk does not decline over time. Although most people have a positive response to initial treatment for the disorder, the risk of recurrence is highest in the first year after recovery. Recurrence rates fall over the next two years and then range from 20 to 30 percent each year thereafter (Coryell, 2002). Continued maintenance treatment is recommended for those who have recently recovered from an episode of bipolar I disorder.

As we have discussed, medication management, treatment, stabilization, and long-term maintenance for people with bipolar disorder are complicated by a variety of factors, including co-occurring disorders, family situation, and medication compliance. Decisions about long-term maintenance of medication should be based on many factors, including severity of manic episodes, level of insight during episodes, side effects of the medication, acuteness of onset, and the person's ability to handle the risk of relapse and its effects on his or her life. As we have already seen, a large cause of treatment failure in people with bipolar disorder is nonadherence to medication regimens (Jefferson, 2003).

Miklowitz (2004) has found that prognosis is worse if the person with bipolar disorder has had multiple prior episodes or has a co-occurring substance use disorder, rapid cycling, or a negative family affective style (high expressed emotion). The primary goal of treatment should be to ensure that mood regulation is maintained while also treating the symptoms of the disorder. Clearly more research is needed on treatment recommendations for people dually diagnosed with bipolar disorder and substance use or other disorders.

Despite these findings, the prognosis for controlling a bipolar disorder with consistent medication and psychotherapy is fairly good. This means that people may need to be on medication for many years. Monitoring of progress, blood tests to assess the effects of the medication, and follow-up are important in obtaining treatment compliance. Although six to nine months of lithium treatment may suffice for a first episode, extended maintenance on lithium or other medication is strongly recommended for most people who have had recurrent episodes, to reduce the likelihood of future recurrences.

Preventive use of therapy is also recommended, although its efficacy has not yet been well documented. Social rhythm therapy, family-focused therapy, and CBT may play an important role in follow-up treatment of people with bipolar disorders. Even though medication will be provided by a psychiatrist or other physician, a nonmedical therapist can monitor progress, encourage appropriate use of the medication, and facilitate the adjustment of people with a history of bipolar disorder. Treatment approaches that combine various medications (such as mood stabilizers with atypical antipsychotics) in an effort to provide targeted, individualized treatment may become the norm, although careful studies of treatment efficacy will need to be documented (Lam, Zis, & Goumeniouk, 2002).

CYCLOTHYMIC DISORDER

Description of the Disorder

Cyclothymic disorder is, in a sense, a longer but milder version of bipolar I and II disorders, just as dysthymic disorder can be thought of as a longer and milder version of major depressive disorder (although any biological relationship between the pairs is unclear). Cyclothymic disorder entails a period of at least two years (one year for children and adolescents) during which a person experiences numerous episodes of hypomania and mild-to-moderate depression (with symptom-free periods lasting no longer than two months). *DSM-IV-TR* (American Psychiatric Association, 2000, p. 398) describes these depressive episodes as being " . . . of insufficient number, severity, pervasiveness, or duration to meet full criteria for a major depressive episode." Similarly, the hypomanic episodes do not meet the criteria for a manic episode. The mood changes tend to be abrupt and unpredictable and to have no apparent cause.

People with cyclothymic disorder have continual mood cycles that are usually briefer (days or weeks rather than months) and less severe than those characteristic of bipolar I or II disorders. The instability and moodiness associated with cyclothymic disorder, however, tend to make people difficult coworkers and companions, so some social and occupational dysfunction typically results. This disorder sometimes resembles and can be confused with a borderline or histrionic personality disorder.

Lifetime prevalence of this disorder ranges from 0.4 percent to 1 percent (American Psychiatric Association, 2000). Like dysthymic disorder, cyclothymic disorder probably is underreported because the long-standing behavior becomes so familiar that it is viewed as normal. Mild hypomania, in which a person feels more energetic, confident, and alert, is particularly unlikely to be viewed as a problem by people experiencing this symptom.

Cyclothymic disorder, like other mood disorders, usually begins in late adolescence or early adulthood and, without treatment, tends to have a chronic course, with no significant symptom-free periods (Sue et al., 2006). This disorder appears to be equally common in males and females.

Typical Client Characteristics

People with cyclothymic disorder and their family members often have other mental disorders. First-degree relatives of people with cyclothymic disorder have an increased incidence of major depressive, substance-related, and bipolar disorders. Some clinicians have noted in people with cyclothymic disorder a common childhood history of poor object relations and of being hypersensitive, hyperactive, and moody. Miklowitz and Goldstein (1997) note that children with parents who have bipolar disorders are more likely to exhibit cyclothymic disorder compared with other children.

This disorder sometimes is accompanied by substance-related, personality, somatoform, and sleep disorders and, in about one-third of cases, is a precursor to another mood disorder, most often bipolar II disorder. Sue and colleagues (2006) report that the risk that a cyclothymic disorder will eventually develop into a bipolar disorder ranges from 15 to 50 percent, although it is difficult to predict who will subsequently develop a bipolar disorder (Miklowitz, 2002).

Substance misuse by people with cyclothymic disorder often reflects an effort at self-medication. People with cyclothymic disorder typically become more severely impaired in response to such substances as marijuana, alcohol, steroids, and antidepressant medication, which may increase depression or precipitate a manic episode (Fawcett, Golden, Rosenfeld, & Goodwin, 2000). Once a person with cyclothymic disorder develops a full manic, mixed, or depressive episode, the diagnosis is changed to bipolar I or II.

Preferred Therapist Characteristics

Little information is available on the therapist's role in the treatment of cyclothymic disorder. Logic suggests the need for stability, patience, structure, and flexibility. Role modeling and feedback may also be useful tools for therapists because people with cyclothymic disorder have no stable sense of themselves and probably will need to clarify their values and direction as symptoms are reduced. Therapists should keep in mind that clients with cyclothymic disorder can vary greatly in presentation from one session to the next. Early intervention is considered crucial. Basco and Rush (2005) report that waiting until symptoms "cluster into a syndrome is more likely to result in a long road back to normalcy" (p. 28).

Intervention Strategies

Little information is available on the treatment of cyclothymic disorder. Life charts in which clients self-report moods over periods of a year or more can help therapists document deviation, severity, polarity, and functional impairment of the mood disorder and assist in diagnosis (Miklowitz, 2001). Treatment seems to be most effective when it includes a combination of medication and psychotherapy. Mood stabilizers such as lithium as well as anticonvulsants, such as carbamazepine (Tegretol), valproic acid (Depakene), gabapentin (Neurontin), and lamotrigine (Lamictal), typically are the first choice of medication for this disorder. These medications effect significant reduction in symptoms as well as stabilization of mood in people with cyclothymic disorder. Antidepressant medication may be indicated, but often triggers a manic episode. Antipsychotics are also sometimes prescribed. No one medication or treatment method has been found highly effective in treating this disorder. Mood stabilizing medications are better for alleviating manic rather than depressive symptoms, whereas psychotherapy appears to be better at doing the opposite. Miklowitz (2001) believes that a combination of the two works best.

Individual psychotherapy usually is important in the treatment of cyclothymic disorder. Treatment goals include education about the disorder, identification of triggers of mood shifts, mood stabilization, amelioration of any work- and family-related concerns, and overall improvement of lifestyle. Individual therapy should probably follow the cognitive-behavioral, interpersonal, and other models that have demonstrated effectiveness in treating major depressive disorder, because depression is a central element in cyclothymic disorder and because behavioral and cognitive deficits are likely to accompany the mood shifts. The depressive cycles of this disorder also tend to produce more dysfunction than do the hypomanic episodes. In addition, although hypomania that presents as irritability and anger, or episodes during which little sleep results in racing thoughts and reckless decisions, can certainly cause problems, people rarely seek treatment for periods during which they experience elevated mood, increased energy and activity levels, and greater self-esteem (S. L. Johnson, 2004).

Family therapy is indicated, as it is for most of the disorders discussed in this chapter, because the unpredictable mood shifts experienced by people with this disorder may well have damaged their family relationships. Educating the family that cyclothymic disorder is a mood disorder rather than willful behavior can help rebuild those relationships. Miklowitz's family-focused therapy (2004; Miklowitz & Goldstein, 1997) is one approach to family counseling that seems likely to help people with cyclothymic disorder. In that treatment model, the role of the clinician is to "coordinate, guide, and assist" the family through three focused modules that include psychoeducation, communication enhancement training, and problem-solving skills training. Goals of family-focused therapy are to reduce stress, help family members develop a nonblaming stance, increase medication compliance, improve communication skills, provide psychoeducation about the disorder, and help the family develop problem-solving strategies.

Career counseling and interpersonal skill development will usually be helpful supplements to the treatment of people with cyclothymic disorder. Their mood changes will probably have made it difficult for them to negotiate a smooth career path and develop a repertoire of positive social skills and coping mechanisms.

Group therapy may also be useful. People with cyclothymic disorder are generally healthy enough to interact with other group members and may benefit from the opportunity to try out new ways of relating, receive feedback, and make use of the role models provided by others.

In general, then, psychotherapy for people with cyclothymic disorder will be multifaceted. Treatment will include individual psychotherapy and may also include group therapy, family therapy, career counseling, and education. If medication is indicated, the treatment will usually include a mood stabilizer. Therapy should be structured and relatively directive to keep clients focused. It generally combines supportive and exploratory elements, to help clients understand their patterns of interaction, and will emphasize cognitive and behavioral strategies.

Prognosis

The combination of psychotherapy and medication has a good likelihood of reducing symptoms and effecting overall improvement in people with cyclothymic disorder. Nevertheless, the long-standing nature of this disorder and the chronicity of related disorders suggest that complete recovery may be difficult. Due to the risk that cyclothymia may evolve into bipolar disorder, long-term treatment is usually indicated for this disorder.

TREATMENT RECOMMENDATIONS: CLIENT MAP

Types of mood disorders discussed in this chapter include major depressive disorder, dysthymic disorder, depressive disorder NOS, bipolar I and II disorders, and cyclothymic disorder. The information presented in this chapter about these disorders is summarized here according to the twelve elements in the Client Map format.

Client Map

Diagnosis

Mood disorders (major depressive disorder, dysthymic disorder, depressive disorder NOS, bipolar I and II disorders, cyclothymic disorder)

Objectives of Treatment

Stabilize mood

Alleviate depression, mania, and hypomania

Teach relapse prevention strategies and prevent relapse

Improve coping mechanisms, family and other relationships, career, and overall adjustment

Establish a consistent and healthy lifestyle

Assessments

Measures of depression and suicidal ideation, such as the Beck Depression Inventory and the Schedule of Affective Disorders and Schizophrenia (Seligman & Moore, 1995)

Measures of hypomania, including the Hypomania Checklist-32

Medical examination for physical symptoms

Broad-based inventory of mental disorders, such as the Minnesota Multiphasic Personality Inventory, to identify comorbid disorders

Clinician Characteristics

High in core conditions of empathy, genuineness, caring, and others

Comfortable with client's dependence and discouragement

Resilient

Able to promote motivation, independence, and optimism

Structured and present-oriented as well as capable of addressing long-standing patterns of difficulty and dysfunction

Location of Treatment

Usually outpatient setting, but inpatient setting if symptoms are severe, if risk of suicide is high, or if there is loss of contact with reality

Interventions to Be Used

Cognitive-behavioral, interpersonal, and related models of treatment

Education about disorder

Relapse prevention

Emphasis of Treatment

Emphasis on cognitions and behavior

Initially directive and supportive

Later on, less directive and more exploratory

Numbers

Primarily individual therapy

Family therapy often indicated

Group therapy useful after symptoms have abated

Timing

Medium duration (at least three to six months)

Moderate pace (one to two sessions per week)

Maintenance and extended follow-up phases common

Medications Needed

Mood stabilizers often indicated in combination with psychotherapy, especially for manic symptoms or severe depression

Adjunct Services

Increased activity

Homework assignments

Career counseling

Development of social and coping skills

Homogeneous support groups

Prognosis

Good for recovery from each episode

Fair for complete remission

Relapses common

Client Map of Karen C.

This chapter began with a description of Karen C., a thirty-year-old woman who began experiencing severe depression after her husband's departure for a tour of duty. Karen's case reflects many of the characteristics of people suffering from depression. Karen's mother had episodes of depression, a disorder that often has a familial component. Karen herself had suffered an early loss with the death of her father, was dependent and low in self-esteem, had few resources and interests, and looked to others for structure and support. Her current depression seemed to be a reactive one, triggered by her perception that her marriage was at risk. Her symptoms were typical of major depressive disorder and included both emotional features (hopelessness, guilt) and somatic features (sleep and appetite disturbances, fatigue). The following Client Map outlines the treatment for Karen.

Diagnosis

Axis I: 296.23 Major depressive disorder, single episode, severe, without psychotic features, with atypical features

Axis II: Dependent personality traits

Axis III: No known physical disorders or conditions, but weight change reported

Axis IV: Separation from husband due to his tour of duty, marital conflict

Axis V: Global assessment of functioning (GAF Scale): current GAF = 45

Objectives of Treatment

Reduce level of depression

Eliminate physiological symptoms

Improve social and occupational functioning

Increase self-esteem, sense of independence, and activity level

Improve communication and differentiation in marital relationship

Reduce marital stress and conflict

Reduce cognitive distortions and unwarranted assumptions

Assessments

Beck Depression Inventory, to be used at the start of each session

Safekeeping contract, in which client agrees not to harm herself (assumption is that client is not acutely suicidal)

Physical examination

Clinician Characteristics

Supportive and patient, yet structured

Able to model and teach effective interpersonal functioning

Able to build a working alliance rapidly with a discouraged and potentially suicidal client

Possibly female (and thereby able to serve as a role model)

Location of Treatment

Outpatient setting

Period of inpatient treatment possible if client does not respond to treatment quickly and remains relatively immobilized by depression

Interventions to Be Used

Interpersonal therapy to explore patterns in client's significant relationships (effects of early loss of her father, dependent and enmeshed relationship with her mother, extended conflict with her husband)

Encouragement of social interactions

Analysis and modification of client's thoughts about herself and her roles and relationships through cognitive therapy

Exploration of her associated emotions

Primary focus on client's present relationship with her husband and her lack of self-direction (interpersonal role disputes and interpersonal deficits)

Attention to helping client clarify and communicate her expectations and wishes to her husband and renegotiate their relationship

Encouragement for client to review strengths and weaknesses of her past and present relationships and to try out improved ways of relating, both at home and in therapy sessions

Encouragement of increased activity and regular exercise to increase client's energy level

Use of such strategies as role playing, examination of logic and belief systems, teaching of communication skills, and modeling

Emphasis of Treatment

High level of directiveness, given client's near-immobilization by her depression

Provision of guidance and structure by the therapist, in view of client's lack of a sense of how to help herself

Reduction of guidance and structure over time, to promote an increase in client's own sense of mastery and competence and to help her take responsibility for her life

High degree of support at the outset, given client's lack of friends and confidants

Shift of focus to include more exploration and education as client's symptoms abate and as she begins to develop some additional outside support systems (but support to remain relatively high)

Attention to both cognitive dysfunction (inappropriate generalizations, self-blame) and behavioral deficits (lack of activities, poor social and interpersonal skills, dependence on others)

Primary emphasis of treatment to be on client's relationships, even though affective symptoms are prominent (focusing on her feelings of depression would probably only further entrench her sense of hopelessness, and the precipitant of her present depression seems to be interpersonal)

Numbers

Individual therapy as the initial approach to treatment

Marital counseling once client's husband returns home

Client's mother may also be invited to attend several sessions if this idea is acceptable to client

Timing

Two sessions per week initially (to facilitate reduction of client's depression and suicidal ideation and improve her functioning)

One session per week after she is able to return to work

Relatively gradual and supportive pace at first (but as fast as client's fragile condition will allow)

Anticipated duration of three to nine months

Possible extension of treatment beyond symptom abatement (for preventive impact, given long history of dependent personality traits, and for possible value in averting recurrences)

Medications Needed

Referral to a psychiatrist for determination of whether medication may be indicated (given client's severe depression and hopelessness, even though hers seems to be a reactive rather than an endogenous depression, and given that medication combined with psychotherapy seems particularly effective in treating major depressive disorder)

Adjunct Services

Suggestion of some nondemanding tasks (such as reading about assertiveness, and increasing and listing pleasurable activities, particularly those involving socialization and physical exercise)

Participation in a women's support group after depression has been reduced

Prognosis

Very good for symptom reduction in major depressive disorder, single episode

Less optimistic for significant modification of underlying dependent personality traits

About a 50 percent probability of another major depressive episode (possibility should be discussed with client and her family and addressed through extended treatment, follow-up, or both)

Recommended Reading

Beck, J. (2005). *Cognitive therapy for challenging problems*. New York: Guilford Press.

Evans, K., & Sullivan, J. M. (2001). *Dual diagnosis: Counseling the mentally ill substance abuser* (2nd ed.). New York: Guilford Press.

Frank, E. (2005). *Treating bipolar disorder: A clinician's guide to interpersonal and social rhythm therapy*. New York: Guilford Press.

Keyes, C.L.M., & Goodman, S. H. (Eds.). (2006). *Women and depression*. Cambridge University Press.

Miklowitz, D. J. (2004). Family therapy. In S. L. Johnson & R. L. Leahy (Eds.), *Psychological treatment of bipolar disorder* (pp. 184–202). New York: Guilford Press.

Miklowitz, D. J. (2002). *The bipolar survival guide*. New York: Guilford Press.

Rosenthal, N. E. (2006). *Winter blues: Everything you need to know to beat seasonal affective disorder* (2nd ed.). New York: Guilford Press.

Sachs, G. S. (2004). *Managing bipolar affective disorder*. London: Science Press.

CHAPTER FIVE

Anxiety Disorders

Roberto M., a twenty-seven-year-old Latino man, sought therapy at the insistence of his fiancée, Luisa. For the past four months, Roberto had been experiencing nightmares and intrusive memories of having been sexually abused during his childhood by his family's housekeeper. Roberto had withdrawn from Luisa as well as from his other friends. He no longer engaged in running and other exercise, which had been a daily activity for him in the past. He refused to visit his parents, who still lived in the house where the abuse had occurred.

Luisa reported that Roberto appeared anxious and irritable. When she encouraged him to get out of the house and do something enjoyable, he became angry and told her that she just did not understand.

The change in Roberto had been triggered by a visit to the dentist. Roberto, who needed extensive dental work, apparently became emotionally and physically uncomfortable during the process. When he sought to leave the dental chair in the middle of the procedure, the authoritarian dentist told Roberto that he would just have to "put up with it." The powerlessness of the situation, the attitude of the dentist, and the reclining position of the chair brought back memories that Roberto had long tried to push out of his mind.

During the time of the abuse, the housekeeper had told Roberto that she would harm his baby sister if he told anyone, so he had kept it to himself. As an adult, he felt ashamed of his experiences and had continued to keep them secret. Although he had never forgotten his mistreatment by the housekeeper, Roberto had done his best to act as if the abuse had never happened, and he had built a rewarding life for himself. Now, however, those experiences could no longer be pushed aside.

Roberto was experiencing an anxiety disorder — posttraumatic stress disorder (PTSD) — typified by both emotional and physiological sensations of tension and apprehension, as well as by a reexperiencing of the trauma and by withdrawal. Although the condition sexual abuse of child (discussed in Chapter Three) would also probably be used to describe Roberto's childhood experiences, the diagnosis of PTSD is used as well, to convey the emotional distress and impairment that he was experiencing. His symptoms cannot accurately be classified as an adjustment disorder because the precipitant happened so long ago and because the nature and severity of Roberto's symptoms do not fit the profile for an adjustment disorder. Roberto did have some underlying depression, but his overriding emotion was anxiety.

OVERVIEW OF ANXIETY DISORDERS

Description of the Disorders

This chapter reviews the diagnosis and treatment of five categories of anxiety disorder:

1. Phobias (including agoraphobia, specific phobia, and social phobia)
2. Panic disorder
3. Obsessive-compulsive disorder
4. Trauma-related stress disorders (posttraumatic stress disorder and acute stress disorder)
5. Generalized anxiety disorder

Although these disorders differ in terms of duration, precipitants, secondary symptoms, and impact, they are all characterized primarily by anxiety.

Anxiety disorders represent one of the most prevalent mental health problems in the United States, with nearly 17 percent of the population experiencing an anxiety disorder in any given year (Barlow, 2002). People with anxiety are more likely to consult physicians than psychotherapists for treatment of anxiety symptoms. In fact, more people consult physicians due to stress-related anxiety than due to bad colds and bronchitis (Barlow, 2002). Social phobia is the most commonly reported anxiety disorder.

Many explanations have been advanced for the causes of anxiety. These explanations differ, but all are valid for some types of anxiety and for some people. In biological terms, anxiety disorders are likely to involve an inherited vulnerability that is activated by stressful life events. The person's ability to cope is then negatively impacted by "a cognitive style that may have both innate and learned origins" (Roy-Byrne & Cowley, 2002, p. 338).

Other theories conceptualize the cause of anxiety in different ways. Psychoanalytic theorists, for example, suggest that anxiety is the product of experiences in which internal impulses, previously punished and repressed, evoke distress that signals danger of further punishment if the impulses are expressed. To restate this theory in cognitive-behavioral terms, a stressor is believed to produce the perception of a threat, and this perception in turn is thought to produce a dysfunctional emotional reaction (anxiety): we learn to view a particular stimulus as frightening, either through our own experiences (conditioning) or through the experiences of others (social learning), so threats of that stimulus evoke apprehension and avoidance behavior. Existential theory explains free-floating or generalized anxiety as reflecting discomfort with the inherent meaninglessness of life.

Anxiety is a common and useful response inherent in everyday experiences. It plays an adaptive role, warning people of potential hazards and risky choices and providing a stimulus for effective action. For example, higher initial levels of distress in response to a diagnosis of cancer have been found to enhance coping (Fawzy et al., 1993). Anxiety becomes a disorder, however, when it is characterized by great intensity or duration and when it causes significant distress and impairment. Anxiety may become problematic at any age (Evans et al., 2005).

Anxiety, like depression, takes many forms, but anxiety usually is not severely debilitating, nor is it usually accompanied by loss of contact with reality. Anxiety may be free-floating and without obvious cause, or it may be what is called signal anxiety, occurring in response to a fear-inducing stimulus (such as recollection of an accident or pictures of snakes). Levels of anxiety fall on a continuum from mild to severe. Most people with anxiety try to manage or conceal their symptoms and go about their lives, often avoiding situations that increase their anxiety. The tendency to avoid anxiety has a circular effect, however, and often contributes to the development or worsening of fears.

Anxiety is characterized by both emotional and physiological symptoms. Fear and apprehension are the primary emotional symptoms but are often accompanied by others, including confusion, impaired concentration, selective attention, avoidance, and, especially in children and adolescents, behavioral problems. Anxiety-related symptoms contribute to suicidal ideation and behaviors as often as depressive symptoms do (Barlow, 2002). Common physiological symptoms of anxiety include dizziness, heart palpitations, changes in bowel and bladder functioning, perspiration, muscle tension, restlessness, insomnia, irritability, headaches, and queasiness. Evans and colleagues (2005) report that children and adolescents experiencing anxiety show an "attentional bias for threat'' (p. 173) just as adults do. In other words, they are hypervigilant for signs of possible danger. They are also likely to present somatic manifestations of their anxiety and are prone to depression later in life.

The symptoms of anxiety, such as heart palpitations and shortness of breath, are in themselves frightening and may lead the person who has them to believe that a heart attack is in progress or that some other serious physical ailment exists. Thus anxiety often breeds further anxiety. Because many medical conditions can be the cause of anxiety-like symptoms, any unexplained physiological symptoms that accompany anxiety warrant a referral for medical evaluation.

Typical Client Characteristics

The onset of severe anxiety is often preceded by financial or relational problems, a bereavement, job loss, or another aversive event that may place stress on an area in which the person is vulnerable, increase the person's responsibilities, or weaken the person's support system. Long-standing anxiety is often linked to an early trauma or a learned fear.

People who are prone to anxiety tend to see themselves as powerless and may view the world as a source of harm and threat. These people typically have few effective support systems and usually have not had a history of successfully coping with stressors. They characteristically have a high level of underlying stress (called trait anxiety), are pessimistic, have a need to overprotect and overcontrol, and react with elevated stress (called state anxiety) to even minor disturbances. Stress has been linked to a pattern of distorted self-evaluation, inability to control negative thoughts, selective attending to critical statements, and hypervigilance for threat or danger (Barlow, 2002). Like depression, anxiety tends to run in families through a combination of genetic predisposition, neurochemical process, and environmental factors (Evans et al., 2005).

More females than males seek treatment for anxiety disorders. Barlow (2002) suggests that the combination of negative life events, external locus of control, and attributional style may account for the increase in anxiety disorders in women. Others have suggested that men who are anxious may turn to alcohol rather than to therapy.

Anxiety is often accompanied by secondary symptoms and disorders. When depression is also present, the result may be what has been termed an agitated depression. About half of those with an anxiety disorder also have a personality disorder. Substance misuse and dependence on others are also common and may represent efforts to control the symptoms through self-medication and overreliance on support systems. Unfortunately, those behaviors seem more likely to worsen the anxiety than to alleviate it.

Assessment

Diagnosis of an anxiety disorder can be facilitated by the use of a brief inventory of anxiety symptoms. Probably the one most widely used is the Beck Anxiety Inventory, which assesses four categories of anxiety symptoms — neurophysiological, subjective, panic related, and autonomic (Beck & Steer, 1990).

When assessing clients with anxiety disorders, clinicians should be aware of any relevant cultural factors. White and Barlow (2002) note that ethnic identity, gender roles within the family, and level of acculturation play important roles in clinical presentation, assessment, and treatment. Eye contact, verbal and nonverbal communication, personal space, and verbal cues, such as tone and volume, may vary from culture to culture. Coping styles may also vary. For example, African Americans tend to use such coping strategies as gratitude and religiosity more than European Americans (White & Barlow, 2002). Some symptoms may also occur more frequently in specific cultural groups. For example, nearly 60 percent of African Americans with panic disorder experience occasional sleep paralysis compared with less than 8 percent of European Americans (White & Barlow, 2002). Some disorders may occur frequently in certain cultures but be nearly nonexistent in others. For instance, Cambodian populations experience "sore neck syndrome," and some Hispanic populations experience *ataque de nervios* (uncontrollable behaviors such as physical or verbal aggression, crying, and shouting) following the death of a loved one or other stressful life events (White & Barlow, 2002, p. 335; Paniagua, 2001).

McCabe and Antony (2002) mention two commonly used and studied semistructured interviews for the assessment of anxiety disorders: the Anxiety Disorders Interview Schedule for DSM-IV (ADIS-IV; Brown, Di Nardo, & Barlow, 1994) and the Structured Clinical Interview for DSM-IV Axis I Disorders (SCID-I; First, Spitzer, Gibbon, & Williams, 1997). Many self-report measures are also available, but the therapist should keep in mind that responses on these measures are not always accurate. Men, in particular, are more likely to underreport fear (McCabe & Antony, 2002). For a complete discussion of assessments for anxiety, the reader is referred to *The Practitioner's Guide to Empirically Based Measures of Anxiety* (Antony, Orsillo, & Roemer, 2001).

Preferred Therapist Characteristics

Although little research is available on the optimal therapist for the anxious client, that therapist is probably one who is stable and calm, untroubled by anxiety, and able to exert a relaxing and reassuring effect on the client. Beck and Emery (1985) suggest that the therapist be a model of patience and persistence, encouraging rather than forcing change.

The therapist treating anxiety, like the therapist treating depression, will probably begin with a moderate level of directiveness and a high level of supportiveness. A person who is anxious typically feels fragile and apprehensive and needs support and encouragement to engage in therapy. Although some directiveness on the part of the therapist is needed to give structure to the sessions, the anxious client is in emotional pain and therefore will usually be eager to collaborate with the therapist in relieving the symptoms. Once the debilitating anxiety has been reduced, the therapist can assume a more probing stance. Most people with anxiety have had a period of relatively healthy functioning before the onset of symptoms and should be able to respond to and grow from some exploration.

The therapist working with an anxious client should be comfortable enough with the client's pain and tension to refrain from taking complete control of the therapeutic process. Nevertheless, the therapist should also have enough concern and compassion to keep searching for an approach that will have a beneficial impact on the client. The therapist should be flexible and able to draw from a variety of therapeutic approaches in finding an optimal combination of techniques.

Intervention Strategies

Common Strategies. Treatments for most anxiety disorders will usually include the following eight elements:

1. *Establishment of a strong therapeutic alliance* that promotes the client's motivation and feelings of safety.
2. *Assessment of the manifestations of anxiety* and of the stimuli for fears. Although treatment of anxiety disorders usually does not emphasize psychodynamic interventions, an anxiety disorder related to a trauma may require considerable processing of affect, as well as exploration of past experiences and patterns.
3. *Referral for medical evaluation* to determine any contributing physical disorders, as well as the need for medication.
4. *The teaching of relaxation skills* and incorporation of regular relaxation into the person's lifestyle. Effective approaches to relaxation include meditation, exercise, visual imagery, and yoga, among others.
5. *Analysis of dysfunctional cognitions* that are contributing to anxiety and substitution of empowering, positive, more accurate cognitions.
6. *Exposure to feared objects*, which can be accomplished in many ways, including in vivo or imaginal desensitization, eye movement desensitization and reprocessing, and flooding.

7. *Homework*, to track and increase the client's progress and to promote the client's responsibility.
8. *Solidification of efforts to cope* with anxiety and prevent a relapse.

Cognitive-Behavioral Therapy. Optimal treatment of anxiety disorders involves multiple components, usually emphasizing cognitive-behavioral therapy (Barlow, 2002; Barlow, Raffa, & Cohen, 2002; Evans et al., 2005). Cognitive-behavioral therapy is not one specific treatment approach; rather it is the generic name given to the combination of cognitive therapy with behavior therapy. Because anxiety disorders vary considerably, treatment must be tailored to the specific nature of the disorder. Exposure-based treatment (developed by Wolpe, 1958), called systematic desensitization, involves teaching clients to relax while exposing them to the feared object or situation. This type of cognitive-behavioral approach can be particularly effective in the treatment of panic or specific phobia. Also effective is stress inoculation training (SIT), in which people learn to develop skills (muscle relaxation, thought stopping, breath control, guided self-dialogue, covert modeling, and role playing) to help them cope with anxiety. SIT includes three phases: (1) conceptualization of the problem and building of rapport, (2) skill acquisition and rehearsal, and (3) application and follow-through. Depending on the particular client and disorder, such techniques as imaginal and in vivo desensitization, relaxation, and hypnotherapy, which are designed to reduce fear and anxiety, may also be used.

Group Therapy. Group therapy is often used along with or in lieu of individual therapy in the treatment of anxiety. People with similar anxiety-related symptoms and experiences (for example, PTSD after a rape or social anxiety in interpersonal situations) can provide each other with a powerful source of encouragement, role models, and reinforcement.

Family Therapy. Family counseling can also be a useful adjunct to treatment. A highly anxious and constricted person may have a strong impact on the life of the family. Family members may benefit from help in understanding the disorder and in learning how to respond supportively and helpfully and without providing the secondary gains that may reinforce the symptoms. In some cases, as in the treatment of agoraphobia, partners may be trained as co-therapists, to encourage and motivate continued change at home.

Medication. Collaboration with a physician is important in treating some people with anxiety disorders because, as previously mentioned, anxiety-like symptoms can be caused by many medical conditions, such as those in the following list:

- Cardiopulmonary disorders (mitral valve prolapse, angina pectoris, and cardiac arrhythmia)
- Endocrine disturbances (hyperthyroidism, hypoglycemia)
- Neurological disorders
- Inflammatory disorders (rheumatoid arthritis, lupus erythematosus)
- Biochemical changes due to substances (diet or cold medications, amphetamines, caffeine, nicotine, or cocaine)

The therapist and the physician must determine whether a physical symptom is causing a psychological symptom or vice versa.

Medication sometimes can accelerate the treatment of certain anxiety disorders, among them panic disorder and obsessive-compulsive disorder, but hospitalization is rarely necessary. Outpatient psychotherapy of medium duration (months rather than weeks or years), combining cognitive and behavioral interventions with between-session practice, will usually be the best approach to treating anxiety disorders.

Prognosis

Two-thirds to as many as 95 percent of people with anxiety disorders show significant improvement after CBT, and some studies indicate that these improvements generally are maintained at seven-year follow-up (Evans et al., 2005). Prognosis for the treatment of specific anxiety disorders varies according to the disorder. Some anxiety disorders, such as phobias, usually respond very well to treatment; others, such as obsessive-compulsive disorder, are sometimes treatment resistant. Recurrences of anxiety disorders, like recurrences of mood disorders, are common. The setting of goals that focus on measurable behavioral and affective change is integral to treatment, and procedures for assessing progress toward goals (such as observation and the use of checklists, diaries, questionnaires, inventories, and even videotapes) often play a role in the monitoring of change. The next sections of this chapter focus on specific anxiety disorders and provide more information on their treatment and prognoses.

PANIC DISORDER

Description of the Disorder

The hallmark of panic disorder, as the name suggests, is attacks of panic that are unexpected. A panic attack is a circumscribed period of intense fear or discomfort that develops suddenly, usually beginning with cardiac symptoms and difficulty in breathing. A full panic attack is accompanied by at least four physiological symptoms, which may include sweating, nausea, and trembling in addition to rapid heartbeat, chest pain, and difficulty in breathing. Panic attacks typically peak within ten minutes, sometimes in as little as two minutes, and rarely last longer than thirty minutes (Eifert & Forsyth, 2005).

Three types of panic attacks have been identified: unexpected or uncued attacks (with no apparent trigger), situationally bound or cued attacks (in anticipation of specific stimuli, such as hearing that a thunderstorm is predicted), and situationally predisposed attacks (usually associated with specific fear-inducing triggers, such as the actual experience of a thunderstorm). By definition, at least some of the panic attacks that accompany panic disorder are unexpected, but people with this disorder may have all three types of attacks.

Panic attacks are common; up to 50 percent of adults will experience at least one panic attack in their lifetime, with only 10 percent developing recurrent attacks and panic disorder (Roy-Byrne & Cowley, 2002). Although most panic attacks occur during the waking hours, a panic attack that occurs during sleep may awaken the sleeping person. A given person may have infrequent panic attacks, with little impact, or may have many attacks each week, resulting in considerable distress and impairment.

Even a small number of panic attacks can be upsetting. The degree of upset depends on the person's interpretation of the symptoms, the person's underlying fears, and the extent of the person's anticipatory anxiety. People sometimes believe that their panic symptoms are indications of having a heart attack, losing control, or going crazy. They often experience a strong urge to escape (Eifert & Forsyth, 2005).

A physiological explanation of an initial panic attack focuses on the pivotal role of the amygdala and an overreaction of the autonomic nervous system to stressful life events (Roy-Byrne & Cowley, 2002). Thus a biological predisposition to stress causes an amplification of body sensations and anxious experiences in response to stressful triggers. In a sense, panic disorder can be viewed as a phobia of bodily sensations. The feelings of panic are caused by fear and stress, those bodily sensations are then misinterpreted, and the outcome is both increased fear and greater likelihood of additional panic attacks, in a self-perpetuating cycle.

According to *DSM-IV-TR* (American Psychiatric Association, 2000), a panic disorder is characterized by at least two unexpected panic attacks, neither of which can be explained by medical conditions or substance use, with one or more followed by at least a month of persistent fear of another attack, worry about the implications of the attack, and/or behavioral change (usually designed to avert future attacks) in response to the attack.

DSM-IV-TR recognizes a connection between panic disorder and phobic avoidance by establishing two subtypes of panic disorder: panic disorder without agoraphobia and panic disorder with agoraphobia. (A subsequent section of this chapter discusses agoraphobia itself, with or without panic disorder.) About half of all people with panic disorder will fall into each of the two groups. People who have panic disorder with agoraphobia typically associate their panic attacks with where they have occurred and avoid those places in an effort to prevent future attacks. They also are likely to misinterpret the attacks as imminent heart attacks or other catastrophes. As the panic attacks occur in more and more places, people with this disorder tend to restrict their activities until, in severe cases, they refuse to leave home; unfortunately, this safety-seeking behavior tends to maintain these people's inaccurate cognitions. Agoraphobia generally occurs within the first year of onset of panic attacks. People who have panic disorder without agoraphobia experience similar physical feelings of dizziness, rapid pulse, and fear of losing control or going crazy, but they tend not to associate those feelings with a particular place. They do, however, develop fear of having another attack, and frequently fear they may have a serious medical condition. They often seek medical treatment to allay their fears of an underlying terminal illness.

Estimates suggest that as many as half of all people with panic disorder have other disorders as well. Substance-related disorders (especially alcohol, used as self-medication in an effort to control panic attacks) is a frequent concomitant of panic disorder. Mood disorders, especially depression, occur in 25 to 65 percent of people with panic disorder (Barlow, 2002). Personality disorders (most commonly avoidant, dependent, or histrionic) are found in 40 to 65 percent of those with panic disorder (Baker, Patterson, & Barlow, 2002). Other kinds of anxiety disorders are also common.

Panic disorder typically has a sudden onset, beginning with a severe panic attack. Approximately 1 to 3.5 percent of the population of the United States will experience a panic disorder at some time in their lives (American Psychiatric Association, 2000). The approximate 2:1 female-to-male ratio has been consistently found in studies conducted around the world (Barlow, 2002). The age of onset for panic disorder peaks between the ages of fifteen and twenty-four, and again between the ages of forty-five and fifty-four, although young children and older adults may also experience initial panic attacks (Baker et al., 2002). Identifiable stressors typically accompany the initial attack, but the panic attacks tend to recur even after the stressor is resolved (Roy-Byrne & Cowley, 2002). In women, panic symptoms may be influenced by hormonal changes postpartum or by the female reproductive cycle (White & Barlow, 2002).

Typical Client Characteristics

Both panic disorder and its close relative, agoraphobia, seem to run in families, yet the results of genetic studies have not been conclusive. Roy-Byrne and Cowley (2002) report that most recent theories of the etiology of panic disorder focus on a genetic predisposition that is then triggered by one or more stressful life events, causing the person to "amplify body sensations and an anxious experience via catastrophic and other cognitive distortions" (p. 338). The risk of developing panic disorder is particularly high for female relatives of people with this disorder, whereas the male relatives of people with panic disorder are at particular risk for problems related to alcohol use (often, as mentioned, a mechanism for coping with anxiety). Panic disorder has also been linked to later-onset depression (Evans et al., 2005).

Assessment

White and Barlow (2002) recommend a comprehensive multimodal approach to the assessment of panic disorder with or without agoraphobia, including a clinical interview, behavioral assessment, self-report, and medical evaluation. Symptoms should be assessed before, during, and following treatment to determine how therapy is progressing (Baker et al., 2002). Such self-monitoring tools as panic diaries, self-report scales, and daily records are important for obtaining an accurate assessment and diagnosis as well as for treatment planning. Although not a formal assessment, establishing a fear and avoidance hierarchy can be helpful. The client is asked to create a list of feared situations. After the list is completed, the client is asked to rate both fear and avoidance for each item, with 0 representing no anxiety/panic or avoidance, and 8 representing a full range of anxiety and avoidance. This fear and avoidance hierarchy and the ADIS-IV mentioned earlier can provide useful measurements of avoidance, severity of panic, and panic-related symptoms, and can help determine the goals and priorities of therapy.

Preferred Therapist Characteristics

The first session with clients experiencing panic disorder is critical in establishing a successful therapeutic alliance. People with this disorder typically have a history of unsuccessful personal and professional efforts to ameliorate their anxiety and may feel demoralized as well as ashamed at not having been successful. These people also may feel angry at having been referred to a psychotherapist for what they believe is a medical or physical problem. Normalizing these reactions, as well as reassuring clients that effective treatments for this disorder are available, can contribute greatly to their motivation to engage in yet another treatment.

Psychoeducation about the symptoms and treatment of panic disorder often is a necessary component of working with clients (Baker et al., 2002). The therapist may need to be directive about the importance of monitoring and assessment of the panic disorder. The recommendations in the preceding section about the ideal therapist to treat anxiety disorders are also pertinent here.

Intervention Strategies

Cognitive-Behavioral Therapy. Many controlled clinical trials support the efficacy of various types of cognitive-behavioral therapy in the treatment of panic disorder (White & Barlow, 2002). Cognitive therapy, enhanced by behavioral interventions and sometimes combined with medication, has been found to be more effective than other interventions, no treatment, or treatment with medication alone (Baker et al., 2002; Evans et al., 2005). White and Barlow (2002) report a meta-analysis that included forty-three controlled studies of treatment for panic with agoraphobia. The results showed that CBT was associated with the largest effect size compared to approaches that combined drug treatment with psychological interventions. These findings make sense, because the disorder stems primarily from misinterpretations of physical symptoms. The cognitive interventions seek to change people's catastrophic and distorted thinking, and such behavioral techniques as distraction, comforting rituals, meditation, and relaxation contribute to the physiological reduction of anxiety that contributes to panic attacks.

Arntz and Van den Hout (1996), having reviewed multiple studies of cognitive therapy in the treatment of panic disorder, found that cognitive therapy has a strong positive impact on both the frequency of attacks and the fear of future attacks. In the studies they reviewed, 75 to 90 percent of people with panic disorder were panic free after treatment.

Panic-Control Therapy. The emphasis of treatment for panic disorder focuses on confronting the mistaken beliefs about the meaning of physical sensations. A multifaceted cognitive-behavioral treatment program for panic disorder has been developed by Barlow and his associates to address this issue (Craske & Barlow, 2006; White & Barlow, 2002). A unique component of Barlow's panic-control therapy (PCT) is progressive evocation of the somatic sensations of panic attacks. People are asked to spin in a chair, hyperventilate, or run up and down stairs (after receiving medical clearance, of course). Treatment interventions, including education, a combination of exposure and desensitization to the panic attacks, and cognitive restructuring, help people recognize that these sensations are not life threatening, and extinguish their fears. Such behavioral techniques as breathing retraining and relaxation enhance people's recovery from the disorder. Inventories and logs are used to assess the severity of the disorder and to track progress.

New Treatment Modalities. Several new therapies that show promise in the treatment of panic disorder include acceptance and commitment therapy (ACT) and sensation-focused intensive treatment (SFIT). SFIT combines treatments for panic and avoidance in an intensive self-study format over eight consecutive days. Treatment involves intentional exposure to the most feared situations without teaching techniques for reducing the anxiety. Initial findings show promise, but further research is needed (White & Barlow, 2002). ACT combines acceptance, compassion, and commitment to goals with interventions drawn from CBT. Clients learn to identify their thoughts and feelings and practice mindful acceptance when fear arises. Because ACT is relatively new, no long-term measures of efficacy are available at this time (Eifert & Forsyth, 2005). ACT is described in more detail in the section on generalized anxiety disorder.

Family and Group Therapy. Both family and group therapy have also received some support in treatment of this disorder. Family interventions, combined with specific treatments for panic attacks, can help ameliorate the impact that this disorder has on family functioning and relationships. Group therapy using cognitive-behavioral interventions has demonstrated high levels of effectiveness.

Medication. Medication is sometimes part of the treatment plan for panic disorder, but it can interfere with the impact of psychotherapy by artificially promoting relaxation and limiting people's ability to self-soothe and credit themselves with overcoming the disorder. Consequently, a referral for medication probably should be made only if psychotherapy alone clearly is not effective or if a person is having many severe panic attacks each week.

Selective serotonin reuptake inhibitors (SSRIs) are the preferred pharmacological treatment for panic disorder because they have few side effects, no dietary restrictions, and absence of tolerance or withdrawal symptoms (Evans et al., 2005; Roy-Byrne & Cowley, 2002). Paroxetine (Paxil) was the first SSRI to receive FDA approval for panic disorder (Evans et al., 2005); others, such as sertraline (Zoloft), have since been approved. Tricyclic antidepressant medications, notably clomipramine (Anafranil) and imipramine (Tofranil), have also contributed to the amelioration of panic disorder, as have monoamine oxidase inhibitors (MAOIs) and benzodiazepines. Two benzodiazepines, alprazolam (Xanax) and clonazepam (Klonopin), have been widely studied and found to be more effective than a placebo (Evans et al., 2005). Although frequently prescribed by physicians for the treatment of panic disorder, benzodiazepines involve the risk of developing physical dependence and withdrawal symptoms and have been shown to be ineffective in the treatment of comorbid depression (Roy-Byrne & Cowley, 2002). Antidepressant medication has been found to suppress panic attacks but not to diminish anticipatory anxiety, whereas anxiolytics have been found to reduce overall anxiety but not to affect panic attacks. Thus, medication should almost never be the sole modality of treatment for panic disorder. Roy-Byrne and Cowley (2002) report that the combination of psychotherapy and medication may enhance efficacy in treating panic attacks, but relapse often occurs when the medication is discontinued. People with this disorder also tend to have concerns (such as low self-esteem and interpersonal difficulties) that precede and underlie their panic attacks, so elimination of the panic attacks may not be sufficient; chronicity and incomplete remission are significant concerns in the treatment of this disorder. Psychotherapy, with or without medication, is necessary in helping effect those personal changes that are likely to prevent future episodes of anxiety disorders. Lifestyle changes can also contribute to relief of panic disorder. For example, caffeine is likely to increase the frequency and severity of panic attacks, so its use should be discouraged in people with this disorder. Regular exercise can help reduce levels of stress and anxiety.

Whether or not a person with panic disorder is referred for medication, the person almost always should be referred for an overall medical evaluation so that the therapist can be sure that the symptoms are indeed of psychological origin. Because people with panic disorder frequently believe their symptoms to be physiological in origin, they are likely to be receptive to the suggestion of a physical examination.

Prognosis

The prognosis for successful treatment of panic disorder, primarily through relatively short-term cognitive-behavioral therapy, is excellent, especially if treatment is sought early in the course of the disorder. One study (Craske & Barlow, 1993) found that 80 to 100 percent of the people treated were panic free after approximately fifteen sessions of treatment, and 50 to 80 percent of that number were viewed as having been cured of the disorder. More recent research is not quite as optimistic, but indicates a 75 to 95 percent success rate at the end of eight to fourteen weeks of treatment for panic disorder, with gains maintained one to two years later (Barlow, 2002). A multicenter study of the efficacy of medication therapy and CBT found that, early on, there was no difference in effectiveness between combined therapy and either CBT or medication alone. However, after treatment ended, CBT alone was found to be superior to medication alone or combined treatment (Evans et al., 2005). This finding is consistent with other studies that have shown a relapse rate of 30 to 90 percent following discontinuation of medication (Roy-Byrne & Cowley, 2002). Treatment of panic disorder without agoraphobia has a slightly higher rate of success than the rate for panic disorder with agoraphobia (Roth & Fonagy, 2005). Likelihood of relapse is strongly related to the presence of comorbid Axis I and II disorders.

PHOBIAS

Description of the Disorders

Phobias are characterized by two ingredients: a persistent, unwarranted, and disproportionate fear of an actual or anticipated environmental stimulus (for example, certain animals or insects, heights, being alone, enclosed places), and a dysfunctional way of coping with that fear, with resulting impairment in social or occupational functioning (such as refusal to leave one's home). People with phobias often experience either limited-symptom or full panic attacks when they are confronted with or expect to encounter the objects of their fear. Unlike attacks associated with panic disorder, panic attacks associated with phobias are usually cued attacks in which triggers can be identified. Anticipatory anxiety often accompanies an established phobia and may be associated with long-standing underlying apprehension and with avoidance behavior. People often react to these exaggerated and disabling fears with self-protective primal reactions (fight, flight, freeze, or faint). People with phobias typically are aware that their reactions are unreasonable yet feel powerless to change them.

DSM-IV-TR describes three categories of phobia: agoraphobia, specific phobia (formerly known as simple phobia), and social phobia. Specific phobia and social phobia are quite common. The *DSM* reports a lifetime prevalence of 3.5 percent for agoraphobia with or without panic disorder (American Psychiatric Association, 2000). Agoraphobia is more common in females, perhaps as much as twice as common as in males.

The incidence of new phobias is highest in childhood and then decreases with maturity, although many phobias have a chronic course. Myriad studies have shown that anxiety in childhood and adolescence often leads to depression at a later date (Barlow, 2002). Most phobias develop suddenly, with the exception of agoraphobia, which tends to have a gradual onset. Phobias, particularly agoraphobia, social phobia, and phobias of the animal type, seem to run in families, but whether this phenomenon is due to learning or to genetics is unclear. People with phobias usually reduce their anxiety by avoiding feared stimuli but simultaneously reinforce their fears through this phobic avoidance. As a result, phobias that have been present for longer than one year are unlikely to remit spontaneously (Antony & Barlow, 2002).

Typical Client Characteristics

The strongest symptoms experienced by people with phobias are racing heart, muscle tension, the urge to run, rapid breathing, an impending feeling of doom, feeling fidgety, shortness of breath, cold hands or feet, trembling, and pounding in the chest (McCabe & Antony, 2002). These symptoms may appear to a greater or lesser extent and in different order of occurrence in the various types of phobias. People with blood and injection phobia may also experience fainting, whereas those with other phobias do not (Antony & Barlow, 2002). Most people encountering a phobic item or situation describe a rush of fear followed by symptoms of arousal. The extent to which the person is sensitive to this physiological response plays a key role in the development of anxiety disorders.

Genetics and biology influence who develops phobias. Antony and Barlow (2002) conclude that what is most likely inherited is a "low threshold for alarm reactions or vasovagal responses which then interact with environmental influences to set the stage for the development of phobia" (p. 405). Thus the interaction of anxiety sensitivity and expected anxiety leads to avoidant behavior in an attempt to reduce the fear. Complicating the situation, people with specific phobias tend to hold distorted beliefs about the situations and objects they fear (Antony & Barlow, 2002).

People with phobias may be apprehensive and tentative, fearing failure and exposure, at the thought of the feared object or situation or when they are approaching new experiences (McCabe & Antony, 2002). They often feel vulnerable and have deficits in social skills and coping mechanisms. The particular nature of their phobias may limit their social and occupational opportunities and cause conflicts in their relationships. One client, for example, a successful lawyer, had a phobia related to driving. His job was accessible via public transportation, but when he and his wife began to discuss buying a house in the suburbs, he told her that she would have to arrange her work hours so that she could drive him to and from work. The resulting marital conflict led this client to seek therapy.

Assessment

In assessing clients for phobias, clinicians must be able to distinguish between phobias and delusional fears (Antony & Barlow, 2002). Assessment instruments, interview questionnaires, and self-reports are helpful for assessing phobias and are discussed in more detail in the section on specific phobias.

Preferred Therapist Characteristics

Exposure therapy is the most frequently used therapy for the treatment of phobias and may sometimes result in the therapist's treating the phobia where it occurs — at the client's home, for example, or other places (such as elevators or dentists' offices) that evoke fear. The therapist needs to be comfortable taking charge of the therapy and providing structure, direction, and suggested assignments while developing a positive working relationship with the client. Butcher, Mineka, and Hooley (2006) report that encouragement, instruction, suggestion, exhortation, support, and modeling on the part of the therapist can all contribute to the client's improvement.

Intervention Strategies

Exposure-based treatments that present people with feared objects or situations have been found to be the most effective and empirically supported treatments of phobia (Barlow et al., 2002; Evans et al., 2005; McCabe & Antony, 2002). Exposure-based therapy may occur in vivo or through imaginal desensitization, which occurs in the therapist's office and may include visualization or pictures of the feared object. Various types of pacing may be used (intensive, spaced, or graduated). Regardless of the location or pacing, all exposure-based treatments share the following five common features:

1. Development of anxiety hierarchies
2. Imaginal or in vivo systematic desensitization, possibly through modeling
3. Cognitive restructuring
4. Encouragement of expressions of feeling, a sense of responsibility, and self-confidence
5. Attention to any family related issues that may be impinging on the phobia or being affected by it and, frequently, inclusion of a partner or significant other in the desensitization process and in communication skills training (especially for the treatment of agoraphobia)

Other components that are frequently added to exposure-based treatment, such as relaxation training, breathing retraining, and paradoxical intention, have been found to be no more effective than the aforementioned combination of interventions alone (Barlow et al., 2002).

Unless the therapist has reason to believe that a person's phobia is linked to a more complex problem (such as a history of abuse), treatment will usually focus primarily on the symptom itself. A range of techniques has been designed to gradually introduce the person into the feared situation and teach fear-reducing techniques while the anxiety is being experienced. Most approaches to treating phobias are structured and directive and include procedures for quantifying and measuring the severity of the presenting problem and monitoring the client's progress. For example, progress in the treatment of agoraphobia can be reflected by the distance from home that a person becomes willing to travel and by the person's degree of anxiety while away from home.

Research has been exploring the effectiveness of spaced exposure versus intensive therapy. Chambless (1990) found that intensive and spaced treatments have the same rate of success, whereas both spaced therapy and graduated methodologies improved compliance rates and decreased relapse rates.

Keane and Barlow (2002) found that long, continuous-exposure sessions are as effective as short, interrupted sessions. Even so, the optimum rate of exposure is not clear. Research currently under way indicates that massed exposure, followed by spaced sessions, could be the most effective (White & Barlow, 2002).

Most theorists advocate exposing people to feared situations long enough for their fears to be aroused and reduced within a single session. Some studies, however, have also substantiated the value of allowing people to leave frightening situations when their anxiety becomes too uncomfortable, as long as they rapidly return to those situations. Encouraging people to focus on their anxiety and control it through coping self-statements, thought stopping, and relaxation techniques is preferable to encouraging the reduction of fear through distraction. The determination of which approach to exposure is likely to be the most successful, as well as of exactly how that approach should be implemented, depends on the nature and severity of the phobia and on the particular client. For example, massed-exposure sessions and spaced-exposure sessions can both be effective, but some people prefer not to participate in massed-exposure sessions, and their preference should be respected.

Flooding or implosion involves prolonged and intensive exposure (usually thirty minutes to eight hours) to the feared object until satiation and anxiety reduction are achieved. Teaching people to use coping self-statements enhances the impact of this exposure because it forces the person to reevaluate the actual threat. Flooding can cause overwhelming initial anxiety, however. If not properly implemented, it can ultimately worsen fears and related physical and emotional conditions, and it is often unappealing to clients. Therefore, it is not often used, but it is sometimes helpful if the feared situation can easily be recreated without causing any danger and when the client can be closely monitored — for example, treating a man with a balloon phobia by having him spend two forty-five-minute sessions in a room filled with balloons. By contrast, flooding would not be recommended for a driving phobia because that approach clearly could create danger.

Graduated exposure involves having a person confront the object of a phobia for a very brief time and then increasing the duration of exposure until the person can remain reasonably calm in the presence of the feared object or situation for approximately one hour. This approach could be very effective, for example, with a person who is able to look at cars and ride in cars while others are driving, but who has the specific fear of driving a car. Initially, the person could be encouraged to drive the car in the driveway or on his or her own street for a few minutes. The driving time would then gradually be increased as the person became more comfortable with driving.

Systematic desensitization begins by setting up an anxiety hierarchy — a list of the person's fears, organized according to severity. The therapist begins with the least frightening presentation of the feared object (often a picture or other image) and uses relaxation techniques to help the person become comfortable with that level of exposure. Presentations of the feared object gradually move up the hierarchy, with the person becoming acclimated to each successive level. For example, a person with a phobia of snakes might be shown a picture of one snake. After becoming comfortable with that level of exposure, a picture of several snakes might be shown in the next session, and so on, until the person reaches the top level of the hierarchy — the ability to look at a live snake. Systematic desensitization can be imaginal (conducted in the imagination), in vivo (conducted in context), or a combination of the two. More complex fears, as well as fears that are not amenable to treatment via in vivo exposure, can often be successfully treated through imaginal systematic desensitization.

Technological advances have widened the delivery options for exposure therapy. For example, videotapes have been used to expose patients to feared stimuli, audiotapes can help client's change negative cognitions, and the use of virtual reality has been used to simulate in vivo exposure for phobias of flying and fear of heights (Antony & Barlow, 2002). Only two controlled studies have been conducted to date on the use of virtual reality to treat phobias. In both studies, virtual reality was found to be equally as effective as in vivo or imaginal therapy (Antony & Barlow, 2002). Clearly, more studies across the entire range of phobias and technological systems (radio, mobile phones, computers, Internet) are needed.

A variety of effective options are also available when it comes to determining the pacing of exposure-based treatments. These include intensive therapy that occurs in one extended two- to three-hour session, treatment spaced out over weeks, and graduated treatment that slowly moves up the hierarchy of anxiety. For example, using graduated treatment, a client with a fear of elevators would move slowly up the fear hierarchy by first approaching an elevator, then standing in an elevator, then using the elevator to go up one floor, and finally taking the elevator to the top of the building. This would occur gradually over the course of several sessions, as the client's anxiety level decreased. In contrast, intensive exposure that occurs in one session would require the client to move through the same hierarchy in one intensive two- to three-hour session. For many phobias (such as animals, blood, dental procedures), one two- to three-hour session of in vivo exposure results in clinically significant improvement in 90 percent of cases (McCabe & Antony, 2002).

Although cognitive therapy can be an important adjunct to exposure therapy, it has not been shown to be effective alone in the treatment of phobias. However, cognitive-behavioral interventions can accelerate the treatment of phobias. For example, Socratic questions are designed by therapists to elucidate clients' cognitive distortions and encourage the testing of their validity, helping clients to understand, normalize, and manage their fears. CBT views inordinate fears as being maintained by mistaken or dysfunctional appraisals of situations. Sessions are structured, directive, and problem-oriented. Manageable homework assignments are another central feature of the treatment and are designed to help people face their fears and test and modify their cognitions. These assignments include such experiences as undergoing gradual exposure to feared stimuli, telling others about fears in order to reduce shame, and assessing the validity of beliefs. CBT stresses the principle of overcoming fears by confronting, rather than avoiding, them.

Prognosis

As already mentioned, childhood phobias often remit without treatment, but phobias that have been present for at least one year are unlikely to do so. Most people with phobias do not seek treatment for their symptoms, however, but tend simply to modify their lifestyles so as to tolerate their phobias. This tendency is unfortunate because specific phobias are among the most effectively treated disorders, and several controlled studies have found that up to 90 percent of people have significant symptom reduction after just two to three hours of therapy (Evans et al., 2005). Barlow and colleagues (2002) report a positive and enduring response to treatment in 60 to 70 percent of people who received exposure-based therapy for phobias. The literature indicates that exposure-based gains are lasting, even when treatment consists of a single three-hour session. In studies of children and adolescents, CBT produces treatment gains even at one-year follow-up (Evans et al., 2005).

No information is available on the effectiveness of pharmacotherapy alone in treating specific phobias. When phobias are not accompanied by severe depression or panic attacks, they generally do not require referral for medication. This point will be expanded on in later sections of this chapter, which deal with the three types of phobias.

Complete remission of a phobia is unusual, and people do tend to retain mild symptoms after treatment, although functioning is much improved. The presence of agoraphobia and personality disorders are frequent predictors of relapse.

Let us turn now to an examination of the three types of phobias described in *DSM-IV-TR:* agoraphobia, specific phobia, and social phobia.

Agoraphobia

Description of the Disorder

Agoraphobia, especially in association with panic disorder, is the most common phobia presented by people seeking treatment. *DSM-IV-TR* reports that 95 percent of people who seek treatment for agoraphobia also have panic disorder (which was discussed earlier). Agoraphobia is defined by *DSM-IV-TR* as "anxiety about being in places or situations from which escape might be difficult (or embarrassing) or in which help might not be available in the event of having an unexpected or situationally predisposed panic attack or panic-like symptom" (American Psychiatric Association, 2000, p. 396). The name of this disorder means "fear of the marketplace" ("marketplace" being the translation of the Greek term *agora*).

People with agoraphobia generally experience fear of losing control and having a limited-symptom panic attack (that is, developing one or a few specific symptoms — for example, loss of bladder control, chest pains, or fainting). As a result of this fear, the individuals restrict their travel and may refuse to enter certain situations without a companion. Places from which escape is difficult (such as cars, tunnels and bridges, supermarket checkout lines, and crowds) are particularly frightening. Exposure to phobic situations typically triggers intense emotional and somatic anxiety, including such symptoms as dizziness, faintness, weakness in the limbs, shortness of breath, and ringing in the ears. People with agoraphobia tend to avoid situations they perceive as dangerous and seek situations where they feel safe. Symptoms can lead to mild to severe restrictions in lifestyle. In severe cases of agoraphobia, people may define a "safe zone" (usually their homes) and be unable to go outside the perimeters (White & Barlow, 2002). This disorder typically begins in the person's twenties or thirties, later than most other phobias.

Typical Client Characteristics

People with agoraphobia tend to be anxious, apprehensive, low in self-esteem, socially uncomfortable, vigilant, concerned about their health, and occasionally obsessive. Depression, anticipatory anxiety, and passivity are common as well; these symptoms not only exacerbate this disorder but are also reactions to the circumscribed lives of the people who suffer from it. Medical problems are often presented, and people with this disorder may view those problems as the reasons for their limited mobility.

People with agoraphobia may avoid caffeine, exercise, and sexual and other activity that produces somatic sensations resembling those associated with panic. White and Barlow term this "interoceptive avoidance" (2002, p. 330). They may also develop substance use problems in an effort to reduce their anxiety, with men more likely than women to self-medicate (Eifert & Forsyth, 2005). Accompanying disorders, particularly avoidant, dependent, and histrionic personality disorders, as well as a history of generalized anxiety disorder, separation anxiety disorder, and social isolation in childhood, are often reported, along with a family history of agoraphobia (Meyer & Deitsch, 1996).

Sometimes a person with agoraphobia feels simultaneously dominated by and dependent on a significant person. This is often the "safe person," the one with whom the person who has agoraphobia feels most comfortable, yet who also often contributes to the dynamics of the disorder. For example, a man's safe person may be his wife, but she may be covertly reinforcing his fears so as to maintain his need for her. Marital difficulties may trigger or exacerbate agoraphobia; the disorder can provide the secondary gain of cementing a marital relationship.

Assessment

The triggering role of stress is common in all anxiety disorders (White & Barlow, 2002). Symptoms can be particularly severe for some women in association with premenstrual dysphoric disorder (White & Barlow, 2002) and are often worsened by caffeine consumption. Such inventories as the Beck Anxiety Inventory (Beck & Steer, 1990), the Mobility Inventory for Agoraphobia (Chambless, Caputo, Gracely, Jasin, & Williams, 1985), and the Agoraphobic Cognitions Questionnaire (Chambless, Caputo, Bright, & Gallagher, 1984) can be useful in assessing symptoms. Suicide risk should also be assessed, as people with agoraphobia often have significant impairment in functioning and quality of life and have an increased rate of suicidal ideation (Baker et al., 2002).

Preferred Therapist Characteristics

Providing support, compassion, acceptance, and empathy is essential in the treatment of all anxiety disorders (Eifert & Forsyth, 2005). This is especially true for agoraphobia. Encouragement and reinforcement can also help the client take risks. The therapist's comfort with providing structure and contextual therapy, as well as with the client's initial dependence, is particularly important. As is true with all phobias, therapist modeling can have a positive effect.

Intervention Strategies

According to White and Barlow (2002), agoraphobia that is seen for treatment is usually a part of panic disorder. If the panic disorder is treated, the agoraphobia often improves, as do any co-occurring mood and personality disorders. The effectiveness of panic-control therapy (PCT) in the treatment of panic disorder with agoraphobia has been well documented in numerous studies and one meta-analysis (Goldstein, de Beurs, Chambless, & Wilson, 2000). White and Barlow (2002) report that more than twenty-five controlled clinical trials support the effectiveness of PCT for the treatment of panic disorder with agoraphobia. A meta-analysis of treatment outcomes in forty-three controlled studies showed that PCT yielded the largest effect size (0.88) in comparison to cognitive therapy or medication alone (Barlow et al., 2002). Approximately 75 percent of the people treated for agoraphobia achieved significant improvement in symptoms and functioning, and 65 percent maintained gains at two-year follow-up (Barlow et al., 2002).

Several new approaches show promise, but more research is needed to determine if they are as effective as PCT. Sensation-focused intensive treatment (SFIT) combines treatments for panic and avoidance in a CBT self-study format that takes place over eight consecutive days (White & Barlow, 2002). Acceptance and commitment therapy (ACT), as explained earlier, is another treatment methodology that shows promise. Clearly, additional studies need to be conducted on the effectiveness of these treatments.

If the agoraphobia is not accompanied by panic attacks, then behavioral methods in combination with cognitive therapy are generally the treatment of choice (White & Barlow, 2002). Not surprisingly, exposure to frightening situations — in sessions and through homework assignments — is the key element of most approaches to treating agoraphobia, and many variations on this strategy have been developed. The client should remain in the exposure situation long enough, and should repeat the exposure frequently enough, for the anxiety to be diminished. This procedure is called habituation. Fear of habituation may precipitate clients' noncompliance with treatment and their premature termination; therefore, a carefully paced and supportive approach is indicated.

One study indicates that clients treated with twelve sessions of graduated, self-paced exposure showed an 87 percent improvement, with 96 percent remaining in remission after two years and 77 percent at five years. The most important predictor of relapse was "residual agoraphobia," suggesting the need to ensure that treatment continues until all symptoms are eliminated (White & Barlow, 2002).

Other behavioral interventions shown to reduce symptoms of agoraphobia include training in relaxation and assertiveness. Cognitive therapy — using thought stopping, restructuring of negative thoughts, and training in positive self-statements about coping abilities — has also contributed to symptom relief, especially in combination with exposure (Goldstein et al., 2000; White & Barlow, 2002). Logs of symptoms and of exposure activities are helpful adjuncts to treatment and can be used to assess and reinforce progress. Skills training has also been shown to be a useful adjunct to CBT.

Both family and group therapy can also enhance the treatment of agoraphobia; indeed, several studies suggest that family dynamics should receive attention in the treatment of people with agoraphobia because the disorder affects the entire family system. White and Barlow (2002) report an uncontrolled clinical trial which indicated that training spouses as co-therapists effected a 90 percent improvement rate in the person with agoraphobia. Other studies showed continuing improvement at four- and nine-year follow-up. Partner involvement, either as coaches or as participants in family therapy, improves communication, educates spouses or significant others about the manner in which their role as a safe person actually reinforces agoraphobic behavior, improves the modification of behavior, and helps maintain continued success after treatment has ended. Husbands who were supportive and involved in their wives' recovery reported concurrent marital improvement. As for group therapy, treatment in a group setting can help reduce dependence on the safe person and can offer models and support, as well as motivation for remaining in the group and practicing behaviors between sessions and after treatment ends (White & Barlow, 2002).

Although little research is available, some movement has been made in the area of self-directed treatments for agoraphobia. Several studies have compared therapist instruction with computer-assisted instruction and text instruction in treatment delivery. No difference in outcomes was found; however, in severe cases of agoraphobia, text instruction was not shown to be effective (White & Barlow, 2002). More research is needed on alternative methods of delivering mental health treatment in general.

Medication, particularly drugs designed to reduce anxiety, is sometimes combined with psychotherapy in the treatment of agoraphobia. Research indicates that although such combination treatment is effective in the short term, high relapse rates occur when the medications are discontinued. Over the long term, medication shows no advantage over cognitive-behavioral therapy alone (White & Barlow, 2002). Such medications as anxiolytics and benzodiazepines may actually reduce the effectiveness of CBT, as they decrease the anxiety necessary for exposure therapy to work. Moreover, withdrawal from medication sometimes triggers a relapse. Medication does have a role in the treatment of agoraphobia, especially when it accompanies panic disorder, but medication alone clearly is inferior to exposure treatment, and, even as an adjunct to psychotherapy, medication should be used with great caution, perhaps only for severe and treatment-resistant cases.

Prognosis

Although many people with agoraphobia continue to have underlying fears, there is no doubt that treatment dramatically improves their quality of life. Effective treatment has also been shown to have a positive impact on co-occurring anxiety and depression and, in one study, was also shown to reduce alcohol misuse (White & Barlow, 2002). Although relapse is not unusual, a relapse seems easier to treat than the original disorder.

Specific Phobias

Description of the Disorders

DSM-IV-TR defines a specific phobia as "a marked and persistent fear that is excessive or unreasonable, cued by the presence or anticipation of a specific object or situation" (American Psychiatric Association, 2000, p. 449). Common specific phobias include fear of dogs, snakes, heights, thunderstorms, flying, injections, and the sight of blood, but they may also involve unusual objects or situations, such as balloons or stairs with openings between the treads.

DSM-IV-TR classifies phobias into five groups:

1. Animal type
2. Natural environment type (such as heights or thunderstorms)
3. Blood-injection-injury type
4. Situational type (such as flying, escalators, bridges, public speaking)
5. Other type (such as fear of choking or contracting an illness)

The situational type, which usually begins in the middle twenties, is most common in adults; the animal type and the blood-injection-injury type are most common in children. Females are more likely to develop phobias, particularly of the animal type. Men are more likely to fear spiders, deep water, and heights. Antony and Barlow suggest that differences in phobia rates between genders may be related to the fact that men tend to underreport their fears. Women are more likely to have learned fearful behavior through modeling. Women, in general, seek treatment at higher rates than men. One study of men and women found that the most frequently feared objects and situations (in descending order) are heights, snakes, closed spaces, spiders, injuries, flying, darkness, and dentists (Antony & Barlow, 2002).

Adults with specific phobias typically recognize the excessive or unreasonable nature of their reactions, but the phobias still may interfere with activities and relationships and may cause considerable distress. Exposure to feared stimuli typically results in high anxiety and perhaps even in a situationally related or cued panic attack. Tantrums and clinging may be manifested by children in frightening situations. A minimum duration of six months is required for the diagnosis of a specific phobia in a person under the age of eighteen.

Phobias in children are relatively common and most remit spontaneously; if a phobia persists into adulthood, however, it is unlikely to remit without treatment. A phobia may stem from a childhood fear that has not been outgrown and has been entrenched by avoidance, or the phobia may have begun in adulthood. Researchers disagree on the exact role that experience, vicarious acquisition, and information learning have on the development of phobias. Genetics and environment both seem to play a role in the development of specific phobias, but the extent that either plays and the differences in their role in causing phobias are yet to be resolved (Antony & Barlow, 2002). Some people present with multiple phobias, but these often involve a common underlying fear that can become the focus of treatment.

Specific phobias are quite common, with a lifetime prevalence rate ranging from 7 to 11 percent (McCabe & Antony, 2002). Nearly 50 percent of the population have a lifetime fear of one sort or another (Antony & Barlow, 2002). However, only a small percentage of people develop a disabling phobia that interferes with daily life, and even fewer will seek treatment for their phobias; instead, the usual responses are modifications in lifestyle and accommodation to avoid episodic anxiety.

Typical Client Characteristics

Very little information is available about common personality patterns in people with specific phobias, probably because the disorder is so pervasive and diverse and tends to be linked more to experiences than to personality traits. Nevertheless, people with specific phobias do have a disproportionate number of first-degree relatives who have similar phobias and who may share a common genetic predisposition toward fear and/or may have communicated these phobias to other family members (Antony & Barlow, 2002).

Anxiety in response to physical sensations may play a role in the development of specific phobias, especially claustrophobia (McCabe & Antony, 2002). When anticipating or confronting feared objects or situations, people with specific phobias typically become agitated and tearful and may experience physical symptoms of anxiety, such as shortness of breath, fear of doom, desire to run, and heart palpitations. People with phobias of the blood-injection-injury type sometimes faint in the presence of the feared stimulus. A medical examination may be a useful safeguard with fragile or highly anxious clients, to ensure that they can handle the temporarily increased stress caused by treatment.

Phobias are often accompanied by other anxiety, mood, and substance-related disorders and may have been preceded by traumatic or very frightening experiences (McCabe & Antony, 2002). The therapist should elicit information on antecedent events, comorbid disorders, and secondary gains that may complicate treatment of the disorder.

Assessment

A variety of assessments that measure phobic reactions to spiders and snakes are available. For example, the Spider Questionnaire (SPQ; Klorman, Hastings, Weerts, Melamed, & Lang, 1974) and the Snake Questionnaire (SNAQ; Klorman et al., 1974) are both thirty-item self-report scales. McCabe and Antony (2002) report that there currently are no published assessments for fears of other animals, such as cats, birds, or rodents. However, a questionnaire for dog phobia is in development. Other assessments for specific phobias include the Medical Fear Survey, a fifty-item self-report scale that measures fear of injections, blood drawing, sharp objects, and medical examination, and the Dental Anxiety Inventory, which measures fear of dental procedures. A more complete discussion of assessment tools for specific phobias can be found in McCabe and Antony (2002).

Preferred Therapist Characteristics

Treatment of specific phobias is often anxiety provoking for clients, and a therapist who models nonfearful behavior can be an important part of treatment. However, Antony and Barlow (2002) report that observational learning is not enough to effect significant change. A therapist who is supportive and optimistic about the outcome of treatment and who can communicate acceptance and empathy while still encouraging people to experience frightening situations is ideal. Creativity and flexibility can be useful in planning exposure and related treatments. When working with clients who are averse to in vivo exposure, especially in phobias related to heights, therapists may need to accompany the client to the location.

Intervention Strategies

Specific phobias are the most treatable of all anxiety disorders. Exposure, typically involving prolonged contact with feared objects or situations, is the empirically supported treatment of choice for this disorder. In this approach, a list (usually including about ten feared stimuli) is developed. To facilitate the establishment of a hierarchy, each of the listed stimuli is then rated on a scale of 1 to 100 for the level of fear and avoidance it provokes. In vivo or imaginal desensitization is then used to lessen fear. This approach to treatment involves relaxation and exposure to one item at a time until the anxiety connected to that item is reduced to a manageable level. In vivo treatment is usually preferable, but imaginal exposure involving visualization and pictures can also be very effective, especially if it is combined with carefully planned actual contact with feared stimuli outside the treatment sessions. Some use is being made of virtual reality techniques to provide exposure treatment for fear of flying and other specific phobias. One extended session (two to three hours) may lead to extremely significant improvement in 90 percent of cases of specific phobia (McCabe & Antony, 2002).

Combining exposure treatment with encouragement to develop a sense of mastery usually contributes to the effectiveness of treatment for specific phobias. Exposure treatment can also be enhanced by the following techniques:

- Imaginal flooding (used carefully)
- Use of positive coping statements
- Paradoxical intention (focusing on anticipatory anxiety)
- Thought stopping
- Thought switching

- Success rehearsal
- Assertiveness training
- Hypnosis
- Cognitive restructuring
- Increased exposure to and awareness of internal cues of anxiety
- Modeling by the therapist or another
- Reinforced practice
- Supportive and family therapy

Cognitive strategies can be integrated into an exposure-based treatment program to enhance treatment effectiveness. However, cognitive approaches alone are usually ineffective in the treatment of specific phobias. One study indicated that cognitive restructuring alone was better than either education or being placed on a wait-list and not receiving treatment for dental phobia. In general, however, exposure-based treatment combined with cognitive restructuring is the most effective treatment approach (Antony & Barlow, 2002).

Massed exposure, which takes place in a single two- to three-hour session, seems to lead to significant fear reduction (Antony & Barlow, 2002), particularly for circumscribed phobias, such as dental phobias or phobias of the animal type. More complex phobias, as well as the blood-injection-injury type (which may cause fainting), usually need somewhat longer and more gradually paced treatment.

Medication is rarely indicated in the treatment of specific phobias, and may actually interfere with the person's ability to benefit from the effects of exposure-based treatments. Benzodiazepines, in particular, tend to reduce anxiety and prevent the person's fear from reaching the level necessary for the client to benefit from exposure-based treatment (Antony & Barlow, 2002). Short-term treatment with benzodiazepines (for example, taking alprazolam during an airplane flight or thirty minutes before dental treatment) was found to be effective for reducing anxiety connected to a specific event. However, in both cases, greater fear was experienced with the next occurrence of the feared situation. In contrast, cognitive-behavioral therapy was associated with fear reduction and further improvements (Antony & Barlow, 2002).

Few studies have looked at the effectiveness of group therapy for specific phobias. One study using exposure and modeling to treat spider phobia yielded significant improvement (Ost, 1996). Groups of three or four were found to be more effective than groups of seven or eight.

Prognosis

The prognosis for treatment of specific phobias is generally excellent, with most people (70 to 85 percent) showing significant improvement. Often, however, some residual apprehension associated with feared stimuli remains or returns years later. If noncompliance is impeding treatment, the presence of secondary gains should be investigated.

Social Phobia

Description of the Disorder

Social phobia, also called social anxiety disorder, is very common. The National Comorbidity Survey Replication indicates a 12 percent lifetime prevalence rate (Kessler, Berglund, et al., 2005). Social phobia is defined by *DSM-IV-TR* as "a marked and persistent fear of one or more social or performance situations in which the person is exposed to unfamiliar situations or to possible scrutiny by others" (American Psychiatric Association, 2000, p. 456). Underlying the situational fear is worry that the person will do or say something that will be humiliating or embarrassing (Hofmann & Barlow, 2002).

Situations involving evaluation are likely to be particularly threatening. Actual or threatened exposure to such situations typically produces an immediate anxiety response that may involve noticeable physical symptoms, such as blushing, perspiration, hoarseness, and tremor (Markway & Markway, 2003). These symptoms can contribute to worsening of the original fear by exacerbating embarrassment. Typically, people with social phobia avoid anxiety-provoking social or occupational situations. Continued avoidance behaviors associated with social phobia can sometimes lead to social isolation.

Social phobias often focus on one or more specific situations, such as public speaking, eating in public, taking tests, writing while observed, and being interviewed. For men, urinating in a public restroom may cause undue anxiety.

People who fear most social situations are described as having a generalized type of social anxiety disorder. One client who was typical of people with social phobia, generalized type, had married the daughter of a family friend and secured stable employment, but his life was still shaped by his phobia. He sought treatment at the age of thirty-five because he saw himself as harming his family; he had turned down several promotions because they involved leading meetings, and he refused to attend events at his child's school because of his fear of meeting new people. He and his wife had little social life outside their immediate families.

Considerable impairment can be evident in people with social phobia. Staying in their comfort zones and avoiding anxiety-producing experiences tend to reduce personal and professional opportunities. People with this disorder are frequently underemployed, have a relatively low rate of marriage, and may have panic attacks and suicidal thoughts related to the phobia. As is true with specific phobias, adolescents and adults typically recognize the excessive nature of their fears. Nevertheless, social phobia is unlikely to remit without treatment.

Children with this disorder often exhibit selective mutism, school refusal, separation anxiety, and excessive shyness. A duration of at least six months is required for the diagnosis of this disorder in a person under the age of eighteen.

Several explanations have been offered for social phobia, including deficits in social skills, conditioned responses to painful experiences, emotional blocks, deficits in perceptual or cognitive processing, and oversensitivity to anxiety. The onset of social phobia may immediately follow a humiliating incident, or it may be insidious (Markway & Markway, 2003). Males and females are equally likely to seek treatment for social phobia, but the disorder seems to be more common in women, at a ratio of 3:2 (Kessler, Berglund, et al., 2005). For both men and women, however, social phobia tends to begin in adolescence; it rarely begins after the age of twenty-five and, without treatment, usually has a chronic course.

Typical Client Characteristics

People with social phobia tend to fear their own emotional reactions to new situations. In social interactions, they rate themselves negatively; exhibit "socially pleasing behaviors," such as smiling, agreeing, apologizing, and making excuses; and typically manifest submissive and avoidant behavior (Hofmann & Barlow, 2002). Because they expect they will not measure up in social situations, they are often hypervigilant for any reactions that reinforce their negative expectations (Markway & Markway, 2003). This excessive focus on their own reactions siphons their attentional resources away from performance of the task at hand, and results in decreased performance on tests, in social interactions, and in interpersonal skills. The outcome is increased anxiety and a vicious loop that includes avoidance of the feared situation and impaired performance.

In addition to exhibiting low self-esteem, people with social phobia may be fragile and easily hurt; sensitive to anger, criticism, or other means of social disapproval; and weak in social skills (Hofmann & Barlow, 2002). These deficits can take many forms. For example, some people with this disorder mask their anxiety with aggression; others seem shy and insecure; and still others participate in avoidant behaviors, such as drinking alcohol before a social event, limiting the time they remain at a social event, or avoiding eye contact (Markway & Markway, 2003).

Both genetic and social factors play a role in the development of social phobia. Twin studies show a 24 percent concordance rate of social phobia in identical twins, suggesting a genetic component. Hofmann and Barlow (2002) report that social phobia occurs at a rate three times higher for relatives of people with the disorder. Inherited temperament characteristics of shyness, timidity, or fearfulness when meeting new people can contribute to the disorder. Behavioral inhibition in childhood is frequently associated with the development of social phobia in adolescence (Hofmann & Barlow, 2002). Social skills, like many others, are learned through family interactions and practice. Thirteen percent of people with social phobia have reported that observational learning was an important part of the development of their disorder (Markway & Markway, 2003).

Social phobia is also associated with a broad range of accompanying disorders. Fifty percent of people with social phobia also have a depressive disorder (Kessler, Chiu, et al., 2005), and as many as one-third also misuse alcohol (Butcher et al., 2006). Other anxiety disorders, avoidant personality disorder, and substance-related disorders commonly co-occur. Educational, marital, occupational, financial, and interpersonal difficulties are also likely to be seen in people with social phobia.

Assessment

Behavioral assessment tests, interview-rated scales, and self-report scales such as the Fear of Negative Evaluation Scale and the Social Interaction Anxiety Scales (SIAS; Mattick & Clarke, 1998) can be very helpful in assessing social anxiety. Journals, logs, and other self-monitoring forms can also be used to assess symptoms and monitor progress. Because of the high incidence of co-occurring disorders, clients should also be assessed for other anxiety disorders, depression, and substance-related disorders in particular.

Preferred Therapist Characteristics

Clients with social phobia typically bring their interpersonal discomfort into the therapy room and are fearful of possible rejection or disapproval by the therapist. An important role for the therapist, then, is to help clients manage the initial anxiety well enough that they do not flee therapy before the process can begin. The development of trust can be a slow process. This is especially true for people with intense social fears (Markway & Markway, 2003). The client with social phobia may not be ready for exposure therapy or may be unable to complete homework assignments due to sensitivity to perceived criticism. Therapists working with such clients must take care not to be rejecting, angry, or critical. They should examine their own beliefs about the process of change, recognize the need to slow down the process, and praise attempts at progress, rather than looking for immediate results or perfection.

Intervention Strategies

The treatment of social phobia is more complex than the treatment of a specific phobia because the impact of social phobia is usually broader and greater.

Although the repertoire of useful behavioral interventions is the same for all phobic disorders, the treatment plan for social phobia is typically multifaceted and is aimed both at reducing fear and at improving socialization and social skills. Cognitive interventions are almost always integrated with behavioral ones.

In vivo desensitization, training in social skills, cognitive restructuring, and relaxation techniques achieve the highest levels of treatment efficacy for social phobia (Barlow et al., 2002). Exposure interventions in the treatment of social phobia generally change the person's beliefs about a situation, even without cognitive restructuring techniques. Hofmann and Barlow (2002) report that "repeated and prolonged exposure to social threat in the absence of all manner of avoidance strategies will lead to an unlearning or extinction of the learned alarm response, improvement of perceived social skills, and decrease in anxious apprehension (including self-focused attention)" (p. 470). They found that either CBT or exposure therapy alone is effective in the treatment of social phobia.

Cognitive therapy is especially useful in improving the accuracy of people's self-ratings, their perceptions of the likelihood of receiving negative reactions from others, and their assessments of the impact of such negative reactions (Foa, Franklin, Perry, & Herbert, 1996). Some form of self-monitoring is also a valuable aspect of the treatment and may involve soliciting feedback from others, role playing, rehearsal with videotaping or audiotaping, self-ratings, and ratings by others. Homework assignments, to facilitate the application of in-session learning, are almost always part of the treatment. Social skills training may focus on communication skills, tone of voice, posture, eye contact, and other aspects of socialization, according to the needs of the individual client. Relaxation techniques, such as abdominal breathing, visualization, and cue-controlled relaxation, can also be helpful in reducing the anxiety associated with social phobia (Markway & Markway, 2003).

Cognitive-behavioral group therapy (CBGT), developed by Heimberg and colleagues (1998) for treatment of social phobia, is included in a list of empirically supported treatments by the American Psychological Association (Hofmann & Barlow, 2002). CBGT is usually conducted in weekly 2.5-hour sessions over a twelve-week period. Clients reported less anxiety posttreatment, which was maintained at six-month follow-up. CBGT (like CBT) is based on the assumption that changes in cognitions are necessary for treatment progress to occur. Group therapy is valuable for people who are not too incapacitated by social phobia. The group interaction gives people the opportunity to learn new skills from others, experiment in a safe setting with new ways of relating, and receive feedback from peers.

Medication does not cure social phobia, but it is sometimes used in combination with psychotherapy, especially to reduce performance anxiety and improve people's ability to participate in therapy. To date, only two SSRIs — paroxetine (Paxil) and sertraline (Zoloft) — and the serotonin-norepinephrine reuptake inhibitor venlafaxine (Effexor) have received FDA approval for the treatment of social anxiety disorder. Other medications, such as MAOIs, beta-blockers, and benzodiazepines, have also been used with some success. To date, only two studies on the effectiveness of benzodiazepines — clonazepam (Klonopin) and alprazolam (Xanax) — on social phobia have been conducted. Both were found to be more effective than placebo at reducing social anxiety symptoms; however, benzodiazepines can lead to physical dependence and a high rate of relapse after discontinuation. They are also contraindicated in people who use alcohol or who have co-occurring depression. Hofmann and Barlow (2002) report that most people returned to pretreatment levels two months after discontinuing medications and that relapse rates are higher when medication is used than in the use of cognitive-behavioral therapy.

Prognosis

Behavioral, cognitive, and combined cognitive-behavioral interventions have been found to be successful in the treatment of social phobia (Evans et al., 2005). Direct comparison has not indicated greater efficacy of any one of these and probably CBT should generally be the treatment of choice. Evans and colleagues note that a variety of medications have been reported to be helpful in 40 to 55 percent of cases, but these clients still retained clinically significant symptoms. A combination of medication management and CBT showed a slightly greater efficacy than either treatment alone.

OBSESSIVE-COMPULSIVE DISORDER

Description of the Disorder

Great strides have been made over the last twenty years in understanding and successfully treating obsessive-compulsive disorder (OCD). According to *DSM-IV-TR*, people diagnosed with OCD have obsessions (recurrent intrusive thoughts, images, or impulses) or compulsions (repetitive, purposeful, driven behaviors or mental acts designed to reduce anxiety or avoid a feared circumstance) or a combination of the two (American Psychiatric Association, 2000). These thoughts and behaviors are distressing and interfere with daily activities and social and occupational functioning. People with OCD typically realize that their thoughts or behaviors are excessive and unreasonable yet are unable to get rid of them. In adolescents or adults who do not see the excessive or unreasonable nature of their thoughts or actions, the disorder is described as "with poor insight." The course of this often chronic disorder is typically static or worsens without treatment, although symptoms may come and go in response to stressors (Taylor, Thordarson, & Sochting, 2002).

Specific obsessions and compulsions are the hallmarks of this disorder and distinguish it from the similarly named but unrelated obsessive-compulsive personality disorder (OCPD), in which obsessions and compulsions are not present; rather, a perfectionistic or compulsive lifestyle characterizes people with OCPD (see Chapter Eight). In OCD, obsessions typically have some content that is unacceptable to the client (because it is immoral, illegal, disgusting, or embarrassing) and that creates considerable anxiety. The client may also engage in magical thinking and believe that having a thought is tantamount to acting on that thought.

Compulsions, as already mentioned, are behavioral or mental acts, often ritualized, that are designed to prevent anxiety, discomfort, or unwanted thoughts and events. People with OCD usually have both obsessions and compulsions, and these are yoked in some way. For example, a woman who had obsessions about accidentally shutting her cat in the refrigerator also had the compulsion of emptying out and replacing the contents of her refrigerator several times a day, to be sure that the cat was not in there.

Four patterns are particularly common in OCD and are listed here in descending order of prevalence (Steketee & Barlow, 2002):

1. Obsessions focused on contamination are accompanied by excessive washing and avoidance of objects viewed as carriers of germs and disease. Anxiety, shame, disgust, and extremely involved rituals are common in people with these symptoms.
2. Obsessive doubts lead to time-consuming and sometimes ritualized counting, repeating, and checking (for example, of appliances or of door and window locks). Guilt and worry about forgetting something important usually characterize these people.
3. Obsessions without compulsions sometimes occur (usually thoughts of a religious nature, or of sexual or violent acts that are horrifying to the person).
4. A powerful need for symmetry or precision can cause the person to perform even routine activities (such as eating and dressing) with extreme slowness.

Common compulsions in addition to those just listed include counting, hoarding, repeating, organizing, asking for reassurance, and touching in some ritualistic fashion. Many people with OCD exhibit multiple symptoms that often overlap, such as checking and contamination-related symptoms (Steketee & Barlow, 2002). Symptoms of OCD tend to wax and wane over time, based on life stress (Franklin & Foa, 2002).

OCD is less common than specific phobias or social phobia. Its incidence in the general population is 2 to 3 percent (Franklin & Foa, 2002). OCD seems equally common in both genders, but it begins earlier in males. The disorder can begin as early as the age of two, but it most often begins in the late teens for males and in the early twenties for females. It rarely begins after age fifty (Steketee & Barlow, 2002). The disorder frequently has a sudden onset, which often follows a stressful or traumatic life event. In 40 percent of cases, however, no precipitant is found.

Current research primarily supports a biological (genetic) cause in the development of OCD, along with the formation of dysfunctional beliefs through verbal instructions, observational learning, or modeling (Taylor et al., 2002). The symptoms of OCD — intrusive thoughts and compulsive actions — are found in mild versions in up to 90 percent of the general population; however, these thoughts do not usually erupt into full-blown OCD (Steketee & Barlow, 2002). In the cases that do develop into OCD, it is important to understand the thoughts and identify the factors that shaped the beliefs, such as parental instructions and modeling, or traumatic experiences. Swedo (2002) found that a very small percentage of childhood OCD can be attributed to PANDAS (pediatric autoimmune neuropsychiatric disorders associated with strep). In these cases, a dramatic onset of OCD immediately follows a strep infection.

Typical Client Characteristics

Many characteristic personality patterns have been identified in people with OCD. People with OCD tend to have rigid consciences and strong feelings of guilt and remorse. They feel driven and pressured, ruminate excessively, doubt themselves, are concerned with control, have a high need for reassurance, and tend to be indecisive and perfectionistic. They typically conceal their symptoms for years before seeking help, and they feel shame and guilt about their symptoms. They sometimes are aggressive and avoid intimacy and affectionate feelings. Compulsive hoarding is found in as many as 30 percent of people with OCD (Steketee & Frost, 2004).

Co-occurring disorders are common. About one-third of people with OCD have a coexisting major depressive disorder or dysthymic disorder; 39 percent have another anxiety disorder, such as social phobia, generalized anxiety disorder, PTSD, or panic disorder (Kessler, Berglund, et al., 2005). Body dysmorphic disorder co-occurs in 12 percent of people with OCD (Butcher et al., 2006). Cluster C personality disorders (especially dependent and avoidant personality disorders) are also common. Eating disorders (particularly bulimia) are found concurrently in nearly 10 percent of people with OCD, and alcohol and substance use may become a problem for people with OCD as they turn to substances to reduce their anxiety. Steketee and Barlow (2002) report that Tourette's disorder seems to be genetically linked with OCD, and research is ongoing in this area. Many people with Tourette's disorder have OCD, but only 4 to 7 percent of people with OCD have Tourette's disorder.

Assessment

Assessment tools for OCD generally involve a clinical interview, as well as self-report and behavioral assessment instruments. Steketee and Barlow consider the Yale-Brown Obsessive Compulsive Scale (Y-BOCS; Steketee, Frost, & Bogart, 1996) as "one of the most useful measures of OCD symptoms from a clinical standpoint" (2002, p. 536). Observations during the interview can further inform assessment of OCD. For example, clients may avoid touching doorknobs, check and recheck items, or continually ask for reassurance. Indecisiveness, perfectionism, and a need for constant reassurance are symptoms of OCD that may hinder the assessment process. Taylor and colleagues (2002) recommend that therapists be gentle but persistent, remind clients of time constraints of the session, and ask more closed rather than open-ended questions. In the course of the interview, thought-action fusion — the belief that a thought will actually happen — can reduce the client's desire to disclose obsessions.

Resistance is especially likely to impede treatment of OCD in people who are depressed and who have poor insight, overvalued ideations, and difficulty seeing the unreasonable nature of their thoughts and behaviors (Franklin & Foa, 2002). In planning treatment for OCD, it is important to assess for symptoms associated with any co-occurring disorders (Taylor et al., 2002).

Preferred Therapist Characteristics

Therapists who work with people with OCD should be well versed in assessment of symptoms, able to distinguish obsessions from delusions, and capable of developing and implementing structured exposure and response prevention treatment protocols. A delicate balance between support and pressure should be maintained by the therapist working with a client who has OCD. The shame, guilt, anxiety, and reluctance to self-disclose that are common in people with this disorder require a therapist who is respectful, encouraging, and flexible. At the same time, the therapist needs to be structured, firm, specific, and able to plan, prompting the client to cooperate with treatment.

Intervention Strategies

The literature on the treatment of OCD is consistent in recommending exposure and response prevention therapy as the first-line treatment of choice for OCD. Prolonged exposure to obsessional cues and strict prevention of rituals have been found to be the most efficacious (Franklin & Foa, 2002; McCabe & Antony, 2002; Taylor et al., 2002). The first step in applying this treatment usually involves obtaining a clear idea of the nature, frequency, and severity of the obsessions, compulsions, and anxiety.

Both the exposure and the response prevention need to be carefully planned and controlled. The exposure typically is graduated, beginning with situations that evoke low anxiety and then moving on to higher levels of anxiety-provoking stimuli as clients become habituated to the lower levels. Franklin and Foa (2002) emphasize the importance of not terminating the exposure while the person's level of distress is still high; thus exposure sessions should last from forty-five minutes to two hours, to allow ample time for anxiety to rise and then fall. Once clients have developed some comfort and familiarity with this procedure, they are encouraged to continue the exposure and response prevention at home, often with the help of friends or family members. Keeping a written diary of these experiences helps the client track and solidify progress.

Although exposure and response prevention are the essential ingredients of treatment for OCD, other treatment approaches and interventions have been combined with those components to enhance treatment. These include cognitive approaches designed to help people challenge their irrational cognitions, stop intrusive thoughts and ruminations, and avoid relapse (Roth & Fonagy, 2005). Other useful strategies include progressive relaxation, stress management, and training in assertiveness, social skills, and relationship improvement.

Therapy for OCD is typically of relatively brief duration (sometimes fewer than ten sessions). Between-session assignments, however, as well as relapse prevention training, are essential in effecting and maintaining improvement (Franklin, & Foa, 2002).

Several studies have found that medication can enhance the impact of exposure and response prevention (Dougherty, Rauch, & Jenike, 2002). The drugs most commonly used include SSRIs, especially fluoxetine (Prozac). It may be six to ten weeks before these medications have a demonstrable impact on the symptoms of OCD, but they can accelerate improvement. Other medications, such as clonazepam (Klonopin) and buspirone (BuSpar), may also be used to augment exposure and response prevention and SSRI treatment, especially if severe depression or anxiety is present.

Prognosis

Therapists should try to set realistic goals for the treatment of OCD. Although a high percentage of people completing treatment do experience significant improvement, incomplete improvement is far more likely than full recovery. However, even a 50 percent reduction in symptoms is likely to make a considerable difference in people's lives.

Factors associated with a positive prognosis include the presence of compulsions, low anxiety and depression, brief duration of the disorder before help is sought, the client's insight into the unrealistic nature of the thoughts and actions, the client's positive social and environmental adjustment, and the presence of an identified precipitant for the onset of the disorder (Franklin & Foa, 2002; McCabe & Antony, 2002; Steketee & Barlow, 2002; Taylor et al., 2002). Compulsions and checking symptoms seem to respond particularly well to treatment. People with early onset, low social functioning, excessive ruminations, persistent symptoms in the years immediately following diagnosis, and co-occurring hoarding behaviors or schizotypal personality disorder are more likely to have worse outcomes (Steketee & Barlow, 2002).

POSTTRAUMATIC STRESS DISORDER AND ACUTE STRESS DISORDER

Description of the Disorders

Both posttraumatic stress disorder (PTSD) and acute stress disorder involve a reaction to an extreme traumatic stressor that has caused or threatened death or severe injury. Extreme stressors include sexual assault, military combat, automobile accidents, violence or threatened violence, and natural disasters, among others. A person's contact with the stressor may involve direct experience, observation (as in the case of a firefighter or a witness to an accident), or vicarious experience (as when a friend, family member, or close associate experiences the stressor). Simply put, PTSD is an understandable response to an extremely stressful situation that results in chronic anxiety (Yehuda, Marshall, Penkower, & Wong, 2002).

DSM-IV-TR includes the following criteria as relevant to the diagnosis of these disorders:

- Great fear and helplessness in response to the traumatic event
- Persistent reexperiencing of the event (for example, through dreams, upsetting recollections, or intense distress on exposure to reminders of the event)
- Loss of general responsiveness, and at least three indications of avoiding reminders of the trauma (for example, feeling detached from others, believing that one's life is foreshortened, and dissociating from or being unable to recall major aspects of the traumatic experience)
- At least two persistent symptoms of arousal and anxiety (such as sleep disturbances, anger or irritability, severe startle responses, and difficulty concentrating) that are apparently due to the stressor and are severe enough to cause significant distress or impairment

Common additional symptoms include shame, survivor guilt or self-blame, lack of interest in usual activities (particularly sexual relationships), alexithymia (inability to identify or articulate emotions), mistrust of others, withdrawal from close relationships, difficulty in self-soothing, fear of losing control or going crazy, and psychosomatic symptoms. People often believe that their previous ways of coping and making sense of the world no longer work, and they are left feeling confused and without direction. Trauma-related disorders involve symptoms of anxiety in all systems — physical, affective, cognitive, and behavioral — but they always reflect the three major characteristics of these disorders: reexperiencing, avoidance and numbing, and increased arousal (Litz, Miller, Ruef, & McTeague, 2002).

The primary differences between PTSD and acute stress disorder are time of onset and duration. Acute stress disorder begins within four weeks of exposure to a traumatic stressor and lasts at least two days but no longer than four weeks; it sometimes develops into PTSD. The symptoms of PTSD, by definition, persist for more than one month. PTSD is described as acute if it lasts for less than three months and as chronic if the symptoms last longer. The disorder is termed PTSD with delayed onset if the symptoms begin more than six months after exposure to the stressor.

The estimated lifetime prevalence rate of PTSD in the general population is approximately 5 to 14 percent, reflecting the high prevalence of life-threatening events in this society (Yehuda et al., 2002). Recent studies show that 60 percent of people in the United States have been exposed to at least one traumatic event over the course of their lives. More than one-third of people who have been raped or assaulted, 20 to 30 percent of U.S. war veterans, as many as 16 percent of survivors of natural disasters, 17 percent of victims of crime, and up to 75 percent of people who survived concentration camps have developed PTSD (Litz et al., 2002; Yehuda et al., 2002). A survey of U.S. military personnel returning from the Iraq War found that one in five reported symptoms of PTSD (Hoge et al., 2004). A national survey reports that 20 percent of adolescents meet the criteria for PTSD. In adolescents, typical traumas involve serious automobile accidents, traumatic exposure to homicide or suicide, life-threatening medical illness, and physical and sexual abuse. Adolescents are twice as likely as adults to be victims of serious violent crime (Evans et al., 2005).

Onset of trauma-related disorders may occur at any age, although children often do not recognize the sources of their symptoms. In children, repetitive themes during play and persistent nightmares reflect the trauma; agitation and confusion reflect their distress. Childhood traumas are often associated with subsequent delays in academic achievement and social and moral development, as well as disruptions in relationships with family and peers. Trauma in adolescents has been correlated with reckless actions, high-risk sexual behavior, substance abuse and dependence, and aggressiveness (Evans et al., 2005).

Although people who have been through traumas initially may seem to have recovered, they are often left with residual and underlying symptoms (such as mistrust, avoidance of close relationships, and psychic numbing). These symptoms can last for many years and may be maintained at a low level by the use of drugs or alcohol, denial, and withdrawal. Reminders of a trauma, however, as well as other stressors or negative life events, can trigger a reexperiencing of the trauma, and the residual symptoms can develop into full-blown PTSD months or even many years after the original trauma (Keane & Barlow, 2002). For example, children who are sexually abused sometimes manifest no symptoms or awareness of the experience in childhood; such prominent symptoms as nightmares, reexperiencing of the trauma, and increased arousal may surface only in adulthood, when they encounter upsetting sexual or interpersonal situations. However, these people's self-images and socialization have probably been adversely affected for many years by the abuse.

The impact of a trauma seems to be particularly severe and long-lasting when it has a human cause. For example, a rape is likely to be more disturbing than a tornado. The impact also seems to be worse if an event is sudden and unexpected, if the person who experiences it has had no prior experience of dealing with such an event and therefore has poor coping skills (Litz et al., 2002), and if people involved in the event are perceived by some as having deserved their fate (for example, if an accident has occurred as a result of engaging in high-risk behavior). If a trauma involves others who did not survive (as in a war or an accident), the survivor often experiences guilt along with the other symptoms of PTSD. Suicidal ideation, depression, somatization, increased impulsivity, substance-related disorders, and other anxiety disorders often develop along with PTSD. Future stressors become inordinately troubling, and people sometimes feel permanently damaged, with little control over their lives.

Typical Client Characteristics

Most people who are exposed to trauma do not develop PTSD. Those who do, typically have an underlying difficulty in dealing with stress. Keane and Barlow (2002) report that a generalized biological vulnerability underlies the development of PTSD. Research verifies that there is a greater occurrence of PTSD in children born of mothers who were pregnant and who escaped from the World Trade Center on September 11. Other contributory factors in the development of PTSD include the severity of the trauma, psychological vulnerability to negative affect and anxiety, little availability of social support, and the number of exposures to the same or similar trauma.

The subjective meaning attached to the stressor, as well as the person's functioning prior to the trauma are also important factors in determining the person's response. Therefore, the therapist needs to understand the client's prior functioning and interpretation of the trauma. Exploration of the client's pretrauma history, as well as the use of such inventories as the PTSD Checklist (Blanchard, Jones-Alexander, Buckley, & Forneris, 1996), can clarify the presenting concerns.

In addition to a biological predisposition, other factors that predispose a person to develop PTSD include childhood trauma, preexisting mental disorders, inadequate support systems, alcohol misuse, recent stressful life changes or circumstances, and an external locus of control. Family history of mental illness, especially of anxiety, mood, or psychotic disorders, is also predictive of PTSD.

A study of residents of Manhattan, conducted three to six months after the terrorist attacks on the World Trade Center, found that 56 percent had one or more symptoms of distress related to the attacks. Why one person developed PTSD while another did not was found to be related to the person's prior history, loss of family or friends, job loss, displacement, and female gender (Resnick, Galea, Kilpatrick, & Vlahov, 2004). Another study of highly exposed Pentagon attack survivors found that 14 percent had PTSD seven months after the attack. Women were five times more likely than men to meet the criteria for PTSD. The researchers also found that people with dissociation, those who experienced more intense emotional reactions, and people who felt less safe prior to their exposure to the trauma were also at increased risk for PTSD (Grieger, Fullerton, & Ursano, 2003).

Another study of psychological responses to September 11 found that people who disengaged from coping efforts or "gave up" had an increased likelihood of developing psychological difficulties up to six months after the trauma (Silver, Holman, McIntosh, Poulin, & Gil-Rivas, 2002). This study also found that female gender; marital separation; being diagnosed with depression, an anxiety disorder, or physical illness prior to September 11; and severity of exposure were positively correlated with the development of PTSD.

Co-occurring disorders include other anxiety disorders, substance use disorders, and depression. Also often present are a variety of disturbances that require attention in treatment: suicidal and parasuicidal behaviors, weak social support, family and marital problems, sexual dysfunction, somatic complaints, and communication skills. People who have experienced multiple traumas across the life span are at increased risk of PTSD and may also exhibit poor self-care, difficulty regulating affect, and perceptual distortions (Litz et al., 2002). Effective coping skills should be developed through treatment, as such skills can help people work through a trauma when it happens and also ward off symptoms of PTSD.

Assessment

The goal of assessment in PTSD is not just to diagnose and measure PTSD symptoms, but also to assess support, coping skills, and the client's strengths and ability to function. The number of assessment tools for PTSD have flourished in the past decade and include checklists, scales, diagnostic interviews, and psychophysiological assessments. Keane and Barlow (2002) report the assessments are "comparable to or better than those available for any disorder in the DSM" (p. 440). A comprehensive discussion of these tools is beyond the scope of this book. Readers are referred to Barlow's *Anxiety and Its Disorders* (2002) for a complete review.

Preferred Therapist Characteristics

The assessment process can be particularly painful for people with PTSD. Therapists should be sensitive to the retraumatization that assessment may cause. Therefore, therapists must be extremely supportive and provide a safe and secure therapeutic environment. Warmth, positive regard, empathy, and consistency are essential in building the client's trust. If the trauma occurred many years before treatment, therapy may be a slow process of gradually building trust and helping the person access the troubling memories. At the same time, the therapist should not reinforce the client's sense of being a victim.

Reluctance to engage productively in treatment — manifested particularly by mistrust of the therapist, noncompliance with treatment recommendations, and missed appointments — is common in people with PTSD or acute stress disorder. People with these disorders may have strong preferences regarding the gender of their therapists; for example, women who have been raped typically prefer to have female therapists. To maximize the development of trust, the client's preferences should be elicited and respected.

Secondary or vicarious trauma can occur in the therapist working with a client who has experienced a trauma. Indications of secondary or vicarious trauma might be shifts in the therapist's sense of safety, view of the world, and feelings of vulnerability. The therapist whose caseload emphasizes trauma-related work is especially prone to these reactions. Awareness of the possibility of these reactions, balance in the therapist's life and caseload, supervision, and peer consultation can help the therapist deal with secondary trauma.

Intervention Strategies

Treatment for acute stress disorder and PTSD should begin as soon as possible after the trauma, and preventive treatment is recommended even before symptoms emerge. In general, effective treatments of trauma-related disorders are designed to promote the accessing and processing of the trauma, the expression of feelings, increased coping with and control over memories (to dilute pain), reduction of cognitive distortions and self-blame, and restoration of self-concept and previous level of functioning.

Jeffrey Mitchell has developed a group intervention — critical incident stress debriefing (CISD) — to provide early help for people who have undergone traumas (Everly, 1995). Designed primarily for groups of people who have experienced the same trauma — for example, the survivors of a natural disaster, an airplane crash, or an act of terrorism — as well as for police and firefighters who are involved in the aftermath of a trauma, CISD is ideally provided twenty-four to seventy-eight hours after the event. Groups of eight to twelve participants meet with facilitators for one or more sessions of ninety minutes to three hours. The emphasis is on caring, peer support, hope, and empowerment of the participants. Typically, facilitators guide the group through the following seven stages:

1. Introductions, information about the process, and guidelines for participation
2. Exploration of facts and information related to the trauma
3. Discussion of thoughts about the event
4. Exploration of emotions and reactions
5. Exploration of symptoms of distress, in order to stabilize, normalize, and facilitate a return to the cognitive domain as a way of coping with overwhelming affect
6. Teaching about reactions to trauma, symptoms, and risk factors
7. Reinforcement of coping skills, presentation of information about stress management, encouragement of reentry (with offer of further help, as needed), and closure

A multifaceted treatment plan that emphasizes cognitive-behavioral interventions seems best for the treatment of PTSD and acute stress disorder, and exposure to the memory of the trauma is an important ingredient of treatment. Other interventions, however, are equally important to the treatment of these disorders. In fact, for people with severe symptoms, or for those who are very distraught or impaired, interventions designed to rebuild a sense of safety and control should precede exposure to the trauma. According to Keane and Barlow (2002), treatments for PTSD that have excellent empirical support include exposure therapy, cognitive therapy, and anxiety management training (AMT).

Cognitive-processing therapy (CPT), developed in 1992 by Resick and Schnicke, combines elements of exposure therapy, AMT, and cognitive restructuring. It has been found to be as effective as exposure therapy in the treatment of rape-related PTSD (Keane & Barlow, 2002). Similar combination treatments have been found to be effective for PTSD related to motor vehicle accidents.

Designed especially for survivors of sexual assault, CPT is a twelve-session structured model in which exposure is combined with cognitive restructuring to change people's disrupted cognitions. Exposure is accomplished through information about the trauma, recollection of responses, and discussion of the trauma's meaning. Exposure must be handled very carefully to ensure that people are not retraumatized. It should include frequent reminders of safety and survival, be conducted in pieces, and continue until anxiety diminishes. Development of coping skills, changes in maladaptive beliefs, and identification of a safe setting all are essential to appropriate processing of the traumatic memories. Writing about the traumatic event is used in CPT but is always paired with training in coping skills. Written recollections of the traumatic event are first read to the therapist, who facilitates understanding, exploration of responses, and expression of emotions. People then are instructed to read their accounts to themselves daily, to habituate themselves to the experience and increase their understanding of the traumatic events and of their reactions.

Other approaches, mentioned earlier in this chapter in the overview of anxiety disorders, have also demonstrated effectiveness in treating people with trauma-related disorders. Anxiety management training (AMT), for example, typically combines prolonged activation of traumatic memories with such strategies as relaxation, cognitive restructuring, and biofeedback, designed to modify these memories and the associated fears (Keane & Barlow, 2002). A study of Vietnam combat veterans with PTSD found AMT to be as effective as exposure-based treatment in decreasing the frequency and intensity of intrusive war memories and avoidance of stimuli reminiscent of war (Pantalon & Motta, 1998).

Stress inoculation training (SIT) has also been used successfully to treat PTSD. SIT includes education and training in six coping skills (muscle relaxation, thought stopping, breath control, guided self-dialogue, covert modeling, and role playing).

Eye movement desensitization and reprocessing (EMDR) is another approach that has proven effective with PTSD (Shapiro, 1989). EMDR pairs visual stimulation (eye movements), kinesthetic stimulation (taps), or auditory stimulation (tones) with a focus on traumatic memories and associated negative beliefs. Reports of the effectiveness of EMDR with Vietnam veterans with PTSD have been encouraging, although EMDR has not been found to be superior to AMT or CBT (Keane & Barlow, 2002). EMDR has been approved by the APA as an empirically supported intervention for PTSD. Research suggests that there is rapid relief of symptoms when EMDR is used in conjunction with other therapeutic interventions.

Other useful ingredients of treatment include education about the nature of trauma-related stress disorders, encouragement for assertiveness and mastery experiences, anger management, stress management, grounding, containment of anxiety, affirmations, and expressive therapies (involving art and movement). Hypnotherapy is often used to help people retrieve and deal with dissociated memories.

Development of support systems is another important ingredient of treatment for acute stress disorder and PTSD. Peer support and therapy groups involving others who have had similar experiences can be particularly helpful in reducing a person's feelings of being stigmatized and alone; for example, group therapy seems to have become the primary mode of treatment for Vietnam veterans. Although a group made up of people who have survived traumas can provide considerable help, it can also contribute to an exacerbation of the trauma; therefore, if group therapy is to be conducted, the therapist should screen participants carefully and should closely control disclosure of and exposure to descriptions of traumatic experiences.

If symptoms of PTSD have been present for an extended period, the disorder has probably had a negative impact on social and occupational pursuits and on family relationships. Therapy with people in this situation should usually take a broad focus. Vietnam veterans with PTSD, for example, have had problems involving self-disclosure and expressiveness with their partners, physical aggressiveness, and overall adjustment (Carroll, Rueger, Foy, & Donahoe, 1985). Therefore, therapy with troubled veterans has to go beyond the exploration of their traumatic wartime experiences and must promote improvement in communication skills, socialization, and trust of others. Similarly, people who were abused as children have a higher than average likelihood of experiencing abuse as adults, and this vulnerability may have to be addressed in therapy (Messman & Long, 1996). Moreover, because the initial abuse often came at the hands of a father or a stepfather, it probably has contributed to family difficulties.

To date, no one medication has been found that addresses the complex sequelae of symptoms of PTSD (Yehuda et al., 2002). Nevertheless, many different medications have been effective in the treatment of symptoms related to PTSD, such as anxiety, sleeplessness, and depression.

Prognosis

Two-thirds of people exposed to a serious trauma do not develop PTSD (Eifert & Forsyth, 2005), and many others have symptoms that quickly remit spontaneously after a trauma. With treatment, the prognosis usually is also very good for recovery for those who have developed PTSD, especially for people whose functioning was positive before exposure to trauma, whose onset of symptoms was rapid, whose symptoms have lasted less than six months, whose social supports are strong, and who have received early treatment (Keane & Barlow, 2002). The prognosis for treatment of delayed-onset PTSD does not seem to be as good, at least in part because that type of PTSD is often accompanied by another psychological disorder (Roth & Fonagy, 2005). Although people's vivid memories of their traumatic experiences cannot be erased through therapy, most people can be helped to resume or even improve on their former levels of functioning. Foa, Davidson, and Rothbaum (1995), for example, report a 91 percent rate of significant improvement after treatment that combined exposure and stress inoculation training. Relapses are not uncommon, especially under stress, but they may be averted through extended follow-up treatment. Evans and colleagues (2005) suggest that future research should focus on whether a combination of medication and CBT would provide greater protection against relapse in PTSD.

GENERALIZED ANXIETY DISORDER

Description of the Disorder

Generalized anxiety disorder (GAD) is a pervasive disorder in which biological and psychological vulnerabilities combine to create ''a diathesis of chronic anxiety'' (Barlow et al., 2002, p. 323). Stress related to negative life events triggers neurobiological reactions. The focus of attention can shift from the negative event to a self-evaluative focus that ultimately creates a negative feedback loop. According to *DSM-IV-TR*, people diagnosed with GAD have had ''excessive anxiety and worry'' about at least two life circumstances for most days during a period of at least six months (American Psychiatric Association, 2000, p. 476). The worry is difficult to control, causes appreciable distress or impairment, and is accompanied by at least three of the following physiological symptoms (at least one in children):

- Edginess or restlessness
- Tiring easily
- Difficulty in concentrating
- Irritability
- Muscle tension
- Difficulty in sleeping

The most common affective and somatic symptoms of GAD (in descending order of frequency) include inability to relax, tension, fright, jumpiness, unsteadiness, apprehension, and uncontrollable worry. Such somatic symptoms as dry mouth, intestinal discomfort, tension-related headache, and cold hands are also common. The most prevalent cognitive and behavioral symptoms include difficulty in concentrating, apprehension about losing control, fear of being rejected, inability to control thinking, confusion, high negative affect, overarousal, and tendency to anticipate the worst (Campbell & Brown, 2002). For the diagnosis to be made, the symptoms should not be substance induced or due to a medical condition.

Anticipatory anxiety is a central manifestation of GAD. This symptom is more likely to be found in people who are homemakers, retirees, or disabled — primarily people who do not work outside the home. According to Barlow (2002), anticipatory anxiety is a future-oriented perspective in which people are in a constant state of hypervigilance and overarousal in expectation of threat-related stimuli. The term *generalized anxiety disorder* is clearly not a misnomer; the anxiety expresses itself through a multitude of pervasive symptoms that typically are without obvious immediate precipitants and that leave people feeling frightened and overwhelmed.

Approximately 80 to 90 percent of people with GAD have had another disorder, most frequently major depressive disorder, social phobia, specific phobia, dysthymic disorder, or panic disorder (Roy-Byrne & Cowley, 2002). Substance-related disorders are also frequent companions of GAD. Worry and anxious apprehension are central features of both anxiety and depression. It is not surprising to find that people who have GAD also experience a 62 percent rate of major depressive disorder and a 39 percent rate of dysthymia over their lifetimes (Campbell & Brown, 2002).

GAD often begins in childhood or adolescence. In early-onset GAD, the client usually cannot identify a precipitant for the disorder or report exactly when it began. Early-onset GAD is associated with a childhood history of fears, avoidant behavior, academic and social difficulties, and a disturbed home environment. People usually seek treatment when they are in their twenties, and the disorder tends to have a chronic course and a poorer treatment outcome (Barlow et al., 2002). Some theorists view GAD as similar to a personality disorder because of its early and insidious onset and its often chronic nature.

Typical Client Characteristics

GAD seems to be especially prevalent among young adults with long-standing feelings of nervousness and a history of physical disease or alcohol or prescription drug misuse (Butcher et al., 2006). Feelings of tension, vulnerability, and early experiences of lack of control over their environments are common in people with GAD, as are insecure attachments to early caregivers (Campbell & Brown, 2002). Some research on people with GAD suggests that they come from disrupted families and have had patterns of adjustment involving dependence and low self-esteem.

In general, anxiety disorders rarely begin in older adults. However, GAD is one of the most likely anxiety disorders to be present in older adults, occurring at a rate of 0.7 to 7.1 percent in older adults, usually after a precipitating event (Roemer, Orsillo, & Barlow, 2002). Lifetime prevalence of GAD is approximately 5 percent of the population (Kessler, Berglund, et al., 2005). GAD is far more common in primary care settings; among low-income, African American women; and among those who seek medical care (Roemer et al., 2002). As with most of the other anxiety disorders, females are twice as likely as males to experience GAD.

Both men and women with GAD are likely to have had one or more negative, important, and unexpected life events associated with the onset of the disorder. For men, the number of such events is also correlated with the likelihood of developing GAD. Many people with GAD report being worried their entire lives.

Assessment

The intake interview for a person believed to have GAD should gather data about the following areas (Barbaree & Marshall, 1985):

- Relevant cognitions (as reflected by self-statements, expectations, fears, attributions, evaluations)
- Somatic and physiological complaints
- Relevant behaviors
- Severity and generalizability of the disorder
- Antecedents and precipitants
- Consequences for relationships and for responses from others
- Family and individual history of emotional disorders
- Previous attempts to manage anxiety
- Overall lifestyle

A comprehensive interview like this one can provide important information about the dynamics of the disorder, and this information can in turn dispel some of the client's fears about the symptoms. Such inventories as the Beck Anxiety Inventory (Beck & Steer, 1990), the Penn State Worry Questionnaire (Meyer, Miller, Metzger, & Borkovec, 1990), and the Anxiety Disorders Interview Schedule (Brown et al., 1994) are also helpful in diagnosing GAD. A key diagnostic question for GAD is, "Do you worry excessively about minor matters?" (Brown, O'Leary, & Barlow, 1993, p. 140).

Preferred Therapist Characteristics

Information in earlier sections dealing with the ideal therapist for a client with an anxiety disorder is also relevant here. The therapist should have a wide repertoire of anxiety management techniques so that those approaches most likely to work with a given client can be selected. People diagnosed with GAD are sometimes reluctant to engage in treatment, primarily because of the ego-syntonic nature of their symptoms or because of their attribution of the symptoms to medical causes. They are often likely to seek medical treatment for their somatic complaints rather than to seek out therapy. Therefore, a collaborative stance and good reasoning abilities on the part of the therapist will also be helpful. Such nonspecific therapeutic qualities as warmth, empathy, acceptance, and the ability to encourage trust and collaboration are important in promoting clients' involvement in treatment.

Intervention Strategies

The two targets of intervention in the treatment of GAD are excessive, uncontrollable worry and the persistent overarousal that accompanies it. Treatment approaches that work tend to be active and multifaceted and to include cognitive therapy, relaxation techniques, training in anxiety management, and other cognitive and behavioral interventions. Several structured approaches to treat GAD have been developed that incorporate these elements and will be discussed in more detail in the next sections. Many other effective approaches are also available for reducing the symptoms of GAD. Clients' and therapists' preferences, clients' lifestyles, and the nature of the disorder should be considered in planning specific approaches to stress management. The cognitive and behavioral approaches can facilitate the development of individualized, multifaceted programs for treatment of GAD.

Cognitive Therapy. The techniques suggested by Beck and Emery in 1985 form the basis of many of the treatments in use today. They include the use of logic and educational (Ericksonian) stories, systematic testing and rational restructuring of beliefs, eliciting and examination of automatic thoughts via free association and behavioral tasks, use of the active voice, emphasis on how rather than why in inquiry, reattribution, decatastrophizing, and induction and modification of visual images. This approach is active, logical, and organized, emphasizing good therapist-client rapport and collaboration, as well as specific interventions.

Beck and Emery (1985) describe a brief, time-limited approach (five to twenty sessions) for treating GAD. This approach emphasizes an inductive/Socratic method of teaching (questions are the primary form of intervention), and homework is an important component. Four stages of treatment are described:

1. Relieving the client's symptoms
2. Helping the client recognize distorted automatic thoughts
3. Teaching the client logic and reason
4. Helping the client modify long-held dysfunctional assumptions underlying major concerns

Behavior Therapy. The primary goal of behavior therapy for GAD is stress management. The following approaches are some of those available for helping people with GAD control stress:

- Progressive muscle relaxation
- Autogenic training (calming the body and mind)
- Guided imagery
- Yoga
- Self-monitoring through logs of anxiety levels and anxiety-reduction activities
- Diaphragmatic breathing
- Meditation
- Biofeedback
- Exercise
- Expressive therapy
- Systematic desensitization

Affective Therapy. Cognitive and behavioral approaches have been shown to be the most effective and are emphasized over affective treatment strategies in the treatment of GAD. Nevertheless, some attention should also be paid to affect, so as to facilitate the decrease of anxiety. Beck and Emery (1985) propose a five-step process, based on the acronym AWARE, for dealing with the affective component of an anxiety disorder:

A: Accept feelings. Normalize, identify, and express them. People are encouraged to go on with life despite their anxiety and to learn such strategies as self-talk to develop some mastery of their anxiety.

W: Watch the anxiety. Seek objectivity and distance. People are encouraged to use diaries and ratings to demonstrate that the anxiety is situational, time-limited, and controllable.

A: Act with the anxiety rather than fight it in dysfunctional ways. People are encouraged to act against their inclinations by confronting fears rather than avoiding them, and to deliberately seek out anxiety-provoking situations in order to inoculate themselves against anxiety.

R: Repeat the steps. People are taught that doing so will establish learning and facilitate the process.

E: Expect the best. People are encouraged to maintain an optimistic outlook.

Cognitive Behavioral Therapy. In the past twenty years, cognitive-behavioral therapy for the treatment of GAD has been validated in more than thirteen controlled studies. CBT successfully reduces symptoms of GAD and results in large changes (Borkovec & Ruscio, 2001). A combined cognitive and behavioral approach described by Brown and colleagues (1993) involves both exposure to worry and prevention of worry-related behavior. CBT was used in both group and individual therapy and typically included twelve to fifteen sessions. Clients were encouraged to confront their worries and to do so without using distraction or any of the other dysfunctional means of avoidance that tend to increase worrying in the long run. The following techniques were used to help people deal with their worries and become habituated to and reduce anxiety:

- Self-monitoring of mood levels
- Analysis and modification of catastrophizing and other cognitive distortions
- Relaxation training, including cue-controlled relaxation
- Problem solving
- Cognitive countering
- Time management

Anxiety Management Training (AMT). Anxiety management training, as discussed earlier, can also be effective in treating GAD. Barlow and colleagues (2002) report two studies of the use of AMT to treat GAD. The first, a controlled clinical trial, involved psychoeducation about anxiety, relaxation, distraction, cognitive restructuring, and exposure. Clients were also encouraged to identify their strengths and to engage in pleasurable activities. The average length of treatment was 8.7 sessions, and those receiving AMT showed significant improvement compared to people on wait-lists who did not receive treatment. A second study, comparing AMT to nondirective counseling or placebo, was not as successful, however. There were few significant differences in effectiveness between AMT and nondirective therapy. However, both were found to be superior to the outcomes for the people who had been wait-listed (Barlow et al., 2002).

Acceptance and Commitment Therapy (ACT). Acceptance and commitment therapy, as developed by Hayes, Strosahl, and Wilson (1999), focuses on helping people create a meaningful life, rather than emphasizing anxiety reduction. One of the core skills learned in ACT is how to recognize and stop self-perpetuating and self-defeating emotional, cognitive, and behavioral avoidance routines. One twelve-week ACT program outlined by Eifert and Forsyth (2005) included the following:

- Psychoeducation about the purpose of anxiety, its benefits, and how it becomes disordered
- Evaluation of clients' strategies for coping with anxiety
- Focus on value-driven behavior as an alternative to anxiety
- In-session experiential exposure exercises that encourage clients to practice mindful observation, acceptance, and cognitive diffusion
- Commitment to engage in actions that are more consistent with clients' values

To date, several studies show promising results of ACT on reducing anxiety and stress.

Medication. Medication is not often necessary in the treatment of GAD. In cases where it is indicated, benzodiazepines such as alprazolam (Xanax) show short-term efficacy in 75 percent of cases (Evans et al., 2005), but usually should be avoided for ongoing, long-term treatment. Buspirone (Buspar) has also been determined to be effective in controlled studies and does not have a sedating side effect. Antidepressants are also sometimes used. Venlafaxine (Effexor) was the first antidepressant to receive FDA approval for the treatment of GAD (Roy-Byrne & Cowley, 2002).

Despite its frequent use in treating anxiety disorders, medication has been found to have a negative effect on the maintenance of improvement after psychotherapy is discontinued. In addition, people who take medication during therapy do not have a full opportunity to experience and deal with their anxiety and so are typically less tolerant of and less able to cope with any return of the anxiety. Therefore, medication for clients experiencing GAD should be used with considerable caution and should be monitored carefully; the inherent risks may not be worth the temporary relief of anxiety. Cognitive-behavioral approaches to anxiety reduction may be safer and have shown to be more effective (Evans et al., 2005), if somewhat slower.

Prognosis

Spontaneous remission of GAD is uncommon, but most people who receive cognitive-behavioral therapy for GAD show significant and consistent improvement. In fact, approximately 71 percent maintain their improvement at six-month follow-up (Evans et al., 2005), although many will not be entirely free of symptoms (as is also the case with most of the other anxiety disorders). Treatment design should take account of the fact that this disorder usually does not remit fully. Indeed, Evans and colleagues report that early trials indicate that only one-third of people treated for GAD achieve full remission, and those who rely solely on medication for treatment experience an 80 percent relapse rate following discontinuation of drugs. Therefore, treatment should include training in the use of preventive and coping mechanisms as well as in the signs of relapse so that clients can be helped to continue managing anxiety and stress effectively on their own.

TREATMENT RECOMMENDATIONS: CLIENT MAP

Treatment recommendations for the anxiety disorders discussed in this chapter are summarized here according to the framework of the Client Map.

Client Map

Diagnoses

Anxiety disorders (panic disorder, agoraphobia, specific phobia, social phobia, obsessive-compulsive disorder, acute stress disorder, posttraumatic stress disorder, and generalized anxiety disorder)

Objectives of Treatment

Reduce anxiety and related behavioral, cognitive, and somatic symptoms of the disorder

Improve stress management, social and occupational functioning, sense of mastery

Assessments

Often will include physical examination to rule out medical disorder

Measures of anxiety or fear

Checklists, interview, and scales specific to each disorder

Clinician Characteristics

Patient

Encouraging

Supportive yet firm and flexible

Concerned but not controlling

Calming and reassuring

Comfortable with a broad range of behavioral and cognitive interventions

Location of Treatment

Generally outpatient, sometimes contextual

Interventions to Be Used

Cognitive-behavioral and behavior therapy, especially modification and replacement of distorted cognitions, in vivo and imaginal desensitization, exposure, and response prevention

Acceptance and commitment therapy

Eye movement desensitization and reprocessing

Training in anxiety management

Stress inoculation

Problem solving

Relaxation

Assertiveness training

Self-monitoring of progress

Homework assignments

Emphasis of Treatment

Usually present-oriented

Moderately directive

Supportive

Usually cognitive and behavioral

Numbers

Individual or group therapy, according to the nature of the disorder

Ancillary family therapy as needed, particularly for heritable disorders and those that have affected family functioning

Timing

Usually weekly treatment of brief to moderate duration (eight to twenty sessions)

Moderate pacing

Possibly flexible scheduling, as necessitated by contextual treatment

Medications Needed

Usually not needed unless anxiety is disabling

May supplement treatment in some forms of anxiety disorders, especially obsessive-compulsive disorder

Adjunct Services

Hypnotherapy

Biofeedback

Meditation

Exercise

Other approaches to stress management

Planned pleasurable activities

Prognosis

Variable according to the specific disorder

Generally good for amelioration of symptoms

Fair for complete elimination of signs of the disorder

Client Map of Roberto M.

This chapter began with a description of Roberto M., a twenty-seven-year-old man who developed symptoms of strong anxiety after a visit to the dentist reactivated memories of childhood sexual abuse. Roberto's diagnosis and treatment plan are presented here according to the format of the Client Map.

Diagnosis

Axis I: 309.81 Posttraumatic stress disorder, delayed onset

Axis II: v71.09 No diagnosis on Axis II

Axis III: Fatigue, difficulty sleeping, other physical complaints reported, but no general medical condition diagnosed

Axis IV: Other psychosocial and environmental problems: childhood abuse; Problems with primary support group: conflict with fiancée

Axis V: Global assessment of functioning (GAF Scale): current GAF — 55

Objectives of Treatment

Reduce level of anxiety and accompanying somatic symptoms

Increase level of self-confidence

Reduce guilt and shame

Increase productivity at work

Improve relationship with fiancée

Help client cope effectively with his history of abuse

Assessments

Referral to a physician for medical examination

Beck Anxiety Inventory

Clinician Characteristics

Male (at client's request)

Supportive and encouraging

Skilled at empowerment

Location of Treatment

Outpatient

Interventions to Be Used

Encouragement for retrieval and discussion of memories at a gradual pace and in a safe fashion

Cognitive restructuring for feelings of guilt, shame, and self-blame

Training in coping skills, including progressive relaxation

Encouragement for resumption of exercise program

Eye movement desensitization and reprocessing

Writing about abuse (after some improvement in therapy) and reading account aloud to the therapist, with use of coping skills to combat anxiety created by this process

Goal setting and realistic planning for resumption of previous lifestyle

Acceptance and commitment therapy to help client focus on creating a lifestyle consistent with his values

Emphasis of Treatment

Moderately directive, to mobilize client's energy and give structure to the treatment in view of client's feeling confused, overwhelmed, and hopeless at the start

Moderately supportive, to bolster self-esteem and avoid adding the experience of even more threat

With abatement of symptoms, increasingly collaborative emphasis

Emphasis on exploration of the past (to help client cope with the abuse), but also on current successes

Numbers

Individual therapy as initial mode of treatment

With lessening of client's anxiety, several joint sessions with him and his fiancée, to help her understand what he was experiencing, encourage her to provide support, and help them both resume their previously close, positive relationship

Timing

Twice a week initially, for rapid reduction of anxiety, and then weekly sessions for at least three to six months

Moderately rapid pace, in view of client's previous high level of functioning and the fact that client was in considerable emotional pain

Medications Needed

None

Adjunct Services

Information about the prevalence and impact of abuse, especially for males

Prognosis

Good for significant reduction of symptoms

Optimistic but less positive for elimination of long-standing mild anxiety

Recommended Reading

Barlow, D. H. (2002). *Anxiety and its disorders: The nature and treatment of anxiety and panic* (2nd ed.). New York: Guilford Press.

Bourne, E. J. (2005). *The anxiety and phobia workbook* (4th ed.). New York: Harbinger.

Eifert, G. H., & Forsyth, J. P. (2005). *Acceptance and commitment therapy for anxiety disorders*. Oakland, CA: New Harbinger.

Markway, B., & Markway, G. (2003). *Painfully shy: How to overcome social anxiety and reclaim your life*. New York: St. Martin's Griffin.

CHAPTER SIX

Disorders of Behavior and Impulse Control

George W., a thirty-six-year-old white male, was referred for therapy by the courts. After his third conviction for driving while intoxicated, George was sentenced to a six-month stay in a work-release program. Therapy was a required part of his participation in that program.

George had begun misusing alcohol when he was fourteen years old and had been drinking excessively ever since. His father, his maternal grandfather, and two of his three brothers also used alcohol in harmful ways.

George had been married to his second wife for two years, and they had a one-year-old child. His first marriage had ended in divorce four years before, partly because his wife would no longer tolerate George's drinking. George had maintained contact with his two children from that marriage.

George was employed as a supervisor for a construction firm. He had been with the same company for more than ten years, despite frequent absences. He consumed little alcohol during the day, but would begin drinking beer as soon as he returned home from work. George reported frequent weekend episodes of binge drinking, as well as occasional blackouts. He had repeatedly tried to stop using alcohol on his own and had been alcohol free for six months at the time of his marriage to his second wife, but he stated that financial difficulties associated with the birth of their child had led him to resume drinking. George said that his wife was unhappy about his drinking and had expressed disappointment that they never went out socially, but he believed that their lack of a social life really mattered little to her because she was so absorbed in caring for their baby.

George reported some mild depression and stated that he was shy and uncomfortable around people. He reported that alcohol had helped him feel more self-confident and establish friendships with a group of men who apparently also drank to excess.

George had been suffering for more than twenty years from alcohol dependence, a disorder of behavior and impulse control. As is common among people with this disorder, George reported a family history of alcohol misuse. As is also typical of people with disorders of behavior and impulse control, George's mental disorder affected most, if not all, areas of his life; he presented with impairment in interpersonal, occupational, and other areas.

The possible diagnosis of an underlying avoidant personality disorder was considered. George's problems otherwise seemed related to his alcohol dependence, which became the focus of treatment.

OVERVIEW OF DISORDERS OF BEHAVIOR AND IMPULSE CONTROL

Description of the Disorders

This chapter focuses on disorders that are characterized primarily by behavioral concerns, behaviors that are engaged in to excess (as in alcohol dependence, bulimia nervosa, and pathological gambling), behaviors that are engaged in too little (as in anorexia nervosa), behaviors that are inappropriate (as in the paraphilias and kleptomania), behaviors that are unrewarding (as in the sexual dysfunctions), and sleep disorders (which can involve sleeping too much, sleeping too little, or unrewarding sleep patterns). All these disorders can cause impairment in social and occupational functioning, and many are life threatening. The following five categories of disorders will be discussed in this chapter:

1. Substance-related disorders
2. Eating disorders (anorexia nervosa and bulimia nervosa)
3. Sexual and gender identity disorders (sexual dysfunctions, paraphilias, and gender identity disorders)
4. Impulse-control disorders not elsewhere classified (pathological gambling, intermittent explosive disorder, pyromania, kleptomania, and trichotillomania)
5. Sleep disorders

This section of the chapter provides an overview of diagnosis and treatment of the entire group of disorders of behavior and impulse control. Subsequent sections of the chapter focus individually on the five categories of disorders.

The prevalence of the behavioral disorders varies considerably. Some of these disorders (such as pyromania and transvestic fetishism) are rarely encountered by most therapists; others, such as the alcohol use disorders, are frequently seen in therapy. The primary symptom of all the disorders discussed in this chapter is undesirable behavior. However, because many of these disorders typically begin in adolescence, persisting and often worsening without treatment, people with these disorders commonly also have serious developmental, occupational, social, and other deficits. Rather than benefiting from the normal developmental experiences of adolescence and early adulthood, people with behavioral disorders sometimes focus their lives around their dysfunctional behavior. When they finally do seek help to change their behavior, their failure to have developed age-appropriate maturity, self-confidence, and life skills complicates the treatment process and becomes an important secondary focus of treatment.

The disorders considered in this chapter almost inevitably affect how the people who suffer from them are viewed by others. People may be able to conceal an anxiety disorder or a depressive disorder from family members, friends, and colleagues, but a behavioral disorder is more difficult to hide because of its external manifestations, such as intoxication or weight loss. Lifestyles and behavioral disorders are interconnected, with each affecting the other. Some of the disorders discussed in this chapter are illegal (such as pyromania and pedophilia); others (such as the sexual dysfunctions) involve a partner. Thus these disorders may damage relationships, career development, and self-image.

The time of onset varies according to the specific disorder. The most common ones, substance-related disorders and eating disorders, usually begin during adolescence. Others, such as kleptomania, tend to begin considerably later. Course and duration also vary. Some people respond to encouragement or exhortation from others to control their behavioral difficulties and may curtail or even eliminate their dysfunctional behaviors without therapy. This pattern is unusual, however, and these disorders generally do not remit spontaneously. Without treatment, most of them tend to become deeply entrenched, and often worsen.

Typical Client Characteristics

Some of these disorders, such as the alcohol use disorders, have a strong genetic or familial component; others, such as anorexia nervosa, are often related to a characteristic pattern of family interactions and expectations that predispose a person to develop a particular set of symptoms. People who present with disorders of behavior and impulse control commonly come from dysfunctional families in which they were not afforded models of positive relationships.

Specific information on the particular personality patterns that characterize people with the various disorders is provided in later sections. Contrary to popular belief, however, people with behavioral disorders do not all have other underlying personality or other emotional disorders. Some may have preexisting conditions that have contributed to the development of their behavioral disorders, and some may develop emotional disorders secondary to their behavioral problems, but many do not have additional diagnoses. This is particularly true of people diagnosed with sexual dysfunctions, gender identity disorders, or sleep disorders.

Assessment

Assessment for impulse-control disorders should consider the symptom severity as well as the impact of the symptoms on quality of life. Stein et al. (2006) recommend that a careful assessment of impulse-control disorders include questions about impulsivity and aggression, repetitive behaviors the person feels compelled to do but later regrets, mood, substance use, and suicidal and homicidal ideation, as well as an inquiry into the client's history of self-harm behaviors (such as skin picking, hair pulling, cutting). Impulse-control disorders frequently co-occur with other impulse-control disorders; thus, the full range of behavior may not be evident without a complete assessment.

Stress plays a key role in the development and continuation of impulse-control disorders. Assessment should include level of stress and its impact on quality of life. Support, including family and peer groups, should also be determined. If there is any indication of childhood abuse, the Childhood Trauma Questionnaire (Bernstein et al., 1994) can help assess the nature and severity of the abuse.

Several useful standardized rating scales are available to assess symptoms of impulse-control disorders including the Minnesota Impulsivity Interview and the Structured Clinical Interview for Diagnosis of Obsessive-Compulsive Spectrum Disorders (Stein et al., 2006, p. 311). Symptoms of aggression and impulsivity also can be evaluated with the Barratt Impulsiveness Scale Version 11 (BIS-11). Hollander and colleagues (2006) report that the BIS-11 is one of the most frequently used measures of impulsivity, is easy to administer, and takes ten to fifteen minutes to complete the thirty questions. Such self-report measures as the Spielberger State-Trait Anger Expression Inventory (STAEI) can be useful in evaluating impulsive aggression. The Overt Aggression Scale-Modified (OAS-M) is a semistructured interview that also is useful in measuring the frequency and severity of aggressive behavior (Coccaro, Harvey, Kupsaw, Herbert, & Bernstein, 1991).

Several different scales and self-report assessments can be useful in the measurement of particular impulse-control disorders. The South Oaks Gambling Screen, the Psychiatric Institute Trichotillomania Scale, and the Kleptomania Symptom Assessment Scale (K-SAS; Grant & Kim, 2002) can be used to screen for specific impulse-control disorders. The Yale-Brown Obsessive-Compulsive Scale (Y-BOCS) has been modified to measure gambling, compulsive shopping, binge eating, and sexual compulsions (Hollander et al., 2006).

Preferred Therapist Characteristics

Therapists treating people with behavioral disorders have diverse educational and experiential backgrounds. Some have doctoral or master's degrees. Others are paraprofessionals (sometimes called mental health technicians or associates) with associate degrees, many of whom have had personal experience with the behavioral difficulties presented by their clients. These treatment providers are especially likely to be involved in the treatment of people with drug and alcohol problems. The establishment of a sound collaborative relationship between professional and paraprofessional therapists is an important element in the treatment of people with substance-related disorders.

Therapists working with this population need to have not only the usual expertise in relationship building and strategies of psychotherapy but also need to pay particular attention to developing a positive therapeutic alliance. Clinicians who rate higher in warmth and empathy have clients who show greater gains in therapy. Miller and Carroll (2006) found that clients' ratings of their working relationship with their clinicians is predictive of treatment outcome.

A good grasp of personal and career development, as well as of family dynamics, is also necessary so that therapists can assess and address the impact that a behavioral disorder has had on a particular client's overall development. These therapists also should have a good understanding of the nature of their clients' disorders, because education is typically an important component in the treatment of behavioral disorders. Therapists should have a treatment style that is directive and structured and involves goal setting and follow-up but that is also supportive and empathic.

Therapists working with people who have problems of behavior and impulse control should be skilled in conducting group and family sessions as well as individual therapy sessions. They should also feel comfortable incorporating self-help groups into treatment plans. Coordination of a multifaceted treatment plan is typically part of the therapist's role in treating behavioral disorders.

Intervention Strategies

Not surprisingly, the treatment of disorders of behavior and impulse control emphasizes such behavioral interventions as behavioral counts, logs, and checklists; goal setting; learning, practicing, and mastering new behaviors; reducing or eliminating dysfunctional behaviors; reinforcement, rewards, and consequences; and between-session tasks. Exercise, relaxation, distraction, desensitization, role playing, and other techniques may also be incorporated into the treatment plan. Information and education are almost always a part of treatment as people are taught about the negative impact of their behaviors on their physical and emotional adjustment and as they learn new and more effective behaviors to replace the old ones.

In treatment of these disorders, group therapy is at least as important as individual therapy. People with behavioral disorders usually benefit from receiving therapy together with others who have experienced similar difficulties. Group therapy allows people to learn from others' successes and failures and to receive feedback and encouragement from other group members. Group therapy also enables people to increase their social interest and involvement and to develop and practice their social skills. It facilitates reality testing and the challenging of defenses, offers points of comparison, promotes self-understanding and self-acceptance, and is often less threatening than individual therapy. Group therapy is particularly useful in the early stages of treatment when motivation may be uncertain, but it usually is not indicated for people who are very fragile or disturbed. Self-help peer groups, such as Rational Recovery, Alcoholics Anonymous, and Overeaters Anonymous, are another important component of treatment.

Family therapy, too, is a salient component of treatment for these disorders. Clients' behavioral concerns typically have had an adverse impact on family relationships, and help may be needed in that arena. Families usually also benefit from education about the nature of these clients' concerns and about how to help these clients maintain desired behavioral changes. Moreover, family members themselves (for example, the enabling husband of a woman who misuses alcohol or the overwhelmed wife who does not know how to cope with her husband's physical abuse) are often participants in patterns that contribute to the perpetuation of these clients' behavioral disorders. When family members are helped to change patterns that maintain, reinforce, and provide secondary gains for these clients, the likelihood of improvement is increased, and the families benefit as well. Multifamily therapy groups, as well as therapy for an individual family or family member, can provide feedback, support, and information, ameliorating family difficulties and improving relationships.

Medication is usually not the primary mode of treatment for behavioral disorders, with the exception of several of the sleep disorders, but it sometimes can contribute to the treatment process. For example, antidepressant medication may reduce hopelessness and inertia in people with bulimia nervosa so that they are able to benefit from psychotherapy.

Many behavioral disorders, including the substance-related disorders and the eating disorders, are physically harmful and even life threatening. Other disorders that have behavioral manifestations, such as the sexual dysfunctions, intermittent explosive disorder, and hypersomnia, sometimes have a physiological cause. For both reasons, many of the disorders discussed in this chapter warrant clients' referral to physicians for evaluation. Medical information can be useful in determining the most appropriate treatment plan for a particular individual.

Prognosis

The prognosis for treatment of the behavioral disorders varies according to the nature of the particular disorder and the motivation and lifestyle of the client. Perhaps the greatest barrier to treatment is the inherently gratifying nature of many of these disorders. For example, even though the eating disorders and substance-related disorders often cause physical, social, and possibly occupational difficulties for the people diagnosed with them, the rewards of being thin or being intoxicated are very powerful and are difficult to counteract in therapy. Relapses are common. The basic course of treatment may be relatively brief, but extended aftercare and follow-up are indicated (through self-help groups, intermittent psychotherapy appointments, drug testing, medical examinations, homework assignments, and family or individual therapy) for consolidation of gains, prevention of relapse, facilitation of adjustment, and assistance in coping effectively if a relapse does occur. With appropriate treatment and follow-up, and with motivation on the part of the client, the prognosis is good for significant improvement if not for complete remission of most behavioral disorders.

SUBSTANCE-RELATED DISORDERS

Description of the Disorders

The category of substance-related disorders, as listed in the *Diagnostic and Statistical Manual of Mental Disorders (DSM-IV-TR)*, includes two substance use disorders — substance dependence and substance abuse — and a wide variety of substance-induced disorders. The substance use disorders describe maladaptive behavioral patterns of using drugs and alcohol; the substance-induced disorders label such symptoms as intoxication, mood changes, and sleep-related problems that stem directly from maladaptive patterns of using drugs or alcohol. Consequently, a substance use disorder often will be accompanied by the diagnosis of one or more substance-induced disorders.

DSM-IV-TR describes substance dependence as "a maladaptive pattern of substance use, leading to clinically significant impairment or distress" (American Psychiatric Association, 2000, p. 197). According to the *DSM*, at least three of the following seven symptoms will be manifested at any time in the same twelve-month period:

1. Signs of tolerance, such as needing more of the substance to obtain the same effect
2. Symptoms of withdrawal
3. Use of more of a substance than was planned
4. Enduring desire or unsuccessful efforts to reduce use of the substance
5. Extensive devotion of time to substance-related activities or to recovering from the effects of the substance
6. Minimal or reduced involvement in career and social activities
7. Continued use of a substance despite the awareness that it is having a negative impact

Substance dependence can be described as being with or without physiological dependence; in a controlled environment (such as a hospital, prison, or halfway house); on agonist therapy (such as Methadone); in early (first twelve months) or sustained (longer than twelve months) remission; and in partial (one or more criteria for dependence have been met but not enough for the diagnosis) or full (no criteria have been met) remission.

The diagnosis of substance abuse also involves recurrent and self-destructive use of drugs or alcohol leading to significant impairment or distress. This disorder is characterized by at least one of the following four substance-related symptoms:

1. Impairment in primary roles (for example, employee, parent, partner, student)
2. Recurrent use of drugs or alcohol in hazardous situations (such as while driving or operating machinery)
3. Recurrent substance-related legal problems (such as arrests for driving while intoxicated)
4. Continued use of a substance despite the awareness that it is having a negative impact

Substance abuse is often characterized by sporadic use of substances (for example, weekend rather than daily use) and entails fewer physiological effects and less consumption of drugs or alcohol than substance dependence. Nevertheless, substance abuse can also have a profound impact on a person's lifestyle and is often a precursor of substance dependence. Substance abuse can be diagnosed only in people who have never met the criteria for substance dependence related to the particular substance in question.

DSM-IV-TR specifies eleven classes of psychoactive substances that are used in maladaptive ways:

1. Alcohol
2. Amphetamines and amphetamine-like substances
3. Caffeine
4. Cannabis
5. Cocaine
6. Hallucinogens
7. Inhalants
8. Nicotine
9. Opioids
10. Phencyclidine (PCP) or phencyclidine-like substances
11. Sedatives, hypnotics, and anxiolytics

DSM-IV-TR also includes other or unknown substance use disorders (such as anabolic steroids, prescription and over-the-counter medications, inhalants, and nitrous oxide) and polysubstance dependence, which involves the use of three or more categories of substances (not including caffeine or nicotine), with no one substance predominating during a twelve-month period. In diagnosing a substance use disorder, the clinician specifies the substance and whether the symptoms meet the criteria for dependence or abuse.

Substance use disorders do not necessarily entail long-standing and pervasive impairment; in fact, most people who misuse drugs or alcohol are employed and have families. Nevertheless, substance use disorders typically have a powerful negative impact on the users, as well as on the people who are close to them.

Substance-induced disorders vary from substance to substance; their manifestations depend on the impact of the specific substances. This category includes the following disorders:

- Substance intoxication
- Substance withdrawal
- Substance-induced delirium
- Substance-induced persisting dementia
- Substance-induced persisting amnestic disorder
- Substance-induced psychotic disorder
- Substance-induced mood disorder
- Substance-induced anxiety disorder

- Substance-induced sexual dysfunction
- Substance-induced sleep disorder
- Hallucinogen persisting perception disorder (flashbacks)

According to Finney and Moos (2002), 18 percent of the U.S. population will meet the criteria for an alcohol-related disorder, and more than 5 percent will meet the criteria for a drug-related disorder at some time in their lives. The annual cost of substance misuse to society is estimated to be $71 billion. When the cost of crime, mental health, and other issues are included, that figure increases to well over $300 billion (Schuckit, 2000). Substance-related disorders are particularly prevalent among young adults between the ages of eighteen and twenty-five, people living in large urban areas, people living in the western part of the United States, and people who are unemployed. Men are twice as likely as women to be dependent on or abuse drugs and alcohol (Substance Abuse and Mental Health Services Administration [SAMHSA], 2003), but there is little difference across racial groups for alcohol or illicit drug use (American Psychiatric Association, 2000; SAMHSA, 1998). Occupational roles can be linked to the prevalence of substance use disorders. For example, medical professionals have an elevated incidence of substance use disorders, perhaps because of their easy access to drugs.

Scientific evidence lends some support to a disease concept of dependence on alcohol, nicotine, and other drugs, such as cannabis and cocaine (Evans et al., 2005). Genetic vulnerability, a neurological basis for many of the symptoms of dependence, and a chronic course that includes relapse underscore the biological bases of misuse. Researchers have mapped the biological effect of substances on the reward centers in the brain, including those influenced by food, sex, and drinking (Evans et al., 2005). Activation of the reward centers has been linked to cravings for drugs or alcohol, tolerance, loss of control, and impaired functioning.

Evans and colleagues (2005) write that vulnerability to substance use disorders probably stems from a triad of contributing factors: drug use, biological characteristics of the user, and environmental factors (physical and psychosocial setting). Certain substances, such as cocaine, amphetamines, heroin, alcohol, nicotine, and marijuana, produce the greatest impact on the brain's reward system. Characteristics of the user, such as clinical depression, low self-esteem, anxiety, or phobias, are initially alleviated by substance use, but the substance use frequently causes more symptoms with continued use. Genetic variations in the person's metabolism and neurological response to a substance are important contributors to how the drug will affect that person, as well as to the risk of dependence. Finally, the role of such environmental factors as familial history of substance use, peer pressure, availability of substances, and living in an environment that triggers cravings are important contributors to substance misuse and relapse after treatment. All three contributing factors (substance use, biological components of the user, and environmental factors) must be taken into account when developing effective treatment and relapse prevention programs. Therapists should also take into account the continuum of symptoms, from occasional use with little or no impact on functioning on one end, to severe dependence and resultant impairment of social, employment, and other functioning on the opposite end.

Typical Client Characteristics

Substance use most often begins in adolescence, peaks in early adulthood, and then decreases with age (Tucker, Vuchinich, & Murphy, 2002). Jessor's problem-behavior theory (Jessor, Donovan, & Costa, 1991) proposes that substance misuse begins as part of a syndrome of adolescent problem behaviors (for example, risky sex, truancy, theft, lying, dangerous driving) that are both maladaptive and adaptive. They serve adolescent developmental needs of individuating from parents, bonding with peers, and coping with failure, boredom, social rejection, and low self-esteem, but can prevent young people from developing healthy social, academic, and adjustment skills. Adults who use drugs or alcohol in maladaptive ways may have learned to cope through dishonesty, manipulation, placating, or abusing others, and these patterns may be carried into their therapy.

Approximately two-thirds of those with substance use disorders have a coexisting disorder. A second substance use disorder is most common, but other disorders that often accompany a substance use disorder include personality disorders (especially antisocial personality disorder), depressive disorders, panic disorder, social phobias, and psychotic disorders (Schuckit, 2000). The coexisting disorders may be preexisting or may be initiated or worsened by substance use. Sometimes the substance use reflects an effort at self-medication for another mental disorder. Studies of people in treatment for mental disorders found co-occurring substance use rates of 40 to 60 percent (Mueser, Drake, Turner, & McGovern, 2006). People with a family history of alcohol misuse, as well as people who use opioids, are particularly likely to have coexisting mental disorders.

This pattern of dual disorders is difficult to treat because it becomes a vicious cycle: the substance use worsens the coexisting disorder, which in turn increases the person's tendency to use drugs or alcohol to self-medicate. Often, moreover, the substance use masks the symptoms of the underlying disorder, further complicating the treatment picture. The bottom line, according to Mueser and colleagues (2006), is that dual diagnosis of a substance use disorder and another mental disorder results in a more severe course of illness and increases the need for treatment.

Suicide and suicidal ideation are common in people with substance use disorders and seem to increase as substance use increases (Evans et al., 2005). This is particularly worrisome because people who misuse substances have an available lethal weapon — drugs or alcohol — and the combination of intoxication and depression may lead a binge to become a suicide attempt. With the use of multiple drugs becoming increasingly common, suicide becomes even easier through the use of a mixture of drugs, such as alcohol and tranquilizers. As many as 25 percent of people entering treatment for substance use have made a previous suicide attempt (Chamberlain & Jew, 2005).

Substance use disorders, particularly alcohol dependence and alcohol abuse, tend to run in families. These familial factors can be either environmental or genetic. Although a gene for substance dependence has not been found, genetic factors might include a biological predisposition that is transmitted from generation to generation that leaves a family more susceptible to substance misuse (Evans et al., 2005).

Nongenetic factors include a pattern of behaviors that may also be passed down. Growing up in a home in which substance use was modeled and accepted may have prompted and entrenched the use of substances. Such a home environment is likely to be dysfunctional and to have serious shortcomings in terms of the life skills that are demonstrated and the values and beliefs that are passed on to the children. People who misuse substances also typically have a negative impact on their partners and children and can contribute to substance use disorders in the next generation. Therapy, then, will have to go beyond the immediate presenting problem and address interpersonal and occupational impairment. It also should reach out to family members who have their own problems with substances or who are being adversely affected by the client's substance use.

Assessment

Because of the prevalence of dual diagnoses in people with substance use disorders, careful assessment and diagnosis are essential before treatment is planned. *DSM-IV-TR* (American Psychiatric Association, 2000) warns against diagnosing a mental disorder based on symptoms observed while a person is intoxicated or withdrawing from substances. Even severe symptoms (such as delirium, dementia, or hallucinations) that have developed as a result of substance use will normally abate within a period of several days to four to six weeks after the substance has been discontinued (Stevens & Smith, 2005). Distinguishing between independent and substance-induced symptoms and disorders requires a careful history taking that includes symptoms, duration, age of onset, relationship to times of substance use, behavior during periods of abstinence from drugs or alcohol, and close observation to determine if symptoms diminish with continued abstinence.

Such inventories as the Michigan Alcoholism Screening Test (Selzer, 1971) and the Addictions Severity Index (McLellan et al., 1992) can facilitate the assessment process. A urinalysis and other laboratory-analyzed tests, a medical examination, and an EEG to look at general brain function can provide further information on the nature of a person's substance use and its physiological impact.

These screening procedures can help determine whether detoxification or a residential treatment program is needed or whether outpatient treatment is sufficient. People's reluctance to leave jobs and families, as well as cutbacks in insurance payments for inpatient treatment of substance use disorders, have led to a reduction in the length and availability of residential treatment. People who are having toxic reactions to a substance, are delusional or having hallucinations without insight into their cause, or are in danger of harming themselves or others probably require hospitalization for protection and safety (Schuckit, 2000). Those who are physiologically dependent on a substance also may require inpatient treatment to detoxify, prior to beginning outpatient treatment for substance use.

Some people seem to deteriorate after detoxification. Memory problems and other mild cognitive deficits emerge, and people may develop anxiety and feelings of being out of control. If these symptoms are not dealt with through education and therapy, they can frighten people into a relapse. The early stages of recovery are tenuous, and close monitoring and support are needed.

Several assessments are available to measure people's readiness and motivation to change. Most are based on the Transtheoretical Model of Change (Prochaska & Norcross, 2006). For those who are not yet in a substance treatment program, the Readiness to Change Questionnaire (RTCQ; Rollnick, Heather, Gold, & Hall, 1992) can be effective. SOCRATES (Stages of Change Readiness and Treatment Eagerness Scale; Miller & Tonigan, 1996) assigns a level of change readiness for people who misuse alcohol, and is based on the Prochaska model. URICA (University of Rhode Island Change Assessment; McConnaughy, Prochaska, & Velicer, 1983) provides a similar assessment for people who misuse drugs.

Tucker and colleagues (2002) report that other tools are available to assess cravings for specific substances, and their use can be an important part of relapse prevention efforts that help people who misuse substances cope with and replace cravings for drugs or alcohol before they relapse. For example, the Desires for Alcohol Questionnaire (DAQ; Love, James, & Willner, 1998) is a thirty-six-item questionnaire that assesses the intention, desire, and anticipated relief from negative affect that a person experiences when contemplating alcohol use. A similar assessment measures such cravings in people who use cocaine (Cocaine Craving Questionnaire; Tiffany, Singleton, Haertzen, & Henningfield, 1993).

Preferred Therapist Characteristics

Therapist characteristics may have a stronger impact on treatment outcome than the type of treatment provided (Finney & Moos, 2002). In general, therapists who are more empathic, less confrontational, and more interpersonally skilled fare better with clients with substance use disorders, possibly due to the creation of better therapeutic alliances.

Therapists working with people who misuse substances must be prepared to deal with lack of motivation, hostility, manipulation, and deception. Indeed, a considerable challenge therapists face is developing an honest relationship with their substance-using client. Therapists need to find appropriate ways of handling their own reactions to clients' reluctance to change and should continue communicating respect, empathy, optimism, and acceptance to even the most hostile and resistant clients.

Building rapport with people who misuse substances is sometimes difficult because support, caring, and empathy have to be combined with a straightforward and realistic approach that may involve confrontation, persuasion, monitoring, and limit setting. Care should always be taken to respect, empower, and support clients and help them feel safe rather than to denigrate and humiliate them. Focusing on the client's behavior, rather than the person, can facilitate a nonjudgmental attitude and the communication of unconditional positive regard (Bishop, 2001).

Therapists' own experiences with drug and alcohol use can enhance rapport and promote client motivation. This supports the use of paraprofessionals' collaborating with therapists who have graduate-level training. Because some of the people providing treatment are themselves recovering from problems with substance use, the therapist's own history is often of interest to the client. Bishop (2001) suggests that some judicious sharing of the therapist's own experiences, whether or not the therapist has had problems with substances, can promote rapport and straightforwardness in the therapeutic relationship. However, the focus should be kept on the client's concerns, and therapists should not assume that what has been personally helpful to them will necessarily be helpful to others.

Intervention Strategies

Motivation can be a problem for many people who misuse substances, especially those who are court ordered into treatment following a DWI or other criminal acts. Motivational interviewing has been shown to increase the effectiveness of programs to treat substance use disorders and was used in Project MATCH to enhance treatment of people who misused drugs and alcohol (Miller, Zweben, DiClemente, & Rychtarik, 1995). Motivational interviewing helps people resolve their ambivalence and recognize and verbalize their internal motivations to change. Through the use of open-ended questions, reflective listening, and affirmations and summarization about behavior change, the therapists skillfully evoke "change talk" that helps people take charge of their desire to change (Miller & Rollnick, 2002). Using the motivational interviewing approach, therapists express empathy for people who misuse substances and for their problems, help them accept their ambivalence about treatment by normalizing commonly expressed feelings, identify discrepancies between people's words and behavior, and create self-efficacy (Springer, McNeece, & Arnold, 2003). Such techniques have been found to increase treatment compliance rates and improve motivation for beginning behavior change (Stasiewicz, Herrman, Nochajski, & Dermen, 2006). Motivational interviewing can become an important part of treatment for substance use disorders, especially with reluctant, court-ordered, and well-defended clients.

Refusal to seek treatment and denial of the severity of their symptoms is common among people who misuse substances. If a person clearly needs treatment for a substance use disorder but is reluctant to obtain help, a therapist often will assist friends and family members in organizing what is called an intervention. Developed by Vernon Johnson (1986), founder of the Johnson Institute, this approach involves having two or more people concerned about someone's substance use meet with that person, usually along with a therapist, to present information on the negative impact of the person's use of substances and encourage the person to accept help. Typically, treatment is prearranged, and consequences (such as loss of a job or a relationship) if the person does not agree to treatment are clearly stated. Interventions have been shown to be highly successful both at involving a person in treatment and at leading to a positive outcome (Schuckit, 2000).

A less formal type of intervention, known as ARISE, has also been found to be effective (Garrett Landau-Stanton, Stanton, Stellato-Kabat, & Stellato-Kabat, 1997). The ARISE model provides an intervention continuum that starts with the first call from families or concerned others and goes through five or six sessions in which family members and friends are encouraged to take steps toward ending the cycle of addiction. Rather than a single confrontation, the intervention matches the family's pressure to the substance user's resistance. Whether or not the person who misuses substances enters treatment, the support needs of the family network are addressed, and the family develops hope that their efforts will make a difference. The ARISE model takes into account that intervention is rarely successful the first time; rather, multiple interventions may be necessary over the course of treatment.

Beginning with an effective assessment screening and continuing through treatment planning, interventions for people with substance use problems should focus on options that offer a continuum of care. Selection of appropriate levels of service should be based on such factors as type of substance, severity of use, degree of physiological and emotional dependence, related biopsychosocial problems, co-occurring disorders, and the person's age and motivation for treatment. Integrating assessment into interventions ensures that people who misuse alcohol or other substances will get individualized attention that focuses on their specific needs. Treatment should be tailored for each person rather than follow a one-size-fits-all approach.

Early assessment and treatment efforts should focus on high-risk behaviors, such as driving while intoxicated, intravenous drug use, polysubstance use, violent and suicidal behavior, and unprotected sex. Intervening to reduce behaviors that pose a risk to self and others should take first priority over other goals, even the immediate goal of abstinence (Tucker et al., 2002).

Next, goals should be established and a system for behavioral change and monitoring set up that reduces the substance use. Although complete abstinence is the goal of most treatment programs, a review of the literature by Tucker and others (2002) indicates many different pathways that can be effective avenues of change for people who misuse substances. For example, reducing problem drinking to nonproblem drinking could be beneficial for people with mild to moderate problems. Those who fail at a trial of reasonable reduction are more likely to be receptive to a subsequent goal of abstinence.

In contrast to programs that take a zero-tolerance approach, the harm reduction approach values any change that results in a reduction of the harm or the risk of harm of substance misuse (Marlatt, 1998). For example, marijuana may be used as a ''reverse gateway drug'' to help people reduce their use of more harmful substances (for example, cocaine, or hypnotics). Harm reduction models focus on positive changes in behavior and lifestyle, such as substituting methadone maintenance for heroin, or on interventions aimed at stopping high-risk drinking and driving.

Research has shown that a wide range of treatments, in different combinations, across a variety of settings and treatment modalities, can be effective in the treatment of substance use disorders. Such interventions are cost-effective in that they reduce substance-related problems and the expenses associated with them (Tucker et al., 2002).

Although not much research is available on the effectiveness of rehabilitation programs, they also have their place in the treatment of substance misuse. Schuckit (2000) delineates the following eleven treatment procedures and characteristics found in most rehabilitation programs:

1. Establish goals that improve physical and mental health, enhance motivation toward abstinence, help the person create a life without substance use, and teach techniques for avoiding and minimizing the duration of relapses when they occur.

2. Assess the best treatment setting and determine if detoxification is necessary. Inpatient care should be reserved for those who are a danger to themselves or others, have not succeeded in outpatient settings, have co-occurring mental disorders, are physiologically dependent on substances, or have chaotic lives that require inpatient treatment.
3. Do not include medication as an integral part of the treatment of substance use unless specifically needed for co-occurring disorders, severe symptoms of withdrawal, or treatment of opioid or nicotine dependence.
4. Use group therapy as an important component of alcohol and substance use programs.
5. Include self-help groups, such as Alcoholics Anonymous, Narcotics Anonymous, and Cocaine Anonymous, to provide inexpensive, helpful peer support.
6. Incorporate a psychotherapy component that includes life skills training.
7. Address issues of family involvement and peer relationships.
8. Improve social support and life situations.
9. Include paraprofessionals in the treatment approach.
10. Build relapse prevention procedures into the treatment and aftercare phases.
11. Maintain follow-up aftercare for at least six to twelve months following treatment.

Marlatt (1998) found that fewer than 25 percent of people who misuse substances seek treatment programs. Those with relatively mild substance use disorders frequently make positive changes on their own, including reduction in substance use, switching to a less addictive substance, abstinence, and modified usage.

If abstinence is the goal, contracts can be useful in affirming the goal and in specifying the steps that people can take when they feel the desire for drugs or alcohol. Motivation, readiness to change, self-efficacy (people's belief in their ability to control their substance use), and controlling urges and cravings are critical elements that are addressed in a treatment program (Marlatt, 1998; Tucker et al., 2002).

Cognitive-behavioral therapy has been found to be an effective component of treatment. Behavior therapy usually is conducted in a group setting so that participants can reinforce and confront each other as appropriate and serve as role models and sources of support and information. Behavioral group therapy for people with substance use disorders includes such approaches as relaxation training, assertiveness training, role playing, stress management, development of other sources of gratification, and enhancement of coping skills.

Therapy with people who have substance use disorders typically follows a series of stages:

1. Identifying the problem
2. Taking a detailed history
3. Providing detoxification, as needed
4. Helping motivate people toward change
5. Setting goals
6. Providing education and interventions to develop coping mechanisms
7. Offering concurrent involvement in family therapy and self-help groups
8. Maintaining change through follow-up and relapse prevention

Pharmacotherapy can enhance the treatment of substance use disorders in two ways. First, it can help alleviate the symptoms of comorbid disorders like schizophrenia or a bipolar disorder, which may be contributing to people's dysfunctional use of substances (for example, if they are using substances as self-medication), and which may also be impairing people's judgment. Second, medication is sometimes used to help in directly modifying a person's use of substances. For example, methadone is used to modify use of heroin, and nicotine patches are effective in helping people stop smoking cigarettes. Although pharmacotherapy does have a place in the treatment of substance use disorders, drugs must be used judiciously with people who already are prone to misuse substances. Moreover, medication as the primary mode of treatment may interfere with people's ability to learn the skills they need in order to remain abstinent and improve their lives.

Education is another important component of most drug and alcohol treatment programs. Understanding the negative effects of drugs and alcohol, as well as recognizing in themselves the triggers and patterns of misuse, can contribute to people's motivation and enable them to deal more effectively with the challenge of abstinence.

Most people who misuse alcohol and other substances also benefit from social skills training that focuses on improving communication and assertiveness skills by helping people initiate social interactions, express thoughts and feelings, and respond appropriately to criticism. The training frequently takes place in a group setting to foster interaction, role plays, and feedback from other group members.

For many people, substance use is reinforced by peer groups, and group counseling as well as self-help programs can counteract that influence. Self-help groups like Alcoholics Anonymous, Rational Recovery, Women for Sobriety, and Narcotics Anonymous are almost always part of the treatment plan for problems of substance use and become a central ingredient of most aftercare programs. Self-help programs also have groups for family members (for example, Al-Anon, Alateen, and Adult Children of Alcoholics) that are useful in helping them deal with another family member's maladaptive substance use and encourage that family member's recovery.

Therapeutic communities or partial hospitalization programs are available for people who are not ready to live independently immediately after detoxification or who have failed to respond positively to outpatient programs in the past. Such transitional programs can help people locate employment and develop the skills and resources necessary for becoming self-sufficient. Token economies, sometimes used in these programs, offer people additional motivation to change and can solidify their resolve to stop using drugs or alcohol. Therapeutic communities can be particularly helpful to people with few resources and support systems, as well as to those whose peer groups and places of residence have promoted such dysfunctional use of substances that a comprehensive life change is required in order to facilitate abstinence.

In addition to direct treatment for substance use, therapy should focus on any developmental or lifestyle deficits that may be present. Many people with substance use disorders need assistance with career development and job seeking, parenting, developing drug-free leisure activities, and improving relationships.

Relapse rates have often been used to judge treatment outcomes. Marlatt (1998) suggests that after an initial lapse following treatment, one of two outcomes is possible. The client either goes back to using substances and is said to have relapsed, or gets back on track in the direction of positive change (prolapse). Lapses are common in any of the impulse-control disorders and are to be expected whenever anyone attempts to change behavior. Therefore, an important piece of any substance use treatment program should be development of relapse prevention skills and an aftercare program to monitor and encourage long-term success (Tucker et al., 2002; Witkiewitz & Marlatt, 2004).

Marlatt (1998) found that regardless of the substance used, three-quarters of all relapses are associated with three contributing factors: negative emotional states, interpersonal conflict, and social pressure. To a lesser extent, positive emotions can also trigger a relapse, especially when combined with socializing. Other conditions that are likely to trigger a relapse are physical pain, urges, and cravings. Therapists can use this list to help clients develop plans to resist relapse and develop coping mechanisms so that they are better prepared to deal with future stress.

No single approach to treatment stands out as ideal for substance use disorders; rather a combination of interventions (including but not limited to detoxification, education, individual and group behavior therapy, general psychotherapy, multifamily group therapy, assertiveness training, self-help groups, and pharmacotherapy), individualized to meet the needs of a particular person, are all part of the therapeutic milieu used in substance abuse treatment. Specific treatment methodologies are covered separately in the sections on alcohol-related disorders and drug-related disorders later in this chapter.

Prognosis

Relapse, especially within the first year after treatment, is common for people who have been treated for substance use disorders. People implementing any type of behavioral change are confronted by cravings, thoughts, and environmental stimuli that remind them of the behaviors they are trying to change. Witkiewitz and Marlatt (2004) describe relapse and relapse prevention as dynamic processes that are complex and unpredictable. Nevertheless, approximately one-third of people who participate in treatment for substance use disorders do remain abstinent, and another third are significantly improved after treatment.

Treatment of substance use disorders has a particularly positive prognosis for people who have stable work and family lives, who manifest little or no accompanying antisocial behavior, and who do not have family histories of alcohol problems. The prognosis is also good for people who comply with treatment; who can see the positive consequences of abstaining from drugs and alcohol; and who rate high on measures of self-efficacy, motivation to change, and coping skills (Witkiewitz & Marlatt, 2004). The prognosis is less optimistic for people with coexisting emotional disorders; in fact, the more severe the accompanying diagnosis, the worse the prognosis. Several studies have found that the main contributing factor to relapse is negative affect. Thus effective regulation of emotions is a necessary component in any treatment or relapse prevention program (Witkiewitz & Marlatt, 2004). The overall emotional health of the client, then, is usually a better predictor of outcome than is the severity of the substance use disorder (McCrady, 2006).

The next two sections of this chapter — on disorders related to alcohol and drugs, respectively — provide an overview of the nature and treatment of some of the specific substance use disorders. In each section, the primary focus will be on the use disorders (abuse and dependence) rather than on the induced disorders, which can vary widely and often require medical intervention. Nevertheless, the therapist must always determine whether a substance use disorder is accompanied by one or more induced disorders, and treatment must take account of the combination of disorders that are present.

Alcohol-Related Disorders

Description of the Disorders

Alcohol-related disorders represent a large and costly health problem in the United States: 10 to 20 percent of men have met the criteria for alcohol dependence at some point in their lives, and an additional 5 to 10 percent meet the diagnostic criteria for alcohol abuse. Figures for women are estimated to be approximately one-third of those for men (Schuckit, 2000, p. 98). Very few of these people are stereotypical "alcoholics"; rather, they are often productive working members of the community.

Approximately two hundred thousand deaths each year are directly attributable to alcohol use, a total that includes 25 percent of all suicides and 50 percent of homicides as well as a large percentage of automobile and other kinds of accidents. McCrady (2006) estimates that 25 percent of all mental health and medical clients are likely to have an alcohol use disorder. On a positive note, alcohol use has declined or remained stable for most age groups for the past twenty-five years.

Alcohol use disorders tend to begin in adolescence or early adulthood, especially for males; they rarely begin after the age of forty-five, and they sometimes remit spontaneously in midlife. People between the ages of twenty and thirty-five are most likely to misuse alcohol.

Men and women typically have different patterns of alcohol use. Women who consume alcohol to excess are more likely to drink alone; to feel guilty and attempt to conceal their drinking; to combine alcohol with other drugs; and to suffer from depression, anxiety, and insomnia. Alcohol problems seem to start later and progress faster in women and are more closely linked to stressful life circumstances (Sullivan, Fama, Rosenbloom, & Pfefferbaum, 2002).

Some ethnic groups have a higher prevalence of alcohol problems than others. People from Hispanic, American Indian, or Eskimo cultures, for example, are overrepresented among those with alcohol problems. In some cases, alcohol consumption could be the result of cultural traditions in which heavy drinking is expected; this is the case in Ireland, Korea, and Japan (Paniagua, 2001). Conversely, alcohol use disorders are less prevalent in groups where alcohol is an accepted part of dining or religion rather than being used primarily for recreation. Several models, described in the paragraphs that follow, have been advanced to explain the development of alcohol use disorders.

Medical or disease model. The medical or disease model suggests that some people have an inborn vulnerability to the physiological effects of alcohol, a vulnerability that is activated when they begin to consume alcohol. This theory is largely based on the belief that brain abnormalities, notably neurotransmitter deficits, can be inherited and may predispose people to maladaptive use of alcohol. The theory that underlies the medical or disease model has received support from studies of twins and seems to be borne out particularly in men. People with first-degree relatives who have an alcohol use disorder are three to four times more likely than people without such a family history to develop an alcohol use disorder. This model is the most widely accepted of those discussed here.

Family systems model. According to this model, dysfunctional use of alcohol is passed on from one generation to the next through modeling. Although the medical or disease model offers the most widely accepted explanation for alcohol misuse, the family systems model is also important in our current understanding of alcohol use disorders. Some factors, such as increased parental involvement with homework, higher levels of religiosity, and the establishment of clear rules that prohibit drinking, can have an apparent protective effect.

Environmental model. This model takes the position that the environment in which one grew up influences later alcohol use. Economic deprivation, low levels of education, and high levels of job stress have been shown to contribute to risk of alcohol dependence. Underachievement in school and failure to complete high school are associated with an increased chance of alcohol misuse in African Americans (Schuckit, 2000).

Behavioral/social learning model. According to this model, alcohol use is reinforced by its immediate social and physiological rewards. Alcohol misuse is particularly prevalent in metropolitan areas and in some college and military environments, where alcohol use is often accepted and perhaps encouraged. Such positive peer attitudes toward drinking have been associated with greater risk for developing alcohol-related problems across the life span, even into the seventh and eighth decades of life (Moos, 2006). Like the family systems model, the behavioral/social learning model occupies an important place in current understanding of alcohol use disorders.

Psychodynamic/psychoanalytic model. This model suggests that alcohol misuse reflects infantile oral dependence needs and unresolved conflict with parents. There is little empirical support for this model, but clearly alcohol is widely used to reduce anxiety and stabilize mood.

Humanistic/existential model. According to this model, using alcohol is a way to garner attention, sympathy, and care, and to avoid responsibility. Less research has been conducted on this model in the treatment of alcohol problems than on most of the others, so its usefulness is still unclear.

These models are mentioned to underscore the interactions among genetic, social, and environmental factors in the development of alcohol abuse and dependence. Understanding of these influences facilitates development of treatment and prevention strategies that take into account individual risk factors and that alter environmental factors that contribute to the vulnerability for this disorder.

Typical Client Characteristics

Nearly 30 percent of men develop alcohol dependence or abuse problems at some point in their lives. Frequently the person who is alcohol dependent is a middle-class man or woman who presents with vague complaints about sleep disturbances, sadness, nervousness, or interpersonal problems (Schuckit, 2000).

Alcohol use disorders have a strong tendency to run in families; males who have grown up in families that have a history of alcohol misuse are three times as likely to develop alcohol use disorders as males from families without that pattern (Schuckit, 2000), and women who have grown up in families that misused alcohol often marry men with alcohol problems. Familial-pattern alcoholism tends to begin earlier and to be more severe than alcohol problems in people from families without a history of the disorder.

People with alcohol-related disorders often have other mental disorders during their lives as well; the incidence of anxiety disorders (especially phobias), mood disorders, antisocial personality disorder, and other substance use disorders is particularly high. Up to 50 percent of males in treatment have co-occurring antisocial personality disorder; 25 to 30 percent of females are likely to have depressive disorders prior to developing an alcohol use disorder (McCrady, 2006). As they do with other substances, people sometimes use alcohol to reduce anxiety, to lessen the severity of a manic or psychotic episode, or to alleviate dysphoria or depression (Laudet, Magura, Vogel, & Knight, 2004).

An early age of first use of alcohol has long been associated with increased alcohol-related problems later in life. The National Longitudinal Alcohol Epidemiological Survey (Stinson et al., 1998) found that more than 40 percent of adults who used alcohol before age fourteen developed alcohol dependence later in life. Alcohol is the most widely used substance during the adolescent years (Evans et al., 2005). By their senior year of high school, 85 percent of students report having used alcohol.

Of adolescents who misuse alcohol, 30 to 50 percent have co-occurring diagnoses of ADHD or conduct disorder (Flory, Milich, Lynam, Leukefeld, & Clayton, 2003). Researchers point to possible common traits that underlie these disorders: poor impulse control, common genetic factors, and similar environmental factors. These factors are not simply additive; they combine exponentially to result in the development of more adverse outcomes and impaired functioning in later life (Flory et al., 2003).

As a result of all these related difficulties, people who misuse alcohol often present with concerns other than alcohol, such as interpersonal, occupational, and legal difficulties; cognitive impairment; and physical problems. Careful interviewing is necessary to determine whether alcohol is the central difficulty, typically the one that must be addressed before the others can be ameliorated.

Some studies have found certain personality patterns to be associated with maladaptive use of alcohol. According to Chamberlain and Jew (2005), people who misuse alcohol tend to receive high scores on the Minnesota Multiphasic Personality Inventory in obsessive-compulsive, depressive, and sociopathic factors. They also tend to score high in imagination, intellectual ability, extroversion, passivity, instability, anxiety, and interpersonal undependability on the California Psychological Inventory (Meyer, 1983).

Problems with alcohol use affect about 4.6 million women in the United States (Sullivan et al., 2002). Women who misuse alcohol are particularly likely to experience depression and anxiety (Evans et al., 2005; Tucker et al., 2002). They typically have special issues that need to be addressed, such as relationship and parenting concerns, partner abuse, a history of trauma, and barriers to treatment (such as finances, transportation, and child care). They often have difficulty in intimate relationships, as well as drinking patterns that are linked to those of significant others in their lives. Women develop drinking problems later in life than men do, frequently in response to a stressful life event, such as divorce or the death of a family member. Women who misuse alcohol are more likely than men who misuse this substance to be single; to have lower self-esteem; to have more severely disturbed personalities; and to be at increased risk for liver disease, depression, physical or emotional abuse, and cognitive deficits resulting from alcohol use (Hommer, Momenan, Kaiser, & Rawlings, 2001). These women have a high incidence of trauma in their backgrounds, including rape, incest, and abuse, and are more likely than men to attempt suicide. Unfortunately, they also are less likely to seek treatment. Some evidence indicates that women are better at concealing their disorder, and thus avoid or delay treatment (Sullivan et al., 2002). Family responsibilities, a lack of empowerment, and the stigma associated with women who misuse alcohol can all be barriers to their seeking treatment.

Women metabolize alcohol differently than men do and tend to be more susceptible to its toxic effects (Lieber, 2000). Research shows that although women consume less alcohol than men and for shorter periods of time, death rates among females who misuse alcohol are 50 to 100 percent greater than their male counterparts. These serious biological, sociological, and behavioral differences between males and females indicate that therapists should tailor treatment to the particular needs of women and should expect slower recovery, greater cognitive impairment, and increased presence of comorbid disorders (Sullivan et al., 2002). Because women do better in programs that focus on female issues, they should be directed toward women's meetings in such support groups as Alcoholics Anonymous and Women for Recovery.

Assessment

The first consideration in treating alcohol use disorders is to assess the extent and severity of the problem, the person's motivation, and social and other factors maintaining the current pattern of use (Bishop, 2001; Tucker et al., 2002). Tucker and colleagues report that screening measures should be brief and easily administered, and should accurately establish the presence of alcohol misuse. Three verbal self-reports that meet these criteria and screen for alcohol problems include the Michigan Alcoholism Screening Test (MAST; Selzer, 1971), the CAGE Screening for Alcohol Abuse (Buchsbaum Buchanan, Centor, Schnoll, & Lawton, 1991; Mayfield, McLeod, & Hall, 1974), and the Alcohol Use Disorders Identification Test (AUDIT; Saunders, Aasland, Babor, DeLaFuente, & Grant, 1993).

Motivation should also be assessed, as it is an important component in behavioral change. Prochaska and colleagues (1992, 2006) developed a five-stage model (discussed in more detail in Chapter One) in which each stage represents a different level of motivational readiness: precontemplation, contemplation, preparation, action, and maintenance. Taking the stage of readiness for change into account can assist the therapist in matching the treatment plan to the client's motivational level and determine whether motivational enhancement is a necessary part of the treatment process. Weaving motivational enhancement approaches into the treatment process has been associated with more positive outcomes (McCrady, 2006).

Preferred Therapist Characteristics

As in the treatment of other substance use disorders, therapists working with people who misuse alcohol should promote optimism, commitment, and a sense of responsibility. They should facilitate reality testing and provide structured treatment and limit setting. Therapists need to be able to tolerate these clients' anger and lack of motivation, to be flexible and patient, to avoid power struggles and negative countertransference, and to inspire hope and motivation. Therapists need to be honest and direct as well as compassionate and empathic (Bishop, 2001). Confrontation and self-disclosure on the part of the therapist should be used judiciously but can sometimes facilitate progress and reduce resistance to treatment. Bishop (2001) emphasizes the importance of the therapist's respect for the considerable challenge that most clients face in remaining abstinent. Therapists should be prepared for clients to engage in some alcohol use while in treatment and should not be discouraged if it occurs. At the same time, a therapy session should not be held if a client arrives intoxicated.

Intervention Strategies

Although *DSM-IV-TR* distinguishes between alcohol abuse and alcohol dependence, treatment is basically the same for the two, with the specific ingredients of the treatment plan being individualized. Current treatment of these disorders has shifted away from intensive residential and rehabilitative programs toward brief, multifaceted interventions or lower-intensity treatment spread out over a longer time period (Finney & Moos, 2002). Nevertheless, more intensive programs sometimes are indicated for people with long-standing misuse of alcohol, especially if they have a history of treatment failures. Withdrawal can be dangerous if alcohol consumption is high, and hospitalization may need to be the first step in treatment. Even if hospitalization is not indicated, a medical examination almost always is, because of the damaging effects of alcohol.

Finney and Moos (2002) examined fifteen psychosocial treatment modalities for treatment effectiveness. The approach shown to be most effective in treating alcohol use disorders was cognitive-behavioral treatment that focused on enhancing coping skills and on improving the balance between environmental demands and the person's abilities, thus reducing stress. Social skills training and the community reinforcement approach, which focuses on the person's drinking behavior and job- and family-related problems, are also important elements of alcohol treatment programs. Other effective treatments for alcohol use disorders include motivational interviewing, behavioral contracting, stress management training, relapse prevention, and aversion conditioning (Finney & Moos, 2002). Lowest ranked in effectiveness of the fifteen treatment modalities were educational lectures and films, confrontational interventions, and general alcohol counseling.

Part of the professional's role is to enhance motivation and increase the client's comfort with life without alcohol. Schuckit (2000) suggests the following process for increasing motivation in those who need treatment for alcohol use:

- Educate the person and his or her family about the course of alcohol use disorders and what they can expect in the future.
- Emphasize the person's responsibility for his or her own actions.
- Motivate the person to remain abstinent through the use of medication that may deter drinking on the spur of the moment.

A typical multifaceted approach to treating alcohol use disorders includes many of the following elements:

- A treatment contract specifying the goals, duration, and ingredients of therapy
- Education on the impact and risks of alcohol use

- Detoxification
- Development of insight into situations and motives that contribute to drinking behavior
- Behavior therapy, usually provided in a group setting and emphasizing decision making, assertiveness training, communication skills, reduction of anxiety and stress, control and redirection of impulses, identification and reduction of cues for drinking, monitoring of drinking behavior, and reinforcement for abstinence (Finney & Moos, 2002)
- Couples and family therapy, to enhance the impact of behavior therapy and help family members with their own alcohol-related difficulties
- Self-help groups
- Change in the client's social context through residence in a halfway house or through distancing from and assertiveness with the peer group that encourages substance use
- Nutritional and recreational counseling
- Naltrexone (ReVia), disulfiram (Antabuse), acamprosate (Campral), or other drugs to discourage alcohol use

Naltrexone (ReVia) was approved by the FDA in 1995 as a safe and effective adjunct to treatments for alcohol use disorders. Research indicates that naltrexone reduces alcohol cravings and alcohol-seeking behavior, and helps those who take it to maintain control over their drinking. Naltrexone can be used in conjunction with an alcohol treatment program to help reduce the frequency and severity of relapse.

Disulfiram (Antabuse) has sometimes been a part of the treatment of alcohol use disorders, particularly for people who have a long history of alcohol problems and who have failed at efforts to maintain sobriety in the past. Antabuse is an alcohol antagonist. If taken regularly, it acts as an emetic when combined with alcohol. Although it has been in use for more than forty years, evidence of its effectiveness is limited. Antabuse has been shown to be more effective than no medication at all, but studies have not always shown Antabuse to be more effective than a placebo in maintaining abstinence (Schuckit, 2000). One study of the use of Antabuse indicated that 46 percent of participants dropped out of treatment. Noncompliance, poor relapse prevention, and the risk of severe reactions associated with the medication suggest that Antabuse should be used cautiously, particularly with people who are depressed or who have heart disease, hypertension, or other serious health problems (Williams, 2005).

Acamprosate (Campral) is the third medication to be approved by the FDA for alcohol dependence. It first became available in the United States in 2005, although it has been used in Europe for years to reduce the unpleasant physical and psychological symptoms associated with withdrawal. Acamprosate is intended to be used as part of a comprehensive relapse prevention plan for those who have already achieved abstinence from alcohol. A meta-analysis of seventeen studies that included more than four thousand people found that continued abstinence (of at least six months) was higher for those treated with acamprosate than for those not receiving the drug (O'Malley & Kosten, 2006). Limited research is available on its effectiveness with people who are still using alcohol at the start of treatment.

Studies of the use of naltrexone (ReVia), acamprosate (Campral), and medications to reduce depression and mania, in conjunction with cognitive-behavioral therapy for alcohol use, are promising but so far inconclusive (O'Brien & McKay, 2002). Although a variety of medications, such as benzodiazepines, antipsychotics, and antidepressants, have been shown to alleviate specific symptoms related to alcohol use (such as anxiety, depression, mood swings, psychosis, and cravings), no medication has been found to be sufficient on its own to effect recovery from alcohol misuse. A large multisite clinical trial being conducted by the National Institute on Alcohol Abuse and Alcoholism (NIAAA) will look at naltrexone and acamprosate, both individually and together, as well as the effect of cognitive-behavioral interventions. The results will add to the knowledge of which treatment approaches are most effective in addressing alcohol use disorders.

Research has not supported the use of an analytic or insight-oriented treatment approach, the use of chemical or electrical aversion therapy, or antianxiety medication. Supportive therapy as a primary intervention also has not proved effective in the treatment of alcohol use disorders (Finney & Moos, 2002).

Some types of interventions for treating alcohol use disorders are unlikely to be effective, but no ideal treatment approach has emerged. One large scale study, Project MATCH, funded by the NIAAA, studied three different treatment approaches, each of which lasted twelve weeks:

1. Twelve-step facilitation, which introduced people to the first three steps of Alcoholics Anonymous and promoted active participation in that organization
2. Cognitive-behavioral therapy, designed to help people manage their thoughts and behaviors, recognize high-risk situations, refuse alcohol, and maintain sobriety
3. Motivational enhancement therapy

At one year follow-up, all three treatments had demonstrated a positive impact: drinking had decreased, and abstinence had increased. Careful matching of clients to treatments was not supported by the outcomes of the research, but each of the approaches did seem best for particular types of people.

The twelve-step approach was best for those with few psychological problems but with severe alcohol use that was encouraged by the social environment. Women, especially those with other significant mental disorders, responded best to the cognitive-behavioral approach. The motivational approach was helpful to those who had low motivation but who had neither social pressure to drink nor significant psychological difficulties (Finney & Moos, 2002).

One of the controversies in the field of alcohol treatment concerns the question of whether controlled drinking can be a viable alternative to abstinence. Those who accept the disease concept of alcohol use disorders generally believe that controlled drinking does not work, and most research suggests that therapy with abstinence as a goal is more effective. However, as discussed earlier, Tucker and colleagues (2002) suggest that moderation of drinking, rather than complete abstinence, is a reasonable first goal for people with mild to moderate alcohol problems. Those who fail at this initial trial are then more likely to consider abstinence. A moderation method allows for incremental steps toward self-care, and people may feel empowered to choose what works for them. Safe alcohol use guidelines are available, as is research on predictors of moderation outcomes (Dawson et al., 2005; Sanchez-Craig, Wilkinson, & Davila, 1995). A study by King and Tucker (2000) of people who met the criteria for alcohol dependence and who spontaneously resolved their drinking problems without treatment found that those who stopped drinking excessively and drank moderately made an average of five attempts at change, whereas those who ultimately became abstinent had made an average of forty-one attempts at moderation. Clearly, moderate drinking does not work for everyone. Sanchez-Craig and colleagues (1995) report that most people eventually use alcohol in moderation and that people find the idea of controlled drinking more acceptable than abstinence.

For maximum effectiveness, peer support groups should be part of a multifaceted treatment plan. Participation in a twelve-step program in conjunction with formal treatment is correlated with greater treatment success (Spiegel & Fewell, 2004). Alcoholics Anonymous (AA) is the most widespread twelve-step program. Its primary tenets are that alcoholism is a progressive disease and that once someone has become an "alcoholic", he or she will always be an alcoholic and cannot stop drinking without help. Alcoholics Anonymous currently has more than fifty thousand groups in the United States. Each AA group has its own focus and personality. It is important for people to attend meetings in which they feel most comfortable.

Some people are uncomfortable with Alcoholics Anonymous because of its strong spiritual component, and dealing with this issue beforehand in therapy may facilitate people's involvement with the program. Rational Recovery is a self-help group based on Ellis's rational emotive behavior therapy (Ellis & Tafrate, 1997). Rational Recovery, as well as other groups, such as Smart

Recovery, LifeRing, Secular Organization for Sobriety (SOS), and Women for Recovery, provide alternatives to Alcoholics Anonymous that de-emphasize religious and spiritual elements and do not insist on abstinence as a goal.

For some people, especially those dually diagnosed with a substance use disorder and a mental disorder, control of their drinking may take longer to achieve. For them, dual diagnosis meetings of AA or NA or a harm reduction support group may be better suited to their needs. Dual Recovery Anonymous (DRA; www.draonline.org) is a twelve-step program specifically for people with chemical dependency and a co-occurring mental disorder (Spiegel & Fewell, 2004).

As with most forms of substance use disorders, treatment of alcohol abuse or dependence should go beyond use of the substance and focus on career development, social and family relationships, and leisure activities. Women who misuse alcohol often need help with parenting skills, past physical and sexual abuse, social support systems, and feelings of low self-esteem. Treatment should encourage development of those skills that are needed to establish a rewarding and alcohol-free lifestyle. People seem to go through a particularly difficult phase during the early months of abstinence, when they are struggling to adjust to sobriety. Halfway houses, day treatment programs, and other follow-up or aftercare programs can facilitate the transition from severe alcohol use to self-sufficiency and abstinence.

Families in which alcohol is misused typically have more than one person who has a strong need for therapy. The children may be suffering the impact of the parents' inconsistent and negative behavior and may manifest emotional and behavioral disorders and early alcohol use themselves, as well as low self-esteem and confused goals and aspirations. Spouses or partners of those who misuse alcohol are sometimes enabling, indirectly encouraging the alcohol use because of their own dependence needs. Therefore, therapy should also address the needs of family members, both to treat their immediate problems and to help them avoid the continuation of patterns that promote alcohol use disorders. Involving the family in the therapy can also increase the accuracy of the available information on the client's drinking. Al-Anon, Alateen, and Adult Children of Alcoholics are programs that can further enhance the treatment of family members.

Prognosis

Long-term outcome for treatment of alcohol use disorders is related primarily to the person's coping skills, social support, and level of stress (Oltmanns & Emery, 2007). These factors appear to be more important than the type of treatment provided (inpatient or outpatient, individual or group, self-help or professional). Other factors related to a positive outcome include increased length of treatment, discovery of substitutes for alcohol (such as pleasurable activities, jobs, new relationships, or involvement in spiritual or self-help groups), and frequency of attendance at self-help meetings.

Lower relapse rates have also been found in people who have created a sense of meaning in their lives, who have lower negativity and a sense of peace and stability, and who experience hope and honesty (Miller & Harris, 2000). Even so, the likelihood of a relapse after treatment is high. Of people who have been treated for alcohol use, 70 to 90 percent relapse within the first year after treatment. Therefore, relapse prevention is an essential element of treatment. Therapists should not give the message that treatment failure is inevitable. However, therapists and clients must recognize that many people will not maintain long-term abstinence after their initial treatment and may need additional treatment, particularly during the first year, in addition to long-term follow-up. Thus the prognosis is good for improvement of alcohol use disorders but fair at best for total abstinence, although approximately 20 percent do achieve long-term sobriety, some even without treatment (American Psychiatric Association, 2000; Schuckit, 2000).

Drug-Related Disorders

Description of the Disorders

Although most people who misuse drugs have a drug of choice, studies have noted an increasing tendency for people to misuse more than one drug. This complicates the treatment picture and makes accidental overdoses more likely. People with comorbid substance use disorders also have a particularly high incidence of suicidal and homicidal behavior.

An important difference between people who misuse drugs and those who misuse alcohol is the illegality of many drugs. People who misuse alcohol may also have legal difficulties, typically due to their having driven while intoxicated, but those who misuse other substances are often involved in felonies and devote extensive time and energy to obtaining the funds needed to purchase drugs. Many people with problems of drug use (and some of those with alcohol problems) come to therapy involuntarily, having been ordered into treatment by the courts, and may be suspicious, guarded, and resentful. With these clients, therapists need to address issues of criminality and anger as well as those of substance use.

Typical Client Characteristics

Like people with alcohol use disorders, people who misuse drugs have a broad range of physical and emotional symptoms and often present with social and occupational impairment. Many people who misuse drugs have difficulty with impulse control. Adolescents who misuse drugs seem to be easily bored and have a high need to take risks and seek excitement (Tarter, Sambrano, & Dunn,

2002). Additional traits often identified in people who misuse drugs include low self-esteem, irritability, and the inability to achieve goals (Evans et al., 2005). Men are more likely to misuse illicit drugs; women are more likely to misuse prescription drugs.

More than 50 percent of people who misuse drugs meet the criteria for an additional psychiatric disorder (Tucker et al., 2002), with a lifetime possibility of developing a major depressive disorder three times that of people who do not use substances. Drug use is also strongly associated with ADHD, conduct disorder, and antisocial personality disorder.

Like the alcohol use disorders, drug abuse and dependence are also familial disorders; people with these disorders often were first exposed to drug use in the home (Tucker et al., 2002). Tarter et al. (2002) report that having had poor parenting is related to drug use and that parent-child conflict is a predictor not only of illegal drug use but of poor school performance and delinquency. Families of people who misuse drugs seem to have a high incidence of impulse-control problems and interpersonal conflict. Antisocial behavior, as well as alcohol use and other substance use disorders, are often found in these families, as are high levels of marital disruption, disciplinary inconsistency, emotional disorders, and lack of child monitoring (Tarter et al., 2002).

Research has indicated a possible association between personality traits and preferred drug. These findings should be viewed as tentative rather than conclusive at present, and overgeneralization should be avoided. Nevertheless, research on the association between personality and drug of choice can help clinicians understand the personality patterns and choices of their clients. The following sections discuss the categories of drugs included in *DSM-IV-TR* in its description of the substance use disorders. Some information on treatment of each of these categories of drugs is included here in order to link that information to the category of drugs.

Amphetamines. Amphetamines typically increase energy and performance and suppress appetite. People who misuse amphetamines often are coping with underlying depression and suicidal ideation. People using amphetamines also tend to be agitated and suspicious, aggressive and violent, and they frequently have little sense of direction. The amphetamines themselves can produce psychotic symptoms.

Amphetamine use is most common among men in their late teens and twenties, but the growing number of young people treated for ADHD with methylphenidate (Ritalin), amphetamine combinations (Adderall), or pemoline (Cylert) has increased the availability and misuse of amphetamine-like drugs among children and adolescents. More than seven million people are estimated to have misused stimulant drugs intended to treat ADHD (Kroutil et al., 2006). The drugs are used recreationally to stay awake, boost academic performance, and finish work faster. However, as many as seventy-five thousand people show signs of dependence (Kroutil et al., 2006). Both men and women misuse these drugs, but women are at greater risk of dependence, whereas men are at greater risk of abuse (Kroutil et al., 2006). Stimulant abuse is highest in the eighteen- to twenty-five-year-old age bracket.

Discontinuation of stimulants can result in symptoms that resemble atypical depression, including impaired mood, oversleeping, and an excessive appetite (Ockert, Baier, & Coons, 2004). Mood swings may continue for months. Amphetamines are the most likely of any drug to produce symptoms that mimic those of mental disorders, such as panic attacks, obsessive-compulsive states, and clinical depression. Continued use may lead to paranoid delusions, hallucinations, suicidal ideation, and violence (Ockert, Baier, & Coons, 2004). Treatment should include individual counseling emphasizing behavioral and cognitive approaches and relapse prevention.

Caffeine. Caffeine increases energy, enhances mental concentration, and produces feelings of well-being in people who consume moderate amounts. Although no caffeine use disorders per se are included in the *DSM*, caffeine-induced disorders are listed and are characterized by anxiety, restlessness, and sleep disturbances. A cycle can evolve in which a person does not get restful sleep because of caffeine but perpetuates the problem by using caffeine to stay awake during the day.

As many as 96 percent of adults have used caffeinated beverages. The average daily intake is 200 to 400 milligrams (roughly the equivalent of three to four eight-ounce cups of brewed coffee). Caffeine use is higher in people who are dependent on other drugs and in those who have a history of mental disorders. There is also a correlation between the amount of caffeine ingested and the use of benzodiazepines and other antianxiety medication (Schuckit, 2000).

Generally, consumption of caffeine begins in childhood, with the use of caffeinated sodas. Use of brewed beverages, including coffee and tea, typically begins in early to late teens. Caffeine usage appears to peak in the twenties and thirties, after which use stabilizes and then declines.

Approximately 40 percent of people who use caffeine have attempted to quit, citing such health reasons as anxiety, insomnia, gastrointestinal problems, heart arrhythmia, and fibrocystic disease of the breast (Schuckit, 2000). Because of caffeine's addictive quality, effects of a sudden withdrawal can include headaches, fatigue, irritability, mild depression, mild anxiety, difficulty concentrating, nausea, and muscle pain. Withdrawal symptoms can range from mild to severe, with as many as 13 percent of people developing symptoms that interfere with work or daily activities (Reid, 2005). Tapering off the use of caffeine over seven to fourteen days is recommended for people who make heavy use of caffeine.

Cannabis. People who use cannabis (including marijuana and hashish) typically value the relaxation, increased sensory awareness, and elevated mood it provides. However, when used in high doses or by particularly susceptible first-time users, marijuana can cause severe anxiety, paranoid thinking, and perceptual distortions similar to those produced by hallucinogens. People with underlying schizophrenia, depression, or another mood disorder are particularly vulnerable to these adverse affects (Evans et al., 2005).

People who chronically use cannabis tend to be passive, lacking in ambition, and prone to depression, anxiety, suspiciousness, and impaired judgment. Long-term use of cannabis can cause neurological impairment, decreased attention span, and reduced cognitive abilities. Cannabis often is used along with other substances, especially nicotine, alcohol, and cocaine (American Psychiatric Association, 2000). Cannabis probably is the most commonly used illegal drug, and its use is particularly prevalent in young adult males.

The potency of marijuana has increased in recent years due to plant breeding and improved growing techniques. Whereas the typical marijuana cigarette in the 1960s contained 10 mg of tetrahydrocannabinol (THC, the psychoactive ingredient in marijuana), current THC content is 150 to 200 mg. The biological effects of higher doses of THC are unknown; most research on marijuana is based on the lower doses found many years ago. Current studies are investigating the toxic effects of marijuana smoke across the life span, including immune system impairment and cardiovascular and pulmonary problems. Marijuana smoke contains more carcinogens than tobacco smoke (National Institute on Drug Abuse [NIDA], 2004). Because those who smoke cannabis tend to hold their breath while smoking, marijuana may be more detrimental to the lungs than cigarettes.

The effects of long-term cannabis use are beginning to show in the aging population. Recent research indicates that although marijuana use has declined among teenagers, there was a 300 percent increase between 1991 and 2001 in marijuana use among adults ages forty-five to sixty-four (NIDA, 2004) and a 22 percent increase in marijuana use disorders during the same time period (Compton, Grant, Colliver, Glantz, & Stinson, 2004). Marijuana has been shown to quadruple the user's risk of heart attacks within the first hour of smoking (NIDA, 2004) and to increase the risk of head and neck cancer. Long-term use of cannabis can cause neurological impairment, including reduction in memory and learning. Problems in fertility, sexual functioning, and low-birth-weight babies born to pregnant women who smoked marijuana have also been reported (Pape, 2004).

Beginning use of marijuana during adolescence may have serious effects, including patterns of use that are similar to addiction (Evans et al., 2005). Longitudinal studies of cannabis use from adolescence through adulthood indicate that weekly usage in adolescents predicts an increased risk of substance dependence as an adult. Early users are also at increased risk of moving on to other illicit drugs, of suicidal ideation, of suicide attempts, and of violence (Evans et al., 2005).

According to the National Institute on Drug Abuse (2004), most people who misuse cannabis are male (76 percent), white (57 percent), and young (46 percent under twenty years old). Fifteen percent of all admissions to substance use treatment facilities in the United States are for marijuana, and marijuana was the third most commonly misused drug mentioned in drug-related hospital emergency room visits in 2002, the latest year that figures are available.

Significant cannabis withdrawal symptoms have been documented; they include restlessness and irritability, chills, nausea, decreased appetite, and headaches. Most symptoms will go away in a day or two, but sleep and mood disturbances that accompany withdrawal can last for weeks. The desire to alleviate these withdrawal symptoms can lead to continued use of cannabis and frequent relapse.

No medication is known to reduce cannabis use. Treatment is similar to that for misuse of other substances. One study found that a fourteen-session cognitive-behavioral group treatment program for marijuana had the same effectiveness as a two-session individual treatment program that included motivational interviewing and advice on ways in which to reduce marijuana use (Stephens, Roffman, & Curtin, 2000). Both treatments educated clients on triggers and helped them develop avoidance strategies. Thirty percent of participants were found to be abstinent after one year.

Cocaine. Cocaine seems initially to boost self-esteem and optimism, increase mental and physical abilities, and convey feelings of power. These symptoms last only as long as brain cocaine levels are rising; within minutes, declining levels promote cravings, cocaine-seeking behavior, depression, and irritability (Evans et al., 2005). Because this drug is highly addictive, use can quickly progress to abuse and then to dependence in a short period of time (American Psychiatric Association, 2000). Extended use of cocaine leads to many negative symptoms, including anxiety, depression, suicidal ideation, weight loss, aggressiveness, sexual dysfunction, sleeping problems, paranoid delusions, and hallucinations. Because of their need for increasingly more cocaine, many who use this substance resort to theft. Stealing from family and friends may be one of the first signs of cocaine use (Schuckit, 2000).

More than 80 percent of those who use cocaine combine the drug with alcohol, resulting in a potentially deadly combination. Death rates are higher for cocaine use than for any other drug, as cocaine increases the risk of death from heart arrhythmia, stroke, and respiratory failure, as well as the risk of accidents, suicide, and homicide (Smith & Capps, 2005). Depressive, bipolar, and anxiety disorders and antisocial personality disorder often co-occur with use of cocaine (NIDA, 2003). In 2002, nearly half of all adult males arrested in Atlanta, New York, and Chicago tested positive for cocaine (NIDA, 2003).

No medication has proven effective in the treatment of cocaine dependence (O'Brien & McKay, 2002). Care should be taken to distinguish between cocaine-induced psychosis, which will remit in several days to a week, and delusions and hallucinations that last for weeks and may signal an underlying psychotic state (schizophrenia spectrum disorder or bipolar disorder). Polysubstance dependence involving benzodiazepines, antidepressants, and other medications should also be considered.

Treatment should include referral to an outpatient drug treatment program if the misuse is recurrent and severe. If individual therapy is indicated, cognitive-behavioral approaches with a relapse intervention component have been shown to be most effective.

Hallucinogens. Hallucinogens, such as lysergic acid diethylamide (LSD) and methylenedioxymethamphetamine (MDMA or ecstasy), can alter perceptions and promote insight, introspection, and feelings of euphoria, but the negative effects of hallucinogens include psychosis, mood changes, illusions (not usually hallucinations), and cognitive impairment. People who misuse hallucinogens often have accompanying interpersonal, academic, and occupational problems. Symptoms of depression, anxiety, and mood swings can last for weeks or months following discontinuation of these substances (Smith & Capps, 2005). Hallucinogen persisting perception disorder — that is, flashbacks, which can occur intermittently for years — is a particularly distressing consequence of hallucinogen use. Hallucinogens are most commonly taken by young white males (Kaplan, Sadock, & Grebb, 1994). Use of LSD, MDMA, and other so-called club drugs has declined in recent years (NIDA, 2003).

Inhalants. Although use of amphetamines and hallucinogens is declining, use of inhalants is increasing. Two million teenagers currently report having sniffed or inhaled substances, such as marking pens, correction fluid, glue, nail polish remover, gasoline, spray paint, lighter fluid, and anesthetic gases (Wu, Pilowsky, & Schlenger, 2004). Misuse of inhalants tends to begin early, typically between the ages of seven and seventeen, because of the ready availability of these substances. These substances produce euphoria and an out-of-body sensation. They also have many short- and long-term side effects ranging from headaches and nausea to irreversible brain damage and death. The use of inhalants is often associated with family, social, and school-related difficulties as well as with depression, anxiety, hostility, suicide attempts, and physiological damage to nerves, organs, and muscles. People typically use inhalants only briefly and then move on to other substances.

Inhalant use has been tied to a cluster of adolescent behaviors including antisocial acts, use of other drugs, and emotional difficulties. Inhalant abuse is particularly common in adolescents and preadolescents, in rural areas, and among Native Americans or people of multiethnic heritage. Smith and Capps (2005) indicate that 17 percent of all teenagers have used inhalants at least once in their lives — girls as often as boys, an unusual finding in drug use statistics (Wu et al., 2004).

Nicotine. Nicotine can increase learning and attention, improve mood, and promote relaxation. For many years, the negative effects of nicotine were minimized, but awareness of the addictive and lethal properties of nicotine, as well as of the difficulty of quitting smoking, has increased over the past three decades. Correspondingly, the number of people in the United States who smoke declined from 44 percent to 23 percent between 1964 and 2003 (Zickler, 2003). Tobacco continues to be associated with 25 percent of all deaths in the United States, however. Lifetime prevalence of nicotine dependence is approximately 20 percent and characterizes 50 to 80 percent of people who currently smoke. Adolescents and women are more vulnerable to becoming dependent on nicotine. Nicotine use is much higher among people with mental disorders than it is in the general population (American Psychiatric Association, 2000) and often coexists with alcohol dependence, schizophrenia, mood disorders, and anxiety disorders.

The most effective treatment for smoking cessation combines nicotine replacement therapy (NRT) with a psychosocial program. The common withdrawal symptoms include irritability, impatience, depressed mood, restlessness, increased appetite, and weight gain (Evans et al., 2005). Five types of NRT have been approved by the FDA (gums, patches, nasal sprays, inhalers, and lozenges) to help relieve some of the symptoms of nicotine withdrawal. When used in combination with behavior therapy, transdermal patches have produced abstinence rates of approximately 60 percent (Syad, 2003).

The connection between smoking and depression has led to treatment recommendations for people who smoke and also are depressed that include antidepressants in combination with smoking cessation programs. Evans and colleagues (2005) also report on the effectiveness of the antidepressant bupropion (Wellbutrin) for improving abstinence in nondepressed people, and a recent study at Yale University (George et al., 2003) found that selegiline (Eldepryl), a medication currently being used to delay the onset of Parkinson's disease symptoms, can also help smokers quit. Symptoms of nicotine withdrawal seem to result from decreased dopamine levels, and selegiline works to increase the level of dopamine in the brain.

A newer medication, varenicline (Chantix), has shown promise in nearly doubling people's chances of quitting smoking (Kuehn, 2006; Thayer, 2006).

Varenicline works by interfering with nicotine receptors in the brain. The medication lessens the pleasurable effects of smoking while reducing the uncomfortable symptoms of nicotine withdrawal.

Smoking cessation is difficult, and relapse is common. The American Cancer Society (2006) reports that about 5 to 16 percent of people quit smoking on their own, without treatment. Another 25 to 33 percent use medication or NRT and remain smoke free for at least six months. As mentioned earlier, combining NRT with psychosocial treatment increases the success rate even more.

Opioids. Opioids, including heroin, morphine, and prescription pain relievers with opioid-like action, produce a rapid sense of intense euphoria. Opioid use typically is preceded by use of other drugs. Opioid tolerance develops rapidly, and use of this substance often leads to theft, prostitution, and other illegal behaviors as means of paying for the substance. Use of opioids can lead to a wide range of negative symptoms, which include psychosis, sleep and sexual difficulties, depression, mania, and such medical conditions as hepatitis, skin infections, and damage to the heart and lungs.

The 2002 National Survey on Drug Use and Health (SAMHSA, 2003) reports that forty-seven thousand people in the twelve- to seventeen-year-old age range actively use heroin, and the age of first use is decreasing. Ten to twenty years ago, people who misused opioids were likely to come from lower socioeconomic urban settings, but greater availability of heroin in the suburbs and even rural areas has resulted in increased use across all age groups (Evans et al., 2005). Twenty-two percent of first-time users become dependent.

Misuse of prescription painkillers has increased markedly. People commonly blame their use on chronic pain, but at least one study has shown that as many as 80 percent of users were already drug dependent before they developed chronic pain, and in some cases the symptoms of drug use (for example, sedation, reduced reaction time) actually led to the accident or other painful condition (Schuckit, 2000).

Most people dependent on heroin have poor motivation to change. Denial is an inherent part of opioid dependence and must be addressed if treatment is to be effective. People who misuse opioids tend to lose sight of daily activities in search of the next fix (O'Brien & McKay, 2002).

Approximately 1.2 million adolescents currently misuse opioid-related pain relievers and other analgesic medications, such as codeine, fentanyl (Sublimaze), hydrocodone (Hycodan), methadone (Dolphine), morphine (Roxanol), oxycodone (Oxycontin, Percocet, Percodan), propoxyphene (Darvocet, Darvon), and others. A newer medication, tramadol (Ultram), has many pain-control properties of the opioids but has a lower risk of dependence.

According to Morrison (2001), approximately 50 percent of people who inject opioids are seropositive for human immunodeficiency virus (HIV). Due to needle sharing and unsafe sexual practices, they are also at increased risk for hepatitis B and C (Tucker et al., 2002). Most people dependent on opioids have at least one co-existing mental disorder, most often major depressive disorder, an alcohol use disorder, antisocial personality disorder, or an anxiety disorder (especially PTSD). Co-existing disorders should be treated with appropriate medication and psychotherapy.

Detoxification and treatment of withdrawal symptoms are the first steps in a long-term treatment approach to opioid dependence. Methadone, used as a less harmful but still addictive opioid, is sometimes substituted for heroin in drug treatment, with success rates that range between 60 and 70 percent in some treatment centers (O'Brien & McKay, 2002). Currently 190,000 people in the United States are on methadone treatment (SAMHSA, 2003). Methadone maintenance is still controversial because it involves substituting one drug for another. However, the benefits of methadone include reducing drug-seeking behavior, blocking symptoms of opiate withdrawal, and stabilizing the person's moods. The duration of methadone treatment can range from 180 days to several years, or methodone maintenance can last indefinitely (O'Brien & McKay, 2002).

O'Brien and McKay (2002) report that people who are misusing opioids benefit more from methadone maintenance when it is provided in combination with psychosocial interventions. This combination results in greater improvement as measured by reduced family problems, decreased drug use, fewer psychiatric symptoms, and higher rates of employment.

Other medications used to treat opioid dependence include levo-alpha-acetylmethadol (LAAM), buprenorphine (Subutex), and naltrexone (ReVia). LAAM has opiate effects similar to methadone, but is longer lasting and needs to be administered only every seventy-two hours. Buprenorphine produces effects similar to heroin, but there is a limit, so that higher doses do not produce greater effects, and overdose is not possible. Naltrexone works by blocking opiate receptors in the brain and is effective only after a person has gone through detoxification. All three of these treatment options have been shown to be effective. O'Brien and McKay (2002) provide a detailed comparison of studies of treatment effectiveness and treatment length for each of these pharmacological treatments. However, additional research is necessary to determine if there is a single most effective course of treatment.

Therapeutic communities are another avenue to treatment, particularly for those with a long history of opioid use. Many of these communities have adopted a highly confrontational model, popularized many years ago by the Synanon program. They encourage responsibility, insist on honesty and self-examination, and exert peer pressure to effect change. People recovering from problems with drugs provide valuable role models. The focus of these communities is on the present, on unlearning and new learning based on education and feedback, and on building responsibility and competence (Friedman & Wilson, 2004; Kennard & Lees, 2001). Longer stays (more than two months) are associated with improved success in therapeutic communities. Few controlled outcome evaluations are available for this approach to treatment. The prognosis for recovery for men and women who use opioids is poor in the short term, with nearly a 90 percent recidivism rate in the first six months following treatment; long-term prognosis is better, with more than a third achieving abstinence (Schuckit, 2000). Traits that improve prognosis are three years or more of abstinence, stable employment, being married, engaging in few antisocial activities, little or no dependence on other substances, and fewer problems with the criminal justice system. Like that of cocaine, the mortality rate among those who use heroin is high, with almost 2 percent per year dying from suicide, homicide, accidents, and such diseases as AIDS, tuberculosis, and other infections (Schuckit, 2000).

Phencyclidines (PCP). Use of phencyclidines (PCP), ketamine, and related substances can produce euphoria and feelings of detachment and dissociation. These drugs also cause many severe psychological problems, however, including rage, disinhibition, panic, mania, unpredictability, psychosis, and flashbacks, as well as such physical problems as seizures, confusion, delirium, coma, and even death from respiratory arrest (Evans et al., 2005). Aggressive behavior and poor judgment are particularly likely consequences of PCP use. Ketamine is odorless and tasteless and is sometimes slipped into drinks and used during sexual assaults and date rape. It produces amnesia and a period of impaired awareness (Evans et al., 2005). PCP use is highest in urban areas, especially Washington, D.C., and Philadelphia. In 2002, 14 percent of adult males arrested in Washington, D.C., tested positive for PCP, a dramatic increase from 2 percent in 1998. Similar figures were reported for juvenile arrests (NIDA, 2003).

Sedatives, Hypnotics, and Anxiolytics. Sedatives, hypnotics, and anxiolytics, including barbiturates, benzodiazepines (such as Ativan, Klonopin, Xanax, and Valium), and other prescription sleeping and antianxiety medications, tend to be misused by people who feel tense, anxious, and inadequate. *DSM-IV-TR* notes that sedative use is often associated with dependence on other substances and may be used to reduce the ill effects of alcohol, cannabis, cocaine, heroin, methadone, and amphetamines (American Psychiatric Association, 2000). These substances have often been prescribed for the people who ultimately misuse them, the sense of well-being and relaxation provided by the drugs having led people to persist in their use. Many of these substances are highly addictive brain depressants. They cause a range of symptoms, among them delirium, psychosis, and amnesia. These substances are potentially lethal, especially in combination with alcohol.

Polysubstance Dependence. According to the Community Epidemiology Work Group (CEWG; NIDA, 2003), polysubstance dependence is increasing at a fast pace with the proliferation of "an ever-growing array of illicit and licit substances" (p. 4) contributing to an increase in health problems and deaths. Polysubstance dependence is defined as the use of at least three types of substances (not including nicotine and caffeine) within a twelve-month period in which the criteria for substance dependence are not met by any one substance but are met by the group of drugs as a whole. The majority of drug-related deaths involve more than one drug, including cocaine (83 percent), heroin (89 percent), and methamphetamine (92 percent). A recent study of oxycodone-related deaths indicated that 97 percent also involved other drugs, such as benzodiazepines, alcohol, cocaine, other opioids, marijuana, or antidepressants (NIDA, 2003).

Other (or Unknown) Substance-Related Disorders. *DSM-IV-TR* (American Psychiatric Association, 2000) includes this category for substance-related disorders not included in the eleven specific drug categories previously mentioned. Other (or unknown) substance-related disorders refer to misuse of anabolic steroids, nitrite inhalants, nitrous oxide, over-the-counter and prescription drugs, and to situations in which the substance is unknown.

Most who misuse anabolic steroids are males who want to increase muscle mass, especially in conjunction with exercise. A 1997 survey indicated that 11 percent of male high school seniors had used anabolic steroids; rates are high among college students, especially men who also use alcohol and other substances (Schuckit, 2000). Steroids come in oral and injectable forms. Signs of steroid use include increase in muscle mass over a short period of time, severe acne, hair growth, development of breasts in men, and lowered voice. Misuse of steroids can result in anxiety, depression, aggression, and medical complications (Schuckit, 2000).

Amyl or butyl nitrite causes a slight euphoria and may slow down time perception as well as dilate the blood vessels. The most common side effects are nausea, dizziness, and anxiety. Use is relatively high among homosexual men (Schuckit, 2000).

Assessment

Treatment for all substance-related disorders should include medical and psychological assessments. Treatment plans can only be developed after a comprehensive assessment has been made, because issues of dependence, motivation, and history of usage will help determine level of treatment.

Preferred Therapist Characteristics

The guidelines for therapists working with people who misuse drugs are similar to those given in the sections on alcohol- and substance-related disorders. Therapists working with this population need a solid understanding of drugs, their current nicknames, their symptoms and prevalence, and the environments that promote their use, as well as an understanding of the legal and medical issues pertinent to people who misuse drugs. Because many people with drug use disorders are referred for treatment from criminal justice sources, these clients may be less cooperative and less likely to be motivated to change. Therapists who use motivational interviewing techniques probably will be more effective with these reluctant clients (Miller & Rollnick, 2002; Stasiewicz et al., 2006).

Intervention Strategies

Treatment goals for people who misuse drugs include abstinence, improved well-being (physical, emotional, social, and occupational), and, as necessary, improved family and overall functioning. Treatment for people who misuse drugs is similar to treatment for people with alcohol use disorders and usually includes the following components:

- Medical and psychological assessment
- Detoxification and, as necessary, treatment for symptoms of withdrawal
- Drug education
- Behavior therapy designed to eliminate drug use
- Psychotherapy to improve motivation, coping, and life skills and to address any coexisting mental disorders
- Self-help groups
- Family therapy
- Relapse prevention

Although behavior therapy has been the most common approach to treating problems of drug use, supportive therapy (promoting impulse control and environmental change) and psychodynamic therapy (focusing on insight), in combination with behavior therapy, have also been used with some success.

Improving interpersonal skills to promote development of a peer group that does not misuse drugs can be an important treatment ingredient for people who may not know how to relate to others without using drugs. Developing leisure activities to fill time previously spent in drug-related activities can also be helpful. People with the typical personality patterns (shyness, anxiety) of those who misuse prescription drugs are particularly likely to benefit from relaxation and assertiveness training.

Group and individual therapy are both often part of the treatment plan, as is involvement in self-help groups, notably Cocaine Anonymous, Narcotics Anonymous, and Alcoholics Anonymous. Participation in structured smoking-cessation programs like those offered by the American Cancer Society has also been effective in helping a substantial number of people stop smoking.

Treatment for people with co-occurring drug use and a significant mental disorder should take into account the fact that these people have more than just two illnesses; they tend to have multiple impairments that permeate all areas of their lives. A dual diagnosis is likely to result in more negative outcomes (hospitalization, suicide attempts, violence, incarceration, homelessness, and serious illnesses, such as HIV and hepatitis), and requires integrated long-term treatment that includes staged interventions, outreach, education, motivational interviewing, CBT, skill development, and social support (Drake et al., 2001). In looking at evidence-based practices, Drake and colleagues found that substance use treatment programs that do not address comorbid disorders are not effective. Integrated services must address both substance use disorders and any comorbid mental disorders concurrently. (See Chapter Nine for additional interventions for dual diagnosis.)

Family therapy is another important part of the treatment plan. Many people begin to use drugs like inhalants and cannabis while still in childhood or adolescence. Family therapy can help empower parents to establish sound values and rules in the home, as well as rewards and consequences that discourage drug use. Such families often could benefit from treatment to improve communication and conflict management skills as well as to provide psychoeducation on boundary setting and relapse prevention (McIntyre, 2004).

Sometimes medications, such as antidepressants and lithium, can be helpful in controlling underlying symptoms and thereby facilitate the treatment of drug problems. However, medication should be used cautiously with people who misuse drugs.

People who misuse drugs seem to respond strongly to life crises, especially those involving arguments and losses. Negative emotions often precipitate a relapse, so therapy should help people who misuse drugs find effective ways of coping with negative events (Witkiewitz & Marlatt, 2004). Extended aftercare, as well as monitoring and building on people's coping mechanisms, are useful in preventing relapses. Periodic blood or urine testing can also be helpful in motivating people to remain drug free and in keeping therapists informed of relapses. Environmental change is yet another intervention that improves relapse prevention, especially for people whose families and peer groups encourage their drug use. It takes several years of abstinence for recovery to be well established; this suggests the need for an equivalent period of aftercare, follow-up, and attendance at meetings of self-help groups.

Prognosis

High relapse rates, often more than 50 percent, are reported for problems of drug use. People who misuse nicotine, in particular, are known to relapse even after years of abstinence. People with stable family backgrounds, intact marriages, jobs, minimal or no criminal activity, less use of drugs and alcohol, and less severe coexisting emotional difficulties have the best prognosis (Schuckit, 2000). A positive prognosis is also associated with clients' attributing the improvement to themselves rather than to a program, involvement in maintenance treatment, and with social support for the effort to stop misusing drugs.

Use of many drugs, such as the opioids, declines with age whether or not treatment is provided. Therefore, middle adulthood may be a time when people who misuse drugs are especially receptive to treatment.

EATING DISORDERS

Description of the Disorders

This section focuses on eating disorders most likely to be found in adolescents and adults. Other eating disorders, found primarily in children, were described in Chapter Two.

Two eating disorders are listed in this section of *DSM-IV-TR:* anorexia nervosa and bulimia nervosa, along with the residual diagnosis of eating disorder not otherwise specified. A third disorder, binge eating disorder (BED), is currently included in the *DSM* appendix and has been proposed for listing as a mental disorder in *DSM-V*, pending further research. Currently this disorder is included under eating disorder not otherwise specified (EDNOS).

Eating disorders are among the most prevalent mental disorders for women and girls. These disorders often are chronic, include marked functional impairment and distress, are associated with increased suicidal ideation, involve repeated and multiple relapses, and may result in severe medical problems and even death (Rivas-Vazquez, Rice, & Kalman, 2003; Stice, Burton, & Shaw, 2004). Anorexia nervosa has the highest mortality rate of any mental disorder, including depression. Approximately 10 percent of people with anorexia nervosa die as a result of the disorder (Costin, 1999).

Overall prevalence rates of 0.5 to 3.7 percent have been reported for anorexia nervosa; rates of 1 to 4.2 percent have been reported for bulimia nervosa (American Psychiatric Association, 2000). The incidence of BED ranges from 0.7 to 4 percent. As many as twenty-five million people have met the criteria for BED at some point in their lifetimes. Since 1960, the incidence of eating disorders has been increasing, and the age of onset is getting younger. The onset of anorexia nervosa is typically between the ages of ten to thirty; for

85 percent of people with this disorder, onset comes between the ages of thirteen and twenty, but children as young as nine have been affected (Costin, 1999). Bulimia nervosa typically has a somewhat later onset and is often preceded by anorexia nervosa, which then evolves into bulimia nervosa in as many as 50 percent of the cases. BED most frequently occurs in young to middle adulthood and has an estimated prevalence rate of 3 percent in adults. About 8 percent of people who meet the criteria for obesity also have BED (Grilo, Sinha, & O'Malley, 2002).

Both anorexia nervosa and bulimia nervosa are most common in young women. These disorders also are being reported with increasing frequency in males and older women. BED is more common among females than males at a ratio of 5:1 (American Psychiatric Association, 2000). Woodside and colleagues (2001) estimate the female-to-male ratio found in anorexia nervosa and bulimia to be 3:1. Males with eating disorders tend not to seek treatment and are more likely to dismiss or ignore symptoms. Friends and family of these men may also attribute symptoms to other causes (such as drug use or excessive exercise to achieve muscle definition) rather than to an eating disorder (Woodside, 2004).

No significant differences were found in eating disorders, obesity, or levels of body image dissatisfaction across cultures or ethnic variables. A study by Mulholland and Mintz (2001) found equal incidence of anorexia nervosa, bulimia nervosa, and EDNOS in African American and white women. However, the incidence of eating disorders was lower for African American women who attended predominantly black versus predominantly white universities. Additional research on cultural patterns of eating disorders is needed.

Negative affect and depressive symptoms in adolescence may be associated with increased risk for the onset of all types of eating problems, including disordered eating, dietary restriction, purging, and recurrent fluctuations in body weight (Johnson, Cohen, Kotler, Kasen, & Brook, 2002). Other early predictors of eating disorders include pica in childhood (predictive of bulimia nervosa), picky eating and eating conflicts around mealtime (predictive of anorexia nervosa), sexual abuse or physical neglect, low social support, low self-esteem, and an avoidant style of coping with stressful events (Jacobi et al., 2004). Many people with eating disorders have a history of anxiety, depression, and maladaptive personality traits (Johnson et al., 2002).

In a study of 320 longitudinal and cross-sectional studies of eating disorders, Jacobi and colleagues (2004) found the following factors predictive of anorexia nervosa: complications with pregnancy and birth, OCD, perfectionism, and negative self-evaluation. The same research found that onset of bulimia nervosa was related to pregnancy complications, childhood obesity, parental problems including alcoholism and obesity, family criticism about weight and body image, and negative self-evaluation. Family heredity is an important factor in the development of obesity and binge eating.

Anorexia Nervosa. Anorexia nervosa, according to *DSM-IV-TR*, involves a person's refusal to maintain normal body weight. As a result, body weight is 85 percent or less of what would be expected for the person's age and height. Other symptoms of the disorder include great fear of becoming fat (even though underweight), a disturbed body image (seeing themselves as overweight even though they are underweight), dread of loss of control, and, in females, amenorrhea (absence of at least three consecutive expected menstrual cycles). In some very young women, the disorder is associated with apprehension about puberty and seems to represent an effort to delay development. Leaving home, as well as other triggers related to separation and maturation, sometimes precipitate this disorder. Twin studies suggest a genetic component for anorexia, possibly as high as 56 percent (Bulik et al., 2006). People with a mother or sister with anorexia nervosa are twelve times more likely to develop the disorder themselves and four times more likely to develop bulimia nervosa. Neurological research indicates that women who develop anorexia nervosa have excess activity in the brain's dopamine receptors, which regulate pleasure (Kaye et al., 2005). New research points to a genetic predisposition for such traits as anxiety, perfectionism, and obsessive-compulsive thoughts and behaviors. People with this underlying genetic predisposition also may be more susceptible to anorexia nervosa.

Common physiological symptoms of anorexia nervosa include cold intolerance, dry skin, an increase in fine body hair, low blood pressure, and edema (Costin, 1999). Metabolic changes, potassium loss, and cardiac damage can result from this disorder and can be lethal.

Two types of anorexia nervosa have been identified. People with the restricting type of the disorder (the more common type) do not engage in binge eating or purging but do maintain low weight by severely limiting their intake of food. People with the binge eating/purging type habitually engage in binge eating and/or purging behavior (such as self-induced vomiting or inappropriate use of laxatives, diuretics, or enemas) and, despite their binge eating, meet the low weight criterion for anorexia.

Bulimia Nervosa. People with bulimia nervosa engage in behaviors similar to those of people with anorexia nervosa, binge eating/purging type, but do not meet the full criteria for that disorder, usually because their weight is more than 85 percent of normal body weight. Bulimia nervosa, according to *DSM-IV-TR*, involves an average of at least two binges per week, usually accompanied by compensatory behavior (such as self-induced vomiting, fasting, laxative use, or extreme involvement in exercise) for at least three months, as well as a sense of being out of control during these episodes. Binges may last anywhere from a few minutes to a few hours. People usually binge when they are alone and, on average, consume approximately fifteen hundred calories in a single binge

(Craighead, 2002). People give many reasons for their binges. These reasons include (in descending order) tension and anxiety, food cravings, unhappiness, inability to control appetite, hunger, and insomnia.

People who binge have many ways of controlling their weight, including purging; fasting; exercising excessively; spitting out food; and using diuretics, laxatives, and diet pills. Combinations of these compensatory behaviors are common. Purging is often learned from friends and seems to have some support among adolescent girls as an acceptable way to control weight. In fact, dieting is often a precursor to the development of bulimia nervosa. The self-induced vomiting seems to increase feelings of self-control and to reduce anxiety, and these secondary gains often make it a difficult behavior to extinguish.

Physical signs usually accompany the self-induced vomiting often associated with binge eating. These signs include swelling of the parotid glands, which produces a chipmunklike appearance; scars on the back of the hand (from the hand's contact with the teeth while vomiting is being induced); chronic hoarseness; and dryness of the mouth. Physiological reactions to purging include dental cavities and enamel loss, electrolyte imbalance, cardiac and renal problems, and esophageal tears (Costin, 1999). Long-term effects of frequent binge eating and purging can include amenorrhea, anemia, dehydration, and acute heart dysrhythmia. Impaired nutrition can also increase the risk for osteoporosis, reproductive problems, diabetes, and high cholesterol (Sagar, 2005).

Binge Eating Disorder (BED). Binge eating disorder consists of a pattern of binge eating episodes on an average of two days per week over a period of at least six months, without the persistent use of compensatory behavior required for a diagnosis of bulimia nervosa (American Psychiatric Association, 2000). People with BED may consume large quantities of food in a short period of time, eat until they are uncomfortably full, feel out of control when eating, feel guilt and embarrassment over the quantity of food they eat, eat alone frequently, and eat even when they are not physically hungry. BED may be the most common eating disorder, and it can lead to obesity and the concomitant health risks associated with being overweight. Loss of control over eating is the primary distinguishing feature of BED. Those who overeat and do not report feelings of lack of control over their eating would not fit the criteria for BED (Craighead, 2002).

Research shows that most binges typically begin with a mood change. People report feeling anxious or tense before a binge, relief of anxiety during the binge eating episode, and absence of anxiety at the conclusion. Several researchers have written about how such affective dysregulation has a bipolar quality (McElroy & Kotwal, 2006). Binge eating may occur on a continuum with normal eating, with "passive overeating" (p. 120) being the least severe form, impulsive or compulsive overeating representing an intermediate form, and recurrent binge eating being the most severe (McElroy & Kotwal, 2006).

Typical Client Characteristics

Eating pathology is rooted in efforts to regulate negative mood states (Stice et al., 2004). Eating has been reported to provide comfort and distraction from negative feelings. However, as with most impulse-control disorders, after the behavior has been completed, it actually leads to more negative affect, assuming a continuing course. Depressive symptoms have been found to be predictive of onset of binge eating. Conversely, feelings of shame, guilt, and negative affect following a binge eating or binge and purging episode increase the risk for depression (Stice et al., 2004).

Low self-esteem, denial, shame, depression, and problems related to socialization, sleeping, and sexual desire are commonly found in people with anorexia nervosa, as are obsessive-compulsive features, especially related to a preoccupation with food (Costin, 1999). People with anorexia nervosa often cook for their families but refuse to eat what they have prepared because of their intense fear of gaining weight. They tend to be resistant to treatment because their disorder is ego-syntonic, and they typically do not want to change their eating behavior.

People with the restricting type of anorexia nervosa commonly are dependent, introverted, compulsive, stubborn, perfectionistic, asexual, and shy. They have low self-esteem and feel ineffectual. They tend to come from affluent homes where food had an important role. They also tend to have been well-behaved children and often played an important part in holding the family together. Many have been parentified children in enmeshed families and were overprotected, constricted, and overregulated. They lack autonomy and a clear sense of their own identity. They had eating problems as children or had one or more family members who displayed some type of disordered eating themselves (Bulik et al., 2006).

Most people with bulimic symptoms report problems with interpersonal relationships. They tend to be anxious, depressed, demoralized, self-critical, and secretive about their eating behaviors. People who binge and purge typically feel shame, guilt, powerlessness, and a sense of being out of control (Stice et al., 2004). Although they usually are sexually active, they tend to have sexual difficulties, as well as conflicted feelings about intimate relationships. They tend to be more extroverted, more emotional, less rigid, more anxious, more guilty, and more depressed than those people with eating disorders who do not habitually binge (Costin, 1999). One study found that multi-impulsivity (defined by three of the following: heavy alcohol use, a suicide attempt, self-mutilation, repeated shoplifting, and sexual disinhibition) was more common in people diagnosed with bulimia (18 percent) than in those with anorexia (2 percent) and people without eating disorders (2 percent) (Nagata, Kawarada, Kirike, & Iketani, 2000). Fischer, Smith, and Anderson (2003) found that people with bulimia had increased scores on impulsive urgency and tended to act rashly in the face of negative emotion.

People with bulimia nervosa tend to see their families as low in cohesiveness and as discouraging of intellectual and recreational activities, independence, assertiveness, and open expression of feelings. These families tend to be highly critical, especially of body image and weight, and have high levels of conflict.

Bulimic behavior, unlike restriction of food intake, tends to be ego-dystonic, and people with this symptom experience considerable hunger and disappointment in connection with their need to binge and purge. As a result, they are more likely to seek treatment than are those with anorexia nervosa, restricting type.

Mothers who have anorexia nervosa, bulimia, or BED tend to deal with children's eating in unhealthy ways by developing odd feeding schedules, using food for rewards and punishment, using food to provide comfort, and being very concerned about their daughters' weight (Agras, Hammer, & McNicholas, 1999). Some parents are overly controlling and restrict their children's food intake; research has shown these children are more likely to eat when they are not hungry, to seek out prohibited foods, and to develop a full-blown eating disorder when they are older (Birch, Fisher, & Davison, 2003). Eating disorders that begin in childhood can be especially difficult to treat.

People with bulimic symptoms are also particularly likely to have first-degree relatives with mood disorders, substance use disorders, and obesity (Jacobi et al., 2004). Their siblings and parents have an unusually high incidence of eating disorders and of major depressive disorders. Lilenfeld et al. (1997) suggested that some people with bulimia nervosa may have a familial vulnerability for impulsivity and affective instability.

Other mental disorders are highly likely to accompany anorexia nervosa, bulimia nervosa, and BED. Most people with these disorders have also experienced a major depressive disorder, and many have met the diagnostic criteria for anxiety disorders and substance use disorders (Johnson et al., 2002; Stice et al., 2004). Perfectionistic traits and obsessive-compulsive disorder are unusually likely to occur in people with anorexia nervosa (Jacobi et al., 2004). More than half of people with eating disorders have accompanying personality disorders (Rosenvinge, Martinussen, & Ostensen, 2000). People with eating disorders, particularly those with a coexisting diagnosis of borderline personality disorder, have a higher than average prevalence of childhood sexual abuse (ranging from 40 to 70 percent of women and 10 percent of men) (Costin, 1999; Woodside, 2004; Woodside et al., 2001). Women with bulimia nervosa also tend to have rates of anxiety, antisocial personality disorder, and familial substance misuse that are higher than in the general population (Grilo et al., 2002).

People with BED tend to have impulsive behavior traits. They often lack deliberation and fail to consider consequences before acting (McElroy & Kotwal, 2006). They also report being outgoing, having a strong appetite, and having engaged in kleptomania. A study by Lacey and Evans (1986) found an increased history of theft (41 percent) among people with eating disorders. The authors concluded that people with eating disorders often have multiple impulse-control disorders.

Assessment

Anorexia nervosa, bulimia nervosa, and BED are physically damaging and potentially lethal disorders. Therefore, the first step in treatment is to assess the client's eating behaviors and any physiological damage by taking a careful history and referring the client for examination by a physician. Craighead (2002) recommends that therapists ask the following questions as part of the initial assessment of eating-disordered clients:

- To what extent is the client motivated for treatment at this point?
- Is the client willing to self-monitor?
- For clients who are binge eating only, is the client willing to focus on reducing binge eating before addressing weight loss? Is the client interested in nondieting interventions?
- Does the client have other mental health problems that might influence the choice of treatment or expected length of treatment?
- What are the functions of the binge eating, the purging, or the eating restriction?

Such inventories as the Questionnaire on Eating and Weight Patterns-Revised (QEWP-R; Yanovski, 1993) and the Eating Disorder Examination Questionnaire, Twelfth Edition (EDEQ; Fairburn & Cooper, 1993) can be useful in obtaining an accurate assessment of the disorder's severity. These self reports screen for the presence of specific eating disorders, provide useful information about the frequency of problem eating and dieting behaviors and attitudes, and are found to be effective tools in the identification of people with possible eating disorders or problems (Craighead, 2002; Grilo et al., 2002).

A life chart can be helpful in determining onset of symptoms, as well as in establishing the relationship between stressful life events and symptoms. Suggested areas to include are a chronology of the client's memories of significant life events throughout the life span, mood and self-esteem, interpersonal relationships, and changes in weight (including any compensatory behaviors). Past treatment should also be included. Documenting eating problems over time can be helpful in pointing out patterns and identifying the usually chronic and fluctuating course of the disorder.

Other useful tools in the assessment of eating disorders include self-reports of eating behavior, assessments of cognitive processing, self-efficacy scales, and body image assessments. Due to the high percentage of people with concomitant eating and personality disorders, care should be taken to assess for relevant personality traits and disorders.

Preferred Therapist Characteristics

Therapists should assume a collaborative approach when working with people diagnosed with eating disorders. People are more motivated to change if they believe a goal can be attained. Thus, early in treatment, therapists should attempt to assess, discuss, and foster clients' expectations of improvement, as part of the development of a positive therapeutic alliance (Constantino, Arnow, Blasey, & Agras, 2005). Positive expectations have been shown to be predictive of positive treatment outcome (Arnkoff, Glass, & Shapiro, 2002).

Therapy for people with eating disorders should address readiness to change and motivational issues (Geller, Brown, Zaitsoff, Goodrich, & Hastings, 2003). For a detailed discussion of motivational interviewing and Prochaska's readiness to change theory, refer to the previous section on the treatment of substance use disorders and to Chapter One.

People with eating disorders typically are very sensitive to disapproval or interpersonal rejection. Consequently, they need considerable support and approval in therapy, to help them disclose symptoms that typically seem shameful to them. Costin (1999) suggests that the following clinician attributes are critical to establishing a positive therapeutic alliance with people who meet the criteria for eating disorders:

- Sustained empathy
- Patience and thinking in the long term
- Limiting battles for control
- Making behavioral agreements and contracts
- Challenging cognitive distortions
- Balancing nurturing with authoritativeness

Costin (1999) reports that early on she tells her clients that the battle will be between the client and the eating disorder, not between the therapist and client. Therapists will need to handle these clients' strong dependence needs by gently encouraging self-control, independence, and active involvement in treatment. At the same time, therapists will also need to be structured, to provide stability and constancy, and to set limits to protect these clients, even hospitalizing them if that becomes necessary.

Because of the high likelihood that people with eating disorders will have at least one other mental disorder, therapists treating these clients need to be knowledgeable not only about eating disorders but also about the many other disorders that may also be present. Assessment of co-occurring disorders will be necessary to planning effective treatments.

Intervention Strategies

Less than one-third of people with eating disorders ever enter into treatment. Of those who do receive treatment, symptom remission occurs in only 40 to 60 percent of cases (Stice et al., 2004). Effective interventions for eating disorders should focus on reducing negative affect, modifying eating behaviors, identifying situations that trigger behavior, and continuing motivation to change (Craighead, 2002; Stice et al., 2004). Relapse prevention is an important part of any program for disordered eating and should be integrated into treatment.

Cognitive-Behavioral Therapy. Cognitive-behavioral therapy has been found to be superior to no treatment, pharmacological treatments, and other forms of psychotherapy, including behavior therapy without a cognitive component (Agras et al., 1999; Grilo et al., 2002; Wilson & Fairburn, 2002). Grilo and colleagues suggest a model of CBT treatment for eating disorders that includes three phases. The first phase involves psychoeducation about the eating disorder and expectations for treatment, including homework, self-monitoring, and a gradual approach to normalized eating. The second phase includes the use of cognitive restructuring to identify, challenge, and change maladaptive thinking. The final stage includes relapse prevention and problem-solving skills to help clients cope with stress and apply their newly found skills to other areas of their lives.

Dialectical Behavior Therapy (DBT). Dialectical behavior therapy has been adapted for use with BED and may prove useful in treating people with chronic eating disorders who are resistant to treatment and those who also have borderline features, such as self-harming behaviors and dissociative episodes (Craighead, 2002). DBT may be especially helpful for those with high negative affect, impulsivity, and difficulty self-regulating their emotions.

One model described by Craighead (2002) for the treatment of BED and bulimia nervosa helps clients identify maladaptive cycles, such as emotional eating, eating when not hungry, restrictive eating, ignoring satiety clues, and planned binges. This information is then used to tailor treatment to the client's specific problems. For example, if a frequent trigger is skipping meals and getting too hungry, people would be advised on how to plan more frequent, low-calorie snacks.

Multidisciplinary Approach. A multidisciplinary approach seems best for working with people with severe anorexia nervosa or bulimia nervosa.

A treatment team consisting of a physician, a nutritionist, and a mental health professional can monitor the impact of the disorder on the person's health. Exposure and response prevention are important components of treatment for people who binge and purge. Presenting people with both prebingeing and purging cues in multiple settings while preventing or delaying those behaviors can enhance treatment, although this approach should also be combined with other treatment interventions.

Manualized Treatment. In 1985, Fairburn developed a structured manual that describes a cognitive-behavioral approach to treating eating disorders. That manual, revised in 2002, has been widely adopted; since that time, manual-based CBT has become the preferred treatment for bulimia nervosa (Wilson & Fairburn, 2002). The approach it describes consists of nineteen sessions of individual therapy that span approximately twenty weeks. The approach emphasizes problem solving and is both present- and future-oriented. The treatment is divided into three stages. The first stage includes information on the treatment approach, on eating disorders, and on nutrition. Self-monitoring is begun, and behavioral techniques to modify behavior are taught, in an effort to restore healthy patterns of eating. Cognitive interventions are emphasized in the second stage, during which people are helped to identify and modify their dysfunctional thoughts about eating, weight, and body size. The third stage emphasizes the maintenance of gains and the prevention of relapses. The treatment program developed by Fairburn is typical of those used to treat eating disorders. The program combines cognitive and behavioral interventions, with some attention to affect, into a structured format that can be used either with individuals or with groups.

Interpersonal Psychotherapy (IPT). Interpersonal psychotherapy also has been shown to be effective in treating eating disorders, but is less effective than cognitive-behavioral therapy (Wilson & Fairburn, 2002). The main emphasis of IPT is on helping people identify and modify current interpersonal problems. Controlled studies on the effectiveness of psychodynamic approaches in the treatment of eating disorders are lacking, yet it still remains a popular therapy for the treatment of bulimia nervosa (Wilson & Fairburn, 2002).

Although research has not established the superiority of group over individual therapy in the treatment of people with eating disorders, group therapy for these clients offers many benefits. These include mutual support, reduction of shame, diffusion of power struggles, feedback from multiple sources, role models, and the opportunity to practice interpersonal skills. At the same time, group therapists must ensure that group members have sufficient empathy to participate successfully in the group and that the group does not encourage competitive weight loss.

Family Therapy. Family therapy may be a useful adjunct in the treatment of eating disorders, particularly for adolescents with anorexia nervosa, whose family dynamics often contribute to the development of the disorder (Wilson & Fairburn, 2002). Family members of people with eating disorders commonly are coping with their own emotional difficulties, and family therapy may help them, in addition to improving the overall functioning of the family. People with eating disorders also often have issues related to separation and individuation from their families of origin, and these too can be addressed through family therapy.

Hospitalization. Hospitalization sometimes is needed for people with eating disorders. The primary goal of hospitalization for the severely underweight person with anorexia is to implement refeeding and weight gain. For the person diagnosed with binge eating or bulimia, it may be necessary to establish control over excessive bingeing and purging (Costin, 1999). Hospitalization may also be necessary to ensure the person's safety in the case of suicide attempts, ideation, or threats, or if severe anxiety or symptoms of depression are interfering with the person's normal ability to function. If the client does not seem to be in immediate danger, however, outpatient treatment may be adequate as long as steps are taken to restore normal weight and to curtail other self-damaging behaviors.

Internet Delivery Methods. The use of the Internet for delivery of treatment interventions for eating disorders is still in its infancy, so few studies exist that document its effectiveness. Yager (2001) used case examples to show how e-mail could serve as an effective adjunct to face-to-face therapy for anorexia nervosa. Clients who communicated via e-mail with their therapists several times a week had increased levels of treatment compliance and reported higher satisfaction with treatment. Luce, Winzelberg, Zabinski, and Osborne (2003) found Internet delivery methods can be used for education, prevention, interventions, and maintenance of therapeutic change. Internet groups often fulfill the same purposes as face-to-face support groups, providing a venue for self-disclosure, giving information, and offering direct emotional support. Internet groups have also been found to be effective in reducing levels of social isolation. However, the Internet must be used cautiously. Some sites promote disordered eating and can worsen symptoms.

Medication. At present, no medication has been approved specifically for the treatment of eating disorders. Research is needed on the effect on symptoms of a variety of medications. For example, atypical antipsychotics such as olanzapine (Zyprexa) have been shown to decrease symptoms of agitation and anxiety and increase weight gain in people with anorexia. Some limited studies have shown that antidepressants can treat underlying serotonin dysregulation and obsessive-compulsive and depressive symptoms (Rivas-Vazquez et al., 2003). In one study, fluoxetine (Prozac) was found to reduce relapse frequency (Kaye et al., 2005).

Antidepressant medication, the anticonvulsant topiramate (Topamax), and opioid antagonists, such as naltrexone (ReVia), have been found to reduce binge eating associated with bulimia nervosa and BED, but relapse is highly likely when medication is withdrawn (Grilo et al., 2002; Rivas-Vazquez, et al., 2003). Several studies and meta-analyses of treatment for bulimia nervosa indicate that a combination of medication and psychotherapy produces "more robust effects" (Rivas-Vazquez et al., p. 565) than either modality alone. Given the high rate of relapse associated with eating disorders, cognitive-behavioral therapy is recommended to help prevent relapse after medication has been discontinued.

Pharmacotherapy may be considered as one component of a more comprehensive treatment strategy for eating disorders. However, until more definitive research is available, medication should be used with care and should not be routinely recommended for people with eating disorders.

Maintaining a dual focus on the eating disorder and other problems the client is facing seems to be an effective way to proceed in therapy. Duration seems to be an important variable in the treatment of eating disorders. Longer treatments, typically lasting at least four to six months, are usually more successful. People with severe eating disorders may need treatment of at least a year in duration.

Prognosis

Improvement of eating disorders has been reported in terms of reductions in binge eating and purging and in terms of the cessation of all disordered eating patterns. Treatment that follows recommended guidelines is likely to have a considerable impact on eating patterns, typically reducing binge eating and purging by a rate of at least 75 percent. The prognosis is less favorable for complete remission of the eating disorder; 44 percent of people with anorexia nervosa recover completely through treatment, 28 percent are significantly improved, 24 percent are unimproved or significantly impaired, and 10 percent die prematurely as a result of the disorder. The prognosis for treatment of bulimia nervosa is somewhat better. Sagar (2005) reports a study in which five to ten years after diagnosis of bulimia, approximately 50 percent of women had recovered completely, 20 percent continued to meet the criteria for the disorder, and about 30 percent had relapsed. Fairburn and colleagues (2000) report higher recovery rates for BED than for bulimia in a five-year follow-up;

51 percent of the bulimia group continued to have a clinical eating disorder, compared with only 18 percent of the BED group.

According to Wilson and Fairburn (2002), early response to treatment is the best predictor of a positive prognosis for treatment of an eating disorder. Good prognosis is also associated with the following factors:

- Good premorbid functioning
- A positive family environment
- The client's acknowledgment of hunger
- Greater maturity (including psychosexual maturity) and self-esteem
- High educational level
- Early age of onset
- Less weight loss
- Shorter duration of the disorder
- Less denial of the disorder
- Overactivity
- Absence of coexisting mental disorders

As with most of the other impulse-control disorders, relapses of eating disorders are common and are often triggered by stressful life events. Moreover, even if people no longer meet the full criteria for an eating disorder, many continue to experience dysphoric moods and to engage in unhealthy eating. Treatment should be extended through follow-up or support groups to prevent and address setbacks. Follow-up treatment should also be helpful in reducing family, social, and occupational difficulties that often persist after the eating disorder has been eliminated.

SEXUAL AND GENDER IDENTITY DISORDERS

Most sexual disorders, like substance-related disorders and eating disorders, involve behavioral patterns that are dysfunctional or self-destructive. Unlike eating disorders or substance use disorders, however, sexual disorders are usually not physically self-injurious, nor do they usually cause pervasive dysfunction. Nevertheless, they are often closely linked to people's satisfaction with their relationships, and these disorders may both reflect and cause impairment in relationships. Some paraphilias may also lead people to break the law in an effort to find sexual gratification.

DSM-IV-TR divides sexual and gender identity disorders into three categories: sexual dysfunctions, paraphilias, and gender identity disorder. In a sense, all three are disorders of behavior involving dysfunctional and inappropriate responses to stimuli, but the people with these three disorders tend to be very different in terms of lifestyle and personality patterns, motivation for treatment, and interactions with their therapists. Their disorders also differ in terms of duration, severity, and impact. The treatments for all three categories have some common ingredients (the primary one being the facilitation of expressions of normal, healthy sexuality), but the three will be discussed separately here because of the important differences among them.

Sexual Dysfunctions

Description of the Disorders

This category of disorders involves disturbances in sexual desire or functioning that cause significant distress and interpersonal difficulties. People with these disorders typically want to have healthy and rewarding sexual relationships but have encountered difficulties in doing so. *DSM-IV-TR* organizes this category according to stages in the sexual response cycle and lists the following disorders:

Sexual desire disorders: hypoactive (deficient) sexual desire disorder and sexual aversion disorder. These disorders are experienced by as many as 50 percent of the population at some point in their lives. Prevalence rates vary from 0 to 7 percent in males to 5 to 46 percent in females. Postmenopausal women have the highest incidence of sexual desire disorders (Wiegel, Wincze, & Barlow, 2002).

Sexual arousal disorders: female sexual arousal disorder and male erectile disorder. Both reflect a lack of physiological arousal and sexual excitement. Sexual arousal disorders are very common, affecting approximately one-third of all women and 10 to 20 percent of men. Age increases the risk of male erectile problems, with one-half of men forty to seventy reporting erectile difficulties (Wiegel et al., 2002). Male erectile disorder is almost always a disorder of the acquired type rather than of the lifelong type.

Orgasmic disorder: female orgasmic disorder, male orgasmic disorder, and premature ejaculation. Female orgasmic disorder is more common than male orgasmic disorder and affects approximately 30 percent of women. Premature ejaculation also is very prevalent, affecting up to 29 percent of men (Wiegel et al., 2002). Together, premature ejaculation and male erectile disorder comprise nearly all the sexual dysfunctions treated in men.

Sexual pain disorders: dyspareunia (genital pain, usually diagnosed in females) and vaginismus (involuntary vaginal contractions). In one study vaginismus was found in 10 to 15 percent of women. It often has a biological basis and may be a conditioned response to previous pain related to sexual relations. Vaginismus is sometimes associated with previous sexual abuse.

Sexual dysfunctions due to a general medical condition. Approximately 50 percent of sexual dysfunctions in men are caused by medical conditions or substances. Diabetes, endocrine disorders, vascular disease, hypertension, and injuries are some of the more common medical causes of these dysfunctions (Segraves & Althof, 2002). Gynecological surgery, vaginitis, and menopause are some of the medical conditions that can cause sexual dysfunctions in women.

Substance-induced sexual dysfunction. Many substances, including alcohol, opioids, anxiolytics, and some medications for hypertension, can cause sexual dysfunction. Most of the antidepressants, with the exception of bupropion (Wellbutrin) and mintazapine (Remeron), are known to cause sexual dysfunction. Benzodiazepines have been found to delay orgasm, and some antipsychotic medications have been found to decrease libido and cause erectile difficulties (Segraves & Althof, 2002).

To warrant a diagnosis of a sexual dysfunction, symptoms must be recurrent and persistent and must cause considerable distress and interpersonal difficulty. The symptoms are not attributable to another Axis I disorder (such as PTSD). In making the diagnosis, the clinician specifies the disorder and indicates whether it is of the lifelong or acquired type, of the generalized or situational type, and due to psychological factors or due to combined factors (psychological and physiological).

Most sexual dysfunctions begin in early adulthood, although some, particularly male erectile disorder, tend to begin later (Segraves & Althof, 2002). Treatment for sexual dysfunctions typically is not sought until people are in their late twenties or early thirties.

The course of these disorders is quite variable. Some are situationally related, precipitated by stress or relationship difficulties, and remit spontaneously once the situation has improved. Others are chronic or progressive, worsening as anxiety about the disorder increases.

Sexual dysfunctions have many possible determinants. Substances or medical conditions should be investigated first. Therapists should also explore the client's cultural and family background, knowledge about sexuality, sexual and relationship history, potential history of sexual abuse, self-image, and the possibility that the client has a coexisting mental disorder. Wiegel and colleagues (2002) report that the sexual dysfunctions are likely to be associated with negative attitudes toward sex on the part of clients and their parents, clients' dissatisfaction with and instability in their intimate relationships, and clients' discomfort with their sexual identities. A history of abuse in childhood and a dysfunctional family background also contribute to the development of these disorders (Segraves & Althof, 2002). Other factors associated with sexual dysfunction include fear of rejection and abandonment, difficulty sharing control and trusting others, poor communication skills, anger and hostility, guilt about sexual thoughts and behaviors, impaired self-esteem, anxiety (especially about sexual performance), depression, and inaccurate information about sexual functioning. These symptoms may be either causes or consequences of sexual dysfunctions.

Typical Client Characteristics

A clear association has not been found between particular personality traits or backgrounds and sexual dysfunctions. However, anxiety is almost always a component of these disorders. Negative attitudes toward sex have been found to be linked to sexual dysfunction in both men and women (Wiegel et al., 2002). Many people with one sexual dysfunction have symptoms of other sexual dysfunctions. For example, in one study, 40 percent of those diagnosed with hypoactive sexual desire disorders also met the criteria for arousal or orgasmic disorders (Segraves & Althof, 2002).

Assessment

A variety of assessment tools are available to assist in the diagnosis of sexual dysfunction. Scales and inventories that measure attitudes toward sexuality can be helpful. Although it does not assess for *DSM-IV-TR* criteria specifically, the Derogatis Interview for Sexual Functioning (DISF; Derogatis, 1997) provides a semistructured interview across five domains: sexual fantasy and cognition, sexual behavior and experiences, orgasm, sexual drive, and sexual arousal.

Because attitudes toward sex have been found to be linked to sexual dysfunction in both men and women, measuring specific attitudes that may adversely affect treatment is helpful. The Sexual Opinion Survey (SOS; White, Fisher, Byrne, & Kingma, 1977) measures responses to sexual stimuli on a range of negative to positive. The survey includes twenty-one items on a 6-point Likert scale. Norms have been established for the SOS based on gender, age groups, countries, and religions. Discrepancies between husbands' and wives' scores on the SOS have been associated with lower sexual satisfaction rates (Wiegel et al., 2002).

Numerous other assessments, such as the Sexual Dysfunction Scale (McCabe, 1998), the Female Sexual Function Index (Rosen et al., 2000), the Sexual Desire Inventory (Spector, Carey, & Steinberg, 1996), and the International Index of Erectile Functioning (IIEF; Rosen, Cappelleri, & Gendrano, 2002), are reviewed in greater detail by Wiegel and colleagues (2002); all provide valid measures of different sexual dysfunctions.

The Early Sexual Experiences Checklist (ESEC; Miller, Johnson, & Johnson, 1991) is a quick, nine-item questionnaire used to detect unwanted sexual experiences that occurred before the age of sixteen. One section asks detailed questions about the most distressing event. Information on the time, duration, frequency, and degree of distress experienced, as well as the amount of coercion involved, is explored. The test can be completed in less than five minutes, and it avoids pejorative labels. The ESEC provides the client with an opportunity to report childhood sexual abuse without having to do so in a face-to-face interview (Wiegel et al., 2002).

Preferred Therapist Characteristics

Treating sexual dysfunctions can be challenging to therapists because they must have expertise in the specific techniques of sex therapy and must also be skilled at providing support and encouragement, communicating empathy, and establishing a relationship with a client who is likely to feel uncomfortable, embarrassed, and exposed. Many people have never talked openly about their sexual attitudes and behaviors before seeking therapy and will have difficulty doing so with a therapist. The client may avoid specific details, minimize the problem, and display unfamiliarity with terminology. The therapist must be sure to conduct a detailed inquiry in terms that are comprehensible to the client and that reduce threat and anxiety as much as possible. Maintaining a nonjudgmental stance is particularly important. Orienting the client quickly to the nature of the treatment may also be useful because the client may be apprehensive about what will be required.

Transference reactions, sometimes of an erotic nature, are frequent in the treatment of sexual dysfunctions because of the intimate nature of the discussions. The therapist should be aware of the development of transference; addressing, discussing, normalizing, interpreting, and diffusing the transference will usually prevent it from undermining psychotherapy. Therapists should be experienced in working with couples. Even if the individual is the only one seeking treatment, therapists must recognize that sexual dysfunction disorders affect the couple as a whole and plan interventions accordingly.

Intervention Strategies

The first step in treating a sexual dysfunction is to determine the cause of the difficulty by taking a history and referring the client for examination by a physician. Although most sexual dysfunctions are psychological in origin, many do have a physiological basis. Prescription medications, for example, as well as other drugs and alcohol, are common physiological causes of sexual dysfunction. Whatever the cause, psychotherapy may still be indicated, but medical treatment may also need to be part of the plan.

Sexual dysfunctions were previously thought to be the result of anxiety, but little empirical research is available to support this notion (Segraves & Althof, 2002). Even so, people often experience sexual difficulties for years before seeking treatment. By the time a client seeks help, the disorder may have been exacerbated by multiple disappointing sexual experiences, avoidance of sexual contact, and long-standing self-blame, all of which may complicate treatment.

A repertoire of techniques for treating these disorders has been developed by Masters and Johnson (1970), Kaplan (1995), Leiblum (2007), Wincze and Carey (2001), and others. Discussion of the specific techniques designed for particular disorders is beyond the scope of this book — the reader is referred to these authors for that information — but some elements are common to most treatment of sexual dysfunctions, and these elements will be reviewed here.

Treatment of these disorders tends to be primarily behavioral. Nevertheless, cognitive and psychodynamic interventions can also be useful in modifying self-damaging thoughts and resolving such long-standing problems as abuse, family dysfunction, and mistrust.

Psychoeducation. Sexual dysfunctions are often exacerbated by inadequate or incorrect information about the process of sexual arousal and about what is considered normal sexual functioning. For example, attitudes about the inappropriateness of sexual activity for older people, or erroneous beliefs about differences between types of female orgasm, can inhibit sexual functioning and cause people to feel uncomfortable with healthy feelings and behaviors. Educating people about sexuality and sexual functioning can help dispel some of their self-blame and modify unrealistic expectations.

Couples Therapy. If the person with a sexual dysfunction has a consistent sexual partner, that partner should almost always be involved in the therapy. Sexual dysfunctions grow out of relationships and affect relationships, so they must be considered in context. Information should be gathered on the couple's interpersonal and sexual relationship to determine whether any difficulties in their interaction have a bearing on the sexual dysfunction. Data should be gathered from the partners while they are together and while they are apart, because they will often have discrepant perceptions of their sexual relationship. In most cases, some couples therapy is helpful, focusing on communication (both verbal and nonverbal), expectations, assertiveness, and sexual desires and behaviors.

Many people develop or exacerbate sexual dysfunctions because of what Masters and Johnson refer to as ''spectatoring'' — the process of watching and monitoring their own sexual performance as well as their partners' responses during sexual relations. Typically, the tension and anxiety associated with this self-monitoring prevent relaxation and comfortable involvement in sexual behaviors, worsening the sexual dysfunction and leading to a vicious cycle in which the sexual dysfunction promotes spectatoring, which in turn increases the severity of the sexual dysfunction.

The first step in the behavioral treatment of a sexual dysfunction, then, is reduction of spectatoring and its accompanying anxiety. To accomplish this step, the couple may be taught nonthreatening relaxation techniques (such as progressive relaxation or nonsexual massage) and may be asked to refrain temporarily from overt sexual activity. Increasing the focus on pleasure can help people gradually resume a more rewarding sexual relationship and apply specific techniques, taught in therapy, that can improve sexual functioning.

Sensate focusing is a common technique used early in treatment. It is designed to help the couple enjoy closeness and intimacy without intercourse, in order to reduce pressure and demands. Other specific techniques that may play a role in the treatment of sexual dysfunction include systematic desensitization, masturbation for women with inhibited orgasm, bridging (making the transition from masturbation or manual stimulation to intercourse), the squeeze technique (to teach control for men with premature ejaculation), and imagery and fantasy to enhance sexual arousal.

Wiegel and colleagues (2002) suggest helping clients create a broader goal of creating pleasurable sexual experiences with their partner, rather than just restoring functioning. Medications can be used to enhance pleasure-focused therapy, but should not be the sole treatment. Effective therapy for sexual dysfunctions should include the following:

- Sensate focus: experiential/sensory awareness exercises
- Stimulus control and scheduling
- Cognitive restructuring, to increase flexibility in attitudes and promote commitment to change
- Communication skills training to address interpersonal concerns as well as promote education on healthy sexuality

Five factors have been found to improve therapeutic outcomes: quality of the couple's relationship, motivation (particularly of male partner) for treatment, absence of severe mental disorders, physical attraction between partners, and early compliance with assigned homework.

Therapy for sexual dysfunctions tends to be relatively brief, although a history of sexual victimization may necessitate longer treatment. Masters and Johnson often conducted their therapy sessions on an intensive daily basis, but weekly therapy has been shown to be equally effective (Segraves & Althof, 2002).

Masters and Johnson (1970) established a model for doing sex therapy that involved a male/female treatment team working with a couple experiencing a sexual dysfunction. This model allows considerable flexibility and does seem ideal, but, of course, it often is not feasible. In general, therapy for sexual dysfunction is conducted with a couple or, if necessary, with an individual.

Group Therapy. Some sexual dysfunctions also seem to benefit from group therapy that is designed to provide support as well as education, role models, and reduction of guilt and anxiety. Group treatment was found to decrease cost, increase motivation, normalize problems, and provide peer support and comfort in discussing private sexual problems (Segraves & Althof, 2002). The downside to group therapy for sexual dysfunctions is the limitation on providing extensive individual attention to specific problems.

Therapy groups have been used for women with orgasmic disorders and for men with erectile disorders. Groups for couples have also been used successfully. Minimal differences in treatment effectiveness for groups versus individual treatment have been found (Segraves & Althof, 2002).

Medication. Medication can be an effective adjunct in the treatment of some types of sexual dysfunctions, particularly in men with erectile dysfunction. FDA approval of sildenafil citrate (Viagra) in 1998 revolutionized the treatment of male erectile dysfunction. Segraves and Althof (2002) report that the efficacy of Viagra has been demonstrated in numerous multisite controlled, double-blind studies. Depending on the cause of the dysfunction, efficacy rates of 40 to 80 percent have been reported, with increased doses associated with increased erectile function. Similar medications for the treatment of erectile dysfunction, tadalafil (Cialis) and vardenafil (Levitra), were approved by the FDA in 2003. Penile implants, transurethral or vacuum therapy, and intracavernosal injection therapy are other medical treatments that are viable options for men who, for health reasons, cannot take sildenafil citrate, tadalafil, or vardenafil for problems of erectile dysfunction.

Estrogen replacement or combined androgen and estrogen replacement therapy have shown promise in the treatment of women with hypoactive sexual desire disorder. One study indicated that bupropion (Wellbutrin) also increased female libido. Despite showing promise, sildenafil citrate (Viagra) was found to be ineffective in restoring sexual functioning in women with sexual arousal disorders and hypoactive sexual desire disorder (Segraves & Althof, 2002). Most people with sexual dysfunctions will be referred for a medical examination, and in those cases where medication seems likely to enhance treatment, the possibility can be raised when the referral is made.

Although therapy for sexual dysfunctions focuses primarily on the couple and on the partners' relationship and sexual difficulties, sometimes a sexual dysfunction is of intrapsychic origin and is linked to other emotional disorders or to underlying pathology. Kaplan (1995), for example, suggests that sexual desire disorders are sometimes associated with hostility and parental transferences in relationships, as well as with guilt and intimacy-related conflicts. In such cases, a treatment plan that combines couples behavior therapy with some individual cognitive, interpersonal, or psychodynamic therapy may facilitate change. The therapist needs to determine the best combination of interventions for treating a person who has both a sexual dysfunction and another mental disorder or emotional difficulty.

Prognosis

In their early research, Masters and Johnson (1970) reported an 80 percent overall success rate for 733 cases in which people received two weeks of intensive treatment for sexual dysfunction. Only 5 percent had a recurrence within five years. Current research, however, suggests that these figures may be too optimistic. Prognosis is particularly good for treatment of vaginismus but fair to poor for treatment of sexual desire disorders. Approximately half of all sexual dysfunctions show improvement in response to treatment, but these gains tend not to be fully maintained. Fifty to 70 percent of men and women with sexual desire disorders achieved modest gains following psychotherapy Those gains were not maintained at three-year follow-up; however, those who had received treatment reported that they had improved their level of satisfaction with their relationship despite their lack of desire (Segraves & Althof, 2002).

All studies with long-term follow-up showed a high incidence of relapses. Better treatment gains are related to improvements in the quality of the relationship between partners. Therapists working with people who have sexual dysfunctions should communicate realistic expectations (improvement rather than cure; likelihood of setbacks) and should plan for follow-up visits and relapse prevention. Problems related to sexual functioning involve a complicated integration of biological, social, relational, and psychological events. Effective interventions will require an appreciation of the complexity of these influences (Segraves & Althof, 2002).

Paraphilias

Description of the Disorders

DSM-IV-TR gives the essential features of a paraphilia as "recurrent, intense, sexually arousing fantasies, sexual urges, or behaviors generally involving (1) nonhuman objects, (2) the suffering or humiliation of oneself or one's partner, or (3) children or other nonconsenting persons" (American Psychiatric Association, 2000, p. 566). These urges or behaviors persist for at least six months and typically lead to impairment in social and sexual relationships and in other important areas of functioning, as well as to considerable distress. *DSM-IV-TR*'s extensive list includes the following paraphilias:

- Exhibitionism (exposing one's genitals to an unsuspecting stranger)
- Fetishism (sexual activity focused on objects)
- Frotteurism (touching and rubbing against others without their consent)
- Pedophilia (sexual activity with children)
- Sexual masochism (enjoyment of humiliation or suffering during sexual activity)
- Sexual sadism (deriving pleasure from causing others to suffer)
- Transvestic fetishism (cross-dressing)
- Voyeurism (covert observation of people who are disrobed or engaged in sexual activity)
- Paraphilia not otherwise specified, including such behaviors as telephone scatologia (lewd telephone calls), necrophilia (sexual interest in corpses), partialism (a focus on part of the body, such as feet), zoophilia (sexual behavior involving animals), coprophilia (sexual behavior involving feces), klismaphilia (sexual behavior involving enemas), and urophilia (sexual behavior involving urine)

Specific criteria are provided in *DSM-IV-TR* for each of these disorders, but discussion of these criteria is beyond the scope of this book. Here, the paraphilias will be considered as an entire class of disorders.

Paraphilias are believed to be more prevalent than the statistics would indicate, largely because only a small percentage of people with these disorders seek help. In general, people with paraphilias do not see themselves as having emotional disorders and tend not to seek treatment on their own initiative; rather, they come into treatment at the urging of a friend or family member (usually the spouse or partner) or because actions associated with their paraphilia have led to their arrest.

People with paraphilias typically commit large numbers of paraphilic acts and, by the time they are identified, may have committed hundreds of sexual offenses, leaving many victims (Seligman & Hardenburg, 2000). These patterns have led to difficulty in estimating the prevalence of these disorders.

People with paraphilias come from all ethnic and socioeconomic backgrounds. Their sexual orientation may be heterosexual, homosexual, or bisexual (Seligman & Hardenburg, 2000).

Paraphilias vary widely in terms of severity. Many disorders of a hypersexual nature lie below the diagnostic line and cannot be classified as a true paraphilia. Such "paraphilia-related disorders" as termed by Kafka (2007, p. 446) may include compulsive masturbation, telephone sex, dependence on pornography, cybersex, and protracted promiscuity, among others. Such behaviors may co-occur with other sexual disorders, or with other Axis I disorders, particularly substance abuse, anxiety or mood disorders, and disorders of impulse control. Paraphilia-related disorders should be accurately identified, assessed, and diagnosed, as they may contribute to partner relationship problems, other sexual-related disorders, and confound or prolong treatment of co-occurring Axis I disorders (Kafka, 2007).

Mild versions of paraphilias may include only disturbing fantasies, perhaps accompanied by masturbation (Seligman & Hardenburg, 2000). The person's ability to control the thoughts, urges, and behavior, and whether the activity or fantasy is required for sexual arousal to occur, are two ways in which severity can be determined. Severe cases of paraphilia may involve the use of threats or force, injury to others, victimization of children, or even murder.

For example, one client, a successful thirty-two-year-old lawyer, had rewarding intimate relationships with women but fantasized a great deal about causing women to suffer. He bought pornographic magazines with sadistic themes and enjoyed films in which women were injured, raped, or killed. He had never hurt a woman, but he sought therapy because he was afraid he would lose control of his fantasies and would injure someone. This client had a mild paraphilia.

By contrast, another client, an accountant, had a severe paraphilia: pedophilia. His only sexual experiences had been with young boys. He had been arrested three times and had received treatment while in prison. Although he, like the other client, also had a professional career, he had lost his job because of his imprisonment, and he feared that his prison record would prevent him from locating future employment in his field.

Expression of paraphilic impulses often follows a cycle that is also common in other disorders of impulse control. Tension builds in the person until it is relieved by a paraphilic act; guilt and regret ensue, with the person often promising a change in behavior. In time, however, tension builds up again, and it is once again released through the undesirable behavior. People with paraphilias may develop a tolerance for their behaviors and require increased frequency or intensity to satisfy their cravings (Seligman & Hardenburg, 2000).

Paraphilias rarely seem to have a biological cause, but they are often linked to early childhood sexual experiences, such as being tied up or forced to cross-dress. Sexual fantasies are likely to have been present since childhood, and paraphilias often develop in adolescence and early adulthood, peaking between ages twenty and thirty and then remitting in later adulthood (Allen & Hollander, 2006). The most common paraphilias are pedophilia, exhibitionism, and voyeurism (American Psychiatric Association, 2000). Paraphilias are seen less often in females; sexual masochism and sexual sadism, for example, are estimated to be found at a 20:1 ratio in males compared to females (Allen &

Hollander, 2006). The diagnosis of two or more paraphilias in one person is not unusual.

Typical Client Characteristics

Although about half of all people with paraphilias are married, most have some impairment in their capacity for intimate relationships (American Psychiatric Association, 2000). Their sexual activities tend to be ritualized and unspontaneous. Most experience some distress and anxiety connected to their disorder, as well as interpersonal difficulties and social rejection. Kafka and Hennen (2002) found that the typical person in outpatient therapy for paraphilia is a thirty-seven-year-old, middle-class, white male with some college education and a job. Many of these men had been abused as children (30 percent); had problems in school (41 percent); and had been in a psychiatric hospital (25 percent). Paraphilias sometimes can be directly attributed to childhood sexual or physical abuse.

Pedophilia, often taking the form of incest, is one of the most common paraphilias treated by psychotherapists. Men who are attracted to young girls typically have marital difficulties, are anxious and immature, and have problems with impulse control. Men who molest young boys tend to avoid any adult sexual experiences and are attracted only to children. Their paraphilia is especially likely to be chronic.

The most commonly co-occurring disorders in people with paraphilias are depressive disorders, substance use disorders, ADHD, social phobia, and other anxiety disorders (Allen & Hollander, 2006). Other impulse-control disorders, OCD, and reckless driving are also found more frequently in people with paraphilias than in the average population.

Assessment

Because of the range of presentations of paraphilias, therapists should conduct a careful assessment to determine the nature and severity of the disorder, other areas of concern, and strengths of the person with a paraphilia. Questions concerning the nature, onset, duration, frequency, and progression of symptoms are important, as is a detailed outline of any arrests, presentence reports, or information from probation or parole officers, as many people with paraphilias have arrest records (Seligman & Hardenburg, 2000). Co-occurring disorders, especially substance-related disorders, other impulse-control disorders, and mood and anxiety disorders, should be assessed prior to developing an effective treatment plan (Kafka, 2007).

Preferred Therapist Characteristics

Therapists will have to deal with the reluctance of many people diagnosed with paraphilias to engage in treatment. People with paraphilias, like those with drug and alcohol problems, generally enjoy the behaviors involved in their disorder. Typically the negative consequences rather than the behaviors themselves lead people with paraphilias to accept treatment. As a result, they may be ambivalent toward or resistant to treatment and, especially if their treatment is court ordered, may be guarded and suspicious. Thus it may be difficult to establish a positive therapeutic relationship with these clients.

Some therapists find that they have strong countertransference reactions to people with paraphilias, particularly paraphilias that involve children. One of the challenges for therapists is to manage their own feelings so that these do not undermine the therapeutic relationship and increase clients' guilt and distress.

Therapists should be aware that many paraphilia-like behaviors are often found in people experiencing psychosis, mania, and substance use disorders. People diagnosed with mental retardation, antisocial personality disorder, and dementia may also engage in unusual sexual behaviors. Behaviors in these cases, and in situations in which symptoms begin in adulthood, are infrequent, and are ego-dystonic. Consequently, a diagnosis of paraphilia may not be appropriate (Seligman & Hardenburg, 2000).

Intervention Strategies

Psychodynamic or insight-oriented treatment has been shown to be ineffective in treating paraphilias. Only cognitive-behavioral therapy has proven effective in the treatment of these disorders (Allen & Hollander, 2006). Although treatments for specific paraphilias vary to some extent, the therapeutic principles and strategies used to modify erotic responses and associated behaviors are generally the same for all paraphilias and typically include the following:

- Identification of triggers and substitution of alternative responses and behaviors
- Stress reduction
- Aversion therapy that pairs paraphilic urges and fantasies with negative experiences, such as undesirable images, electric shocks, or noxious odors
- Covert sensitization, which uses negative images (such as images of imprisonment or humiliation) to discourage paraphilic behavior
- Covert extinction, in which the paraphilic behavior is imagined, but without the anticipated reinforcement or positive feeling
- Orgasmic reconditioning
- Thought stopping
- Cognitive restructuring
- Encouragement of empathy for the victim
- Overall improvement of coping skills and lifestyle

Some people with paraphilias engage in sexual activities with children, animals, or objects because they are afraid of rejection if they seek sexual relationships with adults. Improvement of social and assertiveness skills and education about sexuality can encourage people to engage in sexual activities involving peers. Increasing awareness of the affect of one's behaviors on the victims, promoting empathy for the victims through role playing, and exposure to victims' experiences can also be effective in promoting healthier interpersonal behaviors and responses (Allen & Hollander, 2006; Maletzky, 2002).

Antiandrogenic medication, such as medroxyprogesterone acetate (Depo-Provera), which lowers testosterone, has also been used, particularly in the treatment of people who are sexually attracted to children and who are hypersexual. This medication reduces sexual urges and behavior by reducing testosterone levels. To date, there have been no large controlled trials of such medication, but case reports indicate that antiandrogenic medication is effective in reducing sexual fantasies, thoughts, and behavior, and reducing recidivism in sex offenders (Allen & Hollander, 2006). Surgical interventions, including brain surgery and removal of the testes, have also been used, but their use is still experimental, as well as controversial. Of course, these interventions are only used with the consent of the person diagnosed with a paraphilia.

Selective serotonin reuptake inhibitors (SSRIs) may also be prescribed for paraphilias. SSRIs have been shown to be effective largely due to their antiobsessional effects on thoughts and behavior (Allen & Hollander, 2006). Given that depression and anxiety frequently occur along with paraphilias, SSRIs may be effective in enhancing treatment of both a paraphilia and a comorbid disorder.

Group therapy is a particularly appropriate vehicle for treating paraphilias. People with paraphilias can help one another modify their behaviors, learn and practice better interpersonal skills, and prevent relapse. As with other disorders of impulse control, people with what are often called sexual addictions can benefit from participation in twelve-step programs modeled after Alcoholics Anonymous, such as Sex Addicts Anonymous, Sexual Compulsives Anonymous, and Sex and Love Addicts. Family therapy also can be helpful, especially if the paraphilic behaviors have damaged current family relationships or if sexual abuse has occurred in the family of origin.

An important component of any treatment program for paraphilia is the inclusion of relapse prevention techniques. One meta-analysis found that cognitive-behavioral treatment significantly reduced recidivism rates for paraphilia (Allen & Hollander, 2006).

Prognosis

Paraphilias tend to be treatment resistant, and behaviors tend to increase when the person is under stress. Relapses are also common, so short-term improvement does not provide any assurance of continuing change (Allen & Hollander, 2006; Maletzky, 2002). Long-term treatment and supervision may be needed for these clients. The prognosis seems better for people with good ego strength and flexibility, intrinsic motivation for treatment, and normal adult sexual experiences. The prognosis is worse for people with coexisting mental disorders, early onset and high frequency of paraphilic behaviors, substance misuse, and lack of remorse for their behavior (Seligman & Hardenburg, 2000).

Gender Identity Disorder

Description of the Disorder

Information in this section is based on current knowledge in the *DSM* and the majority of the professional literature on gender identity disorder (GID). However, this is a controversial diagnosis and many believe that it should not be viewed as a mental disorder. Readers should keep in mind the possibility that, like homosexuality, GID will be removed from the *DSM* and will be viewed as simply an uncommon but not unhealthy pattern.

Gender identity disorder (GID), according to *DSM-IV-TR*, is characterized by a strong and enduring cross-gender identification, along with discomfort about one's assigned gender. These symptoms are not due to a physical condition. They are of sufficient severity to cause considerable distress or impairment in functioning. The age of the client determines whether the diagnosis is gender identity disorder in children or gender identity disorder in adolescents or adults.

Two theories have been advanced to explain GID, also known as gender dysphoria, transsexualism or being transgendered. Some believe GID has a biological basis that has not yet been identified; others view GID as a conditioned response. Each of these theories may explain the disorder in some people.

No biological marker has been found for GID at present. However, evidence exists that certain behavioral traits linked to biological processes may be involved. For example, there is evidence that prenatal hormonal variations can affect masculine or feminine behavior. Continued research on this topic will undoubtedly reveal additional relationships among genetic, prenatal, perinatal, and sociological factors in the development of GID.

GID is relatively rare. Carroll (2007) reports two studies in the Netherlands and Scotland that show a consistent prevalence of one in every eleven thousand males and one female out of thirty thousand. Internalizing disorders (anxiety and depression) commonly co-occur with GID. What remains to be determined is whether these feelings contribute to or result from gender dysphoria.

Typical Client Characteristics

People with GID typically prefer activities, occupations, and dress associated with the gender other than their biologically assigned gender. The age of onset of cross-gender behaviors in children with GID is typically during the preschool years, with 55 percent of boys with GID cross-dressing by their third birthday and 90 percent by their fifth birthday (Zucker & Bradley, 2004). Among children with GID, boys typically appear effeminate, whereas girls may be thought of as tomboys. In fact, Zucker and Bradley report that the rigid refusal to wear a dress, under any circumstances, often results in clinical referral of girls. Although many girls without GID may be described as "tomboyish," most are content being a girl. A distinguishing characteristic of girls with GID is a marked unhappiness with their female gender. Boys, too, frequently make verbal statements that they would prefer to be of the other sex. They express displeasure with their sexual anatomy and frequently sit to urinate and otherwise try to conceal their penises (Zucker & Bradley, 2004).

Children with GID often prefer playmates of the opposite sex, and in fantasy play will often take on the role of the other gender. In conjunction with the child's expressed dislike of his or her biological gender and sexual anatomy, these characteristics point to the child's strong cross-gender identification.

Gender identity and gender role are typically viewed as developing before the emergence of sexual orientation (Zucker & Bradley, 2004). If sexual desire is present, it often is directed toward people of the same gender, particularly for males, although most people with GID do not view themselves as homosexual. People with GID may be heterosexual, homosexual, bisexual, or asexual, just like the rest of the population (Langer & Martin, 2004).

Carroll (2007) notes that gender dysphoria is much more common in children than in adults. Basically, people with GID do not show a greater tendency toward psychopathology than the population at large. In fact, they are generally otherwise emotionally healthy people who have the strong belief that they are in the wrong-gendered body.

Considerable social and occupational impairment is associated with GID, at least in part because of societal attitudes and reactions. Egan and Perry (2001) report that the greatest problem for adolescents with GID is the effect of peer pressure for gender conformity and the message they receive that they must avoid cross-gender-type behavior or activities. Peer pressure to conform bears a direct negative relationship to self-esteem, peer relationships, and self-efficacy. Social pressure to behave heterosexually begins in elementary school. This pressure appears to be more intense for boys, whereas nonconforming gender behavior among girls is more socially acceptable (Langer & Martin, 2004; Zucker & Bradley, 2004). Internalizing behaviors, such as depression, anxiety, and social withdrawal, are sometimes presented by people with this disorder (especially by boys). Adolescents often manifest adjustment, self-esteem, and peer relationship difficulties, along with acting-out behavior.

People with GID are more likely to present for treatment because of these associated symptoms than because of their gender discomfort. They also may seek psychotherapy as a condition of being accepted for sex-reassignment surgery.

Assessment

Gender identity is a fluid concept that encompasses four dimensions: social role, gender identification, sexuality, and the body (Carroll, 2007). As with other disorders listed in the *DSM-IV-TR* (American Psychiatric Association, 2000), GID is only a disorder if it causes distress in one or more areas of functioning. Following a medical evaluation, a psychological assessment for gender dysphoria will be similar to other comprehensive psychological assessments, with the additional focus on a complete sexual and gender history. For a more in-depth look at assessing GID, refer to Carroll (2007).

Preferred Therapist Characteristics

Research has shown that therapists' comfort levels and attitudes can affect the client's disclosure of sexual issues and the appropriate handling of sexual topics. Therapists who are not familiar with or not comfortable working with transgendered people should refer them to a qualified therapist with experience in this area.

People with GID typically focus on making the body correspond to the self-image they have in their brains rather than the reverse. They typically are not interested in changing their feelings about their gender. An emphasis on relieving any depression and anxiety and exploring options is usually more successful than focusing treatment on changing the gender dysphoria.

Treatment may be complicated if clients have come as a requirement for gender-reassignment surgery. In this case, therapists may find themselves in the role of "gatekeeper" (Carroll, 2007, p. 505), in determining readiness and referral of transgendered clients for hormones, surgery, or other medical treatment. Therapists need to be aware of and deal with their own counter-transference reactions and any discomfort they may have with these clients and with the surgery clients may be seeking. Whether or not therapists agree with their client's choices, they must respect that the decision of how to resolve gender dysphoria lies within the client.

Intervention Strategies

Treatment for children with GID is controversial. Some suggest early intervention in the hopes of changing GID behavior. However, others believe that gender identification is determined by the age of two or three and has an underlying biological component, so, rather than focusing on the gender issues, therapists should focus on treating the symptoms of depression, anxiety, impaired self-esteem, and social discomfort that frequently result from social ostracism and inappropriate peer relationships.

Children with GID are often brought to therapy to help them with their unhappiness about their biological gender and to work on relationships with family and peers. It seems prudent to focus on alleviating children's current distress rather than on problems the children may encounter in adulthood. Involving children in activities that are not strongly associated with either gender, such as board games, can offer them new and rewarding social opportunities that will not elicit ridicule. Play therapy can be a useful vehicle for introducing children to new activities and role models. The intensity of discomfort with his or her gender varies from person to person, and many children who manifest symptoms of GID in childhood have a lessening of those symptoms with age. For others, however, the development of secondary sex characteristics such as breasts or facial hair during adolescence is a physical reminder of their gender-related unhappiness and leads to a worsening of symptoms.

It is unclear how frequently gender dysphoria continues into adolescence and adulthood. Green (1987) conducted a longitudinal study of sixty-six boys who had received treatment for gender dysphoria in childhood. Only one of the boys continued to express the same feelings in adulthood; however, 75 percent of the boys had developed a clear preference for homosexuality, leading later researchers to conclude that there may be a link between early cross-gender behavior and homosexuality.

If gender dysphoria persists into adolescence and adulthood, the likelihood of changing gender-related attitudes and identifications is low. Therefore, goals should focus on choosing ways to improve adjustment and life satisfaction. Setting realistic goals is essential to the effective treatment of GID. Promoting adjustment or helping people make decisions about biological treatment are usually more viable goals than eliminating the symptoms of GID. In making choices, people should be encouraged to reflect not only on their own preferences but also on the reactions of family members, colleagues, friends, and society at large, and on the clients' own responses to those reactions.

Lifestyle and relationship changes, which may involve clients' living in their preferred gender roles, are one avenue to improved adjustment and satisfaction. Other avenues include hormone therapy and gender-reassignment surgery. In hormone therapy, biological males take estrogen, and biological females take testosterone. These hormones not only effect physiological changes that are gratifying to some people with GID but also improve their sense of well-being. Gender reassignment is a controversial, complex, and multifaceted process that involves hormone treatments, trial cross-gender living, and eventual surgery. Only a small percentage of people with GID pursue this treatment option. Standards of care guidelines that require consultation between mental health professionals and medical professions prior to gender reassignment surgery have been developed by the Harry Benjamin International Gender Dysphoria

Association (HBIGDA, 2001). The guidelines can be followed by practitioners to outline the process of assessment and treatment for GID (Carroll, 2007).

Prognosis

Few controlled studies have been conducted on the treatment of GID. Not all transgendered adolescents have gender dysphoria or seek sex reassignment. In a longitudinal study of adolescent girls with GID, approximately 50 percent developed a homosexual orientation, and 35 to 45 percent persisted in their desire to become the opposite sex. It is not known how many eventually had sex reassignment surgery (Butcher et al., 2006). More research, including longitudinal studies, clearly is needed in this important area.

Some outcome research has focused on the results of gender-reassignment surgery. Many express satisfaction with the results of the surgery, reduced levels of depression and anxiety, and no problems in their new gender (Oltmanns & Emery, 2007). However, some continue to have significant problems of adjustment, and 2 percent of those who undergo this surgery commit suicide. The likelihood of a negative treatment outcome is greatest in people who have coexisting psychological disorders such as severe depression or personality disorders.

IMPULSE-CONTROL DISORDERS NOT ELSEWHERE CLASSIFIED

Description of the Disorders

Substance-related disorders, eating disorders, and paraphilias have already been discussed in this chapter. The remaining impulse-control disorders listed in *DSM IV TR* are included in the present section. This group of disorders includes the following varied array, all characterized by repeated failure to resist an impulse to perform a behavior that is harmful to oneself or to others:

- Intermittent explosive disorder
- Kleptomania
- Pyromania
- Pathological gambling
- Trichotillomania

These disorders typically are characterized by increasing tension or arousal before the harmful behavior is performed, and by feelings of release or pleasure after the act has been completed. Although it may be followed by feelings of guilt and remorse, the behavior itself is usually ego-syntonic.

Although the behaviors associated with the disorders in this section vary considerably, most are similar in terms of age at onset and course (usually chronic but episodic, and worsening under stress). These disorders are also strongly associated with comorbid diagnoses of OCD, substance-related disorders, and mood disorders (Hollander & Stein, 2006).

Some believe that impulse-control disorders have a common underlying dynamic or cause. Possible explanations for these disorders include a biological cause (neurological predisposition) combined with psychosocial causes (such as dysfunctional role models), exacerbated by environmental stress (Hollander, Baker, Kahn, & Stein, 2006). All these possibilities should be considered in seeking to understand a particular person's impulsive behavior.

Intermittent Explosive Disorder. According to *DSM-IV-TR,* this disorder involves "discrete episodes of failure to resist aggressive impulses that result in serious assaultive acts or destruction of property" (American Psychiatric Association, 2000, p. 663). The symptoms are not caused by another mental disorder, a medical condition, or drug or alcohol use, although use of disinhibiting substances such as alcohol often accompany the aggressive episodes.

Intermittent explosive disorder is believed to be more common in males than in females, although one study found the ratio of males to females to be 1:1 (Coccaro, Posternak, & Zimmerman, 2005). Mean age of onset of this disorder is sixteen years of age; it tends to peak in early adulthood and then abates in midlife. Intermittent explosive disorder is found in as many as one-third of first-degree relatives of people with this disorder (Coccaro & Danehy, 2006).

An episode of intermittent explosive disorder tends to occur rapidly, lasts less than thirty minutes, and frequently involves property destruction and verbal or physical assault (Coccaro & Danehy, 2006). Provocation, if any, seems to be minor and is frequently from a person familiar to the person with the disorder.

Forty-four percent of people with intermittent explosive disorder also have other impulse-control disorders (McElroy, Soutullo, Beckman, Taylor, & Keck, 1998). Mood disorders, including bipolar and cyclothymic disorders; anxiety; and substance use are also common in this population. Clinicians should be particularly careful to differentiate between intermittent explosive disorder and bipolar disorder, which may have similar symptoms; the two disorders call for different treatments. As with most of the impulse-control disorders, intermittent explosive disorder appears to have a neurological basis and is often triggered by a stressful life event. People with this disorder often have a history of job loss, relationship conflict, legal difficulties, and injuries resulting from fights or accidents. They may be self-destructive as well as harmful to others and may experience suicidal ideation. A history of reckless behavior often is also present.

Kleptomania. This disorder is characterized by unplanned, solitary, recurrent theft of unneeded objects. The person's goal is the act of stealing, not the objects that are taken.

Prevalence figures are not available; however, more than 60 percent of persons with kleptomania are women. Although this relatively rare disorder often begins in late adolescence, it is most often diagnosed in middle-aged women who are mildly depressed and experiencing interpersonal losses and who feel a sense of injustice and deprivation in their lives (Grant, 2006). Anxiety, shame, and guilt are common in people with kleptomania, with nearly 100 percent reporting they have had depression at one point in their lives. One theory holds that the person with kleptomania is trying to relieve negative affect and depression by participating in high-risk behaviors such as shoplifting (Grant, 2006). Some report pleasure and tension in the beginning of this disorder, which can become a habit as the behaviors become routine.

Many persons with kleptomania have concomitant eating disorders (especially bulimia nervosa), OCD, substance-related disorders, and personality disorders — especially paranoid and histrionic personality disorder (Grant, 2006). Thirty-two percent have attempted suicide. There is also a high rate of extroversion and of hoarding behavior among people who have kleptomania (Grant & Kim, 2002).

Fewer than 5 percent of people who shoplift can accurately be diagnosed as having kleptomania. Conduct disorder or antisocial personality disorder are more common diagnoses for people who frequently steal. Kleptomania is distinguished from shoplifting by the unnecessary nature of the items taken. Most people with this disorder report waiting ten years before seeking treatment, largely due to embarrassment and shame (Grant, 2006). Some enter treatment only because of a court order or arrest.

Pyromania. This disorder describes a small percentage of people who engage in the harmful setting of fires, specifically those who repeatedly set fires for the purposes of pleasure and tension relief rather than for financial gain or revenge. People with this disorder not only set fires but have an interest in anything associated with fires. They set off false fire alarms and associate themselves with fire departments, sometimes becoming firefighters themselves.

Fire setting, which usually begins in childhood, accounted for sixty-five thousand fires in the United States in 1997, and juvenile fire setting accounts for 55 percent of all arson arrests (Hardesty & Gayton, 2002). Separate from pyromania, childhood fire setting is most often associated with conduct disorder, ADHD, or adjustment disorder (Lejoyeux, McLoughlin, & Ades, 2006). Adolescents who set fires were found to be aggressive but also shy and rejected by their peers (Lindberg, Holi, Tani, & Virkkunen, 2005).

Fire-setting recidivism rates vary widely in the literature, ranging from 4 to 60 percent. Those with co-occurring personality disorders, mental retardation, or psychosis were most likely to repeat fire-setting behaviors. However, the incidence of pyromania is rare. Ritchie and Huff (1999) found only three cases of pyromania in 283 cases of arson. Most fire setting is not related to pyromania.

Elliott (2002) divides people who set fires into four groups that can be labeled curious, crisis, delinquent, and pathological. It is only the fourth category in which the multiple fire setting reflects pyromania. These people set fires to fulfill a need and reduce tension. Their involvement with fire can provide a sense of power and social prestige.

Pyromania can occur at any age, from childhood through adulthood. Lejoyeux and colleagues (2006) report that the average age of people diagnosed with pyromania is twenty. Pyromania is often associated with a dysfunctional family background (especially characterized by an absent father and misuse of alcohol), poor social skills, interpersonal difficulties, low self-esteem, alcohol intoxication, enuresis, sexual dysfunction, depression, antisocial behaviors, cruelty to animals, and a history of childhood mental disorders (such as ADHD, conduct disorder, learning disorders, and mild mental retardation). Fifty-four percent of people with pyromania can be diagnosed with alcohol dependence.

Behavior therapy should direct people with pyromania away from their interest in seeing fires and replace these behaviors with more socially acceptable forms of tension reduction and ways of meeting their needs for power, self-esteem, and belonging. Co-occurring disorders, such as mental retardation, psychosis, and alcohol abuse and dependence, must be addressed if treatment is to be effective.

Pathological Gambling. The primary feature of this disorder is persistent preoccupation with self-destructive gambling. This relatively common disorder is found in 2.5 million adults, with an additional 5.3 million at risk for developing the disorder (Ladd & Petry, 2003). Nearly 40 percent of people who seek treatment for problems with gambling are women (Ladd & Petry, 2003; Stinchfield & Winters, 2001). They tend to be depressed, and frequently use gambling to reduce negative affect and dissociate from their problems (Pallanti, Rossi, & Hollander, 2006). Gambling usually begins in adolescence for males but later for females.

Pathological gambling is sometimes accompanied by other mental disorders, notably substance-related disorders, ADHD, other impulse-control disorders, anxiety disorders, mood disorders (especially bipolar disorder), and personality disorders (Pallanti et al., 2006). More than half of people who engage in pathological gambling have been diagnosed with an alcohol or substance use disorder. Several studies have also noted greater incidence of hostility, obsessive-compulsive traits, and paranoia in people who both gamble and misuse substances (Ladd & Petry, 2003; Ledgerwood, Steinberg, Wu, & Potenza, 2005; Petry, 2000).

Seventy-one percent of people who engage in pathological gambling reported experiencing depression at some time in their lives, and 20 to 40 percent reported they had attempted suicide. The severity of the gambling problem, younger age of onset, criminal activity related to gambling, and impulse-control disorders of family members were correlated with increased suicide risk. Several studies note that the suicide rate in cities where gambling is legal is four times higher than in cities without legalized gambling (Ledgerwood et al., 2005; Pallanti et al., 2006). Clearly, an important part of any treatment of pathological gambling will include assessment of suicide risk and the development of an appropriate safety plan.

Similar to those of people with other impulse-control disorders, characteristics of people who gamble include preoccupation with the harmful behavior, loss of control, tolerance, withdrawal-like symptoms, and cycles of abstinence and relapse (American Psychiatric Association, 2000; Ladd & Petry, 2003). People who gamble excessively also tend to be intelligent, overconfident, energetic, extroverted, competitive, restless, and prone to take risks (Pallanti et al., 2006). Gambling, compulsive eating, and alcohol misuse all involve a level of detachment, and Jacobs (1988) suggests that transient dissociative states are likely to occur during these types of addictive activities. Family, financial, occupational, and legal problems are common in people with pathological gambling, as is difficulty in sustaining intimate, emotionally expressive relationships (Ladd & Petry, 2003).

The families of origin of people with this disorder commonly manifest dysfunctional substance use, mood disorders, antisocial behavior, gambling, and an emphasis on material gain. Often people diagnosed with pathological gambling have as children experienced harsh and inappropriate discipline and significant losses.

Pathological gambling typically has three phases (Butcher et al., 2006):

1. Introductory phase, during which winning promotes overconfidence and further involvement in gambling
2. Losing, in which undue risks are taken and financial resources are depleted
3. Desperation, in which gambling becomes frenzied and people borrow or embezzle large sums of money, write bad checks, and engage in other kinds of nonviolent criminal behavior

These phases may extend over as many as fifteen years. Chronicity is usually determined by the amount and frequency of the gambling behavior (Pallanti et al., 2006). Involvement in the twelve-step program Gamblers Anonymous is a valuable adjunct to cognitive-behavioral therapy for people with this disorder because it can offer extensive involvement in self-help and emphasize the need for ongoing self-monitoring and use of coping skills.

Trichotillomania. This disorder is characterized by recurrent plucking of hair from one's own head and body. The practice results in perceptible hair loss, usually from the scalp. Mouthing or eating the hairs is a common feature of the disorder.

Trichotillomania is more common in females and tends to be linked to negative affective states (depression, negative self-evaluation) and hypoarousal (boredom, fatigue, sedentary activities), which serve as cues for hair-pulling behavior (Franklin, Tolin, & Diefenbach, 2006). The hair pulling typically provides feelings of tension release and gratification and perhaps also of stimulation. This disorder typically begins within five years of puberty and often is chronic, although its severity changes, usually in response to changes in stressors. This disorder is rare, and research is limited. A 1991 study of a sample of college students found that 3.4 percent of females and 1.5 percent of males had engaged in clinically significant hair pulling at some point in their lives (Christenson, Mackenzie, & Mitchell, 1991). Other physically self-damaging behavior is common in people with this disorder.

Although trichotillomania is not often presented in treatment, it may be found in as many as six to eight million people (3 to 15 percent of the population). People with trichotillomania often experience significant levels of distress and impairment in social functioning, including loss of intimacy, decreased contact with friends and family, and avoidance of leisure pursuits, such as athletics, swimming, and dating, in part due to embarrassment about their behavior and appearance (Franklin et al., 2006; Stemberger, Thomas, Mansueto, & Carter, 2003).

It is likely that there is a biological basis for the disorder. Trichotillomania is associated with increased rates of OCD in first-degree relatives (Bienvenu et al., 2000). To date, little empirical research is available on treatment interventions for this disorder, although preliminary findings indicate that CBT is effective for many people with trichotillomania (Franklin et al., 2006).

Typical Client Characteristics

In addition to the information already provided about the common characteristics of people with these disorders, most people diagnosed with trichotillomania also have at least one concurrent mental disorder, most often mood or anxiety disorders, although substance-related disorders, OCD, eating disorders, and personality disorders (most often borderline personality disorder) are also common. Overall, impulse-control disorders are typically associated with other mental disorders, including PTSD, Cluster B (dramatic, emotional, or erratic) personality disorders, depressive disorders, anxiety disorders, eating disorders, and substance-related disorders. Suicidal ideation is common, especially among people with pathological gambling. Alcohol and benzodiazepines may be used to reduce self-control and allow people to act on destructive impulses. The impulsive behavior itself is typically used to relieve anxiety and depression.

Although some people with impulse-control disorders may not be severely troubled by their symptoms, others experience considerable shame, embarrassment, and guilt. They recognize that others find their behaviors unacceptable, so they frequently take steps to conceal their actions. These disorders commonly have a negative impact on interpersonal relationships and occupational functioning and are associated with increased carelessness, morbidity, and mortality (Hollander et al., 2006). People with these disorders typically have limited, conflicted, or unrewarding patterns of socialization. Many also tend to be passive and have difficulty expressing their feelings. People with impulse-control disorders often share three key characteristics: failure to defer gratification, distractibility, and disinhibition or impulsiveness. A history of neglect and abuse is often seen in people with impulse-control disorders, as well as a family history of substance misuse, mood disorders, and anxiety.

Preferred Therapist Characteristics

Establishing a therapeutic alliance will be easier with some people with impulse-control disorders than with others, depending on the disorder. For example, people with kleptomania sometimes welcome the opportunity to obtain help with their underlying anger and depression and so are willing clients. However, people with paraphilias are typically reluctant to enter treatment because they do not want to give up their gratifying behaviors. People with these disorders may seek therapy only as a result of a court order or because of pressure from friends and family members. Stein, Harvey, Seedat, and Hollander (2006) suggest that an initial period of negotiating the framework for the therapeutic relationship may be necessary when working with clients with impulse-control disorders. During this time, therapist and client build rapport, work together to establish boundaries, determine client responsibilities, set limits for the relationship, define a structure, and decide whether abstinence versus control will be the treatment goal.

People with impulse-control disorders tend to be defensive, to engage in denial and avoidance, and to resist taking responsibility for the consequences of their behavior. They may perceive others as forcing them to act as they have, and they may view themselves as blameless. In most cases their insight is limited, so engaging them in therapy is likely to present quite a challenge to therapists.

Therapists may view some of the behaviors of people with impulse-control disorders (such as fire setting, paraphilias, or physical abuse of their partners) as distasteful and reprehensible. Another challenge to therapists, then, is managing their own feelings about these clients' behaviors and remaining objective while communicating acceptance and support.

Intervention Strategies

Little research is available on the treatment of many of these impulse-control disorders, so treatment recommendations are tentative and based primarily on theory and on what has been effective in treating individual cases and similar disorders. Developing an appropriate treatment plan involves exploring the behavioral, cognitive, and affective components of the disorder, as well as the impact of the disorder on the person's lifestyle.

Behavioral techniques usually will form the core of treatment for people with impulse-control disorders. Such techniques as stress management, impulse control, distraction, relaxation training, systematic desensitization, contingency contracting, habit reversal training, and aversive conditioning commonly are used to discourage impulsive behavior. Overcorrection through public confession and restitution has been part of the treatment of these clients. People also need help in finding better ways to meet the needs that had been addressed by the impulsive behaviors.

Many other types of interventions can contribute to effective treatment of impulse-control disorders. Because these disorders typically worsen under stress, raising awareness of stressful triggers (such as anniversary dates and family visits) is important, as is an accompanying effort to assist in stress reduction. Reinforcement with praise and tangible rewards can also help modify dysfunctional behaviors and reduce stress. Assertiveness training and improvement of communication skills can help alleviate interpersonal difficulties and increase people's sense of control and power. If an impulsive behavior has reached addictive proportions, people may experience symptoms of withdrawal after its cessation. This withdrawal will also require attention so that a relapse can be prevented.

The specific choice of interventions depends on the nature of the disorder, of course. For example, relaxation training to promote anger management has been effective in treating people with problems involving angry driving (Deffenbacher, Filleti, Lynch, Dahlen, & Oetting, 2002). Improvements in anger and impulsivity scores have also been seen in people with borderline personality disorder as a result of Marcia Linehan's dialectical behavior therapy (Linehan, 1993). This could have implications for people with intermittent explosive disorder, and studies of that are currently under way (Coccaro & Danehy, 2006).

In treatment of trichotillomania, cognitive-behavioral therapy has been shown to be superior to both medication and placebo in two studies. At present, and based on a limited number of studies, habit reversal training, awareness training, and stimulus control seem to form the core cognitive-behavioral intervention strategies for trichotillomania (Franklin et al., 2006).

Treatment for pathological gambling generally follows the model developed to treat substance-related disorders. Treatment interventions might include inpatient treatment and rehabilitation programs, cognitive and behavioral psychotherapy, medication, family therapy, education, and participation in self-help groups. People who engage in pathological gambling and other impulse-control disorders usually need help in coping with their high need for stimulation. Like most impulse-control disorders, the negative behavior is inherently gratifying, so it reinforces itself and makes treatment difficult.

Group therapy with other people who share the same problems can often reduce the attraction of an impulse by providing peer confrontation and support. This approach to treatment is particularly useful for people who engage in pathological gambling and for those who have been diagnosed with intermittent explosive disorder. Gamblers Anonymous, modeled after Alcoholics Anonymous, offers an important avenue to peer support and is often helpful as an adjunct to therapy. However, Gamblers Anonymous has not been found to be helpful when used as the only form of treatment. Dropout rates have been shown to be as high as 70 percent within the first year, and one study indicated that only 8 percent remained abstinent at one-year follow-up (Pallanti et al., 2006). Support groups can help fill the void left when an impulsive behavior is stopped and can offer understanding, concern, role models, peer pressure, inspiration, motivation, and new behaviors. They should not, however, be used as the sole source of treatment.

Although no randomized controlled studies of treatment effectiveness for kleptomania exist, case reports indicate some success with behavior therapy that includes covert sensitization combined with exposure and response prevention for people diagnosed with this disorder. Grant (2006) describes several case reports in which people with kleptomania used covert sensitization to visualize negative consequences of their stealing behavior. For example, one woman who imagined increased nausea and eventual vomiting whenever she had the urge to steal had only one relapse in nineteen months following four sessions of covert sensitization over an eight-week treatment period. Other behavioral techniques, such as imaginal desensitization, learning to substitute alternative sources of satisfaction and excitement, and aversive breath-holding followed by journaling, were also found to be effective in individual case studies (Grant, 2006).

Limit setting is an important component of treatment for impulse-control disorders. Impulsive symptoms often offer short-term positive reinforcement. People must learn to deal with the long-term negative consequences of their behavior, whether these consequences are legal or interpersonal. Family therapy is often indicated as well, particularly for people with pathological gambling or kleptomania, those who abuse family members, and adolescents engaged in pyromania. Often families must be brought into the loop and educated about how their own behaviors may be enabling those of their loved one. For example, bailing people out of trouble seems to reinforce and perpetuate the behavior. Family members may also be called on to help reinforce limits, such as requiring people who engage in pathological gambling to take their mood stabilizing medication or setting curfews for adolescents engaged in fire setting.

Exploration of cognitions can help clients and therapists understand the thinking that promotes these disorders — thoughts like ''Setting fires will show people I'm not really a weakling'' or ''If I can gamble only a little longer, I'm sure I'll get that big win.'' An understanding of the adverse consequences of their behavior can also help people with impulse-control disorders modify their actions. A one-day Trauma Burn Outreach Prevention Program that focused on the medical, financial, legal, and societal impact of fire-setting behavior resulted in a recidivism rate of less than 1 percent, compared to 36 percent recidivism in the control group (Franklin et al., 2002). Underlying depression and anxiety, as well as other coexisting symptoms, also need to be relieved, typically through cognitive therapy, as the impulsive behavior is often a way to manage those feelings.

Some people with impulse-control disorders benefit from psychodynamic treatment designed to help them deal with childhood losses and abuse and to help them gain an understanding of the underlying reasons for their behavior. People who are high in insight and motivation are particularly likely to benefit from therapy with a psychodynamic component. Clients with alexithymia (inability to identify or articulate emotions) and those with high degrees of dissociative behavior, often found in conjunction with trichotillomania and pathological gambling, may benefit from awareness training to help them be more conscious of their behavior and develop insight into stressors and emotional precursors to their maladaptive behavior.

Emotion-focused therapy (Greenberg, 2002) can help people recognize, label, tolerate, and regulate negative affect. Therapists work as emotion coaches to help people use their emotions in healthy ways, rather than dissociating or acting out in an attempt to reduce anxiety and negative affect. Similarly, in acceptance and commitment therapy (Eifert & Forsyth, 2005), therapists help clients ''ACT'': *a*ccept thoughts and feelings, *c*hoose direction, and *t*ake action.

Therapy also needs to attend to the correlates of the disorders, including legal, financial, occupational, and family difficulties. Development of leisure activities and increased involvement with career responsibilities and family members can help replace impulsive behavior.

Medication is sometimes useful in the treatment of impulse-control disorders. Impulsive behaviors sometimes have a neurological component that can be modified by such drugs as mood stabilizers, anticonvulsant medication, or antidepressants. SSRIs, including fluoxetine (Prozac), sertraline (Zoloft), and paroxetine (Paxil), have been shown to reduce impulsivity and have been helpful to people with intermittent explosive disorder, pathological gambling, kleptomania, and trichotillomania (Stein et al., 2006). Mood stabilizers and anticonvulsants such as lithium, valproate, and topiramate have been shown to reduce impulsivity, especially when bipolar disorder is also present. Atypical antipsychotics have also shown promise in the treatment of impulse-control disorders. These medications reduce aggressive symptoms and, although they may not be the first-line treatment, have been beneficial in treating trichotillomania (Stein et al., 2006). Antidepressants and other medications can also have an indirect beneficial impact on impulse-control disorders by alleviating accompanying depression and other symptoms. Some classes of medications, such as the benzodiazepines, tend to reduce inhibitions and would therefore not be appropriate for the treatment of impulse-control disorders.

Prognosis

As with the prognoses for most other impulse-control disorders, the prognosis for the disorders reviewed here is uncertain. Relapse is common, especially at times of stress, loss, or disappointment, and it should be addressed in treatment. Few figures are available on success rates for treatment of these disorders, although research suggests that children treated for pyromania have a good prognosis and that people with late-onset trichotillomania have a poor prognosis (Franklin et al., 2006). Like people with substance use, people with pathological gambling often go through repetitive cycles of abstinence and relapse (Ladd & Petry, 2003). Several of the disorders, however, including intermittent explosive disorder, tend to diminish spontaneously over time. The good news is that in recent years we have learned more about these disorders and have a broader array of evidence-based interventions from which to choose in the treatment of impulse-control disorders.

SLEEP DISORDERS

Description of the Disorders

Sleep disorders are a very different type of behavioral disorder from those disorders discussed previously in this chapter. Unlike most of the others, sleep disorders provide few secondary gains and rewards, and people clearly want to be free of their symptoms. As described in *DSM-IV-TR,* sleep disorders are reflected by disturbances in the restorativeness and continuity of sleep and involve too much sleep, too little sleep, or dysfunctional sleep. They include four major subgroups, distinguished by whether or not they result from another disorder or difficulty:

1. Primary sleep disorders (not caused by a medical condition, a substance, or another mental disorder). These are primary insomnia; primary hypersomnia; narcolepsy; breathing-related sleep disorder; circadian rhythm sleep disorder; and the parasomnias, which are nightmare disorder, sleep terror disorder, and sleep walking disorder.
2. Sleep disorder related to another mental disorder.
3. Sleep disorder due to a general medical condition.
4. Substance-induced sleep disorder.

A review of the specific disorders encompassed by the category of primary sleep disorders will provide familiarity with the major clusters of symptoms included among all the sleep disorders.

Primary Insomnia. This disorder is described by *DSM-IV-TR* as ''difficulty initiating or maintaining sleep or of nonrestorative sleep that lasts for at least one month and causes clinically significant distress or impairment'' (American Psychiatric Association, 2000, p. 599). This fairly common disorder is more prevalent in later life, among women, and in people with personality traits that predispose them to worry and anxiety (Nowell, Buysse, Morin, Reynolds, & Kupfer, 2002). Insomnia has been linked to a constant state of hyperarousal typically reflected by increased metabolic rate, and an overall increase in adrenocorticotropic hormone (ACTH) and cortisol levels (Mahowald & Schenck, 2005). Difficulty falling asleep is its most common manifestation. Secondary symptoms, including mild anxiety, depression, irritability, difficulty concentrating, and fatigue, may interfere with daytime functioning. However, many people with insomnia report less daytime fatigue than people without insomnia, again pointing to a twenty-four-hour cycle of hyperarousal.

Primary Hypersomnia. This disorder is characterized by prolonged sleep (typically nine to twelve hours per night), excessive daytime sleepiness (despite adequate sleep), or sometimes both, for more than one month. It is more common in men than in women, tends to begin in young adulthood, and, without treatment, usually has a chronic course. The tiredness, as well as the napping and the lengthy periods of sleep that characterize the disorder, can have an adverse impact on a person's social or occupational activities. People with this disorder tend to have a first-degree relative who also has primary hypersomnia.

Narcolepsy. This disorder is characterized by at least three months of daily irresistible attacks of sleeping that typically last ten to twenty minutes. Upon awakening, the person is refreshed but may have another attack in two to three hours. Cataplexy, or loss of muscle tone, occurs in about 70 percent of those with this disorder and may cause them to fall or collapse. Cataplexy is often precipitated by an intense emotion such as surprise, anger, or laughter (American Psychiatric Association, 2000). Sleep paralysis, the inability to move, is another troubling symptom of this disorder and most often occurs on waking. Hypnogogic hallucinations occur in 20 to 40 percent of those with narcolepsy. These hallucinations indicate that REM sleep is intruding on the waking state, and they are often the first symptom of this disorder. This disorder has a hereditary component, as does breathing-related sleep disorder. Narcolepsy is relatively rare, affecting only one in ten thousand to twenty thousand people. Slightly more men than women have been diagnosed with this disorder (Savard & Morin, 2002). It usually begins in puberty and rarely has a first occurrence after the age of forty. This chronic disorder can contribute to accidents, depression, and work problems. Co-occurring disorders (primarily mood disorders, substance-related disorders, and generalized anxiety disorder) are found in 40 percent of people with narcolepsy (Savard & Morin, 2002).

Breathing-Related Sleep Disorder. Abnormal respiration during sleep can lead to the excessive daytime sleepiness that is often the presenting problem for this disorder. Loud snoring and gasping during sleep are other clues to the presence of this disorder, although shallow breathing may be present instead. Breathing-related sleep disorder occurs in 2 percent of adult women and 4 percent of adult men. Linked to obstructive sleep apnea, this is not only a condition of middle-aged, obese men, in whom it is especially prevalent; it also can be seen in thin individuals, postmenopausal women, and 3 percent of children (Mahowald & Schenck, 2005; Savard & Morin, 2002). Typically, people with this disorder have as many as three hundred episodes a night in which air flow ceases for ten seconds or longer and is restarted with accompanying arousal. People with this disorder may be unaware of their repeated awakenings, but their bed partners can describe the characteristic breathing and snoring patterns. If left untreated, this disorder can contribute to the development of hypertension and heart failure. This disorder is often hereditary. Breathing-related sleep disorder has increased in children since routine removal of children's tonsils and adenoids was discontinued.

Circadian Rhythm Sleep Disorder. This disorder results from a mismatch between people's natural biological clocks and the demands of their lifestyles. Subtypes — including delayed sleep phase type, in which people have preferred times for sleeping and waking that are significantly later than those of most people and that usually begins in adolescence; jet lag type; and shift work type — reflect common examples of such mismatches. Difficulty falling asleep at prescribed times leads to sleepiness at other times, which in turn often leads to irregular sleeping patterns and use of caffeine and other stimulants, which then exacerbate the disorder.

Parasomnias. Parasomnias are characterized by undesirable physical happenings during sleep and include nightmare disorder, sleep terror disorder, and sleepwalking disorder. All three disorders are particularly common in children. The first two both involve upsetting dreams but are distinguished by the point in the sleep cycle when they occur and by people's reactions upon awakening. Sleep terror disorder, which usually begins between the ages of four and twelve, is characterized by repeated awakening from dreams with a loud scream or cry and accompanying disorientation. People with nightmare disorder, by contrast, are alert upon awakening and can clearly report details of their frightening dreams. Sleepwalking affects 1 to 5 percent of children, with onset typically between the ages of six and twelve and elimination of sleepwalking typically by the age of fifteen; nearly 4 percent of adults also experience sleepwalking (Mahowald & Schenck, 2005). Most parasomnias occur during the transition in the wake-sleep cycle. Mahowald and Schenck (2005) cite current research that considers parasomnias to be ''dissociated sleep states'' (p. 1282) caused by the overlap of wakefulness and either non–rapid eye movement (NREM) sleep (as in the case of arousal disorders such as sleep terrors and sleepwalking) or the combination of wakefulness and REM sleep.

A sleep disorder can also be related to another mental disorder (most often a mood or anxiety disorder). Mahowald and Schenck (2005) point out that in the case of insomnia, the relationship between insomnia and other disorders such as depression or substance use is bidirectional — that is, the other disorder may cause insomnia, and insomnia may contribute to the emotional disorder. Insomnia may also be secondary to a medical condition (such as pain, asthma, fever, or a neurological disorder). Substance-induced sleep disorders can be caused by alcohol, caffeine, nicotine, amphetamines, and other substances.

A diagnostic sleep laboratory that can provide polysomnographic studies of sleep patterns is invaluable in diagnosing most of these sleep disorders, especially breathing-related sleep disorder, primary insomnia, and narcolepsy. These studies should be conducted before a diagnosis of these disorders is finalized. A sleep diary kept by the client can also provide useful information on sleeping patterns.

Typical Client Characteristics

Sleep disorders are quite varied, as are the people who experience them. *DSM-IV-TR* reports that 30 to 45 percent of adults complain of insomnia in any given one-year period. People with sleep disorders are more likely to be female; older; and experiencing health problems, a recent loss, or considerable stress (Savard & Morin, 2002). Sleep problems may be related to environmental cues, as many people with insomnia can sleep well in new surroundings, whereas those without insomnia are more likely to have difficulty sleeping in new environments (Nowell et al., 2002).

People with insomnia report greater muscle tension, greater arousal, and increased incidence of stress-related illnesses (such as headaches and gastrointestinal problems). Problems during the day include poor concentration and reduced energy. Chronic insomnia can lead to increased risk of panic disorder, development of another mental disorder within one year of onset, and alcohol misuse (Nowell et al., 2002). Driving while drowsy has been estimated to be the cause of more than one hundred thousand motor vehicle accidents annually in the United States (Mahowald & Schenck, 2005).

People with a sleep disorder related to another mental disorder typically have difficulty expressing their feelings directly and tend to channel their emotional concerns into somatic symptoms. In some cultures (Southeast Asian, for example), sleep complaints may be viewed as more acceptable than mental disorders and presentation of insomnia or hypersomnia may be a way to seek help for underlying concerns that people are reluctant to acknowledge (Paniagua, 2001).

Assessment

Savard and Morin (2002) recommend the following assessments as part of a thorough evaluation of sleep disorders:

- Semistructured clinical interview
- Use of a sleep diary for at least a week
- Self-report measures
- Laboratory polysomnography if symptoms warrant

The clinical interview should evaluate the type of sleep disorder, symptom severity, frequency, and duration, as well as any daytime symptoms. Sleep habits, contributing factors to the sleep disturbance, family or personal history of sleep problems, triggers (for example, recent loss, divorce, work difficulties), as well as late-night eating and relaxation routines should be included. Medications tried, as well as dysfunctional cognitions that the person has developed in response to the sleep problem, should also be discussed.

Detailed interviewing is particularly indicated with people who present with circadian rhythm sleep disorders, because their lifestyles and their work schedules often contribute to the disorder. Another reason for thorough interviewing is the finding that up to 30 percent of those who complain of difficulty falling or remaining asleep actually do sleep well (Mahowald & Schenck, 2005).

Several assessment measures are available, including the Insomnia Interview Schedule (Morin, 1993), a semistructured interview; the Structured Interview for Sleep Disorders (SIS-D; Schramm et al., 1993), which has a 90 percent concordance rate with a polysomnographic assessment; and the Sleep-EVAL, a computerized assessment that takes upwards of an hour to complete and is consistent with *DSM-IV-TR* criteria (Ohayon et al., 1997). Self-reports, such as a sleep diary that can be maintained for one or two weeks prior to treatment, provide reliable and cost-effective baseline data on symptoms and severity and are less subject to exaggeration of sleep difficulties than an informal self-report (Savard & Morin, 2002).

An important measure of sleep-related cognitions can be found in the Dysfunctional Beliefs and Attitudes about Sleep Scale (DBAS; Morin & Espie, 2003). This thirty-item self-report scale asks for responses to such statements as "I am concerned that chronic insomnia may have serious consequences for my physical health" in an effort to assess how realistic a person's sleep expectations are. The DBAS is a useful tool for focusing cognitive therapy aimed at debunking sleep myths and negative thoughts (Savard & Morin, 2002).

Laboratory polysomnography, an all-night assessment in a sleep lab, is often warranted, particularly when heavy snoring results in gasping and reduced respiration, or leg movements interfere with sleep. The American Academy of Sleep Medicine (AASM) has developed practice guidelines for the use of polysomnography in the evaluation of sleep disorders, as not all sleep problems will require such an extensive assessment (Standards of Practice Committee of the American Academy of Sleep Medicine, 2003).

Preferred Therapist Characteristics

Complaints of insomnia and other sleep disorders are often trivialized or ignored by practitioners (Savard & Morin, 2002). Therapists treating people with sleep disorders seem to be most successful if they take sleep disorders seriously and take a directive yet supportive stance. People with these disorders often have deferred seeking help until the problems felt overwhelming, and they need reassurance and active intervention to modify the symptoms quickly. People with sleep disorders are sometimes reluctant to engage in exploration of their lifestyles and possible underlying concerns, and this reluctance must be addressed and reduced by therapists as part of a comprehensive assessment.

Intervention Strategies

Insomnia and hypersomnia are often related to or caused by other disorders or situations that require attention, such as depression, stress reactions, and substance-related disorders. People with sleep disorders also may have life circumstances — such as a recent loss, a stressful life event, or environmental factors, such as a noisy or an uncomfortable living situation — that interfere with their ability to get a good night's sleep. Therefore, when a person presents with symptoms of a sleep disorder, a careful assessment interview is necessary to ascertain the dynamics of the disorder.

In one study, 40 percent of people with insomnia had another mental disorder (Ford & Kamerow, 1989). If a disorder such as major depressive disorder or a substance-related disorder seems to be causing the sleep disorder, focusing on the underlying disorder usually will take priority. Successful treatment of that disorder may automatically relieve the sleep disorder. However, therapists often will have difficulty shifting the client's focus from the sleeping difficulties to the concerns that underlie them.

Research on the use of psychotherapy to treat sleep disorders is limited. Most of the relevant research has been done by medical researchers working in sleep laboratories. Nevertheless, the literature does provide some guidelines for using psychotherapy to treat sleep disorders once medical causes have been ruled out. If it has been determined that the focus of treatment will be on the sleep disorder, the first steps usually will be to ensure that the person has a sleeping environment conducive to restful sleep and to stabilize the sleep schedule as much as possible, eliminating naps and caffeine and establishing healthy patterns of eating, drinking, and exercising.

As a general rule, people who clearly are not getting enough sleep, typically people with insomnia or circadian rhythm sleep disorder, can be treated primarily via behavior therapy. People who are sleeping too much, however, or who are exhausted even though they seem to have had enough sleep (typically people with narcolepsy, breathing-related sleep disorder, and hypersomnia), usually require medication or medical treatment. People with parasomnias, especially children, require primarily reassurance and help in reducing any stress and anxiety that may be contributing to the disorder.

Generally, behavioral treatments are more effective than medication when long-term outcome for treatment of insomnia is considered (Nowell et al., 2002). A variety of behavioral techniques have been used successfully in the treatment of insomnia: stimulus control therapy, relaxation techniques, sleep hygiene education, and sleep restriction therapy have all proved helpful. Stimulus control therapy consists of a set of instructions to be followed at bedtime to reduce behaviors that are incompatible with sleep and to address circadian factors. Such a list might include the following instructions:

- Go to bed when tired.
- Use the bedroom only for sleep-related activity and sex. Do not eat, watch television, work, or read in the bedroom during the day or night.
- Do not take a nap during the day.

- If unable to sleep after trying for fifteen to twenty minutes, get up and go to another room. Return to bed only when tired again.
- Wake up in the morning at the same time regardless of the amount of sleep the night before.

Relaxation therapy, including progressive muscle relaxation, biofeedback, and cognitive thought-stopping techniques, has been consistently found to be effective in the treatment of insomnia. Sleep hygiene education, although the least effective of the behavior therapies when used on its own, includes health-related practices such as diet, exercise, and control of substance use, and helps people regulate their environment (light, noise, and temperature) so that it is conducive to sleep.

Cognitive-behavioral treatment addresses the maladaptive cognitions that tend to perpetuate insomnia: the difficulty in sleeping causes worry about not sleeping, and the worry in turn exacerbates the difficulty in sleeping. Breaking the cycle is important in reducing the symptoms. Meditation, use of positive imagery, and light therapy are other sleep-enhancing techniques.

Sedative-hypnotic medications were formerly the most commonly used treatment for insomnia; there were forty-two million prescriptions filled in 2005 (della Cava, 2006). Although the research indicates that benzodiazepines with hypnotic effects are efficacious in the short-term management of insomnia (Nowell et al., 2002), the long-term efficacy is unknown, and benzodiazepines have been linked with such side effects as daytime drowsiness, cognitive impairments, and dependence. Elderly people are particularly vulnerable to risk for falls and hip fractures when using long-acting hypnotics (Savard & Morin, 2002). Until longitudinal data is available, the use of hypnotic medications should probably be viewed as a treatment of last resort.

Newer sleep medications, such as ramelteon (Rozerem), zolpidem (Ambien), and zaleplon (Sonata) do not have the addictive properties or side effects of the benzodiazepines. Ramelteon, in particular, works specifically on the suprachiasmatic nucleus — where the body's sleep-wake cycle is located — to inhibit the wake-alerting system. Some people use melatonin and other over-the-counter remedies to help them fall asleep. The long-term impact of these substances has not been fully documented, so these remedies should be used with great care, if at all.

Circadian rhythm sleep disorder, jet lag type and shift work type, are best treated through lifestyle modification that stabilizes sleeping patterns. Chronotherapy, or resetting of the biological clock, is another approach to treatment of this disorder (Mahowald & Schenck, 2005). The delayed sleep phase type of this disorder, for example, can be treated through phase advancing, which systematically, gradually, and progressively schedules earlier bedtimes for people with this disorder. Phototherapy (light therapy), stress management, relaxation, avoidance of alcohol and caffeine, and improved sleep habits can enhance treatment (Mahowald & Schenck, 2005).

Unlike insomnia, excessive sleeping or fatigue usually results from an underlying medical disorder such as sleep apnea (Mahowald & Schenck, 2005). Consequently, treatment of these symptoms should always include a medical evaluation. Medical treatments vary according to the disorder. For example, primary hypersomnia and narcolepsy can be treated successfully with stimulant medication, such as amphetamines. Narcolepsy also benefits from two or three scheduled daily naps of twenty to thirty minutes each. Antidepressant medications can relieve the cataplexy that often accompanies narcolepsy. Breathing-related sleep disorders can be treated with weight loss, nasal continuous positive airway pressure (via CPAP machines) that regulates breathing, and, if all else fails, sometimes by surgery. People with fatigue and chronic sleepiness also can benefit from the establishment of a regular sleeping schedule and healthy eating and exercise. Psychotherapy, addressing both underlying stressors and the stress introduced by the sleepiness, is often indicated.

The parasomnias are usually due to difficulties in the transition from sleep to wakefulness. Rather than having a psychological origin, parasomnias, like sleepwalking, support the concept that wake and sleep are not mutually exclusive states (Mahowald & Schenck, 2005). In children, the parasomnias usually do not reflect underlying pathology and are generally outgrown without any intervention.

Parasomnias may be triggered in adults by alcohol, sleep deprivation, physical activity, emotional stress, or medication. Recurrent frightening or upsetting dreams may also reflect the surfacing of painful memories, which may require therapeutic attention.

In addition to specific treatments for the sleep disorders, people with these disorders also usually benefit from education and attention to any underlying conflicts or sources of excessive arousal. Education as part of treatment can provide people with needed reassurance and dispel myths and cognitive distortions. If the sleep disorder has been long-standing and chronic, it may have damaged a person's career and relationships and caused psychological distress. These issues, too, may need to be addressed in therapy.

Prognosis

The prognosis for reducing sleep disorders is quite good, but an accurate assessment of etiology is critical in determining outcome. Those with a medically or physiologically caused sleep disorder usually respond well to medical treatment or to alleviation of the cause. Those with a psychologically determined sleep disorder are likely to respond well to behavioral psychotherapy as long as any underlying disorders are also addressed. The parasomnias have a high probability of spontaneous remission. Breathing-related sleep disorders and narcolepsy may need lifelong treatment, but usually can be well controlled through that treatment. The prognosis for both primary insomnia and circadian rhythm sleep disorder is uncertain and depends primarily on the people's lifestyles and ability to stabilize their lives to reduce stress and change.

TREATMENT RECOMMENDATIONS: CLIENT MAP

This chapter has focused on the diagnosis and treatment of five groups of disorders of behavior and impulse control: substance-related disorders, eating disorders, sexual and gender identity disorders, impulse-control disorders not elsewhere classified, and sleep disorders. Although the symptoms of these disorders vary widely, they do have an underlying commonality: behavioral dysfunction. The following general treatment recommendations, organized according to the format of the Client Map, are provided for disorders of behavior and impulse control.

Client Map

Diagnosis

Disorders of behavior and impulse control: substance-related disorders, eating disorders (anorexia nervosa and bulimia nervosa), sexual and gender identity disorders (sexual dysfunctions, paraphilias, and gender identity disorders), impulse-control disorders not elsewhere classified (pathological gambling, intermittent explosive disorder, pyromania, kleptomania, and trichotillomania), sleep disorders

Objectives of Treatment

Increased knowledge of the disorder

Reduction of dysfunctional behaviors

Acquisition of new and more positive behaviors

Improved ability to meet own needs

Stress reduction

Lifestyle improvement

Relapse prevention

Assessments

Physical examination (especially important for sleep disorders, sexual disorders, bulimia nervosa, and anorexia nervosa)

Symptom inventories

Establishment of baseline severity of symptoms

Determination of presence of coexisting mental disorders

Clinician Characteristics

Knowledgeable about individual, group, and family therapy

Well informed about specific disorder

Able to be structured and directive yet supportive

Able to manage potential negative feelings about client's behavior

Able to work effectively with client's reluctance, limited motivation, and hostility

Location of Treatment

Usually outpatient setting

Short-term inpatient treatment possible for severe cases of substance-related disorders and eating disorders

Therapeutic communities, day treatment programs also possible

Interventions to Be Used

Multifaceted program emphasizing behavior therapy and cognitive-behavioral therapy

Measurements of change

Education

Improvement of communication and relationship skills

Stress management

Impulse-control strategies

Emphasis of Treatment

Highly directive

Moderately supportive

Primary focus on current behaviors and coping mechanisms

Some attention to past patterns and history

Numbers

Group therapy particularly important when motivation for change is low

Individual and family therapy also important

Timing

Rapid pace

Short to medium duration, with extended aftercare focused on relapse prevention

Medications Needed

Usually not the primary mode of treatment

Medication can accelerate progress in some cases, especially in helping curtail drug and alcohol use, address some sleep disorders, and alleviate underlying depression

Adjunct Services

Peer support groups such as Alcoholics Anonymous, Narcotics Anonymous, Overeaters Anonymous, Gamblers Anonymous, Rational Recovery

Prognosis

Good prognosis for significant improvement if client is (or becomes) motivated to change

Relapse common

Client Map of George W.

This chapter began with a description of George W., a thirty-six-year-old male with a twenty-two-year history of maladaptive alcohol use. George was also experiencing legal, interpersonal, occupational, and marital problems. He reported some underlying depression and social discomfort. George was seen in therapy after his arrest for driving while intoxicated. The following Client Map outlines the treatment provided to George, a course of treatment typical of what is recommended for people who misuse alcohol or have other disorders of behavior and impulse control.

Diagnosis

Axis I: 303.90 Alcohol dependence, severe

Axis II: 799.90 Diagnosis deferred on Axis II. Rule out avoidant personality disorder or avoidant personality traits

Axis III: High blood pressure, intestinal discomfort reported

Axis IV: Incarceration for third DWI conviction, marital conflict, occupational problems

Axis V: Global assessment of functioning (GAF Scale): current GAF = 50

Objectives of Treatment

Establish and maintain abstinence from alcohol

Improve marital relationship

Improve social skills

Improve occupational functioning

Build coping and life skills, as well as enjoyment of life

Obtain diagnosis and treatment for medical complaints

Assessments

Thorough medical evaluation to determine impact of alcohol use on client's physical condition and obtain treatment for physical complaints

Minnesota Alcoholism Screening Test

Clinician Characteristics

Knowledgeable about the development and symptoms of alcohol dependence

Structured and directive

Skilled at setting limits

Location of Treatment

Outpatient setting (rather than inpatient setting with concurrent medical evaluation and supervision), given that client had been alcohol free for several weeks as a result of incarceration

Interventions to Be Used

Group behavior therapy as primary approach

Individual therapy, later family therapy and marital therapy as needed

Cognitive-behavioral therapy

Encouragement for abstinence

Education about stress management, problem solving, communication skills, impact of alcohol, and maladaptive patterns of alcohol use

Development of leisure and social activities not focused on drinking

Emphasis of Treatment

Directive

Focused on current behavior

Elements of both support and exploration

Numbers

Individual, group, family, and couples therapy

Timing

Rapid pace

Medium duration

Extended follow-up and participation in Alcoholics Anonymous

Medications Needed

None

Naltrexone (ReVia) to be considered in case of early relapse

Adjunct Services

Alcoholics Anonymous (at least three meetings per week)

Later participation in Adult Children of Alcoholics

Al-Anon for client's wife

Prognosis

Fair (client internally and externally motivated, acknowledges need to reduce or eliminate drinking, aware that job and marriage are in jeopardy, but reluctant to make the commitment to long-term abstinence)

Better with long-term follow-up and continued participation in Alcoholics Anonymous

Relapse common

Recommended Reading

Agency for Healthcare Research and Quality. (2006). *Management of eating disorders.* AHRQ Publication No. 06-E010. North Carolina: RTI-UNC Evidence-Based Practice Center.

Costin, C. (1999). *The eating disorder sourcebook.* Los Angeles: Lowell House.

Fairburn, C. G., & Brownell, K. D. (2002). *Eating disorders and obesity* (2nd ed.). New York: Guilford Press.

Hollander, E., & Stein, D. J. (Eds.). (2006). *Clinical manual of impulse-control disorders.* Arlington, VA: American Psychiatric Publishing.

Leiblum, S. R. (2007). *Principles and practices of sex therapy* (4th ed.). New York: Guilford Press.

Miller, W. R., & Rollnick, S. (2002). *Motivational interviewing: Preparing people to change addictive behavior.* New York: Guilford Press.

Savard, J., & Morin, C. M. (2002). Insomnia. In. M. M. Antony & D. H. Barlow (Eds.), *Handbook of assessment and treatment planning for psychological disorders* (pp. 523–555). New York: Guilford Press.

CHAPTER SEVEN

Disorders in Which Physical and Psychological Factors Combine

Dr. Martin C., a sixty-two-year-old African American male, was referred for therapy by his physician. Martin had sought medical help for intestinal discomfort. He believed that he had cancer of the small intestine. His father had died of that form of cancer in his sixties when Martin was a teenager.

Over the past year, Martin had consulted three physicians (including an oncologist), had had a thorough medical evaluation, and was found to have nothing more than frequent indigestion and constipation due to poor eating habits. Because Martin had difficulty accepting this diagnosis, his physician referred him for therapy.

Martin had been a history professor for almost thirty-five years. He had been promoted to associate professor about twenty-five years ago, after the publication of an influential book he had written on the history of war, but he had never been able to equal that accomplishment. His efforts to achieve promotion to full professor had been unsuccessful.

Martin was also experiencing stress at home. He had been divorced from his first wife fifteen years ago and had been married for eight years to a woman twenty years younger than he. Martin felt that she was disappointed in him because of his lack of professional success, and he was worried about the future of their marriage. He coped with this worry by working long hours and taking a great deal of nonprescription medication for his gastric symptoms.

He was rarely home, had few friends and leisure activities, and had considerable difficulty verbalizing his feelings.

Martin initially sought help for a physical problem — intestinal discomfort and gastric distress — but his physician believed that Martin's complaints had an emotional cause. Martin was experiencing a disorder called hypochondriasis, which is included in one of four broad groups of disorders considered in this chapter. In these disorders, physical complaints are intertwined with emotional difficulties, and attention must be paid to both groups of symptoms.

OVERVIEW OF DISORDERS IN WHICH PHYSICAL AND PSYCHOLOGICAL FACTORS COMBINE

Description of the Disorders

This chapter begins with an overview of disorders involving an interrelationship of physical and psychological concerns. It goes on to provide information on the diagnosis and treatment of the four groups of disorders that fit this description:

1. Somatoform disorders (somatization disorder, undifferentiated somatoform disorder, conversion disorder, pain disorder, hypochondriasis, and body dysmorphic disorder)
2. Factitious disorders
3. Delirium, dementia, and amnestic and other cognitive disorders
4. Mental disorders due to a general medical condition

People with these disorders typically present for treatment with concerns about a physical or medical complaint. They sometimes seek therapy after referral from a physician who has not been able to find a medical cause for their complaints or who believes that the clients' emotional difficulties would be helped by psychotherapy even though they may stem from a medical condition. These clients may or may not be aware of the dynamics of their disorders. Heightened concerns about physical issues can serve a purpose. Instead of feeling the pain associated with certain emotions, the feelings are translated into physical symptoms. People often are unaware of how or why their emotions are transferred onto physical experiences. Nevertheless, anxiety and other difficult emotions are kept out of conscious awareness and are directed instead to the physical realm of the body. In addition, people may derive benefit from the attention and sympathy their physical symptoms elicit from others. Because clients focus primarily on their physical concerns, they may be surprised by and resistant to the suggestion that they would benefit from psychotherapy.

Typical Client Characteristics

People with disorders in which physical and psychological factors combine typically have difficulty expressing emotions directly and so may channel concerns into the physiological realm, which brings them some rewards. For example, people with factitious disorders or somatoform disorders may have been sickly as children or had a parent who suffered long illnesses, and they learned, through modeling of the sick role, that having medical complaints is a way to receive nurturing and attention.

Often the combination of psychological and biological difficulties began in childhood and persisted into adulthood. People with one of the disorders discussed in this chapter typically have trouble managing environmental stress and tend not to be insightful or psychologically minded. Sometimes people with these disorders have strong dependence needs and want others to take care of them. They frequently have impairment in both the interpersonal and the occupational aspects of their lives, and are often reluctant to discuss their psychological difficulties with others.

Assessment

Effective management of these disorders is dependent on accurate and comprehensive psychological and medical assessments. Simon (2002) notes that special attention should be paid to the development of the therapeutic relationship as well as the following factors: reason for referral, if any; the symptoms and concerns the client identifies; the ability of the therapist to take these symptoms seriously; developing an effective treatment plan that focuses on symptom reduction rather than cure; and effective coordination with medical providers. Other disorders commonly co-occur, and should be assessed as well.

Preferred Therapist Characteristics

Therapists treating people with these disorders benefit from having information on medical conditions and should be comfortable collaborating with physicians. Clients with disorders discussed in this chapter will often be reluctant to engage in therapy and will often dispute the importance of psychological variables. Consequently, their therapists need to be skilled at developing rapport and communicating support and interest so that a helpful therapeutic relationship is established fairly rapidly. If the therapist is harshly confrontational or unsympathetic, the client may well terminate treatment, but if the therapist overemphasizes the physical complaints, little progress will be made. Therefore, the therapist must carefully control discussion of the presenting complaints. Therapy is most likely to be successful if the therapist is understanding of the symptoms and worries that clients have because of their physical complaints, but also uses concrete and structured interventions that are flexible and empowering while involving little in-depth analysis.

Intervention Strategies

Few controlled studies exist on the treatment of the disorders covered in this chapter. Nevertheless, case studies and theoretical articles provide a good indication of effective approaches to treatment.

The first step in treating people who present with interrelated physical and psychological complaints is to obtain a medical consultation (or to confer with physicians whom the client has already consulted) to determine whether a physical disorder really is present. An early assessment of mental status and cognitive functioning also is important. If a medical condition is present, the therapist should become familiar with the impact of the condition on the client and should ensure that appropriate medical treatment is provided if it is needed. Clients should be kept informed about their medical condition and should be involved in decisions about treatment whenever that is possible. Clients who feel that their medical symptoms are being ignored may manifest an increase in somatization.

Therapy for people with interrelated physical and psychological complaints generally de-emphasizes interpretation and analysis, because of the resistance and discomfort those approaches may provoke. Throughout the treatment process, great care should be taken to establish and nurture a positive therapeutic alliance. Holder-Perkins and Wise (2001) advise against telling clients that the problem "is in their head." Rather, a long-term, helpful therapeutic relationship based on trust and collaboration and free of medical evaluations, tests, and measurement of symptoms may be the best approach. Therapy is usually integrative and multifaceted, focusing on affective, cognitive, and behavioral areas to build up the person's coping skills, reduce accompanying depression and anxiety, modify negative cognitions that promote hopelessness and dependence, and help people meet their needs more effectively.

These clients may be receptive to nonverbal therapies, such as meditation, biofeedback, massage, and other relaxation techniques that do not require them to verbalize their feelings, although there is little empirical research on the effectiveness of these treatments with the disorders covered in this chapter. Leisure and career counseling can advance treatment, and family counseling can prevent reinforcement of secondary gains (such as time off from work, and extra attention that the clients receive when they feel ill). Cognitive-behavioral therapy, stress management, and hypnotherapy also are useful in helping people integrate the physical and emotional aspects of themselves and maximize their strengths. If the client is experiencing significant impairment, either cognitive or physical, psychotherapy will need to take that impairment into account.

Medication should be considered for co-occurring disorders such as depression, anxiety, or pain. However, care should be taken, as people with somatoform disorders often are especially sensitive to the effects of medication and their side effects, and are also at increased risk for abusing medication (Holder-Perkins & Wise, 2001).

Prognosis

The prognosis for treating disorders in which physical and psychological factors combine varies greatly according to the nature and dynamics of the client's concerns and the client's receptivity to therapy. If clients can acknowledge having emotional concerns that could benefit from therapy, they may well derive considerable benefit from their treatment: therapy can not only reduce people's focus on their perceived physical complaints but also increase their self-confidence and self-esteem and improve the quality of their lives. Nevertheless, the presence of cognitive impairment or a medical illness, as well as clients' continued emphasis on medical rather than psychological concerns, may limit the progress of therapy.

SOMATOFORM DISORDERS

Description of the Disorders

Somatoform disorders are characterized by physical complaints or symptoms that are not fully explained by a medical condition or by another mental disorder and are believed to be caused (at least in part) by psychological factors. People who have these disorders, however, genuinely believe that they are afflicted with the symptoms and physical illnesses they are presenting. They are not deliberately producing these symptoms, so they are typically very distressed about their physical complaints and about the failure of the medical community to find and address a medical cause for their symptoms. The fourth edition text revision of the *Diagnostic and Statistical Manual of Mental Disorders (DSM-IV-TR)* lists the following six types of somatoform disorders (American Psychiatric Association, 2000).

Somatization Disorder. This disorder, also known as Briquet's syndrome, is one of the most severe of the somatoform disorders (Bond, 2006). In one study, as many as 10 percent of those with somatization disorder were confined to wheelchairs and spent, on average, seven days a month in bed. Somatization disorder is characterized by multiple medically unexplained physical complaints, beginning before the age of thirty and lasting for at least several years, for which a person seeks medical treatment and makes modifications in lifestyle. Over the course of the disorder, by definition, the person has experienced at least four pain symptoms, two gastrointestinal symptoms (usually nausea and bloating), one symptom related to sexual or reproductive activity, and one neurological or conversion symptom. Common symptoms of this disorder include shortness of breath, menstrual complaints, nausea and vomiting, burning sensations in the genitals, limb pain, amnesia, and a sensation of having a lump in the throat (Escobar, 2004). Emotional lability, a susceptibility to anxiety and depression, and overly dramatic and manipulative behavior have also been noted in people with somatization disorder. The combination of multiple physical symptoms and affective dysregulation often results in "disruptive and disrupting lifestyles" (Bond, 2006, p. 262).

More than half of people with somatization disorder were exposed, as children, to illness or physical disease in one or both parents (Bond, 2006). The clients take on the chronic illness behavior they have observed, and secondary gains typically result. This disorder, which often goes unrecognized and untreated (Phillips, 2001), causes considerable distress as well as social and occupational impairment. Somatization disorder is associated with increased absences from work, increased time spent in bed, and reduced life satisfaction (Stuart & Noyes, 1999).

This relatively rare disorder is present in 0.2 to 2.0 percent of women and less than 0.2 percent of men (American Psychiatric Association, 2000). Although it is far more common in women than in men in the United States, increased incidence of the disorder in men in countries such as Greece and Puerto Rico suggest that cultural factors may influence gender ratio (Holder-Perkins & Wise, 2001). Somatization disorder often is accompanied by anxiety, mood, and personality disorders as well as by alcohol use disorders and attentional difficulties. Somatization disorder usually follows a chronic course, beginning in adolescence, although symptoms may wax and wane. This disorder has a familial component, with as many as 10 to 20 percent of female relatives of those with this disorder also experiencing somatization disorder. Male relatives have been found to have increased rates of antisocial personality disorder and alcohol use disorders (Holder-Perkins & Wise, 2001).

Undifferentiated Somatoform Disorder. This disorder involves the presence, for at least six months, of one or more somatic symptoms, not attributable to a medical condition, that cause significant upset or dysfunction. Common complaints include persistent fatigue, loss of appetite, gastrointestinal symptoms, and genitourinary symptoms (American Psychiatric Association, 2000). The diagnosis of undifferentiated somatoform disorder is generally used to describe multiple physical symptoms that resemble but do not meet the full criteria for somatization disorder (American Psychiatric Association, 2000). People with undifferentiated somatoform disorder tend not to be as impaired as those with somatization disorder, but their symptoms often evolve into somatization disorder.

Conversion Disorder. This disorder was well known in Freud's time but is relatively rare today. Prevalence rates vary from eleven to five hundred per one hundred thousand people, and it appears to be more frequent in women than men at a ratio estimated to range from 2:1 to 10:1 (American Psychiatric Association, 2000). Conversion disorder involves a loss or change in motor or sensory functioning, and it results in such symptoms as blindness; tingling, numbness, or paralysis of a limb; impaired balance; inability to speak; and seizures or pseudoseizures. The physical symptom typically has no medical cause but is associated with and symbolic of a conflict, a stressor, or a psychological difficulty that lies outside the person's awareness. For example, a woman who witnessed the killing of her husband and child subsequently developed a conversion disorder in which she became unable to see. Emotional stress, loss of a parent or other close relationship, and divorce often precipitate the development of a conversion disorder (Bond, 2006).

Diagnosing conversion disorder requires great care and consultation with physicians. The literature describes many cases in which this diagnosis was made in error because a medical disorder was overlooked. Thirty percent of people initially diagnosed with conversion disorder were found to have an underlying neurological illness (such as head injury, EEG abnormality, multiple sclerosis, tumors, or petit mal seizures) or were eventually diagnosed with an illness that explained their symptoms (Holder-Perkins & Wise, 2001).

Conversion disorder is most common in adolescents and women who are not medically or psychologically sophisticated and who may have limited education and intellectual ability. This disorder is rarely diagnosed before the age of ten or after the age of thirty-five.

Conversion disorders often are accompanied by another mental disorder. Among people manifesting pseudoseizures, a common symptom of conversion disorder, 77 percent of women had a history of sexual abuse or rape, 70 percent had a coexisting neurological disorder, and the majority had an IQ below 80. Conversion disorder is often associated with childhood sexual abuse (Maldonado & Spiegel, 2001) and with major depressive disorder, with approximately 85 percent of people with conversion disorder meeting the criteria for major depression at some point in their lives (Holder-Perkins & Wise, 2001). Other common co-occurring disorders include somatization disorder, anxiety disorders, alcohol use disorders, dissociative disorders, and personality disorders. Pain is unusual in conversion disorder.

Butcher, Mineka, and Hooley (2006) note that people with conversion disorder are very willing to discuss their symptoms, often at great length and detail. However, people who are deliberately feigning symptoms tend to become defensive, evasive, and suspicious when symptoms or inconsistencies in their behavior are pointed out.

DSM-IV-TR identifies the following subtypes of conversion disorder:

- With motor symptom or deficit (such as impaired balance, difficulty swallowing, paralysis)
- With sensory symptom or deficit (for instance, inability to feel pain or blindness)
- With seizures or convulsions
- With mixed presentation (if more than one category is appropriate)

Pain Disorder. This disorder entails either an excessive reaction to an existing physical pain (pain disorder associated with both psychological factors and a general medical condition) or preoccupation with a pain that is not shown to have any medical origin (pain disorder associated with psychological factors only). According to Bond (2006), in pain disorder associated with both psychological factors and a general medical condition, the level of pain should be "markedly in excess" of what is expected (p. 263). When a pain disorder is suspected, clients should be referred for a complete physical examination, and the therapist should conduct a thorough mental status exam; a diagnosis of pain disorder can be made only in the absence of physical illness or injury that fully explains the symptoms. Bond notes that pain disorder frequently occurs after a minor injury or illness that caused pain and has since improved; nevertheless, the client still reports chronic, severe, disabling pain. This exaggerated pain response is more likely in the presence of secondary gains, including attention from family members or freedom from work or unpleasant experiences or responsibilities. Depression and anxiety sometimes accompany this relatively common disorder, as does impairment in functioning. Pain disorder is most often diagnosed in adolescence and young adulthood. Women with pain disorders are more likely than men to experience certain types of chronic pain, such as severe and persistent headaches and musculoskeletal pain. Pain of a sexual nature (for example, genital pain) is often reported by women who were sexually abused in childhood (Stuart & Noyes, 1999).

This disorder typically begins abruptly and worsens over time. When pain disorder is associated with a medically diagnosed physical condition, it can be exacerbated by physicians' minimization or inadequate treatment of pain. People whose pain is associated with a terminal illness or severe depression are at increased risk of suicide (American Psychiatric Association, 2000).

Hypochondriasis. This is probably the best known variant of somatoform disorder. It is characterized by the belief that minor physical complaints (such as chest pain or a headache) are symptoms of serious conditions, such as a heart attack or a brain tumor. This fear of having a serious medical condition lasts for at least six months, typically begins in early adulthood, and causes marked distress or dysfunction, although the belief is not of sufficient intensity to be described as delusional. Men and women are equally affected by this disorder, which is often accompanied by depressive and anxiety disorders. Hypochondriasis is fairly common and is believed to affect 4 to 9 percent of people who seek medical treatment in outpatient settings (Simon, 2002).

Body Dysmorphic Disorder. This disorder involves preoccupation with an imagined or slight flaw in physical appearance. Facial flaws such as acne or the perception of a larger than average nose are most likely to concern people with this disorder, but they typically have more than one concern; genitalia, hair, and breasts are other common areas of focus. People with this disorder are not delusional and can acknowledge that they may be exaggerating, but they do not have a realistic image of themselves. (A delusional form of this disorder is coded under delusional disorder, somatic type.) This disorder typically causes marked distress or dysfunction. People's self-consciousness can lead them to engage in prolonged grooming and staring into mirrors, to dress in concealing garments, to avoid public situations (sometimes to the point of becoming housebound), and to seek repeated surgeries for perceived flaws (Phillips, 2001).

Body dysmorphic disorder is most likely to begin in adolescence, usually has a gradual onset (American Psychiatric Association, 2000), and is equally common in males and females. Men with body dysmorphic disorder tend to be preoccupied with body build, genitals, thinning hair, and height, whereas women are more likely to focus on hips and weight and have increased incidence of bulimia nervosa and anxiety disorders. For men, dissatisfaction with their physique or musculature may lead to the use of anabolic steroids or overexercising.

Body dysmorphic disorder has high comorbidity with other mental disorders, including mood disorders, anxiety disorders, substance abuse or dependence, and psychotic disorders. Men are also more likely to have avoidant personality disorders, alcohol use disorders, and bipolar disorders (Phillips, 2001). Suicidal ideation is common. People with this disorder are more likely to seek help initially from dermatologists and surgeons than from therapists and to request therapy because of a physician referral.

Typical Client Characteristics

A look at all the somatoform disorders indicates that they typically begin in adolescence or young adulthood and follow a chronic but often inconsistent course. Most types of somatoform disorder are more common in women and in people who live in rural areas, are not well educated, have below-average intellectual functioning and socioeconomic status, are not psychologically minded or insightful, and have difficulty identifying and expressing their feelings. People with these disorders tend to become preoccupied with their illnesses and medical histories and de-emphasize other areas of their lives, often experiencing social and occupational impairment as a result. They tend to feel dependent and helpless and use their physical complaints as a way to relate to others and gain sympathy and attention. Use of both prescription and nonprescription medication to relieve symptoms is common, and these people's lives may revolve around medication schedules and medical appointments and tests. Some become dependent on analgesics.

People with somatoform disorders usually restrict their activities, movement, and levels of stimulation in the belief that if they protect themselves in this way, they may prevent a worsening of their pain or other symptoms (Phillips, 2001). Their preoccupation with their body often leads to social isolation and depression, which in turn may precipitate an intensification of the symptoms. People with somatoform disorders often manifest attitudes of learned helplessness, reinforced by early family and social experiences, and they tend to be discouraged, worried, angry, and low in self-esteem. They commonly have a sense of emptiness; they lack positive emotions and energy, and believe that they cannot build rewarding lives until their physical complaints have been alleviated. Underlying depression may be reflected in problematic sleeping and eating patterns.

Many people with somatoform disorders report a family history of illness, and clients' symptoms may mirror those experienced by family members when the clients were children. The clients themselves may have been sickly when they were younger and may have learned that, in their families, physical illness gained more attention than verbal expressions of emotional discomfort. Stuart and Noyes (1999) found that nearly 20 percent of people with somatization disorder reported experiencing a chronic illness before the age of sixteen. Alexithymia, the inability to identify or articulate emotions, sometimes contributes to and coexists with somatoform disorders, especially with hypochondriasis and somatization disorder (Holder-Perkins & Wise, 2001).

People with pain disorder have often had early exposure to people experiencing pain. Children's reactions of pain tend to mirror their parents' reactions and are more often governed by the parents' affect than by the illness itself (Stuart & Noyes, 1999). As adults, their experience of pain is often connected to a threatened loss or unresolved conflict that raises negative feelings, which are then expressed through somatization (Bond, 2006). Pain disorder often reflects masked depression. Families of people with this disorder also have a high incidence of chronic pain, dysfunctional alcohol use, and depression.

People with hypochondriasis are particularly likely to have symptoms similar to people with OCD, especially obsessive thoughts about illness and the compulsive need to check the Internet for medical information and health sites (Fallon & Feinstein, 2001). Hypochondriasis is often associated with an early bereavement, a history of illness in the family, and overprotective parents. Hypochondriasis commonly is accompanied by anxiety, depression, mistrust, underlying anger and hostility, obsessive-compulsive traits, fear of disease, a low pain threshold, and disturbed early relationships. Personality disorders are present in as many as 61 percent of people with hypochondriasis, with avoidant, paranoid, and obsessive-compulsive personality disorders being the most common (Stuart & Noyes, 1999). Hypochondriasis can be situational or chronic, typically worsening during times of stress or emotional arousal (Fallon & Feinstein, 2001).

People with somatization disorder tend to view themselves as always having been sickly and unhappy. They commonly had problems of adjustment as children and may have been abused. As adults, people with somatization disorder often have major depressive disorder, suicidal ideation, substance misuse, and neurological disorders, and may be dependent, overly emotional, exhibitionistic, narcissistic, disorganized, dependent, and self-centered. Co-occurring personality disorders often include borderline, histrionic, or avoidant personality disorders (Holder-Perkins & Wise, 2001; Stuart & Noyes, 1999).

Somatization disorder seems to have a familial component. The families of origin of people with somatization disorder tend to have a high prevalence of mental disorders, ranging from 44 percent in one study to 70 percent in another (Stuart & Noyes, 1999). The authors found that pathological parenting, child temperament, and genetic influences all contributed to the development of somatization disorders.

Assessment

Depression and anxiety disorders co-occur with somatoform disorders to such an extent that Simon (2002) recommends anxiety and depression be assessed and treated first as an effective treatment for these disorders. Specific assessment tools for anxiety and mood disorders can be found in Chapters Four and Five.

Preferred Therapist Characteristics

Therapists generally should assume a warm, positive, optimistic stance in treating people with somatoform disorders. These clients need a stable relationship that inspires confidence and provides acceptance, approval, and empathy. This requirement may present a challenge because some people with somatoform disorders are frustrated and angry with the medical community's inability to resolve their physical complaints. They may be resentful of a referral for psychotherapy, viewing the referral as a statement that others think their complaints are "all in their minds." These negative feelings are often displaced onto the therapist, who may bear the brunt of these clients' discouragement and unhappiness.

One of the most helpful interventions for the therapist working with a client with somatoform disorder is the development of an accepting and collaborative relationship. Some therapists experience annoyance and even anger with these clients if the clients refuse to let go of the belief that they have serious physical disorders or if the clients view therapists and physicians as adversaries who are refusing to find physical causes for the symptoms. Therapists need to be aware of their own reactions to these clients' behaviors and attitudes so that they can build a positive therapeutic alliance and prevent countertransference reactions from harming the therapeutic relationship.

Stuart and Noyes (1999) recommend that rather than being drawn into a self-defeating interpersonal cycle, therapists should stress accountability and communicate admiration for the suffering these clients have endured. That may be helpful, but the therapist needs to be careful not to reinforce the client's role as a sick person; rather, the therapist should gradually shift the focus off the physical illness and encourage stress management, increased activities and socialization, and positive verbalization. Reinforcement should be used when the client does not dwell on the bodily symptoms but instead takes an active role in self-help.

Intervention Strategies

As with all the disorders in this chapter, a team approach to treatment of somatoform disorders is indicated, with the physician and the therapist working together. The therapist can even be presented as a consultant who will help alleviate the impact of stress on the client's physical complaints while the physician focuses on the medical aspects of those complaints. This stance reassures clients that their physical complaints are being taken seriously and treated appropriately. A collaborative approach also allows the therapist to monitor the client's medical care and discourage unnecessary tests or medical consultations while making sure that the physician does indeed take the client seriously. Bond (2006) reports that it is not the severity of the symptoms that are troublesome, but the person's dramatic and persistent complaints about them. Presenting both the physiological and the psychological component of treatment as an integrated package can promote treatment compliance and increase the chances of a successful outcome.

Overall treatment goals should focus on improving functioning rather than on reducing physical symptoms; if functioning is improved, in most cases, the symptoms will spontaneously decrease. Somatically focused anxiety is a common characteristic of these disorders. Bond (2006) suggests that it is best understood as a cognitive distortion. Thus clients' tendencies toward amplification (their selective perception and exaggeration of physiological symptoms), as well as their withdrawal from relationships and activities, can be reduced through cognitive-behavioral therapy. The focus of therapy should be on the present rather than on the past and should seek to increase skills in stress management and coping, facilitate verbal expression of feelings, promote empowerment, and encourage healthy cognitions as well as increased activity and socialization. Confrontation and emphasis on insight, if used at all, should be reserved for later phases of treatment with these clients.

Medical complaints should be de-emphasized. The therapist should avoid taking a position on the veracity of the medical complaints and certainly should not engage in arguments with the client. People with somatoform disorders genuinely experience and believe in the symptoms they present, and therapists should treat those beliefs gently. Understanding and addressing the social context of people with this disorder is essential because context typically reinforces and explains the presence of the symptoms.

Although information on somatoform disorders is increasing, the empirical research on effective treatment of somatoform disorders is limited. Many approaches and techniques have been suggested and have demonstrated success, such as the following three-stage treatment process. In stage one, therapy begins with a concrete focus on physical symptoms, teaching people strategies for reducing them. Techniques like biofeedback and relaxation training are usually well received because of their emphasis on the body. Stage two emphasizes supportive discussion of symptoms and lifestyle and helps the client make connections between the two, raising awareness of difficulties that may be experienced in the interpersonal, occupational, and leisure areas as well as in self-expression. Stage three employs cognitive and emotive approaches, enabling people to gain deeper awareness of their cognitive distortions; become better able to identify and express their emotions; and make changes in thoughts, feelings, behaviors, relationships, and lifestyle.

Fallon and Feinstein (2001) suggest a comprehensive approach to treating hypochondriasis that has application to the other types of somatoform disorders as well. Therapy begins with the establishment of a trusting relationship that validates the client's experience. Therapists should remain tolerant and sympathetic despite the client's resistance to psychotherapy. Treatment should empathize with and validate the client's experience. Following a careful history taking, the therapist can focus on helping the client understand how stress can aggravate symptoms. The client is asked to keep a self-report log of stressors so that a connection can be made between precipitating events and development and exacerbation of symptoms.

Once that goal has been accomplished, therapy typically includes the following five steps:

1. Exploration of the client's attitudes toward illness
2. Presentation of information on the client's medical condition
3. Perceptual retraining to help the client focus more on external information and less on internal cues
4. Ericksonian suggestions that the client's symptoms will be reduced
5. Encouragement of self-talk and internal dialogue to reduce stress and anxiety

Hypnosis, biofeedback, and relaxation have also contributed to the treatment of hypochondriasis and of pain disorder. One meta-analysis of hypnotic analgesia (Price, 2006) found that hypnosis produced substantial pain relief for 75 percent of the people studied.

Major depression often accompanies chronic pain in 57 to 72 percent of the cases. Depression is more likely to occur in conjunction with physical illness and after physical injuries. Suicidal thoughts also increase as a result of the degree and intensity of pain. Bond (2006) stresses the importance of relieving depression before successful treatment of pain disorder with cognitive-behavioral therapy can begin.

Bond (2006) reports on the results of two meta-analyses of cognitive-behavioral therapy (CBT) used for pain management and relapse prevention. The research shows that CBT and behavior therapy are both effective interventions to help people with pain disorder reduce pain and improve mood. Both types of treatment were also found to be effective when integrated into rehabilitation programs.

An informal 1 to 10 rating scale of pain's severity can be useful in assessing progress that has been made in the treatment of pain disorder. Simon (2002) notes that pain symptoms can be reduced through the combining of strategies to promote pain management (such as imagery and relaxation training) with techniques designed to reduce negative self-talk and increase activity. In this manner, nonpain behaviors are reinforced and cognitive restructuring occurs. Seventy-five placebo controlled trials tested the efficacy of antidepressant medication on pain disorder. Most studies found medication more effective than a placebo (Simon, 2002). Limited studies have been conducted on the combination of pharmacotherapy and psychotherapy. The results indicated a slight benefit when medication is added to therapy in the treatment of pain disorders.

Some hospitals have pain treatment units that facilitate the treatment of people with pain disorder. These programs typically aim at decreasing people's experience of pain as well as their reliance on medication, while increasing their activity levels, their cognitive control over the pain, and their effective use of coping mechanisms (Simon, 2002). Such programs usually offer a multidisciplinary approach to treatment and typically include the following elements:

- Detoxification from medication (if needed)
- Physical, occupational, and recreational therapy
- Acupuncture
- Trigger-point injections
- Transcutaneous electrical nerve stimulation (TENS)
- Group, individual, and family therapy
- Various forms of relaxation

Obsessive features in people with body dysmorphic disorder or hypochondriasis have responded well to behavior therapy. Phillips (2001) suggests the following treatment strategies for body dysmorphic disorder:

- Target body dysmorphic symptoms in the treatment (do not focus exclusively on depression or anxiety).
- Use medication such as SSRIs as a first-line approach for those with severe disorders. Often medication can make cognitive-behavioral therapy possible by reducing depressive and physical symptoms enough so that the person can benefit from therapy.
- For milder forms of the disorder that are not accompanied by co-occurring disorders, use intensive CBT without medication. Schedule frequent sessions with accompanying homework. The cognitive component should include exposure and response prevention.
- Add CBT booster sessions to prevent relapse.
- Include psychoeducation about body image that encourages acceptance and discourages surgery or other medical interventions.

A cognitive-behavioral approach combined with SSRI antidepressants that also reduce anxiety, obsessional thinking, and phobic avoidance has been found to be effective in nearly two-thirds of people in one study of those with somatoform disorders (Simon, 2002).

Group therapy also is an important component of treatment for somatoform disorders, particularly for hypochondriasis, pain disorder, and body dysmorphic disorder (Simon, 2002). It can promote socialization, provide support, and facilitate direct expression of emotions. For those with body dysmorphic disorder, realistic feedback from peers about clients' appearance can be more powerful than feedback from a therapist (Simon, 2002). Group therapy can also change people's expression of symptoms, reduce depression, modify avoidance behaviors, help people assume responsibility for their symptoms, enhance their ability to enjoy life, provide information and support as well as reinforcement, and teach relaxation and other positive behaviors.

Family members usually should be involved in the treatment of somatoform disorders. They can learn to reinforce positive behavior and, as appropriate, to ignore or de-emphasize the client's physical complaints. People diagnosed with somatoform disorders should learn to get attention and affection through means other than physical illness; for most people, this learning is best gained and reinforced in the family environment. People with somatoform disorders tend to be more receptive to therapy when it is endorsed not only by a professional whose opinion is valued but also by a friend or a family member — yet another reason for involving the client's close friends or family members in treatment. If the client has a history of conflicted and dysfunctional family relationships or is still troubled by the illness or death of a family member, therapy may need to pay some attention to those issues in an effort to reduce their present impact.

Because many people with somatoform disorders have neglected the social and occupational areas of their lives, those should receive attention through therapy. People will often need to build support systems, develop leisure activities that may have been avoided before, and establish and work toward realistic and rewarding career goals. Environmental modifications, such as walking to work with a neighbor, may encourage some of these lifestyle changes by reducing secondary gains of physical complaints and altering patterns of activity.

Increasingly, medication has been used to treat somatoform disorders. Although analgesic medication usually does not reduce the pain associated with these disorders, antidepressant medication is often recommended to alleviate the underlying depression and often leads to reduction in the somatic symptoms. For example, SSRIs such as fluoxetine (Prozac) are more effective than other medication in reducing symptoms of body dysmorphic disorder (Phillips, 2001). Although medication generally is not indicated for the treatment of hypochondriasis, several clinical trials have shown improvement ranging from 77 to 80 percent in patients treated with Prozac (Phillips, 2001). Fluoxetine has also been shown to be beneficial for clients with treatment-resistant hypochondriasis (Fallon & Feinstein, 2001).

Pain disorders, too, show significant improvement in response to antidepressant medication. However, the medication does not teach people to develop coping skills and rebuild their lives. Thus, even if medication is helpful, psychotherapy also seems essential to effecting and maintaining a positive response to treatment. Whatever approach to the treatment of somatoform disorders is used, what should be encouraged is healthy, independent, responsible behavior.

Prognosis

Somatoform disorders tend to be persistent and resistant to treatment. Factors associated with a good prognosis are the presence of a stressful precipitant for the symptoms, brief and circumscribed symptoms, the ability to form stable relationships, the capacity to feel and express emotions directly, the ability to form a therapeutic alliance, and the ability to be introspective. A negative prognosis is most likely when people fail to recognize that their concerns are probably excessive.

Prognosis varies according to the specific disorder, the individual client, and treatment methodology. One study conducted at Harvard University found improvement in somatoform disorder after brief, intensive therapy (Holder-Perkins & Wise, 2001). The gains were maintained one year after treatment ended. Conversion disorder almost always spontaneously disappears within a few days or weeks but may recur under stress and tends to be difficult to treat once it becomes entrenched. Conversion symptoms of blindness, aphonia, and paralysis usually respond well to treatment, but pseudoseizures and tremors are less likely to remit (Maldonado & Spiegel, 2001). Pain symptoms can be chronic and disabling, but pain treatment centers report a 60 to 80 percent rate of significant improvement among people with pain disorder, and that improvement is well maintained after discharge. Hypochondriasis can be a chronic and fluctuating disorder, although most people with this disorder do improve significantly.

Body dysmorphic disorder tends to be a chronic and stable disorder that is often difficult to treat, although recent research shows promise for the effectiveness of cognitive-behavioral therapy that focuses on exposure treatment and response prevention (Phillips, 2001). As is the case with other somatoform disorders, insight-oriented therapy does not appear to be effective for body dysmorphic disorder; neither does surgery nor nonpsychological medical treatment. Pharmacotherapy with SSRIs appears to help, but relapse often occurs when the medication is discontinued. Somatoform disorders can be challenging to treat, but most clients do benefit considerably from therapy, sometimes in combination with medication.

FACTITIOUS DISORDERS

Description of the Disorders

Factitious disorders are "characterized by physical or psychological symptoms that are intentionally produced or feigned in order to assume the sick role" (American Psychiatric Association, 2000, p. 513). Unlike people with somatoform disorders, who genuinely experience and believe in their physical complaints, people with factitious disorders purposely simulate symptoms in order to be treated as though they are ill. They are not feigning the symptoms in order to escape work or other obligations; rather, their primary goal is to assume the role of patient and to receive care, nurturance, and attention.

Factitious disorders, also known as Munchausen's syndrome, are among the most difficult disorders to diagnose because of the person's untruthfulness and hidden agendas, as well as the degree to which they will inflict self-harm to substantiate their claims of illnesses (Feldman, Hamilton, & Deemer, 2001). People with this disorder typically feign severe physical or psychological symptoms (for example, psychosis or abnormal bleeding). Their affect tends to be incongruent with these symptoms, often reflecting indifference or lack of concern. They are eager to undergo invasive medical procedures but generally will not allow communication with previous physicians. They avoid accurate diagnosis through changes of residence, physicians, and symptoms.

The onset of a factitious disorder is usually in early adulthood, but the disorder may begin in childhood, often following a medically verified physical illness that places these people in a rewarding patient role in which they are nurtured and receive attention. Sometimes people with factitious disorders have worked in medical settings or are otherwise familiar with medical personnel and illnesses, and this familiarity facilitates their simulation of the symptoms of illness. Alternatively, they sometimes research their feigned disorders so that they can present a convincing story. This disorder is more common in males (American Psychiatric Association, 2000) and is severe in that it typically prevents people's involvement in normal social and occupational activities. Due to the lack of research and people's unwillingness to admit to this disorder, prevalence rates of factitious disorder are unknown, although it seems to be relatively rare (Feldman et al., 2001).

In a variation on this disorder, factitious disorder by proxy (otherwise known as Munchausen's disorder by proxy and diagnosed as factitious disorder not otherwise specified), parents or caregivers deliberately create or exaggerate physical or psychological symptoms in people under their care (such as children or people who are elderly or disabled). Infants and young children are the most likely victims. Caregivers may coach people in their care to confirm or present signs of the illness, or they may harm the people in their care so that they will appear ill. The symptoms bring attention, support, and sympathy to the caregivers.

People with factitious disorder by proxy sometimes cause the deaths of people in their care through suffocation, poisoning, or other means. The estimated death rate for children involved in this pattern ranges from 10 to 60 percent (Schreier, 2002; Sheridan, 2003). Many others are disfigured or impaired, as a result either of harm from their caregivers or of harm from unnecessary medical procedures. In a meta-analysis of published cases, Schreier indicates that these children had as many as "40 to 100 operations for nonexistent conditions" (p. 985) and that 75 percent of the children who died as a result of this disorder died in hospitals.

Typical Client Characteristics

People with factitious disorders tend to be immature, dramatic, grandiose, and demanding; they insist on attention while often refusing to comply with prescribed treatments. In addition to what is usually the primary motivator, the wish for attention and nurturing (Feldman et al., 2001), common underlying motivators are self-punishment, the desire to obtain compensation for past suffering and perceived wrongs, and the desire to obtain drugs. Their behavior may be learned, as people with factitious disorders typically had parents who were normally harsh and demanding but who became caring and loving when their children were ill, thus reinforcing a dysfunctional pattern of behavior. People with this disorder also may have developed positive early relationships with physicians, thereby further reinforcing their symptoms.

Males with factitious disorders tend to be unstable and egocentric, often exaggerating their accomplishments, whereas females tend to be younger, more stable, and more likely to be in the medical field (Schreier, 2002). Factitious disorder has been seen in children and teenagers who induce or claim illness to receive medical attention.

People with factitious disorders typically have other somatoform disorders and have a high incidence of anxiety, mood, and substance use disorders. Men are more likely to have comorbid bipolar disorders; borderline personality disorder more commonly co-occurs in women (Feldman et al., 2001). First-degree relatives of those with factitious disorders also often have mental disorders, chronic medical problems, and poor coping skills. People with factitious disorders may have undergone many surgical procedures and other medical tests and treatments that produced genuine physical complaints that now complicate the treatment picture.

Schreier (2002) notes that people with factitious disorder by proxy usually are young mothers who on the surface appear devoted to their children but are actually hurting their children to meet the mothers' own self-serving needs (such as to gain access to or attention from the medical community). Their backgrounds often include a history of family dysfunction and abuse. Medical settings may be familiar and comfortable to them because of their own illnesses or work experiences. The recidivism rate for these mothers is high and underscores the need to obtain a swift and accurate diagnosis before the child is injured or made sick again. Symptoms on the part of the caregiver include falsification of medical conditions, direct harm induction, inappropriate affect (one mother was reported to be "gleeful" when describing her son's acute life-threatening events), and a wide variety of other symptom presentations (Schreier, 2002).

Assessment

Myriad somatic, cognitive, and behavioral difficulties may be presented by the client with factitious disorder. According to Simon (2002), these symptoms may often be "clearly inconsistent with any known disease" (p. 455). Because the client's goal is frequently to maintain the sick role, accurate assessment of symptoms can be exceedingly difficult.

Preferred Therapist Characteristics

Establishing a therapeutic alliance with a person diagnosed with a factitious disorder will usually be extremely difficult. The therapist should be supportive and empathic but should also gently confront the deception. Strong confrontation should be avoided because typically that will be met with denial and hostility. Schreier (2002) suggests that consulting with the client's physician can be especially effective in working with these clients. Consultation with the physician can confirm whether there is a medical basis for the client's complaints, a past history of repeated unexplained illnesses, or, as often happens, a history of the client's changing doctors frequently. Therapists should avoid power struggles, open conflict, and humiliation of people with factitious disorders and must manage their own feelings of anger and frustration in dealing with the clients' deceptions and manipulations. Viewing the symptoms as a cry for help rather than as hostile or manipulative behavior can be helpful to both therapist and client.

Intervention Strategies

People with factitious disorders are rarely seen for psychotherapy because they typically are not motivated to address their disorder, but they may appear in treatment as a result of pressure from a family member or as part of court-ordered treatment to retain custody of their children. Some may remain in treatment if attention is paid to their feigned complaints and if the treatment meets some of their dependence needs, although most will leave treatment once they realize that they have been found out. While in treatment, people with factitious disorders are likely to be hostile and to resist the formation of a positive therapeutic relationship.

Therapists should try to establish realistic treatment goals with these clients. Personality reconstruction through therapy is unlikely; however, improvement in coping skills, reduction in self-injurious behavior and dangerous medical procedures, and symptom reduction are all realistic goals.

Early detection and treatment are important to prevent unnecessary tests and invasive medical procedures, self-inflicted harm, and suicide. Feldman and colleagues (2001) found that those diagnosed in the early stages of factitious disorder are more amendable to psychotherapeutic interventions.

In factitious disorder by proxy, early detection is essential to prevent injury or death of the child or other target of the harmful behavior. Children whose caregivers can be diagnosed with factitious disorder by proxy may need to be hospitalized or removed from the home for their own protection. Schreier (2002) notes that separating the child from the mother can often be used to demonstrate that the child is disease-free when not under her influence. The available information on the treatment of factitious disorders is nearly all anecdotal or theoretical. It is extremely difficult to obtain a large enough sample size of people with factitious disorders to conduct controlled research. No interventions are now known to be consistently effective in treating factitious disorders (Feldman et al., 2001), so treatment recommendations are based on theory rather than on empirical data. Feldman and colleagues suggest that the treatment approach be nonconfrontational and offer a face-saving means of recovery. Reinforcing appropriate behavior, educating clients on the mind-body connection, addressing stressors that may have precipitated the disorder, developing more effective mechanisms for coping with stress, and improving self-esteem and relationships so clients do not need to look to the medical community for nurturing are all useful ingredients of treatment. Family therapy may be particularly useful for people with factitious disorder by proxy. Many people with factitious disorders who are reluctant to engage in psychotherapy may be more willing to participate in therapeutic stress management and so this may serve as a way to engage them in treatment. These interventions can help those with factitious disorders abandon the sick role and construct a healthier self-image. Eisendrath (1995) suggests a double-bind approach to treatment. In this approach, clients are offered a benign medical intervention (such as biofeedback) and are told that failure of the treatment will confirm a diagnosis of a factitious disorder. This apparently leads some people to choose recovery. One reason for the success of this approach is that it allows people to give up factitious behaviors without embarrassment — an important element of treatment. However, therapists may be uncomfortable with the apparently misleading nature of this intervention.

Prognosis

In some cases a factitious disorder that develops in response to environmental stress will remit spontaneously when the stressor has passed. Once a factitious disorder becomes chronic and part of a person's lifestyle, however, the prognosis for spontaneous recovery is poor. Factors associated with responsiveness to treatment include coexisting Axis I mental disorders (such as depression, anxiety, or substance use), obsessive-compulsive or histrionic personality traits, and the ability to establish a therapeutic alliance. The presence of severe personality disorders reduces the likelihood of a successful treatment outcome (Feldman et al., 2001). Factitious disorder by proxy is difficult to treat, as these caregivers commonly deny any responsibility for producing symptoms in those under their care. Despite treatment efforts, relapse rates remain as high as 50 percent (Simon, 2002).

DELIRIUM, DEMENTIA, AND AMNESTIC AND OTHER COGNITIVE DISORDERS

Description of the Disorders

According to *DSM-IV-TR*, all the cognitive disorders are characterized by ''a clinically significant deficit in cognition that represents a significant change from a previous level of functioning'' (American Psychiatric Association, 2000, p. 125). Common symptoms of cognitive disorders include not only impairment in memory (especially of recent memory) but also impairments in the following areas:

- Abstract thinking
- Perception
- Language
- Ability to concentrate and perform new tasks
- Overall intellectual performance
- Judgment
- Attention
- Spatiotemporal orientation
- Calculating ability
- Ability to grasp meaning and recognize or identify objects
- Perceptions of body and environment

The cognitive disorders are a heterogeneous group with diverse symptoms and origins, although all of these disorders have a genuine physical cause. Common causes include Alzheimer's disease, a systemic illness, a head injury, or deleterious exposure to a psychoactive or toxic substance (such as alcohol).

The symptoms of a cognitive disorder can encompass many of the symptoms associated with other mental disorders, such as depression, anxiety, personality change, paranoia, and confusion. Consequently, other mental disorders may be mistaken for the cognitive disorders that they resemble, and cognitive disorders also can be mistaken for other mental disorders (for example, some people diagnosed as having Alzheimer's disease actually have pseudodementia, a form of depression that has similar symptoms). This error is unfortunate, because effective treatments are available for depression, but an effective treatment for Alzheimer's disease has yet to be found. (However, considerable progress has been made in finding ways to slow disease progression.)

In light of the diagnostic challenge presented by the cognitive disorders, their diagnosis must take account of symptoms as well as of possible causes. The clinician should obtain a psychiatric or neurological evaluation when one of these disorders is suspected. EEGs and other medical tests, as well as such psychological tests as the Wechsler Intelligence Scales and the Halstead-Reitan Neuropsychologic Battery, can determine the likelihood of a cognitive disorder's being present. The therapist may also find the Mini–Mental State Exam useful in making a preliminary diagnosis of a cognitive disorder.

DSM-IV-TR defines three categories of cognitive disorders: delirium, dementia, and amnestic disorder, as well as cognitive disorders not otherwise specified. Cognitive disorders are present in approximately 1 percent of the adult population and are expected to increase in prevalence with the lengthening of the life span (Sue, Sue, & Sue, 2006). Discussion of specific etiologies and related presentations of these disorders is beyond the scope of this book; clinicians treating people with cognitive disorders will want to consult the *DSM* for the detailed descriptions and diagnostic criteria provided there.

Delirium. This disorder is typified by abrupt onset and clouded consciousness, as well as by impairment of recent memory and attention, with accompanying disorientation. Hallucinations and delusions are common (Butcher et al., 2006). Emotional, perceptual, and psychomotor disturbances, as well as changes in the sleep-wake cycle, often accompany this disorder, which can occur at any age but is most common in children and the elderly. Delirium can be caused by a medical condition, by substance use, or by multiple etiologies. Possible specific causes of delirium include central nervous system disease (such as epilepsy), cardiac failure, electrolyte imbalance, head injury, infection, and postoperative states. Butcher and colleagues (2006) report that the most common cause of delirium is drug intoxication or withdrawal. Toxicity from medication may also contribute, as does anesthesia. Postoperative delirium is common in the elderly following surgery. This disorder typically has an inconsistent course and a positive response to appropriate treatment, although it is associated with increased mortality in the hospitalized elderly and those who have an underlying medical illness (American Psychiatric Association, 2000).

Dementia. This disorder is more likely to have an insidious onset and a progressive and pervasive course. It is characterized by multiple cognitive deficits, including memory impairment. Common symptoms of this disorder are decline in language functioning; difficulty in recognizing even familiar people and objects; and impairment in abstract thinking, judgment, and insight. An overall decline in social and occupational functioning nearly always accompanies this disorder. Delusions, especially those of persecution, often are symptoms of this disorder and may lead to aggressive and destructive behavior. Hallucinations and depression also often accompany dementia. Level of consciousness and alertness may be unaffected. The most common causes of dementia are Alzheimer's disease and vascular disease, but many other causes exist as well, including traumatic brain injury, brain tumors, HIV, substances (such as alcohol, inhalants, and sedatives), neurological and endocrine conditions, and vitamin deficiencies. This disorder is most prevalent among people over the age of eighty-five: as many as 25 percent of people in this age group have severe dementia (American Psychiatric Association, 2000).

Amnestic Disorder. This disorder is characterized by memory impairment, especially learning and recall of new information, without other significant accompanying cognitive deficits. This disorder, too, has multiple possible etiologies, including head trauma, encephalitis, alcohol use with accompanying vitamin B1 (thiamine) deficiency, sedative misuse, and brain tumors. Age at onset of amnestic disorder varies, as does the progression of the disorder and length of illness. Transient amnesia may last from several hours to a few days, whereas amnesia caused by head trauma may continue over a period of years.

Typical Client Characteristics

Few generalizations can be drawn about people with cognitive disorders because the causes and symptoms of these disorders vary so greatly. Most people with cognitive disorders will be past midlife, and many will have coexisting medical or substance use disorders. Additional client characteristics are linked to specific disorders.

Dementia is one of the most common cognitive disorders, found in about 5 to 7 percent of people over the age of sixty-five (Sue et al., 2006). Dementia of the Alzheimer's type affects 2 to 4 percent of people over the age of sixty-five and encompasses nearly 80 percent of people with dementia (Butcher et al., 2006). That disorder has a genetic component, with approximately 50 percent of people with a family history of the disease developing Alzheimer's in their eighties and nineties (Sue et al., 2006). Protective factors, such as higher educational and occupational achievement, use of nonsteroidal anti-inflammatory drugs or estrogen replacement therapy, and vitamin E, have been found to delay the onset of Alzheimer's disease (Sue et al., 2006). Vascular dementia is more common in men than women and among people with a history of diabetes and hypertension. It often coexists with depression (Butcher et al., 2006).

Many forms of cognitive disorders have an external cause, such as excessive use of drugs or alcohol, a blow to the head, or exposure to a toxic substance, and will often be associated with habits or lifestyle. For example, substance-induced cognitive disorders usually will be accompanied by concurrent diagnosis of a substance use disorder.

Assessment

Clients presenting with symptoms of dementia or other cognitive-related disorders should first be referred for a comprehensive medical and neurological assessment. Therapists should work closely with medical personnel when establishing and implementing treatment plans.

Preferred Therapist Characteristics

Therapists treating people with cognitive disorders should either have training in the physiological and neurological aspects of these disorders or collaborate with someone who does have that training. The therapeutic relationship that is established with a person who has a cognitive disorder will depend to a large extent on the person's level of functioning. In general, a therapist working with a person who has cognitive deficits will have to be directive, supportive, and reassuring. The therapist may have to take charge of the treatment and determine what psychological and medical interventions are necessary, although client autonomy should be maintained as much as possible. Promoting awareness of reality usually will be an important part of the therapist's role, as will provision of information. Family consultation, education, and intervention, as well as assistance in obtaining adjunct services, such as family support groups, residential treatment facilities, respite care, and medical care may also be necessary. Therapists will also need to deal with their own feelings about treating people whose disorders may have a poor prognosis and limited prospects for improvement.

Intervention Strategies

The goal of treatment of cognitive disorders is to delay the onset of symptoms and slow the progression of the disease while also alleviating symptoms, modifying risk factors, and reducing mortality (Sue et al., 2006). Such treatment involves a multifaceted approach in which psychotherapy is combined with medical and neurological treatment, including drugs or surgery, needed to assess and arrest or reduce the cognitive impairment. Medication may target such symptoms as depression, anxiety, psychosis, and aggressiveness, and it may address the disorder itself. Medications, such as tacrine (Cognex) and donepezi (Aricept), are being used to treat dementia of the Alzheimer's type as well as other cognitive disorders. Although studies show that those who received the medications did better overall compared to those who received a placebo, participants in both groups still manifested considerable decline over the course of the study (Winblad et al., 2001). A relatively new medication approved for the treatment of Alzheimer's disease is memantine (Namenda), which appears to provide some positive cognitive benefits (Forchetti, 2005; Reisberg et al., 2003).

Environmental manipulation may be indicated to help people cope more effectively with their living situation despite their impairment and maintain some form of employment as long as possible. Change in routine, stress, and external stimuli should be reduced so as not to exacerbate symptoms. A person in the advanced stages of one of these disorders may need to be placed in a supervised living situation.

A comprehensive approach to intervention should include support for caregivers, who are at increased risk of depression, stress symptoms, and isolation (Butcher et al., 2006). Support groups, relaxation techniques, and coping skills can help reduce depression, worry, guilt, and the difficulty of caring for family members who have progressive or chronic cognitive disorders. Counseling, information, support, and help with making decisions, expressing feelings, and setting goals can enable family members to cope more effectively with the challenges of caring for someone with a cognitive disorder. Family members may also benefit from help in identifying and making use of community resources, such as respite care and in-home help, that are available to them. Peer support groups are often available in the community and can help share information, normalize feelings, and provide support and a safe and understanding place for caregivers to express themselves.

Although psychotherapy typically plays a secondary role in direct treatment of most cognitive disorders, it can be an important complementary part of the medical treatment. Therapy seems particularly helpful to people in the early or mild stages of dementia of the Alzheimer's type and of vascular dementia. Therapy probably will be most useful if it emphasizes behavioral interventions, encouraging people to remain as active and independent as possible and helping them compensate for changes in their capacities by building on any coping mechanisms that are still accessible to them. Behaviorally oriented therapy can also help these people control their destructive impulses and their emotional lability. Attention should be paid to keeping people appropriately informed about the nature of their disorders, helping them express their feelings about the changes they are experiencing, and maximizing their contact with reality via family pictures, clocks, and other visual and verbal reminders. These therapeutic interventions can help reduce such secondary symptoms as social withdrawal, depression, denial, fear, confusion, impulsive behaviors, and negative feelings about themselves, which are common in people in the early stages of cognitive disorders (Sue et al., 2006).

People with cognitive disorders caused by psychoactive substances often will have a coexisting diagnosis of a substance use disorder. Psychotherapy will play an important role in these people's treatment, helping them eliminate their self-destructive use of drugs or alcohol, a modification that in turn will probably ameliorate the accompanying cognitive disorder and greatly reduce the chances of a recurrence.

Prognosis

The prognosis for recovery from a cognitive disorder is as variable as the disorders themselves and is usually determined by the cause of the disorder. Those disorders stemming from psychoactive substances, metabolic abnormalities, and systemic illnesses tend to be time-limited and usually are followed by full recovery or significant improvement. Dementia of the Alzheimer's type, however, currently has no known cure. Death usually occurs within five years of onset of the disease, which is the fourth leading cause of death in the United States (Sue et al., 2006).

MENTAL DISORDERS DUE TO A GENERAL MEDICAL CONDITION

According to *DSM-IV-TR*, a ''mental disorder due to a general medical condition is characterized by the presence of mental symptoms that are judged to be the direct physiological consequence of a medical condition'' (American Psychiatric Association, 2000, p. 181). In other words, these disorders are caused by a medical condition; they do not reflect people's upset in response to the diagnosis of a medical condition but rather result from the physiological impact of the medical condition. The causative medical condition should be listed on Axis III of the multiaxial assessment.

Nonpsychiatric medical conditions can be direct or physiological causes of a broad range of mental disorders, including psychotic disorders, mood disorders, anxiety disorders, sexual dysfunction, and sleep disorders. Specific diagnoses cited in this section of the *DSM* include catatonic disorder due to a general medical condition (such as neurological and metabolic abnormalities), personality change due to a general medical condition (such as endocrine and autoimmune conditions), and mental disorder not otherwise specified due to a general medical condition. Diagnosis of disorders such as these is usually made by a psychiatrist or a neurologist. Psychotherapists may well collaborate in the treatment of people with these disorders, as well as in the treatment of their family members, but treatment that targets the medical condition will generally be the primary intervention. Because of the scope and diversity of these disorders and their etiologies, further discussion of their diagnosis and treatment will not be provided here. Nevertheless, clinicians should keep these disorders in mind when making diagnoses.

TREATMENT RECOMMENDATIONS: CLIENT MAP

This chapter has discussed the category of disorders in which physical and psychological factors combine. The following summary of treatment recommendations is organized according to the format of the Client Map.

Client Map

Diagnoses

Disorders in which physical and psychological factors combine (somatoform disorders; factitious disorders; delirium, dementia, and amnestic and other cognitive disorders; mental disorders due to a general medical condition)

Objectives of Treatment

Reduce somatization

Promote more constructive expression of feelings

Maximize functioning and coping skills

Improve socialization and use of leisure time

Assessments

Physical examination

Assessments of anxiety, depression, personality, and intellectual functioning as indicated

Clinician Characteristics

Knowledgeable about physical disorders

Willing to collaborate with physicians

Skilled at handling reluctant clients

Structured and concrete

Warm and optimistic

High in tolerance of frustration

Location of Treatment

Usually outpatient setting

Interventions to Be Used

Team approach to treatment involving both medical and mental health professionals

Empathy and reflection of feelings to promote awareness of and ability to verbalize emotions

Holistic approach

Teaching of stress management and coping skills

Encouragement of positive ways to request attention and support

Use of relaxation techniques

Improvement in socialization

Behavioral change strategies to improve functioning

Gentle confrontation as needed

Emphasis of Treatment

Supportive emphasis

Moderately directive emphasis

Some attention to history, with primary orientation toward the present

Integrated focus on cognitive, behavioral, and affective areas (with behavioral interventions usually predominating)

Numbers

Primarily individual therapy

Family therapy to reduce secondary gains and help family members understand and cope with the disorder

Group therapy, as functioning permits, to promote socialization

Timing

Geared to readiness of client

May need to be gradual and long term

Medications Needed

As indicated by the physical disorders and specific emotional symptoms; antidepressant medication often helpful

Adjunct Services

Leisure and career counseling

Prognosis

Fair in general, but widely variable according to disorder

Client Map of Dr. Martin C.

This chapter began with a description of Dr. Martin C., a sixty-two-year-old male who was referred for psychotherapy by his physician after seeking medical help for what Martin was convinced was cancer.

Diagnosis

Axis I: 300.7 Hypochondriasis, moderate, with poor insight

Axis II: V71.09 No diagnosis on Axis II

Axis III: No known physical disorders or conditions, but client reported symptoms of gastric distress

Axis IV: Occupational and financial difficulties, marital conflict, physical concerns

Axis V: Global assessment of functioning (GAF Scale): current GAF = 60

Objectives of Treatment

Improve skills related to stress management and coping

Improve marital relationship and communication

Facilitate development of realistic occupational and financial goals

Improve medical condition

Improve ability to identify and express feelings

Enhance self-esteem and client's enjoyment of life

Assessments

Physical evaluation

Broad-based personality inventory, such as the Minnesota Multiphasic Personality Inventory

Clinician Characteristics

Warm, optimistic

Skilled at handling reluctant clients

Knowledgeable about medical concerns

Mature and experienced

Supportive and accepting throughout, yet directive and structured

Location of Treatment

Outpatient setting

Interventions to Be Used

Multifaceted collaboration between therapist and physician, with therapist and client as primary engineers of treatment (to ensure compatibility of physical and psychological treatments and give client a sense of control missing from other areas of his life)

Education about the impact of stress on gastric functioning

Education about dietary approaches to reducing gastrointestinal discomfort

Supportive and reflective counseling designed to promote awareness of feelings and ability to verbalize them

Techniques of stress management, including progressive relaxation and expansion of leisure activities

Exploration of career-related attitudes, abilities, and opportunities, with goal of establishing more realistic and rewarding career goals

Discussion of partial retirement combined with consulting and half-time teaching (to reduce stress and stabilize client's financial situation)

Marital therapy (to improve communication between client and his wife, help them understand each other's feelings, and define a realistic and mutually acceptable lifestyle)

Emphasis of Treatment

Structured, relatively directive, but encouraging

Client to take appropriate responsibility for his own treatment and his lifestyle

Numbers

Individual and couples therapy

Timing

Weekly sessions

Rapid pace

Medium duration

Medications Needed

Carefully monitored medication as needed for gastrointestinal distress

Adjunct Services

Financial and retirement planning

Leisure counseling

Prognosis

Fair to good

Recommended Reading

Forchetti, C. M. (2005). Treating patients with moderate to severe Alzheimer's disease. *The Primary Care Companion to the Journal of Clinical Psychiatry*, *7*, 155–161.

Mittelman, M. S., Roth, D. L., Coon, D. W., & Haley, W. E. (2004). Sustained benefit of supportive intervention for depressive symptoms in the caregivers of patients with Alzheimer's disease. *American Journal of Psychiatry*, *161*, 850–856.

CHAPTER EIGHT

Personality Disorders

Emily L., a twenty-five-year-old white woman, was referred to a psychotherapist by the hospital where she had been treated after her eighth suicide attempt. The therapist to whom she was referred would be her fourth one; nevertheless, Emily responded with initial optimism to the new therapist and provided an extensive narration of her long-standing difficulties.

Emily was the fourth and last child born to her parents within the first six years of their marriage. Her father abandoned the family a year after Emily's birth, and she had had no contact with him since that time. Emily's mother remarried about five years later, and she and her children had moved into a three-bedroom apartment with her new husband and his two teenage sons.

The older boy, age fifteen, soon began to sexually abuse Emily. He won her silence and cooperation by telling her that he loved her best and by threatening to harm her pets if she did not do what he wanted. The first time Emily balked at complying with his demands, he proved the seriousness of his threats by killing her canary.

After about a year, Emily's stepfather found her undressed in her stepbrother's room. The stepfather became enraged with Emily, now seven years old, and accused her of trying to ruin his family. He also blamed Emily's mother and became increasingly abusive, both emotionally and physically, toward Emily and her mother.

When Emily was ten years old, her mother committed suicide. Emily and her siblings were separated and put in foster homes. Emily remained in her foster home until she dropped out of high school and married at seventeen.

At the time she provided this information, Emily was married to her second husband. Her first husband had been physically abusive, particularly when he was intoxicated. Her current husband was also physically abusive. (''At least he doesn't drink'' was Emily's comment on the situation.)

Emily herself presented with many difficulties. She reported having been depressed for as long as she could remember, with frequent episodes of suicidal ideation and behavior. She often plucked out her eyebrows and eyelashes, as well as the hair on her head, and reportedly spent a great deal of time each day putting on makeup and styling her hair to disguise the hair loss. She was nearly one hundred pounds overweight and often consumed alcohol to excess, a behavior that she blamed on her first husband. She had little contact with her siblings and had no close women friends, but she had engaged in several brief but intense extramarital relationships, one with her husband's brother. She had a spotty employment history, with some computer skills and intermittent work for temporary agencies, but she reported that her depression made it difficult for her to get to work consistently and on time. Emily's principal diagnosis was borderline personality disorder.

OVERVIEW OF PERSONALITY DISORDERS

Personality disorders are a ''pathology that pervades the entire fabric of the person'' (Millon, Grossman, Millon, Meagher, & Ramnath, 2004, p. 78). People with personality disorders generally lack resilience, especially under stress; are inflexible when it comes to change; and engage in vicious cycles of repetitive self-defeating behaviors. Most people with personality disorders have trouble accepting appropriate responsibility for their difficulties; they usually blame others for their problems, but sometimes they blame themselves too much.

People with personality disorders also have poor coping mechanisms and relationship skills. Because their disorders are so enduring and deeply entrenched, and because people with personality disorders typically have little insight and tend to externalize their difficulties, their disorders are difficult to treat (Beck, Freeman, Davis, & Associates, 2004).

Description of the Disorders

Personality disorders are long-standing and are deeply ingrained. They are characterized by maladaptive attitudes and behaviors that show up in at least two of the following areas:

- Perceptions and understanding of oneself and one's environment
- Expression, nature, range, and appropriateness of emotions
- Interpersonal skills and relationships
- Impulse control

The attitudes and behaviors of people with personality disorders typically are rigid and inflexible, causing distress and/or impairment in important areas of their lives (American Psychiatric Association, 2000).

Presenting concerns generally focus on symptoms of depression or anxiety, typically reflecting an additional disorder listed on Axis I of a *DSM-IV-TR* multiaxial assessment. (Personality disorders are listed on Axis II.) These clients typically have little awareness of their underlying dysfunctional personality patterns. Those personality styles generally are ego-syntonic and acceptable to these clients, who are rarely able to grasp the effect of their personalities on others. Even for people whose personality disorders are ego-dystonic or in conflict with their self-image, change is difficult because typically they have never manifested healthy personality patterns and do not have good coping or adjustment skills.

In the past, personality disorders were explained almost exclusively from a psychodynamic perspective, but they are now viewed as resulting from a combination of biological and psychosocial factors (Livesley, 2003). While genetic factors predispose a person to certain traits of temperament, environmental factors can have a favorable or unfavorable impact on those traits. Such psychosocial factors as family dysfunction, physical or sexual abuse in childhood, an invalidating environment, adversity, attachment-related issues, difficulties in early learning, and sociocultural influences can all exacerbate a biological predisposition toward a personality disorder (Beck et al., 2004; Livesley, 2003; Millon, Grossman, Millon, Meagher, & Ramnath, 2004; Paris, 2003). Childhood anxiety and depression are often precursors to adult development of personality disorders (Paris, 2003).

Personality disorders are evident by adolescence or early adulthood, if not earlier, and tend to continue throughout life. Diagnosis of a personality disorder in a person under the age of eighteen is made only if symptoms have been present for at least one year. The only exception is antisocial personality disorder, which, by definition, cannot be diagnosed before the age of eighteen (American Psychiatric Association, 2000).

Personality disorders vary considerably in terms of degree of impairment. Researchers have viewed the borderline, paranoid, and schizotypal personality disorders as the most dysfunctional (Millon et al., 2004). These disorders are characterized by poor social skills, hostility, and fragility. The obsessive-compulsive, dependent, histrionic, narcissistic, and avoidant personality disorders typically involve the least dysfunction. People with these disorders are able to seek out and deal with others in a relatively coherent fashion and can adapt to or control their environments in meaningful ways. Although all personality disorders tend to wax and wane in severity according to life circumstances and stressors, some (for example, obsessive-compulsive, histrionic, narcissistic, and schizotypal personality disorders) worsen with age, whereas others (such as borderline and antisocial personality disorders) tend to improve (American Psychiatric Association, 2000).

Personality disorders are prevalent, although they are often overlooked in clinical settings. No comprehensive figures exist for the total prevalence of personality disorders in the population (Crits-Christoph & Barber, 2002). However, the 2001–2002 National Epidemiologic Survey on Alcohol and Related Conditions reported that 30.8 million adults in the United States (14.8 percent) meet the diagnostic criteria for at least one of seven personality disorders. Three personality disorders — borderline, narcissistic, and schizotypal — were not included in the study. More than forty-three thousand people participated in the survey, which was conducted by the National Institute on Alcohol Abuse and Alcoholism (National Institutes of Health and the National Institute on Alcohol Abuse and Alcoholism [NIH & NIAAA], 2004).

Gender distribution varies from one personality disorder to another. Women are more likely to be diagnosed with borderline personality disorder (80 percent female). Eighty percent of the people diagnosed with antisocial personality disorder are male (Millon et al., 2004). It is unclear whether such gender differences are, at least in part, biases in making the diagnosis or actual variations in gender distribution.

Similar concerns arise in relation to culture and personality disorders. Sue, Sue, and Sue (2006) note that Asians, for example, are more likely to exhibit signs of shyness and collectivism, whereas North Americans and Europeans are more assertive and individualistic. These cultural differences are reflected in the types of personality disorders with which they are most likely to be diagnosed. Being a Native American or African American, having low socioeconomic status, being a young adult, and not being married were found to be risk factors for personality disorders (NIH & NIAAA, 2004). Clearly, cultural, ethnic, and social backgrounds should be considered when diagnosing a personality disorder.

Diagnostic tools can be helpful in identifying personality disorders that sometimes are obscured by other disorders. A number of inventories, including the Millon Clinical Multiaxial Inventory (MCMI), the Minnesota Multiphasic Personality Inventory (MMPI), the Structured Clinical Interview for DSM-IV Axis II Personality Disorders (SCID-II), and projective tests all can be useful in diagnosing these sometimes overlooked disorders (Millon et al., 2004).

In *DSM-IV-TR*, the personality disorders are grouped into the following three clusters:

1. Cluster A (guarded and eccentric): paranoid, schizoid, and schizotypal personality disorders
2. Cluster B (dramatic, emotional, and unpredictable): antisocial, borderline, histrionic, and narcissistic personality disorders
3. Cluster C (anxious and fearful): avoidant, dependent, and obsessive-compulsive personality disorders

DSM-IV-TR also includes the category of personality disorder not otherwise specified (NOS). This category encompasses mixed personality disorders. These do not completely fit the criteria for any one disorder but have symptoms of two or more, which in combination meet the criteria for diagnosis of a personality disorder. Personality disorder NOS also includes other personality disorders that are currently under consideration but are not yet viewed as warranting a full-fledged diagnosis (such as depressive personality disorder or passive-aggressive personality disorder).

Although these clusters do help to organize the array of personality disorders, the literature typically focuses on the specific personality disorders rather than on the clusters. However, recent research suggests that Cluster A (paranoid, schizoid, and schizotypal) personality disorders may be part of a spectrum of disorders genetically related to schizophrenia. Finnish adoption studies indicate that children genetically at risk of developing schizophrenia are also at risk of developing a Cluster A personality disorder, especially schizotypal personality disorder (Tienari et al., 2003).

As is the case with other disorders, caution should be used when diagnosing personality disorders in the presence of a co-occurring mood or substance-related disorder. For a diagnosis of a personality disorder, symptoms must continue to be present after the substance use has been discontinued. The *DSM* also notes that personality traits may not merit the diagnosis of disorder unless they cause ''significant functional impairment or distress and are inflexible and maladaptive'' (American Psychiatric Association, 2000, p. 689).

Typical Client Characteristics

People with personality disorders tend to come from families in which family breakdown or psychopathology of one or both parents is present (Livesley, 2003). The families usually also failed to model healthy interpersonal and coping skills, so identification with family members perpetuates a pattern of impaired functioning. The form taken by a person's personality disorder often makes sense in light of what the parental messages have been.

Personality disorders tend to be proportionally overrepresented among people who have been emotionally abused and neglected in childhood. Such abuse is also related to later self-harming behaviors. Aggressive and antisocial behavior, impulsivity, mood disorders, and substance misuse are often found in the relatives of people with personality disorders as well as in those with personality disorders. These patterns seem to be the result of both genetic and environmental influences (Livesley, 2003).

High levels of sexual abuse have been reported in people with personality disorders. As many as 70 percent of people with borderline personality disorder have a history of childhood sexual abuse (Livesley, 2003). Paris (2003) describes one study in which 73 percent of people with borderline personality disorder reported childhood sexual abuse, compared to 53 percent of people with other personality disorders. A history of sexual abuse also is associated with narcissistic, histrionic, schizotypal, and antisocial personality disorders.

Personality disorders are often accompanied by other, more transient mental disorders and symptoms. Common examples are mood, anxiety, and substance-related disorders. Suicidal ideation is also frequently reported by people with personality disorders. The presence of a personality disorder usually makes the treatment of a coexisting mental disorder more difficult (Paris, 2003). People with personality disorders also usually have long-standing patterns of pervasive dysfunction affecting social and occupational areas.

Achieving intimacy seems particularly difficult for people with personality disorders. The strong sense of entitlement and the lack of empathy characteristic of some people with personality disorders lead them to violate interpersonal boundaries and behave in socially inappropriate ways. People with personality disorders also tend to have an external locus of control, believing they are powerless over life events (Livesley, 2003), as well as strong dependency needs. They frequently have poor self-esteem, low self-efficacy, weak ego strength, and problems with impulse control. Underlying fear and rage are also often present. All these traits impair functioning in many areas.

Each personality disorder seems to be strongly associated with a particular defense mechanism. For example, borderline personality disorder is associated with splitting (viewing people as extremely good or extremely bad), whereas paranoid personality disorder is associated with projection. An understanding of their defenses is essential to an understanding of these clients; helping them manage and modify their defenses is usually necessary for successful treatment.

People with personality disorders also usually have dysfunctional and distorted schemas or belief systems, as well as maladaptive coping strategies (Beck et al., 2004), so they have great difficulty successfully managing stressors and life problems. As a result, people with these disorders typically have a long history of disappointments and come to see the world as a hostile environment. Without help, they are rarely able to make the cognitive shifts and develop the skills that would enable them to control dysregulated affect and manage their lives more successfully.

Avoidance is common in people with personality disorders, and self-acceptance is rare. Livesley (2003) notes that these people often "seem at odds with themselves" (p. 87) in an effort to deny or not acknowledge their participation in their own behavior.

Personality, like intelligence, remains relatively stable over time. From the late twenties on, people may "mellow a little with age and become more reliable" (Livesley, 2003, p. 72), but basically their personality has been formed. Therapists treating personality pathology should begin with the goal of helping people adapt to and better understand their personality traits, develop improved coping skills, and express themselves more effectively, rather than aiming for a complete change in personality.

Assessment

The Millon Clinical Multiaxial Inventory (MCMI), the Minnesota Multiphasic Personality Inventory (MMPI), and the Structured Clinical Interview for DSM-IV Axis II personality disorders (SCID-II; Maffei et al., 1997) can be helpful in diagnosing personality disorders. Co-occurring Axis I disorders, especially substance-related disorders, should also be assessed in order for treatment to be effective.

Preferred Therapist Characteristics

The establishment of a sound therapeutic alliance is viewed as the strongest predictor of successful treatment outcome for people with personality disorders (Meyer & Pilkonis, 2006). The therapist should manifest those conditions that are integral to the development of an effective, collaborative therapeutic alliance: empathy, warmth, compassion, acceptance, respect, and genuineness. Strong confrontation, punishment, criticism, or other expressions of negative feelings can destroy the often fragile therapeutic bond established with a person who has a personality disorder. The therapist should not take sides or argue with the client but should remain supportive while maintaining control of the session.

Patience is an essential ingredient because the treatment of these disorders tends to be long term, with progress and the building of trust often very gradual. The need for patience is especially high in the early stages of treatment, when the client usually exhibits anxiety or depression and when the groundwork for the therapeutic alliance is established.

Many people with personality disorders are not motivated to examine themselves or change. For example, people with paranoid, schizoid, and antisocial personality disorders rarely seek treatment on their own initiative (Meyer & Pilkonis, 2006), and a high proportion of people with personality disorders terminate treatment prematurely (Sue et al., 2006). Blocking or sabotaging treatment; fear of change; transference; and the client's reactions to the therapist, cognitive distortions, and overreactions all can act as barriers to effective treatment of a personality disorder.

Apparent treatment resistance often stems from fear of change or from hopelessness, and the therapist should keep those possibilities in mind when the client fails to keep appointments or to complete agreed-on activities between sessions. The therapist should avoid feeling hurt or angered by these behaviors and should try instead to view them as self-protection on the part of the client.

People with personality disorders tend to have strong transference reactions to their therapists. Some become hostile and resistant; others become needy and dependent. Therapists must monitor and manage any countertransference reactions so that they do not become either overly involved or rejecting toward these clients but instead are appropriately available. Judicious use of limit setting, gentle interpretation, rewards, and modeling also help elicit positive behavior from these clients. Using humor, anecdotes, metaphors, and limited self-disclosure can also help the clients perceive their therapist as genuine and human.

Therapists who are more empathic, interpersonally skilled, and open seem better at developing and maintaining a therapeutic alliance with these clients. A key component, according to Meyer and Pilkonis (2006), is the therapists' ability to adapt their interventions to clients' in-session behavior. An energetic, collaborative relationship seems best.

Intervention Strategies

Despite the prevalence of personality disorders in both general and clinical populations, empirical studies on the treatment of these disorders are limited. Personality disorders received little attention in the research literature until the mid-1980s. The personality inventories developed by Millon, along with the *Journal of Personality Disorders*, initially edited by Millon, spurred interest in the study of personality disorders. However, most of the relevant literature still consists of case studies and theoretical discussions.

During the 1970s and the 1980s, psychodynamic psychotherapy generally was the preferred approach to treatment. The recent literature, however, has focused increasingly on cognitive approaches, as well as on variations of cognitive-behavioral therapy, such as dialectical behavior therapy, schema therapy, and emotion-focused therapy.

In general, therapy for a person with a personality disorder will be multi-faceted, with a psychodynamic or cognitive basis, so as to address the person's core difficulties. Specific interventions are selected to address the client's defenses and individual concerns. The long-standing nature of these disorders, their apparent relationship to family dynamics, and their relatively early origin all suggest an approach that will not only relieve symptoms but also effect change in overall functioning and in the person's view of self and the world.

Leichsenring and Leibing (2003) conducted a meta-analysis of the effectiveness of psychodynamic and cognitive-behavioral therapy. Both were found to be effective treatments for personality disorders. However, the meta-analysis was limited to twenty-two studies of personality disorders. Long-term follow-up and additional research are needed.

Beck and associates (2004) report success in treating personality disorders via cognitive therapy. They begin their treatment approach with standard cognitive therapy to elicit and modify dysfunctional automatic thoughts that are contributing to anxiety and depression. Once affective changes begin, the therapist gradually shifts focus from immediate concerns to dysfunctional core schemas that underlie the personality disorder. Guided discovery helps clients see the impact of these core schemas on their lives. Such techniques as deliberate exaggeration, labeling of distortions, decatastrophizing, and reattribution of responsibility for actions and outcomes gradually help people with personality disorders identify and modify their schemas. Concurrent attention is paid to helping people learn coping, communication, decision-making, and other important life skills. Behavioral strategies, such as relaxation and role playing, along with exploration of childhood experiences that may have entrenched the schemas, enhance treatment. This kind of integrated treatment, with clear goals and treatment strategies, is especially likely to effect positive change in a personality disorder.

Clinicians have been making greater use of control-oriented cognitive strategies in which clients become more mindful. Linehan's dialectical behavior therapy, for example, has been successful in reducing suicidal ideation and self-harm behavior in people with borderline personality disorder (Meyer & Pilkonis, 2006). Emotion-focused therapy, developed by Greenberg (2002), blends Gestalt techniques, psychodrama, and playing the devil's advocate in therapeutic efforts to help clients recognize, regulate, and effectively manage their own emotions. Building on Beck's cognitive therapy, Young (1999) has developed schema therapy that helps clients assess, recognize, and change their own internal schemas.

Behavior therapy has also been used successfully in treating personality disorders, particularly in the initial stages of treatment. Behavior therapy is especially helpful and appealing to people who are reluctant to engage in long-term treatment or who have severely dysfunctional and self-destructive behavioral patterns that require rapid modification. Through behavior therapy, they can learn new social and occupational skills, as well as practical approaches to coping and stress management. Generally, behavior therapy is used to address the Axis I disorders (such as substance-related or mood disorders) and to effect fairly rapid improvement in prominent symptoms, which in turn often increases clients' motivation and confidence in psychotherapy and encourages them to continue treatment, with a focus on underlying personality patterns. Even if these clients do terminate treatment prematurely, at least they are left with positive feelings about their treatment and some initial gains. As a result, they may well return for help if symptoms recur.

Findings on the use of cognitive therapy and CBT to treat personality disorders are promising. However, empirical research on the effects of these approaches on personality disorders remains minimal (Meyer & Pilkonis, 2006). Case studies provide the primary method of substantiation. Continued research on effective treatments for personality disorders is strongly needed.

Several studies have reported on the optimum length of treatment, in general finding greater improvement after longer treatment durations. Typically, effecting changes in personality patterns takes longer than mere symptom changes. Paris (1999) found that treatment duration of 1.3 years or 192 sessions were necessary for a 50 percent reduction in symptoms associated with personality disorders. A 75 percent reduction was achieved after 216 sessions. He concluded that both lengths of treatment are effective in treating personality disorders.

People with personality disorders typically have deficits in many areas of their lives. Therefore, adjunct services such as career counseling, twelve-step programs, and family or couples counseling are often important parts of the treatment package. In severe forms or exacerbations of personality disorders, day treatment, brief hospitalization, or milieu therapy may be indicated, especially for people with borderline or schizotypal personality disorders (Paris, 2003).

Antidepressant medications, mood stabilizers, atypical antipsychotics, and anxiolytics can frequently offer symptom relief. However, medications do not cure personality disorders; they only reduce the severity of their accompanying symptoms (Paris, 2003) and perhaps facilitate a person's involvement in psychotherapy. Moreover, many people with personality disorders are susceptible to becoming dependent on external sources of help and so tend to misuse drugs. Therefore, care must be taken in recommending medication as part of treatment. Empirical data on psychopharmacology for personality disorders has almost exclusively focused on borderline personality disorder. Indeed, in one study, Zanarini, Frankenburg, Hennen, Reich, and Silk (2004) found that people with borderline personality disorder received, on average, four or five different types of medications. Such polypharmacy has not been shown to be effective or helpful (Paris, 2003).

Family therapy can be a useful adjunct to individual therapy for a person with a personality disorder. Family members themselves often present disorders that merit attention, and they can also be helped to understand and react helpfully to the client's personality disorder, thereby reducing the secondary gains of the disorder. The client's social and occupational dysfunctions have probably already damaged family relationships, and family therapy can offer the person an opportunity to improve those relationships and develop new ways of relating to family members (Livesley, 2003). The therapist should be careful not to form separate alliances with family members; doing so could jeopardize the client's tenuous trust in the therapeutic process and could be perceived as a rejection.

Group therapy can be another useful adjunct to individual therapy for people with personality disorders. Empirical data suggests that a combination of individual and group therapy can be effective (Livesley, 2003). However, group therapy should generally be initiated in conjunction with individual therapy or only after some progress has been made in individual therapy. These clients' poor social skills, strong mistrust, and dependence needs can turn premature use of group therapy into another disappointing interpersonal experience for them. Once clients are ready for group involvement, the feedback and support they receive from others can provide encouragement for positive change, as well as a safe place for experimenting with new ways of relating both to peers and to authority figures.

Prognosis

The prognosis for effecting major change in a personality disorder seems fair at best because of the deeply ingrained and pervasive nature of these disorders. Nevertheless, the prognosis for reducing symptoms and improving social and occupational functioning is fair to good if clients can be persuaded to remain in and cooperate with treatment. Unfortunately, however, people with personality disorders often are not motivated to change and may leave treatment abruptly and prematurely. Paris (2003) found that higher-functioning clients and those who are psychologically minded and capable of insight have the best prognosis, but even clients who are more severely troubled can still achieve positive change.

New and more comprehensive approaches to treatment, such as those developed by Young (1999; Young et al., 2003), Greenberg (2002), and Linehan (1993), may yield better outcomes than the earlier treatment approaches were able to produce. The process of therapy with personality disorders entails developing a collaborative working alliance and implementing treatment linked to clients' stages of change, with goals ranging from reducing self-harming behaviors to improving maladaptive relationship patterns. The better the therapeutic alliance, the more likely the client will stay and work toward those goals. Now let's turn to a discussion of each of the personality disorders.

PARANOID PERSONALITY DISORDER

Description of the Disorder

People with paranoid personality disorder have a persistent suspiciousness and expectation that they will be treated badly by others. According to *DSM-IV-TR*

(American Psychiatric Association, 2000), they manifest at least four of the following patterns:

- Unjustly suspecting others of seeking to harm or take advantage of them
- Continually questioning the trustworthiness of others
- Rarely disclosing information about themselves because they believe it will be used against them
- Interpreting benign comments or behaviors as intended to harm them
- Being unforgiving and maintaining long-standing grudges
- Often perceiving themselves, without justification, as under attack
- Being easily motivated to anger or attack
- Frequently questioning the faithfulness of their partners

People with paranoid personality disorder often misinterpret the behavior of others as demeaning or malicious and tend to personalize experiences. As a result of their apprehension about being exploited, criticized, or made to feel helpless, they are constantly on guard. They have little tenderness or sense of humor and can be critical, moralistic, grandiose, insecure, resentful, suspicious, defensive, and jealous. They share little of themselves with others and tend to be rigid and controlling. They are more interested in things than in people or ideas and have little empathy or understanding of others. These clients have a strong sense of hierarchy and typically appear fiercely independent. They crave power and envy those with more influence and success than they have. Sometimes they achieve a sense of authority by becoming leaders of fringe religious or political groups. Generally, they are free of delusions or hallucinations, but when under stress they may experience brief psychotic episodes.

The behavioral dynamics of people with paranoid personality disorder contain elements of projection and projective identification. These people believe that others dislike them and treat them badly; consequently, they take a defensive approach to interpersonal relations and frequently protect themselves by treating others badly. When others respond with disapproval and rejection, it becomes a self-fulfilling prophecy, giving people with this personality disorder the responses that they have feared and yet invited.

People with paranoid personality disorder often have concurrent disorders. The most common are other personality disorders (including narcissistic, avoidant, or obsessive-compulsive personality disorders) and anxiety or mood disorders (Millon et al., 2004). Relatives of people with this disorder have an increased incidence of schizophrenia spectrum disorders. Therefore, the symptoms of a paranoid personality disorder actually may be the premorbid phase of another disorder. Beck and associates (2004) report that there may be an underlying genetic component that contributes to the development of paranoid personality disorder.

Approximately 5 percent of people with personality disorders have paranoid personality disorder, whereas 0.5 to 2.5 percent of the general population can be diagnosed with this disorder (Sperry, 2003). It is more common among men than among women (Millon et al., 2004).

Typical Client Characteristics

Millon and colleagues (2004) describe five subtypes of people with paranoid personality disorder: fanatic, malignant, obdurate, querulous, and insular. The family backgrounds of people with this disorder also vary considerably, although some common antecedents to the disorder have been identified. According to Sperry (2003), people with this disorder "are likely to have grown up in an atmosphere charged with criticism, blame, and hostility, and to have identified with a critical parent" (p. 202). A perfectionistic parent is common, and being the survivor of abuse is not unusual in the histories of people with paranoid personality disorder.

People with this personality disorder are rarely self-referred for treatment and have great difficulty acknowledging a need for help. They have little insight into how their behavior contributes to their problems, and they tend to externalize blame for their difficulties. People with paranoid personality disorder may take pride in what they perceive as their independence and objectivity, and they may view as weak or troubled those who express feelings more easily.

People with personality disorders typically have both interpersonal and occupational difficulties, particularly conflict with family and coworkers. People with this personality disorder typically expect obedience and rigid organization in their family lives and may experience considerable stress when children and partners resist their control. Some can establish a comfortable work or family situation for themselves, as long as they are in charge and do not need to cooperate with others, but that stability may be a tenuous one.

People with this disorder are overly concerned about others' evaluations, and tend to be vigilant in scanning the environment for criticism and malicious intentions of others. They simultaneously believe that they are special and that they are not good enough. They fear being shamed or criticized and spend much time ruminating about their mistreatment by others. To reduce stress and distance themselves from perceived slights, people with paranoid personality disorder tend to isolate themselves, which deprives them of the necessary reality checks that might provide alternative explanations for others' behavior toward them. They tend to avoid intimacy and have considerable difficulty handling stress. They often appear chronically tense due to their constant vigilance (Sperry, 2003). These symptoms are likely to worsen under pressure, failure, or humiliation. Brief psychotic symptoms may even occur in those circumstances.

Preferred Therapist Characteristics

Perhaps the most fundamental goal of therapy for people with paranoid personality disorder is the establishment of trust so that they can become less resistant and more able to engage in therapy. To establish a trusting therapeutic alliance, the therapist should assume a respectful, courteous, and professional stance; be honest though tactful; and not intrude on the client's privacy and independence. Beck and associates (2004) found it helpful to give these clients considerable control over the nature of their treatment, particularly the frequency of their sessions and their between-session tasks. Infrequent sessions, perhaps one every three weeks, can reduce the threat of the therapeutic process. These clients have little respect for people who seem weak or inept, however, so therapists need to communicate confidence and knowledge, but without demeaning these clients.

Because people with paranoid personality disorder are often hostile and abrasive, therapists need to monitor their own reactions and resist being intimidated or angered. Limits may need to be set if clients behave in threatening or aggressive ways. Therapists working with these clients should avoid arguing, communicating excessive warmth and concern, and developing therapeutic plans that may evoke suspicion (such as meeting with a client's family when the client is not present). Clients' questionable beliefs should be accepted but not confirmed.

Intervention Strategies

Individual therapy is usually the treatment of choice for people with paranoid personality disorder. Therapy should not emphasize either interpretation or reflection of feelings; both are likely to be threatening. Rather, a behavioral approach that emphasizes the client's rather than the therapist's control and that focuses on problem solving, stress management, and development of assertiveness and other interpersonal skills is most likely to engage the client in the therapeutic process and effect some positive change. People with paranoid personality disorder often appreciate the logic and organization of behavior therapy. They tend to be more trusting of therapists who focus on actions and experiences than of those who focus on inner dynamics and feelings. Reinforcement, modeling, and education can help these clients develop more effective coping mechanisms and social skills and promote a greater sense of self-efficacy, which in turn should help them engage in the next phase of treatment.

Once progress has been made in establishing a collaborative therapeutic relationship and effecting some behavioral change, cognitive therapy can be introduced (Beck et al., 2004). This model, too, offers the appeal of a logical and clear approach. Because people with paranoid personality disorder are prone to overgeneralization, magnifying the negative, and dichotomous thinking, therapy can help these clients consider alternative explanations. This can modify their defensive stance, encourage them to take more responsibility for the impact they have on others, and reduce their anger and hostility. In this stage of treatment, paranoia often evolves into depression, and cognitive approaches can also be used to reduce those symptoms.

To date, little empirical research exists on the effectiveness of treatment for people with paranoid personality disorder. Beck and colleagues (2004) report promising results with cognitive therapy that helps increase clients' self-efficacy, decrease vigilance and defensiveness, and improve their overall ability to cope with interpersonal problems and concomitant stress. Gentle reality testing can contribute to therapy with these clients. People facing the legal, professional, or relationship consequences of their behavior may need help to appreciate how important it is for them to modify their behavior and attitudes so as to prevent negative consequences.

Some clinicians have reported successful use of a psychodynamic or interpersonal approach that emphasizes understanding in the treatment of people with paranoid personality disorder (Kantor, 2004; Millon et al., 2004). However, research on these treatment approaches is limited.

Group therapy is rarely indicated for people with paranoid personality disorder. Unless they are in charge, they are acutely uncomfortable in group settings, particularly those that are intimate or confrontational, and they tend to sabotage or flee group therapy.

Although family problems are common for people with paranoid personality disorder, family therapy usually is not indicated until considerable progress has been made in individual therapy. Only when people have some awareness of the impact of their behavior and attitudes on others are they ready to talk about family issues and interact productively with family members.

Transient psychotic symptoms and severe anxiety are sometimes present in these clients. Antianxiety agents and atypical antipsychotic agents can ameliorate those symptoms. Pimozide (Orap) and fluoxetine (Prozac) have also been found useful in reducing paranoid ideation (Sperry, 2003). A referral for medication should be presented cautiously, however, lest people feel insulted, manipulated, or controlled.

Prognosis

Therapy for people with paranoid personality disorder is a long, slow process, but real changes can be made if they can be engaged in the process. An integrative approach to treatment that combines a psychodynamic approach with cognitive-behavioral therapy seems best. Providing cognitive restructuring and behavioral change strategies can successfully help clients cope better. Relapse can be prevented by holding occasional follow-up sessions, rather than having a complete termination. However, people with this disorder often refuse to engage in the therapeutic process, and they frequently terminate therapy prematurely. Even if they do cooperate with therapy and manifest some positive change, treatment is unlikely to result in extensive modification of their pervasive patterns of relating. Therefore, limited goals should be set at the outset of treatment so that both therapist and client have a clear direction and can feel a sense of accomplishment even if treatment is not completed. If treatment continues after the initial goals have been achieved, goals can be revised.

SCHIZOID PERSONALITY DISORDER

Description of the Disorder

According to *DSM-IV-TR*, the primary feature of schizoid personality disorder is "a pervasive pattern of detachment from social relationships and a restricted range of expression of emotions in interpersonal settings" (American Psychiatric Association, 2000, p. 694). This pattern is evident by early adulthood, and, in all or nearly all contexts, it characterizes the behavior and attitudes of people with this disorder. They tend to prefer solitary activities, shun family and social activities, and are usually perceived as cold and detached. People with schizoid personality disorder are anhedonic and report few if any sources of pleasure. Interest in sexual or interpersonal closeness is minimal or absent. People with this disorder typically have great difficulty expressing their feelings, may deny having strong emotions, and seem detached and indifferent. When with others, they tend to be guarded and tactless and have a restricted range of emotional response. Most are unaffected by people's reactions to them, although some do acknowledge underlying pain related to their unrewarding social interactions and perceive themselves as social misfits (Beck et al., 2004). Although their reality testing usually is unimpaired, people with schizoid personality disorder often become easily derailed and tangential in their thinking or distracted by irrelevancies (Sperry, 2003).

Such inventories as the Millon Clinical Multiaxial Inventory (MCMI) and the Minnesota Multiphasic Personality Inventory (MMPI) can be helpful in making a diagnosis and in understanding people with schizoid personality disorder. Written responses may be more comfortable for these clients and more informative to therapists than oral responses, especially in the early stages of treatment. Millon and colleagues (2004) suggest that the person's fantasy life could provide rich material for therapy, as any fantasy provides a window into a person's private world of needs and desires. People with schizoid personality disorder should also be assessed for social anxiety.

Schizoid personality disorder is not commonly seen in clinical settings, although it may be present in as many as 7.5 percent of the general population. This disorder seems to be more common among males than among females. However, females with schizoid personality disorder seem to have a higher rate of co-occurring alcohol and drug use disorders than males (Grant et al., 2004).

Typical Client Characteristics

Millon writes that "the schizoid is the personality disorder that lacks a personality" (2004, p. 401). Indeed, from childhood on, people with schizoid personality disorder have few good interpersonal experiences and have the expectation that relationships will be frustrating and disappointing. Early experiences frequently include being subject to bullying, rejection, or abuse (Beck et al., 2004). Rather than expose themselves to what they perceive as more negative experiences, they shun socialization and develop private, isolated lives. Males generally do not date or marry and are not "predisposed to intimate contact" (Sperry, 2003, p. 226). Females may engage in more social and family activities, but they tend to assume a passive role and allow others to make their social decisions. Both men and women with this disorder have poor social skills and few if any close friends. Their capacity for empathy and introspection seems to be severely constricted, and they often view themselves as odd, different, or worthless.

People with schizoid personality disorder have considerable occupational impairment, particularly if their chosen occupations involve interpersonal contact. Some shun employment and continue to live with their parents. Others manage to find stable, secure occupational roles that are congruent with their need for solitude. They may become skilled at scientific, theoretical, creative, or mechanical pursuits, or in endeavors that involve animals rather than people, and may have relatively successful careers. They also may become involved with philosophical or social movements or with extreme health regimes, as long as these pursuits require little interpersonal contact. Although people with schizoid personality disorder typically are not interested in becoming successful or in competing for recognition, they may gain recognition or become successful by accident, as a result of being totally immersed in their work or hobbies and having no social interests to distract them.

In general, people with schizoid personality disorder have a relatively stable existence as long as outside pressures do not intrude. For example, one client with schizoid personality disorder devoted his energy to raising pit bulldogs and collecting poisonous snakes. He had no social life and saw others only for business transactions. He was referred to counseling after his neighbors, feeling endangered by his activities, complained to the police. The client reported contentment with his life; his only concern was his neighbors.

People with this disorder tend to fantasize extensively but almost never lose contact with reality. Their affect is typically flat, and their behavior is lethargic. They tend to be relatively satisfied with their lives, although some engage in considerable intellectualization and denial to justify their lives to themselves and others.

People with schizoid personality disorder typically have been raised in homes that met their physical and educational needs but did not provide emotional interaction, warmth, or social skills (Sperry, 2003). The child may have grown up modeling the parents' aloof, withdrawn style, preferring fantasy or isolation to social interaction. Millon and colleagues (2004) report that a biological predisposition may be reflected in infants who are passive and anhedonic. Schizoid personality disorder usually is not accompanied by other prominent disorders, but some people with this disorder exhibit symptoms of depression, anxiety, depersonalization, obsessional thinking, somatic complaints, or brief manic states. This disorder, like the other Cluster A personality disorders (paranoid and schizotypal), may also be a precursor of a psychotic disorder. Coexisting personality disorders may be present, especially schizotypal, antisocial, and avoidant personality disorders.

Preferred Therapist Characteristics

Building trust is a critical ingredient of treatment with people who have schizoid personality disorder, as it is with those who have paranoid personality disorder. People with schizoid personality disorder have little experience in expressing their feelings, engaging in close and collaborative relationships, or trusting others. Confrontation or scrutiny of their emotions generally makes them uncomfortable and may lead to their premature termination of the therapeutic relationship. What they need instead is a corrective emotional experience to decrease their withdrawal and increase their optimism about relationships. Sperry (2003) suggests that an object relations approach to treatment might prove helpful. The therapist needs to take an active and encouraging stance with this type of client and avoid being critical or threatening. A gentle, consistent, patient, accepting, optimistic, available, and supportive therapist is needed to establish a therapeutic alliance. This is likely to be a slow process because, for this client, anxiety is triggered by interpersonal relationships.

On occasion, people with schizoid personality disorder do take the initiative in seeking therapy, usually when someone breaks through their reserve and increases their anxiety, but they rarely experience an internal wish to change. Usually, however, people with schizoid personality disorder are not self-referred. They are typically encouraged to seek help by concerned family members or employers who are hoping for a change in these people's ability to relate to others. Therefore, these clients are likely to see little need for therapy and to manifest passive resistance. Their eye contact is poor, and they rarely volunteer information, responding only minimally to questions.

Getting past this initial reluctance will be challenging. Therapists will need a high tolerance for distance, for silence, and possibly even for some acting-out behavior. Therapists may also need to manage their own feelings of boredom, irritation, and frustration with this kind of client. If the nature and value of psychotherapy can be clarified for these clients, and if they can be assured that therapists will respect their privacy, they may be able to engage constructively in the therapeutic process.

Intervention Strategies

Little research exists on therapy for people with schizoid personality disorder, but some cautious generalizations can be made. Because these people tend to avoid relationships in general, and intimate relationships in particular, they are not likely to seek therapy, and many terminate early. Thus, any psychotherapy tends to be brief.

Because people with schizoid personality disorder are often ambivalent about therapy, if a supportive therapeutic relationship can be developed, that acceptance by another person may help them to appreciate the value of relationships. Therapists often must first help the client see the benefit of therapy, outlining pros and cons of treatment. Beck and colleagues (2004) suggest that therapist and client collaboratively negotiate a problem list and develop a hierarchy of goals using a Socratic dialogue. Therapists' beliefs must be held in check, as their assumptions are likely to vary greatly from the client's. Their expression could be construed as criticism by these highly sensitive people, thus reinforcing their core beliefs that relationships are "cruel, unfulfilling, and unwelcoming" (Beck, p. 147).

Schema therapy, developed by Young (1999), expands on cognitive therapy to address clients' underlying assumptions and dysfunctional thoughts by using imagery exercises, empathy, limited reparenting, and homework assignments to modify maladaptive schemas. Used with people diagnosed with schizoid personality disorder, these schemas typically include the perception that life is bland and unfulfilling and that human relationships are not worth the trouble. Clients' fantasies and their apprehension about dependence are other areas that can be productively explored through cognitive therapy. Such inventories as Beck's Dysfunctional Thought Record can facilitate identification and modification of such thoughts, as can guided discovery, which helps people determine their interests and increase their involvement in pleasurable activities. Building on interests that are already present can facilitate clients' involvement in additional activities.

Behavioral techniques can help people with schizoid personality disorder improve their social and communication skills and increase their empathy for others. Therapists should keep in mind, however, that people with schizoid personality disorder generally do not respond well to reinforcement, given their lack of reactivity and the limited importance they attach to interpersonal relationships. They may also resent the intrusive and manipulative aspects of some behavioral approaches. An intellectual approach to behavioral change, such as education to increase assertiveness, self-expression, and social skills, is most likely to succeed. Some clients also respond well to environmental changes that afford them increased but still limited exposure to other people and provide them a natural laboratory for practicing their new skills.

The sequencing of the components of a treatment plan for people with schizoid personality disorder is critical. These clients should not be overwhelmed by a multifaceted treatment strategy, nor should they be pushed into group or family therapy before they are ready. A stable therapeutic alliance should first be established through individual therapy. Only when the person is ready should group or family therapy, assertiveness training, career counseling, or other more active and probably more threatening interventions be introduced.

Group therapy can be helpful to these clients, but therapists must assume a protective stance toward them, especially during the initial stages when they are likely to say little and to appear detached from the group. Intrusive interpretations and forced interactions should be avoided. Other group members must also be carefully selected, to ensure that these clients will not feel pressured or attacked. Sperry (2003) recommends a group that is homogeneous in terms of overall functioning but heterogeneous in terms of personality styles. If accepted by the client, group therapy can provide an educational and affirming socialization experience and offer gentle feedback.

Those who are in regular contact with people who have schizoid personality disorder typically have trouble dealing with them because of these clients' limited social interests and skills. Some family or work-site meetings can help others accept the special characteristics of people with schizoid personality disorder, appreciate their strengths, and deal with them more effectively. Pressure from family members or coworkers for the person to date or to socialize more at work, even though the pressure may be the product of good intentions, is likely to exacerbate the person's condition. At the same time, gentle encouragement and increased acceptance on the part of family members and colleagues can help people with schizoid personality disorder socialize more comfortably.

Very few controlled studies have been conducted on pharmacotherapy for the treatment of schizoid personality disorder. In some cases, however, medication to reduce severe anxiety or depression can facilitate therapy (Sperry, 2003). For those with psychotic symptoms, atypical antipsychotic medications such as olanzapine (Zyprexa) or ziprasidone (Geodon) can be helpful.

Relapse prevention is another important ingredient of treatment for people with schizoid personality disorder (Beck et al., 2004). Without help in identifying the signs of a relapse and without periodic follow-up sessions, people with this disorder have a high likelihood of reverting to their previous isolated behaviors.

Prognosis

Schizoid personality disorder can be treated effectively through the use of a combination of treatment approaches and by moving forward slowly. However, premature termination of treatment and failure to benefit or maintain gains from therapy are common (Millon et al., 2004). Many of these clients have established a relatively stable lifestyle and are not motivated to participate in treatment. They may increase their socialization somewhat, especially if required to do so by their employers, but fundamental change is a slow process. With these clients, setting limited goals, becoming comfortable with silence and frustration, and proceeding at a reduced pace can lead to the establishment of a more rewarding therapeutic relationship.

SCHIZOTYPAL PERSONALITY DISORDER

Description of the Disorder

People with schizotypal personality disorder (SPD), like those with paranoid and schizoid personality disorders, have pervasive deficits in interpersonal relations and social skills. They tend to be guarded, suspicious, and hypersensitive. They have few close friends other than first-degree relatives, manifest flat and inappropriate affect, and are uncomfortable and awkward in social situations. In addition, this disorder is characterized by ''cognitive or perceptual distortions and eccentricities of behavior'' (American Psychiatric Association, 2000, p. 697) that may involve ideas of reference, magical thinking, unusual beliefs or perceptual experiences, prominent superstitions, eccentric actions or grooming, and idiosyncratic speech patterns. People with SPD typically are more dysfunctional and unusual in presentation than are those with paranoid or schizoid personality disorders.

SPD is found in approximately 3 percent of the general population (Sperry, 2003). Clear information is not available on gender distribution of this disorder, although recent studies indicate that males with SPD tend to have greater dysfunction than females with the disorder, including more drug and alcohol use, fewer friends, and more disability due to odd thinking and beliefs (Dickey et al., 2005). Men are also more likely to have co-occurring paranoid and narcissistic personality disorders.

Typical Client Characteristics

People with SPD almost always have significant social and occupational impairment, with as many as 40 percent having experienced a period of time during which they were unable to work. They usually do not marry or have children but tend to live alone or with their families of origin. Sometimes they become involved with cults or other groups with unusual beliefs.

According to Dickey and colleagues (2005), the three most frequently occurring symptoms, reported in more than 78 percent of people with SPD, are illusions or unusual perceptual experiences, suspiciousness and paranoid ideation, and magical thinking. Their peculiar habits and attitudes generally are evident to those around them and can contribute to their social isolation. People with SPD are often viewed as strange, odd, and eccentric. Their tendency toward isolation perpetuates the cognitive and social slippage that is commonly found in people with this disorder (Sperry, 2003). People with SPD seem to experience more downward drift than those with any other personality disorder and more than would be expected given their usually average to above-average intelligence (Dickey et al., 2005).

SPD seems to have both genetic and environmental components. People with this personality disorder have a higher percentage of first-degree biological relatives with schizophrenia or mood disorders than does the general population (American Psychiatric Association, 2000; Dickey et al., 2005). Research shows that people with SPD have neurological deficits similar to schizophrenia, and at least some of the dominant symptoms of SPD may be the result of abnormalities in the frontal lobe, similar to what is seen in schizophrenia (Dickey et al., 2005). The parenting received by people with this disorder is generally consistent but often lacks emotional warmth. Sperry notes that at least one study indicates a genetic predisposition to schizotypy and increased passivity in these clients when they were children, which may have contributed to parental indifference and distance. Experiences of humiliation, abuse, bullying, and rejection are commonly found in the backgrounds of people with SPD, as is discouragement of social involvement (Sperry, 2003).

Dickey and colleagues (2005) found that more than half of people with SPD have coexisting major depressive disorder, and 25 percent have anxiety or dysthymia. Transient, stress-related psychotic symptoms also often accompany this disorder. People with SPD tend to somatize and may present vague physical complaints. Suicidal ideation and behavior often accompany this disorder, particularly if a mood disorder or psychotic symptoms are also present. Other personality disorders, including paranoid, avoidant, obsessive-compulsive, and borderline personality disorders, may be present. As is typical of people with schizophrenia spectrum disorders, those with SPD have a high level of suspiciousness, paranoid ideation, and ruminative thought processes that make it difficult for them to establish and maintain social relationships (Dickey et al., 2005). In some cases, SPD is a precursor of schizophrenia.

Preferred Therapist Characteristics

People with SPD, like those with schizoid and paranoid personality disorders, are likely to be resistant to treatment. Building trust is a challenging yet critical ingredient in engaging the person in the therapeutic process. An available, reliable, encouraging, warm, empathic, positive, and nonintrusive stance can help therapists interact effectively with these clients (Sperry, 2003). Because people with SPD tend to ramble and have difficulty making meaningful use of therapy, clinicians will have to be structured and focused and have to teach these clients about psychotherapy. Frequent sessions or telephone calls between sessions can keep clients connected to and involved with treatment. Allowing them to determine the degree of intimacy also can increase their sense of control over and comfort with therapy and can provide a corrective emotional experience.

Several symptoms of SPD, including paranoid ideation and unusual experiences, tend to be treatment resistant, whereas odd behavior and constricted affect were found to be the symptoms most likely to change, according to a two-year study conducted by McGlashan and others (2005). Therapists sometimes will need to provide clients with basic information and advice on taking care of themselves and dealing with the world. Although some therapists may not be comfortable with this role, it can help clients see the value in therapy.

People with SPD have particular difficulty expressing their feelings and dealing appropriately with interpersonal situations. Therefore, therapists should be prepared for unusual reactions and behaviors on the part of these clients. Therapists will need to manage their own discomfort with the strange and possibly offensive mannerisms of these people, as well as with their lack of motivation for treatment. Therapists should communicate acceptance and support while providing some reality testing and education, keeping in mind that 54 is the average global assessment of functioning rating for people with SPD (Skodol et al., 2002).

On the positive side, these clients are usually willing to talk about themselves and their experiences and do not tend to be manipulative. They generally will be sincere, if guarded and cautious (Sperry, 2003).

Intervention Strategies

The research on treatment of SPD is limited, but treatment usually resembles the treatment for schizoid personality disorder, with the addition of medication. People with SPD are unlikely to seek out treatment on their own. Most people with this disorder seem to accept their lifestyles.

Therapy for people with SPD typically is supportive, lengthy, and slow paced, beginning with supportive interventions and medication and subsequently making gentle use of cognitive and behavioral strategies to promote self-awareness, self-esteem, reality testing, and more socially acceptable behavior. The focus of therapy with these people is likely to be very basic, dealing with personal hygiene and daily activities, seeking to prevent isolation and total dysfunction, and establishing some independence and pleasure in their lives (Sperry, 2003).

Cognitive therapy is helpful to people with SPD and typically focuses on four types of thoughts outlined by Beck and colleagues (2004): suspicious or paranoid thoughts, ideas of reference, superstitious and magical thoughts, and illusions. Therapists can encourage these clients to determine whether evidence is available for their beliefs. Cognitive therapy can also help them cope more effectively with perceived criticism and with distorted emotional reasoning, which is a common characteristic of people with SPD.

Behavior therapy can improve speech patterns and personal hygiene as well as social skills. Group therapy may also be useful for milder cases of this disorder, but the group members must be carefully chosen, and these clients must be carefully prepared, so that the experience does not prove too threatening.

A growing body of research underscores the effectiveness of combining medication with therapeutic interventions in the treatment of SPD. In five controlled pharmacological trials, atypical antipsychotics such as risperidone (Risperdal) were found to be beneficial in treating psychotic symptoms (Sperry, 2003). Reductions were effected in cognitive disturbance, derealization, ideas of reference, anxiety, depression, social dysfunction, and negative self-image. Anxiolytics can also be useful in reducing the anxiety that often accompanies this disorder. Nevertheless, although medication may reduce the degree of impairment of people with SPD, it does not change basic personality patterns.

Case management is often an important component of treatment for these clients. They sometimes are seen in treatment programs for the chronically mentally ill, where long-term oversight of their functioning can be provided. These clients often benefit from help in locating housing, finding employment that provides support and supervision and is not emotionally stressful, and obtaining needed medication on a regular basis. It is also helpful for them to have a place to turn to in times of crisis.

Prognosis

The prognosis for treatment of people with SPD seems guarded at best. As a schizophrenia spectrum disorder, SPD has a similar genetic predisposition and clinical presentation as schizophrenia. Indeed, symptoms of severe cognitive and functional deficits, psychotic symptoms, social isolation, and downward drift can all be seen in schizophrenia and, to a milder extent, in SPD. Dickey and colleagues (2005) suggest that SPD might better be called schizophrenia II, similar to bipolar II, in which the symptoms resemble those of a bipolar I disorder but are less extreme. Despite the guarded prognosis for significant positive change, however, most people with this disorder do not deteriorate into schizophrenia and do manage to achieve a stable if marginal existence. Realistic goals, focused on improved adaptive functioning and enjoyment of life rather than on personality restructuring, can help both therapist and client view their work as a success.

ANTISOCIAL PERSONALITY DISORDER

Description of the Disorder

The symptoms of antisocial personality disorder (APD) begin before the age of fifteen with a pattern of behavior that reflects a diagnosis of conduct disorder (see Chapter Two). This pattern is typified by impulsive and aggressive behavior that violates social rules and norms, such as theft, lying, truancy, cruelty to people and animals, vandalism, fighting, and running away from home.

APD is the only personality disorder that, by definition, cannot be diagnosed before the age of eighteen. In people with APD, the symptoms of conduct disorder have persisted beyond the age of eighteen via a pervasive pattern of irresponsible behavior that violates and shows disregard for the rights and feelings of others. Symptoms of the disorder are likely to be most severe in early adulthood and to diminish spontaneously in midlife.

People with APD are typically unable to sustain employment or monogamous relationships and may lead what Millon refers to as a ''parasitic life'' (Millon et al., 2004, p. 154). They are egocentric, impulsive, reckless, angry, irritable, deceptive, and aggressive. They fail to abide by social and legal guidelines for behavior, are often in financial difficulty, behave irresponsibly as employees and parents, lack empathy, and feel little or no guilt or remorse for their actions. Rather, they justify their behavior, perceiving themselves as superior and infallible, and project blame for their difficulties onto others whom they devalue. People with APD are easily bored and have a high need for excitement, stimulation, and new experiences. They typically enjoy life, although they do not want to bear the consequences of their actions. Despite their professed need for independence, people with APD want to impress others and have difficulty with rejection and delayed gratification. They have faith only in themselves and tend to engage in preemptive aggression, attacking in anticipation of being attacked. They are often shrewd judges of others and can use their verbal and interpersonal skills in manipulative ways. At the same time, they rarely engage in introspection and have little sense of themselves.

People with APD disdain generally accepted values and behaviors, although not all actually engage in criminal behavior. Millon and colleagues (2004) report that many find a place for themselves in business, politics, or other settings where a focus on self-interest and accumulation of material goods is rewarded.

APD is approximately three times more common among males than it is among females: approximately 3 percent of men and fewer than 1 percent of women can be diagnosed with this disorder. It has been estimated that 50 to 75 percent of people in prison may have APD (Rogers, Salekin, Sewell, & Cruise, 2000).

Typical Client Characteristics

Genetic and environmental influences both are factors in the development of APD, as they are with many of the personality disorders. People with this personality disorder typically lacked secure and stable parenting and grew up in families in which discipline was inconsistent and erratic, sometimes excessively punitive and sometimes lax. These disrupted families often included others who manifested antisocial behavior (Kazdin, 2002). Fathers of people with this disorder typically manifest antisocial and alcoholic behaviors and often left their families or were otherwise unavailable. Mothers characteristically were overburdened (Millon et al., 2004). Unsupportive and defensive communication patterns are typically seen in families of people with APD (Kazdin, 2002). Therefore, as children, people later diagnosed with APD did not have models of empathic tenderness and failed to develop positive attachments. Instead, they learned that they had to look out for themselves and found that violence and aggression could be used to their advantage to intimidate people. They were typically undeterred by punishment; they manifested behavioral problems early on and engaged in challenging and dangerous activities.

People with APD often have painful underlying symptoms, typically depression and anxiety (Millon et al., 2004). They also are prone to substance-related disorders and are at increased risk of suicide. More than 11 percent of people with APD have attempted suicide, and 5 percent complete a suicide attempt (Verona, Patrick, & Joiner, 2001). APD is sometimes accompanied by other personality disorders, notably narcissistic, paranoid, and histrionic personality disorders, as well as by sadistic and negativistic personality patterns (Millon et al., 2004). Occupational and interpersonal dysfunction is almost always present. People with APD have considerable difficulty sustaining warm, intimate relationships and tend to change partners and jobs frequently.

Preferred Therapist Characteristics

People with APD rarely seek therapy on their own initiative, but often enter treatment because they are court ordered into treatment as a result of breaking the law. Therapy may be a condition of their parole or probation, or they may be treated while incarcerated. The reasons why these clients enter therapy and their motivation to change need to be understood and addressed before treatment can begin (Millon et al., 2004).

Because most people with APD do not initiate or want treatment, developing a therapeutic alliance is not easy. Sperry (2003) suggests that therapists initially empathize and join with the client in his or her hostility, then proceed toward a collaborative relationship. These clients tend to be reluctant to engage in therapy, although some are manipulative and appear superficially cooperative in order to avoid negative consequences. They may afford therapists an initial honeymoon phase, but their opposition to treatment is likely to surface once therapy progresses beyond superficial interactions. These clients typically resent authority figures and may see therapists as part of that group. To reduce the likelihood of being seen in this way, therapists should avoid assuming judgmental and punitive roles, even if they are working in correctional settings. Instead, they should present themselves as specialists and collaborative partners in psychotherapy.

Therapists working with people diagnosed with APD typically encounter a considerable challenge. Once again, the development of trust will be a critical ingredient of successful treatment. Therapists need to be genuine, accepting, and empathic. They also should be self-assured, relaxed, and straightforward and should have a sense of humor.

Directive techniques are often necessary in persuading people with APD to engage in treatment. Beck and colleagues (2004) advise providing these clients with clear explanations of their disorder and setting explicit guidelines and limits for their involvement in therapy. Clear limits in the therapeutic relationship can help prevent clients from becoming hostile and abusive and attempting to engage their therapists in battles; power struggles will only undermine treatment. Therapy should be continued only if clients give some evidence of benefiting from the process.

Therapists working with people with APD often develop countertransference reactions to their clients. Sperry (2003) reports that disbelief and collusion are common. Therapists are liable to rationalize clients' illegal activities and think clients "aren't that bad" (p. 51) or to succumb to their manipulation. Therapists also may be angered or threatened by the histories of clients with APD, as well as frustrated and discouraged by their lack of progress in treatment. All of these reactions must be monitored and managed for treatment to be effective.

Intervention Strategies

The failure to find an effective treatment for APD has not been due to any lack of research; APD is one of the most studied of the personality disorders. Rather, the discouraging results of outcome research reflect the guarded prognosis for treatment of this disorder.

A few approaches have achieved at least some improvement in people with APD. A structured and active approach to therapy is indicated for people with APD. Although research has yet to identify a treatment approach that has a high degree of effectiveness, social skills training has been found helpful in regulating behavior (Sperry, 2003). Milieu and residential approaches, as well as structured group therapy, have achieved some success in strengthening interpersonal skills and prosocial behaviors in people with APD (Sperry, 2003). Therapeutic communities; institutional settings that use token economies; and wilderness programs that involve peer modeling, expectations, and encouragement as well as clear consequences sometimes succeed in breaking through resistance and effecting some change in these clients. For those who are incarcerated, prerelease or halfway programs can also be helpful in facilitating their transition to a more socially acceptable lifestyle. Residential therapeutic programs established specifically for people who have broken the law typically focus on increasing their responsibility, their trust in themselves and others, and their sense of mastery, while instilling an understanding of the consequences of their behavior. An important benefit of these residential programs is that they remove people from their former environments where their antisocial behavior may have been reinforced by peers. Developing new support systems and a sense of belonging through employment or self-help groups (such as Narcotics Anonymous) can accomplish a similar end.

Individual therapy is an essential ingredient of treatment for people with APD. The first steps in individual therapy include establishing a collaborative therapeutic relationship and setting clear and mutually agreed-on goals. Once those steps have been accomplished, behavior, reality, and cognitive therapy can be helpful. Reality therapy can enable people to see the self-destructive nature of their actions, to recognize that their behaviors are not helping them meet their needs, and to make a commitment to change. Behavior therapy can promote positive change by improving problem-solving and decision-making skills, anger management, and impulse control. Beck and associates (2004) recommend cognitive interventions that are designed to promote moral development, abstract thinking, and appreciation for the rights and feelings of others, as well as analysis and modification of dysfunctional thoughts. Millon and colleagues (2004) suggest helping people with APD develop an enlightened self-interest so they can recognize the likely consequences of their actions and determine whether a particular action is in their own best interest. Psychoeducation, often provided in a group format, can be effective at teaching clients self-control and delayed gratification (Sperry, 2003).

As mentioned earlier, schema therapy — which integrates cognitive therapy with imagery, empathic confrontation, homework assignments, and limited reparenting — holds promise in the treatment of personality disorders (Young, Klosko, & Weishaar, 2003). Maladaptive schemas typically found in people with APD include mistrust (fearing that others will abuse or cheat them), a sense of entitlement, lack of self-control, and the belief that they are defective and will be abandoned by others. Although the focus of treatment is generally on current behavior, people with APD are sometimes less defensive when they are talking about the past, and this may provide a useful bridge to a discussion of current activities. Person-centered and insight-oriented therapies are not indicated with these clients, however, even if discussion does focus on past experiences.

An early sign of progress is the emergence of underlying depression (Sperry, 2003). This development can be upsetting to clients and may precipitate a resumption of old patterns of behavior. To encourage clients' persistence in treatment if depression does surface, therapists may need to increase support and empathy. Those whose depression or anxiety are alleviated too quickly, however, may lose motivation to change.

Medication is sometimes combined with therapy in the treatment of people with APD. Lithium, fluoxetine (Prozac), sertraline (Zoloft), and beta-blockers such as propanolol (Inderal) have all demonstrated some effectiveness in helping people control anger and impulsivity (Sperry, 2003). Medication should be prescribed cautiously, however, because of clients' tendency to misuse drugs and because of their reliance on external rather than internal solutions to problems.

Family therapy has also been suggested, especially when clients are young, in an effort to reverse familial patterns that are being transmitted. Therapy may also help family members set limits, be consistent, separate from the client, and deal with their own guilt and anger toward the client.

Treatment specifically for coexisting substance-related disorders can also be helpful to people with APD and can reduce their motivation to engage in antisocial behavior. Messina, Wish, Hoffman, and Nemes (2002) found that completion of treatment for substance use was the most important factor in reducing postdischarge arrests in people with APD.

An issue that often arises in the treatment of people diagnosed with APD is the relationship between therapy and punishment, given that many of these clients come into therapy as a consequence of breaking the law. Millon and colleagues (2004) recommend separating therapy and punishment to increase the likelihood of clients' using therapy constructively and not manipulating or deceiving the therapist. At the same time, the threat of punishment can have a powerful coercive effect and can promote initial involvement in therapy. This issue has not been definitively resolved but must be considered by therapists working with people diagnosed as having APD.

Prognosis

The prognosis for treating APD is not good, primarily because of clients' lack of motivation to change (Millon et al., 2004). Time, according to Sperry, is the greatest healer. As people age, they become less impulsive, and the intensity of antisocial behavior tends to dissipate. The likelihood of successful treatment is higher with people over the age of forty who manifest some remorse for their actions, have a history of some attachments, have not been sadistic or violent, are neither very high nor very low in intelligence, and do not create fear in clinicians (Sperry, 2003). As in the treatment of most of the other personality disorders, realistic and circumscribed goals (such as improvement in prosocial behavior) are likely to lead to a better outcome. Specialized treatment in therapeutic communities and structured programs also seems to help. In most cases, treatment will be long. Sustained treatment aimed at teaching social skills, self-control, and delayed gratification can be helpful in preventing relapse and improving quality of life.

BORDERLINE PERSONALITY DISORDER

Description of the Disorder

People with borderline personality disorder (BPD) are characterized primarily by pervasive instability in mood, relationships, behavior, and self-image, as well as by impulsivity (American Psychiatric Association, 2000). This instability affects all or nearly all areas of their lives. The very name of this disorder reflects the precariousness of people with this condition. (The name was originally intended to indicate that they were on the border between psychosis and neurosis.) By definition, BPD is characterized by at least five of the following patterns:

- Intense and fluctuating interpersonal relationships
- Self-destructive and impulsive behavior (for example, substance misuse, binge eating, excessive spending, promiscuity)
- Labile moods
- Self-mutilation (usually cutting or burning) or suicidal threats and behavior
- Lack of a stable, internalized sense of self
- Persistent sense of emptiness and boredom
- Frantic efforts to avoid loneliness or abandonment
- Inappropriate anger
- Transient stress-related dissociation or paranoid ideation

According to Sperry (2003), BPD can be found in 1.1 to 2.5 percent of the general population, 10 percent of people seen in outpatient mental health clinics, and as many as 50 percent of people receiving inpatient psychotherapy. Approximately 75 percent of people diagnosed with this disorder are females (Johnson, Hurley, Benkelfat, Herpertz, & Taber, 2003).

People with BPD can be high functioning or low functioning, depending on several variables, including the degree of occupational and social impairment, co-occurring disorders, and level of insight. Major depressive disorder is the most common co-occurring disorder. Also common are panic disorder with agoraphobia; PTSD; somatoform, dissociative, substance-related, schizoaffective disorders; and other personality disorders (Johnson et al., 2003). Sleeping, eating, and grooming habits are often erratic, and people with this disorder almost always experience occupational and social impairment.

Typical Client Characteristics

Mothers of people with BPD often have mental disorders themselves, most often BPD, a depressive disorder, or psychosis, which causes them to be inconsistent in their parenting and their availability (Sperry, 2003). Fathers are often unavailable or do not interfere in the mother-child bond (Masterson & Lieberman, 2004). Dysfunctional alcohol use is also very prevalent in the families of these clients, as are other substance-related disorders and antisocial personality disorder (American Psychiatric Association, 2000).

A history of incest, brutality, early loss, neglect, and other traumas are more common among people with BPD than among people with any other disorder. Such early abuse seems to explain the disorganized attachment patterns and negative views of others that are frequently found in people with BPD, as well as the increased incidence of PTSD (Yen et al., 2002). Beck and colleagues (2004) note that it is not the trauma itself that causes BPD, but how the child processes the trauma. Factors such as age, temperament, and other characteristics of the environment at the time of the trauma also contribute to the development of this disorder.

Masterson and Lieberman (2004) note that issues around separation and individuation persist from childhood into adulthood for these clients. People with BPD tend to have little sense of themselves and an external locus of control. They seek to avoid individuation by attaining a symbiotic relationship with another, typically a romantic partner or a therapist. They have considerable difficulty expressing feelings because they often are uncertain of what they are feeling or of how they are expected to be feeling and are fearful of incurring anger and rejection if they make a mistake. They seem to have a sort of false self, built around an effort to please others.

People with BPD seem to have a great deal of underlying anger combined with vengeful impulses. Sometimes these feelings are denied and suppressed lest their expression precipitate abandonment; at other times these feelings are expressed in self-destructive ways that provoke considerable anger in others. This emotional chaos typically leaves people with BPD in a near-constant state of crisis, which they usually attribute to the actions of other people.

Two forms of behavior are common in people with BPD and need to be distinguished: suicidal intent, and self-injuring behavior with no intent to die. More than 75 percent of people with BPD engage in self-injurious behavior, such as cutting or burning, excessive drinking, high-risk sexual behavior, and suicidal gestures (Oldham, 2006). Paradoxically, people with BPD engage in self-injurious behaviors in an effort to make themselves feel better. Such gestures are generally lacking suicidal intent. As can be expected, these behaviors do sometimes result in death or the need for emergency medical care, but these results are generally unintended. Engaging in self-harm or parasuicidal behavior increases the risk of suicide death by 50 percent (Gunderson & Ridolfi, 2001).

Impulsive aggression and affective dysregulation are two behaviors typically linked to suicidal and self-injurious behavior in people with BPD. Axis I comorbidity is common, and major depressive disorder, substance misuse, and bipolar disorder are positively correlated with feelings of hopelessness and an increased number of suicide attempts (Links & Kola, 2005).

Recent research into the neurological roots of emotion regulation have found dysfunction in the neural circuitry of the emotion regulation centers of the brain that relate to impulsive aggression (Johnson et al., 2003). Although the details are beyond the scope of this book, a variety of studies have linked reduced serotonin with impulsivity and depressive symptoms, which are commonly found in BPD, and have also found a link between brain chemistry and affective lability, dissociation, and comorbid mood disorders (Johnson et al., 2003).

BPD tends to be particularly severe in late adolescence and early adulthood, and symptoms gradually improve with age as people with this disorder attain greater stability in their relationships and their vocations. A tendency toward affective instability, strong emotions, and intensity in relationships, however, may be lifelong (American Psychiatric Association, 2000).

Preferred Therapist Characteristics

Therapists who work with people with BPD must provide a "constant, continuing, empathic force" in the person's life, as well as "someone who can listen well and handle being the target of intense rage and idealization while concurrently defining limits and boundaries with firmness and candor" (Goin, 2001, p. 168). In other words, these clients are challenging, and therapists who work with them need to maintain a careful balance. Too much attention to these clients can promote dependence or flight, but too little can promote suicidal threats, panic, anger, and failure to develop a therapeutic alliance.

Therapists should remain compassionate and nonjudgmental and maintain control in the face of these clients' acting-out behaviors. Therapists must be active and involved, providing a stable and safe therapeutic environment. Although therapists should communicate availability, reliability, interest, acceptance, support, genuineness, and empathy to clients with BPD, they must also establish and adhere to clear and consistent limits and guidelines. Extra sessions and supportive telephone calls can be given when they are therapeutically advisable, but they should not be offered as capitulation to clients' manipulations or threats.

Approximately 60 to 70 percent of people with BPD will attempt suicide, and 10 percent will succeed (Oldham, 2006). Especially in the early stages of therapy, addressing suicide risk is often the first priority and focus of treatment. Oldham states that the therapist and client should "meet the preoccupation head-on, as a recognized risk and encourage the client to join forces with the therapist to find a better road to travel" (p. 25).

Because of the self-destructive and potentially lethal behavior of these clients, any approach to therapy that is used must make an effort to reduce acting out and promote more effective functioning and reality testing. Many people with BPD need to be seen several times a week so that stability can be maintained in their lives, suicide can be averted, and the therapeutic alliance can be developed. Therapists need to make clear that they cannot take responsibility for the lives of these clients, and they should not become their rescuers. At the same time, steps must be taken to protect the safety of these clients by providing them with emergency resources, contracting for safety, and developing outside contacts to whom they can turn in times of crisis. Therapists should refer to the American Psychiatric Association's *Practice Guidelines for the Treatment of Borderline Personality Disorder* (2001); this publication defines a treatment framework in which expected roles of the patient and therapist are delineated. The clinician's role includes understanding, empathic feedback, and consistency; it also entails setting clear plans for time and place of meetings, handling emergencies, and billing and payment.

For most of these clients, acting out is a defense against boredom and depression and a way of preventing abandonment. Suicidal ideation and behavior may reoccur following a crisis situation and may accompany depression. Dealing with those concerns can reduce the pressure to engage in self-destructive behavior. Clients must be helped to link their actions with their emotions, to self-soothe, and to find positive ways to reduce disturbing negative affect rather than resort to self-destructive behavior.

Splitting is a common dynamic in the self-images and relationships of people with BPD. They tend to perceive people in extremes, as either idealized or devalued. The client with BPD typically begins a therapeutic relationship by idealizing the therapist. When the therapist fails to yield to demands for special attention, the idealistic view shifts, and the client then harshly criticizes the therapist, often terminating treatment and moving on to the next idealized therapist.

Noncompliance with treatment is a common problem that therapists face in working with people with BPD. In one study, researchers found that more than 50 percent terminated treatment prematurely (Crits-Christoph & Barber, 2002). Instead of blaming these clients or pressuring them to cooperate, therapists need to recognize these clients' underlying struggle with intimacy and fear of abandonment. By acknowledging this fear and helping clients see the benefits that treatment has to offer, therapists can encourage these clients' compliance.

Therapists will need to deal with their own reactions to these often frustrating and complicated clients and should not be lulled into confidence by positive phases of therapy. Because countertransference reactions can be a useful route to understanding these clients, they should be examined. Inevitably, if therapy is to succeed, therapists will need to find gentle and supportive ways to deal with the resistance and transference manifested by people with this disorder. Consultation with colleagues or supervisors is recommended to help therapists maintain their objectivity and equilibrium with these clients. Millon and colleagues (2004) note that many therapists find it helpful to limit the number of clients with BPD in their caseload.

Intervention Strategies

Evidence-based treatment effective for working with people with BPD includes dialectical behavior therapy, psychoanalytic psychotherapy, and psychoeducational approaches (American Psychiatric Association, 2001). Other promising treatments include interpersonal therapy, CBT, cognitive-analytic therapy, systems training for emotional predictability and problem solving, and transference-focused therapy (Oldham, 2006).

Dialectical behavior therapy (DBT), developed by Linehan and her colleagues (Linehan, 1993), not only has yielded empirical evidence of success in treating people with BPD but also has been adapted to treat eating disorders, antisocial personality disorder, and substance use comorbid with BPD (Rizvi & Linehan, 2001). A manualized version of DBT has been used primarily to treat people with BPD who were chronically suicidal and severely dysfunctional. Generally, DBT is carried out over the course of twelve months. However, several studies indicate that DBT may be equally effective in six-month treatment programs (Rizvi & Linehan, 2001).

In DBT, the therapist takes a dialectical stance, accepting and empathizing with the client's emotional pain while also helping the client develop better coping skills. Goals of DBT are grouped into four key stages: (1) development of commitment to therapy; (2) establishment of stability, connection, and safety; (3) exposure to and emotional processing of the past; and (4) synthesis (increasing self-respect, achieving individual goals). DBT takes a holistic, biopsychosocial perspective, emphasizing the use of persuasive dialogue to promote new understanding and change and incorporating many strategies to help clients improve emotion tolerance and affect regulation (including skills training, use of metaphors, and playing devil's advocate). Clients are asked to make a commitment to a combination of individual and group therapy for at least six to twelve months. DBT has been found to be particularly successful in reducing suicidal ideation and self-harming behaviors (Crits-Christoph & Barber, 2002). Improved work and social adjustment have also been reported, as well as reduced anxiety and anger.

Cognitive-behavioral therapy has also been successful with these clients, who typically harbor many strong and maladaptive core beliefs, such as "I'll be alone forever," "I'm a bad person. I deserve to be punished," and "I must subjugate my wants to the desires of others, or they'll abandon me or attack me" (Beck et al., 2004, p. 200). The strategies of cognitive therapy can effect modification in these dysfunctional thoughts.

Building on Beck's work, Young (1999) observed that some pathological emotional states of people with BPD are a regression to similar states in childhood. He identified schema modes that are organized patterns of behavior, cognitions, and feelings reflecting these childhood states. These schemas include the abandoned child, the angry/impulsive child, the primitive parent, and the detached protector.

The person with BPD uses a variety of strategies to avoid feelings and to regulate negative affect, including drugs and alcohol, overeating or excessive sleeping, cutting and other self-harming behaviors, and even attempted suicide. Standard cognitive therapy needs to be adapted to these clients, with initial attention paid to the development of a hierarchy of issues to be addressed. Therapists must first focus on issues of life or death, followed by the development of a collaborative therapeutic relationship. Subsequent attention can then focus on other self-damaging issues and on modifying schemas, reducing dichotomous thinking, teaching adaptive ways to express emotions, and promoting a sense of self (Beck et al., 2004).

Using a developmental approach to the treatment of BPD, Masterson and Lieberman (2004) suggest that the disorder is a failure in separation-individuation, or the development of the self. They incorporate object relations and self-relations in their approach to therapy with these clients and integrate many of the ingredients found effective in their treatment. Masterson and Lieberman outline a long-term plan of treatment that includes the following five phases:

1. Establishment of boundaries through clarification of anger, demands, and manipulativeness

2. Exploration of the therapeutic relationship and the client's history, to provide corrective emotional experiences and promote appropriate expression of feeling and to shift the client from acting-out behavior to verbalization
3. Separation and individuation
4. Development of new feelings, interests, and social skills
5. Termination, carefully planned

For many years, long-term psychodynamic or modified psychoanalytic psychotherapy was viewed as most effective in treating people with this disorder. However, a passive, classical analytic approach is not currently recommended. According to Millon et al. (2004), the psychotherapist is advised to be more direct and to use "gentle confrontation" (p. 518). Supportive therapy may be particularly appropriate for people with BPD who are not high functioning. Emphasis is placed on the importance of the therapeutic relationship in bringing about change. Indeed, research has shown that several years of supportive treatment can effect basic personality changes in people with BPD (Sperry, 2003).

Although all approaches to treating these clients pay some attention to past issues, the primary focus of therapy is usually on the present because, for most of these clients, the present mirrors the past. The therapeutic relationship typically serves as a vehicle to help people work through concerns of separation and individuation and early losses dating back to childhood. Reality testing, rage neutralization, and management of the transference relationship are other important ingredients of therapy with these clients.

Sperry (2003) notes that the most common form of combined treatment for BPD is group therapy in addition to individual therapy. Homogeneous groups, with co-therapists, seem most likely to be effective. These groups can dilute transference reactions, reduce splitting, provide support and friendship, encourage change of manipulative and dysfunctional behaviors, and model coping skills.

Symptom-targeted psychopharmacology combined with psychotherapy can also be beneficial (Oldham, 2006). Antidepressant, antiseizure, antianxiety, and antipsychotic medications sometimes can be useful in treating the secondary symptoms of BPD. SSRIs such as fluoxetine (Prozac) can be helpful in reducing impulsive aggression, depression, and affect dysregulation (Oldham, 2006). Reich (2002) notes that naltrexone (ReVia) has also been found helpful in reducing self-harming behavior. Although benzodiazepines have been used to help calm negative affect, they also reduce inhibitions and actually may lead to additional impulsive behavior; therefore, anxiolytics should probably be avoided in the treatment of BPD. Again, however, medication does not eliminate the basic personality disorder. Use of medication should be closely monitored, given the high suicide risk of these clients, their frequent noncompliance with treatment, and their fear that improvement may lead to abandonment.

Hospitalization, too, may be indicated when clients are experiencing psychotic or suicidal ideation. Typically, hospitalization will be a brief but frequent component of treatment, although crisis intervention and a limited stay in a crisis house can provide safe places for people with BPD.

Family therapy is another useful treatment component for many of these clients. They typically have dysfunctional families of origin and are likely to be in current relationships that are also dysfunctional. Family therapy can have a positive impact on other troubled family members as well and can improve family dynamics and communication.

Prognosis

Sperry (2003) notes considerable difference in the prognosis for people with high-functioning versus low-functioning BPD. A more guarded prognosis is found for those with co-occurring depression or substance misuse. Substance abuse and dependence are the disorders most frequently associated with failure to achieve significant progress in treating BPD (Zanarini et al., 2004). People with BPD have an elevated risk for suicide and death from injury or accident (Oldham, 2006). Fortunately, Linehan's (1983) dialectical behavior therapy has been proven effective at reducing suicidal ideation and self-harming behaviors.

Beck et al. (2004) report that modern CBT tailored to the needs of people with BPD can reduce the rate of early treatment termination and increase efficacy. Treatments of just one year can reduce much of the negative affect and improve anger control and social functioning, although these clients are far from cured and need continued treatment. Increased use of medication and cognitive-behavioral approaches seems likely to yield more encouraging results in the future.

HISTRIONIC PERSONALITY DISORDER

Description of the Disorder

DSM-IV-TR describes histrionic personality disorder as being characterized by "a pervasive pattern of excessive emotionality and attention seeking, beginning by early adulthood and present in a variety of contexts" (American Psychiatric Association, 2000, p. 711). This pattern is characterized by the following features, among others:

- Constant demands for praise or reassurance
- Inappropriate seductiveness
- A need to be the center of attention

- Overemphasis on physical attractiveness
- Exaggerated, shallow, and labile expressions of emotion
- Self-centeredness
- Poor impulse control
- Self-dramatization
- Suggestibility
- A vague, disjointed, general way of speaking

People with this disorder readily become impatient, jealous, manipulative, and volatile. Repression and denial are common defenses. These people also tend to be gullible, to trust others too easily, and to exaggerate the depth of their involvement in their intimate relationships. They usually appear affected and flighty, but their vivacity, imagination, and attractiveness can be engaging. They can also be charming, energetic, and entertaining, especially early in relationships.

People with histrionic personality disorder tend to be other-directed; their moods as well as their feelings about themselves come largely from the reactions they receive from others. They tend to avoid responsibility, feel helpless, and "actively seek out ways that others can be persuaded to take care of them" (Millon et al., 2004, p. 317). Intimate relationships and friendships are both typically impaired. Threats of suicide, although common, are part of these people's exaggerated emotionality and are rarely fatal, but they should nevertheless be taken seriously, as miscalculations can occur and a client may not be rescued as anticipated.

Approximately 2 to 3 percent of the general population and 10 to 15 percent of people in clinical settings meet the criteria for this disorder. Approximately 9 percent of those with personality disorders will be diagnosed as histrionic (Millon et al., 2004). Torgersen, Kringlen, and Cramer (2001) found the disorder to be diagnosed twice as frequently in women as in men. The *DSM* reports that although histrionic personality disorder is more commonly presented by females than males in clinical settings, the actual gender distribution may not differ greatly in the general population (American Psychiatric Association, 2000).

Histrionic personality disorder is often accompanied by other disorders. A particularly strong connection has been found between histrionic personality disorder and somatoform, depressive, dissociative, anxiety, and substance-related disorders, as well as other personality disorders (Millon et al., 2004). Bipolar and cyclothymic disorders have also been reported in people with histrionic personality disorder (Millon et al., 2004). Histrionic personality disorder shares some traits with paranoid personality disorder. People with histrionic personality disorder are particularly likely to develop paranoid traits under conditions of extreme stress (Paris, 2003).

Typical Client Characteristics

People with histrionic personality disorder typically grew up in families that were dramatic and chaotic but not dangerous (unlike the families of those with BPD). These families frequently have a history of antisocial behavior, other personality disorders, and alcohol-related disorders. They typically provide nurturing only when children are ill and give approval primarily for children's attractiveness, talent, and charm (Sperry, 2003). As children, then, people with this disorder were valued for their external presentation rather than for their inner selves.

Sperry (2003) reports that females with histrionic personality disorder often have experienced insufficiency, conflict, and disapproval in their early interactions with their mothers and so have sought attention primarily from their fathers. Consequently, as they mature, these women overemphasize the importance of heterosexual relationships. Males with histrionic personality disorder also experience deprivation from their mothers and may become celibate or engage in compulsive seduction of women.

People with histrionic personality disorder usually are sexually and socially active but may experience sexual difficulties at a higher rate than average (Paris, 2003). They tend to be easily bored; typically, just as they achieve the commitment they seem to be seeking, they shift partners in their quest for the ideal mate. This pattern is exacerbated by the tendency of people with histrionic personality disorder to choose partners who are detached and unemotional and who cannot give them the strong responses they crave. They may have continued difficulties with relationships across the life span, with aging posing a particular challenge to them. People who were overly flirtatious in their youth may need to find another way to be the center of attention as they age (Paris, 2003).

The tendency of people with this disorder to seek out new sources of challenge and stimulation can also interfere with their occupational and social adjustment, and they may have unstable work histories. Their lack of attention to detail and their illogical thinking can also contribute to poor occupational adjustment. If they choose fields that can make accommodations to their unstable temperaments, however, they may be quite successful because they can be driven and energetic in their pursuits.

Preferred Therapist Characteristics

People with histrionic personality disorder tend to be sociable and outgoing and may initially appear to be charming, ingratiating, expressive, and motivated clients, eager to please their therapists. These people do not typically seek therapy voluntarily, and when they do (often after a disappointing end to a relationship), may expect immediate relief from anxiety and depression (Millon et al., 2004, p. 324). Treatment usually begins on a positive note, with the client attempting to charm the therapist, but these clients are externally focused and often want the therapist to retrieve their relationships, fix their problems, or make others (usually a spouse or a partner) change.

As therapy progresses, clients' manipulative and seductive patterns will probably become more evident. They may be annoyed that the therapist has not rescued them, but the secondary gains of therapy — the attention paid by the therapist, and the opportunity to talk about themselves — are often reason enough for them to continue.

Millon and colleagues (2004) report that females with histrionic personality disorder are more likely to seek out male therapists. Their strong need for approval and attention may lead them to seek a romantic relationship with an opposite-sex therapist or to compete with a same-sex therapist.

The therapist must monitor countertransference reactions to these clients, remaining warm, genuine, and accepting yet professional. Clarity and consistency can help build and maintain trust and reduce excessive neediness. The therapist can also make productive therapeutic use of these clients' transference reactions to help clients gain an understanding of how they relate to others and to appreciate the negative impact that their behavior can have.

The therapist should quickly set limits with these clients and must maintain a professional relationship at all times. The clinician should avoid reinforcing dramatic behavior through attention. Millon and colleagues (2004) suggest focusing on process and on the facts of the person's history as a way of setting limits and maintaining appropriate distance. Gentle confrontation also seems to help people with histrionic personality disorder look at the self-destructive nature of their behavior. A detailed agenda, goal setting for each session, and keeping attention focused are necessary, or else the session will be rife with tangential themes and will lack any in-depth problem solving (Millon et al., 2004). Keeping these clients on task will be a challenge because they tend to be distractible and to talk at length in vague, general terms. Their speech may be overly impressionistic; they may resist being introspective, and may avoid tasks that tend to be difficult for them. They are also unable to integrate much of their past, including emotionally upsetting experiences, into their present life, and they have poor reality testing (Millon et al., 2004).

Persuading people with histrionic personality disorder to engage in long-term therapy may be difficult in light of their high need for change, challenge, and stimulation. Such therapeutic strategies as limit setting and confrontation may also make people with histrionic personality disorder feel rejected and unappreciated, and they may become reproachful and demanding, threatening to leave treatment if their needs are not met. Setting a series of clear short-term goals that are meaningful to the client can facilitate extended therapy, as can initiating therapy in an active and engaging fashion and reinforcing even small gains. Empathy should be maintained throughout treatment, as clients who feel that empathy and understanding are slipping away are likely to turn to dramatization for increased effect (Sperry, 2003).

Intervention Strategies

As is the case with most of the other personality disorders, few systematic studies exist on the treatment of histrionic personality disorder (Crits-Christoph & Barber, 2002). Nevertheless, the literature does point to the use of long-term individual psychodynamic or cognitive-behavioral therapy as the core of treatment. People with histrionic personality disorder need help in thinking more systematically, reducing emotional reactivity, improving reality testing, increasing self-reliance and self-esteem, promoting appropriate expression of feeling, and increasing their awareness of the impact of their behavior on others. Thus Millon and colleagues (2004) recommend that therapy be systematic and goal-directed, providing an external structure that will help these clients establish their own sense of identity.

Sperry (2003) notes that therapists need to set professional boundaries and establish the limits of the relationship early in treatment with these clients because of their tendency to be "dramatic, impulsive, seductive, and manipulative, with potential for suicidal gestures" (p. 141). Treatment failure can easily occur with these clients if the therapist mishandles the erotic transference. The use of counterprojection techniques to remind the client that the therapist is not a transference figure of childhood seems helpful, according to Sperry.

Beck and colleagues (2004) found that people with histrionic personality disorder respond well to cognitive therapy, although modifications have to be made to that treatment approach. A sound therapeutic relationship, meaningful goals, and clear limits have to be established before these clients feel comfortable engaging in cognitive exploration, which is typically antithetical to their usual style. According to Beck and colleagues, therapists who take an active role and make extensive use of collaborative and guided discovery are particularly likely to be successful. One way to encourage cooperation is to combine structured tools, such as the Dysfunctional Thoughts Record, with more creative activities. Once the therapeutic process is well under way, clients should be encouraged to challenge such basic assumptions as thinking that they are inadequate or must depend on others to survive (Beck et al., 2004). Training clients in assertiveness and problem solving, increasing clients' awareness of others' feelings, and promoting clients' self-awareness have all been helpful and have contributed to reducing clients' impulsivity (Millon et al., 2004). Helping them find new, safer means of stimulation can also be helpful.

Accompanying disorders also should receive attention. Unless depression, anxiety, or somatic symptoms are relieved, these clients may not be able or willing to modify their pervasive dysfunctional patterns.

Group therapy can be very useful in treating people with histrionic personality disorder (Sperry, 2003). That therapeutic experience can provide helpful feedback, enable people to see that their behavior is not getting them the approval and affection they seek, and provide them with an opportunity to try new ways of establishing both casual and close relationships. Group therapy can dilute transference reactions and offer feedback while still providing attention and support to these clients, but they should be carefully screened for group participation to ensure that they do not monopolize the group.

Couples therapy and family therapy often are indicated because defenses of repression and denial can be more effectively treated in those contexts. People with histrionic personality disorder usually have partners with emotional difficulties; obsessive-compulsive patterns are especially common in the partners of women with these disorders (Sperry, 2003). Family therapy can ameliorate the emotional difficulties of both client and partner and can improve their communication and stabilize their relationship.

Medication is sometimes needed for treatment of the symptoms of people with histrionic personality disorder, especially antidepressants for depressive symptoms, including monoamine oxidase inhibitors (MAOIs) to reduce rejection sensitivity, demanding behavior, and somatic complaints in these clients. Naltrexone (ReVia) may also be helpful for those with self-harming behavior (Sperry, 2003). If medication is recommended, considerable caution should be exercised because these clients are prone to suicidal threats and gestures.

Prognosis

Histrionic personality disorder is one of the milder personality disorders. People with this disorder are likely to benefit from therapy if they can be persuaded to remain in treatment (but persuading them to do so is often a considerable challenge). Unlike most people with paranoid, schizoid, schizotypal, or antisocial personality disorders, people with histrionic personality disorder are motivated to make some changes, and their interpersonal skills are good enough to allow them to engage in therapy. Treatment that combines group with individual therapy can be particularly effective. Medications can be a useful adjunct to therapy.

NARCISSISTIC PERSONALITY DISORDER

Description of the Disorder

Narcissistic personality disorder, according to *DSM-IV-TR*, is characterized by "a pervasive pattern of grandiosity (in fantasy or behavior), need for admiration, and lack of empathy, beginning by early adulthood and present in a variety of contexts'' (American Psychiatric Association, 2000, p. 714). The disorder is characterized by the following features:

- Strong negative reactions to criticism
- Exploitation of others to accomplish one's own goals
- An exaggerated sense of self-importance
- A sense of entitlement
- Constant seeking of attention and praise
- Little appreciation for the feelings of others
- Enviousness, as well as the belief that one inspires envy in others
- Persistent fantasies of high achievement and special endowments, both personally and professionally
- The belief that one can be understood only by special people
- Arrogance and devaluing of others and their accomplishments
- Shallowness and unstable moods

Extensive use of rationalization, denial, and projection are common in people with this disorder (Kernberg, 2000). Most people with narcissistic personality disorder resist looking at their feelings of inferiority and tend to view the cause of their distress as external, failing to see how their own actions and behavior patterns may have contributed. Despite their veneer of superiority, many people with narcissistic personality disorder feel vulnerable and may react even to minor criticisms with depression, violence, or rage. Research shows a link between narcissism and hostile aggression and bullying behavior. Beck and others (2004) report that violent offenders score high on narcissism. People with narcissistic personality disorder believe they must always appear powerful, in control, and superior to others, concealing their real selves from others lest their fraudulence and failure be discovered. They are frequently troubled by an underlying sense of emptiness.

Narcissistic personality disorder is probably more common among men than among women. This disorder is found in less than 1 percent of the general population and in 2 to 16 percent of clinical populations, although the prevalence of narcissistic traits is increasing in the general population (Sperry, 2003). Millon and colleagues (2004) report that narcissism is less prevalent in a collectivist society.

Narcissistic personality disorder is often accompanied by other disorders, including mood disorders, especially hypomania and dysthymic disorder; anorexia nervosa; and substance-related disorders (Beck et al., 2004; Millon et al., 2004). Beck cautions that clinicians should assess for the presence of a delusional disorder, such as erotomanic and grandiose types of that disorder, and also assess to see if the client has decompensated into paranoid delusions as a result of a severe narcissistic injury.

Typical Client Characteristics

Millon and colleagues (2004) note that there are two pathways to the development of narcissistic personality disorder: parental neglect and parental overvaluation in childhood. In the case of neglect, narcissism develops as an attempt to overcompensate for feelings of low self-worth. Lack of empathy and feelings of entitlement often result, and fantasy frequently serves as a substitute for reality. When parents overvalue a child without the child having to work for approval, as frequently occurs with only children, an inflated sense of self-worth develops. As a result, people with narcissistic personality disorder internalize the message that they are superior and deserve special treatment, but also that they will be rejected if they cease to be so exceptional. Shame and humiliation often result when the person with narcissistic personality disorder is confronted with reality.

People with narcissistic personality disorder tend to have a stunted capacity for intimacy, are often shallow and focused on superficial traits, and seek to control and manipulate others. Millon and associates (2004) identify four types of people with narcissistic personality disorder: amorous, elite, compensatory, and unprincipled. Those of the amorous type seek to fulfill their own desires at the expense of others and tend to leave behind a string of sexual conquests as they move from one relationship to the next. They also exhibit scrupulous attention to their own physical appearance and seek out partners who will complement this physical image of themselves. Those of the elite type are self-assured, arrogant, and energetic, and they fear being perceived as an average person. They are adept at self-promotion and may be found moving up the ranks of the military, the medical or legal field, or another profession. These people tend to flaunt their status and accomplishments. The person with compensatory narcissistic personality disorder has developed a mask of superiority to compensate for underlying feelings of inferiority. Sensitive to every slight from others, this person may retreat into fantasy if reality destroys the fragile illusion. The unprincipled type is indifferent to the needs of others, to the point of malicious acting out. This type blends the worst of narcissistic personality disorder with traits of antisocial personality disorder. This person's life is filled with problems in employment and relationships and with the legal system.

People with narcissistic personality disorder may become contentious, arrogant, and demanding if they do not receive the treatment they believe they deserve. Thus their interpersonal relationships typically are impaired. Their quest for the perfect partner to affirm their own perfection can also be extremely damaging to their relationships and can lead to problems later in relationships, when these clients become competitive with their ''perfect'' partners. A dissatisfied partner is often the motivation for these clients to seek treatment.

Some people with narcissistic personality disorder manifest occupational impairment. Fear of rejection or humiliation can inhibit their occupational success, as can their poor interpersonal skills, their intolerance of others' successes, and their disregard of rules or the requests of their supervisors. Some, however, driven by their self-absorption and their fantasies of unlimited success, have an impressive occupational history. Their tendency to be self-reliant and to take control of their own lives contributes to their sense of direction.

People with narcissistic personality disorder tend to deteriorate with age; their loss of youthful vitality and good looks may be extremely painful for them. Nevertheless, as Kernberg (2000) observes, the aging process may weaken their grandiose facade and lead them to be more receptive to therapy.

Preferred Therapist Characteristics

People with narcissistic personality disorder typically are quite resistant to treatment. They typically are intolerant of vulnerability or weakness and fear being viewed as inferior (Beck et al., 2004); therefore, they have difficulty acknowledging that they have any problems or believing that anyone else can help them or understand how uniquely special they are. As in the treatment of most of the other personality disorders, the therapist working with a client who has narcissistic personality disorder needs to communicate acceptance, warmth, genuineness, and understanding in order to engage the client in treatment; any hint of criticism may provoke premature termination.

The therapist should not underestimate the fragility of people with narcissistic personality disorder. These clients may appear powerful, but they must be handled gently. Loss of their defenses can precipitate transient psychotic symptoms and regression.

Although the therapist should not be judgmental, indifference can be as painful to these people as rejection. Therapists might well engage in some cautious sharing of positive reactions to the client, as well as in extensive use of empathy.

People with this disorder tend to be very conscious of authority and are fearful of losing self-determination. These qualities can be used to the therapist's advantage. The therapeutic relationship should be a professional one, with clients accepted as experts on their own concerns and the therapist as the expert on psychotherapy. This collaborative relationship can facilitate clients' acceptance of help and their engagement in a working alliance. Kernberg (2000) emphasizes the importance of giving these clients full credit for any positive changes, to prevent their sabotaging the therapy in order to avoid admitting that another person has helped them.

People with narcissistic personality disorder tend to be concerned with perfection and to seek it in themselves and their relationships. They frequently alternate between idealizing and devaluing others, including the therapist. The development of an idealizing transference, in which the therapist is viewed as an extension of the client or an admiring mirror, is not unusual and will need to be dealt with lest the client subsequently become disillusioned with the therapist's lack of perfection, and leave therapy (Masterson & Lieberman, 2004).

The therapist should avoid being either seduced by the client's flattery or discouraged by the client's deprecating remarks. Instead, the therapist needs to view these transference reactions as therapeutic material and make use of them. With patience, persistence, and the establishment of clear and appropriate limits, the therapist can sometimes succeed in establishing a positive therapeutic relationship with people with narcissistic personality disorder (Beck et al., 2004; Kernberg, 2000).

Intervention Strategies

The literature is lacking in controlled outcome studies on treatment of narcissistic personality disorder (Crits-Christoph & Barber, 2002). As with most of the other personality disorders, however, inferences can be drawn about the types of treatment that are most likely to be successful.

Kernberg (2000), Kohut (1971), and others have used a modified psychoanalytic approach with some success to help people with narcissistic personality disorder develop a more accurate sense of reality and make positive personality changes. Kernberg has focused on such basic issues as anger, envy, self-sufficiency, and demands on the self and others, both in reality and in transference. Kohut has used the transference relationship to explore the client's early development as well as the client's wish for a perfect relationship and an ideal self. In an empathic context, both Kernberg and Kohut have explored defenses as well as needs and frustrations.

A psychodynamic approach seems to have a fair chance of succeeding with people who have narcissistic personality disorder and mild dysfunction and who are motivated to engage in therapy. However, this approach probably is not indicated for those who have significant disturbances of affect or impulse control; these clients seem to respond better to expressive, cognitive, and supportive forms of therapy than they do to analytic approaches (Kernberg, 2000).

Cognitive-behavioral approaches have also shown some success with people with narcissistic personality disorder. Beck and colleagues (2004) recommend that treatment begin with the building of a collaborative relationship, an effort to help clients understand how therapy can help them, and the establishment of goals. A focus on behavioral change typically would be the next phase in this kind of treatment. Behavioral interventions that do not require much self-disclosure or discussion of weaknesses are usually more acceptable to these clients than cognitive interventions. Behavior therapy can alleviate depression and other affective symptoms while beginning to modify the personality disorder; cognitive interventions can subsequently be used to reduce grandiosity and hypersensitivity and increase empathy. Beck suggests using the structured Personality Belief Questionnaire to assess the existence and degree of narcissistic beliefs. The Diagnostic Interview for Narcissism, developed by Gunderson, Ronningstam, and Bodkin (1990), can also be effective.

Building on cognitive-behavioral therapy, Young and colleagues (2003) have developed a detailed treatment model to help people with this disorder recognize, understand, and change early maladaptive schemas. The primary focus of treatment is on the client's intimate relationships and the therapeutic relationship. Through experiential work, cognitive and educational strategies, and the modification of behavioral patterns, clients learn to change core schemas related to entitlement, emotional deprivation, and defectiveness.

Significant change in people with narcissistic personality disorder will usually require long-term treatment, but it is difficult to engage people with this disorder in lengthy, intensive treatment because of their limited insight and their extensive rationalization. Therefore, some therapists advocate a model of brief therapy that sets limited goals and focuses on symptoms and current crises rather than on the underlying disorder itself. Treatment that focuses on rapport, cognitive reorientation, reality testing, improvement in communication skills, rehearsal of new behaviors, and application of those behaviors outside the therapeutic setting seems most likely to be effective. Clients with narcissistic personality disorder often have difficulty with loss and failure and may be particularly amenable to therapy focusing on those issues.

Group therapy, consisting exclusively of people diagnosed with narcissistic personality disorder, can be useful to these clients if they are able to tolerate the exposure and negative feedback of the group experience and do not become disruptive (Sperry, 2003). Group therapy can help these clients develop a more realistic sense of themselves, deal with others in less abrasive ways, and stabilize their functioning, but it should always be combined with individual therapy for these clients.

People with narcissistic personality disorder often come into treatment at the urging of an unhappy partner. In such a case, couples therapy may help the partners understand their roles and patterns of interacting and learn more effective ways of communicating with each other. Schema therapy for couples, for example, helps partners understand each other's and their own core needs and schemas, reparent each other, and develop effective communication and coping skills (Young et al., 2003). Related psychoeducation and skills training are then specifically geared to the needs of people with narcissistic personality patterns.

No medication has been found that really modifies narcissistic personality disorder, but medication can treat the symptoms of this disorder in addition to any underlying disorders. SSRIs, for example, have been shown to decrease vulnerability to criticism, impulsivity, and anger in people with narcissistic personality disorders (Sperry, 2003).

Prognosis

People with narcissistic personality disorder are difficult to treat. Sperry (2003) notes that successful treatment may involve more than one hundred individual sessions. A combination of group and individual or individual and couples therapy can reduce the number of sessions necessary. Nevertheless, despite the challenges presented by these clients, Beck and colleagues (2004), Kohut (1971), Kernberg (2000), Sperry (2003), and others all report some success. Kernberg, for example, reports a favorable prognosis unless clients have strong features of borderline or antisocial personality disorders. Sperry suggests better prognosis for treatment of those who are higher functioning.

AVOIDANT PERSONALITY DISORDER

Description of the Disorder

DSM-IV-TR describes avoidant personality disorder as characterized by "a pervasive pattern of social inhibition, feelings of inadequacy, and hypersensitivity to negative evaluation that begins by early adulthood and is present in a variety of contexts" (American Psychiatric Association, 2000, p. 718). Typical manifestations of this disorder include emotional fragility, reluctance to become involved in interpersonal contact without guarantees of acceptance, fear of being embarrassed by doing something inappropriate or foolish in public, and avoidance of new and challenging activities that might lead to humiliation. People with this disorder typically view themselves as having poor interpersonal skills and as being inferior and unattractive to others.

Unlike people with schizoid personality disorder, those with avoidant personality disorder generally long for companionship and involvement in social activities, but their great anxiety and shyness inhibit their socialization. These people tend to have low self-esteem, to be self-effacing, and to berate themselves for their refusal to take risks in social situations. They fantasize about having a different lifestyle and anguish over their inability to change. Without assistance, however, they typically remain alienated, introverted, mistrustful, and guarded in social situations and avoid them whenever possible. Their need for control and self-protection outweighs their need for companionship.

Males and females are affected by this disorder in approximately equal numbers. About 0.5 to 1 percent of the general population can be diagnosed with avoidant personality disorder, as can about 10 percent of people seen in clinical settings. Millon et al. (2004) have found avoidant personality disorder to be one of the more prevalent personality disorders, representing over 10 percent of those with personality disorders.

Millon notes that "avoidants avoid" unpleasant affect (Millon et al., 2004, p. 205) and are unlikely to disclose the full spectrum of their symptoms. Sperry (2003) has found that people with this disorder have a low tolerance for dysphoria. Thus when people with this disorder are seen in treatment, another disorder, frequently one involving anxiety and depression, is usually the initial focus. Anxiety disorders, particularly social phobia, seem closely related to avoidant personality disorder, and therapists need to conduct a careful assessment to determine which of these is present. Dissociative disorder, somatoform disorders, and schizophrenia have also been reported in combination with avoidant personality disorder (Millon et al., 2004), as have dependent, borderline, paranoid, schizoid, and schizotypal personality disorders.

Typical Client Characteristics

People with avoidant personality disorder typically come from families that did afford some appropriate nurturing and bonding, but these families were also controlling and critical and very concerned with their children's presenting a positive social image (Sperry, 2003). This combination led these clients to value and desire relationships as children but simultaneously to fear and avoid them, believing that others would inevitably reject them. Even as children, people with avoidant personality disorder were temperamentally shy, had limited social experiences and poor peer relationships, and may have experienced parental rejection. As a result, they had little opportunity to develop social competence and instead restricted their social interactions and became introspective (Sperry, 2003). A preoccupied-fearful attachment style is typically found in people with avoidant personality disorder.

By definition, people with avoidant personality disorder have considerable social impairment, which is typically accompanied by occupational impairment. People with this disorder often have jobs well below their abilities, usually because their fear of risk, rejection, and embarrassment prevents them from seeking promotions, taking an active part in meetings, attending business-related social events, and calling attention to their accomplishments. Sperry (2003) notes that this pattern alone can be diagnostic of avoidant personality disorder.

Females with avoidant personality disorder often have a strongly traditional gender identification. They tend to be passive, insecure, and dependent, and look to others to direct their lives. Although they may have underlying anger about the situation in which they find themselves, they are afraid of the consequences of change.

The life of a person with avoidant personality disorder is unsatisfying and disappointing, even if the person does manage to achieve a comfortable occupational situation. Some people with this disorder marry or develop a few close relationships. Typically, however, their friends tend to be distant, shy, and unstable, providing little help to these clients. Although this disorder tends to improve somewhat with age, the avoidant patterns rarely remit significantly without help. Sperry (2003) notes that people with avoidant personality disorder are prone to decompensate.

Preferred Therapist Characteristics

People with avoidant personality disorder rarely seek treatment specifically for the symptoms of this disorder because that process in itself feels threatening and potentially embarrassing. If they do enter treatment, they often have one foot out the door, testing whether the therapist can be trusted, and may leave at any hint of criticism, disapproval, or embarrassment.

These people typically are seen in treatment as a result of another disorder (such as agoraphobia or depression), often at the urging of a family member or an employer. Therapists should proceed gradually in light of the apprehension that people with avoidant personality disorder have about treatment and given the fragile equilibrium they have established. Therapists should communicate concern, availability, empathy, acceptance, support, and protection. Building trust may be slow but is integral to the establishment of an effective therapeutic relationship with these clients. Focusing on their strengths, at least initially, can build self-confidence and contribute to the establishment of rapport. Contracting for a specific number of sessions may increase people's commitment to treatment and prevent them from using therapy to avoid confronting real situations.

Over time, therapists can help clients work at increasing tolerance of negative emotions. Structured social skills training may help guide them in social interactions. Paradoxical intention can also be effective in helping reduce rejection sensitivity (Sperry, 2003). A single woman, for example, who is afraid of being rejected by a man may agree to phone several men and ask them out for coffee. Rejection then becomes part of the goal and reduces the woman's sensitivity.

One advantage that therapists have in working with these clients is that they are in pain, are not happy with themselves, and want to change. They most likely will appreciate the safe environment that the therapist provides. Moreover, these clients generally know how to relate to a select few individuals and have a capacity for introspection. If they can be convinced that therapy can help them and is unlikely to embarrass them, they may have the motivation they need to benefit from treatment and may welcome the opportunity to discuss their concerns.

However, clients with avoidant personality disorder may hesitate to reveal thoughts or experiences that they believe the therapist might criticize or judge, and they may be unwilling to provide direct feedback to the therapist, leaving them at risk for terminating treatment prematurely. Beck and colleagues (2004) suggest that therapists use a feedback form at the end of each session to encourage clients to provide honest assessment of the session. Such forms can help address dissatisfaction, provide a positive model for assertive communication, and help clients give appropriate feedback. Role playing and guided imagery can also help. Therapists may feel frustrated with the apprehensions and slow progress of these clients. Therapists and clients alike will benefit from focusing on progress, no matter how slight. In addition, signs of avoidance can be viewed positively as providing information on impaired behavior and dysfunctional thoughts.

Sperry (2003) has observed two common types of countertransference in therapists working with people who have avoidant personality disorder: overprotectiveness and unrealistic expectations for rapid change. Pacing is important in the treatment of these clients, and therapists should be sure that they are nudging clients forward but not forcing premature confrontation of frightening situations. A gradual shift from general support to selective reinforcement of assertive behavior and positive self-statements can promote progress.

Intervention Strategies

Little empirical research is available to guide treatment of avoidant personality disorder, but guidelines can be drawn from case studies and from research on social phobia. Beck and colleagues (2004) recommend a treatment approach consisting of the following four stages:

1. Building trust and a positive therapeutic relationship and bringing clients to the point where they are willing to discuss their fear of rejection
2. Promoting self-awareness and observational skills so that clients become aware of their self-destructive thoughts and behaviors
3. Using the therapeutic relationship as a "laboratory" (p. 318) to test beliefs and role-play behaviors that clients can implement in the real world
4. Incorporating mood management techniques to help clients tolerate dysphoria and anxiety

Behavioral interventions are essential to successful treatment of avoidant personality disorder. Behavior therapy can begin with fairly safe relaxation exercises and then progress to such techniques as training in assertiveness and social skills, modeling, various kinds of role playing and psychodrama, anxiety management, and graduated exposure or desensitization (using a hierarchy of feared situations). Between-session assignments can accelerate behavioral change as long as they do not cause feelings of failure and humiliation. Comparative research on different kinds of behavioral treatments suggests that treatment designed to fit the specific interpersonal problems of the individual is most likely to prove beneficial. For example, clients with problems related to anger and distrust benefited most from graded exposure exercises that required them to approach and talk to other people. Clients with difficulty saying no benefited from both graded exposure and social skills training (Crits-Christoph & Barber, 2002). As with all personality disorders, assessment of individual needs prior to treatment planning is crucial to achieving positive results.

Beck and colleagues (2004) suggest incorporating a focus on cognitions after some behavioral change has been made. Changes in clients' emotions can be used as opportunities to elicit automatic thoughts. Using standard cognitive-behavioral strategies, such as testing automatic thoughts and assumptions, can help these clients become aware of and change negative self-talk and help them overcome cognitive and emotional avoidance. Using prediction logs to point out any discrepancies between expectations and reality, positive-experience logs, and lists of evidence for and against automatic thoughts (such as "If people really knew me, they would reject me," p. 318) can promote changes in self-critical cognitions.

Because people with avoidant personality disorder tend to avoid negative emotions and thoughts, interventions should include psychoeducation on the processes of exposure and desensitization, and encouragement for clients to tolerate and become more comfortable with negative feelings. The addition of psychodynamic therapy to the treatment plan can promote further gains and help people address issues related to their harsh superegos, underlying shame, and projection of unrealistic self-expectations onto others (Millon et al., 2004). Interpretations should be made with caution, however, because these clients' poor self-concepts and hypersensitivity make them easily hurt by their therapists. Beck and colleagues (2004) suggest that patients rate their discomfort with feedback from their therapists on a scale of 0 to 100 to ensure that the level is perceived as tolerable.

Schema-focused cognitive therapy has also proven effective in working with people with avoidant personality disorder. One study found positive outcomes at the end of treatment that were sustained at one-year follow-up (Crits-Christoph & Barber, 2002). As mentioned earlier, schema therapy incorporates cognitive, experiential, and behavioral interventions, as well as the use of the therapeutic relationship itself, to help clients identify and change maladaptive schemas. Schemas frequently associated with avoidant personality disorder include defectiveness, self-sacrifice, social isolation, and approval seeking. Through the use of imagery exercises, empathic confrontation, homework assignments, and limited reparenting, schema therapy helps people change (Beck et al., 2004; Young, 1999).

As people with avoidant personality disorder improve, group therapy can be an important addition to treatment. It can help clients learn and practice new social skills in a safe context, receive feedback and encouragement, and increase their comfort with others. One limited study of seventeen people in a group behavioral treatment program found that systematic desensitization, behavioral rehearsal, and self-image work conducted in a four-day intensive group setting yielded positive changes that were sustained at one-year follow-up (Crits-Christoph & Barber, 2002). Gains were made primarily in reducing the participants' fear of negative evaluation. Nevertheless, people with avoidant personality disorder should not be placed in group therapy prematurely. Inappropriate placement in a therapy group can be very threatening and can lead these clients to terminate treatment abruptly.

Family therapy can be useful too, if clients are actively involved with family members. The families of people with avoidant personality disorder typically either try to be helpful by protecting these clients or try to effect change by insisting on the clients' greater involvement with others. Beck and colleagues (2004) note that combining couples therapy with social skills training can help decrease social anxiety and encourage people who tend to "hide in the margins of relationships" (p. 320) to break out of patterns that perpetuate avoidant behavior and, instead, to improve and increase their social interactions. These people also often have partner relationships that are characterized by interpersonal distance, and family therapy can modify that pattern, facilitating the establishment of interactions that are more rewarding to both partners.

Medication usually is not needed in the treatment of avoidant personality disorder, and people with this disorder seem uncomfortable with the idea of taking medication (probably because they fear loss of control). These clients also benefit from taking credit for positive changes rather than attributing them to medication. Nevertheless, sometimes medications that have been helpful in the treatment of people with social phobia — such as the SSRIs paroxetine (Paxil) and sertraline (Zoloft), as well as benzodiazepines — can also reduce anxiety, shyness, and sensitivity to rejection in people with avoidant personality disorder.

According to Beck and colleagues (2004), relapse prevention is an important element of treatment for these clients because their avoidant behavior often returns after therapy. Helping clients predict difficulties that may arise after termination and developing a plan to help them cope effectively with those difficulties can be an important part of the termination process. Relapse prevention can include infrequent but ongoing follow-up sessions and may include the agreement that the client will continue using assertive behaviors and pursuing new friendships and challenging tasks. Clients should be instructed to pay continuing attention to situations they are avoiding and to the thoughts underlying such behavior so that they can effectively use what they have learned through therapy after they have completed their treatment.

Prognosis

As with most of the other personality disorders, prognosis for avoidant personality disorder is not very positive and depends on the setting of realistic goals and on clients' finding interpersonal and occupational environments that meet their needs. Most people with avoidant personality disorder can make meaningful changes as long as they are willing to invest in therapy, but they probably will always tend to have self-doubts, as well as some discomfort in new interpersonal situations.

DEPENDENT PERSONALITY DISORDER

Description of the Disorder

Dependent personality disorder, according to *DSM-IV-TR*, is characterized by "a pervasive and excessive need to be taken care of that leads to submissive and clinging behavior and fears of separation" (American Psychiatric Association, 2000, p. 721). People with this disorder typically have great difficulty making decisions independently and without reassurance. They look to others to make major decisions for them, and they avoid disagreeing with others lest they be rejected. They feel uncomfortable, frightened, and helpless when they are alone and when they are required to take initiative. They go out of their way to be helpful in order to be liked, are hypersensitive to criticism and disapproval, fear abandonment, and, if a close relationship ends, feel devastated and driven to quickly find another relationship that provides care and nurturance.

People with dependent personality disorder have very low self-esteem, low self-confidence, and a high need for reassurance. They believe that they have little to offer and so must assume a secondary, even subservient, position with respect to others in order to be accepted. They tend to be inordinately tolerant of destructive relationships and unreasonable requests. They typically are other-directed, and their gratifications and disappointments hinge on the reactions they receive from others. At the same time, they are egocentric in that they are pleasing others to gain appreciation. They tend to think in dichotomous ways, believe in absolutes, and catastrophize (Millon et al., 2004; Sperry, 2003).

According to Millon and associates (2004), dependent personality disorder is the most commonly diagnosed personality disorder, found in approximately

14 percent of those with personality disorders and at least 2.5 percent of the general population (Sperry, 2003). People with dependent personality disorder are frequently seen in treatment. This disorder seems to be more commonly diagnosed among females than among males, but this apparent pattern has raised the question of whether some women who embrace traditional female roles are being discriminated against by being inappropriately diagnosed as having dependent personality disorder. Gender, age, and cultural factors should be taken into account before this diagnosis is made.

The seeds of dependent personality disorder are often seen in an early history of separation anxiety disorder or chronic illness. People with dependent personality disorder also have a predisposition to depression. The two disorders share similar traits, such as hopelessness, helplessness, lack of initiative, and difficulty making decisions (Beck et al., 2004). Other disorders, such as anxiety disorders, somatoform disorders, substance use disorders, eating disorders, and other personality disorders, are also frequently diagnosed along with dependent personality disorder (Beck et al., 2004; Millon et al., 2004; Sperry, 2003). Symptoms are especially likely to emerge or worsen after a loss or an anticipated abandonment.

Typical Client Characteristics

Not surprisingly, many people with dependent personality disorder report a history of having been overprotected. As infants, they were characterized as low in energy, sad, and withdrawn (Sperry, 2003). They typically were pampered as children and were expected to behave perfectly and to maintain strong family ties and loyalties; autonomy was discouraged (Millon et al., 2004). Research shows that the families of these children ranked low on expressiveness and ranked high on need to control. Sperry (2003) found that as children, people with dependent personality disorder were filled with self-doubt, avoided competitive activities, and had peer relationships that left them feeling awkward, unattractive, and incompetent.

People with dependent personality disorder tend to have a small number of significant others on whom they are dependent and who seem to accept their passive and submissive attitudes. Sperry (2003) notes that they cling to those significant others even if they are not happy with the relationships, because they prefer unsatisfying relationships to being alone.

People with this disorder may function satisfactorily in occupations that are consistent with their need to be told what to do and to receive approval. They have difficulty with tasks that require independent action and decisions, however, and may appear fragile, indecisive, placating, and more immature and less competent than others. These traits reinforce these people's sense of inadequacy and weakness, leading them to perpetuate the pattern by turning to those around them for help and support (Millon et al., 2004).

Even when these people's lives seem to be going well, they experience little happiness and seem to have a pervasive underlying pessimistic and dysphoric mood. They typically appear rigid, judgmental, and moralistic, especially under stress. In crisis, despondency increases and suicidal ideation may surface.

Preferred Therapist Characteristics

People with dependent personality disorder may seek therapy voluntarily after an experienced or threatened loss of a relationship (particularly through bereavement or divorce), or they may seek therapy at the suggestion of a partner, another relative, or an employer. These clients also may ask for help with secondary symptoms, such as depression and substance use (Millon et al., 2004). They typically are apprehensive about therapy but want help in averting any threatened loss. Nevertheless, they are unlikely to have much initial interest in becoming more assertive and independent. They tend to be passive clients, waiting for their therapists to ask them questions or give direction to the sessions. They tend to view the therapist as someone else on whom to depend — a magic helper — and probably will work hard to please the therapist rather than themselves.

The challenge for the therapist is to use these dynamics constructively. The client's wish to please may be used to develop rapport and encourage increased independence. Changes made only to please the therapist are not likely to persist outside the sessions, however, and do not reflect internal change.

In working with a person who has a dependent personality disorder, the therapist should probably begin in a directive and structured way, to give focus to the sessions. In order to establish rapport, the therapist will also need to communicate a great deal of support, acceptance, and empathy and should guard against appearing critical. Some initial dependence on the part of the client should be allowed as part of the rapport-building process. With the development of a therapeutic alliance, however, the therapist should gradually assume less responsibility and encourage the client to take more control of the sessions. The therapist should continue to convey empathy, appreciation, and optimism, but should also ask clients to make a commitment to working on their own concerns. The therapist should not give the client feedback on dependence needs, however, or offer interpretations of the transference until less threatening approaches have effected some improvement. The overall goal of treatment will be to promote the client's self-reliance, self-expression, and autonomy in a safe context and then facilitate the transfer of those experiences to settings outside the therapy room. Termination is likely to be particularly difficult, and the therapist will need to be cautious lest the client feel abandoned. Beck and colleagues (2004) recommend tapering off sessions whenever possible and offering continuing booster sessions as a way of easing into termination.

More than any other client, those with dependent personality disorder tend to develop a romantic attachment to the therapist (Beck et al., 2004). The therapist should set clear limits on the relationship with the client, avoid any physical contact, and explain that such romantic feelings are not unusual in therapeutic relationships but that this relationship will remain a professional one.

Strong countertransference reactions to these clients are common (Beck et al., 2004; Livesley, 2003; Sperry, 2003). The therapist may find this type of client frustrating and annoying or may want to protect the client from mistreatment. The therapist needs to manage these feelings and be sure that these feelings do not damage the therapeutic relationship.

Intervention Strategies

Both long-term and short-term psychodynamic approaches have demonstrated effectiveness with people who have dependent personality disorder (Sperry, 2003). Psychodynamic approaches involve allowing the emergence of a dependent transference that is then dealt with in growth-promoting ways. In addition, encouragement and support are used to promote autonomy and improved communication and problem solving. These interventions can help improve clients' self-esteem, increase their sense of autonomy and individuation, teach them to manage their own lives and to ask for help and support without being manipulative, and relieve their fears of harming others or being devastated by rejection. Short-term psychodynamic approaches typically involve weekly therapy for three to five months. These approaches are most likely to succeed when the client presents a clear and circumscribed focal conflict or issue, can rapidly form a therapeutic alliance, and is unlikely to act out or regress (Sperry, 2003). A psychodynamic approach requires both commitment to therapy and introspection and will not be right for everyone with a dependent personality disorder; for example, it would not be indicated for people with considerable separation anxiety and low ego strength.

Cognitive-behavioral therapy has also been used effectively to ameliorate some of the symptoms of dependent personality disorder (Beck et al., 2004; Sperry, 2003). The treatment is similar to that recommended for avoidant personality disorder. It usually includes relaxation and desensitization to help the client handle challenging interpersonal situations, and provides training in assertiveness and communication skills to help the client identify and express feelings and wants in more functional ways. Standard behavioral techniques, such as modeling, reinforcement, and rehearsal, can all contribute to the client's improvement. Homework assignments should be practiced in sessions initially, to reduce the fear of failure. Properly handled, between-session tasks are likely to be completed because these clients typically follow directions and want to please.

Cognitive therapy is generally used to treat dependent personality disorder only after a therapeutic relationship has been formed and some gains have been made through supportive and behavioral interventions. Cognitive therapy can challenge those dichotomous and dysfunctional beliefs that limit clients' autonomy and impair their self-esteem. It can be empowering and reinforcing for clients to gather evidence of their competence and learn to use coping and problem-solving skills. As clients gain experience in these and other skills (such as self-monitoring, accurate self-evaluation, and reinforcement), they can assume greater responsibility for their sessions.

Practical issues like housing and employment sometimes require attention because many people with dependent personality disorder seek therapy after the end of a marriage or long relationship. Helping them successfully reestablish themselves can promote positive behavioral changes, and the tasks involved in their getting reestablished can serve as vehicles for applying what they have learned in therapy.

Family and group therapy are often indicated for these clients. Those treatment settings can afford them the opportunity to try out new ways of expressing themselves and relating to others while receiving support and encouragement along the way. Family therapy may be difficult if the client has a resistant partner, but the family's collaboration can both facilitate progress and improve familial relationships. Therapeutic groups need to be chosen carefully for these clients so as not to overwhelm and threaten them or expose them to undue pressure to leave a harmful relationship. At the same time, shifting a client from individual to group treatment can reduce transference and facilitate termination.

Schema therapy, as mentioned earlier, can help people develop new core cognitions. Those with dependent personality disorder can learn to overcome their approval-seeking dependent pattern, as well as some of their self-doubts.

People with dependent personality disorder sometimes request medication. These clients also sometimes misuse drugs, and the belief that they need medication can detract from their growing sense of competence. Although some medications can reduce dysregulated behavior, depression, and anxiety, Sperry (2003) notes that a similar effect can be achieved through social skills training. He suggests that the building of social skills target five specific areas: cognition, emotional containment and regulation, perceptions, physiology (through meditation and relaxation), and behavior (through assertiveness and communication skills).

Prognosis

Treatment of this disorder has a relatively good prognosis. People with dependent personality disorder are trusting. They can form relationships and make commitments. They want to please, and they can ask for help. All these attributes lead to a somewhat better prognosis and a shorter and more rewarding course of therapy than is found in treating most of the other personality disorders (Sperry, 2003).

OBSESSIVE-COMPULSIVE PERSONALITY DISORDER

Description of the Disorder

Perfectionism and inflexibility characterize obsessive-compulsive personality disorder (OCPD). The following manifestations are typical of this pervasive pattern (American Psychiatric Association, 2000):

- Impaired performance on tasks and activities because of preoccupation with details, rules, order, duties, and perfection
- A strong need to control others
- Avoidance of delegating tasks for fear that they will not be done correctly
- Overinvolvement in work, accompanied by minimal attention to leisure and social activities
- Indecisiveness
- Rigid moral and ethical beliefs
- Restricted expression of emotion
- Reluctance to give to others without the promise of personal gain
- Harsh self-criticism
- Difficulty discarding objects that no longer have value

Although people with OCPD seem indifferent to the feelings of others, they are very sensitive to slights themselves and often overreact to real or imagined insults. These clients tend to be well defended, typically using rules to insulate themselves from their emotions and requiring others to conform to their rules as well. In fact, these clients may become so overly involved with rules that they become rigid and perfectionistic, although they can be quite accomplished and conscientious (Millon et al., 2004).

This disorder differs from obsessive-compulsive disorder (OCD), an anxiety disorder, in that OCPD is a pervasive and ego-syntonic lifestyle, whereas OCD is typically uncomfortable and characterized by specific obsessions and compulsions. Although most people with OCPD do not experience specific unwanted and intrusive obsessions or compulsions, research has found that as many as 44 percent of those with OCD also meet the criteria for OCPD (Beck et al., 2004).

OCPD is approximately twice as common among males as females (American Psychiatric Association, 2000). This disorder is present in approximately

1 percent of the general population and in 3 to 10 percent of people seen at mental health centers.

Anxiety and depression are frequent accompaniments of OCPD (Millon et al., 2004). In people with this disorder, depression often follows a perceived loss or failure and is particularly common in later life (Beck et al., 2004). People with this disorder often seek treatment for psychosomatic disorders or sexual dysfunctions, rather than for obsessive-compulsive behaviors.

Typical Client Characteristics

People diagnosed with OCPD typically experienced strict and punitive parenting that was designed to ensure that they did not cause trouble (Sperry, 2003). The home environments of people with this disorder have usually been rigid, emphasizing control (Beck et al., 2004). Not surprisingly, parents' punitive and authoritarian behavior may be a reflection of their own OCPD. OCPD is more common among first-degree relatives of those with the same disorder than it is in the general population.

People with this disorder almost inevitably have interpersonal and social difficulties. A spouse may insist on couples therapy to help resolve lack of emotional availability, workaholic behavior, and lack of time spent with the family (Beck et al., 2004). People with OCPD tend to be cold, mistrustful, demanding, and uninteresting, and to put little time or effort into building relationships and communicating feelings. They are typically angry and competitive toward others, have difficulty expressing emotions or affection, and are most comfortable in the intellectual realm. Their lives tend to be joyless and focused on work and obligations.

Their occupational development may or may not be impaired, and they typically have greater occupational success than people with other personality disorders because they are tireless and dedicated workers (Millon et al., 2004). Nevertheless, people with OCPD have difficulty delegating, collaborating, and supervising. They tend to be self-righteous and domineering, and they usually have poor relationships with coworkers, whom they tend to view as incompetent and irresponsible. People with OCPD also tend to have difficulty bringing projects to closure because of their indecisiveness, attention to minutia, and perfectionism, and this pattern may cause them to miss deadlines and have work-related difficulties.

Preferred Therapist Characteristics

People with OCPD tend to be difficult clients. They have trouble giving up control and accepting help from others, and they have little facility with insight and self-expression. They often focus on external events and physical rather than psychological complaints in treatment. New situations make them anxious, and they are likely to become even more obstinate and resistant in therapy than they usually are (Millon et al., 2004). If they can become engaged in conversation, they tend to complain bitterly about others' incompetence and how unappreciated they feel. Their interest is in changing others rather than in changing themselves, and they may attack therapists who suggest that they need to make changes. They also may feel competitive with their therapists and may have an investment in sabotaging therapy or proving their therapists incompetent.

Establishing rapport can be difficult with clients who have OCPD, due to their rigidity, discomfort with emotion, and denial of the importance of relationships. Beck notes that therapy with a person with OCPD is likely to be businesslike and problem-focused, with little discussion of emotions. Countertransference issues can revolve around the need for control, and therapists should be aware of their own compulsive traits so that they do not interfere with therapy or result in a power struggle with the client (Beck et al., 2004).

Involving people with this disorder in a productive therapeutic relationship clearly presents a considerable challenge. These clients are respectful of authority, however, as well as persevering, and they usually comply with rules and directions (although they may feel inwardly defiant). Therapists may initially be able to use the authority of their education and position to elicit a short-term commitment to therapy from these clients.

Therapists should be sure not to engage in power struggles and arguments with these clients. Other ways for therapists to earn the admiration of these people and enable them to accept help are to treat them in a respectful and professional way; to refrain from violating their defenses and their need for privacy; to collaborate with them on therapeutic decisions; and to be prompt, organized, and efficient. Too much attention to emotion can be upsetting to these clients, but acceptance, support, and empathy can help convince them that their therapists are not their enemies.

Intervention Strategies

Little clear research exists on effective treatment of OCPD, although some recent studies support the use of cognitive and behavioral interventions with this disorder (Beck et al., 2004). Although long-term psychodynamic or modified psychoanalytic therapy may be ideal for people with this disorder, it is difficult to involve them in therapy that is extended, intensive, and introspective. Emotion is equated with being out of control; thus most people with OCPD will intellectualize, somaticize, or deny affect (Millon et al., 2004). Therefore, more present- and action-oriented approaches, consistent with these clients' limited insight and intolerance of yielding control, will often be used to help these clients establish more realistic expectations for themselves and others.

Cognitive-behavioral therapy is likely to be well received by people with OCPD because that approach is structured, problem-centered, and present-oriented, requiring only limited analysis and expression of emotions. Behavior therapy can be useful in reducing some of the dysfunctional actions of these clients. It can also increase their ability to plan and make decisions, their involvement in leisure and social activities, and their facility in communicating their feelings and reactions positively and assertively. Having a mutually agreed-on list of prioritized goals can keep these clients working productively and can minimize complaining and oppositional tactics. Modeling humor and spontaneity in controlled ways can teach these clients new ways of behaving. Because of their increased anxiety and psychosomatic symptoms, relaxation techniques for stress management can also contribute to the improvement of OCPD, as can thought stopping, social skills training, desensitization, and response prevention.

Beck and colleagues (2004) report success in using a modified version of cognitive therapy with these clients. In this approach, behavioral experiments rather than direct disputation were used to change such characteristic automatic thoughts as "I must avoid mistakes to be worthwhile" (p. 339). Inventories like the weekly activity schedule and the Dysfunctional Thought Record increased structure and, correspondingly, clients' cooperation.

People with OCPD typically are apprehensive about participating in group and family therapy because of their reluctance to disclose their feelings to others and their fear of humiliation. If their commitment to individual therapy can be sustained long enough for them to make some positive changes, however, they may later be able to make productive use of group or family therapy. Those approaches can offer them feedback, as well as the opportunity to learn and experiment with new interpersonal behaviors and to improve relationships. Nevertheless, therapists should be sure that these clients do not monopolize group or family sessions and are ready to listen to others.

Millon and colleagues (2004) note that people with OCPD tend to marry people who have dependent or histrionic personalities — people whose neediness meshes nicely with the need to control on the part of the person with OCPD. Couples therapy can help improve these relationships, resolve sexual issues, and establish rules for handling trouble spots.

Medication generally is not necessary for treatment of people with OCPD, but some medications have demonstrated effectiveness in treating obsessive-compulsive disorder and may be beneficial in the treatment of OCPD as well (Sperry, 2003). The 5-HT antidepressants — fluoxetine (Prozac), sertraline (Zoloft), paroxetine (Paxil), citalopram (Celexa), and escitalopram (Lexapro) — seem to work directly on the brain's 5-HT neurons to reduce symptoms of OCD (Preston, O'Neil, & Talaga, 2005). Medication is also indicated for relief of severe anxiety and depression accompanying OCPD.

Relapse prevention can be helpful to people with OCPD, just as it can be to people with most of the other personality disorders. Beck and colleagues

(2004) suggest teaching people to monitor their own progress and scheduling periodic booster sessions.

Prognosis

Without treatment, OCPD usually is relatively stable over time, neither improving nor worsening. Many case studies report improvement, if not major personality changes, through therapy. As is the case with most of the other personality disorders, a small number of these clients probably make major changes as a result of therapy. A larger number make some important behavioral and attitudinal changes, and another large number either leave therapy prematurely or remain resistant to help. Overall, then, the prognosis is probably only fair for treatment of OCPD.

PERSONALITY DISORDERS NOT OTHERWISE SPECIFIED

DSM-IV-TR includes an NOS (not otherwise specified) category at the end of its section on personality disorders. This category is used by clinicians when the manifestations of a personality disorder are mixed and straddle more than one disorder, not fully meeting the criteria for a specific disorder, or when the clinician determines that a personality disorder included in the *DSM*'s Appendix B (Criteria Sets and Axes Provided for Further Study) is appropriate.

As with other personality disorders, the criteria specify that these disorders must be pervasive and cause significant difficulties in relationships, behavior, and educational or work settings. Johnson and others (2005) discovered that adolescents diagnosed with personality disorder NOS were just as likely to have difficulties in these areas of life and to have co-occurring Axis I disorders as adolescents diagnosed with Cluster A, B, or C personality disorders.

Appendix B also includes two personality disorders under consideration for inclusion in future editions of the *DSM:* passive-aggressive (negativistic) personality disorder and depressive personality disorder. The main feature of passive-aggressive personality disorder is "a pervasive pattern of negativistic attitudes and passive resistance to demands for adequate performance in social and occupational situations" (American Psychiatric Association, 2000, p. 789). Depressive personality disorder is a "pervasive pattern of depressive cognitions and behaviors that begins by early adulthood" (p. 788) and includes worried, negative, and unhappy thoughts; low self-esteem; self-criticism; and feelings of unworthiness that permeate the person's cognitions and become a way of life. The disorder is not better accounted for by a major depressive episode or dysthymic disorder.

Treatment recommendations for the other types of personality disorders provide the basis for determining the treatment of personality disorder NOS, especially when a mixed type includes features of more than one personality disorder. Treatment should be adapted to meet the needs of the particular client.

TREATMENT RECOMMENDATIONS: CLIENT MAP

Recommendations on treating personality disorders are summarized here, according to the framework of the Client Map.

Client Map

Diagnosis

Personality disorders (paranoid, schizoid, schizotypal, antisocial, borderline, histrionic, narcissistic, avoidant, dependent, and obsessive-compulsive)

Objectives of Treatment

Short- to medium-term objectives: improve social and occupational functioning, communication skills, self-esteem, empathy, and coping mechanisms; develop appropriate sense of responsibility; reduce any accompanying depression or anxiety

Long-term objectives: modify underlying dysfunctional personality patterns

Assessments

Broad-based personality inventory (for example, the Millon Clinical Multiaxial Inventory)

Measures of specific symptoms (for example, substance use, depression, anxiety)

Clinician Characteristics

Consistent

Able to set limits

Able to communicate acceptance and empathy in the face of resistance, hostility, or dependence

Good ability to manage transference and countertransference reactions

Patient and comfortable with slow progress

Location

Usually outpatient setting

Emergency and inpatient settings, as necessary, to deal with suicidal ideation or regression

Interventions to Be Used

Psychodynamic (to modify dysfunctional personality)

Behavioral and cognitive (to effect change in coping skills and relationships and to address presenting problems)

Schema-focused therapy

Dialectical behavior therapy for borderline personality disorder as well as some of the other personality disorders

Emphasis of Treatment

Strong emphasis on establishing a therapeutic relationship

Fairly strong emphasis on structure and directiveness

Simultaneous emphasis on fostering client's responsibility

Emphasis balanced between supportive and exploratory elements

Attention to both past and present concerns

Numbers

Individual therapy usually primary, combined later with family or couples therapy

Group therapy often very useful in combination with individual therapy after client is able to tolerate group without becoming frightened or destructive

Timing

Usually long-term, but with development of short-term goals to discourage premature termination

Gradual but steady pace

More than one session per week possible, especially when client is in crisis

Long-term follow-up to address possibility of relapse

Medications Needed

Not effective in modifying basic personality disorder

May sometimes help alleviate depression, anxiety, or psychotic symptoms

Should be used with caution in light of client's tendency to misuse substances or attempt suicide

Adjunct Services

Possibly self-help groups, such as Alcoholics Anonymous, Narcotics Anonymous, social groups

Career counseling

Assertiveness training

Prognosis

Usually fair, but variable

Can be good for short-term behavioral changes

Fair for underlying personality changes

Client Map of Emily L.

This chapter opened with a description of Emily L., a twenty-five-year-old woman who was seen for therapy after a suicide attempt. Emily's background included emotional and physical abuse and loss of both biological parents. She presented a long history of depression, maladaptive substance use, and instability in relationships and employment. Emily was a challenging client because of her multiple symptoms, her previous unsuccessful treatments, her suicidal behavior, her limited sense of self, and her lack of support systems. She initially idealized her therapists, made excessive demands on them, and then left treatment when they failed to meet her demands. Her principal diagnosis was borderline personality disorder. The following Client Map presents recommendations for treating Emily.

Diagnosis

Axis I: 296.33 Major depressive disorder, recurrent, severe

300.4 Dysthymic disorder, severe

305.00 Alcohol abuse, moderate

312.39 Trichotillomania, moderate

Axis II: 301.83 Borderline personality disorder (principal diagnosis)

Axis III: 278.0 Obesity

Axis IV: Marital conflict and abuse; history of childhood sexual, emotional, and physical abuse

Axis V: Global assessment of functioning (GAF scale): current GAF = 25

Objectives of Treatment

Reduction of depression and suicidal ideation

Improvement of coping skills (stress management, verbal self-expression, assertiveness)

Abstinence from alcohol

Reduction of hair pulling

Improved support systems and safety

Establishment of rewarding and realistic goals and direction

Increased stability and sense of competence

Improved and expanded relationships

Modification of self-destructive personality patterns and behaviors, especially suicidal ideation

Working through history of abuse

Assessments

Millon Clinical Multiaxial Inventory

Michigan Alcoholism Screening Test

Beck Depression Inventory

Medical examination

Clinician Characteristics

Stable

Structured

Accepting and supportive

Able to set and maintain clear limits

Able to manage transference and countertransference reactions

Location of Treatment

Outpatient setting

Inpatient and day treatment settings as needed

Interventions to Be Used

Supportive and behavioral therapy at first (to build a therapeutic relationship and enable client to see that therapy could be useful)

Contracts specifying alternative coping behaviors (to prevent suicidal behavior and reduce alcohol consumption)

Development of a safety plan (to protect client from abuse by her husband)

Rewarding activities and between-session tasks (to promote motivation, begin to build feelings of competence, and reduce depression)

Later integration of cognitive and psychodynamic approaches (to help client deal with past losses and profound feelings of hopelessness, emptiness, and worthlessness)

Emphasis of Treatment

Supportive and structured emphasis (but promoting client's responsibility)

Initial emphasis on the present and on behavior

Later emphasis on past issues and underlying dysfunction and dynamics

Numbers

Primarily individual therapy at first

Subsequent marital therapy (to help client and her husband improve their relationship and eliminate abuse)

Group therapy (after amelioration of client's immediate difficulties, and with client's growing ability to participate effectively and benefit from feedback, support, and opportunities for socialization and practice of interpersonal skills)

Timing

Long-term (if client willing)

Steady pace, with communication of clear expectations

Medications Needed

Antidepressant medication probably useful, but with careful monitoring in light of client's suicidal ideation

Adjunct Services

Alcoholics Anonymous

Nutritional counseling

Exercise and weight-control programs

Education about alcohol use, stress management, assertiveness, and job seeking

Prognosis

Fair at best, in light of client's history of treatment failures

Recommended Reading

Beck, A. T., Freeman, A., Davis, D. D., & Associates. (2004). *Cognitive therapy of personality disorders* (2nd ed.). New York: Guilford Press.

Kernberg, O. (2000). *Borderline conditions and pathological narcissism.* New York: Jason Aronson, Inc.

Linehan, M. (1993). *Cognitive-behavioral treatment of borderline personality disorders.* New York: Guilford Press.

Millon, T., Grossman, S., Millon, C., Meagher, S., & Ramnath, R. (2004). *Personality disorders in modern life* (2nd ed.). Hoboken, NJ: Wiley.

Sperry, L. (2003). *Handbook of diagnosis and treatment of DSM-IV-TR personality disorders* (2nd ed.). Philadelphia: Brunner-Routledge.

Young, J. E., Klosko, J. S., & Weishaar, M. (2003). *Schema therapy: A practitioner's guide.* New York: Guilford Press.

CHAPTER NINE

Disorders Involving Impairment in Awareness of Reality: Psychotic and Dissociative Disorders

Victor J., a twenty-two-year-old college senior, was brought to the psychologist in the college counseling center by his roommate, Arnold, who expressed great concern about Victor's thoughts and behaviors. Several months earlier, Victor had spent the winter break in New York City with Arnold and his divorced mother, Vanessa. During that time, Vanessa, a well-known writer of romance novels, had gone out of her way to entertain Victor. She took Victor and Arnold out to dinner and to the theater, introduced them to her friends, and took them shopping.

Upon returning to college, Victor told Arnold that Vanessa and he were in love and would marry in the spring, after graduation. He began writing impassioned letters to Vanessa, calling her frequently, and spending most of his free time reading her novels.

At first Vanessa was amused; she teased Victor about his interest in "an older woman." The teasing only prompted more passionate and graphic letters, however. Vanessa tried repeatedly to let Victor know that she was not romantically interested in him, but even when she returned his letters unopened, he continued his avowals of love. He told Arnold that his mother was concealing her real feelings because she did not want to upset her son.

The week before Victor was brought for counseling, he had borrowed money and traveled to New York, where he went to Vanessa's office. When she told him she was busy and did not want to see him, he refused to leave for several hours and reappeared at her office for the next few days. Vanessa believed that Victor had taken some notes from her desk and had rummaged through her files and her wastebasket.

Victor had dated little in college and generally seemed uncomfortable around women his own age. He had grown up in a lower-middle-class family. His father owned an automobile repair business and had been opposed to Victor's attending college. He expected Victor to join him in the business after graduation. Although Victor's grades had declined somewhat, he was passing all his courses and was due to graduate in two months. Interviews with Victor indicated that he was experiencing delusional disorder, erotomanic type, a mental disorder that involves loss of contact with reality.

OVERVIEW OF PSYCHOTIC AND DISSOCIATIVE DISORDERS

Description of the Disorders

This chapter considers a diverse array of disorders that are characterized by impairment in awareness of reality. They include schizophrenia and other psychotic disorders, as well as dissociative disorders. These disorders differ considerably in terms of origin, duration, treatment, and prognosis. What connects them is similarity in their symptoms: these disorders typically involve a distortion or impairment in memory, awareness of reality, or both. Most significantly impact people's lives, usually producing marked dysfunction in at least one area. People with these disorders are often unable to present a clear picture of their symptoms. Therefore, these disorders can challenge the diagnostician and are sometimes misdiagnosed as cognitive, mood, or substance-induced disorders. Misdiagnosis is unfortunate, of course, because it can lead to inappropriate treatment.

Psychotic Disorders. *DSM-IV-TR* (American Psychiatric Association, 2000) lists the following six psychotic disorders:

1. Schizophrenia
2. Brief psychotic disorder
3. Schizophreniform disorder
4. Delusional disorder
5. Schizoaffective disorder
6. Shared psychotic disorder

Each of the psychotic disorders is considered a separate entity in the *DSM*. However, a growing body of research indicates that these disorders share a similar genetic basis and transmission process and are part of a spectrum of disorders.

More than two-thirds of people hospitalized for a psychotic disorder experienced at least one trauma prior to the event. Half were exposed to life-threatening traumas; almost one-third had been the victims of childhood trauma. As discussed in the section on PTSD (Chapter Five), cumulative trauma can damage personality structures and basic capacities to feel, trust, and relate to others.

Schizophrenia, delusional disorder, and schizoaffective disorder are considered in detail in later sections of this chapter. Brief psychotic disorder and schizophreniform disorder are described and discussed together. Shared psychotic disorder, which involves one or more people adopting the psychotic beliefs of another person, is not discussed here because it is rarely presented in clinical settings and because the dominant member of the dyad or group usually meets the criteria for a diagnosis of schizophrenia.

Dissociative Disorders. The dissociative disorders present a very different picture from that of the psychotic disorders, although they too involve symptoms related to awareness of reality, memory, consciousness, perceptions, and personality integration. In the past twenty years, the study of dissociation has flourished, partially as a result of research connecting dissociation and traumatic life events. Cardena describes dissociation as a process of compartmentalization and alteration of consciousness. Examples of compartmentalization include amnesia and the development of discrete identities as occurs in dissociative identity disorder. In alterations of consciousness, the person or the environment is experienced as unreal or detached, as in the case of depersonalization. Various psychological functions can be dissociated, including emotions, physical sensations, memory, identity, and the sense of self or the environment (Cardena & Weiner, 2004).

Not all dissociative experiences are pathological. Examples of benign episodes of dissociation are the hypnotic states or momentary lapses in awareness that may occur, for example, when people are driving familiar routes. Dissociative episodes are maladaptive only when they become chronic, recurrent, and uncontrollable and when they are severe enough to cause distress or impairment in functioning.

Dissociative disorders are believed to be uncommon, although they do seem to be increasing, perhaps in relation to traumatic, conflicted, or highly stressful life experiences, which also seem to be on the rise. Or perhaps the development of valid and reliable assessment tools and the increasing acceptance of the relationship between trauma and acute and chronic dissociative symptoms have resulted in improved diagnosis of these disorders.

Some dissociative disorders begin and end suddenly, although recurrent episodes are common. They tend to make their initial appearance in childhood or adolescence. Between 80 and 90 percent of abused infants show a type of attachment behavior that resembles dissociation and that is predictive of later development of dissociation (Thomas, 2003). In fact, the majority of people who develop dissociative identity disorder have experienced incest, rape, or physical abuse during childhood.

DSM-IV-TR defines four types of dissociative disorders, in addition to dissociative disorder not otherwise specified:

1. Dissociative identity disorder
2. Dissociative fugue
3. Dissociative amnesia
4. Depersonalization disorder

Dissociative fugue and dissociative amnesia involve a person's temporarily forgetting important components of his or her life, to a more extensive or more extreme degree than would be due to ordinary forgetfulness. By definition, neither disorder is caused by substances or by a general medical condition. Both tend to occur suddenly at times of trauma or unusual stress, are typically of brief duration, and usually remit without recurrence. Both disorders are rare but increase during such circumstances as natural disasters, accidents, or warfare.

Typical Client Characteristics

Just as the disorders in this chapter vary considerably, so do the people who present them. The premorbid functioning of people with psychotic and dissociative disorders varies widely. Some have poor prior adjustment; others previously manifested positive social skills and sound coping mechanisms.

Disturbed family relationships are especially common, and a direct relationship has been found between disordered attachment between parent and child and the later development of dissociative disorders (Cardena & Weiner, 2004). The disorders discussed in this chapter also differ in terms of their development. Some people experience gradual deterioration, whereas others suffer a rapid alteration in consciousness or loss of contact with reality in response to an immediate stressor.

People with dissociative or psychotic disorders typically are aware that something is wrong but may not understand what is happening, may conceal their symptoms for fear of being harmed or hospitalized, and may not be receptive to help that is offered. While their symptoms are present, their social and occupational adjustment is almost invariably affected, although the degree of disturbance ranges from mild and circumscribed to severe and pervasive, according to the particular disorder and its manifestation.

Assessment

Diagnosis of any disorder reflected by impaired memory should involve neurological, medical, and psychiatric evaluations. Because many general medical conditions, as well as substance use, can cause memory impairment, those causes should be ruled out before a diagnosis of a dissociative disorder is made. Clouded consciousness and disorientation, particularly in a person past middle age, suggest that a cognitive disorder or a medical condition rather than a dissociative disorder may be present.

Dissociative identity disorder is described separately in a later section of this chapter, but dissociative fugue, dissociative amnesia, and depersonalization disorder are discussed together.

Preferred Therapist Characteristics

With the exception of dissociative identity disorder and depersonalization disorder, treatment of these disorders generally requires medical as well as psychological intervention. Nevertheless, psychologists, counselors, and other nonmedical mental health professionals often collaborate with physicians and social service professionals to treat clients with all the disorders described in this chapter.

Therapists will need to employ a variety of approaches, often including long-term intensive psychodynamic psychotherapy, hypnotherapy, and cognitive-behavioral therapy. They will need to be comfortable dealing with people who typically do not present a clear and coherent picture of their symptoms or history and who may be reluctant clients. They also need to be able to deal with chronic mental disorders, as well as those that respond rapidly to treatment.

Concern for the client's safety should be the overriding concern of therapists working with people exhibiting dissociative or psychotic symptoms. Thomas (2003) reports that the first stage of treatment for clients who have been injured by their caregivers is the development of a sense of safety, along with reassurance that therapists will not use their position of power to do harm. Creation of a therapeutic alliance will revolve around the client's need for safety. Interventions addressing traumatic memories are generally saved for later in treatment when the client is better able to tolerate intense emotions. Sensitivity, previous clinical experience with people who have been abused, and an ability to proceed at the client's pace rather than exerting their own influence are all necessary attributes of therapists who work with survivors of trauma and abuse, who represent many of the people who experience dissociative disorders.

Intervention Strategies

The nature of the treatment indicated for the disorders discussed in this chapter varies greatly with respect to duration and approach to treatment. Specifics are provided in the sections on the individual disorders.

Prognosis

Prognosis for these disorders is uncertain but bears some relationship to duration. Those disorders that are of shorter duration, such as brief psychotic disorder and dissociative amnesia, typically respond well to relatively brief treatment. Those of longer duration, especially those of insidious onset, such as schizophrenia and dissociative identity disorder, have a less favorable prognosis and usually require long-term treatment.

PSYCHOTIC DISORDERS

Schizophrenia

Description of the Disorder

Schizophrenia is by definition a relatively long-standing and pervasive disorder. *DSM-IV-TR* lists the following symptoms as characteristic of this disorder:

- Bizarre delusions (disturbances in thoughts and logic)
- Hallucinations, usually auditory and commanding or threatening (disturbances in sensory experiences)
- Disorganized speech and behavior
- Flat or very inappropriate affect
- Markedly impaired social and occupational functioning
- A confused sense of self
- Limited insight
- Dependence conflicts
- Loose associations
- Concrete thinking
- Physical awkwardness
- Psychomotor disturbances (for example, catatonic symptoms)
- Dysphoric mood

Schizophrenia typically involves a prodromal (initial) phase, when functioning declines and symptoms begin; an active phase, when so-called positive symptoms such as delusions, hallucinations, and incoherence typically are present; and a residual phase, in which severe symptoms have abated but signs of the disorder are still evident. These signs include such symptoms as flattened affect, restricted thought and speech patterns, and lack of goals or motivation, which have been referred to as the negative symptoms of psychosis. To warrant a diagnosis of schizophrenia, the course of the disorder must be at least six months in duration, including at least one month of the positive symptoms (unless it can be assumed that those symptoms would have persisted for that length of time had treatment not been provided).

DSM-IV-TR describes three major types of schizophrenia. The paranoid type seems to be the most common type in the United States. It typically is characterized by systematized delusions and hallucinations that are related to a theme of grandiosity and persecution. Anger, suspiciousness, and hostility are usually also present (Pratt & Mueser, 2002). Schizophrenia, paranoid type, tends to involve less evidence of incoherence, disorganization, catatonia, and inappropriate affect, as well as a later onset and a better prognosis, than the other types of schizophrenia. The disorganized type, formerly known as the hebephrenic type, is associated with poor previous functioning, an early and insidious onset, extreme impairment, confusion and disorganization in speech and behavior, and flat or inappropriate affect. The catatonic type is uncommon in the United States. It is characterized by some form of catatonia (stupor, rigidity, excitement, or posturing) and by negativity and repetitive imitation of others' words and gestures.

Undifferentiated and residual types of schizophrenia also are included in *DSM-IV-TR*. The undifferentiated type includes a mix of the positive symptoms of schizophrenia but does not meet the criteria for any one of the three types just described. The residual type either follows a full-blown episode of schizophrenia and reflects only the negative symptoms of the disorder or is a circumscribed presentation of at least two positive symptoms.

Schizophrenia usually begins in early adulthood and starts three to four years earlier in males than in females (Evans et al., 2005). Initial episodes of this disorder are unlikely to occur after the age of fifty or before adolescence. Schizophrenia has a prevalence of approximately 1 percent (Pratt & Mueser, 2002). Incidence of this disorder is approximately equal in both genders and across cultures and religions (Jablensky, 1999), but women with schizophrenia tend to have less severe forms of the disorder and a better prognosis than do men.

Early (prodromal) symptoms may include magical thinking, illusions, social withdrawal, mood disorders, lack of motivation, cognitive deficits (lack of concentration), and obsessive behaviors (Pratt & Mueser, 2002). These symptoms may be present for years before overt symptoms of psychosis develop. In fact, Evans et al. (2005) report the average duration of psychotic symptoms before diagnosis and treatment is one year, and three years if earlier, prodromal symptoms are added. Even so, most people will recover from this first episode.

Symptoms of psychosis are delineated as either positive or negative based on comparison to their intensity of occurrence in the average person. Thus positive symptoms (such as delusions, and auditory and visual hallucinations) involve thoughts and perceptions beyond what most people experience, whereas negative symptoms (such as blunted affect, restricted speech, and lack of motivation) are less (of emotion, communication, and drive) than most people experience. In general, negative symptoms occur before positive ones and may linger after positive symptoms have been eliminated (Evans et al., 2005).

Research on the causes of schizophrenia has implicated heredity, environmental factors, and neurological dysfunction. Positron emission tomography (PET) has demonstrated differences between brains of people diagnosed with schizophrenia and those without the disorder. Abnormal dopamine activity has been documented in people with schizophrenia. A high incidence of eye-movement dysfunction and immunological abnormalities has also been noted in people with this disorder. People with schizophrenia are unusually likely to have experienced stressful events in the three weeks prior to onset of the disorder. This and the increase in dopamine activity have led to the stress-diathesis model for the disorder's onset, whereby biological (physical) and psychological (emotional) stress combine to activate a neurological predisposition toward the disorder.

Schizophrenia tends to run in families; first-degree relatives have a risk of developing schizophrenia that is twelve times greater than the general population (Evans et al., 2005). Despite the increased risk, nearly 60 percent of people with schizophrenia do not have a first-degree relative with the disorder, and fewer than 35 percent of the children born to parents diagnosed with schizophrenia eventually develop the disorder (Mjellem & Kringlen, 2001). Clearly, factors other than genetics are at play.

Research into the role of environmental factors found that people with this disorder are likely to come from lower socioeconomic groups and urban environments. They also are likely to have been born during the winter and early spring. The latter correlation may have to do with those months' increased risk of infectious diseases, exposure to which in utero contributes to the development of this disorder. Indeed, due to the way in which the brain develops in utero, several prenatal and perinatal risk factors have been linked to schizophrenia — poor maternal nutrition, smaller head circumference, delivery complications, low birth weight, pre-eclampsia, and maternal stress (Lewis & Levitt, 2002).

New research in molecular genetics indicates that rather than a single gene, many genes may work together to create susceptibility to the symptoms that make up schizophrenia. This may explain why some people develop a milder form, such as schizotypal personality disorder, whereas others develop schizophrenia. Genetics, of course, is not the entire story, as twin studies show the concordance rate for schizophrenia in identical twins to be only 50 percent. Therefore, environmental factors such as stress, prenatal distress, difficult births, and other environmental issues have a significant impact on the development of this disorder. Studies found that children with a family history of schizophrenia were at risk of developing not only schizophrenia but also the Cluster A personality disorders (schizotypal, schizoid, paranoid) as well as avoidant personality disorder (Tienari et al., 2003). These personality disorders sometimes precede the onset of schizophrenia (American Psychiatric Association, 2000). What causes one person to develop a personality disorder and another to develop schizophrenia is the subject of many ongoing studies.

Typical Client Characteristics

Prior adjustment often reflects precursors of the disorder. People with schizophrenia tend to have been socially awkward and isolated, passive, mildly eccentric, impulsive, uncomfortable with competition, and absorbed with fantasy. In adolescence, these symptoms may have led to social isolation, poor social skills, or to use of drugs and alcohol as a means to alleviate social anxiety and to develop a network of peers who were more accepting of such eccentricities (Laudet, Magura, Vogel, & Knight, 2004). Recent research shows that certain drugs (cannabis, amphetamines, and cocaine) may actually promote the onset of psychotic symptoms in vulnerable individuals. Especially when used early in life, cannabis use increases the risk of developing schizophrenic symptoms (Evans et al., 2005).

People with schizophrenia typically have co-occurring mental disorders, especially depression, PTSD, and substance use disorders. PTSD, which co-occurs in 29 to 43 percent of people who have schizophrenia, has been shown to exacerbate symptoms of the disorder, so detection and effective treatment of PTSD may help improve treatment outcomes for schizophrenia. The lifetime prevalence of substance use disorders in people with schizophrenia is also high — reported to be as high as 50 percent (Pratt & Mueser, 2002). Sensitivity to the psychoactive effects of substances tends to be higher in people with schizophrenia than in other people. Substance use is also higher in part because some substances, such as alcohol, apparently reduce psychotic, neurological, and affective symptoms of schizophrenia. Most people with schizophrenia smoke cigarettes, up to 50 percent meet the criteria for an alcohol use disorder, and the incidence of cannabis use also is high.

Such dual diagnosis has important clinical implications and is associated with relapse and increased hospitalizations. Other negative effects of the dual diagnosis of schizophrenia and substance use include depression, suicidal ideation, medication noncompliance, financial and legal problems, violence, victimization, increased risk of developing infectious diseases (for example,

HIV, hepatitis A and B), and homelessness and housing instability (Laudet et al., 2004; Pratt & Mueser, 2002).

An unstable employment history is common for people with a history of schizophrenia. Holding a job may be particularly challenging for people who often do not have the necessary skills to cope with day-to-day stress or social interactions. Especially for the 50 percent of people dually diagnosed with both schizophrenia and substance use problems, recovery may not necessarily result in the ability to live independently or to hold a job (Laudet et al., 2004).

Studies have shown that more than 55 percent of people with schizophrenia do not follow treatment recommendations or take medication as prescribed (Pratt & Mueser, 2002). Medication noncompliance is associated with elevated symptom levels, impairments in executive function, and increased rates of relapse and rehospitalization. Most people with schizophrenia also have significant medical illnesses.

Suicidal ideation is common in people diagnosed with schizophrenia; about half of all those with this disorder make suicide attempts, and, for at least 10 percent of that group, the attempts are completed. Depression, usually most severe immediately after a psychotic episode, has a strong association with suicide risk in people with schizophrenia (Pratt & Mueser, 2002).

In recent years, attention has turned to community fears about the possibility of violence among people with schizophrenia. Several recent empirical studies have looked at the connection between symptoms of psychosis and violence. The results have been mixed. Whereas some studies found that manic symptoms, delusions, paranoia, and impaired overall functioning are correlated with homicidal ideation and intent, eleven other studies found that delusions, especially those of a grandiose nature, can have an ameliorating effect on both violent behavior and suicidal ideation (Grunebaum et al., 2001).

Appelbaum, Robbins, and Monahan (2000) found that delusional motivation for violence is rare; violence is more likely to be associated with anger and impulsivity, rather than delusions. Indeed, Junginger, Parks-Levy, and McGuire (1998) found that only 17 percent of previously violent people acted violently as a result of a delusion. In general, people who have acted violently in the past are likely to be violent in the future.

Other researchers have found that people with schizophrenia run the greatest risk of violence when overall psychopathology increases (Schwartz, Petersen, Reynolds, & Austin, 2003). Repeated use of drugs over time, early symptoms of conduct disorder, persistent violent behavior, and antisocial personality disorder were all found to increase the risk of violence when these behaviors co-occur in people with schizophrenia (Nolan, Volavka, Mohr, & Czobor, 1999; Schwartz et al., 2003). Clearly, more research is needed on this important topic.

Schwartz and colleagues (2003) recommend that therapists working with men with schizophrenia assess clients' overall homicidal ideation and intent and carefully evaluate such symptoms as mania, substance use, and active psychotic symptoms. Impairment in reality testing, judgment, communication, and other areas of cognitive functioning may contribute to violent behavior. Some evidence indicates that violence may be associated with more severe neurological impairments, hostility, suspiciousness, substance abuse, and dysfunctions in self-care and interpersonal behavior.

Assessment

Flexibility and creativity are needed because these clients often will have difficulty reporting their symptoms and previous history in an accurate or clear manner. Evans and colleagues (2005) suggest that an initial assessment may include a combination of interviews with the client, a parent, and a trusted friend. Assessment of positive and negative symptoms, global assessment of functioning, and assessment for co-occurring disorders are important. Equally important is assessment of life domains that may be contributing to negative functioning, such as medication noncompliance, difficulties in occupational performance, and instability of housing, and family environment (Pratt & Mueser, 2002).

Due to the frequency with which substance misuse and PTSD co-occur in people with schizophrenia, Pratt and Mueser (2002) recommend assessing for both concerns and integrating the results into the treatment plan. Levels of anxiety and depression should also be monitored frequently throughout the course of treatment. Useful for this purpose are the Beck Depression Inventory (BDI; Beck, Steer, & Brown, 1996) and the Beck Anxiety Inventory (BAI; Beck & Steer, 1990); both are empirically validated and easy to administer, score, and interpret.

Preferred Therapist Characteristics

Recovery from any adversity involves a psychosocial process of developing hope, learning to manage adversity realistically, and moving on with one's life (Drake & Mueser, 2002). The instillation of hope is particularly important in the case of people with severe mental illness such as schizophrenia. The quality of these people's relationships with their physicians and therapists is an important determinant of treatment outcome. A therapeutic alliance based on compassionate care that reduces anxiety and enhances treatment compliance can be integral to recovery. Therapists working with people with schizophrenia should be available, consistent, patient, and straightforward. Warmth, reassurance, optimism, empathy, genuineness, stability, support, and acceptance on the part of the therapist are all important in forming a positive and trusting working relationship with people diagnosed as having schizophrenia, many of whom are suspicious, guarded, and withdrawn. Limits also need to be established for the protection of these clients and their therapists. Simply sitting with a distraught client, taking a walk, discussing neutral topics of interest (such as a movie), or providing practical assistance can promote a therapeutic alliance and offer support and comfort.

Kantor (2004) suggests that therapists working with people diagnosed with schizophrenia should help them regain contact with reality. At the same time, arguing with or interrogating these clients about their delusions or hallucinations is likely to be nonproductive and harmful to the therapeutic relationship. Part of a therapist's role can be to teach the person with schizophrenia to recognize delusions and hallucinations for what they are — tricks of the mind. This kind of perspective avoids the need to debate the veracity of clients' experiences and can increase understanding and appropriate discussion of the phenomena.

Therapists must find a balance between overwhelming and undersupporting these vulnerable clients. Too much closeness can lead to regression, but too much distance can result in alienation. Therapists should respect clients' privacy and need for distance and should individualize treatment, reducing interpretations and being flexible as the need arises.

Intervention Strategies

Treatment for schizophrenia usually entails a combination of medication and psychosocial interventions that target both the acute psychotic phase of the disorder and the debilitating residual symptoms. Hospitalization is often required, particularly during the active phase of the disorder. The average hospital stay for these clients has declined in length, largely due to pressure from managed care and insurance companies, and is now measured in days rather than weeks. This can pose problems for people with schizophrenia and their families, as many people are being released before they have become stabilized on their medications (Torrey, 2001).

Day treatment centers, partial hospitalization, and halfway houses can be helpful once recovery has begun and acute symptoms have subsided. These transitional settings can promote socialization, ease people's return to independent living, and, as necessary, provide long-term maintenance. Use of these treatment facilities is increasing as the length of hospital stays is decreasing.

Medication. Medication is almost always a component of treatment and is beneficial to most but not all who are diagnosed with schizophrenia. Neuroleptic drugs can effectively alleviate symptoms, particularly the positive symptoms of psychosis (delusions and hallucinations). Medication is less effective in treating the negative symptoms (blunted affect, depression, social withdrawal).

Large numbers of clinical trials (Bradford, Stroup, & Lieberman, 2002) have demonstrated the effectiveness of such atypical antipsychotics as risperidone (Risperdal), olanzapine (Zyprexa), and clozapine (Clozaril) in the treatment of schizophrenia. These newer medications have been found to be as effective as the older antipsychotic medications like chlorpromazine (Thorazine) and haloperidol (Haldol), to have a reduced side-effect profile, and to have a lower risk of causing extrapyramidal symptoms such as tardive dyskinesia. However, recent reports have linked several of the atypical antipsychotics to weight gain and increased risk of diabetes. Careful monitoring of blood glucose levels may prevent diabetes and reduce associated illnesses in people with increased risk (Mahgerefteh, Pierre, & Wirshing, 2006).

Medication is important as well in reducing the risk of relapse. Most people treated for schizophrenia need continued medication after their symptoms have been alleviated. Controlled clinical trials indicate that by one year after treatment, 30 percent of people with schizophrenia will have relapsed while on medication, whereas those who discontinue medication have relapse rates of 65 to 75 percent within one year (Bradford et al., 2002; Harkavy-Friedman, 2006).

Medication compliance is a particular problem for people with schizophrenia, and compliance rates have been reported to be as low as 50 percent. Rehospitalizations, increased suicidality, and premature death may result from medication noncompliance (Harkavy-Friedman, 2006). Medication compliance therapy, including discussion of medication side effects, can be an important part of treatment for people with severe mental illness (Wirshing & Buckley, 2003). Reasons why people with schizophrenia do not take their medication include negative attitudes toward medication, a desire to experience mania or grandiose delusions, apprehension about developing extrapyramidal symptoms such as tardive dyskinesia, and, for those who have paranoid schizophrenia, fear that others are trying to control them through their medication. Providing clients with education about their mental and physical health, discussing and encouraging medication compliance, and educating family members about strategies to help deal with noncompliance issues can help promote treatment compliance as well as provide support, socialization, and practical help (Pratt & Mueser, 2002; Wirshing & Buckley, 2003).

Psychosocial Interventions. The American Psychiatric Association's *Practice Guideline for the Treatment of Patients with Schizophrenia* (2004b) recommends combining psychosocial interventions with medication management for the treatment of schizophrenia. After the person with schizophrenia has become stabilized on medications, psychosocial interventions can begin. Treatments that incorporate behavioral and cognitive-behavioral therapy, social skills training, family education and participation, and substance use treatment (if indicated), and that encourage medication compliance as part of a multifaceted approach, have been found most effective in the treatment of schizophrenia (Bradford et al., 2002; Evans et al., 2005; Mahgerefteh et al., 2006; Pratt & Mueser, 2002).

Behavior therapy. Behavior therapy is the primary approach to psychotherapy for people with schizophrenia. This approach typically focuses on providing the information and skills necessary for people to reduce bizarre and destructive behavior and improve functioning. Development of practical life skills can also be beneficial in facilitating people's resocialization and their adjustment to living with their families or on their own after a period of hospitalization. Adjustment can be facilitated by training in useful occupational skills and by increased involvement in recreational activities. Behavior therapy can be provided via inpatient or outpatient treatment in individual or group formats. Hospitals and day treatment centers sometimes use behavioral models, such as milieu therapy or token economies, to reinforce desirable behaviors.

Skills training. Pratt and Mueser (2002) conducted a meta-analysis of skills training programs and found that the number of weeks of training was positively correlated with size of treatment effect. Skills training programs that take place at least twice a week for a minimum of six months have been found to be most effective in helping people diagnosed with schizophrenia. Although often conducted in groups, such training could also include an individual focus. The group provides a safe setting in which to identify and practice skills without fear of negative consequences.

UCLA's Clinical Research Center for Schizophrenia and Psychiatric Rehabilitation has created several skills training modules that have been empirically validated and have been used in several countries around the world. Module topics include the following:

- Symptom self-management
- Recreation and leisure activities
- Medication self-management
- Community reentry
- Job search
- Basic conversation skills
- Friendship and dating

The UCLA modules include didactic instruction, role plays, problem solving, homework, and in vivo behavioral rehearsal. The modules have proven effective in improving social and independent living skills in people with schizophrenia.

Cognitive-behavioral therapy. CBT has also received support in the treatment of schizophrenia, especially in helping clients challenge and modify delusional beliefs (Dickerson, 2000). In a review of the literature, Dickerson found that cognitive-behavioral therapy could be effective in helping decrease the client's convictions about delusions and the distress they caused. However, CBT was not found effective for reducing negative symptoms or improving social functioning. To date, no evidence has shown that CBT reduces relapse and hospital readmission rates over supportive psychotherapy alone (Evans et al., 2005).

Psychodynamic approaches. Psychodynamic psychotherapy has not received much support in the treatment of schizophrenia. In fact, the emotional intensity of that approach may even be harmful to some people with schizophrenia. For example, one study found that persons living alone who received such therapy actually had elevated relapse rates (Evans et al., 2005).

Family education and counseling. Education and counseling for the family are a particularly important component of treatment for schizophrenia. Family members are often confused and angered by the delusions and hallucinations of the person with schizophrenia and may benefit from understanding the nature of this disorder. In addition, what has been called high expressed emotion (high EE) in the families of people with schizophrenia can contribute to stress and possibly provoke a reemergence of acute symptoms. In recent years, however, researchers have started to look at whether high EE was the cause of symptom exacerbation or whether exacerbation of symptoms produces expressed emotions (King, 2000; Torrey, 2001). Regardless, family training that focuses on reducing critical comments, emotional overinvolvement, and hostility toward the person with schizophrenia has been shown to produce beneficial effects on the course of the disorder (Evans et al., 2005). Relapse rates for schizophrenia are lower when family members participate in family treatment; medication compliance increases; high EE is reduced; and family members learn communication skills, problem solving, and coping skills (Pitschel-Walz, Leucht, Bauml, Kissling, & Engel, 2001). Clearly, family support and education are important components of the effective treatment of this chronic disorder.

Integrated Dual Diagnosis Treatment. Because the co-occurrence of schizophrenia and substance use is so high, integrated treatments in which the same clinical team addresses both disorders simultaneously have become the prevalent therapeutic model for people who are dually diagnosed with these two disorders. Recent studies support the effectiveness of this approach (Drake & Mueser, 2002; Laudet et al., 2004). Successful interventions for dual diagnosis generally take a long-term perspective and involve intensive case management that focuses on substance use counseling, motivational interventions, social support, staged interventions, regular drug screens, and a family counseling component, as well as attention to other needs such as employment, housing, and physical health. Unlike twelve-step programs, most dual diagnosis programs follow a harm-reduction model that advocates a decrease in drug use rather than total abstinence (Mahgerefteh et al., 2006).

Integrated treatments generally take a cautious approach to prescription medication. This includes recognizing signs and symptoms of withdrawal and drug use, and avoiding medication with a high likelihood of addiction (for example, benzodiazepines), while ensuring that psychotic symptoms are adequately treated and drug and alcohol cravings and urges are discussed and addressed. Medication compliance should also be carefully monitored, as many people who are actively using substances discontinue medication to avoid drug interactions (Pratt & Mueser, 2002).

Group Therapy. Group therapy can be helpful in providing information, promoting appropriate use of medication, improving skills (such as communication, problem solving, and socialization), encouraging constructive activities, facilitating reality testing, and providing support and encouragement (Evans et al., 2005). Social skills training programs, vocational rehabilitation programs, and clubhouses can offer camaraderie as well as valuable resources to help people with dual diagnoses develop friendships and obtain employment and housing assistance.

Long-term Management and Relapse Prevention. Long-term management of this disorder requires vigilance with regard to symptom exacerbation, substance use, and relapse (Bradford et al., 2002). Depression, anxiety, and substance use often co-occur with schizophrenia and need to be addressed to reduce suicide risk, improve self-esteem, and increase functioning.

Stress (including trauma; exposure to hostile environments; and instability in family, housing, occupational, or other domains) can precipitate relapses and contribute to impairment in other life functions. Coping resources and the ability to obtain social support can minimize the effects of stress and decrease the need for acute care. Thus, interventions that target vulnerability, stress, and coping can improve the outcome in people with schizophrenia.

Continued case management that includes occupational therapy, supported employment, housing assistance, and assertive community treatment programs are an important part of rehabilitation efforts for people with schizophrenia. Community treatment programs reduce the time that people with schizophrenia spend in hospitals and bridge the gap between in-patient hospitalization and independent living (Mahgerefteh et al., 2006).

Extended contact with helping professionals, often via treatment programs for the chronically mentally ill, also contributes to long-term reduction in relapse rates (Roth & Fonagy, 2005). The Family-to-Family education program, developed by the National Alliance for the Mentally Ill (NAMI), involves a highly structured twelve-week program that increases education and knowledge about the disorder, improves coping strategies, empowers families to take an active role, and reduces stress and family anxiety (Evans et al., 2005). NAMI can be useful to families of people with schizophrenia and other severe mental illnesses (www.nami.org).

Prognosis

A return to full and healthy functioning after an episode of schizophrenia is unusual. Approximately 50 percent of people hospitalized with this disorder are hospitalized again within two years of an initial episode. Although the acute symptoms may be controlled with medication, people are frequently left with psychotic depression, which involves feeling apathetic, socially uncomfortable, depressed, and uneasy in handling emotions. Unfortunately, those who relapse within five years have a 78 percent chance of a second relapse. The risk of personality deterioration increases greatly after the second relapse and worsens with each successive episode, as does the risk of another relapse. The prognosis is particularly poor if the disorder begins with a gradual deterioration that has extended over many years, if the person is dually diagnosed with a drug or alcohol problem in addition to schizophrenia, or if the person with schizophrenia has extensive exposure to a high EE family.

The following factors are some of those associated with a more positive prognosis for the treatment of schizophrenia (and for schizophreniform disorder, discussed later):

- *Premorbid factors:* positive premorbid functioning, especially in social areas; positive work history; intelligence that is average or higher; good neurocognitive functioning; being married or having a stable partner relationship
- *Factors related to characteristics of the disorder:* abrupt onset, particularly when there is an identifiable precipitant; midlife onset; symptoms of confusion and perplexity; depression; absence of flattened affect, psychotic assaultiveness, or schizoid personality disorder
- *Family and environmental factors:* absence of a family history of schizophrenia; family history of depression and mania; positive and supportive environment to which client will return; family involvement in therapy

A positive prognosis also is associated with early, continual intervention; compliance with recommended medication and aftercare; lack of substance use; an adequate financial and living situation; and having social and recreational activities (Kopelowicz, Liberman, & Zarate, 2002).

In addition to relapses and residual symptoms, people with schizophrenia often must cope with extrapyramidal symptoms that are the severe and sometimes permanent side effects of neuroleptic antipsychotic medication. Tardive dyskinesia, for example, resulting from long-term use of antipsychotic medications, is primarily characterized by involuntary smacking and sucking movements of the lips and tongue. This gives people an unusual appearance and can interfere with their social and occupational adjustment.

Brief Psychotic Disorder and Schizophreniform Disorder

Description of the Disorders

Brief Psychotic Disorder. Brief psychotic disorder may resemble schizophrenia, as well as delusional disorder (discussed later). According to *DSM-IV-TR*, the essential feature of brief psychotic disorder is "the sudden onset of at least one of the following positive psychotic symptoms: delusions, hallucinations, disorganized speech . . . , or grossly disorganized or catatonic behavior" (American Psychiatric Association, 2000, p. 329). This disorder lasts at least one day but less than one month, and the person eventually has a full return to premorbid levels of functioning.

Three subtypes of this disorder are described in *DSM-IV-TR*. In the type described as with marked stressor(s), the onset of symptoms is preceded by an identifiable and prominent stressor (for example, loss of a loved one, rape, or combat experience) and typically is accompanied by extreme and rapid emotional shifts and a strong feeling of confusion. Multiple concurrent stressors are particularly likely to precipitate this disorder. The second type, with postpartum onset, begins within four weeks of giving birth. The disorder typically is characterized by depression and thoughts of suicide or infanticide. Due to the unpredictability of such clients, the baby is usually separated from the mother until she improves. In most cases, a mood disorder is ultimately diagnosed, although a small minority will be diagnosed as having schizophrenia (Torrey, 2001). The third type, without marked stressor(s), does not fit either of the other two patterns.

Unlike schizophrenia, brief psychotic disorder usually is not preceded by evidence of prodromal symptoms. This relatively uncommon disorder may begin in adolescence but is more likely to begin in the late twenties or early thirties.

Schizophreniform Disorder. Schizophreniform disorder is usually characterized by symptoms that may be indistinguishable from the most prominent symptoms of schizophrenia. These include impaired reality testing, extremely inappropriate behavior, bizarre delusions and hallucinations, incoherence, and catatonia. Schizophreniform disorder is more like schizophrenia than brief psychotic disorder is, in that it may include a prodromal phase, does not usually have an identifiable precipitant, and includes passive as well as active features of schizophrenia. Agitation and high anxiety are common in schizophreniform disorder, but flat affect is unusual. Unlike schizophrenia, impaired social or occupational functioning is not an essential feature of the disorder but often will be present.

Schizophreniform disorder is distinguished from schizophrenia primarily in terms of duration. Schizophreniform disorder, by definition, has a duration of at least one month but less than six months (including prodromal, active, and residual phases). As mentioned earlier, brief psychotic disorder and schizophreniform disorder share common abnormalities in brain functioning with schizophrenia and are considered to be schizophrenia spectrum disorders. Even so, schizophreniform disorder is currently categorized as a separate disorder, partly because it seems to have a better prognosis than that for schizophrenia. Approximately one-third of those diagnosed with schizophreniform disorder will recover within six months. Of the remaining two-thirds, most will subsequently be diagnosed with schizophrenia or schizoaffective disorder (American Psychiatric Association, 2000).

Schizophreniform disorder and brief psychotic disorder seem to differ from schizophrenia in terms of development, cause, treatment, and prognosis. Schizophreniform disorder may be viewed as a sort of bridge between brief psychotic disorder and schizophrenia, with brief psychotic disorder having the best prognosis and schizophrenia the worst. Schizophreniform disorder can be diagnosed when symptoms originally thought to be brief psychotic disorder persist for at least one month but for less than six months.

If diagnosis of either brief psychotic disorder or schizophreniform disorder is made before recovery, the diagnosis is viewed as provisional and as subject to change if the disorder lasts longer than anticipated. Thus both disorders are sometimes actually the early stages of schizophrenia.

Typical Client Characteristics

Like schizophrenia, both brief psychotic disorder and schizophreniform disorder are more common in people who have had preexisting emotional disorders, particularly personality disorders typified by emotional instability, suspiciousness, and impaired socialization. Depression and suicidal ideation also often coexist with or follow both brief psychotic disorder and schizophreniform disorder. The immediate aftermath of a severe psychotic episode is the most common time for these symptoms to emerge.

As mentioned earlier, substance use has also been found to play a role in the development of psychosis, and brief psychotic episodes often occur after amphetamine, cocaine, or cannabis use. Psychological stress also contributes to the development of psychotic symptoms. A history of traumatic incidents across the life span and recent stressful events can contribute to the development of psychosis.

People who have psychotic experiences show elevated activity in the right hemisphere of the brain. This right hemisphere activation is also found in healthy people who report high levels of paranormal beliefs and in those who report mystical experiences (Pizzagalli et al., 2000). People who are more creative also tend to exhibit a similar pattern of brain activation (Weinstein & Graves, 2002). More research is needed on this phenomenon, but perhaps creative people are more open to such experiences as magical thinking, illusions, and different experiences of reality.

Preferred Therapist Characteristics

People diagnosed with brief psychotic disorder or schizophreniform disorder typically benefit from supportive, safe, and structured therapeutic relationships that avoid casting them in a sick role. Acceptance, respect, genuineness, and empathy can be instrumental in helping these people come to terms with the events that have triggered their disorders and in restoring their awareness of reality. Modeling by therapists and identification with therapists can increase clients' use of effective coping mechanisms, as well as their efforts to take control of their lives.

Intervention Strategies

Initial treatments of brief psychotic disorder and schizophreniform disorder have many similarities to the treatment of schizophrenia. People with these disorders may be so severely incapacitated, aggressive, or disoriented and out of touch with reality that hospitalization and medication are required to protect them, calm them down, and alleviate acute symptoms. Long-term medication or extended inpatient treatment are unusual, however, unless a comorbid mental disorder is present.

Once the psychotic symptoms have subsided, the focus of treatment usually will shift quickly, with psychotherapy rather than medication being the primary ingredient of treatment. In this second phase of treatment, attention should be paid to the nature of any precipitants (including drugs or alcohol), and interventions should be used to help people deal with the events that have triggered their symptoms. People with these disorders often are in crisis, so a crisis-intervention approach to therapy can provide useful direction. According to that model, people are assisted in taking a realistic look at their circumstances, becoming aware of and expressing their feelings and reactions, identifying and mobilizing the coping mechanisms that they have used effectively in the past, and applying them to the current circumstances. Specific additional interventions are determined by the nature of the precipitant, but those interventions generally are short term and symptom-focused, emphasizing cognitive, behavioral, and supportive approaches rather than long-term exploratory ones.

Often people with schizophreniform disorder and brief psychotic disorder experience guilt, loss of self-esteem and self-confidence, and confusion related to their symptoms. They may be troubled by their own reactions and need help to accept and integrate their symptoms into their views of themselves and their lives. Both supportive and educational interventions can facilitate that process.

Group and family treatment also may help clients and their families deal with the aftermath of these disorders, as well as promote effective resolution of any precipitants and restore positive social and occupational functioning. As in the treatment of schizophrenia, encouraging people to draw on support systems, decrease social isolation, and improve interpersonal relatedness is consistently supported as effective in facilitating recovery, crisis resolution, and abatement of residual symptoms (Davidson, O'Connell, Tondora, Lawless, & Evans, 2005; Shahar et al., 2004).

Prognosis

People who are diagnosed with brief psychotic disorder or schizophreniform disorder and whose disorders seem to be related to a severely stressful life event have a good prognosis. Although psychotic episodes may vary in duration and symptoms, brief psychotic disorder frequently remits within a few weeks. Even if a precipitant cannot be identified, psychotic disorders that are brief in nature have a better prognosis than those that are lengthy or recurrent.

The prognosis for a brief psychotic disorder that does not progress to another disorder is by definition excellent. Symptoms of such a disorder typically remit quickly. Nevertheless, the active phase may be followed by temporary symptoms of depression, confusion, and anxiety as clients deal with the stressors that precipitated the disorder and with the experience of having had their functioning severely impaired. Clients often feel embarrassed at having had psychotic symptoms and fear a recurrence and its accompanying loss of control.

According to *DSM-IV-TR*, features associated with a positive prognosis for recovery from schizophreniform disorder are a brief prodromal period (four weeks or less), confusion and perplexity during the active phase of the disorder, good previous functioning, and affect that is depressed rather than flat or blunted.

However, those who have had a psychotic episode are more likely to experience a wide range of biological, social, and environmental influences that contribute to the development of psychosis. Those who have had a psychotic episode, even one of brief duration, are more predisposed to experience another (Johns & van Ohs, 2001).

Delusional Disorder

Description of the Disorder

Delusional disorder typically is less pervasive and disabling than schizophreniform disorder or schizophrenia, but may have some similar symptoms. According to *DSM-IV-TR*, a delusional disorder is characterized by the presence of nonbizarre (possible or believable) delusions of at least one month's duration. The delusions typically are circumscribed, and the person's overall behavior, apart from the delusions, usually does not seem odd or severely impaired. This is a disorder of thoughts rather than of perceptual experiences (auditory, visual, tactile, gustatory, or olfactory hallucinations). Hallucinations are absent or minimal. A history of schizophrenia rules out the diagnosis of this disorder.

The type of delusional disorder experienced by a person should be indicated when this diagnosis is made. The *DSM* identifies the following five types of delusional disorders, in addition to mixed and unspecified types:

1. *Erotomanic type:* unrealistic beliefs about a romantic relationship, often with a stranger or a person in a higher position, and sometimes associated with stalking behavior
2. *Grandiose type:* typically, the inaccurate belief that one has a special talent or has made an important discovery
3. *Jealous type:* unfounded belief that one's partner is unfaithful
4. *Persecutory type:* the most common type of delusional disorder, involving the incorrect belief that others are seeking to harm one, and sometimes associated with violent retaliation or lawsuits based on perceived wrongs
5. *Somatic type:* intense, unrealistic beliefs focused on the body, such as being certain that one has a serious disease

The onset of a delusional disorder typically occurs in middle or late adulthood and may be acute, chronic, or recurrent. Delusional disorder is fairly rare, occurring in approximately 0.03 percent of the population. It occurs with approximately equal frequency in both genders, but the jealous type is more common in men (American Psychiatric Association, 2000).

Typical Client Characteristics

People with delusional disorder typically demonstrate satisfactory premorbid functioning, although they tend to be excessively sensitive, below average in intelligence and insight, and prone to underachievement. People who are recent immigrants and who come from lower socioeconomic backgrounds are more likely to develop a delusional disorder, as are people who are isolated.

Delusional disorder is often preceded by a period of stress and by an experience that evokes strong feelings of insecurity, distrust, and self-doubt — for example, an abortion or divorce. The delusion sometimes is a defense mechanism, particularly one involving denial, projection, or reaction formation, and provides the person a way to preserve self-esteem and be protected from feelings of rejection, inadequacy, or guilt. The delusions may occur as a psychological compensation for the disappointments of life. It would not be unusual, for example, for an actor plagued with self-doubt after losing multiple auditions to develop a grandiose delusion that he was going to win an Oscar®. Ideas of reference (the idea that random events have special meaning) are common in this disorder, as is magical thinking.

A genetic basis for this disorder has not been well established, although first-degree relatives of people with this disorder are more likely to have avoidant or paranoid personality disorders (American Psychiatric Association, 2000). Delusional disorder is often considered on a continuum. People with delusional disorder may appear to be relatively unimpaired when they are not discussing their delusions, and daily functioning, including job-related activities, may not be interrupted. However, those with severe forms of the disorder may act on their delusions and have severe impairments in interpersonal relationships and occupational functioning. Delusions involving guilt are associated with more severe suicidal ideation, yet delusions in isolation do not constitute an independent risk factor for current suicidal ideation or past suicide attempts (Grunebaum et al., 2001). In fact, grandiose delusions were found to provide a protective factor.

People with delusional disorder tend to be low in self-esteem, isolated, easily frustrated, mistrustful, and fearful of intimacy. Irritability and a dysphoric mood are common in people with delusional disorder, although moods vary according to the nature of the delusions to which they are linked. These people view the world as a hostile and unfriendly place. They are very concerned with how they are perceived by others, often feel taken advantage of, and tend to overreact to criticism. People with delusional disorder tend to be defensive and argumentative, particularly with authority figures. They typically project blame for their own failures and shortcomings onto others, sometimes have ideas of reference, and may be perceived as hostile, suspicious, and excessively critical of themselves and others. Their social and sexual adjustment is often flawed, although their occupational adjustment may be satisfactory. People with delusional disorder sometimes have physical problems (for example, a hearing or visual loss) that contribute to their feeling different and isolated. Litigious and aggressive behavior may be manifested in response to delusions.

People with delusional disorder rarely are self-referred for treatment; rather, they present at the instigation of a family member, an employer, or the legal system. Consequently, they typically are reluctant to engage in treatment and do not see how it could help them. They tend to deny affective symptoms, resist acceptance of the idea that stress may have precipitated their symptoms, and have little empathy and insight, but do manifest better organization and overall functioning than those with schizophrenia (Butcher, Mineka, & Hooley, 2006).

Preferred Therapist Characteristics

Therapists should deal gently with people with delusional disorder, respecting their need for privacy and not arguing with them about their delusional beliefs. Instead, therapists should be stable and structured, reliable, reassuring, genuine, supportive, accepting, empathic, fair, and professional, serving as positive role models in an effort to engage these people in treatment and encourage more effective coping methods.

Therapists should discuss the delusions enough to understand their nature and possible functions but should not participate in clients' delusional belief systems. Kantor (2004) recommends that therapists provide affirmation and support when working with delusional clients. Rather than challenging clients' beliefs, therapists can provide alternative explanations and invite client curiosity in validating a hypothesis. In this manner, correcting errors in cognition can be done indirectly, by providing alternative positive interpretations. If clients demand to know whether therapists believe their delusions, therapists can respond, "I don't know, but I know it is very important to you and is having a great impact on your life." The therapeutic focus, then, should be on the immediate precursors and consequences of the delusions and on the personality traits that may have contributed to the development of the delusions rather than on the unrealistic beliefs themselves.

Conditions of the therapeutic relationship are particularly important in treating people with delusional disorder. Without a positive relationship, therapy is not likely to take place, but with a positive relationship, much can be accomplished.

Intervention Strategies

People with delusional disorder rarely seek treatment of their own volition and typically function well enough to avoid involuntary treatment. As a result, they rarely are seen in treatment, and little research is available on the effective treatment of this disorder. Some inferences can be drawn from the literature, however.

Although 1 to 4 percent of people admitted to psychiatric hospitals have delusional disorder (Preston, O'Neal, & Talaga, 2005), medication and hospitalization are less likely to be needed in treating this disorder than in the treatment of schizophrenia. Most people with a delusional disorder can be treated on an outpatient basis, although a day treatment center may provide a helpful change in environment. The suspiciousness that is typical of people with delusional disorder may lead them to refuse medication or fail to comply with prescribed treatments, and to mistrust those who recommend medication. Nevertheless, low doses of antipsychotic and antidepressant medication sometimes are helpful in reducing delusions and accompanying symptoms (Kantor, 2004). Drugs that have shown some effectiveness include pimozide (Orap) and such atypical antipsychotics as risperidone (Risperdal), olanzapine (Zyprexa), and ziprasidone (Geodon). Medication is most likely to be effective in the treatment of somatic delusions and in cases where there has been an apparent precipitant and early diagnosis. Co-occurring mood or anxiety disorders should also be treated with appropriate medication. Delayed treatment of psychosis can result in poorer treatment response and incomplete resolution of delusional thoughts (Preston et al., 2005).

Typically, the amelioration of environmental stressors and the encouragement of improved coping mechanisms will be as essential as medication to the effective treatment of delusional disorder. Establishment of a supportive therapeutic relationship is essential and sometimes sufficient to give these people the courage they need to deal more effectively with their lives. Kantor (2004) found that prognosis improves when people can learn to live with their delusions without the need to act on them. Emphasizing cognitive-behavioral therapy, treatment should focus on modifying core beliefs and schemas, helping clients replace negative thoughts with positive alternatives, and teaching empathy. Treatment should be present-oriented and should focus on maximizing adjustment and helping people deal with loss and frustration. Reality testing should be done gently without blaming, confrontation, or engaging in a power struggle with the client (Kantor, 2004). Encouraging independence and the expression of feelings also can be helpful. An emphasis on clients' strengths, positive behaviors, and improvements can contribute both to establishment of a positive therapeutic alliance and to clients' growth.

Clients' motivation for treatment can be increased with an initial focus on distressing secondary symptoms (such as insomnia or occupational concerns) rather than on delusions, their precipitants, and their consequences. Some attention should also be paid to the delusions themselves because they typically serve a symbolic function that, if understood, could facilitate treatment. For example, the therapist who understands that a narcissistic grandiose delusion is behind a client's belief that the CIA is watching her will not dispel the delusion by confronting the client with reality, but rather should encourage the client to satisfy her need for positive reinforcement and attention via realistic and growth-promoting goals and plans, rather than fantasy (Kantor, 2004).

As people begin to improve, depression and anxiety that were masked by delusional symptoms may emerge. Therapists and clients alike should be prepared for this development and should view it as a sign of progress.

If depression and anxiety do emerge, the focus of treatment should be shifted to amelioration of these affective symptoms.

Family therapy is often an important ingredient of treatment. Because these clients continue to function relatively well, family members may not understand that the clients are experiencing a mental disorder. Particularly if family members have been cast in an unfavorable light by a delusional belief system, they may feel angry and unsympathetic and may benefit from help in understanding the nature of the disorder. Reducing any family-related stress and conflict that are contributing to the delusional disorder can also help alleviate symptoms. Nevertheless, family therapy should be undertaken only with clients' permission, and clients should be reassured that family sessions will be discussed with them if they are not present at family meetings.

Although people diagnosed with delusional disorder often need to improve their social skills and relationships, they typically do not derive much benefit from group therapy. They tend to use their delusions to protect themselves from the group and wind up alienating other group members.

Prognosis

Although delusional disorder has a somewhat better prognosis than schizophrenia and does not have the same pervasive impact on functioning as that disorder does, the prognosis for treatment of delusional disorder is uncertain. Some people recover quickly — particularly women; people with good premorbid functioning; and those for whom the disorder has had a rapid onset, brief duration, and an apparent precipitant. For others, however, the disorder has a chronic course, and these people may experience alternating periods of remission and relapse over many years. Still others go on to develop schizophrenia. Those with delusional disorder of the persecutory, somatic, and erotomanic types seem to have better prospects for recovery than those with delusional disorder of the grandiose and jealous types (Kantor, 2004).

Schizoaffective Disorder

Description of the Disorder

Schizoaffective disorder is one of the most complicated diagnoses listed in *DSM-IV-TR*. By definition, it meets the criteria for a significant mood disorder (either major depressive disorder or bipolar I or II disorder) as well as for the active phase of schizophrenia. The disorder includes at least two weeks of delusions or hallucinations that are not accompanied by prominent mood symptoms, although depression or mania is present throughout most of the course of the disorder. Minimum duration for this disorder is one month. Some view schizoaffective disorder as two discrete disorders — schizophrenia and a mood disorder — or as an atypical form of mania or depression; others believe it is a separate diagnostic entity, a sort of hybrid with its own distinguishing features. Fewer than 1 percent of the population are diagnosed as having this disorder, which is less common than schizophrenia and much less common than mood disorders.

Disorders observed to precede or accompany schizoaffective disorder include substance-related disorders and schizoid, schizotypal, paranoid, and borderline personality disorders. Other disorders may develop later (American Psychiatric Association, 2000).

Typical Client Characteristics

Two types of schizoaffective disorder have been identified. Schizoaffective disorder, bipolar type, most often appears in early adulthood; schizoaffective disorder, depressive type, usually begins later. The age of onset of schizoaffective disorder is later for women than for men, with women particularly likely to manifest the depressive type. This disorder is more prevalent among women and among those with first-degree relatives who have been diagnosed as having schizophrenia or a major mood disorder (American Psychiatric Association, 2000).

In general, the demographic backgrounds and premorbid patterns of adjustment for those with schizoaffective disorder are more like the backgrounds and patterns of people with major depressive disorder than like those of people with schizophrenia or a bipolar disorder. Overall, social and occupational impairment typically accompany schizoaffective disorder. Even after achieving remission from the positive and negative symptoms of schizoaffective disorder, only one-quarter of the people in a four-year longitudinal study achieved sustained social and occupational recovery (Robinson, Woerner, McMeniman, Mendelowitz, & Bilder, 2004). Poor self-care and suicidal ideation often are present, and at least 10 percent of people affected by this disorder commit suicide.

Little clear information is available about the causes of schizoaffective disorder, although the disorder sometimes appears in relatively healthy people after a stressful precipitant; in these cases, onset is usually sudden and is accompanied by marked turmoil and confusion. Although less severe than in schizophrenia, poor insight is also common.

Preferred Therapist Characteristics

Therapist variables discussed in the section on schizophrenia probably also are applicable to schizoaffective disorder. Therapists should provide support, structure, reality testing, empathy, acceptance, and reassurance to allay the resistance and suspiciousness that often accompany psychotic symptoms. Establishing realistic goals and avoiding situations that lead clients to feel demoralized and to blame themselves are important. The relatively strong motivation for treatment that is often found in people with schizoaffective disorder (as it is in people with mood disorders), together with these people's relatively positive previous functioning, may make it easier to form a therapeutic alliance with them than it is to form a therapeutic alliance with people who have a diagnosis of schizophrenia.

Intervention Strategies

Because schizoaffective disorder is both a psychotic disorder and a mood disorder, treatment should focus on affective as well as psychotic symptoms and must be individualized, because the symptom picture associated with this disorder can vary widely. In general, psychotherapy and appropriate medication are the treatments of choice. It seems prudent to base treatment initially on the most prominent symptoms.

Psychotherapy for people diagnosed with schizoaffective disorder usually resembles approaches used to treat schizophrenia. Research on the components of the disorder suggests an interpersonal, cognitive, or cognitive-behavioral approach for the affective symptoms and a supportive and behavioral approach for the psychotic symptoms. Some mix of the two approaches — emphasizing the supportive and the behavioral, with the balance determined by the nature of a particular person's symptoms — is usually a reasonable choice, but because of the limited research, caution should be exercised in planning psychotherapy with these clients. Psychotherapy for people with schizoaffective disorder needs to be concrete, with a focus on social skills building or occupational training. Maniacci (1991) reports success in increasing clients' social interests via a structured program designed to develop life skills and promote insight and motivation; family involvement in this program also contributed to its positive outcome. As in bipolar disorder, family-focused therapy (Miklowitz, 2004) can be helpful in promoting family members' understanding of the disorder and in improving the family environment. Group therapy is generally contraindicated for people with schizoaffective disorder, due to their discomfort in social situations and the frequent occurrence of paranoia.

Medication is often useful in reducing both psychotic and affective symptoms, and a referral for medical evaluation should almost always be made for people with schizoaffective disorder. Determining the appropriate drugs can be challenging, however, because multiple medications may be needed and because the side effects of a medication designed to ameliorate one facet of this disorder may exacerbate symptoms involved in another facet. Therefore, a trial-and-error approach is often necessary in determining the best combination of medications for this disorder. Volavka and colleagues (2002) conducted a fourteen-week double-blind medication trial in which clozapine (Clozaril), rispiridone (Risperdal), and olanzapine (Zyprexa) were shown to be more effective than haloperidol (Haldol) in the reduction of positive and negative symptoms associated with schizoaffective disorder. Maintenance on clozapine (Clozaril) has also yielded positive results; 65 percent of clients in one study had no further hospitalizations or mood episodes (Zarate, Tohen, Banov, & Weiss, 1995). Lithium, antidepressants, atypical antipsychotics, and neuroleptics all have been found useful in treating some cases of schizoaffective disorder (Robinson et al., 2004). Lithium has been particularly helpful in the maintenance of people with the bipolar type of this disorder. Blood chemistry needs to be monitored regularly, as the side effects of Lithium and antipsychotic medications can be severe. Electroconvulsive therapy also has been used to treat people with schizoaffective disorder, especially those who do not have a good response to medication.

Many people diagnosed as having schizoaffective disorder require some period of hospitalization in addition to medication. Extensive treatment after hospitalization is often needed for people with severe forms of the disorder, especially until they are stabilized on medication. Family and social support, a stable schedule and routine, psychotherapy, regular exercise, and a healthy diet can all help maintain treatment gains. Some people may achieve good interepisode recovery, whereas others may remain chronically impaired. Such organizations as the National Alliance for Research on Schizophrenia and Depression and the National Alliance for the Mentally Ill (www.nami.org) offer additional information as well as family education.

Prognosis

The prognosis for schizoaffective disorder, not surprisingly, seems to be better than that for schizophrenia, with less severe residual symptoms (Robinson et al., 2004). Ten-year outcome studies confirm a more promising prognosis in schizoaffective disorder (Harrow, Grossman, Herbener, & Davies, 2000). Mood-incongruent psychotic features are associated with a poor prognosis, as are impaired premorbid functioning, early onset, unremitting course, a family history of schizophrenia, and a predominance of psychotic symptoms. Relapse is common, however, if medication is discontinued.

DISSOCIATIVE DISORDERS

Dissociative Identity Disorder

Description of the Disorder

The dissociative disorder that has received the most attention is dissociative identity disorder (DID), formerly called multiple personality disorder. According to *DSM-IV-TR*, "The essential feature of dissociative identity disorder is the presence of two or more distinct identities" that repeatedly assume control of the person's behavior (American Psychiatric Association, 2000,

p. 526). People with this disorder cannot integrate aspects of their identity, memory, and awareness and often are unable to recall important personal information.

Dramatic cases in which as many as one hundred distinct identities alternate in some way to control a person's identity have been reported, although half of cases report ten or fewer (American Psychiatric Association, 2000). Each identity may claim to have a different history, self-image, gender, name, and other personal features (Butcher et al., 2006). The three most common roles for identities are inadequate or confused protectors, terrified children, and persecutors who violently act out (Ellason & Ross, 1997; Thomas, 2003). Along with the alter identities, pervasive symptoms of DID include the inability to recall important personal information, headaches, erratic behavior, PTSD, and other types of memory loss or fugue symptoms (American Psychiatric Association, 2000).

Prevalence rates are unclear, but incidence of DID ranges from 0.01 to 1 percent of the population (Maldonado, Butler, & Spiegel, 2002). The disorder has been identified across all major racial groups, socioeconomic classes, and cultures. Treatment usually is sought by a primary or host identity or at the urging of family members.

Onset of DID usually is in childhood, after a severe trauma or accompanying negative and abusive experiences in a context involving few support systems. Indeed, more than 90 percent of people diagnosed with DID report histories of childhood abuse (Maldonado et al., 2002; Thomas, 2003). Females are far more likely to be diagnosed with this disorder than are males, although some believe that men with this disorder are more likely to be in prisons than in mental health settings. Although the disorder begins in early childhood, the average age at diagnosis is twenty-nine to thirty five years old. Because of the long-standing and deeply ingrained nature of this disorder, the limited awareness that people with DID have of their condition, and their tendency to conceal their symptoms, this disorder can be mistaken for other dissociative disorders, personality disorders, or psychotic disorders. Diagnosis is also difficult because psychological assessments and physiological tests (such as EEGs, galvanic skin response, and cerebral blood flow) have yielded ambiguous results (Sue, Sue, & Sue, 2006). Few people with DID present their symptoms openly at initial treatment. Consequently, people often spend years in the mental health system before an accurate diagnosis is made. The average time from the appearance of symptoms to an accurate diagnosis is six years, although this is probably changing with the spread of knowledge about DID (Maldonado et al., 2002).

Rifkin and colleagues developed a methodology for diagnosing DID that they believe approaches "the gold standard of diagnosis" (Rifkin, Ghisalbert, Dimatou, Jin, & Sethi, 1998, p. 845). Using a random sampling of one hundred women in a teaching hospital setting, one of two clinicians first interviewed each patient using the Structured Clinical Interview for *DSM-IV* Dissociative Disorders (SCID-D) as an interview guide. Those who tested positive for DID were then interviewed by a second clinician, also using the structured interview technique. Rifkin and colleagues identified a 1 percent occurrence rate of DID among female psychiatric inpatients. The authors report that their results are lower than other studies of psychiatric inpatients, but that their method is superior to the use of self-report measures or fixed questionnaires such as the Dissociative Disorder Interest Scale (DDIS) and the Dissociative Experiences Scale (DES; Bernstein & Putnam, 1986). The methodology may also have implications for outpatient assessment. Clearly, further research is needed on the assessment of DID.

Typical Client Characteristics

The degree of impairment of people with DID varies widely. Symptoms that frequently accompany this disorder include substance misuse, self-mutilation, suicidal and aggressive impulses, eating and sexual difficulties, sleeping problems, time lapses, disorientation, phobias, hallucinatory experiences, feelings of being influenced or changed, and mood swings (Butcher et al., 2006; Ellason & Ross, 1997). People with DID are more likely to have imaginative thoughts, a greater openness to altered states of consciousness, a highly unconventional view of reality, and difficulty integrating information and new learning into their lives. They also score higher on traits of self-transcendence and self-directedness (Maldonado et al., 2002). A history of somatic symptoms is common, especially migraine headaches and intestinal disturbances.

Typically, people with DID have at least two additional mental disorders, with depression being the most common, and PTSD, substance use disorder, and personality disorders (especially borderline personality disorder) being particularly frequent (Ellason & Ross, 1997). Researchers have linked all types of childhood abuse (neglect, confinement, maternal dysfunction, traumatic and stressful life events, physical and sexual abuse) with increased levels of dissociative symptoms. Severity of symptoms appears to be correlated with age of onset; more severe symptoms are associated with an early onset (Maldonado et al., 2002). Twin studies suggest that genetics might also influence the development of dissociative identity disorder.

Preferred Therapist Characteristics

People with dissociative disorders typically are coping with considerable stress and anxiety. They may be confused and frightened by their disorder and fear that they are going insane. They need a warm, supportive therapeutic relationship that provides them clear information on the nature, course, and treatment of their disorder and reassures them that deterioration is unlikely and that the prognosis for improvement is good.

The importance of a strong therapeutic relationship is critical for people with DID, who usually have been abused and violated by their caregivers, making trust and self-disclosure difficult. Therapists should strive to instill realistic hope and promote clients' active participation in recovery, but should at the same time protect them from moving too quickly or dealing with material that may retraumatize them.

Clients' reports of their abuse can be particularly troubling to therapists. Countertransference may occur in which therapists become enraged with those who abused their clients, and want to care for and rescue the clients. This reaction is understandable, but it is, of course, countertherapeutic and can detract from clients' growing self-confidence. Moreover, people's reports of abuse cannot always be proved and may be prone to error and inconsistency. At the same time, however, complete therapist neutrality also is undesirable; this can give clients the message that others will sit passively while they are hurt. Rather, Thomas (2003) suggests that therapists should model appropriate parenting to a client who has lacked appropriate parenting in his or her life.

Intervention Strategies

Treatment of DID typically is a long, slow, challenging process that requires years of therapy and a skillful therapist. General psychotherapy that is not geared to the special needs of this disorder is unlikely to promote improvement. However, controlled studies and comprehensive research on DID are rare. Although numerous case histories are available, they are lacking in empirical research about the most effective treatment outcomes (Butcher et al., 2006). Some believe that individual psychotherapy with hypnosis may be useful in helping people with DID gain a sense of mastery and control over their feelings of depersonalization (Maldonado et al., 2002). Other treatment modalities are based on the research on trauma and on treatment for PTSD (Kihlstrom, 2001). Butcher and colleagues (2006) note that treatment is usually psychodynamic and insight-oriented.

Treatment that focuses on uncovering and working through traumatic memories is important in helping people recover from DID. The early age at which the traumas occurred, the fear induced by the traumatic experiences, and neural changes during stress can all interfere with recall and accuracy of memories. Thus hypnosis is one of the most frequently used techniques in the treatment of DID (Maldonado et al., 2002). An important goal of treatment is to help clients integrate the various aspects of their personality into one identity that can function well (Butcher et al., 2006), but this process must be carefully paced to avoid retraumatization.

Adjunct modes of treatment can be helpful to people with DID. Homogeneous group therapy with a present-oriented focus can be particularly beneficial in helping people with DID understand themselves better and participate with other people in a social context. Group interaction, compassion, tolerance, patience, and sharing can all be experienced firsthand (Maldonado et al., 2002). Expressive therapy can facilitate awareness of emotions, development of insight, and recall of past experiences. Family therapy, focused on the current family, can promote understanding and improve relationships, although therapy with a family of origin that was abusive is generally contraindicated.

No controlled studies were located on the use of cognitive-behavioral therapy in the treatment of DID. However, as in the treatment of PTSD, cognitive-behavioral therapy can be used to develop coping skills and to help people manage or overcome dissociative events (Maldonado et al., 2002).

Medication is not effective in treating the core symptoms of DID. Medication used in the treatment of symptoms such as depression has met with mixed reviews; a recent randomized controlled study of people with DID indicated no difference between treatment with the SSRI fluoxetine (Prozac) versus a placebo (Simeon, Guralnik, Schmeidler, & Knutelska, 2004).

Prognosis

Despite the severity of DID, Ellason and Ross (1997) found that 54 out of 135 people with DID treated in a specialized inpatient unit had improved dramatically at two-year follow-up. Improvement was measured in terms of reducing depression, psychosis, and borderline symptoms. Another follow-up study of twenty-five people was less successful. However, both studies reinforce the need for lengthy treatment, as well as a less optimistic prognosis associated with DID that began early in life.

Dissociative Fugue, Dissociative Amnesia, and Depersonalization Disorder

Description of the Disorders

Dissociative Fugue. Dissociative fugue (and dissociative amnesia, discussed in the next section) involves temporary forgetting of important components of a person's life. The forgetting is more extensive or extreme than would be experienced with ordinary forgetfulness, and often reflects a desire to withdraw from painful emotional experiences, such as severe assault or rape, or natural disasters. According to Maldonado and colleagues (2002), the most common stressors that trigger fugue states are marital discord, financial and occupational difficulties, and war-related situations. Dissociative fugue (as well as dissociative amnesia) is not caused by substances or a general medical condition.

Dissociative fugue most often occurs in adults who have undergone a traumatic or very upsetting experience, such as a natural disaster or a severe interpersonal conflict with a loved one. People with dissociative fugue typically develop sudden confusion about their identity and travel to other places, sometimes for only a few hours but sometimes for months. In a small percentage of cases, a new identity develops, typically that of a more energetic, outgoing, and adventurous personality. Awareness of the old personality and of the amnesia usually is absent.

The behaviors of people with dissociative fugue generally are unremarkable, although their memory loss may cause others to pay attention to them and try to help them. When the fugue state is gone (usually suddenly and spontaneously), people with this disorder typically are confused by what has happened to them, may have amnesia for troubling past events, and cannot recall the details of the fugue state. People with dissociative fugue may experience depression, remorse, anger, and suicidal impulses during the postfugue period and may need to repair the social and occupational consequences of their absence. Dissociative fugue has been associated with alcohol misuse, mood disorders, and personality disorders.

Dissociative Amnesia. Dissociative amnesia involves partial amnesia or forgetting of important personal information, such as the names and identities of significant family members, one's place of employment, or events during a circumscribed period of time. *DSM-IV-TR* describes five types of amnesia that can characterize this disorder:

1. Localized amnesia, focused on events during a limited period
2. Selective amnesia, involving recall of some but not all events during a certain period
3. Generalized amnesia, or inability to recall one's entire life
4. Continuous amnesia, which involves the inability to recall events up to a specific point
5. Systematized amnesia, or failure to recall certain categories of events or information

The first two represent the most common types of this disorder. This diagnosis has been used for some people who report having recovered memories of traumatic childhood experiences.

Like those who have experienced dissociative fugue, people with dissociative amnesia sometimes report a broad range of symptoms after memory has been regained, including depression, aggressive and suicidal impulses, impaired functioning, sexual dysfunction, self-mutilation, trance states, and Ganser's syndrome (presenting approximate answers to questions) (American Psychiatric Association, 2000).

Dissociative amnesia, like dissociative fugue, tends to occur suddenly at times of traumatic events or unusual stress, is typically of brief duration, and may remit without recurrence. For example, after the September 11 attacks on the World Trade Center, several people who had been reported missing were later found alive, but had apparently developed dissociative amnesia (Tucker, 2002). Following such an overwhelming trauma, a person may experience fragmentation or a polarization of their sense of self and may dissociate from affect or painful memories. These symptoms may buffer the full impact of the traumatic experience. However, even though people cannot recall these memories, the memories continue to influence them.

Depersonalization Disorder. *DSM-IV-TR* describes depersonalization disorder as characterized by ''a feeling of detachment and estrangement from one's self'' (American Psychiatric Association, 2000, p. 530). People with this disorder report feeling like robots, feeling as if they were in a dream or a movie, or feeling as though they are outside their bodies, observing themselves. Despite these unusual sensations, delusions and hallucinations are not present, and reality testing is intact. Nevertheless, the symptoms are severe and persistent enough to cause considerable distress or impairment. Symptoms of depression, anxiety, and somatic distress often accompany this disorder, and people sometimes believe that these symptoms are signs that they are crazy.

Nearly 50 percent of people have experienced some form of depersonalization, albeit in a brief, single episode (Maldonado et al., 2002). The symptom of depersonalization has been described as being the third most common psychiatric symptom, after depression and anxiety. The diagnosis of the disorder should be given only when symptoms are severe and cause impairment in functioning as well as marked distress.

Onset of depersonalization disorder tends to be rapid, usually is associated with severe stress or trauma, and can occur at any age including the childhood years, although its onset is most common between the ages of fifteen and thirty. This disorder may be brief or chronic, persistent or episodic. As with all the dissociative disorders, it is more common among females than among males.

Typical Client Characteristics

Depersonalization disorder is particularly common among adolescents. It also seems more prevalent among people with substance-related, anxiety, and somatization disorders. Other co-occurring disorders may include depression, and avoidant, borderline, and obsessive-compulsive personality disorders (Maldonado et al., 2002). Cultural variables should be considered when diagnosing dissociative disorders; culturally sanctioned trance experiences should not be mistaken for depersonalization disorder.

Research on the characteristics of people who experience dissociative fugue or amnesia is limited, but the disorders seem to be more prevalent among people who are highly suggestible, who are easily hypnotized, and who also report symptoms of depression and anxiety (American Psychiatric Association, 2000). Both disorders are rare but increase under circumstances of natural disaster, accidents, or warfare.

Preferred Therapist Characteristics

For many people with dissociative fugue, dissociative amnesia, or depersonalization disorder, a therapeutic relationship based on safety and support is sufficient to promote spontaneous remission. Therefore, therapists working with these clients need to be warm, supportive, consistent, and straightforward. They should be able to establish a stress-free relationship in which their clients can sort through disturbing memories in a psychologically and physically safe environment.

Intervention Strategies

Dissociative Fugue and Dissociative Amnesia. The treatments for dissociative fugue and dissociative amnesia are quite similar (Maldonado et al., 2002). Typically, the first step is to build a positive therapeutic relationship while helping people achieve a safe and stable life situation. Once those goals have been accomplished, the second step is to help people regain any memories that may not yet have been recovered and deal with the traumas or stressors that may have precipitated memory loss or flight. The third step in treatment is to help people integrate their upsetting experiences into their lives, reorder and move on with their lives, and develop coping skills that seem likely to help them manage future stressors more successfully.

Although this process sounds straightforward, people may find it challenging to come to terms with traumatic experiences and their consequences (such as flashbacks and withdrawal), as well as to deal with the feelings (such as shame, self-blame, rage, fear, and hopelessness) that often result not just from traumas but also from having had a dissociative disorder. Careful pacing, grounding, and considerable support are needed to control people's exposure to upsetting material, as well as to help some of these clients recognize and accept their inability to fully process their traumatic experiences. Dissociative disorders often function as defense mechanisms and should not be stripped away before people have developed other ways of taking care of themselves. Maintaining control and a sense of self is usually important to people with dissociative disorders, and that need should be respected.

Many types of interventions can contribute to treatment. In dissociative fugue and dissociative amnesia, hypnosis can facilitate the controlled uncovering of memories, as well as the working through and integration of those memories (Ellason & Ross, 1997; Maldonado et al., 2002). Medication, including barbiturates and benzodiazepines, can also be helpful in restoring lost memories and reducing anxiety. Expressive-supportive psychodynamic psychotherapy, encouraging exploration, coping, the building of confidence, and the expression of feelings, can also help reduce anxiety. Once memory has been regained, psychotherapy can be useful in helping people deal with the precipitants of their amnesia. Other interventions, such as family therapy, free association, environmental change, cognitive therapy, and behavior therapy, also can help ameliorate dissociative fugue and dissociative amnesia and can help people cope with stress-related precipitants. Group therapy, particularly with others who have survived similar traumatic experiences, can be helpful as long as caution is exercised in pacing and in establishing safety (Ellason & Ross, 1997).

Depersonalization Disorder. The overall goal of treatment for depersonalization disorder is to help people regain their sense of reality and develop a feeling of personality integration. A first step toward this goal is to provide education on the nature of depersonalization disorder. Clarifying and normalizing the symptoms of this disorder can often be very therapeutic and can reduce fear about the meaning of the symptoms. The choice of subsequent interventions depends primarily on other disorders and experiences that are associated with the depersonalization. Effective treatment for depersonalization disorder should include assessment and treatment of co-occurring conditions (Maldonado et al., 2002).

Although the most effective treatment for depersonalization disorder has yet to be identified, many forms of treatment have been used successfully with this disorder, including cognitive therapy, behavior therapy, hypnosis, group and family therapy, and antidepressant and antianxiety medications (Maldonado et al., 2002). All have helped some clients and been ineffective with others. Few data-based studies are available to provide general guidance for treatment of this disorder partly because people usually do not seek treatment for its symptoms. Consequently, therapists should determine as accurately as possible what symptoms and past experiences need attention and what treatment approaches are most likely to have a positive impact on those associated difficulties. Finally, improvement of coping skills, life and stress management, and integration of self and experiences almost always are indicated as part of treatment for these clients.

Prognosis

The prognosis is excellent for a rapid and complete recovery from initial episodes of dissociative fugue and dissociative amnesia, particularly if they are linked to specific precipitants (Spiegel, 1996). Recovery is often spontaneous, although it can be facilitated by treatment, but recurrences are common.

Although some do recover from depersonalization disorder, that disorder is more likely to have a chronic course (American Psychiatric Association, 2000). Symptoms may be fairly stable or may wax and wane in response to stressors.

TREATMENT RECOMMENDATIONS: CLIENT MAP

Treatment recommendations for disorders involving impairment in awareness of reality are summarized here according to the Client Map format. Because these disorders do vary widely, readers are also encouraged to review the preceding sections on the specific disorders.

Client Map

Diagnosis

Disorders involving impairment in awareness of reality (schizophrenia, brief psychotic disorder, schizophreniform disorder, delusional disorder, schizoaffective disorder, dissociative identity disorder, dissociative fugue, dissociative amnesia, depersonalization disorder)

Objectives of Treatment

As possible, reduce or eliminate prominent symptoms

Restore client's awareness of reality

Maximize client's coping abilities and emotional and behavioral adjustment to the disorder

Help client deal with any precipitating stressors or traumatic experiences

If needed, improve social and occupational functioning

Prevent relapse

Enable family members to develop understanding of the disorder, deal with their own related needs and feelings, and learn how to help the affected family member

Assessments

Usually medical, neurological, or psychological evaluations, or all three

Inventories of specific symptoms (dissociation, substance use, stress, depression), to clarify diagnosis and provide useful information on level of functioning and secondary symptoms

Clinician Characteristics

Able to communicate caring, consistency, and optimism

Able to establish a trusting and sometimes long-term therapeutic relationship

Knowledgeable about usual nature and course of disorder

Able to manage countertransference reactions, especially with clients who have experienced abuse or other traumatic experiences

Able to collaborate with medical personnel, family and individual psychotherapists, and rehabilitation counselors

Able to provide support and, as necessary, long-term treatment to client and family

Location of Treatment

For psychotic disorders, often inpatient setting initially, with later outpatient setting (sometimes day treatment)

For dissociative disorders, usually outpatient setting, with hospitalization as necessary if client is in crisis or overwhelmed by traumatic memories

Interventions to Be Used

Supportive psychotherapy to maintain stabilization

Family therapy, to promote family members' understanding and client adjustment

Education on the disorder

Medication (especially for the psychotic disorders)

Behavior therapy, to promote development of coping mechanisms and stress management

Hypnotherapy, psychodynamic psychotherapy, and cognitive therapy as indicated for specific disorders

Emphasis of Treatment

Variable according to nature of disorder (for example, focus on behavior and symptom alleviation for psychotic disorders; focus on exploration of background and dynamics of disorder for dissociative identity disorder)

Emphasis on supportiveness and structure typical

Numbers

Primarily individual treatment

Family therapy also useful

Group therapy only in specialized forms (milieu therapy for schizophrenia; homogeneous group therapy for people who experienced abuse and who are diagnosed with dissociative identity disorder)

Timing

Long term, with some exceptions, including brief psychotic disorder and dissociative amnesia

Sometimes several sessions per week

Medications Needed

Almost always indicated for psychotic disorders

Sometimes indicated for dissociative disorders

Should be monitored carefully to minimize side effects and prevent misuse or suicide

Adjunct Services

Rehabilitation counseling

Socialization and development of activities

Respite care for families

Prognosis

Variable, depending on the disorder (for example, excellent for brief psychotic disorder, good for dissociative amnesia and dissociative identity disorder, fair for schizophrenia)

Client Map of Victor J.

This chapter began with a description of Victor J., a twenty-two-year-old college senior who believed that his roommate's mother was in love with him. Victor's poor coping and social skills, his apprehension about graduating from college, and his apparent wish to escape from his family environment all probably contributed to the development of his delusional disorder. Treatment focused on helping him address and alleviate his stressors and improve his coping skills had a rapid effect on Victor's symptoms. His delusional beliefs began to fade in intensity and quickly ceased to become a dominant theme. Victor was then able to invest energy in completing his college studies and seeking employment. Victor made many positive changes within about six months, and his medication was stopped, although he was expected to need continued psychotherapy after the initial interventions. The following Client Map outlines the treatment recommended for Victor.

Diagnosis

Axis I: 297.1 Delusional disorder, erotomanic type, moderate

Axis II: Avoidant personality traits

Axis III: No medical problems reported

Axis IV: Impending college graduation, conflict with family

Axis V: Global assessment of functioning (GAF Scale): current GAF = 52

Objectives of Treatment

Eliminate delusional symptoms

Improve social and relationship skills

Improve communication skills

Establish realistic and rewarding postgraduation plans

Improve socialization, leisure activities, coping mechanisms, support systems, self-confidence, and self-reliance

Facilitate exploration, understanding, and resolution of family issues

Assessments

Referral for medical and neurological tests, to rule out the possibility of a cognitive disorder

Clinician Characteristics

Supportive and patient

Empathic

Skilled at reducing resistance and restoring contact with reality

Preferably male, to serve as a role model for client

Knowledgeable about family dynamics

Location of Treatment

Outpatient setting

Interventions to Be Used

Education about symptoms, communication skills, development of alternative solutions to problems, and effective decision making

Individual therapy combining supportive, cognitive, and behavioral elements

Emphasis on development of strong therapeutic alliance

Behavior therapy, especially to build up client's coping mechanisms

Training in stress management

Assistance in developing plans for after graduation

Validation of client's feelings, but with minimum discussion of client's delusional beliefs

Emphasis of Treatment

Emphasis on structure

Relatively directive emphasis, with supportiveness and orientation to the present also important

Focus on behavioral and affective elements, in holistic context

Numbers

Individual therapy, perhaps followed by group therapy with sufficient abatement of symptoms to permit client to benefit from group feedback and opportunity to practice communication skills

Timing

Gentle yet steady pace, to quickly develop client's commitment to treatment and reduce symptoms

Moderate duration

Medications Needed

Medication prescribed as short-term aid to reducing client's thought disorder and anxiety and facilitating his involvement in therapy

Adjunct Services

Cycling group (to promote client's present enjoyment of biking and facilitate his involvement in a nondemanding, rewarding activity likely to offer increased contact with other young people but unlikely to create discomfort or embarrassment)

Prognosis

Excellent, with combination of medication and psychotherapy

Extended follow-up psychotherapy anticipated

Recommended Reading

Bellack, A. S., Mueser, K. T., Gingerich, S., & Agresta, J. (2004). *Social skills training for schizophrenia: A step-by-step guide* (2nd ed.). New York: Guilford Press.

Graham, H. L., Copello, A., Birchwood, M. J., & Mueser, K. T. (Eds.). (2003). *Substance misuse in psychosis: Approaches to treatment and service delivery*. Hoboken, NJ: Wiley.

Murray, W. H. (2006). *Schizoaffective disorder: New research*. Hauppage, NY: Nova Science.

Spiegel, D. (1996). Dissociative disorders. In R. E. Hales & S. C. Yudofsky (Eds.), *The American Psychiatric Press synopsis of psychiatry* (pp. 583–604). Washington, DC: American Psychiatric Press.

Thomas, P. M. (2003). Protection, dissociation, and internal roles: Modeling and treating the effects of child abuse. *Review of General Psychology*, *7*, 364–380.

Torrey, E. F. (2001). *Surviving schizophrenia: A manual for families, consumers, and providers* (4th ed.). New York: HarperCollins.

CHAPTER TEN

The Future of Diagnosis and Treatment Planning

We have provided, in this third edition of *Selecting Effective Treatments*, a pathway for treatment of mental disorders based on the most recent evidence-based research. At the same time, we recognize that the diagnosis and treatment of mental disorders are part of a dynamic and evolving field, and new and exciting research is currently under way that will inspire innovative theories and practices in the future.

The biological, psychological, and social development of a human being is complex. The next decades will reveal more about how these biopsychosocial influences shape the individual person. More will be learned about the neurobiological underpinnings of behavior, the importance of early life influences and their effects on the person across the life span, and the constantly changing society in which we live and its impact on human behavior. How could these influences not shape and inform our understanding of diagnosis and treatment in fundamentally new and interesting ways?

In an attempt to look at the future of our field, we have included the following brief glimpse into what we believe clinicians can expect in the coming years, based on the research and changes that are currently under way.

NEW UNDERSTANDING OF DIAGNOSIS

Neurobiology

As we learn more about the physiological and biochemical processes of the brain, such neurological tests as computerized axial tomography (CAT), positron emission tomography (PET), and magnetic resonance imaging (MRI) provide increasing diagnostic accuracy for a variety of disorders, such as dementia and schizophrenia. In the future, the refinement of these and even newer tests, taken together with clinical assessments of a person's behavior, thoughts, and emotions, will provide better diagnostic accuracy for a wide range of mental disorders.

Molecular Genetics and Spectrum Disorders

As we become better able to distinguish between biological causes and psychosocial causes of disorders, treatments will become more specific, and prevention will become more focused. This does not mean that a pharmacological or medical approach will be found for every disorder, but rather that research will be better able to determine which psychotherapy treatments, in combination with which medications (if appropriate), are best suited to a particular mental disorder. We need to study and treat both the psychosocial and the biological elements of mental disorders. This is evident in schizophrenia, for example, which has a genetic component, as evidenced by twin studies that show a nearly 50 percent concordance rate among identical twins. Yet the concordance rate is *only* 50 percent, indicating that something more than genetics influences the development of this disorder.

Family, twin, and adoption studies can go only so far. Research in the area of molecular genetics is leading to the identification of multiple contributing genes that work together to create an underlying susceptibility to a particular disorder. For example, rather than there being one gene that causes schizophrenia, multiple genes have been identified that each contribute a degree of pathology. How these genes function and are influenced by environmental and other factors can determine whether the person develops schizophrenia, a milder version of the disorder such as schizotypal personality disorder, or no disorder at all. Current research suggests a spectrum of psychotic disorders that lie on a continuum and include multiple biopsychosocial variables that determine what symptoms, if any, a specific person will develop.

The spectrum disorder concept is being considered for other disorders as well. Some proposed spectra include bipolar spectrum disorders (ranging from cyclothymia to bipolar I disorder); an autism spectrum; and several anxiety spectrum disorders, including a PTSD spectrum, an OCD spectrum, and a panic disorder spectrum. Our understanding of spectrum disorders is still evolving, does not have any hard-and-fast boundaries, and challenges the currently accepted concept of categorical diagnoses that serves as the basis of *DSM-IV-TR* and the *ICD-10* manuals. Look to the future of psychiatric genetics to provide insight into the susceptibility of families to inheriting certain conditions and their accompanying symptoms.

New Diagnoses

The *Diagnostic and Statistical Manual of Mental Disorders* is an evolving document, and work by the American Psychiatric Association committees on the development of the *DSM-V* is currently under way. Clinical experience commonly provides the basis for scientific research and often leads to changes in treatments even before they are scientifically validated. For example, *DSM-IV-TR* contains several diagnoses that have been proposed but that need further study. These include premenstrual dysphoric disorder (emotional and physiological concomitants of premenstrual syndrome), depressive personality disorder, caffeine withdrawal, binge eating disorder, and mixed anxiety-depressive disorder, among others; data are being gathered on these and other disorders to determine whether they should be included as disorders in the next edition of the *DSM*.

Considerable research and discussion informs decisions about the addition of new disorders to the *DSM*. Several that have been under consideration include relational disorder, hypersexuality or sexual addiction, self-mutilation, bullying, excessive spending, and skin-picking. Another diagnosis currently under discussion is executive system dysfunction, which refers to the functioning of the brain's frontal lobe, where executive functions are located.

Whether to continue to include certain diagnoses in the *DSM* is also being debated by American Psychiatric Association committees. Gender identity disorder (GID) is one of the most controversial diagnoses up for debate. Just as homosexuality was determined not to be a mental disorder and was therefore removed from the *DSM*, uncertainty also surrounds the diagnosis of GID. Whether GID is more clearly researched and defined in the next *DSM* or whether its symptoms are changed to "gender dysphoria" or deleted altogether has yet to be determined.

Questions also have been raised about the absence from *DSM-IV-TR* of certain diagnoses, such as one that addresses the impact of maladaptive substance use on families. As one consequence, people who might be described as adult children of alcoholics, codependent, or enabling must be diagnosed according to the language of the *DSM* describing the nature of their symptoms. Thus many people who could be perceived as codependent or enabling are diagnosed as having a dependent personality disorder, a diagnosis that does not reflect the familial or genetic component of the disorder, which might be better captured by a new diagnosis encompassing both the dependence needs and the family origins of those needs.

Revision of the *DSM* is a huge undertaking. Committees have been formed, white papers have been written, and conferences in ten separate interest areas have met. If everything goes according to the current timeline developed by the American Psychiatric Association, *DSM-V* will be published in 2011. In the past, however, revisions of the *DSM* have typically been issued later than anticipated, so we do not know exactly when the next edition will be published.

CHANGES IN TREATMENT

The Therapeutic Alliance

Chapter One covered extensively the importance of the therapeutic alliance in achieving positive treatment outcomes. A plethora of research in the past fifty years has documented that the alliance is important regardless of treatment modality or diagnosis. Two clusters of therapist behaviors are most strongly associated with successful outcomes: the conditions of warmth, empathy, positive regard, and genuineness, first set forth by Rogers, and the formation of a positive and collaborative therapeutic alliance. Without the development of a good working relationship between the therapist and the client, treatment stands little chance of being effective.

The implication of this is that all therapists, new and seasoned, should not underestimate the power involved in creating an effective working alliance. Although having a theoretical orientation is important, and having a variety of effective techniques and strategies at our disposal is wise, nothing has been shown to outweigh the importance of the relationship between the therapist and the client.

Integrative Treatments

Integrative approaches have a growing appeal. Prochaska and Norcross (2006) identified the following twelve trends that have combined over the past several decades to lead clinicians toward integrated treatment approaches:

1. The large and growing number of approaches to treatment. More than four hundred treatment systems have been identified.
2. The increasing diversity and complexity of clients and their concerns.
3. The inability of any one treatment system to successfully address all clients and all problems.

4. The growing importance of solution-focused brief approaches that encourage clinicians to draw on and combine interventions from various systems of therapy to find the most effective and efficient strategy for each treatment situation.
5. The availability of training opportunities, as well as case studies and other informative literature, that give clinicians the opportunity to study, observe, and gain experience in a wide variety of treatment approaches.
6. The requirement of some state and national credentialing bodies that clinicians obtain postgraduate continuing education units. This encourages continued professional growth and development of new skills and ideas.
7. Increasing pressure from managed care organizations (MCOs), governmental agencies, consumers, and others for clinicians to determine the most effective and efficient treatment approach for each client, to plan and document their work, and to maintain accountability.
8. The growing body of compelling research demonstrating which treatment approaches are most likely to be successful in the treatment of particular people, disorders, or problems.
9. The increasing availability of manuals, which provide details and procedures for empirically validated and other treatment plans for specific mental disorders.
10. The development of organizations, such as the Society for the Exploration of Psychotherapy Integration, that focus on studying and promoting treatment integration.
11. The emergence of models providing blueprints or guidelines for logical and therapeutically sound integration of treatment approaches.
12. Clinicians' increasing awareness that such common factors as the nature of the therapeutic alliance are at least as important in determining treatment success as are theoretical orientation and specific strategies (Seligman, 2006, p. 435).

Manualized Treatment

The use of manualized therapy to provide consistent and effective treatment guidelines and interventions has increased in recent years. More than 130 different manualized treatments are available that have been empirically validated and shown to improve consistency in outcomes. Even so, those who use manual-based treatments must keep in mind that therapist effects on outcome are large and that strict adherence to a manual, without thought to development of a therapeutic alliance, can result in poor outcomes and a break in the alliance. The American Psychological Association (Levant, 2005) recommends that clinicians use sound clinical judgment and flexibility, rather than rigid application, in the use of manuals for treatment.

Importance of Accountability

Manualized treatment, clinical guidelines, goal setting and assessment, case tracking, and paperwork are all important elements of efforts to provide cost-effective, empirically based treatments. Therapists are currently required by MCOs to be able to document progress for each client. They accomplish this through assessments, treatment plans, and progress notes. Therapists also increasingly research their own work and provide evidence of their personal effectiveness with a caseload of clients as part of continuing efforts to improve treatment outcomes.

New and Evolving Treatment Modalities

A new wave of humanistic approaches to therapy has brought a postmodern perspective to person-centered therapy. Process-experiential therapies, such as emotion-focused therapy, motivational interviewing, and modified versions of Gestalt therapy, have received support for treatment of many disorders.

Other innovative treatment strategies have emerged, such as family-focused therapy for bipolar disorder, virtual reality for specific phobias, and mindfulness-based therapies and holistic approaches for stress reduction based on Eastern philosophies. Eye movement desensitization and reprocessing (EMDR) has become an accepted form of therapy, especially in the treatment of PTSD. Energy-focused therapies probably will become more acceptable as time goes by.

Medication

As we gain more knowledge of the brain and its chemistry, medication will continue to play an important role in the treatment of mental disorders. This is not to say that medication will eliminate psychotherapy; on the contrary, medication and psychotherapy will continue to work together synergistically for increased effectiveness in the treatment of many disorders. Just as medication for schizophrenia, the bipolar disorders, autism, and ADHD is more effective when combined with a psychotherapeutic component, so too will most future treatments benefit when physicians and mental health therapists work together.

However, research shows that a large number of people do not follow through on medication recommendations or they stop taking medication prematurely. Regular psychotherapy can help; through education, stress reduction, support, and the power of the therapeutic alliance, clinicians can encourage their clients to follow both medical and nonmedical treatment recommendations. In addition, even when therapy appears to be more powerful than medication, the initial use of medication often can increase people's ability to benefit from therapy. An example of this is the combined use of medication and cognitive-behavioral therapy in treatment of some anxiety disorders.

Exciting new medications are being reviewed for treatment of substance use disorders, impulse-control disorders, insomnia, eating disorders, and dementia. More than thirty new medications are under review for schizophrenia alone. A vaccine for nicotine addiction is also being considered. The use of newer medications with fewer side effects will also enhance the impact of therapy.

New Treatment Delivery Methods

Ever since Eliza — a Rogerian-style, nondirective computer response to clients — was first created by Joseph Weizenbaum in 1966, therapists have been examining how technology, and particularly computer technology, could assist in the provision of mental health services. Telephone counseling, online testing, computer-based therapist referrals, and e-mail as an adjunct to therapy are all fairly common elements of present-day therapy. So too is videotherapy, which is much like bibliotherapy, in which a client is asked to read a book relevant to the presenting problem and discuss it in the next session. In videotherapy, people are asked to watch a movie for discussion at their next appointment.

Web-Based Delivery Methods. The manner in which psychotherapy can be delivered is changing, but not as rapidly as the technology. Computerized self-help via online support groups, e-mail, or chats; computer-assisted health education; virtual reality; Internet counseling; and videoconferenced psychotherapy all are in their infancy. As the Internet has grown into one of the leading providers of health care information, special forums have sprouted to meet the educational needs of people with a variety of disorders, such as ADHD, bipolar disorder, and depression. Such forums can provide the latest research on empirically supported treatments and can direct interested parties to online communities that offer support and other information for participants. At the same time, Internet sites can provide erroneous and even destructive information. For example, sites exist for people with anorexia nervosa and bulimia nervosa in which participants share ways to lose weight and conceal their weight loss. Therapists should be careful to check out any sites they recommend and inquire about the specifics of sites that are frequently used by their clients.

Technology-assisted counseling can be an effective and necessary means of enabling counselors and clients to communicate across distances, when circumstances indicate that the approach may be necessary or convenient. The benefits of technology include being able to reach a diverse group of people who would otherwise not be reached, in such settings as forensic and corrections centers and in such locations as rural areas where long distances separate clinicians from their clients. Especially for people for whom transportation or face-to-face meetings present a problem (including people who are elderly, impoverished, hearing impaired, disabled, or reluctant to attend therapy because of anxiety or embarrassment), technology can provide access to therapy they would otherwise never have received (Rees & Stone, 2005).

Cybercounseling. Counseling over the Internet is becoming increasingly popular, although the actual number of people currently offering Internet therapy is unknown. Online counseling is being provided via e-mail, bulletin boards, chat rooms, interactive video, and Web-telephone hookup. Although many therapists express guarded concern about participating in cybercounseling, most seem willing to use it as an adjunct to face-to-face counseling. Some advantages of computer-assisted therapy over face-to-face therapy include reduced cost, increased availability of services to a wider number of people, and the potential for anonymity. Use of the Internet and e-mail is growing as a medium for scheduling appointments and responding to short requests for information. However, no empirical research has been conducted on the efficacy of using e-mail for clinical interventions, and the use of e-mail poses additional questions of security; confidentiality; record keeping; and other clinical, legal, and ethical issues.

Training on the ethical issues involved in all forms of technological delivery of treatment is imperative. In their study of 136 Web sites offering Internet counseling via e-mail and chat rooms, Heinlen, Welfel, Richmond, and Rak (2003) found many ethical violations, but noted that credentialed providers had a higher level of compliance with ethical standards than noncredentialed providers. The researchers reported a lack of standardization in services offered, fees charged, and credentials of the providers. They also found that one-third of the Web sites no longer existed eight months after the study began. Other drawbacks of cybercounseling include difficulty in ensuring client welfare and providing adequate informed consent; instability of Web sites; and concerns about the quality of services provided (National Board for Certified Counselors & Center for Credentialing Education, 2006).

Computer-Assisted Health Education. In a study of female college students at risk for developing eating disorders, Winzelberg and colleagues (1998) showed the effectiveness of using a CD-ROM-based psychoeducational prevention program combined with e-mail discussion groups to improve body image and ward off the development of eating disorders. In a later study, called the Student Bodies program (Winzelberg et al., 2000), treatment was delivered through the Internet over the course of eight weeks. The interactive software featured text, audio, and video components; online self-monitoring journals;

and behavior change exercises. Participants were expected to post a weekly message to the discussion group and were prompted to do so via e-mail reminders. Participants anonymously took part in online discussion moderated by a clinical psychology student. Although there were no differences between intervention and control groups, the intervention participants continued to improve between the postintervention and follow-up assessments.

Telephone-Assisted Therapy. A few studies have shown that good results can be achieved by combining self-help treatment with telephone support. This is particularly hopeful for those who are housebound, such as people who are elderly or have limited mobility, people with agoraphobia, and those who live in rural areas. Specifically, bibliotherapy, relaxation techniques, and symptom monitoring have been shown to be effective in treating specific problems (depression, eating disorders, agoraphobia) when accompanied by regular professional telephone support.

Cuijpers (1997) conducted a meta-analysis of seven studies of bibliotherapy for depression and found improvement of those who were treated compared to wait-listed controls. All clients had at least some telephone contact with a therapist (either weekly or at the beginning and end). Another study, conducted by Scogin, Jamison, and Davis (1990), used media announcements to recruit elderly people with depression. Participants were asked to read one of two books on depression over a four-week period. Each received a telephone call weekly. Both groups achieved decreased Beck Depression Inventory scores in contrast to the wait-listed controls, and the gains were maintained at two-year follow-up. Roth and Fonagy (2005) report several other studies that produced similar results when bibliotherapy using self-help texts was combined with telephone check-in for the treatment of depression (Beutler et al., 1991; Smith, Floyd, Scogin, & Jamison, 1997). Clearly, more research is needed in this area, but for clients who are severely disabled or for whom attending a therapy session is not an option, telephone-assisted therapy may prove to be a useful option.

Virtual Reality. Virtual reality has found a place in the treatment of certain anxiety disorders. Specific phobias, such as dental phobias and fear of flying, spiders, and heights, have all been successfully treated (Sue, Sue, & Sue, 2006). Using videotaped images or computer-generated graphics, the therapist can provide the person with increased exposure to the feared object. Roth and Fonagy (2005) report that virtual reality can be as effective as in vivo exposure in the treatment of certain phobias.

Videoconferencing. Many researchers have compared videoconferencing to face-to-face therapy (Glueckauf et al., 2002; Schopp, Johnstone, & Merrell,

2000). In all these studies, no difference was found in the therapeutic alliance or outcomes. Rees and Stone (2005) conclude that the therapeutic alliance is not compromised by the use of videoconferencing for psychotherapy, but that psychologists rated the alliance more negatively, perhaps because of a negative bias against videoconferencing or possibly because it poses a different and unfamiliar way of working with clients. Therapists are trained to observe both verbal and nonverbal cues during therapy sessions. Rees and Stone suggest that additional published effectiveness research and training of therapists in alternative delivery methods could increase their usage.

Developing Internet Interventions. Ritterband and colleagues (2003) briefly outline important steps involved in developing Internet interventions, reminding therapists that "[a]n effective face-to-face intervention is the gold standard by which an Internet intervention will ultimately be compared" (p. 530). They suggest that therapists use caution when creating such interventions and keep in mind the appropriateness of the disorder for Internet treatment; the effectiveness of Internet treatment; legal and ethical issues such as privacy, confidentiality, and credentialing; and the type of Internet delivery (whether Web-based, PC or Mac), hardware issues, and other considerations. Finally, any such program must first be tested to determine feasibility, usability, and effectiveness. A list of Internet interventions is beyond the scope of this book, but interventions currently in use include support systems for people with life-threatening illnesses, such as HIV and breast cancer (Gustafson et al., 1999, 2001); couples therapy (Jerome et al., 2000); and treatment of childhood encopresis (Ritterband et al., 2003), body image and eating attitudes (Winzelberg et al., 2000), posttraumatic stress, and pathological grief (Lange, van de Ven, Schrieken, & Emmelkamp, 2001); suicide assessment and screening (Haas, Hendin, & Mann, 2003); and many others.

The future promises even more technologies and applications for behavioral health service providers. Evans and colleagues (2005) note that adolescents are frequent media users and that technological skill can be a resource to help reduce stigma for adolescents with mental disorders. Ritterband and others (2003) suggest that if the use of interactive video and colorful graphics could make treatment more fun for young people, it is more likely to be used. Clearly, Internet technologies serve a useful purpose as adjunct treatments for a variety of disorders.

Matching Treatments to Clients

Prochaska and Norcross (2006) write that despite fifty years of research into which type of treatment works best with a particular client, the field is not yet at the stage of development in which the best treatment methodology can be matched with the appropriate client variables. Some of the reasons for the lack of clarity with respect to treatment recommendations are obvious. The challenges of conducting research on something as ill-defined and variable as psychotherapy, without also jeopardizing people's right to the best possible treatment, are enormous. In addition, the various therapies have many underlying similarities, and perhaps these are more important than their overt differences, tending to blur distinctions and thereby leading to inconclusive research. Moreover, as we have seen, client- and therapist-related variables seem to be at least as important as those variables involved in the particular approach to therapy. In the foreseeable future, research can be expected to continue to examine the many approaches to psychotherapy, as well as client- and therapist-related variables and their interaction, and the field can be expected to continue evolving.

Evidence-Based Therapy

Scientific research can assess the impact of various treatment approaches on a particular disorder and can provide invaluable guidelines for treatment planning. Two striking examples of the contribution that data-based research can make to psychotherapy are the research conducted at the National Institute of Mental Health on the treatment of bipolar disorders and the research conducted by Brown, O'Leary, and Barlow on the treatment of anxiety disorders; both bodies of research are discussed elsewhere in this volume. Based on empirical research, the American Psychological Association has developed a list of eighteen empirically supported treatment approaches (Levant, 2005).

At the same time, identifying effective treatments for specific disorders is complicated because many disorders are difficult to diagnose and may be mistaken for other, similar disorders. (For example, the diagnostic challenges presented by childhood bipolar disorder, dissociative identity disorder, schizoaffective disorder, and most of the personality disorders have been discussed elsewhere in this book.) Misdiagnosis is only one possible reason for a treatment failure. Others include lack of expertise on the part of the therapist, inappropriate choice of treatment, a challenging client, or a treatment-resistant disorder.

Occasional treatment failures or setbacks are probably inevitable, but therapists can take steps to maximize the likelihood of a successful treatment. Consulting with other mental health practitioners is one important step. Therapists should not hesitate to refer clients for evaluation by someone from a related discipline (perhaps a neurologist or a psychiatrist) to confirm or clarify a diagnosis. Discussion of a case with colleagues also can be useful in gaining ideas for diagnosis and treatment. Frequent evaluation of the progress attained in meeting the goals established in a Client Map is imperative in monitoring a treatment's effectiveness. As indicated in Chapter One, people typically manifest progress fairly early in therapy; if even slight progress is not made in the first few months of treatment, reevaluation and modification of the goals themselves, the treatment plan, or the therapist-client interaction probably are needed. In addition, keeping up to date with the research on treatment effectiveness can enhance therapists' ability to provide effective treatment.

SOCIAL AND CULTURAL INFLUENCES

Multicultural Influences

Multicultural competency is expected of today's clinicians. Most have been trained with a greater sensitivity to and awareness of diversity, including an expanded definition of diversity that includes not only ethnic and cultural backgrounds but abilities, age, gender, religious and spiritual preferences, socioeconomic status, sexual orientation, and other variables. Awareness of the impact of gender and cultural background on personality and emotional health and pathology has also led to the inclusion in *DSM-IV-TR* and other professional texts of extensive narrative material on the relationship of those variables to many of the diagnoses. (For example, particular caution must be exercised in the diagnosis of disorders like dependent personality disorder that are found much more in one gender or cultural group than in others.) The inclusion of this narrative material is indicative of an effort to help clinicians distinguish patterns reflecting cultural influences from those reflecting pathology and, when appropriate, recognize cultural differences in pathology.

Historical Influences

Historical change is another force that shapes our understanding of the diagnosis and treatment of mental disorders. The events of September 11, 2001, and the devastation of New Orleans by Hurricane Katrina in 2005 left survivors reeling from the effects of destruction on such an unimaginable scale. A growing interest in the effect of trauma and stress on mental, physical, and spiritual well-being and increased interest in PTSD have resulted. Many techniques that were once considered "alternative" (such as meditation, relaxation, EMDR, and mindfulness training) are now finding their way into the mainstream. The impact that historical change will have on future diagnosis and treatment planning, although difficult to predict, is certain to be considerable.

Political, Legislative, and Economic Influences

It is also difficult to predict the impact of political, legislative, and economic change on the funding of programs and on attitudes toward mental illness, but these kinds of change are just as important and just as inevitable as historical change. For example, during the Kennedy-Johnson era, funds were made available to develop a nationwide network of community mental health centers. In more recent years, we have seen a decrease in funding for these programs, and this decrease has contributed to a growing number of chronically mentally ill people being released into the community without sufficient support or follow-up care.

Rapid growth of health maintenance organizations, preferred provider organizations, and employee assistance programs, which are very concerned with cost containment, have further contributed to the emphasis on brief treatment of mental disorders. Some third-party payers offer clients very little choice in who their treatment provider will be, and pay little attention to the need for extended treatment for amelioration and prevention of certain mental disorders. Therefore, some people make the choice either to pay large bills themselves for psychotherapy or not receive the treatment they need.

Legislation has also contributed to a shift in who provides mental health services. For example, the number of psychiatrists has been declining, and the number of doctoral-level psychologists has not grown rapidly; at the same time, the number of mental health counselors and social workers has grown considerably, and legislation has both reflected and facilitated these trends. Moreover, although a long-considered national health insurance plan has been on the drawing board for years and has not yet taken legislative form, current federal legislation mandates third-party payers to provide equity in annual and lifetime limits of payment for treatment of mental and physical disorders. Over the years, legislation to provide true parity in copayments, deductibles, and number of visits between mental health and other medical benefits (known as the Wellstone Bill) has been introduced in Congress. The bill's passage would make psychotherapy increasingly available.

Managed care continues to be a fact of life for clinicians, with the focus maintained on cost-effective and efficient treatment. At the same time, MCOs are also becoming more user friendly, with much of the documentation, including billing, being conducted online.

The future of diagnosis and treatment clearly will be affected by many factors and will continue to evolve through research and practice as well as through clinical, biological, social, historical, legal, political, and economic learning and change. One hopes that most of this change will lead to more accurate diagnosis and more effective treatment. We have already learned a great deal, but the field of psychotherapy is in its late adolescence at best; this book alone probably covers more options for treatment than could be explored in all the doctoral dissertations and research projects that will be conducted in the next decade.

The rapid and often unpredictable changes in the field are both exciting and disconcerting. The challenge to mental health therapists is to stay aware of change, incorporate it wisely and selectively into their own therapeutic practices, and promote positive change in their professions. In so doing, they will be able to maximize the rewards that they receive from the practice of their profession and the benefits that psychotherapy can bring to their clients.

Recommended Reading

Barlow, D. H. (Ed.). (2001). *Clinical handbook of psychological disorders* (3rd ed.). New York: Guilford Press.

Barlow, D. H. (Ed.). (2002). *Anxiety and its disorders: The nature and treatment of anxiety and panic* (2nd ed.). New York: Guilford Press.

Beck, A. T., Freeman, A., Davis, D. D., & Associates. (2004). *Cognitive therapy of personality disorders* (2nd ed.). New York: Guilford Press.

Cain, D. J., & Seeman, J. (Eds.). (2001). *Humanistic psychotherapies: Handbook of research and practice.* Washington, DC: American Psychological Association.

Kazdin, A. E., & Weisz, J. R. (Eds.). (2003). *Evidence-based psychotherapies for children and adolescents.* New York: Guilford Press.

Mash, E. J., & Barkley, R. A. (Eds.). (2006). *Treatment of childhood disorders* (3rd ed.). New York: Guilford Press.

Millon, T., Grossman, S., Millon, C., Meagher, S., & Ramnath, R. (2004). *Personality disorders in modern life* (2nd ed.). Hoboken, NJ: Wiley.

Seligman, L. (2004). *Diagnosis and treatment planning in counseling* (3rd ed.). New York: Kluwer/Plenum.

Sperry, L. (2003). *Handbook of diagnosis and treatment of the DSM-IV-TR personality disorders* (2nd ed.). Philadelphia: Brunner-Routledge.

REFERENCES

Abramowitz, J. S., Whiteside, S. P., & Deacon, B. J. (2005). The effectiveness of treatment for pediatric obsessive-compulsive disorder: A meta-analysis. *Behavior Therapy, 36*, 55–63.

Accordino, M. P., & Guerney, B. G., Jr., (2001). The empirical validation of relationship enhancement couple and family therapy. In D. J. Cain & J. Seeman (Eds.), *Humanistic therapies: Handbook of research and practice* (pp. 403–432). Washington, DC: American Psychological Association.

Achenbach, T. (1991). *Manual for the Child Behavior Checklist.* Burlington: University of Vermont, Department of Psychiatry.

Adams, L., Gouvousis, A., VanLue, M., & Waldron, C. (2004). Social story intervention: Improving communication skills in a child with autism spectrum disorder. *Focus on Autism and Other Developmental Disabilities, 19*, 87–94.

Agency for Healthcare Research and Quality. (2006). *Management of eating disorders.* AHRQ Publication No. 06-E010. North Carolina: RTI-UNC Evidence-Based Practice Center.

Agosti, V., & Stewart, J. W. (2001). Atypical and non-atypical subtypes of depression: Comparison of social functioning, symptoms, course of illness, co-morbidity, and demographic features. *Journal of Affective Disorders, 65*, 75–79.

Agras, W. S., Hammer, L., & McNicholas, F. (1999). A prospective study of the influence of eating-disordered mothers on their children. *International Journal of Eating Disorders, 25*, 327–334.

Ahn, H., & Wampold, B. E. (2001). Where oh where are the specific ingredients? A meta-analysis of component studies in counseling and psychotherapy. *Journal of Counseling Psychology, 48*, 251–257.

Ainsworth, M.D.S., Blehar, M. S., Waters, E., & Wall, S. (1978). *Patterns of attachment: A psychological study of the strange situation*. Mahwah, NJ: Erlbaum.

Akechi, T., Okuyama, T., Sugawara, Y., Nakano, T., Shima, Y., & Uchitomi, Y. (2004). Major depression, adjustment disorders, and post-traumatic stress disorder in terminally ill cancer patients: Associated and predictive factors. *Journal of Clinical Oncology, 22*, 1957–1965.

Albano, A. M., Chorpita, B. F., & Barlow, D. H. (2003). Childhood anxiety disorders. In E. J. Mash & R. A. Barkley (Eds.), *Child psychopathology* (2nd ed., pp. 279–329). New York: Guilford Press.

Alexander, J. F., & Parsons, V. B. (1982). *Functional family therapy: Principles and procedures*. Carmel, CA: Brooks-Cole.

Allen, A., & Hollander, E. (2006). Sexual compulsions. In E. Hollander & D. J. Stein (Eds.), *Clinical manual of impulse-control disorders* (pp. 87–114). Arlington, VA: American Psychiatric Publishing.

Altman, E. (2004). Differential diagnosis and assessment of adult bipolar disorder. In S. L. Johnson & R. L. Leahy (Eds.), *Psychological treatment of bipolar disorder* (pp. 35–57). New York: Guilford Press.

Aman, M. G., Armstrong, S., Buican, B., & Sillick, T. (2002). Four-year follow-up of children with low intelligence and ADHD: A replication. *Research in Developmental Disabilities, 23*, 119–134.

American Academy of Child and Adolescent Psychiatry. (1997). Practice parameters for the assessment and treatment of children and adolescents with conduct disorders. *Journal of the American Academy of Child and Adolescent Psychiatry, 36*(Suppl. 10), 85–121.

American Academy of Child and Adolescent Psychiatry. (2003). *Policy statement: Coercive interventions for reactive attachment disorder*. Washington, DC: Author.

American Academy of Child and Adolescent Psychiatry. (2005). *Practice parameter for the assessment and treatment of children and adolescents with reactive attachment disorders in infancy and childhood* [Online]. Available: www.aacap.org

American Academy of Pediatrics. (2001). *Clinical practice guidelines: Treatment of the school-aged child with attention-deficit/hyperactivity disorder*. American Academy of Pediatrics. [Online.] Available: www.aappolicy.aappublications.org

American Association on Mental Retardation. (2002). *Mental retardation: Definition, classification, and systems of support* (10th ed.). Washington, DC: Author.

American Cancer Society. (2006). Help with physical addiction: Nicotine replacement therapy and other medicines. In *Guide to quitting smoking* [Online]. Available: www.cancer.org

American Psychiatric Association. (2000). *Diagnostic and statistical manual of mental disorders* (4th ed., text rev.). Washington, DC: Author.

American Psychiatric Association. (2001). *Practice guidelines for the treatment of borderline personality disorder*. Washington, DC: Author.

American Psychiatric Association. (2002). *Position statement: Reactive attachment disorder*. Washington, DC: Author.

American Psychiatric Association. (2004a). *Practice guideline for the treatment of patients with bipolar disorder* (2nd ed.). Washington, DC: Author.

American Psychiatric Association. (2004b). *Practice guideline for the treatment of patients with schizophrenia*. Washington, DC: Author.

American Psychological Association Task Force Steering Committee, Division 29. (2001). Empirically supported therapy relationships: Conclusions and recommendations of the Division 29 Task Force. *Psychotherapy, 38*, 495–497.

Anastopoulos, A. D., & Farley, S. E. (2003). A cognitive-behavioral training program for parents of children with attention-deficit/hyperactivity disorder. In A. E. Kazdin & J. R. Weisz (Eds.), *Evidence-based psychotherapies for children and adolescents* (pp. 187–203). New York: Guilford Press.

Anderson, E. M., & Lambert, M. J. (2001). A survival analysis of clinically significant change in outpatient psychotherapy. *Journal of Clinical Psychology, 57*, 875–888.

Angst, J., Adolfsson, R., Benazzi, F., Gamma, A., Hantouche, E., Meyer, T. D., Skeppar, P., Vieta, E., & Scott, J. (2005). The HCL-32: Towards a self-assessment tool for hypomanic symptoms in outpatients. *Journal of Affective Disorders, 88*, 217–233.

Antony, M. M., & Barlow, D. H. (2002). Specific phobias. In D. H. Barlow (Ed.), *Anxiety and its disorders* (pp. 380–417). New York: Guilford Press.

Antony, M. M., Orsillo, S. M., & Roemer, L. (Eds.). (2001). *Practitioner's guide to empirically based measures of anxiety*. New York: Kluwer Academic/Plenum.

Appelbaum, P. S., Robbins, P. C., & Monahan, J. (2000). Violence and delusions: Data from the MacArthur Violence Risk Assessment Study. *American Journal of Psychiatry, 157*, 566–572.

Araoz, D. L., & Carrese, M. A. (1996). *Solution oriented brief therapy for adjustment disorders: A guide for providers under managed care*. New York: Brunner/Mazel.

Arnkoff, D. B., Glass, C. R., & Shapiro, S. J. (2002). Clients' expectations and preferences. In J. C. Norcross (Ed.), *Psychotherapy relationships that work: Therapist contributions and responsiveness to patients* (pp. 335–356). New York: Oxford University Press.

Arntz, M., & Van den Hout, M. (1996). Psychological treatments of panic disorder without agoraphobia: Cognitive therapy versus applied relaxation. *Behaviour Research and Therapy, 34*, 113–121.

Asarnow, J. R., & Asarnow, R. F. (2003). Childhood-onset schizophrenia. In E. J. Mash & R. A. Barkley (Eds.), *Child psychopathology* (2nd ed., pp. 455–485). New York: Guilford Press.

Aschenbrand, S. G., Kendall, P. C., Webb, A., Safford, S. M., & Flannery-Schroeder, E. (2003). Is childhood separation anxiety disorder a predictor of adult panic disorder and agoraphobia? A seven-year longitudinal study. *Journal of the American Academy of Child and Adolescent Psychiatry, 42*, 1478–1485.

Avery, D. H., Holtzheimer, P. E., Fawaz, W., Russo, J., Neumaier, J., Dunner, D. L., Haynor, D. R., Claypoole, K. H., Wajdik, C., & Roy-Byrne, P. (2006). A controlled study of repetitive transcranial magnetic stimulation in medication-resistant major depression. *Biological Psychiatry, 59*, 187–194.

Azar, S. T., & Wolfe, D. A. (2006). Child physical abuse and neglect. In E. J. Mash & R. A. Barkley (Eds.), *Treatment of childhood disorders* (3rd ed., pp. 595–646). New York: Guilford Press.

Azrin, N. H., Sneed, T. J., & Foxx, R. M. (1973). Dry bed: A rapid method of eliminating bedwetting (enuresis) of the retarded. *Behaviour Research and Therapy, 11*, 427–434.

Bagenholm, A., & Gillberg, C. (1991). Psychosocial effects on siblings of children with autism and mental retardation: A population-based study. *Journal of Mental Deficiency Research, 35*, 291–307.

Bagheri, M. M., Kerbeshian, J., & Burd, L. (1999). Recognition and management of Tourette's syndrome and tic disorders. *American Family Physician, 59*, 2263–2272.

Baird, G., Charman, T., Cox, A., Baron Cohen, S., Swettenham, J., Wheelwright, S., & Drew, A. (2001). Screening and surveillance for autism and pervasive developmental disorders. *Archives of Disease in Childhood, 84*, 468–475.

Baker, S. L., Patterson, M. D., & Barlow, D. H. (2002). Panic disorder and agoraphobia. In M. M. Antony & D. H. Barlow (Eds.), *Handbook of assessment and treatment planning for psychological disorders* (pp. 67–112). New York: Guilford Press.

Baldessarini, R. J., & Tondo, L. (2003). Suicide risk and treatments for patients with bipolar disorder. *Journal of the American Medical Association, 290*, 1517–1519.

Barbaree, H. E., & Marshall, W. E. (1985). Anxiety-based disorders. In M. Hersen & S. M. Turner (Eds.), *Diagnostic interviewing* (pp. 55–77). New York: Plenum.

Barber, J. P., Connolly, M. B., Crits-Christoph, P., Gladys, L., & Siqueland, L. (2000). Alliance predicts patients' outcome beyond in-treatment change in symptoms. *Journal of Consulting and Clinical Psychology, 68*, 1027–1032.

Barkley, R. A. (2006). *Attention-deficit hyperactivity disorder: A handbook for diagnosis and treatment* (3rd ed.). New York: Guilford Press.

Barkley, R. A., & Murphy, K. R. (2006). *Attention deficit hyperactivity disorder: A clinical workbook* (3rd ed.). New York: Guilford Press.

Barlow, D. H. (Ed.). (2001). *Clinical handbook of psychological disorders* (3rd ed.). New York: Guilford Press.

Barlow, D. H. (2002). *Anxiety and its disorders: The nature and treatment of anxiety and panic* (2nd ed.). New York: Guilford Press.

Barlow, D. H. (2004). Psychological treatments. *American Psychologist, 59*, 869–879.

Barlow, D. H., Raffa, S. D., & Cohen, E. M. (2002). Psychosocial treatments for panic disorders, phobias, and generalized anxiety disorder. In P. E. Nathan & J. M. Gorman (Eds.), *A guide to treatments that work* (2nd ed., pp. 301–336). New York: Oxford University Press.

Baron-Cohen, S., Allen, J., & Gillberg, C. (1992). Can autism be detected at 18 months? The needle, the haystack, and the CHAT. *British Journal of Psychiatry, 161*, 839–843.

Barrett, P. B., Duffy, A. L., Dadds, M. R., & Rapee, R. M. (2001). Cognitive-behavioral treatment of anxiety disorders in children: Long-term (6-year) follow-up. *Journal of Consulting and Clinical Psychology, 69*, 135–141.

Barrett, P. M., & Shortt, A. L. (2003). Parental involvement in the treatment of anxious children. In A. E. Kazdin & J. R. Weisz (Eds.), *Evidence-based psychotherapies for children and adolescents* (pp. 101–119). New York: Guilford Press.

Basco, M. R., & Rush, A. J. (2005). *Cognitive-behavioral therapy for bipolar disorder*. New York: Guilford Press.

Baumeister, A. A., & Baumeister, A. A. (1995). Mental retardation. In M. Herson & R. T. Ammerman (Eds.), *Advanced abnormal child psychology* (pp. 283–304). Mahwah, NJ: Erlbaum.

Beck, A. T., & Emery, G. (1985). *Anxiety disorders and phobias*. New York: Basic Books.

Beck, A. T., Freeman, A., Davis, D. D., & Associates. (2004). *Cognitive therapy of personality disorders* (2nd ed.). New York: Guilford Press.

Beck, A. T., Rush, A. J., Shaw, B. F., & Emery, G. (1979). *Cognitive therapy of depression*. New York: Guilford Press.

Beck, A. T., & Steer, R. A. (1990). *Manual for the Beck Anxiety Inventory*. San Antonio, TX: Psychological Corporation.

Beck, A. T., Steer, R. A., & Brown, G. K. (1996). *Beck Depression Inventory*, 2nd ed. manual. San Antonio, TX: Psychological Corporation.

Beck, J. (2005). *Cognitive therapy for challenging problems*. New York: Guilford Press.

Beck, M., Friedlander, M. L., & Escudero, V. (2006). Three perspectives on clients' experiences of the therapeutic alliance: A discovery-oriented investigation. *Journal of Marital and Family Therapy, 32*, 355–368.

Becker, K. D., Stuewig, J., Herrera, V. M., & McCloskey, L. A. (2004). A study of firesetting and animal cruelty in children: Family influences and adolescent outcomes. *Journal of the American Academy of Child and Adolescent Psychiatry, 43*, 905–912.

Bellack, A., & Mueser, K. T. (1993). Psychosocial treatment for schizophrenia. *Schizophrenia Bulletin, 19*, 317–336.

Bellack, A., Mueser, K. T., Gingerich, S., & Agresta, J. (2004). *Social skills training for schizophrenia* (2nd ed.). New York: Guilford Press.

Benazon, N. R., & Coyne, J. C. (2000). Living with a depressed spouse. *Journal of Family Psychology, 14*, 71–79.

Benton, T. D., & Lynch, J. (2006, July 13). Adjustment disorders. *EMedicine* [Online]. Available: www.emedicine.com/Med/topic3348.htm

Berardelli, A., Curr, A., Fabbrini, G., Gillio, F., & Manfredi, M. (2003). Pathophysiology of tics and Tourette's syndrome. *Journal of Neurology, 250,* 781–787.

Bergman, R. L., Piacentini, J., & McKracken, J. T. (2002). Prevalence and description of selective mutism in a school-based sample. *Journal of the American Academy of Child and Adolescent Psychiatry, 41,* 938–946.

Berman, J. S., & Norton, N. C. (1985). Does professional training make a therapist more effective? *Psychological Bulletin, 98,* 401–407.

Bernstein, D. P., Fink, L., Handlesman, L., Foote, J., Lovejoy, M., Wenzel, K., Sapareto, E., & Ruggiero, J. (1994). Initial reliability and validity of a new retrospective measure of child abuse and neglect. *American Journal of Psychiatry, 151,* 1132–1136.

Bernstein, E. B., & Putnam, F. W. (1986). Development, reliability, and validity of a dissociation scale. *Journal of Nervous and Mental Disease, 174,* 727–735.

Beutler, L. E., & Consoli, A. J. (1993). Matching the therapist's interpersonal stance to clients' characteristics: Contributions from systematic eclectic psychotherapy. *Psychotherapy, 30,* 417–422.

Beutler, L. E., Crago, M., & Arizmendi, T. G. (1986). Therapist variables to psychotherapy process. In S. L. Garfield & A. E. Bergin (Eds.), *Handbook of psychotherapy and behavior change* (3rd ed., pp. 257–310). Hoboken, NJ: Wiley.

Beutler, L. E., Engle, D., Mohr, D., Daldrup, R., Bergan, J., Meredith, K., & Merry, W. (1991). Predictors of differential response to cognitive, experiential, and self-directed psychotherapeutic procedures. *Journal of Consulting and Clinical Psychology, 59,* 333–340.

Biederman, J., Faraone, S. V., Chu, M., & Wozniak, J. (1999). Further evidence of a bidirectional overlap between juvenile mania and conduct disorder in children. *Journal of the American Academy of Child and Adolescent Psychiatry, 38,* 468–476.

Biederman, J., Newcorn, J., & Sprich, S. (1991). Comorbidity of attention deficit hyperactivity disorder and juvenile mania: An overlooked comorbidity? *Journal of the American Academy of Child and Adolescent Psychiatry, 35,* 997–1009.

Bienvenu, O. J., Samuels, J. F., Riddle, M. A., Hoehn-Saric, R., Liang, K. Y., Cullen, B.A.M., Grados, M. A., & Nestadt, G. (2000). The relationship of obsessive-compulsive disorder to possible spectrum disorders: Results from a family study. *Biological Psychiatry, 48,* 287–293.

Birch, L. L., Fisher, J. O., & Davison, K. K. (2003). Learning to overeat: Maternal use of restrictive feeding practices promotes girls' eating in the absence of hunger. *American Journal of Clinical Nutrition, 78,* 215–220.

Bishop, F. M. (2001). *Managing addictions: Cognitive, emotive, and behavioral techniques.* Northvale, NJ: Aronson.

Black, B., & Uhde, T. W. (1994). Treatment of elective mutism with fluoxetine: A double-blind, placebo-controlled study. *Journal of the American Academy of Child and Adolescent Psychiatry, 33,* 1000–1006.

Black, B., & Uhde, T. W. (1995). Psychiatric characteristics of children with selective mutism: A pilot study. *Journal of American Academy of Child and Adolescent Psychiatry, 34,* 847–856.

Blanchard, E. B., Jones-Alexander, J., Buckley, T. C., & Forneris, C. A. (1996). Psychometric properties of the PTSD checklist. *Behaviour Research and Therapy, 34,* 669–673.

Bloch, C., Crouch, E., & Reibstein, J. (1981). Therapeutic factors in group psychotherapy. *Archives of General Psychiatry, 38,* 519–526.

Bloom, B. (2001). Focused single-session psychotherapy: A review of the clinical and research literature. *Brief Treatment and Crisis Intervention, 1,* 75–86.

Bloom, B. (2002). Brief intervention for anxiety disorders: Clinical outcome studies. *Brief Treatment and Crisis Intervention, 2,* 325–329.

Bohart, A., & Tallman, K. (1999). *How clients make therapy work: The process of active self-healing.* Washington DC: American Psychological Association.

Bolles, R. N. (2006). *What color is your parachute? A practical manual for job hunters and career changers* (Rev. ed.). Berkeley, CA: Ten Speed Press.

Bond, M. R. (2006). Psychiatric disorders and pain. In S. B. McMahon & M. Kottzenburg (Eds.), *Wall and Melzack's textbook of pain* (5th ed., 259–266). Philadelphia: Elsevier Churchill Livingstone.

Bordin, E. S. (1979). The generalizability of the psychoanalytic concept of the working alliance. *Psychotherapy, 16,* 252–260.

Borkovec, T. D., & Ruscio, A. M. (2001). Psychotherapy for generalized anxiety disorder. *Journal of Clinical Psychiatry, 62,* 37–42.

Boss, P. (2000). *Ambiguous loss: Learning to live with unresolved grief.* Cambridge, MA: Harvard University Press.

Boss, P. (2006). *Loss, trauma, and resilience: Therapeutic work with ambiguous loss.* New York: Norton.

Botteron, K. N., & Geller, B. (1995). Pharmacologic treatment of childhood and adolescent mania. *Child and Adolescent Psychiatric Clinics of North America, 4,* 282–304.

Bourne, E. J. (2005). *The anxiety and phobia workbook* (4th ed.). New York: Harbinger.

Bowden, C. L., Kusumakar, V., MacMaster, F. P., & Yatham, L. N. (2002). Diagnosis and treatment of hypomania and mania. In L. N. Yatham, V. Kusumakar, & S. P. Kutcher (Eds.), *Bipolar disorder: A clinician's guide to biological treatments* (pp. 1–16). Philadelphia: Brunner-Routledge.

Bowlby, J. (1982). *Attachment and loss: Vol. 1. Attachment.* New York: Basic Books. (Original work published 1969)

Bowman, D., Scogin, F., Floyd, M., & McKendree-Smith, N. (2001). Psychotherapy length of stay and outcome: A meta-analysis of the effect of therapist sex. *Psychotherapy, 38*, 142–148.

Bozarth, J. D., Zimring, F. M., & Tausch, R. (2001). Client-centered therapy: The evolution of a revolution. In D. J. Cain & J. Seeman (Eds.), *Handbook of research and practice in humanistic psychotherapy* (pp. 147–188). Washington, DC: American Psychological Association.

Bradford, D., Stroup, S., & Lieberman, J. (2002). Pharmacological treatments for schizophrenia. In P. E. Nathan & J. M. Gorman (Eds.), *A guide to treatments that work* (2nd ed., pp. 169–200). New York: Oxford University Press.

Bridges, W. (2001). *The way of transition: Embracing life's most difficult moments*. Cambridge, MA: Perseus.

Brinkmeyer, M. Y., & Eyberg, S. M. (2003). Parent-child interaction therapy for oppositional children. In A. E. Kazdin & J. R. Weisz (Eds.), *Evidence-based psychotherapies for children and adolescents* (pp. 204–223). New York: Guilford Press.

Brooks-Gunn, J., Klebanov, P. K., Smith, J., Duncan, G. J., & Lee, K. (2003). The black-white test score gap in young children: Contributions of test and family characteristics. *Applied Development Science, 7*, 239–252.

Brown, T. A., Di Nardo, P. A., & Barlow, D. H. (1994). *Anxiety Disorders Interview Schedule for DSM-IV (ADIS-IV)*. San Antonio, TX: Psychological Corporation Graywind.

Brown, T. A., O'Leary, T. A., & Barlow, D. H. (1993). Generalized anxiety disorder. In D. H. Barlow (Ed.), *Clinical handbook of psychological disorders* (2nd ed., pp. 137–188). New York: Guilford Press.

Buchsbaum, D. G., Buchanan, R. G., Centor, R. M., Schnoll, S. H., & Lawton, M. J. (1991). Screening for alcohol abuse using CAGE scores and likelihood ratios. *Annals of Internal Medicine, 115*, 774–777.

Budman, S. H. (1981). *Forms of brief therapy*. New York: Guilford Press.

Bulik, C. M., Sullivan, P. F., Tozzi, F., Furberg, H., Lichtenstein, P., & Pedersen, N. L. (2006). Prevalence, heritability, and prospective risk factors for anorexia nervosa. *Archives of General Psychiatry, 63*, 305–312.

Burns, G. L., & Walsh, J. A. (2002). The influences of ADHD hyperactivity/impulsivity symptoms on the development of oppositional defiant disorder symptoms in a 2-year longitudinal study. *Journal of Abnormal Child Psychology, 30*, 245–256.

Butcher, J. N., Mineka, S., & Hooley, J. M. (2006). *Abnormal psychology* (13th ed.). Boston: Pearson Education.

Cain, D. J., & Seeman, J. (Eds.). (2001). *Humanistic psychotherapies: Handbook of research and practice*. Washington, DC: American Psychological Association.

Cameron, P., Leszcz, M., Bebchuk, W., Swinson, R., Antony, M., Azim, H., Doidge, N., Korenblum, M., Nigam, T., Christopher, P., & Seeman, M. (1999). The practice and roles of the psychotherapies: A discussion paper. *Canadian Journal of Psychiatry, 44*(Suppl.), 185–315.

Campbell, J., Cueva, J. E., & Hallin, A. (1995). Autism and pervasive developmental disorders. In G. O. Gabbard (Ed.), *Treatments of psychiatric disorders* (pp. 141–166). Washington, DC: American Psychiatric Press.

Campbell, L. A., & Brown, T. A. (2002). Generalized anxiety disorder. In M. M. Antony & D. H. Barlow (Eds.), *Handbook of assessment and treatment planning for psychological disorders* (pp. 147–181). New York: Guilford Press.

Cantwell, D. P. (1996). Attention deficit disorder: A review of the past 10 years. *Journal of the American Academy of Child and Adolescent Psychiatry, 35*, 978–987.

Cardena, E., & Weiner, L. A. (2004). Evaluation of dissociation throughout the lifespan. *Psychotherapy, 41*, 496–508.

Carrier, J. W., & Ennis, K. (2004). Depression and suicide. In D. Capuzzi (Ed.), *Suicide across the lifespan* (pp. 39–62). Alexandria, VA: American Counseling Association.

Carroll, E. M., Rueger, D. B., Foy, D. W., & Donahoe, C. P., Jr. (1985). Vietnam combat veterans with posttraumatic stress disorder: Analysis of marital and cohabiting adjustment. *Journal of Abnormal Psychology, 94*, 329–337.

Carroll, R. A. (2007). Gender dysphoria and transgender experiences. In S. R. Leiblum (Ed.), *Principles and practice of sex therapy* (4th ed., pp. 477–508). New York: Guilford Press.

Centers for Disease Control and Prevention. (2003). *Web-based Injury Statistics Query and Reporting System (WISQARS)* [Online]. National Center for Injury Prevention and Control. Available: www.cdc.gov/ncipc/wisqars

Chamberlain, L. L., & Jew, C. L. (2005). Assessment and diagnosis. In P. Stevens & R. L. Smith (Eds.), *Substance abuse counseling: Theory and practice* (3rd ed., pp. 123–158). Upper Saddle River, NJ: Pearson Education.

Chamberlain, P., & Smith, D. K. (2003). Antisocial behavior in children and adolescents. In A. E. Kazdin & J. R. Weisz (Eds.), *Evidence-based psychotherapies for children and adolescents* (pp. 282–300). New York: Guilford Press.

Chambless, D. L. (1990). Spacing of exposure sessions in treatment of agoraphobia and simple phobia. *Behavior Therapy, 21*, 217–229.

Chambless, D. L., Caputo, G., Bright, P., & Gallagher, R. (1984). Assessment of fear in agoraphobics: The Body Sensations Questionnaire and the Agoraphobic Cognition Questionnaire. *Journal of Consulting and Clinical Psychology, 52*, 1090–1097.

Chambless, D. L., Caputo, G., Gracely, S., Jasin, E., & Williams, C. (1985). The Mobility Inventory for Agoraphobia. *Behaviour Research and Therapy, 23*, 35–44.

Chambless, D. L., & Ollendick, T. H. (2001). Empirically supported psychological interventions: Controversies and evidence. *Annual Review of Psychology, 52*, 685–716.

Christenson, G. A., Mackenzie, T. B., & Mitchell, J. E. (1991). Characteristics of 60 adult chronic hair pullers. *American Journal of Psychiatry, 148*, 365–370.

Clarke, G., DeBar, L., Ludman, E., Asarnow, J., & Jaycox, L. (2002). *Steady Project intervention manual: Collaborative care, cognitive-behavioral program for depressed youth in a primary care setting* [Online]. Available: www.kpchr.org/public/acwd/acwd.html

Clarkin, J. F., Frances, A. J., & Perry, S. (1992). Differential therapeutics: Macro and micro levels of treatment planning. In J. C. Norcross & M. R. Goldfried (Eds.), *Handbook of psychotherapy integration* (pp. 463–502). New York: Basic Books.

Coccaro, E. F., & Danehy, M. (2006). Intermittent explosive disorder. In E. Hollander & D. J. Stein (Eds.), *Clinical manual of impulse-control disorders* (pp. 19–38). Arlington, VA: American Psychiatric Publishing.

Coccaro, E. F., Harvey, P. D., Kupsaw-Lawrence, E., Herbert, J. L., & Bernstein, D. P. (1991). Development of neuropharmacologically based behavioral assessments of impulsive aggression. *Journal of Neuropsychiatry, 3*, S44–S51.

Coccaro, E. F., Posternak, M. A., & Zimmerman, M. (2005). Prevalence and features of intermittent explosive disorder in a clinical setting. *Journal of Clinical Psychiatry, 66*, 1221–1227.

Coleman, H.K.L., Wampold, B. E., & Casali, S. L. (1995). Ethnic minorities' ratings of ethnically similar and European American counselors: A meta-analysis. *Journal of Counseling Psychology, 42*, 55–64.

Coleman, M. C., & Webber, J. (2002). *Emotional and behavioral disorders: Theory and practice.* Boston: Allyn & Bacon.

Colvin, L., Fyfe, S., Leonard, S., Schiavello, T., Ellaway, C., de Klerk, N., Christodoulou, J., Msall, M., & Leonard, H. (2003). Describing the phenotype in Rett syndrome using a population database. *Archives of Disease in Childhood, 88*, 38–43.

Compton, W. M., Grant, B. F., Colliver, J. D., Glantz, M. D., & Stinson, F. S. (2004). Prevalence of marijuana use disorders in the United States: 1991–1992 and 2001–2002. *Journal of the American Medical Association, 291*, 2114–2121.

Conners, C. K. (1997). *Conners' Rating Scale-Revised manual.* North Tonawanda, NY: Mental Health Systems.

Connors, C. J., Walitzer, K. S., & Dermen, K. H. (2002). Preparing clients for alcoholism treatment: Effects on treatment participation and outcomes. *Journal of Consulting and Clinical Psychology, 70*, 1161–1169.

Constantino, M. J., Arnow, B. A., Blasey, C., & Agras, W. S. (2005). The association between patient characteristics and the therapeutic alliance in cognitive-behavioral and interpersonal therapy for bulimia nervosa. *Journal of Consulting and Clinical Psychology, 73*, 203–211.

Corcoran, K., & Boyer-Quick, J. (2002). How clinicians can effectively use assessment tools to evidence medical necessity and throughout the treatment process. In A. R. Roberts & G. J. Greene (Eds.), *Social workers' desk reference* (pp. 198–204). New York: Oxford University Press.

Coryell, W. H. (2002). Maintenance therapies in bipolar affective disorder. In L. N. Yatham, V. Kusumakar, & S. P. Kutcher (Eds.), *Bipolar disorder: A clinician's guide to biological treatments* (pp. 59–84). Philadelphia: Brunner-Routledge.

Costin, C. (1999). *The eating disorder sourcebook: A comprehensive guide to the causes, treatments, and prevention of eating disorders*. Los Angeles: Lowell House.

Cottone, J., Drucker, P., & Javier, R. A. (2003). Gender differences in psychotherapy dyads: Changes in psychological symptoms and responsiveness to treatment during three months of therapy. *Psychotherapy, 40*, 297–308.

Cowan, P. A., Cohn, D. A., Cowan, C. P., & Pearson, J. L. (1996). Parents' attachment histories and children's externalizing and internalizing behaviors: Exploring family systems models of linkage. *Journal of Consulting and Clinical Psychology, 64*, 53–64.

Cox, D. J., Ritterband, L. M., Quillian, W., Kovatchev, B., Morris, J., Sutphen, J., & Borowitz, S. (2003). Assessment of behavioral mechanisms maintaining encopresis: Virginia Encopresis-Constipation Apperception Test. *Journal of Pediatric Psychology, 28*, 375–382.

Cox, D. J., Sutphen, J., Borowitz, S., Kovatchev, B., & Ling, W. (1998). Contribution of behavior therapy and biofeedback to laxative therapy in the treatment of pediatric encopresis. *Annals of Behavioral Medicine, 20*, 70–76.

Coyne, J. C. (1976). Depression and the response of others. *Journal of Abnormal Psychology, 85*, 186–193.

Craighead, L. W. (2002). Obesity and eating disorders. In M. M. Antony & D. H. Barlow (Eds.), *Handbook of assessment and treatment planning for psychological disorders* (pp. 300–340). New York: Guilford Press.

Craighead, W. E., Hart, A. B., Craighead, L. W., & Ilardi, S. S. (2002). Psychosocial treatments for major depressive disorder. In P. E. Nathan & J. M. Gorman (Eds.), *A guide to treatments that work* (2nd ed., pp. 245–262). New York: Oxford University Press.

Craighead, W. E., Miklowitz, D. J., Frank, E., & Vaik, F. C. (2002). Psychosocial treatments for bipolar disorder. In P. E. Nathan & J. M. Gorman (Eds.), *A guide to treatments that work* (2nd ed., pp. 263–276). New York: Oxford University Press.

Craske, M. G., & Barlow, D. H. (1993). Panic disorder and agoraphobia. In D. H. Barlow (Ed.), *Clinical handbook of psychological disorders* (2nd ed., pp. 1–47). New York: Guilford Press.

Craske, M. G., & Barlow, D. H. (2006). *Mastery of your anxiety and panic: Client workbook for anxiety and panic* (4th ed.). New York: Oxford University Press.

Crits-Christoph, P., Baranackie, K., Kurcias, J. S., Beck, A. T., Carroll, K., Perry, K., Luborsky, L., McLellan, T., Woody, G. E., Thompson, L., Gallagher, D., & Zitrin, C. (1991). Meta-analysis of therapist effects in psychotherapy outcome studies. *Psychotherapy Research, 1*, 81–91.

Crits-Christoph, P., & Barber, J. P. (2002). Psychological treatments for personality disorders. In P. E. Nathan & J. M. Gorman (Eds.), *A guide to treatments that work* (2nd ed., pp. 611–624). New York: Oxford University Press.

Crosson-Tower, C. (2005). *Understanding child abuse and neglect* (6th ed.). Boston: Allyn & Bacon.

Cuddy-Casey, M. (1997). A case study using a child-centered play therapy approach to treat enuresis and encopresis. *Elementary School Guidance and Counseling, 31*, 220–223.

Cuijpers, P. (1997). Bibliotherapy in unipolar depression: A meta-analysis. *Journal of Behavior Therapy and Experimental Psychiatry, 28*, 139–147.

Dalai Lama, & Cutler, H. C. (1998). *The art of happiness: A handbook for living.* New York: Riverhead Books.

Davidson, L., O'Connell, M. J., Tondora, J., Lawless, M., & Evans, A. C. (2005). Recovery in serious mental illness: A new wine or just a new bottle? *Professional Psychology: Research and Practice, 36*, 480–487.

Dawson, D. A., Grant, B. F., Stinson, F. S., Chou, P. S., Huang, B., & Ruan, W. J. (2005). Recovery from *DSM-IV* alcohol dependence: United States, 2001–2002. *Addiction, 100*, 281–292.

Deckersbach, T., Rauch, S., Bulhmann, U., & Wilhelm, S. (2006). Habit reversal versus supportive psychotherapy in Tourette's disorder: A randomized controlled trial and predictors of treatment response. *Behaviour Research and Therapy, 44*, 1079–1090.

Deffenbacher, J. L., Filetti, L. B., Lynch, R. S., Dahlen, E. R., & Oetting, E. R (2002). Cognitive-behavioral treatment of high anger drivers. *Behaviour Research and Therapy, 40*, 895–910.

Delgado, P. L., & Gelenberg, A. J. (2001). Antidepressant and antimanic medication. In G. O. Gabbard (Ed.), *Treatments of psychiatric disorders* (pp. 1137–1179). Washington, DC: American Psychiatric Press.

della Cava, M. R. (2006, February 27). When sleep is just a dream. *USA Today*. p. A-1.

DeLong, R. (1994). Children with autistic spectrum disorder and a family history of affective disorder. *Developmental Medicine and Child Neurology, 36*, 674–688.

Derogatis, L. R. (1997). The Derogatis Interview for Sexual Functioning: An introductory report. *Journal of Sex and Marital Therapy, 23*, 291–304.

de Shazer, S. (1991). *Putting difference to work*. New York: Norton.

Dickerson, F. B. (2000). Cognitive behavioral psychotherapy for schizophrenia: A review of recent empirical studies. *Schizophrenia Research, 43*(2–3), 71–90.

Dickey, C. C., McCarley, R. W., Niznikiewicz, M. A., Voglmaier, M. M., Seidman, L. J., Kim, S., & Shenton, M. E. (2005). Clinical, cognitive, and social characteristics of a sample of neuroleptic-naïve persons with schizotypal personality disorder. *Schizophrenia Research, 78*, 297–308.

Dishion, T. J., & Andrews, D. W. (1995). Preventing escalation in problem behaviors with high-risk young adolescents: Immediate and 1-year outcomes. *Journal of Consulting and Clinical Psychology, 63*, 538–548.

Dishion, T. J., McCord, J., & Poulin, F. (1999). When interventions harm: Peer groups and problem behavior. *American Psychologist, 54*, 755–764.

Dougherty, D. D., Rauch, S. L., & Jenike, M. A. (2002). Pharmacological treatments for obsessive compulsive disorder. In P. E. Nathan & J. M. Gorman (Eds.), *A guide to treatments that work* (2nd ed., pp. 387–410). New York: Oxford University Press.

Dozois, D.J.A., & Dobson, K. S. (2002). Depression. In M. M. Antony & D. H. Barlow (Eds.), *Handbook of assessment and treatment planning for psychological disorders* (pp. 259–299). New York: Guilford Press.

Drake, R. E., Essock, S. M., Shaner, A., Carey, K. B., Minkoff, K., Kola, L., Lynde, D., Osher, F. C., Clark, R. E., & Rickards, L. (2001). Evidence-based practices: Implementing dual diagnosis services for clients with severe mental illness. *Psychiatric Services, 52*, 469–476.

Drake, R. E., & Mueser, K. T. (2002). Co-occurring alcohol use disorder and schizophrenia. *Alcohol: Research & Health, 26*, 99–102.

Durlak, J. A., Fuhrman, T., & Lampman, C. (1991). Effectiveness of cognitive-behavior therapy for maladapting children: A meta-analysis. *Psychological Bulletin, 110*, 204–214.

Duval, S. (2005). Six-year-old Thomas diagnosed with pediatric onset bipolar: A case study. *Journal of Child and Adolescent Psychiatric Nursing, 18*, 38–42.

Eaves, L. C., & Ho, H. H. (2004). The very early identification of autism: Outcome to age $4\frac{1}{2}$–5. *Journal of Autism and Developmental Disorders, 34*, 367–378.

Eells, T. D, Lombart, K. G., Kendjelic, E. M., Turner, L. C., & Lucas, C. P. (2005). The quality of psychotherapy case formulations: A comparison of expert, experienced, and novice cognitive-behavioral and psychodynamic therapists. *Journal of Consulting and Clinical Psychology, 73*, 579–589.

Egan, S. K., & Perry, D. G. (2001). Gender identity: A multidimensional analysis with implications for psychosocial adjustment. *Developmental Psychology, 37*, 451–463.

Eggen, D. (2007, June 2). Violent crime up for a second year. *The Washington Post*, p. A-1.

Ehlers, S., Gillberg, C., & Wing, L. (1999). A screening questionnaire for Asperger syndrome and other high-functioning autism spectrum disorders in school age children. *Journal of Autism and Developmental Disorders, 29*, 129–141.

Eifert, G. H., & Forsyth, J. P. (2005). *Acceptance and commitment therapy for anxiety disorders*. Oakland, CA: New Harbinger.

Eikeseth, S., Smith, T., Jahr, E., & Eldevik, S. (2002). Intensive behavioral treatment at school for 4- to 7-year-old children with autism: A 1-year comparison controlled study. *Behavior Modification, 26*, 49–68.

Eisendrath, S. J. (1995). Factitious disorders and malingering. In G. O. Gabbard (Ed.), *Treatments of psychiatric disorders* (pp. 1803–1818). Washington DC: American Psychiatric Press.

Ellason, J. W., & Ross, C. A. (1997). Two-year follow-up of inpatients with dissociative disorder. *American Journal of Psychiatry, 154*, 832–839.

Elliott, E. J. (2002). Juvenile justice diversion and intervention. In D. Kolko (Ed.), *Handbook on firesetting in children and youth* (pp. 383–394). San Diego: Academic Press.

Elliott, R. (1995). Therapy process research and clinical practice: Practical strategies. In M. Aveline & D. A. Shapiro (Eds.), *Research foundations for psychotherapy practice* (pp. 49–72). Chichester, England: Wiley.

Elliott, R. (2001). Research on the effectiveness of humanistic therapies: A meta-analysis. In D. J. Cain & J. Seeman (Eds.), *Handbook of research and practice in humanistic psychotherapy* (pp. 57–82). Washington, DC: American Psychological Association.

Ellis, A., & Greiger, R. (1996). *What is rational-emotive therapy?* Baltimore: Johns Hopkins University Press.

Ellis, A., & Tafrate, R. C. (1997). *When AA doesn't work for you: Rational steps to quitting alcohol.* Fort Lee, NJ: Barricade.

Erk, R. R. (Ed.). (2004). *Counseling treatment for children and adolescents with* DSM-IV-TR *disorders.* Upper Saddle River, NJ: Pearson Education.

Escobar, J. I. (2004). Transcultural aspects of dissociative and somatoform disorders. *Psychiatric Times, 21,* 5.

Evans, D. L., Foa, E. B., Gur, R. E., Hendin, H., O'Brien, C. P., Seligman, M.E.P., & Walsh, B. T. (2005). *Treating and preventing adolescent mental health disorders.* New York: Oxford University Press.

Evans, K., & Sullivan, J. M. (2001). *Dual diagnosis* (2nd ed.). New York: Guilford Press.

Everly, G., Jr. (1995). The role of the critical incident stress debriefing (CISD) process in disaster counseling. *Journal of Mental Health Counseling, 17,* 278–290.

Eyberg, S. M., & Pinkus, D. (1999). *The Eyberg Child Behavior Inventory and Sutter-Eyberg Student Behavior Inventory: Professional manual.* Lutz, FL: Psychological Assessment Resources.

Fairburn, C. G., & Brownell, K. D. (2002). *Eating disorders and obesity* (2nd ed.). New York: Guilford Press.

Fairburn, C. G., & Cooper, Z. (1993). The Eating Disorders Examination (12th edition). In C. G. Fairburn & G. T. Wilson (Eds.), *Binge eating: Nature, assessment, and treatment* (pp. 317–360). New York: Guilford Press.

Fairburn, C. G., Cooper, Z., Doll, H. A., Norman, P., & O'Connor, M. (2000). The natural course of bulimia nervosa and binge eating disorder in young women. *Archives of General Psychiatry, 57,* 659–665.

Fallon, B. A., & Feinstein, S. (2001). Hypochondriasis. In K. A. Phillips (Ed.), *Somatoform and factitious disorders* (pp. 27–60). Washington, DC: American Psychiatric Association.

Fawcett, J., Golden, B., Rosenfeld, N., & Goodwin, F. K. (2000). *New hope for people with bipolar disorder.* New York: Three Rivers Press.

Fawzy, F. I., Fawzy, N. W., Hyun, C. S., Elashoff, R., Guthrie, D., Fahey, J. L., & Morton, D. L. (1993). Malignant melanoma. *Archives of General Psychiatry, 50,* 681–689.

Feder, B. J. (2006, September 10). Battle lines in treating depression. *New York Times*, p. 21 (Health sec.).

Feldman, M. A., & Werner, S. E. (2002). Collateral effects of behavioral parent training on families of children with developmental disabilities and behavior disorders. *Behavioral Interventions, 17*, 75–83.

Feldman, M. D., Hamilton, J. C., & Deemer, H. N. (2001). Factitious disorder. In K. A. Phillips (Ed.), *Somatoform and factitious disorders* (pp. 129–159). Washington, DC: American Psychiatric Publishing.

Fenster, A. (1993). Reflections on using group therapy as a treatment modality — why, how, for whom and when: A guide to clinicians, supervisors and instructors. *Group, 17*, 84–101.

Field, L. F., & Seligman, L. (2004). Mood disorders in children and adolescents. In R. R. Erk (Ed.), *Counseling treatment for children and adolescents with* DSM-IV-TR *disorders* (pp. 239–272). Upper Saddle River, NJ: Pearson Education.

Findling, R., McNamara, N. K., Youngstrom, E. A., et al. (2005). Young mania rating scale. *Journal of the Academy of Child and Adolescent Psychiatry, 44*, 409–417.

Finney, J. W., & Moos, R. H. (2002). Psychosocial treatments for alcohol use disorders. In P. E. Nathan & J. M. Gorman (Eds.), *A guide to treatments that work* (2nd ed., pp. 157–168). New York: Oxford University Press.

First, M. B., Spitzer, R. L., Gibbon, M., & Williams, J.B.W. (1997). *Structured Clinical Interview for DSM-IV Axis I Disorders (SCID-I): Clinician version*. Washington, DC: American Psychiatric Press.

Fischer, S., Smith, G. T., & Anderson, K. G. (2003). Clarifying the role of impulsivity in bulimia nervosa. *The International Journal of Eating Disorders, 3*, 406–411.

Fletcher, K. E. (2003). Childhood posttraumatic stress disorder. In E. J. Mash & R. A. Barkley (Eds.), *Treatment of childhood disorders* (2nd ed., pp. 330–371). New York: Guilford Press.

Flory, K., Milich, R., Lynam, D. R., Leukefeld, C., & Clayton, R. (2003). Relation between childhood disruptive behavior disorders and substance use and dependence symptoms in young adulthood: Individuals with symptoms of attention-deficit/hyperactivity disorder and conduct disorder are uniquely at risk. *Psychology of Addictive Behaviors, 17*, 151–158.

Foa, E. B., Davidson, J., & Rothbaum, B. O. (1995). Posttraumatic stress disorder. In G. O. Gabbard (Ed.), *Treatments of psychiatric disorders* (pp. 1499–1520). Washington, DC: American Psychiatric Press.

Foa, E. B., Franklin, M. E., Perry, K. J., & Herbert, J. D. (1996). Cognitive biases in generalized social phobia. *Journal of Abnormal Psychology, 105*, 433–439.

Forchetti, C. M. (2005). Treating patients with moderate to severe Alzheimer's disease. *The Primary Care Companion to the Journal of Clinical Psychiatry, 7*, 155–161.

Ford, D. E., & Kamerow, D. B. (1989). Epidemiologic study of sleep disturbances and psychiatric disorders: An opportunity for prevention. *Journal of the American Medical Association, 262*, 1479–1484.

Frank, E. (1999). Interpersonal and social rhythm therapy prevents depressive symptomatology in bipolar I patients. *Bipolar Disorders, 1*(Suppl. 1), 13.

Frank, E. (2005). *Treating bipolar disorder: A clinician's guide to interpersonal and social rhythm therapy*. New York: Guilford Press.

Frank, E., & Swartz, H. A. (2004). Interpersonal and social rhythm therapy. In S. L. Johnson & R. L. Leahy (Eds.), *Psychological treatment of bipolar disorder* (pp. 162–183). New York: Guilford Press.

Frank, J. D., & Frank, J. B. (1991). *Persuasion and healing: A comparative study of psychotherapy* (3rd ed.). Baltimore: Johns Hopkins University Press.

Franklin, G. A., Pucci, P. S., Arbabi, S., Brandt, M., Wahl, W. L., & Taheri, P. A. (2002). Decreased juvenile arson and firesetting recidivism after implementation of a multidisciplinary prevention program. *Journal of Trauma-Injury Infection and Critical Care, 53*, 260–266.

Franklin, M. E., & Foa, E. B. (2002). Cognitive behavioral treatments for obsessive compulsive disorder. In P. E. Nathan & J. M. Gorman (Eds.), *A guide to treatments that work* (2nd ed., pp. 367–386). New York: Oxford University Press.

Franklin, M. E., Tolin, D. F., & Diefenbach, G. J. (2006). Trichotillomania. In E. Hollander & D. J. Stein (Eds.), *Clinical manual of impulse-control disorders* (pp. 149–174). Arlington, VA: American Psychiatric Publishing.

Friedman, E. G., & Wilson, R. (2004). Treatment of opiate addiction. In S.L.A. Straussner (Ed.), *Clinical work with substance-abusing clients* (2nd ed., pp. 187–208). New York: Guilford Press.

Garb, H. N. (1998). Clinical judgment. In H. N. Garb (Ed.), *Studying the clinician: Judgment research and psychological assessment* (pp. 173–206). Washington, DC: American Psychological Association.

Garfield, S. L. (1986). Research on client variables in psychotherapy. In S. L. Garfield & A. E. Bergin (Eds.), *Handbook of psychotherapy and behavior change* (3rd ed., pp. 213–256). Hoboken, NJ: Wiley.

Garrett, J., Landau-Stanton, J., Stanton, M. D., Stellato-Kabat, J., & Stellato-Kabat, D. (1997). ARISE: A method for engaging reluctant alcohol- and drug-dependent individuals in treatment. *Journal of Substance Abuse Treatment, 14*, 235–248.

Geary, D. C. (2003). Learning disabilities in arithmetic: Problem-solving differences and cognitive deficits. In H. L. Swanson, K. R. Harris, & S. Graham (Eds.), *Handbook of learning disabilities* (pp. 199–212). New York: Guilford Press.

Geller, B., & Luby, J. (1997). Child and adolescent bipolar disorder: A review of the past 10 years. *Journal of the American Academy of Child and Adolescent Psychiatry, 36*, 1168–1176.

Geller, J., Brown, K. E., Zaitsoff, S. L., Goodrich, S., & Hastings, F. (2003). Collaborative versus directive interventions in the treatment of eating disorders: Implications for care providers. *Professional Psychology: Research and Practice, 34,* 406–413.

Gendlin, E. T. (1996). *Focusing-oriented psychotherapy: A manual of the experiential method.* New York: Guilford Press.

George, C., Kaplan, N., & Main, M. (1984). *Adult Attachment Interview.* Unpublished manuscript, University of California at Berkeley.

George, T. P., Vessicchio, J. C., Termine, A., Jatlow, P. I., Kosten, T. R., & O'Malley, S. S. (2003). A preliminary placebo-controlled trial of selegiline hydrochloride for smoking cessation. *Biological Psychiatry, 53,* 136–143.

Gillberg, C. (1991). Outcome in autism and autistic-like conditions. Special section: Longitudinal research. *Journal of the American Academy of Child and Adolescent Psychiatry, 30,* 375–382.

Gillberg, C., Gillberg, I. C., & Steffenberg, S. (1992). Siblings and parents of children with autism: A controlled population-based study. *Developmental Medicine and Child Neurology, 34,* 389–398.

Gillies, L. A. (2001). Interpersonal psychotherapy for depression and other disorders. In D. H. Barlow (Ed.), *Clinical handbook of psychological disorders* (3rd ed., pp. 309–331). New York: Guilford Press.

Gintner, G. G. (2004). Treatment planning guidelines for children and adolescents. In R. R. Erk (Ed.), *Counseling treatment for children and adolescents with* DSM-IV-TR *disorders* (pp. 344–380). Upper Saddle River, NJ: Pearson Education.

Girgus, J. S., & Nolen-Hoeksema, S. (2006). Cognition and depression. In C.L.M. Keyes & S. H. Goodman (Eds.), *Women and depression* (pp. 147–175). New York: Cambridge University Press.

Glasser, W. (1990). *The control theory and reality therapy workbook.* Canoga Park, CA: Institute for Reality Therapy.

Gloaguen, V., Cottraux, J., Cucherat, M., & Blackburn, I. M. (1998). A meta-analysis of the effects of cognitive therapy in depressed patients. *Journal of Affective Disorders, 49,* 59–72.

Glueckauf, R. L., Fritz, S. P., Eckland, J., Eric, P., Liss, H. J., & Dages, P. (2002). Videoconferencing-based counseling for rural teenagers with epilepsy: Phase I findings. *Rehabilitation Psychology, 47,* 49–72.

Goin, M. K. (2001). Practical psychotherapy: Borderline personality disorder: The importance of establishing a treatment framework. *Psychiatric Services, 52,* 167–168.

Golden, R. N., Gaynes, B. N., Ekstrom, R. D., Hamer, R. M., Jacobsen, F. M., Suppes, T., Wisner, K. L., & Nemeroff, C. B. (2005). The efficacy of light therapy in the treatment of mood disorders: A review and meta-analysis of the evidence. *American Journal of Psychiatry, 162,* 656–662.

Goldfried, M. R., Greenberg, L. S., & Marmar, C. R. (1990). Individual psychotherapy: Process and outcome. *Annual Review of Psychology, 41*, 659–688.

Goldman, L. S., Genel, M., Bezman, R. J., Slanetz, P. J., for the Council on Scientific Affairs, AMA. (1998). Diagnosis and treatment of attention-deficity/hyperactivity disorder in children and adolescents. *Journal of the American Medical Association, 279*, 1100–1107.

Goldstein, A. J., de Beurs, E., Chambless, D. L., & Wilson, K. A. (2000). EMDR for panic disorder with agoraphobia: Comparison with waiting list and credible attention-placebo control conditions. *Journal of Consulting and Clinical Psychology, 68*, 947–956.

Goleman, D. (Ed.). (2003). *Destructive emotions*. New York: Bantam Books.

Goodman, S. H., & Tully, E. (2006). Depression in women who are mothers: An integrative model of risk for the development of psychopathology in their sons and daughters. In C.L.M. Keyes & S. H. Goodman (Eds.), *Women and depression* (pp. 241–282). New York: Cambridge University Press.

Gottman, J. M., Coan, J., Carrere, S., & Swanson, C. (1998). Predicting marital happiness and stability from newlywed interactions. *Journal of Marriage and the Family, 60*, 5–22.

Gottman, J. M., & Silver, N. (2000). *The seven principles for making marriage work*. New York: Three Rivers Press.

Graham, H. L., Copello, A., Birchwood, M. J., & Mueser, K. T. (Eds.). (2003). *Substance misuse in psychosis: Approaches to treatment and service delivery*. Hoboken, NJ: Wiley.

Grant, B. F., Hasin, D. S., Stinson, F. S., Dawson, D. A., Chou, S. P., Ruan, W. J., & Pickering, R. P. (2004). Prevalence, correlates, and disability of personality disorders in the U.S.: Results from the National Epidemiologic Survey on Alcohol and Related Conditions. *Journal of Clinical Psychiatry, 65*, 948–958.

Grant, J. E. (2006). Kleptomania. In E. Hollander & D. J. Stein (Eds.), *Clinical manual of impulse-control disorders* (pp. 175–202). Arlington, VA: American Psychiatric Publishing.

Grant, J. E., & Kim, S. W. (2002). Clinical characteristics and associated psychopathology of 22 patients with kleptomania. *Comprehensive Psychiatry, 43*, 378–384.

Green, J., & Goldwyn, R. (2002). Attachment disorganization and psychopathology: New findings in attachment research and their potential implication for developmental psychopathology in childhood. *Journal of Child Psychology and Psychiatry, 43*, 835–846.

Green, R. (1987). *The "sissy boy syndrome" and the development of homosexuality*. New Haven: Yale University Press.

Greenberg, L. S. (2002). *Emotion-focused therapy: Coaching clients to work through their feelings*. Washington, DC: American Psychological Association.

Greenberg, L. S., Elliott, R., & Lietaer, G. (1994). Research on humanistic and experiential psychotherapies. In A. E. Bergin & S. L. Garfield (Eds.), *Handbook of psychotherapy and behavior change* (4th ed., pp. 509–539). Hoboken, NJ: Wiley.

Greenberg, L. S., & Johnson, S. M. (1988). *Emotionally focused therapy for couples*. New York: Guilford Press.

Greenberg, L. S., & Watson, J. C. (2005). *Emotion focused therapy for depression*. Washington, DC: American Psychological Association.

Greenberg, L. S., Watson, J. C., Elliott, R., & Bohart, A. (2001). Empathy. *Psychotherapy, 38*, 380–384.

Greenberg, M. T., Lengua, L. J., Coie, J., Pinderhughes, E., & Conduct Problems Prevention Research Group. (1999). Predicting developmental outcomes at school entry using a multiple-risk model: Four American communities. *Developmental Psychology, 35*, 403–417.

Greenhill, L. L., & Ford, R. E. (2002). Childhood attention-deficit hyperactivity disorder: Pharmacological treatments. In P. E. Nathan & J. M. Gorman (Eds.), *A guide to treatments that work* (2nd ed., pp. 25–56). New York: Oxford University Press.

Greenspan, M., & Kulish, N. M. (1985). Factors in premature termination in long-term psychotherapy. *Psychotherapy, 22*, 75–82.

Grieger, T. A., Fullerton, C. S., & Ursano, R. J. (2003). Posttraumatic stress disorder, alcohol use, and perceived safety after the terrorist attack on the Pentagon. *Psychiatric Services, 54*, 1380–1382.

Grilo, C. M., Sinha, R., & O'Malley, S. S. (2002). *Eating disorders and alcohol use disorders: Research update*. Washington, DC: U.S. Government Printing Office.

Grunebaum, M. F., Oquendo, M. A., Harkavy-Friedman, J. M., Ellis, S., Li, S., Haas, G. L., Malone, K. M., & Mann, J. J. (2001). Delusions and suicidality. *American Journal of Psychiatry, 158*, 742–747.

Grunze, H., Kasper, S., Goodwin, G., Bowden, C., Baldwin, D., Licht, R., Vieta, E., & Moller, H. (2002). World Federation of Societies of Biological Psychiatry (WFSBP) guidelines for biological treatment of bipolar disorders, part I: Treatment of bipolar depression. *Biological Psychiatry, 3*, 115–124.

Grunze, H., Kasper, S., Goodwin, G., Bowden, C., Baldwin, D., Licht, R., Vieta, E., & Moller, H. (2003). World Federation of Societies of Biological Psychiatry (WFSBP) guidelines for biological treatment of bipolar disorders, part II: Treatment of mania. *Biological Psychiatry, 4*, 5–13.

Grunze, H., Kasper, S., Goodwin, G., Bowden, C., & Moller, H. (2004). World Federation of Societies of Biological Psychiatry (WFSBP) guidelines for the biological treatment of bipolar disorders, part III: Maintenance treatment. *Biological Psychiatry, 5*, 120–135.

Guerney, B. G., Jr. (1977). *Relationship enhancement: Skill training programs for therapy, problem prevention and enrichment*. San Francisco: Jossey-Bass.

Guerney, B. G., Jr. (1994). The role of emotion in relationship enhancement marital/family therapy. In S. Johnson & L. Greenberg (Eds.), *The heart of the matter: Perspectives on emotion in marital therapy* (pp. 124–150). New York: Brunner/Mazel.

Gunderson, J. G., & Ridolfi, M. E. (2001). Borderline personality disorder: Suicidality and self-mutilation. *Annals of the New York Academy of Sciences, 932*, 61–77.

Gunderson, J. G., Ronningstam, E., & Bodkin, A. (1990). The diagnostic interview for narcissistic patients. *Archives of General Psychiatry, 47*, 676–680.

Gustafson, D. H., Hawkins, R., Oberg, E., Pingree, S., Serlin, R., Graziano, F., & Chan, C. L. (1999). Impact of a patient-centered, computer-based health information/support system. *American Journal of Preventive Medicine, 16*, 1–9.

Gustafson, D. H., Hawkins, R., Pingree, S., McTavish, F., Arora, N. K., Salner, J., Stewart, J., Mendenhal, J., Cella, R., Serlin, R., & Apenteko, F. (2001). Effect of computer support on younger women with breast cancer. *Journal of General Internal Medicine, 16*, 435–445.

Haas, A. P., Hendin, H., & Mann, J. (2003). Suicide in college students. *American Behavioral Scientist, 46*, 1224–1240.

Hagopian, L. P., & Boelter, E. W. (2005). *Applied behavioral analysis: Overview and summary of scientific support.* Baltimore: Kennedy Krieger Institute and Johns Hopkins University School of Medicine. Available: www.kennedykrieger.org

Haley, M. (2004). Risk and protective factors. In D. Capuzzi (Ed.), *Suicide across the lifespan* (pp. 95–138). Alexandria, VA: American Counseling Association.

Hall, S.E.K., & Geher, G. (2003). Behavioral and personality characteristics of children with reactive attachment disorder. *Journal of Psychology, 137*, 145–162.

Hallowell, E. M., & Ratey, J. J. (1994). *Driven to distraction.* New York: Pantheon Books.

Handen, B. L., & Gilchrist, R. H. (2006). Mental retardation. In E. J. Mash & R. A. Barkley (Eds.), *Treatment of childhood disorders* (3rd ed., pp. 411–454). New York: Guilford Press.

Hanna, F., & Hunt, W. P. (1999). Techniques for psychotherapy with defiant, aggressive adolescents. *Psychotherapy, 36*, 1.

Hansen, N. B., & Lambert, M. J. (2003). An evaluation of the dose-response relationship in naturalistic treatment settings using survival analysis. *Mental Health Services Research, 5*, 1–12.

Hanson, R. E., & Spratt, E. G. (2002). Reactive attachment disorder: What we know about the disorder and implications for treatment. *Child Maltreatment, 5*, 137–145.

Harbin, G. L., McWilliam, R. A., & Gallagher, J. J. (2000). Services for young children with disabilities and their families. In J. P. Shonkoff & S. J. Meisels (Eds.), *Handbook of early childhood intervention* (2nd ed., pp. 387–415). New York: Cambridge University Press.

Hardesty, V. A., & Gayton, W. F. (2002). The problem of children and fire: An historical perspective. In D. Kolko (Ed.), *Handbook on firesetting in children and youth* (pp. 1–13). San Diego: Academic Press.

Harkavy-Friedman, J. M. (2006). Can early detection of psychosis prevent suicidal behavior? *American Journal of Psychiatry, 163,* 768–770.

Harrow, M., Grossman, L. S., Herbener, E. S., & Davies, E. W. (2000). Ten-year outcome: Patients with schizoaffective disorders, schizophrenia, affective disorders and mood-incongruent psychotic symptoms. *British Journal of Psychiatry, 177,* 421–426.

Hart, A., & Thomas, H. (2000). Controversial attachments: The indirect treatment of fostered and adopted children via parent therapy. *Attachment and Human Development, 2,* 306–327.

Hart, E. L., Lahey, B. B., Loeber, R., & Hanson, K. S. (1994). Criterion validity of informants in the diagnosis of disruptive behavior disorders in children: A preliminary study. *Journal of Consulting and Clinical Psychology, 62,* 410–414.

Hayes, S. C., Strosahl, K. D., & Wilson, K. J. (1999). *Acceptance and commitment therapy: An experimental approach to behavior therapy.* New York: Guilford Press.

HBIGDA. (2001). Harry Benjamin's International Gender Dysphoria Association's Standards of Care for Gender Identity Disorders, 6th Version. Available at http://wpath.org-documents-socv6.pdf.

Heimberg, R. G., Liebowitz, M. R., Hope, D. A., Schneier, F. R., Holt, C. S., Welkowitz, L. A., Juster, H. R., Campeas, R., Bruch, M. A., Cloitre, M., Falloon, B., & Klein, D. F. (1998). Cognitive behavioral group therapy vs. phenelzine therapy for social phobia. *Archives of General Psychiatry, 55,* 1133–1141.

Heinlen, K. T., Welfel, E. R., Richmond, E. N., & Rak, C. F. (2003). The scope of WebCounseling: A survey of services and compliance with NBCC standards for the ethical practice of WebCounseling. *Journal of Counseling and Development, 81,* 61–69.

Henggeler, S. W., & Lee, T. (2003). Multisystemic treatment of serious clinical problems. In A. E. Kazdin & J. R. Weisz (Eds.), *Evidence-based psychotherapies for children and adolescents* (pp. 301–322). New York: Guilford Press.

Hess, R. S., & Street, E. M. (1991). The effect of acculturation on the relationship of counselor ethnicity and client ratings. *Journal of Counseling Psychology, 38,* 71–75.

Higgins, E. T. (1997). Beyond pleasure and pain. *American Psychologist, 52,* 1280–1300.

Hinkle, J. S. (2004). Anxiety disorders in children and adolescents. In R. R. Erk (Ed.), *Counseling treatment for children and adolescents with* DSM-IV-TR *disorders* (pp. 205–238). Upper Saddle River, NJ: Pearson Education.

Hinshaw, S. P., Klein, R. G., & Abikoff, H. B. (2002). Childhood attention-deficit hyperactivity disorder: Nonpharmacological treatments and their combination with medication. In P. E. Nathan & J. M. Gorman (Eds.), *A guide to treatments that work* (2nd ed., pp. 3–24). New York: Oxford University Press.

Hinshaw, S. P., & Lee, S. S. (2003). Conduct and oppositional defiant disorders. In E. J. Mash & R. A. Barkley (Eds.), *Child psychopathology* (2nd ed., pp. 144–198). New York: Guilford Press.

Hofmann, S. G., & Barlow, D. H. (2002). Social phobia (social anxiety disorder). In D. H. Barlow (Ed.), *Anxiety and its disorders* (pp. 454–476). New York: Guilford Press.

Hoge, C. W., Castro, C. A., Messer, S. C., McGurk, D., Cotting, D. I., & Koffman, R. L. (2004). Combat duty in Iraq and Afghanistan, mental health problems, and barriers to care. *New England Journal of Medicine, 351*, 13–22.

Holder-Perkins, V., & Wise, T. N. (2001). Somatization disorder. In K. A. Phillips (Ed.), *Somatoform and factitious disorders* (pp. 1–21). Washington, DC: American Psychiatric Association.

Hollander, E., Baker, B. R., Kahn, J., & Stein, D. J. (2006). Conceptualizing and assessing impulse-control disorders. In E. Hollander & D. J. Stein (Eds.), *Clinical manual of impulse-control disorders* (pp. 1–18). Arlington, VA: American Psychiatric Publishing.

Hollander, E., & Stein, D. J. (Eds.). (2006). *Clinical manual of impulse-control disorders*. Arlington, VA: American Psychiatric Publishing.

Hollins, S. (2001). Psychotherapeutic methods. In A. Došen & K. Day (Eds.), *Treating mental illness and behavior disorders in children and adults with mental retardation* (pp. 27–44). Washington, DC: American Psychiatric Press.

Hollon, S. D. (2000). Cognitive therapy. In A. E. Kazdin (Ed.), *Encyclopedia of psychology* (Vol. 2, pp. 169–172). Washington, DC, and New York: American Psychological Association/Oxford University Press.

Hollon, S. D., & Beck, A. T. (2004). Cognitive and cognitive behavioral therapies. In M. J. Lambert (Ed.), *Bergin and Garfield's handbook of psychotherapy and behavior change* (pp. 447–492). Hoboken, NJ: Wiley.

Hollon, S. D., Stewart, M. O., & Strunk, D. R. (2006). Enduring effects for cognitive behavioral therapy in the treatment of depression and anxiety. *Annual Review of Psychology, 57*, 285–315.

Hommer, D., Momenan, R., Kaiser, E., & Rawlings, R. (2001). Evidence for a gender-related effect of alcoholism on brain volumes. *American Journal of Psychiatry, 158*, 198–204.

Horvath, A. O., & Laborsky, L. (1993). The role of the therapeutic alliance in psychotherapy. *Journal of Consulting and Clinical Psychology, 61*, 561–573.

Horvath, A. O., & Symonds, B. D. (1991). Relation between working alliance and outcome in psychotherapy: A meta-analysis. *Journal of Counseling Psychology, 38*, 139–149.

Houts, A. C. (2003). Behavioral treatment for enuresis. In A. E. Kazdin & J. R. Weisz (Eds.), *Evidence-based psychotherapies for children and adolescents* (pp. 389–406). New York: Guilford Press.

Howard, K. I., Kopta, S. M., Krause, M. S., & Orlinsky, D. E. (1986). The dose-effect relationship in psychotherapy. *American Psychologist, 41*, 159–164.

Howell, J. C. (2003). *Preventing and reducing juvenile delinquency: A comprehensive framework*. Thousand Oaks, CA: Sage.

Hoyert, D. L., Heron, M., Murphy, S. L., & Kung, H. C. (2006). Deaths: Final data for 2003. *National vital statistics report*, vol. 54. Hyattsville, MD: National Center for Health Statistics.

Hudson, J. L., & Rapee, R. M. (2001). Parent-child interactions and the anxiety disorders: An observational analysis. *Behaviour Research and Therapy, 39*, 1411–1427.

Hunt, J. I., Dyl, J., Armstrong, L., Litvin, E., Sheeran, T., & Spirito, A. (2005). Frequency of manic symptoms and bipolar disorder in psychiatrically hospitalized adolescents using the K-SADS mania rating scale. *Journal of Child and Adolescent Psychopharmacology, 15*, 918–930.

Hurley, A. D. (1989). Individual psychotherapy with mentally retarded individuals. A review and call for research. *Research in Developmental Disabilities, 10*, 261–275.

Jablensky, A. (1999). Schizophrenia: Epidemiology. *Current Opinion in Psychiatry, 12*, 19–28.

Jackson, P. B., & Williams, D. R. (2006). Culture, race/ethnicity, and depression. In C.L.M. Keyes & S. H. Goodman (Eds.), *Women and depression* (pp. 328–359). New York: Cambridge University Press.

Jacobi, C., Hayward, C., de Zwaan, M., Kraemer, H. C., & Agras, W. S. (2004). Coming to terms with risk factors for eating disorders: Application of risk terminology and suggestions for a general taxonomy. *Psychological Bulletin, 130*, 19–65.

Jacobs, D. F. (1988). Evidence for a common dissociative-like reaction among addicts. *Journal of Gambling Behavior, 4*, 27–37.

Jankovic, J. (2001). Tourette's syndrome. *New England Journal of Medicine, 345*, 1184–1192.

Jefferson, J. W. (2003). Bipolar disorders: A brief guide to diagnosis and treatment. *Focus, 1*, 7–14.

Jerome, L. W., DeLeon, P. H., James, L. C., Folen, R., Earles, J., & Gedney, J. J. (2000). The coming of age of telecommunications in psychological research and practice. *American Psychologist, 51*, 407–421.

Jessor, R., Donovan, J. E., & Costa, F. M. (1991). *Beyond adolescence: Problem behavior and young adult development*. New York: Cambridge University Press.

Jindal, R. D., & Thase, M. E. (2003). Integration of care: Integrating psychotherapy and pharmacotherapy to improve outcomes among patients with mood disorders. *Psychiatric Services, 54*, 1484–1490.

Johns, L. C., & van Os, J. (2001). The continuity of psychotic experiences in the general population. *Clinical Psychology Review, 21* (8), 1125–1141.

Johnson, C. R. (2002). Mental retardation. In M. Hersen (Ed.), *Clinical behavior therapy: Adults and children* (pp. 420–433). Hoboken, NJ: Wiley.

Johnson, J. G., Cohen, P., Kotler, L., Kasen, S., & Brook, J. S. (2002). Psychiatric disorders associated with risk for the development of eating disorders during adolescence and early adulthood. *Journal of Consulting and Clinical Psychology, 70,* 1119–1128.

Johnson, J. G., First, M. B., Cohen, P., Skodol, A. E., Kasen, S., & Brook, J. S. (2005). Adverse outcomes associated with personality disorder not otherwise specified in a community sample. *American Journal of Psychiatry, 162,* 1926–1932.

Johnson, J. H., Rasbury, W. C., & Siegel, L. J. (1997). *Approaches to child treatment: Introduction to theory, research, and practice* (2nd ed.). Boston: Allyn & Bacon.

Johnson, P. A., Hurley, R. A., Benkelfat, C., Herpertz, S. C., & Taber, K. H. (2003). Understanding emotion regulation in borderline personality disorder: Contributions of neuroimaging. *Journal of Neuropsychiatry and Clinical Neuroscience, 15,* 397–402.

Johnson, S. (2004). *The practice of emotionally focused couple therapy: Creating connection* (2nd ed.). Philadelphia: Brunner-Routledge.

Johnson, S., & Boisvert, C. (2001). Treating couples and families from the humanistic perspective: More than the symptom, more than solutions. In D. J. Cain & J. Seeman (Eds.), *Humanistic psychotherapies: Handbook of research and practice* (pp. 309–338). Washington, DC: American Psychological Association.

Johnson, S. L. (2004). Defining bipolar disorder. In S. L. Johnson & R. L. Leahy (Eds.), *Psychological treatment of bipolar disorder* (pp. 3–16). New York: Guilford Press.

Johnson, S. P. (2001). Short-term play therapy. In G. L. Landreth (Ed.), *Innovations in play therapy: Issues, process, and special populations* (pp. 217–235). Philadelphia: Brunner-Routledge.

Johnson, V. E. (1986). *Intervention: How to help someone who doesn't want help. A step-by-step guide for families and friends of chemically dependent persons.* Minneapolis: Johnson Institute.

Johnson, W. B., Devries, R., Ridley, C. R., Pettorini, D., & Peterson, D. R. (1994). The comparative efficacy of Christian and secular rational-emotive therapy with Christian clients. *Journal of Psychology and Theology, 2,* 130–140.

Joiner, T. E., Jr. (2000). Depression's vicious scree: Self-propagating and erosive processes in depression chronicity. *Clinical Psychology: Science and Practice, 7,* 203–218.

Jones, S. (2004). Psychotherapy of bipolar disorder: A review. *Journal of Affective Disorders, 80,* 101–114.

Junginger, J., Parks-Levy, J., & McGuire, L. (1998). Delusions and symptom-consistent violence. *Psychiatric Services, 49,* 218–220.

Kabot, S., Masi, W., & Segal, M. (2003). Advances in the diagnosis and treatment of autism spectrum disorders. *Professional Psychology: Research and Practice, 34,* 26–33.

Kadera, S. W., Lambert, M. J., & Andrews, A. A. (1996). How much therapy is really enough? *Journal of Psychotherapy Practice and Research, 5,* 132–151.

Kadesjo, B., & Gillberg, C. (2000). Tourette's disorder: Epidemiology and comorbidity in primary school children. *Journal of the American Academy of Child and Adolescent Psychiatry, 39*, 548–555.

Kafka, M. P. (2007). Paraphilia-related disorders: The evaluation and treatment of non-paraphilic hypersexuality. In S. R. Leiblum (Ed.), *Principles and practice of sex therapy* (4th ed., pp. 442–476). New York: Guilford Press.

Kafka, M. P., & Hennen, J. (2002). A DSM-IV Axis I comorbidity study of males ($n = 120$) with paraphilias and paraphilia-related disorders. *Sexual Abuse: A Journal of Research and Treatment, 14*, 349–366.

Kahng, S., Iwata, B. A., & Lewin, A. B. (2002). Behavioral treatment of self-injury, 1964–2000. *American Journal on Mental Retardation, 107*, 212–221.

Kamphaus, R. W. (2000). Learning disabilities. In A. E. Kazdin (Ed.), *Encyclopedia of psychology*. Washington, DC, and New York: American Psychological Association/Oxford University Press.

Kantor, M. (2004). *Understanding paranoia*. Westport, CT: Praeger.

Kaplan, H. S. (1995). *The sexual desire disorders: Dysfunctional regulation of sexual motivation*. New York: Routledge.

Kaplan, H. S., Sadock, B., & Grebb, J. (1994). *Synopsis of psychiatry* (7th ed.). Baltimore: Williams & Wilkins.

Karel, M. J., Ogland-Hand, S., & Gatz, M. (2002). *Assessing and treating late-life depression*. New York: Basic Books.

Kaslow, N. J., & Thompson, M. P. (1998). Applying the criteria for empirically supported treatments to studies of psychosocial interventions for child and adolescent depression. *Journal of Clinical Child Psychology, 27*, 146–155.

Kaye, W. H., Frank, G. K., Bailer, U. F., Henry, S. E., Meltzer, C. C., Price, J. C., Mathis, C. A., & Wagner, A. (2005). Serotonin alterations in anorexia and bulimia nervosa: New insights from imaging studies. *Physiological Behavior, 85*, 73–81.

Kazdin, A. E. (1990). Premature termination from treatment among children referred for antisocial behavior. *Journal of Child Psychology and Psychiatry, 3*, 412–425.

Kazdin, A. E. (1993). Psychotherapy for children and adolescents: Current progress and future research directions. *American Psychologist, 48*, 644–657.

Kazdin, A. E. (1995). *Conduct disorders in childhood and adolescence*. Thousand Oaks, CA: Sage.

Kazdin, A. E. (1997). Psychosocial treatments for conduct disorder in children. *Journal of Child Psychology and Psychiatry and Allied Professions, 38*, 161–178.

Kazdin, A. E. (2000). *Psychotherapy for children and adolescents: Directions for research and practice*. New York: Oxford University Press.

Kazdin, A. E. (2002). Psychosocial treatments for conduct disorder in children and adolescents. In P. E. Nathan & J. M. Gorman (Eds.), *A guide to treatments that work* (2nd ed., pp. 57–85). New York: Oxford University Press.

Kazdin, A. E. (2003). Problem-solving skills training and parent management training for conduct disorder. In A. E. Kazdin & J. R. Weisz (Eds.), *Evidence-based psychotherapies for children and adolescents* (pp. 241–262). New York: Guilford Press.

Kazdin, A. E., & Weisz, J. R. (Eds.). (2003). *Evidence-based psychotherapies for children and adolescents*. New York: Guilford Press.

Keane, T. M., & Barlow, D. H. (2002). Posttraumatic stress disorder. In D. H. Barlow (Ed.), *Anxiety and its disorders* (pp. 418–453). New York: Guilford Press.

Keck, P. E., & McElroy, S. L. (2002). Pharmacological treatments for bipolar disorder. In P. E. Nathan & J. M. Gorman (Eds.), *A guide to treatments that work* (2nd ed., pp. 277–300). New York: Oxford University Press.

Keijsers, G., Schaap, C., & Hoogduin, C. (2000). The impact of interpersonal patient and therapist behavior on outcome in cognitive behavior therapy: A review of empirical studies. *Behavior Modification, 24*, 264–297.

Kendall, P. C., Aschenbrand, S. G., & Hudson, S. G. (2003). Child-focused treatment of anxiety. In A. E. Kazdin & J. R. Weisz (Eds.), *Evidence-based psychotherapies for children and adolescents* (pp. 81–100). New York: Guilford Press.

Kendall, P. C., & Lipman, A. J. (1991). Psychological and pharmacological therapy: Methods and modes for comparative outcome research. *Journal of Consulting and Clinical Psychology, 59*, 78–87.

Kennard, D., & Lees, J. (2001). A checklist of standards for democratic therapeutic communities. *Therapeutic Communities, 22*, 143–151.

Kernberg, O. (2000). *Borderline conditions and pathological narcissism*. New York: Jason Aronson.

Kessler, R. C. (2006). The epidemiology of depression among women. In C.L.M. Keyes & S. H. Goodman (Eds.), *Women and depression* (pp. 22–40). New York: Cambridge University Press.

Kessler, R. C., Adler, L., Ames, M., Demler, O., Faraone, S. V., Hiripi, E., Howes, M. J., Jin, R., Secnik, K., Spencer, T., Ustun, T. B., & Walters, E. E. (2005). The World Health Organization Adult ADHD Self-Report Scale (ASRS): A short screening scale for use in the general population. *Psychological Medicine, 35*, 245–256.

Kessler, R. C., Berglund, P., Demler, O., Jin, R., Koretz, D. Merikangas, K. R., Rush, A. J., Walters, E. E., & Wang, P. S. (2003). The epidemiology of major depressive disorder: Results from the National Comorbidity Survey Replication. *Journal of the American Medical Association, 289*, 3095–3105.

Kessler, R. C., Berglund, P., Demler, O., Jin, R., Merikangas, K., & Walters, E. E. (2005). Lifetime prevalence and age of onset distributions of DSM-IV disorders in the National Comorbidity Survey Replication. *Archives of General Psychiatry, 62*, 593–602.

Kessler, R. C., Chiu, W. T., Demler, O., & Walters, E. E., (2005). Prevalence, severity, and comorbidity of 12-month DSM-IV disorders in the National Comorbidity Survey Replication. *Archives of General Psychiatry, 62*, 617–627.

Kessler, R. C., Stang, P., Wittchen, H. U., Stein, M., & Walters, E. E. (1999). Lifetime co-morbidities between social phobia and mood disorders in the U.S. National Co-morbidity Survey. *Psychological Medicine, 29*, 555–567.

Keyes, C.L.M., & Goodman, S. H. (Eds.). (2006). *Women and depression*. New York: Cambridge University Press.

Kho, K. H., van Vresswijk, M. F., Simpson, S., & Zwinderman, A. H. (2003). A meta-analysis of electroconvulsive therapy efficacy in depression. *Journal of ECT, 19*, 139–147.

Kihlstrom, J. F. (2001). Dissociative disorders. In P. B. Sutker & H. E. Adams (Eds.), *Comprehensive handbook of psychopathology* (3rd ed., pp. 259–276). New York: Kluwer Academic/Plenum.

Kilpatrick, D. G., Ruggiero, K. J., Acierno, R., Saunders, B. E., Resnick, H. S., & Best, C. L. (2003). Violence and risk of PTSD, major depressive disorder, substance abuse/dependence, and comorbidity. Results from the National Survey of Adolescents. *Journal of Consulting and Clinical Psychology, 71*, 692–700.

King, M. P., & Tucker, J. A. (2000). Behavior change patterns and strategies distinguishing moderation drinking and abstinence during the natural resolution of alcohol problems without treatment. *Psychology of Addictive Behaviors, 23*, 537–541.

King, S. (2000). Determinants of expressed emotion in mothers of schizophrenia patients. *Psychiatry Research, 117*, 211–222.

Klerman, G. L., Weissman, M. M., Rounsaville, B. J., & Chevron, E. S. (1984). *Interpersonal psychotherapy of depression*. New York: Basic Books.

Klorman, R., Hastings, J. E., Weerts, T. C., Melamed, B. G., & Lang, P. J. (1974). Psychometric descriptions of some specific-fear questionnaires. *Behavior Therapy, 5*, 401–409.

Kluger, J. (2003, September 22). Real men get the blues. *Time*, pp. 48–49.

Koegel, L. K. (2000). Interventions to facilitate communication in autism. *Journal of Autism and Developmental Disorders, 30*, 383–391.

Koegel, R. L., Koegel, L. K., & Brookman, L. I. (2003). Empirically supported pivotal response interventions for children with autism. In A. E. Kazdin & J. R. Weisz (Eds.), *Evidence-based psychotherapies for children and adolescents* (pp. 341–357). New York: Guilford Press.

Kohut, H. (1971). *The analysis of self*. Madison, CT: International Universities Press.

Kopelowicz, A., Liberman, R. P., & Zarate, R. (2002). Psychosocial treatments for schizophrenia. In P. E. Nathan & J. M. Gorman (Eds.), *A guide to treatments that work* (2nd ed., pp. 201–228). New York: Oxford University Press.

Korszun, A., Altemus, M., & Young, E. A. (2006). The biological underpinnings of depression. In C.L.M. Keyes & S. H. Goodman (Eds.), *Women and depression* (pp. 41–61). New York: Cambridge University Press.

Kotler, L. A., Cohen, P., Davies, M., Pine, D. S., & Walsh, B. T. (2001). Longitudinal relationships between childhood, adolescent, and adult eating disorders. *Journal of the American Academy of Child and Adolescent Psychiatry, 40,* 1434, 1440.

Kristensen, H. (2000). Selective mutism and comorbidity with developmental disorder/delay, anxiety disorder, and elimination disorder. *Journal of American Academy of Child and Adolescent Psychiatry, 39,* 249–256.

Kristensen, H., & Torgersen, S. (2001). MCMI-II personality traits and symptom traits in parents of children with selective mutism: A case-control study. *Journal of Abnormal Psychology, 110,* 4.

Kronenberger, W. G., & Meyer, R. G. (2001). *The child clinician's handbook* (2nd ed.). Boston: Allyn & Bacon.

Kroutil, L. A., Van Brunt, D. L., Herman-Stahl, M. A., Heller, D. C., Bray, R. M., & Penne, M. A. (2006). Nonmedical use of prescription stimulants in the United States. *Drug and Alcohol Dependence, 84,* 135–143.

Krupnick, J. L., Sotsky, S. M., Elkin, I., Simmens, S., Moyer, J., Watkins, J., & Pilkonis, P. A. (1996). The role of the therapeutic alliance in psychotherapy and pharmacotherapy outcome: Findings in the National Institute of Mental Health treatment of depression collaborative research program. *Journal of Consulting and Clinical Psychology, 64,* 532–539.

Kübler-Ross, E. (1997). *Living with death and dying.* New York: Scribner.

Kübler-Ross, E., & Kessler, D. (2001). *Life lessons.* New York: Scribner.

Kübler-Ross, E., & Kessler, D. (2005). *On grief and grieving.* New York: Scribner.

Kuehn, B. M. (2006). FDA speeds smoking cessation drug review. *Journal of the American Medical Association, 295,* 614.

Kuhn, B. R., Marcus, B. A., & Pitner, S. L. (1999). Treatment guidelines for primary nonretentive encopresis and stool toileting refusal. *American Family Physician, 59,* 2171–2178.

Kushner, H. S. (2004). *When bad things happen to good people.* New York: Anchor Books.

Lacey, J. H., & Evans, D. H. (1986). The impulsivist: A multi-impulsive personality disorder. *British Journal of Addictions, 81,* 641–649.

Ladd, G. T., & Petry, N. M. (2003). A comparison of pathological gamblers with and without substance abuse treatment histories. *Experimental and Clinical Psychopharmacology, 11,* 202–209.

Lam, R. W., Zis, A. P., & Goumeniouk, A. D. (2002). Somatic treatments of bipolar disorder. In L. N. Yatham, V. Kusumakar, & S. P. Kutcher (Eds.), *Bipolar disorder: A clinician's guide to biological treatments* (pp. 241–264). Philadelphia: Brunner-Routledge.

Lambert, M. J. (1982). *The effects of psychotherapy.* New York: Human Sciences Press.

Lambert, M. J., & Anderson, E. M. (1996). Assessment for the time-limited psychotherapies. *American Psychiatric Press Review of Psychiatry, 15,* 23–42.

Lambert, M. J., & Barley, D. E. (2001). Research summary on the therapeutic relationship and psychotherapy outcome. *Psychotherapy, 38,* 357–361.

Lambert, M. J., & Bergin, A. E. (1994). The effectiveness of psychotherapy. In A. E. Bergin & S. L. Garfield (Eds.), *Handbook of psychotherapy and behavior change* (4th ed., pp. 143–189). Hoboken, NJ: Wiley.

Lambert, M. J., & Cattani-Thompson, K. (1996). Current findings regarding the effectiveness of counseling: Implications for practice. *Journal of Counseling and Development, 74,* 601–608.

Lambert, M. J., & Ogles, B. M. (2004). The efficacy and effectiveness of psychotherapy. In M. J. Lambert (Ed.), *Bergin and Garfield's handbook of psychotherapy and behavior change* (pp. 139–193). Hoboken, NJ: Wiley.

Lambert, M. J., Shapiro, D. A., & Bergin, A. E. (1986). The effectiveness of psychotherapy. In S. L. Garfield & A. E. Bergin (Eds.), *Handbook of psychotherapy and behavior change* (3rd ed., pp. 157–212). Hoboken, NJ: Wiley.

Landreth, G. L. (Ed.). (2001). *Innovations in play therapy: Issues, process, and special populations.* Philadelphia: Brunner-Routledge.

Lange, A., van de Ven, J. P., van de Schrieken, B., & Emmelkamp, P. (2001). Interapy. Treatment of posttraumatic stress through the Internet: A controlled trial. *Journal of Behavior Therapy and Experimental Psychiatry, 32,* 73–90.

Langer, S. J., & Martin, J. I. (2004). How dresses can make you mentally ill: Examining gender identity disorder in children. *Child & Adolescent Social Work Journal, 21,* 5–23.

Laudet, A. B., Magura, S., Vogel, H. S., & Knight, E. L. (2004). Perceived reasons for substance misuse among persons with a psychiatric disorder. *American Journal of Orthopsychiatry, 74,* 365–375.

Lavigne, J. V., Cicchetti, C., Gibbons, R., Binns, H. J., Larsen, L., & Devito, C. (2001). Oppositional defiant disorder with onset in preschool years: Longitudinal stability and pathways to other disorders. *Journal of the American Academy of Child and Adolescent Psychiatry, 40,* 1393–1400.

Leahy, R. L. (2004). Cognitive therapy. In S. L. Johnson & R. L. Leahy (Eds.), *Psychological treatment of bipolar disorder* (pp. 139–161). New York: Guilford Press.

Leckman, J. F., & Cohen, D. J. (1994). Tic disorders. In M. Rutter, E. Taylor, & L. Hersov (Eds.), *Child and adolescent psychiatry: Modern approaches* (pp. 455–466). Cambridge, MA: Blackwell.

Leckman, J. F., Zhang, H., Vitale, A., Lahnin, F., Lynch, K., Bondi, C., Kim, Y. S., & Peterson, B. (1998). Course of tic severity in Tourette syndrome: The first two decades. *Pediatrics, 102,* 14–19.

Ledgerwood, D. M., Steinberg, M. A., Wu, R., & Potenza, M. N. (2005). Self-reported gambling-related suicidality among gambling helpline callers. *Psychology of Addictive Behaviors, 19,* 175–183.

Leiblum, S. R. (2007). *Principles and practice of sex therapy* (4th ed.). New York: Guilford Press.

Leichsenring, F., & Leibing, E. (2003). The effectiveness of psychodynamic therapy and cognitive behavior therapy in the treatment of personality disorders: A meta-analysis. *American Journal of Psychiatry, 160*, 1223–1232.

Lejoyeux, M., McLoughlin, M., & Ades, J. (2006). Pyromania. In E. Hollander & D. J. Stein (Eds.), *Clinical manual of impulse-control disorders* (pp. 229–250). Arlington, VA: American Psychiatric Publishing.

Levant, R. F. (2005). *Report of the 2005 presidential task force on evidence-based practice*. Washington, DC: American Psychological Association.

Lewis, D. A., & Levitt, P. (2002). Schizophrenia as a disorder of neurodevelopment. *Annual Review of Neuroscience, 25*, 409–432.

Lieber, C. S. (2000). Ethnic and gender differences in ethanol metabolism. *Alcoholism: Clinical & Experimental Research, 24*, 417–418.

Lieberman, A. F., Silverman, R., & Pawl, J. (2000). Infant-parent psychotherapy. In C. H. Zeanah (Ed.), *Handbook of infant mental health* (2nd ed.). New York: Guilford Press.

Lilenfeld, L. R., Kaye, W. H., Greeno, C. G., Merikangas, K. R., Plotnicov, K., Pollice, C., Rao, R., Strober, M., Bulik, C. M., & Nagy, L. (1997). Psychiatric disorders in women with bulimia nervosa and their first-degree relatives: Effects of comorbid substance dependence. *International Journal of Eating Disorders, 22*, 255–264.

Lindberg, N., Holi, M. M., Tani, P., & Virkkunen, M. (2005). Looking for pyromania: Characteristics of a consecutive sample of Finnish male criminals with histories of recidivist fire-setting between 1973 and 1993. *BMC Psychiatry*, 5(47), 1–5.

Linehan, M. (1983). *Dialectical behavior therapy for treatment of parasuicidal women: Treatment manual*. Seattle: University of Washington.

Linehan, M. (1993). *Cognitive-behavioral treatment of borderline personality disorders*. New York: Guilford Press.

Links, P. S., & Kola, N. (2005). Assessing and managing suicide risk. In J. M. Oldham, A. E. Skodol, & D.S. Bender (Eds.), *The American Psychiatric Publishing textbook of personality disorders* (pp. 449–462). Washington, DC: American Psychiatric Association.

Linscheid, T. R. (1992). Eating problems in children. In C. E. Walker & M. C. Roberts (Eds.), *Handbook of clinical child psychology* (pp. 451–473). Hoboken, NJ: Wiley.

Littrell, J. M., Malia, J. A., & Vanderwood, J. (1995). Single session brief counseling in a high school. *Journal of Counseling and Development, 73*, 451–458.

Litz, B. T., Miller, M. W., Ruef, A. M., & McTeague, L. M. (2002). Exposure to trauma in adults. In M. M. Antony & D. H. Barlow (Eds.), *Handbook of assessment and treatment planning for psychological disorders* (pp. 215–258). New York: Guilford Press.

Livesley, W. J. (2003). *Practical management of personality disorders.* New York: Guilford Press.

Livingston, R. (1991). Anxiety disorders. In M. Lewis (Ed.), *Child and adolescent psychiatry: A comprehensive textbook* (pp. 673–685). Baltimore: Williams & Wilkins.

Lochman, J. E., Barry, T. D., & Pardini, D. A. (2003). Anger control for aggressive youth. In A. E. Kazdin & J. R. Weisz (Eds.), *Evidence-based psychotherapies for children and adolescents* (pp. 263–281). New York: Guilford Press.

Loeber, R., Burke, J. D., Lahey, B. B., Winters, A., & Zera, M. (2000). Oppositional defiant and conduct disorder: A review of the past 10 years, part I. *Journal of American Association of Child and Adolescent Psychiatry, 39,* 1468–1484.

Lord, C., & Rutter, M. (1994). Autism and pervasive developmental disorders. In M. Rutter, E. Taylor, & L. Hersov (Eds.), *Child and adolescent psychiatry: Modern approaches* (pp. 569–593). Cambridge, MA: Blackwell.

Lovaas, O. I. (1987). Behavioral treatment and normal educational and intellectual functioning in young autistic children. *Journal of Abnormal Child Psychology, 20,* 555–566.

Lovaas, O. I., & Smith, T. (2003). Early and intensive behavioral intervention in autism. In A. E. Kazdin & J. R. Weisz (Eds.), *Evidence-based psychotherapies for children and adolescents* (pp. 325–340). New York: Guilford Press.

Love, A., James, D., & Willner, P. (1998). A comparison of two alcohol craving questionnaires. *Addiction, 93,* 1091–1102.

Luborsky, L., Diguer, L., Cacciola, J., Barbar, J. P., Moras, K., Schmidt, K., & De Rubeis, R. J. (1996). Factors in outcomes of short-term dynamic psychotherapy for chronic depression versus nonchronic depression. *Journal of Psychotherapy Practice and Research, 5,* 152–159.

Luce, K. H., Winzelberg, A. J., Zabinski, M. F., & Osborne, M. I. (2003). Internet-delivered psychological interventions for body image dissatisfaction and disordered eating. *Psychotherapy, 40,* 148–154.

Lyon, C., & Schnall, J. (2005). What is the best treatment for nocturnal enuresis in children? *Journal of Family Practice, 54,* 905–909.

Lyon, G. R., Fletcher, J. M., Fuchs, L. S., & Chhabra, V. (2006). Learning disabilities. In E. J. Mash & R. A. Barkley (Eds.), *Treatment of childhood disorders* (3rd ed., pp. 512–594). New York: Guilford Press.

Lyons-Ruth, K., Zeanah, C. H., & Benoit, D. (1996). Disorder and risk for disorder during infancy and toddlerhood. In E. J. Mash & R. A. Barkley (Eds.), *Child psychopathology* (pp. 457–491). New York: Guilford Press.

Ma, S. H., & Teasdale, J. D. (2004). Mindfulness-based cognitive therapy for depression: Replication and exploration of differential relapse prevention effects. *Journal of Consulting and Clinical Psychology, 72,* 31–40.

Mackinaw-Koons, B., & Fristad, M. A. (2004). Children with bipolar disorder: How to break down barriers and work effectively together. *Professional Psychology: Research and Practice*, *35*, 481–484.

Maffei, C., Fossati, A., Agostoni, I., Barraco, A., Bagnato, M., Deborah, D., Namia, C., Novella, L., & Petrachi, M. (1997). Interrater reliability and internal consistency of the Structured Clinical Interview of DSM-IV Axis II personality disorders (SCID-II), version 2.0. *Journal of Personality Disorders*, *11*, 279–284.

Mahgerefteh, S., Pierre, J. M., & Wirshing, D. A. (2006). Treatment challenges in schizophrenia: A multifaceted approach to relapse prevention. *Psychiatric Times* [Online], *23*. Available: www.psychiatrictimes.com/article

Mahowald, M. W., & Schenck, C. H. (2005). Insights from studying human sleep disorders. *Nature*, *437*, 1279–1285.

Maldonado, J. R., Butler, L. D., & Spiegel, D. (2002). Treatments for dissociative disorders. In P. E. Nathan & J. M. Gorman (Eds.), *A guide to treatments that work* (2nd ed., pp. 463–496). New York: Oxford University Press.

Maldonado, J. R., & Spiegel, D. (2001). Conversion disorder. In K. A. Phillips (Ed.), *Somatoform and factitious disorders* (pp. 95–121). Washington, DC: American Psychiatric Association.

Maletzky, B. M. (2002). The paraphilias: Research and treatment. In P. E. Nathan and J. M. Gorman (Eds.), *A guide to treatments that work* (2nd ed., pp. 525–558). New York: Oxford University Press.

Malik, M. L., Beutler, L. E., Alimohamed, S., Gallagher-Thompson, D., & Thompson, L. (2003). Are all cognitive therapies alike? A comparison of cognitive and noncognitive therapy process and implications for the application of empirically supported treatments. *Journal of Counseling and Clinical Psychology*, *71*, 150–158.

Manber, R., Allen, J., & Morris, M. (2002). Alternative treatments for depression: Empirical support and relevance to women. *Journal of Clinical Psychiatry*, *63*, 629–640.

Maniacci, M. P. (1991). Guidelines for developing social interest with clients in psychiatric day hospitals. *Individual Psychology: Journal of Adlerian Theory, Research and Practice*, *47*, 177–188.

Marchi, M., & Cohen, P. (1990). Early childhood eating behaviors and adolescent eating disorders. *Journal of the American Academy of Child and Adolescent Psychiatry*, *29*, 112–117.

Marecek, J. (2006). Social suffering, gender, and women's depression. In C.L.M. Keyes & S. H. Goodman (Eds.), *Women and depression* (pp. 283–308). New York: Cambridge University Press.

Margulies, S. (2001). *Getting divorced without ruining your life*. New York: Fireside.

Maris, R. W. (2002). Suicide. *Lancet*, *360*, 319–326.

Markway, B., & Markway, G. (2003). *Painfully shy: How to overcome social anxiety and reclaim your life*. New York: St. Martin's Griffin.

Marlatt, G. A. (Ed.). (1998). *Harm reduction: Pragmatic strategies for managing high-risk behaviors*. New York: Guilford Press.

Martin, D. J., Garske, J. P., & Davis, M. K. (2000). Relation of the therapeutic alliance with outcome and other variables: A meta-analytic review. *Journal of Counseling and Clinical Psychology, 68*, 438–450.

Mash, E. J. (2006). Treatment of child and family disturbance: A cognitive-behavioral systems perspective. In E. J. Mash & R. A. Barkley (Eds.), *Treatment of childhood disorders* (3rd ed., pp. 3–62). New York: Guilford Press.

Mash, E. J., & Barkley, R. A. (Eds.). (2006). *Treatment of childhood disorders* (3rd ed.). New York: Guilford Press.

Mash, E. J., & Wolfe, D. A. (2005). *Abnormal child psychology* (3rd ed.). Belmont, CA: Wadsworth.

Masters, W. H., & Johnson, V. E. (1970). *Human sexual inadequacy*. Boston: Little, Brown.

Masterson, J. F., & Lieberman, A. R. (Eds.). (2004). *A therapist's guide to the personality disorders: The Masterson approach*. Phoenix: Zeig Tucker & Theisen.

Mattick, R. P., & Clarke, J. C. (1998). Development and validation of measures of social phobia scrutiny fear and social interaction anxiety. *Behaviour Research and Therapy, 36*, 455–470.

Matza, L. S., Revicki, D. A., Davidson, J. R., & Stewart, J. W. (2003). Depression with atypical features in the national comorbidity survey. *Archives of General Psychiatry, 60*, 817–826.

Maurice, C., Green, G., & Foxx, R. M. (1996). *Making a difference: Behavioral interventions for autism*. Austin, TX: Pro-Ed.

Mayes, S. D., & Calhuon, S. L. (2004). Influence of IQ and age in childhood autism: Lack of support for DSM-IV Asperger's disorder. *Journal of Developmental and Physical Disabilities, 16*, 257–272.

Mayfield, D., McLeod, G., & Hall, P. (1974). The CAGE questionnaire: Validation of a new alcoholism instrument. *American Journal of Psychiatry, 131*, 1121–1123.

McCabe, M. P. (1998). Sexual Function Scale: History and current factors. In C. Davis, W. Yarber, R. Bauseman, G. E., Schreer, S. Davis, & G. Schreer (Eds.), *Handbook of sexuality-related measures* (p. 275). Thousand Oaks: Sage.

McCabe, R. E., & Antony, M. M. (2002). Specific and social phobia. In M. M. Antony & D. H. Barlow (Eds.), *Handbook of assessment and treatment planning for psychological disorders* (pp. 113–146). New York: Guilford Press.

McConnaughy, E. A., Prochaska, J. O., & Velicer, W. F. (1983). Stages of change in psychotherapy: Measurement and sample profiles. *Psychotherapy, 20*, 368–375.

McConnaughy, R. (2005). Asperger syndrome: Living outside the bell curve. *Journal of the Medical Library Association, 93*, 139–140.

McCrady, B. S. (2006). Family and other close relationships. In. W. R. Miller & K. M. Carroll (Eds.), *Rethinking substance abuse* (pp. 166–181). New York: Guilford Press.

McDonough, S. (2000). Interaction guidance: An approach for difficult-to-engage families. In C. H. Zeanah (Ed.), *Handbook of infant mental health* (pp. 485–493). New York: Guilford Press.

McEachin, J. J., Smith, T., & Lovaas, O. I. (1993). Long-term outcome for children with autism who received early intensive behavioral treatment. *American Journal on Mental Retardation, 97*, 359–372.

McElroy, S. L., & Kotwal, R. (2006). Binge eating. In E. Hollander & D. J. Stein (Eds.), *Clinical manual of impulse-control disorders* (pp. 115–148). Arlington, VA: American Psychiatric Publishing.

McElroy, S. L., Soutullo, C. A., Beckman, D. A., Taylor, P., Jr., & Keck, P. E. Jr. (1998). DSM-IV-TR intermittent explosive disorder: A report of 27 cases. *Journal of Clinical Psychiatry, 59*, 203–210.

McGlashan, T. H., Grilo, C. M., Sanislow, C. A., Ralevski, E., Morey, L. C., Gunderson, J. G., Skodol, A. E., Shea, M. T., Zanarini, M. C., Bender, D., Stout, R. L., Yen, S., & Pagano, M. (2005). Two-year prevalence and stability of individual DSM-IV criteria for schizotypal, borderline, avoidant, and obsessive-compulsive personality disorders: Toward a hybrid model of Axis II disorders. *American Journal of Psychiatry, 162*, 883–889.

McHolm, A. E. Cunningham, C. E., & Vanier, M. K. (2005). *Helping your child with selective mutism: Practical steps to overcome a fear of speaking*. Oakland, CA: New Harbinger.

McIntyre, J. R. (2004). Family treatment of substance abuse. In S.L.A. Straussner (Ed.), *Clinical work with substance-abusing clients* (2nd ed., pp. 237–263). New York: Guilford Press.

McKenry, P. C., & Price, S. J. (Eds.). (2005). *Families and change: Coping with stressful events and transitions* (3rd ed.). Thousand Oaks, CA: Sage.

McLellan, T. A., Kushner, H., Metzger, D., Peters, R., Smith, I., Grissom, G., Pettinati, H., & Argeriou, M. (1992). The fifth edition of the Addiction Severity Index. *Journal of Substance Abuse Treatment, 9*, 199–213.

McMahon, R. J. (1994). Diagnosis, assessment, and treatment of externalizing problems in children: The role of longitudinal data. Special section: Childhood psychopathology. *Journal of Consulting and Clinical Psychology, 62*, 901–907.

McMahon, R. J., Wells, K. C., & Kotler, J. S. (2006). Conduct problems. In E. J. Mash & R. A. Barkley (Eds.), *Treatment of childhood disorders* (3rd ed., pp. 137–270). New York: Guilford Press.

Meichenbaum, D. H., & Deffenbacher, J. L. (1988). Stress inoculation training. *Counseling Psychologist, 16*, 69–90.

Memon, S. A., Mandhan, P., Qureshi, J. N., & Shairani, A. J. (2003). Recurrent Rapunzel syndrome: A case report. *Medical Science Monitor, 9*(9), 92–94.

Menta, M., Ito, K., Okuma, H., & Nakano, T. (1995). Development and outcome of the Hizen parenting skills training program for mothers of children with mental retardation. *Japanese Journal of Behavior Therapy, 21*(1), 25–38.

Messer, S. B. (2001). What makes brief psychodynamic therapy time efficient. *Clinical Psychology: Science and Practice*, *8*, 5–22.

Messer, S. B., & Warren, C. S. (1995). *Models of brief psychodynamic therapy: A comparative approach*. New York: Guilford Press.

Messina, N., Wish, E., Hoffman, J., & Nemes, S. (2002). Antisocial personality disorder and TC treatment outcomes. *American Journal of Drug and Alcohol Abuse*, *28*, 197–212.

Messman, T. L., & Long, P. J. (1996). Child sexual abuse and its relationship to revictimization in adult women: A review. *Clinical Psychology Review*, *16*, 397–420.

Meyer, B., & Pilkonis, P. A. (2006). Developing treatments that bridge personality and psychopathology. In R. F. Krueger & J. L. Tackett (Eds.), *Personality and psychopathology* (pp. 262–291). New York: Guilford Press.

Meyer, B., Pilkonis, P. A., Krupnick, J. L., Egan, M. K., Simmens, S. J., & Sotsky, S. M. (2002). Treatment expectancies, patient alliance, and outcome: Further analyses from the National Institute of Mental Health treatment of depression collaborative research program. *Journal of Counseling and Clinical Psychology*, *70*, 1051–1055.

Meyer, R. G. (1983). *California Psychological Inventory*. Palo Alto, CA: Consulting Psychologists Press.

Meyer, R. G., & Deitsch, S. E. (1996). *The clinician's handbook* (2nd ed.). Boston: Allyn & Bacon.

Meyer, T. J., & Mark, M. M. (1995). Effects of psychosocial interventions with adult cancer patients: A meta-analysis of randomized experiments. *Health Psychology*, *14*, 101–108.

Meyer, T. J., Miller, M. L., Metzger, R. L., & Borkovec, T. D. (1990). Development and validation of the Penn State Worry Questionnaire. *Behaviour Research and Therapy*, *28*, 487–495.

Miklowitz, D. J. (2001). Bipolar disorder. In D. H. Barlow (Ed.), *Clinical handbook of psychological disorders* (3rd ed., pp. 523–561). New York: Guilford Press.

Miklowitz, D. J. (2002). *The bipolar survival guide*. New York: Guilford Press.

Miklowitz, D. J. (2004). Family therapy. In S. L. Johnson & R. L. Leahy (Eds.), *Psychological treatment of bipolar disorder* (pp. 184–202). New York: Guilford Press.

Miklowitz, D. J. (2006). Psychosocial interventions in bipolar disorders: Rationale and effectiveness. In H. S. Akiskal and M. Tohen (Eds.), *Bipolar psychopharmacotherapy: Caring for the patient* (pp. 313–332). Hoboken, NJ: Wiley.

Miklowitz, D. J., & Goldstein, M. J. (1997). *Bipolar disorder: A family-focused treatment approach*. New York: Guilford Press.

Miller, R. S., Johnson, J. A., & Johnson, J. K. (1991). Assessing the prevalence of unwanted childhood sexual experiences. *Journal of Psychology and Human Sexuality*, *4*(3), 43–54.

Miller, S. D., Hubble, M. A., & Duncan, B. L. (1997). Counseling for change. *Professional Counselor, 12*(1), 15–16, 52–53.

Miller, W. R. (1983). Motivational interviewing with problem drinkers. *Behavioral Psychotherapy, 11*, 147–172.

Miller, W. R., & Carroll, K. M. (2006). Drawing the sciences together: Ten principles, ten recommendations. In. W. R. Miller & K. M. Carroll (Eds.), *Rethinking substance abuse* (pp. 293–311). New York: Guilford Press.

Miller, W. R., & Harris, R. (2000). A simple scale for Gorski's warning signs for relapse. *Journal of Studies on Alcohol, 61*, 759–765.

Miller, W. R., & Rollnick, S. (2002). *Motivational interviewing: Preparing people to change addictive behavior*. New York: Guilford Press.

Miller, W. R., & Tonigan, J. S. (1996). Assessing drinkers' motivation for change: The Stages of Change Readiness and Treatment Eagerness Scale (SOCRATES). *Psychology of Addictive Behaviors, 10*, 81–89.

Miller W. R., Zweben, A., DiClemente, C. C., & Rychtarik, R. G. (1995). *Motivational enhancement therapy manual: A clinical research guide for therapists treating individuals with alcohol abuse and dependence* (Vol. 2, Project MATCH Monograph Series). Rockville, MD: National Institute of Alcohol Abuse and Alcoholism.

Millon, T., Grossman, S., Millon, C., Meagher, S., & Ramnath, R. (2004). *Personality disorders in modern life* (2nd ed.). Hoboken, NJ: Wiley.

Mittelman, M. S., Roth, D. L., Coon, D. W., & Haley, W. E. (2004). Sustained benefit of supportive intervention for depressive symptoms in the caregivers of patients with Alzheimer's disease. *American Journal of Psychiatry, 161*, 850–856.

Mjellem, N., & Kringlen, E. (2001). Schizophrenia: A review, with emphasis on the neurodevelopmental hypothesis. *Nordic Journal of Psychiatry, 55*, 301–309.

Moffitt, T. E., Caspi, A., Harrington, H., & Milne, B. (2002). Males on the life-course-persistent and adolescence-limited antisocial pathways: Follow-up at age 26. *Development and Psychopathology, 14*, 179–206.

Moos, R. H. (2006). Social contexts and substance use. In W. R. Miller & K. M. Carroll (Eds.), *Rethinking substance abuse* (pp. 182–200). New York: Guilford Press.

Morin, C. M. (1993). Insomnia. *Psychological Assessment and Management*. New York: Guilford Press.

Morin, C. M., & Espie, C. A. (2003). *Insomnia: A clinician's guide to assessment and treatment*. New York: Springer.

Morris, T. L., & March, J. S. (2004). *Anxiety disorders in children and adolescents* (2nd ed.). New York: Guilford Press.

Morrison, L. (2001). The global epidemiology of HIV/AIDS. *British Medical Bulletin, 58*, 7–18.

MTA Cooperative Group. (1999). A 14-month randomized clinical trial of treatment strategies for attention-deficit/hyperactivity disorder. *Archives of General Psychiatry, 56*, 1073–1086.

MTA Cooperative Group. (2004). National Institute of Mental Health Multimodal Treatment Study of ADHD follow-up: 24-month outcomes of treatment strategies for attention-deficit/hyperactivity disorder. *Pediatrics, 113,* 754–761.

Mueser, K. T., Drake, R. E., Turner, W., & McGovern, M. (2006). Comorbid substance use disorders and psychiatric disorders. In W. R. Miller & K. M. Carroll (Eds.), *Rethinking substance abuse* (pp. 115–133). New York: Guilford Press.

Mufson, L., Dorta, K. P., Moreau, D., & Weissman, M. M. (2004). *Interpersonal psychotherapy for depressed adolescents* (2nd ed.). New York: Guilford Press.

Mulholland, A. M., & Mintz, L. B. (2001). Prevalence of eating disorders among African American women. *Journal of Counseling Psychology, 48,* 111–116.

Murray, W. H. (2006). *Schizoaffective disorder: New research.* Hauppage, NY: Nova Science.

Myers, I. B., & McCauley, M. H. (1985). *A guide to the development and use of the Myers-Briggs Type Indicator.* Palo Alto, CA: Consulting Psychologists Press.

Nagata, R., Kawarada, Y., Kirike, N., & Iketani, T. (2000). Multi-impulsivity of Japanese patients with eating disorders: Primary and secondary impulsivity. *Psychiatry Research, 94,* 239–250.

Nathan, P. E., & Gorman, J. M. (2002). *A guide to treatments that work* (2nd ed.). New York: Oxford University Press.

National Board for Certified Counselors and Center for Credentialing and Education. (n.d.). *The practice of Internet counseling.* Retrieved December 28, 2006, from http://www.nbcc.org/webethics2

National Center for Health Statistics. (2003). *Health United States 2003 with chartbook on trends in the health of Americans.* Hyattsville, MD: Author.

National Institute on Drug Abuse. (2003). *Epidemiologic trends in drug abuse: Vol. 1. Proceedings of the Community Epidemiology Work Group.* Bethesda, MD: National Institutes of Health.

National Institute on Drug Abuse. (2004). *NIDA InfoFacts: Marijuana* [Online]. Available: www.drugabuse.gov/infofacts/marijuana.html

National Institute of Mental Health. (2002). *Child and adolescent bipolar disorder: An update from the National Institute of Mental Health.* Bethesda, MD: Author.

National Institute of Mental Health. (2004). *Autism spectrum disorders (pervasive developmental disorders)* [Online]. Available: www.nimh.nih.gov/publicat/autism.cfm

National Institute of Mental Health. (2005). *Mental illness exacts heavy toll, beginning in youth* [Online]. Available: www.nimh.nih.gov/press/mentalhealthstats.cfm

National Institutes of Health & the National Institute on Alcohol Abuse and Alcoholism. (2004). *2001–2002 National Epidemiologic Survey on Alcohol and Related Conditions.* Washington, DC: National Institutes of Health.

National Research Council, Committee on Educational Interventions for Children with Autism, Division of Behavioral and Social Sciences and Education. (2001). *Educating children with autism.* Washington, DC: National Academy Press.

National Wellness Institute. (1983). *Lifestyle assessment questionnaire* (2nd ed.). Stevens Point: University of Wisconsin-Stevens Point Institute for Lifestyle Improvement.

Nelson, M. L., & Neufeldt, S. A. (1996). Building on an empirical foundation: Strategies to enhance good practice. *Journal of Counseling and Development, 74*, 609–615.

Nemeroff, C. B., & Schatzberg, A. F. (2002). Pharmacological treatments for unipolar depression. In P. E. Nathan & J. M. Gorman (Eds.), *A guide to treatments that work* (2nd ed., pp. 229–244). New York: Oxford University Press.

Newsom, C., & Hovanitz, C. A. (2006). Autistic spectrum disorders. In E. J. Mash & R. A. Barkley (Eds.), *Treatment of childhood disorders* (3rd ed., pp. 455–511). New York: Guilford Press.

Nolan, K. A., Volavka, J., Mohr, P., & Czobor, P. (1999). Psychopathy and violent behavior among patients with schizophrenia or schizoaffective disorder. *Psychiatric Services, 50*, 787–792.

Nolan, T., Debelle, G., Oberflaid, F., & Coffey, C. (1991). Randomised trial of laxatives in treatment of childhood encopresis. *Lancet, 338*, 523–527.

Nolen-Hoeksema, S. (2006). The etiology of gender differences in depression. In C. M. Mazure & G. P. Keita (Eds.), *Understanding depression in women: Applying empirical research to practice and policy* (pp. 9–43). Washington, DC: American Psychological Association.

Noordsy, D. L., McQuade, D. V., & Mueser, K. T. (2003). Assessment considerations. In H. L. Graham, A. Copello, M. J. Birchwood, & K. T. Mueser (Eds.), *Substance misuse in psychosis: Approaches to treatment and service delivery* (pp. 159–180). Chichester, England: Wiley.

Norcross, J. C. (Ed.). (2002). *Psychotherapy relationships that work: Therapist contributions and responsiveness to patients*. New York: Oxford University Press.

Nowell, P. D., Buysse, D. J., Morin, C., Reynolds, C. F., & Kupfer, D. J. (2002). Effective treatments for selected sleep disorders. In P. E. Nathan & J. M. Gorman (Eds.), *A guide to treatments that work* (2nd ed., pp. 593–609). New York: Oxford University Press.

Oakley, L. D. (2005). Neurobiology of nonpsychotic illnesses. In L. C. Copstead & J. L. Banasik (Eds.), *Pathophysiology: Biological and behavioral perspectives* (3rd ed., pp. 1192–1209). St. Louis: Elsevier Saunders.

O'Brien, C. P., & McKay, J. (2002). Pharmacological treatments for substance use disorders. In P. E. Nathan & J. M. Gorman (Eds.), *A guide to treatments that work* (2nd ed., pp. 125–156). New York: Oxford University Press.

Ockert, D., Baier, A. R., & Coons, E. E. (2004). Treatment of stimulant dependence. In S.L.A. Straussner (Ed.), *Clinical work with substance-abusing clients* (2nd ed., pp. 209–234). New York: Guilford Press.

Ohayon, M. M., Guilleminault, C., Paiva, T., Priest, R. G., Rapoport, D. M., Sagales, T., Smirne, S., & Zulley, J. (1997). An international study on sleep disorders in the general population: Methodological aspects of the use of the Sleep-EVAL system. *Sleep, 12*, 1086–1092.

Ohayon, M. M., & Schatzberg, A. F. (2002). Prevalence of depressive episodes with psychotic features in the general population. *American Journal of Psychiatry, 159,* 1855–1861.

Oldham, J. M. (2006). Borderline personality disorder and suicidality. *American Journal of Psychiatry, 163,* 20–26.

Olfson, M., Marcus, S. C., Tedeschi, M., & Wan, G. J. (2006). Continuity of antidepressant treatment for adults with depression in the United States. *American Journal of Psychiatry, 163,* 101–108.

Oltmanns, T. F., & Emery, R. E. (2007). *Abnormal psychology* (5th ed.). Upper Saddle River, NJ: Pearson Education.

O'Malley, S. S., & Kosten, T. R. (2006). Pharmacotherapy of addictive disorders. In W. R. Miller & K. M. Carroll (Eds.), *Rethinking substance abuse* (pp. 240–256). New York: Guilford Press.

Orlinsky, D. E., Grawe, K., & Parks, B. K. (1994). Process and outcome in psychotherapy: In A. E. Bergin & S. L. Garfield (Eds.), *Handbook of psychotherapy and behavior change* (4th ed., pp. 270–376). Hoboken, NJ: Wiley.

Orlinsky, D. E., & Howard, K. I. (1986). Process and outcome in psychotherapy. In S. L. Garfield & A. E. Bergin (Eds.), *Handbook of psychotherapy and behavior change* (3rd ed., pp. 311–381). Hoboken, NJ: Wiley.

Orr, J. M., Miller, R. B., & Polson, D. M. (2005). Toward a standard of care for child ADHD: Implications for marriage and family therapists. *Journal of Marital and Family Therapy, 31,* 191–205.

Ost, L. (1996). One-session group treatment of spider phobia. *Behaviour Research and Therapy, 34,* 707–715.

Pace, G. M., & Toyer, E. A. (2000). The effects of a vitamin supplement on the pica of a child with severe mental retardation. *Journal of Applied Behavior Analysis, 33,* 619–622.

Pallanti, S., Rossi, N. B., & Hollander, E. (2006). Pathological gambling. In E. Hollander & D. J. Stein (Eds.), *Clinical manual of impulse-control disorders* (pp. 251–289). Arlington, VA: American Psychiatric Publishing.

Paniagua, F. A. (2001). *Diagnosis in a multicultural context: A casebook for mental health professionals.* Thousand Oaks, CA: Sage.

Pantalon, M., & Motta, R. W. (1998). Effectiveness of anxiety management training in the treatment of posttraumatic stress disorder: A preliminary report. *Journal of Behavioral Therapy and Experiential Psychiatry, 29,* 21–29.

Pape, P. A. (2004). Assessment and intervention with alcohol- and drug-abusing women. In S.L.A. Straussner (Ed.), *Clinical work with substance-abusing clients* (2nd ed., pp. 347–369). New York: Guilford Press.

Paris, J. (1999). Borderline personality disorder. In T. Millon, P. H. Blaney, & R. D. Davis (Eds.), *Oxford textbook of psychopathology* (pp. 628–652). New York: Oxford University Press.

Paris, J. (2003). *Personality disorders over time: Precursors, course, and outcome.* Arlington, VA: American Psychiatric Publishing.

Parker, R., & Aldwin, C. M. (1997). Do aspects of gender identity change from early to middle adulthood? Distentangling age, cohort, and period effects. In M. Lachman & J. James (Eds.), *Multiple paths of mid-life development* (pp. 67–107). Chicago: University of Chicago Press.

Patterson, G. R. (1982). *A social learning approach to family intervention*. Eugene, OR: Castalia.

Pavuluri, M. N., Brimaher, B., & Naylor, M. W. (2005). Pediatric bipolar disorder: A review of the past 10 years. *Journal of the American Academy of Child and Adolescent Psychiatry, 44*, 231–235.

Pavuluri, M. N., Graczyk, P. A., Henry, D. B., Carbray, J. A., Heidenreich, J., & Miklowitz, D. J. (2004). Child- and family-focused cognitive-behavioral therapy for pediatric bipolar disorder. *Journal of the American Academy of Child and Adolescent Psychiatry, 43*, 528–537.

Paxon, J. E. (1995). Relapse prevention for individuals with developmental disabilities, borderline intellectual functioning, or illiteracy. *Journal of Psychoactive Drugs, 27*, 167–172.

PDM Task Force. (2006). *Psychodynamic diagnostic manual*. Silver Spring, MD: Alliance of Psychodynamic Organizations.

Penninx, B.W.J.H. (2006). Women's aging and depression. In C.L.M. Keyes & S. H. Goodman (Eds.), *Women and depression* (pp. 129–146). New York: Cambridge University Press.

Penza, K. M., Heim, C., & Nemeroff, C. B. (2006). Trauma and depression. In C.L.M. Keyes & S. H. Goodman (Eds.), *Women and depression* (pp. 360–381). New York: Cambridge University Press.

Perls, F. (1969). *Gestalt therapy verbatim*. Lafayette, CA: Real People Press.

Peterson, L., Reach, K., & Grube, S. (2003). Health-related disorders. In E. J. Mash & R. A. Barkley (Eds.), *Child psychopathology* (2nd ed., pp. 716–749). New York: Guilford Press.

Petry, N. M. (2000). Psychiatric symptoms in problem gambling and non-problem gambling substance abusers. *American Journal of Addictions, 9*, 163–171.

Pettit, J. W., & Joiner, T. E. (2006). *Chronic depression*. Washington, DC: American Psychological Association.

Phillips, K. A. (2001). Body dysmorphic disorder. In K. A. Phillips (Ed.), *Somatoform and factitious disorders* (pp. 67–88). Washington, DC: American Psychiatric Association.

Piacentini, J., & Chang, S. (2005). Habit reversal training for tic disorders in children and adolescents. *Behavior Modification, 29*, 803–822.

Pines, M., & Schlapobersky, J. (2000). Group methods in adult psychiatry. In M. G. Gelder, J. J. Lopez-Ibor Jr., & N. C. Andreasen (Eds.), *New Oxford textbook of psychiatry* (pp. 1442–1462). Oxford: Oxford University Press.

Pinsof, W. M., & Wynne, L. C. (2000). Toward progress research: Closing the gap between family therapy practice and research. *Journal of Marital and Family Therapy, 26*, 1–8.

Pitschel-Walz, G., Leucht, S., Bauml, J., Kissling, W., & Engel, R. R. (2001). The effects of family interventions on relapse and rehospitalization in schizophrenia: A meta-analysis. *Schizophrenia Bulletin, 27,* 73–92.

Pizzagalli, D., Lehmann, D., Gianotti, L., Koenig, T., Tanaka, H., Wackermann, J., & Brugger, P. (2000). Brain electric correlates of strong belief in paranormal phenomena: Intracerebral EEG source and regional omega complexity analyses. *Psychiatry Research, 100,* 139–154.

Pliszka, S. R., Carlson, C. L., & Swanson, J. M. (2001). *ADHD with comorbid disorders: Clinical assessment and management.* New York: Guilford Press.

Polyakova, I., Knobler, H. Y., Ambrumova, A., & Lerner, V. (1998). Characteristics of suicidal attempts in major depression versus adjustment reactions. *Journal of Affective Disorders, 47,* 174–180.

Popper, C. W., & Gherardi, P. C. (1996). Anxiety disorders. In J. M. Wiener (Ed.), *Diagnosis and psychopharmacology of childhood and adolescent disorders* (2nd ed., pp. 294–348). Hoboken, NJ: Wiley.

Portzky, G., Audenaert, K., & van Heeringen, K. (2005). Adjustment disorder and the course of the suicidal process in adolescents. *Journal of Affective Disorders, 87,* 265–270.

Pratt, S. I., & Mueser, K. T. (2002). Schizophrenia. In M. M. Antony & D. H. Barlow (Eds.), *Handbook of assessment and treatment planning for psychological disorders* (pp. 375–414). New York: Guilford Press.

Preston, J. D., O'Neal, J. H., & Talaga, M. C. (2005). *Handbook of clinical psychopharmacology for therapists* (4th ed.). Oakland, CA: New Harbinger.

Price, D. (2006). Do hypnotic analgesic interventions contain placebo effects? *Pain, 124,* 238–239.

Principe, J. M., Marci, C. D., & Glick, D. M. (2006). The relationship among patient contemplation, early alliance, and continuation in psychotherapy. *Psychotherapy, 43,* 238–243.

Prochaska, J. O., DiClemente, C. C., & Norcross, J. C. (1992). In search of how people change: Applications to addictive behaviors. *American Psychologist, 47,* 1102–1114.

Prochaska, J. O., & Norcross, J. C. (2006). *Systems of psychotherapy: A transtheoretical analysis* (6th ed.). Pacific Grove, CA: Brooks/Cole.

Quinn, W. H., Dotson, D., & Jordan, K. (1997). Dimensions of the therapeutic alliance and their associations with outcome in family therapy. *Psychotherapy Research, 7,* 429–438.

Randolph, E. M. (1996). *Randolph Attachment Disorder Questionnaire.* Evergreen, CO: Institute for Attachment.

Rapoport, J. L., & Castellanos, F. X. (1996). Attention-deficit/hyperactivity disorder. In J. M. Wiener (Ed.), *Diagnosis and psychopharmacology of childhood and adolescent disorders* (2nd ed., pp. 265–292). Hoboken, NJ: Wiley.

Rapoport, J. L., & Ismond, D. R. (1996). DSM-IV training guide for diagnosis of childhood disorders. New York: Brunner/Mazel.

Rapport, M. D., & Moffitt, C. (2002). Attention deficit/hyperactivity disorder and methylphenidate. A review of height/weight, cardiovascular, and somatic complaint side effects. *Clinical Psychology Review, 22*, 1107–1131.

Rees, C. S., & Stone, S. (2005). Therapeutic alliance in face-to-face versus videoconference psychotherapy. *Professional Psychology: Research and Practice, 36*, 649–653.

Reich, J. (2002). Drug treatment of personality disorder traits. *Psychiatric Annals, 32*, 590–600.

Reid, T. R. (2005, January). Caffeine. *National Geographic*, pp. 2–33.

Reinecke, M., Ryan, N., & DuBois, D. (1998). Cognitive therapy of depression in adolescence: A review and meta-analysis. *Journal of the American Academy of Child and Adolescent Psychiatry, 37*, 26–34.

Reisberg, B., Doody, R., Stoffler, A., Schmitt, F., Ferris, S., & Mobius, H. J. (2003). Memantine in moderate-to-severe Alzheimer's disease. *New England Journal of Medicine, 348*, 1333–1341.

Resnick, H., Galea, S., Kilpatrick, D., & Vlahov, D. (2004). Research on trauma and PTSD in the aftermath of 9/11. *PTSD Research Quarterly, 15*(1), 1–4.

Rettew, D. C. (2000). Avoidant personality disorder, generalized social phobia, and shyness: Putting the personality back into personality disorders. *Harvard Review of Psychiatry, 6*, 283–297.

Reynolds, C. R., & Kamphaus, R. W. (2002). *Behavior Assessment System for Children.* Circle Pines, MN: American Guidance Service.

Reynolds, C. R., & Richmond, B. O. (1978). Revised Children's Manifest Anxiety Scale. *Journal of Abnormal Psychology, 6*, 271–280.

Reynolds, C. R., & Richmond, B. O. (1985). Revised Children's Manifest Anxiety Scale. Los Angeles: Western Psychological Services.

Richters, M., & Volkmar, F. (1994). Reactive attachment disorder of infancy or early childhood. *Journal of the American Academy of Child and Adolescent Psychiatry, 33*, 328–332.

Rifkin, A., Ghisalbert, D., Dimatou, S., Jin, C., & Sethi, M. (1998). Dissociative identity disorder in psychiatric inpatients. *American Journal of Psychiatry, 155*, 844–845.

Ritchie, E. C., & Huff, T. G. (1999). Psychiatric aspects of arsonists. *Journal of Forensic Science, 44*, 733–740.

Ritterband, L. M., Cox, D. J., Kovatchev, B., McKnight, L., Walker, L. S., Patel, K., Borowitz, S., & Sutphen, J. (2003). An Internet intervention as adjunctive therapy for pediatric encopresis. *Journal of Counseling and Clinical Psychology, 71*, 910–917.

Rivas-Vazquez, R. A., Rice, J., & Kalman, D. (2003). Pharmacotherapy of obesity and eating disorders. *Professional Psychology: Research and Practice, 34*, 562–566.

Rizvi, S. L., & Linehan, M. M. (2001). Dialectical behavior therapy for personality disorders. *Current Psychiatry Reports, 3*, 64–69.

Robbins, M. S., Turner, C. W., & Alexander, J. F. (2003). Alliance and dropout in family therapy for adolescents with behavior problems: Individual and systemic effects. *Journal of Family Psychology, 17*, 534–544.

Roberts, A. R. (2002). Assessment, crisis intervention, and trauma treatment: The integrative ACT intervention model. *Brief Treatment and Crisis Intervention, 2*, 1–21.

Roberts-Harewood, M., & Davies, S. C. (2001). Pica in sickle cell disease: She ate the headboard. *Archives of Disease in Childhood, 85*, 510.

Robins, C. J., Ivanoff, A. M., & Linehan, M. M. (2001). Dialectical behavior therapy. In W. J. Livesley (Ed.), *Handbook of personality disorders* (pp. 437–459). New York: Guilford Press.

Robinson, D. G., Woerner, M. G., McMeniman, M., Mendelowitz, A., & Bilder, R. M. (2004). Symptomatic and functional recovery from a first episode of schizophrenia or schizoaffective disorder. *American Journal of Psychiatry, 161*, 473–479.

Robinson, J. R. (2002). Attachment problems and disorders in infants and young children: Identification, assessment and intervention. *Infants and Young Children, 14*, 6–18.

Rockland, L. H. (2003). *Supportive therapy: A psychodynamic approach*. New York: Basic Books.

Roemer, L., Orsillo, S. M., & Barlow, D. H. (2002). Generalized anxiety disorder. In D. H. Barlow (Ed.), *Anxiety and its disorders* (pp. 477–515). New York: Guilford Press.

Roeser, R. W., Eccles, J. S., & Sameroff, A. J. (2000). School as a context of early adolescents' academic and social-emotional development: A summary of research findings. *Elementary School Journal, 100*, 443–471.

Rogers, C. (1957). The necessary and sufficient conditions of therapeutic personality change. *Journal of Consulting Psychology, 21*, 95–103.

Rogers, C. (1965). *Client-centered therapy: Its current practice, implications, and theory*. Boston: Houghton Mifflin. (Original work published 1951)

Rogers, C. (1980). *A way of being*. Boston: Houghton Mifflin.

Rogers, R., Kropp, P. R., Bagby, R. M., & Dickens, S. E. (1992). Faking specific disorders: A study of the Structured Interview of Reported Symptoms (SIRS). *Journal of Clinical Psychology, 48*, 643–648.

Rogers, R., Salekin, R., Sewell, K., & Cruise, K. (2000). Prototypical analysis of antisocial personality disorder. *Criminal Justice and Behavior, 27*, 234–255.

Rollnick, S., Heather, N., Gold, R., & Hall, W. (1992). Development of a brief "Readiness to Change" questionnaire for use in brief, opportunistic interventions among excessive drinkers. *British Journal of Addictions, 87*, 743–754.

Rosen, R. C., Brown, C., Heiman, I., Leiblum, S., Meston, C., Shabsigh, R., Furguson, D., & Agostino, R. D. (2000). The Female Sexual Function Index (FSFI): A multidimensional self-report instrument for the assessment of female sexual function. *Journal of Sex and Marital Therapy, 26*, 191–208.

Rosen, R. C., Cappelleri, J. C., & Gendrano, N., III. (2002). The International Index of Erectile Function (IIEF): A state-of-the-science review. *International Journal of Impotence Research, 14*, 226–244.

Rosenthal, N. E. (2006). *Winter blues: Everything you need to know to beat seasonal affective disorder* (2nd ed.). New York: Guilford Press.

Rosenvinge, J. H., Martinussen, M., & Ostensen, E. (2000). The comorbidity of eating disorders and personality disorders: A meta-analytic review of studies published between 1983 and 1998. *Eating and Weight Disorders, 5*, 52–61.

Rosenzweig, S. (1936). Some implicit common factors in diverse methods of psychotherapy. *American Journal of Orthopsychiatry, 6*, 412–415.

Ross, E. C. (Ed.). (2001). *Managed behavioral health care handbook*. Gaithersburg, MD: Aspen.

Roth, A., & Fonagy, P. (2005). *What works for whom? A critical review of psychotherapy research* (2nd ed.). New York: Guilford Press.

Roy-Byrne, P. P., & Cowley, D. S. (2002). Pharmacological treatments for panic disorder, generalized anxiety disorder, specific phobia, and social anxiety disorder. In P. E. Nathan & J. M. Gorman (Eds.), *A guide to treatments that work* (2nd ed., pp. 337–366). New York: Oxford University Press.

Sachs, G. S. (2004). *Managing bipolar affective disorder*. London: Science Press.

Sachse, R., & Elliott, R. (2001). Process-outcome research on humanistic therapy variables. In D. J. Cain & J. Seeman (Eds.), *Humanistic psychotherapies: Handbook of research and practice* (pp. 83–115). Washington, DC: American Psychological Association.

Sagar, A. (2005). Long term health risks due to impaired nutrition in women with a past history of bulimia nervosa. *Nutrition Noteworthy* [Online], *7*, Article 8. Available: http://repositories.cdlib.org/uclabiolchem/nutritionnoteworthy/vol7/iss1/art8

Sanchez-Craig, M., Wilkinson, D. A., & Davila, R. (1995). Empirically based guidelines for moderate drinking: 1-year results from three studies with problem drinkers. *American Journal of Public Health, 85*, 823–828.

Sarokoff, R. A., Taylor, B. A., & Poulson, C. L. (2001). Teaching children with autism to engage in conversational exchanges: Script fading with embedded textual stimuli. *Journal of Applied Behavior Analysis, 24*, 81–84.

Saunders, J. B., Aasland, O. G., Babor, T. F., DeLaFuente, J. R., & Grant, M. (1993). Development of the Alcohol Use Disorders Identification Test (AUDIT): WHO collaborative project on early detection of persons with harmful alcohol consumption. *Addiction, 88*, 296–303.

Savard, J., & Morin, C. M. (2002). Insomnia. In M. M. Antony & D. H. Barlow (Eds.), *Handbook of assessment and treatment planning for psychological disorders* (pp. 523–555). New York: Guilford Press.

Saxena, S., & Sharan, P. (2006). Services and treatment for depression: International perspectives and implications for a gender-sensitive approach. In C.L.M. Keyes &

S. H. Goodman (Eds.), *Women and depression* (pp. 417–449). New York: Cambridge University Press.

Schatzberg, A. F. (2005). Recent studies in the biology and treatment of depression. *Focus, 3*, 14–24.

Schopler, E., Reichler, R. J., De Vellis, R. F., & Daly, K. (1991). *Childhood Autism Rating Scale*. Los Angeles: Western Psychological Services.

Schopp, L., Johnstone, B., & Merrell, D. (2000). Telehealth and neuropsychological assessment: New opportunities for psychologists. *Professional Psychology: Research and Practice, 31*, 179–183.

Schramm, E., Hohagen, F., Grasshoff, U., Riemann, D., Hajak, G., Weess, H. G., & Berger, M. (1993). Test-retest reliability and validity of the Structured Interview for Sleep Disorders according to DSM-III-R. *American Journal of Psychiatry, 150*, 867–872.

Schreier, H. (2002). Munchausen by proxy defined. *Pediatrics, 110*, 985–988.

Schuckit, M. A. (2000). *Drug and alcohol abuse: A clinical guide to diagnosis and treatment* (5th ed.). New York: Kluwer Academic/Plenum.

Schwartz, R. C., Petersen, S., Reynolds, C. A., & Austin, J. F. (2003). Homicidality in schizophrenia: A replication study. *American Journal of Orthopsychiatry, 73*, 74–77.

Schwartz, R. H., & Shipon-Blum, E. (2005). Shy child? Don't overlook selective mutism. *Contemporary Pediatrics, 22*, 30–34.

Scogin, F., Jamison, C., & Davis, N. (1990). Two-year follow-up of bibliotherapy for depression in older adults. *Journal of Consulting and Clinical Psychology, 58*, 665–667.

Sedlak, A. J., & Broadhurst, D. D. (1996). *Third national incidence study of child abuse and neglect*. Washington, DC: U.S. Government Printing Office.

Segraves, T., & Althof, S. (2002). Psychotherapy and pharmacotherapy for sexual dysfunctions. In P. E. Nathan & J. M. Gorman (Eds.), *A guide to treatments that work* (2nd ed., pp. 497–524). New York: Oxford University Press.

Seligman, L. (1994). *Developmental career counseling and assessment*. Thousand Oaks, CA: Sage.

Seligman, L. (1996). *Promoting a fighting spirit: Psychotherapy for cancer patients, survivors, and their families*. San Francisco: Jossey-Bass.

Seligman, L. (2004). *Diagnosis and treatment planning in counseling* (3rd ed.). New York: Kluwer/Plenum.

Seligman, L. (2006). *Theories of counseling and psychotherapy: Systems, strategies, and skills* (2nd ed.). Upper Saddle River, NJ: Pearson Education.

Seligman, L., & Hardenburg, S. A. (2000). Assessment and treatment of paraphilias. *Journal of Counseling and Development, 78*, 107–113.

Seligman, L., & Moore, B. (1995). Diagnosis of mood disorders. *Journal of Counseling and Development, 74*, 65–69.

Seligman, M.E.P. (1990). *Learned optimism.* New York: Pocket Books.

Seligman, M.E.P. (1995). The effectiveness of psychotherapy. *American Psychologist, 50,* 965–974.

Seligman, M.E.P., Steen, T. A., Park, N., & Peterson, C. (2005). Positive psychology progress: Empirical validation of interventions. *American Psychologist, 60,* 410–421.

Selzer, M. L. (1971). The Michigan Alcoholism Screening Test: The quest for a new diagnostic instrument. *American Journal of Psychiatry, 127,* 1653–1658.

Shaffer, D., & Craft, L. (1999). Methods of adolescent suicide prevention. *Journal of Clinical Psychiatry, 60*(Suppl. 2), 70–74.

Shahar, G., Trower, P., Iqbal, Z., Birchwood, M., Davidson, L., & Chadwick, P. (2004). The person in recovery from acute and severe psychosis: The role of dependency, self-criticism, and efficacy. *American Journal of Orthopsychiatry, 74,* 480–488.

Shapiro, F. (1989). Efficacy of the eye movement desensitization procedure in the treatment of traumatic memories. *Journal of Traumatic Stress, 2,* 199–223.

Sheperis, C. J., Doggett, R. A., Hoda, N. E., Blanchard, T., Renfro-Michel, E. L., Holdiness, S. H., & Schlagheck, R. (2003). The development of an assessment protocol for reactive attachment disorder. *Journal of Mental Health Counseling, 25,* 291–310.

Sheperis, C. J., Renfro-Michel, E. L., & Doggett, R. A. (2003). In-home treatment of reactive attachment disorder in a therapeutic foster care system: A case example. *Journal of Mental Health Counseling, 25,* 76–89.

Sheridan, M. S. (2003). The deceit continues: An updated literature review of Munchausen syndrome by proxy. *Child Abuse and Neglect, 27,* 431–451.

Siegel, B. (1999). *Pervasive Developmental Disorder Screening Test II.* San Francisco: University of San Francisco, Langley Porter Psychiatric Institute, Pervasive Developmental Disorder Laboratory and Clinic.

Silver, L. B. (2006). *The misunderstood child: Understanding and coping with your child's learning disabilities* (4th ed.). New York: Three Rivers Press.

Silver, R. C., Holman, E. A., McIntosh, D. N., Poulin, M., & Gil-Rivas, V. (2002). Nationwide longitudinal study of psychological responses to September 11. *Journal of the American Medical Association, 288,* 1235–1244.

Silverman, W. K., & Rabian, B. (1999). Rating scales for anxiety and mood disorders. In D. Shaffer, C. P. Lucas, and J. E. Richters (Eds.), *Diagnostic assessment in child and adolescent psychopathology* (pp. 127–166). New York: Guilford Press.

Simeon, D., Guralnik, O., Schmeidler, J., & Knutelska, M. (2004). Fluoxetine therapy in depersonalisation disorder: Randomised controlled trial. *British Journal of Psychiatry, 185,* 31–36.

Simon, G. E. (2002). Management of somatoform and factitious disorders. In P. E. Nathan & J. M. Gorman (Eds.), *A guide to treatments that work* (2nd ed., pp. 447–461). New York: Oxford University Press.

Sinha, R., & Rush, A. J. (2006). Treatment and prevention of depression in women. In C. M. Mazure & G. P. Keita (Eds.), *Understanding depression in women: Applying empirical research to practice and policy* (pp. 45–70). Washington, DC: American Psychological Association.

Skodol, A. E., Gunderson, J. G., McGlashan, T. H., Dyck, I. R., Stout, R. L., Bender, D. S., Grilo, C. M., Shea, M. T., Zanarini, M. C., Morey, L. C., Sanislow, C. A., & Oldham, J. M. (2002). Functional impairment in patients with schizotypal, borderline, avoidant or obsessive-compulsive personality disorder. *American Journal of Psychiatry, 159,* 276–283.

Sledge, W. H., Tebes, J., Rakfeldt, J., Davidson, L., Lyons, L., & Druss, B. (1996). Day hospital/crisis respite care versus inpatient care: Part I: Clinical outcomes. *Journal of Psychiatry, 153,* 1065–1073.

Smith, B. H., Barkley, R. A., & Shapiro, C. J. (2006). Attention-deficit/hyperactivity disorder. In E. J. Mash & R. A. Barkley (Eds.), *Treatment of childhood disorders* (3rd ed., pp. 65–136). New York: Guilford Press.

Smith, E. J. (2006). The strength-based counseling model. *Counseling Psychologist, 34,* 134–144.

Smith, M. L., Glass, G. V., & Miller, T. J. (1980). *The benefits of psychotherapy.* Baltimore: Johns Hopkins University Press.

Smith, N. M., Floyd, M. R., Scogin, F., & Jamison, C. S. (1997). Three-year follow-up of bibliotherapy for depression. *Journal of Consulting and Clinical Psychology, 65,* 324–327.

Smith, R. L., & Capps, F. (2005). The major substances of abuse and the body. In P. Stevens & R. L. Smith (Eds.), *Substance abuse counseling: Theory and practice* (3rd ed., pp. 36–85). Upper Saddle River, NJ: Pearson Education.

Smith-Myles, B., & Simpson, R. L. (2002). Asperger syndrome: An overview of characteristics. *Focus on Autism and Other Developmental Disabilities, 17,* 132–137.

Snyder, H. (2001). Epidemiology of official offending. In R. Loeber & D. P. Farrington (Eds.), *Child delinquents: Development, intervention and service needs* (pp. 25–46). Thousand Oaks, CA: Sage.

Somerset, W., Newport, D. J., Ragan, K., & Stowe, Z. N. (2006). Depressive disorders in women: From menarche to beyond the menopause. In C.L.M. Keyes & S. H. Goodman (Eds.), *Women and depression* (pp. 62–88). New York: Cambridge University Press.

Spector, I. P., Carey, M. P., & Steinberg, L. (1996). The Sexual Desire Inventory: Development, factor structure, and evidence of reliability. *Journal of Sex and Marital Therapy, 22,* 175–190.

Sperry, L. (2003). *Handbook of diagnosis and treatment of DSM-IV-TR personality disorders* (2nd ed.). Philadelphia: Brunner-Routledge.

Spiegel, B. R., & Fewell, C. H. (2004). Twelve-step programs as a treatment modality. In S.L.A. Straussner (Ed.), *Clinical work with substance-abusing clients* (2nd ed., pp. 125–145). New York: Guilford Press.

Spiegel, D. (1996). Dissociative disorders. In R. E. Hales & S. C. Yudofsky (Eds.), *The American Psychiatric Press synopsis of psychiatry* (pp. 583–604). Washington, DC: American Psychiatric Press.

Springer, D. W., McNeece, C. A., & Arnold, E. M. (2003). *Substance abuse treatment for criminal offenders: An evidence-based guide for practitioners*. Washington, DC: American Psychological Association.

Standards of Practice Committee of the American Academy of Sleep Medicine. (2003). Practice parameters for using polysomnography to evaluate insomnia: An update for 2002. *Sleep*, *26*, 754–760.

Staner, L., Luthringer, R., & LeBon, O. (2006). Sleep disturbances in affective disorders. In S. R. Pandi-Perumal & J. M. Monti (Eds.), *Clinical pharmacology of sleep* (pp. 101–124). Basel, Switzerland: Birkhauser Verlag.

Stasiewicz, P. R., Herrman, D., Nochajski, T. H., & Dermen, K. H. (2006). Motivational interviewing: Engaging highly resistant clients in treatment. *Counselor*, *7*(1), 26–32.

Stein, D. J., Harvey, B., Seedat, S., & Hollander, E. (2006). Treatment of impulse-control disorders. In E. Hollander & D. J. Stein (Eds.), *Clinical manual of impulse-control disorders* (pp. 309–325). Arlington, VA: American Psychiatric Publishing.

Steketee, G., & Barlow, D. H. (2002). Obsessive-compulsive disorder. In D. H. Barlow (Ed.), *Anxiety and its disorders* (pp. 516–550). New York: Guilford Press.

Steketee, G., & Frost, R. (2004). Compulsive hoarding: Current status of research. *Clinical Psychology Review*, *23*, 905–927.

Steketee, G., Frost, R., & Bogart, K. (1996). The Yale-Brown Obsessive Compulsive Scale: Interview versus self-report. *Behaviour Research and Therapy*, *34*, 675–684.

Stemberger, R.M.T., Thomas, A. M., Mansueto, C. S., & Carter, J. G. (2003). Personal toll of trichotillomania: Behavioral and interpersonal sequelae. *Journal of Anxiety Disorders*, *14*, 97–104.

Stephens, R. S., Roffman, R. A., & Curtain, L. (2000). Comparison of extended versus brief treatments for marijuana use. *Journal of Consulting and Clinical Psychology*, *68*, 898–908.

Sterling, R. C., Gottheil, E., Weinstein, S. P., & Serota, R. (1998). Therapist/patient race and sex matching. *Addiction*, *93*, 1043–1050.

Stevens, P., & Smith, R. L. (2005). *Substance abuse counseling: Theory and practice* (3rd ed.). Upper Saddle River, NJ: Pearson Education.

Stice, E., Burton, E., & Shaw, H. (2004). Prospective relations between bulimic pathology, depression, and substance abuse: Unpacking comorbidity in adolescent girls. *Journal of Consulting and Clinical Psychology*, *72*, 62–71.

Stinchfield, R., & Winters, K. C. (2001). Outcome of Minnesota's gambling treatment programs. *Journal of Gambling Studies*, *17*, 217–245.

Stinson, F. S., Yi, H., Grant, B. F., Chou, P., Dawson, D. A., & Pickering, R. (1998). *National longitudinal alcohol epidemiological survey*. National Institute on Alcohol Abuse and Alcoholism. Bethesda, MD: National Institutes of Health.

Stone, W. L., Coonrod, E. E., Turner, L. M., & Pozdol, S. L. (2004). Psychometric properties of the STAT for early autism screening. *Behavioral Science*, *34*, 691–701.

Storch, E. A., Murphy, T. K., Geffken, G. R., Sajid, M., Allen, P., Roberti, J. W., & Goodman, W. K. (2005). Reliability and validity of the Yale Global Tic Severity Scale. *Psychological Assessment, 17*, 486–491.

Strain, J. J. (1998). Adjustment disorders. In J. C. Holland, W. Breitbart, R. McCorkle, M. Loscalzo, P. B. Jacobsen, M. S. Lederberg, & M. J. Massie (Eds.), *Psycho-oncology* (pp. 509–517). New York: Oxford University Press.

Strauman, T. J., Vieth, A. Z., Merrill, K. A., Woods, T. E., Kolden, G. G., Klein, M., Schneider, K. L., & Kwapil, L. (2006). Self-system therapy as an intervention for self-regulatory dysfunction in depression: A randomized comparison with cognitive therapy. *Journal of Consulting and Clinical Psychology, 74*, 367–376.

Stricker, G., & Gold, J. (Eds.). (2006). *A casebook of psychotherapy integration*. Washington, DC: American Psychological Association.

Strub, R. L., & Black, F. W. (2000). *The mental status examination in neurology* (4th ed.). Philadelphia: Davis.

Stuart, S., & Noyes, R. (1999). Attachment and interpersonal communication in somatization. *Psychosomatics, 40*, 34–43.

Sturmey, P. (1995). Evaluating and improving residential treatment during group leisure situations: An independent replication. *Behavioral Interventions, 10*, 59–67.

Substance Abuse and Mental Health Services Administration. (1998). *Prevalence of substance use among racial and ethnic subgroups in the United States, 1991–1993*. Washington, DC: National Clearinghouse for Alcohol and Drug Information.

Substance Abuse and Mental Health Services Administration. (2003). *Results from the 2002 National Survey on Drug Use and Health: National findings*. NHSDA Series H–22 (DHHS Pub. No. SMA 03–3836). Rockville, MD: Author. Available: www.oas.samhsa.gov/nhsda/2k2nsduh/Results/2k2Results.htm

Sue, D., Sue, D. W., & Sue, S. (2006). *Understanding abnormal behavior* (8th ed.). Boston: Houghton Mifflin.

Sue, D. W., Ivey, A. E., & Pedersen, P. B. (1996). *A theory of multicultural counseling and psychotherapy*. Pacific Grove, CA: Brooks/Cole.

Sugar, M. (1995). A clinical approach to childhood gender identity disorder. *American Journal of Psychotherapy, 49*, 260–281.

Sullivan, E. V., Fama, R., Rosenbloom, M. J., & Pfefferbaum, A. (2002). A profile of neuropsychological deficits in alcoholic women. *Neuropsychology, 16*, 74–83.

Swedo, S. E. (2002). Pediatric autoimmune neuropsychiatric disorders associated with streptococcal infections (PANDAS). *Molecular Psychiatry, 7*, S24-S25.

Syad, T. (2003). Safety and efficacy of the nicotine patch and gum for the treatment of adolescent tobacco addiction. *Journal of Pediatrics, 147*, 406–407.

Tarter, R. E., Sambrano, S., & Dunn, M. G. (2002). Predictor variables by developmental stages: A Center for Substance Abuse Prevention multisite study. *Psychology of Addictive Behaviors, 16*(45), S3-S10.

Task Force on Promotion and Dissemination of Psychological Procedures. (1995). Training in and dissemination of empirically validated psychological treatments: Report and recommendations. *Clinical Psychologist, 48*(1), 2–23.

Taylor, S., Thordarson, D. S., & Sochting, I. (2002). Obsessive-compulsive disorder. In M. M. Antony & D. H. Barlow (Eds.), *Handbook of assessment and treatment planning for psychological disorders* (pp. 182–214). New York: Guilford Press.

Teasdale, J. D., Segal, Z. V., Williams, J. M., Ridgeway, V. A., Soulsby, J. M., & Lau, M. A. (2000). Prevention of relapse/recurrence in major depression by mindfulness-based cognitive therapy. *Journal of Consulting and Clinical Psychology, 68*, 615–623.

Terman, M., Terman, J. S., & Williams, J.B.W. (1998). Seasonal affective disorder and its treatments. *Journal of Practical Psychiatry and Behavioral Health, 5*, 287–303.

Thayer, A. (2006, September 25). Drugs to fight addictions: A better understanding of the mechanisms of drug and alcohol dependence is helping to further development and use of pharmacotherapies against addictions. *Chemical and Engineering News, 84*(39), 21–44.

Thiedke, C. C. (2003). Nocturnal enuresis. *American Family Physician, 67*, 1499–1506.

Thomas, P. M. (2003). Protection, dissociation, and internal roles: Modeling and treating the effects of child abuse. *Review of General Psychology, 7*, 364–380.

Thompson, C. L., Rudolph, L. B., & Henderson, D. A. (2003). *Counseling children* (6th ed.). Belmont, CA: Wadsworth.

Thompson, V. L., Bazile, A., & Akbar, M. (2004). African American perceptions of psychotherapy and psychotherapists. *Professional Psychology: Research and Practice, 35*, 19–26.

Tienari, P., Wynne, L. C., Laksy, K., Moring, J., Nieminen, P., Sorri, A., Lahti, I., & Wahlberg, K. (2003). Genetic boundaries of the schizophrenia spectrum: Evidence from the Finnish adoptive family study of schizophrenia. *American Journal of Psychiatry, 160*, 1587–1594.

Tiffany, S. T., Singleton, E., Haertzen, C. A., & Henningfield, J. E. (1993). The development and initial validation of a cocaine craving questionnaire. *Drug and Alcohol Dependence, 34*, 19–28.

Torgersen, S., Kringlen, E., & Cramer, V. (2001). The prevalence of personality disorders in a community sample. *Archives of General Psychiatry, 58*, 590–596.

Torrey, E. F. (2001). *Surviving schizophrenia: A manual for families, consumers, and providers* (4th ed.). New York: HarperCollins.

Towbin, K. E., & Cohen, D. J. (1996). Tic disorders. In J. M. Wiener (Ed.), *Diagnosis and psychopharmacology of childhood and adolescent disorders* (2nd ed., pp. 349–369). Hoboken, NJ: Wiley.

Towbin, K. E., Cohen, D. J., & Leckman, J. F. (1995). Tic disorders. In G. O. Gabbard (Ed.), *Treatments of psychiatric disorders* (pp. 201–218). Washington, DC: American Psychiatric Press.

Trafford, A. (1992). *Crazy time: Surviving divorce and building a new life* (Rev. ed.). New York: HarperCollins.

Treating children as young as four for bipolar. (2005, May 26). *Wall Street Journal,* p. D-1.

Tsatsanis, K. D., Foley, C., & Donehower, C. (2004). Contemporary outcome research and programming guidelines for Asperger's syndrome and high-functioning autism. *Topics in Language Disorders, 24,* 249–259.

Tucker, E. (2002, August 28). Two men missing since 9/11 found alive in hospitals. *Houston Chronicle,* p. A-15.

Tucker, J. A., Vuchinich, R. E., & Murphy, J. G. (2002). Substance use disorders. In M. M. Antony & D. H. Barlow (Eds.), *Handbook of assessment and treatment planning for psychological disorders* (pp. 415–451). New York: Guilford Press.

U.S. Department of Health and Human Services, Office of Inspector General. (2000). *Mandatory managed care: Changes in Medicaid mental health services.* Washington, DC: U.S. Department of Health and Human Services.

U.S. Department of Health and Human Services. (2006). *Child maltreatment, 2004* [Online]. Available: www.acf.hhs.gov/programs/cb/pubs/cm04/index.htm

van der Klink, J. J., & van Dijk, F. J. (2003). Dutch practice guidelines for managing adjustment disorders in occupational and primary health care. *Scandinavian Journal of Work and Environmental Health, 29,* 478–487.

Verona, E., Patrick, C. J., & Joiner, T. E. (2001). Psychopathy, antisocial personality, and suicide risk. *Journal of Abnormal Psychology, 110,* 462–470.

Viorst, J. (1998). *Necessary losses.* New York: Free Press.

Volavka, J., Czobor, P., Sheitman, B., Lindenmayer, P., Citrome, L., McEvoy, J., Cooper, T., Chakos, M., & Lieberman, J. (2002). Clozapine, olanzapine, risperidone, and haloperidol in treatment-resistant patients with schizophrenia and schizoaffective disorder. *American Journal of Psychiatry, 159,* 255–262.

Volkmar, F. R. (1996). Childhood and adolescent psychosis: A review of the past 10 years. *Journal of the American Academy of Child and Adolescent Psychiatry, 35,* 843–851.

Wadhwa, P. D., Glynn, L., Hobel, C. J., Garite, T. J., Porto, M., Chicz-DeMet, A., Wiglesworth, A. K., & Sandman, C. A. (2002). Behavioral perinatology: Biobehavioral processes in human fetal development. *Regulatory Peptides, 108,* 149–157.

Wallerstein, R. S. (1986). *Forty-two lives in treatment.* New York: Guilford Press.

Walsh, R. (2000). Asian psychotherapies. In R. Corsini & D. Wedding (Eds.), *Current psychotherapies* (6th ed., pp. 407–444). Itsaca, IL: Peacock.

Walsh, R., & Shapiro, S. L. (2006). The meeting of meditative disciplines and western psychology: A mutually enriching dialogue. *American Psychologist, 61,* 227–239.

Wampold, B. E. (2001). *The great psychotherapy debate: Models, methods, and findings.* Mahwah, NJ: Erlbaum.

Wampold, B. E., & Brown, G. S. (2005). Estimating variability in outcomes attributable to therapists: A naturalistic study of outcomes in managed care. *Journal of Consulting and Clinical Psychology, 73*, 914–923.

Wang, P. S., Berglund, P., Olfson, M., Pincus, H. A., Wells, K. B., & Kessler, R. C. (2005). Failure and delay in initial treatment contact after first onset of mental disorders in the National Comorbidity Survey Replication. *Archives of General Psychiatry, 62*, 603–613.

Watson, J. C. (2006). A reflection on the blending of person-centered therapy and solution-focused therapy. *Psychotherapy, 43*, 13–15.

Weber, M. K., Floyd, R. L., Riley, E. P., & Snider, D. E., Jr. (2002). National task force on fetal alcohol syndrome and fetal alcohol effect: Defining the national agenda for fetal alcohol syndrome and other prenatal alcohol-related effects. *Morbidity and Mortality Weekly Report Recommendations and Reports, 51*(RR-14), 9–12.

Webster-Stratton, C., & Reid, M. J. (2003). The incredible years parents, teachers, and children training series: A multifaceted treatment approach for young children with conduct problems. In A. E. Kazdin & J. R. Weisz (Eds.), *Evidence-based psychotherapies for children and adolescents* (pp. 224–240). New York: Guilford Press.

Wechsler, D. (2001). *Wechsler Individual Achievement Test* (2nd ed.). San Antonio, TX: Psychological Corporation.

Weiner-Davis, M. (2002). *The divorce remedy*. New York: Simon & Schuster.

Weinstein, S., & Graves, R. E. (2002). Are creativity and schizotypy products of a right hemisphere bias? *Brain and Cognition, 49*, 138–151.

Weinstock, L. M., & Whisman, M. A. (2004). The self-verification model of depression and interpersonal rejection in heterosexual dating relationships. *Journal of Social and Clinical Psychology, 23*, 240–259.

Weissman, E. M., Kushner, M., Marcus, S. M., & Davis, D. F. (2003). Volume of VA patients with posttraumatic stress disorder in the New York metropolitan area after September 11. *Psychiatric Services, 54*, 1641–1643.

Weissman, M. M., Markowitz, J. C., & Klerman, G. L. (2000). *Comprehensive guide to interpersonal psychotherapy*. New York: Basic Books.

Weisz, J. R., & Hawley, K. M. (2002). Developmental factors in the treatment of adolescents. *Journal of Consulting and Clinical Psychology, 70*, 21–43.

Weisz, J. R., Weiss, B., Han, S. S., Granger, D. A., & Morton, T. (1995). Effects of psychotherapy with children and adolescents revisited: A meta-analysis of treatment outcome studies. *Psychological Bulletin, 117*, 450–468.

Weller, E. B., Danielyan, A. K., & Weller, R. A. (2004). Somatic treatment of bipolar disorder in children and adolescents. *Psychiatric Clinics of North America, 27*, 155–178.

Whisman, M. A., Weinstock, L. M., & Tolejko, N. (2006). Marriage and depression. In C.L.M. Keyes & S. H. Goodman (Eds.), *Women and depression* (pp. 219–240). New York: Cambridge University Press.

White, K. S., & Barlow, D. H. (2002). Panic disorder and agoraphobia. In D. H. Barlow (Ed.), *Anxiety and its disorders* (pp. 328–379). New York: Guilford Press.

White, L. A., Fisher, W. A., Byrne, D., & Kingma, R. (1977, October). *Development and validation of a measure of effective orientation to erotic stimuli: The Sexual Opinion Survey*. Paper presented at the meeting of the Midwestern Psychological Association, Chicago.

Widiger, T. A., Mullins-Sweatt, S., & Anderson, K. G. (2006). Personality and depression in women. In C.L.M. Keyes & S. H. Goodman (Eds.), *Women and depression* (pp.176–198). New York: Cambridge University Press.

Wiegel, M., Wincze, J. P., & Barlow, D. H. (2002). Sexual dysfunction. In M. M. Antony & D. H. Barlow (Eds.), *Handbook of assessment and treatment planning for psychological disorders* (pp. 481–522). New York: Guilford Press.

Wilhelm, K. (2006). Depression: From nosology to global burden. In C.L.M. Keyes & S. H. Goodman (Eds.), *Women and depression* (pp. 3–21). New York: Cambridge University Press.

Williams, J. W., Barrett, J., & Oxman, T. (2000). Treatment of dysthymia and minor depression in primary care: A randomized controlled trial in older adults. *Journal of the American Medical Association, 284*, 1519–1526.

Williams, S. H. (2005). Medications for treating alcohol dependence. *American Family Physician, 72*, 1775–1780.

Wilson, G. T. (2005). Psychological treatment of eating disorders. *Annual Review of Clinical Psychology, 1*, 439–465.

Wilson, G. T., & Fairburn, C. G. (2002). Treatments for eating disorders. In P. E. Nathan & J. M. Gorman (Eds.), *A guide to treatments that work* (2nd ed., pp. 559–592). New York: Oxford University Press.

Wilson, S. L. (2001). Attachment disorders: Review and current status. *Journal of Psychology, 135*, 37–51.

Winblad, B., Brodaty, H., Gauthier, S., Morris, J. C., Orgogozo, J. M., Rockwood, K., Schneider, L., Takeda, M., Tariot, P., & Wilkinson, D. (2001). Pharmacotherapy of Alzheimer's disease: Is there a need to redefine treatment success? *International Journal of Geriatric Psychiatry. 16*, 653–666.

Wincze, J. P., & Carey, M. P. (2001). *Sexual dysfunction: A guide for assessment and treatment*. New York: Guilford Press.

Wintersteen, M. B., Mensinger, J. L., & Diamond, G. S. (2005). Do gender and racial differences between patient and therapist affect therapeutic alliance and treatment retention in adolescents? *Professional Psychology: Research and Practice, 36*, 400–408.

Winzelberg, A. J., Eppstein, D., Eldredge, K. L., Wilfley, D., Dasmahapatra, R., Dev, P., & Taylor, C. B. (2000). Effectiveness of an Internet-based program for reducing risk factors for eating disorders. *Journal of Consulting and Clinical Psychology, 68*, 346–350.

Winzelberg, A. J., Taylor, C. B., Sharpe, T., Eldredge, K. L., Dev, P., & Constantinou, P. S. (1998). Evaluation of a computer-mediated eating disorder intervention program. *International Journal of Eating Disorders, 24*, 339–349.

Wirshing, D. A., & Buckley, P. (2003, May). Schizophrenia treatment challenges. *Psychiatric Times* [Online], *20*. Available: www.psychiatrictimes.com/p030540.html.

Witkiewitz, K., & Marlatt, G. A. (2004). Relapse prevention for alcohol and drug problems: That was Zen, this is Tao. *American Psychologist, 59*, 224–235.

Wolpe, J. (1958). *Psychotherapy by reciprocal inhibition*. Palo Alto, CA: Stanford University Press.

Wong, E. C., Kim, B. S., Zane, N.W.S., Kim, I. J., & Huang, J. S. (2003). Examining culturally based variables associated with ethnicity: Influences on credibility perceptions of empirically supported interventions. *Cultural Diversity and Ethnic Minority Psychology, 9*, 88–96.

Woodcock, R. W., & Johnson, M. B. (2001). *Woodcock-Johnson-III Tests of Achievement*. New York: Riverside.

Woodside, D. B. (2004). Assessing and treating men with eating disorders. *Psychiatric Times, 11*, 989–990.

Woodside, D. B., Garfinkel, P. E., Lin, E., Goering, P., Kaplan, A. S., Goldbloom, D. S., & Kennedy, S. H. (2001). Comparisons of men with full or partial eating disorders, men without eating disorders, and women with eating disorders in the community. *American Journal of Psychiatry, 158*, 570–574.

World Health Organization. (2005). *ICD-10 classification of mental and behavioural disorders*. Geneva: World Health Organization.

Wu, L. T., Pilowsky, D. J., & Schlenger, W. E. (2004). Inhalant abuse and dependence among adolescents in the United States. *Journal of American Academy of Child and Adolescent Psychiatry, 43*, 1206–1214.

Yager, J. (2001). E-mail as a therapeutic adjunct in the outpatient treatment of anorexia nervosa: Illustrative case material and discussion of the issues. *International Journal of Eating Disorders, 29*, 125–138.

Yalom, I. D. (1995). *The theory and practice of group psychotherapy* (4th ed.). New York: Basic Books.

Yanovski, S. Z. (1993). Binge eating disorder: Current knowledge and future directions. *Obesity Research, 1*, 306–324.

Yatham, L. N., & Kusumakar, V. (2002). Anticonvulsants in treatment of bipolar disorder: A review of efficacy. In L. N. Yatham, V. Kusumakar, & S. P. Kutcher (Eds.), *Bipolar disorder: A clinician's guide to biological treatments* (pp. 201–240). Philadelphia: Brunner-Routledge.

Yatham, L. N., Kusumakar, V., & Kutcher, S. P. (2002). Treatment of bipolar depression. In L. N. Yatham, V. Kusumakar, & S. P. Kutcher (Eds.), *Bipolar disorder: A clinician's guide to biological treatments* (pp.17–32). Philadelphia: Brunner-Routledge.

Yehuda, R., Marshall, R., Penkower, A., & Wong, C. M. (2002). Pharmacological treatments for posttraumatic stress disorder. In P. E. Nathan & J. M. Gorman (Eds.), *A guide to treatments that work* (2nd ed., pp. 411–446). New York: Oxford University Press.

Yen, S., Shea, M. T., Battle, C., Johnson, D. M., Zlotnick, C., Dolan-Sewell, R., Skodol, A. E., Grilo, C. M., Gunderson, J. G., Sanislow, C. A., Zanarini, M. C., Bender, D. S., Rettew, J. B., & McGlashan, T. H. (2002). Traumatic exposure and posttraumatic stress disorder in borderline, schizotypal, avoidant, and obsessive-compulsive personality disorders: Findings from the Collaborative Longitudinal Personality Disorders Study. *Journal of Nervous and Mental Disease, 190*, 510–518.

Young, J. E. (1999). *Cognitive therapy for personality disorders: A schema-focused approach* (Rev. ed.). Sarasota, FL: Professional Resource Press.

Young, J. E., Klosko, J. S., & Weishaar, M. (2003). *Schema therapy: A practitioner's guide.* New York: Guilford Press.

Young, J. E., Wienberger, A. D., & Beck, A. T. (2001). Cognitive therapy for depression. In D. H. Barlow (Ed.), *Clinical handbook of psychological disorders* (3rd ed., pp. 264–308). New York: Guilford Press.

Youngstrom, E., Meyers, O., Demeter, C., Youngstrom, J., Morello, L., Piiparinen, R., Feeny, N., Calabrese, J. R., & Findling, R. L. (2005). Comparing diagnostic checklists for pediatric bipolar disorder in academic and community mental health settings. *Bipolar Disorders, 7*, 507–517.

Zanarini, M. C., Frankenburg, F. R., Hennen, J., Reich, B., & Silk, K. R. (2004). Axis I comorbidity in patients with borderline personality disorder: 6-year follow-up and prediction of time to remission. *American Journal of Psychiatry, 161*, 2108–2114.

Zarate, C. A., & Tohen, M. F. (2002). Bipolar disorder and comorbid Axis I disorders: Diagnosis and management. In L. N. Yatham, V. Kusumakar, & S. P. Kutcher (Eds.), *Bipolar disorder: A clinician's guide to biological treatments* (pp. 115–138). Philadelphia: Brunner-Routledge.

Zarate, C. A., Tohen, M. F., Banov, M. D., & Weiss, M. K. (1995). Is clozapine a mood stabilizer? *Journal of Clinical Psychiatry, 56*, 108–112.

Zeanah, C. H., & Boris, N. W. (2000). Disturbances and disorders of attachment in early childhood. In C. H. Zeanah (Ed.), *Handbook of infant mental health* (2nd ed., pp. 353–368). New York: Guilford Press.

Zeanah, C. H., & Emde, R. N. (1994). Attachment disorders in infancy and childhood. In M. Rutter, E. Taylor, & L. Hersov (Eds.), *Child and adolescent psychiatry: Modern approaches* (pp. 490–504). Cambridge, MA: Blackwell.

Zeanah, C. H., Scheeringa, M. S., Boris, N. W., Heller, S. S., Smyke, A. T., & Trapani, J. (2004). Reactive attachment disorder in maltreated toddlers. *Child Abuse and Neglect, 28*, 877–888.

Zickler, P. (2003). Teen drug use declined in 2002, report shows. *NIDA Notes, 1*(5), 4.

Zucker, K. J., & Bradley, S. J. (2004). Gender identity and psychosexual disorders. In J. M. Wiener & M. K. Dulcan (Eds.), *The American Psychiatric Publishing textbook of child and adolescent psychiatry* (3rd ed., pp. 813–835). Washington, DC: American Psychiatric Association.

ABOUT THE AUTHORS

Linda Seligman received her A.B. degree in English and American literature from Brandeis University, her M.A. degree in guidance and counseling from Teachers College of Columbia University, and her Ph.D. degree in counseling psychology from Columbia University. She is an author, researcher, educator, and practicing psychologist and counselor. All those roles are reflected in the research, discussion, and examples presented in this book.

In her academic role, Seligman currently is a faculty member in psychology at Walden University, where she teaches online courses. In addition, she teaches at Johns Hopkins University. She is also a professor emeritus at George Mason University, Fairfax, Virginia, where she was director of the doctoral program in education and in charge of the Community Agency Counseling Program.

Seligman is licensed as a psychologist in Virginia and Maryland and as a professional counselor in Virginia, and is certified in eye movement desensitization and reprocessing. She is director of the Center for Counseling and Consultation, a private practice in Bethesda, Maryland. Her practice includes people with a broad range of concerns and mental disorders, notably adjustment, mood, and anxiety disorders. Seligman has a particular interest in treating people with chronic and life-threatening illnesses. She also offers training and supervision to people seeking licensure as counselors or psychologists, as well as to practicing clinicians.

Her primary research interests include the diagnosis and treatment of mental disorders, theories of counseling and psychotherapy, and how people cope with chronic and life-threatening illnesses. Seligman has written thirteen books, including *Assessment in Developmental Career Counseling* (1980), *Diagnosis and Treatment Planning in Counseling* (1986, 1996, 2004), *Developmental Career Counseling and Assessment* (1994), *Promoting a Fighting Spirit: Psychotherapy for Cancer Patients, Survivors, and Their Families* (1996), *Systems, Strategies, and Skills in Counseling and Psychotherapy* (2001, 2006), *Technical and Conceptual Skills for Mental Health Professionals* (2004, in press), and the two previous editions of this book (1986, 1998). She has also published more than eighty book chapters and professional articles.

Seligman is a past president of the Virginia Mental Health Counselors Association and was editor of the *Journal of Mental Health Counseling*. She has also served on the editorial boards of the *Journal of Counseling and Development* and the *Virginia Counselors Journal*. She was selected as a Distinguished Professor by George Mason University and, in 1990, was named Researcher of the Year by the American Mental Health Counselors Association. She has consulted to many governmental and human service agencies and has given over one hundred lectures and workshops on diagnosis and treatment planning.

Lourie W. Reichenberg is a licensed professional counselor in private practice in Fairfax, Virginia, and an adjunct faculty member in the School of Education and Human Services at Marymount University. She received her B.A. degree in psychology from Michigan State University and her M.A. degree in counseling psychology from Marymount University.

In addition to individual and couples counseling, she also provides workshops and educational programs on assessing suicide risk, setting personal boundaries, couples communication skills, and adjusting to midlife. Her specific interest areas include adjustment and life transitions, crisis management, and suicide prevention.

Reichenberg is currently on the CrisisLink LOSS team, providing counseling assistance in the community after a suicide has occurred. She also leads a support group for survivors of suicide and is a member of the CrisisLink Advisory Council. She served on the organization's board of directors from 2003 to 2006. She is past editor of the Northern Virginia Licensed Professional Counselors newsletter, served on the editorial board of the *Journal of Counseling and Development*, and was the editor of the *Journal of the College and University Personnel Association* from 1988 to 1993. She has edited more than thirty books and monographs on human resource management. She has also published many professional articles.

NAME INDEX

A
Aasland, O. G., 314
Abikoff, H. B., 91
Accordino, M. P., 39
Achenback, T., 55, 56, 83, 98, 133, 146
Adams, C., 80
Ades, J., 365
Agosti, V., 182
Agras, W. S., 110, 338, 340, 341
Agresta, J., 527
Ahn, H., 11–12, 25
Ainsworth, M. D. S., 54, 131
Akbar, M., 19
Akechi, T., 162
Albano, A. M., 123, 149
Alexander, J. F., 34, 35
Alimohamed, S., 11
Allen, A., 355–359
Allen, J., 77, 201
Altemus, M., 185
Althof, S., 347, 348, 350–353
Altman, E., 214–215
Aman, M. G., 67
Ambrumova, A., 162
Anastopoulos, A. D., 40, 82, 88, 89
Anderson, E. M., 41–43
Anderson, K. G., 198, 338
Andrews, A. A., 42
Andrews, D. W., 102
Angst, J., 215
Antony, M. M., 237, 247–249, 251, 257–260, 268
Appelbaum, P. S., 495
Araoz, D. L., 179
Arizmendi, T. G., 20
Armstrong, S., 67
Arnkoff, D. B., 340
Arnold, E. M., 304
Arnow, B. A., 340
Arntz, M., 244
Arsanow, R. F., 143
Asarnow, J. R., 143
Aschenbrand, S. G., 123, 124
Audenaert, K., 161
Austin, J. F., 495
Avery, D. H., 192
AWARE process, 282
Azar, S. T., 169
Azrin, N. H., 121

B
Babor, T. F., 314
Bagenholm, A., 75, 76
Bagheri, M. M., 113–116
Baier, A. R., 322
Baird, G., 72, 73, 75, 77, 78, 81

Baker, B. R., 364
Baker, S. L., 44, 242–244, 254
Baldessarini, R. J., 211
Banov, M. D., 514
Barbareee, H. E., 280
Barber, J. P., 33, 421, 451, 452, 458, 463, 469, 470
Barkley, R. A., 6, 82, 83, 85, 86, 88, 89, 92, 154, 541
Barley, D. E., 20, 32
Barlow, D. H., 12, 27, 44, 123, 234, 239, 242–249, 251–261, 263–267, 270, 272, 274–280, 289, 346, 538, 541
Baron-Cohen, S., 77
Barrett, P. B., 146
Barrett, P. M., 125
Barry, T. D., 97
Basco, M. R., 224
Baumeister, A. A., 62
Bauml, J., 500
Bazile, A., 19
Beck, A. T., 27, 185, 188, 189, 193, 207, 237, 254, 280–282, 419, 420, 423, 426, 429, 431–434, 436, 438, 441, 444, 448, 452, 454, 458, 460, 462, 463, 465, 468, 469, 472–474, 476–479, 485, 496, 541
Beck, J., 189, 193, 232
Beck, M., 33
Becker, K. D., 96
Beckman, D. A., 364
Bellack, A., 145, 527
Benazon, N. R., 187
Benkelfat, C., 448
Benoit, D., 108
Benton, R. D., 161, 162, 167
Berardelli, A., 112
Bergin, A. E., 24, 25
Berglund, P., 5, 55, 204, 261, 267, 279, 280
Bergman, R. L., 128
Berman, J. S., 20
Bernstein, D. P., 293
Bernstein, E. B., 516
Beutler, L. E., 11, 20, 36, 536
Bezman, R. J., 87
Biederman, J., 84, 86
Bienvenu, O. J., 368
Bilder, R. M., 512
Birch, L. L., 338
Birchwood, M. J., 527
Bishop, F. M., 303, 314
Black, B., 15, 128, 130
Blackburn, I. M., 199
Blanchard, E. B., 273
Blasey, C., 340
Blehar, M. S., 54
Bloch, C., 39
Bloom, B., 41, 42, 165
Bodkin, A., 464
Boelter, E. W., 137
Bogart, K., 268
Bohart, A., 4, 17–18
Boisvert, C., 38–40
Bolles, R. N., 166
Bond, M. R., 391–394, 396, 398, 400
Bordin, E. S., 33
Boris, N. W., 54, 132
Borkovec, T. D., 280, 283
Borowitz, S., 117
Boss, P., 174, 179
Botteron, K. N., 142
Bourne, E. J., 289
Bowden, C. L., 211
Bowlby, J., 54, 94, 131
Bowman, D., 13, 18, 20
Boyer-Quick, J., 43
Bozarth, J. D., 29
Bradford, D., 498, 501
Bradley, S. J., 360
Bridges, W., 179
Bright, P., 254
Brimaher, B., 142
Brinkmeyer, M. Y., 94
Broadhurst, D. D., 168
Brook, J. S., 334
Brookman, L. I., 73
Brooks-Gun, J., 62
Brown, G. K., 188, 496
Brown, G. S., 4, 18
Brown, K. E., 340
Brown, T. A., 237, 278–279, 280, 283, 538
Brownell, K. D., 386
Buchanan, R. G., 314
Buchsbaum, D. G., 314
Buckley, P., 498
Buckley, T. C., 273
Budman, S. H., 26
Buican, B., 67
Bulhmann, U., 115
Bulik, C. M., 335, 337
Burd, L., 113
Burke, J. D., 92
Burns, G. L., 84
Burton, E., 333
Butcher, J. N., 19, 24, 28, 63, 130, 160, 163, 169, 183, 196, 197, 201, 202, 204, 248, 263, 279, 363, 367, 409, 410, 412, 509, 515–517
Buysse, D. J., 374
Byrne, D., 348

C
Cain, D. J., 29, 541
Calhuon, S. L., 75, 76
Cameron, P., 42
Campbell, J., 80
Campbell, L. A., 278–279, 279
Cantwell, D. P., 85
Cappelleri, J. C., 348
Capps, F., 326
Caputo, G., 254
Cardena, E., 488, 489
Carey, M. P., 348, 350
Carlson, C. L., 97
Carrere, S., 29
Carrese, M. A., 179
Carrier, J. W., 183
Carroll, E. M., 277
Carroll, K. M., 294
Carroll, R. A., 359, 361, 362
Carter, J. G., 368
Casali, S. L., 19
Castellanos, F. X., 91
Cattani-Thompson, K., 3, 13, 20
Centor, R. M., 314
Chamberlain, L. L., 301, 313
Chambless, D. L., 39, 249, 254
Chang, S., 114
Chevron, E. S., 190
Chhabra, V., 68, 69
Chiu, W. T., 212, 263
Chorpita, B. F., 123
Christenson, G. A., 368
Chu, M., 84
Clarke, G., 139
Clarke, J. C., 263
Clarkin, J. F., 38
Clayton, R., 312
Coan, J., 29
Coccaro, E. F., 293, 364, 370
Cohen, D. J., 111, 113, 114
Cohen, E. M., 239
Cohen, P., 110, 334
Cohn, D. A., 134
Coie, J., 96
Coleman, H.K.L., 19
Coleman, M. C., 84, 124, 125
Colliver, J. D., 323
Colvin, L., 73, 74
Compton, W. M., 323
Conners, C. K, 56, 83, 98
Connolly, M. B., 33
Connors, G. J., 29
Consoli, A. J., 12, 36
Constantino, M. J., 340
Coon, D. W., 417
Coonrod, E. E., 77
Coons, E. E., 322
Cooper, Z., 339
Copello, A., 527
Corcoran, K., 43
Coryell, W. H., 212, 222
Costa, F. M., 300
Costin, C., 333, 334, 336–338, 340, 343, 386
Cottone, J., 19
Cottraux, J., 199
Cowan, C. P., 134
Cowan, P. A., 134
Cowley, D. S., 235, 241, 242, 245, 246, 279, 284
Cox, D. J., 117
Coyne, J. C., 185, 187
Craft, L., 53
Crago, M., 20
Craighead, L. W., 26, 335–336, 339, 341
Craighead, W. E., 26, 27, 189–191, 194, 199, 202, 206, 207, 213, 215, 216, 218
Cramer, V., 455
Craske, M. G., 244, 246
Crits Christophe, P., 11, 33, 421, 451, 452, 458, 463, 469, 470
Crosson-Tower, C., 179
Crouch, E., 39
Cucherat, M., 199
Cuddy-Casey, M., 117
Cueva, J. E., 80
Cuijpers, P., 536
Cunningham, C. E., 130
Curr, A., 112
Curtain, L., 324
Cutler, H. C., 179
Czobor, P., 495

D
Dadds, M. R., 146
Dahlen, E. R., 370
Dalai Lama, 179
Daly, K., 77
Danehy, M., 364, 370
Danielyan, A. K., 143
Davidson, J., 278
Davidson, J. R., 182
Davidson, L., 506
Davies, E. W., 514
Davies, M., 110
Davies, S. C., 106, 107
Davila, R., 318
Davis, D. D., 419, 485, 541
Davis, M. K., 31

Davis, N., 536
Davison, K. K., 338
Dawson, D. A., 318
de Beurs, E., 254
de Shazer, S., 165
de Zwaan, M., 110
Deacon, B. J., 146
Deckersback, T., 115, 116
Deemer, H. N., 404
Deffenbacker, J. L., 164, 370
Deitsch, S. E., 253
DeLaFuente, J. R., 314
Delgado, P. L., 218
della Cava, M. R., 380
DeLong, R., 74
Dermen, K. H., 29, 304
Derogatis, L. R., 348
DeVellis, R. F., 77
Devries, R., 28
Di Nardo, P. A., 237
Diamond, G. S., 18
Dickerson, F. B., 500
Dickey, C. C., 438–440, 442
DiClemente, C. C., 303
Diefenbach, G. J., 368
Dimatou, S., 515
Dishion, T. J., 59, 102
Dobson, K. S., 198, 200
Doggett, R. A., 132, 133, 135
Donahoe, C. P., Jr., 277
Donehower, C., 80
Donovan, J. E., 300
Dorta, K. P., 26, 190
Dotson, D., 34
Dougherty, D. D., 26
Dozois, D.J.A., 197, 200
Drake, R. E., 300, 332, 496, 500
Drucker, P., 19
DuBois, D., 190
Duffy, A. L., 146
Duncan, B. L., 32
Duncan, G. J., 62
Dunn, M. G., 320–321
Durlak, J. A., 102
Duval, S., 141

E
Eccles, J. S., 97
Eells, T. D., 20
Egan, M. K., 360
Eggen, D., 92
Ehlers, S., 78
Eifert, G. H., 30–32, 241, 245, 253, 254, 277, 283, 289, 372
Eikeseth, S., 79
Eisendrath, S. J., 407
Eldevik,S., 79
Ellason, J. W., 515, 516, 518, 521, 522
Elliott, E. J., 366
Elliott, R., 12, 17–18, 29
Ellis, A., 28
Emde, R. N., 135, 319
Emery, G., 237, 281, 282
Emery, R. E., 53, 319
Engel, R. R., 500
Ennis, K., 183
Erk, R. R., 60, 82, 89, 92, 93, 97
Escobar, J. I., 392
Escudero, V., 33
Espie, C. A., 378
Evans, A. C., 506
Evans, D. L., 40, 44, 125, 127, 139, 144–150, 235, 239, 240, 243–246, 249, 252, 265, 271, 278, 284, 299, 301, 312, 313, 321, 323, 324, 326, 327, 329, 492–502, 537
Evans, K., 232
Everly, G., 275
Eyberg, S. M., 94, 100, 133

F
Fabbrini, G., 112
Fairburn, C. G., 27, 40, 108, 339, 341–345, 386
Fallon, B. A., 397, 399
Fama, R., 310
Faraone, S. V., 84
Farley, S. E., 40, 82, 88, 89
Fawcett, J., 224
Feder, B. J., 221
Feinstein, S., 397, 399
Feldman, M. A., 65
Feldman, M. D., 404–407
Fenster, A., 39
Fewell, C. H., 318, 319
Field, L. F., 60, 138–140
Filetti, L. B., 370
Findling, R. L., 142
Finney, J. W., 299, 303, 315–317
First, M. B., 188, 237
Fischer, S., 338
Fisher, J. O., 338, 348
Fletcher, J. M., 68, 69
Fletcher, K. E., 149
Flory, K., 312
Floyd, M., 13, 18, 536
Floyd, R. L., 64
Foa, E. B., 264, 267–269, 278
Foley, C., 80

Fonagy, P., 11, 26, 29, 43, 221, 246, 278, 501, 536
Forchetti, C. M., 412, 417
Ford, D. E., 379
Ford, R. E., 87, 89–91
Fornerls, C. A., 273
Forsyth, J. P., 30, 31, 241, 245, 253, 254, 277, 283, 289, 372
Foxx, R. M., 80, 121
Foy, D. W., 277
Frances, A. J., 38
Frank, E., 25, 189–190, 220, 232
Frank, J. B., 25
Frank, J. D., 25
Frankenburg, F. R., 427
Franklin, G. A., 368, 371–373
Franklin, M. E., 164, 267–270
Freeman, A., 419, 485, 541
Freud, S., 393
Friedlander, M. L., 33
Friedman, E. G., 329
Fristad, M. A., 139, 142
Frost, R., 267
Fuchs, L. S., 68, 69
Fuhrman, T., 102
Fullerton, C. S., 273

G
Galea, S., 273
Gallagher, D., 11
Gallagher, J. J., 64
Gallagher, R., 254
Garb, H. N., 19, 20
Garfield, S. L., 15
Garrett, J., 304
Garske, J. P., 31
Gatz, M., 206
Gayton, W. F., 365
Geary, D. C., 69
Geher, G., 132, 133
Gelenberg, A. J., 218
Geller, B., 141, 142
Geller, J., 340
Gendlin, E. T., 28
Gendrano, N., 348
Genel, M., 87
George, C., 133
George, T. P., 326
Gherardi, P. C., 123, 124, 130–131
Ghisalbert, D., 515
Gibbon, M., 188, 237
Gilchrest, R. H., 62, 64–66, 140
Gillberg, C., 74, 75, 77, 78, 81, 111–112
Gillberg, I. C., 74
Gillies, L. A., 206
Gillio, F., 112
Gil-Rivas, V., 273
Gingerich, S., 527
Gintner, G. G., 57–60
Girgus, J. S., 187, 188, 198
Gladys, L., 33
Glantz, M. D., 323
Glass, C. R., 340
Glass, G. V., 3
Glasser, W., 103
Glick, D. M., 16
Gloaguen, V., 199
Glueckauf, R. L., 536–537
Goin, M. K., 449
Gold, J., 24
Gold, R., 302
Golden, B., 224
Golden, R. N., 192
Goldfried, M. R., 26
Goldman, L. S., 87
Goldstein, A. J., 254, 255
Goldstein, M. J., 40, 143, 220, 224, 225
Goldwyn, R., 133
Goleman, D., 30
Goodman, S. H., 185–186
Goodrich, S., 340
Goodwin, F. K., 224
Gorman, J. M., 5, 11, 26
Gottheil, E., 19
Gottman, J. M., 29, 174
Goumeniouk, A. D., 223
Gracely, S., 254
Graham, H. L., 527
Granger, D. A., 101
Grant, B. F., 323, 434
Grant, J. E., 365, 371
Grant, M., 314
Graves, R. E., 505
Grawe, K., 17, 20
Grebb, J., 325
Green, G., 80, 362
Green, J., 133
Greenberg, L. S., 17–18, 20, 26, 28, 29, 39, 40, 165, 372, 426, 428
Greenberg, M. T., 96
Greenhill, L. L., 87, 89–91
Greenspan, M., 20
Greiger, R., 28
Grieger, T. A., 28, 273
Grilo, C. M., 334, 338, 339, 341, 344
Grossman, L. S., 514
Grossman, S., 419, 420, 485, 541
Grube, S., 117

Grunebaum, M. F., 495, 508
Grunze, H., 219
Guerney, B. G., Jr., 39, 40
Gunderson, J. G., 449, 464
Guralnik, O., 518
Gustafson, D. H., 537

H
Haas, A. P., 537
Haertzen, C. A., 302
Hagopian, L. P., 137
Haley, M., 140, 183
Haley, W. E., 417
Hall, P., 314
Hall, S.E.K., 132, 133
Hall, W., 302
Hallin, A., 80
Hallowell, E. M., 85
Hamilton, J. C., 404
Hammer, L., 338
Han, S. S., 101
Handen, B. L., 62, 64–66, 140
Hanna, F., 99, 101, 103
Hansen, N. B., 41
Hanson, R. E., 132, 134
Harbin, G. L., 64
Hardenburg, S. A., 354–356, 359
Hardesty, V. A., 365
Harkavy-Friedman, J. M., 498
Harrington, H., 92
Harris, R., 320
Harrow, M., 514
Hart, A. B., 26, 27, 134, 190, 191, 199, 202, 206, 207
Hart, E. L., 98
Harvey, B., 369
Harvey, P. D., 293
Hastings, F., 258, 340
Hawley, K. M., 58, 61
Hayes, S. C., 283
Heather, N., 302
Heim, C., 198
Heimberg, R. G., 264
Heinlen, K. T., 535
Henderson, D. A., 58
Hendin, H., 537
Henggeler, S. W., 99, 100, 102
Hennen, J., 356, 427
Henningfield, J. E., 302
Herbener, E. S., 514
Herbert, J. D., 264
Herbert, J. L., 293
Heron, M., 183
Herpertz, S. C., 448
Herrera, V. M., 96
Herrman, D., 304
Hess, R. S., 19
Higgins, E. T., 192
Hinkle, J. S., 148
Hinshaw, S. P., 91, 92, 94
Hoffman, J., 446
Hofmann, S. G., 261, 263–265
Hoge, C. W., 271
Holder-Perkins, W., 390–393, 396, 397, 403
Holi, M. M., 365
Hollander, E., 293, 294, 355–359, 364, 366, 369, 386
Hollins, S., 58
Hollon, S. D., 27, 191
Hommer, D., 13
Hoogduin, C., 33
Hooley, J. M., 19, 63, 160, 196, 248, 509
Horvath, A. O., 16–17, 32, 33
Houts, A. C., 120, 121
Hovaniz, C. A., 74
Howard, K. I., 42
Howell, J. C., 92
Hoyert, D. L., 183
Huang, J. S., 19
Hubble, M. A., 32
Hudson, J. L., 123, 125
Huff, T. G., 366
Hunt, J. I., 141, 142
Hunt, W. P., 99, 101, 103
Hurley, A. D., 66, 448

I
Iketani, T., 337–338
Ilardi, S. S., 26
Ismond, D. R., 108, 109, 119, 120, 136
Ito, K., 66
Ivanoff, A. M., 28
Ivey, A. E., 19
Iwata, B. A., 65

J
Jablensky, A., 492
Jackson, P. B., 197
Jacobi, C., 110, 334, 338
Jacobs, D. F., 367
Jahr, E., 79
James, D., 302
Jamison, C., 536
Jankovic, J., 111–114
Jasin, E., 254
Javier, R. A., 19
Jefferson, J. W., 209, 222
Jerome, L. W., 537

Jessor, R., 300
Jew, C. L., 301, 313
Jin, C, 515
Jindal, R. D., 43
Johns, L. C., 506
Johnson, C. R., 64
Johnson, J. A., 349
Johnson, J. G., 334, 338
Johnson, J. H., 21, 22, 57, 59
Johnson, J. K., 349
Johnson, M. B., 67, 68
Johnson, P. A., 448, 449
Johnson, S., 39, 40
Johnson, S. L., 29, 213, 225
Johnson, S. M., 40, 480
Johnson, S. P., 58
Johnson, V. E., 304, 350, 351, 353
Johnson, W. B., 28
Johnstone, B., 536–537
Joiner, T. E., 185, 204, 205
Jones, S., 217
Jones-Alexander, J., 273
Jordan, K., 34
Junglinger, J., 495

K

Kabot, S., 73–78, 80, 81
Kadera, S. W., 41
Kadesjo, B., 111–112
Kafka, M. P., 354, 355
Kahn, J., 364
Kahng, S., 65, 66
Kaiser, E., 313
Kalman, D., 333
Kamerow, D. B., 379
Kamphaus, R. W., 56, 69, 83, 98, 133
Kantor, M., 432, 497, 509, 510
Kaplan, H. S., 325, 350, 352
Kaplan, N., 133
Karel, M. J., 206
Kasen, S., 334
Kaslow, N. J., 190
Kawarada, Y., 337–338
Kaye, W. H., 335
Kazdin, A. E., 59, 82, 91, 93, 94, 96–98, 100–105, 119, 145, 154, 541
Keane, T. M., 249, 272, 274–277
Keck, P. E., 213, 364
Keijsers, G., 33
Kendall, P. C., 44, 123, 125–127, 149
Kendjelic, E. M., 20
Kennard, D., 329
Kerbeshian, J., 113
Kernberg, O., 460, 462, 463, 465, 485
Kessler, R. C., 5, 16, 55, 83, 185, 197, 204, 212, 214, 261, 263, 267, 279, 280
Keyes, C.L.M., 232
Kho, K. H., 201
Kihlstrom, J. F., 517
Kilpatrick, D. G., 148, 149, 273
Kim, B. S., 19
Kim, I. J., 19
Kim, S. W., 365
King, M. P., 318
King, S., 500
Kingma, R., 348
Kirike, N., 337–338
Kissling, W., 500
Klebanov, P. K., 62
Klein, R. G., 91
Klerman, G. L., 26, 190, 191
Klorman, R., 258
Klosko, J. S., 446, 485
Kluger, J., 193
Knight, E. L., 312, 494
Knobler, H. Y., 162
Knutelska, M., 518
Koegel, L. K., 73–76, 79
Koegel, R. L., 73, 76
Kohut, H., 463, 465
Kola, L., 449
Kopelowicz, A., 144–146, 502
Kopta, S. M., 42
Korszun, A., 185
Kosten, T. R., 317
Kotler, J. S., 92
Kotler, L. A., 110, 334
Kotwal, R., 336, 337, 339
Kovatchev, B., 117
Kraemer, H. C., 110
Krause, M. S., 42
Kringlen, E., 455, 497
Kristensen, H., 128
Kronenberger, W. C., 107, 109, 110, 114, 128, 130, 149
Kropp, P. R., 170
Kroutil, L. A., 321, 322
Krupnick, J. L., 32, 188
Kübler-Ross, E., 174
Kuehn, B. M., 326
Kuhn, B. R., 116
Kulish, N. M., 20
Kung, H. C., 183
Kupfer, D. J., 374
Kupsaw-Lawrence, E., 293
Kushner, H. S., 179
Kusumakar, V., 211, 219, 221
Kutcher, S. P., 221

L
Laborsky, L., 16–17, 32
Ladd, G. T., 366, 367, 373
Lahey, B. B., 92
Lam, R. W., 223
Lambert, M. J., 3, 13, 19, 20, 24, 25, 32, 34, 41–43
Lampman, C., 102
Landau-Stanton, J., 304
Landreth, G. L., 154
Lang, P. J., 258
Lange, S. J., 537
Langer, S. J., 360
Laudet, A. B., 312, 494, 495, 500
Lavigne, J. V., 92
Lawless, M., 506
Lawton, M. J., 314
Leahy, R. L., 212, 220
LeBon, O., 192
Leckman, J. F., 112–114
Ledgerwood, D. M., 366–367
Lee, K., 62
Lee, S. S., 94
Lee, T., 99, 102
Lees, J., 329
Leibing, E., 426
Leiblum, S. R., 350, 386
Leichsenring, F., 426
Lejoyeux, M., 365, 366
Lengua, L. J., 96
Lerner, V., 162
Leucht, S., 500
Leukefeld, C., 312
Levant, R. F., 11, 12, 538
Levitt, P., 493
Lewin, A. B., 65, 66
Lewis, D. A., 493
Liberman, R. P., 144, 502
Lieber, C. S., 313
Lieberman, A. F., 134
Lieberman, A. R., 448, 452, 463
Lieberman, J., 498
Lietaer, G., 29
Lilenfeld, L. R., 338
Lindberg, N., 365
Linehan, M., 28, 30, 38, 370, 426, 428, 451, 485
Ling, W., 117
Links, P. S., 449
Linscheid, T. R., 109
Lipman, A. J., 44
Littrell, J. M., 42
Litz, B. T., 271–273
Livesley, W. J., 420, 422–424, 428, 474
Livingston, R., 13
Lochmnan, J. E., 97, 103
Loeber, R., 92, 93, 95, 96
Lombart, K. G., 20
Long, P. J., 277
Lord, C., 77
Lovaas, O. I., 78, 79, 81
Love, A., 302
Luborsky, L., 42
Luby, J., 141
Lucas, C. P., 20
Luce, K. H., 343
Luthringer, R., 192
Lynam, D. R., 312
Lynch, J., 161, 162, 167
Lynch, R. S., 370
Lyon, C., 121, 122
Lyon, G. R., 68, 69, 71
Lyons-Ruth, K., 108, 132

M
Ma, S. H., 191, 386
Mackenzie, T. B., 368
Mackinaw-Koons, B., 139, 142
MacMaster, F. P., 211
Maffei, C., 424
Magura, S., 312, 494
Mahgerefteh, S., 498, 499, 501
Mahowald, M. W., 375–377, 380, 381
Main, M., 133
Maldonado, J. R., 393, 403, 515–518, 520, 521
Maletzky, B. M., 358, 359
Malia, J. A., 42
Malik, M., 11, 35, 36, 39
Manber, R., 201
Mandhan, P., 106
Manfredi, M., 112
Maniacci, M. P., 513
Mann, J. J., 537
Mansueto, C. S., 368
Maracek, J., 185, 193, 305
March, J. S., 129, 133, 146
Marchi, M., 110
Marci, C. D., 16
Marcus, B. A., 116
Marcus, S. C., 207
Margulies, S., 166
Marijuana, 305
Maris, R. W., 183
Mark, M. M., 167
Markowitz, J. C., 191
Markway, B., 261, 263, 264, 289
Markway, G., 263, 264, 289

Marlatt, G. A., 305, 306, 308, 309, 332
Marmar, C. R., 26
Marshall, R., 270
Marshall, W. E., 280
Martin, D. J., 31, 32, 34
Martin, J. I., 360
Martinussen, M., 338
Mash, E. J., 12, 62, 64, 67, 68, 96, 107, 108, 118, 122, 144, 148, 149, 154, 541
Masi, W., 73
Masters, W. H., 350, 351, 353
Masterson, J. F., 448, 452, 463
Mattick, R. P., 263
Matza, L. S., 182
Maurice, C., 80
Mayes, S. D., 75, 76
Mayfield, D., 314
McCabe, M. P., 348
McCabe, R. E., 237, 247, 249, 251, 257–259, 268, 270
McCauley, M. H., 162
McCloskey, L. A., 96
McConnaughy, E. A., 302
McConnaughy, R., 75
McCord, J., 59
McCrady, B. S., 309, 310, 314
McDonough, S., 134
McEachin, J. J., 79
McElroy, S. L., 213, 336, 337, 339, 364
McGlashan, T. H., 440
McGovern, M., 300
McGuire, L., 495
McHolm, A. E., 130
McIntosh, D. N., 273
McIntyre, J. R., 332
McKay, J., 317, 326–328
McKendree-Smith, N., 13, 18
McKenry, P. C., 174
McKracken, J. T., 128
McLellan, T., 302
McLoed, G., 314
McLoughlin, M., 365
McMahon, R. J., 92–94, 96–97, 99, 100, 104, 105
McMeniman, M., 512
McNeece, C. A., 304
McNicholas, F., 338
McQuade, D. V., 221
McTeague, L. M., 271
McWilliam, R. A., 64
Meagher, S., 419, 420, 485, 541
Meichenbaum, D. H., 164
Melamed, B. G., 258
Memon, S. A., 106
Mendelowitz, A., 512
Mensinger, J. L., 18
Menta, M., 66
Merrell, D., 536–537
Messer, S. C., 25
Messina, N., 446
Messman, T. L., 277
Metzger, R. L., 280
Meyer, B., 14, 16–17, 20, 28, 424–427
Meyer, R. G., 107, 109, 110, 114, 128, 130, 149, 253
Meyer, T. J., 167, 280, 313
Miklowitz, D. J., 40, 143, 189–190, 193–194, 211, 213–220, 222, 224, 225, 232, 513
Milich, R., 312
Miller, M. L., 280
Miller, M. W., 271
Miller, R. B., 86
Miller, R. S., 349
Miller, S. D., 32
Miller, T. J., 3
Miller, W. R., 17, 29, 294, 302–304, 320, 330, 386
Millon, C., 419, 420
Millon, T., 419–421, 425, 429, 430, 432–434, 436, 438, 442, 444–447, 451, 453, 455, 457, 458, 460, 461, 466, 469, 470, 472, 473, 476–479, 485
Milne, B., 92
Mineka, S., 19, 63, 160, 196, 248, 509
Mintz, L. B., 334
Mitchell, J. E., 275, 368
Mittelman, M. S., 417
Mjellem, N., 496
Moffitt, C., 91
Moffitt, T. E., 92
Mohr, D., 495
Momenan, R., 313
Monahan, J., 495
Moos, R. H., 299, 303, 311, 315–317
Moreau, D., 26, 190
Morin, C., 374
Morin, C. M., 375, 377, 378, 380, 386
Morris, M., 201
Morris, T. L., 129, 130, 146
Morrison, L., 327
Morton, T., 101
Motta, R. W., 276
Mueser, K. T., 43, 145, 221, 300, 492, 494–496, 500, 501, 527
Mufson, L., 26, 190
Mulholland, A. M., 334
Mullins-Sweatt, S., 198
Murphy, J. G., 300

Murphy, K. R., 154
Murphy, S. L., 183
Murray, W. H., 527
Myers, I. B., 162

N
Nagata, R., 337–338
Nakano, T., 66
Nathan, P. E., 5, 11, 26
Naylor, M. W., 142
Nelson, M. L., 32
Nemeroff, C. B., 198, 200
Nemes, S., 446
Neufeldt, S. A., 32
Newcorn, J., 86
Newport, D. J., 187
Newsom, C., 74
Nochajski, T. H., 304
Nolan, T., 495
Nolen-Hoeksema, S., 187, 188, 198
Noordsy, D. L., 221
Norcross, J. C., 13, 14, 26, 30, 57, 302, 531, 537
Norton, N. C., 20
Nowell, P. D., 374, 377, 379, 380
Noyes, R., 392, 396–398

O
Oakley, L. D., 209, 215
O'Brien, C. P., 317, 325, 327, 328
Ockert, D., 322
O'Connell, M. J., 506
Oetting, E. R., 370
Ogland-Hand, S., 206
Ogles, B. M., 34
Ohayon, M. M., 183, 184, 192–193, 378
Okuma, H., 66
Oldham, J. M., 449–451, 453, 454
O'Leary, T. A., 280, 538
Olfson, M., 207
Ollendick, T. H., 11, 39
Oltmanns, T. F., 53, 319, 363
O'Malley, S. S., 317, 334
O'Neal, J. H., 44, 479, 509
Orlinsky, D. E., 17, 20, 42
Orr, J. M., 86, 87
Orsillo, S. M., 237, 279
Osborne, M. I., 343
Ost, L., 260
Ostensen, E., 338
Oxman, T., 207

P
Pace, G. M., 108, 109
Pallanti, S., 366, 367, 371
Paniagua, F. A., 57, 124, 237, 310, 377
Pantalon, M., 276
Pape, P. A., 323
Pardini, D. A., 97
Paris, J., 423, 427, 428, 456
Park, N., 206
Parks, B. K., 17, 20
Parks-Levy, J., 495
Patterson, G. R., 66, 101
Patterson, M. D., 44, 242
Pavuluri, M. N., 142, 143
Pawl, J., 134
Paxon, J. E., 174
Pearson, J. L., 134
Pedersen, P. B., 19
Penkower, A., 270
Penninx, B.W.J.H., 183
Penza, K. M., 198
Perls, F., 28
Perry, D. G., 360
Perry, K. J., 264
Perry, S., 38
Petersen, S., 495
Peterson, C., 206
Peterson, D. R., 28
Peterson, L., 117, 119
Petry, N. M., 366, 367, 373
Pettit, J. W., 185, 204, 205
Pettorini, D., 28
Pfefferbaum, A., 310
Phillips, K. A., 392, 396, 401–403
Piacentini, J., 114, 128
Pierre, J. M., 498
Pilkonis, P. A., 28, 424–427
Pilowsky, D. J., 325
Pinderhughes, E., 96
Pine, D. S., 110
Pines, M., 38
Pinkus, D., 133
Pinsof, W. M., 39
Pitner, S. L., 116
Pitschel-Walz, G., 500
Pizzagalli, D., 505
Pliszka, S. R., 97
Polson, D. M., 86
Polyakova, I., 162
Popper, C. W., 123, 124, 130–131
Portzky, G., 161, 167
Posternak, M. A., 364
Potenza, M. N., 366–367
Poulin, F., 59
Poulin, M., 273
Poulson, C. L., 80
Pozdol, S. L., 77

Pratt, S. K., 43, 492, 494–496, 499, 501
Preston, J. D., 43–45, 479, 509, 510
Price, J. C., 400
Price, S. J., 174
Principe, J. M., 16, 26
Prochaska, J. O., 13, 14, 30, 57, 302, 314, 340, 531, 537
Putnam, F. W., 516

Q
Quinn, W. H., 34
Qureshi, J. N., 106

R
Rabian, B., 139, 146
Raffa, S. D., 239
Ragan, K., 187
Rak, C. F., 535
Ramnath, R., 419, 420, 485, 541
Randolph, E. M., 133
Rapee, R. M., 123, 125, 146
Rapoport, J. L., 91, 108, 109, 119, 120, 136
Rapport, M. D., 91
Rasbury, W. C., 21, 57
Ratey, J. J., 85
Rauch, S. L., 115, 269
Rawlings, R., 313
Reach, K., 117
Rees, C. S., 535, 537
Reibstein, J., 39
Reich, B., 427
Reich, J., 453
Reichler, R. J., 77
Reid, M. J., 93, 94, 100–102, 105
Reid, T. R., 322
Reinecke, M., 190
Reisberg, B., 412
Renfro-Michel, E. L., 132
Resnick, H. S., 273
Rettew, D. C., 128–129
Revicki, D. A., 182
Reynolds, C. A., 83, 495
Reynolds, C. F., 374
Reynolds, C. R., 56, 98, 133, 146, 149
Rice, J., 333
Richmond, E. N., 535
Richters, M., 132
Ridley, C. R., 28
Ridolfi, M. E., 449
Rifkin, A., 515, 516
Riley, E. P., 64
Ritchie, E. C., 366
Ritterband, L. M., 118, 537
Rivas-Vazquez, R. A., 333, 344
Rizvi, S. L., 28, 451
Robbins, P. C., 28, 34, 495
Roberts, A. R., 42
Roberts-Harewood, M., 106, 107
Robins, C. J., 28
Robinson, D. G., 512, 514
Robinson, J. R., 134
Rockland, L. H., 37
Roemer, L., 237, 279, 280
Roeser, R. W., 97
Roffman, R. A., 324
Rogers, C., 17, 18, 21, 25, 28, 29, 33, 531
Rogers, R., 170
Rollnick, S., 17, 300, 302, 304, 331, 386
Ronningstam, E., 464
Rosen, R. C., 348
Rosenbloom, M. J., 310
Rosenfeld, N., 224
Rosenthal, N. E., 183, 201, 232
Rosenvinge, J. H., 338
Rosenzweig, S., 25
Ross, C. A., 515, 516, 518, 521, 522
Ross, E. C., 24
Rossi, N. B., 366
Roth, A., 11, 26, 29, 43, 221, 246, 269, 278, 501, 536
Roth, D. L., 417
Rothbaum, B. O., 278
Rounsaville, B. J., 190
Roy-Byrne, P., 235, 241, 242, 245, 246, 279, 284
Rudolph, L. B., 58
Ruef, A. M., 271
Rueger, D. B., 277
Ruscio, A. M., 283
Rush, A. J., 26, 27, 191, 200, 201, 224
Rutter, M., 77
Ryan, N., 190
Rychtarik, R. G., 303

S
Sachs, G. S., 143, 213, 216–218, 222, 232, 276
Sachse, R., 12, 17
Sadock, B., 325
Sagar, A., 336, 344
Sambrano, S., 320–321
Sameroff, A. J., 97
Sanchez-Craig, M., 318
Sarokoff, R. A., 80
Saunders, J. B., 314
Savard, J., 375, 377, 378, 380, 386
Saxena, S., 182
Schaap, C., 33

Schatzberg, A. F., 181, 183–185, 192–193, 200
Schenck, C. H., 373, 374, 376, 377, 380, 381
Schlapobersky, J., 38
Schlenger, W. E., 325
Schmeidler, J., 518
Schnall, J., 121, 122
Schnoll, S. H., 314
Schopler, E., 77
Schopp, L., 536–537
Schramm, E., 378
Schreier, H., 404–407
Schuckit, M. A., 299, 300, 304, 305, 310–312, 315, 322, 324, 327, 329, 330, 332
Schwartz, R. C., 495, 496
Schwartz, R. W., 129
Scogin, F., 13, 18, 536
Sedlak, A. J., 169
Seedat, S., 369
Seeman, J, 29, 541
Segal, M., 73
Segraves, T., 347, 348, 350–353
Seligman, L., 8, 14–15, 21, 25, 26, 28, 31, 60, 138–140, 166, 174, 354–356, 359, 532, 541
Seligman, M.E.P., 20, 90, 206
Selzer, M. L., 302, 314
Serota, R., 19
Sethi, M., 515
Shaffer, D., 53
Shairani, A. J., 106
Shapiro, C. J., 82
Shapiro, D. A., 24
Shapiro, F., 276
Shapiro, S. J., 340
Shapiro, S. L., 30
Sharan, P., 182
Shaw, B. F., 27
Shaw, H., 333
Sheperis, C. J., 132, 133, 135
Sheridan, M. S., 404
Shipon, Blum, E., 129
Shortt, A. L., 125
Siegel, L. J., 21, 57
Silk, K. R., 427
Sillick, T., 67
Silver, L. B., 9, 68, 70–72
Silver, N., 174
Silver, R. C., 273
Silverman, R., 134
Silverman, W. K., 139, 146
Simeon, D., 518
Simon, G. E., 389, 397, 400, 401, 406
Simpson, R. L., 75
Simpson, S., 201
Singleton, E., 302
Sinha, R., 26, 191, 200, 201, 334
Siqueland, L., 33
Skodol, A. E., 440
Slanetz, P. J., 87
Sledge, W. H., 201
Smith, B. H., 82, 83, 88–91, 206
Smith, E. J., 3, 83, 86–88
Smith, G. T., 338
Smith, J., 62
Smith, N. M., 536
Smith, R. L., 301, 325, 326
Smith, T., 78–81
Smith-Myles, B., 75, 76
Sneed, T. J., 121
Snider, D. E., Jr., 64
Snyder, H., 92
Sochting, I., 266
Somerset, W., 182, 196, 197
Soutullo, C. A., 364
Spector, I. P., 348
Sperry, L., 430, 432, 434, 435, 438–441, 444–448, 453, 456, 458–460, 464–468, 471, 472, 474–477, 485, 541
Spiegel, B. R., 318–320
Spiegel, D., 393, 403, 522, 527
Spitzer, R. L., 188, 237
Spratt, E. G., 132, 134
Sprich, S., 86
Springer, D. W., 304
Staner, L., 192
Stanton, M. D., 304
Stasiewicz, P. R., 304, 331
Steen, T. A., 206
Steer, R. A., 188, 237, 254, 280, 496
Steffernberg, S., 74
Stein, D. J., 293, 364, 369, 373, 386
Steinberg, L., 348
Steinberg, M. A., 366–367
Steketee, G., 266, 267, 270
Stellato-Kabat, D., 304
Stellato-Kabat, J., 304
Stemberger, R.M.T., 368
Stephens, R. S., 324
Sterling, R. C., 19
Stevens, P., 301
Stewart, J. W., 182
Stewart, M. O., 191
Stice, E., 333, 337, 341
Stinchfield, R., 366
Stinson, F. S., 312, 323
Stone, S., 535, 537
Stone, W. L., 77
Storch, E. A., 111

Stowe, Z. N., 187
Strain, J. J., 157, 161
Strauman, T. N., 192
Street, E. M., 19
Stricker, G., 24
Strosahl, K. D., 283
Stroup, S., 498
Strub, R. L., 15
Strunk, D. R., 191
Stuart, S., 392, 394, 396–398
Stuewig, J., 96
Sturmey, P., 65
Sue, D., 212, 218, 219, 224, 409–413, 421, 424, 536
Sue, D. W., 19, 186, 409, 421, 536
Sue, S., 186, 409, 421, 536
Sullivan, E. V., 310, 313
Sullivan, H. S., 26, 190
Sullivan, J. M., 232
Sutphen, J., 117
Swanson, C., 29
Swanson, J. M., 97
Swartz, H. A., 220
Swedo, S. E., 148, 267
Syad, T., 326
Symonds, B. D., 33

T
Taber, K. H., 448
Talaga, M. C., 44, 479, 509
Tallman, K., 4
Tani, P., 365
Tarter, R. E., 320–321
Tausch, R., 29
Taylor, B. A., 80
Taylor, P., Jr., 364
Taylor, S., 266, 267, 269, 270
Teasdale, J. D., 191
Tedeschi, M., 207
Terman, J. S., 183
Terman, M., 183
Thayer, A., 326
Thiedke, C. C., 119–122
Thomas, A. M., 368
Thomas, H., 134
Thomas, P. M., 489, 490, 515, 517, 527
Thompson, C. L., 58
Thompson, L., 11
Thompson, M. P., 190
Thompson, V. L., 19
Thordarson, D. S., 266
Tienari, P., 422, 494
Tiffany, S. T., 134
Tohen, M. F., 214, 215, 514
Tolejko, N., 185
Tolin, D. F., 368
Tondo, L., 211
Tondora, J., 506
Tonigan, J. S., 302
Torgersen, S., 128, 455
Torrey, E. F., 497, 500, 527
Tourette, Gilles de la, 111
Towbin, K. E., 111, 114, 115
Toyer, E. A., 108, 109
Trafford, A., 166, 179
Tsatsanis, K. D., 80
Tucker, E., 300, 302, 305, 306, 308, 313, 314, 318, 321, 328, 520
Tucker, J. A., 318
Tully, E., 185–186
Turner, C. W., 34
Turner, L. C., 20
Turner, L. M., 77
Turner, W., 300

U
Uhde, T. W., 128, 130
Ursano, R. J., 273

V
Vaik, F. C., 189–190
Van den Hout, M., 244
van der Klink, J. J., 164
van Dijk, F. J., 164
van Heeringen, K., 161
van Ohs, J., 506
van Vresswijk, M. F., 201
Vanderwood, J., 42
Vanier, M. K., 130
Velicer, W. F., 302
Viorst, J., 166, 179
Virkkunin, M., 365
Vlahov. D., 273
Vogel, H. S., 312, 494
Volavka, J., 495, 513
Volkmar, F. R., 132
Vuchinich, R. E., 300

W
Wadhwa, P. D., 186
Walitzer, K. S., 29
Wall, S., 54
Wallerstein, R. S., 37
Walsh, B. T., 110
Walsh, R., 30
Wampold, B. E., 4, 11–12, 18, 19, 25
Wan, G. J., 207
Wang, P. S., 16

Warren, C. S., 25
Waters, E., 54
Watson, J. C., 17–18, 28
Webber, J., 14, 84, 92, 125
Weber, M. K., 64
Webster-Stratton, C., 93, 94, 100–102, 105
Wechsler, D., 68, 409
Weerts, T. C., 258
Weinberger, A. D., 189
Weiner, L. A., 488, 489
Weiner-Davis, M., 174
Weinstein, S. P., 19, 505
Weinstock, L. M., 185, 186
Weishaar, M., 446, 485
Weiss, B., 101
Weiss, M. K., 514
Weissman, M. M., 26, 190, 191
Weisz, J. R., 58, 59, 61, 101, 140
Weizenbaum, J., 534
Welfel, E. R., 535
Weller, E. B., 143
Weller, R. A., 143
Wells, K. C., 92
Werner, S. E., 65
Whisman, M. A., 185, 187
White, K. S., 27, 237, 243–245, 249, 253–256
White, L. A., 348
Widiger, T. A., 198
Wiegel, M., 346–349, 351
Wilhelm, K., 183, 196, 197
Wilhelm, S., 115
Wilkinson, D. A., 318
Williams, C., 254
Williams, D. R., 197
Williams, J. W., 207
Williams, J.B.W., 183, 188, 237
Willner, P., 302
Wilson, G. T., 27, 40, 108, 341–343, 345
Wilson, K. A., 254
Wilson, K. J., 283
Wilson, R., 329
Wilson, S. L., 107, 132, 134, 135
Winblad, B., 411
Wincze, J. P., 346, 350
Wing, L., 78
Winters, A., 92
Winters, K. C., 366
Wintersteen, M. B., 18
Winzelberg, A. J., 343, 535
Wirshing, D. A., 498
Wise, T. N., 390–393, 396, 397, 403
Wish, E., 446
Witkiewitz, K., 308, 309, 332
Woerner, M. G., 512
Wolfe, D. A., 62, 64, 67, 68, 95, 96, 107, 108, 118, 122, 144, 148, 149, 169
Wolpe, J., 239
Women for Recovery, 318–319
Wong, C. M., 270
Wong, E. C., 19
Woodcock, R. W., 67
Woodside, D. B., 334, 338
Wozniak, J., 84
Wu, L. T., 325, 326
Wu, R., 366–367
Wynne, L. C., 39

Y
Yager, J., 343
Yalom, I. D., 59
Yanovski, S. Z., 339
Yatham, L. N., 211, 219, 221
Yehuda, R., 270, 271, 277
Yen, S., 448
Young, E. A., 185
Young, J. E., 189, 199, 200, 202, 426, 428, 436, 446, 452, 464, 470, 485

Z
Zabinski, M. F., 343
Zaitsoff, S. L., 340
Zanarini, M. C., 427, 454
Zane, N.W.S., 19
Zarate, C. A., 214, 215, 514
Zarate, R., 144, 502
Zeanah, C. H., 54, 108, 132, 135
Zera, M., 92
Zickler, P., 326
Zimmerman, M., 364
Zimring, F. M., 29
Zis, A. P., 223
Zucker, K. J., 360
Zweben, A., 303
Zwinderman, A. H., 201

SUBJECT INDEX

A
AACAP. See American Academy of Child and Adolescent Psychiatry
Abilify, 44
Abuse, problems related to, 169–170
Academic problems, 171
Academy of Child and Adolescent Psychiatry (AACAP), 100, 104
Acamprosate (Campral), 316, 317
Acceptance and commitment therapy (ACT), 283–284
Accountability, 533
Acculturation problem, 172
Achenbach Child Behavior Checklist (CBCL), 56, 83, 98, 133, 146
Acupuncture, 122
Acute stress disorder. See Posttraumatic stress disorder (PTSD)
Adderall, 321
Adjustment disorders: assessment in, 162–163; description of, 159–162; intervention strategies for, 163–166; preferred therapist characteristics for, 163; prognosis for, 166–167; typical client characteristics in, 162
Adrenocorticotropic hormone (ACTH), 374–375
Adult ADHD Self-Report Scale, 83
Adult Attachment Interview (AAI), 133, 134
Adult Children of Alcoholics, 308
Adult panic disorders, 124
Affective therapy, 282
Agency for Healthcare Research and Quality, 386
Age-related cognitive decline, 171
Agoraphobia, 127; assessment of, 254; description of, 252–253; intervention strategies for, 254–256; medication for, 256; and panic disorder, 240–242; and phobias, 247; preferred therapist characteristics for, 254; prognosis for, 256; typical client characteristics of, 253–254
Agoraphobic Cognitions Questionnaire, 254
Akathisia, 168–169
Al-Anon, 307
Alateen, 307
Alcohol, 329, 330, 347, 369, 376, 408
Alcohol dependence, 291
Alcohol Use Disorders Identification Test (AUDIT), 314
Alcohol use/abuse, 267, 323
Alcoholics Anonymous, 46–47, 295, 306, 307, 313–314, 317–319, 332, 358, 371
Alcohol-related disorders: assessment in, 314; behavioral/social learning model of, 311; description of, 310–312;

Alcohol-related disorders *(continued)* environmental model of, 311; family systems model of, 311; humanistic/existential model of, 311; intervention strategies for, 315–319; medical or disease model for, 310–311; preferred therapist characteristics for, 314; prognosis for, 319–320; psychodynamic/psychoanalytic model of, 311; typical client characteristics in, 312–314
Alprazolam (Xanaz), 45, 245, 265, 284
Alzheimer's disease, 408–413
Ambien, 380
American Academy of Child and Adolescent Psychiatry (AACAP), 87, 134, 135
American Academy of Pediatrics, 87
American Academy of Sleep Medicine (AASM), 378
American Association of Mental Retardation (AAMR), 63
American Cancer Society, 327, 332
American Psychiatric Association, 2, 5, 28, 61, 68, 69, 72–75, 83, 84, 92, 94, 95, 106, 107, 110, 111, 113, 116, 119, 120, 127, 131, 135, 136, 144, 147, 157, 160, 161, 195, 208–211, 213, 223, 242, 247, 256, 261, 265, 278, 296, 298, 323, 324, 326, 329, 333–334, 336, 353, 355, 367, 451, 531
American Psychological Association, 3, 11, 264, 533, 538; Division 12 Task Force, 11, 31, 32; Task Force Steering Committee, 31
Amitriptyline, 45
Amnestic disorder, 410
Amphetamine mixed salts (Adderall), 46, 90
Amphetamines, 144, 321–322, 329, 376
Amyl nitrite, 330
Anabolic steroids, 330
Anafranil, 45, 245
Anhedonia, 195
Anne, 47–48; client map of, 48–49
Anorexia nervosa, 291, 335
Antabuse, 316
Antianxiety drugs, 45–46, 432, 453
Anticholinergic medications, 122
Anticonvulsants, 219, 225, 372–373
Antidepressant medications, 45, 60, 122, 225, 245, 284, 325, 330, 332, 372–373, 381, 453, 479, 514
Antidiuretics, 122
Antihypertensive drugs, 90
Antipsychotic medications, 44, 66, 67, 143, 144, 219, 225, 347, 453
Antiseizure medications, 453
Antisocial personality disorder (APD): description of, 442–443; intervention strategies for, 444–446; preferred therapist characteristics for, 443–444; prognosis for, 447; typical client characteristics in, 443
Anxiety, 161
Anxiety and Its Disorders (Barlow), 274
Anxiety disorders, 64, 84, 128, 146–150, 267; assessment in, 237; description of, 234–236; intervention strategies for, 238–240; preferred therapist characteristics for, 237–238; prognosis for, 240; typical client characteristics in, 236
Anxiety Disorders Interview Schedule for *DSM-IV* (ADIS-IV), 237, 280
Anxiety management therapy (AMT), 275, 276; for generalized anxiety disorder, 283
Anxiolytics, 329–330, 347, 441, 453
Aripiprazole (Abilify), 44
ARISE model, 303
Asperger's disorder, 72, 73, 75, 80
Ataque de nervios, 237
Ativan, 45, 329
Atomeoxetine (Strattera), 46, 67, 90
Attention-deficit and disruptive behavior disorders (ADHD), 81–106; and attention-deficit hyperactivity disorder, 82–84; overview of, 81–82
Attention-deficit/hyperactivity disorder (ADHD), 123, 133, 140–142, 147, 215, 312; description of, 82–84; intervention strategies for, 87–91; preferred therapist characteristics for, 86–87; prognosis for, 91–92; typical client characteristics in, 84–86
Atypical antipsychotics, 60, 144, 219, 373, 432, 437, 441–442, 498, 510, 514
Australian Scale for Asperger's Syndrome, 78
Autism, 136, 137
Autism Behavior Checklist (ABC), 77
Autism Diagnostic Interview-Revised (ADI-R), 77
Autism Screening Questionnaires, 76–77
Autism Spectrum Quotient, 78
Autistic disorder, 59, 72–74, 79, 80
Avoidant personality disorder, 128; description of, 465–466; intervention strategies for, 468–471; preferred therapist characteristics for, 467–468; prognosis for, 471
AWARE process, 282

B
Barbiturates, 329–330, 522
Barratt Impulsiveness Scale Version 11 (BIS-11), 293
Beck Anxiety Inventory, 16, 129, 254, 280
Beck Depression Inventory, 16, 188, 194, 206, 227, 229
Behavior Assessment System for Children-2 (BASC), 16, 56, 83, 99, 133
Behavior modification, 66
Behavior therapy, 26–27; and generalized anxiety disorder, 282; and schizophrenia, 499
Behavioral activation treatment, 191
Behavioral marital therapy (BMT), 206
Benzodiazepine/antianxiety drugs, 45–46, 46, 245, 260, 265, 284, 317, 322, 325, 329–330, 330, 347, 369, 373, 380, 453, 470, 501, 522
Bereavement, 171
Beta-blockers, 265, 446
Beth H., 155–156; client map for, 177–178
Betty, client map of, 50–51
Binge eating disorder (BED), 336–337
Biochemical changes due to substances, 240
Biofeedback, 122
Bipolar disorder, 60; and addressing dual diagnosis, 221–222; assessment in, 215–216; description of, 209; duration of episodes of, 212; and hypomanic episodes of, 211; intervention strategies for, 216–218; manic episodes of, 209–210; medication for, 219; and mixed episodes, 211; preferred therapist characteristics for, 216; prevalence of, 212–213; prognosis for, 222–223; psychotherapy for, 219–221; specifiers, 211; typical client characteristics in, 213–215
Body dysmorphic disorder, 267, 395
Borderline intellectual functioning, 171
Borderline personality disorder (BPD): description of, 447–448; intervention strategies for, 451–454; preferred therapist characteristics, 449–451; prognosis for, 454; typical client characteristics in, 448–449
Breathing-related sleep disorder, 375
Brief Psychiatric Rating Scale, 15
Brief psychotic disorder and schizophreniform disorder: and brief psychotic disorder, 503; description of, 503–504; intervention strategies for, 505–506; preferred therapist characteristics for, 505; prognosis for, 506; and schizophreniform disorder, 503–504; typical client characteristics in, 504–505
Bright light therapy, 192
Briquet's syndrome, 391
Bulimia nervosa, 291, 335–336
Buprenorphine (Subutex), 328
Bupropion (Wellbutrin), 45, 90, 200, 326, 347, 352
BuSpar, 269, 284
Buspirone (BuSpar), 90, 269, 284
Butyl nitrite, 330

C
Caffeine, 322–323, 376
Caffeine restriction, 122
CAGE Screening for Alcohol Abuse, 314
California Psychological Inventory, 15, 313
Cambodian populations, 237
Campral, 316, 317
Cancer, 166
Cannabis, 323–324, 329, 332
Carbamzaepine (Tegretol), 225
Cardiopulmmonary disorders, 240
Career changes, 166
Catapres, 90, 115
CBT. See Cognitive-behavioral therapy
Celexa, 45, 200, 479
Centers for Disease Control and Prevention, 53
Chantix, 326
Checklist for Autism in Toddlers (CHAT), 77
Child- and family-focused cognitive-behavioral therapy (CFF-CBT), 143
Child Assessment Schedule (CAS), 139
Child Depression Inventory, 139
Childhood Autism Rating Scale (CARS), 77
Childhood bipolar disorder, 132
Childhood Depression, 141; assessment, 139; description, 138; intervention strategies, 139–140; preferred therapist characteristics, 139; prognosis, 140; typical client characteristics, 138–139
Childhood disintegrative disorder, 72, 75
Childhood mania, 141
Childhood Trauma Questionnaire, 293
Childhood-onset schizophrenia, 144
Children's Depression Rating Scale-Revised (CDRS-R), 139
Children's Yale-Brown Obsessive-Compulsive Scale, 146
Cialis, 352
Circadian rhythm sleep disorder, 375–376
Citalopram (Celexa), 45, 200, 479

Client Map, 9–10; for anxiety disorders, 285–287; for disorders in which physical and psychological factors combine, 414–415; for disorders involving impairment in awareness of reality, 523–525; for disorders of behavior and impulse control, 382–384; for mood disorders, 226–228; for personality disorders, 481–483; for situationally precipitated disorders and conditions, 175–177
Client map, Shannon, 152–153
Clients: demographic and personal characteristics of, 16–17; expectation for treatment, 14; matching treatments to, 537–538; perception of Psychotherapy, 14; readiness for change, 13–14
Clinical Research Center for Schizophrenia and Psychic Rehabilitation (UCLA), 499
Clomipramine (Anafranil), 45, 245
Clonazepam (Klonopin), 45, 245, 265, 269
Clonidine (Catapres), 90, 115
Clozapine (Clozaril), 44, 219, 338, 498, 514
Clozaril, 44, 219, 513, 514
Cocaine, 144, 323–325, 329, 330
Cocaine Anonymous, 306, 332
Cochrane Incontinence Group Trials, 122
Codeine, 327
Cognex, 411
Cognitive restructuring, 145
Cognitive therapy, 27–28, 189–190, 264, 275, 281
Cognitive-behavioral group therapy (CGBT), 264
Cognitive-behavioral therapy (CBT), 27–28, 88, 91, 125–127, 130, 139, 143, 145, 147, 149, 189–190; and agoraphobia, 256; for anxiety disorders, 239; for eating disorders, 341; for generalized anxiety disorder, 283; for panic disorder, 244; for schizophrenia, 500; and specific phobia, 260
Cognitive-processing therapy (CPT), 275, 276
Community Epidemiology Work Group (CEWG; NIDA), 330
Compliance therapy, 145
Comprehensive Guide to Interpersonal Psychotherapy, A (Weissman, Markowitz, and Klerman), 191
Compulsions, 266
Computer-assisted health education-536, 535
Computerized axial tomography (CAT), 529
Conduct disorder (CD), 55, 59, 64, 84, 90, 93–99, 132, 135, 140, 141
Conduct Problems Prevention Research Group, 96
Congenital heart defects, 64
Conners' Rating Scales-Revised, 83, 91
Conners' Teacher and Parent Rating Scales, 56, 98
Connors' Rating Scale, 16, 56
Continuous performance test (CPT), 83
Conversion disorder, 393–394
Coping Cat model treatment program, 125–127
Corprolalia, 110
Couples therapy, 39–41; for sexual dysfunction, 350–352
Critical incident stress debriefing (CISD), 275
Cybercounseling, 535
Cyclothymic disorder: description of, 223–224; intervention strategies for, 225–226; preferred therapist characteristics for, 224; prognosis for, 226; typical client characteristics in, 224
Cylert, 321
Cymbalta, 45

D

Darvocet, 327
Darvon, 327
Day treatment programs, 104–105
DBT. See Dialectical behavior therapy (DBT)
Delirium, 409
Delirium, dementia, and amnestic and other cognitive disorders: and amnestic disorder, 410; assessment in, 411; and delirium, 409; and dementia, 409–410; description of, 408–410; intervention strategies for, 411–413; preferred therapist characteristics for, 411; prognosis for, 413; typical client characteristics in, 410–411
Delusional disorder: description of, 507; intervention strategies for, 509–511; preferred therapist characteristics for, 509; prognosis for, 511; typical client characteristics, 507–509
Delusions, 144
Dementia, 409–410
Dental Anxiety Inventory, 258
Dental phobia, 260
Depakene, 225
Depakote, 45
Dependent personality disorder: description of, 471–472; intervention strategies for, 474–475; preferred therapist characteristics for, 473–474; prognosis for, 475–475; typical client characteristics in, 472–473

Depersonalized disorder, 520
DepoProvera, 358
Depression, 64, 84, 149, 161, 211; cognitive and cognitive-behavioral therapy for, 189–190; common ingredients of treatments for, 193–194; epidemiology, 186–187; interpersonal psychotherapy for, 190–191; intervention strategies, 189; medication, 193; prognosis, 194–195; relevant predisposing factors of, 185–186; typical client characteristics, 187–188; typical onset, course, and duration of, 184
Depression and Bipolar Support Alliance (DBSalliance), 221
Depressive disorder, not otherwise specified (NOS), 208
Desyrel, 200
Developmental disorders, 128
Dexedrine, 90
Dextroamphetamine (Dexedrine), 90
Diagnostic and Statistical Manual of Mental Disorders (DSM-IV-TR; American Psychiatric Association), 2, 5, 6; and adjustment disorders, 159, 159–161, 161; and agoraphobia, 252–253; and alcohol-related disorders, 315; and anorexia nervosa, 335; and attention-deficit/hyperactivity disorder, 82, 84, 87; and avoidant personality disorder, 465, 466; and bipolar disorder, 141–143; and borderline personality disorder, 447, 448; and brief psychotic disorder, 503; and bulimia nervosa, 335; and conversion disorders, 393–394; and cyclothymic disorder, 223; and delirium, dementia, and other cognitive disorders, 404, 408, 409; and delusional disorder, 507; and dementia, 410; and dependent personality disorder, 471; and depressive disorder NOS, 208; and disruptive behavior disorders, 92–94; and dissociative amnesia, 519; and dissociative disorders, 489, 514; and drug-related disorders, 321, 329, 330; and eating disorders, 333; and encopresis, 116; and feeding and eating disorders of infancy or early childhood, 106; and gender identity disorder, 361; and generalized anxiety disorder (GAD), 278; and histrionic personality disorder, 454, 455; and impulse-control disorders, 363; and intermittent explosive disorder, 364; and learning, motor skills, and communication disorders, 67–69; and major depressive disorder, 195; and mental disorders due to general medical condition, 413; and mental disorders in young people, 53; and mental retardation, 61; and narcissistic personality disorder, 459, 460; and new diagnoses, 530; and obsessive-compulsive disorder, 265; and pain disorder, 394; and panic disorder, 241–242; and paranoid personality disorder, 428, 429; and paraphilias, 353; and personality disorders, 420–422; and phobias, 247; and posttraumatic stress disorder, 270; and primary insomnia, 374; and psychotic disorders, 488; and reactive attachment disorder, 132, 133; and schizoaffective disorder, 338; and schizoid personality disorder, 433, 434; and schizophrenia, 491, 492; and schizophreniform disorder, 503–504; and schizotypal personality disorder, 338; and separation anxiety disorder, 123; and situationally precipitated disorders and conditions, 156–157; and sleep disorders, 373, 376; and social phobia, 261; and somatoform disorders, 391; and specific phobias, 256; and stereotypic movement disorder, 135–136; and substance-related disorders, 296, 297; and undifferentiated somatoform disorder, 392
Diagnostic Interview for Children and Adolescents (DICA), 139
Diagnostic Interview for Narcissism, 464
Diagnostic Interview Schedule for Children (DISC), 139
Dialectical behavior therapy (DBT), 28, 341
Diazepam (Valium), 45
Disabilities Education Act of 1997, 70
Disorders in which physical and psychological factors combine: assessment in, 389; description of, 388–389; and factitious disorders, 403–408; intervention strategies for, 390–391; preferred therapist characteristics for, 389–390; and somatoform disorders, 391–403; typical client characteristics in, 389
Disorders of behavior and impulse control, 290–386; assessment in, 293–294; and conversion disorder, 393–394; description of, 291–292; intervention strategies for, 294–296; overview of, 291–296; preferred therapist characteristics for, 294; prognosis for, 296; and substance-related disorders, 296–309; typical client characteristics for, 291–292

Disruptive behavior disorders, 92–106; assessment in, 98–99; description of, 92–95; intervention strategies for, 100–105; preferred therapist characteristics for, 99–100; prognosis for, 105–106; typical client characteristics in, 95–97
Dissociative amnesia, 519–520; intervention strategies for, 521–522
Dissociative disorder, 132
Dissociative Disorder Interest Scale (DDIS), 516
Dissociative disorders (DID): description of, 514–516; intervention strategies for, 517–518; preferred therapist characteristics for, 516–517; prognosis for, 518; typical client characteristics in, 516
Dissociative Experiences Scale (DES), 516
Dissociative fugue, 518–519; intervention strategies for, 521–522
Disulfiram (Antabuse), 316
Divalproex (Depakote), 45
Divorce, 166
Divorce Remedy, The (Weiner-Davis), 174
Dolphine, 327
Dopamine, 146, 326
Down syndrome, 62
Drogatis Interview for Sexual Functioning (DISF), 348
Drug-related disorders: and amphetamines, 321; assessment in, 330; and caffeine, 322–323; and cannabis, 323–324; and cocaine, 332–325; description of, 320; and inhalants, 325–326; intervention strategies for, 331–333; and nicotine, 326–327; and opioids, 327–329; and polysubstance dependence, 330; preferred therapist characteristics for, 331; prognosis for, 333; and sedatives, hypnotics, and anciolytics, 329–330; typical client characteristics in, 320–330
Dry-bed training, 121
DSM-V, 530, 531
Dual Recovery Anonymous (DRA), 319
Duke University, 192
Duloxetine (Cymbalta), 45
Dyadic therapy, 134
Dysfunctional beliefs and Attitudes about Sleep Scale (DBAS), 378
Dysfunctional Thought Record, 436, 458, 479
Dyspareunia, 346
Dysphoria, 195
Dysthymic disorder, 138–139, 267; description of, 202–204; intervention strategies for, 206–208; preferred therapist characteristics for, 205; prognosis for, 208; typical client characteristics in, 204–205
Dystonia, 168–169

E

Early Sexual Experiences Checklist (ESEC), 349
Eastern philosophy, 533
Eating Disorder Examination Questionnaire, 339
Eating disorders, 59, 147, 267; and anorexia nervosa, 335; assessment in, 339–340; and binge eating disorders (BED, 336–337; and bulimia nervosa, 335–336; and cognitive-behavioral therapy, 341; description of, 333–334; and dialectical behavior therapy, 341; family therapy for, 343; and hospitalization, 343; interpersonal psychotherapy for, 342; intervention strategies for, 341; manualized treatment for, 342; medication for, 343–344; preferred therapist characteristics, 340–341; prognosis for, 344–345; typical client characteristics in, 337–339
Eating Disorders Inventory, 16
Echolalia, 110
Ecstasy (methylenedioxymethamphetamine), 325
Education for All Handicapped Children Act, 70
Effexor, 45, 200, 265, 284
Elavil, 45
Eldepril, 326
Electroconvulsive therapy (ECT), 46, 143, 200–201, 221, 514
Elimination diet, 122
Emily L., 418–419, 481–483; client map for, 483–485
Encorpresis: description of, 116–119; intervention strategies for, 117–119; preferred therapist characteristics for, 117; prognosis for, 119; typical client characteristics in, 117
Endocrine disturbances, 240
Enhanced toilet training, 118
Enuresis: alarm, 121, 122; description of, 119–120; intervention strategies for, 120–122; preferred therapist characteristics for, 120; prognosis for, 122; typical client characteristics in, 120
Epilepsy, 64
Erectile Functioning (IIEF), 348
Ericksonian stories, 281
Escitolopram (Lexapro), 479

Europe, 133, 316
Evelyn R., 210
Evidence-based therapy, 538–539
Exhibitionism, 354
Exposure therapy, 125, 275
Expressive language disorder, 68
Eye movement desensitization and reprocessing (EMDR), 276, 533
Eyeberg Child Behavior Inventory, 133

F

Factitious disorders: assessment in, 406; description of, 403–405; intervention strategies for, 406–407; preferred therapist characteristics for, 406; prognosis for, 407–408; typical client characteristics in, 405–406
Families and Change (McKenry and Price), 174
Family education and counseling, 500
Family therapy, 39–41, 126; for anxiety disorder, 239; for eating disorders, 343; for panic disorder, 245
Family-based psychotherapy, 130
Family-focused therapy (FFT), 220
Family-to-Family education program (National Alliance for the Mentally Ill), 221, 501
Fear of Negative Evaluation Scale, 263
Feeding and eating disorders of infancy or early childhood, 106–110; description of, 106–108; intervention strategies for, 109–110; preferred therapist characteristics for, 108, 108–109; prognosis for, 110; typical client characteristics in, 108
Female Sexual Function Index, 348
Fentanyl (Sublimaze), 327
Fetal alcohol syndrome, 64
Fetishism, 354
Fluoxetine (Prozac), 45, 130, 139, 200, 269, 344, 372–373, 402, 432, 446, 453, 479
Fluvoxamine (Luvox), 45, 200
Fragile X syndrome, 62
Frotteurism, 354
FSHT. *See* Full-spectrum home training
Full-spectrum home training (FSHT), 121, 122
Functional Family Therapy, 103

G

Gabapentin (Neurontin), 225
Gamblers Anonymous, 367–368, 371
Ganser's syndrome, 519
Gender identity disorder: assessment in, 361; description of, 359; *DSM-IV-TR* on, 359; intervention strategies for, 361–363; preferred therapist characteristics for, 361; prognosis for, 363; typical client characteristics in, 359–361
Generalized anxiety disorder (GAD), 149–150, 277; acceptance and commitment therapy and, 283–284; and affective therapy, 282; anxiety management therapy and, 283; assessment for, 280; and behavior therapy, 282; cognitive behavioral therapy and, 283; cognitive therapy and, 281; description of, 278–279; intervention strategies for, 281–285; medication and, 284; preferred therapist characteristics for, 280–281; prognosis for, 284–285; typical client characteristics in, 279–280
Geodon, 44, 219, 437
George W., client map for, 384–386
Gestalt therapy, 28–29, 533
Gilliam Asperger's Disorder Scale (GADS), 78
Global Assessment of Functioning Scale, 10–11
Greece, 392
Group psychotherapy, 38–39, 103–104, 220–221
Group therapy: for anxiety disorder, 239; and panic disorder, 245; for sexual dysfunction, 353
Guanfacine (Tenex), 90, 115

H

Habit-reversal training (HRT), 116
Haldol, 44, 80, 115, 513
Hallucinations, 144
Haloperidol (Haldol), 44, 60, 80, 513
Halstead-Reitan Neuropsychologic Battery, 409
Hamilton Anxiety Scale, 129
Hamilton Rating Scale for Depression, 16, 188
Harry Benjamine International Gender Dysphoria Association (HBIGDA), 362
Harvard University, 403
Hashish, 323
Hepatitis B, 328
Hepatitis C, 328
Heroin, 327, 329, 330
Heterocyclic antidepressants, 45, 122
High School, Children's, and Early School Personality Questionnaire, 15
Historical influences, 539

Histrionic personality disorder: description of, 454–458; intervention strategies for, 458–459; typical client characteristics in, 456
Hizen parenting skill training, 66
Hospitalization, 104–105, 343, 497
Human immunodeficiency virus (HIV), 327
Humanistic-experiential therapy, 28–29
Hycodan, 327
Hydrocodone (Hycodan), 327
Hyperchondriasis, 394
Hypnosis, 122
Hypnotics, 329–330
Hypomania, 210
Hypomania Checklist-32 (HCL-32), 215, 227
Hypomanic episodes, 211

I

ICD-10 Classification of Mental and Behavioral Disorders (World Health Organization), 5–6, 530
IDEA. See Individuals with Disabilities Education Act
Identity problems, 172
Imipramine (Tofranil), 45, 122, 245
Impulse-control disorders not elsewhere classified: description of, 363–369; DSM-IV-TR on, 363; and intermittent explosive disorder, 364; intervention strategies for, 370–373; and kleptomania, 365; and pathological gambling, 366–368; preferred therapist characteristics for, 369–370; and pyromania, 365–366; and trichotillomania, 368; typical client characteristics in, 368–369
Inderal, 446
Indiscriminate sociability, 132
Individual, 103–104
Individual psychotherapy, 38
Individuals with Disabilities Education Act (IDEA), 70
Inflammatory disorders, 240
Inhalants, 325–326
Insomnia Interview Schedule, 378
Integrated dual diagnosis treatment, 500–501
Integrated treatments, 531–532
Intermittent explosive disorder, 364
Internet delivery methods, 343
Interoceptive avoidance, 253
Interpersonal psychotherapy (IPT), 26, 145, 190, 206, 220, 342
Interview Schedule for Children (ISC), 139
Intracavernosal injection, 352
IPT. See Interpersonal psychotherapy (IPT)
IQ tests/scores, 61, 62, 67, 79, 80, 91, 100, 171
Iraq War, 271
Ireland, 310

J

Japan, 66, 310
Johnson Institute, 304
Journal of Personality Disorder, 425

K

Karen C., 180–181; client map for, 228–232
Ketamine, 329
Kleptomania, 291, 365
Kleptomania Symptom Assessment Scale (K-SAS), 294
Klonopin, 45, 245, 329, 369
Korea, 310

L

Lamictal, 225
Lamotrigine (Lamictal), 45, 225
Learning, motor skills, and communication disorders, 67–72; description of, 67–69; intervention strategies for, 70–71; preferred therapist characteristics for, 70; prognosis for, 71–72; typical client characteristics in, 69–70
Levitra, 352
Levo-alpha-acetylmethadol (LAAM), 328
Lexapro, 479
LifeRing, 318–319
Lifestyle Assessment Questionnaire (National Wellness Institute), 162
Lithium, 45, 66, 67, 143, 219, 225, 332, 373, 446, 514
Lorazepam (Ativan), 45
Loss, Trauma, and Resilience (Boss), 174
LSD (lysergic acid diethylamide), 325
Luvox, 45, 200
Lysergic acid diethylamide (LSD), 325

M

Magical thinking, 147
Magnetic resonance imaging (MRI), 84, 529
Major depressive disorder, 123, 138, 267; day treatment programs, 201; description of, 195–197; and electroconvulsive therapy (ECT), 200–201; intervention strategies for, 199; light therapy for, 201; medication for, 200; preferred therapist characteristics for, 199; prognosis for, 202–203; and psychotherapy, 199–200; typical client characteristics in, 195–197

Malingering, 170
Manualized treatment, 342, 532–533
MAOIs. *See* Monoamine oxidase inhibitors (MAOIs)
Marijuana, 144, 323, 330
Marital therapy, 130
Martin C., 387–388; client map of, 415–417
M-CHAT, 77
McMaster Evidence Based Review of ADHD Treatments, 90
MDMA (methylenedioxymethamphetamine), 325
MeCP2 gene, 73
Medical Fear Survey, 258
Medication, 43–46, 533–534; antidepressant, 45; antipsychotic, 44; and anxiety disorder, 239–240; benzodiazepine/anxiety drugs, 45–46; mood stabilizers, 45; and schizophrenia, 497–498
Medication-induced movement disorders, 168–169
Medroyprogesterone acetate (Depo-Provera), 358
Melatonin, 380
Mellaril, 44
Memantine (Namenda), 412
Menninger Foundation, 25
Mental disorders in infants, children, and adolescents: etiology of, 53–56; family interventions for, 59–60; group therapy for, 58; individual therapy for, 57–58; intervention strategies for, 57; mental disorders in, 53–67; play therapy for, 58; preferred therapist characteristics for, 56–57; prevalence and client characteristics in, 55–56; prognosis for, 60
Mental retardation, 60–67, 136–138; description of, 60–63; intervention strategies for, 65–67; preferred therapist characteristics for, 64–65; prognosis for, 67; typical client characteristics in, 63–64
Methadone (Dolphine), 46, 327–329
Methamphetimine, 330
Methylenedioxymethamphetamine (MDMA, ecstasy), 325
Methylphenidate (Ritalin), 46, 90, 91, 321
Michigan Alcoholism Screening Test (MAST), 16, 314
Millon Adolescent Personality Inventory, 15
Millon Clinical Multiaxial Inventory-III (MCMI), 15, 421, 424, 433
Mindfulness, 191
Mini-Mental State Exam, 409
Minnesota Impulsivity Interview, 293
Minnesota Multiphasic Personality Inventory-2, 15, 313, 424
Minnesota Multiphasic Personality Inventory (MMPI), 421, 433
Miracle Question (de Shazer), 164
Mirtazapine (Remeron), 45, 200, 347
Mixed receptive-expressive language disorder, 68
Mobility Inventory for Agoraphobia, 254
Molecular genetics, 529–530
Monoamine oxidase inhibitors (MAOIs), 45, 182, 189–190, 200, 245, 265, 459
Mood disorders, 55, 60; description of, 181–184; and panic disorder, 242
Mood stabilizers, 45, 372–373
Morphine, 327
MTA Cooperative Group, 90
Multicultural influences, 539
Multidimensional Anxiety Scale for Children, 129, 146
Multimodal Treatment Study of ADHD (MTA), 87, 90
Multisystemic Therapy (MST), 102
Myers-Briggs Type Indicator, 15, 162

N

Naltrexone (ReVia), 316, 317, 328, 344, 453, 459
Namenda, 412
Narcissistic personality disorder: description of, 459–461; intervention strategies for, 463–465; preferred therapist characteristics for, 462–463; prognosis for, 465
Narcolepsy, 374–375
Narcotics Anonymous (NA), 46–47, 306–308, 319, 332
Nardil, 45
National Alliance for Research on Schizophrenia and Depression, 514
National Alliance for the Mentally Ill (NAMI), 221, 501–502, 514
National Board for Certified Counselors & Center for Credentialing Education, 535
National Center for Health Statistics, 141
National Comorbidity Survey, 55, 182, 212
National Comorbidity Survey Replication, 212, 261
National Epidemiologic Survey on Alcohol and Related Conditions, 421
National Institute of Mental Health (NIMH), 55, 72, 74, 79, 80, 139, 141, 188, 421, 498, 538
National Institute on Alcohol Abuse and Alcoholism (NIH, NIAAA), 317, 421

National Institute on Drug Abuse (NIDA), 323, 324–325, 329, 330
National Longitudinal Alcohol Epidemiological Survey, 312
National Research Council, 77
National Survey on Drug Use and Health (SAMHSA), 327
National Wellness Institute, 162
Neglect, problems related to, 169–170
Neurobiology, 529
Neuroleptic drugs, 60, 168–169, 497, 514
Neurological disorders, 240
Neurontin, 225
New diagnoses, 530–531
Nicotine, 323, 326–327, 376
Nicotine replacement therapy (NRT), 326, 327
NIH Consensus Development Conference on ADHD, 90
NIMH, 127
NIMH Diagnostic Interview Schedule, 15
Nitrite inhalants, 330
Nitrous oxide, 330
Nocturnal enuresis, 128
Noncompliance with treatment, 170
Normative middle, 220
Norwegian children, study of, 128

O

Obsessive-compulsive disorder (OCD), 136, 146–148, 214, 265; assessment of, 268; DSM-IV, 265–266; four patterns in, 266; intervention strategies for, 268–269; preferred therapist characteristics for, 268; prognosis for, 269; typical client characteristics in, 267–268
Obsessive-compulsive personality disorder (OCPD): description of, 476–47; intervention strategies for, 478–480; prognosis for, 480; typical client characteristics in, 477
Occupational problems, 172
OCD. *See* Obsessive-compulsive disorder
Olanzapine (Zyprexa), 44, 219, 343, 437, 498, 510, 513
Opioids, 327–329, 330, 347
Oppositional defiant disorder (ODD), 55, 59, 64, 84, 88–90, 94, 95, 97–100, 132, 134
Orap, 115, 432, 510
Orgasmic disorder, 346
Overeaters Anonymous, 295
Overt Aggression Scale-Modified (OAS-M), 293
Oxycodone, 327, 330
Oxycontin (oxycodone), 327

P

Pain disorder, 394
Palilalia, 110
PANDAS (pediatric autoimmune neuropsychological disorders associated with streptococcal infections), 148, 267
Panic disorder, 127, 267; and agoraphobia, 240–242; assessment in, 243; cognitive-behavioral therapy for, 244; description of, 240–242; etiology of, 242–243; family and group therapy for, 245; medication for, 245–246; and mood disorder, 242; new treatment modalities for, 244–245; panic-control therapy for, 244; and personality disorder, 242; preferred therapist characteristics for, 243–244; prognosis for, 246; and substance-related disorders, 242; types of, 241; typical client characteristics in, 22–243
Panic-control therapy (PCT), 244; for agoraphobia, 254
Paranoid personality disorder: description of, 428–430; intervention strategies for, 431–432; preferred therapist characteristics for, 431; prognosis for, 432–433; typical client characteristics in, 430–431
Paraphilias, 291, 353–359; description of, 353–356; *DSM-IV-TR* on, 353, 354; intervention strategies for, 357–358; preferred therapist characteristics for, 356–357; prognosis for, 358–359
Parasomnias, 376
Parent management training (PMT), 101–102
Parent, Teacher and Youth Self-Report forms, 83
Parent training (PT), 87, 89
Parkinsonism, 168–169, 326
Parnate, 45
Paroxetine (Paxil), 45, 200, 207, 245, 265, 372–373, 470, 479
Pathological gambling, 291, 366–368
Paxil, 45, 200, 207, 245, 265, 372–373, 470, 479
PDM Task Force, 5–6
PE. *See* Process-experiential therapy (PE)
Pedophilia, 354
Pemoline (Cylert), 90, 321
Penn State Worry Questionnaire, 280
Percocet, 327
Percodan, 327

Personality Belief Questionnaire, 464
Personality disorder, 140; assessment in, 424; description of, 419–422; intervention strategies for, 425–428; and panic disorder, 242; preferred therapist characteristics for, 424–425; prognosis for, 428; typical client characteristics in, 422–424
Personality disorders not otherwise specified, 480
Pervasive developmental disorders, 136
Pervasive developmental disorders (PDD), 72–81; assessment in, 76–78; description of, 72–75; intervention strategies for, 78–81; preferred therapist characteristics for, 78; typical client characteristics in, 75–76
Pervasive Developmental Disorders Questionnaire, 76–77
Pervasive Developmental Disorders Screening Test II (PDDST-II), 76–77
PET scans, 185
Pharmacological interventions, 104
Phase of life problem, 172
Phencyclidines (PCP), 329
Phenelzine (Nardil), 45
Philadelphia, Pennsylvania, 329
Phobias, 125, 150; assessment in, 248; description of, 247; preferred therapist characteristics for, 248; prognosis for, 252; and systematic desensitization, 250–251; types of, 247; typical client characteristics in, 247–247
Phonological disorder, 68
Phototherapy, 380–381
Pica, 106
Pimozide (Orap), 432, 510
Play therapy, 130
Political, legislative, and economic influences, 539–541
Polypharmacy, 200
Polysubstance dependence, 330
Positron emission tomography (PET), 84, 493, 529
Posttraumatic stress disorder (PTSD), 132, 148–149, 214, 234, 267; assessment in, 274; Checklist, 273; description of, 270–272; intervention strategies for, 274–277; preferred therapist characteristics for, 274; prognosis for, 277; typical client characteristics for, 272–273
Practice Guideline for the Treatment of Patients with Bipolar Disorder (American Psychiatric Association), 219
Practice Guideline for the Treatment of Patients with Schizophrenia (American Psychiatric Association), 498
Practice Guidelines for the Treatment of Borderline Personality Disorder (American Psychiatric Association), 40
Practitioner's Guide to Empirically Based Measures of Anxiety (Antony, Orsillo, & Roemer), 237
Primary hypersomnia, 374
Primary insomnia, 374
Problem-solving skills training (PSST), 102–103
Process-experiential therapy (PE), 28–29
Project Match, 303, 317
Prolixin, 44
Propanolol (Inderal), 446
Propoxyphene, 327
Prozac, 45, 130, 139, 200, 267, 344, 372–373, 402, 432, 446, 453, 479
Psychiatric Institute Tricholtillomania Scale, 294
Psychoanalysis, 25
Psychodynamic Diagnostic Manual (PDM Task Force), 5–6
Psychodynamnic psychotherapy, 25, 104, 500
Psychoeducation, 350
Psychopharmacological strategies, 130
Psychosis: and childhood-onset schizophrenia, 144; description of, 143–144; intervention strategies for, 145; preferred therapist characteristics for, 145; prognosis for, 145–146; typical client characteristics in, 144–145
Psychosocial interventions, 498–500
Psychostimulants, 60, 67, 90, 91, 104
Psychotherapy, effectiveness of, 3–4
Psychotherapy Research Project, 25
Psychotic and dissociative disorders, overview: assessment in, 490; description of disorders, 487–489; and dissociative disorders, 488–489; intervention strategies for, 491; preferred therapist characteristics for, 490–491; prognosis for, 491; and psychotic disorders, 487–488; typical client characteristics in, 489–490
Psychotic disorders, 60; and brief psychotic disorder and schizophreniform disorder, 503–506; and delusional disorder, 507–511; and schizoaffective disorder, 511–514; and schizophrenia, 491–503
Psychotropic medication, 60
PTSD, 26
Public Law 94–142 (1975), 70

Puerto Rico, 392
Pyromania, 365–366

Q
Questionnaire on Eating and Weight Patterns-Revised (QEWP-R), 339
Quetiapine (Seroquel), 219

R
RAINBOW program, 143
Ramelteon (Rozerem), 380
Rational emotive behavior therapy (REBT), 28
Rational Recovery, 295, 307, 318
Reauthorized IDEA, 70
Reactive Attachment Disorder Questionnaire, 133
Reactive attachment disorder (RAD): description, 131–132
REBT. *See* Rational emotive behavior therapy (REBT)
Regular exercise, 191
Relaxation techniques, 127, 130, 264
Religious problems, 172
Remeron, 45, 200, 347
Repetitive transcranial magnetic stimulation (rTMS), 192
Residual agoraphobia, 255
Retention control, 122
Rett's disorder, 55–56, 72–74, 78
ReVia, 316, 317, 328, 344, 453, 459
Revised Children's Manifest Anxiety Scale (RCMAS), 146, 149
Risperdal, 44, 115, 219, 441, 498, 510, 513
Risperidone (Risperdal), 44, 219, 441, 498, 510, 513
Ritalin, 91, 104, 321
Roberto M., 233–234; client map for, 287–289
Roxanol, 327
Rozerem, 380
Rumination disorder, 107

S
Safekeeping contract, 229
Schedule for Affective Disorders and Schizophrenia, 15, 227
Schizoaffective disorder: description of, 511–512; intervention strategies for, 513–514; preferred therapist characteristics for, 512–513; prognosis for, 513–514; typical client characteristics in, 512
Schizoid personality disorder: description of, 433–434; intervention strategies for, 436–438; preferred therapist characteristics for, 435–436; prognosis for, 438; typical client characteristics in, 434–435
Schizophrenia: assessment in, 496; and behavioral therapy, 499; and cognitive-behavioral therapy, 500; description of, 491–494; family education and counseling for, 500; group therapy for, 501; integrated dual diagnosis treatment for, 500–501; intervention strategies for, 497; long-term management and relapse prevention for, 501–502; medication for, 497–498; preferred therapist characteristics, 496–497; prognosis for, 502–503; psychodynamic approaches for, 500; psychosocial interventions for, 498–500; and skills training, 499; typical client characteristics in, 494–496
Schizotypal personality disorder (SPD): description of, 438; preferred therapist characteristics, 440; prognosis for, 441–442; typical client characteristics in, 439–440
Schizotypy, 128
School intervention, 130
SCID. See Structured Clinical Interview for DSM
Screening Tool for Autism in Two-Year-Olds (STAT), 77
Seasonal affective disorder (SAD), 197
Secular Organization for Sobriety (SOS), 318–319
Sedatives, 329–330
Selective mutism: assessment for, 129; description of, 127–128; intervention strategies for, 129–131; preferred therapist characteristics for, 129; prognosis for, 131; typical client characteristics in, 128–129
Selective serotonin reuptake inhibitors (SSRIs), 45, 60, 130, 140, 147, 182, 200, 245, 269, 358, 372–373, 400, 402, 403, 453, 465, 470
Selegiline (Eldepryl), 326
Self-injurious behaviors (SIBs), 66, 136, 137, 161
Self-system therapy (SST), 191
Sensation-focused intensive treatment (SFIT), 244–245; for agoraphobia, 255
Separation Anxiety Disorder: assessment in, 124–125; description of, 123; intervention strategies for, 125–127; preferred therapist characteristics for, 125; prognosis for, 127; typical client characteristics in, 124
September 11 terrorist attacks, 273

Serzone, [illegible]
Serotonin and norepinephrine reuptake inhibitors (SNRIs), [illegible], 80, [illegible]
Sertraline (Zoloft), [illegible], 12[illegible], 200, [illegible], 245, 265, 3[illegible]–273, [illegible]46, 4[illegible], 479
Desmopressin (DDAVP), 122
Seven Principles for Making Marriage Work (Gottman and Silver), [illegible]
Sex Addicts Anonymous, 358
Sex and Love Addicts, 358
Sexual and gender identity disorders, 345–371; DSM-IV-TR for, 345; and paraphilias, 353–359; and sexual dysfunctions, 346–353
Sexual arousal disorder, 346
Sexual Compulsives Anonymous, [illegible]
Sexual desire disorders, [illegible]
Sexual Desire Inventory, [illegible]
Sexual Dysfunction Scale, 348
Sexual dysfunctions, 291, [illegible]–35[illegible]; assessment in, 346–[illegible]; description of, 346–348; and group therapy, [illegible]; intervention strategies for, 34[illegible]–35[illegible]; medication for, 352–353; preferred therapist characteristics for, 349; prognosis for, 353; and psychoeducation, 350; typical client characteristics in, 348
Sexual masochism, 354
Sexual Opinion Survey (SOS), 348
Sexual pain disorders, 346
Sexual sadism, 354
Shannon, client map of, 153–154
Sildenafil citrate (Viagra), 352
Situationally precipitated disorders and conditions: description of, 156–157; intervention strategies for, 158–159; preferred therapist characteristics for, 158; prognosis for, 159; typical client characteristics in, 158
Skills training, 499
Sleep disorders, 291; assessment in, 377–378; and breathing-related sleep disorder, 375; and circadian rhythm sleep disorder, 375–376; description of, 373–376; intervention strategies for, 375–381; and narcolepsy, 374–375; and parasomnias, 376; preferred therapist characteristics for, 375; and primary hypersomnia, 374; and primary insomnia, [illegible]; prognosis for, 381; typical client characteristics in, 376–377
Sleep-EVAL, 378
Smart Recovery, 318–319
Snake Questionnaire, 258
SNRIs. *See* Serotonin and norepinephrine reuptake inhibitors (SNRIs)
Social and cultural influences, 539–541
Social Interaction Anxiety Scales (SIAS), 263
Social phobia, 128, 247, 260, 26[illegible]; assessment for, 263; and children, 262; and cognitive-behavioral therapy, 264; description of, 261–262; and exposure therapy, 264; intervention strategies for, 263–26[illegible]; and medication, 264–265; preferred therapist characteristics for, 26[illegible]; prognosis, 265
Social rhythm therapy, [illegible]
Social skills training, [illegible]
Socioeconomic status (SES), 62, 6[illegible], [illegible]
Somatization disorder, 3[illegible]–392
Somatoform disorders: assessment in, 397; and body dysmorphic disorder, [illegible]; and conversion disorder, 39[illegible]–394; description of, 39[illegible]; and hypochondriasis, 395; intervention strategies for, 398–[illegible]; and pain disorder, [illegible]; preferred therapist characteristics, 397–[illegible]; prognosis for, [illegible]; and somatization disorder, 391–392; typical client characteristics in, [illegible] 397; undifferentiated, [illegible]
[illegible], 300
[illegible] syndrome, [illegible]
South Oaks Gambling Screen, 294
Specific phobia, [illegible]; and alcohol abuse, [illegible]; assessment in, [illegible]; classification of, [illegible]; and depressive disorder, 263; description of, [illegible]; intervention strategies for, [illegible]; medication for, [illegible]; prognosis for, [illegible]; typical client characteristics in, 25[illegible]
Spectrum disorders, 529–530
Spider Questionnaire (SPQ), 258
Spielberger State-Trait Anger Expression Inventory (STAEI), 293
Spiritual problems, 172
SSRIs, 182
Standards of Practice Committee (American Academy of Sleep Medicine), 378
Stanford-Binet Intelligence Scales, 60
State-Trait Anxiety Inventory, 16
STEADY intervention model, 139
Steen Happiness Index (SHI), 206
Stelazine, 44
Stereotypic behavior, 137
Stereotypic movement disorder: description of, 135–136; intervention strategies for, 136–137; preferred therapist characteri[illegible]

Stereotypic movement disorder (*continued*)
typical client characteristics in, 136
Steroids, 142
Stimulant abuse, 136
Stimulant medications, 91
Stimulus fading, 131
Strange Situation (attachment theory), 131
Strattera, 40, 45, 90
Stress inoculation training (SIT), 164,
16
Structured Clinical Interview for DSM
(SCID-I), 188, 257, 421, 424
Structured Clinical Interview for *DSM-IV*
Dissociative Disorders (SCID-D), 316
Structured Clinical Interview for
Obsessive-Compulsive Spectrum
Disorders, 265
Structured Interview for Sleep Disorders
(SIS), 378
Structured Interview of Reported Symptoms,
170
Student Bodies program, 535
Stuttering, 68
Sublimaze (fentanyl), 327
Substance Abuse and Mental Health Services
Administration (SAMHSA), 53, 298, 327,
328
Substance Abuse and Mental Health Services
Administration (SAMSA), 53
Substance abuse disorders, 55, 59, 267
Substance-related disorders, 127, 149,
296–309; assessment in, 301–302;
description of, 296–300; in *Diagnostic and Statistical Manual of Mental Disorders*,
296–298; intervention strategies for,
303–309; and panic disorder, 242;
preferred therapist characteristics for, 303;
prognosis for, 309; typical client
characteristics in, 300–301
Subutex, 328
Suicidal ideation, 140, 183, 256, 301
Suicide, 101, 301
Suicide rates, 183
Sutter-Eyberg Student Behavior
Inventory-Revised (SESBI-R), 133
Synanon program, 328
Symptom Checklist-90-R, 15
Systematic desensitization, 130, 250–251

T

Tacrine (Cognex), 411
Tadalafil (Cialis), 352
Tardive dyskinesia, 168–169, 503
Task Force on Promotion and Dissemination
of Psychological Procedures, 3, 17
Tegretol, 225
Telephone-assisted therapy, 536
Tenex, 90, 113
Test of Variables of Attention (TOVA), 83
Tetrahydrocannabinol (THC), 323
THC (tetrahydrocannabinol), 323
Therapeutic alliance, 851
Thorazine, 14, 405
Tic disorders, 60, 84, 91, 110–116, 136, 143;
chronic, 112; description of, 110–112;
intervention strategies, 113–116; preferred
therapist characteristics, 113; prognosis,
116; and Tourette's disorder, 111–112;
transient, 112–113; typical client
characteristics, 113
Tobacco, 323, 326–327
Tofranil, 43, 245
Topamax, 45, 344
Topiramate (Topamax), 45, 3
Tough love, 106
Tourette's disorder, 111–
267, 268
Tourette's syndrome, 136
Tourette's Syndrome Associa
Tramadol, 327
Transvestic fetishism, 354
Tranylcypromine (Parnate), 45
Trauma Burn Outreach Prevention Program,
372
Trazodone (Desyrel), 300
"Treating Children as Young as Four for
Bipolar" (*Wall Street Journal*), 140
Treatment delivery methods, new, 534–537
Treatment modalities, new and evolving, 533
Treatment of Adolescents with Depression
Study (TADS), 139
Treatment of Depression Collaborative
Research Program, 188
Treatment outcome, determinants of, 4–5
Treatment planning: dimensions of, 10–47;
importance of, 1–3; integrated model for,
5–9
Treatment planning, dimensions of: adjunct
services, 46–47; assessments, 14–16;
clinician characteristics, 17–21; diagnosis,
10–12; emphasis, 35–38; interventions,
24–35; location, 21–24; medications,
43–46; numbers, 38–41; objectives of,
12–14; prognosis, 47; timing, 41–43
Trichotillomania, 368
Tricyclic and heterocyclic antidepressants, 45

Let's take a closer look at each light source:

- **Key light**: This is the main light source that will light up your subject from the front.
- **Back light**: This sits behind the subject, directly on the opposite side of your key light. The main purpose of this light is to produce a rim light effect that highlights the edges of your subject.
- **Fill light**: This light source is placed perpendicular to your key light. The main purpose of this light is to control the darkness level of the shadows on the subject.

Adding light nodes

It's finally time to add some lights to your scene, so let there be light! :]

First open up **Game.scn** and create an empty node under the scene graph by clicking the + button. Then, rename this new node to **Lights**. This will act as a group container for all the lights in your scene:

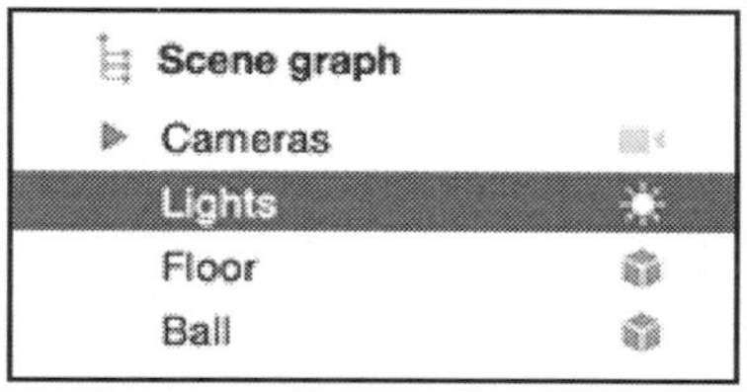

From the Object Library, drag and drop an **Omni light** into your scene. Make sure to move the light under the lights group node:

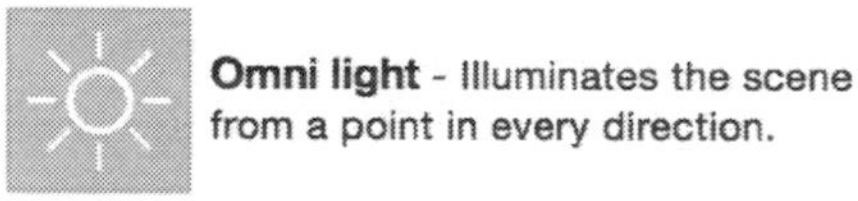

With the light node still selected, open the Node Inspector and rename the node to **Back**. Adjust **Position** so that **x** is **-15**, **y** is **-2** and **z** is **-15**. This represents the back light, so you are positioning it behind the ball. You should have something like this:

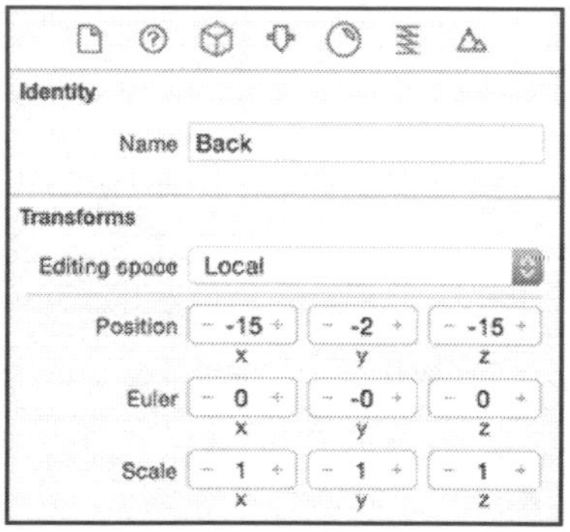

Select the Attributes Inspector to see the different attributes you can adjust for an omni light source:

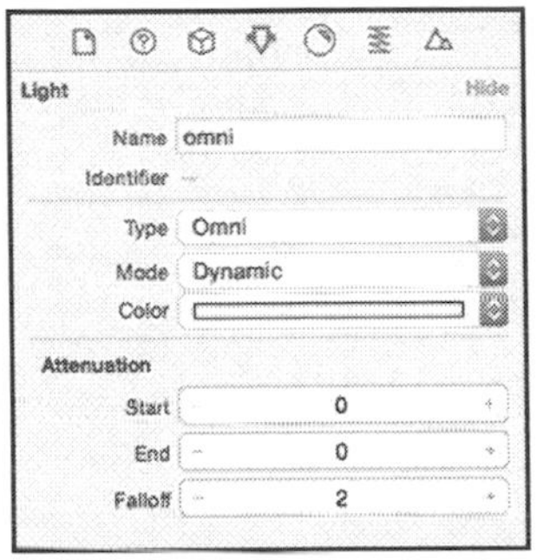

You can leave the default settings as is for this exercise, but you'll want to learn about what they do:

- **Mode**: You can choose from either **Dynamic** or **Baked**. For light sources that move around or apply their effects to nodes that move, you should use a dynamic light. For static lighting, you can use baked lighting where you create a light map texture in an external 3D authoring tool, and then the lighting effects are applied to the textures of the objects in the scene.
- **Color**: This allows you to specify the light's color.
- **Attenuation**: This controls the intensity of the light source over a distance. When a node is closer than the start distance, the light applies its full intensity, whereas a node that is further than the end distance is not affected by the light at all. By default, the value is 0, meaning that attenuation will not apply. Sitting between the start and the end is the falloff, which is an exponetial factor that controls how quickly the intensity diminishes.

Add another light source by dragging and dropping another **Omni light** from the Object Library into your scene. Make sure you move it under the **Lights** group node as well.

Name this new node **Front** and set the **Position** so that **x** is **6**, **y** is **10** and **z** is **15**. This represents the front light, so you are placing it in front of the ball:

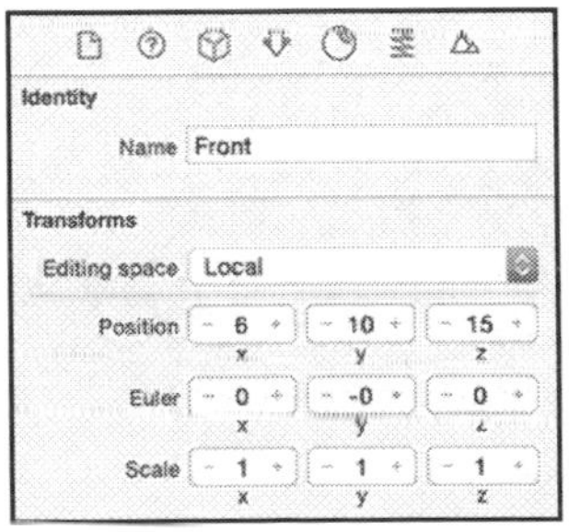

You're almost done, but the scene still needs an ambient light. To add it – you guessed it – drag and drop an **Ambient light** from the Object Library:

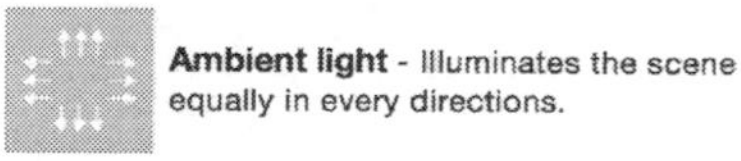

Again, make sure you move this new node into the **Lights** group node. Name it **Ambient**, and simply zero out the **Position** since position for this kind of light source has no effect on the result:

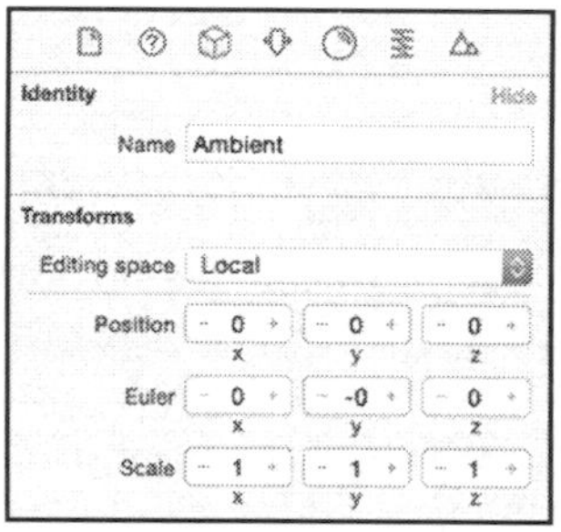

Now take a look at the Attributes Inspector for the ambient light:

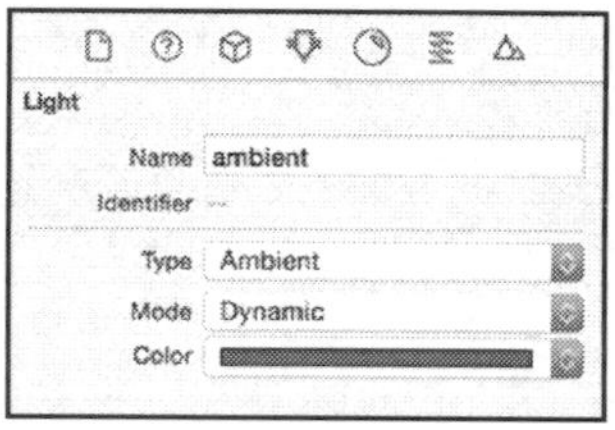

You can leave the settings as the defaults, but take note that only thing you can configure on an ambient light is its color.

Finally! :]

After adding all those lights to your scene, the final result should resemble something like this:

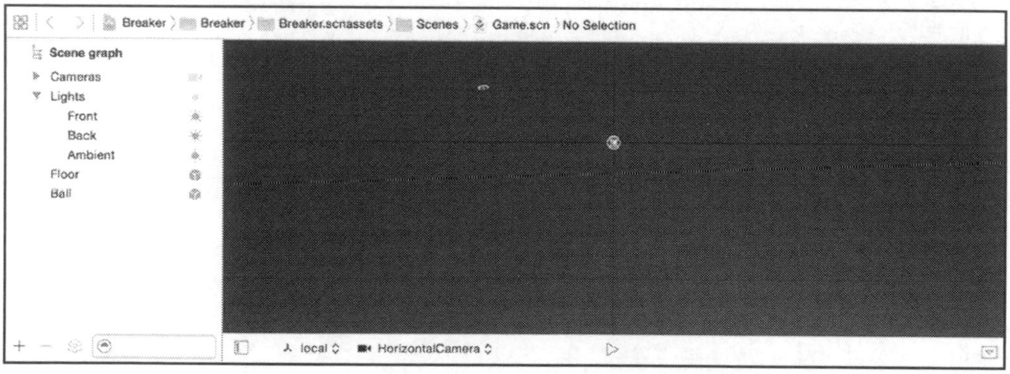

Take particular note of the scene graph structure, where all the lights are grouped under the **Lights** group node.

Conclusion

Not only are you empowered with the knowledge to implement the three point lighting technique, but you also added plenty of lighting to your scene.

To understand what you've just done a bit better, take a look at the following:

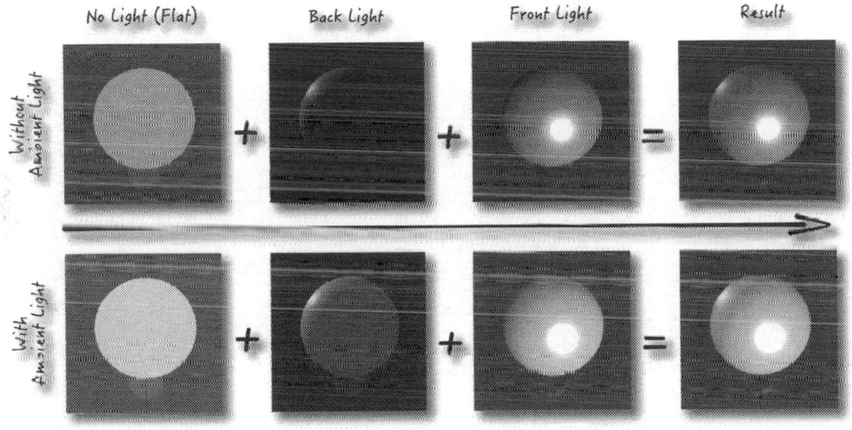

You can see the effect that each individual light has on the ball, as well as the combined effect in the last column. Note that the first row is without an ambient light, while the second row has an ambient light. Let's take a closer look at each step:

- **No light**: When you started off, the ball was flat and dull because the scene had no light source. Scene Kit uses a constant light in the absence of added light sources, hence, you get a very flat looking ball.
- **Back light**: As soon as you add a light to the scene, everything that's not in the light darkens. Scene Kit stops applying a constant light to the whole scene, and starts using the added light sources to apply lighting and shading effects. This particular light is currently acting as your backlight, creating a very subtle rim light effect around the edge of the ball.
- **Front light**: This lights up the ball even more, acting as the key light on the ball. Note that the key light and backlight are across from each other.
- **Ambient Light**: This acts as the fill light in your scene by filling the whole scene with light, especially filling those dark shadowed areas with some light.

Build and run and see the fruits of your labor. :]

Well done, just look at how nice and shiny that ball is! Things are certainly starting to shape up.

Where to go from here?

You just finished yet another chapter. Good job! Clearly there's no stopping you. :]

You've learned quite a mouthful; let's take a moment to recap:

- **Surface normal**: You now know how the surface normal plays its part in light calculations.
- **Sphere node**: You know more about spheres in Scene Kit, and how you can adjust the size of a sphere by adjusting its radius.
- **Lights**: You've learned about all the different types of light sources Scene Kit has to offer. You've also now seen omni lights and ambient lights in action by adding them to you scene.
- **Three point lighting**: As an added bonus, you've also learned about a very cool lighting technique that makes your 3D scenes look more realistic.

> **Note**: You can find the final project for this chapter under the **projects/final/Breaker/** folder.

Chapter 9: Primitives

Chris Language

Your game is making great progress so far. There's a very shiny floor with cameras, lights and even a ball. However, there's still plenty of components missing before it comes close to resembling *Breakout*.

Rest assured, by the end of this chapter you'll have a game because the main focus will be adding walls, bricks and a paddle to the game. But you're not going to take the quick and easy way out here; no, you'll create each component from scratch by using primitive shapes, right in the awesome Scene Kit scene editor.

> **Note**: You can find the starter project for this chapter under the **projects/starter/Breaker/** folder.

Getting started

As you know by now, Scene Kit comes with a whole bunch of primitive shapes out of the box. Here's a nice little grid of all the shapes you'll find under the Object Library:

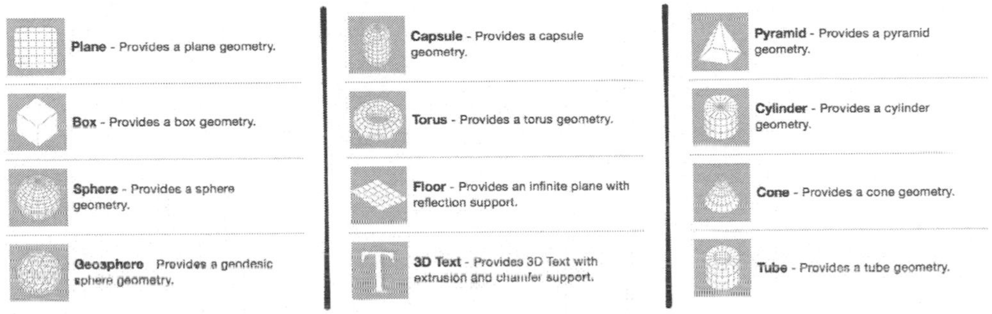

You've encountered a few of these shapes already, and probably found that they're pretty easy to use. Additionally, those pretty little Xcode icons also do a nice job of visually representing them.

The main thing you need to remember is that once you've dragged one of these primitive shapes into your scene, you need to adjust the shape node's properties in the Attributes Inspector.

Stop for just a second and let your imagination run wild and free. Think of all the marvelous creatures you'll be able to create with these basic shapes.

Believe it or not, this little guy comprises only spheres and cones, and was created right inside of Xcode using the Scene Kit designer:

> **Note**: If you're brave enough, go take a closer look at this spider under the **projects/resources/Spider/** folder. Double click the **Spider.scn** file to open it up in **Preview** or **Xcode**.

Just look at the handsome little primitive spider with its shiny, little, beady-red eyes staring right at you. Don't you just love these harmless looking little critters? :]

For your game, you'll make use of the box shape to create the top and bottom barriers as well as the bricks that will be smashed to bits. The cylinder shape will be what you use to make side barriers and the paddle.

Build barriers

In real life, too many barriers can be a bad thing, but in a game, you need plenty of them to make gameplay fun and fair. For instance, think about what would happen in your game, once the ball starts moving.

Right now, there's nothing to stop it – not even resistance – so you could gently tap the ball and send it flying off the screen into a parallel universe; it's an outcome that's exciting for the purposes of discussing theoretical physics, but it sure makes for some lame gameplay.

To stop it from flying off into Neverland, you need barriers! :]

Create a barriers group

You'll make the top and bottom barriers from box nodes.

The first thing you need to do is open up your project and select **Game.scn**. In the Scene Kit editor, use the **+** button on the toolbar create an empty node, and then rename it to **Barriers**.

This will be your group node that contains all the barriers you'll add:

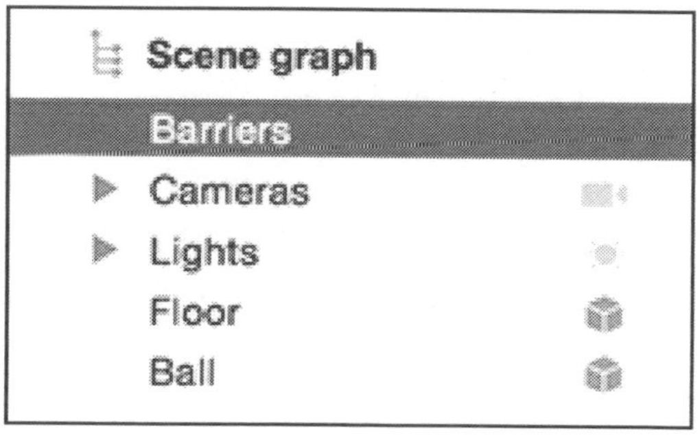

Add the top barrier

From the Object Library, drag and drop a **Box** into your scene:

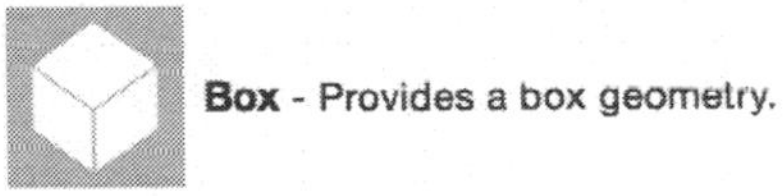

Under the scene graph, drag the new box node into your **Barriers** group node. Next, open the Node Inspector, name this node **Top**, and then set its position to `(x:0, y:0, z:-10.5)`:

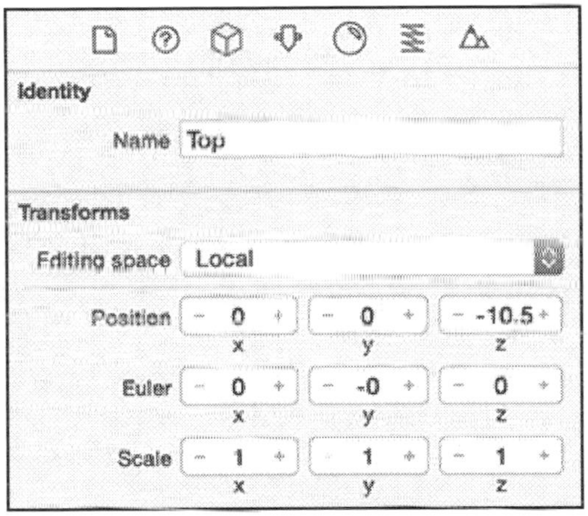

Open the Attributes Inspector and set **Size** to `(width:13, height:2, length:1)`, and then adjust the **Chamfer radius** to `0.3`:

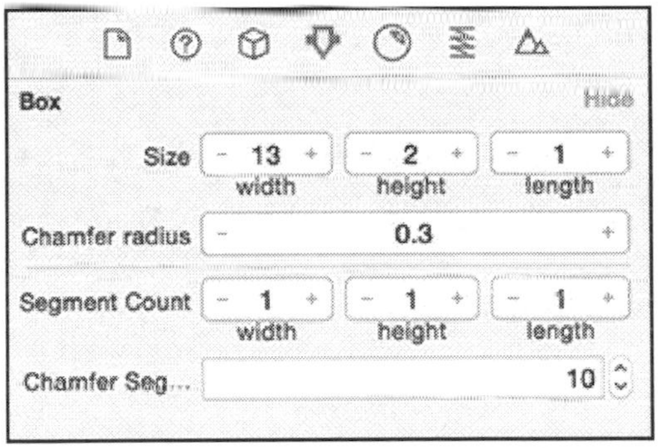

While the width, height and length attributes determine the size of the box, the *Chamfer radius* controls edge and corner rounding on the box.

Next, change the color of the barrier so it isn't just a white box. Bring up the Material Inspector, change the **Diffuse** to a dark gray color by setting the **Hex Color #** to **333333**, and change the **Specular** color to **White**.

You should have something like this:

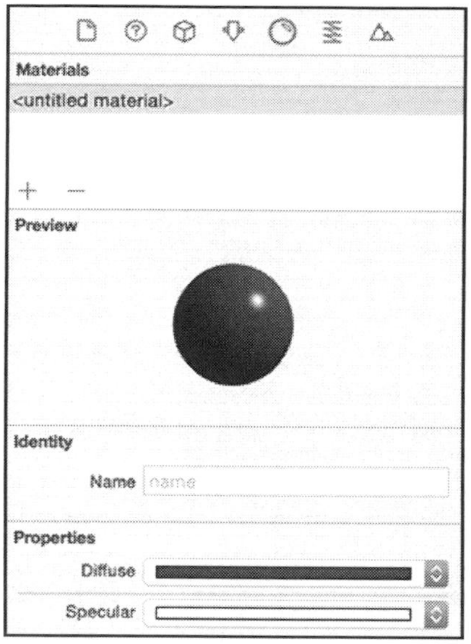

Copy the bottom barrier

The next part involves some trickery, because rather than create another barrier from scratch for the bottom barrier, you'll simply make a copy of the top barrier.

It's a good trick of the trade, so it's worth your time to learn it.

To copy nodes in the Scene Kit editor, you simply drag from the node you want to copy while pressing the Option key.

So, create a copy of **Top** and select it in the editor. While pressing the Option key, click and drag the blue-axis downwards:

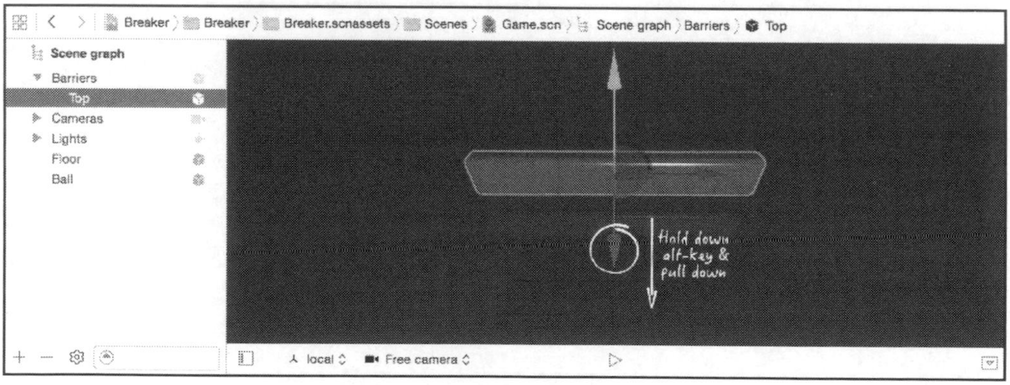

Excellent, now you hace a new copy of the **Top** barrier. Fix it up by renaming the copied node to **Bottom** and drag it under the **Barriers** group:

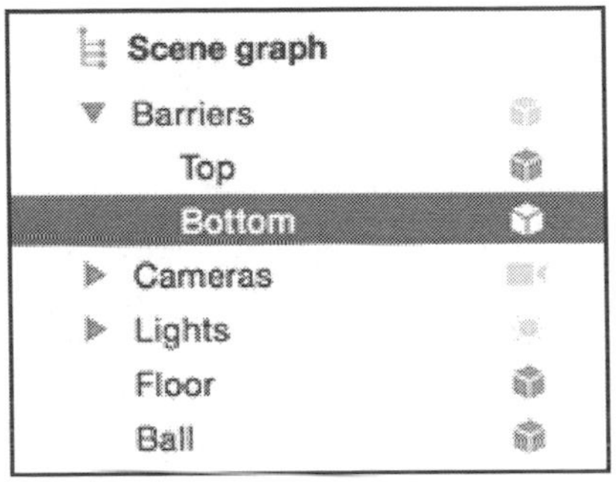

Reposition that bottom barrier so it's in the right place. Open the Node Inspector and change **Position** to `(x:0, y:0, z:10.5)`:

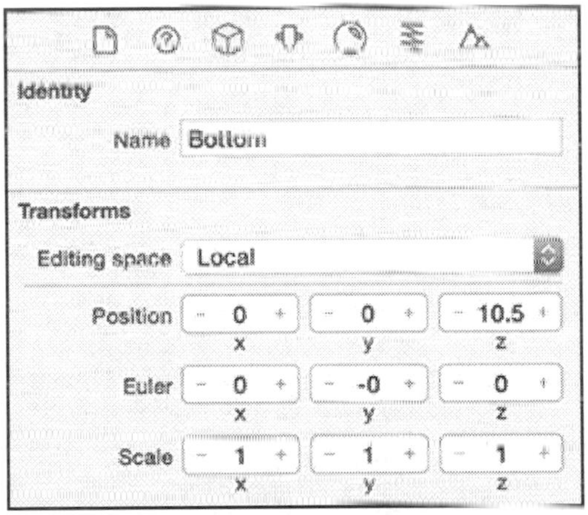

The final result should look like this:

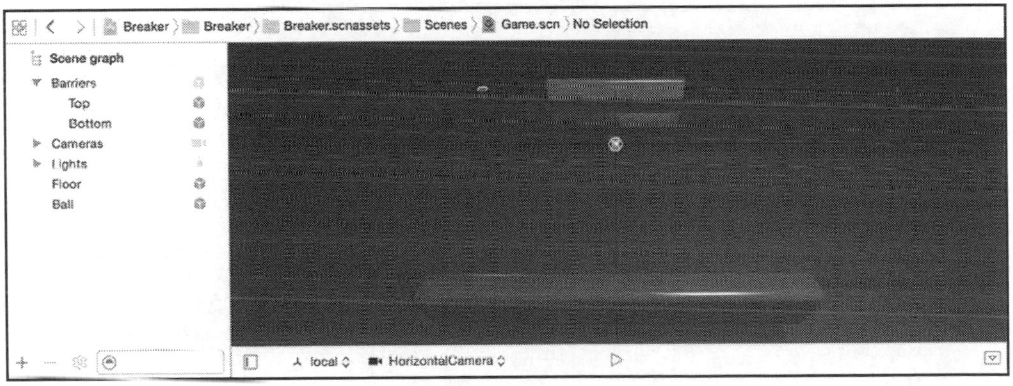

Most importantly, take note of the final scene graph tree structure and how the Barriers group contains both the top and bottom barriers.

Create a left barrier group

Now that you have a top and bottom barrier, you need barriers for the left and right sides of the game. You're going to construct each side barrier with two long cylinders stacked atop one another, and the cylinders for each barrier will be grouped together so that you end up with a **Barriers/Left** group and a **Barriers/Right** group.

You're going to start off with the left barrier first, so highlight your **Barriers** group node and press the **+** button on the toolbar. Rename this new node to **Left**:

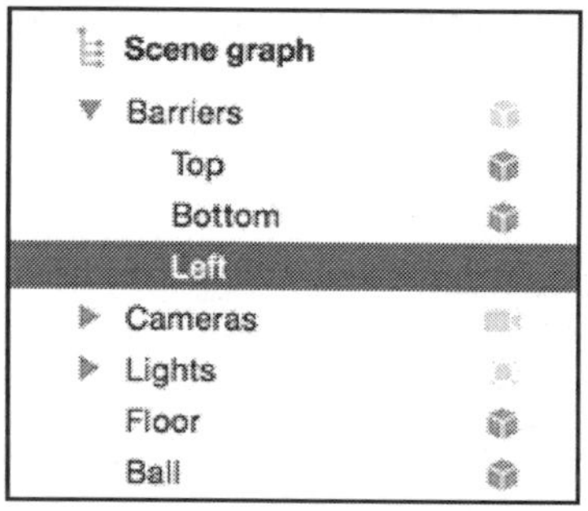

Next, you're going to change the position of this group node. The reason is that because all nodes are positioned relative to their parents. By adjusting the position of the left group node, any child nodes you're adding to the group will get an offset applied to their positions.

With the **Barriers/Left** node still selected, select the Node Inspector and change the **Position** to `(x:-6, y:0, z:0)`:

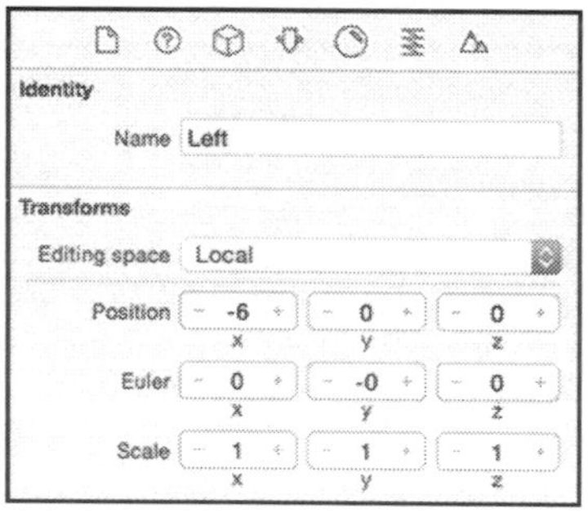

Add the left side top barrier

Here's where you actually get to create the side barrier. Drag and drop a **Cylinder** from the Object Library into your scene:

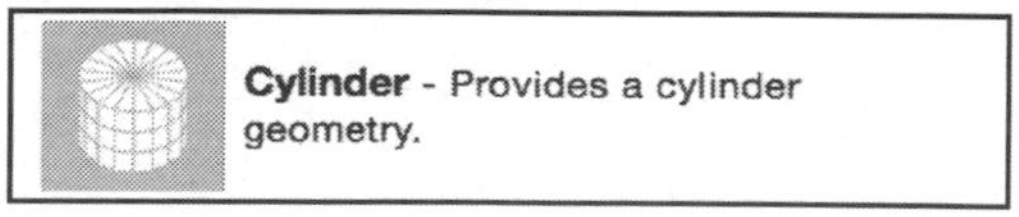

Rename this node to **Top** and fix its position in the scene graph by dragging it under the **Barriers/Left** group node:

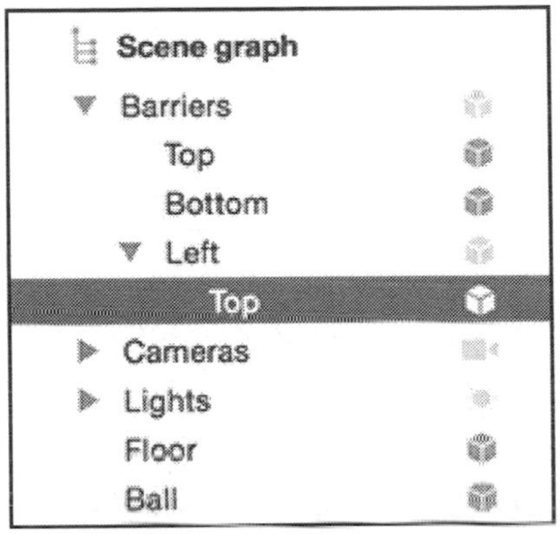

Note: Because a node's position, rotation and scale are relative to its parent, rearranging the scene graph means the Scene Kit editor will automatically recalculate the node's properties to maintain the editor's visuals. This can be both a blessing and a curse, so just be aware of this feature.

Place the node in the right location by going to the Node Inspector and setting its **Position** to `(x:0, y:0.5, z:0)` and **Euler** to `(x:90, y:0, z:0)`:

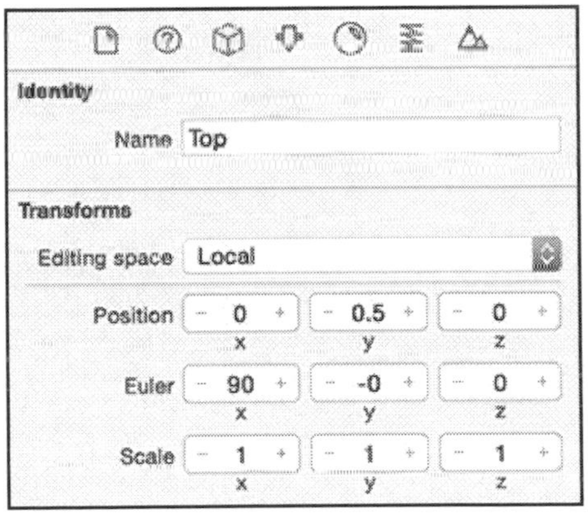

Note: The cylinder node is positioned to the left because it is relative to its parent group node, which has a position of `(x:-6, y:0, z:0)`.

Stretch the cylinder to the correct length and thickness by opening up the Attributes Inspector and setting its **Radius** to **0.3** and **Height** to **22.5**:

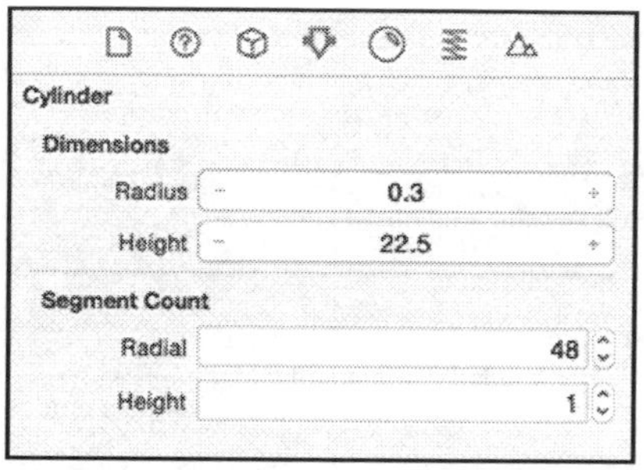

Finally, give the node some color by going to the Material Inspector. Change the **Diffuse** to use a **Hex Color #** of **B3B3B3** which corresponds to a light gray color, and the **Specular** to **White**:

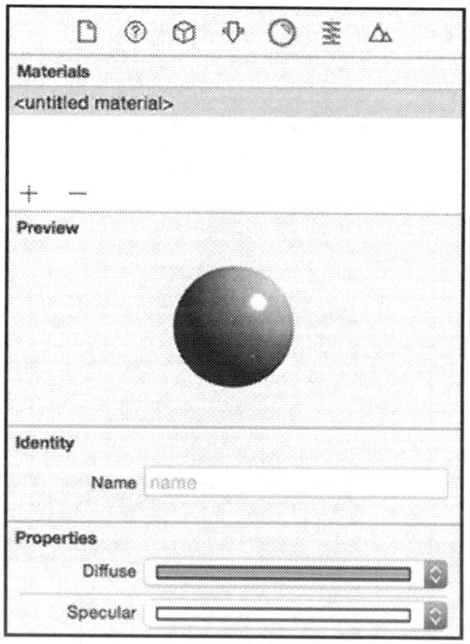

Add the left side bottom barrier

Now that you've got the top left bar of the barrier sorted out, the easiest way to create the bottom bar is to make a copy of it.

Select the **Barrier/Left/Top** node and you should see a little 3D axis on it:

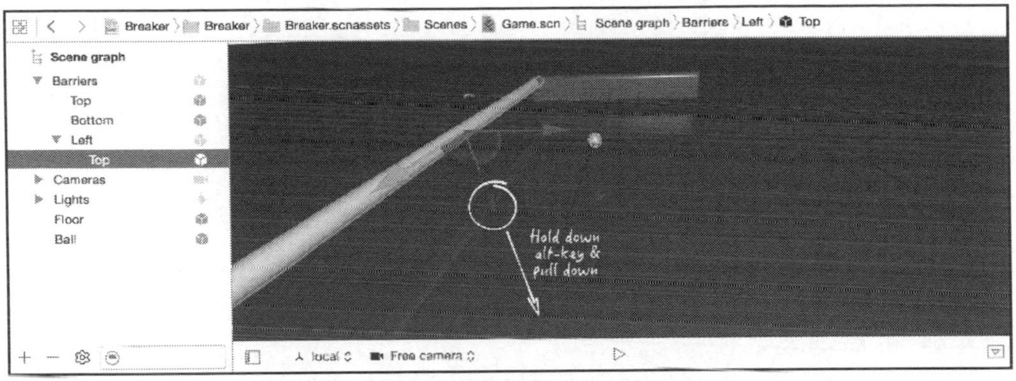

Press and hold the Option key, and then click-drag the blue axis downwards. Once you're done, just let go to create a copy of the bar.

This new copy should be located at the bottom of the scene graph, but that's not where you want it. Move it under the **Barriers/Left** group. Remember to rename it to **Bottom** as well:

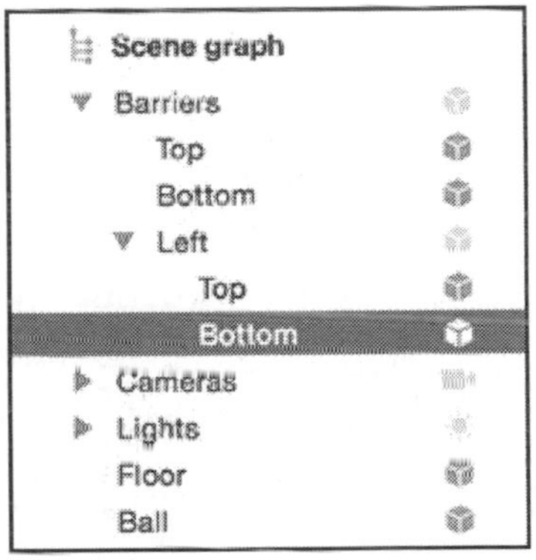

Go into the Node Inspector and adjust **Position** to `(x:0, y:-0.5, z:0)`:

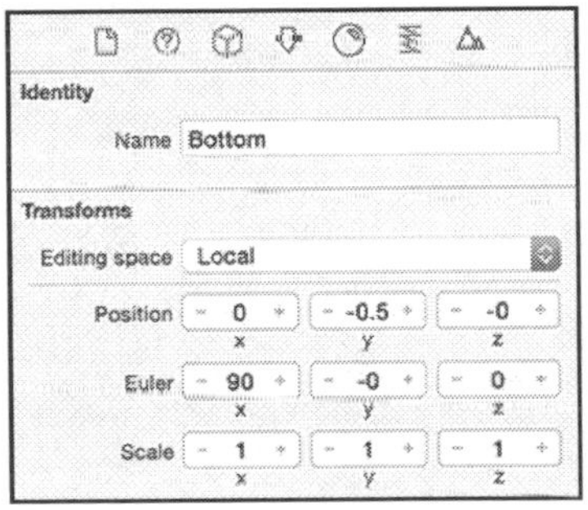

Your final result should look something like this:

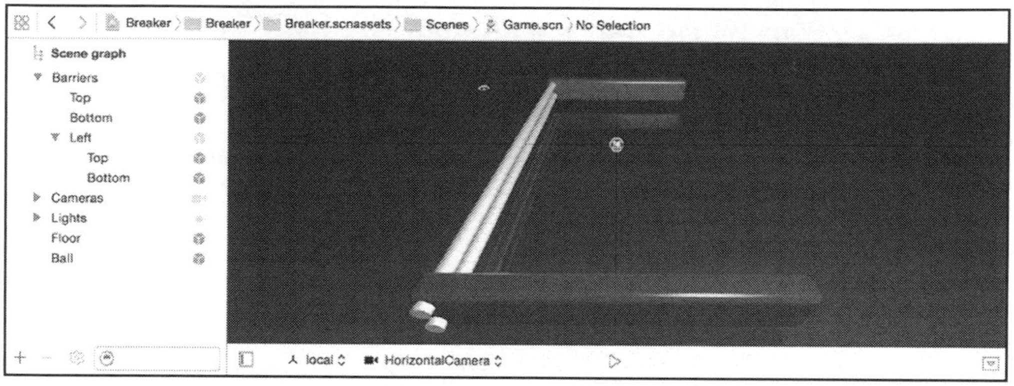

Again, take note of the scene graph and the node tree structure.

Add right side barrier

Look at that left side barrier in its completed state. Looks pretty nice, right? You did quite a bit of work, and it would be a shame to trudge through all that agin.

Good thing you have the ability to copy it all – you've got better things to do than repeat all those steps, like finishing this chapter and having a beer.

What's a little different about copying things this time is that you want to copy the entire group rather than just a single node. So, make sure you select the **Barriers/Left** group in the scene graph:

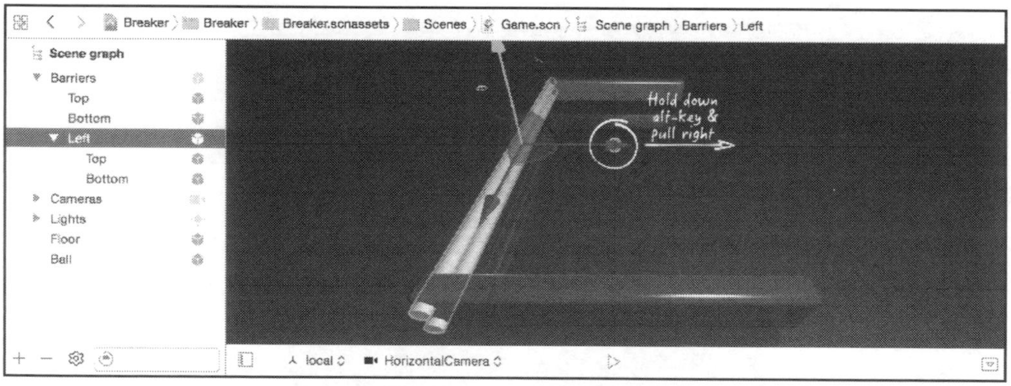

This time, try and do a snap to move and copy, which you do by pressing the Command and Option keys then click-dragging the red axis right. As you drag it to the right, you'll notice how the position snaps to the grid layout.

See if you can place it at position `(x:6, y:0, z:0)`, and with that, you just created a new copy of the left barrier.

Note: When holding down the Command key while dragging, Scene Kit not only snaps the node to the grid, it also snaps to nearby nodes. This useful feature speeds up level design, and it quite possibly makes life in general easier.

Now, rename the group to **Right** and rearrange the scene graph so that the node is a child of the **Barriers** group:

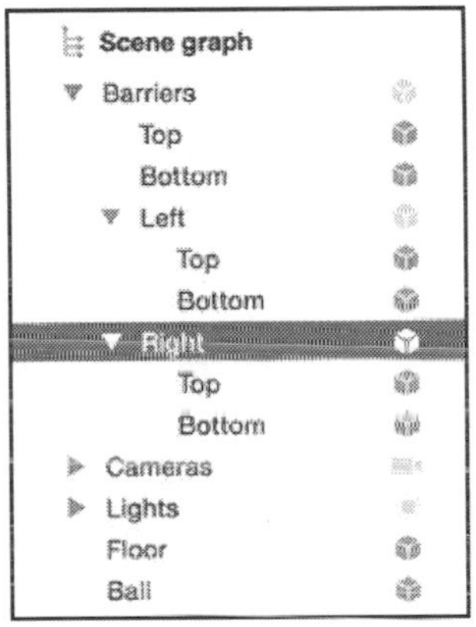

Just to double-check the position, select the Node Inspector, and make sure **Position** is set to `(x:6, y:0 z:0)`:

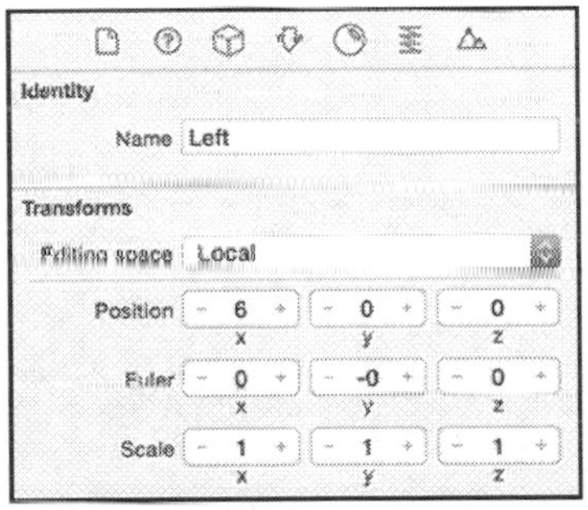

You should end up with the following result:

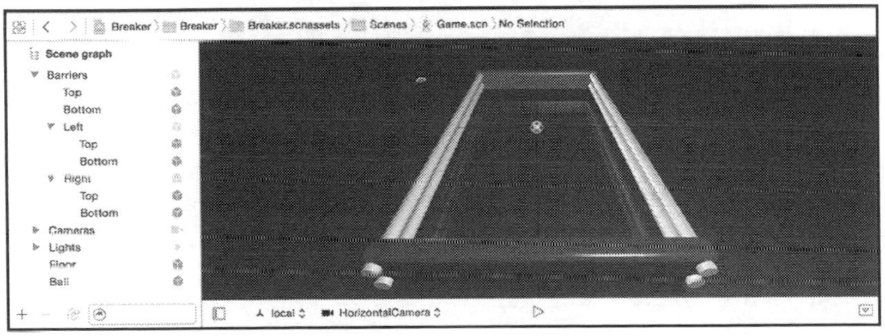

Great job, you're like real-life Bob the Builder! :]

Now is the perfect time to do a quick build and run to see those awesome barriers. Your game should look like this:

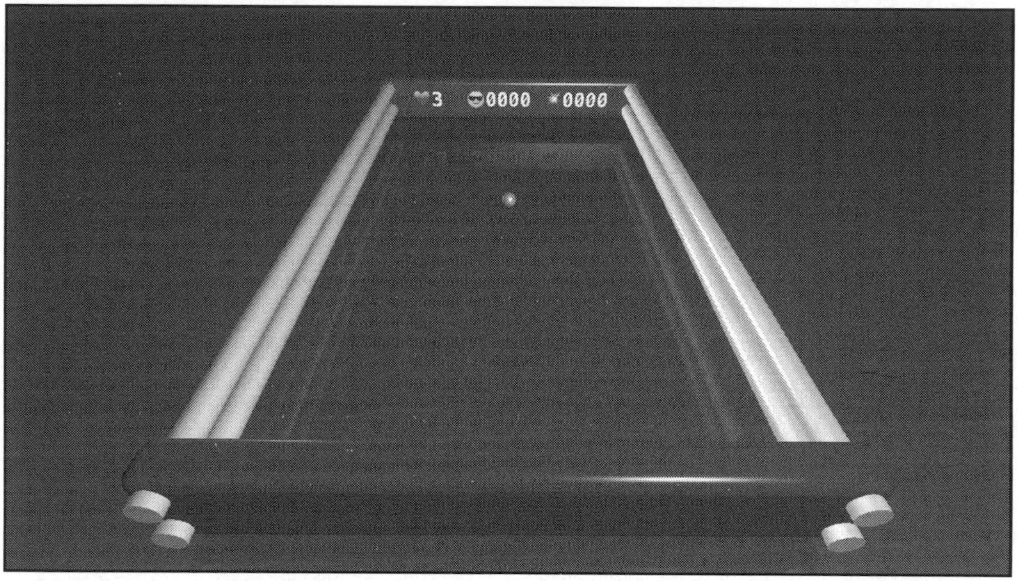

Oh, so pretty and shiny! :]

To top it off, you created all of that by using built-in primitive shapes. However, you're not there just yet. You're missing the bricks you'll bust up and the paddle that controls the ball.

Build the paddle

This game is no fun without some means of destruction. Although the paddle is only one part of the "weaponry", it's essential, and at this point, missing entirely.

Time to change that.

Create the paddle group

Once again, you'll use cylinder shapes – no surprise there, I hope. The first thing you need to do is create an empty node called **Paddle**, which will be your group node for all the paddle's components.

Use the + button in the toolbar and rename the node accordingly:

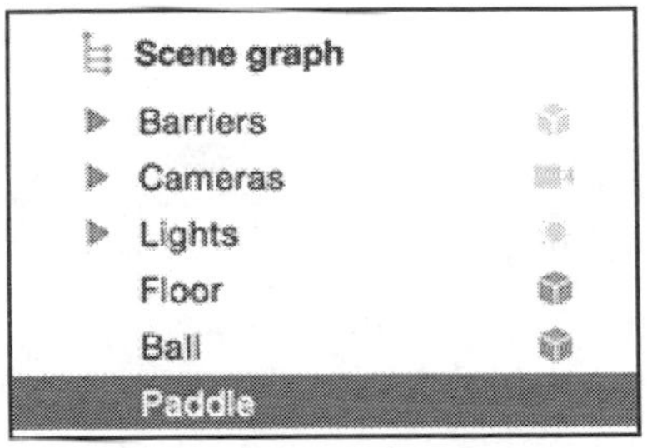

Now set the paddle group's position, so that all of its children are placed relative to that group's location. Open the Node Inspector and set **Position** to `(x:0, y:0, z:8)`:

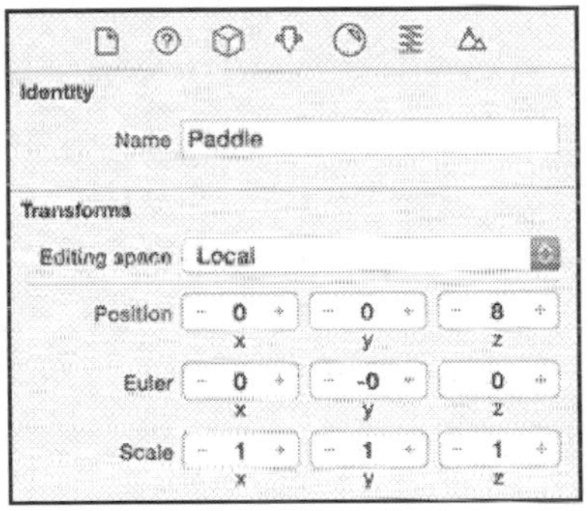

Create the center of the paddle

It's time to build the actual paddle. Start by creating the center part by dragging and dropping a cylinder shape into your scene.

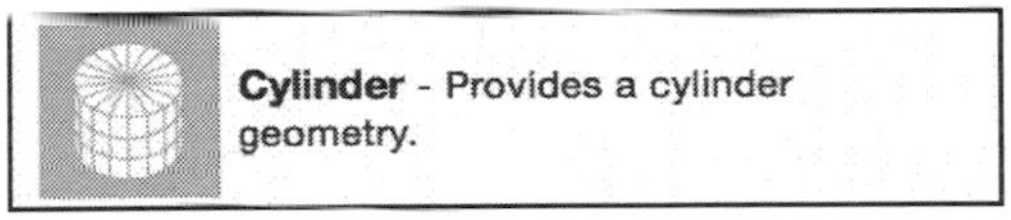

First, rename it to **Center** and sort out its position under the scene graph by dragging it under the **Paddle** group node:

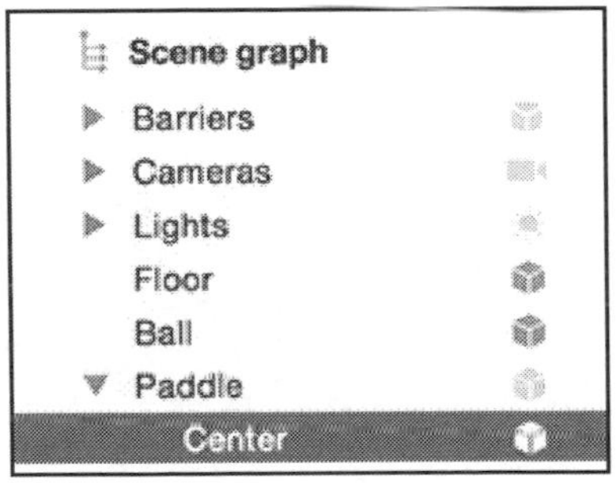

Next, select the Node Inspector and zero out the **x**, **y** and **z** components of the **Position**. Change **Euler** so that it is set to `(x:0, y:0, z:90)`, which will rotate it 90 degrees on the z-axis:

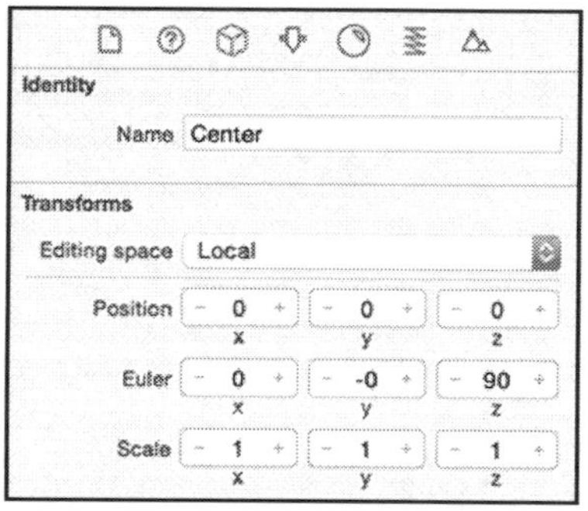

Fix up the size by going to the Attributes Inspector and changing **Radius** to **0.25** and **Height** to **1.5**:

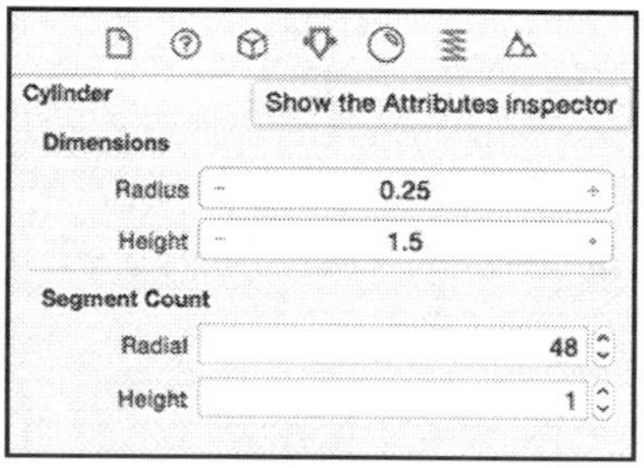

Finally, select the Material Inspector and give this cylinder some color by setting **Diffuse** to a **Hex Color #** of **333333** and **Specular** to **White**:

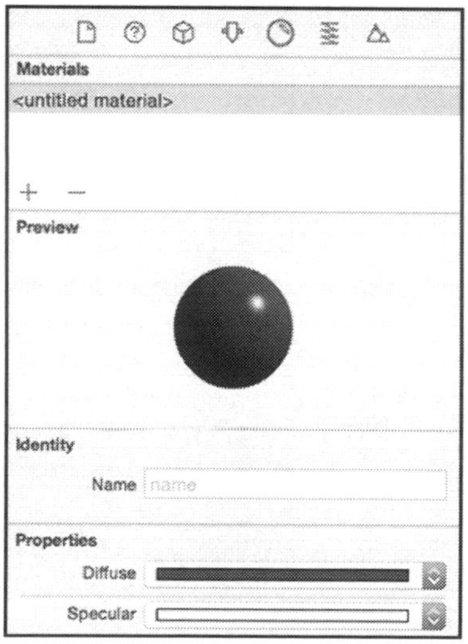

Create the left edge of the paddle

To create the left edge of the paddle, drag and drop a new cylinder shape into your scene. You know the drill by now; name this new node **Left** and drag it under the **Paddle** group node:

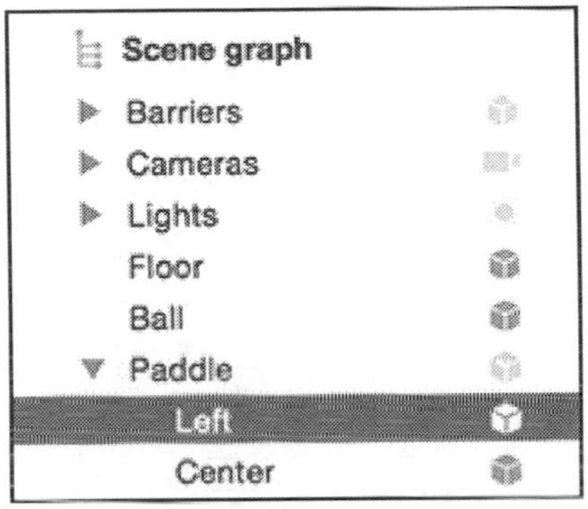

Adjust **Position** to `(x:-1, y:0, z:0)` and **Euler** to `(x:0, y:0, z:90)` to rotate it 90 degrees on the z axis:

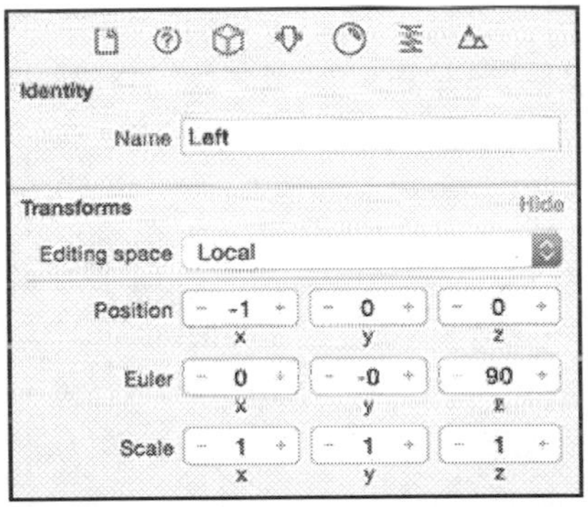

Open the Attributes Inspector and set **Radius** to **0.25** and **Height** to **0.5**:

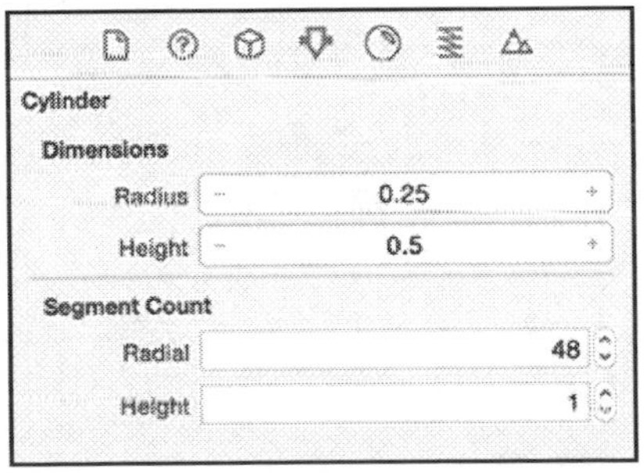

Finally, select the Material Inspector give it a **Diffuse** color using **666666** as the **Hex Color #** and a **Specular** color of **White**:

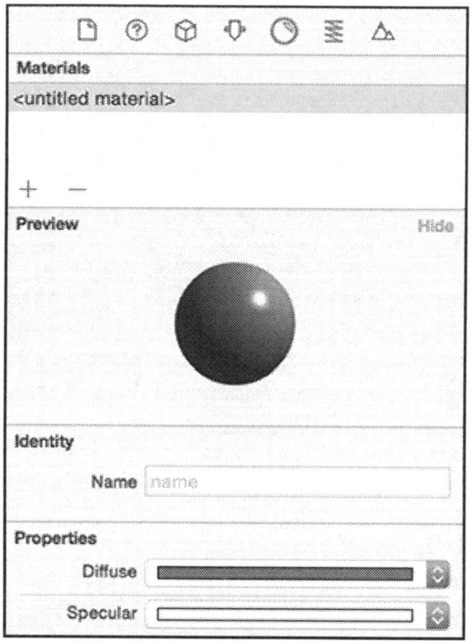

Copy the right edge of the paddle

To create the right edge you can simply copy the left edge of the paddle. Just like before, highlight the **Paddle/Left** node, hold down the Command and Option keys, and drag the green-axis to the right:

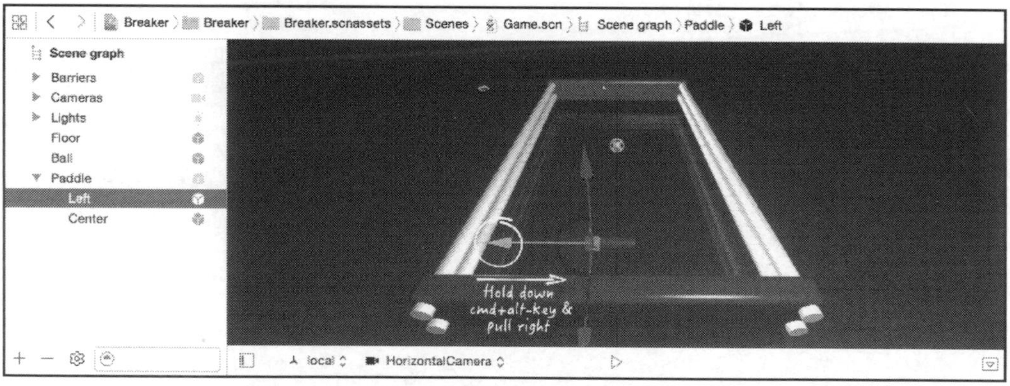

As you move it take note of how the paddle piece snaps to different parts of the center node. See if you can place it at position `(x:1, y:0, z:8)`. If not, you can always go adjust it in the Node Inspector.

Excellent, now that you have a copy the **Left** paddle edge, rename this node to **Right** and rearrange it in the scene graph (which will update its position to be relative to its parent; i.e. `(x:1, y:0, z:0)`).

You should now have the following:

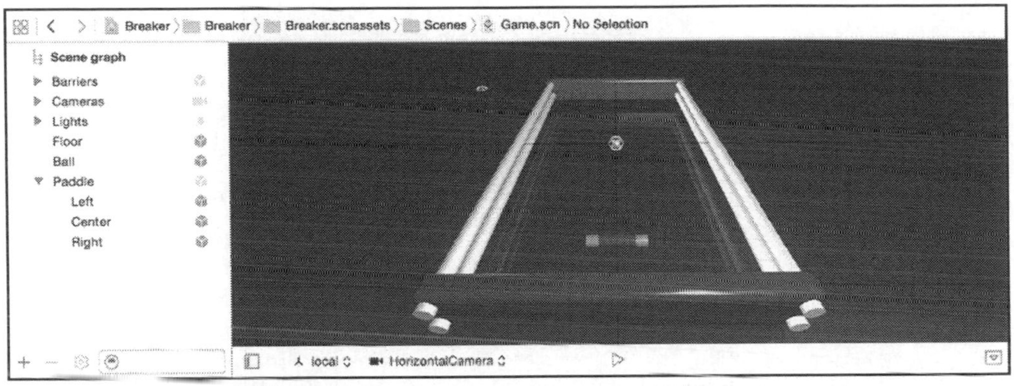

Again, take note of the **Paddle** group and the structure of the nodes within.

Bind to the paddle

So you have a paddle but no way of moving it. That's going to make for some pretty atrocious game play.

The next step is to add some code that will bind to the paddle so you'll be able to control it later on.

Open **GameViewController.swift** and add the following property to `GameViewController` class:

```
var paddleNode: SCNNode!
```

Then bind the paddle in the scene to this property by adding the following line of code to the end of `setupNodes()`:

```
paddleNode =
  scnScene.rootNode.childNodeWithName("Paddle", recursively:
true)!
```

This will bind `paddleNode` to the actual paddle group node in Game.scn.

> **Note**: You can find the final project, including this most recent section, under the **projects/final/Breaker/** folder.

Challenge

Let's take a look at the checklist for your game so far:

- Barriers ✓
- Paddle ✓
- Ball ✓
- Bricks ✗

Of course, to complete your game, you still need something to destroy! :]

This time around, it's going to be a little challenge for you. With all the experience and knowledge you've gained so far – such as how to create groups, shapes and how to set their respective properties – see if you can build the bricks for your game without detailed instructions.

Here are some pointers:

- First create a group node called **Bricks**, and place all your bricks under this group.
- Position the **Bricks** group at position `(x:0, y:0, z:-3.0)`.
- For each brick, use a **Box** with a size of `(width:1, height:0.5, length: 0.5)` and a **Chamfer Radius** of `0.05`.
- Start off by creating a single column of all the various colored bricks using white (#FFFFFF), red (#FF0000), yellow (#FFFF00), blue (#0000FF), purple (#8000FF), and green (#00FF80):

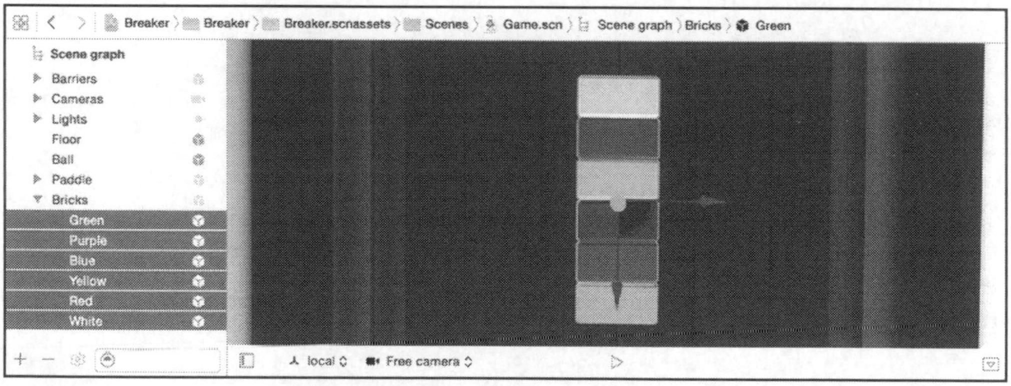

- To help you with positioning, I'll tell you that the white brick should be at position `(x:0, y:0, z:-2.5)`, while the green brick should be at position `(x:0, y:0, z: 0)`.
- Name the bricks according to their color.

- Use the copy techniques learned. (Press the Option key to copy and the Command key to snap.)
- When making copies, remember to use the **Unshare** button when you make color changes to the copied versions under the Material Inspector, so that you don't end up changing the color of the original.
- Once you have one column, use the copy technique to fill up the area from the left to right barrier.

The final result should look like this:

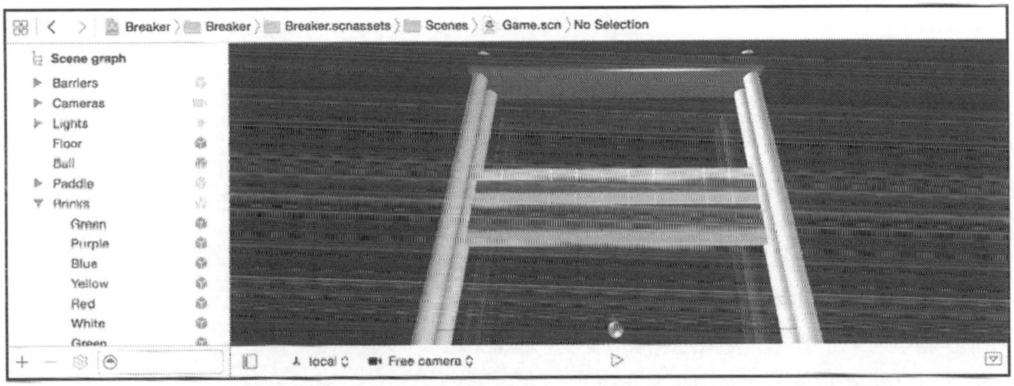

Build and run and see the entire scene all done:

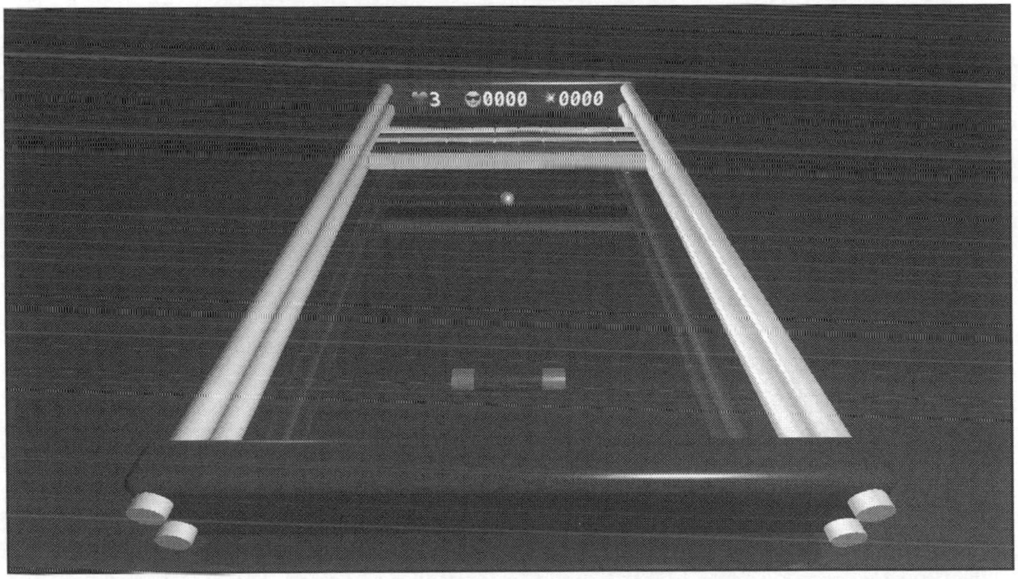

Where to go from here?

Fantastic, you just took your game from barely done to mostly ready.

More importantly, you're a whole lot smarter. Let's recap what you've learned so far:

- **Primitive shapes**: You built an entire scene out of primitive shapes.
- **Practical experience**: You gained valuable practical experience. You built and maintained the scene graph tree structure while keeping all the nodes neat and organized. You learned how to save yourself countless hours by copying nodes. You've also worked with lots of objects together in one scene, and you survived the ordeal! :]

> **Note**: You can find the complete project for this chapter, including the challenge section, under the **projects/challenge/Breaker/** folder.

Chapter 10: Basic Collision Detection

Chris Language

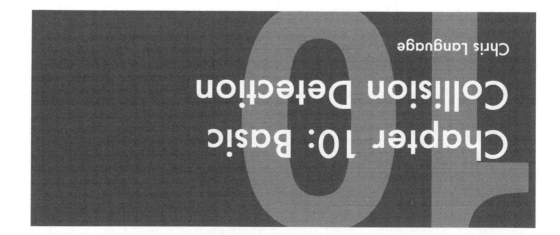

Your game is not quite done yet; there are still a few things standing between you and being a legend in the gaming world:

1. **Physics**: Without any physics for basic collision detection, the ball has no concept of barriers, bricks and paddles. Adding physics to the mix lets that ball detect and collide objects in its path as it bounces about.
2. **A way to move the paddle around**: Without control, you've got no game! You'll add a simple touch control to solve this and learn how to make the camera track the paddle as it moves around, giving the game a very cool 3D feel. :]

By the time you've found the end of this chapter, most loose ends will be neatly tied and you'll be the proud designer of another playable, fun game.

> **Note**: You'll find the starter project for this chapter under the **projects/starter/Breaker/** folder, it continues with the previous chapter's challenge completed.

Add physics

The first step is to add physics for basic collision detection with the game: for the ball, barriers, bricks, and paddle. Let's start with the ball.

Add physics for the ball

A ball without bounce is like a kitten without attitude, so you need to add some physics so the ball behaves as you'd expect. Open up **Game.scn** and select the **Ball**. This time,

open up the **Physics Inspector**, which is denoted by the little spring icon and located to the right of the Material Inspector.

By default, any nodes you add to the scene will be devoid of physics, but adjusting the **Type** of the **Physics Body** to **Dynamic** will bring up a list of settings:

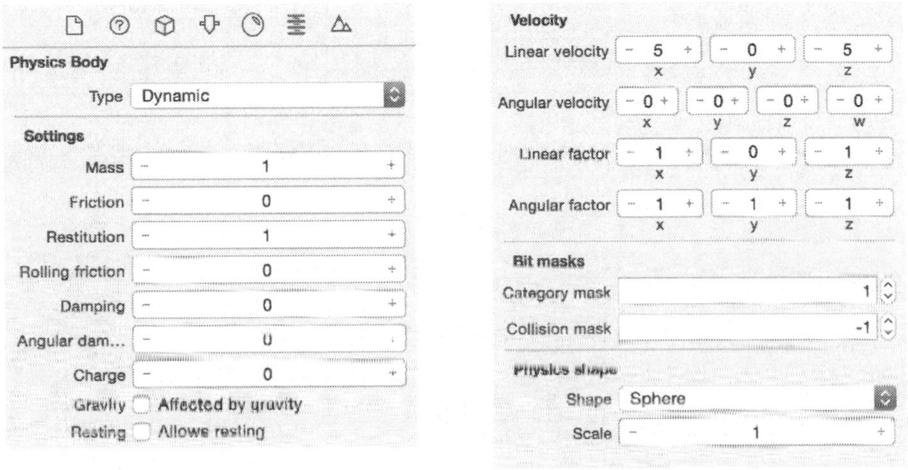

Let's go through each category's properties and how you should set them up:

- **Physics Body**: determines the type of body. Set the ball's **Type** to a **Dynamic** body, which means that the Scene Kit physics engine will take full control over the ball's movement.
- **Settings**: allows you to fine tune the behavior of the physics body. For the ball, set both **Mass** and **Restitution** to **1**. Zero out all the other physics settings, and uncheck both **Affected by gravity** and **Allows resting**. This will set the ball to bounce freely without constraint from gravity.
- **Velocity**: affects the speed and direction of the physics body. Give the ball a **Linear velocity** of `(x:5, y:0, z:5)`. This will give the ball an initial force once the scene starts running. Set the **Linear factor** to `(x:1, y:0, z:1)` which will zero out any physics forces that might be applied to the ball in the y-axis, thus keeping the ball fixed on in the same y position no matter what.
- **Bit Masks**: used to set up collisions later. Set the **Category mask** to **1**. This assigns a bitmask value of 1 to the ball. This mask is used to create collision groups and uniquely identify certain nodes. The physics engine then uses this information to then apply collision calculations based on these masks to determine which objects collides and which ones don't.
- **Physics Shape**: defines the actual shape of the physics body that will be used during collision detections. Set the **Shape** to **Sphere**.

Note: At the time of writing this chapter, there appear to be a few bugs in the Scene Kit Editor relating to physics. Sometimes, when you re-position a node with attached physics, the physics wireframe gets left behind due to some refresh issue. If you run into this problem, the best way around it is to make sure that all your work is saved, then restart Xcode.

Add physics for the barriers

Your barriers are already there and functional, but they're rather static, stiff and antiquated. They'll look out of place once the ball and paddle are finished.

To configure the physics properties for the barriers, you're going to make use of a very cool feature of the Scene Kit editor. Instead of setting up each object individually, you can select multiple nodes and configure them all in one fell swoop.

To select all four parts of the barrier at once, there are two different techniques:

1. Hold down the Command key while clicking each node individually in the scene graph, allowing you to select the desired nodes, one by one.
2. Select a range of nodes in the scene graph at once. Select the **Top** node first, press and hold the Shift key, and then click the **Right** group node; it will also highlight everything between the two nodes you select.

Whichever method you choose, your goal is to select every part of the barrier:

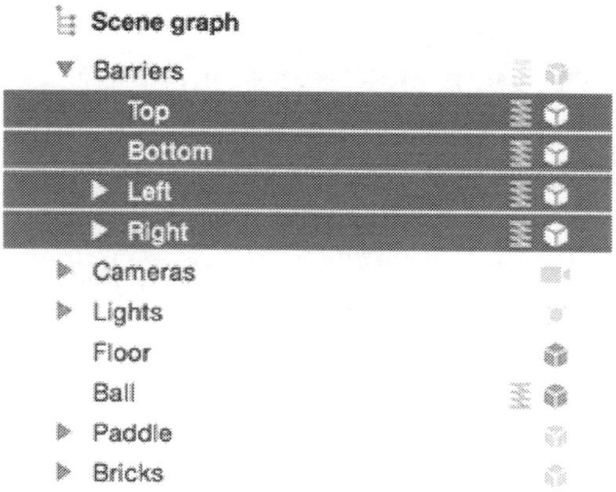

Now, with all the parts still highlighted, open the Physics Inspector. Under the **Physics Body** section, change the **Type** to **Static**, and then this list of settings will show up:

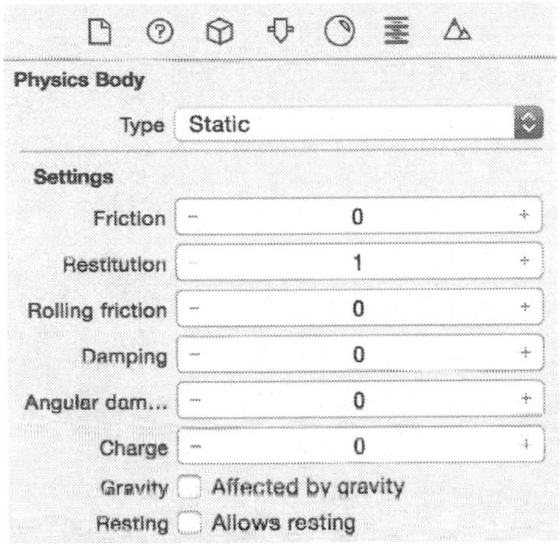

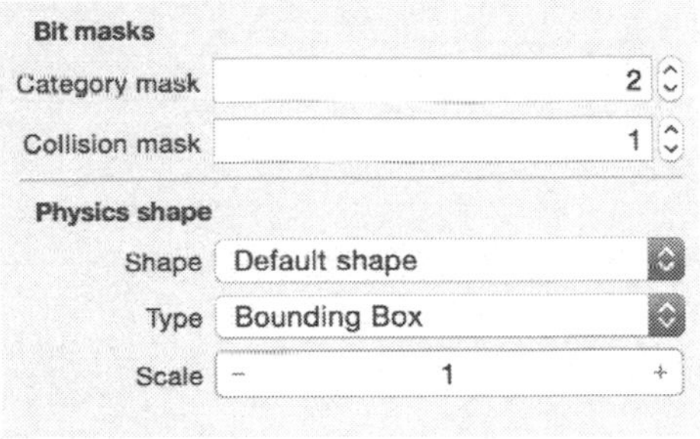

It's broken out into lists, and here's what to do with each part and why you're choosing each setting:

- **Physics Body**: For the **Type**, set it as a **Static** body so the barriers will not move, nor will you move them around with any actions.
- **Settings**: Zero out all the settings and set **Restitution** to **1**, making it so that no energy is lost when collisions happen. Uncheck both checkboxes so the barriers aren't influenced by gravity either.
- **Bit masks**: Set **Category mask** to **2** and **Collision mask** to **1**. This gives the barriers a category bitmask of 2 and sets them to collide with objects that have a category bitmask of 1 – the same category bitmask you gave to the ball.
- **Physics Shape**: Set **Shape** to **Default shape**, and **Type** to **Bounding Box**. Because the two side barriers are nodes with children, this option is more fitting because a bounding box creates a boundary around all the child nodes within the group. If you look at the scene editor, you'll find that there's a red wireframe that shows you how the physics body will look when you run the game.

Do something fun here and press the little play button on the toolbar:

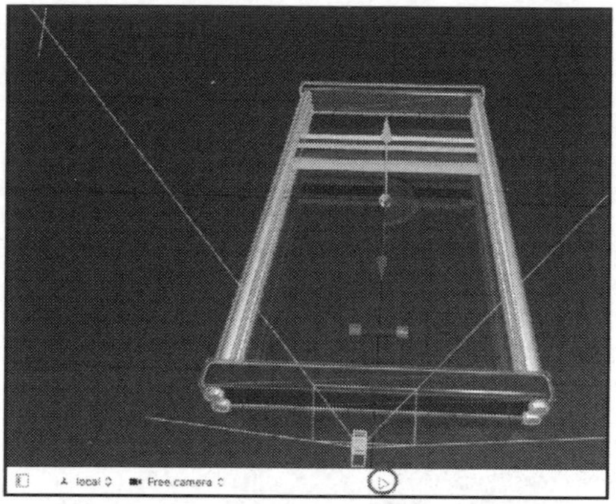

You should see the ball bounce like crazy off all four barriers. Sweet! :]

Here you have a quick simulation of your game's physics. Talk about a handy tool! You're testing out your physics without the hassle of building and running. Stop the animation by pressing the stop button on the toolbar.

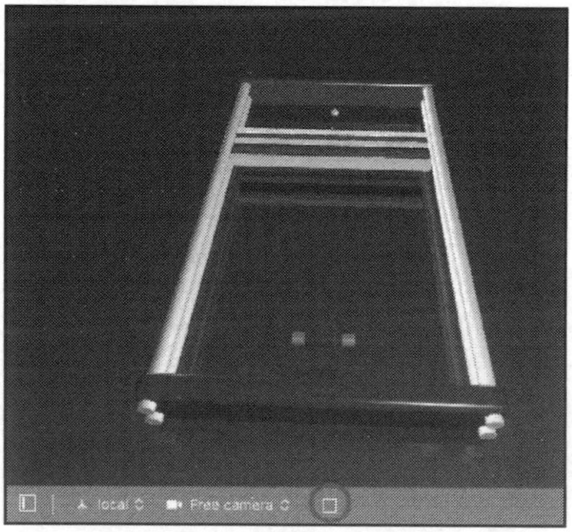

Note: While you could have selected the **Barriers** group itself and applied physics to the entire group, it wouldn't have been the most logical approach. See, it's not the group that has a physics body, rather, it's the fact that you want to apply physics to each section of the barrier.

Add physics for the bricks

Right now each brick is just another boring brick in a wall. If you don't give them some physics, how can you have any collisions?

To configure the physics properties for the bricks, select all the bricks under the scene graph tree.

Use the Shift key technique to select a range by pressing and holding the key, clicking the first brick then selecting the last brick. It sure beats having to click on every single brick node like you would if you used the Command key technique!

This is how it should look when you've selected all the bricks:

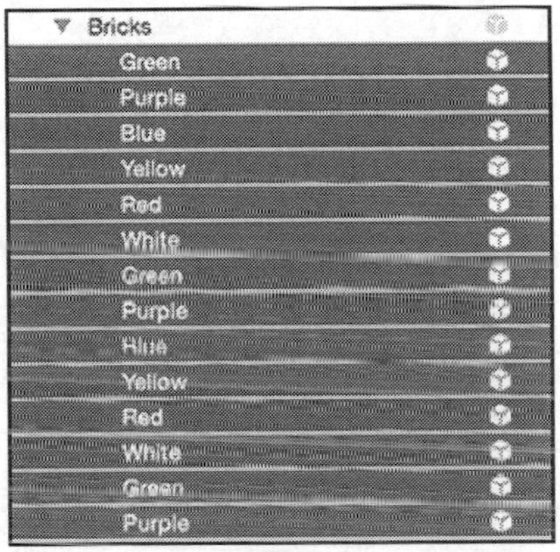

Select the Physics Inspector and change the bricks to be a **Static** body:

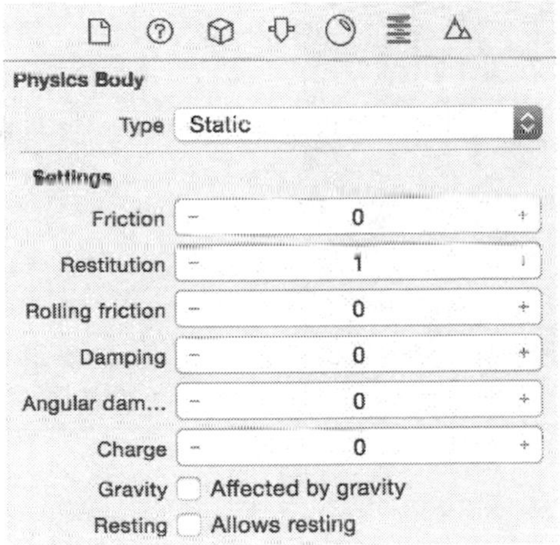

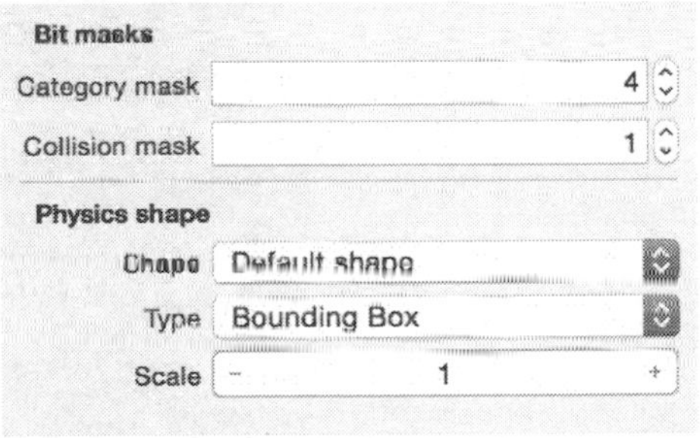

Set the following settings for the bricks:

- **Physics Body**: The bricks are not going to move around and you won't move them with actions, so set the **Type** to **Static**.
- **Settings**: Like you did with the barriers, zero out all the settings and set **Restitution** to **1**. Again, make sure to uncheck the two checkboxes.
- **Bit masks**: This time, set the **Category mask** to **4** and the **Collision mask** to **1**. This

gives the bricks a category bitmask of 4, and makes it so they will collide with objects that have a category mask of 1 – critical because the ball needs to be able to smash bricks.

- **Physics Shape**: Set **Shape** to **Default shape**, and **Type** to **Bounding Box**.

Add physics for the paddle

Now for the last piece of the physics puzzle: the paddle. To configure, start by selecting all the child nodes under the **Paddle** group. You'll configure all three nodes together:

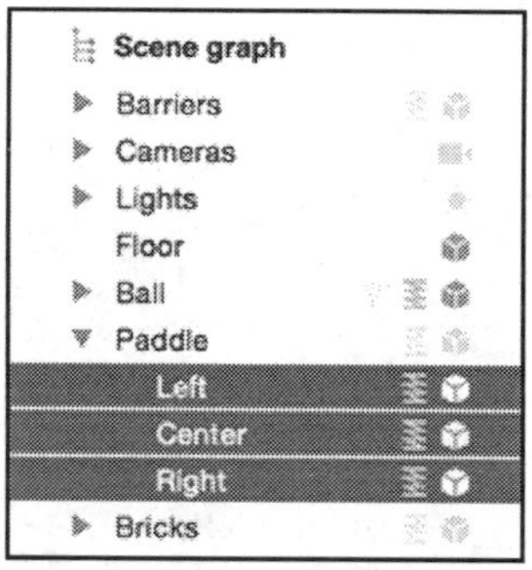

Open the Physics Inspector and adjust the **Type** to **Kinematic**. Oooh, look! Another list of properties to set:

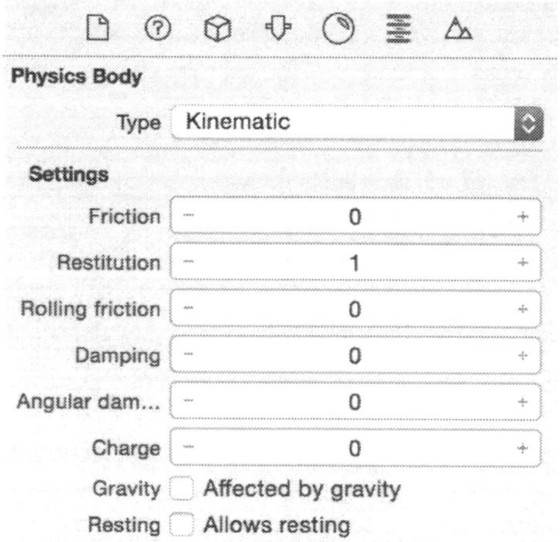

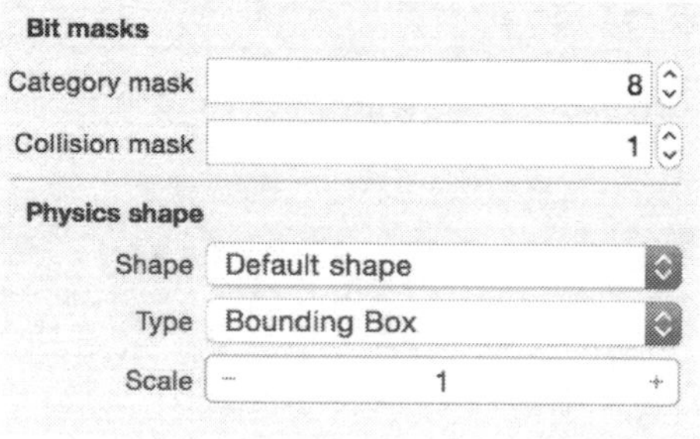

Let's step through the properties you'll need to set for the paddle:

- **Physics Body**: Since the paddle must move around, you set the **Type** to **Kinematic**. This lets the physics engine know that you'll take control of the object's movement, but still allows these nodes to participate in collisions.
- **Settings**: Once again, zero out all the settings, but this time also set **Restitution** to **1**. Make sure to uncheck the checkboxes.

- **Bit masks**: Set the **Category mask** to **8** and the **Collision mask** to **1**. This gives the paddle a category bitmask of 8 and sets it to collide with the ball, which by now you know has a category bitmask of 1.
- **Physics Shape**: Set **Shape** to **Default shape**, and **Type** to **Bounding Box**.

At this point, build and run. You outta be pretty happy with the result:

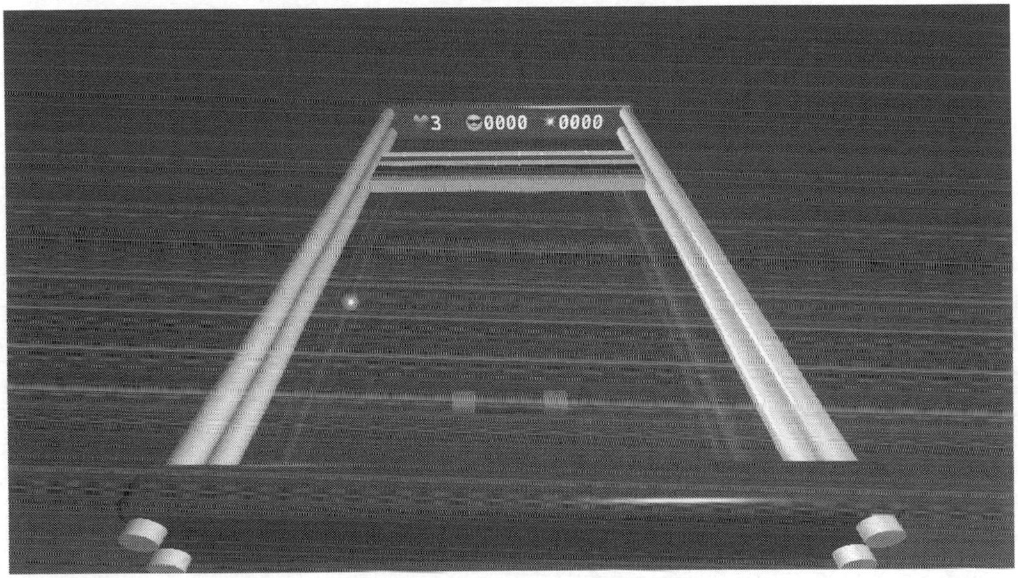

The ball should bounce like crazy off the barriers, bricks and even the paddle.

> **Note**: If performance is slow on the simulator, be sure to run on a physical device instead. Scene Kit apps will often run far slower on the simulator than how it will run on an actual physical device.

Handling collision detection

You're getting closer to applying gameplay logic, but you can't tap into the moments when collisions happen until you've gone through the steps to set up the physics.

So how exactly does one tap into these so-called moments? Meet the **`SCNPhysicsContactDelegate`** protocol! This protocol defines the following methods that you can override to respond to collision events:

- **`physicsWorld(_:didBeginContact:)`**: This method gets called once two physics bodies come into contact with each other.

- **`physicsWorld(_:didUpdateContact:)`**: This method gets triggered after contact has begun and provides additional information about an ongoing collision between two bodies.
- **`physicsWorld(_:didEndContact:)`**: This method gets called once contact between bodies comes to an end.

> **Note**: Each one of these methods will be passed a `SCNPhysicsContact` object that contains the two nodes that are in contact with one another.

Implementing the protocol methods

Before you start implementing the methods in `SCNPhysicsContactDelegate`, you need to set up a helper property to use a bit later.

Open **GameViewController.swift** and add this new property to `GameViewController`:

```
var lastContactNode: SCNNode!
```

You'll use this property to keep track of the last node with which the ball made contact. It's important because there's a little side effect you need to overcome. See, the physics engine will continuously report a collision with the same node if two nodes slide against each other.

Another reason for the property is that although they are still colliding, in *Breaker*, the ball cannot make contact with the same node until it hits another node, so you need it to make sure that you only handle the collision once.

Now that you have this helper set up, it's time to implement the protocol so that you can add gameplay logic for collisions.

Add the following extension to the bottom of **GameViewController.swift**:

```
// 1
extension GameViewController: SCNPhysicsContactDelegate {
  // 2
  func physicsWorld(world: SCNPhysicsWorld,
    didBeginContact contact: SCNPhysicsContact) {
    // 3
    var contactNode: SCNNode!
    if contact.nodeA.name == "Ball" {
      contactNode = contact.nodeB
    } else {
      contactNode = contact.nodeA
    }
    // 4
    if lastContactNode != nil &&
```

```
      lastContactNode == contactNode {
        return
      }
      lastContactNode = contactNode
    }
  }
```

Let's take a closer look at this chunk of code:

1. This extends `GameViewController` to implement `SCNPhysicsContactDelegate`. Pro tip: Using extensions to add protocol conformance is a good way to organize your code.
2. The method you're implementing inside the protocol is `physicsWorld(_:didBeginContact:)`, and it's called when two physics bodies you're interested in start making contact with each other. By default, collisions don't trigger this method, so you'll opt in to it shortly.
3. When this method is called, a `SCNPhysicsContact` is passed to you as a parameter, so you can determine the two nodes that are making contact by accessing `contact.nodeA` and `contact.nodeB`. With Breaker, you know that one of them will be the ball and the other will be a barrier, brick or paddle. This bit of code applies a nifty little trick to filter out which node is which, and once done, `contactNode` end up being the one the ball made contact with.
4. This last bit will also prevent the ball from making contact with the same node more than once per interaction by using `lastContactNode`, which you set up earlier.

Detecting contact with bitmasks

Earlier when you set up the physics properties for the different elements for your game, you put in various numbers for the **Category bitmask**. The values you used were actually numbers chosen to represent a certain value in binary representation.

Take a look at the categories you used for *Breaker* and you should notice a pattern:

```
Ball:       1 (Decimal) = 00000001 (Binary)

Barrier:    2 (Decimal) = 00000010 (Binary)

Brick:      4 (Decimal) = 00000100 (Binary)

Paddle:      8 (Decimal) = 00001000 (Binary)
```

The position of the bits in binary representation is used to store a `1` or `0` when dealing with bitmasks.

First define a new `enum` for the above list, add the following code to the top of

`GameViewController`, just after the imports section, but before the class definition:

```
enum ColliderType: Int {
  case Ball = 0b1
  case Barrier = 0b10
  case Brick = 0b100
  case Paddle = 0b1000
}
```

Now instead of remembering numbers, you can use `ColliderType.Ball.rawValue` as bit mask value for the ball.

To see this in action when dealing with collisions, add the following line of code to the end of `setupNodes()`:

```
ballNode.physicsBody?.contactTestBitMask =
ColliderType.Barrier.rawValue |
  ColliderType.Brick.rawValue | ColliderType.Paddle.rawValue
```

As mentioned previously, the physics engine doesn't call `physicsWorld(_:didBeginContact:)` for every collision by default. To start getting these calls, you need to set the `contactTestBitMask` of a physics body to tell the physics engine that you're interested in notification when collisions happen.

In the line above, you let the physics engine know that you want to call the protocol method whenever the ball collides with nodes that have a category bitmask of either 2, 4, or 8 – respectively, these represent a barrier, brick or paddle.

> **Note**: You can also define more complex scenarios, by making a body part of multiple categories.

Now that you have defined when the protocol method gets called, it's time to jazz things up with more functionality based on the nodes with which your ball will collide.

Add the following lines of code to the bottom of `physicsWorld(_:didBeginContact:)`:

```
// 1
if contactNode.physicsBody?.categoryBitMask ==
ColliderType.Barrier.rawValue {
  if contactNode.name == "Bottom" {
    game.lives -= 1
    if game.lives == 0 {
      game.saveState()
      game.reset()
    }
  }
```

```
}
// 2
if contactNode.physicsBody?.categoryBitMask ==
ColliderType.Brick.rawValue {
  game.score += 1
  contactNode.hidden = true
  contactNode.runAction(
    SCNAction.waitForDurationThenRunBlock(120) {
      (node:SCNNode!) -> Void in
      node.hidden = false
    })
}
// 3
if contactNode.physicsBody?.categoryBitMask ==
ColliderType.Paddle.rawValue {
  if contactNode.name == "Left" {
    ballNode.physicsBody!.velocity.xzAngle -=
(convertToRadians(20))
  }
  if contactNode.name == "Right" {
    ballNode.physicsBody!.velocity.xzAngle +=
(convertToRadians(20))
  }
}
// 4
ballNode.physicsBody?.velocity.length = 5.0
```

Let's take a closer look at the code:

1. Earlier in the method, you added a way to the node the ball makes contact with into a `contactNode`. This section checks whether the ball is making contact with a barrier by looking at the `categoryBitMask` of `contactNode`. Then, you check the name of the node to find out which barrier was hit – remember, you named all your nodes when creating them earlier in the Scene Kit editor. With the barrier now being a known factor, you can tell when the ball hits the bottom. It matters because there's a penalty involved: you reduce the number of lives and if there are zero lives left, you save the high score and reset the game. Game over!
2. This checks whether the ball is making contact with a brick using the same technique as above. The rest of the code lets the brick disappear for 120 seconds then it reappears from the dead like a zombie. Yeah! This basically simplifies the game and makes it endless in nature. Oh yes, contact with the brick increases the score as well.
3. The last type of node to check is the paddle, so this checks which part of the paddle the ball hits. If it hits the left or right side, it adjusts the velocity of the ball by 20 degrees. You do this by first using a helper function from Game Utils to convert the angle from degrees to radians, and then you use this value to adjust the `xzAngle` of the ball's velocity. This added functionality gives the player a little variation in the ball's movement to keep things interesting.

4. Once all checks are performed, this last step brings some control over the physics behavior, forcing the ball to a constant speed of five. Remember that you're dealing with physics simulation, which is somewhat unpredictable, so bringing in adjustments like these puts the player in control of the game.

Setting up the delegate

Now that you have all the pieces ready, the last thing you need to do is hook up the delegate.

Add the following line of code to bottom of `setupScene()`:

```
scnScene.physicsWorld.contactDelegate = self
```

In order to be notified of contact events, you need to tell the physics engine that your class will now take responsibility for handling the protocol methods. You do that by setting the physics world's `contactDelegate` to `self`.

Build and run, and you should see the ball bounce around the screen, destroying bricks along the way!

Add touch controls

What fun is a game without any controls? Not much! In this section, you're going to add some simple touch controls so the player can slide the paddle to and fro.

Start by adding the following properties to `GameViewController`:

```
var touchX: CGFloat = 0
var paddleX: Float = 0
```

These properties simply store the touch's initial x-position and the paddle's x-position.

Next, add the following method to `GameViewController`:

```
override func touchesBegan(touches: Set<UITouch>, withEvent
event: UIEvent?) {
  for touch in touches {
    let location = touch.locationInView(scnView)
    touchX = location.x
    paddleX = paddleNode.position.x
  }
}
```

Here you override `touchesBegan(_:withEvent:)` which gets called every time the user touches the screen. As soon as a touch starts, this code simply stores the touch and paddle's x-position.

Now, you can finally get the paddle moving by adding the following method to `GameViewController`:

```
override func touchesMoved(touches: Set<UITouch>, withEvent
event: UIEvent?) {
  for touch in touches {
    // 1
    let location = touch.locationInView(scnView)
    paddleNode.position.x = paddleX + (Float(location.x -
touchX) * 0.1)

    // 2
    if paddleNode.position.x > 4.5 {
      paddleNode.position.x = 4.5
    } else if paddleNode.position.x < -4.5 {
      paddleNode.position.x = -4.5
    }
  }
}
```

Similar to before, you override `touchesMoved(_:withEvent:)` to detect when the user moves their finger around the screen. Here's a closer look at the code:

1. As the touch location moves, this updates the paddle's position relative to the initial touch location stored in `touchX`. It's a technique that allows the paddle to be moved left and right as if you were using the screen as a touchpad.
2. This simply limits the paddle's movement and confines it between the barrier's limits.

Build and run, and you can now drag to move the paddle across the screen:

Camera tracking

You're thinking in 3D, but the game's cameras are still living in 2D. A really simple, yet effective way to demonstrate the 3D nature of your game would be to let the cameras track the paddle around as it moves across the screen.

Woo-hoo! Let's introduce some larger than life (and possibly motion sickness inducing) effects! :]

Add camera tracking

To add some basic tracking, add the following lines of code to the bottom of `touchesMoved()`:

```
verticalCameraNode.position.x = paddleNode.position.x
horizontalCameraNode.position.x = paddleNode.position.x
```

This updates both cameras' x-position to be the same as the paddle, allowing the cameras to track the paddle's every move. It gives a really cool effect. Build and run to try it out for yourself!

Add camera constraints

You're making progress, but there's problem with the tracking at the moment: The cameras scroll too far to the right and left, leaving the player without a view of the play area.

It's easy to solve this by pointing the cameras to the center of the play area where the floor node is positioned. You'll add constraints to the camera to accomplish this.

Add a new property to store the floor node in `GameViewController`:

```
var floorNode: SCNNode!
```

This will be where you store the floor node once you've found it in the scene.

Next, add the following to the bottom of `setupNodes()`:

```
floorNode =
  scnScene.rootNode.childNodeWithName("Floor", recursively:
true)!
verticalCameraNode.constraints =
  [SCNLookAtConstraint(target: floorNode)]
horizontalCameraNode.constraints =
  [SCNLookAtConstraint(target: floorNode)]
```

This bit of code first finds the node named **Floor** and binds it to `floorNode`. Then, it adds a `SCNLookAtConstraint` to both cameras in the scene, which will force the camera to point towards the targeted node.

Remember that the floor is positioned underneath the center of the play area. So now, no matter where you move the cameras, they're always looking toward the center of the play area.

It's time to try all these awesome new features out, so build and run your game:

Excellent! Slide your finger left and right across the screen, and experience the sheer joy of sliding the paddle across the screen. What's even cooler is how the camera tracks the paddle wherever it goes, but it always keeps on its eye on the center of the scene.

Add a trailing effect

You've probably see the trailing effect in other *Breakout* style games, where the ball leaves a streak in its wake. With a particle system, you can add this effect with relative ease.

Add a particle system to the ball

You're going to use the Scene Kit editor to add a particle system to the ball this time around. It sounds rather futuristic, doesn't it?

Start off by selecting your game scene again under **Breaker.scnassets/Scenes/Game.scn**.

Drag and drop a **Particle System** from the Object Library to your scene:

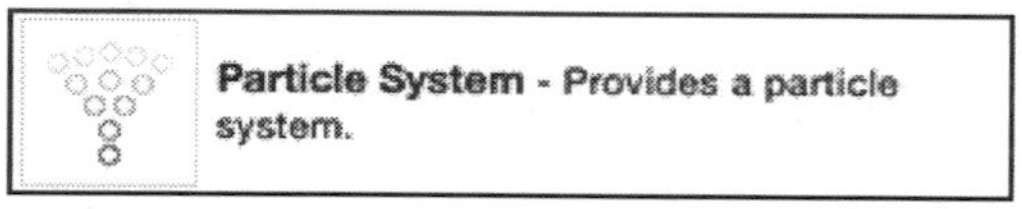

Name this node **Trail** and reorganize the scene graph so that the particle system is a child of **Ball**:

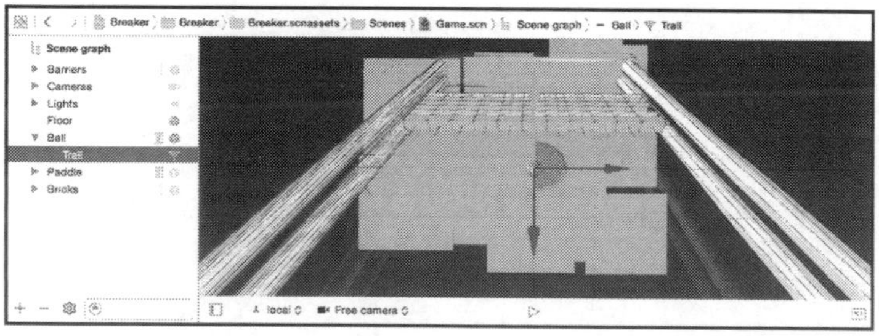

What you're doing is allowing the particle system to be positioned relative to its parent, the ball. So now, when the ball bounces around, the particle system will move along with it.

As soon as you drop the particle system into your scene, it emits big, ugly squares. Don't be alarmed; you've done nothing wrong. :] The reason why it looks like a hot mess is because you still need to give the particle system a proper image to use for each particle it emits.

This is your next bit to fix up, so first make sure your particle system is positioned correctly by opening the Node Inspector:

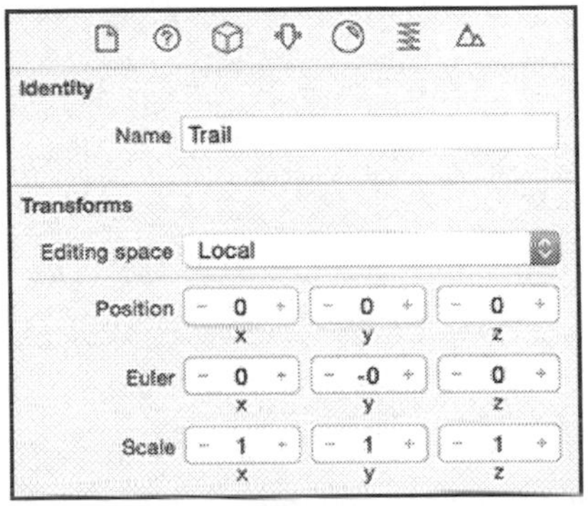

Zero out its position to `(x:0, y:0, z:0)`. Great, now the particle system should start emitting particles smack bang from the center of the ball. Getting better already.

Next, select the Attributes Inspector to configure the properties of the particle system:

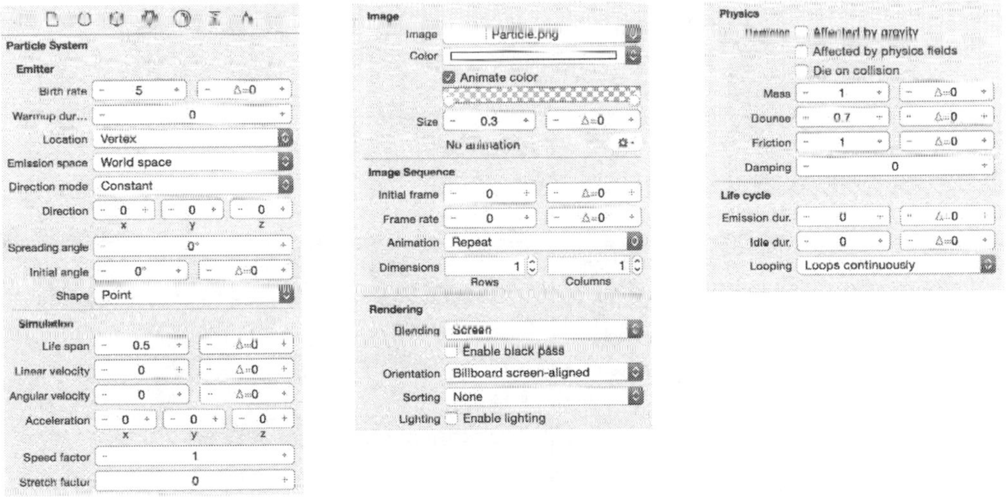

You need to configure the particles so that they fade away and are emitted right from the center of the system. Because the particle system moves with the ball, you'll create the effect of a trail behind the ball.

Let's go through the properties that you'll change from the defaults:

- **Birth rate** to **5**: This controls how often particles spawn. An increase here makes the particles more dense.
- **Location** to **Vertex**: This controls the particles' spawn point.
- **Direction mode** to **Constant**: This controls how to launch the emitted particles from the emitter. **Constant** applies a constant vector to each particle.

- **Direction** to `(x:0, y:0, z:0)`: This zeros out the constant directional vector that gets applied to the particles once they spawn so they stay in place.
- **Life span** to **0.5**: This controls the particles' life span; go ahead and play with this setting to lengthen or shorten the trail.
- **Linear velocity** to **0**: The particles will not move after being spawned.
- **Image** to **Particle.png**: You can find this image under **Breaker.scnassets/Textures**. All particles spawned from this system will use this image as their texture.
- **Color** to **White**: This sets the overall tint color over the particles' texture.
- **Animate color**: Enables the checkbox, and once you enable this, a bar appears to allow you to specify how to animate the tint color over the particle's life span. It's where you create a fade effect! So, create two markers and place them on the beginning and end of the timeline. Set the color for each so that it animates from **White** at 50 percent **Opacity** to **White** at 0 percent **Opacity**. Note that to remove markers, just drag them off the track until an X appears, then release.
- **Size** to **0.3**: This scales the particle down to 30 percent of its original size as determined by the image.
- **Blending** to **Screen**: This controls how the particles are drawn, as well as where multiply mode darkens and screen mode lightens.
- **Emission duration** to **0**. This will control how long the particle system emits particles. Since you really want it to emit perpetually, set it to **0**.

All done! Click the play button at the bottom of the editor to see the resulting effect:

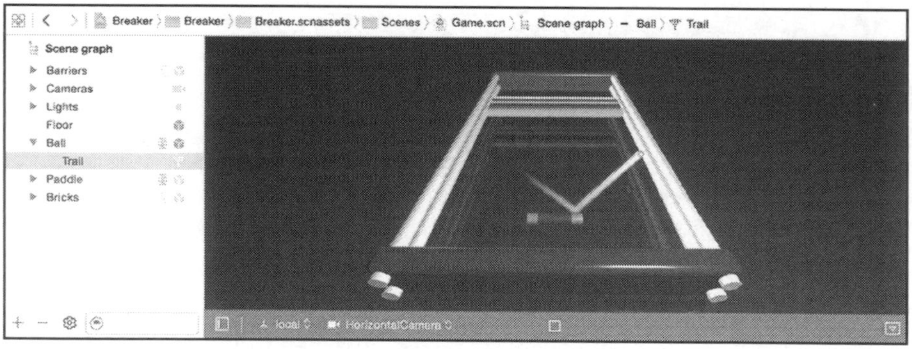

Just look at that pretty tail, it's just like Halley's Comet! :]

Time to build, run and play! :]

Look at all of those little details that you've added to the game: the trailing effect, the camera movement and the gameplay-oriented camera that always keeps its eye on the prize.

> **Note**: You can find the completed project up to this point under the **projects/final/Breaker/** folder.

Challenge

Well-done, your core game is done, but the hardest part is still left: adding juice! A quick juice infusion would be to add some sound effects.

Add the following lines of code to `setupSounds()`:

```
game.loadSound("Paddle",
  fileNamed: "Breaker.scnassets/Sounds/Paddle.wav")
game.loadSound("Block0",
  fileNamed: "Breaker.scnassets/Sounds/Block0.wav")
game.loadSound("Block1",
  fileNamed: "Breaker.scnassets/Sounds/Block1.wav")
game.loadSound("Block2",
  fileNamed: "Breaker.scnassets/Sounds/Block2.wav")
game.loadSound("Barrier",
  fileNamed: "Breaker.scnassets/Sounds/Barrier.wav")
```

This will use a helper method to load a whole bunch of sounds into memory from **Breaker.scnassets/Sounds**. You'll find them stored into a dictionary with named keys for simple access later on.

Now see if you can play the right sound at the precise moment of contact. Here are some hints:

- Use `game.playSound(scnScene.rootNode, name: "SoundToPlay")` to trigger one of the named sound effects that you loaded beforehand.

- Give the **Block** sound effect some randomness by using `random() % 3` to generate a random number from `0` to 2.

Good luck! :]

> **Note**: You can find the completed challenge project for this chapter under the **projects/challenge/Breaker/** folder.

Where to go from here?

You just finished yet another game and had another stellar performance! Are you sure you're not a machine? I think you might just have some machine-like qualities, so well done, T-1000! :]

You've come a long way, and you really have a lot more smarts now when it comes to 3D games, too. In this chapter you've learned a lot of different topics:

- **Physics Inspector**: You learned how to enable and configure physics bodies for all the nodes in your game right inside of the Scene Kit editor.
- **Basic Collision Detection**: You learned how to use the `SCNPhysicsContactDelegate` protocol to listen to collision events in your game and responded by adding game logic in code.
- **Juice!**: You've just scratched the surface of adding "juice" to your game by adding a particle system to display a trail effect on the ball and you had the added challenge of getting sounds to play at the right moments.

With that said, there is always room for improvement and more juice. Here are some ways you could take it up a notch:

- The game still needs some basic state management, which would allow you to transition between different states for your game, for instance, `WaitForTap`, `Playing` and `GameOver` states.
- The physics still needs a bit more tweaking so you can make sure the ball does not fall into an eternal bounce between the side barriers.
- The game definitely needs more juice too! :]

Section III: Intermediate SceneKit

In this section you will create stunning a make belief world, with a shiny wooden relic awaits brave warriors with exceptional balancing skills to guide it through a maze high up in the sky. The game is called **Marble Maze**, and is somewhat based on the *Labyrinth* styled games with a twist.

Chapter 11: Materials

Chapter 12: Reference Nodes

Chapter 13: Shadows

Chapter 14: Intermediate Collision Detection

Chapter 15: Motion Control

Chapter 11: Materials

Chris Language

Take a moment and look around. Pick up something close by and examine it. Aside from its geometrical shape, what makes the object look the way it does? What do you see or feel?

Consider the shiny football below - or for our American friends, the shiny soccer ball:

It looks quite realistic; wouldn't you agree? Believe or not, that's all generated in real time within Scene Kit.

Getting started

Let's see if you picked up on the following qualities of the ball:

- See how each patch bulges out? You can even notice the stitching between the patches.
- Do you see the bumpiness of the leather texture as the light bounces off?
- How about the shiny polished parts that contrast with the matte RW logo on the black patches?
- Do you notice the three rectangular lights from the ceiling reflecting off the ball?
- What about the dark floor reflecting off the bottom of the ball?
- Can you see how light struggles to reach the deep ridges between the patches?

You're probably thinking that all that added detail puts the polygon count off the charts! Well, think again. It's all just eye trickery, because what you're seeing is just a basic primitive sphere wrapped with different types of special materials. Surprised?

The following sections show the details of each material and how it helps contribute to the overall effect.

Lighting models

Scene Kit supports four different lighting models, which define mathematical equations that combine the properties of different materials with the lights in the scene to produce the exact final color of every rendered pixel.

Here's a representation of the different models available in Scene Kit:

Here's each model in detail:

- **Constant**: Uses a flat lighting model that only incorporates the ambient lighting into the equation when calculating the color of a rendered pixel.
- **Lambert**: Incorporates ambient lighting and diffuse information when calculating the color of a rendered pixel.

- **Blinn**: Incorporates ambient, diffuse and specular lighting information, where the specular highlights are calculated using the Blinn-Phong formula.
- **Phong**. Incorporates ambient, diffuse, and specular lighting information, where the specular highlights are calculated using the Phong formula.

> **Note**: You'll use the Phong model in this chapter so you can see all available effects.

Materials

Materials are more commonly known as **textures**; they let you introduce more detail and realism into your scenes without the need for more geometry.

Textures are essentially flat 2D images wrapped around your 3D geometry that use special **texture coordinates** stored within the geometry. All Scene Kit primitive shapes already contain this information out of the box, so all you need to do is provide them with some pretty textures to make them pop.

All the effects on the ball above were created through different types of texture maps: one to give the ball its base color, another to make certain parts bumpy, another to make certain parts shiny or matte, and so forth.

To see how each texture works, you'll see how we created that shiny ball from scratch. Get ready for some material mathematics! :]

> **Note**: Just for fun, there's a little starter project under the **projects/starter/SoccerBall/** folder. Start off with **ball.scnassets/00_Start.scn** scene. Select the **Ball** node, then select the **Material** inspector. See if you can follow the steps below to re-create the final effect yourself. Alternatively, just use the provided solution step to have a more hands-on experience of the resulting effect.

Diffuse map

The diffuse map gives your geometry a base coloring texture. This texture typically defines what your object is, regardless of lights and special effects:

Adding the diffuse map clearly defines the sphere as a football. Looks like one of those cheap $2 plastic balls that wouldn't even last five minutes with your dog, doesn't it? :]

> **Note**: Select the **01_Diffuse.scn** scene to see this effect in action.

Normal map

The normal map feels like sorcery from another planet. Recall the discussion from Chapter 8, "Lights", about how lights use the normal vector to shade and light up a surface. Now combine that single surface normal vector with a whole bunch of detailed normal vectors that define exactly how each pixel on your surface will bend the light, and you've got your normal map.

Think of the normal map as a texture that defines the *bumpiness* of your geometry; you can use it to simulate rough surfaces such as the craters on the surface of the moon, engravings on an ancient stone tablet, or perhaps even the bulging patches and leather pattern on a shiny football:

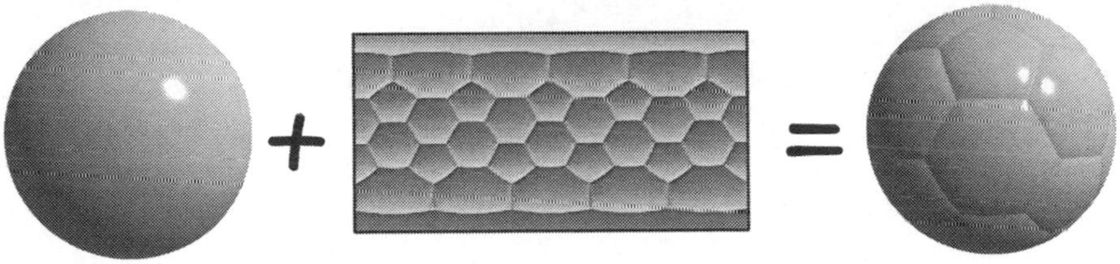

Applying the normal map delivers one heck of a graphics punch; it's taken a basic, dull-looking sphere to a detailed football bulging with awesomeness! :]

> **Note**: Select the **02_Normal.scn** scene to see this effect in action.

Now see what happens when you add the normal effect to the existing diffuse effect:

That certainly makes the ball pop out – no pun intended! Suddenly, your $2 ball becomes a $20 ball. Awesome! But don't celebrate just yet; you can make it look even better.

> **Note**: If you want to generate your own normal maps, there's an awesome tool called *CrazyBump*. You can find it at **crazybump.com**. Hurry, while it's still in beta for Mac owners.

Reflective map

Before diving into reflective maps, you first need to understand the concept of **cube mapping**. You know that a cube consists of six sides. Similarly, a cube map consists of six equally sized textures, all contained within one large map used to texture all sides of a cube.

Scene Kit uses the following pattern to define a cube map, where each tile represents a specific side of the cube:

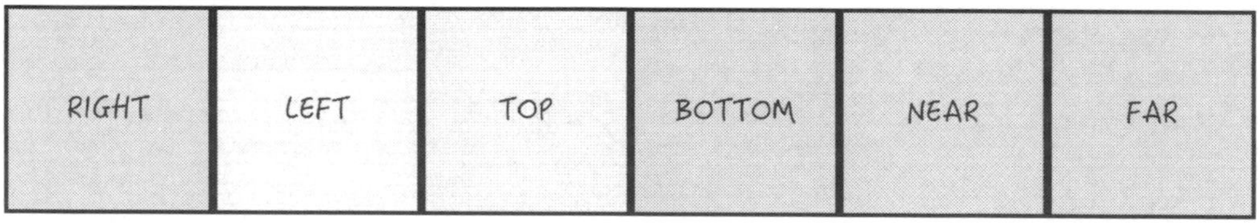

> **Note**: Make a mental note of cube mapping and how Scene Kit uses it, because you'll see it uses again for a different effect.

A reflective map, as the name might suggest, defines reflection. The beauty of using a cube map is that you can define details on your object; the reflectiveness of your object determines how much of this reflection will be visible. For instance, a mirror finish would make your object highly reflective and produce a chrome effect.

Let's create a little light room for the ball:

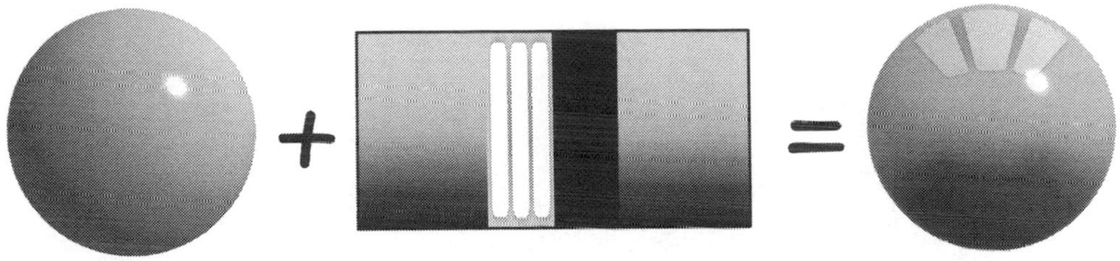

The light room has three ceiling lights and a dark floor. Note that the reflectiveness has been toned down quite a bit; the ball is shiny and reflective, but it's not a mirror ball either.

Note: Select the **03_Reflective.scn** scene to see this effect in action.

See what happens when you combine the results of this effect with the previous effects:

This effect makes the ball even shinier than before. Although subtle, it's still an effective way to provide realism to your objects.

Occlusion map

The occlusion map, also known as the **ambient occlusion map**, is only effective when ambient light exists in your scene. This black-and-white texture map defines how much ambient light reaches certain parts of your geometry; black parts block out ambient light entirely, while white allows all ambient light to shine through.

When it's done well, the occlusion effect lends a lot of realism to a scene. For complex geometrical forms, portions of the geometry will block ambient light from other spots of the geometry, such as the deep ridges around the patches of the ball:

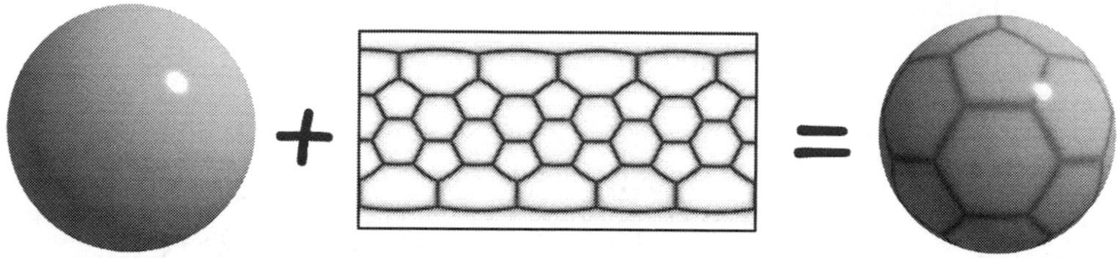

Note: Select the **04_Occlusion.scn** scene to see this effect in action.

Here's what the effect looks like combined with the previous effects:

It's a subtle effect, but it still shows how occlusion mimics the natural properties of light.

Specular map

The **specular map** controls the *shininess* of your geometry. Black sections of the map define matte portions, while white sections indicate a glossy effect:

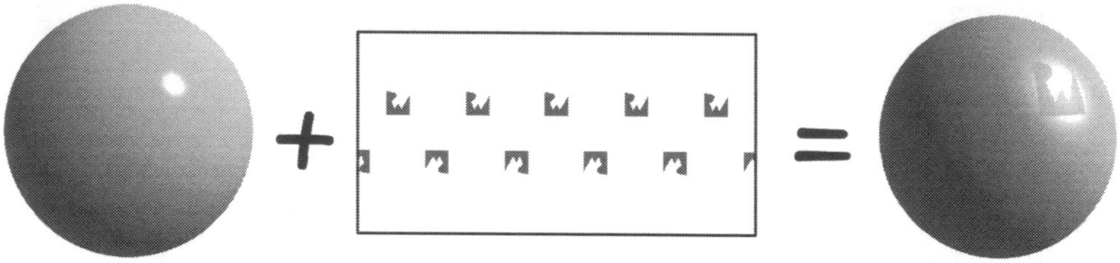

See how the RW logo appears as matte and blocks out all light from the reflective map and the shiny specular light reflection?

Note: Select the **05_Specular.scn** scene to see this effect in action.

You'll get the following effect when you add the specular map to the existing effects in your scene:

Again, it's very subtle, but this effect adds more depth and realism to your scene, bringing you to the final result of a very shiny $50 football! :]

Emission map

In the absence of light, the ball wouldn't be visible at all. But if you slapped some phosphorous paint on it, you could make it glow in the dark!

The **emission map** overrides all lighting and shading information to create a light-emitting effect, which is even more pronounced when you add some blur effects to the map. This is a colorized texture where the brighter colors emit most strongly, darker colors emit less and absolute black emits nothing at all:

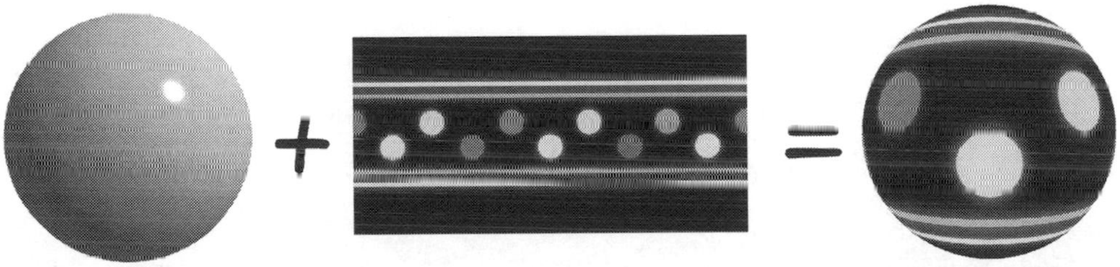

> **Note**: Unlike many 3D authoring tools, the emission map doesn't generate light in Scene Kit; it merely simulates the emission effect. Select the **06_Emission.scn** scene to see this effect in action.

When you dim the lights a bit and apply the emission effect to the ball, you'll see it light right up:

You don't have to worry about lights anymore; this puppy glows in the dark! :]

Multiply map

The **multiply map** is applied after all other effects; it can be used to colorize, brighten or darken the final result:

Add the multiply effect to ball and you'll get the following:

Transparency map

Transparency maps make parts of your geometry transparent, or even completely invisible. Black sections define opaque sections, while white parts end up as transparent:

If you enable double-sided mode, you'll be able to see right through the object.

> **Note**: Select the **07_Transparency.scn** scene to see this effect in action.

If you add the transparency effect to your ball, you'll end up with a ball that defies the laws of physics:

It's like an alien football from a different dimension!

> **Note**: To see the final result select **08_Final.scn**. Also have a look at steps 09, 10 and 11 to see the Multiply, Emission and Transperancy maps in action.

Creating the game project

The good news is that you're all done with materials theory, but the bad news is that you haven't yet begun to build your stunning game! Time to take care of that.

Creating a Scene Kit game project

To keep things easy, you'll start with the built-in Scene Kit Game template. Here's the super-short version of the setup:

1. Open up Xcode, create a new Scene Kit Game project for **iOS** and name it **MarbleMaze**.
2. Delete the **art.scnassets** folder.
3. Drag and drop the new **art.scnassets** folder from the **projects/resources** folder into the project.
4. You'll only play the game in portrait mode, so uncheck **Landscape Left** and **Landscape Right** to disable the other orientations:

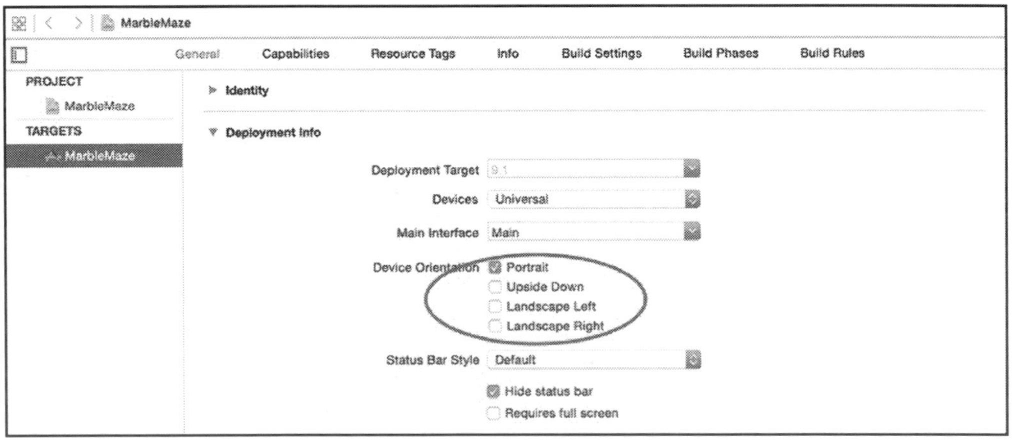

Now you can replace the contents of **GameViewController.swift** with the following lines of code:

```
import UIKit
import SceneKit

class GameViewController: UIViewController {

  var scnView:SCNView!

  override func viewDidLoad() {
    super.viewDidLoad()
```

```
    // 1
    setupScene()
    setupNodes()
    setupSounds()
  }

  // 2
  func setupScene() {
    scnView = self.view as! SCNView
    scnView.delegate = self
    scnView.allowsCameraControl = true
    scnView.showsStatistics = true
  }

  func setupNodes() {
  }

  func setupSounds() {
  }

  override func shouldAutorotate() -> Bool {
    return false
  }

  override func prefersStatusBarHidden() -> Bool {
    return true
  }
}

// 3
extension GameViewController: SCNSceneRendererDelegate {
  func renderer(renderer: SCNSceneRenderer, updateAtTime time:
NSTimeInterval) {
  }
}
```

This code snippet should look familiar; it's the same bare-bones **GameViewController** class you used in the previous sections.

Here's a closer look at the commented sections:

1. These stub methods are called from `viewDidLoad()`; you'll add code to these methods to set up your game.
2. This simply casts **self.view** as an **SCNView** and stores it for convenience. It also sets the render loop **delegate** to **self**.
3. The class now conforms to the **SCNSceneRendererDelegate** render loop protocol and contains a stub that is called on every frame update.

Note: For a more detailed version of these instructions, you can refer to the previous chapters of this book; for the rocket-fuelled approach, simply load up the starter project from the **projects/starter/MarbleMaze/** folder. :]

Creating a skybox

No, it's not the VIP seats at the stadium; rather, a **skybox** is a massive box around your scene that gives the impression of a real backdrop or scenery. Most 3D games today use this clever little trick to create an environment that resembles distant skies and hills for example.

All Scene Kit scene camera nodes have a **background** property. You *could* simply set it to a specific color if that's all you wanted, but it has a hidden superpower: you can set the background to a cube map instead. Scene Kit will detect the cube map and automatically create a massive skybox for you, with your cube map texture applied.

Note: As a reminder, a cube map is constructed of six equally sized images, all combined into one single large image. Scene Kit uses the pattern (right, left, top, bottom, near, and far) for cube maps.

Create a skybox

Inside **art.scnassets** you'll find an empty Scene Kit scene named **game.scn**. Open it and select the default **camera node**, then select **Scene Inspector** on the top right:

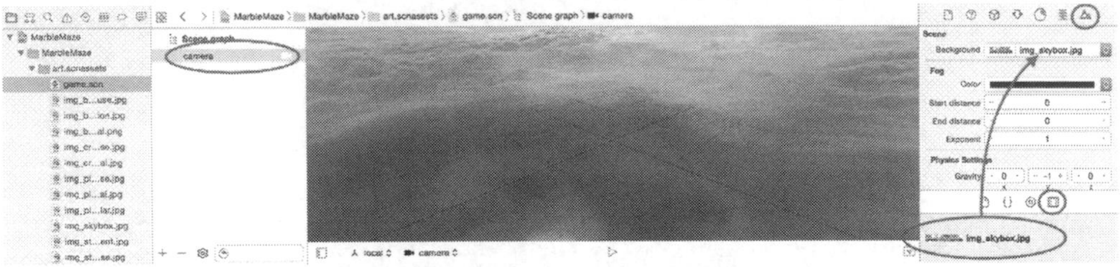

Find **img_skybox.jpg** from the Media Library at the bottom right and drag and drop it into the Background property of the scene.

Load and present the scene

All that's left to do is load and present the scene.

Add the following property to your **GameViewController** class:

```
var scnScene:SCNScene!
```

scnScene provides convenient access to the **SCNScene.scene** property.

Add the following lines code to `setupScene()`:

```
// 1
scnScene = SCNScene(named: "art.scnassets/game.scn")
// 2
scnView.scene = scnScene
```

Taking a closer look at the code:

1. This creates an instance of **SCNScene** using your new scene. Note the specified path **art.scnassets/game.scn** to the scene file.
2. This sets your new scene as the active scene for the view.

Build and run; take a look at the heavenly universe for your game:

Breathtaking, don't you think?

Where to go from here?

You can find the final project for this chapter under the **projects/final/MarbleMaze/** folder.

To recap some highlights from this chapter:

- **Lighting Models**: Scene Kit supports several different lighting models, along with mathematical definitions of how different textures can be combined to determine the color of every rendered pixel.
- **Materials**: Various types of textures used together can create all sorts of special effects and details in your 3D models.
- **Skyboxes**: Cube map textures can create stunning skyboxes in Scene Kit.

In the next chapter you'll get your hands dirty, build game assets from scratch and give them textures to make them look absolutely stunning.

Chapter 12: Reference Nodes

Chris Language

Image for a moment you've created an epic monster, but you can't quite decide what color its eyes should be. Bloodshot red? Werewolf green? Zombie haze? To top it off, you've just spent hours scattering the monster all over your level, so when you *do* finally decide on the color, you'll have to go back and re-color all their eyes with the color you chose!

Fear not – **reference nodes** are here to save you from this scary scenario. :]

Reference nodes let you build your monster in its own little scene; when you're building your level, you can simply pull in a *reference* to that scene that contains the original monster. If you need to modify something on your monster, simply make the change in the original and the change will propagate to all referenced versions.

Using reference nodes saves hours of hard labor, and lets you make those difficult last-minute decisions without driving your graphics artists insane with change requests. In this chapter, you'll learn how to use them in your own games.

Note: You can continue with your project where you left off in the previous chapter, or alternatively you can begin with the starter project for this chapter found in **projects/starter/MarbleMaze/MarbleMaze.xcodeproj**.

Getting started

The most important component of your game is your main character. For Marble Maze, this will be marble - specifically a shiny wooden relic. In the following steps you'll create a primitive sphere inside its own little scene and apply a few different types of textures to

make the relic look quite realistic.

You'll create an empty scene that will hold only the geometry of the main character. Later, you'll reference this scene from another scene so that it becomes a reference node.

Start by dragging and dropping a empty Scene Kit scene file into your project:

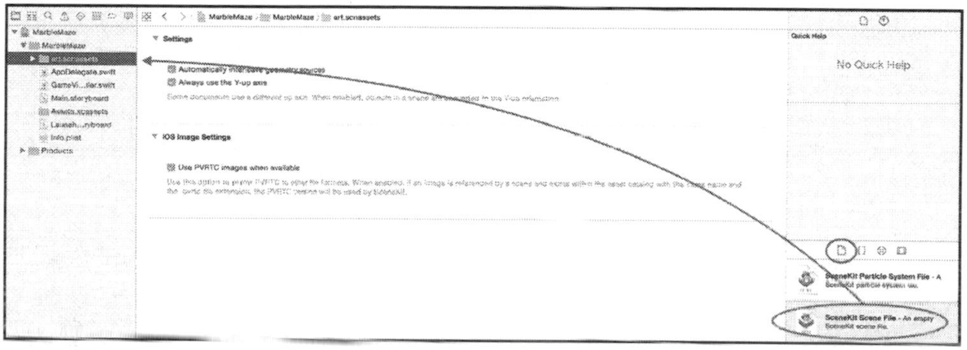

When prompted, select **art.scnassets** as the destination folder for the new scene and name the file **obj_ball.scn**.

Select **art.scnassets/obj_ball.scn**, expand the scene graph, then select the default camera node. All new empty scenes contain this default camera node, which is a real pain when you work with reference nodes. It's best that you get rid of it right away, before you continue. Select the default camera in your scene, then delete it like so:

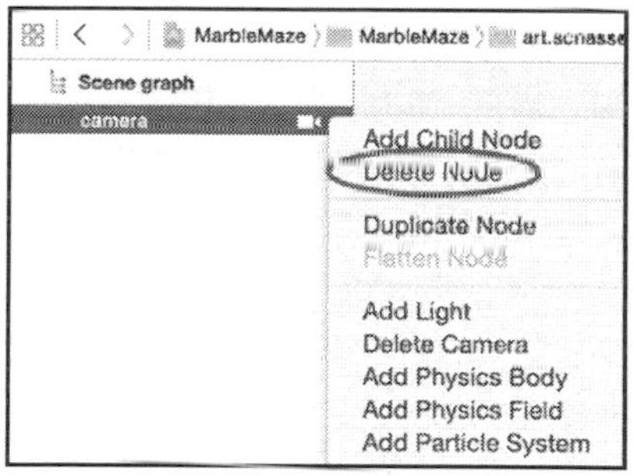

Your wooden relic will start off life as a sphere. Drag a sphere from the Object Library into the scene:

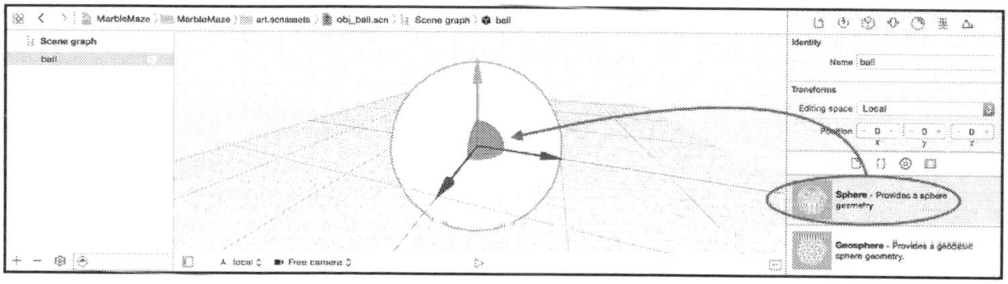

With the sphere still selected, select the Node Inspector. Name your new shape **ball** and place it at position **(x:0, y:0, z:0)** using the inspector:

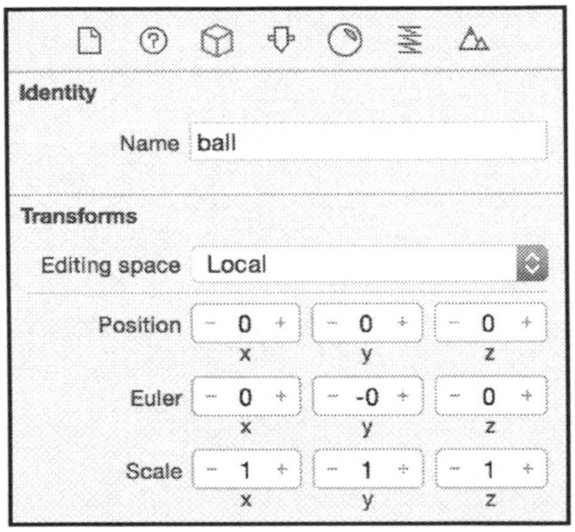

The sphere is much too big at the moment, plus it needs some more detailed geometry.

Select the Attributes Inspector. Change the radius to **0.45** and bump up the segment count to **36**:

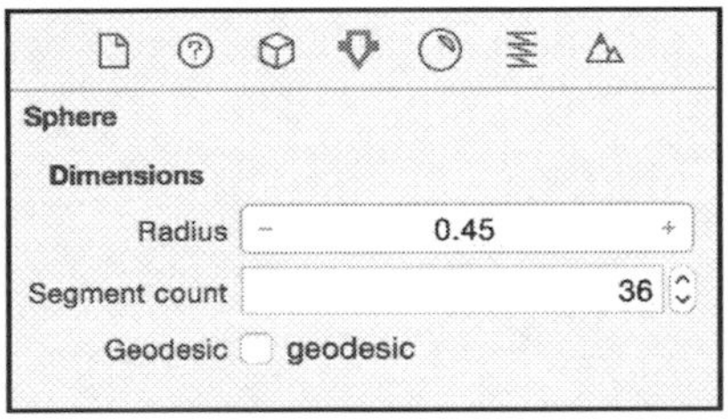

Changing the radius of the ball to 0.45 shrinks it to a size where it would easily fall through a 1x1 gap. Setting the segment count to **36** smooths out the sphere's geometry so that close up views of the sphere will appear more, well, spherical. :]

Materials

Now on to the fun part: adding materials! :]

Select the **Material Inspector** on the top right, and change the Diffuse, Normal, Reflective, and Emission settings as shown in the sub-sections below.

Diffuse

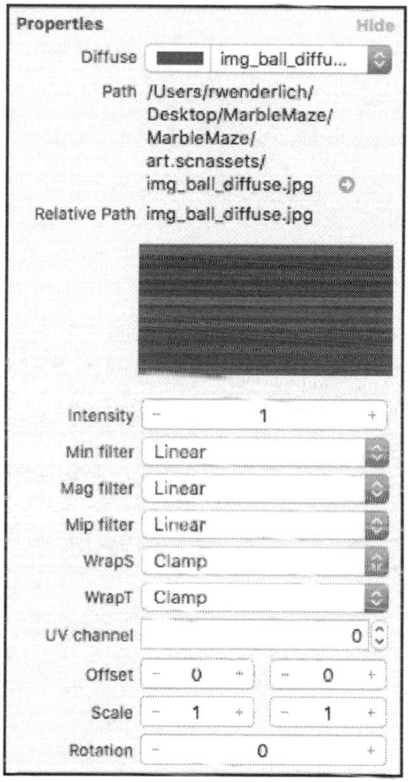

- **Diffuse**: Instead of a solid color, select **img_ball_diffuse** from the dropdown as the diffuse map. Note you must click to the far right of the dropdown where the up/down arrows are for this to work.
- **Intensity**: Leave this set to **1.0**. This controls the brightness level of your base diffuse material; **0.0** would make it completely black.
- **Mip Filter**: Set this to **Linear**, which enables mip mapping for the diffuse texture.

> **Note:** Wondering what *mip* means? This will be discussed along with its brethren *min*, *mag*, *wrapT* and *wrapS* in the next section, so hold tight for a moment – there's need to scream and pull your hair out just yet. :]

Normal

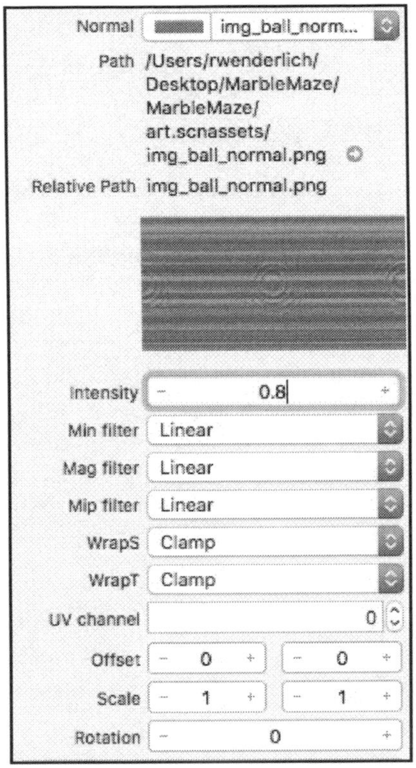

- **Normal**: Select **img_ball_normal** for the normal map.
- **Intensity**: Set this to **0.8** to make the effect just a little less prominent.
- **Mip Filter**: Set this to **Linear**.

> **Note**: If you want to use a different texture, as mentioned in Chapter 11, "Materials", you can use the tool *CrazyBump* to generate a normal map from the diffuse texture.

Specular

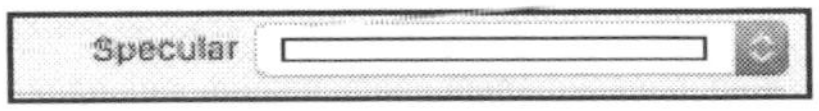

- **Specular**: Change the specular color to pure white, which gives the ball a nice glossy effect.

Reflective

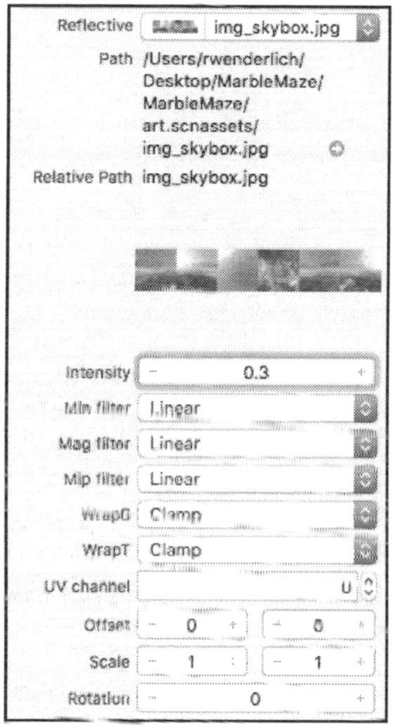

- **Reflective**: Select **img_skybox** for the reflective map. This reflects the environment onto the ball and makes it reflective like a mirror.
- **Intensity**: Set the intensity to **0.3** so it isn't perfectly reflective.
- **Mip Filter**: Set this to **Linear**.

Emission

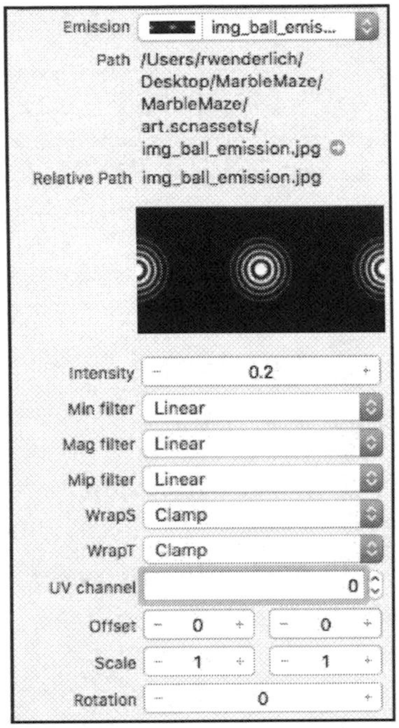

- **Emission**: Select **img_ball_emission** for the emission map.
- **Intensity**: Set this to **0.2** for now; you'll animate the intensity later and change the emission map dynamically.
- **Mip Filter**: Set this to **Linear**.

The images below show the cumulative effect of adding each material type:

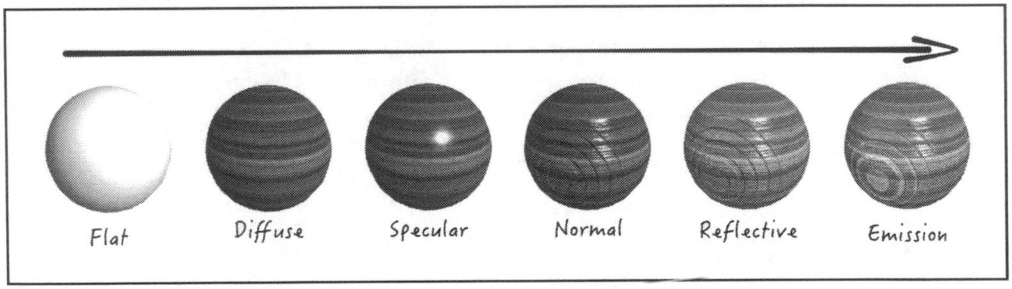

Note: You won't experience the exact same result as above while working in the scene editor. This is due to the lack of lights in your scene.

You've added some great detail to your sphere, but high-resolution textures can come at a serious performance cost. If you're viewing your objects from a distance, isn't it wasteful to use high-resolution textures on objects where the effect is only visible when you're viewing the object up close?

Yes, it can be wasteful, but you can use a technique known as **mip map filtering** to render your objects efficiently.

Texture filtering

3D rendering engines use the mip map filtering technique to speed up the rendering performance of textured objects at a distance; basically, you use smaller pre-generated versions of the original texture.

Scene Kit indeed supports mip mapping; all you need to do is enable it (which it is by default) and decide which technique to use when generating smaller sized textures.

The results of mip mapping can be subtle; you might need a magnifying glass to spot the differences in the following images! :]

The image above shows three versions of the same scene of a patterned floor stretching to the horizon, each using a different mip mapping technique. Look closely at the appearance of the check pattern as it approaches the horizon:

- **None**: This has no mip mapping enabled; note how the pattern generates all sorts of interesting visual artifacts and Moiré patterns near the horizon.
- **Nearest**: This samples pixels from the nearest level mip map when it textures a object.
- **Linear**: This samples pixels from the two nearest-level mip maps and interpolates the result between those two maps when it renders a object. This is the default option that is selected when you choose a texture.

Note: The minification and magnification filters use the exact same techniques when dealing with textures at smaller or larger sizes than the original.

Adding the ball as reference node

Now that you have your relic set up, it's time to pull it into the main game scene.

First select the **art.scnassets/game.scn** scene, then drag and drop the **art.scnassets/obj_ball.scn** into the scene. Set your relic's position to **(x:0, y:0, z:0)** and name it **ball**:

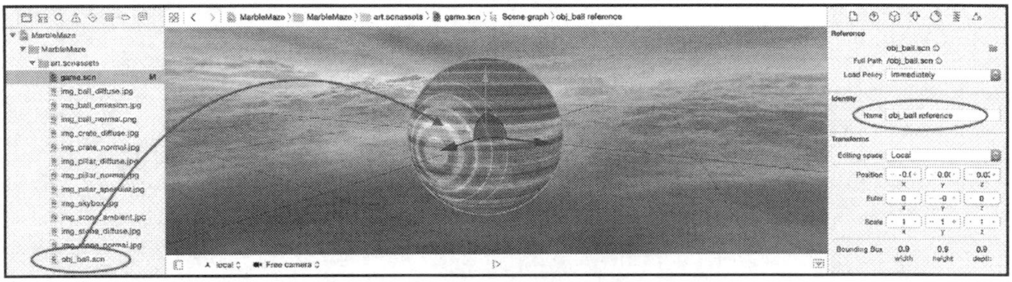

You'll see the wooden relic in your scene, but notice that its identity shows it's been added as a **reference**. Well done – you just mastered the dark art of reference nodes. :]

Build and run your game, and take stock of your scene:

Like magic, the wooden relic defies gravity and hangs in mid-air. Pan around and enjoy the view – but wait a minute. What happened to all those cool texture effects?

That's because there aren't any lights in the scene! Texture effects need light to be visible. You'll need to wait until the next chapter to add some light sources; for now, you'll focus on building the game level with reference nodes. Patience is a virtue. :]

> **Note**: At the time of writing this chapter, there appear to be a few bugs in the Scene Kit Editor relating to reference nodes. When making changes to the origin node, the scene with the referenced version does not always get refreshed properly. If you run into this problem, simply make sure all your work is saved, then restart Xcode.

Challenge

Time for a fun little challenge! Simply read the following hints and apply the skills you've learned so far to create the objects below from scratch:

1. Create each object in its own little empty scene.
2. Delete that pesky default camera node from each empty scene; otherwise it will show up when you create a new reference to your object.

Okay – now try to create the following objects:

- **obj_crate1x1**: Name it **crate** and set its size to **(x:1, y:1, z:1)**. Use the **img_crate_diffuse** texture as diffuse, and **img_crate_normal** as normal. Add a mid-grey specular color; if you make this pure white the crates will look like plastic.
- **obj_stone1x1**: Name it **stone** and set its size to **(x:1, y:1, z:1)**. Use the **img_stone_diffuse** and **img_stone_normal** maps, but lower the normals intensity to

0.5. Give it a nice **white** specular color.

- **obj_stone3x3**: Name this one **stone** as well, but set its size to **(x:3, y:3, z:3)**. This one will be a bit trickier, as you will have to use the texture scale settings and wrapT and wrapS to make it work. Use the same textures as you did for **obj_stone1x1**, and again use a **white** specular color.
- **obj_pillar1x3**: Name it **pillar** and set its size to **(x:1, y:3, z:1)**. Use the **img_pillar_** textures; this one has a specular texture as well, so make use of that. You'll also have to play with the scale and wrap settings a bit.

Note: Don't freak out – you got this! Refer back to the previous section if you get stuck, or take a peek at the finished project located in the **projects/challenge/MarbleMaze** folder. The section below walks you through the creation of the 3x3 stone block in particular.

Scaling and wrapping textures

Here's a little more detail on how to solve the challenge of the 3x3 block:

First off, adjust its size to **(x:3, y:3, z:3)** using the **Attributes Inspector**:

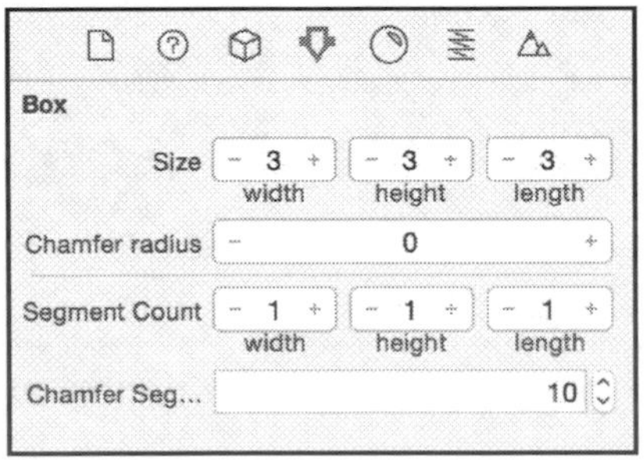

This is where things get interesting. Using the Materials Inspector, change each setting as described below:

- **Diffuse**: Select the diffuse map; the pattern tries to fill the whole block. Since it's such a large block, you need to scale it the texture down to fit the perspective of the smaller stone block.
- **Scale**: Adjust the scaling factor to **(x:3, y:3, z:3)**, which scales down the texture – but to one corner only. To let it fill the block, you have to tell the pattern to repeat.
- **WrapS**: Set wrapS to **repeat**, which enables horizontal texture wrapping; suddenly the texture pattern repeats horizontally.
- **WrapT**: Set wrapT to **repeat**, which enables vertical texture wrapping; the texture pattern repeats vertically and fills the entire block.

Here's how your Materials Inspector will look when you're done:

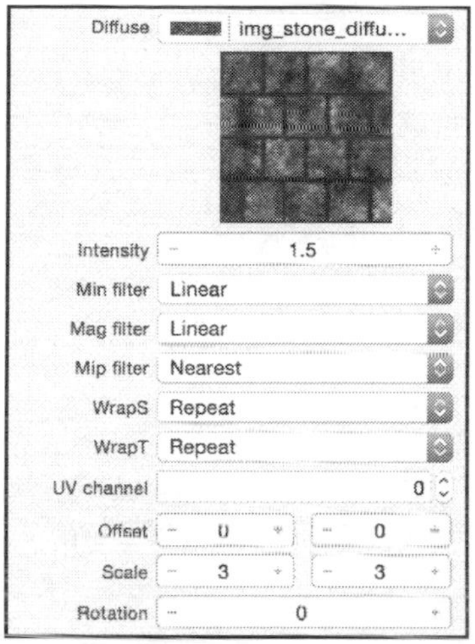

Here's the end result of each step in succession:

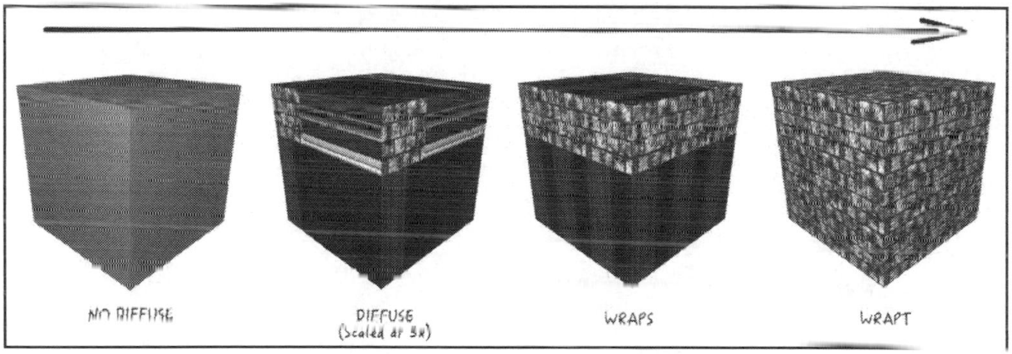

You can use some of these same techniques to solve the 1x3 pillar as well.

Where to go from here?

This brings you to the end of this chapter. Your game is coming along nicely – great job!

Here's a quick recap of what you've learned in this chapter:

- **Reference Nodes**: A reference node is basically a scene all on its own with its own set of objects. The reference part comes in when you've re-used that scene within another scene. Any changes made to the original referenced scene will automatically change all the referenced nodes.
- **Mip Map Filtering**: Mip mapping can make your game look better *and* perform better too.
- **Texture Scaling & Wrapping**: Textures can be scaled, wrapped and repeated to fill in large areas.

In the next chapter, you'll use the objects you created in this chapter to build little mini sets, which you will ultimately reference when you build your main game scene.

Chapter 13: Shadows

Chris Language

If you suffer from Sciophobia, then this chapter's going to be a bit of a challenge for you – but if not, you've got this one in the bag. This chapter deals with a very dark subject matter – shadows! :]

One thing comic books have taught us all is that evil cannot exist without good. One villain in particular pointed this fact out in the movie *Unbreakable*; Mr. Glass knew that an arch-villain can only exist if there's a hero. Well the same goes for shadows – they can only exist in the presence of light.

You've already learned about all the different types of light sources available in Scene Kit. Unfortunately, not all lights are capable of casting shadows; only the **spot** and the **directional** lights have this *dark* ability.

Getting started

In order to demonstrate how lights and shadows work, we had to fabricate a sample scenario, leading you to this very important question: ♫ Do You Want to Build a Snowman? ♫ :]

The neighborhood kids built this little guy on your front lawn, and now he's casting a shadow thanks to the directional light that's simulating sunlight. How sweet; now go grab a shovel and show Olaf's distant cousin what you think about little kids' art projects on your property! :]

Directional shadows

You know how a laser shines a thin beam of light into the distance? You can think of a directional light as a million little laser lights, streaming light in parallel in a given direction.

Unlike a spot light shadow, the size of the shadow cast by the directional light won't change as the distance to the light source changes. However, the length of the shadow is affected by the angle at which the light hits the 3D object, just as your shadow grows longer towards sunset.

Directional lights are somewhat strange when it comes to casting shadows, because the node's scale property plays a big part in determining the area of the shadow it creates. Scene Kit creates a 2D shadow map from the light nodes point of view. Directional lights ignores position information because the light has a constant direction. Directional lights requires an orthographic projection. That's why the scale property controls the visible extents of the orthographic projection.

If you're using a directional light in your scene and you don't see a shadow, you probably need to adjust the node's scale. This can be done by either tweaking the node scale, or the light shadow attributes scale:

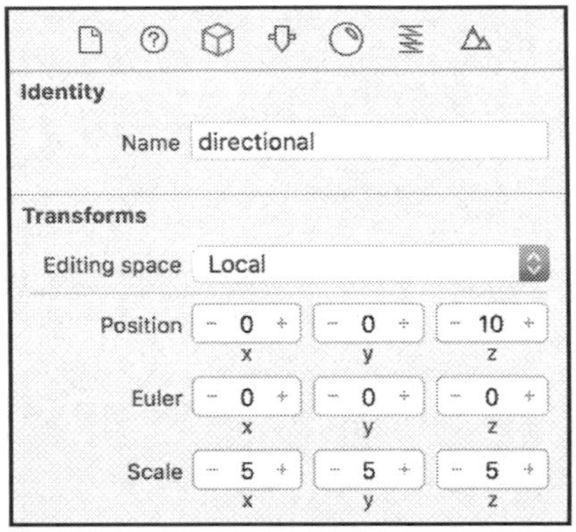

The image below demonstrates the effect that adjusting the directional light's node scale has on the resulting shadow:

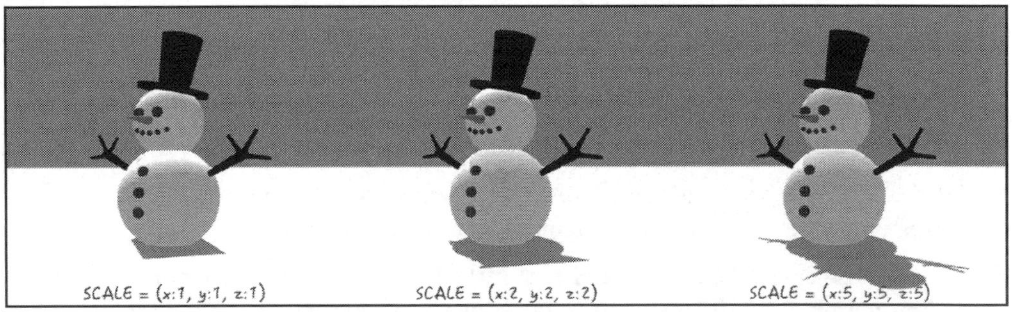

At a scale of 1, you can clearly see a square shadow that's clipped in both the x and y directions. As you increase the scaling to 2, you start to notice the shadow of the rounded body, but still no hands, nose or head. Finally by increasing the scale to 5, you're able to see all the body parts, even the pointy nose.

Note: For a more hands-on experience, have a look under the **projects/resources/Snowman** folder. Double click the **Snowman_Directional.scn** scene file to open it up in Xcode. Select the **directional** light under the scene graph, then press ⌥⌘4 (Option+Command+4) to open up the attributes inspector.

Take a closer look at the directional light's Attributes Inspector; you'll notice there's a **shadow** section at the bottom:

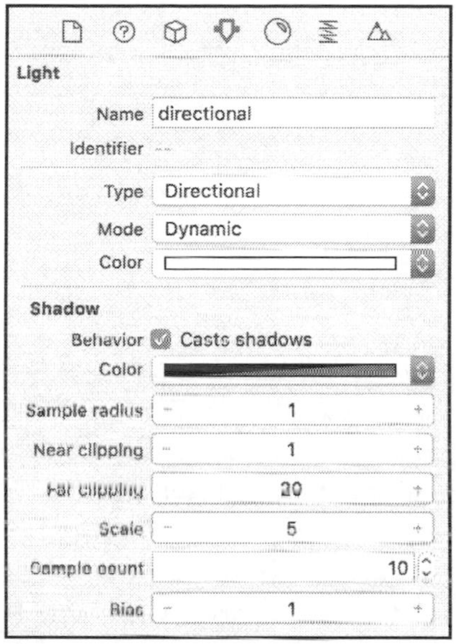

Iterating through all the available shadow properties:

- **Behaviour**: Determines whether the light will cast a shadow.
- **Color**: Determines the color of the shadow cast. You can modify the color and transparency level; this lets other colors show through the shadow.
- **Sample radius**: Scene Kit can produce soft shadows by rendering a silhouette of your 3D object onto a 2D shadow map; this radius is used to generate several sample shadow maps. A lower radius will result in a sharper shadow, while larger radii will produce softer shadows.
- **Near/Far clipping**: Any object outside the range of these values from the light source will not produce a shadow, thus clipping its own shadow. This property can be tweaked when performance starts to become an issue.
- **Scale**: Determines the resolution of the generated shadow maps. A scale of 1 will produce the highest resolution, while higher values produce lower-resolution shadow maps.
- **Sample count**: This property works hand-in-hand with the sample radius property. Specifying higher numbers of shadow samples produces softer shadows.
- **Bias**: Sometimes rendered shadows might not render onto all pixels as expected, causing an effect known as *shadow acne*. You can use this property to fix those types of artifacts.

The image below shows the effect of adjusting the shadow sample count on a spot light shadow with a fairly large sample radius:

With a sample count of 2, you can see two distinct shadows produced. Pushing the sample count higher produces more shadow samples, and eventually ends with a soft shadow on the far right.

The next image shows the impact of shadow scale and reducing the generated shadow map resolution:

With a resolution of 1, you can see a nice crisp shadow edge. Pushing the shadow map resolution lower produces blockier and blockier shadows.

> **Note**: Finding the sweet spot between the shadow Scale and Sample Count plays an important part in tweaking the performance of your games. Crisper shadows are less processor-hungry than soft, smooth shadows. Keep that in mind when you're trying to manage performance issues in your game.

Spot shadows

Arkham City is in trouble; mass riots have broken out, pushing the police force to the breaking point. Arkham has only one hope left – signal the Batman! :]

The Batman signal is a good example of a spot light that casts a shadow. The closer the object is to the light source, the bigger the shadow it casts due to the cone structure of the spot light.

Let's return to Olaf's distant cousin for a moment. Night has fallen upon Winter Wonderland, and a nearby street light now shines its light onto the little snowman, casting a shadow in front of it.

> **Note**: For a more hands-on experience, have a look under the **/projects/resources/Snowman** folder. Double click the **Snowman_Spot.scn** scene file to open it up in Xcode. Select the **spot** light under the scene graph, then press ⌥⌘4 (Option+Command+4) to open up the attributes inspector.

Take a look at the spot light's Attributes Inspector; you'll notice a **shadow** section at the bottom:

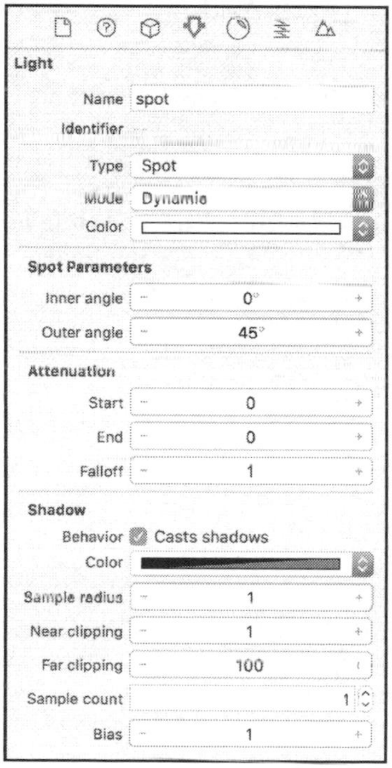

The options for spot lights are similar to the options for directional lights:

- **Behavior**: Determines whether the light will cast a shadow.
- **Color**: The color of the shadow cast. You can choose both color and transparency level, this will allow the shadow to allow other colors through.
- **Sample radius**. Scene Kit can produce soft shadows by rendering a silhouette of your 3D object onto a 2D shadow map, this radius is then used to generate several sample shadow maps. A lower radius will result in a sharper shadow, where larger radiuses will produce softer shadows.
- **Near/Far clipping**. Any object not within the range of these values from the light source will not produce a shadow, thus clipping their shadows. This property can be tweaked when performance starts to become an issue.
- **Sample count**. This property works hand in hand with the sample radius property. Specifying how many shadow samples to generate when generating the shadow map. Higher numbers should produce softer shadows.
- **Bias**. Sometimes rendered shadows might not render onto all pixels as expected, causing an effect known as shadow acne. You can use this property to fix those types of artefacts.

The image below shows the effect of adjusting the sample count of the spot light shadow with a fairly large sample radius:

A sample count of 1 creates a crisp, clean and sharp shadow. With a sample count of 2, you can clearly see two distinct shadows, as if the shadows were produced from two light sources that are close in proximity. Pushing the sample count up to 5 produces a softer, smoother shadow.

OK that's it for your snowman - time to add some shadows to Marble Maze using what you've learned so far!

Note: Before you continue, load up the starter project under the **projects/starter/MarbleMaze** folder. It continues where you left off with the previous chapter.

Organizing the scene

At this point, you need to do some basic housekeeping on the main game scene.

Select the **art.scnassets/game.scn** scene. You should already have a ball and a camera node in the scene. You're going to organize the scene graph so it looks like the following:

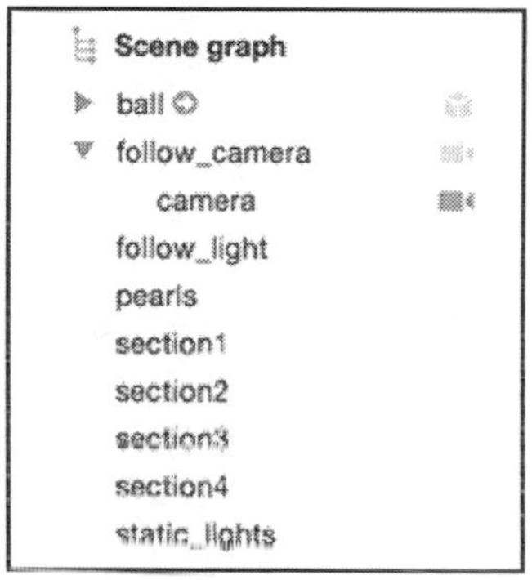

You'll deal with the scene graph first.

Create an empty node named **follow_camera**:

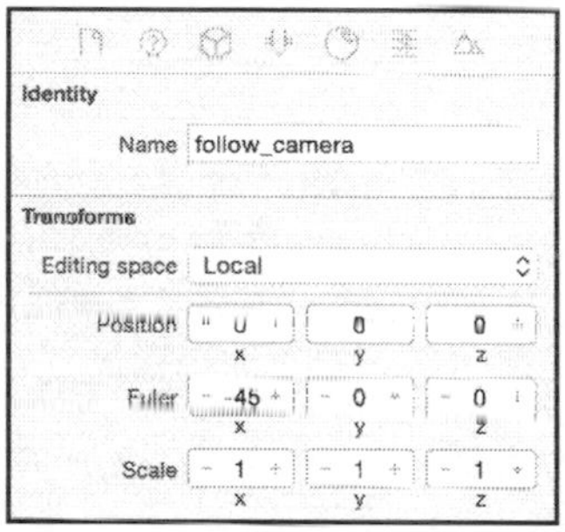

Zero out its position and set its rotation angle to `(x:-45, y:0, z:0)`.

Make the **camera** node a child of **follow_camera**:

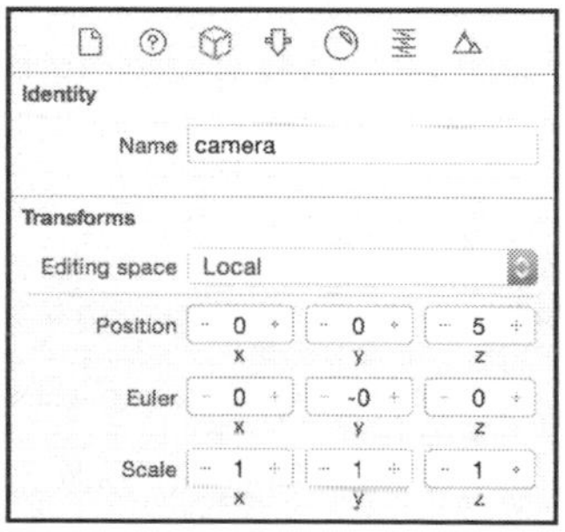

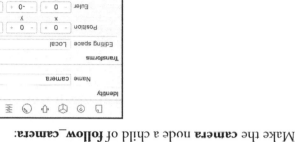

Set the **camera** position to `(x:0, y:0, z:5)`.

Note: By making the **camera** a child node of the **follow_camera** node and placing it at a z-position of 5 units, you have essentially placed it on an imaginary selfie stick. If you move the parent node position, the **camera** will simply follow. If you rotate the parent node, the **camera** will swing around, but it will always face the parent position – it's a neat little trick. Selfie time! :]

Create another empty node named **follow_light**:

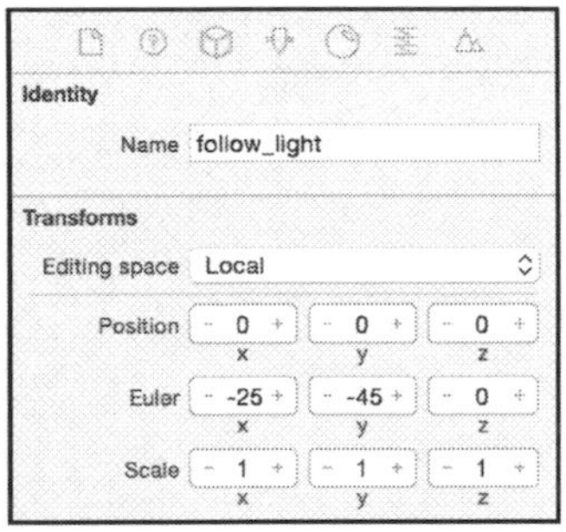

Zero out its position as well. You'll add a spot light to this node that always shines light on its subject. Set the node's rotation to `(x:-25, y:-45, z:0)`. Spin the scene around and you'll notice the background source of light comes from that precise direction.

Add the following empty nodes and zero out their positions; they're simply placeholders for later:

- **pearls**: You'll add collectable pearls under this group.
- **section1**, **section2**, **section3**, **section4**: These groups will hold different sections of the level. This will also help you hide certain sections to simplify level editing.

Create a final empty node and name it **static_lights**:

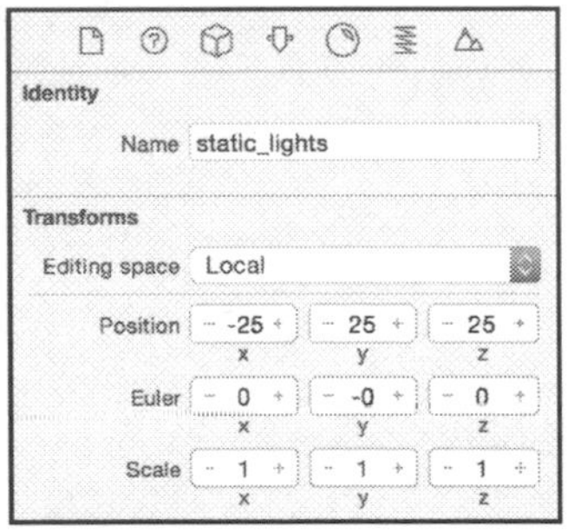

Set its position to `(x:-25, y:25, z:25)`; you'll use this node to group additional lights.

You're all organized and ready to carry on.

Adding lights

You're going to add some static lights to the scene; these are lights that don't move around. You'll also add a spot light to the scene which will move around, following the relic as it rolls through the maze. This spot light will also cast the shadows in your scene.

Add static lights

First you'll add the static lights to the scene. The purpose of these lights is to give the scene some basic lighting, break up the darkness a little and help those normal maps pop.

Drag and drop an omni and an ambient light into the scene and place them under the **static_lights** group node:

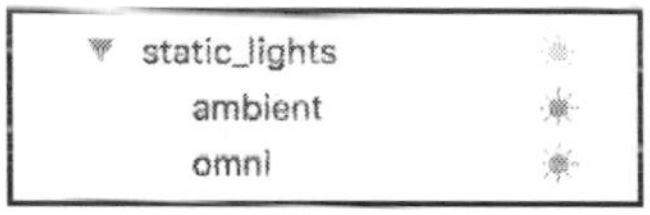

Select the omni light, then select its Node Inspector:

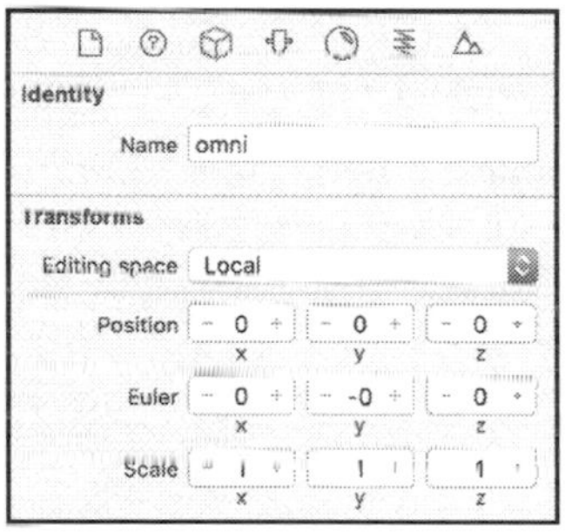

Name the light **omni** and zero out its position and angle; this will place the light right in the middle of its parent node.

Select the Attributes Inspector next:

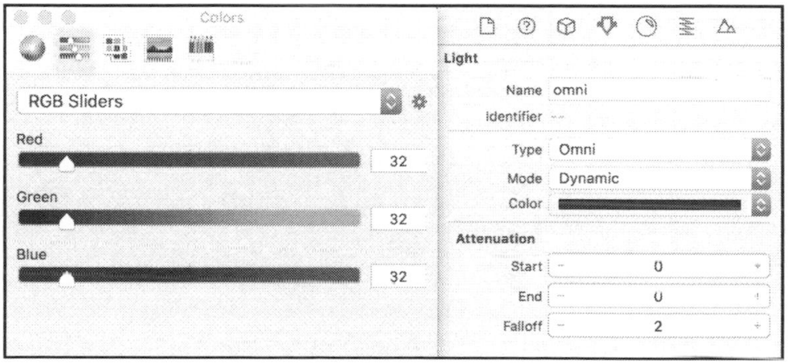

Give the omni light a dark grey color, so that it's not too bright but still has a visible effect.

Select the ambient light next, then select its node inspector.

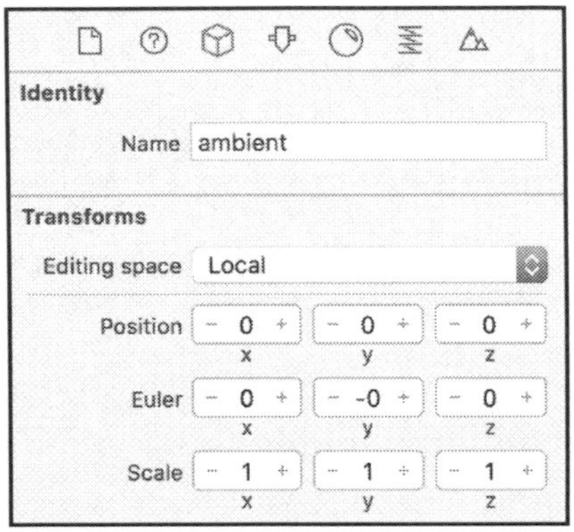

Zero out its position and angle information, which places it right on top of the **omni** light, inside the **static_light** group node parent.

Select its Attributes Inspector:

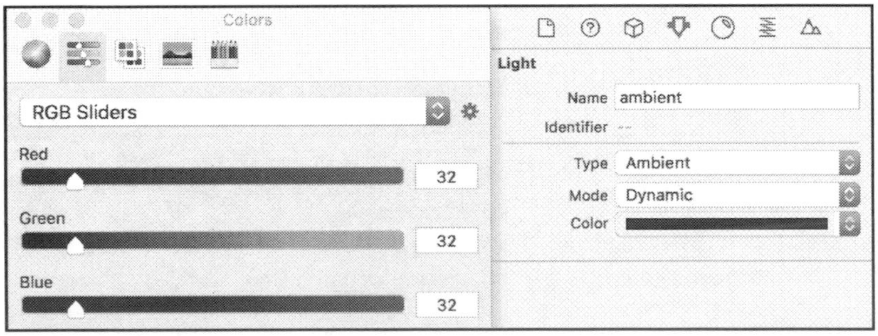

It might seem odd, but give the ambient light a dark grey color as well to lift those dark shadows up a bit.

The final result should resemble the following scene, if you zoom in a bit closer to the ball:

You should be able to see the normal map, and the dark side of the relic shouldn't be black, but softly shaded.

Now to add the light that will follow the relic as it rolls around the scene.

Add the follow light

Drag and drop a spot light into the scene, and place it under the **follow_light** group node:

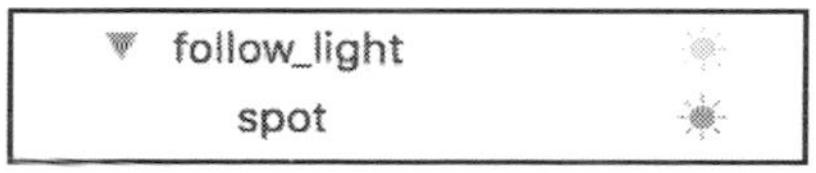

Select the spot light and then select its Node Inspector:

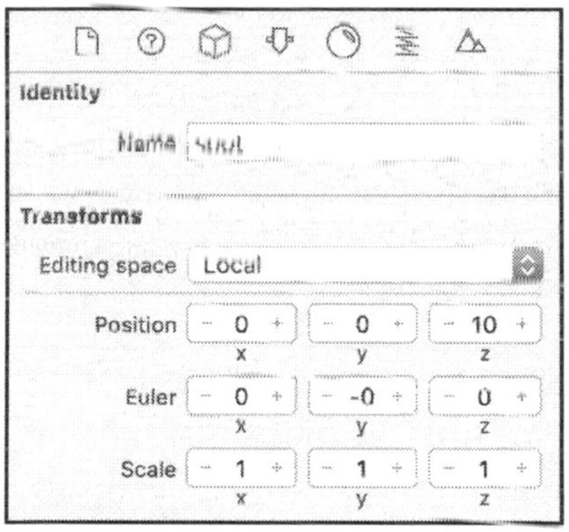

Name the light **spot** and set its position to `(x:0, y:0, z:10)`. This light is a child of the **follow_light** group node, which is at `(x:0, y:0, z:0)` with a angle of `(x: 25, y:-45, z:0)`; therefore the spot light will shine directly on the relic.

> **Note**: This is the selfie stick trick in action, making your life *so* much easier. To keep the light shining on the rolling relic, you simply need to make sure the position of the **follow_light** node matches that of the relic.

Now to add some light and shadow magic. Select the spot light, then select its Attributes Inspector:

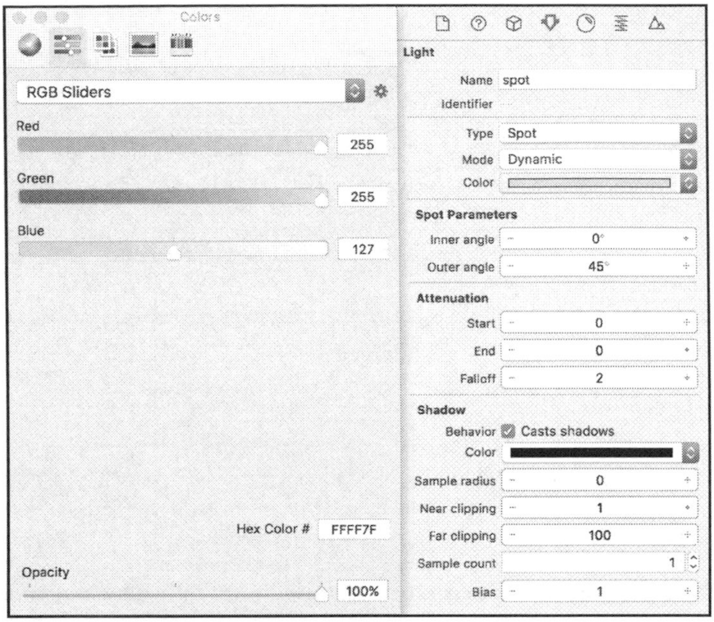

First, set the color of the light to a nice bright golden yellow. This will breathe some warmth into the light and mimic the environmental sunlight shining on the relic.

For a hard-edged shadow, enable **Behavior** so that the light casts shadows. Set **Sample Radius** to `0` to get a crisp shadow. You can leave Near and Far Clipping as they are. Set **Sample Count** to `1` so that you sample the shadow at least once, and leave **Bias** at `1`.

Your scene should now resemble the following:

Behold the glorious golden sun shining warmth onto the relic! :]

Building re-usable sets

Building small little re-usable sets will make your life easier. This way you don't have to manually repeat common patterns and structures, you simply re-use the set where you

need it in the level.

In this section, you'll create a resting point for the relic. It will consist of a nice big 3x3 stone, with 4 pillars stacked on top of it.

Drag an empty **Scene Kit** scene file, from the **File Template** library into the root of your project. Name it **set_restpoint.scn**, then select the group as **art.scnassets** before you hit the **Create** button.

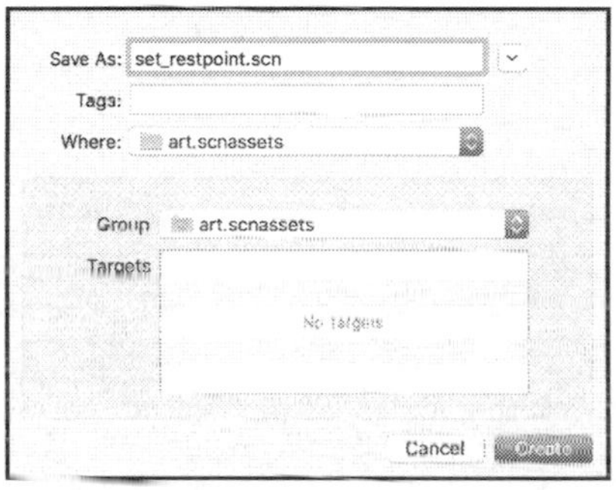

Drag and drop an **obj_stone3x3.scn** reference node into your new empty scene. Make sure to position it at `(x: 0, y: 0, z:0)`.

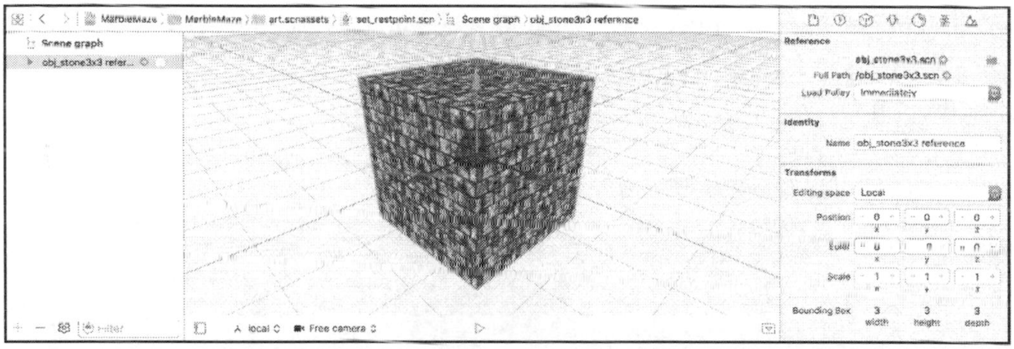

Drag and drop an **obj_pillar1x3.scn** reference node on top of the big stone. Set the position to `(x: -1, y: 3, z: 1)`, so place it right in the corner.

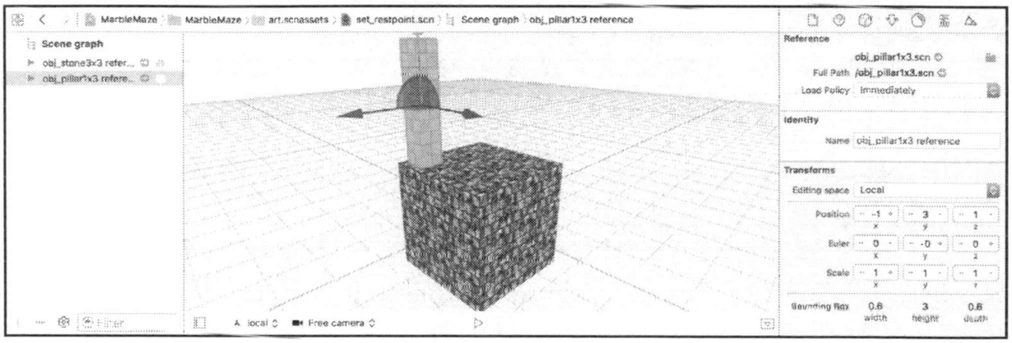

With one pillar down, you still need to create 3 more. Use the ⌥⌘ (Option +Command) key combination to drag copies and place them precisely at the following locations:

- **Top-Left**. Positioned at `(x: -1, y: 3, z: -1)`.
- **Top-Right**. Positioned at `(x: 1, y: 3, z: -1)`.
- **Bottom-Right**. Positioned at `(x: 1, y: 3, z: 1)`.

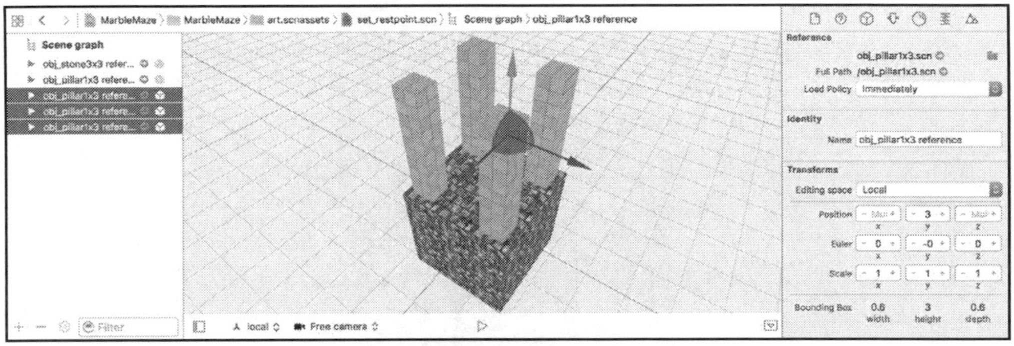

Note: Don't forget to delete that default camera node out of the reference scene before you save it.

Select your **game.scn**, then drag and drop that freshly built **set_restpoint.scn** below the relic. Make sure to position it at `(x: 0, y: 2, z: 0)`

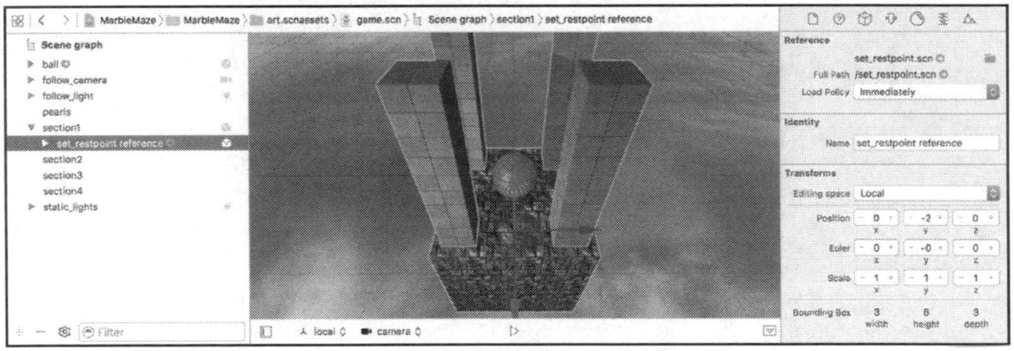

Finally, you can do a build and run, to admire those pretty shadows. :]

Behold the glorious golden sun with a soft cool shadow casted over the relic! :]

Note: You can find a project containing all the work done up to this point under the **projects/final/MarbleMaze** folder.

Challenge

Surprise challenge! You didn't see that one coming, did you? :]

Now that you've mastered the skill of using reference nodes and building small scenes and sets, you'll need to build some more basic sets, which will be referenced in the main game scene.

Build the following sets for the game, making use of the following samples:

The **straight_bridge**:

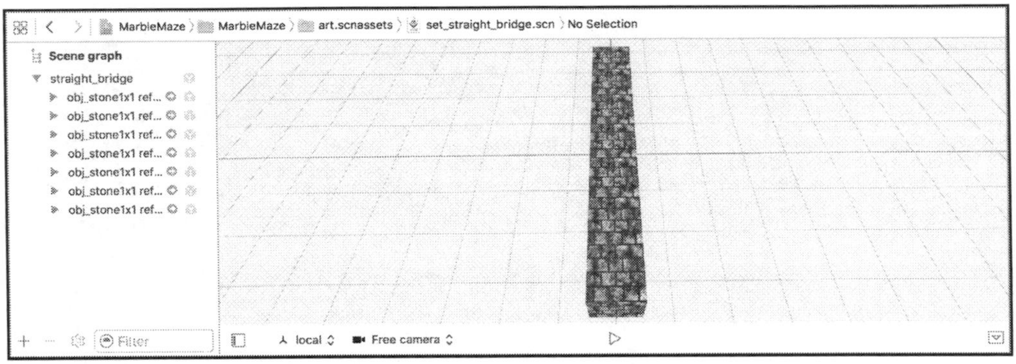

This set consists of seven small **stone1x1** blocks, all neatly packed next to each other.

The **zigzag_bridge**:

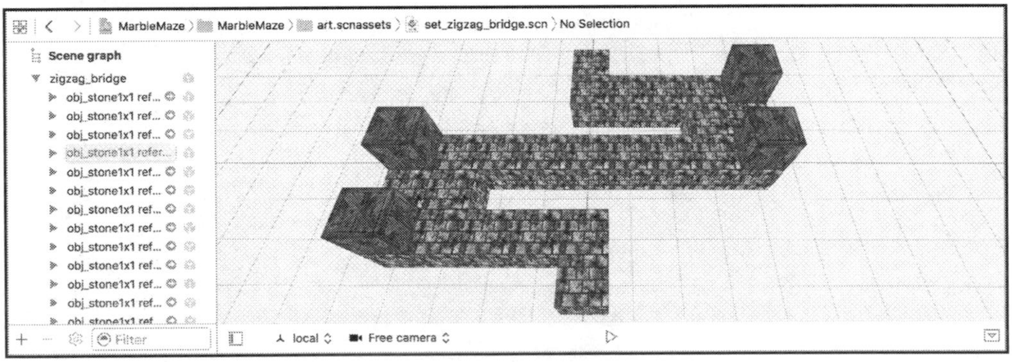

This set might be a bit trickier, but nothing's too tough for you now! :] It's constructed of **stone1x1** blocks and **crate1x1** blocks. It's 9 blocks wide and 7 blocks deep. Make sure to place those crates right on the corner edges.

> **Note**: Each set starts with a blank scene, then uses reference nodes to build up the set. Remember to remove all lights and cameras from these sets as they'll be referenced in your main game scene.

Once you've created all those little sets, see if you can build the first section of the main game scene.

Here's a sample of what the final result should look like:

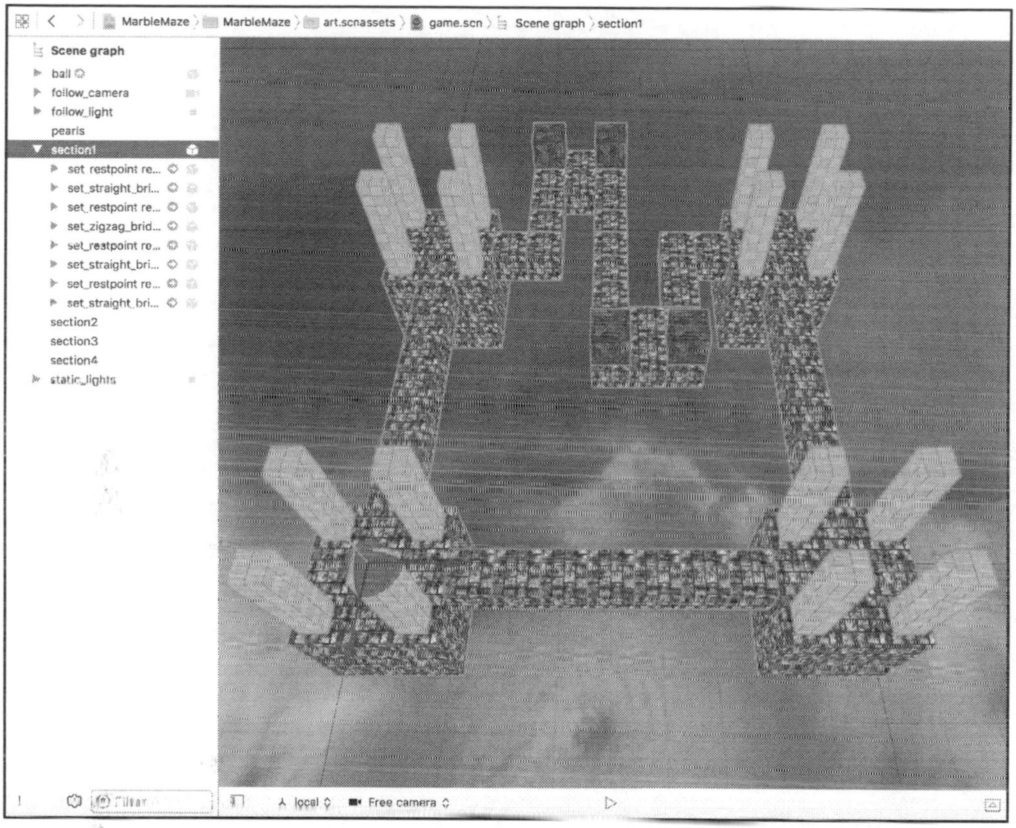

Start at the bottom left corner, place a **restpoint** right underneath the relic positioned at `(x:0, y:0, z:0)`, then pull in the rest of the reference sets to complete the entire scene.

Make sure you place all the sets under the **section1** group node. This is a neat little trick you can apply when you start building large scenes: simply segment the set into sections, then use the **visible** flag to show or hide the set as required. This will definitely speed up the editing process.

> **Note**: Fear not, if this challenge pushed you out of your comfort zone, you can download the final project under the **projects/challenge/MarbleMaze** folder.

Finishing up

To see the stunning result first-hand on a device, build and run and pan the camera around the scene. If you prefer, you can just press the **play** button under the scene:

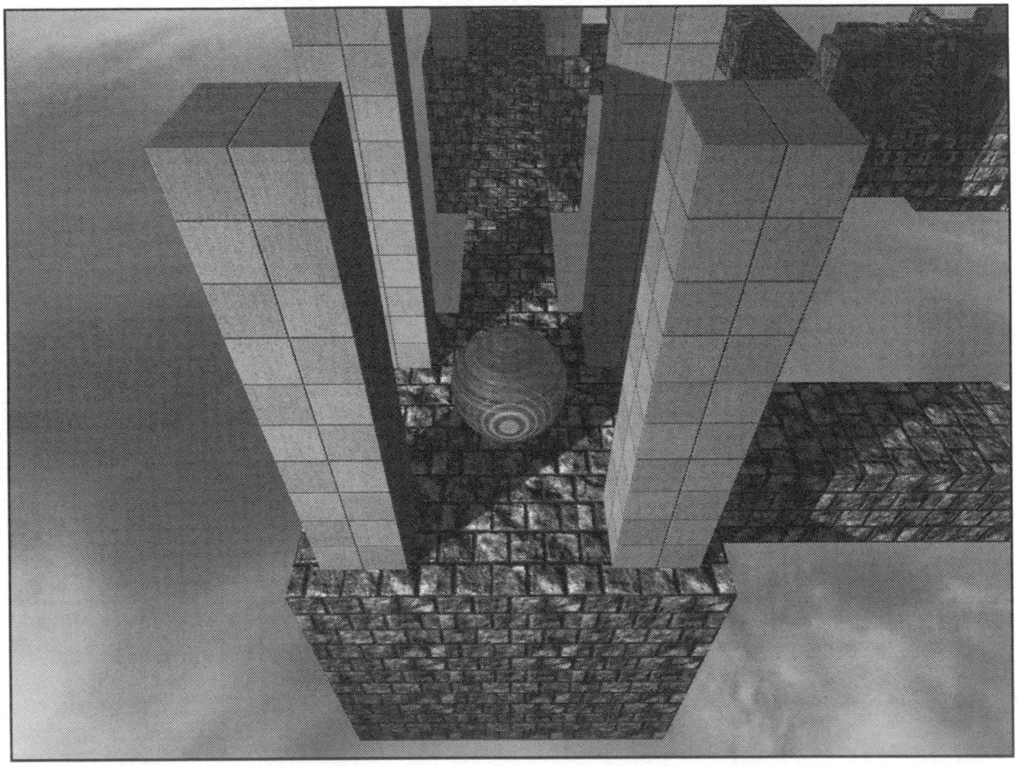

Did your jaw bone just dislodge itself? :] It's an absolutely stunning view.

Before you continue, see if you can spin the view around so that you have the sun light shining in your eyes, like so:

Lights placed at strategic locations in your scene, along with your environmental map, make for some impressive realism. You almost want to squint your eyes, even though your screen can't go any brighter than white. It's all just an illusion – thanks to those stunning silhouetted pillars caused by the shadows.

Where to go from here?

You've reached the end of this chapter; your game is in good shape. In this chapter, you covered the following concepts:

- **Lights**: Shadows needs lights, specifically a spot light or a directional light when dealing with Scene Kit.
- **Soft and hard shadows**: The shadow's Sample Radius and Sample Count settings have a definite effect on the hardness of the shadow edge.

The next chapter will make your game come alive and let your player take control of the relic, rolling it through your maze in the sky!

Chapter 14: Intermediate Collision Detection

Chris Language

In this chapter, you'll enable physics within your game and add collision detection. For the most part, the player will roll the ball around the maze, bumping into stone blocks and crates, while trying to keep the ball from falling off the maze. Although rolling around on a sky maze is pretty cool, it's still lacking that *fun* factor – something that will force the player to take on the maze as fast as possible.

If nothing pushed the player to roll through the maze, then the player could simply park the ball in a corner and take a nap until they felt like tackling the next part of the maze. That's just not acceptable! :]

Therefore, the ball will have to consume pearls of life in order to survive. You'll use the rings of light on the ball as a visual indicator of how much life the player has left; the brighter the rings of light shine, the more life that's left in the ball. The player's life reduces over time, which forces the player to scout for more pearls of life scattered all over the sky maze.

> **Note**: This chapter continues where the previous one left off; you can find the starter project for this chapter under the **projects/starter/MarbleMaze/** folder.

Getting started

Drag an empty Scene Kit file into your project:

Name it **obj_pearl.scn** and save it to the **art.scnassets** folder. Remember to delete the default camera node; you don't want extra lights and cameras in reference nodes

Next, drag and drop a sphere node from the Object Library into your new scene.

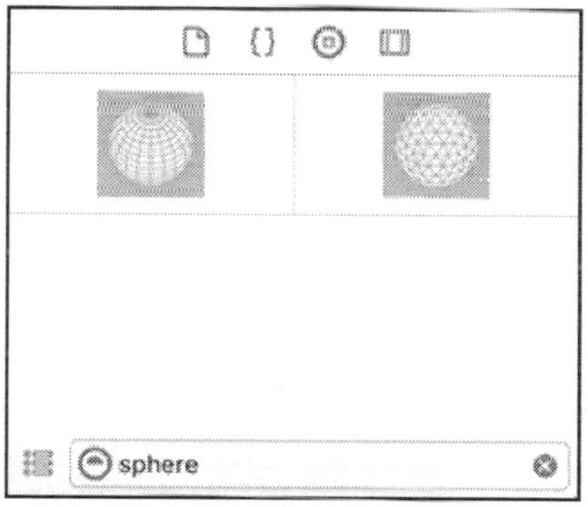

Use the Node Inspector to name the node **"pearl"** and zero out its position and angles:

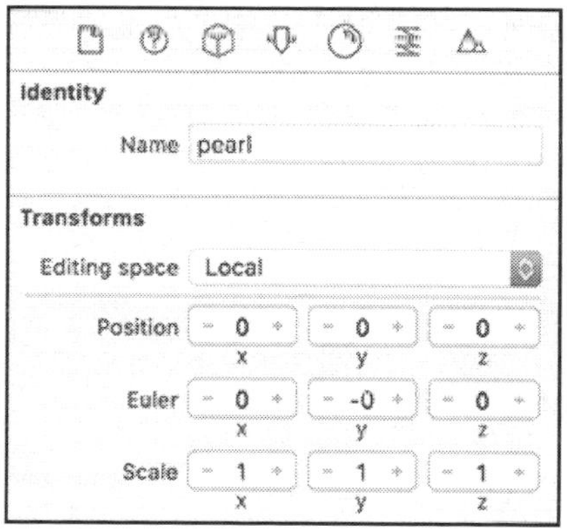

Use the Attributes Inspector to set the radius to `0.2` and reduce the segment count down to `16`:

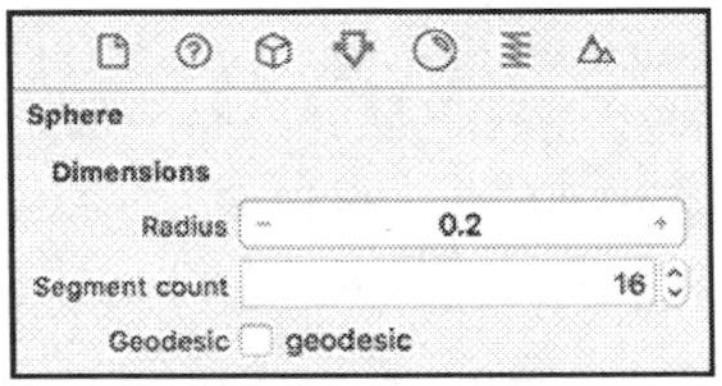

This shrinks the pearl down to a consumable size. :] There's going to be plenty of pearls in the game, so keeping the polygon count low is important.

Your next task is to make the pearl shiny. Use the Materials Inspector to set the diffuse color to black, with a white specular. Pearls are very reflective, so use **img_skybox.jpg** as a reflective map, but drop the intensity down to `0.75`:

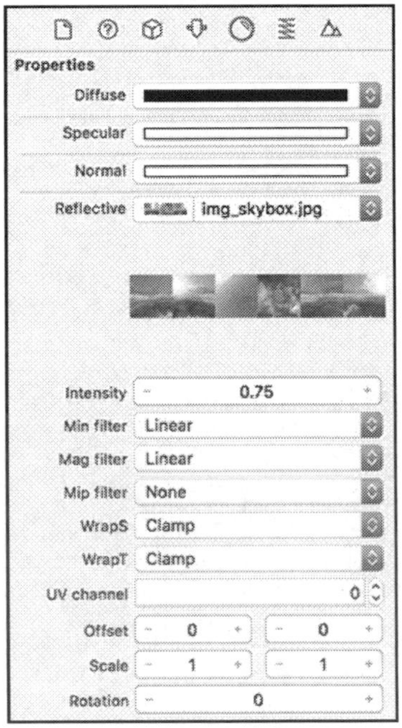

You'll end up with something that resembles this little golden nugget. Just look how shiny it is! :]

Adding game utilities

To keep you focused on collision detection, we've provided a bunch of game utils for you matters outside the focus of this chapter, like some math utility functions, Sprite Kit integration, and so on. All you need to do is add them to the project.

Drag and drop the **GameUtils** folder into your project from the **projects/resources/GameUtils** folder:

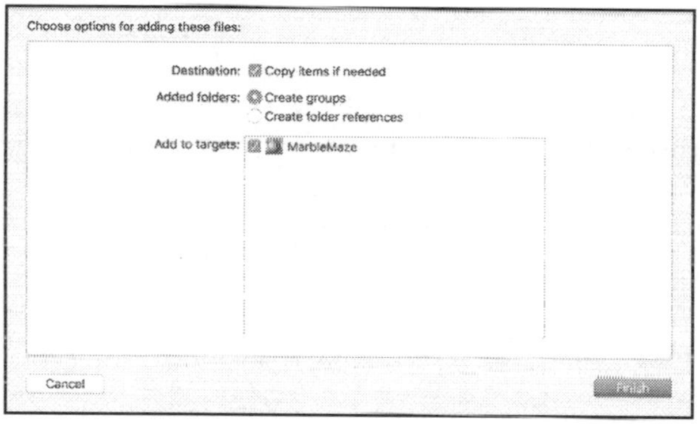

Select **Finish** to complete the process.

Now you'll need to handle the collisions between the ball and the pearls of life. Before you dive into that, you need to understand how bit masks work. The next section covers just that.

Working with bit masks

Bits are those 1's and 0's computers use to represent numbers that looks like this: `00101011`. A collection of 1's and 0's is known as a **binary** number. Each bit represents a specific numerical value and reads in reverse, from the lowest-significant bit to the highest-significant bit. If the bit is 1, it's considered ON, while 0 means it's OFF.

Below is crude example of an 8-bit binary value, counting up from zero to seven:

BIT	7	6	5	4	3	2	1	0	INTEGER
VALUE	128	64	32	16	8	4	2	1	VALUE
1.	0	0	0	0	0	0	0	1	0+0+0+0+0+0+0+1=1
2.	0	0	0	0	0	0	1	0	0+0+0+0+0+0+2+0=2
3.	0	0	0	0	0	0	1	1	0+0+0+0+0+0+2+1=3
4.	0	0	0	0	0	1	0	0	0+0+0+0+0+4+0+0=4
5.	0	0	0	0	0	1	0	1	0+0+0+0+0+4+0+1=5
6.	0	0	0	0	0	1	1	0	0+0+0+0+0+4+2+0=6
7.	0	0	0	0	0	1	1	1	0+0+0+0+0+4+2+1=7

The first row represents the bits 7 to 0 and counts in reverse starting on the right. The next row shows the value each bit represents. The last column adds all the represented values together of the bits that are ON. The binary value `01010101`, where bits 0, 2, 4 and 6 are all ON and the rest are all OFF, represents the following calculation: `64 + 16 + 4 + 1 = 85`. So `01010101` is the binary representation of `85`. Easy!

Bit masks are basically binary numbers in disguise. Bit masking is a clever way of giving all objects in a physics simulation a low-level identity. You can then perform bitwise operations on your objects to quickly filter out which objects can collide with each other. This technique reduces the amount of objects involved when performing collision detection, hence speeding up the collision checking process by quite a bit.

Category masks

The category mask gives an object a unique ID for collision detection. Besides giving an object a unique ID, you can also group objects together.

Consider *Pac-Man* as an example. There are lots of things Pac-Man can collide with; some good, and some bad. So you could create two groups, one for good things to collide with, and one for bad things – like ghosts!

Here's a few category bit mask examples you might see in a typical *Pac-Man* game:

BIT	7	6	5	4	3	2	1	0	INTEGER
VALUE	128	64	32	16	8	4	2	1	VALUE
Good	0	1	0	0	0	0	0	0	0+1+0+0+0+0+0+0=64
Bad	1	0	0	0	0	0	0	0	1+0+0+0+0+0+0+0=128
Blinky	1	0	0	0	0	0	0	1	1+0+0+0+0+0+0+1=129
Pinky	1	0	0	0	0	0	1	0	1+0+0+0+0+0+2+0=130
Inky	1	0	0	0	0	1	0	0	1+0+0+0+0+4+0+0=132
Clyde	1	0	0	0	1	0	0	0	1+0+0+0+8+0+0+0=136
Blue	0	1	0	0	0	0	0	1	0+1+0+0+0+0+0+1=65

Here, the 8th bit is set to 1 to indicate membership in the **Bad** group, and since all the ghosts (Blinky, Pinky, Inky and Clyde) have the 8th bit set, they can be tested for "Badness" in a bitwise check.

For example, you could have a collision test to determine what exactly should happen to Pac-Man when he collides with an object, like the following:

```
// 1
let good = 64
let bad = 128
let blinky = 129
let pinky = 130
let inky = 132
let clyde = 136
let Blue = 65

func testCollision(contactNode:Int) {
  // 2
  if contactNode & bad == bad {
    // Bad things happens to Pacman
  } else if contactNode & good == good {
    // Good things happens to Pacman
  }
}
```

Taking a closer look:

1. This defines all the category masks as depicted in the table above.
2. This uses the bitwise & operator against the `contactNode` to filter out all the other bits. If the result matches **bad**, it means that the **bad** bit was set, which means **contactNode** is a bad guy, and Pac-Man has to die. :[Since the `contactNode` for each of the ghosts in *Pac-Man* has the 8th bit set, it will always match the **bad** category mask in a bitwise & test.

Defining category masks

Marble Maze is a bit simpler than *Pac-Man*; it will use the following set of category masks:

CATEGORY MASK									
BIT VALUE	7 128	6 64	5 32	4 16	3 8	2 4	1 2	0 1	OBJECT VALUE
AIR	0	0	0	0	0	0	0	0	0
BALL	0	0	0	0	0	0	0	1	1
STONE	0	0	0	0	0	0	1	0	2
PILLAR	0	0	0	0	0	1	0	0	4
CRATE	0	0	0	0	1	0	0	0	8
PEARL	0	0	0	1	0	0	0	0	16

All the objects have been defined with their own unique ID, so there's no need to worry about groups in this case. Your next task is to define these category masks somewhere.

Open **GameViewController.swift** and add the following collision categories to the top of the class:

```
let CollisionCategoryBall = 1
let CollisionCategoryStone = 2
let CollisionCategoryPillar = 4
let CollisionCategoryCrate = 8
let CollisionCategoryPearl = 16
```

Collision masks

You use collision masks to tell the physics engine that some objects are allowed to collide with each other; the physics engine will then prevent these objects from simply passing through each other and trigger an effect within the dynamics of the physics engine. To define a collision mask, you'll need to add together all the category masks of objects that collide with your object.

For Marble Maze, you want the ball to collide with everything *except* for the pearls – you don't want the ball to push the pearls out of the way! Conversely, you'll also need to set everything, except for the pearls, to collide with the ball.

You can use the following collision mask table to keep track of things:

COLLISION MASK									
BIT	7	6	5	4	3	2	1	0	MASK
VALUE	128	64	32	16	8	4	2	1	VALUE
AIR	0	0	0	0	0	0	0	0	0
BALL	0	0	0	0	1	1	1	0	14
STONE	0	0	0	0	0	0	0	1	1
PILLAR	0	0	0	0	0	0	0	1	1
CRATE	0	0	0	0	0	0	0	1	1
PEARL	0	0	0	0	0	0	0	1	1

Refer back to the category masks; you'll see the Stone, Pillar, Crate and Pearl collision masks are set to 1, which means they'll collide with the ball. To work out what the ball collision mask should be, you'll have to add all the other categories together to form the following calculation:

```
CollisionMask = Stone + Pillar + Crate = 2 + 4 + 8 = 14
```

Aha – that's why the ball collision mask is set to **14**.

Contact masks

Contact masks tell the physics engine which objects will generate contact events that you'll respond to. These won't automatically have any effect on the physics engine dynamics; they're triggers to which you'll respond programatically. You set up contact masks in exactly the same as you do collision masks.

For Marble Maze, you want the pearl to generate a contact event, but you also want the pillars and crates to generate an event so you can play a "bump" sound when the ball hits them.

You can use the following contact mask table for that:

CONTACT MASK									
BIT	7	6	5	4	3	2	1	0	MASK
VALUE	128	64	32	16	8	4	2	1	VALUE
AIR	0	0	0	0	0	0	0	0	0
BALL	0	0	0	1	1	1	0	0	28
STONE	0	0	0	0	0	0	0	0	0
PILLAR	0	0	0	0	0	0	0	0	0
CRATE	0	0	0	0	0	0	0	0	0
PEARL	0	0	0	0	0	0	0	0	0

You're only interested in contact between the ball and pearls, pillars and crates. This gives you the following calculation:

```
ContactMask = Pearl + Pillar + Crate = 16 + 8 + 4 = 28
```

Now you can configure the contact mask for the ball in code.

Still in **GameViewController.swift**, add the following property to the top of the class:

```
var ballNode:SCNNode!
```

Now add the following code to `setupNodes()`:

```
ballNode = scnScene.rootNode.childNodeWithName("ball",
recursively: true)!
ballNode.physicsBody?.contactTestBitMask =
CollisionCategoryPillar | CollisionCategoryCrate |
CollisionCategoryPearl
```

The first line attaches `ballNode` to the actual **ball** node in the scene. The next line sets up the actual `contactTestBitMask` by performing a bitwise OR on all category masks.

Note: You can set the category mask and collision mask in the Scene Editor, but at the time of writing this chapter you can only set the `contactTestBitMask` in code, hence why you are doing it here. Another benefit of setting it in code is it's easier to work with OR'ing constant values than having to remember what 28 represents in binary!

Now that you've figured out all the bit mask properties for all the game objects, you can enable the physics properties of those objects.

Enabling physics

The ball will be a *dynamic* physics body; this means the physics engine will take full control over the movement of the ball and move it based on its physics properties.

Select the **obj_ball.scn** scene under the **art.scnassets** folder, then select the **ball** node. Use the Physics Inspector to set the **Physics Body** type to **Dynamic**:

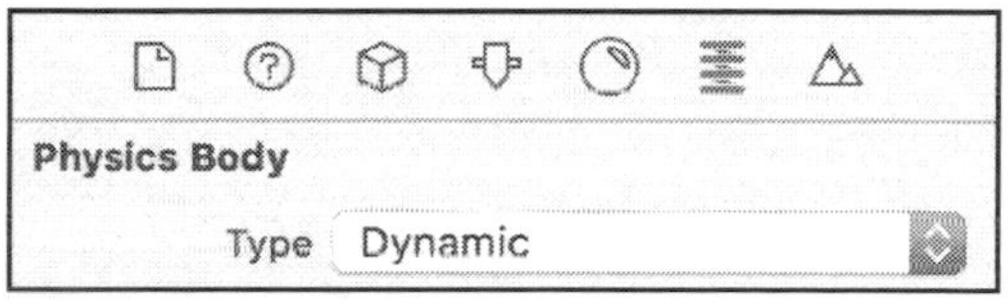

Ensure that **Gravity** is **enabled**; otherwise, the ball would float in space:

Now you can set up the bit masks. Set the **Category mask** to 1 and the **Collision mask** to 14:

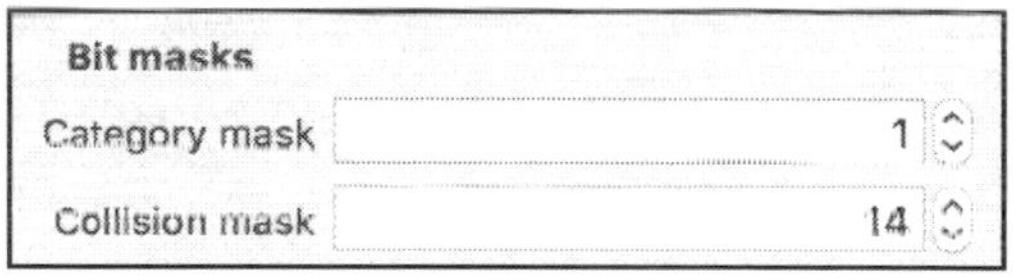

You're going to leave the **Shape** at **Default shape**, and **Type** at **Convex**:

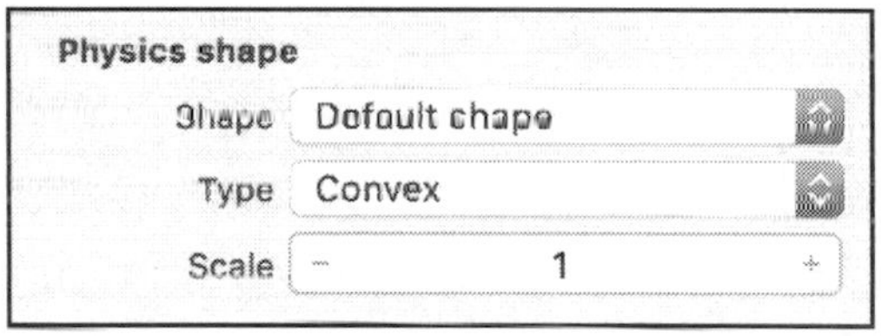

Since this is a spherical object, Scene Kit sets it up as a perfect sphere instead of generating a mesh to represent the shape of the object.

Save the scene changes before you move on.

Return to your main game scene – **game.scn** under **art.scnassets**. Press the **play** button for the scene, and...the ball falls through the stone floor! Don't worry – this is because you haven't set up any of the other physics bodies yet.

Enable static physics objects

The rest of the objects in the game will be *static* objects, which means they can't be moved.

You'll need to repeat the following steps for all of these objects:

- obj_stone1x1.scn
- obj_stone3x3.scn
- obj_pillar1x3.scn
- obj_crate1x1.scn
- obj_pearl.scn

First, select the scene under the **art.scnassets** folder, then make sure the object node itself is selected. Use the Physics Inspector of each object to set their respective **Physics Type** to **Static**:

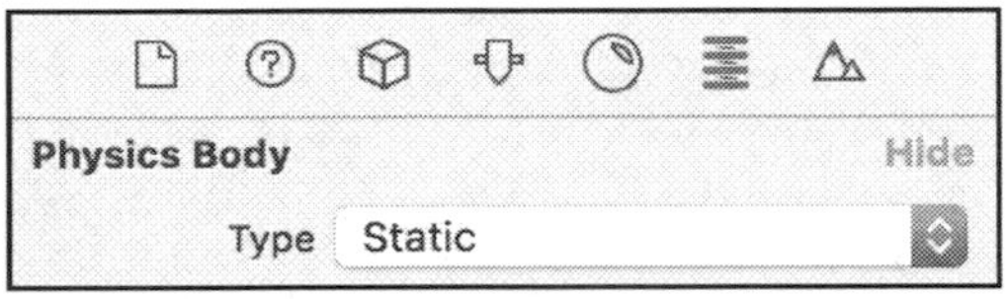

Now for the bit masks. Set the **obj_stone1x1.scn Category mask** to 2, and the **Collision mask** to 1:

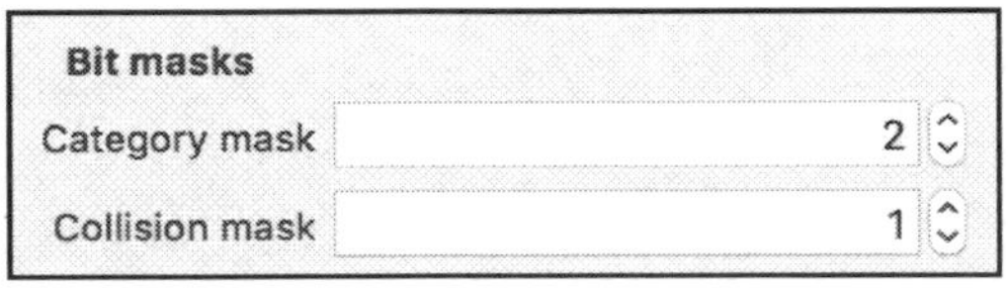

Configure the rest of the objects as follows:

- **obj_stone3x3.scn**: **Category mask** to 2, and **Collision mask** to 1.
- **obj_pillar1x3.scn**: **Category mask** to 4, and **Collision mask** to 1.
- **obj_crate1x1.scn**: **Category mask** to 8, and **Collision mask** to 1.
- **obj_pearl.scn**: **Category mask** to 16, and **Collision mask** to –1.

Note: The pearl is special, and will not cause an actual collision with the ball. That's why it's set to –1.

You're almost done – the only thing left is to configure the physics shapes. The pearl uses a Physics shape of **Default shape**, with a Type of **Convex**:

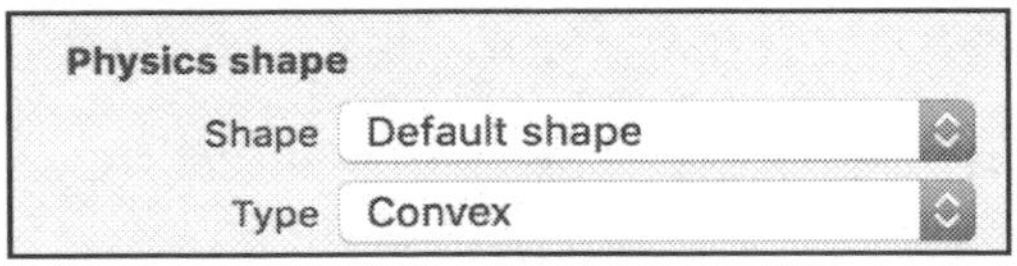

Since the pearl is a sphere, Scene Kit will generate the physics shape as a perfect sphere.

The rest of the objects should be configured as follows, with **Default shape** and **Bounding Box**:

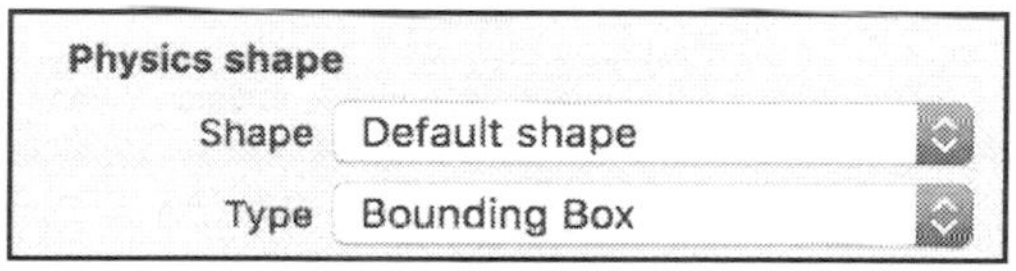

This creates a perfect box around the edges of the object. Since all these bodies are square by nature, the bounding box will fit them perfectly.

Note: The sphere is the most efficient physics shape you can use. The second-most efficient? The bounding box type.

Adding collision detection code

To complete the collision detection, you need to add the code that will handle the actual collision events.

Add the following code to the bottom of **GameViewController.swift**:

```
extension GameViewController : SCNPhysicsContactDelegate {
  func physicsWorld(world: SCNPhysicsWorld, didBeginContact
contact: SCNPhysicsContact) {
    // 1
    var contactNode:SCNNode!
    if contact.nodeA.name == "ball" {
      contactNode = contact.nodeB
    } else {
      contactNode = contact.nodeA
    }

    // 2
    if contactNode.physicsBody?.categoryBitMask ==
CollisionCategoryPearl {
      contactNode.hidden = true

contactNode.runAction(SCNAction.waitForDurationThenRunBlock(30)
{ (node:SCNNode!) -> Void in
      node.hidden = false
      })
    }

    // 3
    if contactNode.physicsBody?.categoryBitMask ==
CollisionCategoryPillar ||
contactNode.physicsBody?.categoryBitMask ==
```

```
CollisionCategoryCrate {
      }
    }
  }
```

This extends the `GameViewController` class with the `SCNPhysicsContactDelegate` protocol. Here's what goes on inside:

1. This is the nifty little trick you learned previously that lets you quickly determine the actual contact node. The `if` block sets `contactNode` to the node that collided with the ball.
2. This section tests to see if the `categoryBitMask` of `contactNode` matches that of `CollisionCategoryPearl`. If so, make the pearl invisible to make it look like the ball "consumed" the pearl. You'll spawn the pearl again after 30 seconds; this is just long enough for the ball to die if the player decides to stick around and wait for the pearl to re-spawn.
3. This section checks whether the ball bounced off of a pillar or off of a crate. This would make a great place to play a "bump" sound later on.

Your final step for this chapter is to ensure that the scene's physics world contact delegate knows that the `GameViewController` class is now responsible for handling these contact events.

Add the following to the bottom of `setupScene()`:

```
scnScene.physicsWorld.contactDelegate = self
```

Make the ball fall from the sky

There's one little thing you need to change, just to add some drama to your game.

Position the ball high up in the air, so that when the game starts, the ball will fall from the sky.

Select the **obj_ball.scn** scene, then adjust the set the y position to 10.

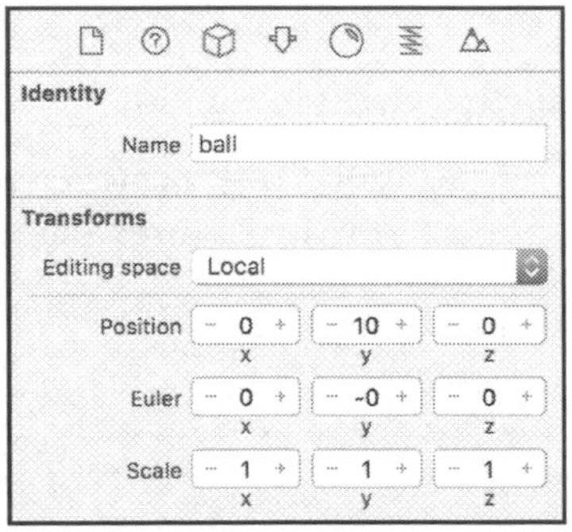

Build and run your game to make sure that everything is still well:

As the game starts up, you'll see the ball fall from above and come to rest on the stone platform below. Hey – it's not falling through the floor any more! Apart from that though, everything still looks pretty much the same as before.

Add a pearl of life

Now to add something special to test out the collisions.

Select the game scene, then drag and drop a **obj_pearl.scn** reference node into the scene. Position it at `(x: 0, y: 0, z: 0)`. Also make sure to move the pearl under the **pearls** group node.

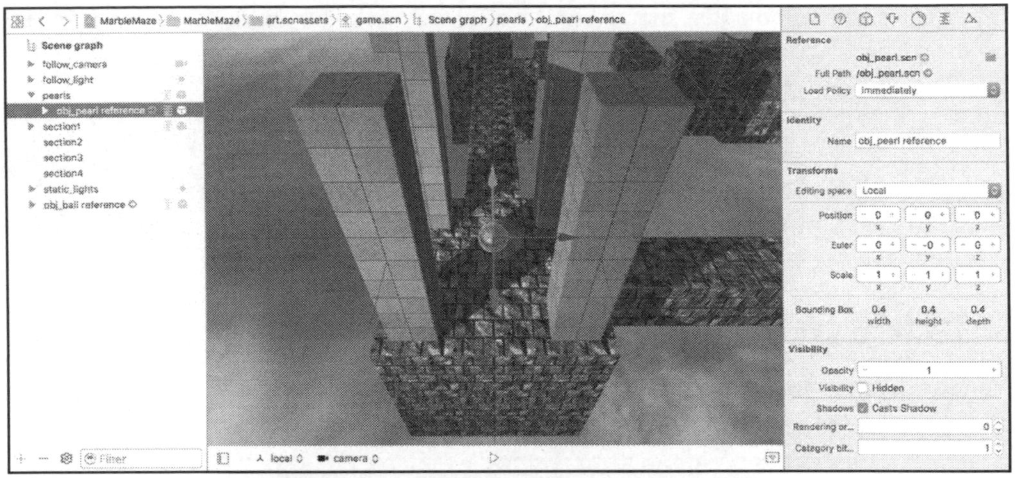

Make sure everything is saved, then do another build and run:

If you take a closer look, you should see the great relic falling from the sky, then gobbles up the pearl. Awesome! :]

> **Note**: You can find the project up to this point under the **projects/final/MarbleMaze/** folder.

Challenge

Time for another fun little challenge; see if you can scatter a few more pearls for the player all over the level. You can use the following image as a reference:

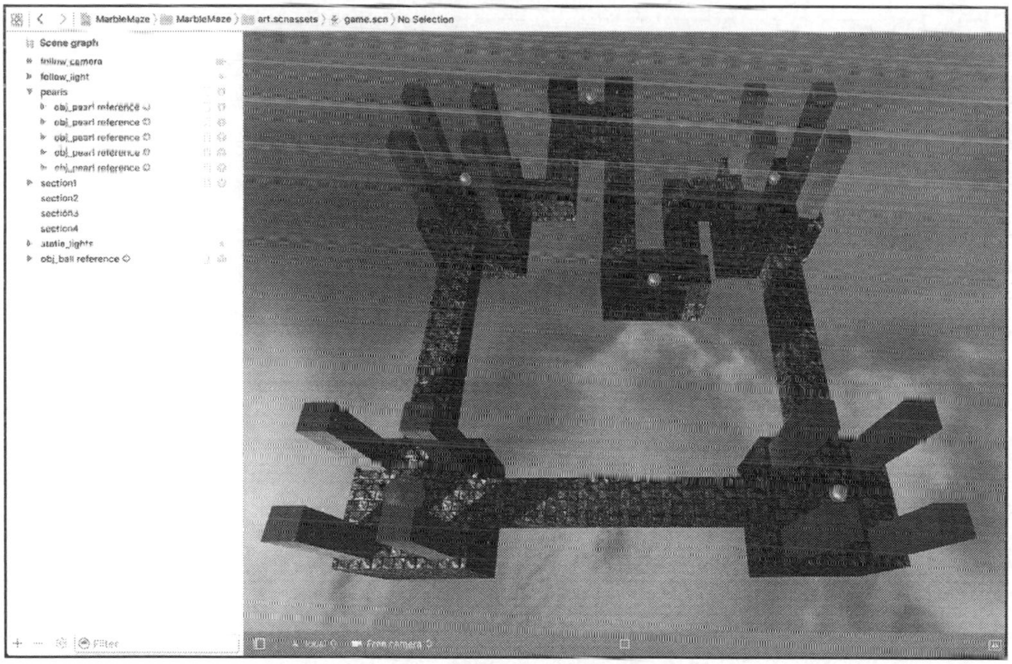

Place a pearl ontop of all the rest points, and between all the crates. Make sure to place the pearls on a y position of `0` – the same plane as the relic. Also make sure you move all the pearls to the **pearls** group node to keep things nice and organized.

> **Note**: You can find the solution for this challenge under the **projects/challenge/MarbleMaze/** folder.

Where to go from here?

You've covered some complex topics in this chapter. To recap:

- **Collectables**: You've added a new element to your game to make it more interesting – the pearl of life. Without it, the ball would simply die a pathetic, lonely death. This also gives the player purpose to navigate the sky maze in search of more pearls.
- **Bit Masks**: You now know all about bit masks; what they look like, how they operate, and most importantly, how to use them in Scene Kit.
- **Category masks**: You've learned that this mask simply gives the object an ID and that you could employ complex grouping strategies should you need to.
- **Collision masks**: You've learned that this mask defines a list of objects that can collide with your object, and physically block them from passing through each other.
- **Contact masks**: You've learned that this mask defines a list of objects that will trigger contact events when they make contact with your object.

In the following and final chapter, you'll add the ability to move the ball. What are you waiting for? It's time to get the ball rolling! :]

Chapter 15: Motion Control

Chris Language

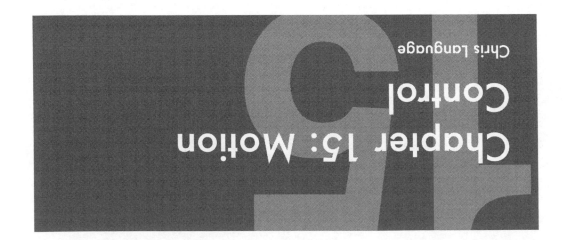

Up to this point, you've focused mostly on the visual aspects of your game – and a fine-looking game it is! This chapter will make a detour from the aesthetics and take you through the code of the game mechanics.

First, you'll add a simple control mechanism to let the player move the ball by tilting the device. You'll then add some logic to the camera and lights to follow the ball wherever it wanders - even if it falls into the abyss! :] Finally, you'll add some basic state management, a HUD for the score, and finally finish it off with some awesome sound effects.

So what are you waiting for? Time to get cracking! :]

Getting started

To start, either load the project where you left it off last time, or laod the starter project under the **projects/starter/MarbleMaze** folder.

In the previous chapter, you added the **GameUtils** folder from the project resources. Now you need to declare a few variables so you can use of those utilities.

Add the following properties to the top of the `GameViewController` class:

```
var game = GameHelper.sharedInstance
var motion = CoreMotionHelper()
var motionForce = SCNVector3(x:0 , y:0, z:0)
```

Here's what these helpers do in detail:

- **game**: A reference to the shared instance of the `GameHelper` class. It provides some simple game state management and a HUD for your game, along with some convenience functions to load and play sound effects.
- **motion**: This creates an instance of the `CoreMotionHelper` class. It gives you a simple way to poll the Core Motion engine for motion data at set intervals.
- **motionForce**: This property will contain a motion vector; you'll use this later as a force vector to put the ball into motion.

Adding sound effects

There's a set of awesome sound effects under the **resources** folder that will bring the game to life. Drag and drop the **Sounds** folder into your project from the **projects/resources** folder:

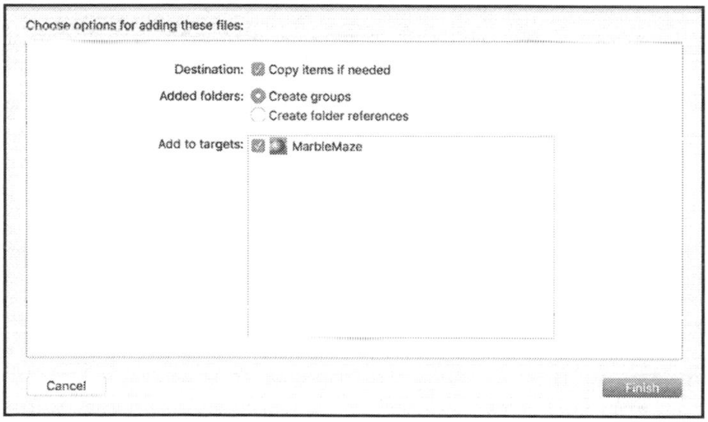

Select **Finish** to complete the import.

Next add the following lines to `setupSounds()` :

```
game.loadSound("GameOver", fileNamed: "GameOver.wav")
game.loadSound("Powerup", fileNamed: "Powerup.wav")
game.loadSound("Reset", fileNamed: "Reset.wav")
game.loadSound("Bump", fileNamed: "Bump.wav")
```

This code is fairly straightforward: it loads the sound files into memory. You'll trigger these sound effects later in this chapter.

Attaching properties to nodes

In this section, you're going to make the camera and lights follow the ball wherever it rolls; this is a common technique in 3rd-person games where the camera trails behind the hero as she runs around the level.

But first, you'll need to attach local properties to the nodes in your game scene.

Attaching to the camera node

Your first task is to make the camera focus continuously on the ball. The camera position won't change, but the camera rotation instead will adjust to follow the ball. To demonstrate this to yourself, hold your head still and roll your eyes around looking at random objects in the room. Are you rolling your eyes at me?! :]

Add the following property to the top of `GameViewController` class:

```
var cameraNode:SCNNode!
```

This will hold your cameraNode once you've attached to it in the game scene.

Next add the following lines to the bottom of `setupNodes()` after the point where you've attached to the `ballNode`:

```
// 1
cameraNode = scnScene.rootNode.childNodeWithName("camera",
recursively: true)!
// 2
let constraint = SCNLookAtConstraint(target: ballNode)
cameraNode.constraints = [constraint]
```

Here's what's going on above:

1. Here you attach **cameraNode** to the actual **camera** in the game scene.
2. This sets up a `SCNLookAtConstraint` to look at the `ballNode` and adds the

constraint to the actual camera's constraints.

Gimbal locking

When the camera has `SCNLookAtConstraint` applied, Scene Kit will do whatever it takes to rotate the camera towards the ball as it rolls around. This "whatever it takes" approach can produce unwanted rotations where the camera might tilt to the left or right.

This wouldn't be a problem if you were controlling a light, but because you're controlling a camera this behavior could cause some odd viewing angles for the player. Instead, you want the camera to stay horizontal at all times.

Scene Kit has you covered, saving you from hours of research and a serious math-related headache. :] Enabling the `gimbalLockEnabled` property on the actual constraint tells Scene Kit to keep the camera aligned horizontally as it follows its target.

Add the following line to the bottom of `setupNodes()`:

```
constraint.gimbalLockEnabled = true
```

This will enable gimbal lock for your camera constraint – and also prevent your viewer from getting motion sick. :]

Attaching to the camera and light follow nodes

Add the following property to the `GameViewController` class:

```
var cameraFollowNode:SCNNode!
var lightFollowNode:SCNNode!
```

This will hold the `cameraFollowNode` and `lightFollowNode` once attached.

Next, add the following to the bottom of `setupNodes()`:

```
// 1
cameraFollowNode =
scnScene.rootNode.childNodeWithName("follow_camera",
recursively: true)!
// 2
cameraNode.addChildNode(game.hudNode)
// 3
lightFollowNode =
scnScene.rootNode.childNodeWithName("follow_light", recursively:
true)!
```

Taking a closer look at the code segment:

1. This attaches `followCameraNode` to the **follow_camera** node in the game scene.
2. This adds the HUD to the camera as a child node so that it remains in view of the camera no matter what direciton it faces.
3. This attaches `followLightNode` to the **follow_light** node in the game scene.

Game state management

Now that you've attached to all the important nodes in the game scene, you need to sort out some basic game states.

You'll be using three states to manage gameplay:

- **WaitForTap**: This is the moment in-between games when the player has not yet started controlling the ball. In this state, you'll let the camera spin around the ball and display a message indicating the game is waiting for input.
- **Playing**: This state triggers when the user taps the screen to start the game. The player can control the ball in this state.
- **GameOver**: This state triggers when the player fails to collect another pearl of life in time or drops into the abyss. This state will automatically move to the **WaitForTap** state after a few seconds.

Next for a few useful functions to help you manage these states. Add the following to the `GameViewController` class:

```
// 1
func playGame() {
  game.state = GameStateType.Playing
  cameraFollowNode.eulerAngles.y = 0
  cameraFollowNode.position = SCNVector3Zero
}
// 2
func resetGame() {
  game.state = GameStateType.TapToPlay
  game.playSound(ballNode, name: "Reset")
  ballNode.physicsBody!.velocity = SCNVector3Zero
  ballNode.position = SCNVector3(x:0, y:10, z:0)
  cameraFollowNode.position = ballNode.position
  lightFollowNode.position = ballNode.position
  scnView.playing = true
  game.reset()
}
// 3
func testForGameOver() {
```

```
    if ballNode.presentationNode.position.y < -5 {
      game.state = GameStateType.GameOver
      game.playSound(ballNode, name: "GameOver")
      ballNode.runAction(SCNAction.waitForDurationThenRunBlock(5)
  { (node:SCNNode!) -> Void in
        self.resetGame()
      })
    }
  }
```

Here's the purpose of each function:

1. **playGame()**: A call to this function switches the game into the `.Playing` state, which starts the game. It also performs some basic cleanup and resets the **cameraFollow** node's angle and position.
2. **resetGame()**: A call to this function puts the game into the `.WaitForTap` state. It also plays a "Reset" sound effect, then does some basic cleanup by resetting the ball's position and velocity. It also resets the `cameraFollowNode` and `lightFollowNode` positions. Note that the `ballNode` position is set to a high y-value; this creates the effect of the ball dropping out of thin air into the sky maze.
3. **testForGameOver()**: A call to this function checks if the ball's y-position has dropped lower than -5 units. If so, the ball has fallen off the edge into the abyss. Whoops! :] It then switches to the `.GameOver` state and plays the "GameOver" sound effect. After five seconds, it automatically triggers a call to `resetGame()`, placing the game back into the `.WaitForTap` state.

> **Note**: During the `.WaitForTap` state, there are no active animations or physics updates, so the renderer stops updating every frame. Later on in this chapter, you will be spinning the camera around the ball during this game state; therefore, the renderer will continue to update every frame. This is why `resetGame()` sets the view's `playing` property to `true`: this forces the renderer to update every frame.

With the basic game state functions in place, you need to set the game's initial state by calling `resetGame()`. Add the following function call to the bottom of `viewDidLoad()`:

```
resetGame()
```

Once everything has been set up, this will set the game into the initial state of `.WaitForTap`.

To start the game, the player simply has to tap on the display. Add the following lines of code to the `GameViewController` class:

```
override func touchesBegan(touches: Set<UITouch>, withEvent
event: UIEvent?) {
  if game.state == GameStateType.TapToPlay {
    playGame()
  }
}
```

This adds a `touchesBegan()` event handler to the `GameViewController` class; if the game is in the `.TapToPlay` state, this will start the game by calling `playGame()`.

Add motion control

Now that you've attached to all the important nodes and have the game states ready, you can set the ball rolling, so to speak! Can you hear the crowd chanting? "Move That Ball! Move That Ball!"" :]

First, add the following to the `GameViewController` class:

```
func updateMotionControl() {
  // 1
  if game.state == GameStateType.Playing {
    motion.getAccelerometerData(0.1) { (x,y,z) in
     self.motionForce = SCNVector3(x: Float(x) * 0.05, y:0, z:
Float(y+0.8) * -0.05)
    }
    // 2
    ballNode.physicsBody!.velocity += motionForce
  }
}
```

Taking a closer look:

1. First, the function updates the `motionForce` vector with the current motion data.
2. Then it adds the `motionForce` vector to the ball's **velocity**.

There's thing left to do: call `updateMotionControl()` from the `SCNSceneRenderDelegate`. Add the following call to `renderer(_, updateAtTime)`:

```
updateMotionControl()
```

This will perform a motion update call 60 times a second, although the actual motion sensor is polled at a much lower pace to preserve energy.

> **Note**: To play, hold the device in a comfortable position, tilted backwards at a 45º angle, just as you would normally look at your phone.

Build and run the game on your device:

The ball spawns out of mid air and drops down onto the sky maze. This is `resetGame()` at work. You'll also hear a loud thundering sound – hopefully you didn't drop your phone when it went off? :]

Touching the display starts the game. Lo and behold, you can control the ball simply by tilting the device left, right, forward and back. Smooth! :]

Try to collect a pearl – careful, don't fall! :]

Adding the health indicator

Recall that the glowing effect you added to the ball was to serve as a health indicator; the ball's health will diminish over time until the emission intensity runs out at `0.0`. If the player collects pearls of life along the way, the health – and emission intensity – will be restored to `1.0`.

You'll need a function to replenish the health bar. To do that, add the following to the `GameViewController` class:

```
func replenishLife() {
  // 1
  let material = ballNode.geometry!.firstMaterial!
  // 2
  SCNTransaction.begin()
  SCNTransaction.setAnimationDuration(1.0)
  // 3
  material.emission.intensity = 1.0
  // 4
  SCNTransaction.commit()
  // 5
  game.score += 1
  game.playSound(ballNode, name: "Powerup")
}
```

Taking a closer look at exactly what the above code does:

1. To access the emission map, you need to get the first and only material for the `ballNode`.
2. This starts a Scene Kit animation transaction sequence by specifying **SCNTransaction.begin()**. At this point, you can set target values for all the animatable Scene Kit properties you want to animate; in this case, the emission intensity. `setAnimationDuration(1.0)` sets the duration of the animation sequence.
3. Here you set the material's emission intensity to `1.0`. This doesn't set the actual value, but sets the value you *want* it to be once the animation completes.
4. This commits the animation transaction. Once committed, Scene Kit will start animating the emission value from its current value to the requested value of `1.0`.
5. The rest of the code increases the score and plays a nice "Powerup" sound effect.

The first spot where you'll need to replenish the health is when you enter the `.Playing` state. Add the following line to the end of `playGame()`:

```
replenishLife()
```

Build and run, and now you'll now hear a cool sound effect and will notice that the indicator on the ball now starts nice and bright:

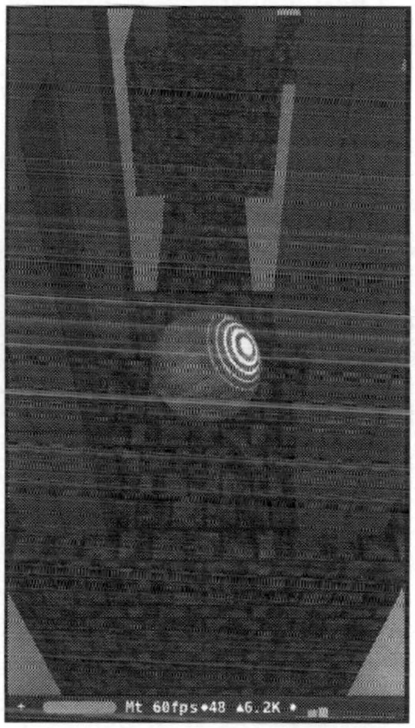

Diminishing life

You have a function that will replenish life, but what about the reverse? Health diminishes over time, so you'll need a function to call for every frame update.

Add the following to the `GameViewController` class:

```
func diminishLife() {
  // 1
  let material = ballNode.geometry!.firstMaterial!
  // 2
  if material.emission.intensity > 0 {
    material.emission.intensity -= 0.001
  } else {
    resetGame()
  }
}
```

Taking each numbered comment in turn:

1. Again, you're accessing the emission map of the ball's first and only material.
2. If the emission intensity is still above `0`, slowly decrease its value by `0.001` units. Once the emission intensity drops below `0`, life has run out for the ball so you trigger the `resetGame()` function.

You'll add a call to `diminishLife()` later in this chapter when you look at checking for the `.GameOver` state.

Other than that, there's still a few obvious problems that needs to be addressed:

- The camera is simply tracking the ball, not following it as you intended.
- The light isn't following the ball.
- There's no HUD, leaving the player wondering what the heck is going on.
- If the ball drops into the abyss, the game gets stuck and you have to restart it in order to play again.

You're so close – time to fix these issues and give your game that final polish!

Updating the camera and lights

`cameraFollowNode` is a special node that acts as a selfie stick for the camera node. But just like a real selfie stick, something needs to "hold" the other end of the stick.

You can't just make the **cameraFollow** node a child node of the ball, because the camera would spin like crazy as the ball rolls around! (Talk about game-induced motion sickness!) Instead, you created the **followCamera** node in the **rootNode**, so you can simply place it at the same position as the ball. Therefore, you need to update the `cameraFollow` position to match that of the ball as it rolls around.

Add the following function to the `GameViewController` class:

```
func updateCameraAndLights() {
  // 1
  let lerpX = (ballNode.presentationNode.position.x -
cameraFollowNode.position.x) * 0.01
  let lerpY = (ballNode.presentationNode.position.y -
cameraFollowNode.position.y) * 0.01
  let lerpZ = (ballNode.presentationNode.position.z -
cameraFollowNode.position.z) * 0.01
  cameraFollowNode.position.x += lerpX
  cameraFollowNode.position.y += lerpY
  cameraFollowNode.position.z += lerpZ
  // 2
```

```
    lightFollowNode.position = cameraFollowNode.position
    // 3
    if game.state == GameStateType.TapToPlay {
        cameraFollowNode.eulerAngles.y += 0.005
    }
}
```

Taking the above function step-by-step:

1. This is a cool set of calculations; instead of simply setting the `cameraFollowNode` position to that of `ballNode`, you calcualate a linearly-interpolated position to slowly move the camera in the direction of ball. This creates a spectacular lazy camera effect.
2. This sets **lightFollowNode** to the exact position as the camera so that whatever is in front of the camera is well lit.
3. Finally, this simply rotates the camera on its y-axis if the game is in a `.TapToPlay` state. This shows off the cool 3D graphics during the short intermission between games.

To call this function, add the following to the bottom of `renderer(_, updateAtTime)`:

```
updateCameraAndLights()
```

This ensures that you update the camera and lights with every single frame.

Build and run your game again to see the effect of your changes:

The ball drops out of the sky into the maze and the camera starts spinning around. This is what the camera will do while the game is in a `.WaitForTap` state. Cool! :]

Tap on the display to start the game:

Hey! Now you can control the ball properly, and the camera and light follows it as it rolls around the maze. Wow – that was even easier than you thought?

Updating the HUD

Time to give the player something to tell them what the heck is going on! The heads-up display is sufficient for this.

Add the following function to `GameViewController` class:

```
func updateHUD() {
  switch game.state {
  case .Playing:
    game.updateHUD()
  case .GameOver:
    game.updateHUD("-GAME OVER-")
  case .TapToPlay:
    game.updateHUD("-TAP TO PLAY-")
  }
}
```

The HUD updates according to the current game state. When the game is in the `.Playing` state, the HUD will display the current score. When in the `.GameOver` state, it will display "-GAME OVER-"; finally, when the game is in the `.TapToPlay` state you'll show "-TAP TO PLAY-".

To make sure you update the HUD accordingly, add the following call to the bottom of `renderer()`:

```
updateHUD()
```

This ensures that the HUD updates with every frame.

Build and run your game; you'll notice the HUD appears and gives the player a little more information than before:

Adding the finishing touches

Marble Maze is *so* close to being done; you just need to add a few final touches.

Testing for the game-over condition

At the moment, the ball is immortal – unless it takes a nose-dive into the abyss, at which point the game gets stuck as the camera continues to track the ball's descent.

To fix that, add the following code to the bottom of `renderer()`:

```
if game.state == GameStateType.Playing {
  testForGameOver()
  diminishLife()
}
```

The game will only test for the game over condition while in the `.Playing` state; you also make a call to `diminishLife()` make the ball's health deteriorate.

Build and run your game; you should be able to transition the game through all available game states without issue. The ball is no longer immortal, and should die after a few seconds. Hm. That's not much fun.

Looks like it's time to add a mechanism to replenish your health!

Replenishing life

At the moment, collecting a pearl of life makes the pearl disappear, but your score doesn't increase, nor does the ball's health. To fix that, simply add a call to `replenishLife()` in `physicsWorld(_, didBeginContact)`, inside the block that handles contact with pearls:

```
replenishLife()
```

Build and run your game; when you collect a pearl, the ball's health is replenished and your score increases by one. Excellent! :]

Adding bump noises

When the ball bumps against the pillars and crates, it would nice to give the player some sort of "bump" noise.

To do that, add the following bit of code to `physicsWorld(_, didBeginContact)`, inside the block that handles contact with pillars and crates:

```
game.playSound(ballNode, name: "Bump")
```

Build and run your game; bonk that ball into a pillar or crate and you'll hear something go bump in the night! :]

Removing debug information

You can now remove the debug information, since you're done building your game. Find the following two lines of code inside `setupScene()` and comment them out like so:

```
//scnView.allowsCameraControl = true
//scnView.showsStatistics = true
```

This will remove the bottom debug information bar from your game and will also remove the ability to rotate the camera freely.

Congratulations! You've completed Marble Maze; build and run and enjoy the fruits of your labor. Just don't get too close to the edge! :]

Where to go from here?

A very famous astronaut once said: "One small step for (a) man, one giant leap for mankind!". Well you just took a massive leap into a bright future of 3D game development with Scene Kit. Well done! :]

Here's a recap of what you covered in this chapter:

- **3D Motion Control**: You've learned how to add basic motion control to your game by using the motion data as a force vector added to the ball velocity.
- **Gimbal locking**: You had a quick introduction to gimbal locking, and how to overcome the issue of camera rotation by enabling a simple property.
- **Animating properties**: You now know how to use `SCNTransaction` to animate properties.
- **Lerping Camera**: You've learned how to do a basic linear interpolation calculation to create a lazy camera effect, which adds a professional feel to the game.

Here are some other ideas you can add to make the game even better:

- **More game elements**: Think about adding bad guys that patrol certain sections of the maze. Maybe add some icy blocks that reduce friction and make the ball slip and slide?
- **More sets and levels**: You can let your imagination go wild here and create some weird and twisted sets, making the game more challenging for the player as they complete each level.
- **More juice**: More sound effects! Camera shaking! Particle effects! What else can you think to add to make the game exciting (and slightly unpredictable) for your player?

Okay, now go and play with your game some more – you know you want to! :]

> **Note:** As always, you can find the final project under the **projects/final/MarbleMaze** folder.

Section IV: Advanced Scene Kit

"The Scene Kit Force is quite strong within you, young apprentice. (Read in a deep, heavy, asthmatic breathing voice. :])

In this section, you'll learn few more advanced techniques, as well as apply all the skills you've learned up to this point, to creating an awesome little voxel style game. By the end of this section you'll know enough to take on the big *Hipster Whales* out there with your very own game: Mr. Pig.

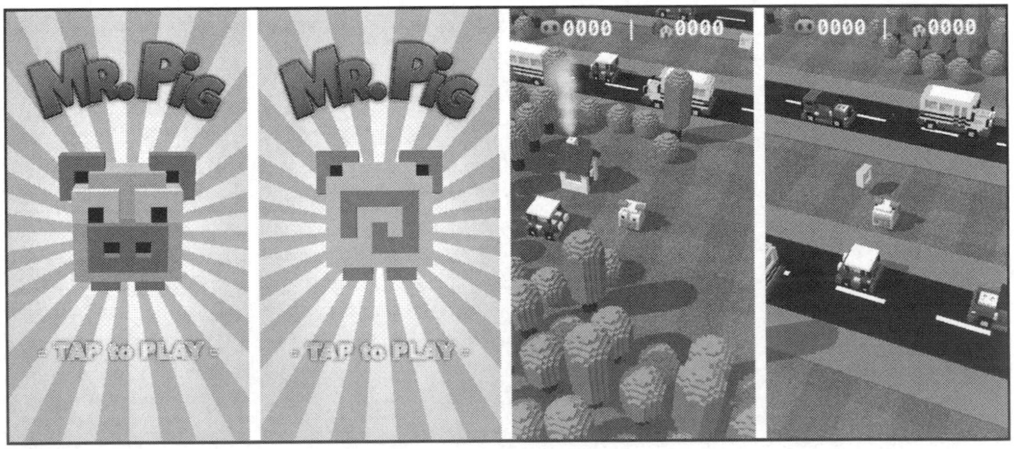

This is a *Crossy Road* style game with stunning voxel graphics, a catchy tune and some cool sound effects.

The premise: Mr. Pig is out and about scouting for lost coins in a nearby park while waiting for his late afternoon tea to heat up on the stove. Unfortunately, some big bad wolf decided to build a massive mall nearby, resulting in a very busy highway straight through his lovely park.

Mr. Pig better watch his step, or he'll end up as pulled pork in the road. :] Our hero can carry quite a few coins with him, but to score, he has to deposit them at his little house.

So what are you waiting for? Get *crackling*! :]

Chapter 16: Transitions

Chapter 17: Advanced Reference Nodes

Chapter 18: Actions

Chapter 19: Advanced Collision Detection

Chapter 20: Audio

Chapter 16: Transitions

Chris Language

In this chapter you'll start off by creating your game project, but in a slightly different way from what you've done in previous sections. Specifically, rather than using the Game template, you'll use the single view application template.

You'll also create the first two main scenes for Mr. Pig; one that will be your main game scene, and one to be your splash scene. Later, you'll also cover how to transition from one scene to the other.

Thankfully, you no longer have to deal with primitive shapes and geometry. This game will use graphics made in the extremely popular voxel style, similar to those more recently used in titles like *Crossy Road*, *Pacman 256* and *Shooty Skies*.

A highly skilled team of graphic artists sweated nights and days away to produce a small set of shiny voxel art just for your game. So, without further ado, please meet the cast of your next game:

From left to right:

- **Trees**. These three little tree types will be used to fill the charming park with lush vegetation. They'll also act as obstacles, so Mr. Pig will have to think on his hooves to move past them.
- **House**: What a pretty little house! This is Mr. Pig's residence, and is also the place where he stores all his found treasures.
- **Mr. Pig**: Meet the hero of your game - Pig, Mr. Pig that is. He's always on a mission to hunt for lost treasures in the nearby park. For a swine, he's rather nimble – you'll build in swiping gestures to make him jump around.
- **Vehicles**: These relentless gas guzzlers are known as Mini's, SUV's and School buses, and they couldn't care less about little pigs that cross the road. They've got places to go and certainly won't stop for our hero.

> **Note**: The voxel graphics were created with a very popular voxel authoring tool known as *MagicaVoxel*. You can download this awesome tool from voxel.codeplex.com for free and play around for yourself!

Working with your game project

Note: Some of the steps in the next few sections are fairly basic, and are unrelated to the main subject of this chapter: Transitions. If you'd like to dive straight ahead into the meat of this chapter, feel free to skip ahead to the "Working with multiple scenes" section, where we'll have a starter project waiting for you.

But if you'd like more practice with project setup, keep reading!

Its template time! As mentioned before, this time around you won't use the built-in Xcode Game template, but you'll make use of the Single View Application template instead.

By now you've made a game template the easy way and you're well acquainted with the steps involved. But you're in the final section. It's time to level up and play around with advanced methods and options to incorporate Scene Kit into existing applications.

Creating a Single View Application game project

Start Xcode and once started, press **Shift+Command+N** to create a new project. This'll launch the **Project Wizard**:

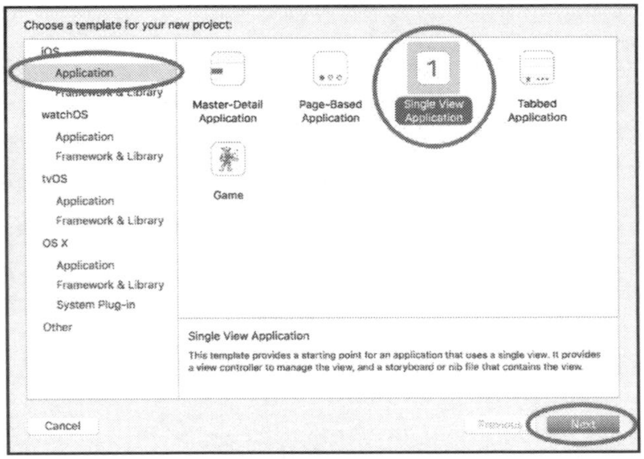

Choose **iOS\Application\Single View Application** template, and click **Next** to continue.

Next set some basic options for your new project.

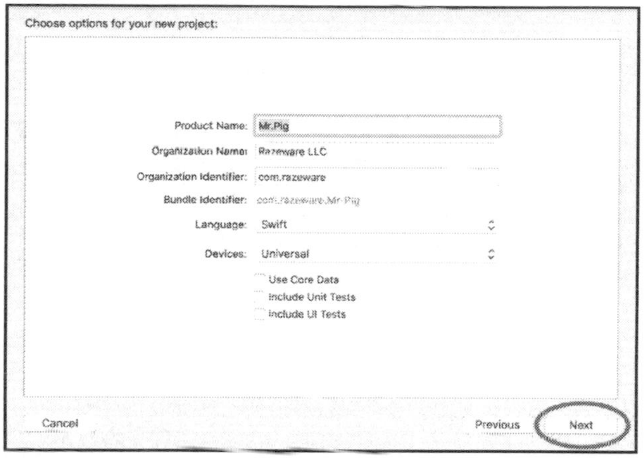

Make sure to set the following options:

- **Product Name**: Name the application **Mr.Pig**.
- **Organization Name**. You can make this whatever you choose.
- **Organization Identifier**: This is your reverse domain identifier.
- **Language**: **Swift** should be your preference by now. :]
- **Devices**: Make this **Universal** so that the application will run on an iPhone or iPad.

Leave the rest unchecked. The final step is to choose a convenient location to save your project. Pick a directory and select **Create**; Xcode will work its magic and generate your project.

Finally set the orientation for **Portrait** only under **Project Settings/General/ Deployment Info**.

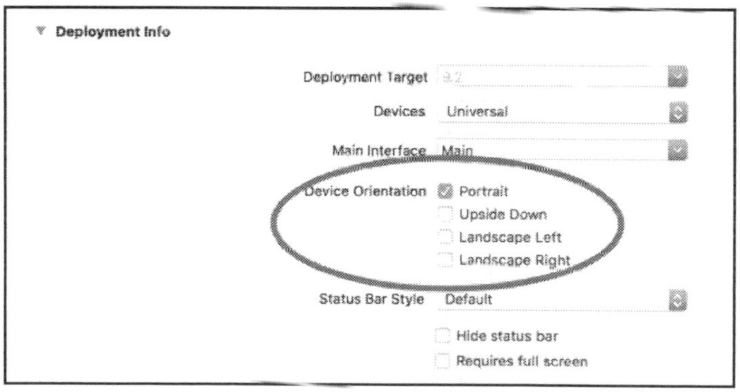

So far so good, nothing much really different from creating a standard game project. Well almost nothing changed, accept for the part where you had to choose **Single View Application**.

Select the Project Navigator to continue.

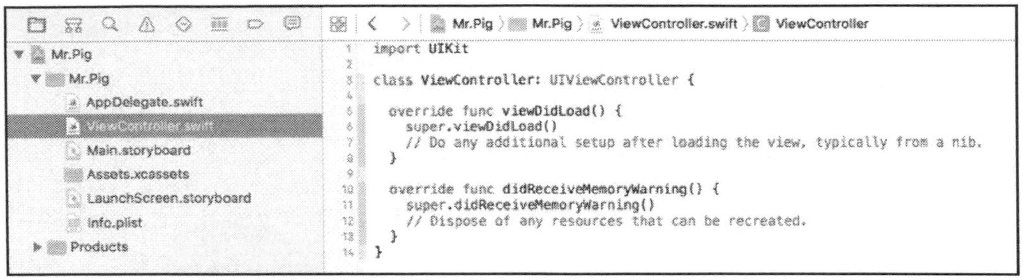

So what's the big difference? Take a closer look:

- **art.scnassets**: The first thing you might notice is that there are no **art.scnassets** folder. That bit is part of the game project template, so it wasn't created for you.
- **ViewController.swift**: This used to be **GameViewController.swift**, so the *Game* prefix fell away. The class still inherrits from `UIViewController` same as before. In this section, you'll reference the `ViewController` class instead of `GameViewController`.

> **Note**: You'll also notice that there's no boilerplate code to start the game. Fear not, you've been training for this, my apprentice.

Adding resources to your project

There are a whole bunch of resources ready to go for your game, you need to add them next.

Start by dragging and dropping the **resources\GameUtils** folder into your project. When prompted, make sure to add the folder as a **Group**:

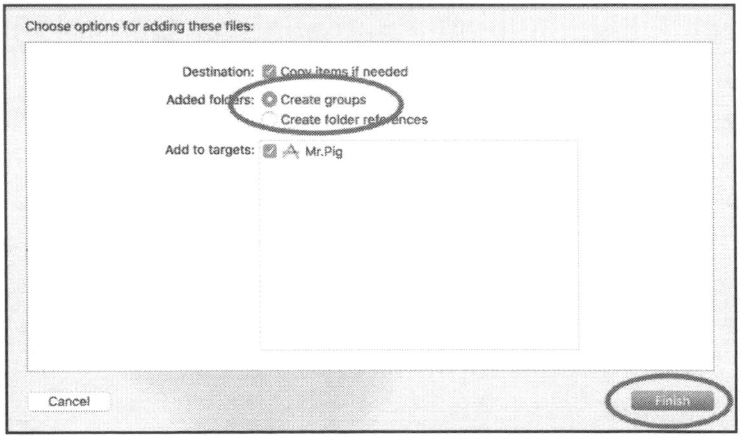

Drag and drop the **resources\MrPig.scnassets** folder into the project next.

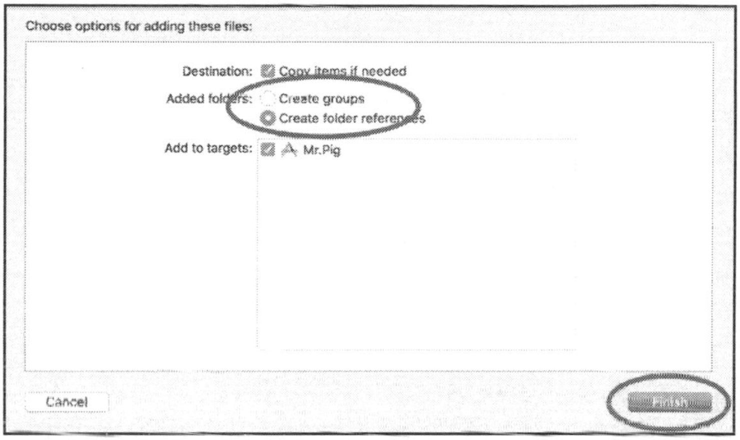

Finally, open the **File Navigator** to take a closer look.

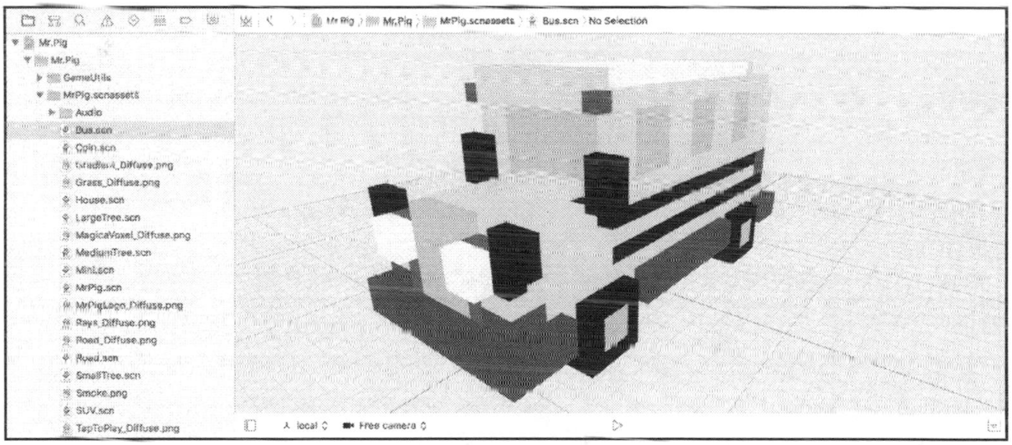

You'll find all sorts of hidden gems under these folders; here's a quick breakdown of what to expect:

- **GameUtils**: These are just a bunch of useful utilities you can use to make everyday tasks a little bit less taxing.
- **MrPig.scnassets**: This contains all the textures, 3D models, sound effects and even music your game will put to use.

> **Note**: Take some time to get yourself familiar with the content inside these folders. You'll be using them extensively in the coming chapters.

Setting up the app icon and launchscreen

You'll find a **LaunchScreen** and **AppIcon** folder under the **resources** folder. These contain a bunch of app icons and a launch screen image for you to use in your project.

Drag and drop the appropriate app icons into the **Assets.xcassets\AppIcon** container.

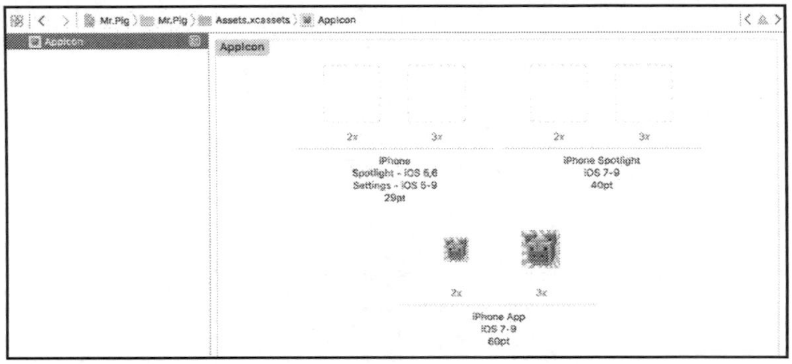

Next drag and drop the **MrPig_Launch.png** into the **Assets.xcassets** folder. This adds the image to your project, making it available from your **Media Library**.

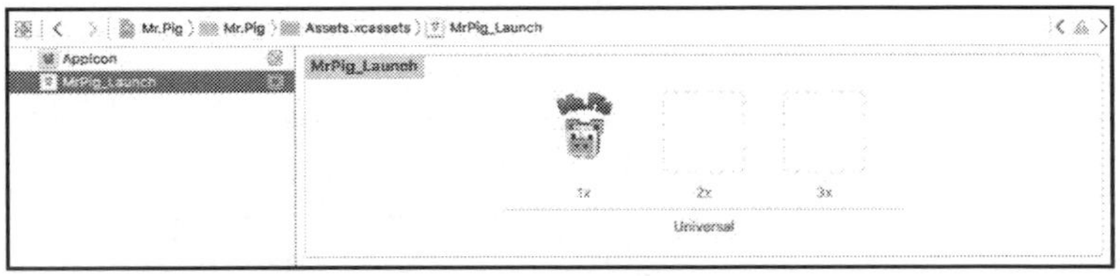

Now you can set up the launch screen with the image.

Here are a few things you need to do right now:

- Set the background color to a nice yellow.
- Drag and drop the launch image from the **Media Library**.
- Remember to add some pin constraints; pinning the image view horizontally and vertically in the container will do.

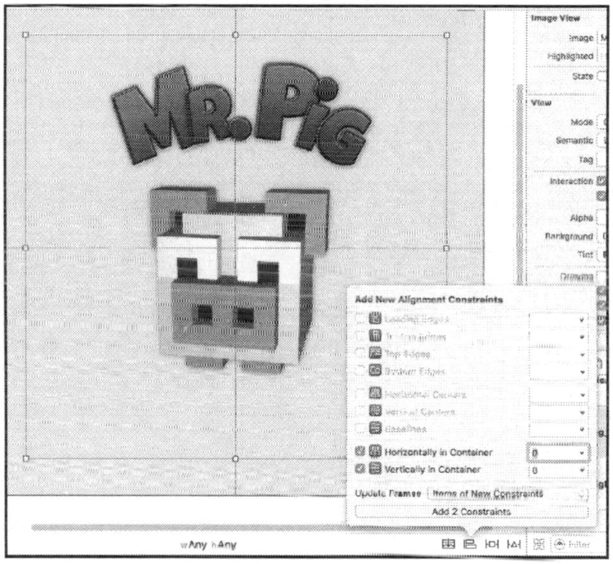

- Finally, make sure you set the **View Mode** of the image view to **Aspect Fill**.

Setting up the Scene Kit view

Now you need to set up the basic view controller, and then create the actual Scene Kit view for your game.

Setting up the View Controller class

Under the **Project Navigator**, select **ViewController.swift** then replace its contents with the following:

```
// 1
import UIKit
import SceneKit
import SpriteKit
// 2
class ViewController: UIViewController {
  // 3
```

```
  let game = GameHelper.sharedInstance

  override func viewDidLoad() {
    super.viewDidLoad()
    // 4
    setupScenes()
    setupNodes()
    setupActions()
    setupTraffic()
    setupGestures()
    setupSounds()
    // 5
    game.state = .TapToPlay
  }

  func setupScenes() {
  }

  func setupNodes() {
  }

  func setupActions() {
  }

  func setupTraffic() {
  }

  func setupGestures() {
  }

  func setupSounds() {
  }

  override func didReceiveMemoryWarning() {
    super.didReceiveMemoryWarning()
  }

  override func prefersStatusBarHidden() -> Bool {
    return true
  }

  override func shouldAutorotate() -> Bool {
    return false
  }
}
```

Let's have a quick look at what happens in here:

1. This part imports the usual suspects, but did you notice that you're now importing **SpriteKit** too? What's up with that? If you'll recall, this chapter actually deals with Transitions, and Scene Kit relies on Sprite Kit functionality to make the transitions. So for now, just make a mental note of this incredibly important import.

2. The class is now known as the `ViewController` that simply inherits from the `UIViewController` with a game template.
3. This declares the `game` object that retrieves the shared instance of the `GameHelper` class. This contains some basic helpful functionality that you'll use throughout the game.
4. The `viewDidLoad()` function is the first to execute once the application starts. Here you're simply calling a whole bunch to stubs that'll set up all the important aspects of your game later on.
5. Finally, you set the game into an initial state of `TapToPlay`.

Setting up the Scene Kit view

Now to tackle the big hole you made for yourself by making use of a **Single View Application** template. You ned to manually create an `SCNView` instance and will start by creating the property that will hold your `SCNView`.

Add the following property to top of `ViewController`:

```
var scnView:SCNView!
```

This is to hold the instance of the SCNView for quick access later on.

Add the following to `setupScenes()`:

```
scnView = SCNView(frame: self.view.frame)
self.view.addSubview(scnView)
```

This creates an instance for `SCNView` by passing in the `view.frame`. Then the key part is to add the Scene Kit view as a sub view of the current view with `addSubView()`.

Feel free to build and run if you'd like, but note you'll end up with a blank white screen because you still need to present a scene in the view.

Working with multiple scenes

> **Note**: If you skipped ahead from earlier in this chapter, you can pick up at this point with the starter project in **projects\starter\Mr.Pig**.

There will be no fun with transitions between scenes until you set some up. You'll create the two main scenes for your game: a splash scene and a game scene.

Create the game scene

The game scene is where all the action will take place. You'll build the entire level inside the game scene. To create a new scene, drag and drop a **SceneKit Scene File** from the **File Template library** into the root of your project.

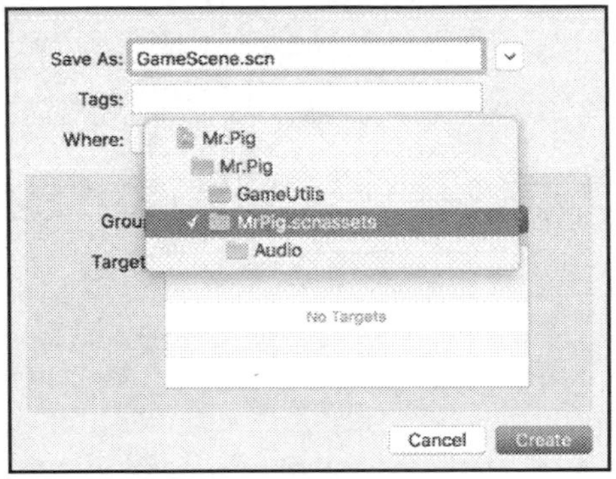

Name the scene **GameScene.scn**, choose **MrPig.scnassets** folder as destination and click **Create**.

Make sure the **MrPig.scnassets\GameScene.scn** is still selected then drag and drop a **Floor Node** into the scene from the **Object Library**. Select its **Node Inspector** to continue.

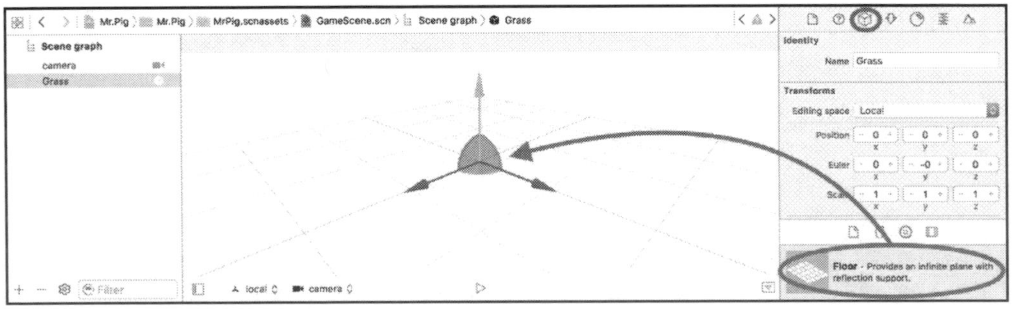

Name the node **Grass**, and zero out the **position** and Euler **rotation**.

Select the **Attributes Inspector**.

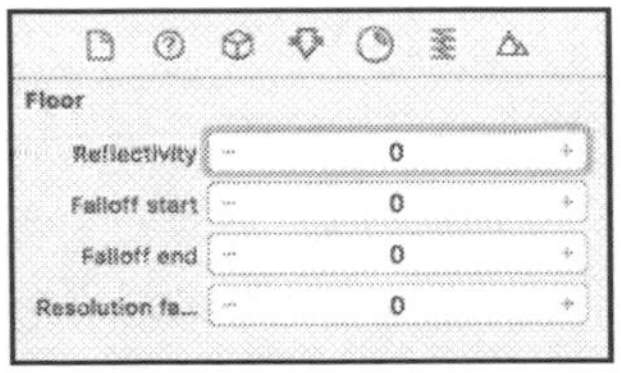

Set the **Floor Reflectivity** to `0`, you definitely don't want the grass to be reflective because, well, grass isn't glass!

Move on to the **Materials Inspector**.

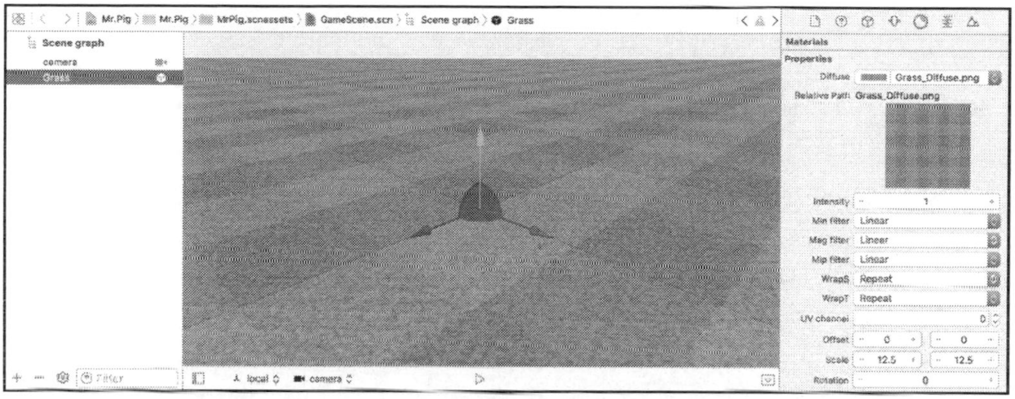

Select the **Grass_Diffuse.png** as the **Material Diffuse** map, then scale it down to `12.5` units vertically and `12.5` units horizontally. This should make a nice repeated grass pattern all over the floor node. It's so realistic you can almost smell the freshly cut grass.

Create the splash scene

The splash scene will be the front scene where Mr. Pig will introduce himself with some some serious dance moves. He's patient, energetic and will keep on rocking until your player initiates a game.

Drag and drop another **SceneKit Scene File** from the **File Template library** into the root of your project.

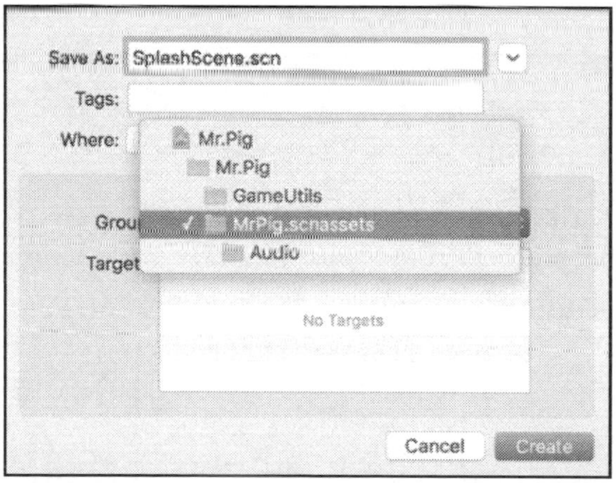

Name the scene **SplashScene.scn**, choose **MrPig.scnassets** folder as destination then click **Create**.

With the **SplashScene.scn** scene still selected, drag and drop a **MrPig** reference node into the scene from the **Media Library**.

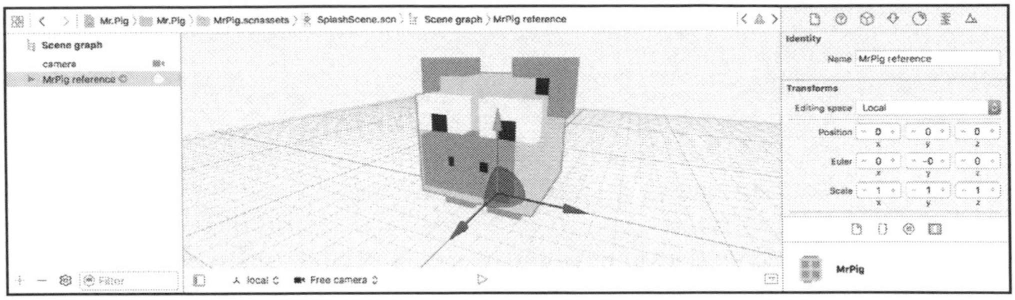

With the **MrPig** node still selected, go into the **Node Inspector** and zero out its position and rotation. Mr. Pig is in position now.

Next you'll give the splash scene an aesthetically pleasing gradient background – solid colors are *so* 2002.

Make sure you still have the **MrPig** reference node selected then select the **Scene Inspector**, the very last inspector. Drag and drop the **Gradient_Diffuse.png** file from the **Media Library** into the **Scene Background** property.

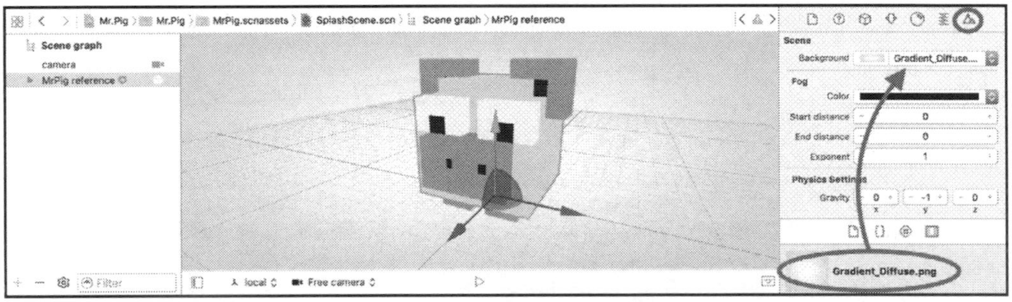

The whole scene background should change to the gradient image. Yes, Mr. Pig loves bright colors. :]

> **Note**: Since you're using a single square image for the background, Scene Kit does something special by stretching it so that it fills the whole scene at all times. Just another cool way you can use some of the hidden features of Scene Kit.

Now to create some sun rays behind Mr. Pig. Drag and drop a **Plane** node into the scene from the **Object Library**.

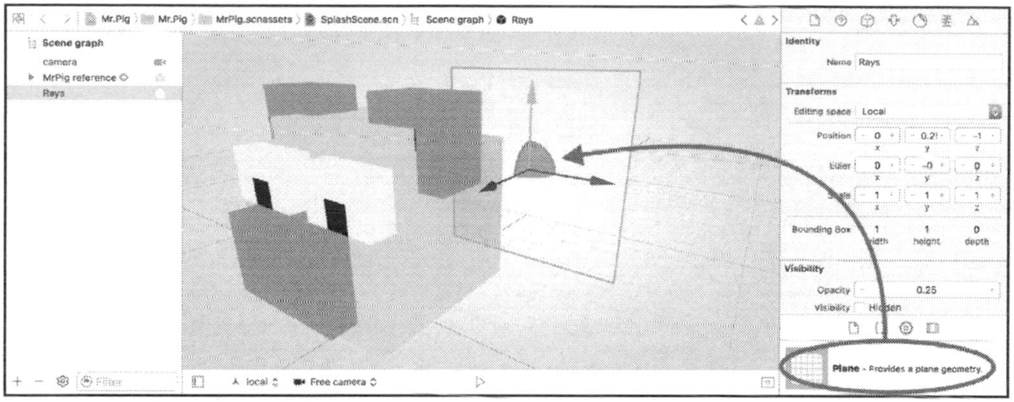

Name the node **Rays**, and set its position to `(x:0, y:0.25, z:-1)` and make sure it has a zero rotation. Also set **Visibility Opacity** to 0.25 to make the plane almost entirely transparent.

Now move on and adjust the plane dimensions under the **Attributes Inspector**.

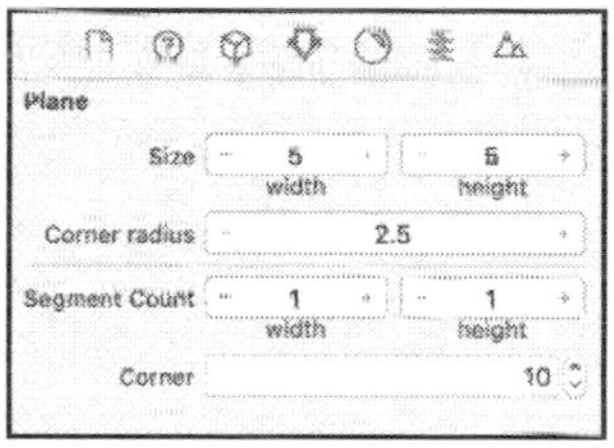

Set the **Size** to `(x:5, y:5)`, and just for the fun of it, make the plane a disc by setting the **Corner Radius** to `2.5`, essentially half of its size.

Now you need to make the plane look like actual rays, and to do that you need to give it a nice little diffuse texture. Select the **Materials Inspector**.

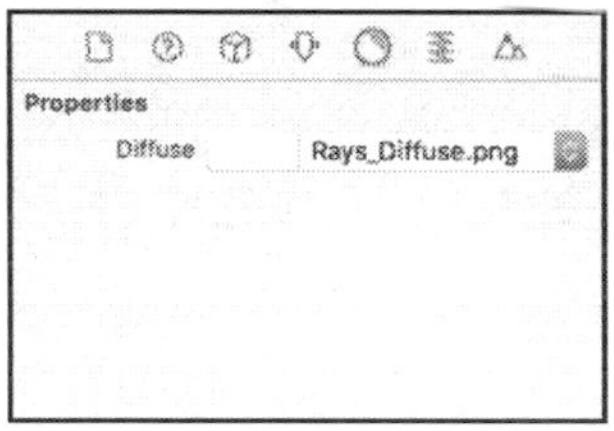

Select the **Rays_Diffuse.png** for a diffuse map. You should notice the plane changing into glorious rays, but there's bound to be a power struggle between the rays of light and your scene lighting.

To fix that, you need to scroll down to the Materials Inspector **Settings** section.

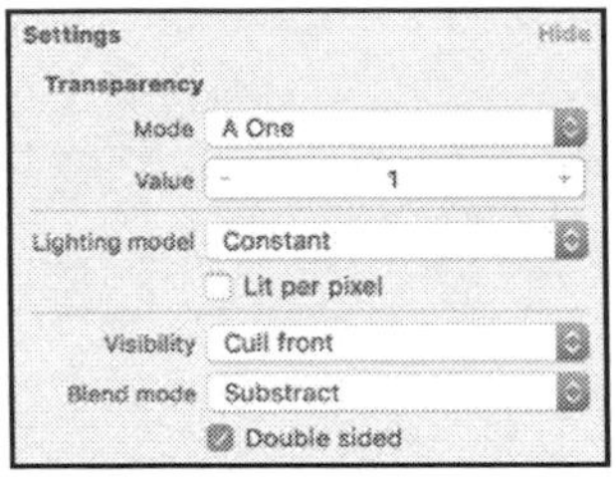

You first need to set the **Lighting Model** to **Constant**. This ensures lighting will have no effect on the rays. Yes, you'll add those to the scene shortly.

Set **Blend Mode** to **Subtract**, which will then darken the scene by using the blend diffuse map by means of subtraction.

Set up camera and lights

What makes the eyes recognize dimension? Lighting, of course. And if you're adding lights you need cameras. Lights, cameras, action!

By default, the splash scene already has a camera. You'll use it *mostly* as-is.

First make sure nothing is selected under your **Scene Graph** tree then click the **+** button to add an **empty node** into the root.

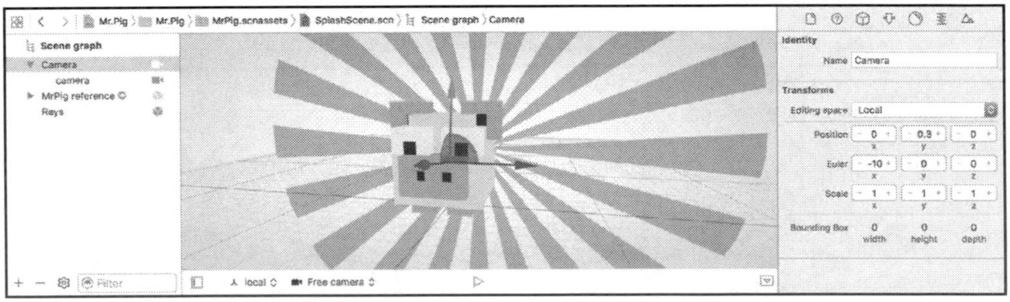

Name the empty node **Camera** and drag the original camera node under it, making it a child node. With the outer **Camera** node selected, use the **Node Inspector** to set its position to `(x:0, y:0.3, z:0)` and its euler angle to `(x:-10, y:0, z:0)`. This will tilt the camera view downwards and aim it straight at the dancing swine almost as if he's holding a selfie stick.

Select the inner **camera** node, so you can set some properties on it too.

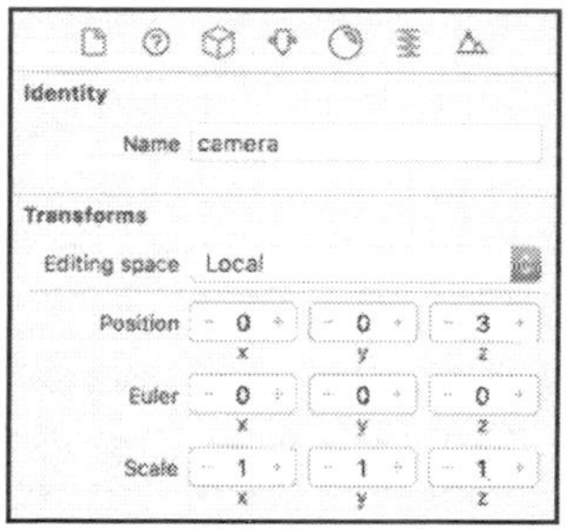

You want to pull the camera back a bit on that selfie stick, but not too far, just far enough to see Mr. Pig, so set its position to `(x:0, y:0, z:3)` and make sure its Euler rotation is `(x:0, y:0, z:0)`.

To make sure the camera is configured correctly, select the **camera** in the dropdown in the bottom left of the scene editor to preview the view:

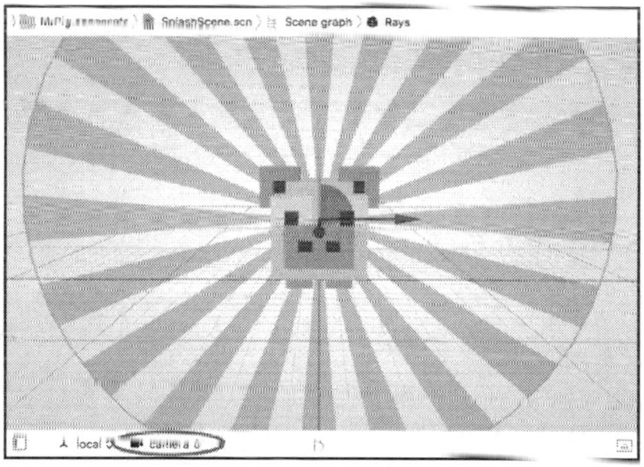

Now add another empty node into the root of the **Scene Graph**, and name it **Lights**. Drag and drop an **Ambient** and an **Omni** light into the scene from the **Object Library**.

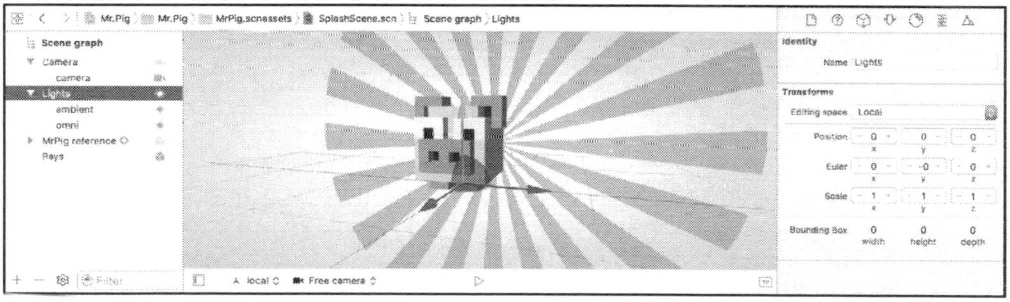

Make sure you move them under the **Lights** node under the **Scene Graph**. You'll leave the attributes as-is, but you need to position the omni light properly, so select it, then select its **Node Inspector**.

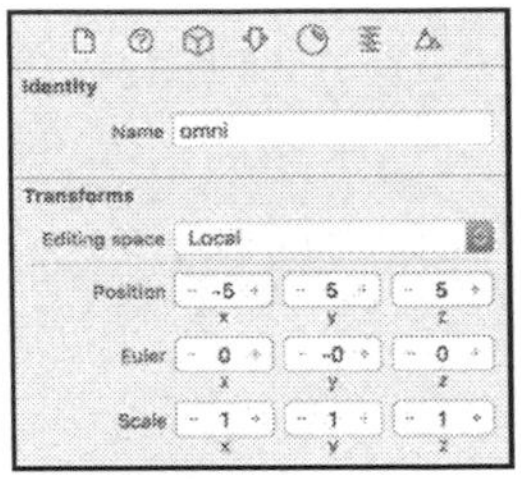

Position the light at `(xL-5, y:5, z:5)`. Looking very dapper! :]

Mini challenge

You're almost done with the entire splash scene, there are just two more components to be added: the logo and tap-to-play nodes. But you're more than capable of handling these two tasks all on your own. :]

Your little challenge is to produce the same results as below. Take special note of the **Scene Graph** structure with the added **Logo** and **TapToPlay** nodes and obviously the precious pink Mr. Pig logo and Tap To Play writing in front of the pig in the scene.

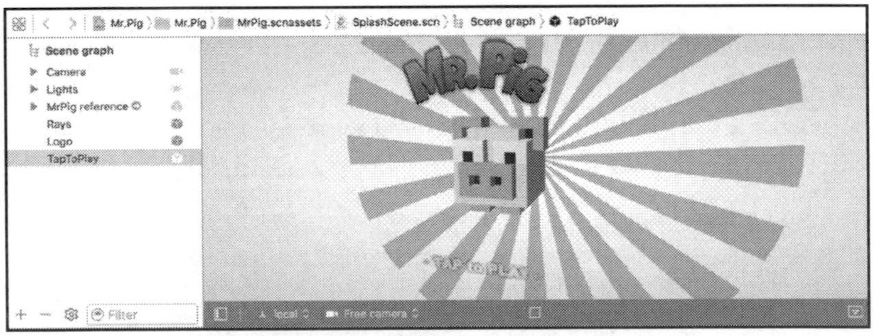

These two nodes are plane nodes with simple diffuse maps on them. Here are a few tips to reference if you need a helping hand:

- **The Logo node**: It uses a basic **plane** node with the **MrPigLogo_Diffuse.png** applied, set to a **size** of `(width:1, height:0.5)`. Make sure to position it in front and above our hero at position `(x:0, y:1, z:0.5)`. Also make sure it's not affected by any light, just like the **Rays** at the back.
- **The TapToPlay node**: Also uses a basic **plane** node with the **TapToPlay_Diffuse.png** applied, set to a **size** of `(width:1, height:0.25)`. Position it in front and below the pig at **position** `(x:0, y:-0.3, z:0.5)`. It also should not be affected by any light.

> **Note**: You can find the solution to this little mini challenge under the **projects \challenge\Mr.Pig** folder.

Load and present the splash scene

Finally you've got your splash scene setup, and the game scene is on its way. What's left now is to load them up and present the splash scene.

You first need objects to hold your scenes, so add the following properties to `ViewController`:

```
var gameScene:SCNScene!
var splashScene:SCNScene!
```

Add the following code to `setupScenes()`:

```
// 1
gameScene = SCNScene(named: "/MrPig.scnassets/GameScene.scn")
splashScene = SCNScene(named: "/MrPig.scnassets/
SplashScene.scn")
// 2
scnView.scene = splashScene
```

Let's take a closer look:

1. This loads both the **GameScene.scn** and the **SplashScene.scn** into memory from the **MrPig.scnassets** folder.
2. This part sets the splash scene up as the initial scene for your game. So once everything is loaded up and the game is started, the splash scene is shown first.

You can do a quick build and run just to make sure all is well.

You're all good if your game started up and showed the splash scene. Oh, yes!

So how do you get from the splash scene to the game scene? Well, if you've just asked yourself that question, then hurry to the next part, because it will show you exactly how.

Creating transition effects

Finally you're ready to learn more about transitions. So what exactly are transitions? To understand this better you'll have to go watch all seven episodes Star Wars again. See you back here in about 14 hours.

Why the Star Wars reference? Well, George Lucas, in all his brilliance, mastered the art of using wipes to transition between scenes. One could even go as far as to say that without these classic sweeping effects, the movies would loose some of their magic. There are many more kinds of transitions, including dissolves, cross fades and cuts.

Scene Kit leverages Sprite Kit's `SKTransition` object for transition effects, and that's precisely why you imported Sprite Kit. So, if you come from a Sprite Kit background, you should feel right at home with these effects.

The `SKTransition` object will help you animate your transition from the active scene to the scene you want to present next by using various transitioning effects.

There's quite a few out of the box transition effects at your disposal:

- **crossFadeWithDuration**: Cross fades from current scene into the new scene.
- **doorsCloseHorizontalWithDuration**: Presents the new scene as a pair of closing horizontal doors.
- **doorsCloseVerticalWithDuration**: Presents the new scene as a pair of closing vertical doors.
- **doorsOpenHorizontalWithDuration**: Presents the new scene as a pair of opening horizontal doors.
- **doorsOpenVerticalWithDuration**: Presents the new scene as a pair of opening vertical doors.
- **doorwayWithDuration**: The current scene disappears as two doors opens up, presenting the new scene from behind opening doors.
- **fadeWithColor**: The current scene first fades into a constant color then presents the new scene by fading into it.
- **fadeWithDuration**: The current scene first fades to black then presents the new scene by fading into it.

- **flipHorizontalWithDuration**: Presents the new scene, flipping away the current scene horizontally.
- **flipVerticalWithDuration**: Presents the new scene, flipping away the current scene vertically.
- **moveInWithDirection**: Presents the new scene by moving it on top of the current scene.
- **pushWithDirection**: Presents the new scene by pushing out the current scene.
- **revealWithDirection**: The current scene moves out, revealing the new scene underneath it.
- **transitionWithCIFilter**: Presents the new scene by making use of Core Image Filters for the transition effect.

Add a transition effect

In this part you're about to kill two birds with one stone.

Relax, that's just an old expression; you're not really going to kill any birds! :]

You're about to add some basic functions that will control the three game states (**Playing**, **WaitForTap** and **GameOver**) your game will go through. Along with that

you'll also add some code to do the actual transition from the one scene to another.

The first function will switch your game into the **Playing** state. It will also transition into the game scene.

Add the following function to `ViewController` class:

```
func startGame() {
  // 1
  splashScene.paused = true
  // 2
  let transition =
SKTransition.doorsOpenVerticalWithDuration(1.0)
  // 3
  scnView.presentScene(gameScene, withTransition: transition,
incomingPointOfView: nil, completionHandler: {
    // 4
    self.game.state = .Playing
    self.setupSounds()
    self.gameScene.paused = false
  })
}
```

Let's see what happens in here:

1. You're assuming that the game can only start from the splash scene. So the first thing you're doing here is manually pausing the splash scene by setting the pause property to true. This will stop all actions and any active physics simulations.
2. Here's how you create a transition effect using the `SKTransition` object. This part simply presents the new scene while the current scene slides away as two vertical doors opens up.
3. You the make a call to the SCNView's `pressentScene()` function by passing in the freshly created transition effect. You can also specify which point of view should be used for the transition, but because all your scenes will only have one camera you simply leave this `nil`. Then you have a completion handler kick in once the transition effect completed.
4. This bit executes after the transition completes and officially sets the game state to **Playing**. It also loads up the correct sounds for the scene and pauses the scene.

The following function switches the game into a GameOver state. This will typically happen once Mr. Pig gets hit by one of the evil gas-guzzling vehicles.

Add it to `ViewController` class:

```
func stopGame() {
  game.state = .GameOver
  game.reset()
}
```

It simply makes sure the game state is set to **GameOver**, and it also resets the scores, readying up for the next game.

The last function switches the game into **WaitForTap** state. This is where the splash scene is presented, and the game waits for the player.

Add the following function to `ViewController`:

```
func startSplash() {
  // 1
  gameScene.paused = true
  // 2
  let transition =
SKTransition.doorsOpenVerticalWithDuration(1.0)
  scnView.presentScene(splashScene, withTransition: transition,
incomingPointOfView: nil, completionHandler: {
    self.game.state = .TapToPlay
    self.setupSounds()
    self.splashScene.paused = false
  })
}
```

Now for a closer look at what's happening here:

1. This simply pauses the game scene, essentially preventing all physics simulations and actions from running.
2. Again as before, this creates a transition effect then performs the actual transition to the splash scene. Once the transition completes, the game state is officially set to WaitForTap, the splash scene sounds are re-configured, and the scene is un-paused.

So, now you have all the basic functions to control the flow of your game setup. There's still one little function left to add, and that's the one that kicks off your game once the user taps to play. Add the following function to `ViewController` class:

```
override func touchesBegan(touches: Set<UITouch>, withEvent
event: UIEvent?) {
  if game.state == .TapToPlay {
    startGame()
  }
}
```

The `touchesBegan()` event will fire once the player taps on the screen. You're only interested in tap events while in a **WaitForTap** state. Once the event fires, you know the player wants to play the game, so you trigger the `startGame()` function.

Time for a build and run to test that transition.

> **Note**: Be sure to test this on a device, not the simulator, as the simulator may be too slow to show the transition.

The game starts up with the splash scene and when you tap to play, the scene transitions into the game scene. Perfect!

Where to go from here?

As usual, you can find the final project for this chapter under the **projects\final\Mr.Pig** folder.

To top it off, you just earned yourself a gold star for completing the first chapter in this section, and your game is already looking mighty fine. :]

Here are some key takeaways from this chapter:

- **Single View Application**: You've now learned how to add Scene Kit to basically any type of application. No more do you need to rely on the Game Template.
- **Transitions**: You've learned that Scene Kit relies on Sprite Kit for transitions, and you added a basic transition effect for your game.

Take a quick break, but hurry back because things will get more interesting in the next chapter where you'll start building the game scene.

Chapter 17: Advanced Scene Creation

Chris Language

Your game is off to a great start. In the previous chapter, your main focus was creating the basic project for your game. Not only that, but you also created the two main scenes for your game - the splash and game scenes. The rest of your focus was on adding making the splash scene pop and setting up a basic transition to the game scene.

In this chapter, your focus will shift towards building out the game scene.

You've already created a massive grass plane that forms the basis of the lovely park in which Mr. Pig lives and collects coins.

There are, of course, some missing details: those two nasty highways filled with traffic running through the park, a whole bunch of trees and the star of the game.

> **Note**: This chapter continues where the previous one left off, so if you followed along you can continue using the same project. Otherwise, you can load up the starter project for this chapter from **projects\starter\Mr.Pig**.

Adding the pig

You'll start off by adding our hero, Mr. Pig, to your game scene so you have a good reference point for where to place the rest of the objects.

Add Mr. Pig

With your Project Navigator open, navigate down and select **MrPig.scnassets\GameScene.scn**.

Drag and drop a **MrPig** reference node from the Media Library into the scene.

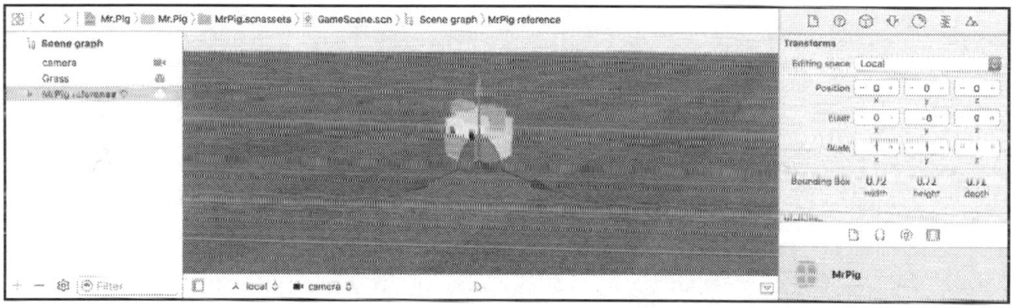

Make sure you zero out his position and rotation. Sweet, that was almost too easy.

Quickly jump over to **ViewController.swift** and add the following property to `ViewController`:

```
var pigNode: SCNNode!
```

This property will hold the instance of Mr. Pig in the game scene. Later on, if you want Mr. Pig to jump, you'd run an action on this node.

Add the following line of code to `setupNodes()`:

```
pigNode = gameScene.rootNode.childNodeWithName("MrPig",
recursively: true)!
```

This method is called after **GameScene.scn** loads, so this line of code is safe to use as a means of binding `pigNode` to the actual object in your game scene.

Note: Although **MrPig** is a reference node, you still access the node in the game scene as if it was a non-reference node.

Set up camera and lights

Now that you have something more than just a massive grass field to look at, it's time to set up a camera and some lights for your scene. Again, you'll make use of the selfie-stick principle by creating an empty node that will act as the focus point for the camera or light – this approach simplifies and eliminates a whole bunch of mathematical issues I'm sure you won't mind skipping. :]

Create the follow camera node

Go back to **MrPig.scnassets\GameScene.scn** to set up the camera.

First, make sure nothing is selected under your scene graph, then click the **+** button to add an empty node into the scene graph. With the node selected, rename it **FollowCamera** under the Node Inspector, zero out its position and set **Euler** to `(x:-45, y:20, z:0)` to adjust the rotation.

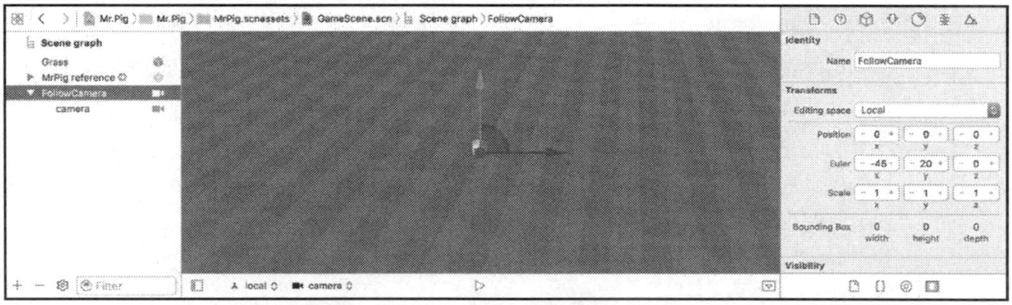

Next, drag and drop the existing **camera** node under the newly added **FollowCamera** node. With **camera** still selected, change its position to `(x:0, y:0, z:14)` and zero out rotation.

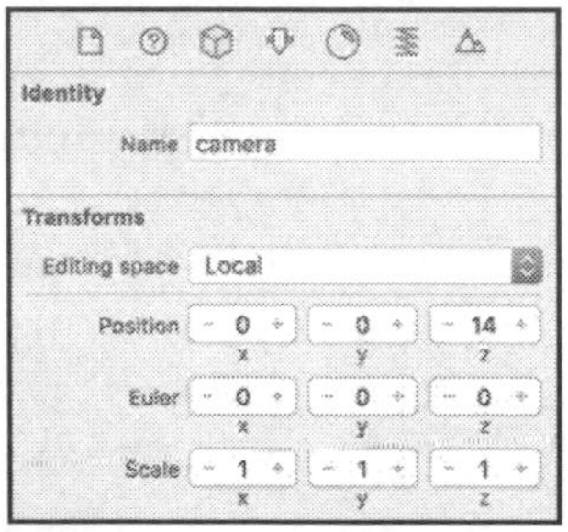

Select **camera** to be your view point at the bottom of the Scene Editor, and then your scene should resemble the image above.

At this point, you're almost done playing around with the camera, but you still need to add some code for it. Select **ViewController.swift** and add the following properties to

`ViewController`:

```
var cameraNode: SCNNode!
var cameraFollowNode: SCNNode!
```

These will hold instances of **camera** and **FollowCamera** in code.

Now add the following to `setupNodes()`:

```
// 1
cameraNode = gameScene.rootNode.childNodeWithName("camera",
recursively: true)!
cameraNode.addChildNode(game.hudNode)
// 2
cameraFollowNode =
gameScene.rootNode.childNodeWithName("FollowCamera",
recursively: true)!
```

What's going on in there?

1. This attaches `cameraNode` to **camera** in the game scene. Then you add `hudNode` as a child node to it, which will keep the HUD in view of the camera at all times. You use the game helper to create `hudNode`, and in turn, it will be used to display information to the player.
2. This attaches `cameraFollowNode` to **FollowCamera** so that when you want the camera to follow the pig around the scene, all you'll need to do is update the position for `cameraFollowNode` to be the same position as the pig.

Create the follow light node

You'll follow a similar process to create the lights for your game scene as you did to set up the camera. This scene will make use of two basic lights: an ambient light, and a directional light to mimic sunlight and cast hard shadows for everything in the view.

First make sure nothing is selected under your game scene scene graph then click the **+** button to add an empty node. Name it **FollowLight** and zero out both the position and rotation.

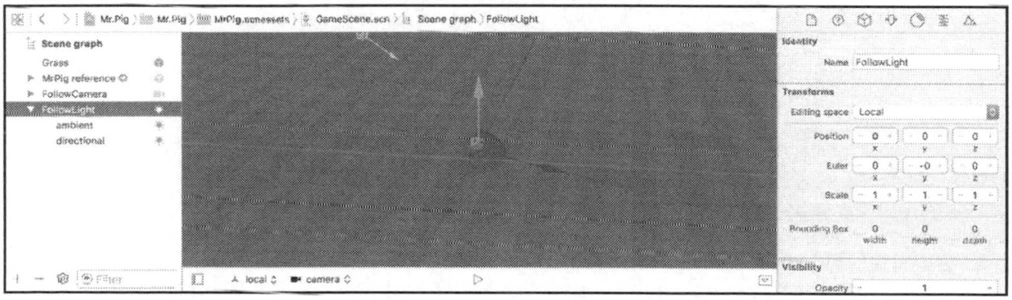

Drag and drop an **Ambient light** and a **Directional light** into the game scene from the Object library. Make sure both lights are children of **FollowLight**.

Select the **ambient** light, and zero out its position and rotation in the Node Inspector.

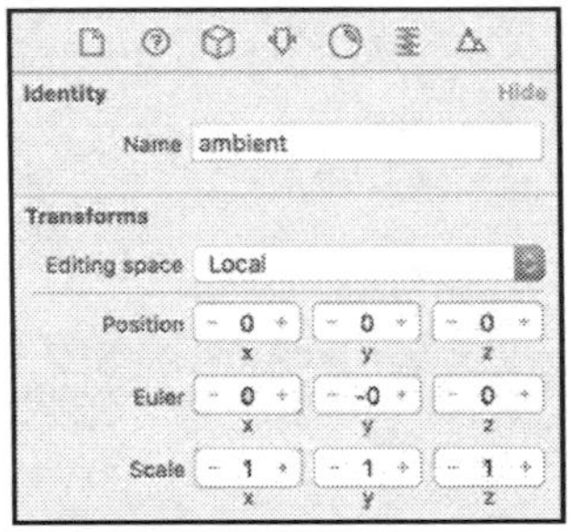

Then, move on to the Attributes Inspector and give the ambient light a mid-grey color by clicking the colored bar next to **Color** to bring up the color picker. Go to the crayons tab, and find the **Aluminum** color to use for the light – this will brighten up the scene a little more.

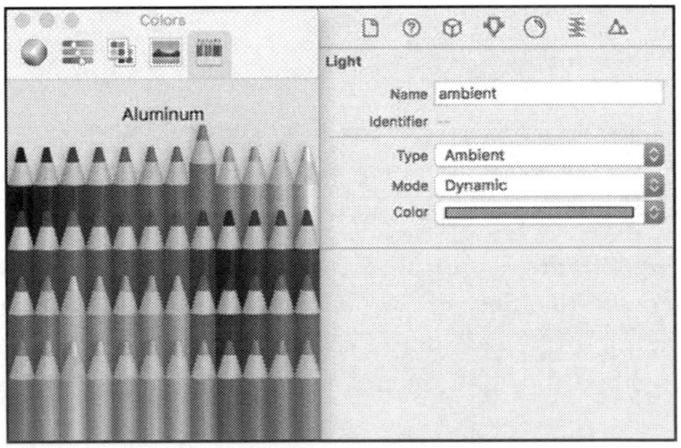

Now select the **directional** light, and bring up its **Node Inspector** again. Set the **Position** to `(x:-5, y:5, z:5)`, and adjust the rotation by setting **Euler** to `(x:-45, y:-60, z:0)`.

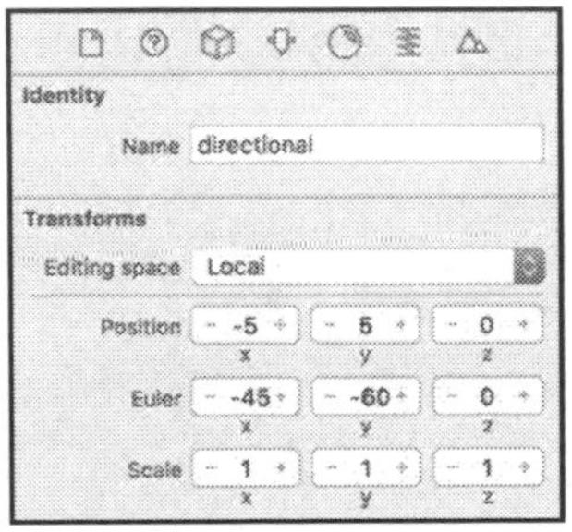

This places the directional light above and to the left of the scene, lighting up everything

nicely.

Move on to the Attribute Inspector to configure **Light** and **Shadow** properties.

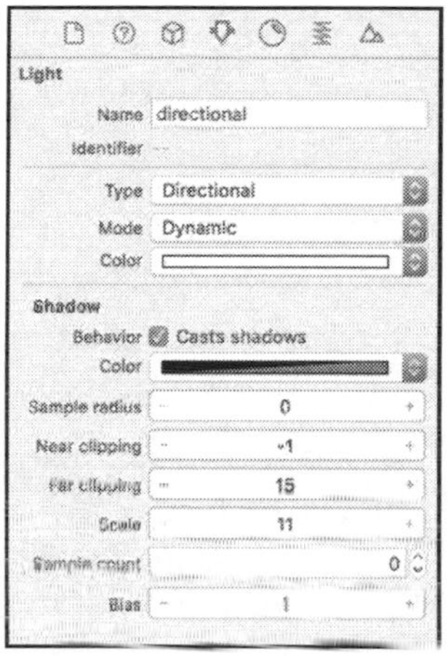

This next list will both tell you what to changes and give you some detail about the properties:

- **Behaviour**: Check this to make the light cast shadows.
- **Sample radius**: Set this to `0` so the edges of shadows cast by this light are not blurred. For this game, which is set outdoors, you want the directional light to mimic the sun and the kinds of crisp shadows it produces.
- **Near/Far clipping**. Specify a value of `-1` for **Near clipping** and `15` for **Far clipping**: Only surfaces between the range of the near and far clippings can have shadows cast upon them. Limiting this range is important for performance, and you calculate how large it will be based on the light source's position
- **Scale**: Set this to `11`. This sets the extents of the orthographic projection for the directional light, large enough so that the casted shadows fills the entire view.
- **Sample count**: Set this to `0`. Again, you want the light to cast a hard shadow. A higher sample count produces softer shadows, so you want to set this to as low as possible.

Once you configure both lights, you should end up with the following result.

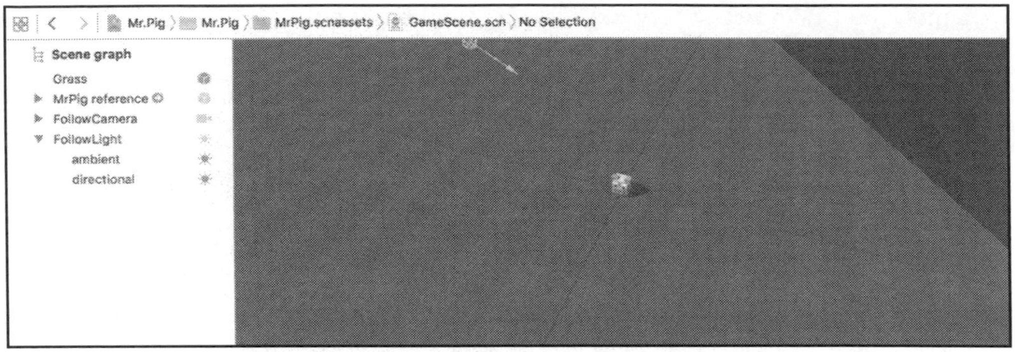

Wait a minute, why on Earth would you want the light to follow the pig around the scene anyway? The answer is simple – performance!

You've already limited the directional light's shadow clipping range, but that range is based on the light's position. When you start panning around the scene, you'll run into parts of the scene that fall outside of the clipping range, and those parts will look very strange without any shadows.

To overcome this issue, you simply set the light to follow the camera view, allowing the shadow clipping region to come along. In short, this approach contrains the task of casting shadows for objects within the camera's *current* point of view.

The alternative is rather expensive and would make this game slow – all in the name of producing shadows the user can't even see. That's why you want the light to follow the pig around the scene.

The only bit left now is to write some code. Start by adding the following property to `ViewController`:

```
var lightFollowNode: SCNNode!
```

This will hold the instance of **FollowLight**.

Add the following code to `setupNodes()`:

```
lightFollowNode =
gameScene.rootNode.childNodeWithName("FollowLight", recursively:
true)!
```

This attaches `lightFollowNode` to **FollowLight**. Now you can move this node to the same position as **FollowCamera** to make sure that the objects in view always cast pretty shadows for the player to see. :]

Do a quick build and run to review what you've done so far.

The game should start up and show the splash scene. Start a game and watch as the scene transitions to the game scene, revealing a very lonesome little pig standing on massive, open grass plane.

Notice that the effect of the hard shadow cast by the sun makes it look hot on that grass. You can almost smell sizzling bacon! :]

Adding highways and traffic

Now to do the bidding of the big bad wolf who built the mall down the street. It seems that his deal included an easement for a new highway straight through Mr. Pig's lovely green park.

Unfortunately, traffic is extremely dangerous for little park-strolling pigs.

Put on your hard hat, it's time to build some highways and a nice big traffic jam while you're at it!

Add the highways

First make sure nothing is selected in your scene graph, then click the + button to add an empty node into the scene. Name it **Highway**.

You'll use this as a container node for the two highways.

Next, drag and drop two **Road** reference nodes from the Media Library into the scene, and make sure to place both of them under **Highway** node.

Select the first road, position it at `(x:0, y:0, z:-4.5)` and zero out the rotation.

Now select the second road and position it at `(x:0, y:0, z:-11.5)`, placing it slightly further away from the first one. Make sure to also zero out the rotation for this road.

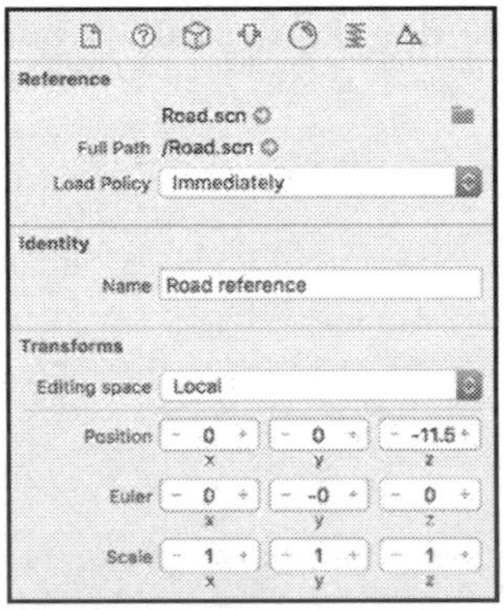

Once you're done positioning both the roads, select **camera** as your point of view in the Scene Editor. You should see something like this:

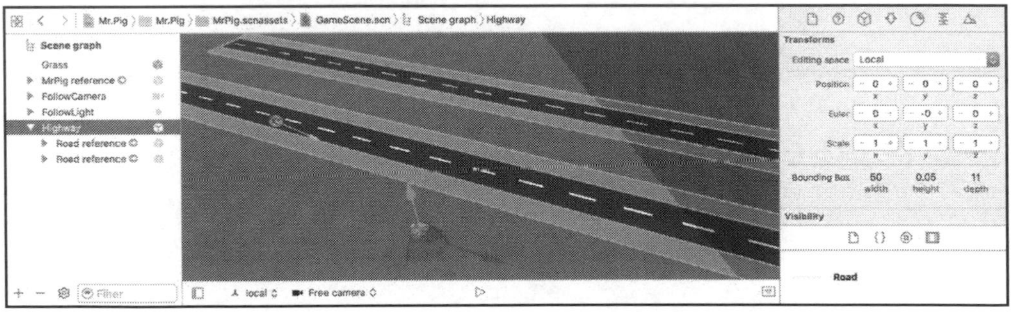

Add the traffic

Build it and they will come, they say. Sure enough, you've built the road and will now make the traffic come. :]

Once again, make sure nothing is selected in your scene graph and add another empty node to the scene to serve as the container node for all the traffic in your game scene. This time around, name it **Traffic**.

Now drag and drop a **Bus** reference node into your scene from the Media Library. Make sure you move the **Bus** node under the **Traffic** node, then set its position to `(x:0, y:0, z:-4)` and give it a rotation of `(x:0, y:-90, z:0)`.

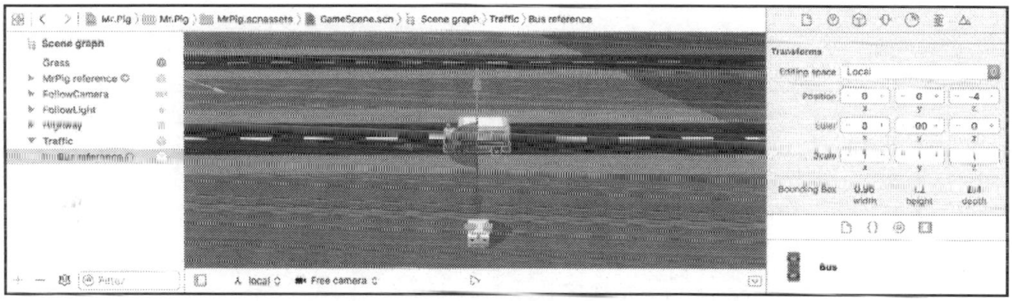

This places the bus nicely on the left lane of the first highway, facing left. Great!

Drag and drop a **Mini** reference node from the Media Library into the scene, and make sure to place it under the **Traffic** node as well. This time, place the Mini on the right lane, at position `(x:3, y:0, z:-5)`, and rotate it to `(x:0, y:-90, z:0)` so that it also faces left, like so:

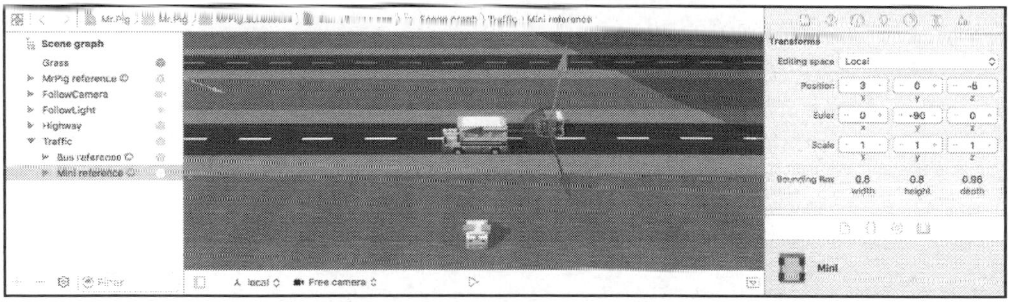

Now drag and drop a **SUV** reference node from the Media Library, and also place it under the **Traffic** node. Place the SUV on the right lane as well – slightly ahead of the Mini – at position `(x:-3, y:0, z:-5)` and rotate it to `(x:0, y:-90, z:0)`.

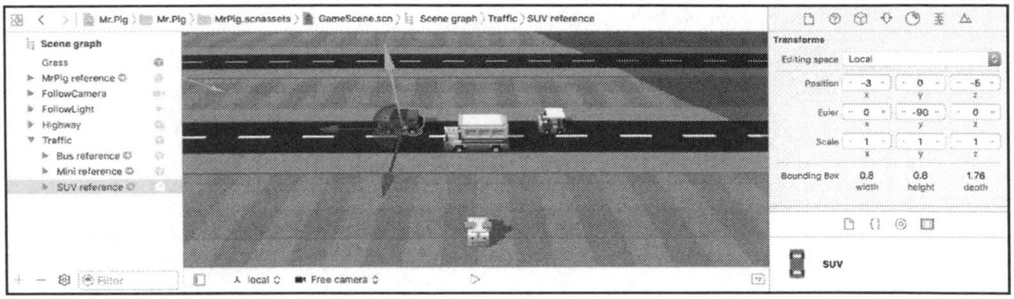

Great job! Now for the coding bit. Select **ViewController.swift** and add the following property to `ViewController`:

```
var trafficNode: SCNNode!
```

This time, instead of making a property for each reference node in traffic, you're going to simply use one container node that holds all the vehicles.

Add the following to `setupNodes()` :

```
trafficNode = gameScene.rootNode.childNodeWithName("Traffic",
recursively: true)!
```

This attaches `trafficNode` to the **Traffic** node in the scene, so now you can easily access all the children of this node to make them drive.

The traffic challenge

Time for a little fun with traffic – no need to drive anywhere for this experience!

Since the vehicles are in place, you should know exactly how to get this challenge done. The challenge is to fill up those highways with even more traffic – lots more.

The final result should look something like this:

Here are some guidelines to follow while adding more traffic:

- Make the left lane a bus lane, and keep the right lane for the smaller, faster vehicles.
- Make one highway's vehicles drive left and the other side's go right.
- To make your life easier, use the **Option** key to make quick copies of something already placed in the scene.
- Also make sure to hold the **Command** key when positioning the cars so they snap to nice round numbers.
- Remember to leave enough space between vehicles for a little pig to run through. You don't want to make the game too difficult.
- Once you've finished the one highway, select all its vehicles and drag them to the other highway while holding **Option** to make a copy. Then, simply rotate them 180 degrees so that they face the other direction.
- Again, while you are rotating the vehicles, hold the **Command** key so that the angles snap into place.

Once you're done adding all the traffic, you can do another build and run just to do a quick sanity check.

Poor little pig is lonely no more! He now shares the once lovely park with two massive highways filled with traffic. :]

> **Note**: If you struggled a bit or want to push ahead, you'll find the completed project after this challenge under **projects\challenge\Mr.Pig**.

Adding trees

At the moment there's one critical element still missing – those cute little trees! It looks like someone built a massive highway across a soccer field, not a green park at the moment.

In this section, you'll create two different groups of trees: a tree line and a tree patch. You'll use the tree line as a border around the whole park, essentially boxing Mr. Pig in.

Then you'll use tree patches to create a few groups of trees to fill in give the scene a park-like look.

Create the tree line

Instead of planting little trees one by one, take a smarter approach and create reusable scenes comprised of a bunch of trees, and then use those as reference nodes in your game scene.

Start off by dragging an empty **Scene Kit Scene File** from the File Template Library into the root folder of your project under the Project Navigator. Name the new scene **TreeLine** and place it under **MrPig.scnassets**:

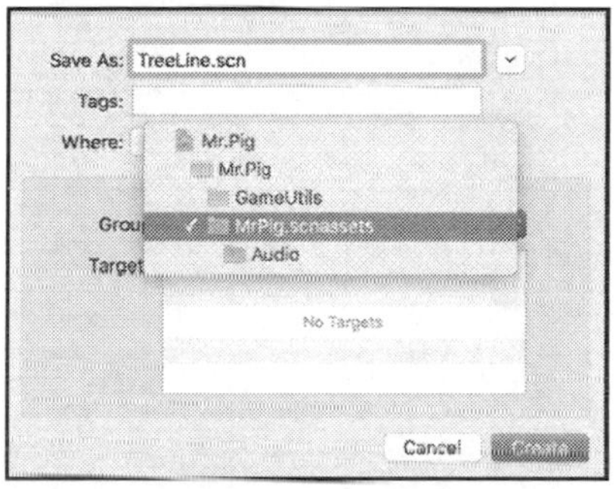

Inside **TreeLine.scn**, create an **empty** node and name it **TreeLine**.

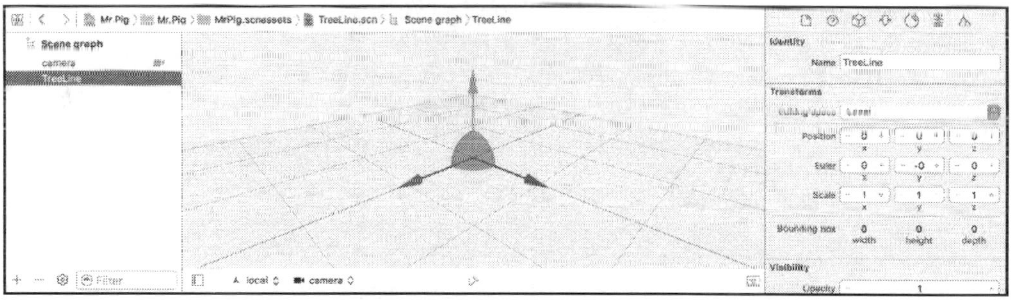

This will be your container node for all the trees in this scene.

Use the following grid pattern to build the tree line.

Z \ X	-5	-4	-3	-2	-1	0	1	2	3	4	5
-1	S	M	S	M	S	M	S	M	S	M	S
0	M	L	M	L	M	L	M	L	M	L	M
1	S	M	S	M	S	M	S	M	S	M	S

What exactly does that grid mean? Each cell holds a tree element and indicates what size of tree to place there.

- **Columns**: indicates the x position for where you'll place the tree element
- **Rows**: indicates the z position for where you'll place the tree element
- **S**: represents a **SmallTree** reference node
- **M**: represents a **MediumTree** reference node
- **L**: represents a **LargeTree** reference node

Thus, as an example, for row 1 and column 1 you need to drag and drop a **SmallTree** reference node from the Media Library into the scene and position it at `(x:-5, y:0, z:-1)`.

To speed things up you can hold the Option and Command keys as you drag to quickly create duplicates that snap to the grid.

Once you're done, your tree line should look something like this:

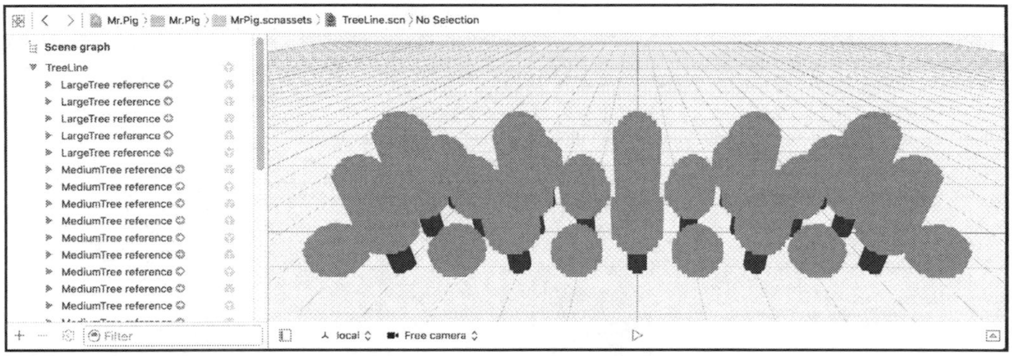

Make sure all the trees are placed under the **TreeLine** container node, and remember to remove that default **camera** because you're going to use this scene as a reference node.

Create the tree patch

You are going to repeat the same steps to create a patch of trees that you can use as a reference node.

Drag another empty **Scene Kit Scene File** from the File Template Library into your project. Name this one **TreePath**, and make sure you place it under **MrPig.scnassets**.

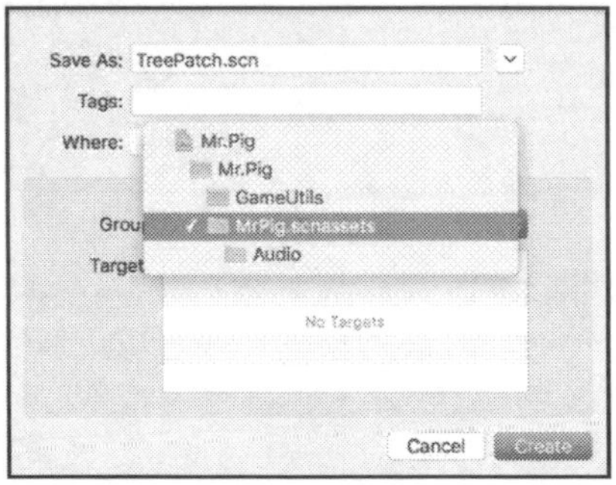

Create an empty node and name it **TreePatch**. This will be your container node for all the trees in this scene.

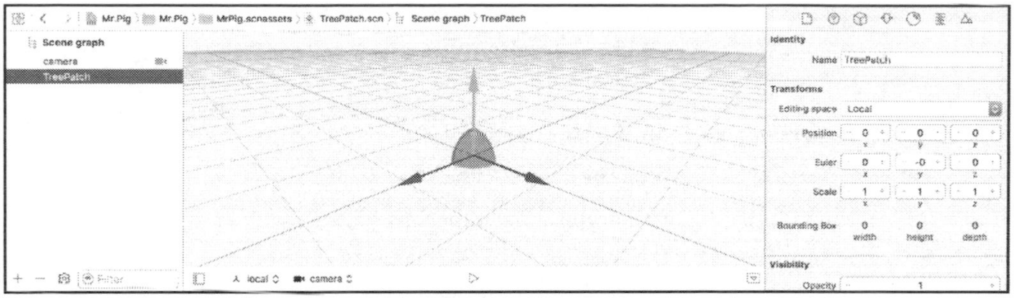

Use the following grid pattern and build the tree patch.

Z \ X	-2	-1	0	1	2
-3			S		
-2		S	M	S	
-1	S	M	I	M	S
0	S	M	I	M	S
1	S	M	L	M	S
2		S	M	S	
3			S		

This works exactly the same as before.

Once done, your tree patch should look something like this:

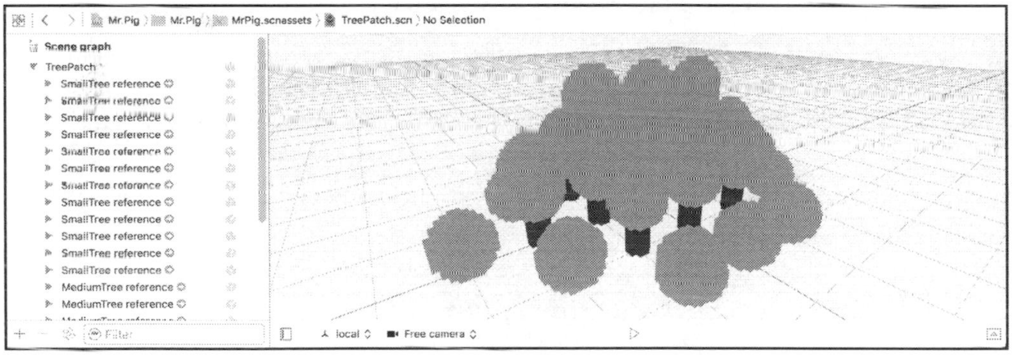

Make sure all the trees are placed under the **TreePatch** container node, and also remember to remove **camera** once you're done because you'll use this scene as a reference node too.

Add the tree line

Now that you got those tree reference nodes ready, you'll need to add them into your game scene so that the lovely park can look and smell like a real park with just a hint of fresh exhaust fumes hanging in the air. :]

Select **MrPig.scnassets\GameScene.scn**, make sure nothing is selected under your scene graph and create an empty node named **Trees**.

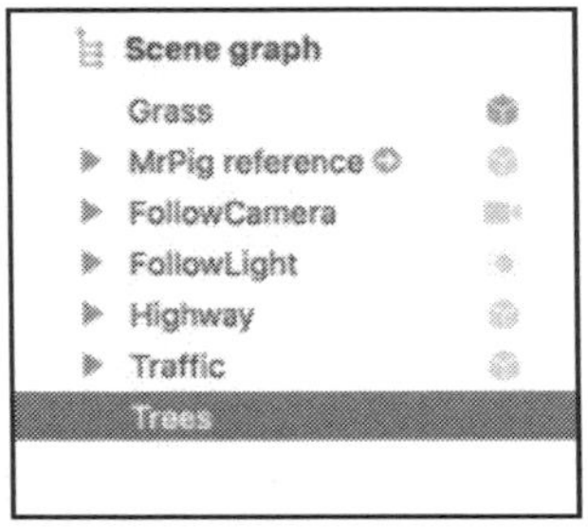

This will be the container node for all the trees you're about to add to the game scene, so make sure you drag all the tree nodes under this container node.

The next bit it going to be somewhat of a challenge, but with settings detailed out all the way through. I think that you're ready for less detail by now. You're about to add the tree lines and you can use the following image as a reference:

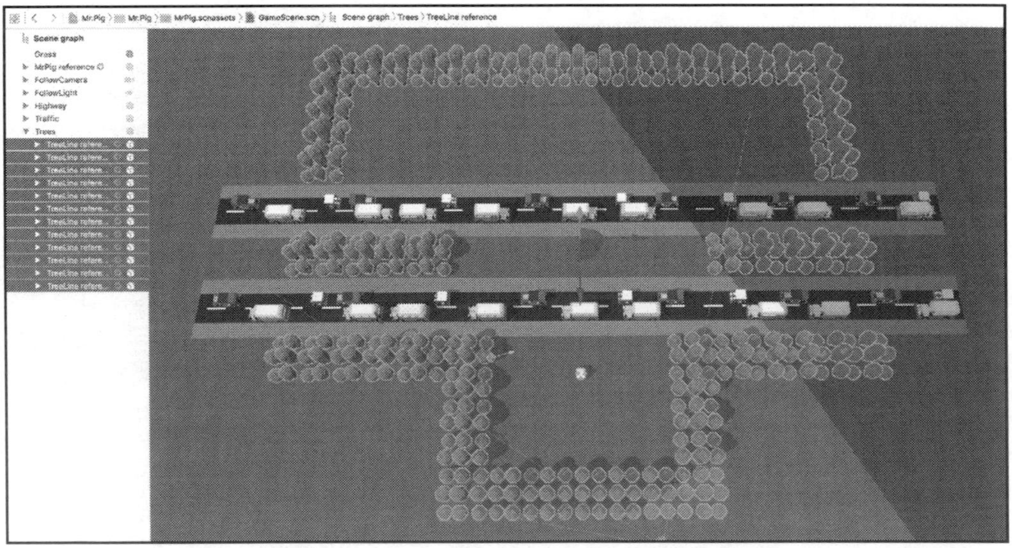

The orange highlighted trees should give you a good indication of the desired result.

Start off by dragging and dropping a single **TreeLine** reference node from the Media Library into your scene. Copy the rest of the tree line from this first reference node by holding Option as you drag. Then use the following positions and rotations to place each one at the correct location and orientation in the game scene.

The tree lines in the front, near Mr. Pig:

- **Position**: `(x:0, y:0, z:7)`, **Euler**: `(x:0, y:0, z:0)`.
- **Position**:`(x:-7, y:0, z:3)`, **Euler**: `(x:0, y:90, z:0)`.
- **Position**: `(x:7, y:0, z:3)`, **Euler**: `(x:0, y:90, z:0)`.
- **Position**: `(x:-14, y:0, z:-1)`, **Euler**: `(x:0, y:0, z:0)`.
- **Position**: `(x:14, y:0, z:-1)`, **Euler**: `(x:0, y:0, z:0)`.

The tree lines between the highways:

- **Position**: `(x:-14, y:0, z:-8)`, **Euler**: `(x:0, y:0, z:0)`.
- **Position**: `(x:14, y:0, z:-8)`, **Euler**: `(x:0, y:0, z:0)`.

The tree lines in the back:

- **Position**: `(x:18, y:0, z:-19)`, **Euler**: `(x:0, y:90, z:0)`.
- **Position**: `(x:-18, y:0, z:-19)`, **Euler**: `(x:0, y:90, z:0)`.
- **Position**: `(x:-11, y:0, z:-23)`, **Euler**: `(x:0, y:0, z:0)`.
- **Position**: `(x:0, y:0, z:-23)`, **Euler**: `(x:0, y:0, z:0)`.
- **Position**: `(x:11, y:0, z:-23)`, **Euler**: `(x:0, y:0, z:0)`.

> **Note**: Remember to put all the copied nodes under the **Trees** container node.

Add the tree patches

Now follow the same process as before to recreate the orange highlighted **TreePatches**.

Start off by dragging and dropping a single **TreePatch** reference node from the Media Library into your scene. Then copy the rest from this node as needed, using the following positions and rotations:

- **Position**: `(x:10, y:0, z:-17)`, **Euler**: `(x:0, y:0, z:0)`.
- **Position**: `(x:-10, y:0, z:-17)`, **Euler**: `(x:0, y:0, z:0)`.
- **Position**: `(x:0, y:0, z:-17)`, **Euler**: `(x:0, y:90, z:0)`.

Again, make sure to move these new tree patch reference nodes under the **Trees** container node you created earlier.

Adding coins

Everybody knows that little piggies are avid coin collectors. Mr. Pig is no different. He even takes his obsession to the next level by risking his own life daily to search for lost coins in the park.

Your mission now is to prevent major disappointment for the little pig by adding some coins to your game scene. :]

Start off by creating an empty node and name it **Coins**. As before, this will be the container node for all the coins you'll add to the scene.

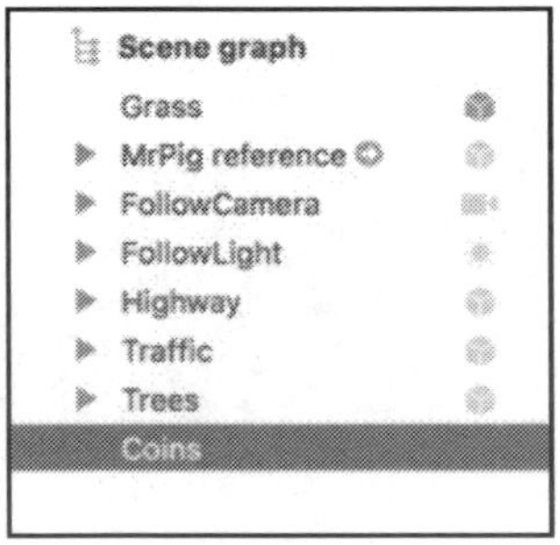

Now drag and drop a **Coin** reference node from the Media Library into the game scene. Make three other copies of this node, and use the following positions for the coins:

- **Position**: `(x:0, y:0.5, z:-8)`.
- **Position**: `(x:0, y:0.5, z:-21)`.
- **Position**: `(x:-14, y:0.5, z:-20)`.
- **Position**: `(x:14, y:0.5, z:-20)`.

Make sure all the coins are under the **Coins** container node. Your scene should now look like this:

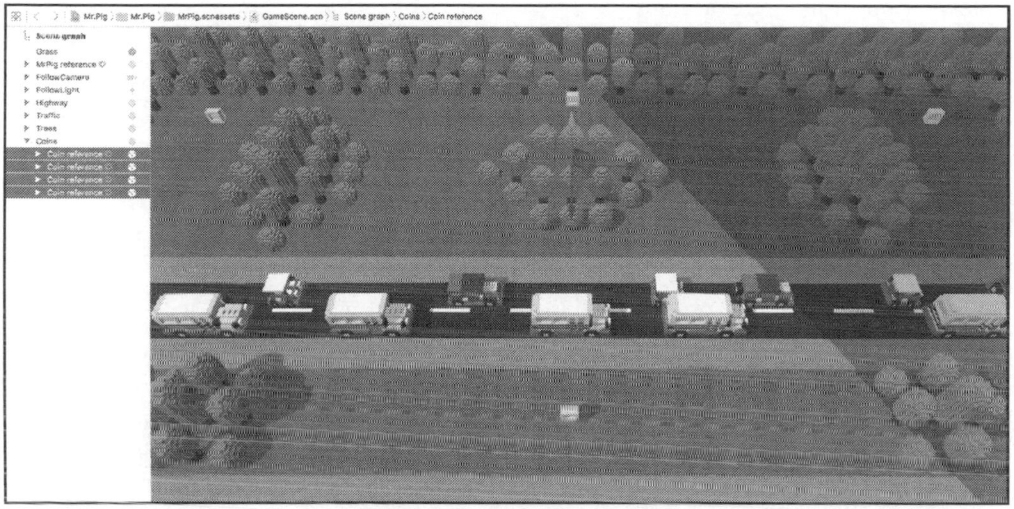

Excellent! You're almost done with this chapter, save for one last build and run that should look like this:

The game now starts up with the splash scene; once the player taps to play, the scene transitions into the game scene, which now has traffic, trees and most importantly, coins for Mr. Pig. :]

Where to go from here?

Good job! You've reached the end of this chapter. You can find the final project for this chapter under **projects\final\Mr.Pig**.

There are a few things in this chapter that you should take away, so let's review:

- You're now starting to apply your skills in a methodical approach when creating complex scenes. This will become second nature – if not already.
- You've learned the importance of using reference nodes inside of reference nodes to turn hard work into child's play. Think back to how you planted a whole bunch of trees in a matter of minutes.
- You've also learned about boosting your game performance by restricting the cast of your shadows. There's also the lesson of moving the light source with the active camera view while keeping the shadows in view.

The game is adorable but still pretty boring at this point because there's nothing to do.

In the next chapter you'll learn all about actions and how to use them within Scene Kit to make traffic move, coins bounce and Mr. Pig jump! So hurry back after a well deserved break. :]

Chapter 18: Actions

Chris Language

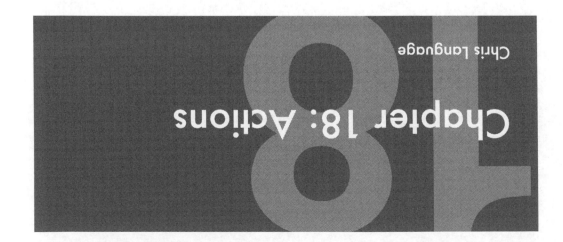

Your game is looking great, but seems to be frozen in time because there isn't any movement. In this chapter, you'll learn all about **actions** in Scene Kit and how to use them to make the nodes in your game move, thus creating a dynamic 3D environment.

You'll start off by making Mr. Pig twerk like *Miley* and head-bang like *Ozzy*! :] Once Mr. Pig has his groove on, you'll add some gestures and actions to make him jump on command so he can navigate to pick up coins as well as bob and weave through traffic.

You'll also make all that traffic flow from one side to another. Then finally, you'll close out this chapter by making shiny coins that spin and bounce.

> **Note**: This chapter picks up where the previous one left off, so if you followed along, you can continue using the same project. Otherwise, you can load up the starter project for this chapter from **projects\starter\Mr.Pig**.

Actions

Actions allow you to manipulate a node's position, scale, rotation and opacity within a scene. For example, when the player swipes left, Mr. Pig should do a leftwards turn while jumping one space to the left. A right swipe should do the opposite.

These basic movements are accomplished by running actions in sequences and groups on the pig node.

You can build action sequences within the Scene Kit editor by dragging and dropping actions from the Object Library into the Secondary Editor, just below the Scene Editor, when you have a node selected. From a coding perspective, you first need to create an

`SCNAction` object, optionally setting its `timingMode` if you want, and then you can execute that action on any `SCNNode` instance by using the `runAction(_:)` method on the node.

There are four basic categories of actions at your disposal for manipulating a node's behaviour in the scene: **Move**, **Scale**, **Rotate** and **Fade**. There are two more special actions used to either run actions in a **Sequence** or as a **Group**.

Note: Think back to when you first learned about physics bodies, and you found out about the three types of physics bodies, which are **dynamic**, **kinematic** and **static**.

If you want the physics engine to take control over a node's movement and rotation, you'd set its physics body to **dynamic**. If you want the node to never move, but still participate within the physics simulation, you'd set its physics body to **static**. When you want to take control of a specific node's movement and rotation, while letting it participate within the physics simulation, you'd to set its physics body type to **kinematic**.

Move actions

When you want to move a node from one point to another point in 3D space, **Move** actions are just the thing to use.

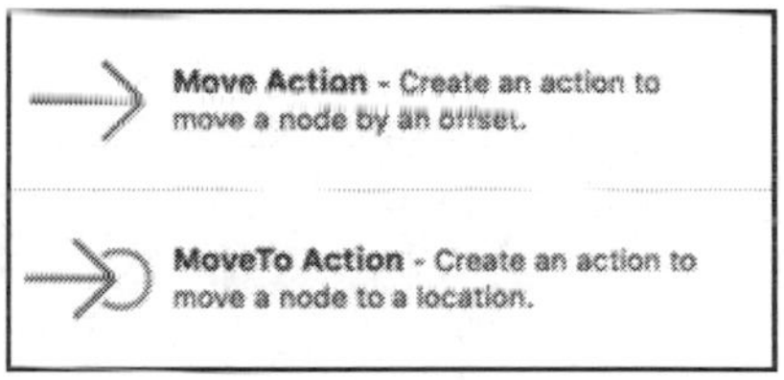

Take a closer look at the two types of move actions:

- **Move Action**: This moves the node by an offset from the node's *current position*.
- **MoveTo Action**: This moves the node to a *specified location* in 3D space *regardless* of the node's current position.

The following image illustrates how you'll use the **Move** action to make Mr. Pig bounce up and down:

For example, the above **Move** action moves the pig to by an offset of `(x:0, y:1, z:0)` from his current position over a period of time, thus moving it upwards along the y-axis. To get the pig back on the ground, you'll have to run another **Move** action, but this time you need to reverse the offset to `(x:0, y−1, z:0)` to get him back on the ground. Awesome! :]

You'll use the same **Move** action to make him move left, right, forward and backward.

Scale actions

Maybe Mr. Pig is extremely allergic to bee stings and you'd like to spice up the game with some bee swarms. :] You could use the **Scale** actions to make him swell up after he becomes a repository for some bee's stinger.

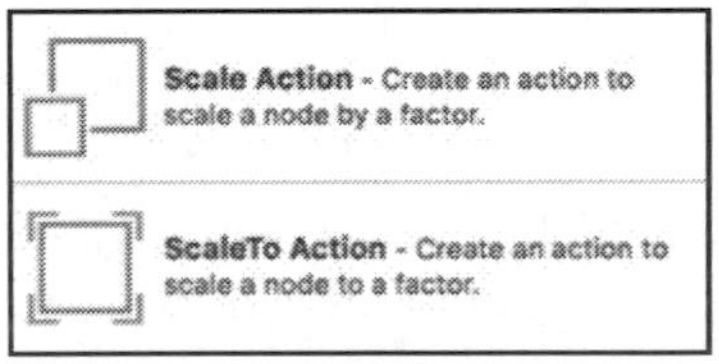

Scale actions work pretty much the same as the move actions.

- **Scale Action**: This scales the node by a factor from the node's current scale.
- **ScaleTo Action**: This scales the node to a specified scale factor, regardless of the node's current scale.

The following image demonstrates how Mr. Pig grows-up from a little piglet to the massive porker he is today:

Did somebody say bacon?

You can also use these **Scale** actions to make nodes wobble by scaling each axis independently. Doing so will distort the geometry, creating an effect that you might want to use when the pig gets stung by a bee, or when he picks up a power-up – like good old Mario after he picked up that magic mushroom! :]

Rotate actions

When Mr. Pig jumps left or right, it makes sense to have him turn towards the same direction; to do that you'll use **Rotate** actions.

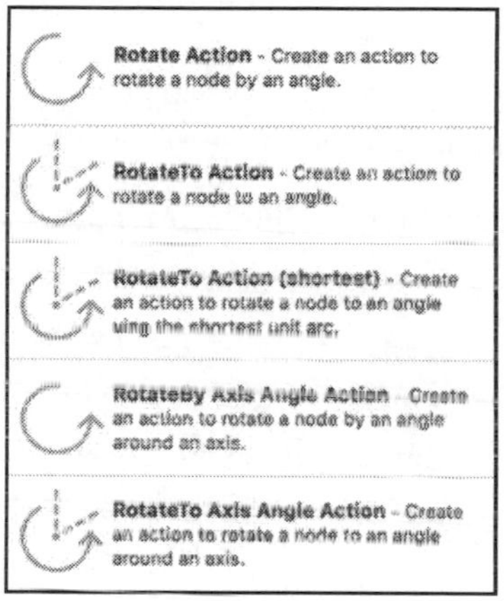

There are a few more options for rotation than there are for move or scale actions:

- **Rotate Action**: Rotates the node by an angle offset from the node's current rotation angle.
- **RotateTo Action**: Rotates the node to a specified angle regardless of its current rotation.
- **RotateTo Action (Shortest)**: Rotates the node to a specified angle, regardless of the node's current rotation, and it'll take the shortest possible rotation to get to the specified angle.
- **RotateBy Axis Angle Action**: This rotates the node by an angle offset on a specified axis from the node's current rotation on that axis.
- **RotateTo Axis Angle Action**: This rotates the node to a specified angle on a specified axis, regardless of the node's current rotation on that axis.

The following image shows how Mr. Pig turns from frontward to backwards by means of using the **RotateTo Action (Shortest)** over a period of time.

From left to right, Mr. Pig spins around, showing you his very cute curly tail. Awww! :]

You can also use **Rotate** actions to make the pig look up or down or even topple over onto his back. Yes, with these controls, Mr. Pig and his world are at your command.

Fade actions

Rarely does a little pink pig fare well when struck by a vehicle. In this scenario, he goes where all pigs go when they die – piggie heaven, where there are countless coins to collect, a never-ending supply of tea, pretty flowers to smell and *no* traffic.

But there's a transition that happens when he leaves this mortal existence. You'll need to represent this with a visual so that the player knows he just killed Mr. Pig.

To turn our hero into a ghost, you'll use the **Fade** actions to make him turn translucent.

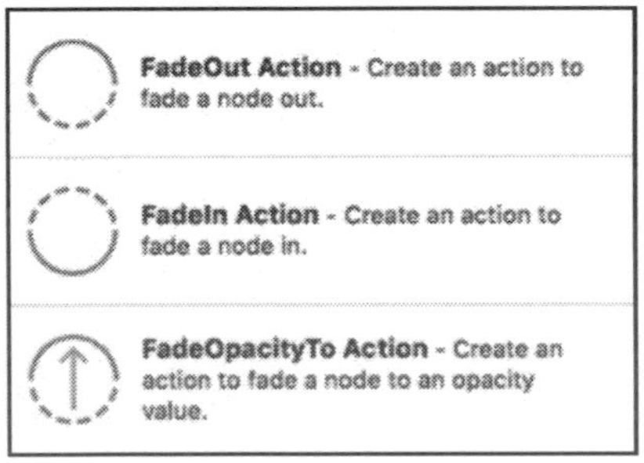

There are a few fade actions at your disposal – take a look:

- **FadeOut Action**: Fades the opacity from its current setting to completely *invisible*.
- **FadeIn Action**: Fades the opacity from its current setting to completely *visible*.
- **FadeOpacityTo Action**: Fades the opacity to a specified value.

The following image demonstrates how Mr. Pig turns into a ghost then vanishes into thin air. From left to right, Mr. Pig fades out from vibrant visible to non-existent. Rest in peace, pig. You lived a good life...

You can also use the **Fade** actions to make nodes pulsate from visible to invisible while they are in a certain state, such as when a spaceship respawns in a shoot-em-up game.

Sequenced and grouped actions

Once you've created a bunch of basic actions, you can combine them together in sequences and groups to make actions run one after another, or together at the same time.

The following diagram shows the relationship between a few basic actions that will play out over a period of two seconds:

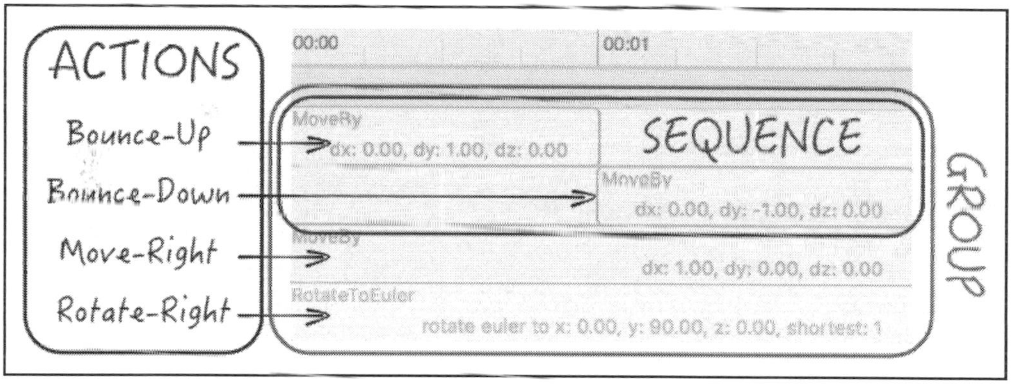

Let's take a closer look:

- **Actions**: The left simply names the four basic actions: bounce-up, bounce-down, move-right and rotate-right.
- **Sequence**: Inside the blue rectangle, you'll see two actions in a *sequence*. So when you move down the timeline, the time cursor will first start the bounce-up action for one second, and once that finishes, it starts running the bounce-down action. This is called a sequence of actions.
- **Group**: Inside the red rectangle is the blue sequence of actions, along with two other actions of *move-right* and *rotate-right*. As you move down the timeline, the time cursor

will start bounce-up, move-right and rotate-right at the same time, in parallel. When the timeline reaches one second, the bounce-up action completes and the bounce-down action starts. At the same time, move-right and rotate-right are still running and halfway done at that point. When the timeline reaches the two-second mark all the actions are complete. By grouping actions together, you can run them all in parallel.

The image below shows the actual animation, as it plays out over time:

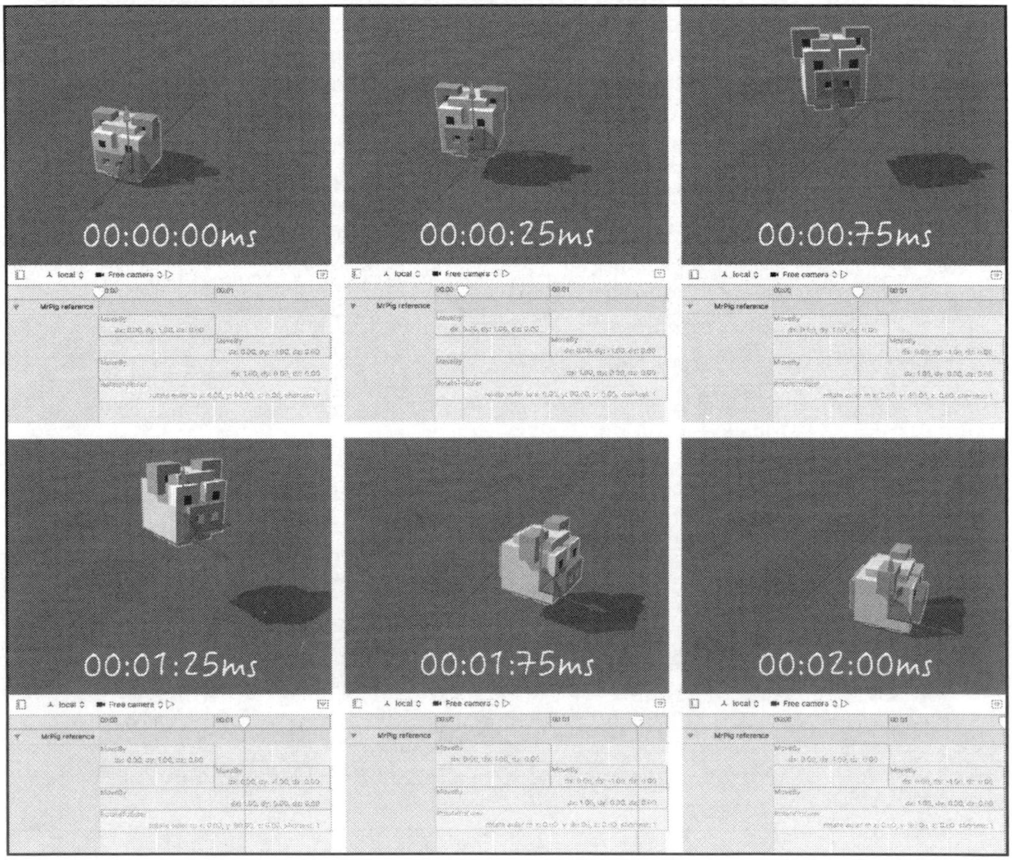

Let's take a closer look at what happens here:

1. First, by running the bounce-up and then the bounce-down actions in a sequence, you make the pig starts on the ground then leap up into the air, only to drop back to the ground again.
2. Although he starts off in one position, over time he moves one space to the right of where he started, by means of the move-right action.
3. At the same time, our hero starts off facing forward, but over time rotates so that he ends up facing right, by means of the rotate-right action.

Action timing functions

Scene Kit provides some basic timing functions you can use to control the progression of the action over time. When Mr. Pig jumps into the air it has to look realistic, and you have some work ahead to make that happen.

At the moment, bounce-up is merely a move action to some defined point in the air, and bounce-down is another move action that takes him to a point on the ground. If you played out these actions in a linear fashion, it would strange because the pig would move up and down in the air in a robotic manner.

This simply is not true when you consider what happens when you toss an egg into the air.

Take the following steps into consideration when you toss an egg into the air:

1. When the egg leaves your hand it's at full velocity, traveling upwards into the air.
2. It continues upwards, but because of gravity's unavoidable pull, its velocity is reduced with time.
3. At some point in time, the egg reaches a point where it comes to a complete stand still in mid-air.
4. It then starts its journey to splatterdom on the ground, falling back to earth with a starting velocity of zero.
5. It continues downwards, all the while its velocity increases thanks to gravity's relentless pull
6. Eventually it reaches maximum velocity, or would if it there wasn't some force acting on it to stop it, like the ground – a collision that is inevitable. Lastly, it shatters to make a terrific mess, which is another physics lesson for another day.

To simulate this bevavior in actions, Scene Kit gives you four basic timing functions to make use of:

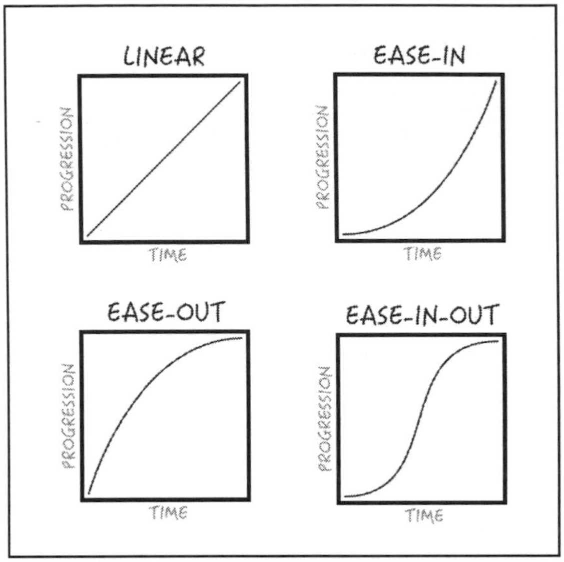

- **Linear**: This is the default timing function used for all actions. The action will play out at the same speed throughout its duration.
- **Ease-In**: This timing function gives the action a slow start, eventually accelerating to its full speed for the rest of the duration.
- **Ease-Out**: This starts the action at its speed and slows as it reaches the end.
- **East-In-Out**: This gives the action a slow start that reaches full speed at its halfway mark. Then it slows as it approaches the end.

To accurately simulate gravity for Mr. Pig's jump action, you'll use a combination of these timing functions.

> **Note**: You can make use of the `timingMode` property on an `SCNAction` to set it's timing function in code.

The action editor

Now that you know all about actions, it's time to see them in action! :]

Xcode has a hidden little feature known as the **Secondary Editor**. In the case of the Scene Kit editor, this secondary editor is the **actions editor** for nodes in a scene.

Take a look at the following image:

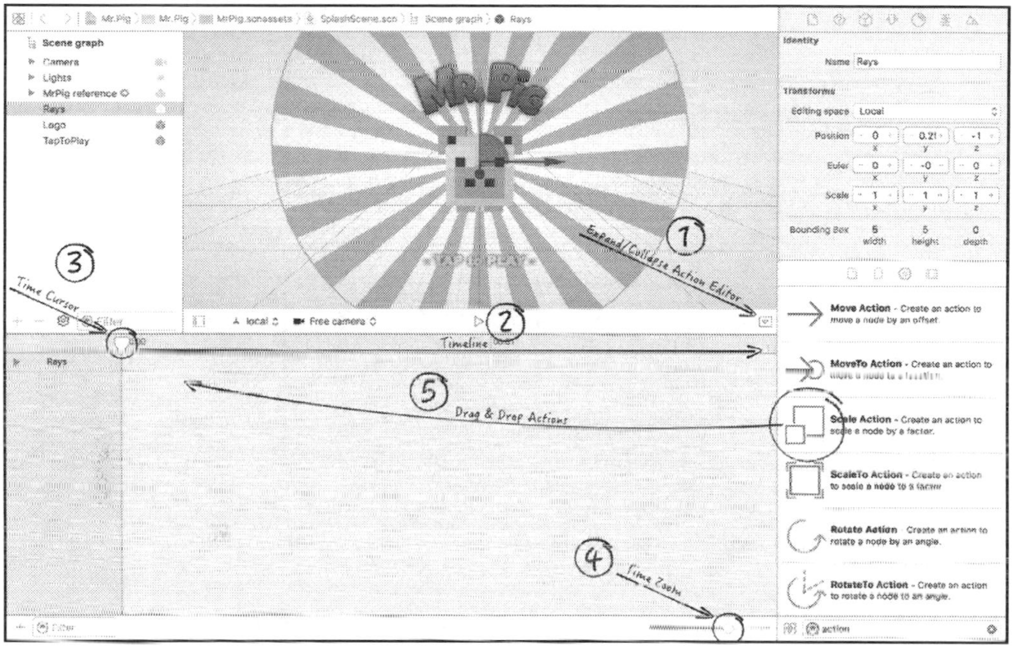

There are a few numbered points to go through:

1. **Expand/Collapse Action Editor**: This is the secondary editor button that you need to press to expand or collapse the actions editor.
2. **Timeline**: This is the timeline, and there's a grid below it that shows when actions take place. Time progression increases as you move to the right.
3. **Time Cursor**: Drag this cursor across the timeline to see the resulting actions running on your nodes in the scene.
4. **Time Zoom**: Use this slider to zoom in or out on the timeline to make editing easier for yourself.
5. **Drag & Drop Actions**: To add actions to a node, you simply drag and drop them from the Object Library into the action editor.

Note: At the time of writing this chapter, there appear to be a few bugs in the Scene Kit Editor relating to actions. Sometimes, when you go back and try to edit existing actions on a node, things can go horribly wrong, and Xcode might even crash on you. If you run into this problem, you may find it best to rather delete the actions and re-create them from scratch.

Animate the rays

Now it's time to apply your knowledge and make the rays spin. :]

Start by opening your project and select **MrPig.scnassets\SplashScene.scn** to bring up the Scene Kit editor. Select the **Rays** node in the scene graph and open up the actions editor for it.

Drag and drop a **Rotate Action** from the Object Library into the actions editor. Make sure to drop it so that the action starts off at time `00:00`:

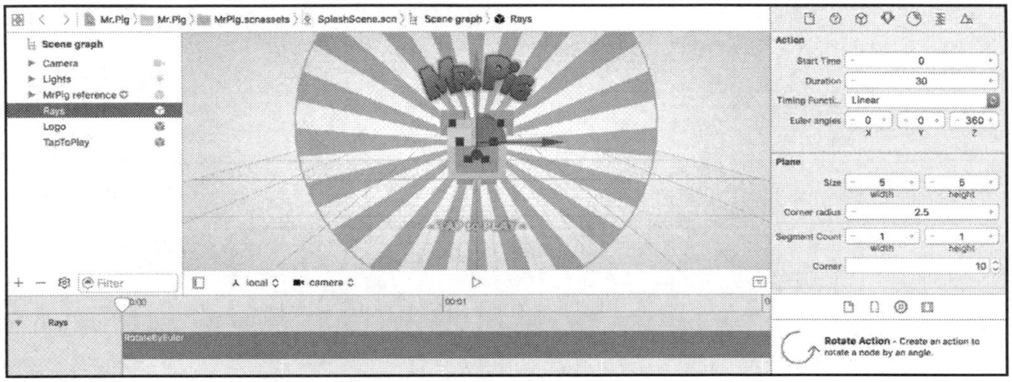

With the action still selected, select the Attributes Inspector:

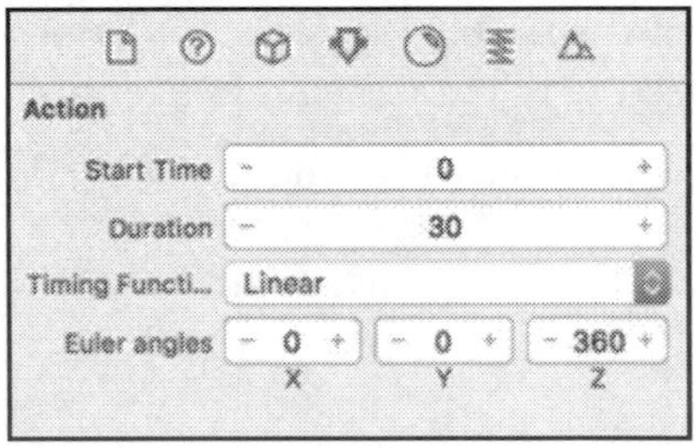

Here you set the properties available for both the action and the node. Let's take a closer look at the available properties you can adjust for this action:

- **Start Time**: This sets the starting point when the action starts to run. Leave this at its default of `0`.
- **Duration**: This sets the duration of how long the action will run for. Set this to `30` so this action runs for 30 seconds in total.
- **Timing Function**: This sets the timing function to use while running the action. Leave this at its default of `Linear`.
- **Euler angles**: This sets the offset of the node's current once the action completes. Leave **X** and **Y** at `0`, but be sure to set the **Z** value to `360`, or else nothing will happen.

Now you want to loop the action so that it runs forever, effectively keeping those rays spinning for an eternity. Right-click on the action and select **Create Loop**:

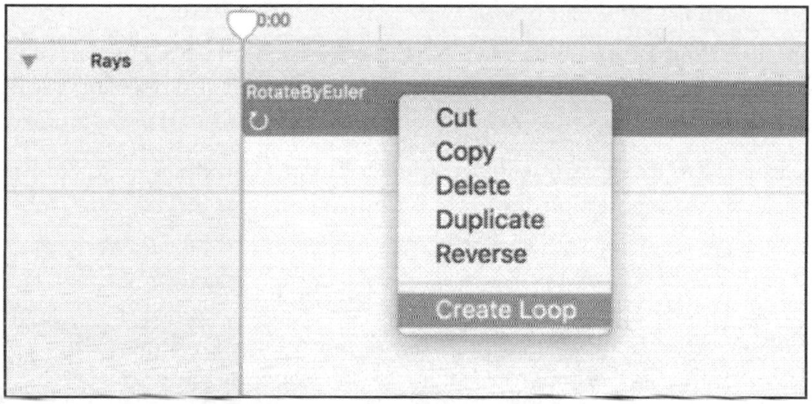

This will show another little **Looping** pop-up:

Click the ∞ (infinite) so that it turns blue and then click outside of the menu to close it. Don't click the **X** button because it'll cancel your loop option selection.

You're all done! Try dragging the time cursor to the right and left to see a preview of your rays spinning:

Note: You can access the looping options again by simply right-clicking on a looping action and selecting **Edit Loop**.

Animate the coins

Another fun little animation you'll add is one that makes the coins in your game scene spin and bounce up and down, making them easy for our hero to see! :]

First select the **MrPig.scnassets\Coin.scn** reference node, then make sure you have the **Coin** node selected and the actions editor open. Drag and drop two instances of **Move Action** one after another. Then, drag and drop a **Rotate Action** parallel in there by placing it below the move actions you added:

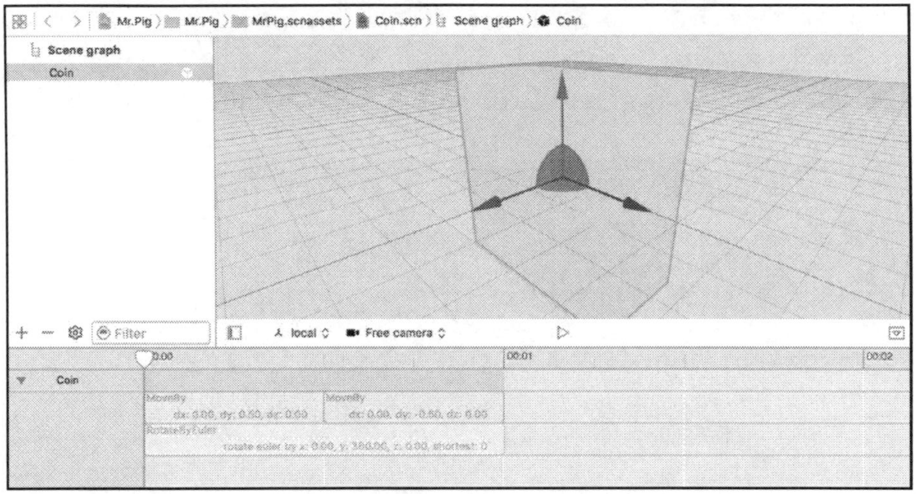

Select the first **Move Action** and set the **Start Time** to `0`, with a **Duration** of `0.5`. Set the **Timing Function** to **Ease In, Ease Out**, and set the **Offset** to `(x:0, y:0.5, z:0)`:

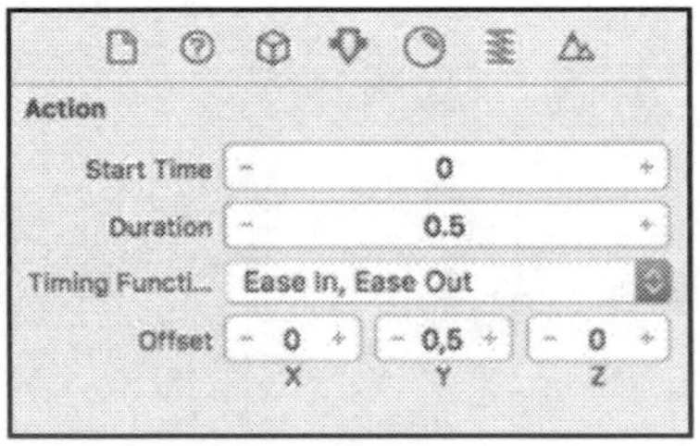

This move action will move the coin upwards, easing in and out as it reaches the end of the action.

Select the next **Move Action**. This time, set its **Start Time** to `0.5`, starting as soon as the previous action ends. Also set its **Duration** to `0.5`, its Timing Function** to **Ease In, Ease Out**, with an **Offset** of `x:0, y:-0.5, z:0`:

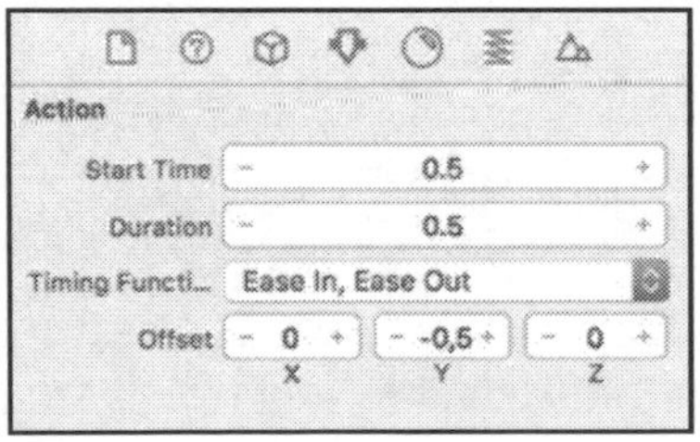

This will move the coin downwards, first easing in then out again as it reaches the end of the action.

Now select the **Rotate Action**. It starts at the same time as the first move action and runs for the same duration as both move actions combined. Set its **Start Time** to `0` and **Duration** to `1`.

Leave its **Timing Function** to **Linear** so that it spins at a constant rate. Finally, set the **Euler Angle** to `(x:0, y:360, z:0)` so that the coin does a full 360 degree spin in one turn of animation:

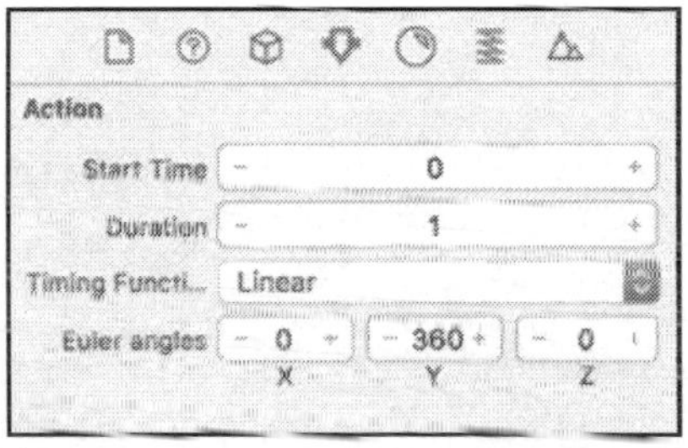

Now to make the coin spin forever.

First, make sure you've got all the actions selected; do this by pressing the Shift key while clicking on each action. Now do a right click to reveal the list of options available.

Select the **Create Loop** option:

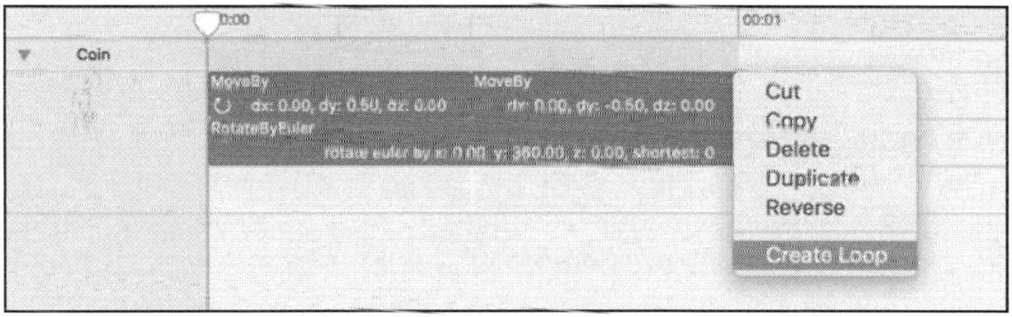

Another little pop-up will appear with the **Looping** options:

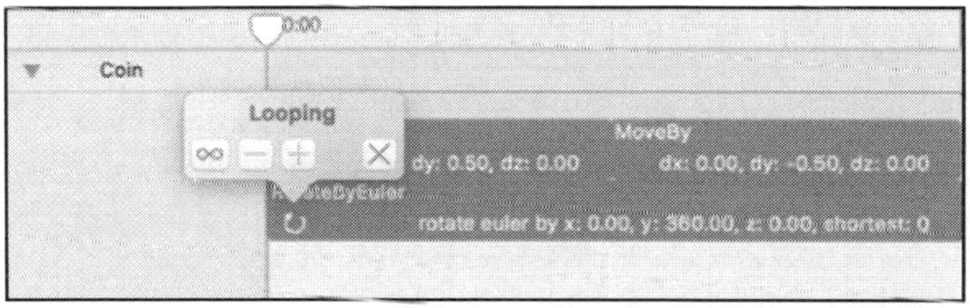

Select the ∞ (infinite) button, which will turn blue. Click outside of this box to confirm your selection. If you click the **X** button, you will delete the loop. This infinite selection

means the actions in the loop run forever.

Again, feel free to use the time cursor to preview your work so far.

Challenge!

Now here's a fun little challenge to test yourself – the twerk challenge! Hey, where are you going? I didn't mean *you* have to twerk. (But kudos if you're one of the select few who can actually do it without looking silly.)

The idea here is to make Mr. Pig twerk and show off that curly little tail, not for you to show off *your* sweet dance moves. :]

Go into **MrPig.scnassets\SplashScreen.scn** to start your challenge. You don't want to make the reference node twerk or else Mr. Pig will be constantly twerking during the game scene and that might be considered obscene.

Twerk it, pig!

Relax, it's much easier than one would think. First, select the **MrPig** reference node in the splash scene and bring up the actions editor.

Next, read through these tips if you need help figuring out how to achieve a twerking pig!

1. Connect 7 **Rotate Actions** in a sequence, and set all of them to a duration of `0.25s`.

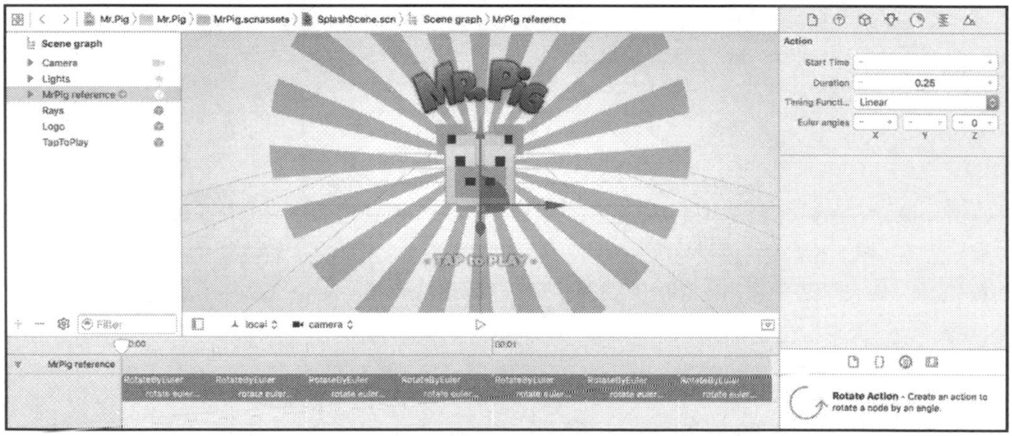

2. Start off by setting the first rotate action to tilt the pig forward by rotating it `30º` on its x-axis.

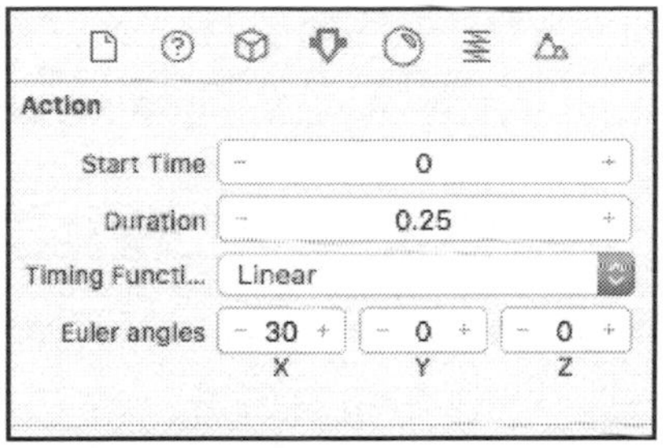

3. Then set the next rotate action to tilt the pig backward by rotating it `-30º` on its x-axis.

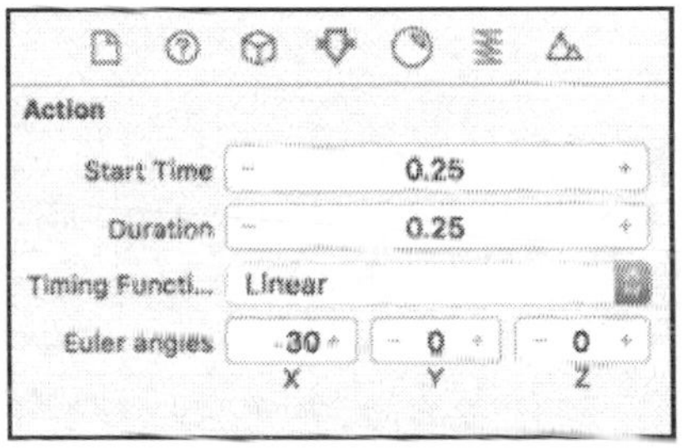

4. Repeat steps two and three for all the following actions except the last one.
5. For the very last rotate action, you want the node to do a full `180º` turn so that the pig shows you its tail-end. Do this by rotating it `180º` on the y-axis.

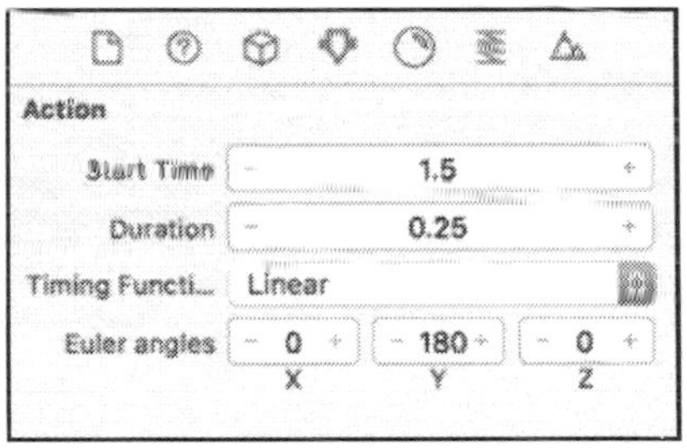

6. If you scrub the time cursor along the timeline, the pig will head-bang, and then flip around to show you his tail. Perfect! :]

The next bit is easy. Simply select all the actions, right-click and select the **Create Loop** option.

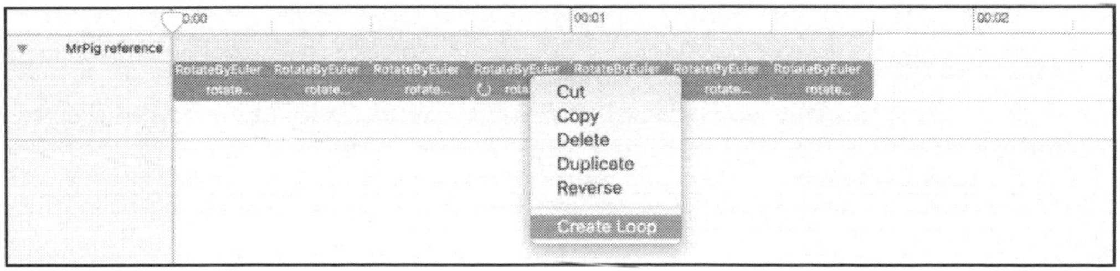

7. Make sure to select the ∞ (infinite) loop option when you see the **Looping** options.

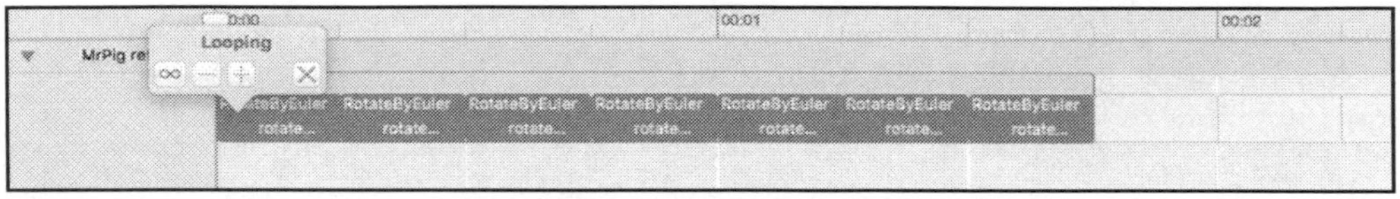

Note: You can find the solution for this little challenge under **projects\challenge \Mr.Pig.**

It's a good time for a build and run.

Your splash scene should look much more attractive now, with the spinning rays and a very energetic twerking Mr. Pig! :]

Now you see that it's really easy to to give your characters a whole lot of attitude with just a few, simple animations.

Coding actions

So now that you know how to create and use actions using the built-in Xcode actions editor, this section will focus more on how to create and use actions in code. That's right, you're getting into the thick of it now!

You'll start by creating two actions that will ultimately make the traffic move. Then you'll create a few basic actions for making the pig jump around the scene using gestures.

Finally, you'll create a game over action to use when Mr. Pig meets his fate against the moving traffic.

Animate the traffic

There are two highways, one with traffic flowing left and another with traffic flowing right.

A **Move Action** should meet the need to make the cars and buses move, as this will move the traffic a certain distance over a period of time.

Remember there's also a bus lane filled with slower moving vehicles. Instead of creating multiple actions for the two speeds, you're simply going to run the same action on the different vehicles and adjust the action's speed.

> **Note**: If you are an Extreme Home Makeover fan, you might find fitting to take a break at this moment and shout: "Move that Bus! Move that Bus! Move that Bus!" :]

In code, actions are represented by instances of the `SCNAction` class and there are, of course, class methods to create all the various actions you looked at in the Object Library.

For instance, **Move Action** can be created in code using the `SCNAction.moveBy( :duration:)` class method.

Open **ViewController.swift** and add the following action properties to `ViewController`:

```
var driveLeftAction: SCNAction!
var driveRightAction: SCNAction!
```

These two properties will store the move left and move right actions so you can reuse them at will.

Add the following to `setupActions()`:

```
driveLeftAction =
SCNAction.repeatActionForever(SCNAction.moveBy(SCNVector3Make(-2
.0, 0, 0), duration: 1.0))
driveRightAction =
SCNAction.repeatActionForever(SCNAction.moveBy(SCNVector3Make(2.
0, 0, 0), duration: 1.0))
```

The `SCNAction.repeatActionForever(_:)` class method creates a special action that will simply loop, or rather repeat, another action forever. The `SCNAction.moveBy(_:duration:)` class method creates an action that will move the node by a specified vector over a certain duration.

Now put these two new actions to good use by adding the following code to `setupTraffic()`:

```
// 1
for node in trafficNode.childNodes {

  // 2 Buses are slow, the rest are speed demons
  if node.name?.containsString("Bus") == true {
    driveLeftAction.speed = 1.0
    driveRightAction.speed = 1.0
  } else {
    driveLeftAction.speed = 2.0
    driveRightAction.speed = 2.0
  }

  // 3 Let vehicle drive towards its facing direction
  if node.eulerAngles.y > 0 {
    node.runAction(driveLeftAction)
  } else {
    node.runAction(driveRightAction)
  }
}
```

The `setupTraffic()` method is already being called from `viewDidLoad()` so you don't need to worry about that, but let's take a closer look at what the actual code does:

1. At this point, `setupNodes()` has already initialized `trafficNode`, which is attached to the **Traffic** node in the game scene. The `childNodes` property of `SCNNode` returns a list of child nodes for you to iterate through. This will essentially be a list of all the vehicle nodes on the highways.
2. If the node is a bus, you set the `SCNAction.speed` to be `1.0`, otherwise you set it to `2.0` to run the action for the smaller vehicles twice as fast.
3. Based on the assumption that you only have traffic moving left and right, this does a crude check to see which direction the vehicle currently faces. It then executes the correct facing drive action on the node.

Do another build and run, then start the game by tapping on the splash scene:

The traffic is moving, oh goody! :]

But wait there's a problem, all of the traffic drives off the screen leaving a safe, empty road for Mr. Pig to cross. At this rate, crossing the road hardly qualifies as heroic.

Don't worry, this is a small little problem that you'll tackle when you're handling updates within the game render loop. That won't be in this chapter, so for now, just accept the current state.

Animate the pig

Your next focus point is to make that pig jump like a little flea. Mr. Pig will need to be quick on his feet, able to jump forwards, backwards, left and right.

To accomplish this, you'll create a whole bunch of little, basic actions that you'll sequence and group together.

Add the following action properties to `ViewController`:

```
var jumpLeftAction: SCNAction!
var jumpRightAction: SCNAction!
var jumpForwardAction: SCNAction!
var jumpBackwardAction: SCNAction!
```

These are the four resulting actions that will perform the jump action in the various directions.

Add the following to bottom of `setupActions()`:

```
// 1
let duration = 0.2

// 2
let bounceUpAction = SCNAction.moveByX(0, y: 1.0, z: 0,
duration: duration * 0.5)
let bounceDownAction = SCNAction.moveByX(0, y: -1.0, z: 0,
duration: duration * 0.5)

// 3
bounceUpAction.timingMode = .EaseOut
bounceDownAction.timingMode = .EaseIn

// 4
let bounceAction = SCNAction.sequence([bounceUpAction,
bounceDownAction])

// 5
let moveLeftAction = SCNAction.moveByX(-1.0, y: 0, z: 0,
duration: duration)
let moveRightAction = SCNAction.moveByX(1.0, y: 0, z: 0,
duration: duration)
let moveForwardAction = SCNAction.moveByX(0, y: 0, z: -1.0,
duration: duration)
let moveBackwardAction = SCNAction.moveByX(0, y: 0, z: 1.0,
duration: duration)

// 6
let turnLeftAction = SCNAction.rotateToX(0, y:
convertToRadians(-90), z: 0, duration: duration,
shortestUnitArc: true)
let turnRightAction = SCNAction.rotateToX(0, y:
convertToRadians(90), z: 0, duration: duration, shortestUnitArc:
true)
let turnForwardAction = SCNAction.rotateToX(0, y:
convertToRadians(180), z: 0, duration: duration,
shortestUnitArc: true)
let turnBackwardAction = SCNAction.rotateToX(0, y:
convertToRadians(0), z: 0, duration: duration, shortestUnitArc:
true)

// 7
jumpLeftAction = SCNAction.group([turnLeftAction, bounceAction,
moveLeftAction])
jumpRightAction = SCNAction.group([turnRightAction,
bounceAction, moveRightAction])
jumpForwardAction = SCNAction.group([turnForwardAction,
bounceAction, moveForwardAction])
jumpBackwardAction = SCNAction.group([turnBackwardAction,
bounceAction, moveBackwardAction])
```

Quite the screen full, so how about a breakdown?

1. Using a variable for the duration will simply make your life easier once you start tweaking action animation times. You'd typically work in fragments of a specific duration, and this simplifies it so that you can use simple math to specify a fragment of the original duration.
2. This creates the two basic actions that bounce the pig up and down, similar to the visual examples demonstrated in the beginning of this chapter.
3. This updates the timing functions for the bounce actions so that when they run in a sequence, the pig will have a realistic jump animation with some hang-time! :]
4. This creates `bounceAction` by using the bounce up and bounce down actions in sequence.
5. This creates four move actions using `SCNAction.moveByX(_:y:z:duration:)` to move in every direction.
6. This creates four rotation actions using `SCNAction.rotateToX(_:y:z:duration:shortUnitArc:)`, one for rotating to each direction.
7. Finally, this creates the four jump actions by combining the turn, bounce and move actions into a group, which will run all three actions in parallel.

Add gesture controls

All the actions are now ready to go. What's left now is to get Mr. Pig to respond to some gestures so that you know what actions to run.

Create four basic gestures for your game by adding the following to `setupGestures()`:

```
let swipeRight:UISwipeGestureRecognizer =
UISwipeGestureRecognizer(target: self, action:
#selector(ViewController.handleGesture(_:)))
swipeRight.direction = .Right
scnView.addGestureRecognizer(swipeRight)

let swipeLeft:UISwipeGestureRecognizer =
UISwipeGestureRecognizer(target: self, action:
#selector(ViewController.handleGesture(_:)))
swipeLeft.direction = .Left
scnView.addGestureRecognizer(swipeLeft)

let swipeForward:UISwipeGestureRecognizer =
UISwipeGestureRecognizer(target: self, action:
#selector(ViewController.handleGesture(_:)))
```

```
swipeForward.direction = .Up
scnView.addGestureRecognizer(swipeForward)

let swipeBackward:UISwipeGestureRecognizer =
UISwipeGestureRecognizer(target: self, action:
#selector(ViewController.handleGesture(_:)))
swipeBackward.direction = .Down
scnView.addGestureRecognizer(swipeBackward)
```

This registers the `handleGesture(_:)` method as the event handler for the swipe up, down, left and right gestures, so that when the player does a swipe gesture, `handleGesture(_:)` will trigger further action.

> **Note**: You're sending all the gestures to the same handler. You'll filter out the exact details of the gesture within the handler method itself, which is up next.

Now add `handleGesture(_:)` to `ViewController`:

```
// 1
func handleGesture(sender:UISwipeGestureRecognizer){
  // 2
  guard game.state == .Playing else {
    return
  }
  // 3
  switch sender.direction {
    case UISwipeGestureRecognizerDirection.Up:
      pigNode.runAction(jumpForwardAction)
    case UISwipeGestureRecognizerDirection.Down:
      pigNode.runAction(jumpBackwardAction)
    case UISwipeGestureRecognizerDirection.Left:
      if pigNode.position.x >  -15 {
        pigNode.runAction(jumpLeftAction)
      }
    case UISwipeGestureRecognizerDirection.Right:
      if pigNode.position.x < 15 {
        pigNode.runAction(jumpRightAction)
      }
    default:
      break
  }
}
```

Take a deeper look at exactly what happens here:

1. This defines a typical gesture handler and receives a `UIGestureRecognizer` as an input. You'll need to inspect this element to determine the exact gesture details.
2. This keeps the game state in mind. Typically you're not interested in any gestures

unless the game is in a `.Playing` state, so ignore all gesture events when the game state is something else.

3. This inspects `direction` of the gesture recognizer to determine the direction the player swiped in. Then, it executes the correct jump action on the pig node, which will make the pig jump in the direction of the swipe. There's also a small check when jumping left and right to prevent Mr. Pig from jumping out of the play area.

Do a build and run and go test out the gesture control system:

Once your game starts, you should be able to swipe in any direction, and Mr. Pig will follow your every command. Excellent! :]

But wait there's another problem, the camera isn't following the pig, so he's able to jump out of sight. Don't worry, this is just another small little problem to sort out when you're handling updates within the game render loop.

Create game over action

You're almost done with this chapter. There's just one more action you need to create that you'll use a little bit later on: the `triggerGameOver` action!

This little action comprises a few sub-actions that will send our beloved hero to piggie heaven, and then finally trigger a call to `startSplash()` to show the splash scene again.

Start off by adding the following action property to `ViewController`:

```
var triggerGameOver: SCNAction!
```

This stores the final action you'll run to trigger the game over sequence.

Add the following to the bottom of `setupActions()`:

```
// 1
let spinAround = SCNAction.rotateByX(0, y:
convertToRadians(720), z: 0, duration: 2.0)
let riseUp = SCNAction.moveByX(0, y: 10, z: 0, duration: 2.0)
let fadeOut = SCNAction.fadeOpacityTo(0, duration: 2.0)
let goodByePig = SCNAction.group([spinAround, riseUp, fadeOut])
// 2
let gameOver = SCNAction.runBlock { (node:SCNNode) -> Void in
  self.pigNode.position = SCNVector3(x:0, y:0, z:0)
  self.pigNode.opacity = 1.0
  self.startSplash()
}
// 3
triggerGameOver = SCNAction.sequence([goodByePig, gameOver])
```

Here's what happens in here:

1. This creates a few basic actions: one to spin the pig 720 degrees, one to move him up into the sky and another to fade him into nothingness. All three actions are put together under a single action group, fittingly named `goodByePig`. This is the animation sequence to make poor Mr. Pig go to the heaven's gate when he meets his fate. :]
2. The `SCNAction.runBlock(_:)` class method creates a special action that allows you to inject code logic into an action, which then can be executed just like any other action. This specific code block simply resets Mr. Pig to his original position and opacity level and then triggers `startSplash()` to bring you back to the splash scene.
3. This creates the final `triggerGameOver` action sequence that first executes the `goodByePig` action, and then once completed, it executes the `gameOver` run block action.

To finish off this chapter, add the following to the bottom of `stopGame()`:

```
pigNode.runAction(triggerGameOver)
```

This will insure that what ever makes a call to the `stopGame()` function will trigger the `triggerGameOver` action sequence, ultimately ending the game. So sad... :[

To test this, add the following temporary code to the top of `handleGesture(_:)`:

```
stopGame()
return
```

Build and run, start the game, then swipe in any direction to trigger the death animation. Poor pig!

Be sure to delete or comment the test code before you continue on:

```
//stopGame()
//return
```

Where to go from here?

Your steller performance has brought you to the end of yet another chapter! Your game is in fantastic shape and there's not too much left to do.

To recap what you've learned in this chapter:

- **Actions**: You learned about actions and how to combine them to build intricate animation sequences.
- **Actions Editor**: You learned all about Xcode's built-in secondary editor for `SCNNode`, aka the actions editor.
- **Timing Functions**: You learned about timing functions that manipulate the progression of an action over time and allow you to simulate realism in action-packed animation sequences.
- **Coding Actions**: You also got your hands dirty by manually creating a whole bunch of different actions for your game in code.

There are a few things that still needs to be addressed, one of the more hilarious being that our hero is unstoppable – neither tree nor car nor bus can stop him. Did you mean to make some kind of mutant pig? :]

The next chapter will focus on solving all that by means of collision detection.

Chapter 19: Advanced Collision Detection

Chris Language

Your game is almost done. It has a vibrant splash scene complete with spinning sun rays, a twerking pig and a game scene that hosts a beautiful park filled with lovely trees, coins and two massive traffic-filled highways.

To top it off, you've added animations to bring the whole thing to life.

In this chapter, your target will be to solve a few problems:

- Nothing can block the little pig right now. Typically obstacles like the trees would fence him in. This poses a little secondary challenge: proactively block movement so that there is no way for the pig to even collide with the tree.
- Traffic isn't a threat, which makes for a most unchallenging game. You'll change all that. The next time the little pig runs in front of a bus it will be his last! :]
- Your poor little pig can only look at the pretty, shiny coins – he can't pick them up. Don't worry, you'll solve that too.

Well, the game isn't to finish itself! Wake up and smell the bacon. It's time to get to it!

> **Note**: There's a starter project for you available under **projects\starter\Mr.Pig**, it continues exactly where the previous chapter left off.

Hidden geometry for collisions

You've already covered basic collision detection and are familiar with collision masks and how they work. To proactively block the little pig's movement before he even collides with an obstacle like a tree, you'll use some ultra-cool, advanced collision detection techniques.

The secret is to make use of hidden geometry that would actually cause an active collision with nearby obstacles, essentially giving Mr. Pig a sixth sense.

He can only move one space forward, backward, left or right. By creating four boxes placed around the pig for each one of those directions, you'll be able to keep track of every box that might find itself in an active collision with an obstacle.

You simply need to block jumps in the direction(s) where these boxes are actively in a collision. Mind blowing stuff, right?

In the below scenario, you can see four boxes placed around the pig, and none are currently in an active collision. For now, Mr. Pig can freely jump in any direction.

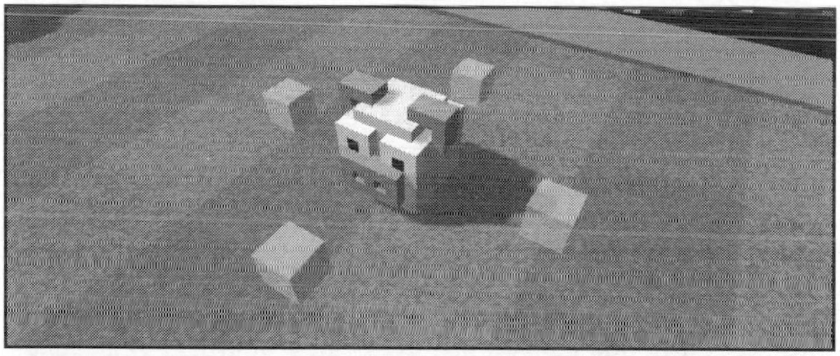

Now consider the next scenario. In this instance, the box to the right finds itself currently in collision with an obstacle. Now you have something substantive to use to prevent the pig from jumping to the right.

Create a hidden collision node

Now that you know how the hidden geometry collision technique will work, you need to create the collision node for your game that will contain the four boxes you'll use for the purpose of collision detection.

Create a collision node

Create a new empty scene by dragging and dropping a **Scene Kit Scene** into the root of your project folder. In the creation wizard, name the new scene **Collision.scn**, and make sure you save it under **MrPig.scnassets**.

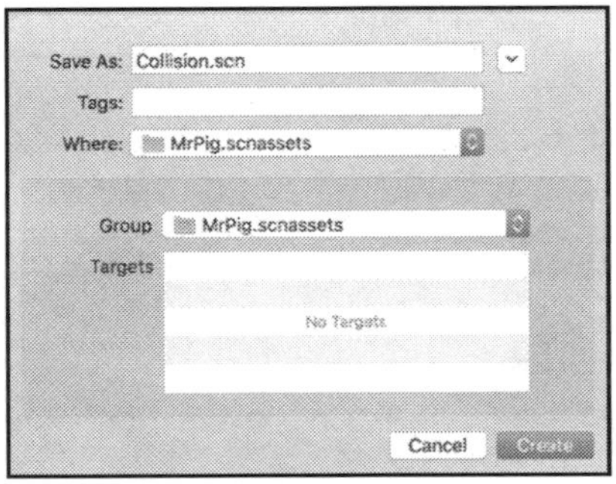

With **Collision.scn** selected, add an empty node to the scene graph and name it **Collision**.

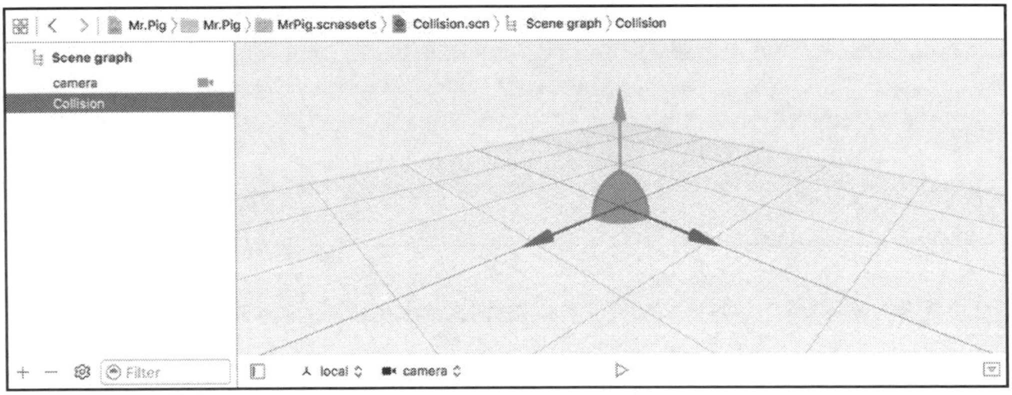

This will be the group node for the collision boxes. Now to create those boxes, drag and drop a **Box** into the scene, and make sure to place it under the **Collision** group node.

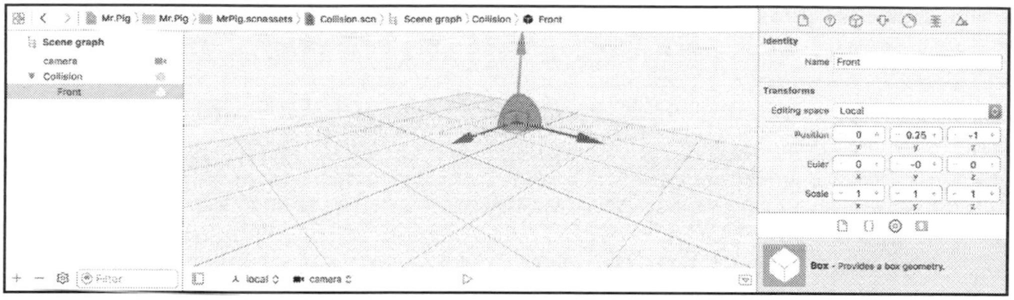

Name the box **Front** and position it at `(x:0, y:0.25, z:-1)` to offset it a bit from the center. Bring up the Attributes Inspector and set the size to be `(x:0.25, y:0.25, z: 0.25)`, a bit smaller than default.

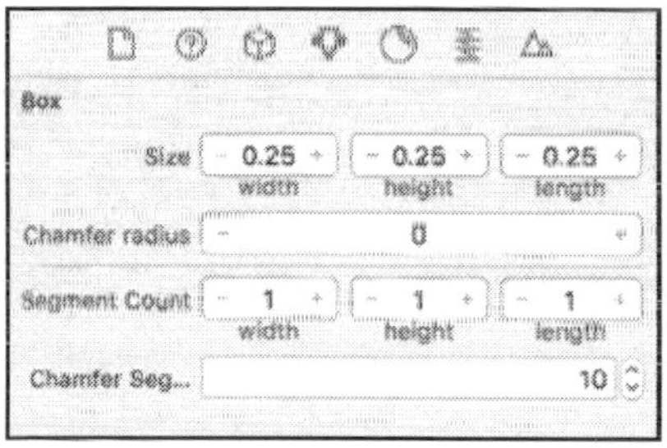

Now simply press the Option key along with Command to drag out three quick copies of the front box for the back, left and right. Make sure that all the new copies are placed under the **Collision** group node, just like the front box node you created.

Once you have three copies of the node, you need to position them correctly. Start off with the back box. Name it **Back**, and position it at `(x:0, y:0.25, z:1)`.

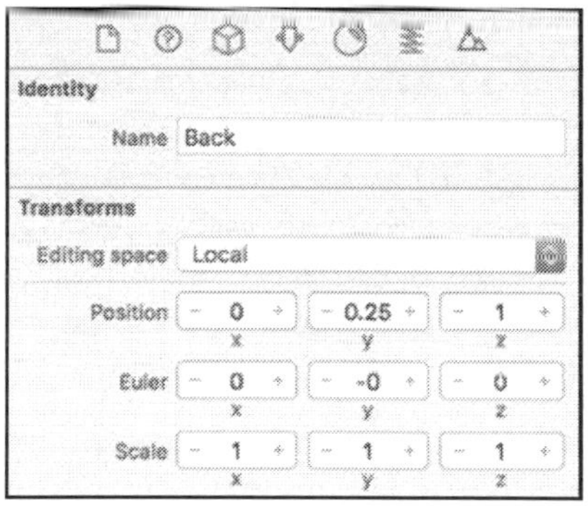

Next, select the node that will be your **Left** box. Name it **Left** and position it at `(x:-1, y:0.25, z:0)`:

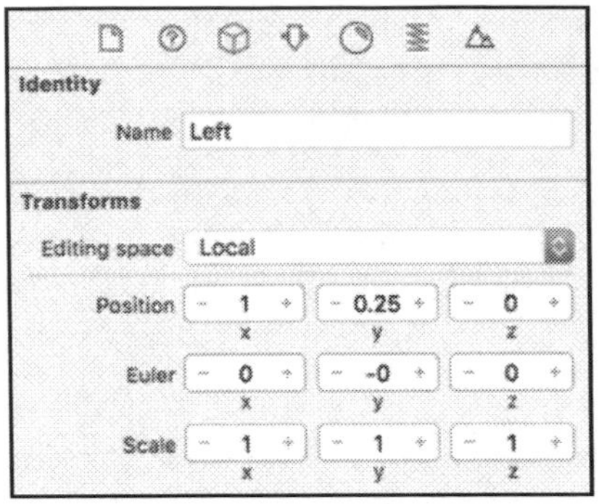

Finally, select the remaining node, name it **Right** and position it at `(x:1, y:0.25, z: 0)`:

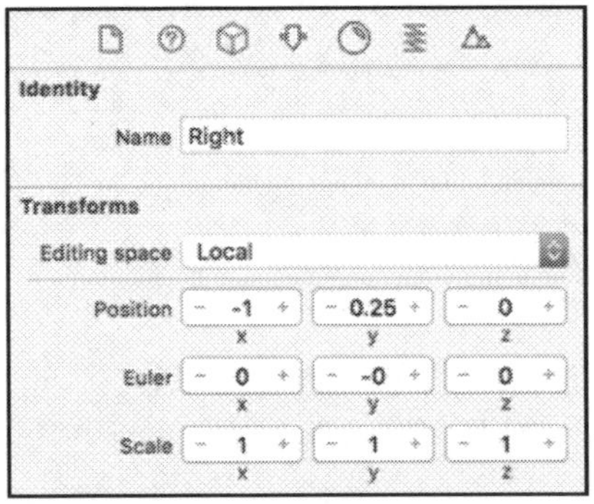

At this point, your scene editor should look like this:

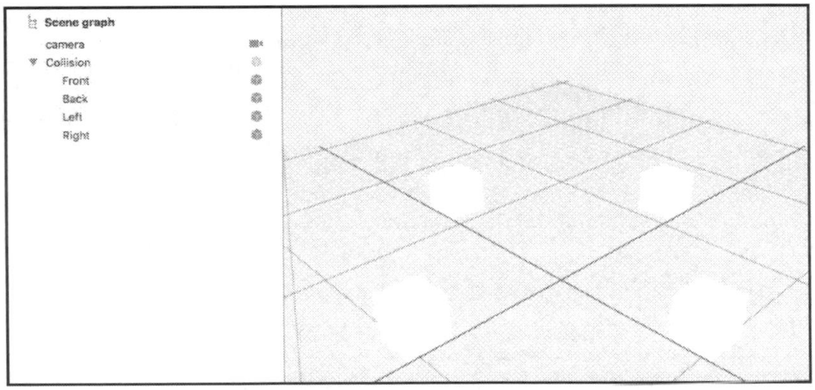

You're halfway done with this part and will play around with physics next.

Enabling physics

Each box needs a category bit mask so that you can tell which one is involved in a collision with an obstacle.

You're about to do a cool little trick that the Scene Kit editor allows you to do – accessing and editing multiple node's attributes and physics properties at the same time. Say what? :]

Start by selecting all the boxes. One quick way to do this is by selecting the first box in the scene graph, and then holding the Shift key while clicking the last box.

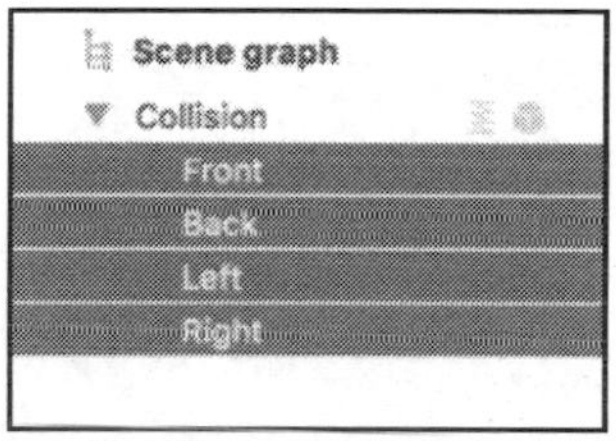

With all the the nodes highlighted, bring up the Physics Inspector. Change the **Type** to **Kinematic**.

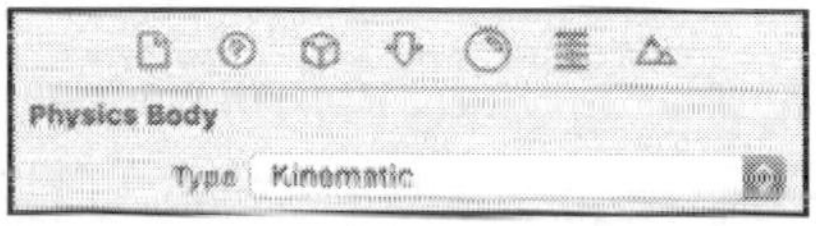

Since you have all four nodes selected, this change will apply to all of the boxes.

Note: This cool little feature works for all the inspectors in the scene editor, so you can use the trick anytime you've got a group of nodes that should have similar properties – obviously, a box node will have different attributes than a sphere node.

Another thing to point out here is that if all of the nodes have the same value for a specific property, then that value would be visible. If one of the selected nodes has a different value than the others, then you would see **Multiple Values** as a value. You can quickly synchronise properties by using this feature.

Here's another little trick to perform. Try licking your own elbow! Just kidding, stop trying, it's impossible. Seriously, stop now! :]

The *actual* trick is to hide the geometry so that your clever little collision trick is concealed from the player.

Besides, it would look pretty silly to have those four boxes showing.

With the four box nodes still selected, select the Node Inspector then scroll down to the **Visibility** section. Set **Opacity** to `0.5`. You need to also disable shadows by unchecking the **Casts Shadow** checkbox, so that the boxes don't give themselves away with shadows.

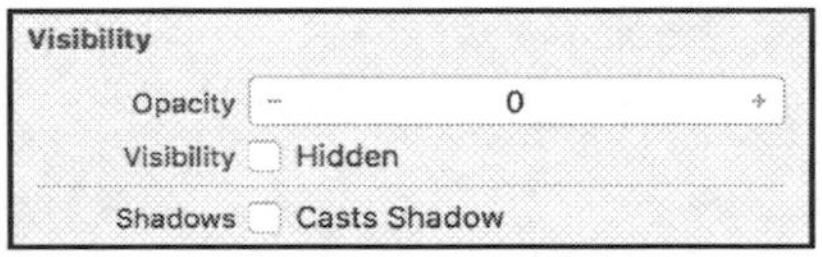

For your purposes, you don't want them to be totally transparent because it'll be helpful to see them in action. In a final version of the game, you would be changing the opacity to `0` to make the boxes fully invisible to the player.

> **Note**: By setting a node's opacity level to `0`, the node is physically still in the scene, it's just invisible. This means that if you have physics properties set on that node, it would still participate in collisions during the physics simulation.
>
> If you were to set the node's visibility to **Hidden**, you would completely remove the node from the scene to such a point that it wouldn't cause any collisions even if it has physics properties.

Things are about to get more granular.

You need to go to each box individually to set up category bit masks because each will have different values. Start with **Front**, bring up the Physics Inspector and set its **Category mask** to 8.

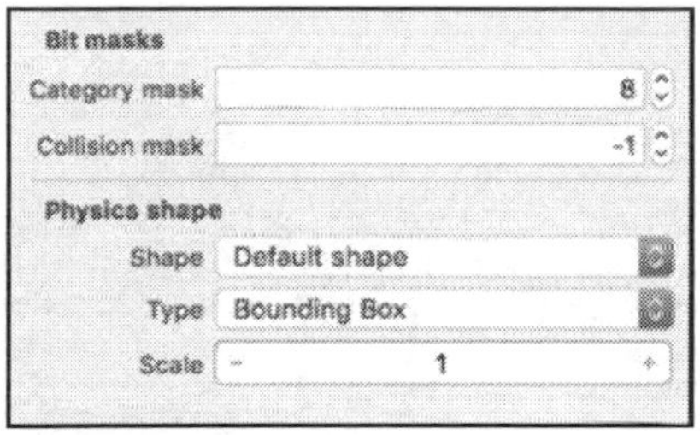

For **Back**, set its **Category mask** to 16.

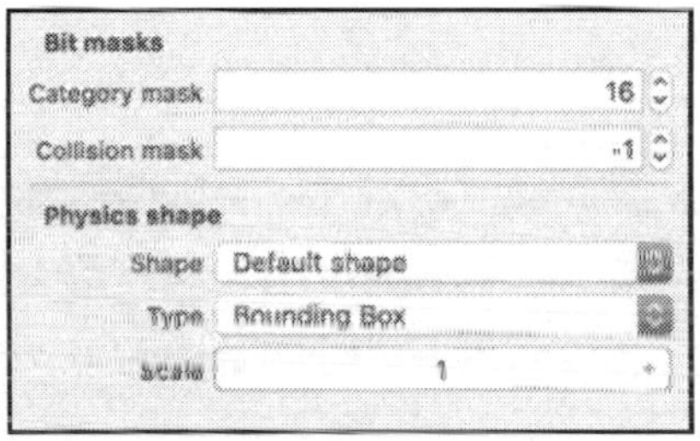

Now for **Left**, set its **Category mask** to 32.

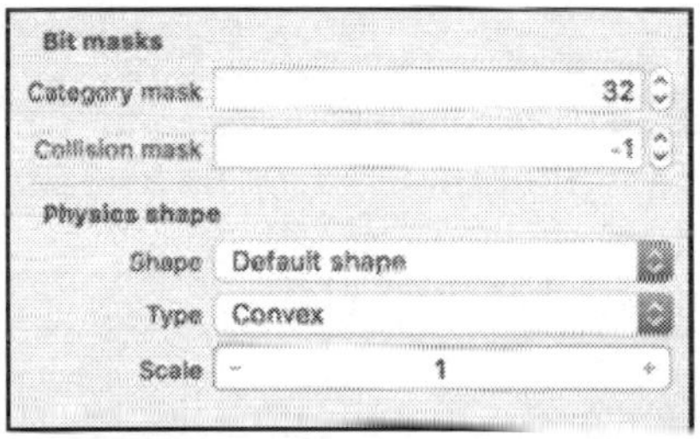

Then finally, set **Right** to have a **Category mask** to 64.

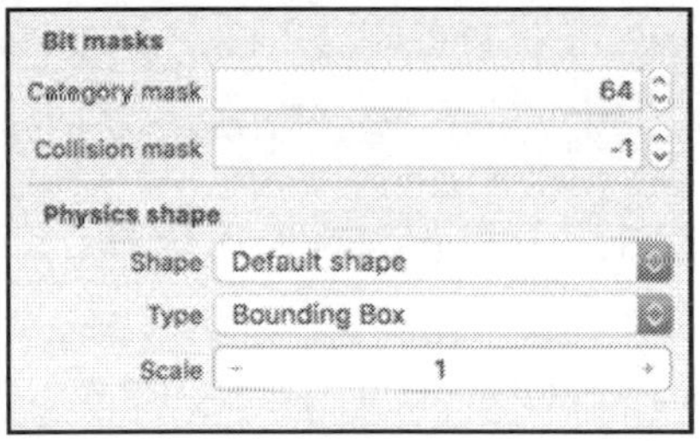

Remember to delete that default **camera**, and then you're all done.

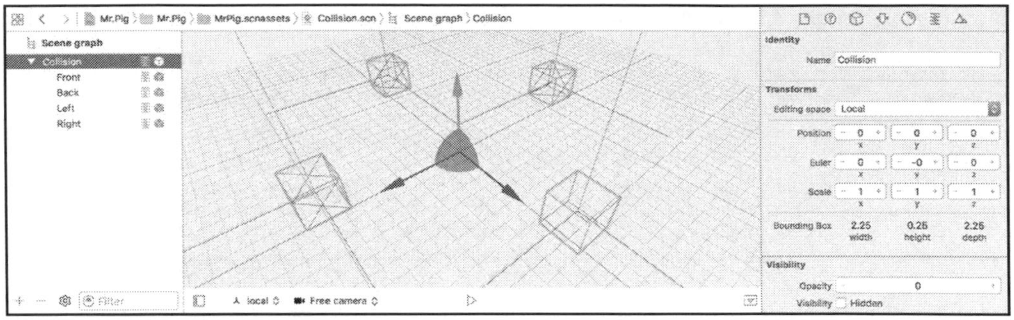

You should now have a **Collision.scn** with four little boxes placed nicely around the middle point of the scene.

Using the collision node

With **Collision.scn** created, what's left for you to do is to actually use this node as a reference node in your game scene.

Add collision reference node

Select **MrPig.scnassets\GameScene.scn**, then drag and drop a **Collsion.scn** reference node into the scene.

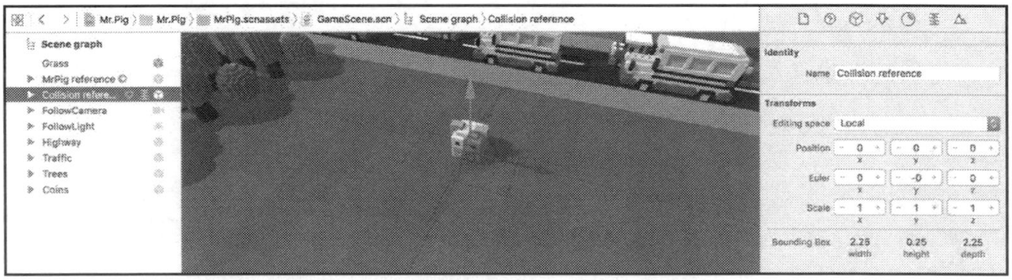

Be sure to position it exactly at position `(x:0, y:0, z:0)`, smack bang on the pig.

Now you need to attach your code to the nodes. Add the following properties to `ViewController` in **ViewController.swift**:

```
var collisionNode: SCNNode!
var frontCollisionNode: SCNNode!
var backCollisionNode: SCNNode!
var leftCollisionNode: SCNNode!
var rightCollisionNode: SCNNode!
```

These are the properties you'll use to access the **Collision** group node as well as each

individual collision box node: **Front, Back, Left and Right**.

To bind the code to the nodes in the scene, add the following code to the bottom of `setupNodes()`:

```
collisionNode =
gameScene.rootNode.childNodeWithName("Collision", recursively:
true)!
frontCollisionNode =
gameScene.rootNode.childNodeWithName("Front", recursively:
true)!
backCollisionNode = gameScene.rootNode.childNodeWithName("Back",
recursively: true)!
leftCollisionNode = gameScene.rootNode.childNodeWithName("Left",
recursively: true)!
rightCollisionNode =
gameScene.rootNode.childNodeWithName("Right", recursively:
true)!
```

This will bind to all the different properties to the **Collision** group node and each collision box node.

Create the render loop

This collision node has to follow Mr. Pig around. The easiest way to do that is to simply update the position of the collision node to the same position as the pig inside the render loop updates.

First, you need to create a new method that will be responsible for updating the node's positions during the render loop of the game. Add the following method to `ViewController`:

```
func updatePositions() {
  collisionNode.position = pigNode.presentationNode.position
}
```

This will keep the position for `collisionNode` in sync with the position for `pigNode`.

Now that you have this method in place, you need to call it in your game's render loop. To do that, you're going to implement the `renderer(_:didApplyAnimationsAtTime:)` delegate method from the `SCNSceneRendererDelegate` protocol.

Add the following to the bottom of **ViewController.swift**:

```
// 1
extension ViewController : SCNSceneRendererDelegate {
  // 2
  func renderer(renderer: SCNSceneRenderer,
didApplyAnimationsAtTime time: NSTimeInterval) {
    // 3
    guard game.state == .Playing else {
      return
    }
    // 4
    game.updateHUD()
    // 5
    updatePositions()
  }
}
```

Take a closer look at that code:

1. This ensures that `ViewController` conforms to the `SCNSceneRenderDelegate` protocol. You use a class extension to organize code from the protocol so that it's separate from the rest of your `ViewController` code.
2. This injects your update game logic just after all the animation actions completed inside the render loop. This way you know exactly the position of each object in your scene, after the applied actions.
3. Again, keeping game states in mind, you only want to do updates while the game is in a `.Playing` state. This `guard` statement will prevent the rest of the method from running if `game.state` is not `.Playing`.
4. This ensures that the HUD node gets updated whenever there is a render update. You added the HUD as a child node to `cameraNode` in a previous chapter.
5. Finally, you make a call to `updatePositions()`, keeping the `collisionNode` position in sync with the `pigNode` position.

Remember to set `ViewController` as the delegate for the view by adding the following line of code to the bottom of the `setupScenes()`:

```
scnView.delegate = self
```

Do a quick build and run and move the pig around to verify the render loop is actually functioning.

If you used an opacity of `0.5` for the boxes, you should see the four boxes follow Mr. Pig whereever he goes, like his own personal security detail. You should also now notice updates that happen in the HUD showing at the top of the screen. Excellent!

> **Note**: Quick clarification of the contents of the HUD: The pig snout shows the total amount of coins collected, and the little house shows the total number of coins banked.

Configure the physics

Define bit masks

Continuing with granular tasks, you'll define a bunch of collision masks next. In `ViewController`, define the following constants:

```
// 1
let BitMaskPig = 1
let BitMaskVehicle = 2
let BitMaskObstacle = 4
let BitMaskFront = 8
let BitMaskBack = 16
let BitMaskLeft = 32
```

```
let BitMaskRight = 64
let BitMaskCoin = 128
let BitMaskHouse = 256
```

Now you have a good idea of all the elements in the game that will play an important role within the collision detection space.

Enable physics

With the bit mask constants defined, you get to move on to a fun little exercise where you'll enable physics for all the important elements of your game, starting with the *most important* element, our hero, Mr. Pig.

Select **MrPig.scnassets\MrPig.scn** to open up the reference node for Mr. Pig. Select the **MrPig** node in the scene graph and open up the Physics Inspector. Change **Type** to **Kinematic** because you'll be running actions on the pig node to change its position.

Under the **Bit masks** section, change **Category mask** to `1`. Then finally, under the **Physics shape** section, change **Type** to **Bounding Box** and set **Scale** to `0.6` to shrink the bounding box down to a smaller size.

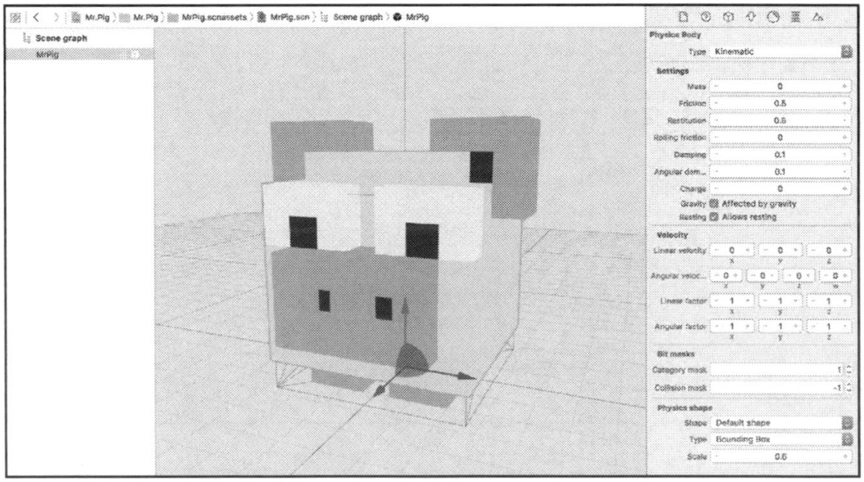

> **Note**: When your game reaches its final stages, you might want to come back and tweak the bounding box size to give the collisions a bit of leeway.

Vehicles are up next, so select **MrPig.scnassets\Bus.scn** and follow the same process as before. Select the **Bus** node in the scene graph, and open the Physics Inspector. Remember that there is already a move action running on the bus node, so you have to change the **Type** to **Kinematic**.

Next, change the **Catergory mask** to 2, which is the same bit mask you'll use for all the vehicles. Then finish off by scrolling down to **Physics shape** and setting **Type** to **Bounding Box** and **Scale** to `0.8`:

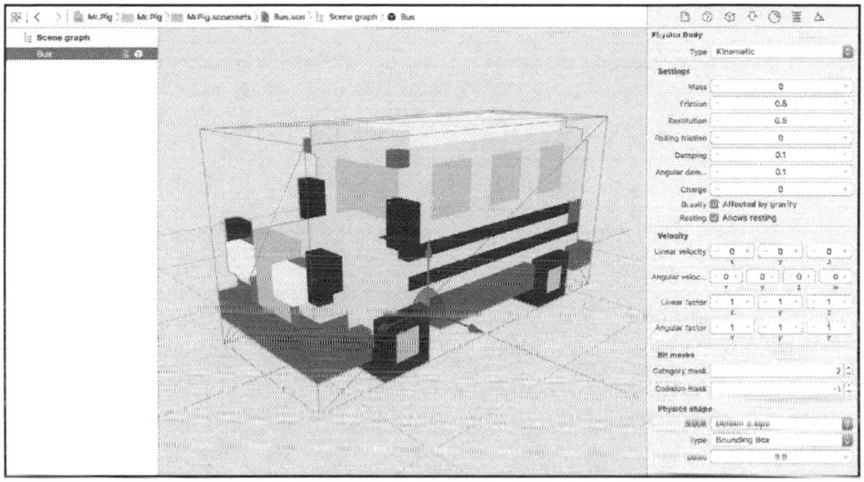

Next in line is **MrPig.scnassets\Mini.scn**. Again, with the **Mini** node selected, set **Type** to **Kinematic** in the Physics Inspector, then set the **Category mask** to 2.

Finally, under **Physics Shape**, set the **Type** to **Bounding Box** with a **Scale** of `0.8`:

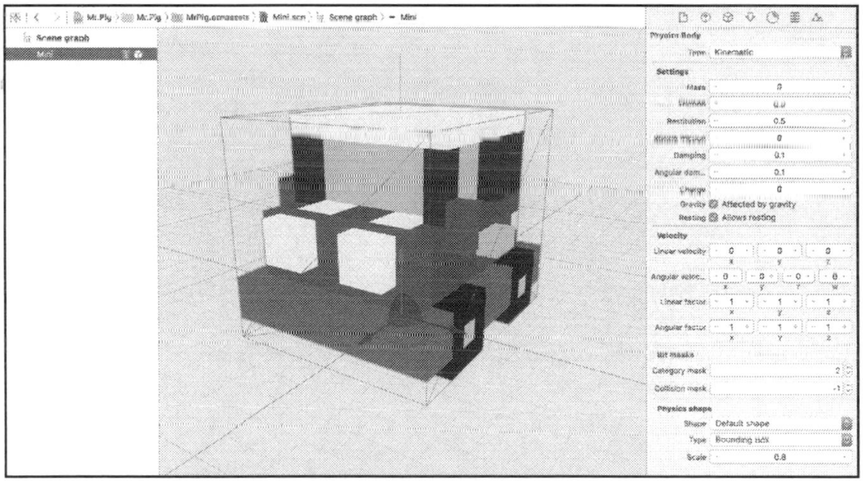

Select the last vehicle, **MrPig.scnassets\SUV.scn**. The SUV will be exactly like the Bus and Mini, so select the **SUV** node and open the Physics Inspector. Set the **Type** to **Kinematic**, then set the **Category mask** to 2.

Finally, under **Physics shape**, set **Type** to **Bounding Box** and **Scale** to `0.8`:

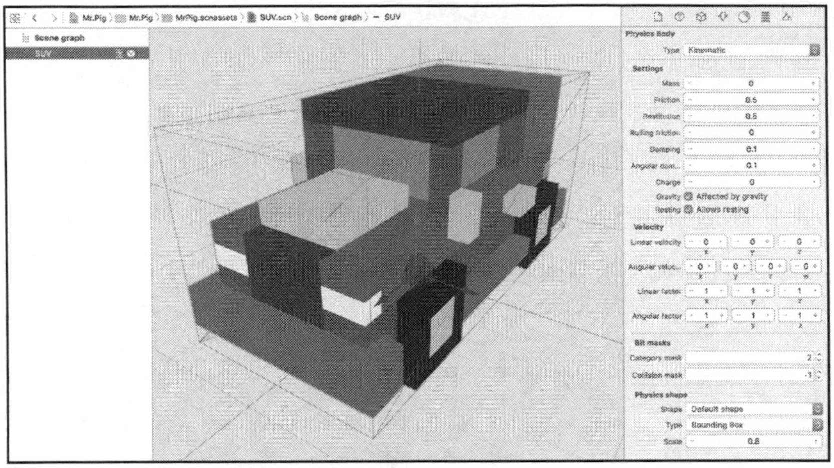

Let's see. Pig? Check. Vehicles? Check. Trees? Not set up yet.

To keep you on your toes, instead of enabling physics on each individual tree, you're going to enable physics on the reference nodes you created in an earlier chapter, **MrPig.scnassets\TreeLine.scn** and **MrPig.scnassets\TreePatch.scn**.

First, select **MrPig.scnassets\TreeLine.scn**. Make sure you have the **TreeLine** node selected and the Physics Inspector open. Trees don't need to move around – unless you're planning to create some kind of fantasy world – so you're going to set the **Type** to **Static**.

Set the **Category mask** to `4`, indicating that the trees are all obstacles. Under **Physics shape**, set **Type** to **Bounding Box** and leave the **Scale** at `1`.

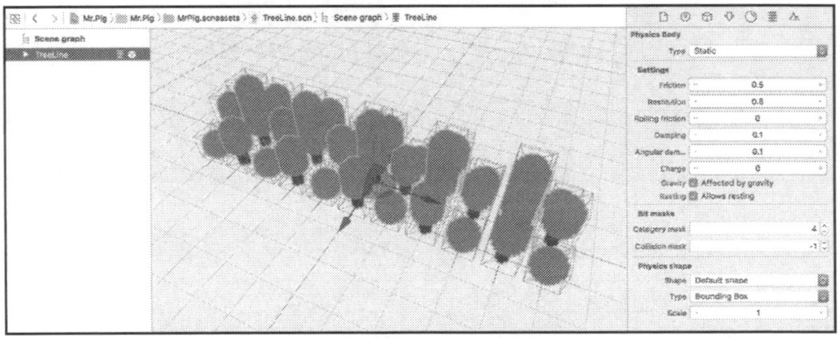

Because the TreeLine node consists of several child tree nodes, you're saving yourself a ton of work once again. The children will inherit the parent's physics properties, saving you from enabling physics on each and every little tree.

Select **MrPig.scnassets\TreePatch.scn** next. This one will work exactly the same as the TreeLine node. With the **TreePatch** node selected, along with the Physics Inspector, set the **Type** to **Static**, **Category mask** to `4`. Under **Physics shape**, set the **Type** to

Bounding Box and leave the **Scale** at 1:

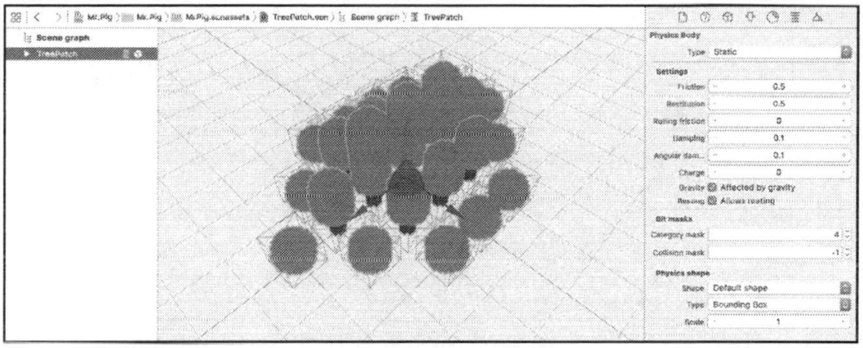

Looks like you're just down to playing around with the coins. Find the **MrPig.scnassets \Coin.scn** reference node.

As it was before, there are actions running on the coin, so you need to set the **Type** to **Kinematic**. Set the **Category mask** to 128, then change the **Type** under **Physics shape** to **Bounding Box** with a **Scale** of `0.8`.

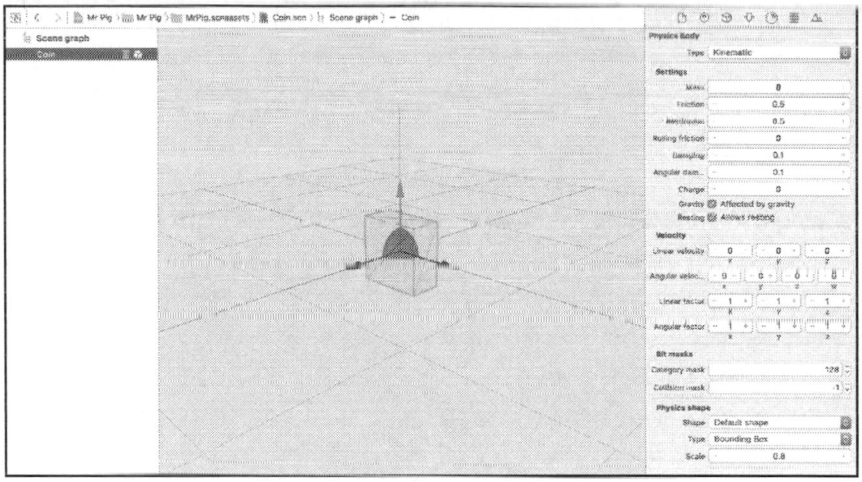

You're finally all done with that. Phew! :]

Set contact bit masks

Now you're back to one of your original objectives: actually blocking the pig when there are obstacles in his way. For this, you'll make use of the contact test between physics bodies.

Oddly enough, the Scene Kit Editor doesn't allow you to modify to the contact test bit mask property yet, so you'll have to manually set that up in code. Fortunately, you don't have to figure it all out on your own!

The following snippet of code has you covered – just open up **ViewController.swift**, add this to the bottom of `setupNodes()` and you're all set:

```
// 1
pigNode.physicsBody?.contactTestBitMask = BitMaskVehicle |
BitMaskCoin | BitMaskHouse
// 2
frontCollisionNode.physicsBody?.contactTestBitMask =
BitMaskObstacle
backCollisionNode.physicsBody?.contactTestBitMask =
BitMaskObstacle
leftCollisionNode.physicsBody?.contactTestBitMask =
BitMaskObstacle
rightCollisionNode.physicsBody?.contactTestBitMask =
BitMaskObstacle
```

There are a couple of things to note:

1. This sets up the contact test bit mask for `pigNode`. From this, you now know that the pig itself will be able to make contact with vehicles, coins and the house.
2. This sets up the contact test bit mask for all the box nodes inside the **Collision** node. The boxes are interested in any object that's an obstacle.

Handle collisions

Collisions with obstacles

As you learned in Chapter 10, "Basic Collision Detection", you set the `contactTestBitMask` of a physics body so that you get notified whenever it touches another physics body with a category mask that matches that mask value.

To keep track of the active collisions in your game, you'll create a special property called `activeCollisionsBitMask`. When one of the four collision boxes makes contact with an obstacle, the `physicsWorld(_:didBeginContact:)` delegate method will be triggered.

You can then use the affected box's category bit mask and add it to the `activeCollisionsBitMask` by means of a bitwise OR (|) operation. This will essentially keep track of all active collisions. Then, the gesture handler can inspect `activeCollisionsBitMask` and ultimately block the gestures based on the active collision directions.

Once the collision ends, the `physicsWorld(_:didEndContact:)` delegate method will be triggered. At that point, you can remove the affected box's category bit mask from `activeCollisionsBitMask`.

This is done by means of first performing a bitwise NOT (~) operation on the category bit mask and then performing a bitwise AND (|) on the result.

Add the following property to `ViewController`:

```
var activeCollisionsBitMask: Int = 0
```

This is the bit mask that will keep track of all the active collisions. Now you need to implement the methods from the `SCNPhysicsContactDelegate` protocol. Add the following code to the bottom of **ViewContoller.swift**:

```
// 1
extension ViewController : SCNPhysicsContactDelegate {
  // 2
  func physicsWorld(world: SCNPhysicsWorld,
    didBeginContact contact: SCNPhysicsContact) {
    // 3
    guard game.state == .Playing else {
      return
    }
    // 4
    var collisionBoxNode: SCNNode!
    if contact.nodeA.physicsBody?.categoryBitMask ==
BitMaskObstacle {
      collisionBoxNode = contact.nodeB
    } else {
      collisionBoxNode = contact.nodeA
    }
    // 5
    activeCollisionsBitMask |=
      collisionBoxNode.physicsBody!.categoryBitMask
  }
  // 6
  func physicsWorld(world: SCNPhysicsWorld,
    didEndContact contact: SCNPhysicsContact) {
    // 8
    guard game.state == .Playing else {
      return
    }
    // 8
    var collisionBoxNode: SCNNode!
    if contact.nodeA.physicsBody?.categoryBitMask ==
BitMaskObstacle {
      collisionBoxNode = contact.nodeB
    } else {
      collisionBoxNode = contact.nodeA
    }
    // 9
    activeCollisionsBitMask &=
      ~collisionBoxNode.physicsBody!.categoryBitMask
  }
}
```

Here's a section-by-section breakdown:

1. This adds a class extension to `ViewController` and makes the class conform to the `SCNPhysicsContactDelegate` protocol.
2. This defines a handler for when a `physicsWorld(_:didBeginContact:)` event gets triggered.
3. You only want to keep track of collisions while the game is in a `.Playing` state.
4. This is a familiar bit of code where you determine whether `nodeA` or `nodeB` is the obstacle, which means that the other node is the collision box.
5. This does a bitwise OR operation to add the colliding box's category bit mask to `activeCollisionsBitMask`.
6. This defines a handler for when a `physicsWorld(_:didEndContact:)` event gets triggered.
7. Again, you only want to keep track of these events while the game is in a `.Playing` state.
8. Again, this is used to determine which node in the contact test is the collision box.
9. Finally, this first does a bitwise NOT operation followed by a bitwise AND operation to remove the collision box category bit mask from the `activeCollisionsBitMask`.

Now you can add code that will inspect the `activeCollisionsBitMask` to block gestures inside the gesture handler.

Add the following code inside `handleGestures()` right after the `block`, making sure you're in a `.Playing` state:

```
// 1
let activeFrontCollision = activeCollisionsBitMask &
BitMaskFront == BitMaskFront
let activeBackCollision = activeCollisionsBitMask & BitMaskBack
== BitMaskBack
let activeLeftCollision = activeCollisionsBitMask & BitMaskLeft
== BitMaskLeft
let activeRightCollision = activeCollisionsBitMask &
BitMaskRight == BitMaskRight

// 2
guard (sender.direction == .Up && !activeFrontCollision) ||
  (sender.direction == .Down && !activeBackCollision) ||
  (sender.direction == .Left && !activeLeftCollision) ||
  (sender.direction == .Right && !activeRightCollision) else {
    return
}
```

Let's look at the code you just added:

1. This uses a bitwise AND to check for active collisions in each direction stored in `activeCollisionsBitMask` and saves them in individual constants.
2. This `guard` statement makes sure that you only continue on to the rest of the gesture handler code when there is no active collision in the direction of the gesture. For example, if the gesture direction is up and there is an active collision, the entire condition will evaluate to `false` and code execution will go to the `else` clause of the `guard` statement which will end the gesture handler.

One last thing you need to do is to set your `ViewController` up as the contact delegate for your game scene's physics world by adding the following line of code to the bottom of `setupScenes()`:

```
gameScene.physicsWorld.contactDelegate = self
```

This sets `self` as the `contactDelegate` for `gameScene.physicsWorld`.

Time for a quick build and run to test things out.

Try and jump as far down as possible. If all sanity is intact, then Mr. Pig will not be able to jump into the tree anymore. Yay!

Collisions with vehicles

The next bit is easy. You need to make sure that he doesn't survive when he throws himself in front of a bus.

Add the following code to bottom of `physicsWorld(_:didBeginContact:)`:

```
// 1
var contactNode: SCNNode!
if contact.nodeA.physicsBody?.categoryBitMask == BitMaskPig {
  contactNode = contact.nodeB
} else {
  contactNode = contact.nodeA
}

// 2
if contactNode.physicsBody?.categoryBitMask == BitMaskVehicle {
  stopGame()
}
```

1. You should now be very familiar with how this snippet of code determines which node is the pig and which is not. Once done, you know for a fact that the `contactNode` is not the pig.
2. If the node the pig made contact with is indeed a vehicle, then it's the end of the game.

Build, run and throw that pig under a bus!

If you're fast enough, you can catch some traffic. Once the bus collides with the poor little pig, he flies off to heaven and the game transitions back to the splash scene, exactly as it was designed to do.

Collisions with coins

Next up, Mr. Pig needs to be able to actually collect those coins.

Add the following code to the bottom of `physicsWorld(_:didBeginContact:)`:

```
// 1
if contactNode.physicsBody?.categoryBitMask == BitMaskCoin {
  // 2
  contactNode.hidden = true

contactNode.runAction(SCNAction.waitForDurationThenRunBlock(60)
{ (node: SCNNode!) -> Void in
    node.hidden = false
  })
  // 3
  game.collectCoin()
}
```

Let's look at the code:

1. You check if the node the pig made contact with is a coin.
2. If it is, you hide the coin node, then run an action on it that will unhide the coin after 60 seconds.
3. Then you call the `collectCoin()` method on `game`, which will update the score.

Build and run and go grab that coin!

Be careful though – Mr. Pig is a mere mortal now. Watch out for that bus! :]

If you manage to cross the road, you'll see coins disappear once Mr. Pig jumps on them. You should notice the score increase as well. Excellent!

Where to go from here?

You've now conquered the hardest tasks of your game, and the end is in sight! Reaching this point means you deserve a pat on the back.

You can continue to administer said back-patting for yourself as I'm stuck behind the print here; feel free to sneak in another attempt to lick your elbow while you're at it. :]

Understanding how to use hidden geometry to assist your game with collision detection is the primary concept to take away from this chapter.

It's a technique that can be applied to many use cases, including these:

- In an FPS game, it can be used to determine if your hero was stabbed from the front or back.
- In a platform game, it can be used to flip a nearby switch or check if your hero is standing close to the edge.
- You can also use hidden geometry for particle systems, like a campfire for example, so you can respond accordingly when someone steps into it.

There are quite a few bits that are left unattended, so in the next chapter you'll add those much needed finishing touches. For now, go and take a well deserved break, but hurry back!

Chapter 20: Audio

Chris Language

This is the final chapter in which you'll conclude the 3D Scene Kit game you've been building since Chapter 16 – Mr. Pig. Don't worry, that light at the end of the tunnel isn't a bus about to hit you, it's success barreling down on you!

The main focus of this chapter will be on audio and Scene Kit. Along the way, you'll get to put some final touches on the game too.

Only a few more steps to go before all is done. Good luck! :]

> **Note**: There's a starter project for you available under **projects\starter\Mr.Pig**, it continues where the previous chapter ended.
>
> There is one small difference: the opacity of the collision boxes are now set to `0` to make them invisible to the player. If you want to continue using your current project, just make that same change before continuing.

Adding finishing touches

Mr. Pig's habit of jumping out of the camera's view is pretty annoying, and where the heck is all the traffic disappearing to?

Don't worry. You're about to resolve all these little annoyances by working with render loop updates for your game.

Update camera position

It's time to unleash Big Brother and follow that little pig's every move. Surely the authorities are wondering where on earth he gets all his money, and you need to keep a sharp eye on him so you can usher him and his coins safely across traffic. Killing off that darn static camera is the best thing for all parties involved.

Open up **ViewController.swift** and add the following code to bottom of `updatePositions()`:

```
let lerpX = (pigNode.position.x - cameraFollowNode.position.x) *
0.05
let lerpZ = (pigNode.position.z - cameraFollowNode.position.z) *
0.05
cameraFollowNode.position.x += lerpX
cameraFollowNode.position.z += lerpZ
```

In the previous chapter, you already created the `updatePositions()` method, which gets called 60 times per second as part of your game's render loop update.

So the first two lines calculate a linearly interpolated x and z value between `pigNode` and `cameraFollowNode`, with a factor of `0.05`. The results are then added to the position of `cameraFollowNode`. In turn, this moves the camera towards the pig's position over a period of time.

Instead of simply updating `cameraFollowNode` to the same position as that of the `pigNode`, this technique creates a smooth, lazy camera tracking effect.

Note: To make the camera less lazy and more responsive, you can tweak the factor. Setting the factor to `1.0` will make the camera tracking 100 percent real-time.

Do a build and run and see if you can get the little pig to escape the eye in the sky.

At last, the camera follows the pig everywhere, and now he can explore the entire park under your watchful eye. Hey, did Mr. Pig just discover another coin? Awesome! :]

Hang on, after moving Mr. Pig around the park for a bit, did you notice something odd with the scene?

Is that large shadow on the top-right an alien mothership about to land? And why the heck does that coin have no shadow? Is it impervious to sunlight?

Relax, there are no aliens in this game and the shadow mystery will soon be resolved. All will be revealed in the next little section.

Update light position

In order to make your game as efficient as possible, one of the applied techniques was tweaking your light settings so that only the visible areas in view cast shadows.

And this is the culprit for all those weird things you noticed. Specifically, it's because of the shadow clipping range that you configured on the directional light that you configured earlier.

Now that you know the problem, the fix is elementary: just make the light follow the camera around. Thank goodness, sanity restored! :]

Add the following line to the bottom of `updatePositions()`:

```
lightFollowNode.position = cameraFollowNode.position
```

This simply updates `lightFollowNode`'s position to the exact same position of `cameraFollowNode`, thus keeping the light in sync with the camera's point of view.

Do another build and run to see if the shadow issue has been resolved.

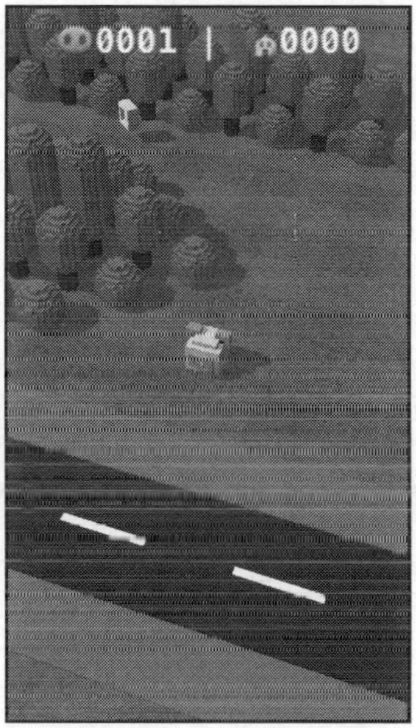

Hey, that coin is still there, and everything now has shadows. It looks like you successfully foiled an alien invasion too.

What a lovely, sunny day indeed!

Update traffic bounds

On to your next problem – where is all that traffic going? Something is seriously wrong here; traffic never just disappears, unless there's a black hole in the road ahead. :]

What you really want to accomplish here is the effect of endless traffic with only a few cars. Fortunately, the solution is quite simple.

By introducing a bounds check for each moving vehicle, you can actively monitor for when a vehicle drives past a defined boundary and then reset the vehicle's position to the opposite side of the scene.

Once you do that, the vehicle has to travel from the beginning again, thus driving through the scene in an endless loop of madness.

Add the following `updateTraffic()` method to `ViewController`:

```
func updateTraffic() {
  // 1
  for node in trafficNode.childNodes {
    // 2
    if node.position.x > 25 {
      node.position.x = -25
    } else if node.position.x < -25 {
      node.position.x = 25
    }
  }
}
```

1. You are iterating through all the vechicle nodes placed under `trafficNode` group node.
2. Once the node's x-position crosses the 25 unit mark, you reset it to −25 and vice versa for nodes moving in the opposite direction.

Don't forget to actually call the `updateTraffic()` method inside the render loop update. Add the following code to the bottom of `renderer(_:updateAtTime:)`:

```
updateTraffic()
```

Build and run, and review the changes.

Wow, look at that traffic flow. It just never stops, as you'd expect. How on earth did the poor little pig manage to get himself trapped on that island between the highways? Now the traffic flows forever and ever, just like in real life! :]

Challenge!

Why did the little pig cross the road? Because he got *boared*!

Granted, that was pretty weak, the real answer is because he wanted to *score*...points.

Speaking of scoring, it's time to reward yourself by proving you've got the skills to crack this challenge. What? Huh?

That's right, it's challenge time, and this one is specifically designed to give your game some *purpose*.

When you think about it, what happens if Mr. Pig runs across the road, then simply stays in the park, never to cross the road again? He's a smart little pig; he would totally try to do something like that just to avoid a run-in with an SUV.

But, there's an incentive for him to make that dangerous trek across the highway: points.

Once the little pig has collected a few coins, in order to actually score, he has to bank them somewhere. Plus, they get heavy after a while.

Back in Chapter 16, you read about how Mr. Pig banks coins in his house (most likely under the mattress) and that he's got a kettle of tea on the ready.

Your challenge, dear reader, is to build that home.

Fear not, most of the hard work is done and you won't have to pick up a hammer. All you need to do is build a small reference scene with a little house, car and garden in it. Doesn't that sound like fun?

Here's a high level look at the steps ahead:

1. Start by creating an empty Scene Kit scene named **Home.scn** and deleting the default camera.
2. Add a little **House.scn** into the scene, right in the middle.
3. Create an empty group node named **Obstacles**. Make sure you place all the rest of the objects for this scene under this node.
4. Add a few trees – big, medium and small. (See reference image below)
5. Add a little **Mini.scn** too.

You can use the following reference image for building Mr. Pigs little **Home.scn**:

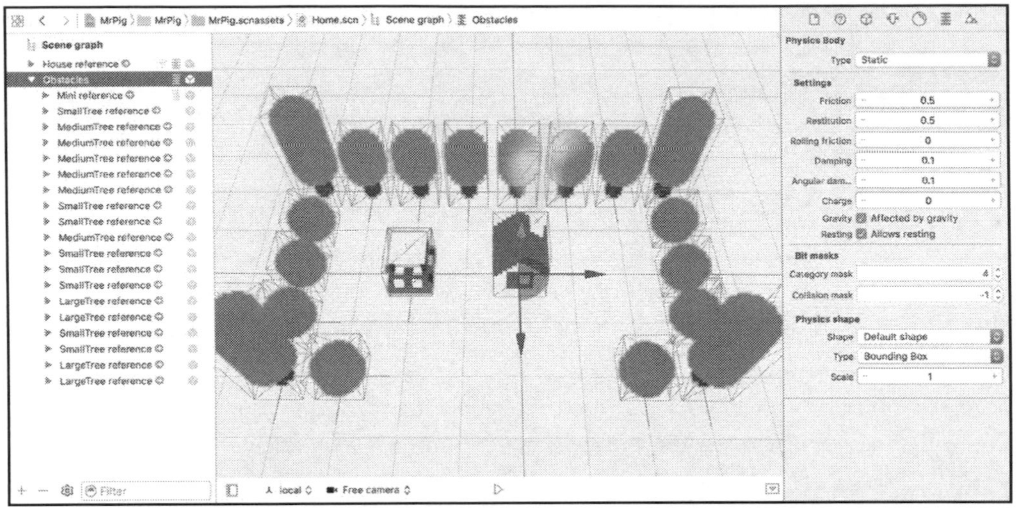

7. You need to set up the physics for all **Obstacles** too; make sure they are static physics bodies with a category bit mask of `4`. For the little **House**, use a category bit mask of `256`. Remember to change their physics shapes to a bounding box as well.

8. Once you're done with the home scene, you have to add a reference to it in the game scene.

9. Finally, you can use the following code inside of `physicsWorld(_:didBeginContact:)` to make sure all the game correctly credits Mr. Pig when he brings coins into his little house.

```
if contactNode.physicsBody?.categoryBitMask == BitMaskHouse {
  if game.bankCoins() == true {
  }
}
```

Once a collision with a house occurs, you use the provided `game.bankCoins()` function to tally all the collected coins and add them to the actual score.

Note: As always, you'll find the solution for this challenge under **projects \challenge\Mr.Pig**.

Audio in Scene Kit

Mr. Pig is nearly done, but there's one crucial missing element. Where are the sound effects? The worst thing a game developer can do is to underestimate the power of audio.

Sound is so powerful that the scariest movie ever made would turn into a comedy of note. Go ahead, put in a classic suspense film like "Rear Window" and mute it. Tell me how long you manage to stay interested. Three minutes – five, maybe?

In particular, ambient sounds create atmosphere, giving your game environment life. Sound effects bring actions to life by letting your audience experience every little jump, bump or crash. Music taps into that deep, dark, scary place inside all of us, just as easily as it pulls out the happy, giddy inner child.

In fact, even before there were games and movies with elaborate audio tracks, the screening of silent movies were accompanied by a lovely little ivory-tickling piano player.

Thank goodness the good folks at Apple also realized the importance of sound because they added some really cool sound capabilities into Scene Kit for you to use.

Here are a few important elements in Scene Kit you can use for audio:

- **`SCNAudioSource`**: An *audio source* is an object that represents an audio file such as music or a sound effect. It can be preloaded into memory or streamed in real-time.
- **`SCNAudioPlayer`**: With an *audio player* you can play back an *audio source* as 3D spatialized audio using the position of an **SCNNode** object.
- **`SCNAction.playAudioSource(_:waitForCompletion:)`**: Is a special action you can run on an **SCNNode** that will play back an *audio source*.

Add music

To start your exploration of sound, the first sound element you'll add is music to set the overall tone for your game.

Scene Kit puts a few special objects at your fingertips, especially for playing music.

In **ViewController.swift**, add the following code to `setupSounds()`:

```
// 1
if game.state == .TapToPlay {
  // 2
  let music = SCNAudioSource(fileNamed: "MrPig.scnassets/Audio/
Music.mp3")!
  // 3
  music.volume = 0.3;
  music.loops = true
  music.shouldStream = true
  music.positional = false
  // 4
  let musicPlayer = SCNAudioPlayer(source: music)
  // 5
  splashScene.rootNode.addAudioPlayer(musicPlayer)
}
```

Take a deeper look at what this code does:

1. This makes sure that the music only plays while on the splash scene.
2. This creates an `SCNAudioSource` object from **MrPig.scnassets/Audio/Music.mp3**.
3. What follows are a few properties that configure the audio source.

- `volume`: Controls the volume at which the audio source is played back.
- `loops`: Controls whether the audio source is played back in a loop or not.
- `shouldStream`: This controls whether the audio source is streamed from its source or preloaded into memory. Typically music and large audio files should be streamed, but for small sound effects it's better to preload them into memory for faster playback.
- `positional`: Controls whether the audio source will make use of 3D spatialized playback.

4. This section creates an audio player that will make use of the music audio source for playback.
5. By adding the audio player to the `rootNode` of the scene, this will start the audio player, and the music will start to stream from its audio source.

Do a build and run, and this time around look *and* listen.

Hey, it's really hard to visualize music, but you get the idea. Now you also know why Mr. Pig's been twerking his little tail off! :]

Add ambiance

Do you really think a park with two massive highways through its heart could be so peaceful?

Add the following `else if` block to the bottom of `setupSounds()`:

```
// 1
else if game.state == .Playing {
  // 2
  let traffic = SCNAudioSource(fileNamed: "MrPig.scnassets/
Audio/Traffic.mp3")!
  traffic.volume = 0.3
  traffic.loops = true
  traffic.shouldStream = true
  traffic.positional = true
  // 3
  let trafficPlayer = SCNAudioPlayer(source: traffic)
  gameScene.rootNode.addAudioPlayer(trafficPlayer)
  // 4
  game.loadSound("Jump", fileNamed: "MrPig.scnassets/Audio/
Jump.wav")
  game.loadSound("Blocked", fileNamed: "MrPig.scnassets/Audio/
Blocked.wav")
  game.loadSound("Crash", fileNamed: "MrPig.scnassets/Audio/
Crash.wav")
```

```
  game.loadSound("CollectCoin", fileNamed: "MrPig.scnassets/
Audio/CollectCoin.wav")
  game.loadSound("BankCoin", fileNamed: "MrPig.scnassets/Audio/
BankCoin.wav")
}
```

Here's what's happening in there:

1. This time around you check if the game is in a `.Playing` state.
2. This sets **MrPig.scnassets/Audio/Traffic.mp3** as a streaming audio source.
3. Then you start to play the audio source as soon as it's added to the `rootNode`.
4. This preloads a whole bunch of sound effects that you'll use in the next section.

Build and run, start a game and then look and listen.

Suddenly the park springs to life. You can hear the traffic with sounds of little cars, big cars and even those noisy old squeaky buses too. Yippee!

Add sound effects

For your final act, you just need to unlock the sound effects so the player can hear every jump, bump and crash.

Start off by giving life to every jump. Add the following line to the bottom of `handleGesture(_:)`:

```
game.playSound(pigNode, name: "Jump")
```

This will play a nice little *boing* sound effect every time a valid gesture is handled.

> **Note:** This uses a helper method found in `GameHelper` to play a sound. Under the hood, all it does is simply run a `playAudioSource(_:waitForCompletion:)` action on the node you pass it by using a preloaded audio source. You can take a look at how it does this by browsing **GameHelper.swift**.

What about when Mr. Pig stumbles into an obstacle? To solve that, add the following sound effect code inside the second `guard` statement that will block gestures matching the `activeCollisionBitMask` at top of `handleGesture()`, just before the `return` statement:

```
game.playSound(pigNode, name: "Blocked")
```

Now blocked gestures will make a short little *thump* when the player tries to jump into an obstacle.

Coins need sound too! Add the following line just after the call to `game.collectCoin()` inside of `physicsWorld(_:didBeginContact:)`:

```
game.playSound(pigNode, name: "CollectCoin")
```

Collecting coins certainly sounds much cooler, but the sound effect is somewhat muted. The reason is because the player hasn't really scored yet; he needs to bank that coin in order to get the full audio experience.

Add the following sound effect to that moment when the pig makes contact with the little house.

You'll go back into `physicsWorld(_:didBeginContact:)`, where there's an `if` statement checking the return value of `game.bankCoins()`, so that you only play a sound if there are actual coins available to bank:

```
game.playSound(pigNode, name: "BankCoin")
```

Ah, yes! Once the pig jumps into his little house, that familiar, yet satisfying coin sound effect lets the player know that some valuable points were just added to the score board.

Cha-ching! :]

Last but not least is the moment of impact when pig meets bumper and fades away on his way to piggie heaven.

Still inside of `physicsWorld(_:didBeginContact:)`, add the following line of code inside the `if` statement that handles the moment when `pigNode` makes contact with a vehicle, but place the code just before the call to `stopGame()`:

```
game.playSound(pigNode, name: "Crash")
```

Do a final build and run, and enjoy the full Mr. Pig experience, now with music, ambiance and sound effects!

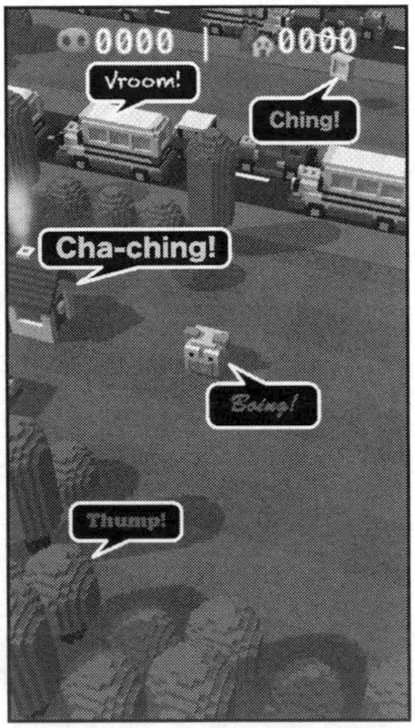

And with that, you just finished your last game and this book. Congratulations! :]

Where to go from here?

The final project for this chapter can be found under the **projects\final\Mr.Pig** folder.

In this chapter, you've learned the value and impact of sound. Thanks to Scene Kit, it's easy to add sounds to all of your future titles.

Mr. Pig certainly has so much unexplored potential just waiting for you to discover, here are a few ideas for you to consider:

- **Voxel Graphics**: Voxel graphics look sharp and are super easy to create. It's the perfect style for someone who's wanting to make something in 3D but not ready to go into

great detail.

- **More characters**: You should definitely add more characters to your game. Mr. Wolf, the menacing figure behind that atrocious mall and traffic, is a big bad bully, and he would love nothing more than to troll Mr. Pig from time to time. Rumor has it that he's got his eyes on the park and cute little house. He could be a good motivator to stay away from certain parts of the park or take on the role of an evil boss Mr. Pig must defeat.
- **More obstacles**: Go and explore a nearby park and see what else you could add into the park. There could be a fountain, some park benches and even birds!
- **More actions**: Use actions to add juice to your game. The more elaborate and fun the animations, the more players will enjoy playing it.
- **Go big**: At the moment it's such a small little park – surely you can think up some other clever designs to make the park bigger and more interesting. Why not add power-ups and traps to keep our hero on his hooves?

Now for your final challenge; free your mind, think outside the box and unleash your newly found Scene Kit powers onto the world! :]

Conclusion

We hope you've enjoyed your journey through this book. If you followed it from top to bottom, you've created four epic games from scratch using SceneKit and Swift — from colorful, exploding geometry, to a shiny paddle with a bouncing ball; a beautiful maze, up high in the sky, right down to a cute little pig that twerks.

You now have the knowledge to make your very own hit game. Why wait any longer?

Got a great idea? With SceneKit, prototyping your app is child's play. Share it with your friends, then use their feedback as inspiration to keep on improving it. Don't forget about adding juice: music, sound effects and stunning graphics. Keep on pushing, until you make that final push and publish your game for the whole world to enjoy!

We can't wait to see what you come up with! Be sure to stop by our forums and share your progress at www.raywenderlich.com/forums.

You might also be interested to know that we have a monthly blog post where we review games written by fellow readers like you. If you'd like to be considered for this column, please visit this page after you release your game: www.raywenderlich.com/reviews

Thank you again for purchasing this book. Your continued support is what makes the tutorials, books and other things we do at raywenderlich.com possible. We truly appreciate it.

Best of luck in all your iOS adventures,

— Chris L., Ken, Wendy, Toby, Chris B. and Ray

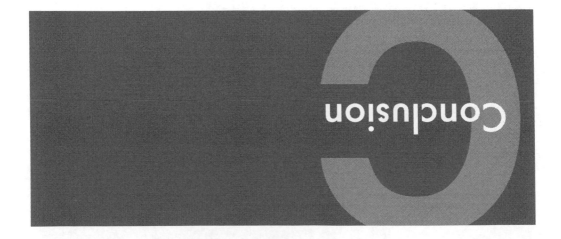

The *3D iOS Games by Tutorials* Team

52093214R00211

Made in the USA
Lexington, KY
21 May 2016